新华字典

（汉英双语版）

XINHUA DICTIONARY

（Chinese-English Edition）

商務印書館
创于1897 The Commercial Press
2014年·北京

图书在版编目(CIP)数据

新华字典:汉英双语版.—北京:商务印书馆,2013(2014.1重印)

ISBN 978-7-100-04555-1

Ⅰ.①新… Ⅱ. Ⅲ.①汉语—字典 Ⅳ.①H163

中国版本图书馆CIP数据核字(2012)第276904号

新 华 字 典

(汉英双语版)

商 务 印 书 馆 出 版

(北京王府井大街36号 邮政编码100710)

商 务 印 书 馆 发 行

山东鸿杰印务集团有限公司印刷

ISBN 978-7-100-04555-1

2013年7月新1版 开本787×960 1/32

2014年1月第2次印刷 印张37¼

定价:69.90元

新华字典（汉英双语版）

XINHUA DICTIONARY（Chinese-English Edition）

主审 Chief Reviser：汪榕培 Wang Rongpei

主译 Chief Translator：门顺德 Men Shunde

译者 Translators（以姓氏笔画为序 surname stroke order）：

王太林 Wang Tailin　刘江 Liu Jiang

宋建华 Song Jianhua　郑雪青 Zheng Xueqing

英文顾问 English Advisor：William W. Moss

目　录

Contents

出版说明

《新华字典》是新中国最有影响、最权威的一部现代汉语字典，1953 年首版后历经数次修订，一直畅销不衰，累计发行突破 4 亿册。

跨入新世纪以来，世界范围内的汉语热持续升温，这本中国小学生入学后几乎人手一册的权威汉语字典也就成为更多国际读者关注的对象，于是《新华字典》（汉英双语版）便应运而生。

《新华字典》（汉英双语版）是在《新华字典》第 10 版的基础上进行翻译编纂的。在保留《新华字典》原书全文的同时，提供英文对译，兼具中文和英文工具书的功能，既可用于外国人学习汉语和了解中国文化，也可用于我国读者阅读原字典汉语内容或学习英文。

在出版之际，我们谨向《新华字典》第 10 版的修订者中国社会科学院语言研究所，向本双语版的主审汪榕培教授、主译门顺德教授和其他译者深表敬意。翻译如此权威的《新华字典》绝非易事，纰漏之处还望读者指正。

商务印书馆辞书研究中心

2012 年 8 月

Foreword

With a total print run of well over 400 million copies and having been revised for several times, the Xinhua Dictionary has been a best seller and the most influential and authoritative dictionary for the Chinese language in China since its first publication in 1953.

As an authoritative dictionary of the Chinese language, the Xinhua Dictionary is a must for almost every pupil in China who first goes to school, and has drawn the attention of Chinese learners all over the world since the beginning of the new century in an increasing world-wide craze of learning the Chinese language. Hence the Xinhua Dictionary (English-Chinese Edition) comes into being.

The Xinhua Dictionary (Chinese-English Edition), compiled on the basis of the tenth edition of the Xinhua Dictionary, has preserved the full text of the original dictionary and provided English explanations. It can serve as a reference book for the foreigners in learning the Chinese language and the Chinese culture, as well as for the Chinese people in learning the Chinese and English languages.

At the publication of this dictionary, we would like to extend our sincere thanks to the Language Research Institute of the Chinese Academy of Social Sciences (the reviser of the Xinhua Dictionary), Professor Wang Rongpei (the chief English reviser of this Chinese-English Edition), Professor Men Shunde (the chief translator) and all the other translators. We all know that it is no easy task to translate such an authoritative dictionary as the Xinhua Dictionary. We would greatly appreciate the readers' comments and suggestions for the Xinhua Dictionary (Chinese-English Edition).

Lexicographical Research Center
of The Commercial Press
August 2012

第 10 版修订说明

《新华字典》1953 年首次出版，此后经多次修订再版，深受广大读者欢迎。为了使《新华字典》在新世纪更好地服务于社会，我们在第 9 版的基础上，对字典进行了修订。

修订中我们认真研究了 1953 年原版的风格特点，对比参考了历次修订版本，在加强规范性和科学性的同时，特别注重保持原书的简明性和实用性。

本次修订的主要方面有：根据中华人民共和国教育部、国家语言文字工作委员会发布的《第一批异形词整理表》对本字典中所涉及的异形词作了相应处理；增补了部分新词、新义、新例和少量字头，删除了部分陈旧的词条和例证；订正了一些过时的内容和个别的错误以及表述不够准确的地方；统查整理了部分体例；调整了个别字头和部分复音词的顺序；增补了几幅插图和一个附录《地质年代简表》；按照国家有关规定重新编制了《部首检字表》。

本次修订吸收了一些读者意见，得到了有关专家和商务印书馆的热情帮助和支持，在此谨表谢意。欢迎广大读者继续提出宝贵意见。

中国社会科学院语言研究所

2003 年 10 月

About the 10th Revised Edition

The Xinhua Dictionary, first published in 1953 and revised for many editions, has been well received by the reading public. The present revision is done on the basis of the 9th edition in order to better serve the society in the new century.

In doing the revision, we have made a serious study of styles and features of the 1953 edition and made comparisons and references to all the other successive editions. Special attention has been paid to preserving the conciseness and practicality of the original edition, in addition to its further conformity to the criteria and the scientific spirit.

In the present revision, the variant forms of the same word in the dictionary are adjusted according to the First Batch of Standardized Forms of Chinese Words with Non-Standardized Variant Forms issued by the Ministry of Education and the State Language Working Committee of the

PRC. Some new words, new meanings, new examples, and a few headwords are added, while some obsolete entries and examples are deleted. Some out-of-date material, errors and inaccuracies are corrected. Some format guidelines are checked and rearranged throughout the dictionary. The order of some headwords and multi-syllabic words are adjusted. Some illustrations and an appendix the Table of Geological Time Scale are added. The Radical Index is re-compiled according to the relevant national stipulations.

We would like to extend our thanks to the readers for their suggestions, and to the experts and The Commercial Press for their assistance and support during our revision process. We sincerely hope that the readers will continue to offer their comments and suggestions to the dictionary.

Language Research Institute

Chinese Academy of Social Sciences

October 2003

第 9 版修订说明

1. 本字典是一部小型语文工具书，主要供中小学教师和学生使用，中等文化程度以上的读者也可参考。

2. 本次修订是在 1992 年重排本的基础上进行的。保持字典原有规模和特点，同时，全面认真地贯彻执行国家颁布的语言文字法令、法规以及有关规范的国家标准，注意吸收了语言文字研究及相关学科的最新成果，对字形、字音、释义、例证、体例以及附录内容作了较为全面的修改和调整。

3. 本次修订根据《简化字总表》、《现代汉语通用字表》、《第一批异体字整理表》增删、调整了字头，明确区分了字头后的繁体字、异体字；根据《普通话异读词审音表》改动了少数字音；根据《现代汉语通用字笔顺规范》调整了部首的排列顺序、检字表和字头的字的排列顺序。

4. 本次修订还根据最新资料修改了附录，增加了《我国各省、直辖市、自治区及省会(或首府)名称表》。

5. 修订后的字典计收单字(包括繁体字、异体字)10 000余个，带注解的复音词3 500余个，附录 9 种，综合插图 9 幅。

6.《新华字典》原由新华辞书社编写。1956 年，新华辞书社并入当时的中国科学院语言研究所词典编辑室。中国社会科学院语言研究所负责本次修订。

1998 年 5 月

About the 9th Revised Edition

1. This is a pocket-sized dictionary of Chinese words, chiefly for teachers and students in primary and secondary schools, and also for readers above the intermediate level.

2. This revision is done on the basis the 1992 reprinting of the dictionary with its original scale and features. A comparatively whole-scale revision and adjustment have been made to update the word-forms, pronunciations, definitions, examples, formats and appendices in the light of the latest achievements in linguistics and other related disciplines and in conformity with the decrees, statutes and criteria concerning the Chinese language and written characters, as well as the national standards issued by the government.

3. Headwords in this revised edition are added, deleted or adjusted in accordance with the Final List of Simplified Characters, the Table of Frequently Used Characters in Modern Chinese

and the First Batch of Standardized Forms of Chinese Characters with Non-Standardized Variant Forms, to distinguish clearly the traditional characters and the variant forms of characters listed after the headwords. Pronunciations of a few characters are altered according to the Table of Authorized Pronunciation for Variants in Putonghua. The arrangement of the radicals, the arrangement of characters in the Radical Index, and the headwords are adjusted in accordance with the Criteria for the Stroke Order of Frequently Used Characters in Modern Chinese.

4. The appendices of the dictionary are revised in the light of the latest material, with the addition of the Table of Provinces, Municipalities, Autonomous Regions and Provincial Capitals in China.

5. This revised dictionary contains 10,000 odd Chinese characters (including characters of complex forms and variant forms), 3,500 odd multi-syllabic words with definitions, 9 appendices, and 9 comprehensive illustrations.

6. The Xinhua Dictionary was originally compiled by Xinhua Lexicographical Publishing House, which was annexed into the Dictionary Editing Department of the Language Research Institute of the Chinese Academy of Sciences in 1956. The Language Research Institute of the Chinese Academy of Social Sciences takes charge of the present revision of the dictionary.

May 1998

凡例

一、本字典的字头用大字排印。繁体字、异体字附在字头后面，外加圆括弧。不带＊号的为繁体字，带一个＊号的为《第一批异体字整理表》中的异体字，带两个＊号的是《第一批异体字整理表》以外的异体字。有些繁体字、异体字的左上方附有义项数码，表示只适用于某义项；有些繁体字、异体字的左上方带个小三角（△），表示另外也做字头。

二、一个字头有几个音的，就列为几个字头，各在注音前面分别用㈠㈡㈢等表明次第，注解之末附列有其余的音及其所见页码。

三、字头下所收的带注解的复音词或词组，外加［ ］号，按音序排列。意义上有联系的，分别放在重点字的相关义项之下；意义上联系不明确的，放在本字注解最后，并另起行。对于《第一批异形词整理表》中的非推荐词形，在左上角加＊号，外加圆括号，附列于推荐词形之后。

四、本字典的字音依据普通话的语音系统，用汉语拼音字母及注音字母标音。

五、有些字头连注两个音，第二个音后面附注“(又)”字，表示“又音”。有时某义项内注“又某音”，表示“又音”用于某义。

六、有些字头注有“旧读”，表示旧来读法不同。有时某义项内注“旧读”，表示某义旧读不同。

七、对行文中一些生僻字、多音字或复音词中读轻声的字加注读音。

八、字头的意义不止一项的，分条注解，用❶❷❸等表示义项。一个义项下如再分条，用1、2、3等表示。[ ]中的复音词或词组，如分条注解，也用1、2、3等表示。

九、注解中㊀、喻、转的用法如下：

㊀表示由原义引申出来的意义。如312页“急jí”字条❶义下，“㊀气恼，发怒”是由“焦躁”引申出来的。

喻表示由比喻形成的意义。如359页“晶jīng”字条[结晶]下注“喻成果”。

转表示由原义、故事、成语等转化而成的意义。如330页“简jiǎn”字条❶义下注“转书信”，765页“推tuī”字条❶义下[推敲]条注“转斟酌文章字句”。

十、注解中的（一子）、（一儿）、（一头）表示本字可以加上这类词尾，构成大致同义的词，不另加注解。

十一、注解中的（叠）表示本字可以重叠。放在注解前的表示必须叠用，如343页“喈”字；放在注解后的表示可叠也可不叠，如451页“凛”字❷。

十二、注解中的连表示本字可以跟一个意义相同或相近的字并列起来构成大致同义的词，不另加注解。

十三、注解中的〈方〉表示本字是方言地区用的字或者本义项所注的是方言地区的用法。〈古〉表示本字是古代用的字或者本义项所注的是古代的用法。

十四、从兄弟民族语言中来的词，加注民族简称。如260页“哈 hǎ”字条[哈达]是从藏语来的，注“(藏)”。

十五、有些词的后面注“(外)”字，表示是近代的外来语。历史上相沿已久的外来语，一般不注来源。

十六、在注解后举例中，用“～”号代替本字。一个“～”号只代替一个字。

十七、“—”和“-”(短横)的用法如下：

1. 在“—子、—儿、—头”中，在“㊟”字后，“—”代替本字。

2. 在拼音字母标音中，“—”代替省略的音节，“-”(短横)表示连接转行的音节。

十八、“·”(圆点)用于注音字母的标音时，表示后面的音节读轻声。

Guide to the Text

1. The headwords in the dictionary are printed in the larger type. The Chinese characters of the original complex forms or variant forms are placed in the parentheses following the headwords. If a character without an asterisk (*) following it, it is of the complex form; if it has an asterisk (*) following it, it is of the variant form collected in the First Batch of Standardized Forms of Chinese Characters with Non-standardized Variant Forms (FBSFCCNVF); if it has two asterisks, it is of the variant form not collected in FBSFCCNVF. The small number to the upper left of some complex-formed or variant-formed characters indicates that these characters are applicable only in certain senses while a small triangle (△) to the upper left of some complex-formed or variant-formed characters indicates that these characters are also used as headwords.

2. A headword with more than one pronunciation is treated as separate entries with marks ㊀, ㊁, ㊂ etc. before the pronunciation to indicate its sequence. At the end of its definition, the other pronunciations and their

page numbers therein are listed for cross references.

3. The multi-syllabic words or phrases with definitions under a headword are placed in square brackets [ ] in the order of their phonetic sequences. The words semantically related to the headword are placed under their relevant senses and those not closely related semantically are placed at the end of the definitions in a separate line. The non-recommended forms of the characters in the First Batch of Standardized Forms of Chinese Words with Non-standardized Variant Forms are placed after the recommended ones with an asterisk (*) in the parentheses to its upper left.

4. The pronunciation system adopted in this dictionary is that of mandarin Chinese (*putonghua*) and every entry is noted with the Chinese phonetic transcription (*hanyu pinyin*) and the Phonetic Symbols of the Chinese Language (*hanyu zhuyin*).

5. Some headwords have two phonetic transcriptions and the second one is noted with (又 also), which means "also pronounced". Sometimes in certain senses there is a label "又某音", which indicates that the pronunciation is only applicable to this sense of the character.

6. Some headwords are noted with "(旧读 formerly

pronounced)", which indicates that there was a different pronunciation in the former times. When this label appears in a certain sense of a character, it indicates that the former pronunciation is only applicable to this sense of the character.

7. Rarely used characters, polysyllabic characters or multi-syllabic words with a neutral-tone character are specially noted in the pronunciation.

8. When there are more than one sense in the definition of the headword, these senses are respectively marked with ❶, ❷, ❸ etc. If there are sub-senses under a sense, they are marked with 1, 2, 3 etc. If polysyllabic characters or multi-syllabic words in the square brackets [ ] need to be noted with different sense items, they are also marked with 1, 2, 3 etc.

9. The use of labels, "㉄ extension, ㊟ metaphor, ㉟ transfer", is as follows:

The label "㉄ extension" indicates that the meaning of the character here is extended from its original meaning. For instance, "㉄ extension 气恼，发怒 irritated; annoyed" under the definition ❶, entry "急 jí", on page 312 is extended from "焦躁 impatient; anxious."

The label "㊟ metaphor" indicates that the meaning of the character here is used figuratively. For instance, [结

晶] under the entry of "晶 jīng" on page 359 is defined as "[喻] metaphor 成果 achievement."

The label "[转] transfer" indicates that the meaning of the character here is transferred from its original meaning, a story, or a proverb, etc. For instance, the definition under the entry of "简 jiǎn" on page 330 is noted with "[转] transfer 书信 letters" and the definition of [推敲] under the entry of "推 tuī" on 765 is noted with "[转] transfer 斟酌文章字句 to weigh (one's words); to deliberate."

10. Such Chinese suffixes as (一子), (一儿), and (一头) in the definition mean that they can be added to the headword to form its synonymous word without a further definition.

11. The label (叠 reduplication) in the definition means that the character can be reduplicated. When it is placed before the definition, it indicates that the character must be reduplicated in use, such as in the case of "喈" on page 343. When it is placed after the definition, it indicates that the character can be either reduplicated or used singly such as in the case of "凛" on page 451.

12. The label "[连] doublet" in the definition indicates that the character can be used together with a synonymous or near synonymous character to form a near-synonymous expression without a further definition.

13. The label "〈方 dialect〉" in the definition indicates that the character is used in dialect areas or this sense defines its use in a dialect area. The label "〈古 archaism〉" means that the character is an archaic one, or this sense defines its use in the ancient times.

14. If a character is borrowed from the language of an ethnic minority of China, it is marked with the shortened form of its ethnic group. For instance, the word [哈达] under the entry of 哈 hǎ on page 260 marked with (藏 of Tibetan ethnic group) indicates that it is borrowed from Tibetan.

15. Some characters followed by (外 loanword) means that they are modern loanwords. Loanwords that have become common through long usage are not given their origins.

16. In the illustration examples after a definition, the sign "～" replaces the illustrated character. One "～" replaces only one character.

17. The use of "一" and "-" is as follows:

1) When used in "一子, 一儿, and 一头" or after the label "㊥ doublet", the sign "-" replaces the headword.

2) The sign "-" in the phonetic transcriptions replaces the omitted syllable and the hyphen "-" is used to connect the syllable which is moved to the next line.

18. The dot "·" used in the phonetic symbols of the Chinese characters shows that the following symbol is in the neutral tone.

汉语拼音音节索引

Index of Syllables of Hanyupinyin

1. 每一音节后举一字做例，可按例字读音去查同音的字。
There's an example character after each syllable. Characters with the same pronunciation shall be consulted in accordance with the pronunciation of this example character.
2. 数字指本字典正文页码。
The numeral indicates the page number of the text in this dictionary.

新旧字形对照表

（字形后圆圈内的数字表示字形的笔画数）

Old and New Forms of Characters

(Numbers in circles indicate number of strokes)

旧字形 Old form	新字形 New form	新字举例 Example
艹④	艹③	花草
辶④	辶③	连速
幵⑥	开④	型形
丰④	丰④	艳沣
巨⑤	巨④	苣渠
屯④	屯④	纯顿
瓦⑤	瓦④	瓶瓷
反④	反④	板饭
丑④	丑④	纽杻
犮⑤	犮⑤	拔茇
印⑥	印⑤	茚
耒⑥	耒⑥	耕耘
呂⑦	吕⑥	侣营
攸⑦	攸⑥	修倏
爭⑧	争⑥	净静
产⑥	产⑥	彦産
𦍌⑦	𦍌⑥	差养
幷⑧	并⑥	屏拼
吳⑦	吴⑦	蜈虞
角⑦	角⑦	解确
奐⑨	奂⑦	换痪
㡀⑧	㡀⑦	敝弊
𠭥⑧	𠭥⑦	敢嚴
者⑨	者⑧	都著

旧字形 Old form	新字形 New form	新字举例 Example
直⑧	直⑧	值植
黽⑧	黾⑧	绳鼋
咼⑨	咼⑧	過蝸
垂⑨	垂⑧	睡郵
飠⑨	飠⑧	飲飽
郎⑨	郎⑧	廊螂
彔⑧	录⑧	渌箓
𥁕⑩	昷⑨	温瘟
骨⑩	骨⑨	滑骼
鬼⑩	鬼⑨	槐嵬
俞⑨	俞⑨	偷渝
既⑪	既⑨	溉厩
蚤⑩	蚤⑨	搔骚
敖⑪	敖⑩	傲遨
莽⑫	莽⑩	漭蟒
眞⑩	真⑩	慎填
䍃⑩	䍃⑩	摇遥
殺⑪	殺⑩	摋鎩
黃⑫	黄⑪	廣横
虛⑫	虚⑪	墟歔
異⑫	異⑪	冀戴
象⑫	象⑪	像橡
奧⑬	奥⑫	澳襖
普⑬	普⑫	谱氆

部首检字表
Radical Index

〔说明〕1. 本表采用的部首依据《汉字统一部首表(草案)》,共201部;编排次序依据《GB13000.1字符集汉字笔顺规范》和《GB13000.1字符集汉字字序(笔画序)规范》,按笔画数由少到多顺序排列,同画数的,按起笔笔形横(一)、竖(丨)、撇(丿)、点(丶)、折(乛)顺序排列,第一笔相同的,按第二笔,依次类推。2. 在《部首目录》中,主部首的左边标有部首序号;附形部首大多加圆括号单立,其左边的部首序号加有方括号。3. 在《检字表》中,繁体字和异体字加有圆括号;同部首的字按除去部首笔画以外的画数排列。4. 检字时,需先在《部首目录》里查出待查的字所属部首的页码,然后再查《检字表》。5. 为方便读者查检,有些字分收在几个部首内。如“思”字在“田”部和“心”部都能查到。6.《检字表》后面另有《难检字笔画索引》备查。

[Directions] 1. The radicals in this Radical Index is adopted from The Uniform Chinese Character Radical Index (draft), which totals 201 volumes; the layout sequence is based on The Criterion on Stroke Orders of the Chinese Character in GB13000.1 Character Set and The Criterion on Character Orders (Stroke Orders) of the Chinese Character in GB13000.1 Character Set, and arranged in accordance with the stroke numbers increasingly; as to characters with the same stroke number, the layout sequence is arranged in accordance with the starting stroke of horizontal (一), vertical (丨), left-falling stroke(丿), dot (丶) and the turning stroke(乛). If the first starting stroke is still the same, the second will in turn function. 2. In List of Radicals, the sequence number of the radicals is marked on the left of the major radical; the form-attached radicals are most listed solely with parenthesis, and the radical numbers to the left are marked with square brackets. 3. In Character Index, the original complex form of a simplified Chinese character and the variant form of a Chinese character are both marked with parenthesis; characters of the same radical shall be arranged in accordance with the stroke numbers except the same radical number. 4. When consulting a character, one shall get to know the radical page number of the will-be-consulted characters in List of Radicals, then to consult Character Index. 5. For readers' convenience, some characters are listed under separate radicals, e. g., 思 is listed under both radicals 田 and 心. 6. Following Character Index, Stroke Index for Difficult Characters is provided.

(一) 部首目录
List of Radicals

(部首左边的号码是部首序号;右边的号码指检字表的页码。)
(The number to the left of the radicals is the sequence number of the radical and the number to the right is the page number of the *Index*.)

（二）检字表

Character Index

（字右边的号码指正文的页码；带圆括号的字是繁体字或异体字。）

(The number to the right of each character indicates the page number in the dictionary. Characters in parentheses are the original complex forms or variant forms.)

9 画

10—12 画

13 画以上

［75］
⺜部

76
贝部

2—4 画

5 画

6—7 画

8 画

9 画以上

［76］
貝部

5—8 画

9 画以上

77
水部

[77] 氵部

[88]
⺝部

89
氏部

90
欠部

91
风部

[91]
風部

92 殳部

93 文部

94 方部

95 火部

［98］
忄部

103
龙部

［103］
龍部

104
业部

105
目部

106 田部

107 罒部

108 皿部

109 生部

110 矢部

111 禾部

(癉) 129
癌 3
(癆) 419
癞 413
(癤) 343
(癒) 922
癔 893
癜 148
癖 563

14 画以上

(癟) 48
49
癣 850
(癡) 88
(癢) 872
(癥) 971
癫 145
(癧) 432
(癮) 898
癯 619
(癰) 904
(癱) 727

116 立部

立 433

1 画

产 74

3—6 画

妾 605
竖 695
亲 606
612
竑 278
彦 868
飒 644
站 954
竞 362
(竝) 52
(竚) 996
章 955
竟 362
(産) 74
翊 892
翌 892

7 画以上

竦 707
童 755
(竢) 706
竣 379
(豎) 695
靖 363
意 893
竭 347
端 163
(競) 362
(贑) 219
赣 219

117 穴部

穴 851

1—6 画

(穵) 771
究 364
穷 613
空 394
395
帘 438
穸 799
穹 614
(穽) 360
突 760
穿 100
窀 1005
窃 605
窆 43
窍 603
窅 876
窄 951
窌 444
窎 149
窈 876
窒 982
窑 874
窕 748
(窓) 102

7 画以上

窜 112
窝 791
窖 342
窗 102
窘 363
窥 404
窦 159
窠 388
(窩) 791
窣 710
窟 397
窬 917
窨 854
899
窭 372
(窪) 771
(窮) 613
窳 919
(窯) 874
(窰) 874
(窶) 372
(窻) 102
窸 802
窿 461
窾 401
(竄) 112
(竅) 603
(竇) 159
(竈) 942
(竊) 605

118 疋部

(疋) 562
胥 844
疍 128
蛋 129
楚 98
疐 986
疑 885

[118] ⺪部

(疎) 691
疏 691

119 皮部

皮 560
皱 991
(皰) 554
皲 377
颇 573
皴 114
(皺) 991
(皷) 948

120 癶部

癸 254
登 137
(發) 179
凳 138

121 矛部

矛 489
柔 636
矜 248
351
607
(務) 797
矞 923
(穫) 607
(矟) 636
蟊 489

122 耒部

耒 424
耔 1011
耕 229
耘 932
耖 80
耗 268
耙 14
546
耜 706
耞 321
耠 302
耢 421
(耡) 97
耥 730
732
耦 545
耧 463
耩 336
耨 541
耬 14
耪 552
(耬) 463
(耮) 421
耰 908
(耰) 14
穰 289
耱 517

123 老部

老 419
耆 585
耄 490
耋 151

[123] 耂部

考 386
老 419
孝 825
者 964
(煑) 995
煮 995
翥 998

124 耳部

耳 177

2 画

耵 152
耶 877
878
取 620

3 画

耷 118

132 肉部

133 缶部

134 舌部

135 竹(⺮)部

136 臼部

[136] 𦥑部

137 自部

138 血部

139 舟部

140 色部

141 齐部

[141] 齊部

142 衣部

[142] 衤部

2—5 画

[145] 肀部

[145] 𦘒部

[145] 聿部

146 艮部

[146] 皀部

147 羽部

3—8 画

9 画以上

148 糸部

1 画

4—6 画

8 画以上

[148] 纟部

2—3 画

4 画

5 画

6 画

7 画

[148] 糹部

149 麦部

[149] 麥部

150 走部

151 赤部

7—8 画

9—10 画

11 画

12 画

13 画以上

159 邑部

[159] 阝(在右)部

2—4 画

5 画

6 画

7 画

8 画

9 画

10—11 画

12 画以上

160 身部

161 采部

162 谷部

163 豸部

164 龟部

[164] 龜部

165 角部

166 言部

2—7 画

8—12 画

13 画以上

[166] 讠部

2 画

3 画

176 金部

[176] 钅部

177 鱼部

183 香部

184 鬼部

185 食部

[185] 饣部

2—4 画

5—6 画

7—8 画

9—11 画

12 画以上

[185] 飠部

186 音部

187 首部

188 髟部

189 鬲部

190 鬥部

（三）难检字笔画索引
Stroke Index for Difficult Characters

（字右边的号码指正文的页码；带圆括号的字是繁体字或异体字。）
(The number to the right of each character indicates the page number in the dictionary. Characters in parentheses are the original complex forms or variant forms.)

A Y

A Y

阿 ㊀ ā Y 〈方 ***dialect***〉词头 ***prefix*** **1** 加在排行、小名或姓的前面(used before a number denoting order of seniority in a family, a monosyllabic pet name or a surname):～大 *Ah Da* (*The Eldest*) | ～根 *Ah Gen* | ～王 *Ah Wang* **2** 加在某些亲属称谓的前面(used before some kinship terms):～妹 *sis* | ～公 *grandpa; granddad* [阿姨] **1** 称跟父母同辈的女性(term of address for a woman of one's parent's generation) auntie; aunt **2** 对保育员或保姆等的称呼(term of address for a nanny or a housemaid) *Ayi* **3** 〈方 ***dialect***〉姨母 auntie; aunt [阿昌族]我国少数民族,参看附表(see the appendix) the Achang ethnic group, one of the ethnic minorities of China

㊁ ē 见 172 页 see p172

呵 ㊀ ā Y 同"啊㊀"same as 啊㊀

㊁ á 见 1 页 see p1

㊂ ǎ 见 2 页 see p2

㊃ à 见 2 页 see p2

㊄ a 见 2 页 see p2

㊅ hē 见 269 页 see p269

啊 ㊀ ā Y 叹词 ***interjection***, 表示赞叹或惊异(used to express surprise or admiration) ah; oh:～,这花多好哇! *Ah, what a lovely flower!* | ～,下雪了! *Oh, it's snowing!*

㊁ á 见 1 页 see p1

㊂ ǎ 见 2 页 see p2

㊃ à 见 2 页 see p2

㊄ a 见 2 页 see p2

锕 ā Y 一种放射性元素(符号 Ac) actinium (Ac)

腌 ㊁ ā Y [腌臜](—za) 〈方 ***dialect***〉不干净 dirty; filthy

㊀ yān 见 862 页 see p862

呵 ㊁ á Ý 同"啊㊁"same as 啊㊁

㊀ ā 见 1 页 see p1

㊂ ǎ 见 2 页 see p2

㊃ à 见 2 页 see p2

㊄ a 见 2 页 see p2

㊅ hē 见 269 页 see p269

啊 ㊁ á Ý 叹词 ***interjection***, 表示追问(used to press for an answer or to ask for a repetition of sth just said) pardon; what; well:～,你说什么? *Pardon, what did you say?* | ～,你再说! *Well, say it again!*

㊀ ā 见 1 页 see p1

㊂ ǎ 见 2 页 see p2

㊃ à 见 2 页 see p2

㊄ a 见 2 页 see p2

嗄 ㊀ á Ý 同"啊㊁" same as 啊㊁

A

㊁ shà 见 651 页 see p651

呵 ㊂ ǎ ㄚˇ 同"啊㊂" same as 啊㊂
㊀ ā 见 1 页 see p1
㊁ á 见 1 页 see p1
㊃ à 见 2 页 see p2
㊄ a 见 2 页 see p2
㊅ hē 见 269 页 see p269

啊 ㊂ ǎ ㄚˇ 叹词 ***interjection***，表示疑惑(used to express doubt) eh; what:～，这是怎么回事？*Eh, what's the matter?*
㊀ ā 见 1 页 see p1
㊁ á 见 1 页 see p1
㊃ à 见 2 页 see p2
㊄ a 见 2 页 see p2

呵 ㊃ à ㄚˋ 同"啊㊃" same as 啊㊃
㊀ ā 见 1 页 see p1
㊁ á 见 1 页 see p1
㊂ ǎ 见 2 页 see p2
㊄ a 见 2 页 see p2
㊅ hē 见 269 页 see p269

啊 ㊃ à ㄚˋ 叹词 ***interjection*** **1** 表示应诺或醒悟(音较短)(used to express agreement or sudden realization in a shorter syllable) er; yeah:～，好吧。*Yeah, agreed.* | ～，原来是你呀！*Oh, it's you!* **2** 表示惊异或赞叹(音较长)(used to express surprise or admiration in a longer syllable) ah; oh:～，伟大的祖国！*Ah, our great motherland!*
㊀ ā 见 1 页 see p1
㊁ á 见 1 页 see p1
㊂ ǎ 见 2 页 see p2
㊄ a 见 2 页 see p2

呵 ㊄ a ·ㄚ 同"啊㊄" same as 啊㊄
㊀ ā 见 1 页 see p1
㊁ á 见 1 页 see p1
㊂ ǎ 见 2 页 see p2
㊃ à 见 2 页 see p2
㊅ hē 见 269 页 see p269

啊 ㊄ a ·ㄚ 助词 ***auxiliary*** **1** 用在句末，表示赞叹、催促、嘱咐等语气(常因前面字音不同而发生变音，可用不同的字来表示)[used at the end of a sentence to express admiration, urging, exhortation, etc (often changed into variant pronunciations or forms owing to the pronunciation of the word before it)]: 快些来～(呀)！*Hurry up!* | 您好～(哇)！*How are things with you?* | 同志们加油干～(哪)！*Work harder, comrades!* **2** 用在列举的事项之后(used after each item enumerated): 纸～、笔～，摆满了一桌子。*The table is littered with paper and pens.*
㊀ ā 见 1 页 see p1
㊁ á 见 1 页 see p1
㊂ ǎ 见 2 页 see p2
㊃ à 见 2 页 see p2

AI ㄞ

哎 āi ㄞ 叹词 ***interjection***，表示不满或提醒(used to express disapproval or to remind sb of sth) hey; why:～，你怎么能这么说呢！*Why, how can you talk like this?* | ～，你们

看，谁来了！*Hey, look and see who's coming!* ［哎呀］叹词***interjection***，表示惊讶(used to express surprise) Oh, my! ［哎哟］(—yō)叹词***interjection***，表示惊讶、痛苦(used to express astonishment or pain) oh, dear, ouch

哀 āi ㄞ ❶悲痛 sorrow; grief (连 ***doublet*** 悲— sadness; woe)：喜怒～乐 *happiness, anger, sorrow and joy — the whole gamut of human emotions; joy and anger, weal and woe* ❷悼念 to condole; to mourn：默～ *to stand in silent tribute* ❸怜悯，同情 to feel pity for; to sympathize：～怜 *to feel pity for*｜～其不幸 *to feel pity for sb's misfortune*

锿 āi ㄞ 一种人造的放射性元素(符号 Es) einsteinium (Es)

埃 āi ㄞ 灰尘 dirt; dust (连 ***doublet*** 尘— dirt; dust)

挨 ㊀ āi ㄞ ❶靠近 near; close to; next to：居民区～着一条河。*The residential area is close to a river.* ❷顺着(一定次序) in sequence; in the order of：～家查问 *to make enquiries from door to door*｜～着号叫 *to call in numerical order*

㊁ ái 见 3 页 see p3

唉 ㊀ āi ㄞ 叹词 ***interjection*** **1** 表示答应(used to express response) yeah：～，听见了。*Yeah, I've heard it.* **2** 表示叹息(used to express regret) alas：～，一天的工夫又白费了。*Alas! Another day's work is wasted.* **3** 表示招呼(used to hail sb) hi; hey：～，你来一下。*Hey! you come here!*

㊁ ài 见 4 页 see p4

娭 āi ㄞ ［娭毑］(—jiě)〈方 ***dialect***〉**1** 称祖母(used as a form of address for one's paternal grandmother) grandma **2** 尊称年老的妇人(used as a respectful form of address for elderly women) grandma

嗳(噯) ㊂ āi ㄞ 同"哎" same as 哎

㊀ ǎi 见 4 页 see p4

㊁ ài 见 5 页 see p5

挨(**捱) ㊁ ái ㄞ ❶遭受，亲身受到 to suffer; to endure：～饿 *to be starved; to go hungry*｜～打 *to be beaten; to catch (or get) a toco*｜～骂 *to be scolded* ❷困难地度过(岁月) to drag out (one's life)：～日子 *to drag out a miserable existence* ❸拖延 to delay; to stall：别～磨了，快走吧。*Stop stalling and get going!*

㊀ āi 见 3 页 see p3

騃 ái ㄞ 傻 foolish; stupid：痴～ *idiotic*

皑(皚) ái ㄞ 白 pure-white; snow-white (叠 ***reduplication***)：～～白雪 *dazzling white snow*

癌 ái ㄞ(旧读 formerly yán) 生物体细胞由于某些致癌因素的作用，变成恶性增生细胞所形成的恶性肿瘤 cancer;

malignant tumour：胃～ *stomach cancer*｜肝～*liver cancer*

毐 ǎi ㄞ 用于人名（Ai，used in a given name）嫪毐（Lào—），战国时秦国人 Lao Ai，a man of the Qin state during the Warring States Period

欸 ㊄ ǎi ㄞ［欸乃］（—nǎi）拟声词 ***onomatopoeia***，摇橹声（used to express the sound of sculling）：～～一声山水绿。*The boat sculls past the green river and mountain.*

㊀ ē 见 174 页 see p174

㊁ é 见 175 页 see p175

㊂ ě 见 175 页 see p175

㊃ è 见 175 页 see p175

嗳（噯）㊀ ǎi ㄞ 叹词 ***interjection***，表示否定或不同意（used to express negation or disagreement）no：～，别那么说。*No，don't talk like this.*｜～，不是这样放。*No，that's not the right way to put it.*

㊁ ài 见 5 页 see p5

㊂ āi 见 3 页 see p3

矮 ǎi ㄞ 人的身材短（of stature）short：他比他哥哥～。*He is shorter than his elder brother.* ㊊ ***extension*** **1** 高度小的（of height）short；low：几棵小～树 *a few short trees* **2** 等级、地位低（of rank or status）low；inferior to：我比他～一级。*I'm a grade younger than he.*

蔼 ǎi ㄞ 和气，和善 amiable；friendly：对人很和～*to be amiable to others*｜～然可亲 *amiable*

霭 ǎi ㄞ 云气 mist；haze：云～*thin，floating clouds*｜暮～*evening mist；evening haze*

艾 ㊀ ài ㄞ ❶多年生草本植物，开黄色小花，叶制成艾绒，可供灸病用 Chinese mugwort（*Artemisia argyi*）❷止，绝 to halt；to end：方兴未～*to be fast unfolding；to be in the ascendant* ❸漂亮，美 pretty；beautiful：少～（年轻漂亮的人）*handsome young man* ❹姓 Ai，a surname

［艾滋病］获得性免疫缺陷综合征的通称。由人类免疫缺陷病毒引起，常并发多种感染及恶性肿瘤的疾病。主要通过性接触、血液和母婴等途径迅速传播，病死率高 AIDS（acquired immune deficiency syndrome）

㊁ yì 见 888 页 see p888

砹 ài ㄞ 一种放射性元素（符号 At）astatine（At）

唉 ㊁ ài ㄞ 叹词 ***interjection***，表示伤感或惋惜（used to express sadness or regret）alas：～，病了两个月，把工作都耽搁了。*Alas，the work was delayed as I was ill for two months.*

㊀ āi 见 3 页 see p3

爱（愛）ài ㄞ ❶喜爱，对人或事物有深挚的感情 to love；to have profound affection for：拥军～民 *to support the army and cherish the people*｜～祖国 *to love one's motherland*｜～人民 *to love the people*｜友～ *friendly af-*

fection; fraternal love ❷喜好 to be fond of; to like: ～游泳 *to be fond of swimming* | ～干净 *to like cleanliness* | ～劳动 *to enjoy physical labour* ❸爱惜，爱护 to cherish; to take good care of: ～集体荣誉 *to cherish the honour of the collective* ❹容易 to be apt to; to be likely to: 铁～生锈。*Iron rusts easily.*

嗳(噯) ㊀ ài ㄞ 叹词 ***interjection***，表示懊恼、悔恨(used to express regret or annoyance) alas; oh: ～，早知道是这样，我就不来了。*Oh! I wouldn't have come if I had known it.*
㊁ ǎi 见 4 页 see p4
㊂ āi 见 3 页 see p3

嫒(嬡) ài ㄞ [令嫒][令爱]对对方女儿的尊称(used as a respectful form of address for sb's daughter) your daughter

瑷(璦) ài ㄞ [瑷珲](—huī)地名，在黑龙江省。今作"爱辉"(now written as 爱辉) Aihui (*or* Aigun), a place in Heilongjiang Province

叆(靉) ài ㄞ [叆叇](—dài)云彩很厚的样子 overcast; enveloped in clouds

暧(曖) ài ㄞ 日光昏暗(of daylight) dim (叠 ***reduplication***) [暧昧] **1** 态度不明朗(of attitude, intention, etc) ambiguous; ambivalent **2** 行为不光明(of behaviour) dubious

餲 ㊀ ài ㄞ 食物经久而变味(of food) spoiled in flavour
㊁ hé 见 272 页 see p272

隘 ài ㄞ ❶险要的地方 pass: 要～*strategic pass* ❷狭小 narrow (㊟ ***doublet*** 狭 — narrow): 气量狭～*narrow-minded*

嗌 ㊀ ài ㄞ 噎，食物塞住嗓子 to be choked (with food)
㊁ yì 见 892 页 see p892

碍(礙) ài ㄞ 妨害，阻挡 to hinder; to be in the way of: ～口(不便说) *to be too embarrassed to mention sth* | ～事不～事? *Am I in the way?* | ～手～脚 *to be in the way*

AN ㄢ

厂 ㊀ ān ㄢ 同"庵"(多用于人名)(an, usually used in a given name) same as 庵
㊁ chǎng 见 77 页 see p77

广 ㊁ ān ㄢ 同"庵"(多用于人名)(an, usually used in a given name) same as 庵
㊀ guǎng 见 251 页 see p251

安 ān ㄢ ❶平静，稳定 calm; stable: ～定 *stable* | ～心(心情安定) *to be at ease; to set one's mind at rest* | ～居乐业 *to live and work in peace and contentment* ❷使平静，使安定(多指心情)(usually used to denote one's mood) to stabilize; to set at ease: ～神 *to soothe one's nerves* | ～民告示 *a notice to reassure the public* ❸

安全，平安，跟“危”相对（the opposite of 危）safe; secure: ～康 *safe and sound* | 治～ *public security; public order* | 转危为～ *to pull through a crisis and restore security* ❹安置，装设 to fix; to install（[连] ***doublet*** 一装 to install）: ～排 *to arrange* | ～营扎寨 *to pitch a camp* | ～电灯 *to install electric lights* ❺存着，怀着（多指不好的念头）（usually used to denote a bad intention）to be up to; to harbour: 你～的什么心？*What on earth are you up to?* ❻代词 **pronoun**，哪里 where; how: 而今～在？*Where is it now?* | ～能如此？*How can you behave like this?* ❼电流强度单位名安培的简称（符号 A）ampere (A)

桉 ān ㄢ 桉树，常绿乔木，树干高而直，木质坚韧，供建筑用，树皮和叶都可入药，叶又可提桉油，树皮又可提鞣料。也叫“有加利树”(also called 有加利树) eucalyptus (*Eucalyptus*)

氨 ān ㄢ 一种无机化合物，分子式 NH_3，是无色而有剧臭的气体。在高压下能变成液体，除去压力后吸收周围的热又变成气体，人造冰就是利用氨的这种性质制成的。氨又可制硝酸、肥料和炸药 ammonia

鮟 ān ㄢ [鮟鱇](—kāng) 鱼名。生在深海里，体前半部平扁，圆盘形，尾部细小，头大，口宽，全身无鳞，能发出像老人咳嗽的声音。俗叫“老头儿鱼”(popularly called 老头儿鱼) anglerfish (*Lophiiformes*)

鞍(*鞌) ān ㄢ （一子）放在骡马等背上承载重物或供人骑坐的器具 saddle

庵(*菴) ān ㄢ ❶圆形草屋 round thatched hut ❷小庙（多指尼姑居住的）(usually used to denote a nunnery) Buddhist temple: ～堂 *Buddhist nunnery*

鹌 ān ㄢ [鹌鹑](—chun) 鸟名。头小尾短，羽毛赤褐色，杂有暗黄色条纹，雄的好斗。肉、卵可以吃 quail (*Coturnix*)

谙 ān ㄢ 熟悉 to know well; to be familiar with: 不～水性 *not to know how to swim* [谙练]熟习，有经验 to be skilled in; to be proficient in

盦 ān ㄢ ❶古代一种器皿 *an*, a kind of container in ancient China ❷同“庵”(多用于人名)(an, usually used in a given name) same as 庵

垵 ǎn ㄢˇ 同“埯” same as 埯

铵 ǎn ㄢˇ 铵根，化学中一种阳性复根，以NH_4^+表示，在化合物中的地位相当于金属离子，如化肥硫铵和碳酸铵的分子中，都含有它 ammonium

俺 ǎn ㄢˇ 〈方 ***dialect***〉代词 **pronoun**，我，我们 I; we: ～村 *my village; our village* | ～们 *we* | ～那里出棉花。*We grow cotton in our village.*

埯 ǎn ㄢ ❶点播种子挖的小坑 hole for dibbling seeds ❷挖小坑点种 to dibble: ～瓜 *to dibble the melon seeds* | ～豆 *to dibble the beans* ❸(～儿)量词 ***quantifier***,用于点种的植物 (of seedlings) cluster; handful: 一～儿花生 *a cluster of peanut seedlings*

唵 ǎn ㄢ ❶ 把食物放在手里吞食 to press (sth held in one's hand) into one's mouth; to swallow: ～了几口炒米 *to swallow mouthfuls of dry-cooked rice* ❷ 佛教咒语的发声词(word used in Buddhist incantations) om; aum

揞 ǎn ㄢ 用手指把药粉等按在伤口上 to apply (medicinal powder, etc) onto a wound

犴 ㊁ àn ㄢ 见 38 页"狴"字条"狴犴"(bì—) see 狴犴 on p38

㊀ hān 见 262 页 see p262

岸 àn ㄢ ❶江、河、湖、海等水边的陆地 bank; shore; coast: 河～ *river bank* | 船靠～了。*The ship has pulled in to the shore.* ❷高大 tall; high: 伟～(*of man*) *tall and sturdily built*

按 àn ㄢ ❶用手压或摁(èn) to press; to push down: ～脉 *to feel the pulse* | ～电铃 *to ring an electric bell* [按摩]一种医术,推、按、揉或抚摩人体的一定部位,帮助血液循环。也叫"推拿"(also called 推拿) massage ❷止住,压住 to stop; to keep under control: ～兵不动 *to hold one's troops where they are; to sit by, watching idly* | ～下此事先不表。*Set this topic aside for the moment.* ❸介词 ***preposition***, 依照 according to: ～理说你应该去。*Normally you ought to go.* | ～人数算 *to count according to the number of people* | ～部就班(依照程序办事) *to follow the prescribed order; to keep to the conventional way of doing things* | ～图索骥(本喻拘泥,转为根据线索去寻求) *to look for a fine horse with the aid of its picture* (to be overcautious)—*to look for sth by following up a clue* ❹经过考核研究后下论断 to make a comment after careful studies: ～语 *comment; note* | 编者～ *editor's note*

案 àn ㄢ ❶长形的桌子 long, narrow table ❷机关或团体中记事的案卷 files; archives: 备～ *to put on file; to enter* (*a case*) *in the records* | 有～可查 *to be on the record; to be documented* ❸提出计划、办法等的文件 document for a proposal: 提～ *motion; proposal* | 议～ *proposal; bill* ❹事件 incident; event: 五卅惨～ *May 30th Massacre* 特指涉及法律问题的事件(used specially for a law case): ～情 *details of a case* | 犯～ *to commit a crime* | 破～ *to solve a* (*criminal*) *case* ❺古时候端饭用的木盘 *an*, a wooden tray for serving meals in ancient

A

China：举～齐眉(形容夫妇互相敬重)(*of man and wife*) *to respect each other* ❻同"按❹" same as 按❹

胺 àn ㄢ 有机化学中，氨(NH_3)的氢原子被烃(tīng)基代替所成的化合物(通式是 $R\text{-}NH_2$) amine

暗(❶❸*闇) àn ㄢ ❶不亮，没有光，跟"明"相对(the opposite of 明) dark; dim：～中摸索 *to grope in the dark; to explore by oneself* | 这间屋子太～。*This room is too dark.* [暗淡] 昏暗，不光明 dim; gloomy：颜色～～*to be faint in colour* | 前途～～*to have a dismal future* ❷不公开的，隐藏不露的，跟"明"相对(the opposite of 明) hidden; secret：～号 *secret signal; countersign* | ～杀 *to assassinate* | 心中～喜 *to feel secretly pleased* ❸愚昧，糊涂 muddled; confused：明于知彼，～于知己 *to have a good knowledge of others but a poor knowledge of oneself; to understand others but not oneself*

黯 àn ㄢ 昏黑 obscure; gloomy [黯然] 昏暗的样子 dim; faint ⑩ ***figurative*** 心神沮丧 to be dejected; to feel low-spirited：～～泪下 *to shed tears in dejection*

ANG 尢

肮(骯) āng 尢 [肮脏](—zāng)不干净 dirty; filthy

昂 áng 尢 ❶仰，高抬 to raise (one's head)：～首挺胸 *with one's chin up and chest out; vigorous; full of vigour* ❷高，贵 high; expensive：～贵 *expensive; costly* | 价～*costly; expensive* ❸情绪高 to be in high spirits (叠 ***reduplication***)：斗志～扬 *to have a high morale; to be militant* | 慷慨激～ *to be enthusiastic and fervent* | 气～～*full of vigour*

盎 àng 尢 ❶古代的一种盆，腹大口小 *ang*, vessel of ancient China (with a big belly and a small mouth) ❷盛(shèng) brimming; abundant：春意～然。*Spring is in the air.*

AO 幺

凹 āo 幺 洼下，跟"凸"相对(the opposite of 凸) concave; hollow：～透镜 *concave lens* | ～凸不平 *bumpy; uneven*

熬(**爊、**熝) ㊁ āo 幺 煮 to stew; to boil：～菜 *to stew vegetables*

㊀ áo 见9页 see p9

敖 áo 幺 ❶同"遨" same as 遨 ❷姓 Ao, a surname

嶅 áo 幺 嶅山，山名，一在山东省新泰，一在广东省东北部 Aoshan Mountain, one in Xintai, Shandong Province, and the other in the northeast of Guangdong Province［嶅阳］地名，在山东省新泰 Aoyang, a place in Xintai, Shandong Province

遨 áo ㄠ 遨游，游逛 to stroll; to roam

嗷 áo ㄠ 拟声词 ***onomatopoeia***，嘈杂声，喊叫声 (sound of crying in pain or suffering) ow（叠 ***reduplication***）：～～待哺 (*of starving children or young animals*) *to cry for food*

廒（＊＊厫）áo ㄠ 收藏粮食的仓房 granary; barn：仓～ *granary; barn*

璈 áo ㄠ 古代的一种乐器 *ao*, a stringed musical instrument in ancient China

獒 áo ㄠ 一种凶猛的狗，比平常的狗大，善斗，能帮助人打猎 mastiff

熬 ㊀ áo ㄠ ❶久煮 to stew; to boil for a long time：～粥 *to make gruel; to cook porridge*｜～药 *to decoct medicine by boiling medicinal herbs* ❷忍受，耐苦支撑 to endure; to put up with：～夜 *to stay up late at night; to burn the midnight oil*｜～红了眼睛 *one's eyes become bloodshot* (*because he stays up late at night*)

㊁ āo 见 8 页 see p8

聱 áo ㄠ 话不顺耳 (of words) unpleasant to the ears［聱牙］文句念着不顺口 (of writings) full of awkward words and sentences：诘屈～～ *to be full of awkward words and sentences*

螯 áo ㄠ 螃蟹等甲壳动物变形的第一对脚，形状像钳子，能开合，用来取食、自卫 (of crabs, etc) pincers; chelae

謷 áo ㄠ 诋毁 to slander; to vilify：訾(zǐ)～ *to defame*［謷謷］**1** 不考虑别人的话 to ignore others' words **2** 悲叹声 lamentation with deep sorrow

鳌（＊鼇）áo ㄠ 传说中海里的大鳖 *ao*, a huge sea-turtle in legends

翱（＊翶）áo ㄠ［翱翔］(—xiáng) 展开翅膀回旋地飞 to soar; to hover：雄鹰在天空～～。*An eagle is hovering in the sky.*

鏖 áo ㄠ 鏖战，激烈地战斗 to fight hard; to be engaged in a fierce battle：赤壁～兵 *the Battle of Chibi, an important battle in the Three-Kingdoms Period*

拗（＊抝）㊀ ǎo ㄠ〈方 ***dialect***〉弯曲使断，折 to bend and break; to break：竹竿～断了。*The bamboo pole was bent and broken.*

㊁ ào 见 10 页 see p10

㊂ niù 见 540 页 see p540

袄（襖）ǎo ㄠ 有衬里的上衣 Chinese-style coat (*or* jacket)：夹～ *lined jacket*｜棉～ *cotton-padded jacket*｜皮～ *fur coat*

媪 ǎo ㄠ 年老的妇人 old woman

A

A

岙（**嶴） ào ㄠ 浙江、福建等沿海一带把山间平地叫"岙"（ao，used in a place name in Zhejiang，Fujian and other coastal provinces） strip of level land in a mountain

坳 ào ㄠ 地名用字（ao，used in a place name）：黄～（在江西省井冈山市）*Huang'ao （a place in Jinggangshan，Jiangxi Province）*

坳（*坳） ào ㄠ 山间平地 col；mountain pass：山～ *col*

拗（*抝） ㊂ ào ㄠ 不顺，不顺从 to defy；to disobey［拗口令］用声、韵、调相近的字编成的话，说快了容易错。也叫"绕口令"（also called 绕口令） tongue-twister

㊀ ǎo 见 9 页 see p9

㊂ niù 见 540 页 see p540

奡 ào ㄠ ❶同"傲" same as 傲 ❷矫健 strong and vigorous：排～（文章有力）（*of writings*） *vigorous and powerful* ❸上古人名 Ao，a person in ancient China

傲 ào ㄠ ❶自高自大 haughty and arrogant（[连] ***doublet*** 骄一 arrogant；conceited）：～慢无礼 *arrogant and insolent* ❷藐视，不屈 to defy；to refuse to yield to：红梅～霜雪。*Braving snow and frost，the red plums blossomed defiantly.*

骜 ào ㄠ ❶快马 fine horse；steed ❷马不驯良（of horses） intractable [喻] ***figurative*** 傲慢，不驯顺 arrogant；haughty：桀～不驯 *to be haughty and arrogant*

鏊 ào ㄠ 一种铁制的烙饼的炊具，平面圆形，中间稍凸 *ao*，a griddle for baking pancakes

奥 ào ㄠ 含义深，不容易懂 profound；difficult to comprehend：深～ *unfathomable；abstruse* ｜ ～妙 *mysterious；wondrously incomprehensible*

墺 ào ㄠ 可居住的地方 place fit to live in

澳 ào ㄠ ❶海边弯曲可以停船的地方 bay；indented coast for mooring ❷指澳门 Macao：港～（香港和澳门）同胞 *compatriots in Hong Kong and Macao* ❸指澳洲（现称大洋洲），世界七大洲之一（now Oceania） Australia

懊 ào ㄠ 烦恼，悔恨 to regret；to be remorseful：～悔 *to repent；to feel remorseful*［懊丧］（－sàng） 因失意而郁闷不乐 to feel depressed out of disappointment

B ㄅ

BA ㄅㄚ

八 bā ㄅㄚ 数目字 eight

扒 ㊀ bā ㄅㄚ ❶抓住,把着 to hold on to; to cling to: ～着栏杆 *to hold on to the railing*|～着树枝 *to clutch the branch of a tree* ❷刨开,挖 to dig: 城墙～了个豁口。*A breach was made in the city wall.* [扒拉](— la) 拨动 to push lightly: ～～算盘 *to click abacus beads*|～～开众人 *to push one's way through a crowd* ❸剥,脱 to strip off; to take off: ～皮 *to skin; to peel*|～下衣裳 *to take off one's clothes*

㊁ pá 见546页 see p546

叭 bā ㄅㄚ 拟声词 ***onomatopoeia***, snap: ～的一声,弦断了。*The string broke with a snap.*

朳 bā ㄅㄚ 无齿的耙子 toothless rake

巴 bā ㄅㄚ ❶黏结着的东西 crust that adheres to sth else: 锅～ *rice crust* ❷〈方 ***dialect***〉粘住,依附在别的东西上 to stick to; to cling to sth else: 饭～锅了。*The rice has stuck to the pot.*|爬山虎～在墙上。*The ivy clings to the wall.* ❸〈方 ***dialect***〉贴近 to be close to; to be next to: 前不～村,后不～店 *with neither village ahead nor inn behind; to be stranded* (or *held up*) *in a desolate place* [巴结](— jie) 奉承,谄媚 to flatter; to fawn on ❹巴望,盼,期望 to hope; to look forward to: ～不得马上到家 *to be very anxious to arrive home immediately* ❺古代国名,在今重庆市一带 Ba, an ancient state around the area in present Chongqing ❻(ba) 词尾 ***suffix*** **1** 在名词后(used after a noun): 尾～*tail* **2** 在动词后(used after a verb): 眨～眼 *to blink*|试～试～*to have a try* **3** 在形容词后(used after an adjective): 干～*dried up; shriveled*|皱～*crumpled; rumpled; wrinkled* ❼压强的非法定计量单位,1巴等于10^5帕(符号bar) bar, an unofficial unit of pressure equal to 10^5 pascal

芭 bā ㄅㄚ [芭蕉](— jiāo) 多年生草本植物,叶宽大,叶和茎的纤维可编绳索。果实也叫芭蕉,跟香蕉相似,可以吃 Japanese banana (*Musa basjoo*)

吧 ㊀ bā ㄅㄚ ❶拟声词 ***onomatopoeia***,同"叭" same as 叭: ～嗒(dā) *to patter*| ～唧(jī) *to squelch*|～的一声 *with a squelch* ❷(外 **loanword**)具备特

定功能或设施的休闲场所 bar：酒～*bar*|网～*Internet bar*；*cybercafé*|氧～*oxygen bar*|～台 *bar counter*；*pub counter*

㊁ ba 见 15 页 see p15

岜 bā ㄅㄚ （壮 *Zhuang*）石山 rocky mountain［岜关岭］地名，在广西壮族自治区扶绥 Baguanling，a place in Fusui，Guangxi Zhuang Autonomous Region

疤 bā ㄅㄚ ❶疤瘌（la），伤口或疮平复以后留下的痕迹 scar：疮～*scar*|好了伤～忘了疼（喻不重视经验教训）*to forget the pain as soon as the wound has healed — to neglect the lessons of the past*|伤口结～了。*The wound has scarred.* ❷器物上像疤的痕迹 scar-like mark on a vessel

笆 bā ㄅㄚ 用竹子、柳条等编成的一种东西，用途和席箔差不多 wicker ware；articles woren from wickers，bamboo strips，etc.：～篓 *wicker*（or *bamboo*）*basket*|荆～*interlaced chaste-tree twigs*

粑 bā ㄅㄚ 〈方 **dialect**〉饼类食物 cake（叠 ***reduplication***）：玉米～～ *corn cake*

鲃 bā ㄅㄚ 鱼名。体侧扁或略呈圆筒形，生活在淡水中，分布在我国华东、华南和西南地区 common barbel（*Barbus barbus*）

捌 bā ㄅㄚ "八"字的大写 eight，capital form of 八

拔 bá ㄅㄚˊ ❶抽，拉出，连根拽（zhuài）出 to pull out；to root up：～草 *to pull up weeds*|～牙 *to extract a tooth*|一毛不～（喻吝啬）*unwilling to give up even a hair — very stingy*|不能自～*too deeply involved to quit* 㘃 ***extension*** 夺取军事上的据点 to capture（*or* seize）a military stronghold：连～数城 *to capture several cities in succession*|～去敌人的据点 *to seize an enemy stronghold*［拔河］一种集体游戏，人数相等的两队，对拽一条大绳，把对方拽过界线（代替河），就算胜利 tug-of-war ❷吸出 to suck out；to draw：～毒 *to draw out poison*|～火罐 *cupping* ❸挑选，提升 to select；to promote：选～人才 *to select talented people*［提拔］挑选人员使担任更重要的职务 to promote；to select sb to fill a more important post ❹超出 to surpass；to stand out：出类～萃（人才出众）*outstanding*；*above the average*［海拔］地面超出海平面的高度 elevation；height above sea level

茇 bá ㄅㄚˊ 草根 grass roots

胈 bá ㄅㄚˊ 大腿上的毛 hairs on the thigh

菝 bá ㄅㄚˊ ［菝葜］（—qiā）落叶藤本植物，叶子多为卵圆形，茎有刺，花黄绿色，浆果红色。根茎可入药 sarsaparilla；smilax（*Smilax*）

跋 bá ㄅㄚˊ ❶翻过山岭 to cross mountains：～山涉水

to scale mountains and ford streams; to travel across mountains and rivers — indicating a difficult journey [跋涉]爬山趟水，形容行路辛苦 to trudge：长途～～*to trudge over a long distance* ❷写在文章、书籍等后面的短文，多是评介内容的 postscript

[跋扈](—hù)骄傲而专横 bossy; domineering

魃 bá ㄅㄚˊ [旱魃]传说中造成旱灾的鬼怪 *hanba*, a legendary demon of drought

鼥 bá ㄅㄚˊ 见 769 页"鼧"字条"鼧鼥"(tuó—) see 鼧鼥 on p769

把 ㊀ bǎ ㄅㄚˇ ❶拿，抓住 to hold; to grasp：～盏 *to raise a wine cup*｜两手～住门 *to hold the door with both hands* ❷控制，掌握 to control：～舵 *to operate the rudder; to steer*｜～犁 *to handle a plough* [把持]专权，一手独揽，不让他人参与 to dominate; to monopolize：～～财权 *to monopolize financial power* [把握] **1** 掌握，控制，有效地处理 to grasp; to seize：～～时机 *to grasp an opportunity; to seize the right time* **2** 事情成功的可靠性 assurance; certainty：这次试验，他很有～～。*He is quite sure of this experiment.* ❸把守，看守 to guard; to watch：～门 *to guard a gate*｜～风(守候，防有人来) *to be on the lookout* ❹手推车、自行车等的柄 handlebar：车～*handlebar of a cycle* ❺(一儿)可以用手拿的小捆 bundle：草～儿 *bundle of straw* ❻介词 ***preposition***，和"将"相当(equal to 将)：～一生献给党 *to devote one's whole life to the Party*｜～更多的工业品供应给农民 *to provide more industrial products for farmers* ❼量词 ***quantifier*** **1** 用于有柄的(used for sth with a handle)：一～刀 *a knife*｜一～扇子 *a fan* **2** 用于可以一手抓的 handful of：一～粮食一～汗。*A drop of sweat brings a handful of grain.* **3** 用于某些抽象的事物(used for sth abstract)：一～年纪 *to get on in years*｜努～力 *to make an effort* ❽放在量词或"百、千、万"等数词的后面，表示约略估计(used after quantifiers or numerals such as 百，千，万，etc) about; or so：丈～高的树 *tree about ten feet high*｜个～月以前 *about a month ago*｜有百～人 *about a hundred people* ❾指拜把子(结为异姓兄弟)的关系 sworn brotherhood：～兄 *sworn brother*

[把势][把式](—shi) **1** 武术 *wushu*, martial arts **2** 专精一种技术的人 skilled person：车～～(赶车的) *cart-driver*

[把头] **1** 旧时香会(迷信组织)的头目(of superstitious organizations in former times) chieftain **2** 旧社会里把持某一种行(háng)业，从中剥削工人的人 gangmaster; labour contractor who exploited workers in former times

[把戏] 1 魔术、杂耍一类的技艺 acrobatics; jugglery 2 ⑩ ***figurative*** 手段,诡计 trick:你又想玩什么~~? *What tricks are you up to now?*

㊁ bà 见 14 页 see p14

钯 ㊀ bǎ ㄅㄚˇ 一种金属元素,符号 Pd,银白色,富延展性,能吸收多量的氢,可用来提取纯粹的氢气。又可制催化剂。它的合金可制电器仪表等 palladium (Pd)

㊁ pá 见 546 页 see p546

靶 bǎ ㄅㄚˇ (一子)练习射击用的目标 target:打~ *to practise target-shooting*

坝(壩) bà ㄅㄚˋ ❶截住河流的建筑物 dam:拦河~ *diversion dam* ❷河工险要处巩固堤防的建筑物 dyke; embankment ❸(一子)平地。常用于西南各省地名 (ba, usually used in a place name in provinces of southwest China) flatland; plain

把(**欛) ㊁ bà ㄅㄚˋ (一儿)物体上便于手拿的部分,柄 handle; grip:刀~儿 handle of a knife|茶壶~儿 handle of a teapot [话把儿]被人作为谈笑资料的言论或行为 subject for ridicule

㊀ bǎ 见 13 页 see p13

爸 bà ㄅㄚˋ 称呼父亲 papa; father (叠 ***reduplication***)

耙 ㊀ bà ㄅㄚˋ ❶把土块弄碎的农具 harrow ❷用耙弄碎土块 to harrow:地已经~过了。*The field has been harrowed.*

㊁ pá 见 546 页 see p546

齙 bà ㄅㄚˋ 〈方 ***dialect***〉牙齿外露(of front teeth) projecting:~牙 *bucktooth*

罢(罷) ㊀ bà ㄅㄚˋ ❶停,歇 to stop; to cease (连 ***doublet*** 一休 to give up):~工 *to go on strike*|~手 *to give up*|欲~不能 *to find it hard to stop; to be unable to stop even though one wants to* ❷免去(官职) to dismiss (from office) (连 ***doublet*** 一免 to dismiss):~官 *to dismiss from office*|~职 *to remove from a position; to dismiss* ❸完了,毕 to finish:吃~饭 *after the meal*

〈古 ***archaism***〉又同"疲"(pí) also same as 疲

㊁ ba 见 15 页 see p15

䎬(䎱) bà ㄅㄚˋ 同"耙㊀" same as 耙㊀

鲅 bà ㄅㄚˋ 鲅鱼,鱼名。背部黑蓝色,腹部两侧银灰色,生活在海洋中 Chinese mackerel (*Scomberomorus sinensis*)

鲌 ㊁ bà ㄅㄚˋ 同"鲅" same as 鲅

㊀ bó 见 55 页 see p55

霸(*覇) bà ㄅㄚˋ ❶依靠权势横行无忌,迫害人民的人 tyrant; bully:他过去是码头上的一~。*He used to be a bully at the wharf.* ⑪ ***extension*** 以武力或经济力量侵略、压迫别国,扩大自己势力的国家 hegemonic power; hegemony [霸道] 1 蛮横 overbearing:横行~~ *to tyrannize*

over; to ride roughshod over **2** (—dao) 猛烈的,厉害的 strong; potent:这药够～～的。*This medicine is really strong.* ❷强占 to seize; to occupy by force:～住不让 *to occupy by force and refuse to give up* ❸ 我国古代诸侯联盟的首领 leader of an alliance of princedoms in ancient China:春秋五～ *the Five Overlords in the Spring and Autumn Period*

灞 bà ㄅㄚˋ 灞河,水名,在陕西省西安 Bahe River, in Xi'an, Shaanxi Province

吧 [二] ba ·ㄅㄚ 助词 ***auxiliary***,用在句末,也作"罢"(also written as 罢 and used at the end of a sentence) **1** 表示可以,允许(used to express consent or approval):好～,就这么办～。*All right, let's do it this way.* **2** 表示推测,估量(used to express supposition):今天不会下雨～。*Looks like it won't rain today.* **3** 表示命令,请求(used to express a command or a request):快出去～!*Come on and get out, will you?* | 还是你去～!*It would be better for you to go!* **4** 用于停顿处(used to mark a pause):说～,不好意思;不说～,问题又不能解决。*To say is embarrassing, but not to say will leave the problem unsolved.*

[一] bā 见 11 页 see p11

罢(罷) [二] ba ·ㄅㄚ 同"吧[二]" same as 吧[二]

[一] bà 见 14 页 see p14

BAI ㄅㄞ

B

刯 bāi ㄅㄞ [刯划](—huai)〈方 ***dialect***〉**1** 处置,安排 to deal with; to arrange:这件事让他～～吧。*Let him deal with it.* **2** 修理,整治 to repair; to fix:这孩子把闹钟～～坏了。*The child damaged the alarm clock with his tinkering.*

掰 bāi ㄅㄞ 用手把东西分开或折断 to break off; to snap off:～月饼 *to break a moon-cake into pieces* | ～老玉米 *to break off corn cobs* | 把这个蛤蜊～开。*Split the clam open.*

擘 [二] bāi ㄅㄞ 同"掰" same as 掰

[一] bò 见 57 页 see p57

白 bái ㄅㄞˊ ❶雪或乳汁那样的颜色 white:～面 *wheat flour* | 他头发～了。*His hair has turned grey.* [白领]一般指从事脑力劳动的管理人员、技术人员、政府公务员等 white-collar worker [转] ***transfer*** **1** 有关丧事的 concerning a funeral:办～事 *to manage funeral affairs* **2** 反动的 reactionary:～军 *the White Army* | ～匪 *White bandits* ❷清楚 clear ([连] ***doublet*** 明— clear):真相大～。*The truth has come out.* | 蒙受不～之冤 *to suffer an unredressed injustice* ❸亮 bright:东方发～。*It dawns in the east.* ❹空空的,没有加上其他东西的 blank; plain:～卷

(juàn) *unanswered examination paper* | ～水 *plain boiled water* | ～地(没有庄稼的地) *unplanted land* ㊀ **extension** 副词 **adverb** **1** 没有效果地 in vain:这话算～说。*The words have fallen on deaf ears.* | 烈士们的鲜血没有～流。*The martyrs did not shed their blood in vain.* **2** 不付代价地 free of charge: ～给 *to give away for free* | ～饶 *to give as an extra* | ～吃 *to eat without paying* ❺陈述,说明 to state; to explain: 自～ *to make clear one's meaning or position* | 表～ *to explain oneself; to vindicate oneself* | 道～(戏曲中不用唱的语句)(in Chinese opera) *spoken parts* [白话]口头说的话,跟"文言"相对(the opposite of 文言) vernacular ❻指字形或字音有错(of Chinese characters) wrongly written or pronounced: 写～了 *to write a word wrongly* | 念～了 *to mispronounce a word* [白字]别字 wrongly written or pronounced word

[白族]我国少数民族,参看附表(see the appendix) the Bai ethnic group, one of the ethnic minorities of China

百 bǎi ㄅㄞˇ ❶数目,十个十 hundred ㊀ **extension** 众多,所有的 numerous; all kinds of: ～花齐放,～家争鸣。*Let a hundred flowers blossom and a hundred schools of thought contend.* | ～战～胜 *to fight a hundred battles and always emerge victorious; to be ever-victorious* [百分率](——lǜ)百分之几,符号为"%",如百分之七十五写作75% percentage (%) [百姓]人民 common people ❷法定计量单位中十进倍数单位词头之一,表示10^2(符号h) hecto-(h)

佰 bǎi ㄅㄞˇ "百"字的大写 hundred, capital form of 百

伯 ㊁ bǎi ㄅㄞˇ [大伯子](——zi)丈夫的哥哥 elder brother of one's husband; brother-in-law

㊀ bó 见54页 see p54

柏(*栢) ㊀ bǎi ㄅㄞˇ ❶常绿乔木,有侧柏、圆柏、罗汉柏等多种。木质坚硬,纹理致密,可供建筑及制造器物之用 Chinese weeping cypress (*Cupressus funebris*) ❷姓 Bai, a surname

㊁ bó 见55页 see p55

㊂ bò 见57页 see p57

捭 bǎi ㄅㄞˇ 分开 to divide; to separate: ～阖(hé)(开合) *to manoeuvre to divide or unite*

摆(擺、❺襬) bǎi ㄅㄞˇ ❶陈列,安放 to put; to arrange: 把东西～整齐。*Put things in order.* ㊟ **transfer** 故意显示 to show off; to assume: ～阔 *to parade one's wealth* | ～架子 *to put on airs* [摆布]任意支配 to order about; to manipulate: 受人～～ *to be ordered about; to be at sb's beck and call* ❷陈述,列举 to state; to spell out: ～事实,

讲道理 *to present the facts and reason things out* ❸来回地摇动 to sway; to wave: ～手 *to wave one's hand* | 摇头～尾 *to shake the head and wag the tail — to assume an air of complacency or levity* | 大摇大～ *to strut; to swagger* [摆渡] **1** 用船运载过河 to ferry **2** 过河用的船 ferry; ferryboat [摆脱]挣脱，甩开 to shake off; to break away from: ～～贫困 *to shake off poverty* ❹摇动的东西 sth that sways: 钟～ *pendulum* ❺衣裙的下边 lower hem: 下～ *lower hem of a garment, etc* (图见 882 页"衣"picture on p882)

呗 ㊁ bài ㄅㄞˋ [梵呗](fàn—) 佛教徒念经的声音 *Pathaka*; eulogy to the Buddha ㊀ bei 见 31 页 see p31

败 bài ㄅㄞˋ ❶输，失利，跟"胜"相对 (the opposite of 胜) to lose; to be defeated: 一～涂地 *to fail completely; to suffer a crushing defeat* | 敌军～了。*The enemy troops have been defeated.* ❷打败，使失败 to defeat; to beat: 人民军队大～侵略军。*The people's army inflicted a crushing defeat on the invading troops.* ❸做事没有达到目的，不成功 to fail: 功～垂成 *to fail on the verge of success* ❹败坏，毁坏 to spoil; to ruin: ～血症 *septicaemia* | 身～名裂 *to bring disgrace and ruin upon oneself; to lose all standing and reputation* ❺解除，消散 to relieve; to disappear: ～火 *to relieve internal heat* | ～毒 *to counteract a toxin* ❻衰落，使衰落 to wither: 花开～了。*The flowers faded.* | ～兴(xìng)(情绪低落) *to be disappointed* | ～家子儿 *black sheep; spendthrift*

拜 bài ㄅㄞˋ ❶过去表示敬意的礼节 respectful formality in the past [转] ***transfer*** 恭敬地 courteously: ～托 *to entrust* | ～访 *to pay a visit* | ～望 *to call on* | ～请 *to invite* [礼拜]宗教徒对神敬礼或祷告 liturgy [转] ***transfer*** 周、星期的别称 another term for week ❷行礼祝贺 to send greetings; to extend congratulations: ～年 *to pay a New Year call; to wish sb a Happy New Year; to extend New Year greetings* | ～寿 *to present birthday greetings* ❸用一定的礼节授与某种名义或结成某种关系 to confer a title or establish a relationship with ceremony: ～将(jiàng) *to confer the title of general* | ～把子 *to become sworn brothers*

稗 bài ㄅㄞˋ (一子)一年生草本植物，长在稻田里或低湿的地方，形状像稻，但叶片毛涩，颜色较浅，主脉清楚，是稻田的害草。果实可以做饲料、酿酒 common barnyard grass (*Echinochloa curs-galli*) [喻] ***figurative*** 微小的，琐碎的 insignificant; unofficial: ～史(记载轶闻琐事的书) *unofficial history; book containing historical anecdotes*

B

擓(韛) bài ㄅㄞˋ 〈方 ***dialect***〉风箱 bellows: 风～*bellows* | ～拐子(风箱的拉手) *bellows handle*

呗 bai ·ㄅㄞ 助词 ***auxiliary***, 相当于"呗"(bei) equal to 呗

BAN ㄅㄢ

扳 bān ㄅㄢ ❶把一端固定的东西往下或往里拉,使改变方向 to pull; to turn: ～枪栓 *to unlock a rifle bolt* | ～着指头算 *to count on one's fingers* ❷把输了的赢回来 to win back: ～回一局 *to win back a game*

攽 bān ㄅㄢ 分给,发给 to distribute; to issue

颁 bān ㄅㄢ 发下 to issue: ～布命令 *to issue an order* | ～发奖章 *to award a medal*

班 bān ㄅㄢ ❶一群人按次序排成的行(háng)列 queue (of people): 排～ *to queue up* ❷工作或学习的组织 unit organized for the purpose of work or study: 学习～ *studying class* | 机修～ *maintenance team* ❸工作按时间分成的段落,也指工作或学习的场所 shift; work or study place: 上～*to go to work* | 下～*to come off work* | 值～ *to be on duty* ❹定时开行的regularly-run; scheduled: ～车 *regular bus; shuttle bus* | ～机 *airliner; flight* ❺军队编制中的基层单位,在排以下 squad (in the army) ❻量词 ***quantifier*** **1** 用于人群(used to refer to a group of people): 这～年轻人真有力气。*These young people are really strong*. **2** 用于定时开行的交通运输工具(used to refer to scheduled means of transportation): 我搭下一～飞机走。*I'll leave by the next flight*. ❼调回或调动(军队)(of troops) to withdraw or redeploy: ～师 *to order troops to withdraw from the front* | ～兵 *to redeploy troops*

斑 bān ㄅㄢ 一种颜色中夹杂的别种颜色的点子或条纹 spot; stripe (㊈ ***doublet*** 一驳 mottled): ～马 *zebra* | ～竹 *mottled bamboo* | ～白(花白) *grizzled; greying* | 脸上有雀～。*There are freckles on the face*. [斑斓](-lán)灿烂多彩 gorgeous; bright-coloured multi-coloured: 色彩～～*riot of colour*

瘢 bān ㄅㄢ 皮肤上生斑点的病 freckles

般 bān ㄅㄢ ❶样,种类 way; kind: 如此这～ *so and so; thus and thus* | 百～照顾 *to show every possible consideration* | 兄弟～的友谊 *fraternal friendship* [一般] **1** 同样 same as; as ... as: 我们两个人～～高。*The two of us are of the same height*. **2** 普通的,普遍的 ordinary; common: ～～的读物 *general reading materials* | ～～人的意见 *general opinion* ❷古同"搬"same as 搬 in ancient Chinese

搬 bān ㄅㄢ 移动，迁移 to move; to relocate; to remove：把这块石头～开。*Move the rock away.* | ～家 *to move (one's household)*

瘢 bān ㄅㄢ 疤瘌（bāla）scar：～痕 *scar*

阪 bǎn ㄅㄢˇ 同"坂" same as 坂

[大阪]地名，在日本 Osaka, a place in Japan

坂（*岅）bǎn ㄅㄢˇ 山坡，斜坡 hillside; slope：～上走丸（喻迅速）*like a ball rolling down a hillside — speedy; fast*

板（❹闆）bǎn ㄅㄢˇ ❶（～子、～儿）成片的较硬的物体 board; plank：～材 *plank stuff* | 铁～ *iron plate* | 玻璃～ *plate glass* | 黑～ *blackboard* ❷演奏民族音乐或戏曲时打节拍的乐器（used to beat time in Chinese national music or traditional operas）clappers：檀～ *hardwood clappers* [引] ***extension*** 歌唱的节奏（in singing）rhythm：一～三眼 *one accented beat followed by three unaccented ones; in a methodical way* | 离腔走～ *off the beat; out of tune* [板眼]民族音乐或戏曲中的节拍（in traditional Chinese music or opera）metre [喻] ***figurative*** 做事的条理 orderliness in doing things [快板儿]曲艺的一种，词句合辙押韵，说时用竹板打拍子 *kuaiban*, a rhythmic comic talk or monologue to the accompaniment of bamboo clappers; clapper talk ❸不灵活，少变化 stiff; inflexible：表情太～ *to look too stiff* | ～起面孔 *to put on a stern expression* ❹[老板] 1 私营工商业的业主 proprietor; boss 2 过去对著名戏曲演员的尊称 *laoban*, a respectful form of address for well-known opera actors in former times

版 bǎn ㄅㄢˇ ❶上面有文字或图形，用木板或金属等制成供印刷用的东西 printing plate; block：木～书 *block-printed book* | 活字～ *movable-type plate* [引] ***extension*** 底版，相片的底片 negative; photographic plate：修～ *to retouch; to touch up* ❷印刷物排印的次数 edition：第一～ *first edition* | 再～ *second edition* [出版]书刊杂志等编印发行 to publish; to come out ❸报纸的一面叫一版 page (of a newspaper)：头～头条新闻 *headline news on the front page* ❹打土墙用的夹板（for making an earthen wall）clamping board：～筑 *to build a wall with clamping boards* ❺户籍 household register [版图]户籍和地图 books recording registration of residents and maps [转] ***transfer*** 国家的疆域 domain; territory

钣 bǎn ㄅㄢˇ 金属板材 metal plate：铅～ *lead plate* | 钢～ *steel plate*

舨 bǎn ㄅㄢˇ 见652页"舢"字条"舢舨"（shān—）see 舢

B

粄 on p652

办(**辦**) bàn ㄅㄢˋ ❶处理 to handle; to deal with: ～公 *to handle official business* | ～事 *to handle affairs* | 好,就这么～。*OK, let's do it this way.* ㊉ **extension** 处分,惩治 to punish: 重(zhòng)～ *to punish severely* | 首恶者必～。*The chief criminals shall be punished without fail.* ❷创设 to set up: ～工厂 *to set up a factory* ❸置备 to prepare: ～货 *to buy goods* | ～酒席 *to prepare a feast*

半 bàn ㄅㄢˋ ❶二分之一 half: 十个的一～是五个。*Half of ten is five.* | ～米布 *half a metre of cloth* | 一吨～ *one and a half tons* | 分给他一～。*Give him half of it.* ❷在中间 in the middle: ～夜 *midnight* | ～路上 *midway; halfway* | ～途而废 *to give up halfway* ❸不完全的 partly; semi-: ～透明 *semitransparent* | ～脱产 *partly released from one's regular work*

伴 bàn ㄅㄢˋ ❶(一儿)同在一起而能互助的人 companion; partner (㊟ **doublet** 一侣 partner): 找个～儿学习 *to find a companion to study with* ❷陪着,伴随 to accompany: ～游 *to accompany sb on sightseeing* | ～奏 *to accompany (by musical instruments); to play while sb is singing or dancing*

拌 bàn ㄅㄢˋ 搅和 to mix: 搅～ *to stir and mix* | ～种子 *to dress seeds* | ～草喂牛 *to prepare fodder for cattle (by mixing hay with bran, etc)*

绊 bàn ㄅㄢˋ 行走时被别的东西挡住或缠住 to stumble: ～马索 *rope for tripping a horse; heel rope* | 走路不留神被石头～倒了 *to stumble over a stone by accident while walking* [羁绊](jī一)束缚 trammels; fetters: 不受～～ *free from fetters*

柈 bàn ㄅㄢˋ (一子)大块的木柴 large piece of firewood

靽 bàn ㄅㄢˋ 驾车时套在牲口后部的皮带 breeching; croup strap

扮 bàn ㄅㄢˋ 化装成(某种人物) to dress up as; to play the part of; to be disguised as (㊟ **doublet** 装一 to dress up): ～老头儿 *to dress up as an old man* | ～演(化装成某种人物出场表演) *to play the role of; to act the role of* [打扮] **1** 化装,装饰 to do up; to make up; to deck out **2** 装束穿戴 the way one is dressed

瓣 bàn ㄅㄢˋ ❶(一儿)花瓣,组成花冠的各片 petal; pieces that form the corolla: 梅花五～。*A plum blossom has five petals.* ❷(一儿)植物的种子、果实或球茎可以分开的片状物 segment; section; piece: 豆～儿 *bean segments* | 蒜～儿 *clove of garlic* | 橘子～儿 *tangerine wedge*

BANG ㄅㄤ

邦(**邦) bāng ㄅㄤ 国 nation; state; country: 友～ *friendly country; friendly nation* | 盟～ *allied nation; ally* [邦交]国与国之间的正式外交关系 diplomatic relations between two countries: 建立～～ *to establish diplomatic relations*

帮(幫) bāng ㄅㄤ ❶辅助 to help; to assist (㊌ **doublet** 一助 to help; to assist): ～你做 *to help you* [帮忙]帮助别人做事 to give sb a hand; to do sb a favour: 请大家来～～ *to ask everybody to help* [帮手]帮助工作的人 assistant [帮凶]帮助坏人行凶作恶的人 accomplice; accessory ❷集团, 帮会 clique; underworld gang; secret society: 匪～ *bandit gang* | 青红～ *the Blue Gang and the Red Gang* ❸(一子、一儿)旁边的部分 out part of sth: 船～ *side of a boat; gunwale* | 鞋～儿 *upper of a shoe* | 白菜～子 *outer leaves of Chinese cabbage* ❹量词 **quantifier**, 群, 伙 group; gang; band: 大～人马 *a large group of people*

啷 bāng ㄅㄤ 拟声词 **onomatopoeia**, 敲打木头等的声音 bang; sound of rapping on wood: ～～的敲门声 *the knocking sound on the door; bang on the door*

梆 bāng ㄅㄤ ❶梆子, 打更用的响器, 用竹或木制成 watchman's bamboo (*or* wooden) clapper 又指戏曲里打拍子用的两根短小的木棍, 是梆子腔的主要乐器 *bangzi*, the main musical instrument of clapper operas [梆子腔]戏曲的一种, 敲梆子加强节奏。简称"梆子"。有陕西梆子、河南梆子、河北梆子等(梆子 for short, a kind of traditional opera strengthening the rhythm through beating clappers, such as Shaanxi clapper opera, Henan clapper opera, Hebei clapper opera, etc) clapper opera ❷拟声词 **onomatopoeia**, 同"啷" same as 啷

浜 bāng ㄅㄤ 〈方 **dialect**〉小河沟 creek; brook

绑 bǎng ㄅㄤˇ 捆, 缚 to bind; to tie (up): 把两根棍子～在一起 *to fasten two sticks together*

榜 bǎng ㄅㄤˇ 张贴出来的文告或名单 notice; poster containing a list of names: 张～招贤 *to put up a proclamation to recruit talented people; to post a notice to summon men of worth* | 光荣～ *honour roll* [榜样]样子, 行动的模范 good example; model for others to follow: 雷锋是我们学习的～～。*Lei Feng is a fine example for us to follow.*

膀 ㊀ bǎng ㄅㄤˇ ❶(一子)胳膊上部靠肩的部分 upper arm: 他的两～真有劲。*He has*

B

strong arms. ❷（一儿）鸟类等的翅膀 wing (of a bird, etc)

㊁ pāng 见 551 页 see p551
㊂ páng 见 552 页 see p552

B

蚌（**蜯）㊀ bàng ㄅㄤˋ 生活在淡水里的一类软体动物，贝壳长圆形，黑褐色，壳内有珍珠层，有的可以产出珍珠 freshwater mussel; clam (*Cyclina sinensis*)

㊁ bèng 见 34 页 see p34

棒 bàng ㄅㄤˋ ❶棍子 stick; club; cudgel：棍～ *stick; rod; cudgel* [棒子]（一zi）**1** 棍子 stick **2**〈方 ***dialect***〉玉蜀黍的俗称 popular name for corn：～～面 *corn flour; corn meal* ❷体力强，能力高，成绩好等 strong; outstanding; excellent：这小伙子真～。*This young fellow is terrific.* | 画得～。*The painting is excellently done.*

傍 bàng ㄅㄤˋ ❶靠 to be close to; to draw near：依山～水 *situated at the foot of a hill near a stream* ❷临近（多指时间）(usually used to denote time) close to：～亮 *at dawn; at daybreak* | ～晚 *at dusk; at nightfall*

谤 bàng ㄅㄤˋ ❶恶意攻击 to slander; to defame; to vilify (㊊ ***doublet*** 诽— to slander; to defame; to vilify | 毁 — to slander; to malign; to calumniate) ❷公开指责 to condemn publicly; to denounce publicly：国人～王。*The countrymen condemned the king publicly.*

搒 ㊀ bàng ㄅㄤˋ 摇橹使船前进，划船 to row a boat; to paddle a boat

㊁ péng 见 558 页 see p558

蒡 bàng ㄅㄤˋ [牛蒡]多年生草本植物，叶子是心脏形，很大，夏季开紫红色小花，密集成头状。果实瘦小，果、根、叶可入药 greater burdock (*Arctium lappa*)

磅 ㊀ bàng ㄅㄤˋ（外 ***loanword***）❶英美制重量单位。1 磅等于 453.6 克 pound, a unit of weight in the British and US system equal to 453.6 grams ❷磅秤 scale：过～（*on a scale*）*to weigh*

㊁ páng 见 552 页 see p552

镑 bàng ㄅㄤˋ（外 ***loanword***）英国、埃及等国家的货币单位 pound, a unit of currency in Britain, Egypt, etc

稖 bàng ㄅㄤˋ [稖头]〈方 ***dialect***〉玉米。也作"棒头"(also written as 棒头) maize; corn

BAO ㄅㄠ

包 bāo ㄅㄠ ❶用纸、布等把东西裹起来 to wrap; to envelop：把书～起来 *to wrap up a book* ❷（一儿）包好了的东西 parcel; package; packet：邮～ *postal parcel* | 行李～ *luggage pack* [包裹] **1** 缠裹 to wrap up; to bind up：把伤口～～起来 *to bandage a wound* **2** 指邮寄的包 postal parcel ❸装东西的袋 bag; sack：书～

school bag | 皮～ *leather handbag; briefcase; portfolio* ❹量词 ***quantifier***,用于成包的东西 a bundle of; a pack of; a package of:一～花生米 *a pack of peanuts* ❺(一子、一儿)一种带馅蒸熟的食物 *baozi*, a steamed bun with filling:糖～儿 tangbao, *a steamed bun with sugar filling* | 肉～子 roubaozi, *a steamed bun with meat filling* ❻肿起的疙瘩 swelling; lump:腿上起个大～ *to have a bump on one's leg* ❼容纳在内,总括在一起 to include; to contain (㊈ ***doublet*** 一含 to contain | 一括 to include):无所不～ *all-embracing; all-inclusive* | 这几条都～括在第一项里。*These points are all included in the first item.* [包涵](—han) 客套话,请人宽容,原谅 (a polite expression, asking to be excused or forgiven) to excuse; to forgive ❽总揽,负全责 to undertake the entire task:～销 *to have exclusive selling rights* | ～换 *to guarantee replacement of goods* [包办]总负全责 to take full responsibility for everything; to take sole charge of ㊕ ***transfer*** 专断独行,不让别人参与 to monopolize; to arrange arbitrarily ❾保证 to guarantee:～你喜欢。*I bet you'll like it.* or *Satisfaction guaranteed.* | ～你玩得痛快。*I'm sure you'll have a good time.* ❿约定专用 to hire; to charter:～饭 *to get meals at a fixed rate; to board* | ～场 *to book a whole theater* (or *cinema*); *to make a block booking* | ～了一辆车 *to hire a car* (or *a bus*); *to rent a car*

苞 bāo ㄅㄠ ❶花苞,苞片,植物学上称花或花序下面像叶的小片 bud:含～未放 *in bud; budding* ❷茂盛 profuse; luxuriant:竹～松茂 *bamboos and pines growing in profusion*

孢 bāo ㄅㄠ 孢子,某些低等生物在无性繁殖或有性生殖中所产生的生殖细胞 spore

胞 bāo ㄅㄠ ❶胞衣,包裹胎儿的膜和胎盘 afterbirth [细胞]生物体的基本结构和功能单位 cell ❷同一父母所生的 born of the same parents:～兄 *full elder brother* | ～叔(父亲的同父母的弟弟) *paternal uncle* (*father's full brother*) [同胞] **1** 同父母的兄弟姊妹 siblings; blood brothers and sisters **2** 同祖国的人 compatriot; fellow countryman

炮 ㊂ bāo ㄅㄠ ❶把物品放在器物上烘烤或焙 to dry with heat:把湿衣服搁在热炕上～干 *to spread damp clothes on the heated* kang (*brick bed*) *for drying* ❷烹调方法,在旺火上急炒 to quick-fry; to sauté:～羊肉 *to sauté mutton*

㊀ páo 见 553 页 see p553

㊁ pào 见 554 页 see p554

龅 bāo ㄅㄠ 龅牙,突出唇外的牙齿 bucktooth

剥 ㊁ bāo ㄅㄠ 去掉外面的皮、壳或其他东西(常用于口语)(usually used colloquially) to shell; to peel; to skin:～花生 *to shell peanuts*|～皮 *to peel the skin off*

㊀ bō 见 54 页 see p54

煲 bāo ㄅㄠ〈方 ***dialect***〉❶壁较陡直的锅 deep pot:沙～ *casserole*|瓦～ *earthen pot*|电饭～ *electric rice cooker* ❷用煲煮或熬 to cook in a deep pot:～粥 *to cook gruel*|～饭 *to cook rice*

褒(*襃) bāo ㄅㄠ 赞扬,夸奖,跟"贬"相对(the opposite of 贬) to praise; to commend(㊥ ***doublet*** 一奖 to praise and honour; to commend and award):～扬 *to praise; to commend*|～义词 *commendatory term; ameliorative word*

雹 báo ㄅㄠ (一子)空中水蒸气遇冷结成的冰粒或冰块,常在夏季随暴雨下降 hail; hailstone

薄 ㊀ báo ㄅㄠ ❶厚度小的 thin; flimsy:～片 *thin slice*|～饼 *thin pancake*|～纸 *tissue paper*|这块布太～。*This piece of cloth is too flimsy.* ❷(感情)冷淡 (of emotions) indifferent; cold ❸(味道)淡 (of taste) insipid; light:酒味很～。*The wine tastes light.* ❹不肥沃 infertile; poor:土地～。*The land is infertile.*

㊁ bó 见 57 页 see p57

㊂ bò 见 57 页 see p57

饱 bǎo ㄅㄠ ❶吃足了,跟"饿"相对(the opposite of 饿) to have eaten one's fill; to be full ㊞ ***extension*** 足,充分 fully; to the full:～学 *learned; erudite; scholarly*|～经风霜 *weather-beaten; having experienced the hardships of life* [饱和]在一定的温度和压力下,溶液内所含被溶解物质的量已达到最大限度,不能再溶解 saturation ㊞ ***extension*** 事物发展到最高限度 (of things) having reached the ultimate limit [饱满]充实,充足 full; plump:谷粒长得很～～。*The grains are very plump.*|精神～～ *full of vigour and vitality* ❷满足 to feel satisfied:大～眼福 *to feast one's eyes on sth*

宝(寶、*寳) bǎo ㄅㄠ ❶珍贵的 precious; treasured:～刀 *precious (or treasured) sword; rare, fine sword*|～石 *precious stone* 敬辞 ***polite***:～地 *your (honourable) place*|～眷 *your (honourable) wife and children; your (respected) family* ❷珍贵的东西 treasures; valuables:珠～ *pearls and jewels; jewelry*|国～ *national treasures*|粮食是～中之～。*Grain is the treasure of all treasures.* [宝贝] **1** 珍贵的东西 treasured object; treasure **2**(一儿)对小孩儿亲昵的称呼 (endearment for young child) darling; dear; baby [元宝]一种金、银锭,两头翘起,中

间凹下 shoe-shaped gold or silver ingot

保 bǎo ㄅㄠˇ ❶看守住,护着不让受损害或丧失 to protect; to defend (㊥ ***doublet*** 一卫 to defend|一护 to protect): ～家卫国 *to protect our homes and defend our country*|～健 *health care; health protection* [保持]维持,使持久 to maintain; to keep:～～艰苦奋斗的作风 *to preserve the style of plain living and hard struggle* [保守] **1** 保住,使不失去 to guard; to keep: ～～机密 *to keep secret* **2** 守旧,不改进 conservative:这个想法太～～了。*The idea is too conservative.* [保育]对幼儿的抚养教育 childcare; nursing [保障] **1** 维护 to ensure; to guarantee: 婚姻法～～了男女双方和下一代儿女的利益。*The Marriage Law guarantees the interests of both husband and wife, and those of their children as well.* **2** 作为卫护的力量 guarantee: 强大的中国人民解放军是祖国安全的～～。*The powerful PLA of China is the guarantor of the safety of our homeland.* ❷负责,保证 to assure; to guarantee: ～荐 *to recommend*|我敢～他一定做得好。*I can assure you that he'll do it well.* [保险] **1** 因自然灾害或意外事故等造成损失而给付保险金的一种经济补偿制度。参与保险的个人或企业按期向保险公司交保险费,发生灾害或遭受损失时,由保险公司按预定保险数额赔偿 insurance **2** 靠得住 sure; secure; reliable:这样做～～不会错。*Surely it is safe to do it this way.* [保证]担保(做到) to pledge; to ensure:～～完成任务 *to pledge to fulfill the task* ❸旧时户口的一种编制,若干户为一甲,若干甲为一保 *bao*, a former administrative system organized on the basis of households, each *bao* being made up of several *jia* and each *jia* of several households

[保安族]我国少数民族,参看附表(see the appendix) the Bonan ethnic group, one of the ethnic minorities of China

葆 bǎo ㄅㄠˇ ❶草木繁盛 (of grass and trees) luxuriant ❷保持 to preserve; to keep:永～青春 *to keep alive the vigour of youth; to remain youthful forever; to stay young forever*

堡 ㊀ bǎo ㄅㄠˇ ❶堡垒 fort; fortress: 桥头～ *bridgehead; bridge tower* [堡垒]军事上防守用的建筑物 fort; fortress; stronghold: 打下敌人最坚固的～～ *to capture the enemy's strongest fortress* ㊙ ***figurative*** 难于攻破的事物 hard nut to crack: 攻克科学～～ *to scale a height of science; to surmount a scientific obstacle* ❷小城 small town

㊁ bǔ 见 59 页 see p59

㊂ pù 见 578 页 see p578

B

褓(*緥) bǎo ㄅㄠˇ 见 599 页"襁"字条"襁褓"(qiǎng —) see 襁褓 on p599

鸨 bǎo ㄅㄠˇ ❶大鸨,一种鸟,比雁略大,背上有黄褐色和黑色斑纹,不善于飞而善于走 bustard (*Otididae*) ❷指鸨母 bawd:老～(开设妓院的女人) *procuress; brothel keeper*

报(報) bào ㄅㄠˋ ❶传达,告知 to announce; to report:～喜 *to announce good news; to report success*|～信 *to notify; to inform* [报告]向上级或群众陈述,也指向上级或群众所做的陈述 to report:～～大家一个好消息。*I have some good news for you all.*|起草～～ *to draft a report* ❷传达消息和言论的文件或信号 documents or signals that transmit news or speeches:电～ *telegram; cable*|情～ *information; intelligence*|警～ *warning; alarm* ❸报纸,也指刊物 newspapers; journals:日～ *daily paper; daily*|晚～ *evening paper*|画～ *pictorial*|黑板～ *blackboard newspaper* ❹回答 to reply; to respond:～恩 *to pay a debt of gratitude; to requite sb's kindness*|～仇 *to avenge; to revenge* [报酬] **1** 由于使用别人的劳动或物件而付给的钱或实物 remuneration; payment **2** 答谢 to requite [报复]用敌对的行动回击对方 to make reprisals; to retaliate

刨(*鉋、*鑤) ㊀ bào ㄅㄠˋ ❶(一子)推刮木料等使平滑的工具 plane [刨床]推刮金属制品使平滑的机器 planer; planing machine ❷用刨子或刨床推刮 to plane:～得不光 *not well planed*|～平 *to plane sth smooth*

㊁ páo 见 553 页 see p553

抱(❸**菢) bào ㄅㄠˋ ❶用手臂围住 to hold in the arms (㊇ ***doublet*** 拥— to embrace; to hug):～着孩子 *to hold a child in one's arms*|～头鼠窜 *to cover the head with one's hands and run away like a rat — to turn tail and scurry away; to flee helter-skelter* ㊄ ***extension*** 围绕 to surround:山环水～ *surrounded by mountains and rivers* [抱负]愿望,志向 aspiration; ambition:做有志气有～～的青年 *to become a young man with aspiration and ambition* [合抱]两臂围拢(多指树木、柱子等的粗细)(of a tree, pillar, etc) circumference big enough to wrap one's arms around ❷心里存着 to cherish; to harbour:～不平 *to be outraged by an injustice*|～歉 *to feel sorry; to feel apologetic*|～着必胜的决心 *full of confidence in success* ❸孵(fū) to hatch:～窝 *to hatch; to sit (on eggs)*|～小鸡 *to hatch (out) chickens*

鲍 bào ㄅㄠˋ ❶一种软体动物,肉味鲜美。俗叫"鲍鱼",古称"鳆"(fù)(commonly called

鲍鱼，formerly called 鳆）abalone（*Haliotis*）❷鲍鱼，盐腌的干鱼 salted fish

趵 bào ㄅㄠˋ 跳 to spring forth; to bounce：～突泉（在山东省济南）*Baotu Spring, in Jinan, Shandong Province*

豹 bào ㄅㄠˋ 像虎而比虎小的一种野兽，毛黄褐或赤褐色，多有黑色斑点，善跳跃，能上树，常捕食鹿、羊、猿猴等 leopard（*Panthera pardus*）

暴 ㊀ bào ㄅㄠˋ ❶强大而突然来的，又猛又急的 sudden and fierce：～风雨 *rainstorm; storm; tempest* | ～病 *sudden serious disease* [暴动]为推翻原有的国家政权，破坏当时的政治制度和社会秩序而采取的集体武装行动 rebellion; uprising; insurrection ❷过分急躁的，容易冲动的 hot-tempered; short-tempered; irritable：这人脾气真～。*This person is really quick-tempered.* ❸凶恶残酷的 fierce; cruel（㊈ ***doublet*** —虐 tyrannical| 凶—brutal）：～行（xíng）*outrage; ferocity* | ～徒 *rioter; thug* | ～虐的行为 *savage act; outrage* ❹糟蹋，损害 to spoil; to ruin：自～自弃 *to be self-abandoned; to give oneself up as hopeless* ❺姓 Bao, a surname

[暴露]（—lù）显露 to expose：～～目标 *to give away one's position*

㊁ pù 见 579 页 see p579

瀑 ㊁ bào ㄅㄠˋ ❶暴雨 torrential rain; downpour ❷瀑河，水名，一在河北省东北部，一在河北省中部 Baohe River, one in the northeast, and the other in the middle, of Hebei Province

㊀ pù 见 579 页 see p579

曝 ㊁ bào ㄅㄠˋ [曝光]使感光纸或摄影胶片感光（in photography）to expose ㊅ ***figurative*** 隐蔽的事情暴露出来，被众人知道 to lay bare; to expose

㊀ pù 见 579 页 see p579

爆 bào ㄅㄠˋ ❶猛然破裂 to burst; to explode（㊈ ***doublet*** —炸 to explode; to blow up）：豆荚熟得都～了。*The pods are so ripe that they burst open.* [爆竹]用纸卷火药，点燃引线爆裂发声的东西。也叫"爆仗"、"炮仗"（also called 爆仗 or 炮仗）firecrackers ❷突然发生 to crop up; to happen unexpectedly：～冷门 *to have an unexpected turn of events* [爆发]突然发生 to erupt; to break out：火山～～。*The volcano erupted.* ❸烹调方法，用滚水稍微一煮或用滚油稍微一炸 to quick-fry; to quick-boil：～肚（dǔ）儿 *quick-boiled tripe* | ～炒 *to quick-fry and stir*

BEI ㄅㄟ

陂 ㊀ bēi ㄅㄟ ❶池塘 pond; pool：～塘 *pond* | ～池 *pond* ❷池塘的岸 waterside;

bank ❸山坡 mountain slope

㊁ pí 见 561 页 see p561

㊂ pō 见 573 页 see p573

杯(*盃) bēi ㄅㄟ (一子)盛酒、水、茶等的器皿 cup; glass; mug: 酒～ *wine glass*|玻璃～ *glass*|～水车薪(用一杯水救一车着火的柴。喻无济于事) *to try to put out a burning cartload of faggots with a cup of water—an utterly inadequate method in dealing with a severe situation*

卑 bēi ㄅㄟ 低下 low-lying; low: 地势～湿 *low-lying and damp terrain*|自～感 *sense of inferiority; inferiority complex* ㊈ ***extension*** 低劣 inferior; substandard; low-grade (㊈ ***doublet*** —鄙 base; mean; despicable): ～劣 *base; mean; despicable*|～鄙无耻 *mean and shameless; base and brazen*

庳 bēi ㄅㄟ bì ㄅㄧˋ (又 *also* bì) ❶低下 low: 堕高堙～(削平高丘,填塞洼地) *to level the mounds and fill up the low-lying land* ❷矮 low

椑 bēi ㄅㄟ [椑柿]柿子的一种,果实小,色青黑,可制柿漆 kaki persimmon (*Diospyros kaki*)

碑 bēi ㄅㄟ 刻上文字纪念事业、功勋或作为标记的石头 stele; upright stone tablet: 人民英雄纪念～ *Monument to the People's Heroes*|里程～ *milestone*|有口皆～(喻人人都说好) *to be praised by everyone—to win universal praise; to be universally acclaimed*

鹎 bēi ㄅㄟ 鸟名。羽毛大部分为黑褐色,腿短而细,吃昆虫、果实等 bulbul (*Pycnonotidae*)

背(*揹) ㊁ bēi ㄅㄟ 人用背(bèi)驮(tuó)东西 to carry sth on one's back: 把小孩儿～起来 *to carry the child on one's back*|～包袱 *to carry baggage—to have a load on one's mind; to take on a mental burden*|～枪 *to shoulder a rifle*

㊀ bèi 见 29 页 see p29

悲 bēi ㄅㄟ ❶伤心,哀痛 sadness; sorrow; grief (㊈ ***doublet*** —哀 sadness; sorrow; grief): ～喜交集 *mixed feelings of grief and joy; grief mingled with joy* ❷怜悯 compassion: 慈～ *mercy; benevolence*

北 běi ㄅㄟˇ ❶方向,早晨面对太阳左手的一边,跟"南"相对 (the opposite of 南) north: ～门 *north gate*|由南往～ *from south to north* ❷败北,打了败仗往回跑 to suffer a defeat; to lose a battle; to run back after being defeated: 三战三～ *to lose three battles in succession*|追奔逐～(追击败走的敌人) *to pursue routed enemy forces*

贝(貝) bèi ㄅㄟˋ ❶古代称水中有介壳的动物,现在称软体动物中蛤蜊、珠蚌、刀蚌、文蛤等为贝类 shellfish ❷古代用贝壳做的货币 ancient shell currency; cowrie

狈 bèi ㄅㄟˋ 传说中的一种兽 *bei*, a legendary animal:狼～ *wolf and bei — to be in a difficult position; to be embarrassed*

钡 bèi ㄅㄟˋ 一种金属元素,符号 Ba,颜色银白,燃烧时发黄绿色火焰 barium (Ba)

孛 bèi ㄅㄟˋ 古书上指彗星(in ancient Chinese texts) comet

悖 bèi ㄅㄟˋ 混乱,违反 to be confused; to go against:并行不～ *to run parallel and not contrary to each other; not to be mutually exclusive*

邶 bèi ㄅㄟˋ 周代诸侯国名,在今河南省汤阴东南 Bei, a princedom of the Zhou Dynasty, in the southeast of today's Tangyin, Henan Province

背 ㊀ bèi ㄅㄟˋ ❶背脊,脊梁,自肩至后腰的部分 back of the human body(图见 741 页"体"picture on p741)[背地]不当人面 privately; behind sb's back; on the sly:不要当面不说,～～乱说。*When you won't say it to his face, don't gossip behind his back.* [背景] **1** 舞台上的布景 stage setting; backcloth; backdrop **2** 图画上或摄影时衬托主体事物的景物 background [喻] ***figurative*** 对人物、事件起作用的环境或关系 background:政治～～ *political background* | 历史～～ *historical background* [背心]没有袖子和领子的短上衣 waistcoat; vest; sleeveless garment ❷物体的反面或后面 back of an object:～面 *back; reverse side* | 手～ *back of a hand* | 刀～ *back of a knife* ❸用背部对着,跟"向"相对(the opposite of 向) with one's back towards:～水作战 *to fight with one's back to the river — to fight a last-ditch battle* | ～光 *with one's back to the light — in a poor light* | ～灯 *backlight* [引] ***extension*** **1** 向相反的方向 towards the opposite direction:～道而驰 *to run in the opposite direction; to run counter to* | ～地性(植物向上生长的性质) *apogeotropism; the response by an organism of turning away from the earth; bending up or away from the ground* **2** 避 to do sth behind sb's back:～着他说话 *to talk about sb behind his back* **3** 离开 to leave; to go away:离乡～井 *to abandon one's hometown* ❹凭记忆读出 to recite from memory; to learn by heart:～诵 *to recite; to repeat from memory* | ～书 *to recite a passage from memory* ❺违背,违反 to violate; to break; to act contrary to:～约 *to break a contract; to violate a treaty* | ～信弃义 *to break faith with sb* [背叛]投向敌对方面,反对原来所在的方面 to betray; to forsake ❻不顺 unlucky:～时 *unlucky* ❼偏僻,冷淡 out-of-the-way; remote:这条胡同太

～。*This alley is out-of-the-way.*｜～月（生意清淡的季节）*slack business season* ❽听觉不灵 hard of hearing：耳朵有点儿～ *to be a little hard of hearing*

㊁ bēi 见 28 页 see p28

褙 bèi ㄅㄟˋ 把布或纸一层一层地粘在一起 to glue layers of cloth or paper together：裱～ *to mount*

备（備、*俻） bèi ㄅㄟˋ ❶具备，完备 to have；to possess：德才兼～ *to have both ability and moral integrity*｜求全责～ *to be too particular about (sth)；to be fastidious about (sth)*｜爱护～至 *to take utmost care of* ❷预备，防备 to prepare；to provide against；to take precautions against：～耕 *to make preparations for ploughing and sowing*｜～荒 *to get prepared against crop failure (or famine)*｜～课 *(of a teacher) to prepare lessons (before a lecture or class)*｜准～ *to prepare；to get ready*｜有～无患。*Where there is precaution, there is no danger.* or *Preparedness averts peril.*［备案］向主管机关做书面报告，以备查考 to put on record or on file；to enter a case in the records［备份］备用的重(chóng)份文件、数据或资料等 backup ❸设备 equipment：装～ *equipment*｜军～ *arms；armaments；military equipment*

惫（憊） bèi ㄅㄟˋ 极度疲乏 exhausted；fatigued：疲～ *weary；exhausted；tired out*

糒 bèi ㄅㄟˋ 干饭 cooked rice (as distinct from porridge)

鞴 bèi ㄅㄟˋ 把鞍辔(pèi)等套在马身上 to saddle a horse：～马 *to saddle a horse*

倍 bèi ㄅㄟˋ ❶跟原数相同的数，某数的几倍就是用几乘某数 times；-fold：二的五～是十。*Five times two is ten.*｜精神百～（精神旺盛）*full of vigour* ❷加倍 to double；to redouble；to put in more effort：事半功～ *half work, double result*｜勇气～增。*One's courage is redoubled.*｜～加努力 *to redouble one's effort；with redoubled effort*

焙 bèi ㄅㄟˋ 把东西放在器皿里，用微火在下面烘烤 to bake over a slow fire：把花椒～干研成细末 *to bake the seeds of Chinese pepper over a fire and grind them into powder*

蓓 bèi ㄅㄟˋ［蓓蕾］(－lěi)花骨朵儿，还没开的花 bud

碚 bèi ㄅㄟˋ［北碚］地名，在重庆市 Beibei, a place in Chongqing

被 bèi ㄅㄟˋ ❶(－子)睡觉时覆盖身体的东西 quilt：棉～ *duvet；cotton-padded quilt*｜夹～ *quilt without padding* ❷盖，遮盖 to cover：～覆 *to cover* ❸介词 ***preposition***，引进主动的人物并使动词含有受动的意

义(used to introduce an active agent and to make the verb passive) by:他～大家评选为生产能手。*He was elected a model worker by all*. ❹放在动词前,表示受动(used before a verb to express a passive meaning):～压迫 *to be oppressed* | ～批评 *to be criticized*

〈古 **archaism**〉又同"披"(pī) also same as 披(pī)

鞁 bèi ㄅㄟˋ ❶古时套车用的器具 saddle and bridle in ancient China ❷同"鞴" same as 鞴

琲 bèi ㄅㄟˋ 珠子串儿 string of beads

辈 bèi ㄅㄟˋ ❶代,辈分 generation; generational hierarchy:长～ *eldership; member of elder generation; senior* | 晚～ *member of younger generation; junior* | 革命前～ *revolutionary predecessors* [辈子](—zi)人活着的时间 lifetime:活了半～～了 *to have lived half of one's lifetime* ❷类(指人) people of a certain kind; the like:无能之～ *the incompetent; incapable people* ㊀ **extension** 表示多数(指人)[used to denote plurality (of people)]:彼～ *they* | 我～ *we*

鐾 bèi ㄅㄟˋ 把刀在布、皮、石头等物上反复摩擦几下,使锋利 to whet; to strop; to sharpen:～刀 *to sharpen a knife; to whet a knife* | ～刀布 *canvas strop*

呗 ㊀ bei ·ㄅㄟ 助词 ***auxiliary*** **1** 表示"罢了"、"不过如此"的意思(used to show that sth is just so-so):这就行了～。*Well, that'll do*. **2** 表示勉强同意的语气,跟"吧"相近(used to express reluctant agreement) similar to 吧:你愿意去就去～。*Well, go if you like*.

㊁ bài 见 17 页 see p17

臂 ㊁ bei ·ㄅㄟ 见 223 页"胳"字条"胳臂"(gē—) see 胳臂 on p223

㊀ bì 见 41 页 see p41

BEN ㄅㄣ

奔(*犇) ㊀ bēn ㄅㄣ 急走,跑 to run quickly; to dash (㊈ **doublet** —跑 to run; to race):狂～ *to run like mad; to dash headlong* | ～驰 *to speed; to dash; to gallop* | 东～西跑 *to run about here and there* [奔波]劳苦奔走 to be busy running about; to rush about

㊁ bèn 见 33 页 see p33

锛 bēn ㄅㄣ ❶(—子)砍平木料的一种工具,用时向下向内用力 adze ❷用锛子一类东西砍 to chop with an adze, etc:～木头 *to cut wood with an adze* | 用镐～地 *to dig earth with a pickaxe*

贲 ㊀ bēn ㄅㄣ ❶奔走,快跑 to run fast; to dash [虎贲]古时指勇士 ancient warrior ❷姓 Ben, a surname

[贲门]胃与食管相连的部分 cardia

㊁ bì 见 39 页 see p39

栟 ㊀ bēn ㄅㄣ [栟茶]地名,在江苏省如东 Bencha, a place in Rudong, Jiangsu Province

㊁ bīng 见 51 页 see p51

本 běn ㄅㄣˇ ❶草木的根,跟"末"相对(the opposite of 末) root of a plant:无～之木 *tree without roots* | 木～水源 *the root of a tree and the source of a river* ㊀ **extension** 事物的根源 foundation; basis; origin:翻身不忘～ *not to forget one's past after emancipation* [本末]头尾,始终,事情整个的过程 ins and outs (of sth); course of events from beginning to end:～～倒置 *to put the incidental before the fundamental; to put the cart before the horse* | 纪事～～(史书的一种体裁)(*a form of traditional Chinese historical writing*) *history presented in separate accouts of imperial events* [根本] **1** 事物的根源或主要的部分 foundation; base ㊉ **transfer** 彻底 thoroughly; radically:～～解决 *to solve problems once and for all* **2** 本质上 in essence; in nature:～～不同 *completely different* [基本] **1** 主要的部分 main part:～～建设 *capital construction* **2** 大体上 on the whole; by and large:大坝～～上已经建成。*The dam has been mostly completed.* ❷草的茎或树的干 stem of grass or trunk of a tree:草～植物 *herbaceous plants* | 木～植物 *ligneous plants* ❸中心的,主要的 central; principal:校～部 *main campus* ❹本来,原来 original:～意 *original meaning; real intention* | 这幅画～来是我的,后来送给他了。*It was my painting, but I gave it to him.* ❺自己这方面的 on one's own side:～国 *one's own country* | ～厂 *this factory* [本位] **1** 自己的责任范围 one's responsibility:做好～～工作 *to do one's own job well* **2** 计算货币用作标准的单位(used as calculating criterion of monetary value) monetary standard:～～货币 *standard or basic unit of a national currency* ❻现今的 current; this; present:～年 *this year* | ～月 *this month* ❼(－儿)本钱,用来做生意、生利息的资财 capital; principal:老～儿 *principal; capital* | 够～儿 *to gain enough to cover the cost* ❽根据 according to; in line with:有所～ *to be well based on; to be well founded* | ～着负责的态度去做 *to do sth conscientiously* ❾(－子、－儿)册子 book; notebook:日记～*diary; journal* | 笔记～*notebook* ❿(－儿)版本或底本 edition; version; script:刻～ *block-printed edition* | 稿～ *manuscript* | 剧～儿 *script; play* ⓫量词 **quantifier**:一～书 *a book*

苯 běn ㄅㄣˇ 一种有机化合物，分子式 C_6H_6，无色液体，有特殊的气味，工业上可用来制染料，是多种化学工业的原料和溶剂 benzene

畚 běn ㄅㄣˇ 簸箕，用竹、木、铁片等做的撮土器具（made of bamboo, wood or iron sheet）dustpan

夯 ㊁ bèn ㄅㄣˋ 同"笨"（见于《西游记》、《红楼梦》等书）（seen in such books as *Record of a Journey to the West*, *Dream of the Red Chamber*, etc）same as 笨

㊀ hāng 见 265 页 see p265

坌 bèn ㄅㄣˋ ❶灰尘 dust ❷聚集 to gather; to collect

奔（*逩）㊁ bèn ㄅㄣˋ ❶直往，投向 to go straight to; to head for：投～ *to go (to a friend or a place) for shelter*｜直～工厂 *to head directly for the factory*｜党指向哪里，就～向哪里。*Go where the Party directs.* ㊂ ***extension*** 接近（某年龄段）（of one's age）to approach; to get close to; to be getting on for：他是～七十的人了。*He is almost seventy.* ❷为某种目的而尽力去做 to go about (some business); to be after：～材料 *to be busy procuring materials*｜～命 *to be in a desperate hurry*

㊀ bēn 见 31 页 see p31

倴 bèn ㄅㄣˋ［倴城］地名，在河北省滦南 Bencheng, a place in Luannan, Hebei Province

笨 bèn ㄅㄣˋ ❶不聪明 stupid; foolish; dull（㊃ ***doublet*** 愚— stupid）❷不灵巧 clumsy; awkward：嘴～ *inarticulate*｜～手～脚 *to be clumsy (with one's hands and feet)* ❸粗重，费力气的 cumbersome; awkward; unwieldy：箱子太～。*The suitcase is too cumbersome.*｜～活 *heavy unskilled work*

BENG ㄅㄥ

伻 bēng ㄅㄥ 〈古 ***archaism***〉使，使者 envoy

祊（**鬃）bēng ㄅㄥ ❶古代宗庙门内的祭祀，也指门内祭祀之处 offering of sacrifices to ancestors inside the gate of an ancestral temple in ancient China, or the spot for such offerings ❷祊河，水名，在山东省中部偏南，沂（yí）河支流 Benghe River, a tributary of Yihe River, in the south central part of Shandong Province

崩 bēng ㄅㄥ ❶倒塌 to collapse：山～地裂。Mountains collapse and the ground cracks.［崩溃］垮台，彻底失败 to collapse; to crumble; to fall apart：敌军～～了。*The enemy collapsed.* ❷破裂 to burst; to crack; to split：把气球吹～了 *to blow the balloon up so hard that it bursts* ❸被弹（tán）射出来的东西突然打中 to be hit by sth bursting：放爆竹～了手。*The firecrackers hurt his hand* *when it went off.* ❹崩症,一种妇女病。也叫"血崩"(also called 血崩) metrorrhagia ❺封建时代称帝王死 (of an emperor) to die

嘣 bēng ㄅㄥ 拟声词 ***onomatopoeia***,东西跳动或爆裂声(sound of sth bouncing, snapping, or bursting) bang:气球～的一声破了。*The balloon burst with a bang.*

绷(*綳) ㊀ bēng ㄅㄥ ❶张紧,拉紧 to stretch tight; to strain:衣服紧～在身上。*The coat is tight-fitting.*|～紧绳子 *to stretch the rope tight* [绷带]包扎伤口的纱布条 bandage [绷子](—zi)刺绣用的架子,把绸布等材料张紧在上面,免得皱缩 embroidery frame; hoop; tambour ❷粗粗地缝上或用针别上 to baste; to pin; to tack:～被头 *to sew a cover onto the head of a quilt*

㊁ běng 见34页 see p34

甭 béng ㄅㄥˊ 〈方 ***dialect***〉副词 ***adverb***,不用 don't; needn't:你～说。*You needn't say it.*|～惦记他。*Don't worry about him.*

绷(*綳) ㊁ běng ㄅㄥˇ ❶板着 to pull (a long face):～着个脸 *to pull a long face* ❷强忍住 to strain oneself:他～不住笑了。*He could not but burst out laughing.* or *He could not stifle a laugh.*

㊀ bēng 见34页 see p34

琫 běng ㄅㄥˇ 古代刀鞘近口处的装饰 ornaments on the rim of an ancient sheath for a knife

泵 bèng ㄅㄥˋ (外 ***loanword***)把液体或气体抽出或压入用的一种机械装置 pump:气～ *air pump*|油～ *oil pump*

迸 bèng ㄅㄥˋ 爆开,溅射 to burst forth; to spout:火星儿乱～。*Sparks flew about.*

蚌 ㊁ bèng ㄅㄥˋ [蚌埠](—bù)地名,在安徽省 Bengbu, a place in Anhui Province

㊀ bàng 见22页 see p22

甏 bèng ㄅㄥˋ 〈方 ***dialect***〉瓮、坛子一类的器皿 jar; vat

镚 bèng ㄅㄥˋ (—子、—儿)原指清末发行的无孔的小铜币,今泛指小的硬币(formerly late-Qing small copper coin without a hole in it) small coin:金～子 *gold coin*|钢～儿 *coin*

蹦 bèng ㄅㄥˋ 两脚并着跳 to leap; to jump:欢～乱跳 *healthy and vivacious; alive and kicking*|～了半米高 *to jump as high as half a metre* [蹦跶](—da)蹦跳 to jump about; to bounce about ㊗ ***figurative*** 挣扎 to struggle; to battle:秋后的蚂蚱～～不了几天了。*In late autumn, grasshoppers are on their last legs.* or *A grasshopper in late autumn — nearing its end.*

BI ㄅㄧ

逼(*偪) bī ㄅㄧ ❶强迫,威胁 to force; to compel; to threaten (㊄ *doublet* —迫 to force; to compel):~债 *to dun; to press for debt repayment* | ~上梁山 *to have no alternative but to join the Liangshan Marsh rebels—to be driven to revolt* | 寒气~人。*There is a nip in the air.* ❷切近,接近 to press on towards; to close in on:~近 *to close in on; to approach* | ~真 *lifelike; true to life* ❸狭窄 narrow

鲾 bī ㄅㄧ 鲾鱼,鱼名。体小而侧扁,青褐色,鳞细,口小。生活在近海中 ponyfish (*Leiognathidae*)

荸 bí ㄅㄧˊ [荸荠](—qi)多年生草本植物,生在池沼或栽培在水田里。地下茎也叫荸荠,球状,皮赤褐色,肉白色,可以吃 water chestnut (*Eleocharis tuberosa*)

鼻 bí ㄅㄧˊ ❶(—子)嗅觉器官,也是呼吸的孔道 nose (图见 758 页"头"picture on p758) ❷(—儿)器物上面突出带孔的部分或带孔的零件 (protruding) part of an implement or a utensil with a hole:门~儿 *bolt staple* | 针~儿 *eye of a needle* | 扣~儿 *buttonhole*
[鼻祖]始祖,创始人 (of a tradition, school of thought, etc) earliest ancestor; originator

匕 bǐ ㄅㄧˇ 古代一种类似汤勺的餐具 *bi*, a ladle-like tableware in ancient China [匕首]短剑 dagger

比 bǐ ㄅㄧˇ ❶比较,较量 to compare; to contrast; to compete:~干劲 *to compete with each other in drive* | ~大小 *to compare the size of objects or the age of people* | ~优劣 *to compare the quality* [比赛]用一定的方式比较谁胜谁负 to match; to compete ❷表示比赛双方得分的对比 (of a score) to:三~二 *3 to 2* ❸两个数相比较,前项和后项的关系是被除数和除数的关系,如3∶5,3是前项,5是后项,比值是 3/5 ratio; proportion [比例] **1** 表示两个比相等的式子,如6∶3=10∶5 proportion; scale **2** 数量之间的关系 ratio [比重] **1** 一定体积的物体的重量跟在4℃时同体积的纯水重量的比值,现常改用相对密度表示 specific gravity **2** 某一事物在整体中所占的分量 proportion:青年工人在基本建设队伍中的~~迅速上升。*The proportion of young people in the capital construction work force is increasing rapidly.* | 我国工业在整个国民经济中的~~逐年增长。*The proportion of industry within the national economy as a whole is growing year by year.* ❹比方,模拟,做譬喻 to compare to; to liken to; to draw a analogy (㊄ *doublet* —喻 metaphor; analogy):

B

～拟不伦 *illogical analogy*｜用手～了一个圆形 *to make a circle with one's hands* [比画](-hua)用手做样子 to gesture; to gesticulate：他一边说一边～～。*He was gesticulating as he talked.* [比照]大致依照 according to; in the light of：你～～着这个做一个。*Make one after this model.* ❺介词 ***preposition***，用来比较程度或性状的差别 than; (superior or inferior) to：他～我强。*He is superior to me.*｜今天的雨～昨天还大。*The rain is heavier than it was yesterday.* ❻(旧读 formerly bì)靠近，挨着 close together; next to：～邻 *to be in the neighbourhood of; to be located close to*｜～肩 *shoulder to shoulder* [比比]一个挨一个 one by one：～～皆是 *can be seen everywhere; can be found here, there and everywhere* [比及]等到 when; at the time when; by the time that：～～敌人发觉，我们已经冲过火线了。*We had already crossed the front-line before the enemy realized what had happened.* [比来]近来 recently; of late [朋比]互相依附，互相勾结 to gang up：～～为奸 *to gang up (with others) for evil ends*

吡 bǐ ㄅㄧˇ [吡啶](-dìng)有机化合物，无色液体，有臭味，用作溶剂、化学试剂 pyridine

沘 bǐ ㄅㄧˇ 沘江，水名，在云南省西北部，澜沧江支流 Bijiang River, a tributary of Lancang River, in the northwest of Yunnan Province

妣 bǐ ㄅㄧˇ 原指母亲，后称已经死去的母亲 (formerly one's mother) one's deceased mother：先～ *my deceased mother*｜如丧考～(像死了父母一样) *very sad or sorrowful (as if one had lost one's parents)*

秕(*粃) bǐ ㄅㄧˇ 子实不饱满 (of grain) not plump; blighted [秕子](-zi)不饱满的子实 blighted grain

彼 bǐ ㄅㄧˇ 代词 ***pronoun*** ❶那，那个，跟"此"相对(the opposite of 此) that; those; the other; another：～岸 *other side of a river; opposite shore*｜～处 *that place*｜顾此失～ *to attend to one thing while ignoring the other* ❷他，对方 he; the other (party)：知己知～ *to know both one's opponent and oneself* [彼此]那个和这个。特指对方和自己两方面 this and that; each other; one another：～～有深切的了解。*They know each other well.*｜～～互助 *to help each other*

笔(筆) bǐ ㄅㄧˇ ❶写字、画图的工具 pen; pencil; writing or painting brush：毛～ *writing brush*｜画～ *painting brush*｜钢～ *pen* ❷笔画，组成汉字的横竖撇点折，一画就是一笔 strokes that form Chinese characters, such as horizontal, vertical, left-falling, dot and turning strokes ❸

写 to write：亲～ *to write in one's own hand* | 代～ *to write (a letter, etc) for sb; to write on sb's behalf* | ～之于书 *to put down in black and white* [笔名]著作人发表作品时用的别名 pen name; pseudonym ❹(写字、画画、作文的)笔法 (of calligraphy, drawing, writing) techniques：败～ *faulty stroke in calligraphy or painting; flaw in a piece of writing* | 伏～ *foreshadowing clues; foreshadowing* | 工～画 *Chinese painting made with fine, delicate strokes; meticulous brushwork* ❺像笔一样(直) straight as a ramrod：～直 *perfectly straight; straight as a ramrod* | ～挺 *trim* ❻量词 ***quantifier***：收到一～捐款 *to receive a sum of donated money* | 写一～好字 *to write a good hand*

俾 bǐ ㄅㄧˇ 使 in order to; so that; so as to：～便考查 *so as to make assessment easy*

鄙 bǐ ㄅㄧˇ ❶粗俗，低下 low; mean; vulgar：～陋 *shallow; ignorant* 谦辞 ***humble***：～人 *your humble servant; I* | ～意 *my humble opinion; my opinion* | ～见 *my humble view; my idea* ❷低劣 mean; base：卑～ *mean; base; despicable* ❸轻蔑 to despise; to disdain; to scorn：可～ *despicable; contemptible* | ～视 *to look down upon; to despise* | ～薄 *to disdain* | ～夷 *to scorn* ❹边远的地方 out-of-the-way place：边～ *remote area*

币(幣) bì ㄅㄧˋ 钱币，交换各种商品的媒介 money; currency：银～ *silver coin* | 纸～ *paper currency; note* | 硬～ *coin* | 人民～ *RMB; Renminbi*

必 bì ㄅㄧˋ 副词 ***adverb*** ❶必定，一定 certainly; surely; necessarily：～能成功 *will surely succeed* | 骄兵～败。*An arrogant army is doomed to defeat.* [必然]必定如此 inevitable; certain：种族歧视制度～～要灭亡。*The racial discrimination system will certainly perish.* [必需]不可少的 indispensable; necessary; essential：～～品 *necessities; necessaries* ❷必须，一定要 must; ought to; have to：事～躬亲 *to attend everything in person* | 不～着急。*There is no need to worry.* [必须]副词 ***adverb*** 一定要 must; have to：个人利益～～服从整体利益。*Personal interests must be subordinated to the overall interests.*

邲 bì ㄅㄧˋ 古地名，在今河南省荥(xíng)阳东北 Bi, an ancient place, in the northeast of today's Xingyang, Henan Province

苾 bì ㄅㄧˋ 芳香 fragrant; aromatic

闭 bì ㄅㄧˋ ❶闭门，关闭 to close (the door) ❷谨慎 prudent

泌 ㊁ bì ㄅㄧˋ [泌阳]地名，在河南省 Biyang, a place in

B

Henan Province

㊁ mì 见501页 see p501

毖 bì ㄅㄧˋ 谨慎 to caution：惩前～后 *to punish past wrongdoing so as to caution those to come; to learn from past mistakes to avoid future ones*

铋 bì ㄅㄧˋ 一种金属元素，符号Bi。银白色或粉红色。合金熔点很低，可做保险丝和汽锅上的安全塞等 bismuth (Bi)

秘（*祕） ㊀ bì ㄅㄧˋ 姓 Bi, a surname

［秘鲁］国名，在南美洲 Peru, a country in South America

㊁ mì 见501页 see p501

毕（畢） bì ㄅㄧˋ ❶完，完结 to finish; to complete; to conclude：话犹未～。*His remark sounds as if he still has sth to say in his mind.*［毕竟］副词 ***adverb*** 究竟，到底 after all; all in all; in the final analysis：他的话～～不错。*After all, he has not said anything wrong.*［毕业］学生学习期满，达到一定的要求 to graduate; to finish school ❷全，完全 fully; completely; altogether：～生 *all one's life; lifetime* | 真相～露 *to show one's true colours* ❸星宿名，二十八宿之一 *bi*, 19th of the 28 constellations

荜（蓽） bì ㄅㄧˋ ❶［荜拨］（—bō）多年生藤本植物，叶卵状心形，雌雄异株，浆果卵形。果穗可入药 long pepper (*Piper longum*) ❷同"筚" same as 筚

哔（嗶） bì ㄅㄧˋ［哔叽］（—jī）（外 ***loanword***）一种斜纹的纺织品 serge

筚（篳） bì ㄅㄧˋ 用荆条、竹子等编成的篱笆或其他遮拦物 wicker fence or other barriers：蓬门～户（喻穷苦人家）*thatched hut with a wicker door — humble household*

跸（蹕） bì ㄅㄧˋ ❶帝王出行时清道，禁止行人来往 to keep the road clear for the emperor to pass：警～ *to stop all traffic for the imperial carriage* ❷帝王出行的车驾 emperor's carriage on tours：驻～（帝王出行时沿途停留暂住）(*of emperor on a tour*) *to stay temporarily; to stop over*

庇 bì ㄅㄧˋ 遮蔽，掩护 to shelter; to protect; to shield（㊇ ***doublet*** —护 to shelter; to shield; to put under the aegis of）：包～ *to shelter; to harbour; to cover up*

陛 bì ㄅㄧˋ 宫殿的台阶 flight of steps leading to a palace hall［陛下］对国王或皇帝的敬称 Your Majesty

毙（斃） bì ㄅㄧˋ 死 to die; to get killed：～命 *to meet violent death; to get killed* | 击～ *to shoot* (or *strike*) *dead*

狴 bì ㄅㄧˋ［狴犴］（—àn）传说中的一种走兽。古代牢狱门上常画着它的形状，因此又用为牢狱的代称 *bi'an*, a legendary beast often painted on prison doors in ancient China; another name for prison (*or* jail)

梐 bì ㄅㄧˋ [梐枑](-hù)古代官署前拦住行人的东西，用木条交叉制成。也叫"行马"(also called 行马) railings in front of government offices in ancient China to keep out pedestrians, made of crisscross wooden slats

闭 bì ㄅㄧˋ ❶关，合 to shut; to close：～上嘴 *to shut one's mouth*｜～门造车(喻脱离实际) *to make a cart behind closed doors — to shut oneself off from reality* ㊀ ***extension*** 结束，停止 to stop; to end：～会 *to close* (or *finish*) *a meeting* ❷塞，不通 to obstruct; to stop up; to block up：～气 *to hold one's breath* [闭塞](-sè)堵住不通 to block; to stop up ㊀ ***extension*** 交通不便，消息不灵通 hard to get to; out-of-the-way; unenlightened：这个地方很～～。*This is an out-of-the-way place.*

诐 bì ㄅㄧˋ 偏颇，邪僻 biased; evil; sinister

畀 bì ㄅㄧˋ 给与 to give; to confer

痹(*痺) bì ㄅㄧˋ 中医指由风、寒、湿等引起的肢体疼痛或麻木的病(caused by wind, cold, damp, etc according to traditional Chinese medicine) disease with symptoms of pains or numbness in limbs and trunk

箅 bì ㄅㄧˋ (-子)有空隙而能起间隔作用的片状器物，如竹箅子、铁箅子、纱箅子、炉箅子(such as bamboo sieve, iron grid, muslin, stove grate, etc) grate; grid

贲 ㊀ bì ㄅㄧˋ 装饰得很好 well adorned：～临(客人盛装光临)(*of distinguished guests*) *to come in grand attire*

㊁ bēn 见31页 see p31

庳 bì ㄅㄧˋ (又 also bēi) 见28页 bēi see bēi on p28

婢 bì ㄅㄧˋ 旧时被有钱人家役使的女孩子 servant girl：～女 *maid; servant girl*｜奴～ *maidservant female slave*

睥 bì ㄅㄧˋ (又 also pì) 见563页 pì see pì on p563

裨 ㊀ bì ㄅㄧˋ 补益，益处 benefit; advantage：无～于事。*It won't be of any help.*｜对工作大有～益 *to be of great benefit to one's work*

㊁ pí 见562页 see p562

髀 bì ㄅㄧˋ 大腿，也指大腿骨 thigh; thighbone

敝 bì ㄅㄧˋ 破旧 shabby; worn-out; ragged：～衣 *shabby clothes* 谦辞 ***humble***，称跟自己相关的事物 my; our; this：～姓 *my surname*｜～处 *my place*｜～公司 *our company*

蔽 bì ㄅㄧˋ ❶遮，挡 to cover; to shelter; to hide (㊌ ***doublet*** 遮一 to hide｜掩一 to cover)：旌旗～日。*The banners and flags are fluttering and screening off the sun.* ❷概括

to sum up; to summarize; to generalize: 一言以～之 *to sum up in a word*

弊 bì ㄅㄧˋ ❶欺蒙人的行为 fraud; abuse; malpractice: 作～ *to practise fraud; to cheat* | 营私舞～ *to engage in malpractice for selfish ends* ❷弊病,害处,跟"利"相对 (the opposite of 利) disadvantage; harm: 兴利除～ *to promote what is beneficial and abolish what is harmful* | 流～ *corrupt practices; abuses*

皕 bì ㄅㄧˋ 二百 two hundred

弼 bì ㄅㄧˋ 辅助 to assist

赑 bì ㄅㄧˋ [赑屃](－xì) ❶用力的样子 straining hard ❷传说中的一种动物,像龟。旧时大石碑的石座多雕刻成赑屃形状 *bixi*, a legendary animal like a tortoise (in former times the bases of many steles were carved in the shape of such legendary animal)

愎 bì ㄅㄧˋ 乖戾,固执 willful; self-willed: 刚～自用(固执己见) *self-willed; opinionated; headstrong*

蓖(**萆) bì ㄅㄧˋ [蓖麻](－má)一年生或多年生草本植物。种子可榨油,医药上用作轻泻剂,工业上用作润滑油等 castor-oil plant; palma christi (*Ricinus communis*)

篦 bì ㄅㄧˋ ❶(－子)齿很密的梳头用具 double-edged fine-toothed comb ❷用篦子梳 to comb with such a comb: ～头 *to comb one's hair with a double-edged fine-toothed comb*

滗(潷) bì ㄅㄧˋ 挡住渣滓或泡着的东西,把液体倒出 to decant; to strain; to drain: 壶里的茶～干了。*The teapot has been drained dry.* | 把汤～出去。*Decant the soup out.*

辟 ㊀ bì ㄅㄧˋ ❶君主 monarch; sovereign [复辟]失位的君主恢复君位 to restore a dethroned monarch ㊉ ***extension*** 被打垮的统治者恢复原有的统治地位或被推翻的制度复活 to restore one's original ruling position, or to revive a toppled system ❷旧指君主召见并授予官职 (of a sovereign) to summon sb and confer on him an official post in former times ❸古同"避" same as 避 in ancient Chinese

㊁ pì 见563页 see p563

薜 bì ㄅㄧˋ [薜荔](－lì)常绿灌木,爬蔓,花小,叶卵形,果实球形,可做凉粉,叶及乳汁可入药 climbing fig (*Ficus pumila*)

壁 bì ㄅㄧˋ ❶墙 wall (㊥ ***doublet*** 墙一 wall): 四～ *four walls of a room* | ～报 *wall newspaper* | 铜墙铁～ *bastion of iron; impregnable fortress* [壁虎]爬行动物,身体扁平,尾巴圆锥形,四肢短,趾上有吸盘,捕食蚊、蝇等 house gecko (*Hemidactylus*) ❷陡峭的山石 wall-like stone; cliff: 绝～ *cliff*;

precipice|峭～ *cliff*; *precipice*; *steep* ❸壁垒,军营的围墙 rampart; breastwork; military barrier:坚～清野 *to strengthen the defences and clear the fields*; *to fortify the defense works and to leave nothing usable to the invading enemy*|作～上观(坐观双方胜败,不帮助任何一方) *to be an onlooker*; *to sit by and watch*; *to watch the fighting from behind the rampart* ❹星宿名,二十八宿之一 *bi*, 14th of the 28 constellations

避 bì ㄅㄧˋ ❶躲,设法躲开 to avoid; to evade; to shun (㊋ **doublet** 躲— to hide oneself; to avoid): ～暑 *to get away from summer heat*; *to get away for the summer holidays*|～雨 *to take shelter from the rain*|不～艰险 *to be undaunted by danger and hardship*; *to face danger and hardship squarely* ❷防止 to prevent; to keep away; to repel: ～孕 *contraception*|～雷针 *lightning rod*

嬖 bì ㄅㄧˋ ❶宠幸 to show favour to:～爱 *to dote on* ❷被宠幸 to be in favour (with sb); to enjoy favour: ～臣 *favourite courtier*|～人 *monarch's favourite*

臂 ㊀ bì ㄅㄧˋ 胳膊,从肩到腕的部分 arm:振～高呼 *to raise one's arms and shout*[臂助] **1** 帮助 assistance **2** 助手 assistant

㊁ bei 见 223 页"胳"字条"胳臂"see 胳臂(gē—) on p223

璧 bì ㄅㄧˋ 古代玉器,平圆形,中间有孔 round flat piece of jade with a hole in its centre used in ancient China[璧还](—huán)㊕ ***transfer*** 敬辞 ***polite***,用于归还原物或辞谢赠品 to return (a borrowed object) with thanks; to decline (a gift) with thanks: 谨将原物～～。*Please allow me to return your object with sincere thanks.*

襞 bì ㄅㄧˋ 古代指给衣裙打褶(zhě)子,也指衣裙上的褶子(in ancient China) to make folds in clothes; to pleat; pleats (*or* folds) in clothes

躄(**躃) bì ㄅㄧˋ ❶腿瘸(qué),不能行走 to be lame in the leg; to limp ❷仆倒 to fall down

碧 bì ㄅㄧˋ ❶青绿色的玉石 green jade; jasper ❷青绿色 bluish green; blue: ～草 *green grass*|～波 *blue waves*|金～辉煌 (*of a building*, *etc*) *resplendent and magnificent*

觱(**篳) bì ㄅㄧˋ [觱篥](—lì)古代的一种管乐器 *bili*, a bamboo pipe with a reed mouthpiece in ancient China

濞 bì ㄅㄧˋ [漾濞](yàng—)地名,在云南省 Yangbi, a place in Yunnan Province

BIAN ㄅㄧㄢ

边(邊) biān ㄅㄧㄢ ❶(—儿)物体周围的

部分 margin; side; edge; brim: 纸～儿 *margin*|桌子～儿 *edge of a table* ⑤ ***extension*** 旁边,近旁,侧面 side; edge; flank: 身～ *by one's side*|马路～ *by the roadside* ❷国家或地区之间的交界处 border; boundary; frontier: ～防 *frontier* (*or border*) *defence*|～境 *border; frontier*|～疆 *border area; borderland; frontier* ❸几何学上指夹成角的射线或围成多边形的线段 side of a geometrical figure; lines that form an angle or a multi-angle figure in geometry ❹方面 side; party: 双～会谈 *bilateral talks*|两～都说定了。*Both sides have reached an agreement.* ❺(一)边…(一)边…,用在动词前,表示动作同时进行(used before verbs, to express the simultaneous progression or development of two actions): ～干～学 *to learn while working; to learn on the job*|～走～说 *to talk while walking* ❻(bian)表示位置、方向,用在"上"、"下"、"前"、"后"、"左"、"右"等字后(used after 上,下,前,后,左,右,etc, to express position or direction): 东～ *the east*|外～ *the outside*|左～ *the left*

笾(籩) biān ㄅㄧㄢ 古代祭祀或宴会时盛(chéng)果品等的竹器 (used at banquets or sacrifices in ancient China) bamboo container for fruit or other things

砭 biān ㄅㄧㄢ 古代用石针扎皮肉治病 to perform acupuncture with stone needles in ancient China [针砭]㊥***figurative*** 指出过错,劝人改正 to criticize and admonish; to point out sb's errors and offer salutary advice

萹 biān ㄅㄧㄢ [萹蓄](－xù)又叫"萹竹"。多年生草本植物,叶狭长,略似竹叶,夏季开小花。全草可入药 (also called 萹竹) common knotgrass (*Polygonum aviculare*)

编 biān ㄅㄧㄢ ❶用细条或带子形的东西交叉组织起来 to weave; to plait: ～草帽 *to weave a straw hat*|～筐子 *to weave a basket* ❷按一定的次序或条理来组织或排列 to organize; to group; to arrange: ～号 *to number*|～队 *to form into columns; to organize into teams*|～组 *to group; to organize* (*people, vehicles, etc*) *into groups* [编辑]把资料或现成的作品加以适当的整理、加工做成书报等,也指从事这一工作的人 to edit; to compile; editor; compiler [编制]军队或机关中按照工作需要规定的人员或职务的配置 authorized strength or size; establishment ❸成本的书,书里因内容不同自成起讫的各部分 part of a book; volume: 正～ *main part* (*of a book*); *the book proper*|下～ *last part* (*of a book*)|简～ *concise edition* ❹创作 to write; to compose: ～歌 *to* *compose a song* | ～剧本 *to write a play* ❺捏造，把没有的事情说成有 to fabricate; to invent; to make up：～了一套瞎话 *to fabricate a story; to invent a lie*

煸 biān ㄅㄧㄢ 把蔬菜、肉等放在热油里炒 to stir-fry (vegetables or meat in hot oil)

蝙 biān ㄅㄧㄢ ［蝙蝠］(—fú) 哺乳动物，头和身体的样子像老鼠。前后肢都有薄膜和身体连着，夜间在空中飞，捕食蚊、蛾等 bat (*Chiroptera*)

鳊 biān ㄅㄧㄢ 鳊鱼，鱼名。身体侧扁，头尖，尾巴小，鳞细，生活在淡水中，肉可以吃 white bream (*Blicca bjoerkna*)

鞭 biān ㄅㄧㄢ ❶(—子)驱使牲畜的用具 whip; lash ❷用鞭子抽打 to lash; to whip ［鞭策］㊗ ***figurative*** 督促前进 to spur on; to urge on; to give impetus to ❸一种旧式武器，用铁做成，没有锋刃，有节 nodular iron-staff with no blade used as a weapon in former times ❹编连成串的爆竹 stringed firecrackers：～炮 (*a string of*) *firecrackers*

贬 biǎn ㄅㄧㄢˇ ❶给予不好的评价，跟"褒"相对 (the opposite of 褒) to depreciate; to belittle：一字之～ *to censure with one word* ［褒贬］**1** 评论好坏 to assess; to appraise **2** (—bian)指出缺点 to speak ill of; to point out the shortcomings ❷减低，降低 to reduce; to devalue：～价 *to reduce the price* | ～值 *to devalue* | ～职 *to demote*

窆 biǎn ㄅㄧㄢˇ 埋葬 to bury

扁 ㊀ biǎn ㄅㄧㄢˇ 物体平而薄 flat and thin：鸭子嘴～。*The duck has a flat beak.*

㊁ piān 见564页 see p564

匾 biǎn ㄅㄧㄢˇ 匾额，题字的横牌，挂在门、墙的上部 (hanging over a door or on the upper part of a wall) horizontal inscribed board：金字红～ *red board with golden words on it* | 光荣～ *board of honour*

碥 biǎn ㄅㄧㄢˇ 在水旁斜着伸出来的山石 rock sticking out obliquely by the side of a river

褊 biǎn ㄅㄧㄢˇ 狭小，狭隘(ài) narrow; cramped

藊 biǎn ㄅㄧㄢˇ ［藊豆］一年生草本植物，爬蔓，开白色或紫色的花，种子和嫩荚可以吃。现作"扁豆"(now written as 扁豆) hyacinth bean (*Lablab purpureus*)

卞 biàn ㄅㄧㄢˋ 急躁 irritable; irascible (㊐ ***doublet*** 一急 hot-tempered; irascible)

抃 biàn ㄅㄧㄢˋ 鼓掌 to applaud; to clap one's hands

苄 biàn ㄅㄧㄢˋ ［苄基］也叫苯甲基。有机化合物的基。结构式为

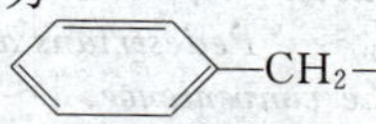

(also called 苯甲基) benzyl

汴 biàn ㄅㄧㄢˋ 河南省开封的别称 Bian, another name for

Kaifeng, in Henan Province

忭 biàn ㄅㄧㄢˋ 高兴,喜欢 happy; glad

弁 biàn ㄅㄧㄢˋ ❶古代男子戴的一种帽子 man's cap worn in ancient China [弁言]书籍或长篇文章的序文,引言 foreword; preface ❷旧时称低级武官 low-ranking military officer in former times: 马~ *officer's bodyguard*

昪 biàn ㄅㄧㄢˋ ❶日光明亮 (of sunlight) bright ❷欢乐 joyful; merry

变(變) biàn ㄅㄧㄢˋ 性质、状态或情形和以前不同,更改 to become different (㊟ **doublet** 一更 to change; to alter; to modify | 一化 to change; to vary):沙漠~良田。*The deserts have been turned into cultivated land.* |天气~了。*The weather has changed.* |他的思想~了。*He has changed his view.* ㊞ **extension** 事变,突然发生的非常事件 incident; unexpected turn of events:政~ *coup* [变通]改动原定的办法,以适应新情况的需要 to be flexible; to make changes according to specific conditions

便 ㊀ biàn ㄅㄧㄢˋ ❶方便,顺利,没有困难或阻碍 convenient; smooth; handy; easy (㊟ **doublet** 一利 convenient):行人称~。*Pedestrians appreciate the convenience.* |~于携带 *portable; easy to carry* ❷简单的,非正式的 simple; informal:家常~饭 *homely (or simple) meal* |~衣 *plain (or civilian) clothes* |~条 *note* [便宜]根据实际需要而灵活、适当地 flexibly:~~行事 *to act as one sees fit; to act at one's discretion* (另 piányi,见"便"pián see also 便 pián for piányi) [随便]不勉强,不拘束 casual; at ease ❸便利的时候 at one's convenience: ~中请来信。*Please write to me at your convenience.* |得~就送去。*I will send it to you at a convenient time.* ❹屎尿或排泄屎尿 urine or faeces; to urinate or defecate: 粪~ *excrement* |小~ *urine; to urinate; to pee* ❺副词 **adverb**,就 then; in that case:没有一个人民的军队,~没有人民的一切。*The people would have none of what they have now without an army of the people.*

㊁ pián 见 565 页 see p565

缏 biàn ㄅㄧㄢˋ [草帽缏]用麦秆等编成的扁平的带子,用来编草帽、提篮、扇子等。也作"草帽辫"(also written as 草帽辫)(for making hats, baskets, fans, etc) plaited straw

遍(*徧) biàn ㄅㄧㄢˋ ❶普遍,全面 all over; everywhere:我们的朋友~天下。*We have friends all over the world.* |~布全国 *all over the country* |满山~野 *over hill and down dale; all over the mountains and plains* ❷量词 ***quantifier***,次,回 time:念一~ *to read (a book) through* |问了

两～ *to have asked (sb) twice*

辨 biàn ㄅㄧㄢˋ 分别，分析 to distinguish; to differentiate（㊀ ***doublet*** 一别 to distinguish|分一 to differentiate）：明～是非 *to make a clear distinction between right and wrong*|不～真伪 *to fail to distinguish between truth and falsehood; to be unable to tell the true from the false*|～认笔迹 *to identify sb's handwriting*

辩 biàn ㄅㄧㄢˋ 说明是非或真假，争论 to argue; to debate（㊀ ***doublet*** 一论 to argue; to debate）：～驳 *to refute; to rebut*|～护 *to defend; to plead* [辩证法]事物矛盾的运动、发展、变化的一般规律，也指阐明这种规律的哲学。唯物辩证法认为，事物运动和发展的根本原因在于事物内部的矛盾性。对立统一规律是宇宙的根本规律，是唯物辩证法的实质和核心 dialectics

辫（辮） biàn ㄅㄧㄢˋ ❶（一子）把头发分股编成的带状物 plait; braid ❷（一子、一儿）像辫子的东西 sth resembling a plait or braid：草帽～儿 *plaited straw (for making hats)*|蒜～子 *braid of garlic*

BIAO ㄅㄧㄠ

杓 ㊀ biāo ㄅㄧㄠ 古代指北斗柄部的三颗星 ancient term for the three stars forming the handle of the Big Dipper

㊁ sháo 见 660 页 see p660

标（標） biāo ㄅㄧㄠ ❶树木的末梢 tip of a tree; treetop ㊀ ***extension*** 表面的，非根本的 surface; superficial; outward sign：治～不如治本。*It's better to treat the disease than the symptoms.* or *To seek a permanent cure is better than temporary treatment.* ❷记号 mark; sign：浮～（浮在水上的行船航线标志）*buoy*|商～ *trade mark*|～点符号 *punctuation* [标榜]吹捧，夸耀 to flaunt; to advertise：互相～～ *to boost each other*|～～民主 *to flaunt democracy* [标的]（一dì）目标 objective; target; aim [标语]用文字写出的有鼓动宣传作用的口号 slogan; poster [标准]衡量事物的准则 standard; criterion：实践是检验真理的唯一～～。*Practice is the sole criterion of truth.* [锦标]授给竞赛优胜者的锦旗、奖杯等 prize; trophy [指标]计划中规定达到的目标 target; quota; norm：数量～～ *quota*|质量～～ *quality index* ❸用文字或其他事物表明 to mark; to label：～题 *title*|～价 *marked price; to mark a price*|～新立异 *to start sth new just in order to be different; to do sth unconventional or unorthodox* [标本]保持原样供学习研究参考的动物、植物、矿物 sample; specimen ❹发承包工程或买卖大宗货物时公布的标准和条件 bid; tender：投～ *to enter a bid; to*

B

submit a tender｜招～ *to invite tenders*｜竞～ *to compete for a bid*
[标致](—zhi)容貌美丽,多用于女子 (usually of women) beautiful; pretty

飑 biāo ㄅㄧㄠ 气象学上指风向突然改变,风速急剧增大且常伴有阵雨的天气现象 squall

彪 biāo ㄅㄧㄠ 小虎 young tiger 喻 ***figurative*** 躯干魁梧 hefty; burly:～形大汉 *tall and strong man; hefty fellow; burly guy*

骠 ㊀ biāo ㄅㄧㄠ [黄骠马]—种黄毛夹杂着白点子的马 white-spotted yellow horse
㊁ piào 见 568 页 see p568

膘(*臕) biāo ㄅㄧㄠ 肥肉(多指牲畜)(usually of a domestic animal) fat:～满肉肥 *plump and fat*｜上～(长肉) *to get fat; to put on flesh*

镖 biāo ㄅㄧㄠ 旧时以投掷方式杀伤敌人的武器,形状像长矛的头 (weapon thrown to kill or injure the enemy in former times) dart; dart-like weapon

瘭 biāo ㄅㄧㄠ [瘭疽](—jū)手指头肚儿或脚指头肚儿发炎化脓的病,症状是局部红肿,剧烈疼痛,发烧 felon; pyogenic infection of the pad of a finger or toe

飙(**飊、**飇) biāo ㄅㄧㄠ 暴风 violent wind; whirlwind:狂～*hurricane*

藨 biāo ㄅㄧㄠ 藨草,多年生草本植物,茎可织席、编草鞋,又可用来造纸及人造纤维等 bulrush (*Scirpus*)

瀌 biāo ㄅㄧㄠ [瀌瀌]形容雨雪大 (of rain or snow) heavy

镳 biāo ㄅㄧㄠ ❶马嚼子两头露在嘴外的部分 two ends of a bit (of a bridle); curb bit:分道扬～(喻趋向不同) *to separate and go different ways—to part company, each going his or her own way* ❷同"镖" same as 镖

表(❺錶) biǎo ㄅㄧㄠˇ ❶外部,跟"里"相对 (the opposite of 里) surface; outside 1 在外的 outside:～面 *surface; appearance*｜～皮 *epidermis* 2 外面,外貌 outside look; appearance:外～ *outward appearance*｜～里如一 *to think and act in the same way*｜虚有其～ *to look impressive but to be inwardly worthless; to be striking only in appearance* ❷表示,显示 to show; to demonstrate:略～心意。*It is only a token of our regard*.[表白]说明自己的心意对人进行解释,分清责任 to explain oneself; to clarify; to profess [表决]会议上用举手、投票等方式取得多数意见而做出决定 to vote; to decide by vote:这个议案已经～～通过了。*This motion has been voted through*. [表现] 1 显露 to show; to display:医疗队的行动充分～～了救死扶伤的人道主义精神。*The action of the medical team fully displayed the humanitarianism of healing the wounded and rescuing the dying.* **2** 所显露出来的行为,作风 performance; behaviour:他在工作中的～～还不错。*He is doing quite well in his work.* [表扬]对集体或个人,用语言、文字公开表示赞美、夸奖 to praise; to commend:～～好人好事 *to praise good people and good deeds* ❸中医指用药物把感受的风寒发散出来(of traditional Chinese medicine) to administer medicine to drive out the cold ❹分类分项记录事物的东西 table; form:历史年～ *chronological table of history*|时间～ *time-table*|统计～ *statistic table* ❺计时间的器具,通常比钟小,可以带在身边 watch; timepiece:手～ *wrist watch; watch*|怀～ *pocket watch* ❻计量某种量的器具 metre; gauge:温度～ *thermometre*|电～ *kilowatt-hour metre; electric metre*|水～ *water metre* ❼树立的标志 model; example [表率](—shuài)榜样 model:他是新中国青年的～～。*He is a model for the youth of New China.* [华表]古代宫殿、陵墓等大建筑物前面做装饰用的巨大石柱,柱身多雕刻龙凤等图案,顶端有云板和蹲兽,是我国民族形式的艺术建筑物的一种 *huabiao*, an ornamental pillar (erected in front of palaces, tombs, etc) ❽称呼父亲或祖父的姊妹、母亲或祖母的兄弟姊妹生的子女,用来表示亲属关系 relationship between the children or grand-children of a brother and those of a sister:～兄弟 *male cousins*|～叔 *male cousin of one's father; son of one's grandfather's sister, or son of one's grandmother's sister or brother*|～姑 *female cousin of one's father; daughter of one's grandfather's sister, or daughter of one's grandmother's sister or brother* ❾封建时代称臣子给君主的奏章 memorial to an emperor in feudal times

婊 biǎo ㄅㄧㄠˇ [婊子](—zi)对妓女的称呼。多用作骂人的话 whore; prostitute

裱 biǎo ㄅㄧㄠˇ 用纸、布或丝织物把书、画等衬托装饰起来 to mount (a piece of calligraphy or picture on paper, cloth or silk to embellish it):双～纸 *double mount*|揭～字画 *to remove a piece of calligraphy or picture and then mount it anew* [裱糊]用纸或其他材料糊屋子的墙壁或顶棚 to paper (the walls or ceiling of a room):把这间屋子～～一下。*Please paper this room.*

俵 biào ㄅㄧㄠˋ 〈方 **dialect**〉俵分,把东西分给人 to distribute; to hand out

摽 biào ㄅㄧㄠˋ ❶紧紧地捆在器物上 to tie fast; to fasten:

把口袋～在车架子上 *to fasten a sack to the carrying rack of a bicycle* ❷用手、胳膊钩住 arm in arm; hand in hand:他俩～着膀子走。*The two of them are walking arm in arm.* ❸由于利害相关而互相亲近、依附或纠结 to be locked together; to cling to one another:他们老～在一块儿。*They are always locked together.*

鳔 biào ㄅㄧㄠˋ ❶鱼体内可以胀缩的气囊,通称"鱼泡",膨胀时鱼上浮,收缩时鱼下沉。有的鱼类的鳔有辅助听觉或呼吸等作用(commonly called 鱼泡) swim bladder; air bladder ❷鳔胶,用鳔或猪皮等熬成的胶,很黏 isinglass; fish glue ❸用鳔胶粘上 to stick sth on with fish glue:把桌子腿儿～一～ *to stick the table-leg on with isinglass*

BIE ㄅㄧㄝ

瘪(癟) ㊂ biē ㄅㄧㄝ [瘪三]〈方 **dialect**〉旧时上海人对城市中无正当职业而以乞讨或偷窃为生的游民的称呼(appellation used in Shanghai before 1949 for a wretched-looking tramp who lived by begging or stealing) tramp; bum

㊀ biě 见 49 页 see p49

憋 biē ㄅㄧㄝ ❶气不通 to suffocate; to stifle:门窗全关着,真～气。*It is stifling in the room with all the doors and windows closed.* [憋闷](—men)心里不痛快 to be depressed; to be dejected:这事真叫人～～。*This is downright depressing.* ❷勉强忍住 to suppress; to hold back:把嘴一闭,～足了气 *to close one's mouth and hold one's breath*|心里～了许多话要说 *to be bursting with unspoken words*

鳖(*鼈) biē ㄅㄧㄝ 也叫"甲鱼"、"团鱼",俗叫"王八"。爬行动物,形状像龟,背甲无纹,边缘柔软。肉供食用,甲可入药(also called 甲鱼 or 团鱼; popularly called 王八) Chinese soft-shelled turtle (*Pelodiscus sinensis*)

别 ㊀ bié ㄅㄧㄝˊ ❶分离 to leave; to part; to depart(㊟ **doublet** 分— to part; to depart|离—to leave; to part):告～ *to say goodbye to; to bid farewell to*|临～赠言 *parting words of advice; words of encouragement given at parting* ❷分辨,区分 to differentiate; to distinguish(㊟ **doublet** 辨— to differentiate; to distinguish):分门～类 *to classify; to put into different categories*|分～清楚 *to make a clear distinction* ㊂ **extension** 差别,差异 difference; distinction:天渊之～ *world of difference; poles apart* [区别] **1** 划分 to differentiate:正确～～和处理敌我矛盾和人民内部矛盾 *to correctly distinguish and handle the two different types of contradictions, contradictions between* *ourselves and the enemy, and contradictions among the people* **2** 差异 difference：～～不大。*There is little difference.* or *The difference is not remarkable.* ❸类别，分类 category；classification：性～*gender*｜职～*official rank* ❹另外的 other；another：～人 *somebody else；other people*｜～名 *alternative name；another name；alias*｜～开生面 *to develop a new style；to break fresh ground*［别致］跟寻常不同的，新奇的 original；novel；exquisite：式样～～。*The style is unique.*［别字］写错了的或念错了的字。也叫"白字"（also called 白字）incorrectly written or mispronounced character；malapropism ❺副词 ***adverb***，不要（表示禁止或劝阻）(used to give command or advice against doing sth) don't；had better not：～动手！*Don't touch it!* or *Hands off!*｜～开玩笑！*Don't joke!* ❻绷住或卡(qiǎ)住 to pin；to fasten：用大头针把两张表格～在一起 *to pin the two forms together*｜～针 *pin；brooch*｜腰里～着旱烟袋 *with a long-stemmed Chinese pipe stuck in one's belt* ❼姓 Bie，a surname

㊁ biè 见 49 页 see p49

蹩 bié ㄅㄧㄝˊ 扭了脚腕子 to sprain (one's ankle)［蹩脚］〈方 ***dialect***〉质量不好，本领不强 inferior；shoddy；poor：～～货 *inferior goods；shoddy goods*

瘪（癟）㊀ biě ㄅㄧㄝˇ 不饱满，凹下 shriveled；shrunken；deflated：～花生 *blighted peanuts*｜干～ *dry and shriveled；wizened*｜车带～了。*The tyre is flat.*

㊁ biē 见 48 页 see p48

别（彆）㊁ biè ㄅㄧㄝˋ［别扭］(—niu) **1** 不顺，不相投 awkward；uncomfortable：心里～～ *to feel awkward and uncomfortable*｜闹～～ *to be at odds with sb；to fall out with sb* **2** 难对付 hard to get along with；hard to deal with：这人脾气很～～。*This person has an eccentric temper.*

㊀ bié 见 48 页 see p48

BIN ㄅㄧㄣ

邠 bīn ㄅㄧㄣ 邠县，在陕西省。今作"彬县"（now written as 彬县）Binxian County，in Shaanxi Province

玢 ㊀ bīn ㄅㄧㄣ 玉名 a kind of jade

㊁ fēn 见 194 页 see p194

宾（賓）bīn ㄅㄧㄣ 客人 guest（㊣ ***doublet*** 一客 guest；visitor）：来～ *guest；visitor*｜外～ *foreign guest*｜～馆 *guesthouse；hostel；hotel*｜喧～夺主（喻次要事物侵占主要事物的地位）*a noisy or presumptuous guest usurps the host's role — the secondary supercedes the primary*

傧（儐）bīn ㄅㄧㄣ 引导 to usher；to lead：～

者 usher [傧相](—xiàng)旧指为主人接引宾客的人,今指婚礼时陪伴新郎新娘的人(usher in former times) groomsman or bridesmaid

滨(濱) bīn ㄅㄧㄣ ❶水边 water's edge; bank; shore:湖～ *lakefront; lakeside*|海～ *seashore; seaside* ❷靠近 to be close to; to border on:～海 *coastal; bordering on the sea*

缤(繽) bīn ㄅㄧㄣ [缤纷](—fēn)繁盛而交杂的样子 in riotous profusion:五彩～～ *riot of colours; multi-coloured*

槟(檳、**梹) ㊀ bīn ㄅㄧㄣ 槟子,苹果树的一种,果实也叫槟子,比苹果小,熟的时候紫红色,味酸甜 *binzi*, a species of crab apple, yielding purplish-red fruits, which tastes sour and sweet; crabapple(*Malus*)

㊁ bīng 见51页 see p51

镔(鑌) bīn ㄅㄧㄣ [镔铁]精炼的铁 wrought iron

彬 bīn ㄅㄧㄣ [彬彬]形容文雅 elegant; refined; urbane:文质～～ *suave; urbane; quiet and scholarly*

斌 bīn ㄅㄧㄣ [斌斌]同"彬彬" same as 彬彬

濒 bīn ㄅㄧㄣ ❶紧靠(水边) to be close to (a sea, a river, etc); to border on:～海 *to border the sea* ❷接近,将,临 to be on the verge of; to be on the brink of:～危 *to be in imminent danger*|～死 *to be on the verge of death*

豳 bīn ㄅㄧㄣ 古地名,在今陕西省旬邑一带 Bin, an ancient place, now in Xunyi, Shaanxi Province

摈(擯) bìn ㄅㄧㄣˋ 排除,遗弃 to discard; to reject; to exclude:～斥异己 *to exclude those who hold different opinions; to get rid of those who differ from oneself*

殡(殯) bìn ㄅㄧㄣˋ 停放灵柩或把灵柩送到墓地去 to lay a coffin in a memorial hall; to carry a coffin to the burial place:出～ *to carry a coffin to the cemetery; to hold a funeral procession*|～仪馆(代人办理丧事的场所) *funeral parlour; the undertaker's*

膑(臏) bìn ㄅㄧㄣˋ 同"髌" same as 髌

髌(髕) bìn ㄅㄧㄣˋ ❶膝盖骨(图见241页"骨" see the picture of 骨 on p241) kneecap; patella ❷古代削去膝盖骨的酷刑(a cruel torture in ancient China) chopping off the kneecaps

鬓(鬢) bìn ㄅㄧㄣˋ 脸旁边靠近耳朵的头发 hair over the temples:两～斑白 *to grey at the temples; to have grey temples*

BING ㄅㄧㄥ

冰(*氷) bīng ㄅㄧㄥ ❶水因冷凝结成的固体

ice［冰毒］一种毒品，像小冰块的白色结晶体。常用成瘾，会对人的生理平衡造成严重破坏，甚至可导致狂躁而死亡 ice, a common name for methamphetamine used in the form of crystalline hydrochloride, a deadly addictive stimulant drug ❷使人感到寒冷 to feel cold：河里的水有点～手。*The water in the river is somewhat icy*. ❸用冰贴近东西使变凉 to ice; to put sth near or on ice to make it cool：把汽水～上 *to ice the soda water*

并 ㊁ bīng ㄅㄧㄥ 并州，山西省太原的别称 Bingzhou, another name for Taiyuan in Shanxi Province

㊀ bìng 见 52 页 see p52

栟 ㊁ bīng ㄅㄧㄥ［栟榈］(—lǘ) 古书上指棕榈 (in ancient Chinese texts) palm

㊀ bēn 见 32 页 see p32

兵 bīng ㄅㄧㄥ ❶武器 weapons; arms：～器 *weapons; arms*｜短～相接 *to fight at close quarters* ❷战士，军队 soldier; army; troops：官～一致 *unity between officers and men*｜步～*infantry*｜～民是胜利之本。*Unity between the army and the people is the foundation of victory*. ❸与军事或战争有关的 related to war or military affairs：～法 *art of war; military strategy and tactics*｜纸上谈～ *to be an armchair strategist; to engage in idle theorizing; to talk about fighting battles only on paper*

槟（檳、**梹）㊁ bīng ㄅㄧㄥ［槟榔］(—lang) 常绿乔木，生长在热带、亚热带。果实也叫槟榔，可以吃，也可入药 betel palm; areca nut palm (*Areca catechu*)

㊀ bīn 见 50 页 see p50

丙 bǐng ㄅㄧㄥˇ ❶天干的第三位，用作顺序的第三 *bing*, the 3rd of the 10 Heavenly Stems; third in order：～等 *third grade; grade C* ❷指火 fire：付～(烧掉) *to burn (up); to put to fire*

邴 bǐng ㄅㄧㄥˇ 姓 Bing, a surname

柄 bǐng ㄅㄧㄥˇ ❶器物的把(bà)儿 handle (of sth)：刀～ *handle of a knife*［把柄］可被人作为要挟或攻击的事情 handle (against sb); excuse［笑柄］被人当作取笑的资料 laughingstock：一时传为～～ *to become a standing joke for a period of time; to spread far and wide as a joke* ❷植物的花、叶或果实跟枝或茎连着的部分 stem：花～ *stem of a flower*｜叶～ *footstalk; leafstalk; stem of a leaf*｜果～ *stem of a fruit* ❸执掌 to control; to be in power：～国 *to rule a country*｜～政 *to hold political power* ❹权 power; authority：国～ *national power*

炳 bǐng ㄅㄧㄥˇ 光明，显著 bright; splendid; remarkable

秉 bǐng ㄅㄧㄥˇ ❶拿着，持 to hold; to grasp：～烛 *to*

B

hold a candle | ~笔 *to hold a pen* ㊀ ***extension*** 掌握,主持 to control; to preside over: ~公处理 *to act with justice; to handle impartially* ❷古代容量单位,合十六斛(hú) *bing*, a unit of capacity in ancient China, equal to 16 *hu*

饼 bǐng ㄅㄧㄥˇ ❶扁圆形的面制食品 cake; pie: 肉~ *meat pie* | 大~ *large flatbread; big flat pie* ❷像饼的东西 sth shaped like a cake: 铁~ *discus* | 豆~ *bean cake*

屏 ㊁ bǐng ㄅㄧㄥˇ ❶除去,排除 to eliminate; to reject; to get rid of (㊇***doublet*** 一除 to eliminate; to get rid of): ~弃不用 *to discard; to throw away* | ~退左右 *to dismiss one's attendants* ❷抑止(呼吸) to hold (one's breath): ~气 *to hold one's breath* | ~息 *to hold one's breath*

㊀ píng 见 572 页 see p572

禀(*稟) bǐng ㄅㄧㄥˇ ❶承受,生成的 to receive; to be endowed with (㊇***doublet*** 一受 to be born with; to possess): ~性 *natural disposition* ❷下对上报告 to report (to one's superior): ~明一切 *to report everything in detail*

鞞 bǐng ㄅㄧㄥˇ 刀鞘 sheath of a knife or sword

并(❶*併、❷-❹*並、❷-❹*竝) ㊀ bìng ㄅㄧㄥˋ ❶合在一起 to combine; to merge; to incorporate (㊇***doublet*** 合一 to combine; to amalgamate): ~案办理 *to merge related cases and deal with them altogether* ❷一齐,平排着 side by side: ~驾齐驱 *to run neck and neck; to keep abreast of sb* | ~肩作战 *to fight shoulder to shoulder* | ~排坐着 *to sit side by side* ❸连词 ***conjunction***, 表示进一层 and also; besides: 讨论~通过了这项议案。*The motion was discussed and adopted.* [并且] 连词 ***conjunction***, 表示进一层,常跟"不但"相应 (used to express an increasing degree often in collocation with 不但) but also; furthermore; in addition; moreover: 他不但赞成,~~愿意帮忙。*He not only agreed but also offered to help.* ❹副词 ***adverb*** **1** 放在否定词前面,加强否定语气,表示不像预料的那样 (used before a negative for emphasis, indicating that sth is not as expected): ~不太冷 *not so cold* | ~非不知道。*It is not the case that he does not know it.* **2** 同时,一起 simultaneously; side by side; equally: 齐头~进 *to advance simultaneously; to do two or more things at once* | 相提~论 *to mention in the same breath; to be named in the same day with; to take rank with* | 二者~重。*Both are equally important.*

㊁ bīng 见 51 页 see p51

摒 bìng ㄅㄧㄥˋ 排除 to get rid of (㊀ *doublet* —除 to eliminate; to discard)

病 bìng ㄅㄧㄥˋ ❶生物体发生不健康的现象 (to suffer from) illness; (to catch) disease (㊀ *doublet* 疾— disease; illness; sickness): 害了一场～ *to suffer from a disease* | 他～了。*He is ill.* [毛病](—bing) **1** 疾病 disease; illness **2** 缺点 shortcoming; defect **3** 指器物损坏或发生故障 trouble; breakdown: 勤检修，机器就少出～～。*When regularly maintained, the machine will seldom go wrong.* ❷弊端，错误 fault; error: 语～ *faulty wording* | 通～ *common mistake* ❸损害，祸害 to do harm to; to injure: 祸国～民 *to bring calamity to the country and the people*

BO ㄅㄛ

拨(撥) bō ㄅㄛ ❶用手指或棍棒等推动或挑动 to move; to turn; to poke (with one's fingers or a stick): 把钟～一下 *to set a clock* [拨冗](—rǒng)推开杂事，抽出时间 to find some time in the midst of pressing affairs: 务希～～出席。*Your presence is cordially requested.* ❷分给 to allocate; to assign: ～款 *to allocate funds* | ～点儿粮食 *to allocate some grain* ❸(—儿)量词 **quantifier**，用于成批的，分组的 batch; group: 一～儿人 *a batch of people; a group of people* | 分～儿进入会场 *to go into the conference hall in groups*

波 bō ㄅㄛ ❶江、河、湖、海等因振荡而一起一伏的水面 wave (㊀ *doublet* —浪 waves | —涛 great waves; billows | —澜 billows; great waves) [波动]㊀ *figurative* 事物起变化，不稳定 to undulate; to fluctuate [波及]㊀ *figurative* 牵涉到，影响到 to spread to; to affect; to involve ❷物理学上指振动在物质中的传播，是能量传递的一种形式 (in physics) wave: 光～ *light wave* | 声～ *sound wave* | 电～ *electric wave* [微波]一般指波长从 1 米到 1 毫米(频率 300 兆赫—300 000 兆赫)的无线电波。包括分米波、厘米波和毫米波。广泛应用于导航、遥感技术、通信、气象、天文等方面 microwave

玻 bō ㄅㄛ [玻璃](—li) ❶一种质地硬而脆的透明物体，是用沙子、石灰石、碳酸钠等混合起来，加高热熔解，冷却后制成的 glass ❷透明像玻璃的质料 transparent and glass-like substance: 有机～～ *plexiglass; perspex* | ～～纸 *cellophane; glassine*

菠 bō ㄅㄛ [菠菜]一年生或二年生草本植物，根带红色，果实分无刺和有刺两种，茎叶可以吃 spinach (*Spinacia oleracea*)

B

锇 bō ㄅㄛ 一种人造的放射性元素（符号 Bh）bohrium (Bh)

钵（*缽）bō ㄅㄛ ❶盛饭、菜、茶水等的陶制器具 earthen bowl：饭～*rice bowl*［乳钵］研药使成细末的器具（used to grind medical herbs into powder）pestle and mortar ❷梵语“钵多罗”的省称，和尚用的饭碗（short for “钵多罗” in Sanskrit）alms bowl (of a Buddhist monk)：～盂 *alms bowl* (*of a Buddhist monk*)［衣钵］原指佛教中师父传授给徒弟的袈裟和钵盂，后泛指传下来的思想、学术、技能等（formerly used to denote *kasaya* and alms bowl handed down by a Buddhist monk to his favorite disciple）inherited thinking, learning, skills, etc

饽 bō ㄅㄛ［饽饽］(—bo)〈方 *dialect*〉**1** 馒头或其他块状的面食 *bobo*, steamed buns such as *mantou* **2** 甜食，点心 sweet pastry

剥 ㊀ bō ㄅㄛ 义同“剥㊁”，用于复合词（used in compound words）same as 剥㊁［剥夺］**1** 用强制的方法夺去 to rob sb of sth; to take away by force **2** 依照法律取消 to deprive by law：～～政治权利 *to deprive sb of his* (or *her*) *political rights*［剥削］(—xuē) 凭借生产资料的私人所有权、政治上的特权无偿地占有别人的劳动或产品 to exploit

㊁ bāo 见 24 页 see p24

播 bō ㄅㄛ ❶撒种 to sow (seeds); to seed：条～*to sow in furrows*｜点～*to dibble seeds; to dibble* ❷传扬，传布 to spread：～音 *to transmit; to broadcast over the radio or TV*［广播］利用电波播送新闻、文章、文艺节目等 to broadcast

嶓 bō ㄅㄛ［嶓冢］(—zhǒng) 古山名。在今甘肃省成县东北 Bozhong, an ancient mountain, now in the northeast of Chengxian County, Gansu Province

伯 ㊀ bó ㄅㄛˊ ❶兄弟排行(háng)常用“伯”、“仲”、“叔”、“季”做次序，伯是老大 the eldest in the order of seniority among brothers［伯仲］㊕ ***transfer*** 不相上下，好坏差不多 about the same; not much different ❷伯父，父亲的哥哥，大爷(ye) uncle; elder brother of one's father 又对年龄大、辈分高的人的尊称（respectful form of address for a man of one's father's generation who is older than one's father）：老～*uncle* ❸我国古代五等爵位（公、侯、伯、子、男）的第三等 earl; count; the third of the five ranks of nobility in ancient China ❹姓 Bo, a surname

㊁ bǎi 见 16 页 see p16

帛 bó ㄅㄛˊ 丝织品的总称 silk fabrics［玉帛］古代往来赠送的两种礼物，表示友好交往（used as gifts presented to friendly states in ancient China）jade objects and silk fabrics:化干戈为～～ *to turn hostility into friendship*

泊 ㊀ bó ㄅㄛˊ ❶停船靠岸 to berth; to moor (㊟ ***doublet*** 停一 to cast anchor):～船 *to berth a ship* ❷恬静 tranquility [淡泊](*澹泊)不贪图功名利禄 to seek no fame nor wealth

㊁ pō 见573页 see p573

柏 ㊂ bó ㄅㄛˊ [柏林]德国的首都 Berlin, capital of Germany

㊀ bǎi 见16页 see p16

㊁ bò 见57页 see p57

铂 bó ㄅㄛˊ 一种金属元素,符号Pt,富延展性,导电传热性都很好,熔点很高。可制坩埚、蒸发皿。化学上用作催化剂 platinum (Pt)

舶 bó ㄅㄛˊ 大船 oceangoing ship:船～ *ships* | ～来品(旧称外国输入的货物)(former term for goods from abroad) *imports*

鲌 ㊀ bó ㄅㄛˊ 鱼名。身体侧扁,嘴向上翘,生活在淡水中 topmouth culter (*Culter alburnus*)

㊁ bà 见14页 see p14

箔 bó ㄅㄛˊ ❶用苇子、秫秸等做成的帘子 (of reeds, sorghum stalks, etc) screen ❷养蚕的器具,多用竹制成,像筛子或席子。也叫"蚕帘"(also called 蚕帘) sieve or mat-like tray (usually made of bamboo for rearing silkworms) ❸金属薄片 foil; tinsel:金～*gold foil* | 铜～*copper foil* ❹敷上金属薄片或粉末的纸 paper pasted with thin sheet metal or metal powder; paper tinsel:锡～*tin foil*

魄 ㊂ bó ㄅㄛˊ "落魄"(luòpò)的"魄"的又音 (another pronunciation for "魄" in "落魄")

㊀ pò 见574页 see p574

㊁ tuò 见770页 see p770

驳(❶❸*駁) bó ㄅㄛˊ ❶说出自己的理由来,否定别人的意见 to refute; to present one's own opinion to refute another's:真理是～不倒的。*Truth fears no refutation.* | 反～*to refute* | 批～*to refute; to criticize* ❷大批货物用船分载转运 to transport by barge or lighter:起～*to start shipment by lighter* | 把大船上的米～卸到堆栈里 *to unload rice from a big ship to a storehouse by barge* [驳船]转运用的小船。也叫"拨船"(also called 拨船) barge; lighter ❸马的毛色不纯。泛指颜色不纯,夹杂着别的颜色(of the colour of a horse) parti-coloured; mottled (㊟ ***doublet*** 斑一 mottled)

勃 bó ㄅㄛˊ 旺盛(叠 ***reduplication***) vigorous; thriving:～起 *to have an erection* | 蓬～*vigorous; thriving* | 生气～～ *full of vitality* | 英姿～～ *dashing and spirited* [勃然] **1** 兴起旺盛的样子 vigorously; prosperously:～～而兴 *to spring up* **2** 变脸色的样子

B

agitatedly; excitedly: ～～大怒 *to fly into a rage; to flare up*

浡 bó ㄅㄛˊ 〈古 ***archaism***〉兴起,涌出 to cheer up; to display vigour

脖 bó ㄅㄛˊ ❶(－子)颈,头和躯干相连的部分 neck ❷像脖子的 neck-shaped: 脚～子 *ankle*

鹁 bó ㄅㄛˊ [鹁鸪](－gū)鸟名。羽毛黑褐色,天要下雨或天刚晴的时候,常在树上咕咕地叫。有的地方叫"水鸪鸪"(also called 水鸪鸪 in some areas) common wood-pigeon (*Columba palumbus*)

渤 bó ㄅㄛˊ 渤海,由辽东半岛和山东半岛围抱着的海 Bohai Sea (Bohai Gulf), surrounded by the Liaodong Peninsula and the Shandong Peninsula

钹 bó ㄅㄛˊ 铜质圆片形的乐器,中心鼓起,两片相击作声 cymbals

亳 bó ㄅㄛˊ [亳州]地名,在安徽省 Bozhou, a place in Anhui Province

袯(襏) bó ㄅㄛˊ [袯襫](－shì) ❶古蓑衣 straw or palm-bark rain cape in ancient China ❷粗糙结实的衣服 coarse but durable clothes

博 bó ㄅㄛˊ ❶多,广 rich; abundant; extensive (㊟ ***doublet*** 广－extensive): 地大物～ *vast territory with abundant resources; large territory that abounds in natural resources* | ～学 *learned; erudite* | ～览 *to read extensively* [博士] **1** 学位名,在硕士之上 doctor, academic degree higher than a master's degree **2** 古代掌管学术的官名 court academician in ancient China [博物]动物、植物、矿物、生理等学科的总称 natural science ❷知道得多 well-informed; erudite: ～古通今 *to have both ancient and modern knowledge; to be erudite and well-informed* ❸用自己的行动换取 to win; to gain: ～得同情 *to win sympathy (from sb)* ❹古代的一种棋戏,后泛指赌博 (chess game in ancient China) gambling

搏 bó ㄅㄛˊ ❶对打 to wrestle; to fight: ～斗 *to wrestle; to fight with hands* | ～击 *to fight with; to struggle with* | 肉～(打交手仗) *to fight hand to hand* ❷跳动 to beat; to throb: 脉～ *pulse*

馎 bó ㄅㄛˊ [馎饦](－tuō)古代的一种面食 *botuo*, a kind of cooked wheaten food in ancient China

膊 bó ㄅㄛˊ 胳膊(bo),肩膀以下手腕以上的部分 arm [赤膊]光膀子,赤裸上身 bare to the waist; to be stripped to the waist: ～～上阵 *to go into battle bare-chested*

镈 bó ㄅㄛˊ ❶大钟,古代乐器,形圆 *bo*, a large round bell, used as a musical instrument in ancient China ❷古代锄一类的农具 *bo*, a hoe-like tool in ancient China

薄 ㊁ bó ㄅㄛˊ ❶同"薄㊀"用于合成词或成语,如厚薄、单薄、淡薄、浅薄、薄田、薄弱、尖嘴薄舌、厚古薄今等(used in compound words or idioms, such as 厚薄 "thickness", 单薄 "thin and weak", 淡薄 "to become indifferent", 浅薄 "superficial", 薄田 "infertile land", 薄弱 "weakness", 尖嘴薄舌 "to have a caustic and flippant tongue", 厚古薄今 "to stress the past, not the present", etc) same as 薄㊀ ❷轻微,少 slight; meagre: ～技 *slight skill* | ～酬 *small reward; meagre remuneration* ❸不庄重 frivolous: 轻～ *frivolous; flirtatious* ❹看不起,轻视,慢待 to despise; to look down upon: 鄙～ *to despise* | 厚此～彼 *to favour one and disfavour the other* | 不可妄自菲～。*Don't belittle yourself.* ❺迫近 to approach: ～暮(天快黑) *dusk; twilight* | 日～西山 *declining rapidly as the sun is setting beyond the western hills; nearing one's end* ❻姓 Bo, a surname

㊀ báo 见 24 页 see p24

㊂ bò 见 57 页 see p57

礴 bó ㄅㄛˊ 见 552 页"磅"字条"磅礴"(páng—) see 磅礴 on p552

僰 bó ㄅㄛˊ 我国古代西南地区的少数民族 the Bo ethnic group, an ancient ethnic minority in southwest China

踣 bó ㄅㄛˊ 跌倒 to fall; to tumble: 屡～屡起 *to fall down and get up repeatedly*

跛 bǒ ㄅㄛˇ 瘸(qué),腿或脚有毛病,走路身体不平衡 lame; limping: 一颠一～ *to walk with a limp; to limp along* | ～脚 *lame*

簸 ㊀ bǒ ㄅㄛˇ ❶用簸(bò)箕颠动米粮,扬去糠秕和灰尘 to winnow ❷颠动得像米粮在簸箕里簸起来一样 to toss up and down: 船在海浪中颠～起伏。*The ship was tossed roughly in the sea.*

㊁ bò 见 57 页 see p57

柏 ㊂ bò ㄅㄛˋ [黄柏]即黄檗 i.e. 黄檗

㊀ bǎi 见 16 页 see p16

㊁ bó 见 55 页 see p55

薄 ㊂ bò ㄅㄛˋ [薄荷](—he) 多年生草本植物,叶和茎有清凉香味,可入药 mint (*Mentha*)

㊀ báo 见 24 页 see p24

㊁ bó 见 57 页 see p57

檗 bò ㄅㄛˋ 黄檗,落叶乔木,羽状复叶,开黄绿色小花,木材坚硬,茎可制黄色染料。树皮可入药 amur corktree (*Phellodendron amurense*)

擘 ㊀ bò ㄅㄛˋ 大拇指 thumb [巨擘][喻] ***figurative*** 杰出的人物 giant among equals; authority in a certain field

㊁ bāi 见 15 页 see p15

簸 ㊁ bò ㄅㄛˋ [簸箕](—ji)扬糠除秽的用具 winnowing basket; dustpan

㊀ bǒ 见 57 页 see p57

卜(蔔) ㊁ bo ·ㄅㄛ 见476页"萝"字条"萝卜" see 萝卜 on p476
㊀ bǔ 见58页 see p58

啵 bo ·ㄅㄛ 助词 ***auxiliary***, 相当于"吧" equal to 吧

BU ㄅㄨ

逋 bū ㄅㄨ ❶逃亡 to flee (㊥ ***doublet*** 一逃 to flee; to escape) ❷拖欠 to be behind in payment; to default: ～租 *to fail to pay one's rent in time*

晡 bū ㄅㄨ〈古 ***archaism***〉申时,指下午三点到五点 period of the day from 3 p. m. to 5 p. m.

醭 bú ㄅㄨˊ (旧读 formerly pú)(一儿)醋、酱油等表面上长(zhǎng)的白色的霉 (on the surface of soy sauce, vinegar, etc) mildew

卜 ㊀ bǔ ㄅㄨˇ ❶占卜,古时用龟甲、兽骨等预测吉凶的一种迷信活动。后泛指用其他方法预测吉凶 fortune-telling; divination ㊕ ***transfer*** 料定,先知道 to foretell; to predict: 预～*to foretell* | 吉凶未～。*No one knows how it will turn out*. [卜辞]商代刻在龟甲、兽骨上记录占卜事情的文字 oracle inscriptions concerning the writings of divination on tortoise shells or animal bones in the Shang Dynasty ❷姓 Bu, a surname
㊁ bo 见58页 see p58

卟 bǔ ㄅㄨˇ [卟吩]有机化合物,结构式为

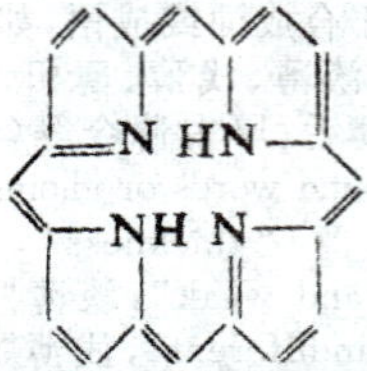

是叶绿素、血红蛋白等的重要组成部分 porphin

补(補) bǔ ㄅㄨˇ ❶把残破的东西加上材料修理完整 to mend; to repair: ～衣服 *to mend clothes* | ～锅 *to mend a pot* ❷把缺少的充实起来或添上 to fill; to supply; to make up for (㊥ ***doublet*** 一充 to replenish | 贴一 to replenish): ～空(kòng)子 *to fill a vacancy* | ～习 *to attend make-up lessons; to take remedial courses* | 候～委员 *alternate member* | 滋～ *nourishing; nutritious* [补白]报刊上填补空白的短文 (in a newspaper or magazine) filler ❸益处 benefit: 不无小～*not to be without some benefit; to be of some help (if not much)*

捕 bǔ ㄅㄨˇ 捉,逮 to catch; to seize; to arrest: ～获 *to catch; to capture* | ～风捉影(喻言行没有事实根据) *to chase the wind and clutch at shadows—to speak or act on unsubstantiated evidence; to speak or act on hearsay*

哺 bǔ ㄅㄨˇ ❶喂不会取食的幼儿 to feed (a baby): ～养 *to nurse; to raise* | ～育 *to*

feed; to nurture｜～乳 *to breast-feed; to suckle* ❷嘴里嚼着的食物 food in one's mouth：一饭三吐～（*as showing one's preoccupation with public affairs*）*to be unable to eat at leisure*

堡 ㊁ bǔ ㄅㄨˇ 堡子，有围墙的村镇。又多用于地名（*bu*，usually used in a place name）town or village surrounded with earthen walls：吴～（在陕西省榆林）*Wubu, a place in Yulin, Shaanxi Province*｜柴沟～（在河北省张家口）*Chaigoubu, a place in Zhangjiakou, Hebei Province*

㊀ bǎo 见25页 see p25

㊂ pù 见578页 see p578

不 bù ㄅㄨˋ 副词 ***adverb*** **1** 表示否定的意义（used to express negation）not；no：他～来。*He is not coming.*｜～好 *not good*｜～错 *not bad*｜～简单 *not simple; not ordinary* **2** 表示否定对方的话（used as a negative reply）no：他刚来农村吧？～，他到农村很久了。*He has just arrived in the countryside, hasn't he? Yes, he has been here for a long time.* **3** 表示否定效果，跟"得"相对（the opposite of 得）（used to express a negative effect）：拿～动（*sth*）*too heavy to carry*｜说～明白 *to fail to make oneself understood*｜跑～很远 *to be unable to run very far* **4** 跟"就"搭用，表示选择（used in collocation with 就 to express alternation）if not…（then）；either…or：他在休息的时候，～是看书，就是看报。*When he is having a rest, he would read either a book or a newspaper.* **5** 〈方 ***dialect***〉用在肯定句末，构成问句（used as a question tag）：他来～？*Is he coming or not?*｜你知道～？*Do you know it?*［不过］**1** 副词 ***adverb***，仅仅，不超过 only；merely；no more than：一共～～五六个人 *only about five or six people altogether* **2** 连词 ***conjunction***，但是，可是 but；however：困难虽然很多，～～我们能克服它。*There are a lot of difficulties, but we can overcome them.*

吥 bù ㄅㄨˋ 见234页"唝"字条"唝吥"（gòng—）see 唝吥 on p234

钚 bù ㄅㄨˋ 一种放射性元素，符号Pu，化学性质跟铀相似，是原子能工业的重要原料 plutonium（Pu）

布（❷—❹ *佈）bù ㄅㄨˋ ❶用棉纱、麻纱等织成的、可以做衣服或其他物件的材料 cloth；textiles［布匹］布的总称 cloth ❷宣布，宣告，对众陈述 to declare；to announce；to proclaim：发～ *to issue; to release*｜开诚～公 *to be frank and sincere; to be open-hearted*［布告］张贴出来通知群众的文件 notice；bulletin ❸散布，分布 to spread；to disseminate：阴云密～ *covered with dark clouds; overcast*｜星罗棋～ *to be dotted like stars in*

B

the sky and scattered like the pieces on a chessboard; *to spread all over the place* ❹布置，安排 to dispose; to arrange; to deploy：～防 *to deploy troops for defence* | ～局 *overall arrangement*; *composition* (*of an article, painting, etc*); *opening moves* (*in a chess game*) ❺古代的一种钱币 *bu*, a kind of coin in ancient China

[布朗族]我国少数民族，参看附表 (see the appendix) the Blang ethnic group, one of the ethnic minorities of China

[布依族]我国少数民族，参看附表 (see the appendix) the Bouyei ethnic group, one of the ethnic minorities of China

埗 bù ㄅㄨˋ [茶埗]地名，在福建省建阳 Chabu, a place in Jianyang, Fujian Province

怖 bù ㄅㄨˋ 惧怕 to be afraid of; to fear (㊟ ***doublet*** 恐一 terror; horror)：情景可～。*It was a horrible sight.* or *The scene was frightful.* | 白色恐～(反动统治者迫害人民造成的情势) (a situation brought about by the persecution by the reactionary rulers) White Terror

步 bù ㄅㄨˋ ❶脚步，行走时两脚之间的距离 step; pace：一～跟不上，～～跟不上。*One step behind means never catching up with others.* | 稳～前进 *to move forward steadily* [步伐]队伍行进时的脚步 step; pace：～～整齐 *to march in step with each other* ❷阶段 stage; step：初～*tentative; initial* [步骤]事情进行的程序 steps; measures ❸行，走 to walk; to go on foot：～其后尘(追随在人家后面) *to follow in sb's footsteps — to trail along behind others* [步兵]陆军里步行或乘战车作战的兵种 infantry ❹用脚步量地面 to measure by paces; to pace out：～一～看这块地有多长。*Pace out this piece of land and see how long it is.* ❺旧制长度单位，一步等于五尺 *bu*, a former unit of length, equal to five *chi* ❻地步，境地，表示程度 condition; situation; state：没想到他竟会落到这一～。*No one expected him to have got into such a state.* ❼古同"埠" same as 埠 in ancient Chinese

埔 ㊁ bù ㄅㄨˋ [大埔]地名，在广东省 Dabu, a place in Guangdong Province

㊀ pǔ 见577页 see p577

部 bù ㄅㄨˋ ❶部分，全体中的一份 part; section：内～*inside; interior* | 南～*southern part* | 局～*part; locality* [部位]位置 position; location; place ❷机关企业按业务范围分设的单位 unit; ministry; department：农业～*Ministry of Agriculture* | 编辑～*editorial department; editorial board* | 门市～*retail department* [部队]军队 army; armed forces; troops [部首]按汉字形体偏旁所分的门类，如"山"部、"火"部

等 radicals by which characters are arranged in traditional Chinese dictionaries ❸统属 to control; to command: ～领 *commander* | 所～三十人 *thirty people under one's command* [部署]布置安排 to deploy; to organize; to delegate (human resources, tasks) ❹ 量词 ***quantifier*** **1** 用于书籍(for books):一～小说 a novel | 两～字典 *two dictionaries* **2** 用于车辆或机器(for machines and vehicles):一～收割机 *a reaper* | 三～汽车 *three cars*

瓿 bù ㄅㄨˋ 小瓮 small jar

篰 bù ㄅㄨˋ 〈方 ***dialect***〉竹篓 bamboo basket

埠 bù ㄅㄨˋ 埠头,停船的码头。多指有码头的城镇(usually used to denote a town or city with a port) port; wharf; pier:本～*this town; this city* | 外～*other cities; city or town other than where one is* [商埠]旧时与外国通商的城镇(in former times) commercial port

簿 bù ㄅㄨˋ (一子)本子 book; notebook: 账～ *account book* | 发文～*register of outgoing documents, letters, etc* [簿记]根据会(kuài)计学原理记账的技术 bookkeeping

C ㄘ

CA ㄘㄚ

拆 ㊁ cā ㄘㄚ 〈方 *dialect*〉排泄(大小便) to discharge (faeces or urine); to void:～烂污(喻不负责任,以致把事情弄糟) *to do things sloppily and leave a mess — to be irresponsible; to do sloppy work*

㊀ chāi 见72页 see p72

擦 cā ㄘㄚ ❶抹(mā),揩拭 to wipe; to mop:～桌子 *to wipe the table* | ～脸 *to wipe (or mop) one's face* ❷摩,搓 to rub:摩拳～掌 *to be eager to have a try* (or *go*); *to itch for action* ❸贴近 to approach; to touch lightly; to brush past:～黑儿(傍晚) *dusk; sunset* | ～着屋檐飞过 *to brush past the eaves*

嚓 ㊀ cā ㄘㄚ 拟声词 ***onomatopoeia***:摩托车～的一声停住了。*The motorcycle screeched to a halt.*

㊁ chā 见70页 see p70

礤 cā ㄘㄚ [礓礤儿](jiāngcār)台阶 steps

礤 cǎ ㄘㄚˇ 粗石 coarse stone [礤床儿]把瓜、萝卜等擦成丝的器具 vegetable grater

CAI ㄘㄞ

偲 ㊀ cāi ㄘㄞ 有才能 talented; competent

㊁ sī 见703页 see p703

猜 cāi ㄘㄞ ❶推测,推想 to guess; to speculate:～谜 *to solve a riddle; to guess a riddle* | 你～他来不来? *Do you think he'll come?* ❷疑心 to doubt (㊟ ***doublet*** 一疑 to have a suspicion; to have misgivings):～忌 *to be suspicious and jealous of* | ～嫌 *to be suspicious of*

才(❸纔) cái ㄘㄞˊ ❶能力 talent; ability(㊟ ***doublet*** 一能 competence; faculty):口～*eloquence* | 这人很有～干。*He's very capable.* or *He has great ability.* ❷从才能方面指称某类人 people of talent and ability:干(gàn)～*capable person* | 奇～*wizard; genius* | 庸～*mediocre person* ❸副词 ***adverb*** **1** 方,始 not ... until; only after; only then (㊟ ***doublet*** 刚一 just now; a moment ago | 方一 just now; a moment ago):昨天～来 *not to come until yesterday* | 现在～懂得这个道理 *not to understand this until now* **2** 仅仅 only:～用了两元 *to have spent only two yuan* | 来了～十天 *to have been here for only ten days*

材 cái ㄘㄞˊ ❶木料 timber:美木良～ *fine timber* ㊇

extension 材料，原料或资料 material，raw material or data：器～ *equipment*｜教～*teaching material* ❷资质，能力 endowment；aptitude：因～施教 *to teach in accordance with student aptitude，disposition，interest，etc* ❸棺木 coffin：一口～*a coffin*

财 cái ㄘㄞˊ 金钱或物资 money or belongings（㊟***doublet*** 一产 property｜资一assets｜钱一 wealth；riches）：理～*to manage finances；to manage money*｜～务 *finance*［财富］具有价值的东西 wealth；riches：物质～～*material wealth*｜精神～～*non-material wealth*［财政］国家的收支及其他有关经济的事务 finance；fiscal administration

裁 cái ㄘㄞˊ ❶用剪子剪布或用刀子割纸 to cut：～衣服 *to cut out clothes*｜对～（把整张纸平均裁为两张）*to cut a sheet of paper into two of the same size；to cut in folio*［裁缝］（—feng）以做衣服为职业的人 tailor；dressmaker ❷削减，去掉一部分 to cut down；to reduce；to curtail：～军 *disarmament*｜～员 *to reduce the staff* ❸决定，判断 to judge；to decide：～夺 *to decide*｜～判 *referee；umpire* ❹安排取舍 to select；to choose；to opt：独出心～*to be original；to be ingenious*｜《唐诗别～》*A Novel Guide to the Tang Poetry*

采（❶❷＊採）㊀ cǎi ㄘㄞˇ ❶摘取 to pick；to pluck：～莲 *to pluck lotus seeds*｜～茶 *to pick tea* ❷选取 to choose；to select：～用 *to adopt*｜～矿 *to mine for ore；mining*［采访］搜集寻访，多指记者为搜集材料进行调查访问 to interview［采纳］接受（意见）to accept；to adopt：～～群众的意见 *to accept public opinion* ❸神采，神色，精神 mien；countenance；vigour：兴高～烈 *elated；jubilant* ❹同"彩" same as 彩

㊁ cài 见 64 页 see p64

彩（❷＊綵）cǎi ㄘㄞˇ ❶各种颜色 multicolour：～色影片 *colour film*｜～排（化装排演）*dress rehearsal*［挂彩］㊗ ***figurative*** 在战斗中受伤 to get wounded in the battle ❷彩色的绸子 coloured silk：悬灯结～*to hang lanterns and festoons；to decorate with lanterns and coloured streamers* ❸指赌博或某种竞赛中赢得的东西 lottery prize：得～*to win a lottery prize*｜～金 *lottery prize* ❹称赞、夸奖的欢呼声 cheer；acclamation：喝（hè）～ *to cheer；to acclaim*

睬（＊倸）cǎi ㄘㄞˇ 理会，答理 to heed；to pay attention to；to take notice of：不理不～ *to turn a blind eye to*｜～也不～ *to disregard；to turn a deaf ear to*

踩（＊跴）cǎi ㄘㄞˇ 用脚登在上面，踏 to step on；to tread：～了一脚泥 *to get one's feet all muddied*

C

采(*寀、**埰) ㊁ cài ㄘㄞˋ 采地，采邑，古代卿大夫的封地 fief; feoff

㊀ cǎi 见 63 页 see p63

菜 cài ㄘㄞˋ ❶蔬菜，供作副食品的植物 vegetable; greens ❷主食以外的食品，如经过烹调的鱼、肉、蛋等 dish; non-staple food

蔡 cài ㄘㄞˋ ❶周代诸侯国名，在今河南省上蔡、新蔡一带 Cai, a princedom of the Zhou Dynasty, covering today's Shangcai and Xincai and nearby areas in Henan Province ❷〈古 ***archaism***〉大龟 big tortoise：蓍(shī)～(占卜用的东西) *yarrow and tortoise plectrum — things used in divination*

CAN ㄘㄢ

参(參) ㊀ cān ㄘㄢ ❶参加，加入 to join; to enter：～军 *to join the army; to enlist*｜～战 *to enter a war; to take part in a battle* [参半]占半数 half; fifty-fifty：疑信～～ *half-believing and half-doubting* [参观]实地观察(事业、设施、名胜等) to visit [参考]用有关的材料帮助了解、研究某事物 to consult; to refer to [参天]高入云霄 towering：古木～～ *old towering tree* ❷进见 to call on：～谒 *to pay respect to; to pay homage to*｜～拜 *to pay respect to; to pay homage to* ❸封建时代指弹劾(tánhé) to impeach an official before the emperor：～他一本 *to impeach him in a memorial to the emperor*

㊁ shēn 见 666 页 see p666

㊂ cēn 见 68 页 see p68

骖(驂) cān ㄘㄢ 古代驾在车前两侧的马 outside horses in a team drawing a carriage in ancient China

餐(**飡、**湌) cān ㄘㄢ ❶吃 to eat; to dine：饱～一顿 *to eat one's fill*｜聚～ *to dine together; to have a dinner party* ❷饭食 food; meal：一日三～ *three meals a day*｜午～ *lunch*｜西～ *Western-style food*

残(殘) cán ㄘㄢˊ ❶毁坏，毁害 to damage; to injure ([连] ***doublet*** —害 to kill; to maltreat)：摧～ *to wreck; to damage*｜自～ *to mutilate oneself; to hurt oneself* ❷凶恶 savage ([连] ***doublet*** —暴 ferocious｜—忍 brutal) ❸不完全的，有毛病的 incomplete; defective ([连] ***doublet*** —缺 fragmentary)：～疾 *disabled; handicapped*｜～品 *defective goods*｜～破不全 *dilapidated* [引] ***extension*** 余下的 remaining ([连] ***doublet*** —余 remnant)：～局 *end-game; final phase of a chess game; situation after the failure of an undertaking* (or *after social unrest*)｜～茶剩饭 *left-overs*

蚕(蠶) cán ㄘㄢˊ 家蚕，又叫"桑蚕"。昆虫，吃桑叶长大，蜕（tuì）皮时不食不动，俗叫“眠”。蚕普通经过四眠就吐丝做茧，蚕在茧里变成蛹，蛹变成蚕蛾。蚕吐的丝可织绸缎。另有“柞（zuò）蚕”，也叫“野蚕”，吃柞树的叶子。柞蚕的丝可织茧绸（also called 桑蚕，and there is another term 柞蚕 or called 野蚕 “tussah”）silkworm（*Bombyx mori*）

惭（*慚）cán ㄘㄢˊ 羞愧 ashamed; abashed（㊟**doublet** 一愧 ashamed; abashed）：自～*to feel ashamed*｜大言不～ *to boast shamelessly*

惨（慘）cǎn ㄘㄢˇ ❶凶恶，狠毒 merciless; ruthless：～无人道 *inhumane* ❷使人悲伤难受 miserable; tragic（㊟ **doublet** 凄一wretched｜悲一deplorable; miserable）：她的遭遇太～了。*How tragic it was for her!*［惨淡］**1** 暗淡无色 somber; dim **2** 指辛苦 painstaking：～～经营 *to run (a business) painstakingly* ❸程度严重 terribly; exceedingly：敌人～败。*The enemy was devastated.* or *The enemy suffered a crushing defeat.*｜可累～了 *exhausted; tired out; worn out*

䅟（穇）cǎn ㄘㄢˇ 䅟子，一种谷类植物，子实可以吃，也可以做饲料 finger millet（*Eleusine coracana*）

篸（簝）cǎn ㄘㄢˇ〈方 **dialect**〉一种簸箕 dustpan

灿（燦）càn ㄘㄢˋ［灿烂］鲜明，耀眼 bright; brilliant：阳光～～。*The sun is shining brightly.*｜光辉～～ *splendid; glorious*

孱 ㊁ càn ㄘㄢˋ 同“孱㊀”，只用于“孱头”same as 孱㊀，only used in 孱头［孱头］（一tou）〈方 **dialect**〉软弱无能的人 weakling

㊀ chán 见 73 页 see p73

粲 càn ㄘㄢˋ 鲜明的样子 bright; brilliant［粲然］笑的样子 bright; beaming：～～一笑 *to show a beaming smile*

璨 càn ㄘㄢˋ ❶美玉 fine jade ❷同“粲” same as 粲

CANG ㄘㄤ

仓（倉）cāng ㄘㄤ 收藏谷物的建筑物 barn; granary：米～ *rice barn*｜谷～ *granary; grain barn*［仓库］储藏东西的房子 storehouse; warehouse

［仓促］［仓猝］（一cù）匆忙 hurried; hasty

伧（傖）㊀ cāng ㄘㄤ 古代讥人粗俗，鄙贱（used in ancient China to show contempt for a vulgar person）：～俗 *vulgar; uncouth*

㊁ chen 见 84 页 see p84

苍（蒼）cāng ㄘㄤ ❶青色 blue：～天 *heaven* ❷草色，深绿色 dark green：～松 *green pines* ❸灰白色 grey：面色～白 *pale*｜两鬓～～。*His (or Her) hair is grey at the*

C

temples.［苍老］**1** 容貌、声音老 old; decrepit **2** 书画笔力雄健 (of calligraphy and painting) vigorous

沧(滄) cāng ㄘㄤ ❶暗绿色(指水)(of water) dark green:～海 *deep blue sea*［沧海桑田］大海变成农田，农田变成大海。Seas change into fields and fields change into seas. ㊗ ***figurative*** 世事变化很大 *great changes in the world; vicissitude of life* ❷寒，冷 cold:～～凉凉 *bleak*

鸧(鶬) cāng ㄘㄤ［鸧鹒］(— gēng)黄鹂。也作"仓庚"(also written as 仓庚) oriole

舱(艙) cāng ㄘㄤ 船或飞机的内部，用于载人或物 cabin:货～*cargo hold*｜客～*passenger cabin*｜底～*bilge*

藏 ㊀ cáng ㄘㄤˊ ❶隐避 to hide; to conceal:埋～*to bury*｜他～在树后头。*He's hiding himself behind a tree.* ❷收存 to collect; to store:～书处 *depository library*｜储～室 *storage room*｜把这些东西收～起来。*Store away these things.*

㊁ zàng 见 940 页 see p940

CAO ㄘㄠ

操 cāo ㄘㄠ ❶拿，抓在手里 to hold; to seize:～刀 *to wield a knife*｜～戈 *to take up arms; to start a fight* ㊀***extension*** 掌握，控制 to grasp; to control:～舟 *to sail a boat; to steer a ship*｜～必胜之券 *to be sure to win; to have full assurance of success*［操纵］随着自己的意向来把持支配 to operate; to manipulate ❷拿出力量来做 to strive to do:～劳 *to work hard*｜～持家务 *to do household chores; to manage a household*［操作］按照一定的程序和技术要求进行活动，也泛指劳动 to operate; to handle:田间～～ *to work in the fields* ❸从事，做某种工作 to do; to act:重～旧业 *to resume one's former job* ❹用某种语言或方音说话 to speak:～俄语 *to speak Russian*｜～闽语 *to speak Fujian dialect* ❺操练，指体力上的锻炼，军事演习等 to drill; to manoeuvre:体～ *gymnastics*｜徒手～ *free exercise*｜下～ *to finish drilling* ❻行为，品行 conduct; behaviour:节～ *moral integrity*｜～行 *behaviour; conduct*

糙 cāo ㄘㄠ ❶糙米，脱壳未去皮的米 brown rice; unrefined rice ❷不细致，粗 rough; coarse (㊣ ***doublet*** 粗—coarse):这活做得太～。*What a crude piece of work!*

曹 cáo ㄘㄠˊ ❶等，辈 people of the same kind:尔～*you; you and your kind*｜吾～ *we; us* ❷古代分科办事的官署(in ancient China) department of government:部～ *office; department*｜功～ *administrator*

嘈 cáo ㄘㄠˊ 杂乱(多指声音)(usually used to denote noise) noisy; clamorous:人声～杂 *hubbub; din*

漕 cáo ㄘㄠˊ 利用水道转运食粮 to transport grain by water:～运 *to transport grain by water to the capital or for military use*|～河(运粮的河道) *watercourse* (or *waterway*) *for transporting grain*

槽 cáo ㄘㄠˊ ❶一种长方形或正方形的较大的容器 trough:石～ *stone trough*|水～ *gutter* 特指喂牲畜食料的器具 manger:猪食～ *pig's trough*|马～ *manger* ❷(一儿)东西上凹下像槽的部分 groove; slot:挖个～儿 *to cut a groove*|河～ *channel*

碏 cáo ㄘㄠˊ 地名用字 cao, used in a place name [斫碏](zhuó—)地名,在湖南省邵东 Zhuocao, a place in Shaodong, Hunan Province

螬 cáo ㄘㄠˊ 见583页"蛴"字条"蛴螬"(qí—) see 蛴螬 on p583

艚 cáo ㄘㄠˊ (一子)载货的木船 wooden cargo boat

草(❶*艸、❺**騲) cǎo ㄘㄠˇ ❶普通对高等植物中除了树木、庄稼、蔬菜以外茎干柔软的植物的统称 grass [草本植物]茎比较柔软的植物,如小麦、豌豆等 herb ❷草率,不细致(叠 ***reduplication***) careless; sloppy; slipshod:～～了(liǎo)事 *to rush the work; to rush things*|～率从事 *to do sth perfunctorily* [草书]汉字形体的一种,汉代初期就已经流行,笔画牵连曲折 (in Chinese calligraphy) cursive script ❸草稿,文稿 draft:起～ *to draw up; to draft* ㉠ ***extension*** 还没有确定的(文件等) rough draft; manuscript:～约 *draft treaty; draft agreement*|～案 *draft bill*|～图 sketch ❹打稿 to make a draft:～拟 *to draw up; to draft*|～檄 *to draft a war proclamation* [草创]开始创办或创立 to start; to begin; to initiate ❺雌性的(指某些家禽、家畜)(of domestic fowl or cattle) female:～鸡 *hen*|～驴 *jennet; female donkey*

CE ㄘㄜ

册(*冊) cè ㄘㄜˋ ❶古时称编串好的许多竹简,现在指装订好的纸本子 (bamboo slips strung together in ancient China) volume; book:第三～ *the third volume; volume three*|纪念～ *autograph album* ❷量词 ***quantifier***,用于书籍 (for books) copy

厕(*廁) cè ㄘㄜˋ ❶厕所,大小便的地方 toilet; washroom; lavatory:公～ *toilet; washroom; restroom* ❷参与(yù),混杂在里面 to mingle with; to participate in:～身其间 *to work in* (or *among*)

侧 ㊀ cè ㄘㄜˋ ❶旁 side：楼～ *the side of a building*｜～面 *profile*；*flank* ❷斜着 to incline；to lean：～耳细听 *to listen attentively*；*to keep one's ears open*｜～身而入 *to sidle into* [侧目]斜着眼睛看，表示畏惧而又愤恨 to look askance at；to cast a sidelong glance (with fear or indignation)：世人为之～～。*The world looked askance at it*. [侧重](—zhòng)偏重 to emphasize；to stress

㊁ zhāi 见 950 页 see p950

㊂ zè 见 945 页 see p945

测 cè ㄘㄜˋ ❶测量，利用仪器来度量 to measure；to survey；to gauge：～角器 *goniometer*｜～绘 *survey and mapping*｜～一下高度 *to measure the height* [测验]用一定的标准检定 to examine；to test ❷推测，料想 to speculate；to conjecture；to infer：预～ *to predict*；*to forecast*｜变幻莫～ *unpredictable*；*changeable*

恻 cè ㄘㄜˋ 悲痛 sorrowful；sad [恻隐]指对遭难(nàn)的人表示同情 compassion；pity

策(*筞、*筴) cè ㄘㄜˋ ❶计谋，主意 plan；scheme (㊟ ***doublet*** 计—plan)：决～ *to make a decision*｜献～ *to make suggestions*｜下～ *the worst plan*｜束手无～ *at a loss*；*at one's wits' end* [策动]设法鼓动或促成 to instigate；to stir up [策略]根据形势发展而制定的行动方针和方法 tactics ❷古代的一种马鞭子，头上有尖刺 (in ancient China) spur；pointed stick used to spur a horse ❸鞭打 to whip：～马 *to whip a horse*｜鞭～ *to spur* ❹古代称编连好的竹简 a string of bamboo slips in ancient China：简～ *bamboo slip* ❺古代考试的一种文体 expository writing required in imperial examinations in ancient China：对～ *to write an essay on a way or means to cope with a situation*｜～论 *essay on a political issue*

CEN ㄘㄣ

参(參) ㊂ cēn ㄘㄣ [参差](—cī)长短不齐 uneven；erose；irregular：～～不齐 *uneven*

㊀ cān 见 64 页 see p64

㊁ shēn 见 666 页 see p666

岑 cén ㄘㄣˊ 小而高的山 high hill；tor

涔 cén ㄘㄣˊ 连续下雨，积水成涝 waterlogged [涔涔] **1** 雨多的样子 rainy **2** 流泪的样子 (of tears) shedding；weeping

CENG ㄘㄥ

噌 cēng ㄘㄥ 拟声词 ***onomatopoeia***：～的一声，火柴划着了。*The match was lit with a scratch*.

层(層) céng ㄘㄥˊ ❶重复，重叠 overlapping：～出不穷 *to emerge in an endless stream*｜～峦叠翠 *range upon range of green hills* ❷重叠的事物或其中的一部分 layers; tiers：云～*cloud layer*｜大气～ *atmosphere*｜基～ *grass roots* ❸量词 ***quantifier***，重(chóng) storey; floor; tier：二～楼 *two-storey building*｜三～院子 *compound with three rows of houses*｜絮两～棉花 *to wad two layers of cotton*｜还有一～意思。*It has got a further implication.*

曾 ㊁ céng ㄘㄥˊ 曾经，表示从前经历过(used to indicate that something happened or was the case at sometime in the past) once：未～ *never*｜何～*ever*｜他～去北京两次。*He's been to Beijing twice.*｜～几何时(表示时间过去没多久) *not long before*

㊀ zēng 见 946 页 see p946

嶒 céng ㄘㄥˊ 见 425 页"崚"字条"崚嶒"(léng—) see 崚嶒 on p425

蹭 cèng ㄘㄥˋ 摩擦 to rub; to scratch; to graze：～了一身泥 *to be daubed all over with mud*｜～破了皮 *to be skin grazed* ㉄ ***extension*** 拖延 to dawdle：快点，别～了。*Hurry up! You're too slow!*｜走路老磨～(ceng) *to be always dawdling when walking*

[蹭蹬](—dèng)遭遇挫折 to be frustrated; to suffer a setback

CHA ㄔㄚ

叉(❷**扠) ㊀ chā ㄔㄚ ❶(—子)一头有两个以上长齿便于扎取东西的器具 fork：鱼～ *harpoon*｜三齿～ *three-pronged fork*｜粪～子 *dung-fork* ❷用叉子扎取 to fork：～鱼 *to spear fish* ❸交错 to cross; to crisscross：～着手站着 *standing with arms crossed*

㊁ chá 见 70 页 see p70

㊂ chǎ 见 71 页 see p71

杈 ㊀ chā ㄔㄚ 一种用来挑(tiǎo)柴草等的农具 hayfork; pitchfork

㊁ chà 见 71 页 see p71

差 ㊀ chā ㄔㄚ ❶不同，不同之点 difference; disparity (㊈ ***doublet*** —别 disparity; difference｜—异 discrepancy｜偏—deviation) ❷大致还可以 passable：～强人意 *to be just so-so* ❸错误 mistake; error：～错 *mistake; slip*｜阴错阳～ *accidental mistake* ❹差数，两数相减的余数 remainder; quantity left after subtraction

㊁ chà 见 72 页 see p72

㊂ chāi 见 72 页 see p72

㊃ cī 见 106 页 see p106

插 chā ㄔㄚ 扎进去，把细长或薄的东西扎进、放入 to insert; to pierce：～秧 *to transplant rice seedlings*｜把花～在瓶子里 *to place flowers in a vase* ㉄ ***extension*** 加入，参与 to join; to take part in：～班 *to*

join a class or a course in the middle of the school year | ～嘴 *to cut in; to get a word in; to interject*

锸(**臿) chā 彳丫 铁锹(qiāo),掘土的工具 spade

C

喳 ⊜ chā 彳丫 [喳喳](— cha)拟声词 ***onomatopoeia***:打～～(低声说话) *to whisper*

⊖ zhā 见947页 see p947

馇 chā 彳丫 ❶拌煮猪、狗的食料 to cook and stir mast for pigs and dogs:～猪食 *to cook and stir mast for pigs* ❷〈方 ***dialect***〉熬(粥) to cook (gruel):～锅豆粥 *to cook bean porridge*

嚓 ⊜ chā 彳丫 见380页"喀"字条"喀嚓"(kā—) see 喀嚓 on p380

⊖ cā 见62页 see p62

叉 ⊜ chá 彳丫́ 挡住,堵塞住,互相卡住 to block; to jam:车把路口～住了。*Vehicles blocked traffic at the crossroads.*

⊖ chā 见69页 see p69

⊜ chǎ 见71页 see p71

垞 chá 彳丫́ 小土山。多用于地名(*cha*, usually used in a place name) mound

茬 chá 彳丫́ ❶(—儿)庄稼收割后余留在地上的短根和茎 stubble:麦～儿 *wheat stubble* | 豆～儿 *bean stubble* ❷(—儿)在同一块土地上庄稼种植或收割的次数 crop; times of yield of any farm product in one place:换～ *to change crops* | 头～ *first crop* | 二～ *second crop* ❸短而硬的头发、胡子 stubble hair and moustache

茶 chá 彳丫́ ❶茶树,常绿灌木,开白花。嫩叶采下经过加工,就是茶叶 tea (the plant or its leaves) ❷用茶叶沏成的饮料 tea (the drink) ㊀ ***extension*** 某些饮料的名称 name of some beverage:果～ *fruit tea* | 杏仁～ *almond tea*

搽 chá 彳丫́ 涂抹 to apply:～药 *to apply medicine* | ～粉 *to powder*

查 ⊖ chá 彳丫́ ❶检查 to check; to examine; to inspect:～账 *to examine* (*or audit*) *accounts* ❷翻检着看 to look up; to consult; to refer to:～地图 *to try to locate a place on the map; to consult a map* | ～字典 *to consult a dictionary*

⊜ zhā 见947页 see p947

嵖 chá 彳丫́ [嵖岈山](— yá —)山名,在河南省遂平 Chaya Mountain, in Suiping, Henan Province

猹 chá 彳丫́ 獾类野兽,喜欢吃瓜(见于鲁迅小说《故乡》) badger-like wild animal, fond of eating melons (seen in *My Old Home* by Lu Xun)

楂 ⊜ chá 彳丫́ 同"茬" same as 茬

⊖ zhā 见948页 see p948

碴 chá 彳丫́ ❶(—儿)小碎块 shard; bit; fragment:冰～儿 *broken ice; small pieces of*

ice | 玻璃～儿 *shards of glass* ❷(一儿)东西上的破口 cut:碗上还有个破～儿。*There's still a sharp edge on the bowl*. [喻] ***figurative*** 争执的事由 the cause of a quarrel:找～儿打架 *to pick a fight* ❸皮肉被碎片碰破 (of skin, flesh) to be cut by broken pieces:手让碎玻璃～破了。*The hand was cut by shards of glass*.

槎 chá ㄔㄚˊ ❶木筏 raft:乘～ *to ride on a raft* | 浮～ *floating raft* ❷同"茬" same as 茬

察(*詧) chá ㄔㄚˊ 仔细看,调查研究 to examine; to investigate:考～ *investigation* | 视～ *inspection*

檫 chá ㄔㄚˊ 檫木,落叶乔木,木材坚韧,供建筑、造船等用 sassafras (*Sassafras albidum*)

叉 ㊂ chǎ ㄔㄚˇ 分开,张开 to part; to separate:～腿 *to open one's legs; to be with legs apart*

㊀ chā 见 69 页 see p69

㊁ chá 见 70 页 see p70

衩 ㊁ chǎ ㄔㄚˇ [裤衩]短裤 underpants; undershorts:三角～～ *panties; briefs*

㊀ chà 见 71 页 see p71

蹅 chǎ ㄔㄚˇ 踩,在泥水里走 to trudge (*or* tramp) in mud:～雨 *to trudge in rain* | 鞋都～湿了 *to get one's shoes wet and muddy*

镲 chǎ ㄔㄚˇ 钹(bó),一种打击乐器 cymbals

汊 chà ㄔㄚˋ 河流的分支 tributary; river branch

杈 ㊁ chà ㄔㄚˋ (一子、一儿)植物的分枝 branch:树～儿 *branch* | 打棉花～ *to prune cotton plants*

㊀ chā 见 69 页 see p69

衩 ㊀ chà ㄔㄚˋ 衣服旁边开口的地方 (in the sides of a garment) vent; slit

㊁ chǎ 见 71 页 see p71

岔 chà ㄔㄚˋ ❶分歧的,由主干分出的 divergent:～道 *divergent path; side-road* | 三～路 *junction of three roads; fork in the road* ❷转移主题 to change the topic:拿话～开 *to change the topic by saying sth different* | 打～ *to interrupt; to butt in* ❸互相让开(多指时间) to stagger; to space out:把这两个会的时间～开。*The two meetings should be scheduled at different times*. ❹(一子、一儿)乱子,事故 accident; trouble:别出～子。*May nothing go wrong!*

侘 chà ㄔㄚˋ [侘傺](一chì)形容失意 frustrated; disappointed

诧 chà ㄔㄚˋ 惊讶,觉着奇怪 surprised; astonished:～异 *astounded* | 惊～ *astonished*

姹 chà ㄔㄚˋ 美丽 beautiful:～紫嫣红(形容百花艳丽) *colourful with beautiful flowers*

刹 ㊀ chà ㄔㄚˋ 梵语,原义是土或田,转为佛寺 (in Sanskrit, original meaning earth or

C

field and later transferred to mean Buddhist temple)：宝～ *Buddhist pagoda*｜古～ *ancient Buddhist temple*
[刹那]梵语，极短的时间(Sanskrit) instant; split second
㊁ shā 见 649 页 see p649

C

差 ㊀ chà 彳丫 ❶错误 wrong; mistaken：说～了。*What you said is wrong.* ❷不相当，不相合 to fall short of：～得远 *to fall far short of*｜～不多 *to differ slightly* ❸缺欠 to be wanting：～一道手续。*One formality is wanting.*｜还～一个人。*There is one person short.* ❹不好，不够标准 inferior：成绩～ *low grades*
㊁ chā 见 69 页 see p69
㊂ chāi 见 72 页 see p72
㊃ cī 见 106 页 see p106

CHAI 彳丂

拆 ㊀ chāi 彳丂 把合在一起的弄开，卸下来 to take apart：～信 *to open a letter*｜～卸机器 *to dismantle a machine*
㊁ cā 见 62 页 see p62

钗 chāi 彳丂 妇女发髻上的一种首饰 hairpin：金～ *gold hairpin*｜荆～布裙(旧喻妇女装束朴素)(*of women in former times*) *plainly dressed*

差 ㊂ chāi 彳丂 ❶派遣去做事 to dispatch (㊟ **doublet** 一遣 to dispatch) ❷旧时称被派遣的人，差役 errand man in former times ❸差事，被派遣去做的事 errand：兼～ *part-time job; moonlighting*｜出～ *to go on business*
㊀ chà 见 72 页 see p72
㊁ chā 见 69 页 see p69
㊃ cī 见 106 页 see p106

侪(儕) chái 彳丂 同辈，同类的人们 people of the same generation or kind：吾～(我们) *we; people like us*

柴 chái 彳丂 烧火用的草木 firewood [火柴]用细木条蘸上磷、硫等制成的能摩擦生火的东西 match

豺 chái 彳丂 一种像狼的野兽，嘴比狼的短，性贪暴，常成群侵袭家畜 jackal [豺狼] ㊕ ***figurative*** 贪心残忍的恶人 cruel and evil person

茝 chǎi 彳丂 古书上说的一种香草，即白芷(zhǐ) (aromatic plant mentioned in ancient Chinese texts, i.e. 白芷) dahurian angelica

䶪 chǎi 彳丂 (一儿)碾碎了的豆子、玉米等ground beans, maize, etc：豆～儿 *ground beans*

虿(蠆) chài 彳丂 古书上说的蝎子一类的毒虫 a kind of scorpion mentioned in ancient Chinese texts

瘥 ㊀ chài 彳丂 病愈 to recover from illness：久病初～ *to have just recovered from a lingering illness*
㊁ cuó 见 116 页 see p116

CHAN 彳马

觇 chān 彳马 看，窥视 to survey; to observe; to peep

[觇标]一种测量标志。标架用木料或金属制成，高几米到几十米，架在被观测点上作为观测目标 surveyor's rod

掺(摻) chān ㄔㄢ 混合 to mix; to blend; to mingle (㊟ **doublet** —杂 to mix; to mingle): 里面～糖了。*Sugar has been blended in it.*

搀(攙) chān ㄔㄢ ❶用手轻轻架住对方的手或胳膊 to support sb by the hand or arm (㊟ **doublet** —扶 to support sb by the hand or arm): 你～着那位老人吧。*Please support the old man by the arm.* ❷同"掺" same as 掺

襜 chān ㄔㄢ 古代系在身前的围裙 (in ancient China) apron

单(單) ㊂ chán ㄔㄢˊ [单于](—yú)古代匈奴的君主 *Chanyu*, the Hun's ruler in ancient China

㊀ dān 见 125 页 see p125

㊁ shàn 见 654 页 see p654

婵(嬋) chán ㄔㄢˊ [婵娟](—juān) **1** (姿态)美好 graceful **2** 旧时指美人 (in former times) beauty **3** 古诗文中指明月 (in ancient verses and poems) moon

禅(禪) ㊀ chán ㄔㄢˊ ❶梵语"禅那"的省称，佛教指静思 (short for 禅那 in Sanskrit) meditation in Buddhism: 坐～ *to sit in meditation with crossed legs* ❷关于佛教的 related to Buddhism: ～杖 *Buddhist monk's staff* | ～师 *Zen master, honorific title for a Buddhist monk*

㊁ shàn 见 654 页 see p654

蝉(蟬) chán ㄔㄢˊ 昆虫名，又叫"知了"。雄的腹面有发声器，叫的声音很大 (also called 知了) cicada

[蝉联] ㊞ **figurative** 接续不断 to continue to hold (a post or title)

鋋 chán ㄔㄢˊ 古代一种铁把(bà)儿的短矛 short spear with an iron shaft (in ancient China)

谗(讒) chán ㄔㄢˊ 在别人面前说陷害某人的坏话 to slander; to calumniate: ～言 *calumny; slander*

馋(饞) chán ㄔㄢˊ ❶贪吃，专爱吃好的 greedy; gluttonous: 嘴～ *greedy; gluttonous* | ～涎欲滴 *salivating with greed* ❷贪，羡慕 to be greedy for; to be envious of: 眼～ *to covet*

巉 chán ㄔㄢˊ 山势险峻 precipitous; abrupt: ～岩 *crag*

镵 chán ㄔㄢˊ ❶古代铁制的一种刨土工具 (digging tool made of iron in ancient China) shovel; trowel ❷刺 to prick; to stick: 以刃～腹 *to stab one's belly with a knife; hara-kiri*

孱 ㊀ chán ㄔㄢˊ 懦弱，弱小 weak; frail (㊟ **doublet** —弱 weak; feeble)

㊁ càn 见 65 页 see p65

C

潺 chán ㄔㄢˊ ［潺潺］拟声词 ***onomatopoeia***，溪水、泉水等流动的声音 babbling; burbling; murmuring; gurgling：～～流水 *babbling brook* ［潺湲］（—yuán）水慢慢流动的样子 slow flowing of water：溪水～～。*The brook burbles on.*

缠（纏） chán ㄔㄢˊ ❶绕，围绕 to wind; to twine（㊥ ***doublet*** — 绕 to wind; to twine）：头上～着一块布。*A turban is twined around the head.* ［缠绵］纠缠住不能解脱（多指感情或疾病）abiding; lingering ❷搅扰 to pester; to disturb：胡搅蛮～ *to harass; to hassle*

廛 chán ㄔㄢˊ 古代指一户人家占用的房子和宅院，泛指城邑民居（civilian residence in general）house and courtyard of a commoner's family in ancient China ［市廛］店铺集中的地方 marketplace

瀍 chán ㄔㄢˊ 瀍河，水名，在河南省洛阳 Chanhe River, in Luoyang, Henan Province

躔 chán ㄔㄢˊ ❶兽的足迹 footprints of beasts ❷日月星辰的运行 orbiting of celestial bodies

澶 chán ㄔㄢˊ ［澶渊］古地名，在今河南省濮阳西南 Chanyuan, an ancient place in the southwest of today's Puyang, Henan Province

蟾 chán ㄔㄢˊ 指蟾蜍 toad：～宫（指月亮）moon ［蟾蜍］（—chú）俗叫"癞蛤蟆"或"疥蛤蟆"。两栖动物，皮上有许多疙瘩，内有毒腺。吃昆虫等，对农业有益（popularly called 癞蛤蟆 or 疥蛤蟆）toad ［蟾酥］（—sū）蟾蜍表皮腺体和耳后腺的分泌物，可入药 dried venom of toads

产（產） chǎn ㄔㄢˇ ❶人或动物生子 to give birth to：～子 *to give birth to its young* | 母鸡～卵（*of a hen*）*to lay eggs* ［产生］生 to produce ㊂ ***extension*** 由团体中推出 to select out of a group：每个小组～～一个代表。*Each group selects one representative.* ❷有关生孩子的 related to giving birth to a child：～科 *maternity*（or *obstetrical*）*department; obstetrics* | 妇～医院 *maternity hospital* ❸制造、种植或自然生长 to produce：沿海盛～鱼虾。*Coastal areas abound in*（or *teem with*）*fish and shrimp.* | 我国～稻、麦的地方很多。*Many places in China abound in rice and wheat.* | 增～大量工业品和粮食 *to increase industrial products and the yield of grain in large quantity* ❹制造、种植或自然生长的东西 product：土特～ *local specialty*（or *product*）| 出口鱼虾等水～ *to export aquatic products such as fish and shrimp* ❺财产 property; estate：房～ *real estate* | 地～ *landed estate* | 遗～ *legacy; heritage* ［产业］**1** 家产 property;

estate **2** 生产事业，特指工业生产 industry：～～革命 *industrial revolution*｜～～工人 *industrial worker*

浐(滻) chǎn ㄔㄢˇ 浐河，水名，在陕西省西安 Chanhe River，in Xi'an，Shaanxi Province

铲(鏟、*剗) chǎn ㄔㄢˇ ❶(－子、－儿)削平东西或把东西取上来的器具 shovel：铁～ *iron shovel*｜饭～儿 *rice turner* ❷用锹(qiāo)或铲子削平或取上来 to shovel：把地～平 *to level the ground with a spade*｜～土 *to shovel dirt*｜～菜 *to remove vegetables；to ladle dish from a pot* [铲除]去掉 to eradicate；to remove

刬(剗) ㊁chǎn ㄔㄢˇ 同"铲❷" same as 铲❷

㊀ chàn 见 75 页 see p75

谄 chǎn ㄔㄢˇ 巴结，奉承 to flatter；to fawn on：～媚 *to flatter；to fawn on*｜不骄不～ *neither conceited nor obsequious*

啴(嘽) ㊀ chǎn ㄔㄢˇ 宽舒，和缓 lenient；relaxed：～缓 *mild and lenient*

㊁ tān 见 726 页 see p726

阐(闡) chǎn ㄔㄢˇ 说明，表明 to clarify；to expound：～述 *to illustrate；to elaborate*｜～明 *to expound；to clarify* [阐发]深入说明事理 to elucidate

冁(囅) chǎn ㄔㄢˇ 笑的样子 smiling：～然而笑 *to give a smile*

蒇 chǎn ㄔㄢˇ 完成，解决 to finish；to complete：～事(把事情办完)to finish the work

骣 chǎn ㄔㄢˇ 骑马不加鞍辔 to ride bareback：～骑 *to ride bareback*

忏(懺) chàn ㄔㄢˋ 梵语"忏摩"的省称。佛教指请人宽恕。又指佛教、道教讽诵的一种经文 (short for 忏摩(*kama*) in Sanskrit，also used to denote a kind of Buddhist sutra and Taoist scripture) to ask for pardon in Buddhism [忏悔]悔过 to repent

刬(剗) ㊀ chàn ㄔㄢˋ [一刬]〈方 ***dialect***〉全部，一律 all；every：～～新 *brand-new*｜～～都是平川。*A vast plain appears.*

㊁ chǎn 见 75 页 see p75

颤 ㊀ chàn ㄔㄢˋ 物体振动 to vibrate；to quiver：这条扁担(dan)担上五六十斤就～了。*The shoulder pole shakes when it carries a load of fifty to sixty* jin.｜～动 *to vibrate*

㊁ zhàn 见 954 页 see p954

羼 chàn ㄔㄢˋ 掺杂 to mix；to mingle；to adulterate：～入 *to mix in*

韂 chàn ㄔㄢˋ 马鞍子下面垫的东西 saddle blanket：鞍～ *saddle and blanket*

CHANG ㄔㄤ

伥(倀) chāng ㄔㄤ 古代传说中被老虎咬死的

C

人变成的鬼，它常助虎伤人（in ancient legend）a person devoured by a tiger turned into a ghost, helping the tiger to devour other people：为（wèi）虎作～（喻帮恶人作恶）*to play the jackal to the tiger—to help a villain do evil*

昌 chāng 彳尢 兴盛 prosperous; flourishing; thriving：祖国繁荣～盛。*Ours is a prosperous country.*｜科学～明。*Science is flourishing.*

菖 chāng 彳尢 [菖蒲]多年生草本植物，生在水边，地下有根茎，花穗像棍棒。根茎可作香料，也可入药 calamus; sweet flag (*Acorus calamus*)

猖 chāng 彳尢 凶猛，狂妄 ferocious; outrageous [猖狂]狂妄而放肆 savage; ferocious; outrageous：打退了敌人的～～进攻。*The enemy's savage onslaught was repulsed.* [猖獗](－jué)放肆地横行，闹得很凶 rampant：～～一时 *to be rampant for a time*

阊 chāng 彳尢 [阊阖](－hé) **1** 传说中的天门 the gate of Heaven in legend **2** 宫门 palace gate [阊门]苏州城门名 Changmen, a city gate of Suzhou

娼 chāng 彳尢 妓女 prostitute（㊌ ***doublet*** 一妓 prostitute; streetwalker）

鲳 chāng 彳尢 鲳鱼，鱼名。身体短，没有腹鳍，背部青白色，鳞小，产在海中。肉细腻鲜美。也叫"镜鱼"、"平鱼"（also called 镜鱼 or 平鱼）butterfish (*Stromateidae*)

长（長）㊀ cháng 彳尢 ❶长度，两端的距离 length：这块布 3 米～。*The piece of cloth is three metres long.*｜那张桌子～1 米，宽 70 厘米。*That table is 1 metre long and 70 centimetres wide.* ❷长度大，跟"短"相对（the opposite of 短）long **1** 指空间（of space）long：这条路很～。*The road is very long.*｜～篇大论 *lengthy speech* (*or article*) **2** 指时间（of time）long：天～夜短。*Days are long and nights short.*｜～远利益 *long-term interest* [长短] **1** 长度 length **2** 意外的变故 accident; mishap：万一有什么～～ *if anything should happen* ❸长处，专精的技能，优点 forte; merit：特～ *forte; speciality*｜一技之～ *speciality; professional skill* ❹对某事做得特别好 to be good at; to be proficient in：他～于写作。*He's good at writing.*

㊁ zhǎng 见 956 页 see p956

苌（萇）cháng 彳尢 姓 Chang, a surname

场（場、*塲）㊀ cháng 彳尢 ❶平坦的空地，多半用来打庄稼 level clearing (*or* ground) often used for threshing crops：打～ *to thresh*｜～院里堆满了粮食。*Mounds of grain are everywhere on the threshing floor.*

❷量词 ***quantifier***，常用于一件事情的经过 process; course: 经历了一～激烈搏斗 *to have experienced a fierce fight*｜下了一～大雨。*There was a heavy rainfall.*

㊁ chǎng 见 78 页 see p78

肠(腸) cháng ㄔㄤˊ (～子)内脏之一，呈长管形，是消化和吸收的主要器官，分大肠、小肠两部分 intestine; bowel: 断～(喻非常悲痛) *heart-broken; grief-stricken*｜牵～挂肚(喻挂念) *to be very worried; to be deeply concerned* (图见 940 页"脏" picture on p940)

尝(嘗、❶*嚐) cháng ㄔㄤˊ ❶辨别滋味 to taste; to savour; to sample: ～～咸淡 *to taste a dish* [喻] ***figurative*** 经历，体验 to experience; to taste: 备～艰苦 *to have experienced untold hardships* [尝试]试 to attempt; to try: ～～一下 *to have a try* ❷曾经 once; ever: 未～ *never*

偿(償) cháng ㄔㄤˊ ❶归还，补还 to return; to compensate ([连] ***doublet*** 赔一 to repay; to redeem): ～还 *to repay; to redeem*｜赔～损失 *to pay for the loss*｜得不～失。*The loss outweighs the gain.* ❷满足 to satisfy; to fulfil: 如愿以～ *to have one's wish fulfilled*

鲿(鱨) cháng ㄔㄤˊ 毛鲿鱼，鱼名。侧扁，体长 1 米多，头较大，眼小，产在海中。也叫"大鱼"(also called 大鱼) Megalonibea fusca

徜 ㊁ cháng ㄔㄤˊ [倘佯](-yáng)旧同"徜徉" same as 徜徉 in former times

㊀ tǎng 见 732 页 see p732

徜 cháng ㄔㄤˊ [徜徉](-yáng)自由自在地来回走 to roam; to stroll; to saunter: ～～湖畔 *to roam leisurely on the lakeshore*

常 cháng ㄔㄤˊ ❶长久 constant; invariable: ～绿树 *evergreen trees*｜冬夏～青 *evergreen* ❷经常，时时(叠 ***reduplication***) often; frequently: ～～见面 *to see each other quite often*｜～和工人一起劳动 *to work often with labourers* ❸平常，普通的，一般的 ordinary; common; average: ～识 *common sense*｜～态 *normality*｜～事 *common occurrence*｜反～ *abnormal*｜习以为～ *to be used to; to be accustomed to*

嫦 cháng ㄔㄤˊ [嫦娥]神话中月宫里的仙女 Chang'e, the goddess of the moon in Chinese fairy tales

裳 ㊀ cháng ㄔㄤˊ 遮蔽下体的衣裙 skirt

㊁ shang 见 659 页 see p659

厂(廠、**厰) ㊀ chǎng ㄔㄤˇ ❶工厂 factory; mill; plant: 机械～ *mechanical plant*｜造纸～ *paper mill*｜纱～ *cotton mill* ❷有空地可以存货或进行加工的场

C

所 yard; depot：木～ *timber yard*｜煤～ *coal yard* ❸跟棚子类似的房屋 shack; shed

㊁ ān 见 5 页 see p5

场(場、*塲) ㊁ chǎng 㐬 ❶(一子、一儿)处所，能适应某种需要的较大地方 place：会～ *meeting place; conference hall*｜市～ *marketplace*｜广～*square*｜飞机～ *airport* ㊞ ***extension*** 特定的地点或范围 site; spot; scene：当～ *on the spot*｜现～ *on the spot*｜情～ *man-woman relationship in love; arena of love*｜生意～ *business world* [场合]某时某地或某种情况 occasion; situation ❷戏剧的一节 scene：三幕五～ *three acts and five scenes* ❸量词 ***quantifier***，用于文体活动(used in sports and recreation)：一～电影 *a film*｜一～球赛 *a match; a ball game* ❹物质相互作用的范围 field：电～ *electric field*｜磁～ *magnetic field*｜引力～ *gravitational field*

㊀ cháng 见 76 页 see p76

昶 chǎng 㐬 ❶白天时间长 (of the day) long ❷舒畅，畅通 relaxed and easy; unimpeded

惝 chǎng 㐬 (又 also tǎng) 见 732 页 tǎng see tǎng on p732

敞 chǎng 㐬 ❶没有遮蔽，宽绰 spacious; roomy：～亮 *bright and spacious*｜这房子很宽～。*The house is very spacious.* ❷打开 to open：～开大门 *to leave the door open*

氅 chǎng 㐬 大氅，大衣 cloak; overcoat

怅(悵) chàng 㐬 失意，不痛快(叠 ***reduplication***) disappointed; frustrated：～～离去 *to depart with regret*｜～然 *depressed*

韔(韔) chàng 㐬 古代盛(chéng)弓的袋子 bow case (in ancient China)

畅(暢) chàng 㐬 ❶没有阻碍 smooth; unimpeded：～达 *smooth; fluent*｜～行 *to pass without hindrance*｜～销 *best-selling* ❷痛快，尽情地 free; to one's heart's content：～谈 *to chat freely*｜～饮 *to drink one's fill*

倡 chàng 㐬 发动，首先提出 to initiate; to start：～议 *to propose*｜～导 *to advocate*

唱 chàng 㐬 ❶歌唱，依照音律发声 to sing; to vocalize：～歌 *to sing (a song)*｜～戏 *to sing an opera; to sing in an opera*｜～曲 *to sing a song (or tune)* ㊞ ***extension*** 高呼 to call out; to cry：～名 *to call (or read) the roll*｜～票 *to call out the names on votes while recording their corresponding number of votes* ❷(一儿)歌曲 song：唱个～儿 *to sing a song*

鬯 chàng 㐬 ❶古代祭祀用的一种酒 sacrifice wine in ancient China ❷同"畅" same as 畅：一夕～谈 to have an overnight talk

CHAO 彳幺

抄 chāo 彳幺 ❶誊写，照原文写 to copy; to transcribe: ～文件 *to copy a document* | ～书 *to copy (from) a book* ❷把别人的文章或作品照着写下来当自己的 to plagiarize; to lift: ～袭 *to plagiarize; to lift* ❸搜查并没(mò)收 to search and confiscate: ～家 *to search sb's house and confiscate his property* ❹走近便的路 to take a short cut: ～小道走 *to take a short cut* ❺同"绰㊁❷" same as 绰㊁❷: ～起镰刀就去割麦子 *to grab a sickle to harvest wheat*

吵 ㊁ chāo 彳幺 [吵吵](— chao) 吵嚷 to make a noise; to have a row

㊀ chǎo 见 80 页 see p80

钞 chāo 彳幺 ❶同"抄❶" same as 抄❶ ❷钞票，纸币 banknote: 外～ *foreign banknote*

怊 chāo 彳幺 悲伤失意 sad and disappointed

弨 chāo 彳幺 ❶弓解弦后弓背反过来 (of the back of a bow) reversed when the string is removed ❷弓 bow

超 chāo 彳幺 ❶越过，高出 to exceed; to surpass: ～龄 *overage* | ～额 *to overfulfil the quota* | ～声波 *ultrasonic wave; ultrasound* ❷在某种范围以外，不受限制 to transcend; to go beyond: ～现实 *surreal; surrealistic* | ～自然 *supernatural*

绰 ㊁ chāo 彳幺 ❶同"焯㊁" same as 焯㊁ ❷匆忙地抓起 to grab; to take up; to seize: ～起一根棍子 *to grab a stick*

㊀ chuò 见 105 页 see p105

焯 ㊁ chāo 彳幺 把蔬菜放在开水里略微一煮就拿出来 (of cooking) to blanch; to scald: ～菠菜 *to scald spinach*

㊀ zhuō 见 1006 页 see p1006

剿(*勦) ㊁ chāo 彳幺 因袭套用别人的语言文句作为自己的 to plagiarize; to lift: ～说 *plagiarize*

㊀ jiǎo 见 341 页 see p341

晁(**鼂) cháo 彳幺 姓 Chao, a surname

巢 cháo 彳幺 鸟搭的窝，也指蜂蚁等的窝 nest; beehive; anthill

朝 ㊀ cháo 彳幺 ❶面对 to face: 坐北～南 *to face south* | 这个窗户～着大街。*The window faces the street.* ㊉ ***extension*** 介词 ***preposition***，向着，对着 towards; to: ～前看 *to look ahead* | ～着宏伟的目标奋勇前进 *to proceed courageously towards the grand goal* ❷封建时代臣见君 to have an audience with the monarch in feudal times ㊉ ***extension*** 宗教徒参拜 to worship; to make a pilgrimage to: ～圣团 *pilgrim group* ❸朝廷，皇帝接见官吏、发号施令的地方 royal court [在朝]㊕ ***transfer*** 当政 to be in power; to be on the throne ❹朝代，称一姓帝王世代连续统治的时代 dynasty：唐～ *Tang Dynasty*｜改～换代 *dynastic changes* ❺姓 Chao, a surname [朝鲜族] **1** 我国少数民族，参看附表（see the appendix）the Korean ethnic group, one of the ethnic minorities of China **2** 朝鲜和韩国的主要民族 the main ethnic group of the Democratic People's Republic of Korea and Republic of Korea

㊁ zhāo 见 959 页 see p959

嘲（**謿）㊀ cháo 彳幺（旧读 formerly zhāo）讥笑，取笑 to sneer at; to ridicule（㊥ ***doublet*** 一笑 to sneer｜一讽 to ridicule）：冷～热讽 *to satirize; to make sarcastic remarks*

㊁ zhāo 见 960 页 see p960

潮 cháo 彳幺 ❶海水因为受了日月的引力而定时涨落的现象 tide：～水 *tide*｜～汐 *tide* ❷像潮水那样汹涌起伏的事物 tide; current; upsurge：思～ *trend of thoughts*｜风～ *agitation; unrest*｜革命高～ *a wave of revolution* ❸湿（程度比较浅）damp; moist：～气 *moisture; humidity*｜受～了 *to become damp*｜阴天返～。*Things get damp easily on cloudy days.* ❹成色差，技术低 inferior：～金 *impure gold ingot*｜手艺～ *not skilled*

吵 ㊀ chǎo 彳幺 ❶声音杂乱搅扰人 noisy; tumultuous：～得慌 *too noisy*｜把他～醒了。*He was awakened by the noise.* ❷打嘴架，口角 to quarrel; to squabble：～架 *to quarrel*｜争～ *to quarrel*｜他俩～起来了。*The two of them started quarreling.*

㊁ chāo 见 79 页 see p79

炒 chǎo 彳幺 把东西放在锅里搅拌着弄熟 to stir-fry; to sauté：～鸡蛋 *scrambled eggs*｜～菜 *stir-fried vegetables*｜糖～栗子 *roasted sweet chestnuts*

耖 chào 彳幺 ❶在耕、耙（bà）地以后用的一种把土弄得更细的农具 *chao*, a harrow-like implement for pulverizing soil ❷用耖弄细土块，使地平整 to level land with a *chao*

CHE 彳さ

车（車）㊀ chē 彳さ ❶陆地上有轮子的交通工具 vehicle：火～ *train*｜汽～ *car; motorcar*｜马～ *carriage; chariot*｜轿～ *car; sedan; limousine* ❷用轮轴来转动的器具 instrument with pivot and wheel：纺～ *spinning wheel*｜水～ *waterwheel*｜滑～ *pulley* ㊂ ***extension*** 指机器 machine：开～ *to run a machine*｜试～ *to make a trial run* [车间]工厂里在生产过程中能独立完成一个工作阶段的单位 workshop：翻砂～～ *foundry workshop*｜加工～～ *processing workshop*｜装配～～ *assembling workshop* ❸用旋（xuàn）床旋东西 to lathe：～圆 *to make sth round* *on a lathe* | ～光 *to smooth sth on a lathe* ❹用水车打水 to lift water with a waterwheel：～水 *to lift water with a waterwheel* ❺姓 Che, a surname

㊁ jū 见 366 页 see p366

砗 chē ㄔㄜ [砗磲](－qú) 一种软体动物，比蛤蜊大，生活在热带海中。壳略呈三角形，很厚，可做装饰品 giant clam (*Tridacna gigas*)

尺 ㊁ chě ㄔㄜˇ 旧时乐谱记音符号的一个，相当于简谱的"2" a note of the scale in musical notation in former times, corresponding to 2 (re) in numbered musical notations

㊀ chǐ 见 90 页 see p90

扯(*撦) chě ㄔㄜˇ ❶拉 to drag; to pull：～住他不放 *to grab at him* ❷不拘形式、不拘内容地谈 to chat; to gossip：闲～ *to chitchat* | 不要把问题～远了。*Don't stray from the subject.* ❸撕，撕破 to tear; to rip：～几尺布 *to buy several* chi *of cloth* | 他把信～了。*He tore the letter into pieces.*

彻(徹) chè ㄔㄜˋ 通，透 penetrating：冷风～骨。*The cold wind chills one to the bone.* | ～头～尾（自始至终，完完全全）*thorough; out-and-out* | ～夜（通宵）*all night; through the night* [彻底]根本的，不是表面的 thorough; downright：～～解决问题 *to solve the problem once and for all*

坼 chè ㄔㄜˋ 裂开 to split open; to crack：天寒地～。*The ground cracked in the severe cold.*

掣 chè ㄔㄜˋ ❶拽(zhuài)，拉 to pull; to drag：～后腿 *to hold sb back* | 风驰电～（喻迅速）*swift as wind and lightning* [掣肘]拉住别人的胳膊 to hold sb back by the elbow ⓜ ***figurative*** 阻碍旁人做事 to impede; to hinder ❷抽 to draw：～签 *to draw lots; to cast lots*

撤 chè ㄔㄜˋ ❶除去，免除 to remove; to dismiss：～职 *to remove sb from office; to dismiss sb from his* (or *her*) *post* | ～销 *to cancel; to revoke* ❷向后转移，收回 to withdraw; to retreat：～兵 *to withdraw troops* | ～资 *to recall the investment* | ～回 *to retract*

澈 chè ㄔㄜˋ ❶水清 (of water) clear; limpid：清～可鉴 *crystal clear; crystalline* ❷同"彻" same as 彻

CHEN ㄔㄣ

抻(**捵) chēn ㄔㄣ 扯，拉 to stretch：～面（抻面条或抻的面条）*to make noodles by stretching the dough by hand; hand-pulled noodles* | 把衣服～～ *to give the clothes a stretch* | 把袖子～出来 *to stretch out the sleeves*

郴 chēn ㄔㄣ 郴州，地名，在湖南省 Chenzhou, a place in

Hunan Province

琛 chēn ㄔㄣ 珍宝 treasure

嗔(△*瞋) chēn ㄔㄣ 生气 to be angry (㊣ *doublet* 一怒 to get angry; to be enraged): ～怪 *to complain* | ～责 *to blame* | 转～为喜 *to go from anger to pleasure* [嗔着] (—zhe)对人不满,嫌 to be displeased: ～～他多事 *to blame him for being meddlesome*

瞋 chēn ㄔㄣ ❶睁大眼睛瞪人 to stare angrily (at sb): ～目而视 *to glare (at sb or sth)* ❷同"嗔" same as 嗔

臣 chén ㄔㄣˊ ❶奴隶社会的奴隶 slave in the slave society ❷帮助皇帝进行统治的官僚 official helping the emperor to rule ❸封建时代官吏对君主的自称 (form of self-address used by officials when speaking to the king or emperor) I; your vassal; your servant

辰 chén ㄔㄣˊ ❶地支的第五位 *Chen*, 5th of the 12 Earthly Branches ❷辰时,指上午七点到九点 the period from 7 am to 9 am ❸指时日 day: 生～ *time and date of birth* | 诞～ *birthday* [辰光]〈方 *dialect*〉时候,时间 time ❹日、月、星的总称 (general term for the sun, the moon, and the stars) celestial bodies

宸 chén ㄔㄣˊ ❶屋宇,深邃(suì)的房屋 mansion ❷旧指帝王住的地方 (in former times) imperial palace ㊉ *extension* 王位、帝王的代称 substitutive designation for throne or emperor

晨 chén ㄔㄣˊ 清早,太阳出来的时候 morning: 清～ *early morning* | ～昏(早晚) *morning and evening; dawn and dusk*

尘(塵) chén ㄔㄣˊ ❶尘土,飞扬的灰土 dust; dirt ❷尘世(佛家道家指人间,和他们所幻想的理想世界相对) (earthly or practical world in the eyes of a Buddhist or Taoist believer, as the opposite of their imagined world) this world; this mortal life: ～俗 *worldly; earthly; mundane* | 红～ *world of mortals; human world*

沈 ㊁ chén ㄔㄣˊ 同"沉" same as 沉

㊀ shěn 见 668 页 see p668

忱 chén ㄔㄣˊ 真实的心情 true feelings: 热～ *zeal; zest; enthusiasm* | 谢～ *gratitude; thankfulness*

沉 chén ㄔㄣˊ ❶没(mò)入水中,跟"浮"相对 (the opposite of 浮) to sink; to submerge: 船～了。*The ship sank.* ㊉ *extension* 落下,陷入 to subside; to sink: 地基下～。*The foundation has subsided.* [沉淀] **1** 液体中不溶解的物质往下沉 to precipitate **2** 沉在液体底层的物质 sediment ❷重,分量大 heavy: ～重 *heavy* | 铁比木头～。*Iron is heavier than wood.* [沉着](—zhuó)镇静,不

慌张 calm; composed:～～应(yìng)战 *to meet the attack calmly* ❸深入,程度深 deep; profound:～思 *to contemplate; to ponder*|～醉 *intoxicated*|天阴得很～。*What a gloomy day!*

陈(陳) chén ㄔㄣˊ ❶排列,摆设 to display; to arrange(㊥ ***doublet*** —列 to display; to exhibit|—设 to display; to exhibit):古物～列馆 *antiques exhibition hall* ❷述说 to state; to explain(㊥ ***doublet*** —述 to state; to explain):详～ *to explain in detail* ❸旧的,时间久的 old; stale(㊥ ***doublet*** —旧 oldfashioned; out of date):～腐 *antiquated; obsolete*|～酒 *mellow wine*|新～代谢 *metabolism* ❹周代诸侯国名,在今河南省淮阳一带 Chen, a princedom of the Zhou Dynasty, covering today's Huaiyang and nearby areas, Henan Province ❺朝代名,南朝之一,陈霸先所建立(公元 557—589 年) Chen Dynasty, one of the Southern Dynasties, founded by Chen Baxian (557－589)

〈古 ***archaism***〉又同"阵"(zhèn) also same as 阵

谌 chén ㄔㄣˊ ❶相信 to have faith in; to believe in ❷的确,诚然 indeed; truly

碜(磣、硶)** chěn ㄔㄣˇ ❶东西里夹杂着沙子 gritty [牙碜](—chen)食物中夹杂着沙子,嚼起来牙不舒服 gritty:面条有些～。*The noodles are a bit gritty.* ❷丑,难看 ugly [寒碜](*寒伧)(—chen) **1** 丑,难看 ugly **2** 使人没面子 disgraceful; shameful; disreputable:说起来怪～～人的。*I feel a bit ashamed to say this.*

衬(襯) chèn ㄔㄣˋ ❶在里面再托上一层 to line; to place a layer underneath:～绒 *lining cotton flannel*|～上一张纸 *to place a piece of paper underneath* ❷搭配上别的东西 to serve as a foil for:红花～着绿叶。*Green leaves set off red flowers.*

疢 chèn ㄔㄣˋ 热病。也泛指病(also disease in general) febrile disease

龀 chèn ㄔㄣˋ 小孩儿换牙(乳牙脱落长出恒牙)(of a child) to grow permanent teeth (milk teeth fall out and permanent teeth grow)

称(稱) ㊁ chèn ㄔㄣˋ 适合 to fit; to match; to suit:～心 *to feel contented*|～职 *to be qualified*|相～ *compatible; suitable* [对称]两边相等或相当 symmetric; symmetrical

㊀ chēng 见 84 页 see p84

㊂ chèng 见 87 页 see p87

趁 chèn ㄔㄣˋ ❶利用机会 to take advantage of; to avail oneself of:～热打铁 *to strike while the iron is hot*|～着晴天打场(cháng) *to thresh the grain when it's sunny; to make hay while the sun shines* ❷〈方

C

dialect〉富有 to be rich; to possess: ～钱 *to have lots of money*

榇(櫬) chèn ㄔㄣˋ 棺材 coffin

谶 chèn ㄔㄣˋ 迷信的人指将来要应验的预言、预兆 augury; prophecy

伧(傖) ㊀ chen ·ㄔㄣ [寒伧]旧同"寒碜"。参看 83 页"碜"(chěn)(see 碜 on p83) same as 寒碜 in former times

㊁ cāng 见 65 页 see p65

CHENG ㄔㄥ

柽(檉) chēng ㄔㄥ 柽柳,又叫"三春柳"或"红柳"。落叶小乔木,老枝红色,花淡红色,性耐碱抗旱,适于盐碱地区造林防沙。枝叶可入药(also called 三春柳 or 红柳) Chinese tamarisk (*Tamarix chinensis*)

蛏(蟶) chēng ㄔㄥ (一子)一种软体动物,贝壳长方形,淡褐色,生活在沿海泥中,肉味鲜美 razor clam

琤 chēng ㄔㄥ 拟声词 ***onomatopoeia***,玉石碰击声、琴声或流水声(叠 ***reduplication***) jangling (of jade); twanging (of string instrument); gurgling (of flowing water)

称(稱) ㊀ chēng ㄔㄥ ❶量轻重 to weigh: 把这包米～一～。*Weigh this bag of rice, please.* ❷叫,叫作 to name; to address: 自～ *to call oneself; to style oneself as* | ～得起英雄 *to deserve the title of hero* ❸名称 name; designation; appellation: 简～ *abbreviation; short for* | 别～ *another name; alternative name* ❹说 to say: ～病 *to plead illness; to claim to be ill* | 连声～好 *to hail repeatedly* | 拍手～快 *to clap and cheer* ❺赞扬 to praise; to commend: ～许 *commendation; praise* | ～道 *to acclaim; to commend* ❻举事 to start: ～兵 *to launch a military attack; to take military action*

㊁ chèn 见 83 页 see p83

㊂ chèng 见 87 页 see p87

铛(鐺) ㊀ chēng ㄔㄥ 烙饼或做菜用的平底浅锅 pan; griddle: 电饼～ *electric pan*

㊁ dāng 见 130 页 see p130

赪 chēng ㄔㄥ 红色 red

撑(*撐) chēng ㄔㄥ ❶抵住,支撑 to prop up; to support: ～竿跳高(田径运动项目之一) *pole-vault* | ～腰 *to back up; to bolster up* | ～门面 *to keep up an appearance; to maintain an outward show of property* ❷用篙使船前进 to pole; to punt: ～船 *to pole a punt; to punt a boat* ❸充满到容不下的程度 to fill to the point of bursting: 少吃些,别～着。*Don't eat too much, otherwise you'll be bursting at the seams.* | 麻袋装得太满,都～圆了。*The sack is stuffed so full* *that it is bursting.* ❹使张开 to open; to unfurl:～伞 *to open an umbrella* | 把口袋～开 *to hold open a bag*

瞠 chēng ㄔㄥ 直看,瞪着眼 to stare:～目结舌 *to stare stunned and speechless* | ～乎其后(喻赶不上) *to stare at from behind, despairing of catching up*

成 chéng ㄔㄥˊ ❶做好了,办好了 done; finished (㊎ ***doublet*** 完— to finish):～事 *to succeed; to accomplish* | 大功告～。*The great mission has been accomplished.* | 完～任务 *to accomplish one's task* ❷事物生长发展到一定的形态或状况 mature:～虫 *imago* | ～人 *adult; grown-up* | 五谷～熟。*All food crops are ripe.* ❸成为,变为 to become:他～了飞机驾驶员了。*He became a pilot.* |雪化～水。*The snow has melted.* ❹成果,成绩 harvest; achievement:坐享其～ *to sit idle and enjoy the fruits of others' work* | 到头来一事无～ *only to accomplish nothing in the end* ❺可以,能行 all right; ok:这么办可不～。*It just won't do to act like this.* | ～,就那么办吧。*OK! Go ahead!* ❻称赞人能力强 able; capable:你们小组真～,这个月又超额了。*Your group has surpassed the production target again, terrific!* ❼够,达到一定的数量 to amount to:～千上万 *thousands upon thousands; tens of thousands* | ～车的慰问品 *cartloads of gifts* [成年累月](— — lěi —)形容经历的时间长 all year round; year after year ❽已定的,定形的 established; existing:～规 *convention* | ～见 *prejudice; bias* ❾(—儿)十分之一 one tenth:八～ *80 percent* | 提出一～做公益金 *to draw ten percent for a public welfare fund*

诚 chéng ㄔㄥˊ ❶真心 sincere (㊎ ***doublet*** —实 honest; upright):～心～意 *sincerely; in all sincerity* | ～恳 *earnest; genuine* ❷实在,的确 indeed; truly:～然 *indeed; really* | ～有此事。*Something like this really happened.*

城 chéng ㄔㄥˊ ❶城墙 city wall:万里长～ *Great Wall* ❷城市,都市 city; town; metropolis:～乡互助 *mutual aid between town and country*

宬 chéng ㄔㄥˊ 皇帝的藏书室 imperial archives:皇史～(明清两代保藏皇室史料的处所,在北京) *the Imperial Archives (located in Beijing, where imperial records were kept in the Ming and Qing dynasties)*

盛 ㊀ chéng ㄔㄥˊ ❶把东西放进去 to ladle; to fill:～饭 *to fill a bowl with rice* ❷容纳 to hold; to contain:这礼堂能～几千人。*This auditorium holds thousands of people.*

㊁ shèng 见 673 页 see p673

C

C

铖 chéng ㄔㄥˊ 用于人名 cheng, used in a given names

丞 chéng ㄔㄥˊ ❶帮助,辅佐 to help; to assist:～辅 *to assist* [丞相](－xiàng)古代帮助皇帝处理政务的最高一级官吏 prime minister in ancient China ❷封建时代帮助主要官员做事的官吏 assistant to an official in feudal times:县～ *county magistrate's assistant* | 府～ *petty official in a prefectural magistrate's office*

呈 chéng ㄔㄥˊ ❶显出,露出 to appear; to look:皮肤～红色。*The skin appears to be red.* | ～现一片新气象 *to take on a new look* ❷恭敬地送上去 to submit:送～ *to deliver and submit* | 谨～ *to submit respectfully* ❸呈文,下级报告上级的书面文字 petition:辞～ *resignation*

埕 chéng ㄔㄥˊ ❶蛏埕,福建、广东沿海一带饲养蛏类的田 razor clam farm ❷〈方 **dialect**〉酒瓮 wine jar

程 chéng ㄔㄥˊ ❶里程,道路的段落 distance; leg of a journey (㊤ **doublet** 路一 journey):起～ *to set out* | 登～ *to start* (or *embark*) *on a journey* | 送他一～ *to accompany him on the first leg of his journey* [过程]事物变化、发展的经过 process; procedure ❷进度,限度 progress; limit:日～ *agenda; schedule* | ～序 *procedure* ❸法式 form; modality (㊤ **doublet** 一式 formula; pattern):操作规～ *operating rules* ❹计量,计算 to measure; to calculate:计日～功。*Progress can be measured by days.* or *Success is drawing near.*

裎 chéng ㄔㄥˊ 脱衣露体 naked; nude

酲 chéng ㄔㄥˊ 喝醉了神志不清 fuddled; drunken:忧心如～ *extremely worried*

枨(棖) chéng ㄔㄥˊ ❶古时门两边竖的木柱,泛指支柱 (pillar in general) wooden pillars at each side of a gate in ancient China ❷触动 to touch:～触 *to move*

承 chéng ㄔㄥˊ ❶在下面接受,托着 to support; to hold:～尘(天花板) *ceiling* ❷承担,担当 to bear; to undertake:～应(yìng) *to agree to do; to accept; to promise* | 这工程由建筑公司～包。*The contracted project has been undertaken by a construction company.* | 责任由我～当。*I'll shoulder the responsibility.* ㊂ **extension** 蒙,受到,接受(别人的好意) to be honoured; to be accorded (a title, approval, etc):～情 *to be indebted* | ～教(jiào) *to be grateful for sb's instructions* | ～大家热心招待。*I'm deeply grateful for your hospitality.* [承认] **1** 表示肯定,同意,认可 to admit; to consent; to recognize:～～错误 *to acknowledge one's mistake* | 他～～有这么回事。*He admitted it.* **2** 国际上指肯定新国家、新政权的法律地位 to give diplomatic recognition; to recognize ❸继续，接连 to continue; to carry on:～上启下 *transitional; a connecting link between the preceding and the following* | 继～ *to inherit; to succeed* | ～接 *to undertake; to carry on*

乘 ㊀ chéng ㄔㄥˊ ❶骑，坐 to ride; to take:～马 *to ride a horse* | ～车 *to take a bus* (or *train*) | ～飞机 *to take a plane* ❷趁，就着 to take advantage of:～便 *at one's convenience* | ～机 *to seize the opportunity* | ～势 *to avail oneself of a favourable situation* | ～兴(xìng) *while in excitement* ❸算术中指一个数使另一个数变成若干倍 to multiply; to time:五～二等于十。*5 times 2 is 10.* or *5 multiplied by 2 makes 10.* ❹姓 Cheng, a surname

㊁ shèng 见 673 页 see p673

惩(懲) chéng ㄔㄥˊ 处罚，警戒 to punish; to penalize:严～ *to punish severely* | ～前毖(bì)后 *to learn a lesson from the past to avoid future mistakes; to learn from past errors to avoid future ones*

塍 chéng ㄔㄥˊ 田间的土埂子 path between fields:田～ *path between fields*

澄(*澂) ㊀ chéng ㄔㄥˊ 水清 (of water) clear; limpid [澄清]清澈，清亮 crystal clear; crystalline:溪水～～。*The creek is clear.* ⑩ ***figurative*** 搞清楚，搞明白 to clarify; to elucidate:把问题～～一下 *to elucidate a problem*

㊁ dèng 见 139 页 see p139

橙 chéng ㄔㄥˊ ❶常绿乔木，果实叫橙子，品种很多，可以吃，果皮可入药 orange (*citrus*) ❷红和黄合成的颜色 orange (colour)

逞 chěng ㄔㄥˇ ❶炫耀，卖弄 to show off; to display:～能 *to parade one's ability* | ～强 *to flaunt one's superiority* ❷施展，实现 to carry out; to succeed:决不让敌人的阴谋得～。*Never let the enemy's plot succeed.*

骋 chěng ㄔㄥˇ 骑马奔驰，奔跑 to gallop (㊟ ***doublet*** 驰— to gallop):汽车在公路上驰～。*A car is speeding down the road.* ㊞ ***extension*** 放任，尽量展开 to give free rein to:～目 *to look into the distance* | ～望 *to look as far as one's eyes can see*

秤 chèng ㄔㄥˋ 衡量轻重的器具 balance; scales

称(稱) ㊂ chèng ㄔㄥˋ 同"秤" same as 秤

㊀ chēng 见 84 页 see p84

㊁ chèn 见 83 页 see p83

牚 chèng ㄔㄥˋ ❶斜柱 tilting pillar ❷(一儿)桌椅等腿中间的横木 rung

CHI ㄔ

吃(*喫) chī ㄔ ❶咀嚼(jǔjué)食物后咽下(包括喝、吸) to eat:～饭 *to have meals*|～奶 *to suck milk*|～药 *to take medicine* ❷靠某种事物生活 to live on; to live off:～老本 *to rest on one's laurels*|靠山～山,靠水～水 *to live off local resources* ❸吸 to absorb; to take in:～墨纸 *blotting paper; blotter* ❹感受 to feel:～惊 *surprised; astonished*|～紧 *crucial; critical* [吃力]费力气 arduous; strenuous ❺承受,支持 to withstand; to endure:这个任务很～重。*It's arduous work.*|～不住太大的分量 *cannot bear too much* ❻消灭 to annihilate:～掉敌人一个团 *to wipe out an enemy regiment* ❼介词 ***preposition***,被(宋元小说戏曲里常用)(word indicating passiveness in novels and operas of the Song and Yuan dynasties) by:～那厮骗了 *to have been deceived by that fellow*

[吃水]船身入水的深度。根据吃水的深浅可以计算全船载货的重量 draught

[口吃](“吃”旧读 formerly jī)结巴 to stutter; to stammer

哧 chī ㄔ 拟声词 ***onomatopoeia***:～～地笑 *to titter; to chuckle*

蚩 chī ㄔ 无知,痴愚 ignorant; stupid

嗤 chī ㄔ 讥笑 to ridicule; to jeer at:～之以鼻 *to sneer at; to sniff at*

媸 chī ㄔ 面貌丑 ugly

鸱 chī ㄔ 鹞(yào)鹰 sparrow hawk [鸱鸮](－xiāo) **1** 猫头鹰一类的鸟 birds of the owl family **2** 古代指“鷦鷯”(jiāoliáo) referring to 鷦鷯 in ancient China [鸱鸺](－xiū)一种凶猛的鸟,俗叫“猫头鹰”或“夜猫子”。眼大而圆,头上有像耳的毛角。昼伏夜出,捕食小鸟、兔、鼠等,是益鸟(popularly called 猫头鹰 or 夜猫子) owl

絺 chī ㄔ 细葛布 fine kohemp cloth; fine hemp cloth

瓻 chī ㄔ 古代的一种酒器 wine pot in ancient China

眵 chī ㄔ 眼眵,眼睛分泌出来的液体凝结成的淡黄色东西。也叫“眵目糊”或“眼屎”(also called 眵目糊 or 眼屎) eye secretion

笞 chī ㄔ 用鞭、杖或竹板打 to whip; to flog; to thrash

痴(*癡) chī ㄔ 傻 silly; foolish:～人说梦(喻完全胡说) *idiotic nonsense*

螭 chī ㄔ 古代传说中一种没有角的龙。古代建筑或工艺品上常用它的形状作装饰 legendary hornless dragon in ancient China; ancient decorative motif (in the shape of this legendary animal)

魑 chī ㄔ [魑魅](－mèi)传说中山林里能害人的怪物 legendary man-eating monster in mountains and forests

池 chí ㄔˊ ❶(一子)水塘,多指人工挖的 pool; pond (㊟ **doublet** 一沼 large pond): 游泳～ *swimming pool*|养鱼～ *fish pond*|❷像水池的东西 pond-shaped thing: 便～ *urinal*|花～ *flower bed* ❸护城河 moat:城～ *city*|金城汤～(喻极为坚固,不易攻破) *impregnable fortress; strongly fortified city*

弛 chí ㄔˊ (旧读 formerly shǐ)放松,松懈,解除 to relax; to slacken:一张一～ *to alternate tension with relaxation*|废～ *to be neglected*|～禁 *to annul a ban*

驰 chí ㄔˊ ❶快跑(多指车马)(of vechicles, horses, etc) to drive at a high speed; to gallop (㊟ **doublet** 一骋 to gallop):背道而～ *to run in the opposite direction; to go against*|风～电掣 *swift as wind and lightning* ㊞ **extension** 向往 to crave for:神～ *to yearn for*|情～ *to long for* ❷传播 to spread: ～名 *famous; well-known*

迟(遲) chí ㄔˊ ❶慢,缓 slow; tardy:说时～,那时快 *in an instant; in a twinkling; in the wink of an eye*|行动～缓 *slow in action*|～～不去 *lingering* ㊞ ***extension*** 不灵敏 slow; blunt:心～眼钝 *slow in reaction* [迟疑]犹豫不决 to hesitate ❷晚 late:不～到 *not to be late*|睡得太～ *to stay up late; to sit up late*

坻 ㊀ chí ㄔˊ 水中的小块高地 sandbank; sandbar

㊁ dǐ 见141页 see p141

茌 chí ㄔˊ [茌平]地名,在山东省 Chiping, a place in Shandong Province

持 chí ㄔˊ ❶拿着,握住 to hold; to grasp: ～笔 *to hold a pen*|～枪 *to hold a gun* ❷遵守不变 to adhere; to maintain:坚～真理 *to uphold the truth* [持久]保持长久 abiding; lasting: ～～战 *protracted warfare*|绿肥肥效能～～,还能松地抗旱。*Green manure can not only have long-lasting effect, but also loosen the soil and resist draught.* [持续]延续不间断 continuous; sustained [相持]各不相让 at a stalemate; in a deadlock:～～不下 (*both sides*) *unyielding* ❸治理,主管 to manage; to be in charge of:勤俭～家 *to be industrious and thrifty in running one's household*|这件事由你主～好了。*You'll take charge of the matter.*

匙 ㊀ chí ㄔˊ 舀(yǎo)汤用的小勺子。也叫"调羹"(tiáogēng) (also called 调羹) soup spoon

㊁ shi 见686页 see p686

漦 chí ㄔˊ lí ㄌㄧˊ (又 also lí) 涎沫 saliva; spit

墀 chí ㄔˊ 台阶上面的空地。又指台阶(also sidestep or step) landing on top of a flight of steps

踟 chí 彳 [踟蹰](—chú)心里犹豫,要走不走的样子 to hesitate; to falter; to waver:～～不前 *to hesitate to move forward; to linger*

篪(**箎、**竾) chí 彳 古代一种用竹管制成的乐器 bamboo flute in ancient China

尺 ㊀ chǐ 彳 ❶市制长度单位,10 寸是 1 尺,10 尺是 1 丈 *chi*, a traditional Chinese unit of length, 10 *cun* is one *chi*, and 10 *chi* is one *zhang*:1 米等于 3 市～。*One metre is 3 chi*.[尺寸](—cun)衣物的大小长短 size; length:开个～～好照着做 *to take a size for making clothes*|～～要量得准确。*The measurements should be taken accurately*.[尺牍]书信(因古代的书简长约 1 尺)(the bamboo strip, about one *chi* long, on which characters were written in ancient China) letter; correspondence ❷尺子,一种量长短的器具 ruler ❸画图的器具 tool for drawing:放大～ *pantograph* ❹像尺的东西 sth like a ruler:计算～ *slide-rule*

㊁ chě 见 81 页 see p81

呎 chǐ 彳 也读作 yīngchǐ。英美制长度单位,1 呎是 12 吋,合 0.3048 米。现写作"英尺"(also pronounced yīngchǐ, now written as 英尺, a unit of length in Britain, US, etc. One foot is 12 inches, equal approximately to 0.3048 metre.) foot

齿(齒) chǐ 彳 ❶牙齿,人和动物嘴里咀嚼食物的器官 tooth[挂齿]谈及,提及(只用在否定的句子里)(only used in negative sentences) to speak of; to mention:不足～～ *not worth mentioning* (or *speaking of*)|何足～～ *not worth mentioning* (or *speaking of*) ❷(一儿)排列像牙齿形状的东西 tooth-like or dentate part of anything:锯～ *saw teeth*|梳子～儿 *teeth of a comb*|～轮 *gear* ❸年龄 age:马～徒增(自谦年长无能) *to grow old with nothing accomplished* [不齿]㊕ ***transfer*** 不认为是同类的人,表示鄙弃 to despise

侈 chǐ 彳 ❶浪费,用财物过度 wasteful; extravagant (㊇ ***doublet*** 奢— extravagant):生活奢～ *to live in extravagance* ❷夸大 to exaggerate:～谈 *to prate about; to prattle about*

耻(*恥) chǐ 彳 羞愧,耻辱 shame; disgrace (㊇ ***doublet*** 羞— disgraceful):雪～ *to avenge an insult*|浪费可～。*Waste is a shame*. or *A waste and a shame!*

豉 chǐ 彳 豆豉,一种用豆子制成的食品 (food made of soya beans) fermented soya beans

褫 chǐ 彳 剥夺 to deprive:～职 *to remove sb from office*|～夺 *to deprive; to dispossess*

彳 chì 彳[彳亍](—chù)小步慢走或走走停停的样子 to

stroll; to saunter

叱 chì ㄔˋ 呼呵(hē),大声斥骂 to rebuke; to shout at [叱咤](—zhà)发怒吆喝 to flare up; to bawl angrily:～～风云 *to ride the whirlwind*

斥 chì ㄔˋ ❶责备 to blame; to scold (㊥ ***doublet*** —责 to reprimand):遭到～责 *to be denounced* | 痛～这种荒谬的论调 *to denounce the fallacy sharply* ❷使退去,使离开 to repel; to dismiss:排～ *to repel; to exclude* | ～退 *to expel* ❸多,广 numerous; broad [充斥]多得到处都是(含贬义)(with derogatory sense) to flood; to be full of

[斥候]旧时军队称侦察(敌情)。也指进行侦察的士兵(also denoting a scout) to reconnoiter (*or* scout) in former times

[斥资]支付费用,出资 to fund; to invest:～～百万 *to invest a million dollars*

赤 chì ㄔˋ ❶比朱红稍暗的颜色,泛指红色 red:～小豆 *red bean* | ～铜矿 *cuprite; red copper core* [赤子]初生婴儿 newborn baby [赤字]财政上亏空的数字 deficit; shortfall ❷忠诚 loyal; faithful:～诚 *absolutely sincere* | ～心 *loyalty* | ～胆忠心 *utter devotion; ardent loyalty* ❸空无所有 bare; empty:～手空拳 *barehanded; barefisted* | ～贫 *impoverished; penniless* ❹裸露 bare; naked:～脚 *barefooted* | ～背(bèi) *barebacked*

饬 chì ㄔˋ ❶整顿,使整齐 to rectify; to readjust (㊥ ***doublet*** 整— to rectify):整～纪律 *to strengthen discipline* ❷旧时指上级命令下级 order from one's superior in former times:～知 *to inform* | ～令 *to order*

炽(熾) chì ㄔˋ 旺盛 flaming; ablaze:～热 *scorching; fervent*

翅(*翄) chì ㄔˋ ❶翅膀,鸟和昆虫等用来飞行的器官 wing ❷鱼翅,指鲨鱼的鳍,是珍贵的食品 shark's fin ❸古同"啻" same as 啻 in ancient Chinese

敕(*勅、*勑) chì ㄔˋ 帝王的诏书、命令 imperial edict; imperial decree

鶒 chì ㄔˋ 见 802 页"鸂"字条"鸂鶒"(xī—) see 鸂鶒 on p802

啻 chì ㄔˋ 但,只 but; only; merely [不啻] **1** 不只,不止 not only; not less than:～～如此。*There's much more than this.* **2** 不异于,如同 as; like:～～兄弟 *just like brothers*

傺 chì ㄔˋ 见 71 页"侘"字条"侘傺"(chà—) see 侘傺 on p71

瘈 ㊁ chì ㄔˋ 同"瘛" same as 瘛

㊀ zhì 见 986 页 see p986

瘛 chì ㄔˋ [瘛疭](—zòng)中医指手脚痉挛、口眼歪斜的症状。也叫"抽风"(also

called 抽风) clonus; clonic convulsion

CHONG ㄔㄨㄥ

冲(❸❹衝、❶❷**沖)

㊀ chōng ㄔㄨㄥ ❶用开水等浇,水流撞击 to pour boiling water on; to rinse; to flush:~茶 *to make tea* | 用水~服 *to take medicine after dissolving it with water; to take medicine with water* | 这道堤不怕水~。*The embankment will withstand the flood surge.* [冲淡] 加多液体,降低浓度 to dilute ㊗ ***figurative*** 使某种效果、气氛等减弱 to weaken ❷向上钻 to soar:~入云霄 *to soar into the sky* ❸通行的大道 thoroughfare:要~ *place of strategic importance* | 这是~要地方。*This is a place of strategic importance.* ❹快速向前闯 to charge; to dash:~锋 *to charge; to assault* | ~入敌阵 *to rush at the enemy's positions* | 横~直撞 *to barge about; to jostle* [冲动] 没经过仔细思考而突然产生的情绪或行动 impulse; urge [冲突] **1** 互相撞击或争斗 to crash; to collide **2** 意见不同,互相抵触 to conflict; to contradict ❺互相抵消 to counterbalance; to counteract:~账 *to strike a balance; to balance an account; to balance one's books*

㊁ chòng 见93页 see p93

忡(**㤝) chōng ㄔㄨㄥ 忧虑不安(叠 ***reduplication***) worried; anxious:忧心~~ *careworn*

翀 chōng ㄔㄨㄥ 鸟向上直飞 (of bird) to soar

充 chōng ㄔㄨㄥ ❶满,足 sufficient; full (㊦ ***doublet*** 一足 adequate; abundant):~其量 *at most; at best* | 理由~分 *to have sound reasons* | 内容~实 *with substantial content* ❷填满,装满 to fill; to stuff:~电 *to charge* | ~耳不闻 *to turn a deaf ear to* | ~满愉快的心情 *to be imbued with pleasure* ❸当,担任 to serve as; to act as:~当 *to serve as; to act as* | ~任 *to fill the position of* ❹假装 to pretend to be; to pose as:~行家 *to pose as an expert* | ~能干 *to pretend to be capable*

茺 chōng ㄔㄨㄥ [茺蔚](一wèi)就是益母草,一年或二年生草本植物,茎方柱形,叶掌状分裂,花红色或白色。茎、叶、子实都入药 (i.e.益母草) Chinese motherwort (*Leonurus japonicus*)

舂 chōng ㄔㄨㄥ 捣去皮壳或捣碎 to pound; to pestle:~米 *to husk rice with a mortar and pestle* | ~药 *to pound medicinal herbs in a mortar*

憧 chōng ㄔㄨㄥ 心意不定 uneasy; disquieted [憧憧] 往来不定,摇曳不定 flickering:人影~~ *shadows of people moving about*

[憧憬](一jǐng)向往 to long

for; to yearn for

艟 chōng ㄔㄨㄥ 见 497 页"艨"字条"艨艟"(méng —) see 艨艟 on p497

虫(蟲) chóng ㄔㄨㄥˊ 虫子,昆虫 worm; insect [大虫]老虎 tiger

种 ㊂ chóng ㄔㄨㄥˊ 姓 Chong, a surname

㊀ zhǒng 见 987 页 see p987

㊁ zhòng 见 988 页 see p988

重 ㊁ chóng ㄔㄨㄥˊ ❶重复,再 to repeat; to duplicate: 书买~了 *to have bought two copies of the same book by mistake* | 旧地~游 *to revisit a once familiar place* | ~整旗鼓 *to rally one's forces after a defeat; to resume work after failure* | ~来一次 *to try again* [重阳][重九]夏历九月九日。是我国传统节日(9th day of the 9th lunar month, a traditional Chinese festival) Double Ninth Festival ❷层 layer; level: 双~领导 *dual leadership* | ~~围住 *to encircle ring upon ring; to besiege*

㊀ zhòng 见 989 页 see p989

崇 chóng ㄔㄨㄥˊ ❶高 lofty; sublime: ~山峻岭 *towering mountains and high ridges; precipitous mountains* | ~高的品质 *noble character* ❷尊重 to respect; to esteem: 推~ *to hold sb in esteem* | ~拜 *to worship* | 尊~ *to revere; to adore*

宠(寵) chǒng ㄔㄨㄥˇ ❶偏爱,过分地爱 to indulge; to spoil; to dote on: 不能老~着孩子。*Don't indulge your children's every whim.* ❷光耀,荣耀 glory; honour: ~辱不惊 *to be unmoved by favour or disgrace; to keep one's head cool whether favoured or humiliated; to remain indifferent to other's opinions*

冲(衝) ㊁ chòng ㄔㄨㄥˋ ❶对着,向 facing; towards: ~南的大门 *gate facing south* | 别~着我说。*Don't direct these remarks to me.* ❷猛烈 vigorously; bluntly: 这小伙子有股~劲儿。*The young fellow has vigorous drive.* | 水流得真~。*How swift is the torrent!* | 大蒜气味~。*Garlic has a pungent odour.* ❸介词 ***preposition***,凭,根据 because of; according to: ~他这股子钻劲儿,一定能完成这项技术革新任务。*Working with such vigour, he'll surely be able to accomplish this task of technical innovation.*

㊀ chōng 见 92 页 see p92

铳 chòng ㄔㄨㄥˋ ❶旧时指枪一类的火器 (in former times) blunderbuss; shotgun ❷(一子)用金属做成的一种打眼器具 punching pin ❸用铳子打眼或除去 to punch (a hole); to remove with a punching pin

CHOU ㄔㄡ

抽 chōu ㄔㄡ ❶从事物中提出一部分 to pull; to draw: ～签 *to draw lots; to cast lots* | ～调干部 *to transfer administrators* | ～空儿 *to manage to find time* [抽象] **1** 从事物中抽取本质并形成概念的思维活动 to abstract **2** 笼统,不具体 abstract: 问题这样提太～～了,最好举一个实例。*To such an abstract question, a concrete example is preferable.* ❷长出 to put forth: 谷子～穗。*The millet is earing.* ❸吸 to absorb; to inhale: ～水 *to draw water; to pump water* | ～气机 *air extractor; air exhauster* | ～烟 *to smoke* ❹减缩,收缩 to shrink: 这布一洗～了一厘米。*The cloth shrank by one centimetre after the first wash.* [抽风]手足痉挛,口眼歪斜的症状 convulsion ❺用细长的、软的东西打 to whip; to lash: 他不再用鞭子～牲口了。*He didn't whip the livestock any more.*

紬 ㊀ chōu ㄔㄡ 引出,缀辑 to expound; to compose [紬绎][抽绎](－yì)引出头绪 to sort out

㊁ chóu 见 94 页 see p94

瘳 chōu ㄔㄡ ❶病愈 to recover ❷损害 to harm; to damage

犨 chōu ㄔㄡ ❶牛喘息声 wheezing; panting of an ox ❷突出 protruding; protuberant

仇(*讐) ㊀ chóu ㄔㄡ 深切的怨恨 hatred; enmity; grudge: ～人 *foe; enemy* | 报～ *to revenge; to avenge* | 恩将～报 *to return evil for good; to repay love with hate* | ～视侵略者 *to be hostile to invaders*

㊁ qiú 见 615 页 see p615

紬 ㊁ chóu ㄔㄡ 同"绸" same as 绸

㊀ chōu 见 94 页 see p94

俦(儔) chóu ㄔㄡ 同伴,伴侣 companion; partner; mate

帱(幬) ㊀ chóu ㄔㄡ ❶帐子 bed curtain ❷车帷 carriage curtain

㊁ dào 见 134 页 see p134

畴(疇) chóu ㄔㄡ ❶田地 field; farmland ❷类,同类 kind; category

[畴昔]过去,以前 past; former times; bygone days

筹(籌) chóu ㄔㄡ ❶计数的用具,多用竹子制成 (usually made of bamboo) chip; counter ❷谋划 to plan: ～款 *to raise money; to raise funds* | ～备 *to prepare; to arrange* | 统～ *to make overall plans* | 一～莫展 *at one's wits' end; at a loss*

踌(躊) chóu ㄔㄡ [踌躇](－chú) **1** 犹豫,拿不定主意 hesitant; faltering: 他～～了半天才答应了。

He agreed after hesitating for a long time. **2** 自得的样子 complacent; smug: ～～满志 *complacent; enormously proud of one's success*

惆 chóu 彳ㄡˊ [惆怅](—chàng)失意,伤感 disconsolate; melancholy

绸 chóu 彳ㄡˊ (—子)一种薄而软的丝织品 silk (fabric)

稠 chóu 彳ㄡˊ ❶密 dense (㊀ ***doublet*** —密 dense): 人烟～密 *densely-populated* | 棉花棵很～。*Cotton is densely planted.* ❷浓 thick: 这粥太～了。*The porridge is too thick.*

酬(*酧、*醻) chóu 彳ㄡˊ ❶向客人敬酒 to propose a toast; to toast [酬酢](—zuò)主客互相敬酒。泛指交际往来 (to socialize in general) to exchange toasts [应酬](yìngchou) **1** 交际往来 to socialize; to entertain **2** 表面应付 to treat with courtesy ❷用财物报答 to reward; to repay: ～劳 *reward; payment; remuneration* ❸报酬 payment; remuneration: 同工同～ *equal pay for equal work*

愁 chóu 彳ㄡˊ 忧虑 to worry; to be anxious (㊀ ***doublet*** 忧— worried; anxious): 发～ *to get worried; to be anxious* | 不～吃,不～穿 *to have no worry about food or clothing*

雠(*讐) chóu 彳ㄡˊ ❶校(jiào)对文字 to collate; to proofread (㊀ ***doublet*** 校— to collate) ❷同"仇㊀" same as 仇㊀

丑(❹❺醜) chǒu 彳ㄡˇ ❶地支的第二位 *Chou*, 2nd of the 12th Earthly Branches ❷丑时,指夜里一点到三点 the period from 1 am to 3 am ❸(—儿)戏剧里的滑稽角色 clown; comedian ❹相貌难看 ugly; unsightly: 长得～ *to have an ugly figure* ❺可厌恶的,可耻的,不光彩的 scandalous; shameful; disgraceful: ～态 *abominable appearance; disgusting performance* | ～名 *notoriety; infamy* | 出～ *to bring shame on oneself; to make a fool of oneself*

杻 ㊀ chǒu 彳ㄡˇ 古代刑具,手铐之类 instrument of custody, such as handcuffs in ancient China

㊁ niǔ 见 540 页 see p540

瞅(*矁) chǒu 彳ㄡˇ 〈方 ***dialect***〉看 to look at: 我没～见他。*I didn't see him.*

臭 ㊀ chòu 彳ㄡˋ ❶气味难闻的,跟"香"相对 (the opposite of 香) smelly; stinking: ～气熏人 *foul; stinky* ㊗ ***figurative*** **1** 惹人厌恶的 disgusting; detestable: 遗～万年 *to earn eternal notoriety* | 放下～架子 *to give up one's disgusting airs* **2** 低劣 inferior; poor: ～棋 *bad move* | 这球踢得真～。*What a lousy kick!* ❷狠狠地 severely: ～骂 *tongue-lashing*

C

㊂ xiù 见 843 页 see p843

CHU 彳乂

C

出(⑩齣) chū 彳乂 ❶ 跟"入"、"进"相对 (the opposite of 入 and 进) **1** 从里面到外面 to go or come out: ～门 *to go out* | 从屋里～来 *to come out of the room* | ～汗 *to sweat* **2** 支付,往外拿 to offer; to give: ～一把力 *to make an effort* | ～主意 *to offer advice* | 量入为～ *to make both ends meet; to live within one's means* ❷ 来到 to show one's appearance: ～席 *to attend; to be present* | ～勤 *attendance at work* ❸ 离开 to leave: ～轨 *to derail* ❹ 产,生长 to produce; to grow: ～品 *to manufacture; to make* | 这里～米。*Rice grows in this region.* ❺ 发生 to happen; to occur: ～事 *to have an accident; to meet with a mishap* | ～问题了。*Something has gone wrong.* ❻ 显得量多 to rise well (in cooking); to appear in big quantity: 这米很～饭。*This kind of rice is very expandable.* ❼ 显露 to be made known: ～名 *well-known; celebrated* | ～头 *to take the lead* ❽ 超过 to surpass: ～众 *outstanding* | ～人头地 *to distinguish oneself* [出色](-sè) 特别好,超出一般的 excellent; remarkable: ～～地完成了任务 *to have accomplished the task with flying colours* ❾ 放在动词后,表示趋向或效果 (used after a verb to indicate tendency or effect): 提～问题 *to raise a question* | 作～贡献 *to make a contribution* ❿ 传(chuán)奇中的一回,戏曲的一个独立剧目 a scene from a play

初 chū 彳乂 开始,表示时间、等级、次序等都在前的 beginning; initial; inceptive: ～一 *the first day of each lunar month* | ～伏 *first fu, first ten days of the hottest period in summer* | ～稿 *the first draft* | ～学 *to be a beginner* | ～等教育 *elementary education* | 红日～升。*The sun has just risen.* ㉕ ***extension*** 原来的,原来的情况 original; original situation: ～衷 *original intention* | 和好如～ *to be on good terms again*

樗 chū 彳乂 樗树,即臭椿树 (i.e. 臭椿树) tree of heaven (*Ailanthus altissima*)

刍(芻) chú 彳乂 ❶ 喂牲畜的草 hay; fodder ❷ 割草 to cut grass; to weed

鸰(鶵) chú 彳乂 ❶ 同"雏" same as 雏 ❷ 见 923 页"鹓"字条"鹓鸰"(yuān—) see 鹓鸰 on p923

雏(雛) chú 彳乂 幼小的鸟,生下不久的 young bird; newborn bird: ～鸡 *chick; chicken* | ～莺乳燕 *newborn warbler and young swallow; the young* [雏形] ㊗ ***figurative*** 事物初具的规模 embryo; embryonic form: 略具～～ *to come into shape basically*

除 chú ㄔㄨˊ ❶去掉 to remove; to get rid of: ~害 *to eliminate evils* | 斩草~根 *to eradicate the source of trouble* ❷不计算在内 except; apart from: ~此以外 *besides* | ~了这个人,我都认识。*I know everyone except him* (or *her*). [除非] **1** 连词 ***conjunction***,表示唯一的条件,只有 only if: 若要人不知,~~己莫为。*If you don't want others to know about it, don't do it.* or *Whatever one does is sure to leave a trace.* **2** 表示不计算在内,除了 unless; except: 那条山路,~~他,没人认识。*No one except him knows the mountain path.* [除夕]一年最后一天的夜晚,也指一年最后的一天 New Year's Eve ❸算术中用一个数去分另一个数 to divide: 用二~四得二。*4 divided by 2 is 2.* ❹台阶 door steps: 庭~ *courtyard*

滁 chú ㄔㄨˊ 滁州,地名,在安徽省 Chuzhou, a place in Anhui Province

蜍 chú ㄔㄨˊ 见74页"蟾"字条"蟾蜍"(chán—) see 蟾蜍 on p74

篨 chú ㄔㄨˊ 见619页"籧"字条"籧篨"(qú—) see 籧篨 on p619

厨(*廚、*厨) chú ㄔㄨˊ 厨房,做饭做菜的地方 kitchen

橱(*櫥) chú ㄔㄨˊ (一子、一儿)一种放置东西的家具,前面有门 cupboard; cabinet: 衣~ *wardrobe* | 碗~儿 kitchen cupboard

蹰(*躕) chú ㄔㄨˊ 见90页"踟"字条"踟蹰"(chí—) see 踟蹰 on p90

锄(*鉏、*耡) chú ㄔㄨˊ ❶弄松土地及除草的器具 hoe: 三齿耘~ *hoe fork; hoe with three teeth* ❷耪(pǎng),弄松土地,除草 to hoe: ~田 *to hoe the field* | ~草 *to hoe up weeds* ❸铲除 to eradicate; to uproot: ~奸 *to eliminate traitors*

躇 chú ㄔㄨˊ 见94页"踌"字条"踌躇"(chóu—) see 踌躇 on p94

处(處、**處、**処) ㊀ chǔ ㄔㄨˇ ❶居住 to dwell; to reside; to inhabit: 穴居野~ *to dwell in caves and live in the wild* [处女]没有发生过性行为的女子 virgin; maiden [处女地]未开垦的土地 virgin land [处女作]作者的最初的作品 maiden work; first effort ❷存在,置身 to be situated in: 设身~地 *to put oneself in sb else's place or position* | ~在有利位置 *to be in a favourable position* ❸跟别人一起生活,交往 to get along with: 他们相~得很好。*They are on good terms with each other.* ❹决定,决断 to make a decision [处分](—fèn)对犯错误或有罪过的人给予相当的惩戒 to punish; to

C

take disciplinary action against [处理]办理,解决 to handle; to deal with:这事情难~~。*It's hard to handle.*

㊀ chù 见 98 页 see p98

杵 chǔ 彳ㄨˇ ❶舂米或捶衣的木棒 pestle ❷用长形的东西戳或捅 to pound; to pestle:用手指头~他一下 *to give him a poke (with one's finger)*

础(礎) chǔ 彳ㄨˇ 础石,垫在房屋柱子底下的石头 plinth [基础] **1** 柱脚石 plinth **2** 事物的根本或起点 base; foundation:~~教育 *elementary education*

楮 chǔ 彳ㄨˇ 就是构树(i. e. 构树) paper mulberry (*Broussonetia papyrifera*) 参看 237 页"构❹" see 构❹ on p237 [转] ***transfer*** 纸 paper

储 chǔ 彳ㄨˇ (旧读 formerly chú) ❶储蓄,积蓄 to save; to reserve:~存 *to store; to keep* | ~藏 *to keep in store; to lay in* | ~备 *to stock; to lay up* ❷已经确定为继承皇位等最高统治权的人 crown prince:立~ *to designate a crown prince* | 王~ *crown prince*

褚 ㊁ chǔ 彳ㄨˇ 姓 Chu, a surname

㊀ zhǔ 见 995 页 see p995

楚 chǔ 彳ㄨˇ ❶牡荆,落叶灌木,开青色或紫色的穗状小花,鲜叶可入药 five-leaved chaste tree (*Vitex negundo*) ❷周代诸侯国名,它的疆域在今湖北省,后来扩展到湖南省北部,河南省南部及江西、安徽、江苏、浙江等省 Chu, a princedom of the Zhou Dynasty, which first covered today's Hubei Province, and later expanded to today's northern Hunan, southern Henan, Jiangxi, Anhui, Jiangsu and Zhejiang provinces ❸痛苦 pain; pang ([连] ***doublet*** 苦— suffering; distress | 凄— wretched; miserable)

[楚楚] **1** 鲜明,整洁 neat; tidy:衣冠~~ *neatly dressed; decently dressed* **2** 娇柔,秀美 delicate; pretty:~~动人 *delicate and charming*

亍 chù 彳ㄨˋ 见 90 页"彳"字条"彳亍"(chì —) see 彳亍 on p90

处(處、虜、**処)** ㊀ chù 彳ㄨˋ ❶地方 place:住~ *accommodation; residence* | 各~ *everywhere* [引] ***extension*** 部分,点 part; point:长(cháng)~ *forte; merit* | 好~ *benefit; advantage* | 益~ *benefit; profit* ❷机关,或机关、团体里的部门 office; department; division:办事~ *agency; office* | 总务~ *general affairs department*

㊁ chǔ 见 97 页 see p97

怵 chù 彳ㄨˋ 恐惧 to fear; to dread:~惕(恐惧警惕) *to feel apprehensive and alert*

绌 chù 彳ㄨˋ 不足,不够 insufficient; inadequate:经费支~ *insufficient funds* | 相形见~ *to prove inferior by contrast*

黜 chù 彳ㄨˋ 降职或罢免 to demote; to remove:~退 *to*

discharge | ～职 *to dismiss from one's post*

俶 ㊀ chù ㄔㄨˋ〈古 ***archaism***〉开始 to start [俶尔]忽然 suddenly; abruptly:～～远逝 *to disappear into the distance suddenly*

㊁ tì 见 742 页 see p742

畜 ㊁ chù ㄔㄨˋ 禽兽,有时专指家养的兽类 beast; domestic animal:家～ *livestock* | 牲～ *cattle; livestock* | 幼～ *young animal* | ～力 *animal power*

㊀ xù 见 846 页 see p846

搐 chù ㄔㄨˋ 牵动 to twitch; to jerk [抽搐]肌肉不自主地、剧烈地收缩 to have a tic

滀 chù ㄔㄨˋ 水聚积 (of water) to accumulate

触(觸) chù ㄔㄨˋ ❶抵,顶 to prop; to sustain:羝羊～藩 *like a ram butting a hedge and getting its horns caught in it—on the horns of a dilemma; between the devil and the deep blue sea* ❷碰,遇着 to touch:～礁 *to hit a rock* | ～电 *to get an electric shock* | ～景生情 *to rouse old memories at familiar sights* | 一～即发 *imminent* [触觉](－jué)皮肤、毛发等与物体接触时所产生的感觉 tactile sensation; sense of touch

憷 chù ㄔㄨˋ 害怕,畏缩 to fear; to flinch:他遇到任何难事,也不发～。*He never shrinks from any difficulties.*

矗 chù ㄔㄨˋ 直立,高耸 tall and upright; towering:～立 *to tower over* | 高～ *to stand tall and upright*

CHUA ㄔㄨㄚ

欻 ㊀ chuā ㄔㄨㄚ 拟声词 ***onomatopoeia***, (sound of steady steps) tramp

㊁ xū 见 845 页 see p845

CHUAI ㄔㄨㄞ

揣 ㊁ chuāi ㄔㄨㄞ 藏在衣服里 to hide or carry in one's clothes; to tuck:～手 *to tuck each hand in the opposite sleeve* | ～在怀里 *to hide in the bosom; to tuck into the bosom*

㊀ chuǎi 见 99 页 see p99

㊂ chuài 见 100 页 see p100

搋 chuāi ㄔㄨㄞ 用拳头揉,使掺入的东西和(huó)匀 to knead:～面 *to knead dough*

膗 chuái ㄔㄨㄞˊ〈方 ***dialect***〉肥胖而肌肉松 fat and flabby:看他那～样。*See, how fat and flabby he is!*

揣 ㊀ chuǎi ㄔㄨㄞˇ 估量,忖度 to estimate; to conjecture:我～测他不来。*I guess he won't come.* | 不～浅陋 *to venture; to take the liberty* [揣摩] **1** 研究,仔细琢磨 to fathom; to figure out:仔细～～写作的方法 *to study writing techniques carefully* **2** 估量,推测 to surmise:我～～你也能做。*I guess you can do it as well.*

㊁ chuāi 见 99 页 see p99
㊂ chuài 见 100 页 see p100

阘 chuài ㄔㄨㄞˋ 见 974 页"阐"字条"阐阘"(zhèng—) see 阐阘 on p974

啜 ㊁ chuài ㄔㄨㄞˋ 姓 Chuai, a surname
㊀ chuò 见 105 页 see p105

揣 ㊂ chuài ㄔㄨㄞˋ [挣揣](zhèng—)挣扎 to struggle; to strive
㊀ chuǎi 见 99 页 see p99
㊁ chuāi 见 99 页 see p99

踹 chuài ㄔㄨㄞˋ 践踏,用脚底踢 to kick:一脚把门~开 *to kick the door open*

嘬 ㊁ chuài ㄔㄨㄞˋ 咬,吃 to bite; to eat
㊀ zuō 见 1021 页 see p1021

膗 chuài ㄔㄨㄞˋ [囊膗](nāng—)猪的胸腹部肥而松软的肉 flabby meat from a pig's belly and breast

CHUAN ㄔㄨㄢ

川 chuān ㄔㄨㄢ ❶河流 river:高山大~ *high mountains and big rivers* | ~流不息 *flowing past in an endless stream; never-ending* ❷平地,平原 flat land; plain:平~ *plain; level land* | 米粮~ *rich rice-producing area* ❸指四川 Sichuan Province:~马 *Sichuan horse* | ~贝 *Sichuan fritillary bulb*
[川资]旅费 travelling expenses

氚 chuān ㄔㄨㄢ 氢的同位素之一,符号 T,质量数 3,有放射性,应用于热核反应 tritium (T)

穿 chuān ㄔㄨㄢ ❶破,通透 to penatrate; to pierce:屋漏瓦~。*The roof is leaking and the tiles are broken.* |用锥子~一个洞 *to poke a hole with an awl* ❷放在动词后,表示通透或揭开(used after a verb) penetrating; uncovered:说~ *to speak one's mind; to put it bluntly* | 看~ *to read one's mind; to see through* ❸通过孔洞 to pass through a hole:~针 *to thread a needle* | 把这些铁环用绳子~起来 *to string the iron hoops* ㊕ ***extension*** 通过 to pass:从这个胡同~过去 *to go through this alley* |横~马路 *to cross a street* ❹把衣服鞋袜等套在身上 to wear; to don; to put on:~衣服 *to put on clothes; to get dressed*

传(傳) ㊀ chuán ㄔㄨㄢˊ ❶递,转授 to pass; to hand down; to transmit (㊐ ***doublet*** —递 to transmit; to deliver):~球 *to pass (a ball); to push a pass* | ~令 *to transmit orders; to dispatch orders* | 言~身教(jiào) *to teach by personal example as well as verbal instruction; to teach by precept and example*
[传统]世代相传,具有特点的风俗道德、思想作风等 tradition:发扬艰苦奋斗的优良~~ *to carry on the fine tradition of plain living and hard work*
❷推广,散布 to spread; to

circulate：～单 *leaflet; handbill*｜宣～ *to publicize; to propagate*｜胜利的消息～遍了全国。*The news of triumph spread all over the country.* [传媒]传播的媒介，多指报纸、广播、电视等 media; mass media [传染]因接触或由其他媒介而感染疾病 to infect; to be contagious ❸叫来 to summon：～人 *to call sb in*｜～呼电话 *relay telephone; neighbourhood telephone service* ❹传导 to conduct; to transmit：～电 *to conduct current*｜～热 *to conduct heat* ❺表达 to express; to convey：～神 *vivid; lifelike*｜眉目～情 *to give sb the eye; to make (sheep's) eyes at sb*

㊁ zhuàn 见 1000 页 see p1000

船(*舩、**舡) chuán ㄔㄨㄢˊ 水上的主要交通工具，种类很多 boat; ship; vessel：帆～ *sailboat*｜轮～ *steamer; steamboat*

遄 chuán ㄔㄨㄢˊ ❶往来频繁 to come and go frequently ❷快，迅速 rapidly; quickly：～往 *to go in haste*

篅 chuán ㄔㄨㄢˊ 一种盛粮食等的器物，类似囤(dùn) grain bin

椽 chuán ㄔㄨㄢˊ (一子)放在檩上架着屋顶的木条 rafter (图见 188 页 picture on p188)

舛 chuǎn ㄔㄨㄢˇ ❶舛错，错误，错乱 error; mistake; slip ❷违背 to run counter to; to be against

喘 chuǎn ㄔㄨㄢˇ ❶急促地呼吸 to breathe heavily; to gasp：～息 *to pant; to puff*｜累得直～ *to pant from exertions*｜苟延残～ *to linger on in a steadily worsening condition; to be on one's last leg* [喘气]呼吸 to breathe ❷气喘的简称 short for 气喘

踳 chuǎn ㄔㄨㄢˇ 同"舛" same as 舛 [踳驳]舛谬杂乱 jumbled; disorderly; messy

串 chuàn ㄔㄨㄢˋ ❶许多个连贯成一行(háng) to string：把珠子～起来 *to thread pearls on a string*｜～联 *to contact; to link* ㊂ **extension** (一儿)连贯起来的东西 string：珠子～儿 *string of beads*｜羊肉～儿 *shish kebab* ❷(一儿)量词 ***quantifier***，用于成串儿的东西 a string of：一～儿项链 *a necklace*｜两～钥匙 *two bunches of keys* ❸互相勾结、勾通 to collaborate; to conspire：～通 *to collude; to gang up*｜～骗 *to gang up* [串供](-gòng)互相串通，捏造口供 to collude to make each other's confessions identical ❹由这里到那里走动 to go about：～亲戚 *to go visiting relatives*｜～门儿 *to drop in* ❺指演戏剧、杂耍等 to act in a play or variety show：客～ *to be a guest performer*｜反～ *to play a reverse role*

钏 chuàn ㄔㄨㄢˋ (一子)用珠子或玉石等穿起来做成的镯子 bracelet of beads or jade

CHUANG ㄔㄨㄤ

创(創) ㊁ chuāng ㄔㄨㄤ 伤 wound (㊎ **doublet** 一伤 wound; trauma):刀～ *knife wound* | 予以重(zhòng)～ *to deal sb a heavy blow; to inflict heavy casualties (on the enemy)*

㊀ chuàng 见 102 页 see p102

疮(瘡) chuāng ㄔㄨㄤ 皮肤上肿烂溃疡的病 skin ulcer; decubital ulcer

窗(*窓、*牎、*牕) chuāng ㄔㄨㄤ (一子、一儿)窗户,房屋通气透光的装置 window:～明几(jī)净 *with bright windows and clean tables; bright and clean* (图见 188 页 picture on p188)

床(*牀) chuáng ㄔㄨㄤˊ ❶床铺 bed ❷像床的东西 bed-shaped thing:车～ *lathe* | 河～(河身) *riverbed* | 琴～ *musical instrument stand*

噇 chuáng ㄔㄨㄤˊ 〈方 **dialect**〉大吃大喝 to eat and drink greedily

幢 ㊀ chuáng ㄔㄨㄤˊ ❶古代指旗子一类的东西 (in ancient China) flag; banner ❷佛教的经幢。在绸伞上写经的叫经幢,在石柱上刻经的叫石幢(silk umbrella with a scriptural inscription is called 经幢; stone pillar with a scriptural inscription is called 石幢) Buddhist dharani banner

㊁ zhuàng 见 1003 页 see p1003

闯 chuǎng ㄔㄨㄤˇ ❶猛冲 to dash; to charge:往里～ *to rush in; to break in* | 刀山火海也敢～。*Be there seas of fire and forests of knives, yet will I charge ahead.* [闯祸]惹祸,招乱子 to get into trouble; to bring disaster ❷历练,经历 to experience:～练 *to temper oneself* [闯荡]旧时指离家在外谋生 (in former times) to make a living away from home; to leave home to make a living:～～江湖 *to roam about to make a living*

创(創、*剏、*剙) ㊀ chuàng ㄔㄨㄤˋ 开始,开始做 to start; to initiate:～办 *to found; to set up* | ～造 *to create* | 首～ *to originate; to initiate* [创举]从未有过的举动或事业 unprecedented undertaking; pioneering work [创刊号]报刊开始刊行的一期 first issue; first number [创意]独创、新颖的构思 originality; original idea:颇具～～ *rather original in concept*

㊁ chuāng 见 102 页 see p102

怆(愴) chuàng ㄔㄨㄤˋ 悲伤 sorrowful:凄～ *pathetic; wretched* | ～然泪下 *to shed sad tears*

CHUI ㄔㄨㄟ

吹 chuī ㄔㄨㄟ ❶合拢嘴唇用力出气 to blow; to puff:

～灯 *to blow out a lamp*｜～笛 *to play the flute* ❷夸口 to boast; to brag:瞎～ *to brag* [吹牛]说大话,自夸 to boast; to brag [吹嘘]自夸或替人夸张 to lavish praise on sb; to boast ❸奉承 to flatter:～捧 *to flatter; to adulate* ❹类似吹的动作 action similar to blowing:～风机 *hairdryer; blower*｜氢氧～管 *oxyhydrogen blowpipe*｜不怕风～日晒 *to fear neither the wind nor the scorching sun* ❺(事情)失败,(感情)破裂 (of things) to fail; (of feelings) to break up:事情～了。*The matter fell through.*｜他们俩～了。*The couple have broken up.*

炊 chuī ㄔㄨㄟ 烧火做饭 to cook:～烟 *cooking smoke*｜～事员 *cook; chef*｜～帚(zhou)(刷洗锅碗等的用具) *kitchen brush*

垂 chuí ㄔㄨㄟˊ ❶东西一头挂下来 to droop; to hang:～杨柳 *weeping willow*｜～钓 *to go angling*｜～涎(喻羡慕) *to slaver; to drool; to salivate* 敬辞 ***polite***:～询 *to condescend to enquire; to deign to enquire*｜～念 *to show kind concern for* [垂直]几何学上指两根直线、两个平面或一根直线和一个平面相交成直角 perpendicular; vertical ❷传下去,传留后世 to hand down; to bequeath to posterity:永～不朽 *to be immortal; to live forever*｜名～千古 *to go down in history* ❸接近,快要 to near; to be on the verge of:～危 *dying*｜功败～成(快要成功的时候遭到失败) *to fail on the verge of success; to suffer defeat on the verge of victory; to fall through when victory is within reach*

陲 chuí ㄔㄨㄟˊ 边疆,国境,靠边界的地方 frontier; border:边～ *frontier; border*

捶(*搥) chuí ㄔㄨㄟˊ 敲打 to beat; to thump:～衣裳 *to pound clothes when washing them*｜～腿 *to beat on the leg (as in massage)*

棰(❸❹*箠) chuí ㄔㄨㄟˊ ❶短棍子 cudgel ❷用棍子打 to beat with a cudgel; to cudgel ❸鞭子 whip ❹鞭打 to whip

锤(❷❸*鎚) chuí ㄔㄨㄟˊ ❶秤锤,配合秤杆称分(fèn)量的金属块 steelyard weight ❷(一子、一儿)敲打东西的器具 hammer:铁～ *iron hammer*｜木～ *wooden hammer* ❸用锤敲打 to hammer:千～百炼 *to temper thoroughly; to go through many trials*

椎 ㊁ chuí ㄔㄨㄟˊ ❶敲打东西的器具 hammer:铁～ *iron hammer* ❷敲打 to beat; to thump; to pound:～鼓 *to beat drums* ❸愚钝 stupid:～鲁 *slow-witted*

㊀ zhuī 见1003页 see p1003

槌 chuí ㄔㄨㄟˊ (一子、一儿)敲打用具 beetle; gavel; mallet:棒～(chui) *wooden club*｜鼓

～儿 *drumstick*

CHUN ㄔㄨㄣ

春 chūn ㄔㄨㄣ ❶春季,四季的第一季 spring [春秋] **1** 春季和秋季,泛指岁月 (years in general) spring and autumn:不知过了多少～～ *to be unaware of the passing of years* **2** 年龄,年岁 age:～～已高 *to be advanced in years* **3** 我国古代最早的一部编年体史书 *The Spring and Autumn Annals*, the first chronological history book in ancient China **4** 泛指历史 history in general **5** 我国历史上的一个时代(公元前 770—公元前 476 年)。因鲁国编年体史书《春秋》而得名 the Spring and Autumn Period (770BC－476BC), which got its name from the chronicle *The Spring and Autumn Annals* compiled in the state of Lu [青春]青年时代 youth ❷指男女情欲 love; lust:～情 *stirring of love* | ～心 *amorous feeling; desire for love* ❸生气,生机 life; vitality:大地回～。*Spring has come.* | 妙手回～ *(of a doctor) to effect a miraculous cure and bring the dying back to life*

椿 chūn ㄔㄨㄣ 植物名 name of a plant **1** 香椿,落叶乔木,叶初生时,有香气,可作菜吃,木材坚实细致 Chinese toon (*Toona sinensis*) **2** 臭椿,又叫"樗"(chū)。落叶乔木,夏天开花,白色。叶子有臭味,木材不坚固 (also called 樗) tree of heaven (*Ailanthus altissima*)

蝽 chūn ㄔㄨㄣ 椿象,昆虫,圆形或椭圆形,头部有单眼。种类很多,有的能放出恶臭,多数是害虫 stink bug; shield bug

䲠 chūn ㄔㄨㄣ 鱼名,即马鲛,有的长达 1 米多,生活在海中 (i.e.马鲛) Chinese seerfish (*Scomberomorus sinensis*)

纯 chún ㄔㄨㄣˊ ❶专一不杂 pure; unadulterated ([连] ***doublet*** — 粹 pure; genuine):～洁 *innocent; pure* | ～钢 *pure steel* | ～蓝 *pure blue* ❷熟练 skillful:～熟(shú) *skillful; versed* | 工夫不～ *unskilled; clumsy*

莼(*蒓) chún ㄔㄨㄣˊ 莼菜,多年生水草,叶子椭圆形,浮生在水面,开暗红色的小花。茎和叶表面都有黏液,可以做汤吃 water shield (*Brasenia schreberi*)

唇(*脣) chún ㄔㄨㄣˊ 嘴唇,嘴的边缘红色部分 lip [唇齿][喻] ***figurative*** 关系密切 closely related; mutually dependent:～～相依 *to be as interdependent as lips and teeth; to be closely related and mutually dependent like lips and teeth*

淳 chún ㄔㄨㄣˊ 朴实,厚道 simple; honest:～朴 *simple; unsophisticated* | ～厚 *simple and honest; unsophisticated*

鹑 chún ㄔㄨㄣˊ 即鹌(ān)鹑(i. e. 鹌鹑) quail [鹑衣]⑩ *figurative* 破烂的旧衣服 ragged clothes; tattered clothes

醇 chún ㄔㄨㄣˊ ❶酒味浓厚,纯 rich mellow; strong: ～酒 *mellow wine* | 大～小疵(优点多,缺点少) *have great merits despite minor blemishes* ❷同"淳" same as 淳 ❸有机化合物的一大类,主要的通式是 $C_nH_{2n+1}OH$,医药上常用的酒精,就是醇类中的乙醇 alcohol [木糖醇]从玉米芯、甘蔗渣等物中提取的有机化合物,味甜,可作为糖尿病人使用的甜味剂,并可预防龋(qǔ)齿 xylitol

蠢(❶*惷) chǔn ㄔㄨㄣˇ ❶愚笨,笨拙 stupid; clumsy (㊣ *doublet* 愚—foolish): ～才 *idiot; fool* ❷虫子爬动 to wriggle; to squirm [蠢动]⑩ *figurative* 坏人的扰乱活动 disruptive activities

CHUO ㄔㄨㄛ

逴 chuō ㄔㄨㄛ 远 far; distant

踔 chuō ㄔㄨㄛ ❶跳 to jump; to leap: ～腾 *to leap; to bound* ❷超越 to transcend; to go beyond; to surpass

戳 chuō ㄔㄨㄛ ❶用尖端触击 to poke; to jab; to stab: 用手指头～了一下 *to poke (with one's finger)* ❷因猛触硬物而受伤 to sprain: 打球～伤了手 *to sprain one's hand while playing a ball game* ❸竖立 to erect; to stand: 把秫秸～起来 *to stand the bundle of sorghum stalks on end* ❹(—子、—儿)图章 stamp; seal: 邮～ *postmark* | 盖～子 *to stamp*

娖 chuò ㄔㄨㄛˋ 谨慎(叠 *reduplication*) cautious; prudent

龊 chuò ㄔㄨㄛˋ 见 792 页"龌"字条"龌龊"(wò—) see 龌龊 on p792

啜 ㊀ chuò ㄔㄨㄛˋ ❶饮,吃 to sip; to sup; to suck: ～茗(喝茶) *to sip tea* | ～粥 *to eat porridge* ❷哭泣的时候抽噎的样子 sobbing; whimpering: ～泣 *to sob; to whimper*

㊁ chuài 见 100 页 see p100

惙 chuò ㄔㄨㄛˋ ❶忧愁(叠 *reduplication*) worried; depressed ❷疲乏 fatigued; exhausted

辍 chuò ㄔㄨㄛˋ 中止,停止 to stop; to cease: ～学 *to drop out of school* | 岂能中～? *How could you stop halfway?* or *How could it be stopped halfway?*

绰 ㊀ chuò ㄔㄨㄛˋ 宽裕 spacious; roomy: ～～有余 *ample; abundant; more than enough* | 这间屋子很宽～(chuo)。*The room is spacious.*

[绰号]外号 nickname; sobriquet

㊁ chāo 见 79 页 see p79

歠 chuò ㄔㄨㄛˋ ❶吸,喝 to suck; to drink ❷指可以喝的汤、粥等 soup; porridge

CI ㄘ

C

刺 ㊁ cī ㄘ 拟声词 ***onomatopoeia***:～棱(－lēng)(动作迅速的声音) *swish; sound of a swift movement* | ～溜(－liū)(脚底下滑动的声音) *sound of sliding* | ～～地冒火星儿 *to be ignescent; to keep spattering sparks*

㊀ cì 见 108 页 see p108

差 ㊃ cī ㄘ 见 68 页"参"字条"参差"(cēn－) see 参差 on p68

㊀ chà 见 72 页 see p72

㊁ chā 见 69 页 see p69

㊂ chāi 见 72 页 see p72

疵 cī ㄘ 毛病 fault; defect; blemish:吹毛求～(故意挑剔) *to find fault; to nitpick*

跐 ㊁ cī ㄘ 脚下滑动 to slip; to slide:登～了(脚没有踏稳) *to slip*

㊀ cǐ 见 107 页 see p107

词 cí ㄘ ❶在句子里能自由运用的最小的语言单位,如"人"、"马"、"水"、"商品"、"竞争"等 word; term [词组] 两个或两个以上的词的组合,也叫短语 (also called 短语) phrase ❷语言,特指有组织的语言、文字 wording; expression:歌～ *lyrics of a song* | 演讲～ *speech* | 义正～严 *to speak sternly out of a sense of justice* ❸一种长短句押韵的文体 *ci* poem, a form of classical Chinese poetry written to certain tunes with strict tonal patterns and rhyme schemes in fixed numbers of lines and words

祠 cí ㄘ 旧时供奉祖宗、鬼神或有功德的人的庙宇或房屋 (in former times) ancestral temple; memorial temple:～堂 *ancestral hall* | 先贤～ *memorial temple for the sages*

茈 ㊀ cí ㄘ [凫茈](fú－)古书上指荸荠 (in ancient Chinese texts) water chestnut

㊁ zǐ 见 1012 页 see p1012

雌 cí ㄘ (旧读 formerly cī) 母的,阴性的,跟"雄"相对 (the opposite of 雄) female:～花 *female flower; pistillate flower* | ～鸡 *hen* | ～蕊 *pistil* [雌黄]矿物名,橙黄色,可做颜料,古时用来涂改文字 (a mineral with orange colour used as a pigment and it was used in ancient China to cover something written and make some alteration) orpiment:妄下～～(乱改文字,乱下议论) *to make irresponsible comments; to make irresponsible remarks* | 信口～～(随意讥评) *to indulge in irresponsible talk; to talk sheer nonsense* [雌雄] ㊗ ***figurative*** 胜负 victory and defeat; success and failure:一决～～ *to fight it out; to have it out with sb*

茨 cí ㄘ ❶用茅或苇盖房子 to thatch (a roof) ❷蒺藜 puncture vine; puncture weed

瓷 cí ㄘ 用高岭土(景德镇高岭产的黏土,现泛指做瓷器的土)烧成的一种质料,所做

器物比陶器细致而坚硬 porcelain; china; chinaware

兹(**茲) ㊁ cí ㄘˊ 见614页"龟"字条"龟兹"(qiū—) see 龟兹 on p614

㊀ zī 见1009页 see p1009

甆 cí ㄘˊ 同"瓷" same as 瓷

慈 cí ㄘˊ ❶慈爱,和善 affectionate; genial: 敬老～幼 *to respect the old and care for the young* | 心～面善 *tender-hearted and benign* ❷指母亲 mother: 家～ *my mother*

磁 cí ㄘˊ ❶磁性,物质能吸引铁、镍等的性质 magnetism [磁卡]表面带有磁性物质、可存储信息的卡片。如银行磁卡 magnetic card [磁盘]表面带有磁性物质、可存储信息的圆盘,分为硬磁盘和软磁盘 (magnetic) disc [磁石]一种带有磁性的矿物。磁铁矿的俗称。又叫"吸铁石"。化学成分是四氧化三铁 (popular name for 磁铁矿, also called 吸铁石) magnetite ❷同"瓷" same as 瓷

鹚(*鷀) cí ㄘˊ 见465页"鸬"字条"鸬鹚"(lú—) see 鸬鹚 on p465

糍(*餈) cí ㄘˊ 一种用江米(糯米)做成的食品 food made of glutinous rice: ～粑(bā) *glutinous rice cake* | ～团 *dumpling made of glutinous rice*

辞(辭、*辤) cí ㄘˊ ❶告别 to take leave; to bid farewell: ～行 *to take one's leave; to say goodbye* ❷不接受,请求离去 to decline; to resign: ～职 *to resign* ㊕ ***transfer*** 躲避,推托 to elude; to decline: 虽死不～ *never to shirk even at the cost of one's life* | 不～辛苦 *to spare no pains; to brave difficulties* ❸解雇 to fire; to dismiss; to discharge: 他被老板～了。*He was fired by the boss.* ❹同"词❷" same as 词❷: ～藻 *ornate diction; rhetoric; flowery language* ❺古典文学的一种体裁 *ci*, a form of poetry in classical Chinese literature: ～赋 *cifu; rhyme prose; poetic prose*

此 cǐ ㄘˇ 代词 ***pronoun*** ❶这,这个,跟"彼"相对 (the opposite of 彼) this; this one: 彼～ *each other* | ～人 *this person* | ～时 *now; at present* | 特～布告。*Notice is hereby given that …* ❷这儿,这里 here: 由～往西 *to go west from here* | 到～为止 *hereto; hereunto; That's all.*

泚 cǐ ㄘˇ ❶清,鲜明 limpid; lucid ❷用笔蘸墨 to dip a writing brush in ink: ～笔作书 *to dip the writing brush in ink to begin a work of calligraphy*

跐 ㊀ cǐ ㄘˇ 踩,踏 to step on: 脚～两只船 *to straddle two boats; to have a foot in each camp*

㊁ cī 见106页 see p106

次 cì ㄘ ❶第二 second; next:～日 *the second day*|～子 *the second son* ❷质量或品质较差 inferior; second-rate:～货 *substandard goods; faulty commodities*|～品 *shoddy products; defective goods*|这东西太～。*It's really no good.* ❸等第,顺序 rank; order (㊥ ***doublet*** 一序 order):名～ *place in a contest*|车～ *train number*|依～前进 *to proceed in order* ❹量词 ***quantifier***,回 time:第一～来北京 *to be in Beijing for the first time* ❺临时驻扎,也指途中停留的处所 stopover:舟～ *to stay overnight in a boat*|旅～ *lodging in one's journey; hotel*

佽 cì ㄘ 帮助 to help; to aid:～助 *to aid*

伺 ㊀ cì ㄘ 同"伺㊀",用于"伺候"(same as 伺㊀, used in 伺候)[伺候](—hou) **1** 旧指侍奉或受役使 (in former times) to wait on; to serve **2** 照料 to wait on; to attend:～～病人 *to nurse a patient; to look after a patient*

㊀ sì 见706页 see p706

刺 ㊀ cì ㄘ ❶用有尖的东西穿进或杀伤 to pierce; to thrust; to stab:～绣 *to embroider; embroidery*|～杀 *to assassinate*[刺激] **1** 光、声、热等引起生物体活动或变化的作用 stimulation ㊞ ***extension*** 一切使事物起变化的作用 stimulation; incentive; fillip **2** 精神上受到挫折、打击 irritation; frustration:这件事对他～～很大。*He was terribly upset by this.* ❷暗杀 to assassinate:～客 *assassin*|被～ *to be assassinated* ❸打听,侦探 to pry; to spy:～探 *to spy* ❹用尖刻的话指摘、嘲笑 to criticize; to ridicule:讽～ *to satirize* ❺尖锐像针的东西 thorn; sting:鱼～ *fishbone*|～猬 *hedgehog*|～槐 *locust tree* ❻名片 visiting card; card:名～ *visiting card*

[刺刺]说话没完没了 to chatter; to rattle on:～～不休 *to chatter; to rattle away*

㊁ cī 见106页 see p106

赐 cì ㄘ ❶给,指上级给下级或长辈给晚辈 to grant; to bestow; to confer (㊥ ***doublet*** 赏— to award; to bestow):恩～ *to bestow; to grant* 敬辞 ***polite***:～教(jiào) *to grant instruction*|希～回音。*RSVP; Please favour me with a reply.* ❷赏给的东西,给与的好处 gift; favour:皆受其～。*Everyone receives a gift.*|受～良多 *to have been granted many favours and gifts*

CONG ㄘㄨㄥ

匆(*悤、*怱) cōng ㄘㄨㄥ 急促(叠 ***reduplication***) hastily; hurriedly:～忙 *hurriedly*|来去～～ *to come and go in a hurry*

葱(*蔥) cōng ㄘㄨㄥ ❶多年生草本植物,叶圆筒状,中空,开白色小花。

茎叶有辣味，是常吃的蔬菜 scallion ❷ 青色 green：～翠 *luxuriantly* (or *fresh*) *green*

苁(蓯) cōng ㄘㄨㄥ [苁蓉] (— róng) 植物名 name of a plant 1 草苁蓉，一种寄生植物，叶、茎黄褐色，花淡紫色 northern ground cone (*Boschniakia rossica*) 2 肉苁蓉，一种寄生植物，茎和叶黄褐色，花紫褐色，茎可入药 desert-broomrape (*Cistanche deserticola*)

玐(瑽) cōng ㄘㄨㄥ [玐瑢] (— róng) 拟声词 ***onomatopoeia***，佩玉相碰的声音 tinkling of jade

枞(樅) ㊀ cōng ㄘㄨㄥ 又叫"冷杉"。常绿乔木，果实椭圆形，暗紫色。木材供制器具，又可用作建筑材料 (also called 冷杉) fir (*Abies*)

㊁ zōng 见 1014 页 see p1014

囱 cōng ㄘㄨㄥ 烟囱，炉灶、锅炉出烟的通路 chimney

骢 cōng ㄘㄨㄥ 青白色的马 piebald horse

璁 cōng ㄘㄨㄥ 像玉的石头 jadelike stone

熜 cōng ㄘㄨㄥ ❶微火 slow-fire ❷热气 steam

聪(聰) cōng ㄘㄨㄥ ❶听觉灵敏 (of hearing) acute; sharp：耳～目明 *to have good ears and eyes*; *to be sharp at hearing and seeing* ❷聪明，智力强 clever; intelligent：～颖 *bright*; *intelligent* | ～慧 *intelligent*; *smart*

从(從) cóng ㄘㄨㄥˊ ❶跟随 to follow：愿～其后 *to volunteer to follow* ❷依顺 to obey; to comply with：服～ *to obey*; *to submit*; *to be obedient to* | 胁～ *accomplice under duress*; *person forced into wrong doing* | 言听计～ *to be at sb's beck and call* ❸参与 to participate in：～政 *to be engaged in politics* | ～军 *to join the army* ❹介词 ***preposition***，自，由 from：～南到北 *from north to south* | ～古到今 *from ancient to modern times* [从而] 连词 ***conjunction***，由此 thus：坚持改革开放，～～改变了贫穷和落后的面貌。*Perseverance in the reform and opening-up policy has changed the poor and backward situation.* [从来] 副词 ***adverb***，向来，一向 always; ever：他～～不为个人打算。*He has never acted to pursue selfish interests.* ❺采取某种态度或方式 in a certain attitude or manner：～速解决 *to solve as soon as possible* | 一切～简 *to be as simple as possible* | ～宽处理 *to be lenient in punishment* ❻跟随的人 follower：仆～ *retainer* | 随～ *entourage* ❼指堂房亲属 relationship between cousins, etc of the same paternal grandfather or great grandfather：～兄弟 *male cousins on the paternal side* | ～伯叔 *father's male cousins* ❽次要的 secondary：主～ *principal and subordinate* | 分别首～ *to differentiate the primary from the secondary* (❻❼❽三义旧

读 zòng formerly pronounced zòng）
［从容］不慌不忙 calm；unhurried：举止～～ *to carry oneself with ease*｜～～不迫 *confident and without haste* [引] **extension** 充裕 sufficient；ample：手头～～ *to be well-off*｜时间～～ *plenty of time*

〈古 **archaism**〉又同纵横的"纵" also same as 纵 in 纵横

从（叢、**菆）cóng ㄘㄨㄥˊ ❶聚集，许多事物凑在一起 to cluster；to crowd：草木～生 *overgrown with bushes and trees*｜百事～集。*A multitude of things crops up.* ❷聚在一起的人或物 crowd；collection：人～ *crowd of people*｜草～ *thick growth of grass*

淙 cóng ㄘㄨㄥˊ 拟声词 **onomatopoeia**，流水声（叠 **reduplication**）gurgling；babbling

悰 cóng ㄘㄨㄥˊ ❶快乐 joy ❷心情 mood

琮 cóng ㄘㄨㄥˊ 古时的一种玉器，筒状，外边八角，中间圆形（in ancient China）octagonal piece of jade with a long hollow

賨 cóng ㄘㄨㄥˊ 秦汉时期今湖南、重庆、四川一带少数民族所缴的一种赋税。后也指这部分少数民族 tax that the ethnic minorities in today's Hunan，Chongqing and Sichuan had to pay in the Qin and Han dynasties；（later it refers to）the ethnic minorities there

潨 cóng ㄘㄨㄥˊ ❶小水汇入大水 small river flowing into a bigger one ❷水声 gurgling；babbling

COU ㄘㄡ

凑（*湊）còu ㄘㄡˋ ❶聚合 to gather；to collect：～在一起 *to gather together*｜～钱 *to pool money* ［凑合］（—he）1 同"凑❶" same as 凑❶ 2 将就 to make do；to make shift：～～着用吧 *to make do with it* ❷接近 to approach：～上去 *to move closer*｜往前～ *to come up* ［凑巧］碰巧 by chance；by coincidence；as luck would have it

辏 còu ㄘㄡˋ 车轮的辐聚集到中心 to converge：辐～ *to converge*

腠 còu ㄘㄡˋ 肌肤上的纹理 skin texture

CU ㄘㄨ

粗（*觕、*麤、**麁）cū ㄘㄨ ❶跟"细"相对（the opposite of 细）1 颗粒大的 coarse；crude：～沙子 *coarse sand*｜～面 *unrefined flour* 2 长条东西直径大的 wide（in diameter）；thick：～线 *thick thread*｜这棵树长（zhǎng）得很～。*The tree has a thick trunk.*｜～枝大叶（喻疏忽）*crude and careless；sloppy* 3

毛糙,不精致的 coarse; rough; unrefined: 板面很～。*The board has a rough surface.* | ～瓷 *rough chinaware* | ～布 *coarse cloth* | 去～取精 *to discard the dross and select the essence* **4** 声音低而大 gruff; husky:嗓音很～ *husky voice* **5** 疏忽,不周密 careless; negligent: ～心 *thoughtless; inadvertent* | ～～一想 *after a little thinking* ❷鲁莽 rude (㊣ ***doublet*** —鲁 rude):～暴 *brutal; savage* | ～人 *uneducated person; unrefined person* | 这话太～。*The words are too rude.*

徂 cú ㄘㄨˊ ❶往 to go ❷过去 to pass ❸开始 to start ❹同"殂" same as 殂

殂 cú ㄘㄨˊ 死亡 to die; to pass away: 崩～ *to pass away*

卒 ㊁ cù ㄘㄨˋ 同"猝" same as 猝

㊀ zú 见 1018 页 see p1018

猝 cù ㄘㄨˋ 忽然 sudden; abrupt; unexpected: ～生变化 *to change suddenly* | ～不及防 *to be taken by surprise*

促 cù ㄘㄨˋ ❶靠近 to be close to; to be near: ～膝谈心 *to sit side by side and talk intimately; to have a heart-to-heart talk* ❷时间极短,急迫 (of time) short; urgent: 急～ *hurried; pressing* | 短～ *of very short duration; very short or brief* ❸催,推动 to urge; to promote: 督～ *to supervise and urge* | ～进 *to promote; to accelerate* | ～销 *to promote sales*

酢 ㊁ cù ㄘㄨˋ 同"醋" same as 醋 [酢浆草] 多年生草本植物,匍匐茎,掌状复叶,茎、叶有酸味,开黄色小花,结蒴果,圆柱形。全草可入药 creeping woodsorrel (*Oxalis corniculata*)

㊀ zuò 见 1023 页 see p1023

醋 cù ㄘㄨˋ 一种调味用的液体,味酸,用酒或酒糟发酵制成,也可用米、麦、高粱等直接酿制 vinegar

蔟 cù ㄘㄨˋ 蚕蔟,用麦秆等做成,蚕在上面做茧 small bundle of straw for silkworms to spin cocoons on

簇 cù ㄘㄨˋ ❶丛聚,聚成一团 to crowd; to cluster: ～拥 *to cluster round* | 花团锦～ *with bouquets of flowers and piles of brocade—(of decorations) splendid* ❷量词 ***quantifier***,用于聚成团的东西 cluster; bunch: 一～鲜花 *a bunch of flowers*

踧 cù ㄘㄨˋ ❶形容惊惧不安 timid and uneasy [踧踖] (—jí)恭敬而不安的样子 deferential; respectful and uneasy ❷同"蹙" same as 蹙

蹙 cù ㄘㄨˋ ❶急促 pressed: 气～ *breathless; short of breath* ❷困窘 poverty-stricken; destitute: 穷～ *in straitened circumstances; in dire straits* ❸缩小,收敛 to gather sth into folds: ～眉 *to frown* | 颦～(皱眉头) *to knit one's brow(s)*

C

蹴（*蹵） cù ㄘㄨˋ ❶踢 to kick：～鞠（jū）（踢球）*to kick a ball*；*to play football* ❷踏 to tread：一～而就（一下子就成功）*to accomplish in an action*；*to accomplish one's aim in one move — to achieve immediate success*

C

CUAN ㄘㄨㄢ

汆 cuān ㄘㄨㄢ ❶把食物放到开水里稍微一煮 to quick-boil：～汤 *to quick-boil sth in soup*｜～丸子 *quick-boiled meat ball* ❷（一子、一儿）烧水用的薄铁筒，能很快地把水煮开 small cylindrical pot of thin metal ❸用汆子把水烧开 to boil water with a plating kettle：～了一汆子水 *to boil a pot of water*

撺（攛） cuān ㄘㄨㄢ〈方 **dialect**〉 ❶抛掷 to throw；to fling ❷匆忙地做，乱抓 to do in haste：事先没准备，临时现～ *to improvise on the spot* ❸（一儿）发怒，发脾气 to fly into a rage：他～儿了。*He flared up*.

［撺掇］（—duo）怂恿，劝诱别人做某种事情 to urge；to instigate；to egg on：你就是～～他，他也不去。*Even if you egg him on, he is not going*.｜你自己不干，为什么～～我呢？*Why do you press me to do what you won't do yourself?*

镩（鑹） cuān ㄘㄨㄢ 冰镩，一种铁制的凿冰器具 ice pick；ice chisel

蹿（躥） cuān ㄘㄨㄢ 向上跳 to leap up；to leap forward：猫～到房上去了。*The cat leapt onto the roof*.

攒（**欑） ⊖ cuán ㄘㄨㄢˊ 聚，凑集，拼凑 to collect；to piece together：～凑 *to gather together*｜～钱 *to pool money*｜～电视机 *to assemble a television*

⊜ zǎn 见 938 页 see p938

窜（竄） cuàn ㄘㄨㄢˋ ❶逃走，乱跑 to flee；to scurry；to scamper：东跑西～ *to flee in all directions*｜打得敌人抱头鼠～。*The enemy was put to rout*. ❷放逐，驱逐 to exile；to banish；to expel ❸修改文字 to reword：～改 *to alter*；*to falsify*｜点～ *to make alterations in wording*

篡 cuàn ㄘㄨㄢˋ ❶封建时代指臣子夺取君位（in feudal times）to usurp the throne ❷用阴谋手段夺取地位或权力 to usurp

爨 cuàn ㄘㄨㄢˋ ❶烧火做饭 to make a fire and cook；to cook：分～（旧时指分家）（*dividing up family property and living apart in former times*）*to split the family property*｜同居各～ *to live together but cook separately* ❷灶 earthen cooking stove

CUI ㄘㄨㄟ

衰 ⊜ cuī ㄘㄨㄟ〈古 **archaism**〉❶等衰，等差，等次，

等级 grade; rank ❷同"缞" same as 缞

㊀ shuāi 见 697 页 see p697

缞 cuī ㄘㄨㄟ 古时用粗麻布制成的丧服。也作"衰"(also written as 衰) funeral garment made of coarse linen cloth in ancient China

榱 cuī ㄘㄨㄟ 古代指椽子(in ancient China) rafter

崔 cuī ㄘㄨㄟ 姓 Cui, a surname

[崔嵬](—wéi)山高大不平(of mountains) lofty and rocky

催 cuī ㄘㄨㄟ ❶催促,使赶快行动 to urge; to press:~办 *to press sb to do sth*|~他早点动身 *to urge him to set out early* ❷使事物的产生、发展变化加快 to speed up; to expedite; to accelerate:~生 *to hasten parturition*|~化剂 *catalyst*

摧 cuī ㄘㄨㄟ 破坏,折断 to destroy; to break:~毁 *to destroy; to smash; to devastate*|~残 *to wreck; to destroy*|无坚不~ *to overrun all fortifications*|~枯拉朽(喻腐朽势力很容易打垮) *as easy as crushing dry weeds and smashing rotten wood — destroying sth already in a state of ruin; to inflict a crushing defeat on*

璀 cuǐ ㄘㄨㄟˇ [璀璨](—càn)形容玉石的光泽鲜明夺目(of jade) resplendent; brilliant; splendid

脆 cuì ㄘㄨㄟˋ ❶容易折断,容易碎,跟"韧"相对(the opposite of 韧) fragile; brittle:~枣 *crisp dates*|这纸太~。*The paper is too fragile.* [脆弱]懦弱,不坚强 fragile; frail ❷声音响亮、清爽(of voice) crisp; clear:嗓音挺~。*The voice is very crisp.* ❸〈方 ***dialect***〉干脆,说话做事爽利痛快 neat:办事很~ *to do a neat job*

萃 cuì ㄘㄨㄟˋ 草丛生(of grass) to grow densely ㊉ ***extension*** 聚在一起的人或物 crowd of people; collection of things:出类拔~(超出同类) *outstanding; out of the ordinary*

啐 cuì ㄘㄨㄟˋ 用力从嘴里吐出来 to spit:~一口痰 *to spit sputum*

淬(**焠) cuì ㄘㄨㄟˋ 淬火,金属和玻璃的一种热处理工艺,把合金制品或玻璃加热到一定温度,随即在水、油或空气中急速冷却,一般用以提高合金的硬度和强度。通称"蘸火"(generally called 蘸火) to temper; to chill; to quench [淬砺]㊥ ***figurative*** 刻苦锻炼,努力提高 to temper oneself through severe trials

悴(*顇) cuì ㄘㄨㄟˋ 见 602 页"憔"字条"憔悴"(qiáo—) see 憔悴 on p602

瘁 cuì ㄘㄨㄟˋ 过度劳累 exhausted; fatigued:鞠躬尽~ *to bend one's body and exhaust one's energy — to spare no effort in the performance of one's duty*|心力交~ *to be mentally and physically exhausted*

C

粹 cuì ㄘㄨㄟˋ ❶不杂 pure：纯～ pure ❷精华 essence；cream（㊣ *doublet* 精～ essence；quintessence）：国～（指我国传统文化的精华，曾经含有盲目崇拜旧文化的保守意味）（*referring to the quintessence of traditional Chinese culture，which once had a sense of conservativeness as a result of blind worship of old culture*）*quintessence*（or *best*）*of Chinese culture*

翠 cuì ㄘㄨㄟˋ ❶翠鸟，鸟名，又叫"鱼狗"。羽毛青绿色，尾短，捕食小鱼（also called 鱼狗）kingfisher ❷绿色的玉，翡翠 green jade；emerald：珠～ *pearls and jade*；*jewellery* ❸绿色 green：～绿 *emerald green*；*jade green*｜～竹 *green bamboo*

膵（**脺） cuì ㄘㄨㄟˋ 膵脏（zàng），胰腺的旧称（former term for 胰腺）pancreas

毳 cuì ㄘㄨㄟˋ 鸟兽的细毛 fine hair on birds or animals；down［毳毛］就是寒毛，人体表面生的细毛 fine hair on the human body；down

CUN ㄘㄨㄣ

村（*邨） cūn ㄘㄨㄣ ❶（～子、～儿）乡村，村庄 village；hamlet ❷粗俗 vulgar：～话 *vulgar words*

皴 cūn ㄘㄨㄣ ❶皮肤因受冻或受风吹而干裂 cracked；chapped：手都～了。*His hands are chapped.* ❷皮肤上积存的泥垢和脱落的表皮 grime；dirt：一脖子～ *a grimy neck* ❸中国画的一种画法，涂出山石的纹理和阴阳向背（technique of showing the shade and texture of mountain rocks by light ink strokes in traditional Chinese landscape painting）textual stroke

存 cún ㄘㄨㄣˊ ❶在，活着 to exist；to live；to survive：～在 *to exist*｜～亡 *to live or die* ❷保留，留下 to keep；to preserve：～留 *to remain*；*to reserve*｜去伪～真 *to remove the false and retain the true*［存盘］把计算机中的信息存储到磁盘上 to save［存心］居心，怀着某种想法 to harbour certain intentions：～～不良 *to harbour evil intentions* ❸储蓄 to save：～款 *to deposit*｜整～整取 *lump-sum deposit*；*fixed and withdrawal*；*deposit of fixed amount and period* ❹寄放 to check；to park：～车 *to park a bicycle* ❺停聚 to accumulate；to stuff：小孩儿～食了。*The baby has indigestion from being over-stuffed.*｜下水道修好，街上就不～水了。*Water will not accumulate in the street if the sewer is repaired.* ❻慰问 to express sympathy and solicitude for：～问 *to extend regards*｜～慰 *to express sympathy and solicitude for*｜～恤 *to express sympathy for* *and give relief to (a bereaved family)*

蹲 ㊁ cún ㄘㄨㄣˊ 脚、腿猛然落地受伤 to sprain：他跳下来～了腿了。*He sprained his leg when he jumped down.*

㊀ dūn 见 167 页 see p167

忖 cǔn ㄘㄨㄣˇ 揣度(chuǎi duó)，思量 to ponder; to speculate：～度(duó) *to conjecture*｜自～ *to turn over in one's mind*

寸 cùn ㄘㄨㄣˋ 市制长度单位，一尺的十分之一，约合3.33厘米 *cun*, a Chinese unit of length, equal to one tenth of a *chi*, approximately 3.33 centimetres ㊞ ***figurative*** 短小 very short; very little：～阴 *very short time*｜～步 *tiny step; very short distance*｜手无～铁 *barehanded; unarmed*｜鼠目～光 *short-sighted*

吋 cùn ㄘㄨㄣˋ 也读作 yīngcùn 英美制长度单位，一呎的十二分之一，合2.54厘米。现写作"英寸"(also prouounced yīngcùn and now written as 英寸) inch, a unit of length in Britain and US, equal to one twelfth of one foot, approximately 2.54 centimetres

CUO ㄘㄨㄛ

搓 cuō ㄘㄨㄛ 两个手掌相对或把手掌放在别的东西上反复揉擦 to rub one's hands together; to rub with hands：～手 *to rub one's hands*｜～绳子 *to make cords by twisting hemp fibres between the palms*

磋 cuō ㄘㄨㄛ 把骨、角磨制成器物 to grind (bones or horns into utensils, implements, wares, etc)［磋商］商量 to consult; to negotiate; to confer

蹉 cuō ㄘㄨㄛ ❶跌，倒 to slip and fall; to fall down ❷失误，差错 slip; mistake

［蹉跎］(—tuó)把时光白耽误过去 to idle away; to waste time：岁月～～。*Months and years are turned to empty waste.*

撮 ㊀ cuō ㄘㄨㄛ ❶聚起，现多指把聚拢的东西用簸箕等物铲起 to bring together; to scoop up：～成一堆 *to scoop into a pile*｜把土～起来 *to scoop up dirt*［撮合］给双方拉关系 to make a match; to act as a go-between［撮口呼］ü 韵母和拿 ü 开头的韵母叫作"撮口呼"[class of syllables with ü as the final or a final beginning with ü] round-lip vowel ❷取，摘取 to extract; to summarize：～要(摘取要点) *to make an abstract; to write a gist* ❸市制容量单位，一升的千分之一 *cuo*, a traditional unit of capacity, equal to one thousandth of a *sheng* ❹(—儿)量词 ***quantifier***：一～米 *a pinch of rice*｜一～儿土 *a pinch of dirt*

㊁ zuǒ 见 1022 页 see p1022

嵯 cuó ㄘㄨㄛˊ ［嵯峨］(—é)山势高峻 (of mountains)

lofty and rugged

瘥 ㊁ cuó ㄘㄨㄛˊ 病 disease; illness

㊀ chài 见72页 see p72

鹾(鹺) cuó ㄘㄨㄛˊ ❶盐 salt ❷咸 salty:～鱼 *salted fish*

矬 cuó ㄘㄨㄛˊ 〈方 ***dialect***〉矮 short:他长得太～。*He's too short.*

痤 cuó ㄘㄨㄛˊ 痤疮,一种皮肤病,多生在青年人的面部,通常是有黑头的小红疙瘩。俗称"粉刺"(popularly called 粉刺) acne

酂 cuó ㄘㄨㄛˊ [酂阳][酂城] 地名,都在河南省永城西 Cuoyang and Cuocheng, two places both in the west of Yongcheng, Henan Province

脞 cuǒ ㄘㄨㄛˇ 小而繁 trivial and numerous; trivial; trifling [丛脞]细碎,烦琐 trivial; trifling

挫 cuò ㄘㄨㄛˋ ❶挫折,事情进行不顺利,失败 setback; defeat:经过了许多～折 *to have experienced many setbacks*|事遭～阻。*The project met with a setback.* ❷按下,使音调降低 to tone down:语音抑扬顿～ *cadence*

莝 cuò ㄘㄨㄛˋ 莝草,铡碎的草 chopped fodder

锉(*剉) cuò ㄘㄨㄛˋ ❶用钢制成的磨铜、铁、竹、木等的工具 file; rasp ❷用锉磨东西 to file; to rasp:把锯～一～ *to file the teeth of a saw* ❸折伤 to be defeated

厝 cuò ㄘㄨㄛˋ ❶放置 to lay; to place:～火积薪(把火放在柴堆下,喻隐患) *to put fire under faggots—to have a hidden danger* ❷停柩(jiù),把棺材停放待葬,或浅埋以待改葬 to place a coffin in a temporary shelter pending burial, or to bury a coffin in a shallow pit before moving it to a permanent grave

措 cuò ㄘㄨㄛˋ ❶安放,安排 to arrange; to handle:～辞 *wording*|～手不及(来不及应付) *to be caught unawares; to be taken by surprise* ❷筹划办理 to make plans to handle sth:～借 *to raise money or resources; to arrange a loan*|筹～款项 *to raise funds*|～施(对事情采取的办法) *measures; steps*

错 cuò ㄘㄨㄛˋ ❶不正确,不对,与实际不符 incorrect; wrong; erroneous (㊀ ***doublet*** —误 mistake; error):你弄～了。*You have made a mistake.*|没～儿。*No mistakes.* [错觉](—jué)跟事实不符的知觉,视、听、触各种感觉都有错觉 illusion ❷差,坏(用于否定式)(used in negative sentences) bad; poor:今年的收成～不了。*We're sure to have a good harvest this year.*|他的身体真不～。*He's really healthy.* ❸交叉着 interlocked:～杂 *mixed; heterogeneous; jumbled*|～落 *scattered and interlocked*|～综

复杂 *perplexing*; *intricate* | 犬牙交～ *jigsaw-shaped*; *jagged* ❹岔开 to make way; to miss: ～车（*of vehicles*）*to make way for each other* | ～过机会 *to miss an opportunity*; *to blow a chance* ❺磨玉的石 grindstone for polishing jade: 他山之石，可以为～。*As stones from other hills may serve to polish the jade of this mountain, advice from other people may help one to overcome one's shortcomings.* ❻古同"措" same as 措 in ancient Chinese

D ㄉ

D

DA ㄉㄚ

哒 dā ㄉㄚ （发音短促）吆喝牲口前进的声音 to gee (up)

耷 dā ㄉㄚ 大耳朵 big ear [耷拉]（—la）向下垂 to droop; to hang down: 狗～～着尾巴跑了。*The dog ran away with its tail drooping.* | 饱满的谷穗～～着头。*The plump grain ears droop heavily.*

哒(嗒) dā ㄉㄚ 同"嗒㊁" same as 嗒㊁

搭 dā ㄉㄚ ❶支起，架起 to put up; to build: ～棚 *to put up a shed* | ～架子 *to put up scaffolds; to build a framework* | ～桥 *to build a bridge* [搭救]帮助人脱离危险或灾难 *to rescue* ❷共同抬 *to lift up together*: 把桌子～起来。*Let's lift up the table together.* ❸相交接 **1** 连接，接触 to touch: 两根电线～上了。*The two wires are touching.* **2** 凑在一起 to join: ～伙 *to join as partners* **3** 搭配，配合 to combine; to mix: 两种材料～着用。*The two kinds of materials can be used in combination.* **4** 放在支撑物上 to hang over; to drape over: 把衣服～在竹竿上 *to hang the clothes on a bamboo pole* | 身上～着一条毛毯 *with a blanket draped over one's shoulder* ❹乘坐车船、飞机等 to take (a train, bus, plane, etc): ～载(zài) *to carry* | ～车 *to get a lift* | ～船 *to take a ship* | ～班机 *to take a scheduled flight*

嗒 ㊁ dā ㄉㄚ 拟声词 ***onomatopoeia***，马蹄声、机关枪声等 clatter; rattle (叠 ***reduplication***)

㊀ tà 见 723 页 see p723

铬 dā ㄉㄚ 铁铬，翻土的农具 iron rake

褡 dā ㄉㄚ [褡裢](—lian)一种口袋，中间开口，两头装东西 *dalian*, a long, rectagular bag with two openings cut in the middle, through which things are put into its ends

答(**荅) ㊁ dā ㄉㄚ 同"答㊀"，用于口语"答应"、"答理"等词 same as 答㊀, used in colloquial Chinese 答应，答理，etc [答理](—li)打招呼，理睬 to acknowledge sb's greeting [答应](—ying) **1** 应声回答 to respond; to answer **2** 允许 to agree; to promise: 我们坚决不～～。*We definitely won't permit it.*

㊀ dá 见 119 页 see p119

打 ㊁ dá ㄉㄚˊ （外 **loanword**）量词 ***quantifier***，12 个为 1 打 dozen

㊁ dǎ 见 119 页 see p119

达(達) dá ㄉㄚˊ ❶通,到达 to reach; to extend; to lead to: 抵～*to reach*|四通八～*to extend in all directions*|火车从北京直～上海。*It is a through train from Beijing to Shanghai.* ❷通达,对事理认识得透彻 to understand thoroughly: 通～事理 *to be reasonable*|通权～变(不拘常规,采取变通办法) *to be adaptable to changing circumstances; to be flexible* [达观]对不如意的事情看得开 philosophical; resilient ❸达到,实现 to achieve; to attain: 目的已～ *to have achieved the goal*|～成协议 *to come to an agreement* ❹告知,表达 to express; to convey: 转～ *to pass on; to convey*|传～命令 *to deliver an order*|词不～意。*The words fail to convey the meaning.* ❺旧时称人得到有权有势的地位(of one's position in former times) eminent; distinguished; prominent (㊃ **doublet** 显— distinguished; prominent): ～官 *senior official; high ranking officer*

[达斡尔族](—wò——) 我国少数民族,参看附表 (see the appendix) the Daur (*or* Tahur) ethnic group, one of the ethnic minorities of China

荙(薘) dá ㄉㄚˊ 见 378 页"莙"字条"莙荙菜"(jūn——) see 莙荙菜 on p378

鞑(韃) dá ㄉㄚˊ [鞑靼](—dá)我国古代对北方少数民族的统称 Tartar, a general term for the northern ethnic minorities in ancient China

沓 ㊀ dá ㄉㄚˊ (—子、—儿)量词 **quantifier**,用于叠起来的纸张或其他薄的东西 (of paper or other thin things) pile; stack; pad: 一～子信纸 *a pad of letter paper*

㊁ tà 见 722 页 see p722

怛 dá ㄉㄚˊ 忧伤,悲苦 grieved; distressed

妲 dá ㄉㄚˊ 用于人名 da, used in a given name 妲己,商纣王的妃子 Daji, a concubine of King Zhou, in the Shang Dynasty

炟 dá ㄉㄚˊ 用于人名 da, used in a given name 刘炟,东汉章帝 Liu Da, Emperor Zhang of the Eastern Han Dynasty

笪 dá ㄉㄚˊ ❶用粗竹篾编的像席的东西,用来晾晒粮食等 bamboo-strip mat for sun-drying grains ❷拉船的竹索 bamboo tow rope ❸姓 Da, a surname

靼 dá ㄉㄚˊ 见 119 页"鞑"字条"鞑靼"(dá—) see 鞑靼 on p119

答(**荅) ㊀ dá ㄉㄚˊ ❶回答,回复 to answer; to reply (㊃ **doublet** —复 to reply): 问～ *questions and answers*|～话 *to answer; to re-*

spond ❷还报 to requite; to reciprocate: 报～ *to reward; to requite* | ～谢 *to express appreciation; to express gratitude* | ～礼 *to take the salute*

㊁ dā 见 118 页 see p118

瘩 ㊀ dá ㄉㄚˊ ［瘩背］中医称生在背部的痈。也叫"搭手"(also called 搭手) carbuncle on the back in traditional Chinese medicine

㊁ da 见 122 页 see p122

D

打 ㊀ dǎ ㄉㄚˇ ❶击 to hit; to strike: ～铁 *to forge iron* | ～门 *to knock at the door* | ～鼓 *to beat a drum* | ～靶 *to shoot at a target* | ～垮 *to defeat; to destroy* ㊞ ***extension*** 放射 to shoot: ～枪 *to fire a gun* | ～闪(*of lightening*) *to flash* ［打击］使受到挫折 to crack down on: ～～侵略者 *to fight the invaders* ❷表示各种动作,代替许多有具体意义的动词 used to denote kinds of actions in place of many specific verbs **1** 除去 to get rid of: ～虫 *to get rid of intestinal parasites by taking medicine* | ～沫(把液体上面的沫去掉) *to skim off the scum* | ～食(服药帮助消化) *to take medicine to relieve indigestion* **2** 毁坏,损伤,破碎 to damage; to injure: 衣服被虫～了。*The clothes are moth-eaten.* | 碗～了。*The bowl is broken.* **3** 取,收,捕 to fetch; to gather; to catch: ～鱼 *to catch fish* | ～粮食 *to reap grains* | ～柴 *to gather firewood* | ～水 *to fetch water* **4** 购买 to purchase: ～车票 *to buy a train* (or *bus*) *ticket* | ～酒 *to buy some liquor* (or *wine*) **5** 举 to lift; to raise: ～伞 *to hold up an umbrella* | ～灯笼 *to carry a lantern* | ～旗子 *to hold up a flag; to raise a banner* **6** 揭开,破开 to open; to uncover: ～帐子 *to open a bed-curtain* | ～西瓜 *to cut open a watermelon* | ～鸡蛋 *to whisk eggs; to beat eggs* **7** 建造 to build: ～井 *to dig a well* | ～墙 *to build a wall* **8** 制作,编织 to make; to knit: ～镰刀 *to forge a sickle* | ～桌椅 *to make desks and chairs* | ～毛衣 *to knit a sweater* **9** 捆扎 to tie up; to pack: ～铺盖卷 *to pack up bedding* | ～裹腿 *to wind puttees* **10** 涂抹 to draw; to paint: ～蜡 *to wax* | ～桐油 *to paint with tung oil* **11** 玩耍,做某种文体活动 to play: ～秋千 *to play on the swing* | ～球 *to play a ball game* **12** 通,发 to dispatch; to send; to project: ～一个电报去 *to go to send a telegram* | ～电话 *to make a telephone call* **13** 计算 to calculate: 精～细算 *to do careful calculation and strict budgeting; to pinch pennies* | 设备费～二百元 *to estimate the cost of the equipment at 200 yuan* **14** 立,定 to set (up); to work out (in one's mind): ～下基础 *to lay a foundation* | ～主意 *to think out a plan* | ～草稿 *to work out a draft; to write a draft* **15** 从事或担任某些工作 to do; to be engaged in: ～杂儿 *to do odds and ends* | ～前站 *to act as an* *advance party; to set out in advance to make arrangements; to arrange ahead* (*for travel accommodations*) **16** 表示身体上的某些动作 used to denote some physical action: ～手势 *to make a gesture* | ～冷战 *to shiver; to shudder* | ～哈欠 *to yawn* | ～前失(马前腿跌倒)(*of horses*) *to stumble* | ～滚儿 *to roll about* ❸ 与某些动词结合为一个动词 used to form a new verb with some verbs: ～扮 *to dress up* | ～扫 *to clean up* | ～搅 *to pester; to bother* | ～扰 *to break in; to disturb* ❹ 介词 ***preposition***, 从, 自 from; since: ～去年起 *from last year* | ～哪里来? *Where are you from?*

㊁ dá 见118页 see p118

大 ㊀ dà ㄉㄚˋ ❶ 跟"小"相对(the opposite of 小) **1** 占的空间较多, 面积较广, 容量较多 large; vast; great: ～山 *big mountain* | ～树 *big tree* | 这间房比那间～。*This room is larger than that one.* **2** 数量较多 in great number: ～众 *the masses* | ～量 *great number; great amount* **3** 程度深, 范围广 high in degree; vast in range: ～冷天 *very cold day* | ～干社会主义 *to work for socialism energetically* | ～快人心 *to afford great satisfaction to the people* **4** 声音较响 loud: ～声说话 *to speak loudly* **5** 年长, 排行第一 eldest: ～哥 *the eldest brother* | 老～ *the eldest* (*child*) **6** 敬辞 ***polite***: ～作 *your work; your book; your script* | 尊姓～名 *your name* [大夫] 古代官职名称 senior official in feudal China (另 dàifu, 见"大" dài see also 大 dài for dàifu) [大王] **1** 古代尊称国王 (term of respect in ancient China) Your (or His) Majesty; king **2** 指最长于某种事情的人 person of the highest class or skill in sth: 爆破～～ *ace dynamiter* **3** 指垄断某种行业的人 monopoly capitalist: 钢铁～～ *steel magnate* (另 dàiwang, 见"大" dài see also 大 dài for dàiwang) ❷ 时间更远 further in time: ～前年 *three years ago* | ～后天 *three days from now* ❸ 不很详细, 不很准确 not detailed; not very precise: ～略 *general; rough; approximate* | ～概 *general; rough; approximate* | ～约 *about; approximately* ❹ 〈方 ***dialect***〉 称父亲或伯父 father or father's elder brother

[大黄] (dà—) (dài—) (又 **also** dài—) 又叫"川军"。多年生草本植物, 夏季多数开黄白色小花, 根及根状茎粗壮, 黄色, 可入药 (also called 川军) Chinese rhubarb (*Rheum officinale*)

〈古 ***archaism***〉 又同"太"、"泰", 如"大子"、"大山"等 also same as 太, 泰 such as 大子, 大山, etc

㊁ dài 见122页 see p122

垯 (墶) da · ㄉㄚ 见223页"圪"字条"圪垯" (gē—) see 圪垯 on p223

D

纮(縒) da ·ㄉㄚ 见 223 页"纥"字条"纥纮"(gē—) see 纥纮 on p223

跶(躂) da ·ㄉㄚ 见 34 页"蹦"字条"蹦跶"(bèng—) see 蹦跶 on p34

瘩 ⊜ da ·ㄉㄚ 见 223 页"疙"字条"疙瘩"(gē—) see 疙瘩 on p223

⊖ dá 见 120 页 see p120

D

DAI ㄉㄞ

呆(*獃) dāi ㄉㄞ ❶傻,愚蠢 stupid; silly ❷死板,发愣 blank; wooden:两眼发～*to be in a daze*|他～～地站在那里。*He stood frozen to the spot.*|～板 *stiff; rigid* ❸同"待⊜" same as 待⊜

呔 dāi ㄉㄞ 叹词 ***interjection***,突然大喝一声,使人注意 hey

待 ⊜ dāi ㄉㄞ 停留,逗留,迟延,也作"呆"(also written as 呆)to stay:你～一会ㄦ再走。*Why not stay for a while?*

⊖ dài 见 124 页 see p124

歹 dǎi ㄉㄞˇ 坏,恶 evil; vicious:～人 *villain*|～意 *malice*|为非作～*to do evil*[好歹] **1** 好和坏 good and evil:不知～～*to be unable to tell good from evil* **2** 危险(多指生命危险)(usually used to denote life in peril) mishap; disaster; risk:他要有个～～,就惨了。*The world would come to an end if something should happen to him.* **3** 无论如何 in any case; at any rate; anyhow:～～你得(děi)去一趟。*You should go there anyhow.*

逮 ⊜ dǎi ㄉㄞˇ 捉,捕,用于口语(used colloquially) to catch; to hunt:～老鼠 *to catch mice*|～蝗虫 *to catch locusts*

⊖ dài 见 125 页 see p125

傣 dǎi ㄉㄞˇ [傣族]我国少数民族,参看附表(see the appendix) the Dai (*or* Tai) ethnic group, one of the ethnic minorities of China

大 ⊜ dài ㄉㄞˋ [大城]地名,在河北省 Daicheng, a place in Hebei Province [大夫](—fu)医生 doctor (另 dàfū,见"大"dà see also 大 dà for dàfū)[大王](—wang)旧戏曲、小说中对国王、山寨头领或大帮强盗首领的称呼(in old Chinese novels or operas) Your (*or* His) Majesty; king; (bandit) chief (另 dàwáng,见"大"dà see also 大 dà for dàwáng)

⊖ dà 见 121 页 see p121

轪 dài ㄉㄞˋ 包在车毂端的铜皮、铁皮 hubcap; copper or iron plate covering the hub of a wheel

代 dài ㄉㄞˋ ❶替 to replace; to substitute (㊀ ***doublet*** 一替、替一 to replace):～理 *to act as an agent*|～办 *to act as an agent; to act on sb's behalf*|～耕 *to do farmwork for others*[代表] **1** 受委托或被选举出来替别人或大家办事 to represent:我～～他去。*I'll go*

on his behalf.｜他～～一个单位。*He represents a unit*. **2** 被选派的人 representative：工会～～ *representative of the trade union*｜全权～～ *plenipotentiary* ［代词］代替名词、动词、形容词、数词或量词的词，如"我、你、他、谁、什么、这样、那么些"等 pronoun ［代价］获得某种东西所付出的价钱 price；cost ⑪ ***extension*** 为达到某种目的所花费的精力和物质 price；cost ❷历史上划分的时期，世 historical period（㊄ ***doublet*** 世 — for generations；from generation to generation｜时 — times）：古～ *ancient times*｜近～ *modern times*｜现～ *contemporary times*；*modern times*｜清～ *the Qing Dynasty* ［年代］**1** 泛指时间 time：～～久远 *age-old*；*of remote antiquity* **2** 十年的时期（前面须有确定的世纪）decade：20 世纪 50 ～～（1950—1959）*1950s*；*1950's* ❸世系的辈分 generation：第二～ *the second generation*｜下一～ *the next generation*；*the coming generation* ［代沟］指两代人之间在思想观念、心理状态、生活方式等方面的巨大差异 generation gap ❹地质年代分期的第二级，在"宙"之下、"纪"之上 era：古生～ *Palaeozoic Era*｜中生～ *Mesozoic Era*｜新生～ *Cenozoic Era*

岱 dài ㄉㄞˋ 五岳中东岳泰山的别称，又叫"岱宗"、"岱岳"，在山东省 *Dai*，another name for Mount Taishan，the eastern mountain among the five Sacred Mountains，also called 岱宗 or 岱岳，in Shandong Province

玳（*瑇） dài ㄉㄞˋ ［玳瑁］（— mào）（旧读 formerly — mèi）一种爬行动物，跟龟相似。甲壳黄褐色，有黑斑，很光滑。生在海中 hawksbill sea turtle（*Eretmochelys imbricata*）

贷 dài ㄉㄞˋ ❶借贷，借入或借出（簿记学上专指借出）（especially credit in bookkeeping）to borrow or lend money：～款 *to extend credit*；*to obtain a loan* ❷贷款 loan：农～ *agricultural loans* ❸推卸给旁人 to shift；to shirk：责无旁～ *duty-bound*；*with unshirkable duty* ❹宽恕，饶恕 to forgive；to pardon：严惩不～ *to punish without mercy*；*to punish without leniency*

袋 dài ㄉㄞˋ（—子、—儿）衣兜或用布、皮等做成的盛（chéng）东西的器物 bag；sack；pocket；pouch：布～ *cloth bag*｜衣～ *pocket*｜面口～ *flour sack* ［烟袋］抽旱烟或水烟的用具 Chinese tobacco pipe：水～～ *water pipe*｜～～锅儿 *bowl of a long-stemmed pipe*

黛 dài ㄉㄞˋ 青黑色的颜料，古代女子用来画眉（used to black eyebrows by ancient females）black pigment：～眉 *to black eyebrows*｜粉～ *face powder and black eye pigment* — *beautiful woman*

甙 dài ㄉㄞˋ 有机化合物的一类，多存在于植物体中。中药车前、甘草、陈皮等都是含甙的药物。现叫"苷"(gān)(now called 苷)glucoside

迨 dài ㄉㄞˋ ❶等到，达到 till; until ❷趁 when

绐 dài ㄉㄞˋ 欺哄 to coax; to cajole; to wheedle

殆 dài ㄉㄞˋ ❶几乎，差不多 almost; nearly: 敌人伤亡～尽。*The enemy was practically wiped out.* ❷危险 dangerously: 危～*danger*｜知彼知己，百战不～。*Knowing the enemy and yourself, you can fight a hundred battles with no danger of defeat.*

怠 dài ㄉㄞˋ 懒惰，松懈 idle; slack (㊥ ***doublet*** 一惰 indolent; lazy｜懒一slothful｜懈一sluggish; remiss)

带(帶) dài ㄉㄞˋ ❶(一子、一儿)用皮、布或纱线等物做成的长条 belt; band; tape: 皮～*leather belt*｜腰～*girdle; waist band*｜鞋～儿 *shoe lace* ㊀ **extension** 轮胎 tyre: 外～*tyre*｜里～*inner tube (of a tyre)* ❷地带，区域 zone; area; belt: 温～*temperate zone; variable zone*｜寒～*frigid zone*｜沿海一～*coastal area* ❸携带 to carry: 腰里～着盒子枪 *with a Mauser pistol tucked under one's belt*｜～着行李 *to take one's luggage along* ❹捎，顺便做，连着一起做 to take; to do sth in passing: 你给他～个口信去。*Would you please take him a message?*｜把门～上。*Close the door behind you.*｜连送信～买菜 *to send letters as well as buy vegetables* ❺显出，有 to bear; to wear; to have: 面～笑容 *with a smile; all smiles*｜～花纹的 *figured* ❻领，率领 to lead; to head (㊥***doublet*** 一领 to lead; to guide): ～路 *to lead the way*｜～兵 *to command troops*｜起～头作用 *to take the lead* ❼白带，女子阴道流出的白色黏液，如量过多是阴道或子宫发炎的一种症状，白带有血的叫"赤带"leucorrhoea［带下］中医指女子赤、白带症 (in traditional Chinese medicine) morbid leucorrhoea

待 ㊀ dài ㄉㄞˋ ❶等，等候 to wait (㊥ ***doublet*** 等一 to wait): ～业 *unemployed*｜～机出击 *to bide one's time to launch an attack*｜尚～研究 *to remain to be studied* ❷对待，招待 to treat; to entertain: ～人接物 *the way of getting along with people*｜大家～我太好了。*You're so kind to me.*｜～客 *to entertain guests*［待遇］在社会上享有的权利、地位等 social rights and position one enjoys; treatment: 政治～～ *political treatment*｜物质～～ *material treatment; remuneration* 特指工资、食宿等 remuneration; salary or wages and accommodations: 调整～～ *to improve remuneration* ❸需要 to need: 自不～言 *it goes without saying* ❹将，要(古典戏曲小说和

现代某些方言的用法）to be about to; to be going to：正～出门，有人来了。*I was about to leave when someone came.*

㊁ dāi 见 122 页 see p122

埭 dài ㄉㄞˋ 土坝 dam

逮 ㊀ dài ㄉㄞˋ ❶到，及 to reach：力有未～ *beyond one's reach; beyond one's power*｜～乎清季（到了清代末年）*by the end of the Qing Dynasty* ❷逮捕，捉拿 to arrest; to apprehend

㊁ dǎi 见 122 页 see p122

叇（靆） dài ㄉㄞˋ 见 5 页"叆"字条"叆叇"（ài—）see 叆叇 on p5

戴 dài ㄉㄞˋ ❶加在头、面、颈、手等处 to adorn; to wear：～帽子 *to put on* (or *wear*) *a hat*｜～眼镜 *to wear glasses*｜～红领巾 *to wear a red scarf*｜～笼头 *to put a headstall on* (*a horse*)｜披星～月（喻夜里赶路或在外劳动）*to travel* (or *work outdoors*) *at night* ❷尊奉，推崇 to respect; to support：推～ *to support* (*sb in assuming leadership*)｜拥～ *to support* (*sb as a leader*)｜爱～ *to love and esteem*

襶 dài ㄉㄞˋ 见 524 页"褦"字条"褦襶"（nài—）see 褦襶 on p524

DAN ㄉㄢ

丹 dān ㄉㄢ ❶红色 red：～心 *loyal heart; loyalty*｜～砂（朱砂）*cinnabar* ❷一种依成方配制成的中药，通常是颗粒状或粉末状的（of traditional Chinese medicine）pellet; powder：丸散（sǎn）膏～ *pills, powder, extract and pellets*｜灵～妙药 *panacea*

担（擔） ㊀ dān ㄉㄢ ❶用肩膀挑 to carry on a shoulder pole：～水 *to carry water* (*with pails hanging from a carrying pole*)｜～着两筐青菜 *to carry two baskets of vegetables on a shoulder pole* [担心]忧虑，顾虑 to worry; to be anxious about：我～～他身体受不了。*I'm worried about his health.* ❷担负，承当 to undertake; to take on：～风险 *to run the risk of; to take a risk*｜～责任 *to shoulder the responsibility*

㊁ dàn 见 128 页 see p128

㊂ dǎn 见 127 页 see p127

单（單） ㊀ dān ㄉㄢ ❶种类少，不复杂 lacking in variety; simple：简～ *simple*｜～纯 *simple; unsophiscated*｜～式簿记 *single entry bookkeeping* ㊀ **extension** 副词 **adverb**，只，仅 only; alone：做事～靠热情不够。*Enthusiasm alone does not work.*｜不提别的，～说这件事。*Don't talk about anything else. Let's focus on this matter.* or *Let's talk about nothing but this matter.* [单位] **1** 计算物体轻重、长短及数量的标准 unit (as a standard of measurement) **2** 指机关、团体或属于一

个机关、团体的各个部门 unit (as an organization, department, division, section, etc): 那里有五个直属～～。*There are five units directly under the jurisdiction.* ❷独,一 alone; single: ～身 *single* | ～打一 *to concentrate on one thing at a time; to have a one-track mind; to be single-minded* | ～枪匹马 *single-handed; all by oneself* | ～数(跟"复数"相对) *singular (the opposite of* 复数) ❸奇(jī)数的 odd: ～日 *odd-numbered days* | ～号 *odd numbers* | ～数(一、三、五、七等,跟"双数"相对) *odd numbers (such as one, three, five, seven, etc, the opposite of* 双数) [单薄](-bó) **1** 薄,少 thin: 穿得很～～ *to be thinly dressed* **2** 弱 weak: 他身子骨太～～。*He's thin and weak.* | 人力～～ *short of manpower* ❹(一子、一儿)记载事物用的纸片 bill; list: ～据 *receipt; voucher* | 传～ *leaflet; handbill* | 账～儿 *bill* | 清～ *detailed list; checklist; inventory* | 药～ *medical prescription* ❺衣服被褥等只有一层的 unlined: ～衣 *unlined garment* | ～裤 *unlined pants* ❻(一子、一儿)覆盖用的布 sheet: 被～ *coverlet* | 床～ *bedsheet; bedspread* | 褥～儿 *sheet*

㊁ shàn 见 654 页 see p654

㊂ chán 见 73 页 see p73

郸(鄲) dān ㄉㄢ [郸城]地名,在河南省 Dancheng, a place in Henan Province

殚(殫) dān ㄉㄢ 尽,竭尽 to exhaust: ～力 *to do one's utmost* | ～心 *to be dedicated to* | ～思极虑 *to rack one's brains*

箪(簞) dān ㄉㄢ 古代盛(chéng)饭的圆竹器 ancient round bamboo utensil for containing cooked rice: ～食壶浆(古代百姓用箪盛饭、用壶盛汤来慰劳所爱戴的军队) *to receive soldiers with food and drink; to welcome soldiers with food and drink*

眈 dān ㄉㄢ [眈眈]注视的样子 glaring: 虎视～～(凶狠贪婪地看着) *to cast a fierce and covetous look at*

耽(❶ *躭) dān ㄉㄢ ❶迟延 to delay [耽搁](-ge)迟延,停止没进行 to delay: 这件事～～了很久。*It has been delayed for a long time.* [耽误](-wu)因耽搁或错过时机而误事 to delay; to hold up: 不能～～生产。*Production should never be held up.* ❷沉溺,入迷 to indulge in: ～乐(lè) *to indulge in pleasure* | ～于幻想 *to indulge in fantasies*

酖 ㊀ dān ㄉㄢ 同"耽❷" same as 耽❷

㊁ zhèn 见 969 页"鸩" see 鸩 on p969

聃(**聸) dān ㄉㄢ 古代哲学家老子的名字 Dan, name of Laozi, ancient Chinese philosopher

儋 dān ㄉㄢ 儋州,地名,在海南省 Danzhou, a place in Hainan Province

担 ㊂ dǎn ㄉㄢˇ 拂,拂拭。后作"掸"(later written as 掸) to whisk; to flick

㊀ dān 见 125 页 see p125

㊁ dàn 见 128 页 see p128

胆(膽) dǎn ㄉㄢˇ ❶胆囊,俗叫"苦胆",是一个梨状的袋子,在肝脏右叶的下部,内储黄绿色的汁液,叫胆汁,味很苦,有帮助消化、杀菌、防腐等作用(popularly called 苦胆) gallbladder (图见 940 页"脏"picture on p940) ❷(一子、一儿)胆量 courage:~怯 *timid* | ~子小 *cowardly; timid* | ~大心细 *brave but not reckless* ❸某些器物的内层 inner layer of some containers: 球~ *rubber bladder of a ball* | 暖瓶~ *glass liner inside a thermos flask*

疸 dǎn ㄉㄢˇ 黄疸,病人的皮肤、黏膜和眼球的巩膜等都呈黄色,是由胆红素大量出现在血液中所引起的,是多种病(肝脏病、胆囊病、血液病等)的症状 jaundice; icterus

掸(撣、**撢) ㊀ dǎn ㄉㄢˇ 拂,打去尘土 to dust; to brush: ~桌子 *to dust the table* | ~衣服 *to flick the dust off one's clothes*

㊁ shàn 见 654 页 see p654

赕 dǎn ㄉㄢˇ (傣 Dai) 奉献 to denote; to offer: ~佛 *to make a donation to Buddhist temples*

亶 dǎn ㄉㄢˇ 实在,诚然 indeed; truly

石 ㊁ dàn ㄉㄢˋ 市制容量单位,1 石是 10 斗,合 100 升 *dan*, a unit of dry measure, equal to ten *dou*, or 100 *sheng* (此义在古书中读 shí,如"二千石"pronounced as *shi* in ancient Chinese texts, such as two thousand *shi*)

㊀ shí 见 676 页 see p676

旦 dàn ㄉㄢˋ ❶早晨 morning: ~暮 *morning and evening* | 枕戈待~ *sleep with one's head on his sword and wait for dawn; to keep battle-alert all night* ㊀ **extension** 天,日 day; daytime: 元~ *New Year's Day* | 一~发现问题,立刻想法解决。*Once a problem is noticed, we should find a solution immediately.* [旦夕] **1** 早晨和晚上 morning and evening **2** 在很短的时间内 in a short time: 危在~~ *to hang by a thread; to be in imminent danger* ❷传统戏曲里扮演妇女的角色 female role in traditional Chinese opera

但 dàn ㄉㄢˋ ❶只,仅 only; merely: ~愿能成功。*All I desire is success.* or *May success be true.* | 我们不~保证完成任务,还要提高质量。*We guarantee not only to accomplish the task, but also to improve the quality.* [但凡]只要 as long as; at any time: ~~我有工夫,我就去看他。*I'll visit him whenever I'm free.* ❷连词 **conjunction**, 但是,不过 but;

nevertheless：我们热爱和平，～也不怕战争。*We love peace but never fear war.*

担（擔） ㊂ dàn ㄉㄢˋ ❶扁担，挑东西的用具，多用竹、木做成（made of bamboo or wood to carry a load on the shoulder） shoulder pole；carrying pole ❷（一子）一挑儿东西 shoulder pole and the loads at its ends：货郎～*street vendor's goods carried on a shoulder pole* ㊀喻 ***figurative*** 担负的责任 responsibility：重～*heavy task* | 不怕～子重 *not to fear a heavy task* ❸市制重量单位，1 担是 100 斤，合 50 千克 *dan*，a traditional unit of weight，equal to 100 *jin*，i.e. 50 kilos ❹量词 ***quantifier***：一～水 two buckets of water on a shoulder pole

㊀ dān 见 125 页 see 125

㊁ dǎn 见 127 页 see p127

疍 dàn ㄉㄢˋ［疍民］过去广东、广西、福建内河和沿海一带的水上居民。多以船为家，从事渔业、运输业 boat dweller

诞 dàn ㄉㄢˋ ❶诞生，人出生 to be born：～辰（生日）*birthday* ❷生日 birthday：华～*birthday* ❸荒唐的，不合情理的 absurd；fantastic：荒～不经 *absurd and unreasonable* | 怪～*fantastic；ridiculous；grotesque*

萏 dàn ㄉㄢˋ 见 265 页“菡”字条“菡萏”（hàn—） see 菡萏 on p265

啖（*啗、*噉） dàn ㄉㄢˋ ❶吃或给人吃 to eat；to feed ❷拿利益引诱人 to entice with some benefit：～以私利 *to lure with benefits*

淡 dàn ㄉㄢˋ ❶含的盐分少，跟“咸”相对（the opposite of 咸） bland；tasteless：菜太～。*The dish is too bland.* | ～水湖 *freshwater lake* ❷含某种成分少，稀薄，跟“浓”相对（the opposite of 浓） thin；light：～绿 *light green* | ～酒 *light liquor* | 云～风轻 *thin clouds and light breeze* ❸不热心 indifferent；cold：态度冷～*remote and cold；aloof* | 他～～地说了一句话。*He uttered some words indifferently.* ❹营业不旺盛 slack；stagnant；sluggish：～月 *slow month* | ～季 *slack season*

氮 dàn ㄉㄢˋ 一种化学元素，在通常条件下为气体，符号 N，无色、无臭、无味，化学性质不活泼。可制氮肥 nitrogen (N)

惮（憚） dàn ㄉㄢˋ 怕，畏惧 to fear；to dread：不～烦 *to spare no trouble* | 肆无忌～ *unbridled；unscrupulous*

弹（彈） ㊀ dàn ㄉㄢˋ ❶可以用弹（tán）力发射出去的小丸 ball；pellet：～丸 *pellet* ❷装有爆炸物可以击毁人、物的东西 bullet；bomb：炮～*shell；cannon-shot；cannon ball* | 炸～*bomb* | 手榴～*grenade*

㊁ tán 见 727 页 see p727

瘅(癉) dàn ㄉㄢˋ ❶因劳累造成的病 illness resulting from overwork ❷憎恨 to detest; to hate: 彰善～恶 *to praise good and denounce evil*

蛋 dàn ㄉㄢˋ ❶鸟、龟、蛇等生的带有外壳的卵，受过精的可以孵出小动物 egg: 鸡～ *egg* | 鸭～ *duck's egg* | 蛇～ *snake's egg* ❷(～子、～儿)形状像蛋的东西 egg-shaped thing: 山药～ *potato* | 驴粪～儿 *donkey's dung*

澹 ㊀ dàn ㄉㄢˋ ❶(叠 ***reduplication***)水波起伏的样子 rippling; undulating ❷安静 tranquil; quiet: 恬～ *peaceful; serene; tranquil*

㊁ tán 见 728 页 see p728

DANG ㄉㄤ

当(當、❼噹) ㊀ dāng ㄉㄤ ❶充，担任 to work as; to serve as: 开会～主席 *to act as the chairman of the conference* | 人民～了主人。*The people have become masters of the country.* ㊂***extension*** 承担 to undertake: 好汉做事好汉～。*A true man has the courage to accept the consequences of his own deeds.* [当选] 选举时被选上 to be elected; to win an election: 他～～为人民代表。*He was elected a representative of the people.* ❷掌管，主持 to run; to be in charge of: ～家 *to run a household* | ～权 *to be in power* | ～局 *the authorities* ❸介词 ***preposition***，正在那时候或那地方 at the time or place: ～学习的时候，不要做别的事。*Do not do anything else when you are studying.* | ～胸就是一拳 *to punch sb in the chest* | ～面说清 *to make clear face to face* | ～初 *originally; at the outset* [当即]立刻 immediately: ～～散会 *to end the meeting at once* [当年][当日]从前 at that time: 想～～我离家的时候，这里还没有火车。*When I left home, trains were still unavailable here.* (另 dàng—，见"当"dàng see also 当 dàng for dàng—) [当前]目前，眼下，现阶段 present; current: ～～任务 *current task* [当下]马上，立刻 at once; immediately: ～～就去 *to go at once* ❹相当，相称(chèn)，相配 to equal; to match: 旗鼓相～ *well-matched; well-matched in strength* | 门～户对 *well-matched in social and economic status* ❺应当，应该 ought to; should: ～办就办。*Do at once whatever ought to be done.* | 不～问的不问。*Do not ask what you should not ask.* ❻顶端，头 tip; top; end: 瓜～(瓜蒂) *the base of a melon* | 瓦～(屋檐顶端的盖瓦头，俗叫"猫头")(popularly called 猫头) *tile end; eaves tile* ❼拟声词 ***onomatopoeia***，撞击金属器物的声音 clanking; clanging: 小锣敲得～～响。*The clang*

of the small gong is resounding.［当啷］(— lāng) 拟声词 ***onomatopoeia***,摇铃或其他金属器物撞击的声音 clanking; clanging:～～～～,上课铃响了。*The bell rang* (or *clanged*) *for class*.
［当心］留心,小心 to take care; to be careful; to watch out

㊁ dàng 见 130 页 see p130

珰(璫) dāng ㄉㄤ ❶妇女戴在耳垂上的装饰品 earing; eardrop ❷汉代武职宦官帽子上的装饰品。后来借指宦官(adornment on military eunuchs' hats in the Han Dynasty) eunuch

铛(鐺) ㊀ dāng ㄉㄤ 同"当㊀❼" same as 当㊀❼

㊁ chēng 见 84 页 see p84

裆(襠) dāng ㄉㄤ 裤裆,两裤腿相连的地方(of trousers) crotch; crutch: 横～ *transverse crotch* | 直～ *straight crotch* | 开～裤 *open-seat pants* (图见 882 页"衣" picture on p882) [引] ***extension*** 两腿相连的地方(of the human body) crotch

筜(簹) dāng ㄉㄤ 见 932 页"筼"字条"筼筜" (yún—) see 筼筜 on p932

挡(擋、*攩) ㊀ dǎng ㄉㄤˇ ❶阻拦,遮蔽 to keep off; to ward off ([连] ***doublet*** 阻— to block; to obstruct | 拦— to hold back; to bar): 水来土～ *to stem the flow of water with earth* | 把风～住 *to keep off the wind* | 拿芭蕉扇～着太阳 *to shut out the sun with a palm-leaf fan* ❷(—子、—儿) 用来遮蔽的东西 blind; fender: 炉～ *fire screen*; *grate* | 窗户～儿 *window blind* (or *shade*)

㊁ dàng 见 131 页 see p131

党(黨) dǎng ㄉㄤˇ ❶政党 political party 在我国特指中国共产党 (in China) the Chinese Communist Party ❷由私人利害关系结成的集团 clique; clan; gang: 死～ *sworn followers* | 结～营私 *to gang up for selfish interests* ［党羽］附从的人(指帮同作恶的) members of a gang; henchmen ❸偏袒 to be partial to; to take sides with: ～同伐异 *to shield those who agree and attack those who differ* ❹旧时指亲族(in former times) kinfolk; relative: 父～ *father's kinfolk* | 母～ *mother's kinfolk* | 妻～ *wife's relatives* (or *kinfolk*)

谠(讜) dǎng ㄉㄤˇ 正直的(言论)(of opinions) upright; unbiased: ～言 *impartial remarks* | ～论 *unbiased comments*

当(當) ㊁ dàng ㄉㄤˋ ❶恰当,合宜 appropriate; proper: 处理得～ *to handle properly* | 用词不～ *inappropriate wording* | 妥～的办法 *appropriate method* | 适～的休息 *adequate rest* ❷抵得上,等于 equal; match: 一个人～俩人用。*One can do the work of*

two people. ❸当作,作为 to regard as; to take for:安步～车 *to walk rather than ride* | 不要把他～外人。*Don't treat him as an outsider.* ㊞ ***extension*** 认为 think:你～我不知道吗?*Do you think I don't know it?* ❹表示在同一时间 that very (day, year, etc):他～天就走了。*He left that very day.* [当年]本年,在同一年 that very year; the same year:～～种,～～收。*We can harvest the crops we have planted the same year.* | ～～受益 *to benefit in the same year* (另 dāng—,见"当"dāng see also 当 dāng for dāng—) [当日]本日,在同一天 that very day; the same day:～～的火车票 *that day's train ticket* (另 dāng—,见"当"dāng see also 当 dāng for dāng—) ❺用实物作抵押向当铺借钱 to pawn ❻押在当铺里的实物 pledge

[上当]吃亏,受骗 to be taken in; to be fooled

㊀ dāng 见 129 页 see p129

垱(壋) dàng ㄉㄤˋ 〈方 ***dialect***〉为便于灌溉而筑的小土堤 irrigation dyke

挡(擋) ㊁ dàng ㄉㄤˋ [摒挡](bìng—)收拾,料理 to arrange; to put in order

㊀ dǎng 见 130 页 see p130

档(檔) dàng ㄉㄤˋ ❶存放案卷用的带格子的橱架 shelf; pigeon hole:归～*to file a document* ❷档案,分类保存的文件、材料等 files; records; archives:查～*to consult the records* ❸等级 grade; class:～次 *grade* | 高～商品 *merchandise of high quality; high-grade goods* ❹(—子、—儿)量词 ***quantifier***,件,桩 piece:一～子事 *the same thing (as)*

凼(**氹) dàng ㄉㄤˋ 〈方 ***dialect***〉塘,水坑 pond; pool:水～*waterpool* | ～肥 *wet compost*

砀(碭) dàng ㄉㄤˋ [砀山]地名,在安徽省 Dangshan, a place in Anhui Province

荡(蕩、❶-❸*盪) dàng ㄉㄤˋ ❶清除,弄光 to clear away; to sweep off:倾家～产 *to lose all the family fortune* ❷洗涤 to rinse; to wash away:涤～*to cleanse; to rinse* ❸摇动 to sway; to swing (㊇ ***doublet*** 摇— to sway):～舟 *to row a boat* | ～秋千 *to play on the swing* [荡漾](—yàng)水波一起一伏地动 rippling; undulating ❹不受约束或行为不检点 to loaf about; debauched (㊇ ***doublet*** 浪— to loiter about; to idle about; to loaf about | 放—debauched; licentious) ❺浅水湖 shallow lake; marsh:芦花～*reed marshes* | 黄天～*Huangtian Marshes*

宕 dàng ㄉㄤˋ 延迟,拖延 to delay:延～*to delay*

菪 dàng ㄉㄤˋ 见 418 页"莨"字条"莨菪"(làng—) see 莨菪 on p418

DAO ㄉㄠ

刀 dāo ㄉㄠ ❶(一子、一儿)用来切、割、斩、削、刺的工具 cutting tool; knife: 镰～*sickle* | 菜～*kitchen knife* | 刺～*bayonet* | 旋～*cutting tool of a turning lathe* | 铅笔～儿 *pencil sharpener* ❷量词 **quantifier**,纸张单位,通常为 100 张 unit of paper (=100 sheets of paper) ❸古代的一种钱币(in ancient China) knife-shaped coin

叨 ㊁ dāo ㄉㄠ [叨叨](—dao)话多 to chatter away [叨唠](—lao)翻来覆去地说 to chatter away; to babble

㊀ tāo 见 733 页 see p733

忉 dāo ㄉㄠ [忉忉]忧愁,焦虑 worried; anxious

鱽 dāo ㄉㄠ 鱽鱼(现多写作"刀鱼")(now usually written as 刀鱼) **1** 我国北方也称带鱼为刀鱼,体长而侧扁,银白色,无鳞,牙齿发达,肉可吃(also called 带鱼 in the north) hairtail **2** 就是刀鲚(jì),平时生活在海里,产卵时进入长江下游(i.e.刀鲚) coilia ectenes

氘 dāo ㄉㄠ 氢的同位素之一,符号 D,质量数 2,用于热核反应 deuterium (D)

捯 dáo ㄉㄠˊ 两手不住倒换着拉回线、绳子等 to pull thread or string with allernating hands: 把风筝～下来 *to reel the kite in* ㊂ **extension** 追溯,追究原因 to look into; to investigate: 这件事到今天还没～出头儿来呢。*To this day, we still haven't found a clue to the mystery.*

[捯饬](—chi)〈方 **dialect**〉打扮,修饰 to dress up; to decorate

导(導) dǎo ㄉㄠˇ ❶指引,带领 to lead; to guide: 领～*leader* | ～游 *tour guide* | ～航 *navigation; pilot* ㊂ **extension** 指教,教诲 to instruct; to teach: 开～*to enlighten; to give guidance to* | 教～*to teach; to instruct* | 劝～*to advise* [导言]绪论 introduction [导演]指导排演戏剧或指导拍摄电影,也指担任这种工作的人 director ❷疏导 to dredge: ～管 *catheter; conduit; vessel* | ～尿 *catheterization* | ～淮入海 *to channel the Huaihe River into the sea* ❸传导 to conduct; to transmit: ～热 *to transmit heat* | ～电 *to conduct electricity* | ～体 *conductor*

岛(島) dǎo ㄉㄠˇ 海洋或湖泊里四面被水围着的陆地叫岛。三面被水围着的陆地叫半岛 island(半岛 peninsula)

捣(搗、*擣) dǎo ㄉㄠˇ ❶砸,舂,捶打 to crush; to smash; to pound: ～蒜 *to pound garlic* | ～米 *to husk rice* | ～衣 *to beat clothes in washing* ㊂ **extension** 冲,攻打 to charge; to assault: 直～敌巢 *to make a swift assault on the enemy camp* ❷搅扰 to disturb; to harass: ～乱 *to dis-*

turb; to make trouble | ～鬼 *to play tricks*

倒 ㊀ dǎo ㄉㄠˇ ❶竖立的东西躺下来 to fall over; to topple; to tumble: 墙～了。*The wall tumbled down.* | 摔～ *to fall over* ㊂ ***extension*** 指工商业因亏累而关门 to close down; to go bankrupt: ～闭 *to go bankrupt; to close down* [倒霉](*倒楣)事情不顺利,受挫折 to have bad luck; to be out of luck ❷转移,更换 to shift; to exchange: ～手 *to change hands* | ～车 *to transfer from one vehicle to another* | ～换 *to rotate; to take turns; to exchange* ❸倒买倒卖,进行投机活动 to speculate; to profiteer: ～汇 *to speculate in foreign currencies* | ～邮票 *to speculate in stamps* ❹指食欲变得不好 to spoil (one's appetite): 老吃白菜,真～胃口。*Too much Chinese cabbage spoils my appetite.*

㊁ dào 见 133 页 see p133

祷(禱) dǎo ㄉㄠˇ 教徒或迷信的人向天、神求助 to pray for help: 祈～ *to pray* 敬辞 ***polite***(书信用语 used in correspondence): 为～ *to pray for your answer* | 盼～ *to hope earnestly*

蹈 dǎo ㄉㄠˇ ❶踩,践踏 to tread; to step: ～白刃而不顾(喻不顾危险) *to take no notice of danger* | 赴汤～火 *to go through fire and water — to defy all difficulties and dangers* ㊂ ***extension*** 实行,遵循 to adopt; to follow: 循规～矩 *to observe rules and conventions* ❷跳动 to jump: 手舞足～ *to dance for joy*

到 dào ㄉㄠˋ ❶达到,到达 to reach; to arrive: ～北京 *to arrive in Beijing* | ～十二点 *up to 12 o'clock* | 不～两万人 *no more than 20,000 people* | 坚持～底 *to stick out; to carry through; to hold on to the last* (or *end*) [到处]处处,不论哪里 everywhere; anywhere ❷往 to go to; to leave for: ～祖国最需要的地方去。*Go to the places where our motherland needs us the most.* ❸周到,全顾得着 considerate; thoughtful: 有不～的地方请原谅。*Please excuse me if I have been inconsiderate in any way.* ❹表示动作的效果(used as a verb complement to show the result of an action): 办得～ *to be able to do* | 做不～ *to be unable to do* | 达～先进水平 *to reach an advanced level*

倒 ㊁ dào ㄉㄠˋ ❶上下或前后颠倒 inverted; reverse; upside down: 这面镜子挂～了。*The mirror hangs upside down.* | 把那几本书～过来 *to turn over those books* | ～数第一 *the last one* [倒粪]把堆着的粪来回翻动弄碎 to turn over a heap of manure repeatedly to smash it ❷把容器反转或倾斜使里面的东西出来 to pour: ～茶 *to pour tea* | ～水 *to pour*

D

water ❸向后，往回退 to move backwards：～退 *to go backwards；to retrograde*｜～车（车向后退）*to back a car* ❹副词 **adverb**，反而，却，相反 but；yet；on the contrary：这～好了。*On the contrary，that's great.*｜跑了一天，～不觉得累。*I don't feel tired at all though I have run about for a whole day.*

D

㊀ dǎo 见 133 页 see p133

帱（幬）㊁ dào ㄉㄠˋ 覆盖 to cover

㊀ chóu 见 94 页 see p94

焘（燾）dào ㄉㄠˋ tāo ㄊㄠ（又 also tāo）覆盖 to cover

盗 dào ㄉㄠˋ ❶偷 to steal（[连] **doublet** 一窃 to steal）：～卖 *to steal and sell*｜～取 *to steal*｜掩耳～铃 *to plug one's ears while stealing a bell — to deceive oneself* [引] **extension** 用不正当的方法谋得 to embezzle；to usurp：欺世～名 *to win popularity by deception*［盗版］未经版权所有者同意，大量偷录或偷印，非法牟利 copyright piracy；piracy［盗汗］因病在睡眠时出汗 night sweat：患肺病的人常常夜间～～。*People with lung diseases often have night sweats.* ❷偷窃或抢劫财物的人 thief（[连] **doublet** 一贼 robber）：强～*robber；burgler*｜海～*pirate*

悼 dào ㄉㄠˋ 悲伤，哀念 to mourn（for）；to grieve over（sb's death）（[连] **doublet** 哀一 to mourn；to grieve）：追～（追念死者）*to mourn*

道 dào ㄉㄠˋ ❶（一儿）路 road；way；path（[连] **doublet** 一路 road；way）：火车～*railway*｜水～*water course* ❷方向，途径 orientation；way：志同～合 *to share the same orientation and aspirations；to have a common goal* ❸道理，正当的事理 principle；justice：无～*unprincipled*｜治世不一～。*There are various ways to run a state.*［道具］佛家修道用的物品 things used by Buddhists when practicing self-cultivation [转] **transfer** 演剧等用的一切设备和用具 stage property；prop ❹（一儿）方法，办法，技术 way；method；technique：门～*knack*｜医～*medical expertise；medical skill*｜照他的～儿办。*Follow his practice.* ❺道家，我国古代的一个思想流派，以老聃和庄周为代表（an ideological system in ancient China with Laodan and Zhuangzhou as the representatives）Taoist school；Taoists ❻道教，我国主要宗教之一，创立于东汉（one of the chief religions in China founded in the Eastern Han Dynasty）Taoism：～观（guàn）（道教的庙）*Taoist temple* ❼指某些迷信组织 certain superstitious sects：一贯～ *Yiguandao，a secret society*｜会～门 *superstitious sects and secret societies* ❽说 to speak：说长～短 *to gos-*

sip｜一语～破 *to lay bare the truth with one penetrating remark; to hit the nail on the head*｜常言～*as the saying goes* ㊂ ***extension*** 用话表示情意 to express; to extend：～贺 *to congratulate*｜～谢 *to thank*｜～歉 *to apologize*｜～喜 *to congratulate on a happy occasion* ❾历史上的行政区域 administrative division in history **1** 唐太宗时分全国为十道 *dao*, an administrative division of the country used during the regime of Emperor Taizong of the Tang Dynasty when the country was divided into ten *daos* **2** 清代和民国初年每省分成几个道 *dao*, an administrative division under a province in the Qing Dynasty and in the early years of the Republic of China ❿(一子、一儿)线条 line：红～儿 *red line*｜铅笔～儿 *pencil line* ⓫量词 ***quantifier*** **1** 用于长条状的(for long and narrow things)：一～河 *a river*｜画一～红线 *to draw a red line* **2** 用于路上的关口，出入口(used for pass, exit and entrance)：两～门 *two entrances*｜过一～关 *to pass a barrier* **3** 则，条(for orders, questions, etc)：三～题 *three questions*｜一～命令 *an order* **4** 次(for number of times or layers)：洗了三～*to have washed three times*

稻 dào ㄉㄠˋ (一子)一种谷类植物，有水稻、旱稻之分，通常指水稻。子实椭圆形，有硬壳，去壳后就是大米 paddy; rice

纛 dào ㄉㄠˋ 古代军队里的大旗(in ancient China) big army banner

DE ㄉㄜ

嘚 dē ㄉㄜ 拟声词 ***onomatopoeia***，马蹄踏地声 clatter of horses [嘚啵](—bo)〈方 ***dialect***〉唠叨 to chatter：别瞎～～了，赶紧干活儿吧。*Shut up! Go on with your work!*

得 ㊀ dé ㄉㄜˊ ❶得到 to get; to obtain(㊃ ***doublet*** 获一 to acquire; to attain; to achieve)：大～人心 *to win popular sympathy*｜～奖 *to win a prize*｜～胜 *to triumph; to succeed* ㊂ ***extension*** 遇到 to have; to get：～空(kòng) *to have leisure; to be free (with time)*｜～便 *when it's convenient; at one's convenience* ❷适合 fit; proper：～当(dàng) *proper; suitable*｜～法 *to work in the proper way; to be properly managed; to get the knack*｜～手(顺利) *to go smoothly; to do fine*｜～劲 *to feel well* ❸得意，满意 satisfied; pleased：扬扬自～*complacent* ❹完成 to finish：衣服做～了。*The coat is done.*｜饭～了。*Dinner is ready.* ❺用于某种语气(used for certain tones) **1** 表示禁止(used to express no)：～了，别说了。*That's enough. Let it go at that.* **2** 表示同意(used to express approval):～,就这么办。*All right, let's do it this way.* **3** 表示无可奈何(used to express helplessness):～,今天又迟到了。*Oh, dear! Late again!* ❻可以,许可 to permit; to allow:不～随地吐痰。*No spitting!* | 正式代表均～参加表决。*Every full representative should take part in the vote.*

㊁ děi 见 137 页 see p137

㊂ de 见 136 页 see p136

D

锝 dé ㄉㄜˊ 一种放射性元素,符号 Tc,是第一种人工制成的元素 technetium (Tc)

德(*悳) dé ㄉㄜˊ ❶好的品行 virtue:～才兼备 *virtuous and talented* ❷道德,人们共同生活及其行为的准则、规范 morality:公～ *public morality* ❸信念 mind; heart:同心同～ *to be of one heart and one mind; to be dedicated to the same cause* ❹恩惠 favour:感恩戴～ *to be deeply grateful; to be overwhelmed with gratitude* ❺指德国 Germany

[德昂族]原名"崩龙族",我国少数民族,参看附表(see the appendix) the De'ang ethnic group, originally named 崩龙族, one of the ethnic minorities of China

地 ㊁ de ·ㄉㄜ 助词 ***auxiliary***,用在状语后,主要修饰动词、形容词(used after an adverbial mainly modifying verbs and adjectives):胜利～完成任务 *to carry out the task successfully* | 天色渐渐～黑了。*It's getting dark.*

㊀ dì 见 142 页 see p142

的 ㊂ de ·ㄉㄜ 助词 ***auxiliary*** ❶用在定语后(used after an attributive) **1** 主要修饰名词(used mainly to modify nouns):美丽～风光 *beautiful scenery* | 宏伟～建筑 *grand building* | 光荣而艰巨～任务 *honourable but hard task* **2** 表示所属的关系,旧时也写作"底"(used to denote a possessive relation, also written as 底 in former times):我～书 *my book* | 社会～性质 *the nature of the society* ❷用在词或词组后,表示人或事物(used after a word or a phrase to denote someone or something):吃～ *something to eat* | 穿～ *something to wear* | 红～ *the red* | 卖菜～ *one who sells vegetables* ❸用在句末,表示肯定的语气,常跟"是"相应(used at the end of a sentence to denote an affirmative tone, and usually used correspondingly with 是):他是刚从北京来～。*He's just come from Beijing.*

㊀ dì 见 143 页 see p143

㊁ dí 见 140 页 see p140

底 ㊁ de ·ㄉㄜ 助词 ***auxiliary***,同"的㊂❶**2**" same as 的㊂❶**2**

㊀ dǐ 见 141 页 see p141

得 ㊂ de ·ㄉㄜ 助词 ***auxiliary*** ❶在动词后表可能(used after a verb denoting possibility) **1** 再接别的词(followed by other words):冲～出去。*It's*

quite possible to break out from here. | 拿～起来 *to have the ability to do (sth); to be able to lift (sth)* **2** 不再接别的词(followed with no words):要～*all right* | 要不～*no* | 说不～*unspeakable; unmentionable* ❷用在动词或形容词后连接表结果或程度的补语(used after a verb or adjective to link to a complement denoting the result or degree):跑～快 *to run fast* | 急～满脸通红 *to blush with anxiety* | 香～很 *very sweet-smelling*

㊀ dé 见 135 页 see p135

㊁ děi 见 137 页 see p137

脦 de·ㄉㄜ te·ㄊㄜ (又 **also** te) 见 421 页"肋"字条"肋脦"(lē—) see 肋脦 on p421

DEI ㄉㄟ

得 ㊁ děi ㄉㄟ ❶必须,需要 must; have to:你～用功。*You must study hard.* | 这活儿～三个人才能完成。*Three people are needed to finish the job.* | 那事～你去做。*You are to do the job.* ❷会,估计必然如此 to be sure to:时间不早了,要不快走,就～迟到。*Time is running out. If we don't hurry, we'll be late.* ❸〈方 **dialect**〉满意,高兴,舒适 satisfied; contented:挺～*quite satisfied*

㊀ dé 见 135 页 see p135

㊂ de 见 136 页 see p136

DEN ㄉㄣ

扽(**撜) dèn ㄉㄣ 用力拉 to tug:把绳子～一～*to give a tug to the rope* | ～线 *to tighten the thread*

DENG ㄉㄥ

灯(燈) dēng ㄉㄥ 照明或利用光线达到某种目的的器具 light; lamp; lantern:电～*electric light* | 路～*street lamp* | 探照～*searchlight* | ～箱广告 *illuminated advertisement*

登 dēng ㄉㄥ ❶上,升 to mount; to ascend:～山 *mountaineering; mountain climbing* | ～高 *to ascend a height* | ～峰造极(喻达到顶峰) *to reach the peak of perfection; to reach the acme of perfection* ❷踩,践踏,也作"蹬"(also written as 蹬) to tread; to step:～在凳子上 *to step on a stool* ㊁ ***extension*** 脚向下用力 to pedal:～三轮车 *to pedal a tricycle* | ～水车 *to pedal a waterwheel* ❸刊载,记载 to publish; to record; to carry:～报 *to publish in a newspaper* | 把这几项～在簿子上 *to record these items in the registry* [登记]为了特定的目的,向主管机关按表填写事项 to register; to check in; to enter one's name:～～买票 *to book a ticket* ❹(谷物 of corn)成熟 ripen:五谷丰～*bumper*

harvest; abundant harvest of all crops
[登时]即时，立刻 at once; immediately

噔 dēng ㄉㄥ 拟声词 ***onomatopoeia***，重东西落地或撞击物体的响声 thumping; thudding

簦 dēng ㄉㄥ 古代有柄的笠，类似现在的雨伞 (in ancient China) bamboo or straw hat with a conical crown, broad rim serving also the same function as a modern parasol or umbrella

蹬 ㊀ dēng ㄉㄥ 同"登❷" same as 登❷
㊁ dèng 见 139 页 see p139

等 děng ㄉㄥˇ ❶数量一般大，地位或程度一般高 equal: 相～ *equal*｜一加二～于三。*One plus two is three.*｜男女权利平～。*Men and women are endowed with equal rights.*[等闲]平常 ordinary ㊉ ***figurative*** 轻易地，不在乎地 easily; casually: 莫作～～看！*Don't look down on him!* ❷级位，程度的分别 rank (㊊ ***doublet*** 一级 rank; grade): 立了一～功 *to win a first class merit citation*｜特～英雄 *special-class hero*｜何～快乐！*How happy I am!* ❸类，群 kind; group **1** 表示多数 (used to denote a plural number of people): 我～ *we*｜你～ *you*｜彼～*they; the others* (*usually referring to those who are opposed*) **2** 列举后煞尾(used to denote the end of an enumeration): 北京、天津、武汉、上海、广州～五大城市 *the five major cities — Beijing, Tianjin, Wuhan, Shanghai and Guangzhou* **3** 表示列举未完(叠 ***reduplication***) (used to denote an unfinished enumeration) and so on; and so forth; etc: 张同志、王同志～五人 *five comrades including Zhang and Wang*｜煤、铁～～都很丰富 *rich in coal, iron and so on* ❹待，候 to wait (㊊ ***doublet*** 一待 to wait; to await｜一候 to wait; to await): ～一下再说。*Let's wait and see.*｜～不得。*It can't wait.* ❺同"戥" same as 戥

戥 děng ㄉㄥˇ ❶(一子)一种小型的秤，用来称金、银、药品等分量小的东西 small steelyard for weighing gold, silver, medicine, etc ❷用戥子称 to weigh with a small steelyard: 把这包药～一～。*Weigh this package of medicine.*

邓(鄧) dèng ㄉㄥˋ 邓州，地名，在河南省 Dengzhou, a place in Henan Province

僜 dèng ㄉㄥˋ 僜人，住在我国西藏自治区察隅一带 Deng, people living near Chayu in the Tibet Autonomous Region

凳(*櫈) dèng ㄉㄥˋ (一子、一儿)有腿没有靠背的坐具 stool; bench: 板～ *wooden bench; wooden stool*｜小～儿 *small stool*

嶝 dèng ㄉㄥˋ 山上可攀登的小路 hill path

澄 ㊁ dèng ㄉㄥˋ 让液体里的杂质沉下去 to settle; to become clear: 水～清了再喝。*Settle the water before drinking.*

㊀ chéng 见 87 页 see p87

磴 dèng ㄉㄥˋ ❶石头台阶 stone step ❷量词 ***quantifier***, 用于台阶或楼梯的层级 (used to refer to the number of steps, stairs, etc)

瞪 dèng ㄉㄥˋ 睁大眼睛 to open one's eyes wide: 把眼一～*to give sb a stare* | 你～着我做什么? *Why are you staring at me?* | ～眼 *to stare; to glare*

镫 dèng ㄉㄥˋ 挂在马鞍子两旁的东西, 是为骑马的人放脚用的 stirrup

〈古 ***archaism***〉又同"灯"(dēng) also same as 灯

蹬 ㊁dèng ㄉㄥˋ 见 69 页"蹭"字条"蹭蹬"(cèng—) see 蹭蹬 on p69

㊀ dēng 见 138 页 see p138

DI ㄉㄧ

氐 ㊁ dī ㄉㄧ ❶我国古代西部的少数民族名 Di, an ethnic minority in the west of ancient China ❷星宿名, 二十八宿之一 *di*, the 3rd of the 28 constellations

㊀ dǐ 见 141 页 see p141

低 dī ㄉㄧ ❶跟"高"相对(the opposite of 高) **1** 矮 low; short: 这房子太～。*The house is too low.* | 弟弟比哥哥～一头。*He's a head shorter than his elder brother.* **2** 地势洼下 low-lying: ～地 *lowlands* **3** 声音细小 low in voice: ～声讲话 *to speak in a low voice* **4** 程度差 low in degree: ～能 *mentally deficient; feeble-minded* | 眼高手～*to have grandiose aims but puny abilities; to be fastidious but incompetent* | 政治水平～*low in political consciousness* **5** 等级在下的 low in grade: ～年级学生 *students of lower grades* ❷俯, 头向下垂 to droop: ～头 *to lower one's head*

羝 dī ㄉㄧ 公羊 ram; billy goat

堤(*隄) dī ㄉㄧ 用土、石等材料修筑的挡水的高岸 embankment: 河～*river embankment* | 修～*to build dykes* [堤防]堤 dyke; embankment

提 ㊁ dī ㄉㄧ [提防](—fang) 小心防备 to be on one's guard against [提溜](—liu)手提(tí) to carry in the hand; to hold in one's hand

㊀ tí 见 739 页 see p739

鞮 dī ㄉㄧ 古代的一种皮鞋(in ancient China) leather shoe

䃅(磾) dī ㄉㄧ 用于人名。金日䃅, 汉代人 di, used in a given name, such as Jin Ridi, a person in the Han Dynasty

滴 dī ㄉㄧ ❶落下的少量液体 to drop: 汗～*bead of sweat* | 水～*drop of water* [点滴]零星, 少 a bit ❷液体一点一点地落下, 使液体一点一点

地落下 to drip：汗水直往下～。*Sweat kept dripping down.* | ～眼药 *to put eyedrops in one's eyes* [滴沥](—lì)拟声词 ***onomatopoeia***，雨水下滴的声音 pattering
[滴溜](—liū) **1** 滚圆的样子 perfectly round：～～圆 *perfectly round* **2** 形容很快地旋转 to turn very quickly：～～转 *to spin fast*

D

镝 ㊀ dī ㄉㄧ 一种金属元素，符号 Dy，用于原子能工业等 dysprosium (Dy)
㊁ dí 见 141 页 see p141

奀 ㊁ dí ㄉㄧˊ 〈方 ***dialect***〉小 small
㊀ ēn 见 175 页 see p175

狄 dí ㄉㄧˊ 我国古代对北部少数民族的统称 Di, a general term for the northern ethnic minorities in ancient China

荻 dí ㄉㄧˊ 多年生草本植物，生长在水边，叶子长形，跟芦苇相似，秋天开紫花 Amur silvergrass (*Miscanthus sacchariflorus*)

迪 dí ㄉㄧˊ 开导 to enlighten (㊃ ***doublet*** 启— to enlighten)

笛 dí ㄉㄧˊ (—子、—儿)管乐器名，通常是竹制的，有八孔，横着吹 (bamboo) flute ㊅ ***extension*** 响声尖锐的发音器 whistle：汽～ *hooter; steam whistle* | 警～ *siren*

的 ㊁ dí ㄉㄧˊ 真实，实在 truly; really：～当(dàng) *proper; appropriate* | ～确如此 *indeed; really*
㊀ dì 见 143 页 see p143
㊂ de 见 136 页 see p136

籴(糴) dí ㄉㄧˊ 买粮食 to buy (grain)：～米 *to buy rice*

敌(敵) dí ㄉㄧˊ ❶敌人 enemy; foe：划清～我界限 *to make a clear distinction between friend and foe* ❷相当 to match; to equal：势均力～ *to match in strength* ❸抵挡 to fight against：军民团结如一人，试看天下谁能～。*Who in the world can match them when the army and the people are united as one?*

涤(滌) dí ㄉㄧˊ 洗 to wash (㊃ ***doublet*** 洗— to wash)：～除旧习 *to do away with old habits*

觌(覿) dí ㄉㄧˊ 相见 to meet：～面 *to meet*

髢 dí ㄉㄧˊ (旧读 formerly dì) 假头发(叠 ***reduplication***) wig

嘀(**啾) dí ㄉㄧˊ [嘀咕](—gu) **1** 小声说私话 to whisper：他们俩～～什么呢？*What are those two whispering?* **2** 心中不安，犹疑不定 unsettled：拿定主意别犯～～。*Don't hesitate! Make up your mind!*

嫡 dí ㄉㄧˊ ❶封建宗法制度中称正妻 legal wife, as distinguished from a concubine under the feudal-patriarchal system ㊅ ***extension*** 正妻所生的

born of the legal wife：～子 *son born of the legal wife* | ～嗣 *eldest son born of the legal wife* ❷亲的，血统最近的 of lineal descent；closely related：～亲哥哥 *elder blood brother* | ～堂兄弟 *paternal male cousins* ㊀ **extension** 系统最近的 orthodox；authentic：～系 *direct line of descent*

镝 ㊀ dí ㄉㄧˊ 箭头 arrowhead：锋～ *swords and arrows* | 鸣～(响箭) *whistling arrow*

㊁ dī 见 140 页 see p140

蹢 ㊀ dí ㄉㄧˊ 〈古 **archaism**〉蹄子 hoof

㊁ zhí 见 979 页 see p979

翟 ㊀ dí ㄉㄧˊ ❶长尾山雉 pheasant ❷古代哲学家墨子名翟 Di，given name of Mozi，ancient Chinese philosopher

㊁ zhái 见 951 页 see p951

氐 ㊀ dǐ ㄉㄧˇ 根本 foundation；base

㊁ dī 见 139 页 see p139

邸 dǐ ㄉㄧˇ 高级官员的住所，现多用于外交场合 residence of a high official，now often used on diplomatic occasions：官～ *official residence*

诋 dǐ ㄉㄧˇ 毁谤 to slander (㊀ **doublet** 一毁 to defame)：丑～(辱骂) *to insult；to abuse*

坻 ㊁ dǐ ㄉㄧˇ 山坡 mountain slope

［宝坻］地名，在天津市 Baodi，a place in Tianjin

㊀ chí 见 89 页 see p89

抵(❷*牴、❷*觝) dǐ ㄉㄧˇ ❶挡，拒，用力支撑着 to support；to prop；to sustain (㊀ **doublet** 一挡 to withstand)：～挡一阵 *to withstand for a time* | ～住门，别让风刮开。*Prop something against the door so that it won't get blown open by the wind.* ［抵制］抵抗，阻止，不让侵入 to boycott；to resist ❷牛、羊等有角的兽用角顶、触 (of animals with horns such as bulls or sheep) to butt ［抵触］发生冲突 conflict；contravene：他的话前后～～。*What he said was self-contradicting.* ❸顶，相当 equal：～债 *to pay a debt in kind or by labour* | ～押 *mortgage* | 一个～俩。*One can do the work of two.* ［抵偿］用价值相等的事物作为赔偿或补偿 to compensate for；to make up for ❹到达 to arrive：～京 *to arrive in Beijing* ❺抵消 to offset；to counteract：收支相～ *to make both ends meet*

［大抵］大略，大概 approximately；more or less：～～是这样，详细情况我说不清。*That's the case on the whole. I'm not very clear about the details myself.*

底 ㊀ dǐ ㄉㄧˇ ❶(一子、一儿)最下面的部分 bottom：锅～ *bottom of a pot* | 鞋～儿 *sole of a shoe* | 海～ *bottom of the sea* ㊀ **extension** 末了 end：月～ *end of a month* | 年～ *end of a year* ❷(一子、一儿)根基，基础，留作根据的 base；basis；

foundation:～稿 *draft; manuscript*|～账 *original accounts; record-copy of an account book*|刨(páo)根问～ *to get to the root of something*|那文件要留个～儿 *to keep a copy of the document on file* [底细]内情,详情,事件的根底 ins and outs; detail ❸(一儿)图案的底子 background of patterns:白～儿红花碗 *a white bowl with red flowers on it* ❹达到 to end up with; to come to:终～于成 *to succeed in the end* ❺何,什么 what; which:～事 *What?*|～处 *Where?*

㊁ de 见 136 页 see p136

柢 dǐ ㄉㄧˇ 树木的根 root ([连] ***doublet*** 根－ root):根深～固 *deep-rooted*

砥 dǐ ㄉㄧˇ (旧又读 formerly zhǐ)细的磨刀石 fine whetstone [砥砺]磨炼 to temper:～～意志 *to temper one's will*

骶 dǐ ㄉㄧˇ 腰部下面尾骨上面的部分 sacrum (图见 241 页"骨" picture on p241)

地 ㊀ dì ㄉㄧˋ ❶地球,太阳系九大行星之一,人类居住的星球 the earth:天～ *heaven and earth; sphere (or field) of activity*|～心 *earth's core*|～层 *stratum* [引] ***extension*** **1** 指土地、地面 land; land surface:～大物博 *vast territory and abundant natural resources*|草～ *lawn; grassland; meadow*|两亩～ *two* mu *of land* **2** 指某一地区,地点 place; area; location:此～ *this area*|华东各～ *all over the eastern China*|目的～ *destination* **3** 指路程,用在里数或站数后(used after the number of stops or *li*) distance:三十里～ *distance of 30* li|两站～ distance between three stops; distance of two stops [地道] **1** 地下挖成的隧道 tunnel:～～战 *tunnel warfare* **2** (－dao)有名产地出产的,也说"道地"(also called 道地) genuine; authentic:～～药材 *genuine (medicinal) herb* [转] ***transfer*** 真正的,纯粹 pure; genuine:一口～～北京话 *to speak a pure Beijing dialect* [地方] **1** 各省、市、县,对全国和中央说 local government; local administration:～～各级人民代表大会 *local People's Congress at various levels*|～～服从中央。*Local authorities should obey the central government.* **2** (－fang) 区域 space; place:飞机在什么～～飞? *Where is the plane flying?*|那～～出高粱。*That place produces Chinese sorghum.* **3** (－fang)点,部分 point; part:他这话有的～～很对。*Part of what he said is right.* [地位]人在社会关系中所处的位置 status [地下] **1** 地面下,土里 underground; subterranean:～～铁道 *(the) underground; subway; tube* [喻] ***figurative*** 秘密的,不公开的 secret; underground:～～工作 *underground work* **2** (－xia)地面上 on the ground:掉在～～了 *to drop to* *the ground* ❷表示思想活动的领域 insight; mind: 见～ *insight; judgement* | 心～ *heart; character* ❸底子 ground (㊀ **doublet** 质— texture; ground; background): 蓝～白花布 *a piece of blue cloth with white flowers*

㊁ de 见136页 see p136

弟 dì ㄉㄧˋ ❶同父母的比自己年纪小的男子(叠 ***reduplication***) younger brother [弟兄] (—xiong) **1** 包括所有的兄和弟 brothers (口语里跟"兄弟(dì)"有分别,"兄弟(dì)"专指弟弟) (different from 兄弟 which means younger brother in spoken Chinese): 我们～～三个 *we three brothers* **2** 同辈共事的朋友间亲热的称呼 (used to denote an intimate address between colleagues of the same generation) brother ❷称同辈比自己年纪小的男性 (used to address a younger man of the same generation) brother: 小～～ *little brother* | 师～ *junior male fellow apprentice* [弟子]学生对老师自称或别人指称 disciple; pupil ❸古同"第❶❷❹" same as 第❶❷❹ in ancient Chinese

〈古 ***archaism***〉又同"悌"(tì) also same as 悌

递(遞) dì ㄉㄧˋ ❶传送,传达 to pass; to hand on (㊀ **doublet** 传— to transmit): 投～ *to deliver* | 你把书～给我。*Pass me the book.* | ～眼色(以目示意) *to wink at* ❷顺着次序 successively: ～补 *to fill the vacancies in the proper order* | ～加 *to increase progressively* | ～进 *to go forward one by one*

娣 dì ㄉㄧˋ ❶古代称丈夫的弟妇 (in ancient China) wife of one's husband's younger brother: ～姒(sì)(妯娌) *wives of husband's younger and elder brothers; sisters-in-law* ❷古时姐姐称妹妹为娣 form of address for a woman to call her younger sister in ancient China

睇 dì ㄉㄧˋ 斜着眼看 to look askance; to cast a sidelong glance

第 dì ㄉㄧˋ ❶次序 sequence; order (㊀ **doublet** 等— rank; grade | 次— sequence; order) ㊂ ***extension*** 科举时代考中(zhòng)叫及第,没考中叫落第 (in imperial examinations, passing the examination is called 及第, failing to pass is called 落第) ❷表次序的词头 prefix used to denote ordinal numbers: ～一 *the first* | ～二 *the second* ❸封建社会官僚贵族的大宅子 mansion (*or* residence) of a ranking official in feudal society (㊀ **doublet** 宅— mansion | —宅 residence): 府～ *mansion* ❹仅,只 only; but: 此物世上多有,～人不识耳。It's very common in the world, but people don't know it.

的 ㊀ dì ㄉㄧˋ 箭靶的中心 bull's eye; target: 中(zhòng)～ *to hit the target* | 有

～放矢 *to shoot an arrow at the target*; *to have a definite object in view* [目的]要达到的目标、境地 purpose; goal:我们的～～一定能够达到。*We're sure to attain our goal.*

㊁ dí 见 140 页 see p140

㊂ de 见 136 页 see p136

菂 dì ㄉㄧˋ〈古 ***archaism***〉莲子 lotus seed

帝 dì ㄉㄧˋ ❶古代指天神(in ancient China) Supreme Being:上～*God* ❷君主,皇帝 emperor; monarch:称～*to proclaim oneself emperor*|三皇五～*three rulers and five emperors* (*three rulers — the ruler of heaven "Fuxi", the ruler of earth "Suiren", the ruler of humanity "Shennong"; five emperors — Huangdi, Zhuanxu, Diku, Tangyao and Yushun*) ❸帝国主义的简称 short for 帝国主义

谛 dì ㄉㄧˋ ❶仔细 attentively; carefully:～听 *to listen attentively*|～视 *to examine closely* ❷意义,道理(原为佛教用语 from Buddhism) significance; reason:妙～*subtlety*|真～*essence*

蒂(*蔕) dì ㄉㄧˋ 花或瓜果跟枝茎相连的部分 base:瓜熟～落。*A ripe mellon falls off its stalk — things will be easily settled when conditions are ripe.* [蒂芥][芥蒂]细小的梗塞,比喻嫌隙或不满 unpleasantness; grudge:毫无～～*to hold no grudge against*

缔 dì ㄉㄧˋ 结合 to combine; to unite (㊀ ***doublet*** —结 to combine):～交 *to establish diplomatic relations*|～约 *to conclude a treaty* [缔造]创立,组织 to found; to create; to establish:毛泽东同志和他的战友们～～和培育了伟大、光荣、正确的中国共产党。*Mao Zedong and his comrades-in-arms founded and cultivated the great, glorious and correct Chinese Communist Party.*

禘 dì ㄉㄧˋ 古代一种祭祀 a kind of ancient sacrifice

碲 dì ㄉㄧˋ 一种非金属元素,符号 Te,对热和电传导不良,是半导体材料。用于钢铁工业。碲的化合物有毒,可作杀虫剂 tellurium (Te)

棣 dì ㄉㄧˋ ❶植物名 name of a plant **1** 唐棣,也作"棠棣",古书上说的一种植物(also written as 棠棣) shadberry **2** 棣棠,落叶灌木,花黄色,果实黑色 kerria (*Kerria japonica*) ❷同"弟",旧多用于书信(usually used in correspondence in former times) same as 弟:贤～my worthy brother

踶 dì ㄉㄧˋ 踢,踏 to kick; to tread

DIA ㄉㄧㄚ

嗲 diǎ ㄉㄧㄚˇ〈方 ***dialect***〉形容撒娇的声音或姿态 voice or posture of a person acting as a pampered child:～声～气 *to*

speak in the manner of a pampered child | ～得很 *affectedly sweet*

DIAN ㄉㄧㄢ

战 diān ㄉㄧㄢ [战敠](—duo) 同"掂掇" same as 掂掇

掂 diān ㄉㄧㄢ 用手托着东西估量轻重 to weigh in the hand: ～一～ *to weigh in the hand* | ～着不轻。*It feels quite heavy in the hand.* [掂掇](—duo) **1** 斟酌 to consider; to think over **2** 估量 to estimate; to reckon

滇 diān ㄉㄧㄢ ❶滇池,湖名,在云南省昆明。也叫"昆明湖"(also called 昆明湖) Dianchi Lake, in Kunming, Yunnan Province ❷云南省的别称 Dian, another name for Yunnan Province

颠 diān ㄉㄧㄢ ❶头顶 crown (of the head): 华～(头顶上黑发白发相杂) *grizzled hair; grey-headed* ㉄ ***extension*** 最高最上的部分 summit; top: 山～ *mountain peak* | 塔～ *top of a tower* ❷始 beginning: ～末 *beginning and ending* ❸倒,跌 to collapse; to topple (㊟ ***doublet*** —覆 to overturn; to subvert): ～扑不破(指理论正确不能推翻) *irrefutable; indisputable* [颠倒](—dǎo) **1** 上下或前后的次序倒置 to invert; to reverse: 书放～～了。*The book is upside down.* | 这两个字～～过来意思就不同了。*The meaning will be different if we reverse the two characters.* **2** 错乱 confused; disordered: 神魂～～ *infatuated* [颠沛] **1** 倒下 to fall; to collapse **2** 穷困,受挫折 destitute; frustrated: 他以前过着～～流离的生活。*He used to lead a vagrant life.* ❹颠簸,上下震动 to jolt; to bump: 山路不平,车～得厉害。*The car bumped along the rough mountain path.* ❺同"癫" same as 癫

攧 diān ㄉㄧㄢ 跌 to fall

巅 diān ㄉㄧㄢ 山顶。也作"颠"(also written as 颠) mountaintop

癫 diān ㄉㄧㄢ 精神错乱、失常 deranged; insane (㊟ ***doublet*** —狂 deranged; demented | 疯— insane)

典 diǎn ㄉㄧㄢˇ ❶可以作为标准、典范的书籍 standard work of scholarship: ～籍 *ancient book; ancient records* | 词～ *dictionary* | 字～ *dictionary* | 引经据～ *to quote the classics; to quote authoritative works* ㉄ ***extension*** 标准,法则 standard; regulations: ～范 *model; example; paragon* | ～章 *institutions; decrees and regulations* | 据为～要 *to quote as a criterion* [典礼]郑重举行的仪式 ceremony: 开学～～ *school-opening ceremony* | 开幕～～ *opening ceremony* [典型] **1** 有概括性或代表性的人或事物 model; example; paragon **2** 文艺作品中,用典型化的方法创造出来的能

D

够反映一定社会本质而又具有鲜明个性的艺术形象 typical character (in literature) ❷ 典故,诗文里引用的古书中的故事或词句 literary quotation; classical allusion: 用～ *use of allusion* ❸ 旧指主持,主管(in former times) to be in charge: ～试 *examiner* | ～狱 *warden* ❹ 活买活卖,到期可以赎 to mortgage; to pawn: ～当(dàng) *to pawn* | ～押 *to pawn*

D

碘 diǎn ㄉㄧㄢˇ 一种非金属元素,符号I,黑紫色鳞片状,有金属光泽,供制医药染料等用。人体中缺少碘能引起甲状腺肿 iodine (I)

点(點) diǎn ㄉㄧㄢˇ ❶ (～子、～儿)细小的痕迹或物体 dot; speck; spot: 墨～儿 *ink spot* | 雨～儿 *raindrop* | 斑～ *spot* ㊀ ***extension*** 少量 a little; a bit: 一～小事 *a trifle* | 吃～儿东西 *to have something to eat* ❷ 几何学中指只有位置而没有长、宽、厚的图形 point ❸ 一定的处所或限度 place; point: 起～ *starting point* | 终～ *terminal point* | 据～ *stronghold* | 焦～ *focal point; focus* | 沸～ *boiling point* ❹ 项,部分 item; part: 优～ *strong point; merit* | 重～ *emphasis; stress* | 要～ *gist* | 补充三～ *to add three points* ❺ (～儿)汉字的一种笔形(丶) dot stroke: 三～水(*basic structural part in Chinese characters formed by three dot strokes*) *water radical* ❻ 加上点子 to put a dot: ～句 *to punctuate sentences* | 评～ *to comment* | 画龙～睛 *to add eyes to a painted dragon — to put the finishing touches to a piece of work to brighten it up* [点缀](－zhuì) 在事物上略加装饰 to adorn; to embellish: ～～风景 *to embellish the scenery* ❼ 一落一起地动作 to touch on briefly: ～头 *to nod* | 蜻蜓～水。*Dragonflies skim (over) the water.* ❽ 使一点一滴地落下 to drip: ～眼药 *to put drops in the eyes* | ～种牛痘 *to give small pox vaccination* | ～播种子 *to dibble* ❾ 引火,燃火 to kindle; to burn: ～灯 *to light a lamp* | ～火 *to light a fire* ❿ 查数(shǔ) to check one by one: ～收 *to check and accept* | ～数(shù) *to count* | ～验 *to examine item by item* ⓫ 指示,指定 to instruct; to point (㊈ ***doublet*** 指－ to instruct): ～破 *to point out; to lay bare* | ～菜 *to order dishes* | ～歌 *to request a song* ⓬ 旧时夜间计时用更点,一夜分五更,一更分五点 one fifth of the watch (the night was formerly divided into five watches and each covered two hours): 三更三～ *about 2:12 am* ⓭ 钟点,规定的时间 o'clock; appointed time: 保证火车不误～。*Be sure that the train will not run behind schedule.* ⓮ 点心 refreshments; pastry: 糕～ *cake; pastry* | 早～ *breakfast*

踮(**跕) diǎn ㄉㄧㄢˇ 也作"点"(also written as 点）❶跛足人走路用脚尖点地（of a lame person）to limp：～脚 *to limp* ❷提起脚跟，用脚尖着地 to tiptoe；to stand on tiptoe：～着脚向前看 *to stand on tiptoe and look ahead*

电（電） diàn ㄉㄧㄢˋ ❶物质中存在的一种能，人利用它来使电灯发光、机械转动等 electricity［电脑］指电子计算机 computer［电子］物理学上称构成原子的一种带阴电的粒子 electron ❷阴雨天气空中云层放电时发出的光。也叫"闪电"、"闪"（also called 闪电，闪）lightning ❸电流打击，触电 to give or get an electric shock：电门有毛病，～了我一下。*Something is wrong with the switch for I got an electric shock when touching it.* ❹指电报 telegram；telegraph：急～ *urgent telegram；express telegraph*｜通～*to send a telegraph* ❺打电报 to telegraph：～汇 *to remit by telegram*｜～告 *to inform by telegraph*

佃 ㊀ diàn ㄉㄧㄢˋ 一般指旧社会无地或少地的农民，被迫向地主、富农租地耕种（in the old society）tenant farmer：～户 *tenant*｜～农 *tenant farmer*

㊁ tián 见 744 页 see p744

甸 diàn ㄉㄧㄢˋ 古时称郊外的地方（in ancient China）suburbs；outskirts［甸子］〈方 **dialect**〉放牧的草地 pasture；meadow

钿 ㊀ diàn ㄉㄧㄢˋ ❶把金属、宝石等镶嵌（qiàn）在器物上作装饰 to inlay pieces of metal or gems on utensils for ornament：宝～ *women's hair ornament inlaid with sth like gold or jade*｜螺～（一种手工艺，把贝壳镶嵌在器物上）*mother-of-pearl inlay；shell-inlaid flower pattern* ❷古代一种嵌金花的首饰 women's hair ornament inlaid with gold flowers in ancient China

㊁ tián 见 744 页 see p744

阽 diàn ㄉㄧㄢˋ yán ㄧㄢˊ（又 **also** yán）临近（危险）on the verge of（danger）

坫 diàn ㄉㄧㄢˋ ❶古时室内放东西的土台子 indoor earthern platform for placing objects on in ancient China ❷屏障 protective screen

玷 diàn ㄉㄧㄢˋ 白玉上面的污点 flaw in a piece of jade［玷污］使有污点 to blemish；to tarnish

店 diàn ㄉㄧㄢˋ ❶商店，铺子 store；shop：书～ *bookstore*｜零售～ *retail shop*｜～员 *shop assistant*［饭店］**1** 较大的卖饭食的铺子 restaurant **2** 都市中的大旅馆 hotel ❷旧式的旅馆 old-fashioned inn：住～ *to stop at an inn*｜大车～ *inn for carters*

惦 diàn ㄉㄧㄢˋ 惦记，记挂，不放心 to be concerned about：请勿～念。*Don't worry yourself about me.*｜心里老～着工作。*The work is the very con-*

D

cern of him. or *He's always concerned about his work.*

垫(墊) diàn ㄉㄧㄢˋ ❶衬托,放在底下或铺在上面 to pad; to put sth under (*or* above) sth else:～桌子 *to put sth under the legs of a table to make it level*|～上个褥子 *to put a cotton-padded mattress on the bed*|路面～上点儿土 *to spread earth on the road to make it level* ❷(一子、一儿)衬托的东西 cushion; pad; mat:草～子 *straw mat*|鞋～儿 *insole*|椅～子 *chair cushion* ❸替人暂付款项 to pay for sb and expect to be repaid later:～款 *to advance money*|～钱 *to advance money*

淀(❷澱) diàn ㄉㄧㄢˋ ❶浅的湖泊 shallow lake:白洋～*Baiyang Lake* ❷渣滓,液体里沉下的东西 sediment [淀粉]一种不溶于水、很微小的颗粒,米、麦、甘薯、马铃薯中含量很多 starch

靛 diàn ㄉㄧㄢˋ ❶靛青,蓝靛,用蓼蓝叶泡水调和石灰沉淀所得的蓝色染料 indigo ❷蓝色和紫色混合而成的一种颜色 indigo blue

奠 diàn ㄉㄧㄢˋ ❶陈设祭品向死者致敬 to make offerings to the dead ([连] ***doublet*** 祭一 to hold a memorial service):～酒 *to offer libation*|～仪 *condolence money* ❷奠定,稳稳地安置 to establish; to settle:～基 *to lay a foundation*|～都(dū) *to establish a capital*

殿 diàn ㄉㄧㄢˋ ❶高大的房屋,特指封建帝王受朝听政的地方,或供奉神佛的地方 hall; palace; temple ❷在最后 at the rear; in the rear:～后 *to bring up the rear* [殿军] **1** 行军时走在最后的部队 rearguard **2** 体育、游艺竞赛中的最末一名,也指入选的最末一名 person who comes last in a contest; the last of the successful candidates

癜 diàn ㄉㄧㄢˋ 皮肤病名,常见的是白癜,俗叫"白癜风",皮肤生斑点后变白色(popularly called 白癜风) leucoderma; vitiligo

簟 diàn ㄉㄧㄢˋ 竹席 bamboo mat

DIAO ㄉㄧㄠ

刁 diāo ㄉㄧㄠ 狡猾,无赖 cunning; tricky; sly:～棍(恶人)*villain*|这个人真～。*This person is very cunning.* [刁难](一nàn)故意难为人 to make things difficult for sb on purpose

叼 diāo ㄉㄧㄠ 用嘴衔住 to hold in the mouth:猫～着老鼠。*The cat held a rat in its mouth.*

汈 diāo ㄉㄧㄠ [汈汊]湖名,在湖北省汉川 Diaocha Lake, in Hanchuan, Hubei Province

凋 diāo ㄉㄧㄠ 草木零落,衰落 to wither; to wilt; to fade ([连] ***doublet*** 一谢 to wither|一零 to wilt):松柏后～。*The pine and cypress are known as the last to fade away.*|百业～

敝。*All businesses languished.*

碉 diāo ㄉㄧㄠ 碉堡，防守用的建筑物 blockhouse

雕（❶＊鵰、❷❸❹＊彫、❷❸＊琱）diāo ㄉㄧㄠ ❶老雕，一类很凶猛的鸟，羽毛褐色，上嘴钩曲，捕食野兔、鼠类等 vulture; eagle ❷刻竹、木、玉、石、金属等 to carve; to engrave; to sculpt：木～泥塑 *wood carving and clay modelling*｜浮～*relief (sculpture); relievo*｜～版 *wood block for printing* ❸用彩画装饰 to decorate with colourful paintings：～弓 *elaborate bow*｜～墙 *wall with sculptures* ❹同"凋" same as 凋

鲷 diāo ㄉㄧㄠ［真鲷］鱼名，通称"加吉鱼"。身体红色，有蓝色斑点，是黄海、渤海重要的海产鱼之一，肉味鲜美（generally called 加吉鱼）porgy (*Calamus*)

貂 diāo ㄉㄧㄠ 哺乳动物，嘴尖，尾巴长，毛皮黄黑色或带紫色，生活在我国东北 marten

吊（＊弔）diào ㄉㄧㄠˋ ❶祭奠死者或对遭到丧事的人家、团体给予慰问 to condole; to mourn：～丧(sāng) *to offer condolences to the bereaved*｜～唁 *to condole* ❷悬挂 to hang：房梁上～着四盏光彩夺目的大红灯。*Four dazzlingly bright red lanterns hang down from the beams of the house.* ❸把毛皮缀在衣面上 to put in a fur lining：～皮袄 *to line a coat with fur* ❹提取，收回 to revoke; to withdraw：～卷 *to ask for files or examination papers*｜～销执照 *to revoke a licence* ❺旧时货币单位，一般是一千个制钱叫一吊 former monetary unit, equal to 1,000 copper coins

铞 diào ㄉㄧㄠˋ 见446页"钌"字条"钌铞儿"(liàodiàor) see 钌铞儿 on p446

钓 diào ㄉㄧㄠˋ 用饵诱鱼上钩 to angle; to fish：～鱼 *to go fishing; to angle* ㊞ ***figurative*** 施用手段取得 to fish for; to angle for：沽名～誉 *to fish for fame and compliments*

莜（蓧）diào ㄉㄧㄠˋ 古代除草用的农具 *diao*, a weeding implement in ancient China

窎 diào ㄉㄧㄠˋ 深远 remote; distant (㊁ ***doublet*** 一远 distant)

调 ㊁ diào ㄉㄧㄠˋ ❶调动，安排 to transfer; to shift：～职 *to be transferred to a new post*｜～兵遣将 *to deploy forces* ❷(一子)曲调，音乐上高、低、长、短配合和谐的一组音 tune; melody (㊁ ***doublet*** 腔一tune)：这个～子很好听。*The tune sounds lovely.* ❸多指调式类别和调式主音高度 key; scale; mode：C大～*the key of C major* ❹语言中字音的声调 tone; tune：～号 *tone mark*｜～类 *tone category*［声调］**1** 字音的高低升降。古汉语的声调是平、上、

去、入四声。普通话的声调是阴平、阳平、上声、去声 the tone of Chinese characters (Classical Chinese had four tones: level tone, rising tone, falling tone and entering tone, while standard Chinese pronunciation has five tones: high and level tone, rising tone, falling-rising tone, falling tone and neutral tone) **2** 读书、说话、朗诵的腔调 tone

㊁ tiáo 见 747 页 see p747

掉 diào ㄉㄧㄠˋ ❶落 to fall; to drop; to shed: ～眼泪 *to shed tears* | ～在水里 *to fall into water* ❷落在后面 to lag behind; to fall behind: ～队 *to drop out* ❸〈方 ***dialect***〉遗漏, 遗失 to lose; to be missing: 文章～了几个字。*There are a few characters* (or *words*) *missing in the article.* | 钱包～了。*The purse is missing.* ❹减损, 消失 to decrease; to decline; to reduce: ～膘儿 *to lose weight* | ～色 *to lose colour; to fade* ❺回转 to turn; to turn round; to turn back: ～头 *to turn around; to turn back* | ～过来 *to turn around* ❻摇摆 to wag: 尾大不～(喻指挥不灵) *the tail is too heavy to wag — (of an organization) too cumbersome to be effective; leadership rendered ineffectual by recalcitrant subordinates* ❼对换 to exchange; to swap: ～一个个儿 *to swap places* ❽在动词后表示动作的完成 (used after certain verbs to indicate completion): 丢～ *to throw away* | 卖～ *to sell* | 改～坏习惯 *to get rid of bad habits*

铫 ㊀ diào ㄉㄧㄠˋ (～子、～儿) 煮开水熬东西用的器具 kettle; pot: 药～儿 *medicine pot* | 沙～ *earthern pot*

㊁ yáo 见 874 页 see p874

DIE ㄉㄧㄝ

爹 diē ㄉㄧㄝ ❶父亲(叠 ***reduplication***) papa; dad; daddy ❷对老人或长(zhǎng)者的尊称 (polite term of address for elderly men): 老～ *old pa*

跌 diē ㄉㄧㄝ 摔倒 to fall; to tumble: ～了一跤 *to have a fall* | ～倒 *to tumble; to topple* ㊊ ***extension*** 下降, 低落 to drop; to fall: ～价 *to fall* (or *drop*) *in price; to go down in price* [跌足] 顿足, 跺脚 to stamp one's foot

迭 dié ㄉㄧㄝˊ ❶交换, 轮流 to alternate: 更～ *to change; to alternate* | ～为宾主 *to be a guest and a host alternately* ❷屡, 连着 repeatedly: ～次会商 *to consult time and again* | 近年来, 地下文物～有发现。*Discoveries of underground cultural relics have been made in recent years one after another.* ❸及, 赶上 to be in time for: 忙不～ *hurriedly*

昳 ㊀ dié ㄉㄧㄝˊ 〈古 ***archaism***〉日过午偏西 (of the sun) to go to the west after noon time

㊁ yì 见 890 页 see p890

D

瓞 dié ㄉㄧㄝˊ 小瓜 small melon

垤 dié ㄉㄧㄝˊ 小土堆 mound; molehill (㊟ **doublet** 丘— mound; hillock): 蚁～*anthill*

咥 ㊀ dié ㄉㄧㄝˊ 咬 to bite
㊁ xì 见 807 页 see p807

绖 dié ㄉㄧㄝˊ 古代丧服用的麻带儿 linen sash on ancient mourning garment: 首～*linen band around one's head for mourning* | 腰～*linen sash around one's waist for mourning*

耋 dié ㄉㄧㄝˊ 年老,七八十岁的年纪 old; in one's seventies or eighties

谍 dié ㄉㄧㄝˊ 秘密探察军事、政治及经济等方面的消息 espionage: ～报 *intelligence* [间谍](jiàn—)为敌方或外国刺探国家秘密情报的特务分子 intelligence agent; spy

堞 dié ㄉㄧㄝˊ 城墙上呈⎍⎍形的矮墙 battlements

喋 ㊀ dié ㄉㄧㄝˊ [喋喋]啰唆,语言烦琐 to chatter away; to rattle on: ～～不休 *to rattle away; to chatter on* [喋血]流血满地 bloodshed
㊁ zhá 见 948 页 see p948

牒 dié ㄉㄧㄝˊ 文书,证件 official document; certificate: 通～(两国交换意见用的文书) *diplomatic note*

碟 dié ㄉㄧㄝˊ (—子、—儿)盛(chéng)食物等的器具,扁而浅,比盘子小 small plate; saucer; dish

蝶(*蜨) dié ㄉㄧㄝˊ 蝴蝶,昆虫名。静止时四翅竖立在背部,喜在花间、草地飞行,吸食花蜜。幼虫多对作物有害。有粉蝶、蛱蝶、凤蝶等多种 butterfly

蹀 dié ㄉㄧㄝˊ 蹈,顿足 to stamp; to step [蹀躞](—xiè)迈着小步走路的样子 to mince

鲽 dié ㄉㄧㄝˊ 鱼名。比目鱼的一类,体形侧扁,两眼都在身体的右侧,有眼的一侧褐色,无眼的一侧大都为白色,常见的有星鲽、高眼鲽等。肉可以吃 righteye flounder; flatfish (*Pleuronectidae*)

嵽(**嵽**) dié ㄉㄧㄝˊ [嵽嵲](—niè)形容山高 (of a mountain) lofty; towering

叠(*曡、*疊) dié ㄉㄧㄝˊ ❶重复地堆,累积 to pile up (㊟ **doublet** 重— overlapping): ～床架屋(喻重复累赘) *needless duplication; repetitiousness* | ～假山 *to pile up rocks into rockeries* | ～罗汉 *human pyramid* ❷重复 to repeat: 层见～出 *to appear repeatedly; to occur frequently* ❸折叠 to fold: ～衣服 *to fold clothes* | 铺床～被 *to make the bed and fold up the quilt*

氎 dié ㄉㄧㄝˊ 细棉布 fine cotton cloth

DING ㄉㄧㄥ

丁 ㊀ dīng ㄉㄧㄥ ❶天干的第四位 *ding*, the 4th of the 10 heavenly stems 常用作顺序的第四 the fourth ❷成年男子

D

male adult; man: 壮～*able-bodied man* ㊀ ***extension*** **1** 旧指人口(in former times) population: 人～*population* | ～口 *population* **2** 指从事某种劳动的人 person engaged in certain types of manual work: 园～*gardener* ❸当,遭逢 to incur: ～兹盛世 *born into this prosperous age* | ～忧(旧指遭父母丧)(*in former times*) *to be in mourning for one's parent* ❹(一儿)小方块 cube: 肉～儿 *meat cubes* | 咸菜～儿 *diced salted vegetables* [丁点儿]表示极少或极小 a tiny bit: 一～～～毛病都没有。*There isn't the slightest flaw.* or *It's flawless.* ❺姓 Ding, a surname

[丁当](一dāng)拟声词 ***onomatopoeia***, 金属等撞击的声音 dingdong; jingling; clinking

㊁ zhēng 见 970 页 see p970

仃 dīng ㄉㄧㄥ 见 452 页"伶"字条"伶仃"(líng一) see 伶仃 on p452

叮 dīng ㄉㄧㄥ ❶叮嘱,再三嘱咐 to exhort ❷蚊子等用针形口器吸食 to sting; to bite: 被蚊子～了一口 *to get a mosquito bite* ❸追问 to inquire: ～问 *to question persistently; to make a detailed inquiry*

[叮当]同"丁当" same as 丁当

[叮咛](*丁宁)反复地嘱咐 to exhort repeatedly: ～～再三 *to exhort repeatedly*

玎 dīng ㄉㄧㄥ [玎玲](一líng)拟声词 ***onomatopoeia***, 玉石等撞击的声音 clinking; tinkling; jingling

盯 dīng ㄉㄧㄥ 注视,集中视力看 to gaze at: 大家眼睛直～着他。*We all fixed our eyes on him.*

町 ㊀ dīng ㄉㄧㄥ 见 775 页"畹"字条"畹町"(wǎn一) see 畹町 on p775

㊁ tǐng 见 752 页 see p752

钉 ㊀ dīng ㄉㄧㄥ ❶(一子、一儿)竹、木、金属制成的可以打入他物的细条形的东西 nail: 螺丝～儿 *screw* | 碰～子(喻受打击或被拒绝) *to receive a serious rebuff; to suffer setbacks; to meet with rejection* ❷紧跟着不放松 to tail: ～住对方的前锋(*in sports*) *to shadow the forward from the opposing side* (*in football*) ❸督促,催问 to urge; to press: 这事得～着他点儿。*You'd better keep pressing him to do that.* or *You must keep reminding him of the matter.*

㊁ dìng 见 154 页 see p154

疔 dīng ㄉㄧㄥ 疔毒,疔疮,一种毒疮 malignant boil; malignant furuncle

耵 dīng ㄉㄧㄥ [耵聍](一níng)耳垢,耳屎,皮脂腺分泌的蜡状物质 earwax; cerumen

酊 ㊀ dīng ㄉㄧㄥ (外 ***loanword***)医药上用酒精和药配合成的液剂 tincture: 碘～*tincture of iodine*

㊁ dǐng 见 153 页 see p153

靪 dīng ㄉㄧㄥ 补鞋底 to mend the sole of a shoe

顶 dǐng ㄉㄧㄥˇ ❶(一儿)人体或物体的最高最上的部分 crown; top: 头～ *the crown; top* (or *crown*) *of the head*|山～*mountaintop*|房～*roof* ❷用头支承 to carry on the head: 用头～东西 *to carry sth on the head*|～天立地(喻英雄气概) *indomitable; heroic* ㊀ ***extension*** **1** 用东西支撑 to prop up: 用门杠把门～上 *to prop up the door with a bar* **2** 冒 against; in the teeth of: ～着雨走了 *to leave despite the rain* ❸用头或角撞击 to gore; to butt; to head: ～球 *to head a ball*|公牛～人。*Bulls gore people.* ❹自下而上用力拱起 to jack up: 用千斤顶把汽车～起来 *to jack up a car*|麦芽～出土来了。*The malt has sprouted from the earth.* ❺相逆,对面迎着 against: ～风 *to head into the wind* ❻顶撞(多指下对上) to retort; to talk back: 他气冲冲地～了班长两句。*He said a few words angrily to the monitor in retort.* ❼代替 to replace (㊀ ***doublet*** 一替 to take the place of): ～名 *to assume sb else's name*|冒名～替 *to assume the identity of another person* ❽相当,等于 to equal; to be equivalent to: 一个人～两个人工作。*One can do the work of two.* ㊀ ***extension*** 担当,抵得过 to undertake; to stand up to: 他一个人去不～事。*He alone is not enough.* ❾〈方 ***dialect***〉直到 until: 昨天～十二点才到家。*He didn't go back home until twelve o'clock yesterday.* ❿副词 ***adverb***, 最,极 most; extremely: ～好 *excellent; superb*|～多 *at most*|～会想办法 *to be always ready with an idea* ⓫量词 ***quantifier***: 两～帽子 *two caps*

酊 ㊁ dǐng ㄉㄧㄥˇ 见 511 页"酩"字条"酩酊"(mǐng—) see 酩酊 on p511

㊀ dīng 见 152 页 see p152

鼎 dǐng ㄉㄧㄥˇ ❶古代烹煮用的器物,一般是三足两耳 *ding*, an ancient cooking vessel with two loop handles and three legs [鼎立]三方并立 tripartite confrontation; tripartite balance of forces: 三国～～*the tripartite balance of power of the three states—Wei, Shu and Wu* ❷大(叠 ***reduplication***) great; grand: ～力 *great effort*|～～大名 *famous; celebrated* ❸〈方 ***dialect***〉锅 pot: ～间(厨房) *kitchen* ❹正当,正在 during; in the course of: ～盛 *in a period of great prosperity; at the height of power and splendour*

订 dìng ㄉㄧㄥˋ ❶改正,修改 to correct; to revise: ～正初稿 *to revise the first draft*|考～*to do textual research*|校(jiào)～*to revise; to blue-pencil* ❷立(契约),约定 to conclude; to agree on: ～报 *to subscribe to a newspaper*|～货 *to order goods*|～婚 *to be en-*

D

gaged to | ～合同 *to conclude a contract* ❸用线、铁丝等把书页等连在一起 to staple; to bind: 装～*to staple* | ～一个笔记本儿 *to staple a notebook*

饤 dìng ㄉㄧㄥˋ 见159页"饾"字条"饾饤"(dòu—) see 饾饤 on p159

钉 ㊁ dìng ㄉㄧㄥˋ ❶把钉子或楔(xiē)子打入他物 to nail: 拿个钉子～～*to fetch a nail and drive it in* | 墙上～着木橛。*There's a wood peg in the wall*. ❷连接在一起 to sew on: ～扣子 *to sew a button on*

㊀ dīng 见152页 see p152

定 dìng ㄉㄧㄥˋ ❶不可变更的,规定的,不动的 fixed; settled: ～理 *theorem* | ～论 *final conclusion* | ～量 *ration* | ～期 *periodic* ㊂ **extension** 副词 ***adverb***,必然地 surely; certainly: ～能成功 *to be sure to succeed* [定义]对事物本质或范围的扼要说明 definition ❷使确定,使不移动 to fix; to set: ～案 *to decide on a verdict* | ～胜负 *to judge the winner* | 否～*to deny* | 决～*to decide* | ～章程 *to make rules* | ～制度 *to set regulations* ❸安定,平靖(多指局势)(usually of a situation) to settle; to pacify: 大局已～。*The overall situation is already irreversible*. ❹镇静,安稳(多指情绪)(usually of mood) calm; placid: 心神不～*agitated; restless* | ～～神再说 *to wait until one calms down* ❺预先约妥 to subscribe; to order; to book: ～金 *deposit* | ～做 *to have sth made to order*

啶 dìng ㄉㄧㄥˋ 见36页"吡"字条"吡啶"(bǐ—)、501页"嘧"字条"嘧啶"(mì—) see 吡啶 on p36; see 嘧啶 on p501

腚 dìng ㄉㄧㄥˋ 〈方 ***dialect***〉屁股 buttocks: 光～*naked*

碇(*椗、*矴) dìng ㄉㄧㄥˋ 系船的石礅 small anchor; killock; killick: 下～(停船) *to cast anchor; to anchor* | 起～(开船) *to weigh anchor; to lift anchor*

锭 dìng ㄉㄧㄥˋ ❶(—子)纺车或纺纱机上绕纱的机件 spindle: 纱～*spindle* ❷(—子、—儿)金属或药物等制成的块状物 ingot; ingot-shaped tablet: 钢～*steel ingot* | 金～儿 *gold ingot* | 紫金～ zijin ding, *a kind of medicine*

DIU ㄉㄧㄡ

丢 diū ㄉㄧㄡ ❶失去,遗落 to lose; to be missing: ～了一枝钢笔 *to have lost a pen* | ～脸(失面子) *to lose face; to be disgraced* | ～三落(là)四 *forgetful; scatterbrained* ❷放下,抛开 to put aside; to throw away: 这件事可以～开不管。*It can be put aside*.

铥 diū ㄉㄧㄡ 一种金属元素,符号 Tm,银白色,质软。可用来制 X 射线源等 thulium (Tm)

DONG ㄉㄨㄥ

东(東) dōng ㄉㄨㄥ ❶方向,太阳出来的那一边,跟"西"相对(the opposite of 西) east:~方红,太阳升。*The east is turning red and the sun is rising.*|面朝~*to face east*|黄河以~*to the east of the Huanghe River*|华~*east China* [东西](-xi)物件,有时也指人或动物 thing; creature ❷主人 host; owner:房~*landlord* ❸东道(请人吃饭,出钱的叫"东道",也简称"东")(one who treats sb else to dinner is called 东道, or 东 for short) host:做~*to be the host*
[东乡族]我国少数民族,参看附表(see the appendix) the Dongxiang ethnic group, one of the ethnic minorities of China

岽(崬) dōng ㄉㄨㄥ [岽罗]地名,在广西壮族自治区扶绥。今作"东罗"(now written as 东罗) Dongluo, a place in Fusui, Guangxi Zhuang Autonomous Region

鸫(鶇) dōng ㄉㄨㄥ 鸟名。种类很多,羽毛多淡褐色或黑色,叫得很好听,食昆虫,是益鸟 thrush (*Turdidae*)

冬(❷鼕) dōng ㄉㄨㄥ ❶四季中的第四季,气候最冷 winter:过~*to pass the winter*|隆~*midwinter* ❷拟声词 ***onomatopoeia***,敲鼓、敲门的声音(叠 ***reduplication***)(sound of beating a drum or knocking at a door) rub-a-dub; rat-a-tat; thump-thump
[冬烘]思想迂腐,知识浅陋(of one's thinking and knowledge) shallow but pedantic

咚 dōng ㄉㄨㄥ 同"冬❷" same as 冬❷

氡 dōng ㄉㄨㄥ 一种放射性元素,在通常条件下为气体,符号 Rn,无色无臭,不易跟其他元素化合,在真空玻璃管中能发荧光 radon (Rn)

董 dǒng ㄉㄨㄥˇ 监督管理 to supervise; to superintend; to direct [董事]某些企业、学校等推举出来代表自己监督和主持业务的人,也省称"董"(also 董 for short) director:~~会 *board of directors*

懂 dǒng ㄉㄨㄥˇ 了解,明白 to know; to understand:一看就~*to understand at the first sight*|~得一点医学 *to know a little medicine*

动(動) dòng ㄉㄨㄥˋ ❶从原来位置上离开,改变原来的位置或姿态,跟"静"相对(the opposite of 静) to move; to stir:站住别~!*Stand still and don't move!*|风吹草~*rustle of grass in the wind — a sign of disturbance or trouble; sign of anything untoward brewing* ㊞ ***extension*** **1** 能动的 capable of movement; mobile:~物 *animal* **2** 可以变动的 movable:~产 *personal property; movables* [动弹](-tan)身体或物体动 to move ❷

行动，动作，行为 movement; action; act：一举一～ *every move* [动词]表示动作、行为、变化的词，如走、来、去、打、吃、爱、拥护、变化等 verb [动静](—jing)动作或情况 activity; movement：没有～～。*There's no sign of activity.* | 侦察敌人的～～ *to reconnoiter the enemy's movements* ❸使动，使有动作 to cause to move or do：～手 *to start work; to get to work* | ～脑筋 *to rack one's brains* [动员] **1** 战争要发生时，把国家的武装力量由和平状态转入战时状态，把所有的经济部门转入供应战争需要的工作 national mobilization **2** 号召大家或说服别人做某种工作 to mobilize; to call upon people to participate in a certain activity ❹感动，情感起反应 to move; to touch：～心 *to have one's feelings aroused* | ～人 *moving; touching* ❺开始做 to start：～工 *to start construction* | ～身(起行) *to set out; to start off* ❻往往 frequently：观众～以万计 *to draw audiences of tens of thousands* [动不动]表示很容易发生，常跟"就"连用(often used in collocation with 就 to express something apt to happen) frequently; always; easily：～～～就引古书 *to be always citing from classic works* | ～～～就争吵 *to be apt to quarrel* ❼放在动词后，表示效果(used after a verb to express result)：拿得～ *to be able to carry (sth with one's hands)* | 搬不～ *to be unable to move (sth)*

冻(凍) dòng ㄉㄨㄥˋ ❶液体或含水分的东西遇冷凝结 to freeze：河里～冰了。*The river is frozen.* | 天寒地～ *freezing* ❷(—儿)凝结了的汤汁 jelly：肉～儿 *meat jelly; aspic* | 鱼～儿 *fish jelly* | 果子～儿 *jelly* ❸感到寒冷或受到寒冷 to feel cold; to freeze：外面很冷，真～得慌。*It's so cold outside that I am freezing.* | 小心别～着。*Take care so you won't catch cold.*

栋(棟) dòng ㄉㄨㄥˋ ❶古代指房屋的脊檩(in ancient China) ridgepole [栋梁] ㊟ ***figurative*** 担负国家重任的人 pillar of a state ❷量词 ***quantifier***：一～房子 *a house*

胨(腖) dòng ㄉㄨㄥˋ 蛋白胨，有机化合物，医学上用作细菌的培养基 peptone

侗 ㊀ dòng ㄉㄨㄥˋ [侗族] 我国少数民族，参看附表(see the appendix) the Dong ethnic group, one of the ethnic minorities of China

㊁ tóng 见 754see p754

㊂ tǒng 见 756 页 see p756

垌 ㊀ dòng ㄉㄨㄥˋ ❶田地 field：田～ *field* ❷地名用字 dong, used in a place name：麻～(在广西壮族自治区桂平) *Madong (a place in Guiping, Guangxi Zhuang Autonomous Region)* | 中～(在广东省化州)

Zhongdong (*a place in Huazhou, Guangdong Province*)

㊁ tóng 见 755 页 see p755

峒 ㊀ dòng ㄉㄨㄥˋ 山洞，石洞 cave; cavern

㊁ tóng 见 755 页 see p755

洞 dòng ㄉㄨㄥˋ ❶洞穴，窟窿 hole; cavity: 山～ *cave; cavern*|老鼠～*rat hole*|衣服破了一个～。*There's a hole in the garment.* ❷透彻，清楚 thoroughly; penetratingly: ～察一切 *to have a keen insight into matters*|～若观火 *to see sth as clearly as a blazing fire — to understand sth thoroughly at a glance* ❸说数字时用来代替零 (used as a code word for 零) naught

恫 dòng ㄉㄨㄥˋ 恐惧，恐吓 to frighten; to threaten [恫吓](—hè)吓(xià)唬 to scare; to intimidate

胴 dòng ㄉㄨㄥˋ ❶躯干，整个身体除去头部、四肢和内脏余下的部分 trunk; torso; body ❷大肠 large intestines

硐 dòng ㄉㄨㄥˋ 山洞、窑洞或矿坑 cave; cave dwelling; pit

DOU ㄉㄡ

都 ㊁ dōu ㄉㄡ 副词 ***adverb*** ❶全，完全 all; completely: 事情不论大小，～要做好。*Everything big or small, we should do it well.* ❷表示语气的加重 for emphasis: ～十二点了还不睡。*Why don't you go to bed? It's already 12 o'clock!*|连小孩子～搬得动。*Even a small child can move it.*

㊀ dū 见 160 页 see p160

哣 dōu ㄉㄡ 斥责声，多见于旧小说或戏曲中 exclamation of scolding in old novels or operas

兜 dōu ㄉㄡ ❶(—子、—儿)作用和口袋相同的东西 pocket; bag: 裤～*trousers pocket*|～儿布 *cloth used to make inner pockets* ❷做成兜形把东西拢住 to wrap up in a piece of cloth folded like a bag, etc: 用手巾～着 *to wrap it up in a towel*|船帆～风。*Sails can catch the wind.* ㊀ ***extension*** 兜揽，招揽 to tout: ～售 *to peddle; to hawk* ❸承担 to take responsibility: 没关系，有问题我～着。*Don't worry! Should anything go wrong, I'll see to it.* ❹环绕，围绕 to move around: ～抄 *to round up*|～圈子 *to circle*

蔸 dōu ㄉㄡ 〈方 ***dialect***〉❶指某些植物的根和靠近根的茎 root and stem of some plants: 禾～*roots of rice*|树～脑(树墩儿) *tree stump* [坐蔸] 稻子的幼苗发黄，长不快 (of rice seedlings) to turn yellow, and grow very slowly ❷量词 ***quantifier***, 相当于"丛"或"棵" (similar to 丛 or 棵): 一～草 *a clump of grass*|两～白菜 *two heads of Chinese cabbage*

篼 dōu ㄉㄡ ❶(—子)走山路坐的竹轿 bamboo chair tied to two bamboo poles serving as a sedan chair ❷竹、藤、柳条等做成的盛东西的器物 basket made of bamboo, cane, or wicker, etc

斗 ㊀ dǒu ㄉㄡˇ ❶市制容量单位,1斗是10升 *dou*, a traditional unit of capacity, equal to ten litres ❷量(liáng)粮食的器具,容量是1斗,多为方形 *dou*, a square grain-measuring container with a capacity of one litre [喻] ***figurative*** **1** 形容小东西的大(of a small thing) big: ～胆 *to venture*; *to be bold* **2** 形容大东西的小(of a big thing) small: ～室 *small room* | ～城 *small town* ❸像斗的东西 *dou*-shaped object: 漏～ *funnel* | 熨～ *iron* [斗拱](*科栱)(－gǒng)拱是建筑上弧形承重结构,斗是垫拱的方木块,合称斗拱 *dougong*, a tier of unique Chinese architectural structure, comprising of a bow-shaped bracket (called 拱) cushioned with a trapezoidal block (called 斗), which is inserted between the top of a pillar and a crossbeam; corbel bracket ❹呈圆形的指纹 whorl of a fingerprint ❺星宿名,二十八宿之一 *dou*, the 8th of the 28 constellations

㊁ dòu 见158页 see p158

抖 dǒu ㄉㄡˇ ❶使振动 to shake; to flick: ～床单 *to spread the sheet with a flick* | ～空竹 *to play with a diabolo* | ～～身上的雪 *to shake the snow off one's clothes* [抖搂](－lou) **1** 同"抖❶"same as 抖❶: ～～衣服上的土 *to shake the dust off one's clothes* **2** 任意挥霍 to squander; to waste: 别把钱～～光了。*Don't waste every penny you have.* **3** 揭露 to expose: ～～老底儿 *to bring sb's past to light* ❷哆嗦,战栗 to tremble; to shiver: 冷得发～ *to tremble with cold* ❸讽刺人突然得势或生活水平突然提高(used sarcastically) to preen oneself; to get on in the world; to feel puffed up with self-importance: 他最近～起来了。*He seems to be preening himself recently.* or *He seems to be taking on airs recently.*

枓 dǒu ㄉㄡˇ [枓栱]旧同"斗拱"same as 斗拱 in former times 参看158页"斗㊀❸"see 斗㊀❸ on p158

钭 dǒu ㄉㄡˇ (又 also tǒu) 见760页 tǒu see tǒu on p760

蚪 dǒu ㄉㄡˇ 见388页"蝌"字条"蝌蚪"(kē－) see 蝌蚪 on p388

陡(**阧) dǒu ㄉㄡˇ ❶斜度很大,近于垂直 steep; precipitous: 这个山坡太～。*The hillside is too steep.* ❷突然 abruptly; suddenly: 气候～变。*The climate changed abruptly.*

斗(鬥、*鬭、*鬪)

㊁ dòu ㄉㄡˋ ❶对打 to fight; to tussle ([连] ***doublet*** 战— to battle; to combat): 搏～ *to combat* [斗争] **1** 矛盾的双方互相冲

突,一方力求战胜另一方 to struggle; to strive:思想~~ *ideological struggle* **2** 用说理、揭露、控诉等方式打击 to denounce; to accuse:开~~会 *to have a public accusation meeting* **3** 奋斗 to strive:为实现四个现代化而~~ *to strive for the four modernizations* [奋斗]为了达到一定的目的而努力干 to strive ❷比赛胜负 to compete with; to contest with:~智 *to battle with wits* | ~力 *to battle with strength* ❸〈方 ***dialect***〉拼合,凑近 to fit together; to put together:那条桌子腿还没有~榫(sǔn)。*The leg tenons of the table haven't been fitted into the mortises.* | 用碎布~成一个口袋 *to make a sack with small pieces of cloth*

㊀ dǒu 见158页 see p158

豆(❶*荳) dòu ㄉㄡˋ ❶豆科,双子叶植物的一科,草本木本都有,如绿豆、黄豆、落花生、槐树、紫檀等都属这一科。通常统称豆类植物,有大豆、豌豆、蚕豆等。又指这些植物的种子 legume; bean ❷(一儿)形状像豆粒的东西 bean-shaped thing:山药~儿 *Chinese yam* | 花生~儿 *peanut kernel* ❸古代盛(chéng)肉或其他食品的器皿(in ancient China) stemmed cup or bowl

逗 dòu ㄉㄡˋ ❶停留 to stay; to stop ([连] ***doublet*** 一留 to stay; to tarry) ❷引,惹弄 to tease; to toy with:~笑 *amusing; funny* | ~趣 *to amuse* ❸同"读"(dòu) same as 读

饾 dòu ㄉㄡˋ [饾饤](—dìng) 供陈设的食品 food for display [喻] ***figurative*** 文辞堆砌 ornate writing

脰 dòu ㄉㄡˋ 脖子,颈 neck

痘 dòu ㄉㄡˋ ❶水痘,一种传染病,小儿容易感染 pox ❷痘疮,即天花。参看285页"花"字条"天花"(i.e.天花, see 天花 on p285) smallpox [牛痘]牛身上的痘疮,制成牛痘苗,接种在人身上,可以预防天花。也省称"痘"(also 痘 for short) cowpox

读(讀) ㊁ dòu ㄉㄡˋ 旧指文章里一句话中间念起来要稍稍停顿的地方(in former times) slight pause in reading to mark the end of a phrase, clause, or sentence (when reading unpunctuated ancient writing):句~(*at the end of a phrase* or *sentence*) *pause; sentences and phrases*

㊀ dú 见161页 see p161

窦(竇) dòu ㄉㄡˋ 孔,洞 hole:鼻~ *paranasal sinus* | 狗~ *kennel* [疑窦]可疑的地方 suspicion:顿生~~ *to feel suspicious suddenly*

DU ㄉㄨ

厾(**毅) dū ㄉㄨ 用指头、棍棒等轻击轻点 to touch or tap lightly with a finger, stick, etc:~一个点儿 *to make a dot* [点厾]画

D

家随意点染 to add a few touches to a painting

都 ㊀ dū ㄉㄨ ❶首都，全国最高领导机关所在的地方 capital：建～*to establish a capital* ❷大城市 major city（㊟ **doublet** 一市 city）：通～大邑 *metropolis* ❸姓 Du，a surname

㊁ dōu 见157页 see p157

阇 ㊀ dū ㄉㄨ 城门上的台 platform over a city gate

㊁ shé 见662页 see p662

嘟 dū ㄉㄨ 拟声词 ***onomatopoeia***，toot：喇叭～～响。*The horn is tooting*.［嘟囔］（—nang）连续地自言自语，常带有抱怨的意思 to mutter；to mumble：别瞎～～啦！*Don't mumble to yourself anymore!*［嘟噜］（—lu）**1** 向下垂着 to sag；to dangle：～～着脸，显得很不高兴。*He put on a long face, looking very unhappy*. **2** 量词 ***quantifier***，用于连成一簇的东西 bunch；cluster：一～～钥匙 *a bunch of keys*｜一～～葡萄 *a bunch of grapes* **3**（—儿）舌或小舌连续颤动发出的声音 trill：打～～儿 *to trill*

㞘（**启）dū ㄉㄨ（—子、—儿）〈方 ***dialect***〉❶屁股 buttocks ❷蜂或蝎子等尾部的毒刺 sting

督 dū ㄉㄨ 监督，监管，察看 to superintend；to oversee：～师 *to supervise military operations*｜～战 *to supervise military operations*｜～促 *to supervise and urge*

毒 dú ㄉㄨˊ ❶对生物体有危害的性质，或有这种性质的东西 poison：～气 *poisonous gas*｜中（zhòng）～*poisoning*｜消～*to disinfect；to sterilize*｜砒霜有～。*Arsenic is poisonous*. 㘾 **extension** 对思想品质有害的事物 things harmful to one's mind：肃清流～ *to eradicate pernicious influences* ❷毒品 drugs；narcotics：吸～ *to take drugs*｜贩～*to traffic in drugs*｜禁～*to prohibit drugs* ❸用有毒的东西使人或物受到伤害 to poison：用药～老鼠 *to poison rats*｜～杀害虫 *to poison pests* ❹毒辣，凶狠，厉害 malicious；cruel；fierce：心～*cruel-hearted*｜～计 *venomous scheme*｜下～手 *to lay murderous hands on sb*｜太阳真～。*The sun is scorching*.

独（獨）dú ㄉㄨˊ ❶单一 single（㊟ **doublet** 单一 on one's own；by oneself）：～唱 *solo*｜～幕剧 *one-act play*｜～生子女 *the only child*｜无～有偶 *it is not unique；do not come singly, but in pairs* ❷没有依靠或帮助 alone；by oneself（㊟ **doublet** 孤—lonely）［独立］自立自主，不受人支配 independent ❸没有子孙的老人 old people with no offspring：鳏寡孤～ *widowers, widows, orphans and the childless* ❹只，惟有 only；merely：大家都到了，～有他没来。*He's the only one who has not come yet*.

［独龙族］我国少数民族，参看附表（see the appendix）the Dulong (*or* Drung, Derung) ethnic group, one of the ethnic minorities of China

顿 ㊁ dú ㄉㄨˊ 见 515 页"冒"字条"冒顿"(mò—) see 冒顿 on p515
㊀ dùn 见 168 页 see p168

读(讀) ㊀ dú ㄉㄨˊ 依照文字念 to read: 宣～ *to read out in public* | 朗～ *to read aloud* | ～报 *to read a newspaper* [引] ***extension*** **1** 阅读,看书,阅览 to read: ～书 *to read a book* | ～者 *reader* **2** 求学 to attend school: ～大学 *to attend university*
㊁ dòu 见 159 页 see p159

渎(瀆、❷**黷) dú ㄉㄨˊ ❶水沟,小渠 ditch; drain ([连] ***doublet*** 沟一 ditch) ❷亵渎,轻慢,对人不恭敬 to show disrespect or contempt to [渎职]不尽职,在执行任务时犯错误 malfeasance; dereliction of duty

椟(櫝) dú ㄉㄨˊ ❶柜子 casket ❷匣子 case; box

犊(犢) dú ㄉㄨˊ (一子、一儿)牛犊,小牛 calf: 初生之～不怕虎。*Newborn calves are not afraid of tigers — young people are fearless.*

牍(牘) dú ㄉㄨˊ 古代在上面写字的木简 (in ancient China) wooden tablets or slips for writing [引] ***extension*** **1** 文牍,公文 archives; official documents: 文～ *official documents and correspondence* | 案～ *official documents or correspondence* **2** 尺牍,书信 correspondence (of an eminent writer)

讟(讟) dú ㄉㄨˊ 诽谤,怨言 slander; complaint

黩(黷) dú ㄉㄨˊ ❶污辱 to disgrace; to blacken ❷随随便便,不郑重 to act rashly; to act wantonly [黩武]好(hào)战 militaristic; warlike: 反对穷兵～～,扩军备战 *to object to militarism, arms expansion and war preparations*

髑 dú ㄉㄨˊ [髑髅](—lóu)死人头骨 skull (of a dead person)

肚 ㊁ dǔ ㄉㄨˇ (一子、一儿)动物的胃作食品时叫肚 tripe: 猪～子 *pork tripe* | 羊～儿 *mutton tripe*
㊀ dù 见 162 页 see p162

笃 dǔ ㄉㄨˇ ❶忠实,全心全意 sincere; earnest: ～学 *to study diligently* | ～信 *to believe in sincerely* ❷病沉重 (of illness) serious; critical: 病～ *seriously ill*

堵 dǔ ㄉㄨˇ ❶阻塞(sè),挡 to block; to plug: 水沟～住了。*The ditch is blocked.* | ～老鼠洞 *to plug mouse holes* | 别～着门站着! *Don't stand in the doorway!* [喻] ***figurative*** 心中不畅快 unhappy: 心里～得慌 *to feel suffocated* ❷墙 wall: 观者如～。*There were crowds of spectators.* [安堵]安定,不受骚

扰 to live in peace and security ❸量词 ***quantifier***，用于墙 (used of walls)：一～高墙 *a high wall*

赌 dǔ ㄉㄨˇ 赌博，用财物作注争输赢 to gamble：～钱 *to gamble* ㊀ ***extension*** 争输赢 to bet：打～ *to bet* [赌气]因不服气而任性做事 to be discontented and act rashly：他～～走了。*He left in a fit of pique.*

D

睹（*覩） dǔ ㄉㄨˇ 看见 to see：耳闻目～ *what one sees and hears*｜熟视无～ *to turn a blind eye to；to pay no attention to a familiar sight；to be ignorant of*

芏 dù ㄉㄨˋ 见334页"茳"字条"茳芏"(jiāng—) see 茳芏 on p334

杜（❷ **敱） dù ㄉㄨˋ ❶杜梨树，落叶乔木，果实圆而小，味涩可食。是嫁接梨的主要砧(zhēn)木 birchleaf pear ❷阻塞(sè)，堵塞 to stop：以～流弊 *so as to put an end to abuses* [杜绝]堵死，彻底防止 to put an end to：～～漏洞 *to plug (up) the loopholes*｜～～事故发生 *to put an end to accidents*

[杜鹃](—juān) **1** 鸟名。一般多指大杜鹃(又叫"布谷"、"杜宇"或"子规")上体黑灰色，胸腹常有横斑点，吃害虫，是益鸟 (also called 布谷，杜宇 or 子规) cuckoo (*Cuculidae*) **2** 植物名，又叫"映山红"。常绿或落叶灌木，春天开花，红色，供观赏(also called 映山红) azalea (*Rhododendron*)

[杜撰](—zhuàn)凭自己的意思捏造 to fabricate；to make up

肚 ㊀ dù ㄉㄨˋ ❶(—子)腹部，胸下腿上的部分 belly；abdomen ㊀ ***extension*** (—儿)器物中空的部分 hollow central part of some utensils：大～儿坛子 *big-bellied earthen jar* ❷(—子、—儿)圆而凸起像肚子的 belly-shaped thing：腿～子 *calf*｜手指头～儿 *inner side of the top section of a finger*

㊁ dǔ 见161页 see p161

钍 dù ㄉㄨˋ 一种人造的放射性元素(符号 Db) dubnium (Db)

妒（*妬） dù ㄉㄨˋ 因为别人好而忌恨 to be jealous of；to envy：嫉～ *to be jealous of；to envy*｜嫉贤～能 *to envy the good and capable；to be jealous of the talented and the able*

度 ㊀ dù ㄉㄨˋ ❶计算长短的器具或单位 linear measure：～量(liàng)衡 *length，capacity and weight* ❷依照计算的标准划分的单位 degree：温～ *temperature*｜湿～ *humidity*｜经～ *longitude*｜用了20～电 *to have consumed 20 kilowatt-hour electricity* ❸事物所达到的程度 degree；extent：知名～ *popularity*｜高～的爱国热情 *strong sense of patriotism* ❹法则，应遵行的标准 rule；code (㊟ ***doublet*** 制—regulation｜法—law) ❺度量，能容受的量 tolerance；magnanimity：气～

deportment | 适～*moderate* | 过～*excessive* ❻过，由此到彼 to spend; to pass: ～日 *to pass one's days; to subsist on* ❼所打算或考虑的 consideration: 置之～外 *to give no thought to* ❽量词 ***quantifier***，次 time: 一～*once* | 再～*once again* | 前～*the time before the last*

㊁ duó 见 170 页 see p170

渡 dù ㄉㄨˋ ❶横过水面 to cross: ～河 *to cross a river* | ～江 *to cross a river* ㉄ ***extension*** 过，由此到彼 to pass (㊃ ***doublet*** 过— transition): ～过难关 *to pull through; to tide over a difficulty* | 过～时期 *transitional period* ❷渡口，渡头，过河的地方 ferry

镀 dù ㄉㄨˋ 用物理或化学方法使一种物质附着在别的物体的表面上 to plate: ～金 *to gild* | 电～*to electroplate* | ～膜镜头 *coated-lens*

蠹(**蝨、**蠧) dù ㄉㄨˋ ❶蛀蚀器物的虫子 moth: 木～*wood moth* | 书～*bookworm* | ～鱼 *fish moth; silverfish* ❷蛀蚀，侵害 moth-eaten; worm-eaten: 流水不腐，户枢不～。*Running water is never stale and a door-hinge is never worm-eaten — things in use never rot.* or *Practice keeps one always fit.*

DUAN ㄉㄨㄢ

端(*耑) duān ㄉㄨㄢ ❶端正，不歪斜 proper; upright: 五官～正 *to have regular features* | ～坐 *to sit up straight* ㉄ ***extension*** 正派 upright: 品行不～*morally loose; ill-behaved* ❷东西的一头 end: 两～*both ends* | 末～*tip; end* | 笔～*tip of a pen* ㉄ ***extension*** **1** 事情的开头 beginning: 开～*beginning* **2** 项目，点 item; point: 不只一～*not only one point* | 举其大～*to take for example the crux of the matter* [端底][端的](-dì) **1** 事情的经过，底细 ins and outs: 不知～～*not to know the whole story* **2** 的确，果然 indeed; really: ～～是好！*Truly remarkable!* **3** 究竟 actually; truly: ～～是谁？*Who on earth is this person?* [端午][端阳]夏历五月初五日。民间在这一天包粽子、赛龙舟，纪念两千多年前的楚国诗人屈原 Duanwu (or Dragon Boat) Festival, a traditional Chinese festival on the 5th day of the 5th lunar month on which dragon boat races are held and *zongzi* are eaten to cherish the memory of Qu Yuan, a great poet of the Chu State over two thousand years ago [端详] **1** 从头到尾的详细情形 details: 听～～*to listen to the whole story* | 说～～*to give a full account of* **2** 仔细地看 to look at carefully: 她静静地～～着孩子的脸。*Quietly, she looked closely at the child's face.* ❸用手很平正地拿着 to hold sth level: ～碗 *to carry a bowl* | ～茶 *to* *serve tea*

"耑"又 zhuān 见 999 页 "专" also zhuān see 专 on p999

短 duǎn ㄉㄨㄢˇ ❶长度小，跟"长"相对(the opposite of 长) short **1** 空间 of space：～距离 *short distance* | ～裤 *pants; shorts* | ～视(目光短浅) *short-sighted* **2** 时间 of time：～期 *short term* | 天长夜～。*The days are long and nights short.* | ～工(指短期雇用的工人、农民) *casual labourer* ❷缺少，欠 to lack(㊟ ***doublet*** 一少 to lack)：别人都来了，就～他一个人了。*All are here except him.* ❸短处，缺点 shortcoming; deficiency：不应该护～。*It's wrong to shield a fault.* | 取长补～ *to learn from others' strong points to offset one's own weakness*

段 duàn ㄉㄨㄢˋ ❶量词 ***quantifier***，用于事物、时间的一节，截 section; segment; part：一～话 *a passage of a speech* | 一～时间 *a period* | 一～木头 *a log* [段落]文章、事情等根据内容划分成的部分 part; paragraph：工作告一～～。*The work comes to an end for the time being.* | 这篇文章可以分两个～～。*The article can be divided into two parts.* [段位]根据围棋棋手的技能划分的等级，共分九段，棋艺越高，段位越高(of ranks in *weiqi*) level; dan ❷工矿企业中的行政单位(as an administrative level in a mine or factory) section：工～ *work section; workshop* | 机务～ *locomotive department*

塅 duàn ㄉㄨㄢˋ〈方 ***dialect***〉指面积较大的平坦地形。多用于地名(duan, usually used in a place name)：李家～(在湖南省汨罗) *Lijiaduan (a place in Miluo, Hunan Province)*

缎 duàn ㄉㄨㄢˋ (一子)质地厚密，一面光滑的丝织品，是我国的特产之一 satin

椴 duàn ㄉㄨㄢˋ 椴树，落叶乔木，像白杨，我国南北均产。木材细致，可以制家具等 lime; (Chinese) linden (*Tilia*)

煅 duàn ㄉㄨㄢˋ ❶同"锻" same as 锻 ❷放在火里烧，减少药石的烈性(中药的一种制法) to calcine：～石膏 *plaster of Paris*

锻 duàn ㄉㄨㄢˋ 把金属加热，然后锤打 to forge (metal)：～件 *forging* | ～工 *forging; forger* | ～造 *to forge* [锻炼] **1** 通过体育活动，增强体质 to exercise：～～身体，保卫祖国 *to build up a good physique and defend one's motherland* **2** 通过生产劳动、社会斗争和工作实践，使思想觉悟、工作能力提高 to temper：在工作中～～成长 *to get mature through working practices*

断(斷) duàn ㄉㄨㄢˋ ❶长形的东西截成两段或几段 to break; to snap：棍子～了。*The stick snapped.* | 风筝线～了。*The kite string broke.* | 把绳子剪～了 *to have the rope cut* ❷断绝，不继续 to break off; to cut off:～奶 *to wean*｜～了关系 *to break off relations* ㊀ ***extension*** 戒除 to give up; to quit:～酒 *to give up drinking*｜～烟 *to quit smoking* [断送]丧失、毁弃、败坏原来所有而无可挽回 to forfeit; to ruin:～～前程 *to ruin one's future* ❸判断,决定,判定 to judge:诊～*to diagnose*｜～案 *to settle a lawsuit*｜当机立～*to make a prompt decision*｜下～语 *to make a conclusion* ❹一定,绝对 surely; absolutely:～无此理 *definitely unreasonable*｜～然做不得 *absolutely cannot do*

簖(籪) duàn ㄉㄨㄢˋ 插在水里捕鱼、蟹用的竹栅栏 bamboo weir (for catching fish, crabs, etc)

DUI ㄉㄨㄟ

堆 duī ㄉㄨㄟ ❶(一子、一儿)累积在一起的东西 heap; pile:土～*mound*｜草～*haystack*｜柴火～*firewood stack* ❷累积,聚集在一块 to heap (㊀ ***doublet*** 一积 to pile up; to heap up):粮食～满仓。*The barns were bursting with grain.* [堆肥]聚集杂草、泥土等,腐烂发酵而成的肥料 compost [堆砌]㊀ ***figurative*** 写文章用大量华丽而无用的词语 to write in an ornate and redundant style [堆栈]临时存放货物的地方 storehouse; warehouse ❸量词 ***quantifier***,用于成堆的事物 heap; pile:两～土 *two piles of earth*｜一～事 *a pack of things*｜一～人 *a crowd of people*

队(隊) duì ㄉㄨㄟˋ ❶有组织的集体或排成的行(háng)列 team; group; line (of people); queue:乐～*band; orchestra*｜工程～*construction brigade*｜排～*to line up; to stand in a queue* [队伍](—wu) **1** 军队 troops **2** 有组织的群众行列或群体 parade; contingent:游行～～过来了。*Here comes the parade.*｜干部～～*contingent of public functionaries* ❷量词 ***quantifier***,用于排成队列的人或物 file:一～人马 *a file of soldiers and horses; a file of troops*

对(對) duì ㄉㄨㄟˋ ❶答话,回答 to answer; to respond:无词可～*to have nothing to say in reply*｜～答如流 *to answer fluently* ❷向着 to face:面～太阳 *to face the sun* [对象] **1** 思考或行动(如研究、批评、攻击、帮助等等)所及的事物或人 target; object **2** 特指恋爱的对方 prospective partner in marriage; boyfriend (*or* girlfriend) ❸对面的 opposite:～门(*of two houses*) *to face each others; the opposite room* (or *building*)｜～岸 *the opposite bank* ❹互相 mutual:～调 *to exchange*｜～流 *convection* [对比]不同的事物放在一块比较 to contrast; to compare [对照]不同的事物放在一块,互相比较参照 to contrast ❺介词 ***preposition*** **1** 向,跟 to:可以～

D

他说明白 *to be able to make clear to him*｜～人很和气 *to be amiable to others* **2** 对于，说明事物的关系 concerning，with regard to：我～这件事情还有意见。*I still have my own opinions on this matter.*｜他～祖国的历史很有研究。*He's an expert in the history of his motherland.* ❻对待，看待，对付 to treat；to counter：～事不～人 *to concern oneself with facts and not with individuals — Business is business.*｜刀～刀，枪～枪 *sword against sword and spear against spear；tit for tat；an eye for an eye* [对得起][对得住]不亏负 to treat sb fairly ❼照着样检查 to check：～笔迹 *to identify the handwriting*｜校(jiào)～ *to proofread* ❽相合，适合 to fit：～劲 *to be to one's liking*｜～症下药 *to prescribe the right medicine for an illness；to take proper steps* [对头] **1** 相合，正确 to be on good terms；right **2** (—tou)互相对立，有仇恨的人，合不来的人 enemy；opponent ❾正确 right：这话很～。*It's quite true.* ㊞ ***extension*** 用作答语，表示同意 yes：～，你说得不错！*Yes，what you said is not bad.* ❿双，成双的 pair；couple：～联 *antithetical couplet*｜配～ *to pair* ㊞ ***extension*** **1** (—子、—儿)联语 antithetical phrases：喜～ *wedding couplet* **2** 平分，一半 half：～开 *to divide into two halves；to go fifty-fifty*｜～成 *one half* ⓫掺和(多指液体) to mix：～水 *to add some water* ⓬(—儿)量词 ***quantifier***，双 pair：一～鸳鸯 *a pair of mandarin ducks*｜两～夫妻 *two couples*

怼(懟) duì ㄉㄨㄟˋ 怨恨 resentment

兑 duì ㄉㄨㄟˋ ❶交换 to exchange(㊟ ***doublet*** 一换 to exchange)：～款 *to exchange for money*｜汇～ *to remit*｜～现 *to cash* ❷掺和，混合 to mix；to blend：勾～ *to mix；to blend* ❸八卦之一，符号为☱，代表沼泽 *dui*，one of the Eight Diagrams with a symbol of ☱ representing marsh

敦 ㊁ duì ㄉㄨㄟˋ 古时盛黍稷的器具(in ancient China) grain container

㊀ dūn 见167页 see p167

憝 duì ㄉㄨㄟˋ ❶怨恨 resentment ❷坏，恶 wicked；evil：元凶大～ *arch-criminal*

镦 ㊁ duì ㄉㄨㄟˋ 古代矛戟柄末的金属箍 flat-bottom metal hood at the end of a spear or halberd

㊀ dūn 见167页 see p167

碓 duì ㄉㄨㄟˋ 捣米的器具，用木、石制成 wood or stone husking device

DUN ㄉㄨㄣ

吨(噸) dūn ㄉㄨㄣ (外 ***loanword***) ❶质量单位，法定计量单位中1吨等于1 000千克(公斤)。英制1吨

（长吨）等于 2 240 磅，合 1 016.05千克（公斤），美制 1 吨（短吨）等于 2 000 磅，合907.18 千克（公斤）ton，a unit of weight equal to 1,000 kilogramms，and in the British system，one ton（long ton）is 2,240 pounds，or 1,016.05 kilogramms while in the American system，one ton（short ton）is 2,000 pounds，or 907.18 kilogramms ❷指登记吨，计算船只容积的单位，1 吨相当于 100 立方英尺，合 2.83 立方米（in shipping）tonnage，equal to 2.83 cubic metres or 100 cubic feet

惇 dūn ㄉㄨㄣ 敦厚 honest and sincere

敦 ㊀ dūn ㄉㄨㄣ ❶敦厚，厚道 honest and sincere：～睦邦交 *to promote friendly diplomatic relations between two countries* ❷诚心诚意 sincere：～聘 *to offer to engage；to invite cordially*｜～请 *to request sincerely；to invite cordially* ❸姓 Dun，a surname

㊁ duì 见 166 页 see p166

墩 dūn ㄉㄨㄣ ❶土堆 mound ❷（一子、一儿）厚而粗的木头、石头等，座儿 stand：门～儿 *gate pier*｜桥～*bridge pier* ❸量词 ***quantifier***，用于丛生的或几棵合在一起的植物 cluster：栽稻秧两万～*to plant 20,000 clusters of rice seedlings*｜每～五株 *five plants for each cluster*

撴 dūn ㄉㄨㄣ〈方 ***dialect***〉揪住 to catch hold of；to seize

礅 dūn ㄉㄨㄣ 厚而粗的石头 thick and heavy stone：石～*stone block*

镦 ㊀ dūn ㄉㄨㄣ 冲压金属板，使其变形。不加热叫冷镦，加热叫热镦 stamping；punching；cold or hot punching

㊁ duì 见 166 页 see p166

蹾（**撉）dūn ㄉㄨㄣ 猛地往下放，着（zháo）地很重 to lay down heavily：篓子里是鸡蛋，别～。*Please lay the basket down gently as there are eggs in it.*

蹲 ㊀ dūn ㄉㄨㄣ 两腿尽量弯曲，像坐的样子，但臀部不着地 to squat：大家都～下。*Squat down，everybody.* ㊕ ***transfer*** 闲居 to live an idle life：不能再～在家里了。*Don't be idle at home any longer.*［蹲班］留级 to fail to advance to the next grade：～～生 *student failing to go up to the next grade*［蹲点］深入到基层单位，参加实际工作，进行调查研究等（of leaders，etc）to stay at a selected grass-roots unit，take part in the practical work，and carry out surveys and research so as to improve the overall level of work there

㊁ cún 见 115 页 see p115

不 dǔn ㄉㄨㄣˇ［不子］（一 zi）〈方 ***dialect***〉**1** 墩子 wood block or stone block **2** 特指做成砖状的瓷土块，是制造瓷器

的原料 brick-shaped block of porcelain clay

盹 dǔn ㄉㄨㄣˇ (一儿)很短时间的睡眠 doze; nap:打～儿(打瞌睡) *to doze off; to take a nap*

趸(躉) dǔn ㄉㄨㄣˇ ❶整,整数 wholesale:～批 *wholesale*|～卖 *to sell wholesale* ❷整批地买进 to buy wholesale:～货 *to buy goods wholesale*|～菜 *to buy vegetables wholesale*|现～现卖 *to buy wholesale and sell immediately*

D

囤 ㊀ dùn ㄉㄨㄣˋ 用竹篾、荆条等编成的或用席箔等围成的盛粮食等的器物 bin:大～满,小～流。*All the grain bins, either big or small, are bursting with grain.*

㊁ tún 见 767 页 see p767

沌 dùn ㄉㄨㄣˋ 见 302 页"混"字条"混沌"(hùn—) see 混沌 on p302

炖(**燉) dùn ㄉㄨㄣˋ ❶煨煮食品使熟烂 to stew:清～鸡 *water-boiled chicken without salt or soy sauce*|～肉 *stewed meat* ❷〈方 **dialect**〉把汤药、酒等盛在碗里,再把碗放在水里加热 to warm sth in a container in boiling water

砘 dùn ㄉㄨㄣˋ ❶(一子)耩(jiǎng)完地之后用来轧(yà)地的石磙子 stone-roller ❷用砘子轧地 to roll loose soil with a stone-roller

钝 dùn ㄉㄨㄣˋ ❶不锋利,不快 blunt; dull:这把刀真～。*The knife is very blunt.*|镰刀～了,磨一磨吧。*The sickle is dull. Sharpen it.* ❷笨,不灵活 stupid; dull-witted:脑筋迟～ *slow; dull-witted*|拙嘴～舌 *clumsy-tongued; clumsy in expressing oneself*

顿 ㊀ dùn ㄉㄨㄣˋ ❶很短时间的停止 short pause (㊀ **doublet** 停— to pause):抑扬～挫 *cadence*|念到这个地方应该～一下。*Pause briefly when reading here.* ❷忽然,立刻,一下子 suddenly; immediately:～悟 *to be suddenly enlightened*|～时紧张起来 *to be nervous all of a sudden* ❸叩,碰 to touch one's head to the ground:～首 *to kowtow* ㊇ **transfer** 跺 to stamp:～足 *to stamp one's feet* ❹处理,放置 to handle; to place:整～ *to rectify; to readjust*|安～ *to settle down; to settle in* ❺书法上指运笔用力向下而暂不移动 (in Chinese calligraphy) to pause in writing in order to reinforce the beginning or ending of a stroke ❻疲乏 tired; exhausted:劳～ *fatigued*|困～ *tired out* ❼量词 **quantifier**,次 time:一天三～饭 *three meals a day*|说了一～ *to give sb a dressing down*|打了他一～ *to give sb a good beating* ❽姓 Dun, a surname

㊁ dú 见 161 页 see p161

盾 dùn ㄉㄨㄣˋ ❶古代打仗时防护身体,挡住敌人刀、箭等的牌 shield [后盾]指后方护卫、支援的力量 backing; backing force ❷盾形的东西 shield-shaped thing:金～*gold shield*|银～*silver shield* ❸越南等国的货币单位 unit of currency of Vietnam (dong), etc

遁(*遯) dùn ㄉㄨㄣˋ 逃走,逃避 to escape; to flee:～去 *to run away*|夜～*to escape into the night* [遁词][遁辞]理屈词穷时所说的应付话 subterfuge; quibble

楯 ㊀ dùn ㄉㄨㄣˋ 同"盾" same as 盾

㊁ shǔn 见 700 页 see p700

DUO ㄉㄨㄛ

多 duō ㄉㄨㄛ ❶跟"少"相对 (the opposite of 少) **1** 数量大的 many; much; a lot of:人很～*many people*|～生产 *to produce a great deal* **2** 有余,比一定的数目大 more; greater; -odd (following a quantity)(㊟ ***doublet*** 一余 surplus):十～个 *more than ten*|一年～*more than one year*|只预备五份,没有～的。*Only five, no more*. **3** 过分,不必要的 excessive; unnecessary:～嘴 *to shoot off one's mouth; to have a big mouth*|～心 *oversensitive; over suspicious* [多亏]幸亏 thanks to; luckily:～～你来帮忙 *thanks to your help*|～～他加一把力量,推动了这工作。*But for his effort, the work wouldn't have progressed*. [多少] **1** 未定的数量 unspecified amount or number:你要～～拿～～。*Take as many as you like*. **2** 问不知道的数量 how many; how much:这本书～～钱? *How much is this book?*|这班有～～学生? *How many students are there in this class?* **3** 许多 many; much:没有～～ *not many; not much* **4** 或多或少 more or less:～～有些困难。*It's somewhat difficult*. ❷表示相差的程度大 much more; much less; far more; far less:好得～*much better*|厚～了 *much thicker* ❸副词 ***adverb*** **1** 多么,表示惊异、赞叹(used in exclamatory sentences to indicate a high degree) how; what:～好! *How wonderful!*|～大! *How big!*|～香! *How delicious!* **2** 表疑问(used in questions) how:有～大? *How old?* [多会儿](—huìr)[多咱](—zan)什么时候,几时 when

哆 duō ㄉㄨㄛ [哆嗦](—suo)发抖,战栗 to shiver; to tremble:冷得打～～*to tremble with cold*

咄 duō ㄉㄨㄛ 表示呵叱或惊异(used to show disapproval or to berate) to tut-tut [咄咄]表示惊怪(used to show disapproval) tut-tut:～～怪事 *absurdity* [咄嗟](—jiē)吆喝 to shout:～～立办(马上就办到) *to get things done immediately as ordered; to get sth done straight away*

剟 duō ㄉㄨㄛ ❶刺,击 to sting; to stab ❷削,删除 to cut; to delete

D

掇 duō ㄉㄨㄛ ❶拾取 to pick up (㊟ *doublet* 一拾 to pick up) ❷〈方 *dialect*〉用双手拿(椅子、凳子等),用手端 to hold (a chair, stool, etc) with both hands

敠 duō ㄉㄨㄛ 见145页"战"字条"战敠"(diānduo) see 战敠 on p145

裰 duō ㄉㄨㄛ ❶缝补破衣 to patch:补～*to patch up* ❷直裰,古代士子、官绅穿的长袍便服,也指僧道穿的袍子(in ancient China) long flowing robe

夺(奪) duó ㄉㄨㄛˊ ❶抢,强取 to seize (㊟ *doublet* 抢一 to grab; to snatch):把敌人的枪～过来 *to wrest a gun from the enemy* [夺目]耀眼 brilliant; dazzling:光彩～～*splendid; radiant* ❷争取得到 to strive for:～丰收 *to strive for a good harvest* ❸冲出 to rush out:泪水～眶而出 *to burst into tears* ❹做决定 to decide:定～*to make a final decision*|裁～*to consider and decide* ❺漏掉(文字) to be missing:讹～*error or omission* ❻失去,使失去 to lose:勿～农时。*Don't miss the farming season.*

度 ㊁ duó ㄉㄨㄛˊ 忖度,揣度,计算,推测 to conjecture; to estimate:～德量力 *to appraise oneself by standards of morality and ability*

㊀ dù 见162页 see p162

踱 duó ㄉㄨㄛˊ 慢慢地走 to pace; to stroll:～来～去 *to pace up and down*

铎(鐸) duó ㄉㄨㄛˊ 大铃,古代宣布政教法令时或有战事时用的 big bell (used in ancient China in times of war or when a proclamation was issued)

朵(*朶) duǒ ㄉㄨㄛˇ ❶花朵,植物的花或苞 flower; blossom; bud ❷量词 ***quantifier***,用于花或成团的东西 for flowers, clouds, etc:三～花 *three flowers*|两～云彩 *two clouds*

垛(*垜) ㊀ duǒ ㄉㄨㄛˇ (一子)用泥土、砖石等筑成的掩蔽物 buttress; battlement:箭～子 *arrow crenel*|门～子 *gate buttress*|城墙～口 *crenel; battlement*

㊁ duò 见171页 see p171

哚(**哚) duǒ ㄉㄨㄛˇ 见897页"吲"字条"吲哚"see 吲哚(yǐn—) on p897

躲(**躱) duǒ ㄉㄨㄛˇ 隐藏,避开 to hide; to avoid (㊟ *doublet* 一藏 to hide; to conceal|一避 to dodge; to duck; to elude):～雨 *to take shelter from the rain*|他～在哪里? *Where is he hiding?*|明枪易～,暗箭难防。*It's easy to dodge an overt spear, but hard to guard oneself against a covert arrow — hidden attacks are more dangerous than open acts of enmity.*

埵 duǒ ㄉㄨㄛˇ 坚硬的土 hard soil

痑 duǒ ㄉㄨㄛˇ 马疲劳(of a horse) tired

亸(軃、**躲) duǒ ㄉㄨㄛˇ 下垂 to droop; to hang down

驮 ㊁ duò ㄉㄨㄛˋ (一子)骡马等负载的成捆的货物 load carried by a pack animal; pack: 把～子卸下来,让牲口休息一会儿。*Unload the animal and let it rest for a while.*

㊀ tuó 见 768 页 see p768

剁(**刴) duò ㄉㄨㄛˋ 用刀向下砍 to chop; to cut: ～碎 *to chop up* | ～饺子馅 *to chop the stuffing of* jiaozi

垛(*垜、**稞) ㊁ duò ㄉㄨㄛˋ ❶ 整齐地堆成的堆 pile; stack: 麦～ *wheat stack* | 砖～ *brick pile* ❷整齐地堆积 to pile up neatly: 柴火～得比房还高。*The pile of firewood is higher than the house.*

㊀ duǒ 见 170 页 see p170

跺(*跥) duò ㄉㄨㄛˋ 顿足,提起脚来用力踏 to stamp: ～脚 *to stamp one's foot*

饳 duò ㄉㄨㄛˋ 见 241 页"馉"字条"馉饳"(gǔ—) see 馉饳 on p241

柮 duò ㄉㄨㄛˋ 见 241 页"榾"字条"榾柮"(gǔ—) see 榾柮 on p241

沲 duò ㄉㄨㄛˋ [淡沲]荡漾 to ripple; to undulate

柁 ㊁ duò ㄉㄨㄛˋ 同"舵" same as 舵

㊀ tuó 见 769 页 see p769

舵 duò ㄉㄨㄛˋ 控制行船方向的设备,多装在船尾 rudder; helm: 掌～ *to steer (a boat); to take the helm* | ～手 *steersman; helmsman* ㊞ ***extension*** 飞机等交通工具上控制方向的装置 rudder; helm

堕(墮) duò ㄉㄨㄛˋ 掉下来,坠落 to fall; to drop: ～地 *to fall on the ground* [堕落] ㊥ ***figurative*** 思想行为向坏的方向变化 to degenerate: ～～分子 *degenerate* | 腐化～～ *corruptive and degenerate*

惰 duò ㄉㄨㄛˋ 懒,懈怠,跟"勤"相对(the opposite of 勤) lazy; indolent (㊟ ***doublet*** 懒— lazy | 怠—idle)

D

E ㄜ

E ㄜ

阿 ㊁ ē ㄜ ❶迎合,偏袒 to pander to; to play up to: ～附 *to fawn on and echo* | ～其所好 *to cater to* | ～谀逢迎 *to curry favour with* ❷凹曲处 winding area: 山～ *mountain range that twists and turns*

[阿胶]中药名,用驴皮加水熬成的胶,有滋补养血的作用,原产山东省东阿 E-gelatin; donkey-hide gelatin; Ejiao, a traditional Chinese tonic for nourishing the blood, made by stewing donkey hide with water, originally produced in Dong'e, Shandong Province

㊀ ā 见1页 see p1

屙 ē ㄜ 排泄大小便 to discharge (faeces or urine): ～屎 *to shit*

婀 ē ㄜ [婀娜](—nuó)姿态柔美的样子 lithe and graceful

讹(❶*譌) é ㄜ ❶错误 mistake; error: 以～传～*to circulate erroneous reports* ❷敲诈,假借某种理由向人强迫索取财物或其他权利 to blackmail: ～人 *to blackmail; to swindle* | ～诈 *to blackmail; to swindle*

囮 é ㄜ (—子)捕鸟时用来引诱同类鸟的鸟。也叫"圝(yóu)子"(also called 圝子) decoy bird

俄 é ㄜ ❶俄顷,短时间 all of a sudden; in a moment: ～而日出,光照海上。*In a moment, the sun rises, shining splendidly over the sea.* ❷指俄罗斯 Russia

[俄罗斯族]**1** 我国少数民族,参看附表(see the appendix) the Russian ethnic group, one of the ethnic minorities of China **2** 俄罗斯联邦的主要民族 the main nationality in the Russian Federation

莪 é ㄜ 莪蒿,草名,生在水边 sagebrush (*Artemisia*)

[莪术](—zhú)多年生草本植物,产于我国南方,根状茎可入药 curcuma (*Curcuma phaeocaulis*)

哦 ㊂ é ㄜ 吟哦,低声地唱 to chant softly

㊀ ó 见544页 see p544

㊁ ò 见544页 see p544

峨(*峩) é ㄜ 高 lofty: 巍～ *lofty; towering* | ～冠 *high-topped hat*

[峨眉][峨嵋]山名,在四川省 Emei Mountain, in Sichuan Province

娥 é ㄜ ❶美好(指女性姿态) graceful ❷指美女 beauty:

宫～*palace maid*［娥眉］指美女的眉毛，也指美女。也作"蛾眉"(also written as 蛾眉)beautiful eyebrows; beauty

锇 é ㄜ 一种金属元素，符号Os，青白色，很坚硬。可制催化剂，其合金可用来制耐腐蚀、耐磨部件 osmium (Os)

鹅（*鵞）é ㄜ 一种家禽，比鸭子大，颈长，脚有蹼，头部有黄色或黑褐色的肉质突起，雄的突起较大 goose

蛾 é ㄜ （一子、一儿）像蝴蝶的昆虫，静止时，翅左右平放 moth：灯～*moth*｜蚕～*silk moth*｜飞～投火 *a moth darting into a flame—to seek one's own doom*

〈古 ***archaism***〉又同"蚁"(yǐ) also same as 蚁

额（*額）é ㄜ ❶俗叫"脑门子"，眉上发下的部分。(popularly called 脑门子) forehead（图见 758 页"头" picture on p758）❷规定的数量 specified number or amount：定～*quota*｜名～*quota; vacancy*｜超～完成任务 *to overfulfil (a task)*［额外］超出规定以外的 additional; extra：～～的要求 *additional requirement* ❸牌匾 inscribed board：横～*horizontal inscribed board*｜匾～*horizontal inscribed board*

恶（惡、噁）㊂ ě ㄜ［恶心］(一 xin) 要呕吐 sick ㊕ ***transfer*** 厌恶(wù) to be disgusted with; to abhor; to abominate

㊀ è 见 173 页 see p173
㊁ wù 见 798 页 see p798
㊃ wū 见 794 页 see p794

厄（*阨）è ㄜ ❶困苦，灾难 adversity; hardship：～运 *misfortune; disaster* ❷阻塞，受困 to be stranded：～于海上 *to be stranded at sea* ❸险要的地方 strategic point：险～*strategic point*

扼（*搤）è ㄜ 用力掐着，抓住 to clutch; to grip：力能～虎 *to have the strength to clutch a tiger*［扼守］把守要地，防止敌人侵入 to hold (a strategic point); to guard (a place of strategic importance)［扼要］抓住要点 to the point：文章简明～～。*The article is brief and to the point.*

苊 è ㄜ 有机化合物，分子式 $C_{12}H_{10}$，无色针状结晶，溶于热酒精，有致癌作用，可作媒染剂 acenaphthene

呃 è ㄜ 呃逆，因横膈膜痉挛引起的打嗝儿 hiccup

轭 è ㄜ 驾车时搁在牛颈上的曲木 yoke

垩（堊）è ㄜ ❶粉刷墙壁用的白土 chalk ❷用白土涂饰 to whitewash

恶（惡）㊀ è ㄜ ❶恶劣，不好 evil; wicked：～感 *ill feeling; malice*｜～习 *bad (or vicious) habit* ❷凶狠 ferocious; vicious（㊣ ***doublet*** 凶一 ferocious)：～狗 *ferocious dog*｜～战 *fierce battle*｜～霸 *local tyrant* ❸犯罪的事，极坏

的行为，跟"善"相对（the opposite of 善）evil；wickedness：罪～*crime；evil*｜无～不作 *to stop at nothing in doing evil*

㊁ wù 见 798 页 see p798

㊂ ě 见 173 页 see p173

㊃ wū 见 794 页 see p794

饿 è ㄜ 肚子空，想吃东西 hungry：肚子～了。*I'm hungry.*

鄂 è ㄜ 湖北省的别称 E，another name for Hubei Province

［鄂伦春族］我国少数民族，参看附表（see the appendix）the Oroqen（or Olunchun）ethnic group，one of the ethnic minorities of China

［鄂温克族］我国少数民族，参看附表（see the appendix）the Ewenki（or Owenk）ethnic group，one of the ethnic minorities of China

谔 è ㄜ 言语正直（of speech）righteous［谔谔］直言争辩的样子 outspoken

萼 è ㄜ 花萼，在花瓣下部的一圈绿色小片 calyx

愕 è ㄜ 惊讶 stunned；astounded：～然 *stunned；astounded*｜惊～*astounded*

腭（*齶）è ㄜ 口腔的上膛，分为两部，前面叫硬腭，后面叫软腭 palate

鹗 è ㄜ 鸟名，又叫"鱼鹰"。性凶猛，背暗褐色，腹白色，常在水面上飞翔，捕食鱼类（also called 鱼鹰）osprey

锷 è ㄜ 刀剑的刃 blade

颚 è ㄜ ❶某些节肢动物摄取食物的器官 mandible ❷同"腭"same as 腭

鳄（*鱷）è ㄜ 俗叫"鳄鱼"。一类凶恶的爬行动物，皮和鳞很坚硬，生活在热带、亚热带的沿海和河流、池沼中，主要捕食小动物（popularly called 鳄鱼）crocodile（*Crocodylidae*）

遏 è ㄜ 阻止 to check；to hold back：怒不可～*to fly into a rage；to be in a towering rage*［遏制］制止，控制 to restrain；to contain：～～敌人的进攻 *to restrain the enemy's momentum of attack*｜～～不住满腔的激情 *to fail to hold the passion in check*

頞 è ㄜ 鼻梁（nose）bridge

噩 è ㄜ 可怕而惊人的 shocking：～梦 *nightmare*｜～耗（指亲近或敬爱的人死亡的消息）（*news of the death of a person close or dear to one*）*evil tidings*

Ê ㄝ

诶 ㊀ ē ㄝ ēi ㄟ（又 also ēi）同"欸㊀"same as 欸㊀

㊁ é 见 175 页 see p175

㊂ ě 见 175 页 see p175

㊃ è 见 175 页 see p175

欸 ㊀ ē ㄝ ēi ㄟ（又 also ēi）叹词 ***interjection***，表示招呼（used to call attention）hey：～，你快来！*Hey，come over here!*

㊁ ế 见 175 页 see p175
㊂ ě 见 175 页 see p175
㊃ è 见 175 页 see p175
㊄ ǎi 见 4 页 see p4

诶 ㊁ ế ㄝ éi ㄟ (又 also éi) 同"欸㊁"same as 欸㊁
㊀ ē 见 174 页 see p174
㊂ ě 见 175 页 see p175
㊃ è 见 175 页 see p175

欸 ㊁ ế ㄝ éi ㄟ (又 also éi) 叹词 ***interjection***,表示诧异(used to express surprise) why:～,怎么回事! *Why, what's the matter?*
㊀ ē 见 174 页 see p174
㊂ ě 见 175 页 see p175
㊃ è 见 175 页 see p175
㊄ ǎi 见 3 页 see p3

诶 ㊂ ě ㄝ ěi ㄟ (又 also ěi) 同"欸㊂"same as 欸㊂
㊀ ē 见 174 页 see p174
㊁ é 见 175 页 see p175
㊃ è 见 175 页 see p175

欸 ㊂ ě ㄝ ěi ㄟ (又 also ěi) 叹词 ***interjection***,表示不以为然(used to express disapproval) huh:～,你这话可不对呀! *Huh, you shouldn't say that!*
㊀ ē 见 174 页 see p174
㊁ é 见 175 页 see p175
㊃ è 见 175 页 see p175
㊄ ǎi 见 4 页 see p4

诶 ㊃ è ㄝ èi ㄟ (又 also èi) 同"欸㊃"same as 欸㊃
㊀ ē 见 174 页 see p174
㊁ é 见 175 页 see p175
㊂ ě 见 175 页 see p175

欸 ㊃ è ㄝ èi ㄟ (又 also èi) 叹词 ***interjection***,表示应声或同意(used to express approval or consent) OK; all right:～,我这就来! *OK, I'm coming!* |～,就这么办! *All right, go ahead.*
㊀ ē 见 174 页 see p174
㊁ é 见 175 页 see p175
㊂ ě 见 175 页 see p175
㊄ ǎi 见 4 页 see p4

EI ㄟ

唉 éi ㄟ 叹词 ***interjection***,表示诧异或忽然想起(used to express surprise or sudden remembrance) why; oh:～,他怎么病了! *Why, he's ill!* |～,我三点钟还有一场电影呢! *Oh, I am going to see a movie at three o'clock.*

EN ㄣ

奀 ㊀ ēn ㄣ 〈方 ***dialect***〉瘦小(多用于人名)(usually used in a given name) small and thin
㊁ dí 见 140 页 see p140

恩 ēn ㄣ 好处,深厚的情谊 favour (㊣ ***doublet*** 一惠 grace|一德 benevolence):共产党的～情说不完。*We shall never say enough about our gratitude to the Chinese Communist Party.* [恩爱]形容夫妻亲爱 affectionate

蒽 ēn ㄣ 一种有机化合物,分子式 $C_{14}H_{10}$,无色晶体,发

紫色荧光，是染料工业的原料 anthracene

摁 èn ㄣˋ 用手按压 to press: ～电铃 *to ring an electric bell*

ENG ㄥ

鞥 ēng ㄥ 马缰 reins

ER ㄦ

儿(兒) ér ㄦˊ ❶小孩子 child（㊀ ***doublet*** —童 child）：六一～童节 *International Children's Day*（*June 1st*）|小～科 *paediatrics*|别把这件事当作～戏。*Don't trifle with this matter.* ❷年轻的人（多指青年男子）youth; youngster：健～*excellent athlete* ❸儿子，男孩子 son：他有一～一女。*He has a son and a daughter.* ㊀***extension*** 雄性的 male：～马 *male horse* ❹父母对儿女的统称，儿女对父母的自称 son; daughter ❺词尾 ***suffix***，同前一字连成一个卷舌音 added to the proceeding word to form a retroflex sound **1** 表示小 small：小孩～*kid*|乒乓球～*table-tennis ball*|小狗～*little dog* **2** 使动词、形容词等名词化（used to turn verbs, adjectives into nouns）：没救～*hopeless*|拐弯～*to make a turn*|挡着亮～*to shut out the light*|叫好～*to shout "bravo"*

而 ér ㄦˊ 连词 ***conjunction*** ❶连接同类的词或句子 and; as well as **1** 顺接 and：聪明～勇敢 *clever and brave*|通过实践～发现真理，又通过实践～证实真理和发展真理 *to discover the truth through practice and verify and develop the truth through practice* **2** 转接 but; and yet：有其名～无其实 *to exist in name but not in reality; to be merely nominal*［而且］连词 ***conjunction*** **1** 表示平列 and also：文章写得长～～空，群众见了就摇头。*The article is long-winded and lacks substance, so when people read it, they will shake their heads with disapproval.* **2** 表示进一层，常跟"不但"相应（usually used correspondingly with 不但）but also：鲁迅不但是伟大的文学家，～～是伟大的思想家和革命家。*Lu Xun was not only a great writer, but also a great thinker and revolutionary.*［而已］助词 ***auxiliary***，罢了 that's all：不过如此～～。*That's all.* ❷把表时间或情状的词连接到动词上（used to link an adverbial element of time and situation to a verb）：匆匆～来 *to come in a hurry*|侃侃～谈 *to talk with ease and fluency*|挺身～出 *to step forward bravely* ❸（从）…到…（from）… to …：自上～下 *from top to bottom; up and down*|由小～大 *from small to large*

洏 ér ㄦˊ 见 438 页"涟"字条"涟洏"(lián—) see 涟洏 on p438

鸸 ér ㄦˊ [鸸鹋](—miáo)鸟的一种,形体像鸵鸟,嘴短而扁,有三个趾。善走,不能飞,生活在澳大利亚的草原和沙漠地区 emu (*Dromaius novaehollandiae*)

尔(爾) ěr ㄦˇ ❶代词 ***pronoun*** **1** 你,你的 thou; you; your:~辈 *you* |~父 *your father* |出~反~(喻无信用)to go back on one's words; to contradict oneself [尔汝]你我相称,关系亲密 on very close terms with each other:相为~~*to be on close terms with each other* |~~交 *to be close friends* **2** 如此(叠 ***reduplication***)like that:果~*if so* |偶~*occasionally*|不过~~*just so-so* **3** 那,其(指时间)that:~时 *at that time*|~日 *that day*|~后 *thereafter* ❷同"耳❸" same as 耳❸ ❸词尾 ***suffix*** 相当于"然" corresponding to 然:卓~*preeminent; outstanding*|率~(轻率)*rash; hasty*

迩(邇) ěr ㄦˇ 近 near; close:遐~闻名 *to be well-known far and near; to enjoy widespread renown* |~来(近来)*recently; lately*

耳 ěr ㄦˇ ❶耳朵,听觉器官 ear:~聋 *deaf*|~熟(听着熟悉)*to sound familiar* |~生(听着生疏) *to sound strange*|~语(嘴贴近别人耳朵小声说话)*to whisper* ❷像耳朵的 ear-shaped **1** 指形状 of shape:木~*edible fungus* |银~*tremella* **2** 指位置在两旁的 on either side; side:~房 *smaller room on either side of the main room; wing room* |~门 *smaller door on either side of a gate, or beside the main entrance* ❸〈古 ***archaism***〉助词 ***auxiliary***,表示"罢了"的意思,而已 only; just:前言戏之~。*What has been said is only a joke.* |此无他,唯手熟~。*It requires nothing special. It only needs repeated practice.*

饵 ěr ㄦˇ ❶糕饼 cake; pastry:香~*savoury cakes* |果~*candies and pastries* ❷钓鱼用的鱼食 bait:鱼~*bait* ❸引诱 to entice:以此~敌。*Use this to entice the enemy.*

洱 ěr ㄦˇ [洱海]湖名,在云南省大理 Erhai Lake, in Dali, Yunnan Province

珥 ěr ㄦˇ 用珠子或玉石做的耳环 jade or pearl earrings

铒 ěr ㄦˇ 一种金属元素,符号 Er,银白色,质软。可用来制特种合金、激光器等 erbium (Er)

二 èr ㄦˋ ❶数目字 two:十~个 *twelve*|两元~角 *two yuan and twenty fen* ("二"与"两"用法不同,参看 441 页"两"字注)(for the difference between 二 and 两, refer to the entry of 两 on p441)❷第二,次的 second; inferior:~等货 *second-rate goods*|~把刀(指技术不高)*to have but a smattering*

of a subject; to have half-baked knowledge or *imperfect skill* [二手] **1** 旧的，用过的 used; second-hand：～～车 *second-hand car* | ～～货 *second-hand goods* **2** 间接的 indirect：～～资料 *second-hand material* ❸两样 different：心无～用 *One cannot keep one's mind on different things at the same time.*

贰（**弍） èr 儿 "二"字的大写 two, capital form of 二

佴 ㊀ èr 儿 置，停留 to place; to stay

㊁ nài 见 524 页 see p524

E

F ㄈ

FA ㄈㄚ

发(發) ㊀fā ㄈㄚ ❶交付，送出，跟"收"相对(the opposite of 收) to deliver; to dispatch; to send out: ～选民证 *to distribute voters' certificates*｜～货 *to deliver goods*｜信已经～了。*The letter has been posted* (or *sent*). [发落]处理，处分 to deal with: 从轻～～ *to deal with sb leniently* [打发](－fɑ) **1** 派遣 to send; to dispatch: ～～专人去办 *to assign a special person to a task* **2** 使离去 to send away: 好不容易才把他～～走了。*It takes much effort to send him away.* **3** 消磨(时日) to kill time: 病人们靠聊天儿～～时光。*The patients chatted to kill time.* ❷表达，说出 to express; to utter: ～言 *to speak; to make a speech*｜～问 *to ask a question*｜～誓 *to vow* [发表]用文字或语言表达意见 to express; to publish ❸放射 to fire; to radiate: ～炮 *to fire shells*｜～光 *to give off light* ㊂ **extension** 量词 **quantifier**，枪弹、炮弹一枚称一发(of bullets and shells): 五十～子弹 *fifty bullets* ❹散开，分散 to disperse: ～汗 *to induce perspiration*｜挥～ *to volatilize*｜蒸～ *to evaporate* [发挥]把意思尽量地说出，把力量尽量地用出 to bring into play: 借题～～ *to seize a pretext to air one's views*｜～～题意 *to elaborate on a subject*｜～～群众的智慧和力量 *to bring the intelligence and strength of the masses into full play* ❺开展，扩大，膨胀 to develop; to expand: ～扬 *to keep up; to carry on*｜～展 *to develop*｜～海带 *to soak dried kelp in water*｜面～了。*The dough has risen.* [发达]兴旺，旺盛 flourishing: 工业～～ *thriving industry*｜交通～～ *well-developed traffic* [发育]生物逐渐长成壮大 to grow: 身体～～正常 *normal physical development* [发展]事物内部的矛盾运动，通常指事物由小而大，由弱而强，由低级到高级，由简单到复杂的变化 to develop: 形势迅速～～。*The situation develops rapidly.*｜～～生产 *to develop production* ❻因得到大量资财而兴旺 to make a fortune: 暴～户 *upstart*｜这几年他做买卖～了。*He has made a fortune through business in recent years.* ❼打开，揭露 to open; to expose: ～掘潜力 *to tap potentials*｜揭～阴谋 *to bring schemes to light* [发明]创造出以前没有的事物

to invent：印刷术是我国首先～～的。*Printing was first invented in China.*［发现］**1** 找出原先就存在而大家不知道的事物或道理 to discover：～～新油田 *to discover a new oil-field* **2** 发觉 to notice：～～问题就及时解决 *to solve the problem as soon as it is noticed* ❽显现，显出 to look；to appear：脸上～黄。*The face appears sallow.* ❾产生，发生 to come into existence：～芽 *to sprout*｜～病 *to come down with an illness* ❿觉得 to feel：～麻 *to feel numb*｜～烧 *to have a fever* ⓫开始动作，起程 to start：～端 *to make a start*｜朝～夕至 *to start at dawn and arrive at dusk*｜～动机器 *to start a machine*｜队伍出～。*The troops set out.*

㊁ fà 见181页 see p181

乏 fá ㄈㄚˊ ❶缺少 lack（㊟ ***doublet*** 缺一 lack）：～味 *tasteless；dull*｜不～其人。*There's no lack of such people.* ❷疲倦 tired（㊟***doublet*** 疲一 tired）：人困马～。*The men wore out and the horses were jaded — tired out；exhausted*｜跑了一天，身上有点～*to feel a bit tired after running about for a whole day*

伐 fá ㄈㄚˊ ❶砍 to fell；to chop：～树 *to cut down trees*｜采～木材 *to lumber* ❷征讨，攻打 to attack（㊟***doublet*** 讨一 to go on a punitive expedition）：北～*the Northern Expedition*

垡 fá ㄈㄚˊ ❶耕地，把土翻起来 to turn up soil：秋～地（秋耕）*autumn ploughing* 也指翻起来的土块 upturned soil：晒～*to sun the upturned soil* ❷量词 ***quantifier***，相当于次、番 time ❸地名用字 fa，used in a place name：榆～（在北京市大兴）*Yufa (a place in Daxing, Beijing)*｜落～（在河北省廊坊）*Luofa (a place in Langfang, Hebei Province)*

阀 fá ㄈㄚˊ ❶封建时代指有权势的家庭、家族 powerful and influential family in feudal times：门～*influential family*｜～阅之家 *powerful and influential family* ❷凭借权势造成特殊地位的个人或集团 person or group achieving special status through one's power and influence：军～*warlord*｜财～*financial magnate；plutocrat* ❸（外 ***loanword***）又叫"活门"、"阀门"或"凡尔"。管道、唧筒或其他机器中调节流体的流量、压力和流动方向的装置（also called 活门，阀门 or 凡尔）valve

筏（*栰） fá ㄈㄚˊ（一子）用竹、木等平摆着编扎成的水上交通工具 raft

罚（*罸） fá ㄈㄚˊ 处分犯错误的人 to punish；to penalize（㊟***doublet*** 惩一 to punish；to penalize｜责一 to punish）：他受～了。*He's punished.*

法 fǎ ㄈㄚˇ ❶由国家制定或认可，以强制力保证其实施

的行为规范的总称 law; statute:婚姻～*marriage law*|犯～*to break the law*|合～*legal; lawful; legitimate*|依～治国 *to govern the state by law*[法院]独立行使审判权的国家机关 court ❷(－子、－儿)方法,处理事物的手段 method; way:写～*writing style*|办～*method; approach*|用～*usage; use*|没～儿办 *to be impossible to do* ❸仿效 to imitate:效～*to follow sb's example; to follow sb's lead*|师～*to model oneself after (a great master)* ❹标准,模范,可仿效的 standard; model:～书 *model calligraphy*|～绘 *model painting*|～帖 *model calligraphy*[法宝][喻]***figurative*** 特别有效的工具、方法或经验 magic weapon, formula or experience:统一战线、武装斗争、党的建设,是中国革命的三大～～。*There are three magic weapons in the Chinese revolution — united front, armed struggle and Party building.* ❺佛教徒称他们的教义,民间传说的所谓"超人力"的本领 dharma; sutra:佛～*Buddhist doctrine*|～术 *witchcraft; black magic* ❻指法国 France

砝 fǎ ㄈㄚˇ [砝码](－mǎ)天平和磅秤上用作重量标准的东西,用金属制成 weight

发(髮) ㊁ fà ㄈㄚˋ 头发 hair:理～*to have one's hair cut*|脱～*to lose hair*|令人～指(喻使人非常气愤)*to make one's hair stand on end; to make sb boil with rage*

㊀ fā 见 179 页 see p179

珐(*琺) fà ㄈㄚˋ [珐琅](－láng)用硼砂、玻璃粉、石英等加铅、锡的氧化物烧制成像釉子的物质。涂在铜质或银质器物的表面作为装饰,又可防锈。一般的证章、奖章等多为珐琅制品。珐琅制品景泰蓝是我国特产的手工艺品之一 enamel

FAN ㄈㄢ

帆(*颿) fān ㄈㄢ 利用风力使船前进的布篷 sail:一～风顺 *plain sailing; in smooth waters*

番 ㊀ fān ㄈㄢ ❶称外国的或外族的 foreign; of foreign nationality:～茄 *tomato*|～薯 *sweet potato*|～椒 *hot pepper* ❷代换 turn:轮～*by turns; in rotation*|更～*in turn; alternatively* ❸量词 ***quantifier*** **1** 遍,次 time:三～五次 *time and (time) again*|费了一～心思 *to have done a lot of thinking*|解说一～*to give an explanation* **2** 倍 time; -fold:产量翻了一～。*The output has doubled.*

㊁ pān 见 549 页 see p549

蕃 ㊁ fān ㄈㄢ 同"番(fān)❶" same as 番❶

㊀ fán 见 183 页 see p183

幡(**旛) fān ㄈㄢ 用竹竿等挑起来直着挂的长条形旗子 streamer

藩 fān ㄈㄢ 藩篱,篱笆 fence; hedge [喻]***figurative*** 作保卫

F

的屏障 screen; barrier 封建时代用来称属国、属地(in feudal times) vassal; feudatory: ～国 *vassal state; feudatory* | ～属 *vassal state; feudatory*

翻(*飜) fān ㄈㄢ ❶歪倒(dǎo),或上下、内外移位 to reverse; to overturn: 车～了。*The car overturned.* | ～修马路 *to rebuild a road* | 把桌上的书都～乱了。*The books on the table are in a mess after being rummaged.* [翻砂]把熔化的金属倒(dào)入用潮湿砂子制成的模型里,铸造成器具或机件 founding; moulding; casting [翻身] **1** 翻转身体 to turn over **2** 比喻从被压迫的情况下解放出来 to be liberated; to be freed: 劳动人民～～当家做主人。*The labouring people have stood up and become the masters of their own fate.* ❷改变 to change: ～改 *to remake* | ～案 *to reverse a verdict* ❸数量成倍增加 to multiply; to double: 生产～一番。*The production has doubled.* ❹翻译,把一种语文译成另一种语文 to translate; to interpret: 把外国名著～成中文 *to translate foreign masterpieces into Chinese* ❺(一儿)翻脸 to fall out; to split up: 闹～了 *to split up*

F

凡(*凢) fán ㄈㄢˊ ❶平常的,不出奇的 common; ordinary: ～人 *ordinary person; man of mould* | 在平～的工作中做出惊人的成绩 *to make extraordinary achievements in ordinary work* ❷宗教、神话或迷信的人称人世间 mundane world; earth: 神仙下～。*The fairy came to the mundane world.* ❸凡是,所有的 all; every: ～事要跟群众商量。*The masses should be consulted in all matters.* ❹概要,要略 outline; gist: 发～起例 *introduction and guide* [凡例] 书前面说明内容和体例的文字 guide ❺总共 altogether: 全书～十卷。*The book comprises 10 volumes altogether.* ❻旧时乐谱记音符号的一个,相当于简谱的"4" note in the traditional Chinese musical scale, corresponding to 4 in numbered musical notation

矾(礬) fán ㄈㄢˊ 含水复盐的一类,是某些金属硫酸盐的含水结晶。最常见的是明矾(硫酸钾铝,也叫"白矾"),还有胆矾(硫酸铜)、绿矾(硫酸亚铁)等 vitriol

钒 fán ㄈㄢˊ 一种金属元素,符号 V,银白色。熔合在钢中,能增加钢的强度、弹性和耐热耐蚀性,工业上用途很大 vanadium (V)

烦 fán ㄈㄢˊ ❶苦闷,急躁 depressed; irritated: ～恼 *annoyed; upset* | 心～意乱 *perturbed* | 心里有点～*to be a little annoyed* ❷厌烦 bored; tired: 不耐～*impatient* | 这些话都听～了 *to get tired of these words* ❸又多又乱 redundant and confusing: 要言不～ *suc-*

cinct; pithy | 话多真絮 ～ *to be too long-winded* [烦琐] 琐碎，不扼要 tedious ❹ 敬辞 ***polite***，表示请托 to trouble; to bother: ～你做点事。*May I bother you to do something for me?*

墦 fán ㄈㄢˊ 坟墓 tomb; grave

蕃 ㊀ fán ㄈㄢˊ 茂盛 luxuriant; lush: 草木～盛 *luxuriant vegetation* ㊙ ***figurative*** 繁多 to proliferate; to multiply: ～衍(逐渐增多或增广，现作"繁衍")(now written as 繁衍) *to proliferate; to multiply*

㊁ fān 见 181 页 see p181

璠 fán ㄈㄢˊ 美玉 fine jade

膰 fán ㄈㄢˊ 古代祭祀时用的熟肉 sacrificial meat in ancient China

燔 fán ㄈㄢˊ ❶ 焚烧 to burn ❷ 烤 to roast; to bake

蹯 fán ㄈㄢˊ 兽足 animal's paw: 熊～(熊掌) *bear's paw*

樊 fán ㄈㄢˊ 篱笆 fence [樊篱] ㊙ ***figurative*** 对事物的限制 restriction; barrier

繁 (*緐) ㊀ fán ㄈㄢˊ ❶ 复杂，跟"简"相对 complicated (㊥ ***doublet*** — 杂 miscellaneous) (the opposite of 简): 删～就简 *to simplify sth by cutting out the superfluous* ❷ 许多，不少 numerous; manifold: 实～有徒(这种人实在很多)。*There's no lack of such people.* | ～殖(生长成许多) *to breed; to reproduce* [繁华] 市面热闹，工商业兴盛 bustling; busy [繁荣] 兴旺发展或使兴旺发展 flourishing; thriving: 市场～～ *booming market* | ～～经济 *to promote economic prosperity*

㊁ pó 见 574 页 see p574

蘩 fán ㄈㄢˊ 白蒿。草本植物，可入药 wormwood (*Artemisia absinthium*); artemisia

反 fǎn ㄈㄢˇ ❶ 翻转，颠倒 to reverse; to overturn: ～败为胜 *to turn defeat into victory; to turn the tide* | ～守为攻 *to turn defence into offence* | 易如～掌 *as easy as ABC* ㊀ ***extension*** 翻转的，颠倒的，跟"正"相对 (the opposite of 正) reverse; inverse: 这纸看不出～面正面。*It's impossible to differentiate the reverse side from the obverse side of the paper.* | ～穿皮袄 *to wear the fur-lined jacket inside out* | 放～了。*It's placed upside down.* | 图章上刻的字是～的。*The characters on the seal are reversed.* [反复] **1** 翻来覆去 changeable: ～～无常 *changeable; capricious* **2** 重复 repeatedly; again and again: ～～练习 *to practise repeatedly* [反间] (—jiàn) 利用敌人的间谍，使敌人内部自相矛盾 to sow discord among the enemies [反正] **1** 指平定混乱局面，恢复原来秩序 to restore things to order: 拨乱～～ *to bring order out of chaos* **2** 敌方的军队或人员投到己方 to come over from the enemy's side **3** 副词 ***ad-***

F

verb，无论如何，不管怎么样 anyway；in any case：～～我要去，你不去也行了。*I'll go there anyway；so it's all right if you don't.*［反刍］（—chú）倒嚼（dǎojiào）。牛、羊、骆驼等动物把粗粗吃下去的食物再回到嘴里细嚼 to ruminate ❷和原来的不同，和预想的不同 different：～常 *abnormal；eccentric*｜画虎不成～类犬 *to try to draw a tiger but end up with the likeness of a dog — to make a poor imitation*｜我一劝，他～而更生气了。*I tried to smooth him，but on the contrary，he became angrier.*［反倒］（—dào）正相反，常指和预期相反 on the contrary；contrary to one's expectation：希望他走，他～～坐下了。*We wished he would leave，but on the contrary，he took a seat.* ❸反对，反抗 to resist；to be against：～浪费 *to oppose extravagance*｜～腐败 *to combat corruption*｜～封建 *to fight against feudalism*｜～法西斯 *to be anti-fascist*［反动］**1** 指思想上或行动上维护旧制度，反对新制度，反对革命的 reactionary：～～势力 *reactionary forces*｜～～行为 *reactionary action* **2** 相反的作用 counteraction：从历史来看，党八股是对于五四运动的一个～～。*From the historical perspective，Party jargon is a reaction to the May 4th Movement.*［反对］不赞成，抵制 to resist：坚决～～贪污、盗窃 *to oppose resolutely corruption and larceny* ❹类推 to analogize：举一～三 *to draw inferences about other cases from one instance* ❺回，还 to return；to counter：～攻 *to counterattack*｜～求诸己 *to seek the cause in oneself*［反省］（—xǐng）对自己的思想行为加以检查 to reflect on oneself；to introspect ❻古同"返" same as 返 in ancient Chinese

返 fǎn ㄈㄢˇ 回，归 to return：往～*to go to and fro*｜一去不复～*to be gone forever*［返工］工作没有做好再重做 to do poorly done work over again

犯 fàn ㄈㄢˋ ❶抵触，违反 to violate；to offend：～法 *to violate the law*｜～规 *to break the rule* ❷犯罪的人 criminal：战～*war criminal*｜要～*principal criminal*｜贪污～*embezzler* ❸侵犯，进攻 to invade；to attack：人不～我，我不～人；人若～我，我必～人。*We will not attack unless we are attacked.* or *We will surely counterattack if we are attacked.* ❹发作，发生 to recur；to attack：～病 *to have a relapse；to fall ill again*｜～脾气 *to flare up*｜～错误 *to make a mistake；to commit an error*［犯不着］（—zháo）［犯不上］不值得 not worth doing；not worthwhile：你～～～和他生气。*It's not worthwhile for you to be angry with him.*

F

范（範） fàn ㄈㄢˋ ❶模(mú)子 mould; matrix: 钱～*coin mould*［范畴］**1** 概括性最高的基本概念，如化合、分解是化学的范畴；矛盾、质和量等是哲学的范畴 category **2** 类型，范围 domain; scope［范围］一定的界限 limit; range: 责任的～～*sphere of responsibility*｜活动～～*scope of activities* ❷模范，榜样 model; example: 示～*to demonstrate; to set an example*｜师～*model; normal school; teacher-training*｜～例 *example; paradigm*

饭 fàn ㄈㄢˋ ❶煮熟的谷类食品。多指大米饭(usually used to denote cooked rice) cooked cereals ❷每日定时吃的食物 meal: 午～*lunch*｜开～*to serve a meal*

贩 fàn ㄈㄢˋ ❶指买货出卖 to buy to sell: ～货 *to transport goods for sale*｜～了一群羊来 *to buy a herd of sheep for sale* ❷(一子)买货物出卖的行商或小商人 pedlar; vendor: 菜～子 *vegetable trader*｜摊～*vendor; street pedlar*

畈 fàn ㄈㄢˋ〈方 **dialect**〉田地，多用于村镇名(fan, usually used in a name of a village or a town) field; land

泛（❶—❸*汎、❸❹*氾） fàn ㄈㄢˋ ❶漂浮 to float: ～舟 *to go boating* [引]**extension** 透出 to be suffused with: 脸上～红 *with one's cheeks suffused with blushes* ❷浮浅，不深入(叠 **reduplication**) shallow; superficial: ～～之交(友谊不深) *casual acquaintance*｜这文章做得浮～不切实。*This is a superficial article.* ❸广泛，一般地 extensive; general: ～览 *to browse*｜～问 *to ask broad questions*｜～论 *general survey* (or *discussion*)｜～称 *general term* ❹水向四处漫流 to overflow; to flood: ～滥 *to overflow; to inundate*

梵 fàn ㄈㄢˋ 梵语"梵摩"的省称，意思是清静，常指关于佛教的(short for 梵摩 in Sanskrit, used usually to denote Buddhism) Brahma; peace and quiet: ～宫 *Buddhist temple*｜～刹 *Buddhist temple*［梵语］印度古代的一种语言 Sanskrit, a language in ancient India

FANG ㄈㄤ

方 fāng ㄈㄤ ❶四个角全是直角的四边形或六个面全是方形的六面体 square; cube: 正～*square*｜长～*rectangle*｜见～(长宽或长宽高相等) *square*｜平～米 *square meter*｜立～米 *cubic meter* [引] **extension** 乘方，求一个数目自乘若干次的积数 involution; power: 平～(自乘两次，即本数×本数) *square*｜立～(自乘三次，即本数×本数×本数) *cube*［方寸］[喻] **figurative** 心 heart: ～～已乱 *greatly agitated*［方圆］周围 circumference: 这个城～～有四五十里。*The city has a circumference of* *forty to fifty* li. ❷正直 upright; honest：品行～正 *to behave with integrity* ❸一边或一面 side：对～*the other party*｜前～*the front*｜四～*four directions; four sides*｜四面八～*in all directions; everywhere* 引 **extension** 一个区域的，一个地带的 local; regional：～言 *dialect*｜～志 *local records; local annals*［方向］**1** 东、西、南、北的区分 direction：航行的～～*the direction of sailing* **2** 目标 target：做事情要认清～～。*People should have a clear understanding of their goal in doing things.* ❹方法，法子 method; way：教导有～*to know how to teach and guide*｜千～百计 *by every means; by hook or crook* 引 **extension**（一子、一儿）药方，配药的单子 prescription：偏～*folk prescription*｜秘～*secret recipe*｜开～子 *to give a prescription*［方式］说话、做事所采取的方法和形式 way ❺副词 **adverb**，才 only when：书到用时～恨少。*Books are not enough when they are needed.* ❻副词 **adverb**，正，正当 just; at the time when：来日～长。*There will be a time for this.* ❼量词 ***quantifier*** **1** 旧制 former unit：a. 指平方丈（用于地皮、草皮）square *zhang* b. 指一丈见方一尺高的体积，即十分之一立方丈（用于土、沙、石、碎砖）one tenth cubic *zhang* c. 指一尺见方一丈长的体积，即百分之一立方丈（用于木材）one hundredth cubic *zhang* **2** 指平方米（用于墙、地板等）或立方米（用于土、沙、石、木材等）square metre or cubic metre **3** 用于方形的东西 square-shaped objects：一～图章 *a stamp; a seal*｜三～砚台 *three inkstones*

邡 fāng ㄈㄤ［什邡］地名，在四川省 Shifang, a place in Sichuan Province

坊 ㊀ fāng ㄈㄤ ❶里巷，多用于街巷的名称（fang, usually used in street names）lane; alley 引 **extension** 街市，市中店铺 downtown streets; shops in downtown areas：～间 *in the streets* ❷牌坊，旧时为旌表"功德"、宣扬封建礼教而建造的建筑物 memorial archway (or gateway)：忠孝牌～*memorial archway of loyalty and filial piety*｜贞节～*chastity archway*

㊁ fáng 见187页 see p187

芳 fāng ㄈㄤ 芳香，花草的香味 fragrant 喻 ***figurative*** 美好的德行或声名 virtue or fame：流～百世 *to leave a fine reputation to posterity; to leave a good name forever*

枋 fāng ㄈㄤ 方柱形木材 timber shaped like a square pillar

钫 fāng ㄈㄤ ❶一种放射性元素（符号 Fr）francium (Fr) ❷古代一种酒壶，方口大腹（in ancient China）square-mouthed and big-bellied wine vessel

防 fáng ㄈㄤˊ ❶防备,戒备 to defend; to guard:～御 *to defend*|～守 *to defend; to guard*|预～*to prevent*|军民联～*army-civilian defence*|冷不～*unexpectedly; suddenly*|谨～假冒 *to beware of counterfeits*[国防]为了保卫国家的领土、主权而部署的一切防务 national defence:～～军 *national defence forces*|～～要地 *strategic point in national defence* ❷堤,挡水的建筑物 dyke; embankment

坊 ㊁ fáng ㄈㄤˊ 作(zuō)坊,某些小手工业的工作场所 workshop; mill:染～*dyehouse*|油～*oil mill*|粉～*flour mill*|磨～*mill*

㊀ fāng 见 186 页 see p186

妨 fáng ㄈㄤˊ 妨害,阻碍 to hinder; to impede (㊟**doublet**—碍 to hamper):这样做倒无～。*There is no harm in doing that.*|开会太多反而～害生产。*Too many meetings will impede production.*[不妨]没有什么不可以 might as well; may as well:～～试试。*You might as well have a try.*[何妨]用反问语气表示"不妨"why not:你～～去看看。*Why not go and have a look?*

肪 fáng ㄈㄤˊ 厚的脂膏,特指动物腰部肥厚的油 fat (㊟**doublet** 脂—fat)

房 fáng ㄈㄤˊ ❶(—子)住人或放东西的建筑物 house (㊟**doublet** —屋 house):楼～*building*|瓦～*tile-roofed house*(图见下页 picture on the next page)|库～*warehouse* ❷形状、作用像房子的 structure like a house or for housing:蜂～*honeycomb; beehive*|莲～*lotus pod*|心～*atrium* ❸称家族的一支 branch of an extended family:大～*the first branch; the branch of the eldest son*|长(zhǎng)～*the first branch* ❹星宿名,二十八宿之一 *Fang*, the 4th of the 28 constellations

鲂 fáng ㄈㄤˊ 鲂鱼,跟鳊(biān)鱼相似,银灰色,背部隆起,味鲜美 triangular bream (*Megalobrama terminalis*)

仿(❶❷*倣、❸*髣) fǎng ㄈㄤˇ ❶效法,照样做 to imitate; to copy (㊟**doublet**—效 to imitate):～造 *to imitate*|～制 *to model on* ❷依照范本写的字 characters written after a calligraphy model:写了一张～*to have written a page of characters after a calligraphy model* ❸[仿佛](*彷彿、*髣髴)(—fú) **1** 好像 as if:这个字我～～在哪里见过。*I seemed to have seen the character somewhere.* **2** 类似 to resemble; to be similar:弟兄俩长得相～～。*The two brothers look alike.*

访 fǎng ㄈㄤˇ ❶向人询问调查 to investigate; to inquire:～查 *to investigate*|～贫问苦 *to call on the impoverished and wretched*|采～新闻 *to gather*

F

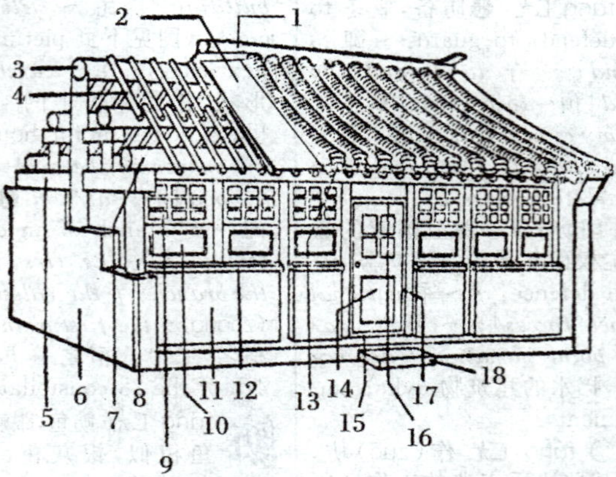

房屋的构造 *structure of a house*

1 屋脊 *roof ridge*
2 苫背 *thatch with straw mat, tarpaulin, etc*
3 脊檩 *ridgepole*
4 椽子 *rafter*
5 梁 *roof beam*
6 山墙 *gable*
7 檩 *purlin*
8 柱子 *pillar*
9 窗格子 *window lattice*
10 窗户 *window*
11 墙 *wall*
12 窗台 *windowsill*
13 檐 *eaves*
14 门 *door*
15 门槛 *threshold*
16 门楣 *lintel*
17 门框 *doorframe*
18 台阶 *doorstep*

news ❷探问，看望 to visit; to call on：～友 *to visit a friend*｜～古（古迹）*to search for ancient relics; to look for places of historic interest*［访问］有目的地看望，探问 to visit; to call on：～～劳动模范 *to visit a model worker*｜出国～～ *to pay a visit abroad*

彷 ㊁ fǎng ㄈㄤˇ［彷佛］旧同"仿佛"。参看 187 页"仿❸"（see 仿 ❸ on p187）same as 仿佛 in former times

㊀ páng 见 551 页 see p551

纺 fǎng ㄈㄤˇ ❶把丝、棉、麻、毛或人造纤维等做成纱 to spin：～纱 *to spin yarn*｜～棉花 *to spin cotton* ❷纺绸，一种绸子 a soft and thin plain-weave silk fabric：杭（杭州）～ *Hangzhou silk*｜富春～ *Fuchun silk*

昉 fǎng ㄈㄤˇ ❶明亮 bright ❷起始 beginning

舫 fǎng ㄈㄤˇ 船 boat：画～（装饰华美专供游览用的船）

gaily-painted pleasure boat | 游～*tour boat*

放 fàng ㄈㄤˋ ❶解除约束，得到自由 to free; to release：～行 *to let pass* | 释～*to set free*; *to release* | 把笼子里的鸟～了 *to let the bird out of the cage* ㊊***extension*** **1** 赶牲畜、家禽到野外去觅食 to put out to pasture：～牛 *to graze cattle* | ～羊 *to herd sheep* | ～鸭子 *to tend ducks* **2** 散 to dismiss：～工 *to knock off* | ～学 *to dismiss class*［放晴］阴雨后转晴 to clear up ❷任意，随便 to indulge in：～任 *to let alone* | ～纵 *to give loose to* | ～肆 *unbridled* ❸发出 to let off：～枪 *to fire a gun* | ～光 *to give off light* | ～电 *to discharge electricity* ㊕***transfer*** 借钱给人，收取利息 to loan：～款 *to loan* ❹点燃 to light; to kindle：～火 *to set fire to* | ～鞭炮 *to set off firecrackers* ❺扩展 to expand：～大 *to enlarge* | ～宽 *to widen* | 把领子～出半寸 *to let the collar out for half an inch* ㊊***extension*** 花开 to blossom：芦花～，稻谷香。*The reed catkins come into bloom, and the paddies are fragrant.* | 心花怒～*to burst with joy* ❻搁，置 to put at a place; to lay：存～*to store* | ～在箱子里 *to put in the case*［放心］安心，解除忧虑和牵挂 to set one's mind at rest; to rest assured：～～吧，一切都准备好了！*Rest assured! Everything is ready!* ❼流放，旧时把人驱逐到边远的地方去 to exile：～逐 *to banish*

FEI ㄈㄟ

飞（飛） fēi ㄈㄟ ❶鸟类或虫类等用翅膀在空中往来活动 to fly：～行 *to fly* | ～鸟 *flying bird* | ～虫 *winged insect* ㊊***extension*** 物体在空中飘荡或行动 to hover; to flutter：～沙走石 *sand flying and pebbles hurling* | 飞机向东～。*The plane is flying eastward.* ❷快，像飞似的 to move swiftly：～奔 *to dash*; *to run like split* | ～跑 *to streak* ❸极，特别地 extremely：这把刀～快。*The knife is very sharp.* ❹指无根据的，无缘无故的 groundless：～语 *gossip* | ～灾 *unexpected disaster* ❺（外 ***loanword***）法定计量单位中十进分数单位词头之一，表示 10^{-15}（符号 f）femto-(f)

妃 fēi ㄈㄟ ❶古代皇帝的妾，地位次于皇后 imperial concubine ❷太子、王、侯的妻 wife of a prince or a marquis：王～*princess*

非 fēi ㄈㄟ ❶跟"是"相对（the opposite of 是）**1** 不，不是 no; not：莫～*Can it be that …?* or *Is it possible that …?* | ～卖品 *articles not for sale* | ～但要生产得多，而且要提高质量。*Not only the output but also the quality should be enhanced.* **2** 不合理的，不对的 unreasonable; wrong：明辨是

F

～ *to make a clear distinction between right and wrong* | 为～作歹 *to do evil* | 痛改前～ *to repent thoroughly of one's misdeeds*［非常］1 异乎寻常的 extraordinary:～～时期 *time of emergency* 2 副词 ***adverb***, 十分,极 very:～～光荣 *very glorious* | ～～高兴 *very glad* ❷副词 ***adverb***,跟"不"搭用,表示必须,一定(有时后面没有"不"字)(used in collocation with 不 to express necessity, but sometimes without 不):～组织起来不能发挥力量。*We shall not bring our energy into full play unless we get organized.* | 他～去不可。*He must go.* | 不让他去,他～去。*He was told not to go, but he insisted on going.* ❸以为不对,不以为然 to censure; to oppose; to find fault with:～笑(讥笑) *to ridicule* | ～议 *to reproach; to censure*［非难］(—nàn)责备 to reprimand ❹指非洲,世界七大洲之一 Africa, one of the seven continents in the world

菲 ㈠ fēi ㄈㄟ 花草茂盛 luxuriant; lush: 芳～ *fragrance of flowers and grass*

㈡ fěi 见 191 页 see p191

啡 fēi ㄈㄟ 见 481 页"吗"字条"吗啡"(mǎ—)、380 页"咖"字条"咖啡"(kā—) see 吗啡 on p481, and 咖啡 on p380

騑 fēi ㄈㄟ 古时一车驾四马,中间两马叫服马,服马两旁的马叫騑马,也叫"骖马"(also called 骖马) a team of four horses to a cart in ancient China, among which the two in the middle were called 服马, while the other two were called 騑马

绯 fēi ㄈㄟ 红色 red:两颊～红 *blush; flush*

扉 fēi ㄈㄟ 门 gate:柴～ *faggot door* | ～页(书刊封面之内印着书名、著者等项的一页) *head* (or *title*) *page* | ～画(书籍正文前的插图) *front illustration placed before the full text of a book*

蜚 ㈠ fēi ㄈㄟ 古同"飞"same as 飞 in ancient Chinese

㈡ fěi 见 191 页 see p191

霏 fēi ㄈㄟ ❶(雨、雪、云气等)很盛的样子(叠 ***reduplication***) (of rain, snow, cloud, etc) thick and fast: 雨雪～～。*There is a heavy snowstorm.* ❷云气 mist; cloud: 日出而林～开。*The sun rose and the mists in the forest dispersed.* ❸飘扬 to float:烟～云敛。*Smoke diffuses and clouds disperse.*

鲱 fēi ㄈㄟ 鲱鱼,鱼名。种类超过 200 种,其中包括沙丁鱼,大部分生活在海洋中,肉可吃 Pacific herring (*Clupea pallasii*)

肥 féi ㄈㄟˊ ❶含脂肪多的,跟"瘦"相对(the opposite of 瘦) fat:～猪 *hog* | ～肉 *fat* | 牛～马壮。*The cows are fat and the horses are strong.*［肥差］(—chāi)可以从中多得好处的差事 lucrative errand ❷肥沃,土质含养分多的 fertile; rich:

地很～。*The soil is very fertile.* ❸肥料,能增加田地养分的东西,如粪、豆饼、化学配合剂等 fertilizer:上～ *to apply manure to fields*|施～*to apply fertilizer*|追～*to apply additional fertilizer*|基～*base manure*|化～*chemical fertilizer* ❹使田地增加养分 to fertilize:用草灰～田 *to fertilize the soil with plant ash* ❺宽大(指衣服鞋袜等)(clothes, shoes, socks, etc) loose; large:袖子太～了。*The sleeves are too loose.*

淝 féi ㄈㄟˊ 水名,南淝河、北淝河、东淝河、西淝河等,都在安徽。东淝河古称淝水 fei, name of rivers in Anhui Province such as Nanfei River, Beifei River, Dongfei River, Xifei River, etc (Dongfei River was called Feishui in ancient China):～水之战 *the Battle of Feishui*

蜚 féi ㄈㄟˊ 臭虫 bedbug; bug

腓 féi ㄈㄟˊ 腓肠肌,胫骨后的肉。俗叫"腿肚子"(popularly called 腿肚子) calf [腓骨]小腿外侧的骨头,比胫骨细小 fibula(图见 241 页"骨" picture on p241)

匪 fěi ㄈㄟˇ ❶强盗,抢劫财物的坏人 bandit; robber:惯～ *hardened bandit*|土～ *bandit; brigand* ❷不,不是 no; not:获益～浅 *to reap no little benefit; to benefit a lot*|～夷所思(不是常人所能想到的)*fantastic; eccentric; grotesque*

诽 fěi ㄈㄟˇ 说别人的坏话 to defame; to slander (㊀ *doublet*－谤 to defame; slander):腹～心谤 *to harbour unspoken criticism*

菲 ㊁ fěi ㄈㄟˇ ❶微,薄 humble; unworthy (㊀*doublet*－薄 humble; poor):～礼 *my humble gift*|～材 *my humble talent* ❷古书上说的一种像蔓菁的菜 radish or red turnip in ancient Chinese texts

㊀ fēi 见 190 页 see p190

悱 fěi ㄈㄟˇ 想说可是不能够恰当地说出来 to be at a loss for words

棐 fěi ㄈㄟˇ ❶辅助 assistance ❷古同"榧"、"篚" same as 榧 or 篚 in ancient Chinese

斐 fěi ㄈㄟˇ 有文采 rich in literary grace[斐然]**1** 有文采的样子 of striking literary talent:～～成章 *to show striking literary talent* **2** 显著 striking:成绩～～*brilliant achievements*

榧 fěi ㄈㄟˇ 常绿乔木,种子叫榧子,种仁可以吃,可以榨油,又可入药。木材供建筑用 Chinese torreya (*Torreya grandis*)

蜚 ㊁ fěi ㄈㄟˇ [蜚蠊](－lián)蟑螂(zhāngláng)的别称 another name for 蟑螂

㊀ fēi 见 190 页 see p190

翡 fěi ㄈㄟˇ [翡翠](－cuì) **1** 翡翠鸟,嘴长而直,有蓝色和绿色的羽毛,捕食鱼和昆虫

F

common kingfisher (*Alcedo atthis*) **2** 绿色的玉,半透明,有光泽,很珍贵 jadeite

篚 fěi ㄈㄟˇ 古代盛(chéng)东西的竹器(in ancient China) round bamboo basket

芾 ㊀ fèi ㄈㄟˋ [蔽芾]形容树干及树叶小(of trunk and leaves) small

㊁ fú 见 203 页 see p203

肺 fèi ㄈㄟˋ 肺脏,人和某些高等动物体内的呼吸器官(图见 940 页"脏" picture on p940)[肺腑]㊣***figurative*** 内心 bottom of one's heart:～～之言 *heart-to-heart talk; words from the bottom of one's heart*

吠 fèi ㄈㄟˋ 狗叫 bark; yap; yelp:狂～ *to bark ferociously*|蜀犬～日(喻少见多怪)*dogs in Sichuan bark at the sun (because it's a rare sight in that misty region) — an ignorant person making a fuss about something which he has not seen before*

狒 fèi ㄈㄟˋ [狒狒]猿一类的动物,面形似狗,面部肉色,光滑无毛,体毛褐色,食果实及鸟卵等。多产在非洲 baboon

沸 fèi ㄈㄟˋ 开,滚,液体受热到一定温度时,内部汽化形成气泡,冲出液体表面的现象 to boil; to bubble:在标准大气压下,水的～点是 100 摄氏度。*The boiling point of water is 100 degrees centigrade under standard atmospheric pressure.*|热血～腾 *with one's blood boiling; burning with righteous indignation*

怫 fèi ㄈㄟˋ (又 also fú) 见 202 页(fú) see p202

费 fèi ㄈㄟˋ ❶花费,消耗 to spend; to consume:～力 *to exert great efforts; to be strenuous*|～心 *to take much trouble; may I trouble you (to do sth); would you mind (doing sth)*|～神 *to tax one's energy; to be exhausting*|～事 *troublesome*|～工夫 *time-consuming*|反浪～ *to oppose extravagance*|这孩子穿鞋太～。*The child wears out his shoes much too quickly.* ❷费用,为某种需要用的款项 expenses; fee:学～ *tuition fees*|办公～ *administrative expenses*

镄 fèi ㄈㄟˋ 一种人造的放射性元素(符号 Fm) fermium (Fm)

废(廢) fèi ㄈㄟˋ ❶停止,放弃 to abandon; to give up:半途而～ *to give up halfway*|～寝忘食(*to be so absorbed as*) *to forget food and sleep*|～除不平等条约 *to abrogate unequal treaties* ㊀ ***extension*** 失去效用的,没有用的 waste; useless:～纸 *wastepaper*|～物利用 *recycling of wastes*|修旧利～ *to repair and utilize old or discarded things* ❷荒芜,衰败 to decline:～园 *garden lying waste; abandoned garden*|～墟 *ruins* ❸残疾 disabled:～疾 *disability*

剕 fèi ㄈㄟˋ 古代把脚砍掉的酷刑(in ancient China) cruel

F

punishment of amputating the feet

痱(*疿) fèi ㄈㄟˋ 痱子,由于暑天出汗过多,引起汗腺发炎,皮肤表面生出来的小红疹,很刺痒 prickly heat

FEN ㄈㄣ

分 ㊀ fēn ㄈㄣ ❶分开,区划开,跟"合"相对(the opposite of 合) to divide; to separate:~离 *to separate* | ~类 *to classify; to categorize* | ~工合作 *to have division of labour as well as cooperation* | ~别处理 *to deal with separately* ㊞ ***extension*** **1** 由整体中取一部分 to distribute; to allot:他~到了一千斤粮食。*He has been allotted 1,000* jin *of grains*. **2** 由机构分出的部分 branch:~会 *branch* | ~队 *contingent; detachment* | ~局 *sub-bureau* | ~社 *branch agency*[分化]由一种事物演变成几种不同的事物 to divide; to break up:"他"字~~成"他"、"她"、"它"。*The character* 他 *has developed into three forms*: 他, 她 *and* 它. [分解]**1** 一种化合物分成两种以上的元素或化合物 to decompose; to resolve **2** 调解,排解 to patch up; to reconcile:~~纠纷 *to reconcile a quarrel* | 难以~~ *to be difficult to mediate* **3** 细说 to explain:且听下回~~ *to be disclosed in the next episode*[分析]把事物、现象、概念等划分成简单的部分,找出它的本质、属性或相互联系 to analyze:~~问题 *to analyze a problem* | 化学~~ *chemical analysis* ❷分配 to allot:~粮食 *to allot grains* | ~工作 *to assign a task* ❸辨别 to distinguish; to tell (㊟ ***doublet*** 一辨 to differentiate):不~青红皂白 *to make no distinction between black and white* (or *right and wrong*) | ~清是非 *to make a distinction between right and wrong* ❹表示分数 fraction:二~之一 *one half* | 百~之八 *eight percent*[分数]数学中表示除法的式子,画一道横线,把被除数写在线上面叫分子,把除数写在线下面叫分母 fraction formed by a numerator, a fraction line and a denominator[分子]**1** 物体分成的最细小而不失原物性质的颗粒 molecule:水的一个~~,含有两个氢原子和一个氧原子。*One molecule of water has two hydrogen atoms and one oxygen atom*. **2** 见本字条"分数" see 分数 on this page (另 fènzǐ,见"分"fèn also see 分 fèn for fènzǐ) ❺法定计量单位中十进分数单位词头之一,表示 10^{-1}(符号 d) deci-(d) ❻计量单位名 *fen*, a traditional Chinese system of weights and measures **1** 市制长度,10 分是 1 寸,1 分约合 3.33 毫米 *fen*, a traditional Chinese unit of measures equal to 0.1 cun, approximately 3.33 millimetres **2**

F

市制地积，10 分是 1 亩，1 分约合66.67平方米 *fen*, a traditional Chinese unit of area equal to 0.1 *mu*, approximately 66.67 square metres **3** 市制重量，10 分是 1 钱，1 分合0.5 克 *fen*, a traditional Chinese unit of weight equal to 0.1 *qian*, approximately 0.5 grams **4** 币制，10 分是 1 角 *fen*, a unit of currency equal to 0.1 *jiao* **5** 时间，60 分是 1 小时 minute (equal to one sixtieth of an hour) **6** 圆周或角，60 分是 1 度 minute (equal to one sixtieth of a degree of circumference or angle) **7** （一儿）表示成绩 point; mark: 赛篮球赢了三～ *to win the basketball match by three points* | 考试得了一百～ *to get 100 marks in the examination* **8** 利率，月利一分按百分之一计算，年利一分按十分之一计算 *fen*, an alternative interest rate, which is one percent when used as a monthly interest rate or ten percent as a yearly interest rate tenth [分寸](—cun) ㊥ ***figurative*** 说话或办事的适当标准或限度 sense of propriety: 说话要有～～。*We should speak with a good sense of propriety.*

㊁ fèn 见 195 页 see p195

芬 fēn ㄈㄣ 芬芳，花草的香气 fragrance of plants

吩 fēn ㄈㄣ [吩咐](*分付)(—fu) 口头指派或命令 to tell; to order: 母亲～～他早去早回。*His mother told him to start off early and come back early.*

纷 fēn ㄈㄣ 众多，杂乱 tangled (㊨***doublet***—乱 chaotic | —杂 disorderly) (叠 ***reduplication***): 众说～纭。*People hold diverse and confused opinions.* | 大雪～飞。*It's snowing heavily.* | 议论～～ *to provoke much disputation*

玢 ㊁ fēn ㄈㄣ 见 644 页"赛"字条"赛璐玢" see 赛璐玢 on p644

㊀ bīn 见 49 页 see p49

氛（△*雰）fēn ㄈㄣ 气 mist ㊞ ***extension*** 气象，情势 atmosphere: 战～ *atmosphere of war* | 会场充满团结的气～。*The conference hall is filled with an atmosphere of solidarity.*

棻 fēn ㄈㄣ 有香味的木头 fragrant wood

酚 fēn ㄈㄣ 苯酚（也叫"石炭酸"），是医药上常用的防腐杀菌剂 (also called 石炭酸) phenol

雰 fēn ㄈㄣ 雾气 mist

[雰雰] 形容霜雪很盛的样子 (of snow, frost) heavy

餴 fēn ㄈㄣ 〈方 ***dialect***〉不曾，没 haven't; didn't

坟（墳）fén ㄈㄣˊ 埋葬死人之后筑起的土堆 tomb (㊨ ***doublet***—墓 tomb)

汾 fén ㄈㄣˊ 汾河，水名，在山西省 Fenhe River, in Shanxi Province

棼 fén ㄈㄣˊ 纷乱 confused; disorderly: 治丝益～（整理

丝不找头绪,越理越乱。比喻做事没有条理,越搞越乱)*to try to sort out silk threads only to tangle them further — to try to do sth only to make it worse; to add disorder to confusion*

鼢(**蚡) fén ㄈㄣˊ 鼢鼠,哺乳动物,身体灰色,尾短,眼小。在地下打洞,损害农作物和树木的根,甚至危害河堤。也叫"盲鼠"、"地羊"(also called 盲鼠,地羊) zokor (*Myospalacinae*)

焚 fén ㄈㄣˊ 烧 to burn:~毁 *to burn down* | 忧心如~ *to be burning with anxiety* | 玩火自~。*He who plays with fire will get burnt.*

濆 fén ㄈㄣˊ 水边 waterside; water margin

豮 fén ㄈㄣˊ 〈方 **dialect**〉雄性的牲畜 male livestock:~猪 *boar*

粉 fěn ㄈㄣˇ ❶细末ㄦ powder:药~*medicinal powder* | 藕~ *lotus-root starch* | 漂白~ *bleaching powder* 特指化妆用的粉末 cosmetic powder:香~ *face powder* | 涂脂抹~*to apply powder and paint; to embellish; to whitewash* ❷粉刷,用涂料抹刷墙壁 to whitewash:这墙是才~的。*The wall has just been whitewashed.*[粉饰]装饰表面,掩盖污点或缺点 to whitewash; to prettify:门面~~一新。*The shop front is newly whitewashed.* | ~~太平 *to present a picture of false peace and prosperity* ❸使破碎,成为粉末 to break into pieces:~碎 *to break into pieces; to smash* | ~身碎骨 *to have one's body smashed to pieces and one's bones ground to powder* ❹浅红色 pink:这朵花是~的。*The flower is pink.* ❺白色的或带粉末的 white (or with white powder):~蝶 *white butterfly* | ~墙 *white wall* ❻用豆粉或别的粉做成的食品 food made from starch:~条 *starch noodles; starch vermicelli* | 凉~*bean jelly* | 米~*rice-flour noodles*

分 ㊁ fèn ㄈㄣˋ ❶名位、职责、权利的限度 extent of one's obligation, right:~所当然。*That's what one ought to do as part of one's duty.* | 本~ *one's duty; one's obligation* ❷成分 ingredient; composition:水~*moisture content; moisture* | 糖~*sugar content* | 养~*nutrient* ❸同"份"same as 份[分子](—zǐ)属于一定阶级、阶层、集团或具有某种特征的人 member; element:积极~~*activist*(另 fēnzǐ 见"分"fēn also see 分 fēn for fēnzǐ)

㊀ fēn 见193页 see p193

份 fèn ㄈㄣˋ ❶整体分成几部分,每一部分叫一份 share; part; portion:分成三~ *to divide into three parts* | 每人一~*a share for each person* | 股~*share; stock* ❷量词 **quantifier**,用于成组成件的 set:一~报 *a copy of newspaper* | 一~ㄦ礼 *a gift* ❸用在"省、县、

F

年、月”后面，表示划分的单位(used after 省，县，年 or 月 to denote a unit)：省～*province*｜年～*year*

〈古 ***archaism***〉又同“彬”(bīn)also same as 彬

忿 fèn ㄈㄣˋ 生气，恨 angry；indignant (㊥***doublet*** —怒 angry｜—恨 indignant)(叠 ***reduplication***)：～～不平 *indignant；resentful* 现多作“愤”now usually written as 愤[不忿]不服气，不平 to be resentful [气不忿儿]看到不平的事，心中不服气 to feel unhappy about what is unjust or unfair

奋(奮) fèn ㄈㄣˋ 振作，鼓劲 to exert oneself；to bestir oneself：～翅 *to flap the wings vigorously*｜～斗 *to strive*｜兴～*excited*｜～不顾身 *to do sth regardless of one's safety*｜～发图强 *to go all out to achieve success；to exert oneself for a better result*

偾 fèn ㄈㄣˋ 败坏，破坏 to ruin；to spoil：～事 *to ruin things*｜～军之将 *a general who ruined the army*

愤 fèn ㄈㄣˋ 因为不满意而感情激动，发怒(叠 ***reduplication***) indignant；resentful：气～*indignant*｜～～不平 *indignant；resentful*[发愤]自己感觉不满足，努力地做 to strive：～～图强 *to strive for the best*

鲼 fèn ㄈㄣˋ 鱼名。身体扁平，呈菱形，尾部像鞭子，生活在热带及亚热带海洋中 eagle ray (*Myliobatidae*)

粪(糞) fèn ㄈㄣˋ ❶屎，粪便，可作肥料 excrement；dung；droppings ❷施肥，往田地里加肥料 to fertilize；to manure：～地 *to spread manure onto the fields*｜～田 *to apply manure to the fields* ❸扫除 to clear away (㊥***doublet*** —除 to wipe out；to clear away)

瀵 fèn ㄈㄣˋ 水从地面下喷出漫溢(of underground water) to gush out and overflow

FENG ㄈㄥ

丰(❷❸豐) fēng ㄈㄥ ❶容貌、姿态美好 good looks；fine appearance；graceful carriage [丰采][丰姿]见197页“风”字条“风采”、“风姿”see 风采 and 风姿 on p197 ❷盛，多 lavish；sumptuous (㊥***doublet*** —盛 abundant；plentiful)：～年 *abundant year；bumper harvest year*｜～衣足食 *to have ample food and clothing；to live an abundant life* ❸大 great：～功伟绩 *great achievements；magnificent contributions*

沣(灃) fēng ㄈㄥ 沣河，水名，在陕西省西安 Fenghe River，in Xi'an，Shaanxi Province

风(風) fēng ㄈㄥ ❶跟地面大致平行的流动着的空气 wind；breeze；gale：北～*north wind*｜旋(xuàn)～*whirlwind*｜刮一阵～*to blow a*

gust of wind ㊀**extension** 像风那样快、那样普遍地 swift; far and wide as the wind is blowing: ～行 *to be popular; to come into vogue* (or *fashion*) [风化] **1** 风俗教化 decency: 有伤～～ *offence against decency* **2** 地质学上称岩石因在地表长期受风雨等侵蚀而分解崩溃 weathering **3** 化学上称结晶体在空气中因失去结晶水而分解 efflorescence [风头] (－tou) **1** 指形势的发展方向或有关个人利害的情势 trend; circumstance: 不要看～～办事。*Don't act according to the temporary circumstances favourable to you.* **2** 出头露面，当众表现自己 publicity; limelight: 出～～ *to seek the limelight* ❷ 消息 news: 闻～而至 *to come without delay upon hearing the news* ❸ 没有确实根据的 hearsay; rumour: ～传 *rumour; hearsay* | ～闻 *to get wind of* ❹ 表现在外的景象或态度 scene; view: ～景 *scenery; landscape; view* | ～光 *scene; view; sight* | 作～ *style; attitude; conduct* | ～度 *bearing; manner* [风采] 风度神采。也作"丰采" (also written as 丰采) mien; charisma [风姿] 风度姿态。也作"丰姿" (also written as 丰姿) elegant charm; graceful bearing ❺ 风气，习俗 habit; custom: 世～ *public morals* | 勤俭成～。*Thrift is prevailing.* | 移～易俗 *to change established habits and customs* | ～土人情 *local conditions and customs* ❻ 病名 name of diseases: 抽～ *convulsions* | 羊痫(xián)～ *epilepsy* ❼ 古代称民歌 folk song in ancient China: 国～ *folk songs of various states* | 采～ *to collect folk songs*

〈古 **archaism**〉又同"讽" (fěng) also same as 讽

沨 fēng ㄈㄥ 水声 gurgling

枫 fēng ㄈㄥ 又叫"枫香"。落叶乔木，春季开花。叶子掌状三裂，秋季变红色 (also called 枫香) Chinese sweet gum; maple (*Acer*)

砜 fēng ㄈㄥ 硫酰(xiān)基与烃(tīng)基或芳香基结合成的有机化合物，如二甲砜、二苯砜 sulphone (such as diphenyl sulphone and dimethyl sulphone)

疯 fēng ㄈㄥ 一种精神病，患者精神错乱、失常 lunacy (㊀**doublet** 一癫 insane; mad | 一狂 insane; crazy) ㊀**figurative** **1** 指农作物生长旺盛不结果实 (of crops) to grow tall and thin without bearing fruits; to spindle: 长～杈 *to spindle with fruitless branches* | 棉花长～了。*The cotton plants are spindling.* **2** 言行狂妄 (of talk) wild: ～言～语 *ravings; slanderous gossips*

封 fēng ㄈㄥ ❶ 密闭 to seal; to close: ～瓶口 *to seal a bottle* | ～河 (河面冻住) *The river has frozen over.* [封锁] 采取军事、政治、经济等措施使

F

跟外界断绝联系 to blockade：～～港口 *to blockade a harbour*｜～～消息 *information blackout*｜军事～～线 *military blockade* ❷(一儿)封起来的或用来封东西的纸袋、纸包 envelope：信～ *envelope*｜赏～ *gratuity or small gift wrapped in red paper* ❸古代帝王把土地或爵位给予亲属、臣属 to grant：～侯 *to grant a title of nobility*［封建社会］地主阶级依靠土地所有权和反动政权残酷剥削、统治农民的社会制度 feudal society ❹指疆界，范围 boundary：～疆 *boundary; frontier*

葑 ㊀ fēng ㄈㄥ 即芜菁。也叫“蔓(mán)菁”(also called 蔓菁) turnip

㊁ fèng 见 199 页 see p199

犎 fēng ㄈㄥ 一种野牛 a kind of wild ox; buffalo

峰(*峯) fēng ㄈㄥ 高而尖的山头 peak; summit：山～ *peak; summit*｜顶～ *peak; summit*｜～峦 *ridges and peaks*

烽 fēng ㄈㄥ 烽火，古时边防报警的烟火，有敌人来侵犯的时候，守卫的人就点火相告 signal fire; beacon-fire

锋 fēng ㄈㄥ 刃，刀剑等器械的锐利或尖端部分 a sharp point or cutting edge of a knife, sword, etc (㊉***doublet***—刃 edge; blade)：交～(双方作战或比赛) *to cross swords; to engage in a battle*｜刀～ *edge; blade* ㊊***extension*** **1** 器物的尖锐部分 point：笔～ *tip of a writing brush* **2** 在前面带头的人 vanguard：先～ *pioneer*｜前～ *vanguard; forward*

蜂(*蠭) fēng ㄈㄥ 昆虫名。会飞，多有毒刺，能蜇(zhē)人。有蜜蜂、熊蜂、胡蜂、细腰蜂等多种，多成群住在一起 wasp (*Apoidea*) 特指蜜蜂 honeybee; bee (*Apis mellifera*)：～糖 *sediment of honey*｜～蜡 *beeswax*｜～蜜 *honey* ㊋***figurative*** 众多 in swarms：～起 *to rise in swarms*｜～拥 *to swarm; to flock*

酆 fēng ㄈㄥ［酆都］地名，在重庆市。今作“丰都”(now written as 丰都) Fengdu, a place in Chongqing

冯 féng ㄈㄥˊ 姓 Feng, a surname

〈古 ***archaism***〉又同“凭”(píng) also same as 凭

逢 féng ㄈㄥˊ ❶遇到 to meet; to encounter：～人便说 *to tell whoever happens to come one's way*｜每～星期三开会。*A meeting is to be held each Wednesday.* ❷迎合 to fawn on［逢迎］迎合旁人的意图，巴结人 to curry favour with; to fawn on

缝 ㊀ féng ㄈㄥˊ 用针线连缀 to stitch; to sew：把衣服的破口～上 *to sew up the opening on the dress*［缝纫］裁制服装 tailoring; sewing：学习～～ *to learn tailoring*

㊁ fèng 见 199 页 see p199

讽 fěng ㄈㄥˇ (旧读 formerly fèng)❶不看着书本念，背

书 to recite（㊣*doublet*—诵 to chant; to intone）❷用含蓄的话劝告或讥刺 to expostulate implicitly; to satirize（㊣***doublet*** 讥—to satirize; to mock）：～刺 *to satirize*｜冷嘲热～ *burning satire and frigid irony*

唪 fěng ㄈㄥˇ 唪经，佛教徒、道教徒高声念经（of Buddhists or Taoists）to chant scriptures in a loud voice

凤（鳳）fèng ㄈㄥˋ 凤凰（huáng），传说中的鸟王。又说雄的叫"凤"，雌的叫"凰"（古作"皇"），通常单称作"凤" phoenix, legendary king of birds, the male is called 凤，the female called 凰（written as 皇 in ancient Chinese text），but the latter is also called 凤 when mentioning it singly：～毛麟角（喻罕见而珍贵的东西）*phoenix feathers and unicorn horns — rarity of rarities*

奉 fèng ㄈㄥˋ ❶恭敬地用手捧着 to hold in hands with respect ㊀***extension*** 尊重，遵守 to esteem; to revere; to abide by：～行 *to pursue*｜～公守法 *to be law-abiding* 敬辞 ***polite***：～陪 *to keep sb company*｜～劝 *to offer a piece of advice*｜～送 *to offer as a gift*｜～还 *to return* [奉承]恭维，谄媚 to flatter ❷献给（多指对上级或长辈）to present; to submit：双手～上 *to present respectfully with both hands* ❸接受（多指上级或长辈的）to receive（orders from superiors or elders）：～命 *at sb's orders*｜昨～手书。*Your letter came to hand yesterday.* ❹信奉，信仰 to believe in：素～佛教 *faithful belief in Buddhism* ❺供养，伺候 to wait on; to attend to（㊣***doublet***—养 to take care of｜供— to enshrine and worship｜侍— to support and wait on）

俸 fèng ㄈㄥˋ 旧时称官员等所得的薪金（in former times）pay; salary：～禄 *official's salary*｜薪～*salary; pay*

覅 fèng ㄈㄥˋ〈方 **dialect**〉不用 needn't

葑 ㊁ fèng ㄈㄥˋ 古书上指菰的根 root of wild rice in ancient texts

㊀ fēng 见 198 页 see p198

赗 fèng ㄈㄥˋ 古时指用财物帮助人办丧事（in ancient China）to help handle affairs associated with a funeral by presenting gifts or money to the bereaved family：赙（fù）～*to present funeral gifts*

缝 ㊁ fèng ㄈㄥˋ ❶（—子、—儿）缝隙，裂开或自然露出的窄长口子 slit; crevice：裂～*crack*｜墙～*crack in the wall* ❷（—儿）接合处的痕迹 seam：这道～儿不直。*The seam is not straight enough.*

㊀ féng 见 198 页 see p198

FO ㄈㄛ

佛 ㊀ fó ㄈㄛˊ 梵语"佛陀"的省称，是佛教徒对修行圆满的人的称呼。特指佛教的创始人释迦牟尼(short for 佛陀) Buddha [佛教]宗教名。相传公元前 6 世纪—公元前 5 世纪释迦牟尼所创 Buddhism

㊁ fú 见 202 页 see p202

FOU ㄈㄡ

缶 fǒu ㄈㄡˇ 瓦器,大肚子小口 earthen jar with big belly and small mouth

否 ㊀ fǒu ㄈㄡˇ ❶不 no; not **1** 用在表示疑问的词句里(used in an interrogative sentence):是~? *Whether … or not …*; *if …* | 可~? *Can I …?* or *Can we …?* | 能~? *Can I …?* or *Can we …?* or *Can you …?* **2** 用在答话里,表示不同意对方的意思(used in negative response):~,此非吾意。*No. That's not what I mean.* [否定] **1** 反面的 opposite; reverse **2** 不承认,作出相反的判断 to negate; to deny [否决]对问题作不承认、不同意的决定 to vote down; to veto [否认]不承认 to deny; to repudiate ❷不如此,不然 otherwise:必须确定计划,~则无法施工。*A plan must be drawn first; otherwise the construction cannot be started.*

㊁ pǐ 见 563 页 see p563

FU ㄈㄨ

夫 ㊀ fū ㄈㄨ ❶成年男子的通称 general term for a male adult:农~ *farmer* | 渔~ *fisherman* ㊞ **extension** 旧时称服劳役的人,也作"伕"(also written as 伕) conscripted labourer in former times (㊟ ***doublet*** — 役 servant; coolie) ❷丈夫(fu),跟"妻"、"妇"相对(the opposite of 妻 or 妇) husband:~妻 *husband and wife; man and wife* | ~妇 *man and wife; married couple* | 姐~ *brother-in-law* | 姑~ *uncle*

[夫人]对别人妻子的敬称 term of respect for another person's wife

[夫子] **1** 旧时尊称老师或学者 term of respect for a scholar or a teacher in former times **2** 旧时妻称丈夫(used in former times) my husband

㊁ fú 见 201 页 see p201

伕 fū ㄈㄨ 同"夫㊀❶㊞" same as 夫㊀❶㊞

呋 fū ㄈㄨ [呋喃](—nán)有机化合物,分子式 C_4H_4O,无色液体。供制药用,也是重要的化工原料 furan [呋喃西林]有机化合物,分子式 $C_6H_6O_4N_4$,浅黄色粉末,对多种细菌有抑制和杀灭作用。外用药,可作皮肤、黏膜的消毒剂 nitrofuran

肤(膚) fū ㄈㄨ 皮肤,人体表面的皮 skin:~色 *skin colour* | 肌~ *skin and muscle* | 切~之痛 *sharp pain; deep grief* ㊗ ***figurative*** 表面的,浅薄的 superficial; shallow:内容~浅 *shallow content*

铁 fū ㄈㄨ 铡刀 straw cutter; fodder chopper

麸(*麬) fū ㄈㄨ (一子)麸皮,小麦磨面过罗后剩下的皮儿和碎屑 bran

趺 fū ㄈㄨ 同"跗",脚背(same as 跗) instep

跗 fū ㄈㄨ 脚背 instep:~骨 *tarsus; tarsal bones* | ~面 *instep* 也作"趺"(also written as 趺)(图见 241 页"骨" picture on p241)

稃 fū ㄈㄨ 小麦等植物的花外面包着的硬壳 husk; chaff:内~*bran* | 外~*husk; chaff*

孵 fū ㄈㄨ 鸟类伏在卵上,使卵内的胚胎发育成雏鸟。也指用人工的方法使卵孵化 to hatch; to brood

鄜 fū ㄈㄨ 鄜县,地名,在陕西省。今作"富县"(now written as 富县) Fuxian County, in Shaanxi Province

敷 fū ㄈㄨ ❶涂上,搽上 to apply:~粉 *to apply powder* | 外~药 *medicine for external use* ❷布置,铺开 to spread; to lay:~设路轨 *to lay a railway track* ❸足够 sufficient:~用 *to be sufficient for use* | 入不~出 *to be unable to make both ends meet; to run behind one's expenses*

[敷衍](—yǎn)做事不认真或待人不真诚,只是表面应酬 to be perfunctory; to muddle through:~~了(liǎo)事 *to muddle through sth; to gloss over sth* | 这人不诚恳,对人总是~~。*The man is not sincere, for he always takes a perfunctory attitude towards others.*

夫 ㊁ fú ㄈㄨˊ ❶文言发语词 (used in classical Chinese at the beginning of a sentence to introduce a new subject):~天地者 *the heaven and the earth* ❷文言助词 ***auxiliary in classical Chinese***:逝者如斯~。*Thus do things flow away.*

㊀ fū 见 200 页 see p200

扶 fú ㄈㄨˊ ❶搀,用手支持人或物使不倒 to support with the hand:~老携幼 *to help the aged and the young* | ~犁 *to put one's hand to the plough; to follow the plough* ❷用手按着或把持着 to place a hand on sb or sth for support:~墙 *to support oneself against the wall* | ~栏杆 *to hold onto the railings*[扶手]手扶着可以当倚靠的东西,如楼梯旁的栏杆等 banister; handrail ❸帮助,援助 to help; to assist:~贫 *to aid the poor; to give support to poor households in developing production and changing the conditions of poverty* | 救死~伤 *to heal the wounded and rescue the dying* | ~危济困 *to help those in danger and relieve those in need*

芙 fú ㄈㄨˊ [芙蓉](—róng) **1** 落叶灌木,花有红、白等色,很美丽,为别于荷花,也叫"木芙蓉"(also called 木芙蓉) cottonrose hibiscus; cotton rosemallow (*Hibiscus mutabilis*) **2** 荷花的别名 another name for 荷花 (lotus)

蚨 fú ㄈㄨˊ 青蚨,古代用作铜钱的别名 *qingfu*, another name for copper coins in ancient China

弗 fú ㄈㄨˊ 副词 ***adverb***,不 not:～去 *do not leave*|～许 *do not permit*

佛(*彿、*髴) ㊁ fú ㄈㄨˊ 见 187 页"仿"字条"仿佛"(fǎng—) see 仿佛 on p187

㊀ fó 见 199 页 see p199

拂 fú ㄈㄨˊ ❶掸(dǎn)去,轻轻擦过 to whisk; to flick:～尘 *to whisk the dust*|春风～面。*A spring breeze caresses the cheeks.*[拂晓]天将明的时候 daybreak; dawn [拂袖]甩袖子,表示生气 to flick one's sleeve in anger ❷违背,不顺 to go against:～意(不如意)*to go against sb's wishes*

〈古 ***archaism***〉又同"弼"(bì) also same as 弼

茀 fú ㄈㄨˊ 道路上草太多,不便通行 inconvenient for people to pass with tangled and bushy grass on the road

怫 fú ㄈㄨˊ fèi ㄈㄟˋ(又 **also** fèi) 忧郁或愤怒的样子 gloomy or indignant:～郁 *gloomy and indignant*|～然作色 *to flush with anger*

绋 fú ㄈㄨˊ 大绳,特指出殡时拉棺材用的大绳(especially thick cords fastening the coffin, or used for pulling the hearse) thick rope:执～(送殡) *to serve as a pallbearer*

氟 fú ㄈㄨˊ 一种化学元素,在通常条件下为气体,符号 F,淡黄色,味臭,性毒。液态氟可作火箭燃料的氧化剂。含氟塑料和含氟橡胶有特别优良的性能 fluorine (F)

艴 fú ㄈㄨˊ 艴然,生气的样子 looking angry

伏 fú ㄈㄨˊ ❶趴,脸向下,体前屈 to lie prostrate:～在地上 *to lie prostrate on the ground*|～案读书 *to bend over a desk reading* ❷低下去 to fall; to subside:此起彼～。*As one falls, another rises in succession.*|时起时～ *now rise, now down; up and down* ❸隐藏 to hide:～兵 *ambush*|～击 *to ambush*|潜～期 *delitescence; latent period* ❹屈服,承认错误或受到惩罚 to yield:～辜(承认自己的罪过)*to admit one's guilt*|～法 *to be executed* ❺伏日,夏至后第三个庚日叫初伏,第四个庚日叫中伏,立秋后第一个庚日叫末伏,统称三伏。初伏到中伏相隔十天,中伏到末伏相隔十天或二十天。通常也指夏至后第三个庚日起到立秋后第二个庚日前一天的一段时间 dog days; hottest season ❻电压单位名伏特的简称,符号 V (short for 伏特) volt (V)

茯 fú ㄈㄨˊ [茯苓](—líng)寄生在松树根上的一种真菌,外形呈球状,皮黑色,有皱纹,内部白色或粉红色,包含松根的叫茯神,都可入药 *fu ling* (*Wolfiporia extensa*)

洑 ㊀ fú ㄈㄨˊ ❶旋涡 eddy; whirl ❷水在地下潜流(of water) to flow underground

㊁ fù 见 210 页 see p210

栿 fú ㄈㄨˊ 古书上指房梁 beam of a roof in ancient Chinese texts

袱(**襆) fú ㄈㄨˊ 包裹、覆盖用的布单 cloth wrapper [包袱](-fu) **1** 包裹衣物的布单 cloth wrapper **2** 用布单包成的包裹 cloth pack: 白布~~ *white-cloth bundle* ㊗ ***figurative*** 思想上的负担或使行动受到牵制的障碍 burden; weight; load: 放下~~,轻装前进 *to drop one's burden and march forward with a relieved mind* **3** 指相声、快书等曲艺中的笑料(of cross talk, quick-patter) punchline; laughing stock: 抖~~ *to crack a joke*

凫(鳧) fú ㄈㄨˊ ❶水鸟,俗叫"野鸭",形状像鸭子,雄的头部绿色,背部黑褐色,雌的黑褐色。常群游湖泊中,能飞(popularly called 野鸭) wild duck ❷在水里游 to swim: ~水 *to swim in water*

芾 ㊀ fú ㄈㄨˊ ❶草木茂盛 lush; luxuriant ❷同"黻"。宋代书画家米芾,也作米黻(same as 黻; 米芾 also written as 米黻) Mi Fu, a painter and calligrapher in the Song Dynasty

㊁ fèi 见 192 页 see p192

芣 fú ㄈㄨˊ [芣苢](-yǐ)古书上指车前,多年生草本植物,花淡绿色,叶和种子可入药(in ancient Chinese texts) Asiatic plantain (*Plantago asiatica*)

罘 fú ㄈㄨˊ [罘罳][罦罳](-sī) **1** 一种屋檐下防鸟雀的网 net under eaves for warding off birds **2** 古代一种屏风 folding screen in ancient China [芝罘]山名,靠黄海,在山东省烟台 Zhifu Mountain, by the Yellow Sea, in Yantai, Shandong Province

孚 fú ㄈㄨˊ ❶信用 credit ❷使人信服 to inspire confidence (in sb): 深~众望 *to enjoy high prestige*

俘 fú ㄈㄨˊ ❶打仗时捉住的敌人 captive (㊤***doublet***—虏 captive): 战~ *prisoner of war* | 遣~ *to repatriate prisoners of war* ❷打仗时捉住敌人(㊤***doublet***—虏 to take sb captive) to capture; to hold sb prisoner: 被~ *to be taken prisoner* | ~获 *to capture; to seize*

郛 fú ㄈㄨˊ 古代城圈外围的大城 outer wall of a city in ancient China

莩 ㊀ fú ㄈㄨˊ 芦苇秆子里面的薄膜 thin membrane inside a reed stalk

㊁ piǎo 见 567 页 see p567

浮 fú ㄈㄨˊ ❶漂,跟"沉"相对(the opposite of 沉) to float (㊤***doublet*** 漂— to float): ~萍 *duckweed* | ~桥 *pontoon bridge* | ~在水面上 *to float on water* ❷表面的 superficial: ~

F

面 *surface* | ～皮 *epidermis; cuticle; surface* | ～土 *surface dust; surface soil* [浮雕]雕塑的一种,在平面上雕出凸起的形象 relief; bas-relief ❸暂时的 temporary; provisional: ～记 *to keep a temporary account; to tally sth for the time being* | ～支 *temporary account of expenses* ❹不沉静,不沉着(zhuó) frivolous: 心粗气～*hot-headed* | 心～气躁 *restless and fretful* ❺空虚,不切实 empty; hollow: ～名 *empty name; vain reputation* | ～华 *ornate; florid* | ～泛 *superficial; shallow* ❻超过,多余 to exceed: 人～于事 *overstaffed* | ～额 *surplus number*

[浮屠][浮图] **1** 佛教徒称释迦牟尼(used by Buddhists to address Sakyamuni) **2** 古时称和尚(used to address a monk in ancient China) **3** 塔 pagoda: 七级～～*seven-tiered pagoda*

桴(❷**枹) fú ㄈㄨˊ ❶小筏子 small raft ❷鼓槌 drumstick

罘 fú ㄈㄨˊ 古书上指捕鸟的网 net for catching birds in ancient Chinese texts [罘罳](—sī)同"罘罳"same as 罘罳(参看203页"罘"(fú) see 罘 on p203)

蜉 fú ㄈㄨˊ [蜉蝣](—yóu)昆虫,幼虫生在水中,成虫褐绿色,有翅两对,在水面飞行。成虫生存期极短,交尾产卵后即死 mayfly (*Ephemeroptera*)

苻 fú ㄈㄨˊ ❶同"莩㊀"same as 莩㊀ ❷姓 Fu, a surname

符 fú ㄈㄨˊ ❶朝廷传达命令或征调(diào)兵将用的凭证,用金、玉、铜、竹、木制成,刻上文字,分成两半,一半存朝廷,一半给外任官员或出征将帅 tally issued in ancient China by a ruler to his general or envoy as a credential: 兵～*military tally* | 虎～*tiger-shaped tally* ❷代表事物的标记,记号 symbol; mark: 音～*musical note* | 星～*astrologic omen* [符号] **1** 同"符❷"same as 符❷ **2** 佩带在身上表明职别、身份等的标志(sign that shows one's rank or status) insignia ❸相合 to accord with; to tally with (㊟ ***doublet*** —合 to conform to; to be in line with): 言行相～*to match one's actions with one's words* | 完全～合人民的利益 *to accord totally with the people's interests* ❹道士、巫婆等画的驱使鬼神的东西(迷信)(superstitious) magic figure or sign drawn by a Taoist priest to invoke or expel spirits and bring good or ill fortune: 护身～*amulet; talisman*

服 ㊀ fú ㄈㄨˊ ❶衣服,衣裳 clothes; dress (㊟ ***doublet*** —装 clothing): 制～*uniform* | ～装整齐 *neatly dressed* 旧时特指丧服 mourning (apparel) in former time ❷穿(衣裳) to wear; to be dressed in ❸承当,担任 to serve: ～刑 *to serve* *one's term of imprisonment* | ～兵役 *to serve in the army* ❹信服，顺从 to be convinced; to be obedient (㊥ ***doublet*** 一 从 to obey; to submit to)：说～ *to convince* | 心悦诚～ *to have a heartfelt admiration* | 心里不～ *not to be convinced* | ～软(认输，认错) *to acknowledge defeat; to admit a mistake* | ～从党的领导 *to follow the leadership of the Party* ❺习惯，适应 to be used to; to be accustomed to：水土不～ *to be not acclimatized to the local environment* ❻吃(药) to take：～药 *to take medicine*

㊁ fù 见 209 页 see p209

菔 fú ㄈㄨˊ ［莱菔］(lái—)萝卜 radish

箙 fú ㄈㄨˊ 古代盛(chéng)箭的器具 utensil for keeping arrows in ancient China; quiver

绂 fú ㄈㄨˊ 古代系(jì)印章或佩玉用的丝带 silk ribbon used to tie a seal or a jade pendant in ancient China

韨(韍) fú ㄈㄨˊ ❶古代朝见或祭祀时遮在衣前的一种服饰，用熟皮制成 knee-length, cured leather apron tied over the ceremonial or sacrificial gown in ancient China ❷同"绂"same as 绂

祓 fú ㄈㄨˊ 古代迷信的习俗，用斋戒沐浴等方法除灾求福 (superstitious practice in ancient China) sacred ablution for getting rid of disasters and praying for blessings ㊊ ***extension*** 清除 to wash away; to get rid of

黻 fú ㄈㄨˊ ❶古代礼服上绣的半青半黑的花纹 embroidered pattern of black and blue on ancient grande toilette ❷同"韨"same as 韨 ❸同"绂"same as 绂

匐 fú ㄈㄨˊ 见 577 页"匍"字条"匍匐"(pú—)see 匍匐 on p577

幅 fú ㄈㄨˊ ❶幅面，布匹、呢绒等的宽度 width of cloth：这块布的～面宽。*The piece of cloth is of wide breadth.* | 这种布是双～的。*This cloth is of double breadth.* ［幅度］物体振动或摇摆所展开的宽度 extent; range ㊞ ***figurative*** 事物变动的大小 degree or extent of change：产品质量大～～提高。*The quality of products has improved greatly.* ［幅员］宽窄叫幅，周围叫员 dimensions ㊕ ***transfer*** 疆域 territory：我国～～广大。*China has a vast territory.* ［振幅］振动的物体，从往复运动的中点到运动所能达到的最大距离 amplitude ❷边缘 margin; edge ❸量词 ***quantifier***：一～画 *a piece of painting*

辐 fú ㄈㄨˊ 连接车辋和车毂的直条 spoke(图见 475 页"轮" picture on p475)［辐辏］［辐凑］(—còu)车辐聚于车毂 to converge ㊞ ***figurative*** 人、物聚集 to converge; to cluster［辐射］光、热、粒子等向四周放射的现象 radiation

F

福 fú ㄈㄨˊ 幸福，跟"祸"相对(the opposite of 祸) bliss; happiness：为人类造～*to benefit mankind*［福利］幸福和利益 welfare：职工的～～*the welfare of the staff*｜～～事业 *welfare project; welfare service*

蝠 fú ㄈㄨˊ 见43页"蝙"字条"蝙蝠"(biān—) see 蝙蝠 on p43

涪 fú ㄈㄨˊ 涪江，发源于四川省，入嘉陵江 Fujiang River, rising in Sichuan Province and joining the Jialing River

幞(**襆) fú ㄈㄨˊ 同"袱" same as 袱［幞头］古代男子用的一种头巾 headdress for men in ancient China

F

父 ㊁ fǔ ㄈㄨˇ ❶老年人 elderly man：田～*old farmer*｜渔～*old fisherman* ❷同"甫❶" same as 甫❶

㊀ fù 见208页 see p208

斧 fǔ ㄈㄨˇ ❶(一子、一头)砍东西用的工具 axe; hatchet ❷一种旧式武器 battleax, an old-fashioned weapon

釜(**鬴) fǔ ㄈㄨˇ ❶古代的一种锅 cauldron in ancient China：～底抽薪(喻从根本上解决) *to take away firewood from under the cauldron — to tackle a problem at the root; to take a drastic measure to deal with a situation*｜破～沉舟(喻下决心去干，不留后路) *to break the cauldrons and sink the boats* (after crossing a river); *to throw away the scabbard; to cross* (or *pass*) *the Rubicon* ❷古代量器名 *fu*, measuring tool in ancient China

滏 fǔ ㄈㄨˇ［滏阳河］水名，在河北省西南部 Fuyang River, in the southwest of Hebei Province

抚(撫) fǔ ㄈㄨˇ ❶慰问 to console：～恤(xù) *to console and compensate*｜～慰 *to soothe; to comfort* ❷扶持，保护 to rear; to protect：～养成人 *to bring sb up*｜～育孤儿 *to foster an orphan* ❸轻轻地按着 to caress; to stroke：～摩 *to stroke; to caress* ❹同"拊" same as 拊

甫 fǔ ㄈㄨˇ ❶古代在男子名字下加的美称。也作"父"(also written as 父) male courtesy name in ancient China［台甫］旧时询问别人名号的用语(used in asking sb's courtesy name in former times) your honoured style; your name ❷刚，才 just now：～入门 *to have just entered the house*｜年～十岁 *to have just reached the age of ten*

辅 fǔ ㄈㄨˇ ❶帮助，佐助 to help; to assist (㊟***doublet*** 一助 to assist)：～导 *to coach*｜相～而行 *to go together; to complement each other*［辅音］发音的时候，从肺里出来的气，经过口腔或鼻腔受到障碍所成的音，也叫"子音"。拼音字母b、d、g等都是辅音(also called

子音)consonant ❷人的颊骨 cheekbone:~车相依(车:牙床。喻二者关系密切,互相依存)*interdependent*

脯 ㊀ fǔ ㄈㄨˇ ❶肉干 dried meat:鹿~ *dried venison* ❷果脯,蜜饯果干 preserved fruit:桃~*preserved peach*|杏~*preserved apricot*

㊁ pú 见577页 see p577

蜅 fǔ ㄈㄨˇ [螟蜅鲞](míng—xiǎng)墨鱼干 dried inkfish; dried cuttlefish

簠 fǔ ㄈㄨˇ 古代祭祀时盛稻、粱的器具。长方形,有盖和耳 rectangular sacrificial grain vessel with a lid and ears in ancient China

黼 fǔ ㄈㄨˇ 古代礼服上绣的半黑半白的花纹 embroidered pattern of black and white on ancient grande toilette

拊 fǔ ㄈㄨˇ 拍,也作"抚"(also written as 抚)to clap:~掌大笑 *to clap hands and laugh heartily*

府 fǔ ㄈㄨˇ ❶储藏文书或财物的地方 government repository(㊃***doublet*** 一库 government repository):~库充实。*The government repository is full.*|天~(喻物产富饶的地方)*Nature's storehouse; land of abundance* ❷贵族或高级官员办公或居住的地方 government office; official residence:王~*prince residence*|总统~*presidential residence*|相(xiàng)~*mansion of a prime minister*[府上](—shang)对对方的籍贯、家庭或住宅的敬称(term of respect for one's home) your home ❸旧时行政区域名,等级在县和省之间 prefecture which ranks between a province and a county in former times

俯(*頫、*俛) fǔ ㄈㄨˇ 向下,低头,跟"仰"相对(the opposite of 仰) to bow; to bend:~视山下 *to overlook the mountain*|~仰之间(很短的时间)*in a flash; in the twinkling of an eye*

腑 fǔ ㄈㄨˇ 脏腑,中医对人体胸、腹内部器官的总称。心、肝、脾、肺、肾叫"脏",胃、胆、大肠、小肠、膀胱等叫"腑"(in traditional Chinese medicine) cover term for internal organs (the heart, liver, spleen, lungs and kidneys are called 脏; the stomach, gall, large intestine, small intestine and bladder are called 腑)

腐 fǔ ㄈㄨˇ 烂,变质 rotten; stale (㊃***doublet*** 一败 decayed; corrupt|一烂 rotten; decomposed|一朽 decadent; putrid):流水不~。*Running water never goes stale.*|鱼~肉败。*The fish and meat rotted.*|这块木头已经~朽不堪了。*The piece of wood has already decayed.* ㊂***extension*** 思想陈旧或行为堕落 corrupt; rotten:观点陈~*outdated idea* (*in traditional Chinese medicine*) *cover term for internal organsout-worn concept*|生活~化 *to lead*

F

a corrupt life[腐蚀]通过化学作用使物体逐渐消损或毁坏 to corrode：～～剂 *corrosive* (*in traditional Chinese medicine*) *cover term for internal organ-sescharotic* [喻]***figurative*** 使人腐化堕落 to corrupt[豆腐](—fu)用豆子制成的一种食品，也省称"腐"(also 腐 for short) tofu；bean curd：～～皮 *thin sheets of dried bean curd*｜～～乳 *fermented bean curd*

父 ㊀ fù ㄈㄨˋ ❶父亲，爸爸 father；dad ❷对男性长辈的称呼 term of respect to address a man of a senior generation：叔～*uncle* (*on the paternal side*)｜姨～ *uncle* (*on the maternal side*)｜师～*master*｜～老 *elders*

㊁ fǔ 见 206 页 see p206

讣 fù ㄈㄨˋ 报丧，也指报丧的通知 obituary：～闻 *obituary*｜～告 *obituary; obituary notice*

赴 fù ㄈㄨˋ 往，去 to go；to attend：～北京 *to go to Beijing*｜～宴 *to attend a banquet*｜～汤蹈火(喻不避艰险) *to go through fire and water — to defy all difficulties and dangers*

付 fù ㄈㄨˋ ❶交，给 to hand over；to submit；to give：～款 *to pay*｜～印 *to send to the press*｜～表决 *to put to the vote*｜～诸实施 *to put into practice*｜～出了辛勤的劳动 *to put in a lot of hard work* ❷量词 ***quantifier*** **1** 同"副❹"same as 副❹：一～手套 *a pair of gloves*｜一～笑脸 *a smiling face* **2** 同"服㊁"same as 服㊁

附(*坿) fù ㄈㄨˋ ❶另外加上，随带着 to add；to attach；to enclose：～录 *appendix*｜～设 *to have as an attached agency*｜～注 *annotation*｜信里面～着一张相片。*A photo is enclosed in the letter.*[附和](—hè)盲目地同意别人的主张 to echo：不要随声～～。*Don't echo others' views.*[附会](*傅会)把不相关联的事拉到一起，把没有某种意义的事物说成有某种意义 to make a strained interpretation：牵强～～ *to draw a forced analogy; to make a farfetched comparison*[附议]对别人的提议或动议表示同意 to second a motion；to support a proposal[附庸]古代指附属在诸侯大国下面的小国 dependency；vassal [引] ***extension*** 从属的地位或依赖的关系 to depend on；to comply with ❷靠近 to be close to：～近 *nearby*｜～耳交谈 *to whisper in one's ear*

驸 fù ㄈㄨˋ 几匹马共同拉车，在旁边的马叫"驸"horse hitched by the side of the shaft horse (to assist the pulling of a vehicle)[驸马]驸马都尉，汉代官名。后来帝王的女婿常做这个官，因此驸马专指公主的丈夫 *fuma*，the emperor's son-in-law，a term derived from *Fumaduwei*，an official title in the Han Dynasty

鲋 fù ㄈㄨˋ 古书上指鲫鱼 crucian carp (*Carassius carassius*) in ancient Chinese texts:涸(hé)辙之～(喻处在困难中急待援助的人)*fish stranded in a dry rut — person in a predicament*

负 fù ㄈㄨˋ ❶背 to carry:～重 *to carry a heavy load*|～荆请罪 *to proffer a bunch of birch sticks and ask for a flogging — to make a humble and sincere apology* ㊀ ***extension*** 担任 to shoulder; to bear:～责 *to be responsible for; to take charge of*[负担] **1** 担当 to undertake **2** 责任,所担当的事务 responsibility; duty:减轻～～*to lessen a burden* ㊁ ***figurative*** 感到痛苦的不容易解决的思想问题 mental burden; weight on the mind ❷仗恃,倚靠 to have sb at one's back; to rely on:～险固守 *to rely on one's strategic position for a stubborn defence*|～隅(yú)顽抗 *to put up a desperate resistance with one's back against the wall*[负气]赌气 to be in a fit of pique[自负]自以为了不起 conceited ❸遭受 to suffer:～伤 *to be wounded; to be injured*|～屈 *to be wronged* ❹具有 to enjoy:～有名望 *to enjoy a good reputation*|素～盛名 *to have long enjoyed a good reputation* ❺欠(钱)to owe; to be indebted:～债 *to be indebted* ❻违背,背弃 to betray:～盟 *to betray the alley*|忘恩～义 *to be ungrateful*|不～人民的希望 *to live up to the expectations of the people* ❼败,跟"胜"相对(the opposite of 胜) to fail; to be defeated:不分胜～ *to play to a draw; to draw even* ❽小于零的 minus; negative:～数 *negative number* ❾指相对的两方面中反的一面,跟"正"相对(the opposite of 正) negative:～极 *negative pole; cathode*|～电 *negative electricity*

妇(婦) fù ㄈㄨˋ ❶已经结婚的女子 married woman ㊀ ***extension*** 女性的通称 general term for women:～科 *gynaecology*|～女翻身 *women's emancipation* ❷妻,跟"夫"相对(the opposite of 夫) wife:夫～ *man and wife* ❸儿媳 daughter-in-law:长～ *wife of the eldest son*|媳～ *daughter-in-law*

阜 fù ㄈㄨˋ ❶土山 mound ❷盛,多 abundant:物～民丰。*Products abound and the people live in plenty.*

服 ㊁ fù ㄈㄨˋ 量词 ***quantifier***,用于中药,也作"付"(used in traditional Chinese medicine, also written as 付) dose:吃～药就好了。*A dose of Chinese medicine will make you recover.*

㊀ fú 见 204 页 see p204

复(❶—❺復、❺❻複) fù ㄈㄨˋ ❶回去,返 to turn around; to return:反～ *to chop and change; to relapse*|循环往～ *to recur time and again* ❷回

答，回报 to reply; to return: ～仇 *to revenge* | ～命 *to report on the completion of a task* | 函～ *to reply by a letter* ❸还原，使如旧 to recover; to resume: 光～ *to restore; to recover* | 身体～原 *to recover one's health* | ～员军人 *demobilized soldier; ex-serviceman* ❹副词 ***adverb*** 又，再 again: 死灰～燃 *to revive; to resurge* | 一去不～返 *to be gone for ever; never to be found again* ❺重复，重叠 to repeat: ～习 *to review; to go over* | ～印 *to duplicate; to copy* | 山重水～ *winding mountains and meandering streams; over hills and rills* ❻不是单一的，许多的 compound; complex: ～姓 *two-character surname; compound surname* | ～杂 *complicated; complex* | ～分数 *complex fraction* | ～式簿记 *double entry bookkeeping*

腹 fù ㄈㄨˋ 肚子，在胸部的下面 belly: ～部 *belly* | ～背(前后)受敌 *to be attacked front and rear* [腹地] 内地，中部地区 hinterland; interior

蝮 fù ㄈㄨˋ 蝮蛇，蛇名。体色灰褐，头部略呈三角形，有毒牙 Pallas' pit viper (*Crotalinae*)

鳆 fù ㄈㄨˋ 鳆鱼，鲍(bào)的古称(former term of 鲍) abalone 参看 26 页"鲍❶" see 鲍❶ on p26

覆 fù ㄈㄨˋ ❶遮盖，蒙 to cover: 天～地载 *covered by heaven and carried by earth — all-embracing* | 大地被一层白雪～盖着。*The earth is blanketed with snow.* ❷翻，倒(dào)过来 to overturn; to upset: ～舟 *capsized boat* | 天翻地～ *snafu; earth-shaking* [覆没] (－mò) 船翻沉 to capsize; to sink ㊗ ***figurative*** 军队被消灭 to be annihilated [覆辙] 在那里翻过车的车辙 rut of an overturned cart ㊗ ***figurative*** 失败的道路、方法 previously unsuccessful method [颠覆] 车翻倒(of cart) to overturn ㊗ ***figurative*** 用阴谋推翻合法政权，也指政权垮台 to subvert ❸同"复❶❷" same as 复❶❷

馥 fù ㄈㄨˋ 香气 fragrance [馥郁] 香气浓厚 richly fragrant; sweet-scented

洑 ㊁ fù ㄈㄨˋ 在水里游 to swim: ～水 *to swim*
㊀ fú 见 203 页 see p203

副 fù ㄈㄨˋ ❶居第二位的，辅助的(区别于"正"或"主") (in contrast with 正 or 主) deputy; assistant; vice: ～主席 *vice-chairman* | ～排长 *assistant platoon leader* ❷附带的或次要的 subsidiary: ～食 *non-staple food* | ～业 *sideline* | ～作用 *side effect* | ～产品 *by-product* [副本] **1** 书籍原稿以外的誊录本 copy; duplicate **2** 重要文件正式的、标准的一份以外的若干份 transcript; copy [副词] 修饰动词或形容词的词，如都、也、很、太、再三等 adverb ❸相称(chèn)，符合 to correspond to; to fit: 名不～实

to have an undeserved reputation｜名实相～。*Name conforms to reality*. ❹量词 ***quantifier*** **1** 用于成组成套的东西 group; set：一～对联 *a pair of antithetical couplets*｜一～担架 *a stretcher*｜全～武装 *to be fully armed; to be armed to the teeth* **2** 用于面部表情、态度等(used in facial expression, attitude, etc)：一～笑容 *a broad smile*｜一～庄严而和蔼的面孔 *a solemn but genial face*

富 fù ㄈㄨˋ ❶富有,跟"贫"、"穷"相对(the opposite of 贫 and 穷) rich：～人 *rich man; the rich*｜～豪 *rich and powerful person; plutocrat*｜新中国走向繁荣～强。*The People's Republic of China is developing into a prosperous and strong country*. [富丽]华丽 gorgeous; magnificent：～～堂皇 *gorgeous; splendid* ❷资源、财产 resource; property：～源 *natural resources*｜财～ *wealth; riches* ❸充裕,多,足 sufficient; abundant(㊀ ***doublet*** —裕 ample｜—足 affluent｜—饶 abundant in natural resources｜丰— sumptuous)：我国人民～于创造精神。*The Chinese people are highly creative*.｜西红柿的维生素C很丰～。*Tomatoes are rich in vitamin C*.

赋 fù ㄈㄨˋ ❶旧指田地税 land tax in former times：田～ *land tax*[赋税]旧时田赋和各种捐税的总称 taxes and levies ❷我国古典文学中的一种文体,盛行于汉魏六朝 *fu*, an intricate literary form combining of elements of poetry and prose, which prevailed in the Han and the Wei dynasties and the Six Dynasties period; versified prose ❸念诗或作诗 to read or compose a poem：登高～诗 *to ascend high and compose a poem* ❹交给,给予 to grant; to bestow：完成党～予的任务 *to accomplish the task the Party has entrusted us with*

傅 fù ㄈㄨˋ ❶辅助,教导 to tutor; to instruct ❷师傅,教导人的人 instructor ❸附着,使附着 to attach; to adhere：～粉 *to powder; to apply powder*

缚 fù ㄈㄨˋ 捆绑 to tie up; to bind fast：束～*to bind up; to fetter; to shackle*

赙 fù ㄈㄨˋ 拿钱财帮人办理丧事 to present money or a gift to a bereaved family：～金 *money presented to a bereaved family*｜～仪 *gift presented to a bereaved family*

咐 fu · ㄈㄨ 见194页"吩"字条"吩咐"(fēn —)、996页"嘱"字条"嘱咐"(zhǔ—) see 吩咐 on p194 and 嘱咐 on p996

F

G ㄍ

GA ㄍㄚ

夹(夾) ㊂ gā ㄍㄚ [夹肢窝](—zhiwō)胳窝 armpit
㊀ jiā 见 321 页 see p321
㊁ jiá 见 322 页 see p322

旮 gā ㄍㄚ [旮旯](—lá)(—子、—儿)角落 corner; nook: 墙～～*corner of a wall* | 门～～*corner behind a door* ㊣ *figurative* 偏僻的地方 out-of-the-way place: 山～～*mountain recess* | 背～～儿 *secluded spot*

伽 ㊂ gā ㄍㄚ [伽马射线]又叫"丙种射线"。波长极短,一些放射性元素的原子能放出这种射线,在工业和医学上用途很广。通常写作"γ射线"(also called 丙种射线, usually written as γ射线) gamma ray
㊀ qié 见 603 页 see p603
㊁ jiā 见 320 页 see p320

咖 ㊀ gā ㄍㄚ [咖喱](—lí)(外 **loanword**)用胡椒、姜黄等做的调味品 curry
㊁ kā 见 380 页 see p380

嘎 ㊀ gā ㄍㄚ 拟声词 ***onomatopoeia*** [嘎吧][嘎叭](—bā)拟声词 ***onomatopoeia***, snap; crack [嘎吱](—zhī)拟声词 ***onomatopoeia***, creak; squeak; squish

[嘎巴](—ba) **1** 黏东西凝结在器物上 to crust **2** (—儿)凝结在器物上的东西 crust; that which adheres to sth else: 衣裳上有好多～～。*There are a lot of crusts on the clothes.*

[嘎渣](—zha) **1** 疮伤结的痂 scab **2** (—儿)食物烤黄的焦皮 crust: 饭～～ *rice crusts* | 饼子～～儿 *pancake crusts*
㊁ gá 见213页 see p213
㊂ gǎ 见213页 see p213

轧 ㊂ gá ㄍㄚˊ 〈方 ***dialect***〉❶挤,拥挤 to squeeze; to press ❷结交(朋友) to make friends (with) ❸查对(账目) to check (the accounts)
㊀ yà 见860页 see p860
㊁ zhá 见948页 see p948

钆 gá ㄍㄚˊ 一种金属元素,符号Gd,用于微波技术、原子能工业等 gadolinium (Gd)

尜 gá ㄍㄚˊ [尜尜](—ga) **1** 一种儿童玩具,两头尖中间大。也叫"尜儿"(also called 尜儿) *gaga*, a spindle-shaped toy with a bulging middle and pointed at both ends **2** 像尜尜的 spindle-like: ～～枣 gagazao, *spindle-like jujube* (or *date*) | ～～汤(用玉米面等做的食品) gagatang, *soup cooked with maize flour*

嘎 ㊁ gá ㄍㄚˊ [嘎嘎](—ga) 同"尜尜"same as 尜尜
㊀ gā 见212页 see p212
㊂ gǎ 见213页 see p213

噶 gá ㄍㄚˊ 译音用字(used in transliteration)

尕 gǎ ㄍㄚˇ〈方 ***dialect***〉❶乖僻 eccentric; odd ❷调皮 naughty; mischievous

尕 gǎ ㄍㄚˇ〈方 ***dialect***〉小 little; small:～娃 *little child*|～李 *Xiao Li; Young Li*

嘎 ㊂ gǎ ㄍㄚˇ 同"尕"(gǎ) same as 尕
㊀ gā 见212页 see p212
㊁ gá 见213页 see p213

尬 gà ㄍㄚˋ 见216页"尴"字条"尴尬"(gān—) see 尴尬 on p216

GAI ㄍㄞ

该 gāi ㄍㄞ ❶应当,理应如此 should; ought to (㊫ ***doublet*** 应— should; ought to):～做的一定要做。*What should be done must be done.* ❷表示根据情理或经验推测必然的或可能的结果 most likely; probably:不学习,思想就～落后了。*If you don't study, your thinking will be outdated.* ❸指前面说过的人或事物,多用于公文(usually used in official documents) this; that; the above-mentioned:～地 *that place*|～员 *this* (or *that*) *member*|～书 *this book* ❹欠,欠账 to owe:～他几块钱 *to owe him a few yuan* ❺同"赅"same as 赅

陔 gāi ㄍㄞ ❶近台阶的地方 place near the stairs ❷级,层,台阶 step; layer; stair ❸田埂 footpath in a field; ridge

垓 gāi ㄍㄞ ❶垓下,古地名,在今安徽省灵璧东南,是汉刘邦围困项羽的地方 Gaixia, an ancient place in today's southeastern Lingbi, Anhui Province, where Liu Bang, the Lord of Han and his army besieged Xiang Yu, the Lord of Chu ❷古代数目,是京的十倍,指一万万(an ancient numeral) ten *jing*; one hundred million

荄 gāi ㄍㄞ 草根 grass roots

赅 gāi ㄍㄞ 完备 complete; full:言简意～ *brief but sufficient; concise but comprehensive*

改 gǎi ㄍㄞˇ ❶变更,更换 to change; to transform (㊫ ***doublet*** —革 to reform|—变 to change|更— to change):～天换地 *to transform nature; to change the world* ❷修改 to alter; to revise:～文章 *to revise an article*|～衣服 *to alter clothes* ❸改正 to correct; to rectify:知过必～ *to be ready to correct an error when one becomes aware of it*

丐 gài ㄍㄞˋ ❶乞求 to beg ❷乞丐,讨饭的人 beggar ❸给予 to give; to grant

钙 gài ㄍㄞˋ 一种金属元素,符号 Ca,银白色。动物的骨骼、蛤壳、蛋壳都含有碳酸钙和

G

磷酸钙。它的化合物在工业上、建筑工程上和医药上用途很大 calcium (Ca)

芥 ㊁ gài ㄍㄞˋ 芥菜(也作"盖菜"),是芥(jiè)菜的变种。叶子大,表面多皱纹,是普通蔬菜(also written as 盖菜) leaf mustard (*Brassica juncea*) [芥蓝菜]一种不结球的甘蓝,叶柄长,叶片短而宽,花白色或黄色。嫩叶和菜薹是普通蔬菜 Chinese kale (*Brassica alboglabra*)

㊀ jiè 见349页 see p349

盖(葢) ㊀ gài ㄍㄞˋ ❶(一子、一儿)器物上部有遮蔽作用的东西 lid; cover:锅～ *pot cover* (or *lid*)|瓶～ *bottle top* ❷伞 umbrella:华～(古代车上像伞的篷子) *canopy* (umbrella-like cover over an ancient carriage) ❸由上向下覆 to cover (㊟ ***doublet*** 覆一 to cover):～上锅 *to put a lid over a pot*|～被 *to put a quilt over* ㊕ ***transfer*** **1** 压倒 to surpass; to top:～世无双 *unparalleled anywhere in the world* **2** 用印打上 to affix (a seal):～章 *to stamp*|～印 *to affix a seal; to stamp* ❹建造 to build:～楼 *to construct a building*|～房子 *to build a house* ❺动物的甲壳 shell:螃蟹～ *crab shell* ❻文言虚词 ***function word in classical Chinese*** **1** 发语词(used to begin a sentence):～有年矣。*Many years have passed since then.* **2** 表不能确信,大概如此 approximately; about:～近之矣。*That's about it.* **3** 连词 ***conjunction***,表原因 for; because:有所不知,～未学也。*There are things we don't know, because we haven't learnt about them.* ❼姓 Gai, a surname

〈古 ***archaism***〉又同"盍"(hé) also same as 盍

㊁ gě 见226页 see p226

溉 gài ㄍㄞˋ 浇灌 to irrigate; to water (㊟ ***doublet*** 灌一 to irrigate)

概 gài ㄍㄞˋ ❶大略,总括 general:～论 *outline; introduction*|大～ *generally; approximately*|不能一～而论。*You should not treat them all alike.* [概念]人们在反复的实践和认识过程中,将事物共同的本质特点抽出来,加以概括,从感性认识飞跃到理性认识,就成为概念 concept; conception; notion ❷情况,景象 general situation; scenery:胜～ *beautiful scenery* ❸气度 deportment; bearing:气～ *spirit; lofty quality* ❹刮平斗、斛用的小木板 *gai*, a small board used to level the top layer of grains in *dou* or *hu*

戤 gài ㄍㄞˋ〈方 ***dialect***〉冒牌图利 to counterfeit

GAN ㄍㄢ

干(❼－⓭△乾) ㊀ gān ㄍㄢ ❶关联,涉及 to have to do with; to be concerned with:不相～ *to have*

nothing to do with | 这事与你何～? *What has it to do with you?* ❷冒犯,触犯 to offend:～犯 *to offend; to encroach upon* | 有～禁例 *to violate the prohibitions* [干涉]过问或制止,常指不应管硬管 to interfere; to intervene:互不～～内政 *not to interfere in each other's internal affairs* ❸追求,旧指追求职位俸禄(formerly used to denote seeking official positions, emoluments, etc) to seek:～禄 *to seek official emoluments* ❹盾 shield:动～戈(喻战乱)*to start wars* [干城][转] ***transfer*** 捍卫者 defender; defending army ❺天干,历法中用的"甲、乙、丙、丁、戊、己、庚、辛、壬、癸"十个字,也作编排次序用(used in the Chinese lunar calendar, also used as serial numbers) 10 Heavenly Stems [干支]天干和地支,历法上把这两组字结合起来,共配成六十组,表示日子或年份,周而复始,循环使用(Each of the 10 Heavenly Stems pairs up alternatively with each of the 12 Earthly Branches to form 60 pairs that are used in a recurrent cycle to designate days or years in the Chinese lunar calendar.) Heavenly Stems and Earthly Branches ❻水边 waterside; bank:江～*river bank* | 河～*riverside* ❼没有水分或水分少的,跟"湿"相对(the opposite of 湿) dry ([连] ***doublet*** 一燥 dry):～柴 *firewood* | ～粮 *solid food; field* (or *marching*) *rations* [干脆][喻] ***figurative*** 爽快,简捷 straightforward; clear-cut:说话～～,做事也～～*to be straightforward in speaking and efficient in doing* ❽(一儿)干的食品或其他东西 dried food:饼～*biscuits* | 豆腐～儿 *dried bean curd* ❾枯竭,净尽,空虚 to dry up; to empty; to hollow:大河没水小河～。*The tributaries dry up when there is no water in the main stream.* | ～杯 *cheers; bottom-up; to drink a toast* | 外强中～*outwardly strong but inwardly weak* ❿空,徒然 in vain; for nothing:～着急 *to be anxious but unable to do anything* | ～等 *to wait idly* | ～看着 *to look on without giving any help* ⓫拜认的亲属关系 taken into nominal kinship:～娘 *godmother* ⓬说怨恨、气愤的话使对方难堪 to embarrass sb by making offensive remarks:今天,我又～了他一顿。*Today, I embarrassed him once again.* ⓭慢待,不理睬 to leave sb in the cold; to give sb the cold shoulder:没想到,他把咱们～起来了。*Unexpectedly, he left us in the cold.* ⓮量词 ***quantifier***,伙 group; band:一～人 *a group of people* ⓯姓 Gan, a surname

[干将](—jiāng)古宝剑名 *ganjiang*, an ancient double-edged sword

㊁ gàn 见218页 see p218

"乾"又 qián 见595页(also

qián) see p595

玕 gān ㄍㄢ [琅玕](láng—) 像珠子的美石 pearl-like stone

杆 ㊀ gān ㄍㄢ (—子、—儿) 较长的木棍 pole: 旗～ *flagpole* | 电线～子 *telegraph-(or telephone-) line pole* | 栏～儿 *railing; banister*

㊁ gǎn 见216页 see p216

肝 gān ㄍㄢ 肝脏,人和高等动物主要内脏之一。是分泌胆汁的器官,可储藏糖原,进行蛋白质、脂肪和碳水化合物的代谢及解毒等 liver (图见940页"脏" picture on p940) [肝胆] ㊃ ***figurative*** **1** 诚心,诚意 open-heartedness; sincerity: ～～相照(喻真诚相见) *to be devoted to each other heart and soul — to treat each other with sincerity* **2** 勇气,血性 courage; heroic spirit

矸 gān ㄍㄢ 矸子,夹杂在煤里的石块 gangue; attal; attle

竿 gān ㄍㄢ (—子、—儿) 竹竿,竹子的主干,竹棍 bamboo pole

酐 gān ㄍㄢ 酸酐,是含氧的无机或有机酸缩水而成的氧化物,如二氧化硫、醋酸酐 anhydride

甘 gān ㄍㄢ ❶甜,味道好,跟"苦"相对(the opposite of 苦) sweet: ～苦 *sweetness and bitterness; weal and woe* | ～泉 *sweet spring* | 苦尽～来。*After sufferings comes happiness.* ㊃ ***figurative*** 美好 pleasant; good: ～雨 *timely rain* ❷甘心,自愿,乐意 willingly; of one's own accord: ～心情愿 *willingly and gladly* | 不～失败 *unwilling to accept the defeat*

坩 gān ㄍㄢ 盛(chéng)东西的陶器 earthenware [坩埚](—guō)用来熔化金属或其他物质的器皿,多用陶土或铂制成,能耐高热 crucible

苷 gān ㄍㄢ 有机化合物的一类,旧叫甙(dài) (formerly called 甙) glucoside

泔 gān ㄍㄢ 泔水,洗过米的水 water from washing rice ㊄ ***extension*** 洗碗洗菜用过的脏水 swill; slops

柑 gān ㄍㄢ 常绿灌木或小乔木,初夏开花,白色。果实圆形,比橘子大,赤黄色,味甜。种类很多 mandarin orange (*Citrus reticulata*)

疳 gān ㄍㄢ 病名 disease name **1** 疳积,中医称小儿的肠胃病 infantile malnutrition due to improper feeding **2** 马牙疳,又叫"走马疳"。牙床和颊部急性溃疡,流脓和血,小儿容易患这种病(also called 走马疳) noma **3** 下疳,性病的一种 chancre

尴(尷、****尲**) gān ㄍㄢ [尴尬](—gà) **1** 处境窘困,不易处理 in a dilemma **2** 神态不自然 embarrassed; uneasy

杆(*桿) ㊁ gǎn ㄍㄢˇ ❶(—子、—儿)较小的圆木条或像木条的东西(指作为器物的把儿的) shaft or

淦 gàn ㄍㄢˋ 淦水，水名，在江西省 Ganshui River in Jiangxi Province

赣（*贛、*灨） gàn ㄍㄢˋ ❶赣江，水名，在江西省 Ganjiang River in Jiangxi Province ❷江西省的别称 Gan, another name for Jiangxi Province

GANG ㄍㄤ

冈（岡） gāng ㄍㄤ 山脊(of a hill) ridge：山～ *low hill* | 景阳～ *Jingyang Ridge* | 井～山 *Jinggang Mountain*

刚（剛） gāng ㄍㄤ ❶坚强，跟"柔"相对 (the opposite of 柔) firm; strong; hard (㊀ ***doublet*** —强 firm; staunch)：性情～正 *staunch and upright* ❷副词 ***adverb***，正好，恰巧(叠 ***reduplication***) just; exactly：～～合适 *to fit perfectly; to be just right for* | ～好一杯 *just a cup* ❸副词 ***adverb***，才，刚才 just now; a moment ago：～来就走 *to leave as soon as one arrives* | ～说了一句话 *to have just said a word*

掆（掆） gāng ㄍㄤ 同"扛"(gāng) same as 扛

岗（崗） ㊁ gāng ㄍㄤ 同"冈" same as 冈

㊀ gǎng 见220页 see p220

纲（綱） gāng ㄍㄤ ❶提网的总绳 head-rope of a fishing net ㊀ ***extension*** 事物的关键部分 prime part; guiding principle：大～ *outline* | ～目 *detailed outline; compendium* | ～领 *programme; guiding principle* ❷从唐朝起，转运大量货物时，把货物分批运行，每批的车辆、船只计数编号，叫作一纲(guarded transportion of certain goods in large quantities by vehicles and ships, which started in the Tang Dynasty) convoy：盐～ *salt convoy* | 茶～ *tea convoy* | 花石～ *ornamental rock and rare plant convoy* ❸生物的分类单位之一，在"门"之下、"目"之上(category in biological taxonomy, which is under 门 and above 目) class：鸟～ *the class of birds* | 单子叶植物～ *the class of monocotyledons*

㭎（棡） gāng ㄍㄤ 青㭎，又叫"槲栎"(húlì)。落叶乔木，叶椭圆形，木质坚实，供建筑用 (also called 槲栎) oriental white oak (*Quercus aliena*)

钢（鋼） ㊀ gāng ㄍㄤ 经过精炼，不含磷、硫等杂质的铁，含碳量低于2%，比熟铁更坚硬、更富于弹性，是工业上极重要的原料 steel [钢精][钢种](—zhǒng)指制造日用器皿的铝(as used for utensils) aluminium [钢铁] iron and steel; steel ㊃ ***figurative*** 坚强，坚定不移 strong; firm：～～的意志 *iron will*

㊁ gàng 见220页 see p220

G

扛 ㊁ gāng ㄍㄤ ❶两手举东西（with both hands）to lift：～鼎 *to lift a* ding（*an ancient cooking vessel with two loop handles and three or four legs*）❷〈方 **dialect**〉抬东西（of two or more people）to carry together

㊀ káng 见385页 see p385

肛 gāng ㄍㄤ 肛门，直肠末端的出口 anus

缸（**瓨）gāng ㄍㄤ 盛东西的陶器，圆筒状，底小口大 vat；jar

罡 gāng ㄍㄤ ［天罡星］即北斗星（i. e. 北斗星）the Big Dipper；the Plough

堽 gāng ㄍㄤ ［堽城屯］地名，在山东省宁阳 Gangchengtun，a place in Ningyang，Shandong Province

岗（崗）㊀ gǎng ㄍㄤˇ ❶（一子、一儿）高起的土坡 hillock；mound：黄土～儿 *loess hill* ❷（一子、一儿）平面上凸起的一长道 welt；ridge：肉～子 *flesh welt* ❸守卫的位置 sentry；post：站～*to stand sentry；to keep guard*｜门～ *gate sentinel*｜布～*to post a sentinel* ［岗位］守卫、值勤的地方。也指职位（also used to denote 职位）sentinel post；position：工作～～*job；position*

㊁ gāng 见219页 see p219

港 gǎng ㄍㄤˇ ❶江河的支流 tributary of a river ❷可以停泊大船的江海口岸 port；harbour：军～*naval port*｜商～*commercial port*｜不冻～*ice-free port* ❸指香港 Hong Kong：～澳（香港和澳门）同胞 *compatriots from Hong Kong and Macao*｜～人治～*Hong Kong people administering Hong Kong*

杠（*槓）gàng ㄍㄤˋ（一子）较粗的棍子 thick rod：铁～*iron rod*｜木～*stick*｜双～（一种运动器具）*parallel bars* ［杠杆］（一gǎn）一种简单助力器械，如剪刀、辘轳、秤，都是利用杠杆的原理制作的 lever

钢（鋼）㊁ gàng ㄍㄤˋ 把刀在布、皮、石或缸沿上用力摩擦几下使它锋利 to sharpen；to whet：这把刀钝了，要～一～。*This knife is blunt and needs sharpening*.

㊀ gāng 见219页 see p219

筻 gàng ㄍㄤˋ ［筻口］地名，在湖南省岳阳 Gangkou，a place in Yueyang，Hunan Province

戇 ㊁ gàng ㄍㄤˋ〈方 **dialect**〉鲁莽 rash；reckless：～头～脑 *to be muddle-headed*

㊀ zhuàng 见1003页 see p1003

GAO ㄍㄠ

皋（*臯）gāo ㄍㄠ 水边的高地 highlands by a waterside：汉～*highland by the Hanshui River*｜江～*river bank*

槔（**槹）gāo ㄍㄠ 见347页“桔”字条“桔槔”（jié—）see 桔槔 on p347

高 gāo ㄍㄠ ❶跟“低”相对(the opposite of 低) **1** 由下到上距离远的 tall; high:～山 *high mountain*|～楼大厦 *high buildings and large mansions; tall buildings* **2** 等级在上的 of a high level or degree:～年级学生 *senior students; seniors*|～等学校 *colleges and universities; institutions of higher learning* **3** 在一般标准或平均程度之上 superior; above the average:质量～ *superior quality*|～速度 *high speed*|～价 *high price* **4** 声音响亮 loud:～歌 *to sing loudly*|～声 *loud voice*［高低］**1** 高低的程度 height **2** 优劣 relative superiority or inferiority **3** 深浅轻重(指说话或做事)(of words or deeds) discretion; sense of propriety:不知～～ *to have no sense of propriety* **4** 到底,终究 at long last:～～做好了 *to have finished it at last* **5** 无论如何 on any account:再三请求,他～～不答应。*We made repeated requests, but he simply refused to agree.* ❷敬辞 **polite**:～见(高明的见解) *your farsighted opinion*|～寿(问老人的年纪)(*used to ask the age of old people*) *your venerable age*

［高山族］我国少数民族,参看附表(see the appendix) the Gaoshan ethnic group, one of the ethnic minorities of China

膏 ㊀ gāo ㄍㄠ ❶肥或肥肉 fat:～粱(肥肉和细粮) *fat meat and fine grain—rich food*［膏腴］(—yú)土地肥沃(of land) fertile ❷脂,油 grease; oil ❸很稠的、糊状的东西 paste; cream:梨～ *pear syrup*|牙～ *toothpaste*|～药 *plaster*

㊁ gào 见222页 see p222

篙 gāo ㄍㄠ 用竹竿或杉木等做成的撑船的器具 punt-pole

羔 gāo ㄍㄠ (—子、—儿)羊羔,小羊 lamb:～儿皮 *lambskin* 泛指幼小的动物 young animal:狼～ (*wolf*) *cub; wolfkin; wolfling*

糕(*餻) gāo ㄍㄠ 用米粉或面粉等掺和其他材料做成的食品 cake; pudding:鸡蛋～ *sponge cake*|年～(*made of glutinous rice flour*) *New Year cake*

睾 gāo ㄍㄠ 睾丸,雄性脊椎动物生殖器官的一部分,在体腔或阴囊内,能产生精子。也叫“精巢”或“外肾”(also called 精巢 or 外肾) testis; testicle

杲 gǎo ㄍㄠˇ 明亮 bright:～～出日。*The sun is rising, shining brightly.*

搞 gǎo ㄍㄠˇ 做,弄,干,办 to do; to carry on; to be engaged in:～工作 *to do one's job; to work*|～通思想 *to straighten out one's thinking*|～清问题 *to get a clear understanding of the question*

缟 gǎo ㄍㄠˇ 一种白色的丝织品 thin white silk:～衣

white silk dress [缟素]白衣服,指丧服 white mourning apparel

槁(*稾) gǎo ㄍㄠˇ 枯干 withered (㊀ **doublet** 枯 — withered):～木 *withered tree*

镐 ㊀ gǎo ㄍㄠˇ 刨土的工具 pick; pickaxe

㊁ hào 见269页 see p269

稿(*稾) gǎo ㄍㄠˇ ❶谷类植物的茎秆 straw; grain stalk:～荐(稻草编的垫子) *straw mattress* ❷(一子、一儿)文字、图画的草底 draft; sketch:文～儿 *manuscript*|打～儿 *to make a sketch* ㊇ ***figurative*** 事先考虑的计划 plan; idea:做事没有准～子不成。*It won't do to have no definite plan.*

藁 gǎo ㄍㄠˇ 藁城,地名,在河北省 Gaocheng, a place in Hebei Province

告 gào ㄍㄠˋ ❶把事情说给别人,通知 to tell; to inform (㊀ **doublet** 一诉 to tell):报～ *to report*|奔走相～ *to run around spreading the news* [告白]对公众的通告 public notice [忠告]规劝 to advise sincerely; to admonish ❷提起诉讼 to sue; to accuse (㊀ **doublet** 控— to accuse):～发 *to inform against; to report* (*an offender*); *to denounce*|原～ *plaintiff; prosecutor*|被～ *defendant; the accused* ❸请求 to ask for; to request:～假 *to ask for leave*|～饶 *to beg for mercy* ❹表明 to declare; to announce:～辞 *to say goodbye to; to make one's farewells*|自～奋勇 *to volunteer to undertake* (*a difficult task*) ❺宣布或表示某种情况的出现 to announce a particular stage reached:大功～成 *to be crowned with success*|～急 *to report an emergency; to ask for emergency help*

郜 gào ㄍㄠˋ 姓 Gao, a surname

诰 gào ㄍㄠˋ 古代帝王对臣子的命令 imperial mandate:～命 *imperial decree*|～封 *conferment of honorary titles by the sovereign*

锆 gào ㄍㄠˋ 一种金属元素,符号 Zr,银灰色,耐蚀性好。应用于原子能工业,或用作气体吸收剂 zirconium (Zr)

膏 ㊁ gào ㄍㄠˋ ❶把油加在车轴或机械上 to lubricate:～油 *to lubricate*|～车 *to lubricate the cart axle* ❷把毛笔蘸上墨汁在砚台边上掭 to dip a writing brush in ink and smooth it on an ink-stone before writing:～笔 *to smooth a wet writing brush on an ink-stone*|～墨 *to dip a writing brush in ink*

㊀ gāo 见221页 see p221

GE ㄍㄜ

戈 gē ㄍㄜ 古代的一种兵器,横刃长柄 (an ancient weapon) dagger-axe [戈壁](蒙 *Mongolia*)沙漠地区 go-bi; desert

仡 ㊀ gē ㄍㄜ ［仡佬族］(—lǎo—)我国少数民族，参看附表(see the appendix) the Gelao ethnic group, one of the ethnic minorities of China

㊁ yì 见889页 see p889

圪 gē ㄍㄜ ［圪垯］(—da) **1** 同"疙瘩 **2**"same as 疙瘩 **2** 多用于土块等(usually used for a lump of earth, etc) lump：土～～*lump of earth*；*clod*｜冰～～*lump of ice* **2** 小土丘，多用于地名(ge, usually used in a place name) mound

纥 ㊀ gē ㄍㄜ ［纥繨］(—da) 同"疙瘩 **2**"same as 疙瘩 **2** 多用于纱线、织物等(usually used for yarn, thread and fabric, etc) knot：线～～*thread knot*｜解开头巾上的～～*to undo the knot in the scarf*

㊁ hé 见271页 see p271

疙 gē ㄍㄜ ［疙瘩］(—da) **1** 皮肤上突起或肌肉上结成的病块 pimple; lump：头上起了个～～。*There is a pimple on the head*. **2** 小球形或块状的东西 lump; knot：面～～*dough-ball*｜芥菜～～*swede* **3** 不易解决的问题 hang-up; (in one's heart) knot：思想～～*hang-up*｜这件事有点儿～～。*It is a little bit hard to deal with this matter*. **4** 不通畅、不爽利的话(of language) not fluent：文字上有些～～。*The writing somehow lacks fluency*. **5** 〈方 ***dialect***〉量词 ***quantifier***：一～～石头 *a stone*｜一～～糕 *a cake*

咯 ㊂ gē ㄍㄜ ［咯噔］(—dēng) 拟声词 ***onomatopoeia***, click：～～～～的皮鞋声 *clicking noise of leather shoes* ［咯咯］拟声词 ***onomatopoeia***, chuckles; chortles：传来一阵～～的笑声。*There comes a wave of chortles*.｜牙齿咬得～～响 *to grind one's teeth* ［咯吱］(—zhī) 拟声词 ***onomatopoeia***, creak：～～～～地直响 *to creak*

㊀ kǎ 见380页 see p380

㊁ lo 见460页 see p460

胳(*肐) gē ㄍㄜ ［胳膊］(—bo)［胳臂］(—bei)上肢，肩膀以下手腕以上的部分 arm (图见741页"体" picture on p741)

袼 gē ㄍㄜ ［袼褙］(—bei)用纸或布裱糊成的厚片，多用来做纸盒、布鞋等 pasteboard

搁 ㊀ gē ㄍㄜ 放，置 to put (at a place); to place：把书～下 *to place the book aside*｜盐～在水里就化了。*Salt dissolves in water*. ㊀引 ***extension*** 耽搁，放在那里不做 to leave over; to put aside：这事～了一个月。*The matter has been put aside for a month*. ［搁浅］船停滞在浅处，不能进退 to get stranded ㊀喻 ***figurative*** 事情停顿 to reach a deadlock

㊁ gé 见225页 see p225

哥 gē ㄍㄜ ❶兄，同父母或亲属中同辈而年龄比自己大的男子(叠 ***reduplication***) elder brother; elder male cousin：大～*eldest brother*｜表～*cousin*;

G

elder male cousin ❷称呼年龄跟自己差不多的男子(term of address for a male of approximately one's age) brother:张大～*Brother Zhang*

歌 gē ㄍㄜ ❶(一儿)能唱的文辞 song:山～(*sung in the fields or mountains*) *folk song*|唱～to sing a song ❷唱 to sing(㊟ ***doublet*** 一唱 to sing|一咏 singing):高～*to sing loudly*|～咏队 *singing group; chorus* [歌颂]颂扬 to sing praise of; to eulogize:～～伟大的祖国 *to eulogize one's great motherland*

鸽 gē ㄍㄜ (一子)鸟名。有野鸽、家鸽等多种,常成群飞翔。有的家鸽能够传递书信。常用作和平的象征 pigeon; dove(*Columbidae*)

割 gē ㄍㄜ 切断,截下 to cut:～麦 *to cut wheat*|～草 *to cut grass*|～阑尾 *to have one's appendix removed; to have an appendectomy* ㊂ ***extension*** 舍去 to give up:～舍 *to give up; to abandon; to part with*|～爱 *to give up what one treasures* [割据]一国之内拥有武力的人占据部分地区,形成分裂对抗的局面(a nation) torn apart by armed separatist forces [割线]数学上称跟圆或曲线在两点或多点相交的直线 secant [交割]一方交付,一方接收,双方结清手续 to complete a business transaction [收割]把成熟的庄稼割下收起 to reap; to harvest; to gather in

革 ㊀ gé ㄍㄜˊ ❶去了毛,经过加工的兽皮 leather; hide(㊟ ***doublet*** 皮一leather):制～*to process hides; to tan* ❷改变 to change(㊟ ***doublet*** 改一to reform):～新 *to innovate*|洗心～面 *to turn over a new leaf* ㊂ ***extension*** 革除,撤销(职务)to abolish; to expel; to dismiss [革命] **1** 被压迫阶级用暴力夺取政权,摧毁旧的腐朽的社会制度,建立新的进步的社会制度 revolution **2** 事物的根本变革 radical change; revolution:思想～～*ideological revolution*|技术～～*technological revolution*

㊁ jí 见312页 see p312

阁(閤) gé ㄍㄜˊ ❶小门,旁门 small (or side) door ❷见224页"阁"see 阁 on p224

"閤"又 hé 见270页"合"(also hé) see 合 on p270

蛤 ㊀ gé ㄍㄜˊ 蛤蜊(li),软体动物,生活在近海泥沙中。体外有双壳,颜色美丽。肉可吃 clam (*Mactridae*) [蛤蚧](一jiè)爬行动物,即大壁虎,头大,尾部灰色,有红色斑点。中医用作强壮剂(i. e. 大壁虎) giant gecko (*Gekko gecko*)

㊁ há 见260页 see p260

颌 ㊀ gé ㄍㄜˊ 口 mouth

㊁ hé 见271页 see p271

阁(*閤) gé ㄍㄜˊ ❶类似楼房的建筑物 pavilion:亭台楼～(*general reference to the elaborate Chi-*

nese architecture) *pavilions, terraces and towers*［阁下］对人的敬称，今多用于外交场合（term of respect, now usually used on diplomatic occasions）Your Excellency; His (*or* Her) Excellency［阁子］小木头房子 small wooden house［内阁］明清两代大臣在宫中处理政务的机构。民国初年的国务院和现在某些国家的最高行政机关也叫内阁，省称"阁"（阁 for short）cabinet：组～*to form a cabinet*｜入～*to become a cabinet member or minister* ❷闺房 boudoir：出～(*of a woman*) *to get married; to marry*

格（❹**挌）gé ㄍㄜˊ ❶(一子、一儿)划分成的空栏和框子(formed by crossed lines) squares; check：方～儿布 *checked fabric*｜～子纸 *squared paper*｜打～子 *to square off*｜架子上有四个～。*There are four shelves in the rack*. ❷规格，标准 standard：～言 *maxim; motto*｜合～*qualified; up to standard* ㊉ **extension** 人的品质 character; quality (㊈ ***doublet*** 品一character)：人～*personality*［格外］副词 **adverb**，特别地 especially; particularly：～～小心 *to be especially careful; to exercise extra caution*｜～～帮忙 *to give special help* ❸阻碍，隔阂(叠 ***reduplication***) to obstruct; to impede：～～不入 *incompatible with; out of tune with* ❹击，打 to hit; to fight：～斗(dòu) *to grapple; to wrestle*｜～杀 *to kill* ❺推究 to examine; to study：～物致知(推究事物的道理取得知识) *to study natural phenomena in order to acquire knowledge*

搁 ㊁ gé ㄍㄜˊ 禁(jīn)受，承受 to bear; to stand; to endure：～不住这么沉。*It can't bear such a weight*.｜～不住揉搓。*It can't stand rubbing*.

㊀ gē 见223页 see p223

骼 gé ㄍㄜˊ 骨头 bone：骨～*skeleton*

鬲 ㊁ gé ㄍㄜˊ［鬲津河］古水名，旧称四女寺减河，即今漳卫新河，是河北、山东两省的界河(formerly called 四女寺减河, now called 漳卫新河) Gejin River, an ancient river marking the boundary between Hebei Province and Shandong Province

㊀ lì 见436页 see p436

隔 gé ㄍㄜˊ ❶遮断，隔开 to separate; to partition：～着一条河 *to be separated by a river*｜～靴搔痒(喻不中肯) *to scratch an itch from outside one's boot—to fail to get to the root of the matter*［隔阂］(—hé)义同"隔膜 **1**"same as 隔膜 **1** in meaning［隔离］使互相不能接触，断绝来往 to keep apart; to isolate［隔膜］**1** 情意不相通，彼此有意见 estrangement **2** 不通晓，外行 unfamiliar：我对于这种技术实在～～。*I know very little about this technique*. **3** 同"膈膜"same as

膈膜 ❷距，离 at a distance from：相～很远 *at a great distance from each other*

塥 gé ㄍㄜˊ 〈方 **dialect**〉水边的沙地，多用于地名（ge，usually used in a place name）sands：青草～（在安徽省桐城）*Qingcaoge*，*a place in Tongcheng*，*Anhui Province*

嗝 gé ㄍㄜˊ （一儿）胃里的气体从嘴里出来而发出的声音，或横膈膜痉挛，气体冲过关闭的声带而发出的声音 belch；hiccup：打～*to belch*；*to hiccup*

滆 gé ㄍㄜˊ 滆湖，湖名，在江苏省南部 Gehu Lake，in the south of Jiangsu Province

膈 gé ㄍㄜˊ 旧称"膈膜"或"横膈膜"。人或哺乳动物胸腔和腹腔之间的膜状肌肉（formerly called 膈膜 or 横膈膜）diaphragm

镉 gé ㄍㄜˊ 一种金属元素，符号 Cd，银白色，在空气中表面生成一层保护膜。用于制合金、釉料、颜料，并用作原子反应堆中的中子吸收棒 cadmium（Cd）

葛 ㊀ gé ㄍㄜˊ 多年生藤本植物，花紫红色。茎可编篮做绳，纤维可织葛布。根可提制淀粉，又供药用 kudzu（*Pueraria lobata*）

㊁ gě 见226页 see p226

个（個）㊁ gě ㄍㄜˇ ［自个儿］自己 oneself；by oneself

㊀ gè 见226页 see p226

合 ㊁ gě ㄍㄜˇ ❶市制容量单位，一升的十分之一 *ge*，unit of dry measure for grain，equal to one-tenth *sheng* ❷旧时量粮食的器具（in former times）container for measuring grains

㊀ hé 见270页 see p270

各 ㊁ gě ㄍㄜˇ 〈方 **dialect**〉特别，与众不同 peculiar；queer：那人挺～。*That man is quite eccentric*.

㊀ gè 见226页 see p226

哿 gě ㄍㄜˇ 表示赞许，可，嘉 to approve；to praise

舸 gě ㄍㄜˇ 大船 barge

盖（蓋）㊁ gě ㄍㄜˇ 姓 Ge，a surname

㊀ gài 见 214 页 see p214

葛 ㊁ gě ㄍㄜˇ 姓 Ge，a surname

㊀ gé 见226页 see p226

个（個、*箇）㊀ gè ㄍㄜˋ ❶量词 ***quantifier***：洗～澡 *to have a bath*｜一～人 *a person*｜一～不留神 *by accident*｜打他～落花流水 *to put sb to rout* ❷单独的 single：～人 *individual*｜～体 *individual* ❸（一子、一儿）身材或物体的大小 height；stature；size：高～子 *a tall person*｜小～儿 *a short person*｜馒头～儿不小。*The* mantou *is big*.

㊁ gě 见226页 see p226

各 ㊀ gè ㄍㄜˋ 每个，彼此不同的 every；different：～种职业 *various professions*｜～处都有 *to be found everywhere*｜～不相同 *to differ from each other*；*to have nothing in com-*

G

mon with each other

㊁ gě 见226页 see p226

硌 ㊁ gè ㄍㄜˋ 凸起的硬东西跟身体接触使身体感到难受或受到损伤(of sth hard or bulging) to press or rub against: ～脚 *to hurt the foot* | ～牙 *to hurt the teeth*

㊀ luò 见478页 see p478

铬 gè ㄍㄜˋ 一种金属元素,符号Cr,银灰色,质硬而脆。主要用于制不锈钢和高强度耐腐蚀合金钢。又可用于电镀,坚固美观,胜于镀镍 chromium (Cr)

虼 gè ㄍㄜˋ [虼蚤](—zao)见942页"蚤"(zǎo) see 蚤 on p942

GEI ㄍㄟ

给 ㊀ gěi ㄍㄟˇ ❶交付,送与 to give; to grant: ～他一本书 *to give him a book* | 是谁～你的? *Who gave it to you?* ㊂ ***extension*** 把动作或态度加到对方 to impose an action or attitude on sb: ～他一顿批评 *to give him a dressing down* ❷介词 ***preposition*** **1** 替,为 for: 医生～他看病。*The doctor gave him treatment.* | ～大家帮忙 *to do a favour for everyone* **2** 被,表示遭受(used in a passive sentence to describe a bitter experience): ～火烧掉了 *to be burnt up* (or *out*) | ～拉走了 *to be dragged away* **3** 向,对(used to introduce the recipient of an action): 快～大伙儿说说。*Come on and tell us all about it.* | ～人家赔不是 *to apologize to him* (or *her*) ❸助词 ***auxiliary***,跟前面"让"、"叫"、"把"相应,可有可无(used correspondingly to the preceding word such as 让,叫 or 把, and sometimes it can be omitted): 窗户叫风(～)吹开了。*The window was blown open by the wind.* | 羊让狼(～)吃了。*The sheep was devoured by a wolf.* | 狼把小羊(～)叼走了。*The wolf ran off with a lamb in its mouth.*

㊁ jǐ 见315页 see p315

GEN ㄍㄣ

根 gēn ㄍㄣ ❶植物茎干下部长在土里的部分。有从土壤里吸收水分和溶解在水中的无机盐的作用,还能把植物固定在地上,有的植物的根还有储藏养料的作用 root (㊄ ***doublet*** 一柢 root): 树～ *tree roots* | 草～ *grass roots* | 直～(如向日葵、甜菜的根)(*of sunflowers or beets*) *tap roots* | 须～(如小麦、稻的根)(*of wheat or rice*) *fibrous roots* | 块～(如甘薯等可以吃的部分)(*the edible part of sweet potatoes, etc*) *root-tuber* ㊂ ***extension*** (一儿) **1** 比喻后辈儿孙 offspring: 他是刘家一条～。*He is an offspring of the Lius.* **2** 物体的基部和其他东西连着的部分 root; foot; base (㊄ ***doublet*** 一基 foundation; basis): 耳～ *base of the*

G

ear｜舌～*root of the tongue*｜墙～儿 *base of a wall* **3** 事物的本源 cause; origin; source：祸～ *the cause of the disaster*｜斩断穷～*to do away with the root cause of poverty* **4** 彻底 thoroughly; completely：～绝 *to eradicate*｜～治 *to perform a radical cure; to cure once and for all* ［根据］凭依，依据 on the basis of; according to：～～什么？*What is the basis?*｜有什么～～？*Do you have any reason?* ❷量词 ***quantifier***，用于长条的东西(used for a long, thin object) piece：一～木料 *a piece of firewood*｜两～麻绳 *two hemp ropes* ❸代数方程式内未知数的值 solution of an algebraic equation ［方根］数学上，任何次自乘幂(mì)的底数，也省称“根”(also 根 for short) root ❹化学上指带电的基 radical：氢～*hydrogen radical*｜硫酸～*acid radical*

跟 gēn ㄍㄣ ❶(一儿)踵，脚的后部 heel：脚后～*heel* ㊂ ***extension*** 鞋袜的后部 heel of a sock or a shoe：袜后～儿 *heel of a sock* ❷随在后面，紧接着 to follow：一个～一个别掉队。*Follow one after another and don't lag behind.*｜开完会～着就参观。*The meeting was followed by a visit.* ㊂ ***extension*** 赶，及 to catch up with：后续部队也～上来了。*The follow-up troops have caught up too.* ❸连词 ***conjunction***，和，同 and; with：我～他都是山东人。*He and I are both from Shandong.* ❹介词 ***preposition***，对，向 to; with：已经～他说过了。*I've talked to him about it.*

［跟头］(一tou) **1** 身体摔倒 to tumble; to fall：摔～～*to have a fall*｜栽～～*to have a fall* **2** 身体向下翻转的动作 somersault：翻～～*to turn* (or *do*) *a somersault*

哏 gén ㄍㄣˊ 〈方 ***dialect***〉❶滑稽，可笑，有趣 amusing; comical; funny：这话真～。*What he says is really funny.* ❷滑稽的话或表情 comical speech or expression：捧～(*of the supporting role in a cross talk*) *to help the leading role to make the audience laugh by funny words or gestures*｜逗～(*of the leading role in a cross talk*) *to make the audience laugh by saying sth funny or by playing the fool*

艮 ㊁ gěn ㄍㄣˇ 〈方 ***dialect***〉食物韧而不脆 (of food) tough; leathery：～萝卜不好吃。*Tough radishes are not good to the taste.*

㊀ gèn 见228页 see p228

亘(*亙) gèn ㄍㄣˋ 空间或时间上延续不断 (of space or time) to extend; to stretch：绵～数十里 *to extend for tens of* li｜～古及今 *from time immemorial down to the present day*

艮 ㊀ gèn ㄍㄣˋ 八卦之一，符号为☶，代表山 *gen*, one of the Eight Diagrams, symbolized by 亖，indicating a mountain

㊁ gěn 见228页 see p228

茛 gèn ㄍㄣˋ［毛茛］多年生草本植物，喜生在水边湿地，夏天开五瓣黄花，果实集合成球状。全草有毒，可作外用药 buttercup (*Ranunculus*)

GENG ㄍㄥ

更 ㊀ gēng ㄍㄥ ❶改变，改换 to change; to replace (㊣ **doublet** 一改 to alter|一换 to replace|变一 to change)：～动 *to change; to alter*|万象～新。*Everything takes on a new look.*|～番（轮流调换）*by turns; alternately*|～正错误 *to make corrections of errors (in published statements or articles)* ❷经历 to experience：少(shào)不～事 *to be a spring chicken* ❸旧时一夜分五更 watch; one of the five two-hour periods into which the night was formerly divided：三～半夜 *at midnight; in the dead of night*|打～(打梆敲锣报时巡夜) *to beat the watches*

㊁ gèng 见230页 see p230

庚 gēng ㄍㄥ ❶天干的第七位，用作顺序的第七 *geng*, the 7th of the 10 Heavenly Stems; seventh ❷年龄 age：同～*to be of the same age*

赓 gēng ㄍㄥ 继续 to continue (㊣ **doublet** 一续 to continue)

鹒 gēng ㄍㄥ 见66页"鸧"字条"鸧鹒"(cāng一) see 鸧鹒 on p66

耕 gēng ㄍㄥ ❶用犁把土翻松 to plough; to till：深～细作 *deep ploughing and intensive cultivation* ❷指从事某种劳动 to work (for a living)：笔～*to earn a living by writing*|舌～*to make a living by teaching*

羹 gēng ㄍㄥ 煮或蒸成的汁状、糊状、冻状的食品 thick soup; custard：鸡蛋～*egg custard*|肉～*meat broth*|豆腐～*beancurd custard*［调羹］(tiáo一)喝汤用的小勺子。也叫"羹匙(chí)"(also called 羹匙) soup spoon

埂 gěng ㄍㄥˇ ❶(一子、一儿)田间稍稍高起的小路 ridge; low bank of earth between fields：田～儿 *ridge (of field)*|地～子 *ridge* ❷地势高起的地方 long, narrow mound

哽 gěng ㄍㄥˇ 声气阻塞 to choke：～咽(yè) *to choke with sobs; to sob*

绠 gěng ㄍㄥˇ 汲水用的绳子 well rope：～短汲深(喻才力不能胜任) *a short rope for a deep well—ability not equal to an important post*

梗 gěng ㄍㄥˇ ❶(一子、一儿)植物的枝或茎 stalk; stem：花～*flower stem*|荷～*lotus stem*［梗概］大略的情节 broad outline; gist ❷直，挺立 to straighten：～着脖子 *to stiffen one's neck* ❸阻塞，妨碍 to obstruct; to block (㊣ **dou-**

G

blet 一塞 to block)：从中作～*to hinder sb from carrying out a plan; to put a spoke in sb's wheel*

鲠(*骾) gěng ㄍㄥˇ ❶鱼骨 fishbone ❷骨头卡在嗓子里(of a fishbone) to get stuck in one's throat [骨鲠]正直 upright

耿 gěng ㄍㄥˇ ❶光明 bright ❷正直 upright：～介 *upright; honest and straightforward* [耿直](*梗直、*鲠直)直爽，正直 honest and frank; upright

[耿耿] **1** 形容忠诚 devoted; dedicated：忠心～～*to be extremely loyal and devoted* **2** 心里老想着不能忘怀 to have sth on one's mind; to be troubled with sth：～～于怀 *to take sth to heart*

颈(頸) ㊁ gěng ㄍㄥˇ 义同"颈㊀"，用于"脖颈子" same as 颈㊀ in meaning, used in 脖颈子

㊀ jǐng 见360页 see p360

更 ㊁ gèng ㄍㄥˋ 副词 ***adverb*** ❶再，又 further; what is more：～上一层楼 *to climb* (or *go up*) *one storey higher — to make further progress* ❷越发，愈加 more; even more：～好 *better*|～明显了 *more distinct*

㊀ gēng 见229页 see p229

晅 gèng ㄍㄥˋ 晒。多用于人名(geng, usually used in a given name) to bask; to dry in the sun

GONG ㄍㄨㄥ

工 gōng ㄍㄨㄥ ❶工人 worker：矿～*miner*|技～*skilled worker; mechanic*|～农联盟 *worker-peasant alliance* ❷工业 industry：化～*chemical industry*|～商界 *industrial and commercial circles* ❸工作，工程 work; project; construction：做～*to work*|～具 *tool*|手～*handwork*|兴～*to start construction* [工程]关于制造、建筑、开矿等，有一定计划进行的工作 engineering; project：土木～～*civil engineering*|水利～～*water conservancy project; irrigation works* ❹一个工人一个劳动日的工作 a man-day：这件工程需要二十个～才能完成。*This project will take 20 man-days to complete.* ❺精细 fine; exquisite：～笔画 *traditional Chinese meticulous painting* ❻善于，长于 to be good at：～书善画 *to be versed in calligraphy and painting* ❼旧时乐谱的记音符号，相当于简谱的"3" *gong*, a note of the scale in *gongchepu* in former times, corresponding to 3 in numbered musical notation [工尺](－chě)我国旧有的音乐记谱符号，计有合、四、一、上、尺(chě)、工、凡、六、五、乙，相当于简谱的5̣、6̣、7̣、1、2、3、4、5、6、7。"工尺"是这些符号的总称 *gongche*, term for the traditional Chinese musical scale with the symbols of 合，四，一，上，尺，工，凡，六，五，乙，which correspond respectively to 5, 6, 7, 1, 2, 3, 4, 5, 6, 7 in numbered musical notation

［工夫］［功夫］（－fu）**1** 时间（多用“工夫”）（usually written as 工夫）time：有～～来一趟。*Come here if you have time.* **2** 长期努力实践的成果，本领（多用“功夫”）（usually written as 功夫）skill：～～深 *to have a great skill*

功 gōng ㄍㄨㄥ ❶功劳，贡献较大的成绩 meritorious service：记大～一次 *to cite sb for outstanding service*｜立～*to render meritorious service* ［功臣］封建时代指为皇帝效劳有功的官吏，现在指对某项事业有特殊功劳的人 one who has rendered outstanding service; meritorious person ❷功夫 effort; work：用～*hardworking*｜下苦～*to work very hard* ❸成就，成效 achievement; effect：成～*to succeed*｜徒劳无～*to make a futile effort* ❹物理学上指度量能量转换的量。在外力作用下使物体顺力的方向移动，机械功的大小就等于这个力和物体移动距离的乘积 work

红 ㊁ gōng ㄍㄨㄥ ［女红］旧指女子所做的缝纫、刺绣等工作。也作“女工”（also written as 女工）（in former times）needlework

㊀ hóng 见277页 see p277

攻 gōng ㄍㄨㄥ ❶攻击，打击，进击，跟“守”相对（the opposite of 守）to attack; to take the offensive：～守同盟 *offensive and defensive alliance; pact to shield each other*｜～势 *offensive*｜～城 *to attack a city* ㊀ ***extension*** 指摘别人的错误 to accuse：～人之短 *to attack someone at his weakest point* ❷致力研究 to study; to major in：～读 *to study diligently; to specialize in*｜专～化学 *to major in chemistry*

弓 gōng ㄍㄨㄥ ❶射箭或发弹（dàn）丸的器具 bow：弹～*catapult*｜～箭 *bow and arrow* ❷（－子）像弓的用具（of a stringed instrument）bow：胡琴～子 *bow of huqin* ❸旧时丈量地亩的器具，也是计量单位。1弓约等于5市尺。240平方弓为1亩 *gong*, land-measuring instrument in former times; unit of length for measuring land（one *gong* is about 5 *chi* and 240 square *gong* is equal to one *mu*）❹弯曲 to bend; to bow：～腰 *to hunch*

躬（*躳）gōng ㄍㄨㄥ ❶身体 body ㊀ ***extension*** 自身，亲自 personally：～行 *to practise personally*｜～耕 *to do farming personally* ❷弯曲身体 to bend forward; to bow：～身 *to bend forward*

公 gōng ㄍㄨㄥ ❶属于国家或集体的，跟“私”相对（the opposite of 私）public; state-owned; collective: ～物 *public property* | ～务 *public affairs; official business* | 大～无私 *selfless* ❷公平,公道 fair; impartial: ～允 *fair and just* | ～正 *fair; just; impartial* | 秉～办事 *to handle affairs impartially* ❸让大家知道 to make public: ～开 *to make public; to make known to the public* | ～告 *public notice; announcement* | ～布 *to announce; to promulgate* [公示]公开宣布示知,让公众了解并征求意见(for soliciting opinions) to make public ❹共同的,大家承认的,大多数适用的 common; general: ～海 *high seas* | 爱国～约 *patriotic pledge* | 几何～理 *geometric axiom* [公司]合股(或单股)经营的一种工商业组织,经营产品的生产、商品的流转或某些建设事业 company; corporation; firm: 百货～～ *department store* | 运输～～ *transport company* | 煤气～～ *gas company* ❺公制的 metric: ～里 *kilometre* | ～尺 *metre* | ～斤 *kilogram* ❻属于国家的或集体的事 public affairs; official business: ～文 *official document* | 办～ *to handle official business* | 因～出差 *to go on a business trip* ❼雄性的 male: ～鸡 *cock* | ～羊 *ram* ❽对祖辈和老年男子的称呼(叠 ***reduplication***) (term of address for one's grandfather's generation or an old man): 外～ *maternal grandfather* | 老～～ *grandpa* ❾丈夫的父亲(叠 ***reduplication***) husband's father; father-in-law: ～婆 *husband's parents; parents-in-law* ❿我国古代五等爵位(公、侯、伯、子、男)的第一等 duke, the first rank of the five ranks of nobility (公,侯,伯,子,男) in ancient China ⓫对年长男子的尊称(respectful term of address for an elderly man): 诸～ *all the gentlemen* | 丁～ *the revered Mr Ding*

蚣 gōng ㄍㄨㄥ 见795页"蜈"字条"蜈蚣"(wúgong) see 蜈蚣 on p795

供 ㊀ gōng ㄍㄨㄥ 供给(jǐ),准备着东西给需要的人应用 to supply; to provide: ～养 *to support; to provide for (one's parents or elders)* | 提～ *to provide* | ～销 *supply and marketing* | ～求相应 *balance between supply and demand* | ～参考 *for your reference* [供给制]对工作人员不给工资,只供给生活必需品的一种制度 supply system, a system of payment in kind, providing the working personnel with primary necessities of life

㊁ gòng 见234页 see p234

龚(龔) gōng ㄍㄨㄥ 姓 Gong, a surname

肱 gōng ㄍㄨㄥ 胳膊由肘到肩的部分,泛指胳膊 upper arm; arm: 曲～ *to bend one's arm* [股肱][喻] ***figurative*** 旧指得力的助手(in former times) right-hand assistant

G

宫 gōng ㄍㄨㄥ ❶房屋，封建时代专指帝王的住所 palace：故～*Imperial Palace* ❷神话中神仙居住的房屋或庙宇的名称(house in which supernatural beings live or name of temples) palace ❸一些文化娱乐场所的名称(place for cultural activities and recreation) palace：少年～*Children's Palace*｜文化～*Cultural Palace* ❹宫刑，古代阉割生殖器的残酷肉刑(punishment in ancient China) castration ❺古代五音"宫、商、角、徵(zhǐ)、羽"之一 *gong*, one of the five notes (宫，商，角，徵，羽) of the ancient Chinese scale

恭 gōng ㄍㄨㄥ 肃敬，谦逊有礼貌 respectful (㊟ ***doublet*** 一敬 respectful)：～贺 *to congratulate* [出恭]排泄大小便 (for bowel movement) to go to the lavatory

塨 gōng ㄍㄨㄥ 用于人名。李塨，清代人(gong, used in a given name) Li Gong, a scholar in the Qing Dynasty

觥 gōng ㄍㄨㄥ 古代用兽角做的一种饮酒器皿 *gong*, an ancient wine vessel made of horn

巩(鞏) gǒng ㄍㄨㄥˇ 坚固，结实，使牢固 to consolidate; to strengthen：基础～固。*The foundation is solid.*｜～固学习成果 *to consolidate the achievement in studies*｜～固人民民主专政 *to consolidate the people's democratic dictatorship*

汞(**銾) gǒng ㄍㄨㄥˇ 通称"水银"。一种金属元素，符号 Hg，银白色的液体，能溶解金、银、锡、钾、钠等。可用来制温度表、气压计、水银灯等(commonly called 水银) mercury; hydrargyrum (Hg) [汞溴(xiù)红]俗叫"二百二"或"红药水"，是敷伤口的杀菌剂(popularly called 二百二 or 红药水) mercurochrome

拱 gǒng ㄍㄨㄥˇ ❶拱手，两手向上相合表示敬意 to cup one hand in the other before the chest in salutation ❷两手合围(with two arms) to surround：～抱 *to surround; to encircle*｜～木 *to embrace the tree* ㊀ ***extension*** 环绕 to surround; to encircle：～卫 *to surround and protect* ❸肩膀向上耸 to shrug (shoulders)：～肩膀 *to hunch one's shoulders* ❹建筑物上呈弧形的结构，大多中间高两侧低 arch：～门 *arched door*｜～桥 *arched bridge*｜连～坝 *multi-arch dam* ❺顶动，向上或向前推 to push upward or forward：～芽(*of buds*) *to sprout up through the earth*｜虫子～土(*of earthworms*) *to wriggle through the earth*｜猪用嘴～地。*Pigs dig up the earth with their snouts.*

珙 gǒng ㄍㄨㄥˇ ❶大璧 a kind of jade ❷珙县，地名，在四川省 Gongxian County, a place in Sichuan Province

G

栱 gǒng ㄍㄨㄥˇ ［枓栱］(dǒu—)旧同"斗拱"。参看158页"斗㊀❸"(see 斗㊀❸ on p158) same as 斗拱 in former time

共 gòng ㄍㄨㄥˋ ❶同，一齐 together(㊣ *doublet* —同 together)：和平～处五项原则 *the Five Principles of Peaceful Coexistence*｜干部和战士同甘～苦。*The officers shared the joys and sorrows of the soldiers.*｜取得～识 *to come to a common understanding* ❷副词 ***adverb***，总，合计 altogether; in all (㊣ ***doublet*** —总 altogether)：～二十人 *altogether 20 people*｜～计 *to add up to* ❸共产党的简称 short for the Communist Party：中～ *the CPC*

〈古 ***archaism***〉又同"恭"(gōng) also same as 恭

〈古 ***archaism***〉又同"供"(gōng) also same as 供

供 ㊁ gòng ㄍㄨㄥˋ ❶向神佛或死者奉献祭品 to lay (offerings)：～佛 *to give offerings to Buddha; to enshrine and worship Buddha* ❷指奉献的祭品 offerings：上～*to lay offerings on the altar* ❸被审问时在法庭上述说事实 statement made by the person on trial：招～*to confess*｜口～*oral confession*｜～状 *written confession*｜～认 *to confess*

㊀ gōng 见232页 see p232

贡 gòng ㄍㄨㄥˋ ❶古代指属国或臣民向君主献东西 (in ancient China) to pay tribute to the sovereign by a vassal state or a subject ［贡献］**1** 拿出力量或财物来给国家和人民 to contribute; to dedicate; to devote：～～出自己的一切 *to contribute all one has; to dedicate oneself heart and soul* **2** 对人民、人类社会所做的有益的事 contribution：马克思、恩格斯创立的学说，是对人类的伟大～～。*The theory founded by Marx and Engels is a great contribution to mankind.* ❷贡品 tribute：进～*to pay tribute* ❸封建时代指选拔人才，推荐给朝廷 to recommend scholars or suitable persons to the imperial court in feudal times：～生 *scholars recommended by local governments to the Imperial College in the capital city*｜～举 *to recommend suitable persons to the imperial court for national service*

唝 gòng ㄍㄨㄥˋ ［唝吥］(—bù) 地名，在柬埔寨 Kampot, a place in Cambodia

GOU ㄍㄡ

勾 ㊀ gōu ㄍㄡ ❶用笔画出符号，表示删除或截取 to tick off; to cancel; to cross out：～了这笔账 *to cancel the debt*｜一笔～销 *to write off at one stroke; to cancel totally*｜把精彩的文句～出来 *to put a tick at the excellent sentences* ❷描画，用线条画出形象的边

缘 to delineate; to draw:～图样 *to draw a draft* (or *pattern*) [转] ***transfer*** 用灰涂抹建筑物上砖、瓦或石块之间的缝 to point; to fill up the joints of brickwork with mortar or cement:～墙缝 *to point a brick wall*｜用灰～抹房顶 *to point the roof with mortar* ❸招引，引 to induce; to evoke ([连] ***doublet*** 一引 to induce):～结 *to collude with*｜～通 *to collude with*｜～搭 *to gang up with; to be in collusion with*｜这一问～起他的话来了。*This question prompted his talking.* ❹我国古代称不等腰直角三角形中构成直角的较短的边 *gou*, used in ancient China for the shorter leg of a right triangle

[勾留]停留 to stop over:在那里～～几天 *to stop over there for several days*

㊁ gòu 见236页 see p236

沟(溝) gōu ㄍㄡ ❶流水道 ditch; channel; trench:阴～ *sewer; underground ditch*｜阳～ *ditch; open sewer*

[沟通]使两方通达 to link up; to connect:～～文化 *to promote cultural exchanges* ❷像沟的东西 sth like a ditch:车～ *rut*

钩(*鉤) gōu ㄍㄡ ❶(～子、～儿)悬挂或探取东西用的器具，形状弯曲，头端尖锐 hook:秤～儿 *steelyard hook*｜钓鱼～儿 *fishhook*｜挂～儿 *hook*｜火～子 *poker; fire hook* ❷(～子、～儿)形状像钩子的 hooklike thing:蝎子的～子 *sting of a scorpion* ❸(～儿)汉字的一种笔形(乛㇂乚等)(in Chinese characters, such as 乛,㇂,乚, etc) hook stroke ❹用钩状物探取 to hook:把床底下那本书～出来。*Hook out the book from under the bed.* [引] ***extension*** 研究，探寻 to search; to seek:～深致远 *to seek the profound truth* ❺同"勾㊀❷" same as 勾㊀❷ ❻一种缝纫法，多指缝合衣边(usually used to denote sewing up an edging) a way of sewing:～贴边 *to sew on an edging*

句 ㊁ gōu ㄍㄡ 古同"勾" same as 勾 in ancient Chinese

[高句丽][高句骊](一一lí)古族名，古国名 Koguryo, an ancient race or country

[句践]春秋时越王名 Goujian, the king of the state of Yue during the Spring and Autumn Period

㊀ jù 见371页 see p371

佝 gōu ㄍㄡ [佝偻](一lóu)佝偻病，俗叫"小儿软骨病"。由于食物中缺少钙、磷和维生素D，并缺乏日光照射而引起的骨骼发育不良。症状有方头、鸡胸、两腿弯曲等。(popularly called 小儿软骨病) rickets

枸 ㊀ gōu ㄍㄡ [枸橘](一jú)就是枳(zhǐ)。参看979页"枳"(i. e. 枳) trifoliate orange (*Poncirus trifoliata*) (see 枳 on p979)

㊁ gǒu 见236页 see p236
㊂ jǔ 见370页 see p370

缑 gōu ㄍㄡ 刀剑等柄上所缠的绳 string round the handle of a knife, sword, etc

韝(鞲) gōu ㄍㄡ 古代的套袖 ancient oversleeves

篝 gōu ㄍㄡ 熏笼 cage［篝火］原指用笼子罩着的火，现指在野外或空旷的地方燃烧的火堆(originally used to denote a fire covered by a cage) bonfire; campfire

鞴 gōu ㄍㄡ ［鞴鞴］(—bèi) 活塞，唧筒里或蒸汽机、内燃机的汽缸里往复运动的机件 piston

苟 gǒu ㄍㄡˇ 姓 Gou, a surname

苟 gǒu ㄍㄡˇ ❶姑且，暂且 temporary：～安 *to seek momentary ease*｜～延残喘 *to linger on in a worsening condition* ❷马虎，随便 careless; casual：一丝不～ *to be conscientious and meticulous* ❸文言连词 ***conjunction in classical Chinese***，假如 if：～可以利民，不循其礼。*If it benefits the people, the rules of etiquette can be neglected.* ❹姓 Gou, a surname

岣 gǒu ㄍㄡˇ［岣嵝］(—lǒu)山峰名，衡山的主峰，也指衡山，在湖南省中南部(also used to denote Hengshan Mountain) Goulou, the highest peak of Hengshan Mountain, in the south central of Hunan Province

狗 gǒu ㄍㄡˇ 一种家畜，听觉、嗅觉都很灵敏，有的善于看守门户 dog［狗腿子］㊕ ***figurative*** 走狗，为有权势的人奔走做坏事的人 lackey; hired thug; henchman

枸 ㊁ gǒu ㄍㄡˇ［枸杞］(—qǐ) 落叶灌木，夏天开淡紫色花。果实红色，叫枸杞子，可入药 Chinese wolfberry (*Lycium chinense*)

㊀ gōu 见235页 see p235
㊂ jǔ 见370页 see p370

笱 gǒu ㄍㄡˇ 竹制的捕鱼器具 bamboo basket trap for fishing

勾 ㊁ gòu ㄍㄡˋ ❶勾当(dang)，事情(多指坏事)(derogatory) business; deal ❷同"够"same as 够 ❸姓 Gou, a surname

㊀ gōu 见234页 see p234

构(構、❶-❸ *搆) gòu ㄍㄡˋ ❶构造，组合 to construct; to form：～屋 *to build a house*｜～图 *composition of a picture*｜～词 *to form a word*［构造］各组成部分及其相互关系 structure; construction：人体～～ *structure of the human body*｜飞机的～～ *construction of a plane*｜句子的～～ *sentence construction* ❷结成(用于抽象事物)(used for sth abstract) to fabricate; to make up：～怨 *to incur hatred; to be at feud*｜虚～ *to fabricate; to make up*［构思］做文章或进行艺术创作时

运用心思 to conceive; to work out the plot of a literary work or the composition of a painting ❸作品 literary composition:佳～*good piece of writing*|杰～*masterpiece* ❹构树,落叶乔木,开淡绿色花。果实红色。树皮纤维可造纸。也叫"榖"(gǔ)或"楮"(chǔ)(also called 榖 or 楮) paper mulberry (*Broussonetia papyrifera*)

购(購) gòu ㄍㄡˋ 买 to buy; to purchase (㊟ ***doublet*** 一买 to buy; to purchase):～物 *to go shopping*|～置 *to buy*|采～原料 *to purchase* (or *buy*) *raw materials*

诟 gòu ㄍㄡˋ ❶耻辱 shame; humiliation ❷辱骂 to abuse; to revile

垢 gòu ㄍㄡˋ ❶污秽,脏东西 dirt; filth:油～ *grease stain*|牙～*tartar*|藏污纳～*to harbour the wicked and evil* ❷耻辱。也作"诟"(also written as 诟) humiliation

够(*夠) gòu ㄍㄡˋ ❶足,满足一定的限度 enough; sufficient:～数 *sufficient in quantity; enough*|～用 *enough for use; sufficiency*|～多 *enough in quantity* ㊕ ***transfer*** 腻,厌烦 to be tired of:这个话我真听～了。*I'm tired of these remarks.* ❷达到,及 to reach:～得着 *to be able to reach*|～格 *to be qualified; to be up to the standard*

遘 gòu ㄍㄡˋ 相遇 to meet; to come across

媾 gòu ㄍㄡˋ ❶结合,交合 coition:婚～(亲上做亲)(between two relatives) *marriage*|交～(雌雄配合) *copulation* ❷交好 to reach an agreement:～和(讲和) *to make* (or *negotiate*) *peace*

觏 gòu ㄍㄡˋ 遇见 to meet:罕～(很少见) *rarely seen*

彀 gòu ㄍㄡˋ ❶同"够" same as 够 ❷使劲张弓 to draw a bow to the full [彀中](—zhōng)箭能射及的范围 shooting range ㊗ ***figurative*** 牢笼,圈套 snare; trap [入彀]㊗ ***figurative*** 进牢笼,入圈套 to fall into a trap; to be caught in a trap

GU ㄍㄨ

估 ㊀ gū ㄍㄨ 揣测,大致地推算 to estimate; to appraise:～计 *to estimate; to appraise*|～量 *to appraise; to estimate*|不要低～了群众的力量。*Don't underestimate the potentiality of the masses.*|～一～价钱 *to estimate the price*

㊁ gù 见242页 see p242

咕 gū ㄍㄨ 拟声词 ***onomatopoeia***, coo:布谷鸟～～地叫。*The cuckoo is coo-cooing.* [咕咚](—dōng)拟声词 ***onomatopoeia***,重东西落下声 thud; plump [咕嘟] **1** (—dū)拟声词 ***onomatopoeia***,水的响声 bubble; gurgle **2** (—du)煮,煮得滚滚的 to boil for a long time:东西～～烂了吃,容易消化。

Overcooked food is easier to digest. **3** (—du)鼓起 to purse one's lips; to pout:他气得把嘴～～起来。*He sulkily pursed his lips.*[咕唧](—ji)小声说话 to whisper; to murmur[咕噜][—lū]拟声词 ***onomatopoeia***,形容水流动或东西滚动的声音 rumble; roll[咕哝](—nong)小声说话 to murmur

沽 gū ㄍㄨ ❶买 to buy:～酒 *to buy wine*|～名钓誉(有意做使人赞扬的事,捞取个人声誉) *to fish* (or *angle*) *for fame and compliments* ❷卖 to sell:待价而～(喻等候有了较高的待遇再贡献自己的才智) *to wait to sell at a good price; to wait for higher pay to the contribution of one's wisdom*

姑 gū ㄍㄨ ❶父亲的姊妹(叠 ***reduplication***) aunt; father's sister ❷丈夫的姊妹 husband's sister; sister-in-law:～嫂 *woman and her elder brother's wife; sisters-in-law*|大～子 *husband's elder sister; sister-in-law* ❸妻称夫的母亲 husband's mother; mother-in-law:翁～(公婆)*husband's parents; parents-in-law* ❹姑且,暂且 for the time being:～妄言之 *to tell sb sth for what it's worth*|～置勿论 *to leave sth aside for the moment*[姑息]暂求苟安 to appease ㊕ ***transfer*** 无原则地宽容 to indulge; to tolerate:对错误的行为绝不～～。*We tolerate no wrong behaviour.*

轱 gū ㄍㄨ [轱辘](—lu) **1** 车轮 wheel **2** 滚动,转(zhuàn) to roll; to turn:别让球～～了。*Don't let the ball roll away.*

鸪 gū ㄍㄨ 见965页"鹧"字条"鹧鸪"(zhè—)、56页"鹁"字条"鹁鸪"(bó—) see 鹧鸪 on p965 and 鹁鸪 on p56

菇 gū ㄍㄨ 蕈(xùn) mushroom:香～ *fragrant mushroom*|金针～*Flammulina velutipes*

蛄 gū ㄍㄨ 见463页"蝼"字条"蝼蛄"(lóu—)、300页"蟪"字条"蟪蛄"(huì—) see 蝼蛄 on p463 and 蟪蛄 on p300

辜 gū ㄍㄨ ❶罪 guilt; crime:无～ *innocent*|死有余～。*One's crimes deserve more than death.* or *Even death would not expiate all his crimes.* ❷亏负,违背 to let down; to disappoint:～负了他的一番好意 *to waste his kindness*

酤 gū ㄍㄨ ❶买酒 to buy wine ❷卖酒 to sell wine

呱 ㊂ gū ㄍㄨ [呱呱]古书上指小儿哭声 (in ancient Chinese texts) cry of a baby

㊀ guā 见244页 see p244

㊁ guǎ 见245页 see p245

孤 gū ㄍㄨ ❶幼年丧父或父母双亡(of a child) fatherless or orphaned ❷单独 alone; solitary (㊈ ***doublet*** 一独 lonely; solitary):～雁 *solitary wild goose*|～掌难鸣(喻力量单薄,难以有所作为) *It is impossible to clap with one*

hand — *It is hard to succeed without support.* | ～立 *isolated* ❸古代君主的自称(used by an emperor to call himself in ancient China) I:～家(*used by an emperor in ancient China*) *I* | ～王(*used by an emperor in ancient China*) *I* ❹同"辜❷" same as 辜❷:～恩负义 *to be ungrateful*

轱 gū ㄍㄨ 大骨 big bone

菰(❶**苽) gū ㄍㄨ ❶多年生草本植物,生在浅水里,开淡紫红色小花。嫩茎经黑穗病菌寄生后膨大,叫茭白,果实叫菰米,都可以吃 wild rice (*Zizania*) ❷同"菇"same as 菇

觚 gū ㄍㄨ ❶古代一种盛酒的器具 ancient wine vessel ❷古代写字用的木板 ancient wooden writing tablet:操～(执笔写作) *to write* ❸棱角 edge and corner

骨 ㊀ gū ㄍㄨ [骨朵](—duo)(—儿)没有开放的花朵 flower bud [骨节](—jie)泛指长条形东西的一段 (of a long object) section [骨碌](—lu)滚动 to roll

㊁ gǔ 见240页 see p240

蓇 gū ㄍㄨ [蓇葖](—tū) **1** 果实的一种,成熟时在一面开裂,如芍药、八角的果实 follicle **2** 骨朵儿 flower bud

箍 gū ㄍㄨ ❶用竹篾或金属条束紧器物(with a bamboo or metal strip) to bind tightly; to hoop:～木盆 *to bind a wooden basin* ❷(—儿)紧束器物的圈 hoop:铁～*iron hoop*

古 gǔ ㄍㄨˇ ❶时代久远的,过去的,跟"今"相对(the opposite of 今) ancient (㊟ **doublet** —老 ancient):～书 *ancient book* | ～迹 *historic site; place of historic interest* | ～为今用 *to make the past serve the present; to apply old traditions for modern purposes* [古板]守旧固执,呆板 old-fashioned and inflexible [古怪]奇怪,罕见,不合常情 strange; odd; eccentric ❷古体诗 ancient poetry; form of classical poetry:五～ *five-character-line poem* | 七～ *seven-character-line poem*

[古董](*骨董)古代留传下来的器物 antique; curio ㊙ ***figurative*** 顽固守旧的人或过时的东西 old-fashioned person or article; old fogey

诂 gǔ ㄍㄨˇ 用通行的话解释古代语言文字或方言字义 to explain archaic or dialectal words in the contemporary language:训～ *explanation of words in ancient books; exegesis* | 解～ *explanatory notes in ancient books; exegesis* | 字～ *word for word explanation of a text in ancient books*

牯 gǔ ㄍㄨˇ 牯牛,指公牛 bull:黄～*ox* | 黑～*black bull*

罟 gǔ ㄍㄨˇ 〈古 **archaism**〉捕鱼的网 fishnet

钴 gǔ ㄍㄨˇ 一种金属元素,符号 Co,银白色。有延展性,熔点高,可以磁化,是制造

G

超硬耐热合金和磁性合金的重要原料。钴的放射性同位素钴-60在机械、化工、冶金等方面都有广泛的应用,在医疗上可以代替镭治疗癌症 cobalt (Co)

嘏 gǔ ㄍㄨˇ jiǎ ㄐㄧㄚˇ (又 **also** jiǎ) 福 felicity; good fortune

鼓 gǔ ㄍㄨˇ (一子)烹饪用具,周围陡直的深锅 deep pot: 瓷~子 *china pot* | 沙~子 *earthenware pot*

谷(❷-❹穀) ㊀ gǔ ㄍㄨˇ ❶山谷,两山中间的水道。又指两山之间 (also used to denote land between two hills or mountains) valley; gorge: 万丈深~ *fathomless ravine; bottomless chasm; very deep valley* ❷庄稼和粮食的总称 cereal crops; grain: 五~ *five cereals* ❸(一子)一种禾本科植物,子实碾去皮以后就成小米,供食用,茎可喂牲口 millet (*Setaria italica*) ❹〈方 ***dialect***〉稻,也指稻的子实 paddy: 糯~ *glutinous rice* | 粳(jīng)~ *round-grained non-glutinous rice* | 轧(yà)~机 *thresher; threshing machine* ❺姓 Gu, a surname

㊁ yù 见920页 see p920

汩 gǔ ㄍㄨˇ 水流的声音或样子(叠 ***reduplication***) (of running water) gurgle

股 gǔ ㄍㄨˇ ❶大腿,自胯至膝盖的部分 thigh (图见741页"体" picture on p741) ❷事物的一部分 part of sth **1** 股份,指集合资金的一份 share; stock: ~东 *shareholder; stockholder* | ~票 *share; stock* | ~市 *stock market* **2** 机关团体中的一个部门 section: 总务~ *general affairs section* | 卫生~ *hygiene section* **3** 合成绳线等的部分 strand; ply: 合~线 *plied yarn* | 三~绳 *three-strand rope* ❸指不等腰直角三角形中构成直角的长边 longer leg of a right triangle ❹量词 ***quantifier*** **1** 用于成条的东西(used for a long and narrow thing): 一~道(路) *a road* | 一~线 *a skein of thread* | 一~泉水 *a stream of spring water* **2** 用于气味、力气(used for smell, strength, etc): 一~香味 *a whiff of fragrance* | 一~劲 *a burst of energy* **3** 用于成批的人(多指匪徒或敌军)(used for a group of people, usually of bandits or enemy): 一~残匪 *a gang of remnants of the bandits*

骨 ㊀ gǔ ㄍㄨˇ ❶骨头,脊椎动物身体里面支持身体的坚硬组织 bone: 脊椎~ *vertebra; spine* [骨骼]全身骨头的总称 skeleton [骨干](-gàn) diaphysis ㊗ ***figurative*** 中坚有力的 backbone: ~~分子 *key (or core) member* | ~~作用 *to act as the mainstay* [骨节]两骨(或更多)相连接的关节 joint [骨肉] flesh and blood ㊗ ***figurative*** 最亲近的有血统关系的人,指父母、子女、兄弟、姊妹 kindred ❷像骨的东西 sth like a bone: 钢~水泥 *reinforced con-*

crete ❸ 品格，气概 character; quality; spirit：～气 *strength of character; moral integrity* | 媚～*obsequiousness*

㊁ gū 见239页 see p239

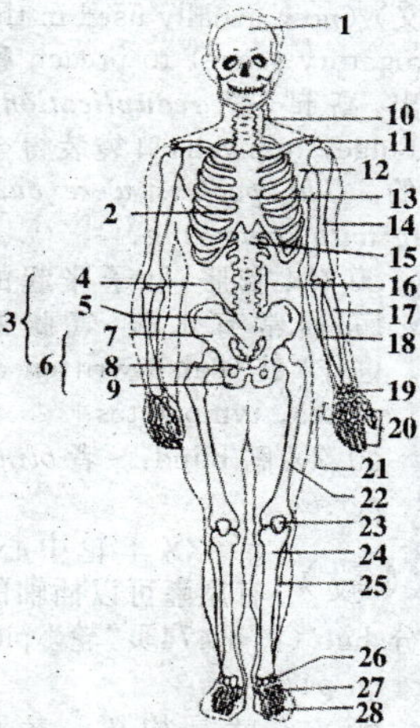

人体骨骼 Human Bone Structure

1 颅 cranium
2 肋骨 ribs
3 骨盆 pelvis
4 骶骨 sacrum
5 尾椎 coccyx
6 髋骨 hip bone
7 髂骨 ilium
8 耻骨 pubis
9 坐骨 ischium
10 颈椎 vertebrae
11 锁骨 clavicle
12 肩胛骨 scapula
13 胸骨 sternum
14 肱骨 humerus
15 胸椎 thoracic vertebra
16 腰椎 lumbar vertebra
17 桡骨 radius
18 尺骨 ulna
19 腕骨 carpus
20 指骨 phalanx
21 掌骨 metacarpus
22 股骨 femur
23 髌骨 patella
24 胫骨 tibia
25 腓骨 fibula
26 跗骨 tarsus
27 跖骨 metatarsus
28 趾骨 phalanx

馉 gǔ ㄍㄨˇ［馉饳］(－duò)(－儿)一种面制食品 *guduo*, a kind of food made of flour

榾 gǔ ㄍㄨˇ［榾柮］(－duò)截成一段一段的短木头 wood block; stump

鹘 ㊁ gǔ ㄍㄨˇ［鹘鸼］(－zhōu)古书上说的一种鸟，羽毛青黑色，尾巴短 *guzhou*, a kind of bird mentioned in ancient Chinese texts

㊀ hú 见283页 see p283

贾 ㊁ gǔ ㄍㄨˇ ❶ 商人 merchant (㊟ ***doublet*** 商－merchant)。古时特指坐商 (specially used to denote shopkeeper in ancient China) ❷ 卖 to sell：余勇可～(喻还有多余的力量可以使出) *with plenty of strength left in one － with strength yet to spare*

㊀ jiǎ 见324页 see p324

羖(**𦍩) gǔ ㄍㄨˇ 公羊 ram

蛊(蠱) gǔ ㄍㄨˇ 旧时传说把许多毒虫放在器皿里，使互相吞食，最后剩下不

G

死的毒虫叫蛊，可用来毒害人 *gu*, a legendary venomous insect (Legend has it that someone had put many venomous insects in a utensil so that they ate each other, and he mixed the one that survived, called *gu*, with food to poison people in former times.) [蛊惑]使人心意迷惑 to bewitch

鹄 ⊖ gǔ ㄍㄨˇ 射箭的靶子 (in archery) target [鹄的](—dì)箭靶子的中心，练习射击的目标 bull's eye; centre of the target

⊜ hú 见283页 see p283

鼓 gǔ ㄍㄨˇ ❶打击乐器。多为圆柱形，中空，两头蒙皮，有军鼓、腰鼓、拨浪鼓等多种 drum [大鼓][大鼓书][鼓儿词]曲艺的一种，一人打着鼓说唱故事，另一人弹弦子伴奏 *dagu*, *dagushu* or *gurci*, a folk art form with one person singing a versified story to the accompaniment of a small drum performed by himself and a three-stringed plucked instrument played by another person ❷敲鼓 to beat a drum: 一～作气 *to be stimulated at the sound of the first drum; to get sth done in one vigorous effort* ㊀ ***extension*** **1** 击，拍，弹 to beat; to clap; to play: ～掌 *to clap one's hands; to applaud* | ～琴 *to play the zither* **2** 发动，使振作起来 to rouse; to agitate: ～足干劲 *to go all out* | ～励 *to encourage* | ～动 *to agitate; to rouse* | ～舞 *to inspire; to encourage* [鼓吹] **1** 打击乐和管乐合奏 ensemble of percussion instruments and wind instruments **2** 传播，宣扬(现多用于贬义) (now usually used in the derogatory sense) to preach ❸凸出，高起(叠 ***reduplication***) to bulge; to swell: 口袋装得～～的。*The pockets were bulging with something.*

臌 gǔ ㄍㄨˇ 膨胀，肚子胀起的病，通常有水臌、气臌两种。也作"鼓"(also written as 鼓) ascites; tympanites

瞽 gǔ ㄍㄨˇ 瞎 blind: ～者 *blind person*

毂(轂) gǔ ㄍㄨˇ 车轮中心，有窟窿可以插轴的部分 hub (图见474页"轮" picture on p474)

穀 gǔ ㄍㄨˇ 就是构树。参看236页"构"(i. e. 构树) paper mulberry (*Broussonetia papyrifera*) (see 构 on p236)

瀔 gǔ ㄍㄨˇ [瀔水]地名，在湖南省湘乡。今作"谷水" (now written as 谷水) Gushui, a place in Xiangxiang, Hunan Province

估 ⊖ gù ㄍㄨˋ [估衣](—yi)旧指贩卖的旧衣服。贩卖旧衣的行业叫估衣业 (the trade of selling second-hand clothes, which is called 估衣业) second-hand clothes on sale in former times

⊖ gū 见237页 see p237

G

故 gù ㄍㄨˋ ❶意外的事情 accident：变～*unforeseen event*｜事～*accident*［故障］机器等发生的毛病 breakdown ❷缘故，原因 reason; cause：不知何～。*The reason is unknown.*｜无缘无～*without rhyme or reason; for no reason at all* ❸故意，存心 intentionally; deliberately; on purpose：明知～犯 *to violate on purpose*｜～弄玄虚 *to turn simple things into mysteries deliberately* ❹老，旧，过去的 old; former：～书 *used book*｜～人（老朋友）*old friend*｜～宫 *Imperial Palace* ❺本来，原来的 original：～乡（老家）*hometown* ❻死（指人）(of people) to die：～去 *to die; to pass away*｜病～*to die of illness*［物故］指人死(of people) to die; to pass away ❼连词 **conjunction**，所以 therefore; hence：他有坚强的意志，～能克服困难。*He was able to overcome the difficulty because he has a strong will.*

固 gù ㄍㄨˋ ❶结实，牢靠 solid; firm（㊀ **doublet** 坚－solid; firm）：稳～*firm; stable* ❷坚定，不变动 firmly; resolutely：～请 *insistent request*｜～守阵地 *to defend one's position tenaciously* ❸本，原来 originally：～有 *intrinsic; inherent*［固然］连词 **conjunction**，表示先承认原来的意思，后面还要否定那个意思或者转到另一方面去(admitting a certain fact for transition in the context) no doubt; true：这项工作～～有困难，但是一定能完成。*For all its difficulties, this task will surely be completed.* ❹坚硬 solid; hard：～体 *solid*

堌 gù ㄍㄨˋ 堤。多用于地名(gu, usually used in a place name) dyke：牛王～（在河南省夏邑）*Niuwanggu (a place in Xiayi, Henan Province)*｜青～集（在山东省曹县）*Qingguji (a place in Caoxian County, Shandong Province)*

崮 gù ㄍㄨˋ 四周陡峭而顶部较平的山。多用于地名(gu, usually used in a place name) mountain with a flat top and steep cliffs：孟良～（在山东省临沂）*Menglianggu (a place in Linyi, Shandong Province)*｜抱犊～（在山东省枣庄和临沂交界的地方）*Baodugu (a place at the juncture of Zaozhuang and Linyi, Shandong Province)*

锢 gù ㄍㄨˋ ❶把金属熔化开浇灌堵塞空隙 to plug with molten metal ❷禁锢，禁闭起来不许跟人接触 to imprison; to hold in custody

痼 gù ㄍㄨˋ 痼疾，积久不易治的病 chronic disease ㊁ **extension** 长期养成不易克服的 inveterate：～习 *deep-rooted habit*｜～癖 *inveterate weakness; addiction*

鲴 gù ㄍㄨˋ 鱼名，又叫“黄鲴”。体长约0.3米，侧扁，口小无须，银白带黄色。以藻类等为食。生活在江河湖泊中(also called 黄鲴) silvery xenocypris (*Xenocypris argentea*)

G

顾(顧) gù ㄍㄨˋ ❶回头看,泛指看 to turn round and look at; to look at: 回～*to look back; to retrospect*|环～*to look round*|～视左右 *to look right and left* ❷拜访 to visit; to call on: 三～茅庐 *three visits to show sincerity — to solicit the service of a wise man thrice in succession* ❸照管,注意 to take care of; to attend to: ～面子 *to save one's face; to spare one's feelings*|～全大局 *to take the interest of the whole into account*|奋不～身 *to dash ahead regardless of one's own safety* ⑳ **transfer** 商店称来买货物 to patronise: 惠～*patronage*|～客 *customer*|主～*patron* [照顾] **1** 照管,特别关心 to look after; to take care: ～～群众的生活 *to take care of the livelihood of the masses* **2** 旧时商店称顾客来买货(in former times) to patronise ❹文言连词 **conjunction in classical Chinese**,但,但是 but

梏 gù ㄍㄨˋ 古代束缚罪人两手的木制刑具 ancient wooden handcuffs

雇(*僱) gù ㄍㄨˋ ❶出钱让人给自己做事 to hire; to employ: ～工 *to hire labour*|～保姆 *to hire a housemaid* ❷租赁交通运输工具 to hire means of transportation: ～车 *to hire a car*|～牲口 *to hire a beast of burden*

GUA ㄍㄨㄚ

瓜 guā ㄍㄨㄚ 蔓生植物,叶掌状,花大半是黄色,果实可吃,种类很多,有西瓜、南瓜、冬瓜、黄瓜等 melon (*Cucurbitaceae*) [瓜分] 像切瓜一样地分割 to carve up; to divide up [瓜葛] (—gé) melon and vine ⑳ **figurative** 亲友关系或相牵连的关系 connection; implication

呱 ㊀ guā ㄍㄨㄚ [呱哒](—dā) 拟声词 **onomatopoeia**, clip-clop; clack [呱哒板儿] **1** 唱莲花落(lào)等打拍子的器具 bamboo clappers **2** 木拖鞋 clogs [呱呱] 拟声词 **onomatopoeia**,鸭子、青蛙等的响亮叫声 (of ducks) quack; (of frogs) croak ⑳ **transfer** 形容好 top-notch; excellent: ～～叫 *top-notch*|顶～～*tip-top; first-rate*

㊁ gū 见238页 see p238

㊂ guǎ 见245页 see p245

胍 guā ㄍㄨㄚ 有机化合物,分子式 CH_5N_3,无色结晶体,易潮解。是制药工业上的重要原料 guanidine

刮(❷颳) guā ㄍㄨㄚ ❶用刀子去掉物体表面的东西 to scrape: ～脸 *to shave*|～冬瓜皮 *to peel a white gourd* ⑳ **figurative** 搜刮民财 to plunder; to fleece; to extort: 贪官污吏只会～地皮。*Corrupt officials are only overlords who extort money from the people.* ❷风吹动(of wind) to blow: ~倒了一棵树。*A tree has been blown down.*

括 ⊜ guā ㄍㄨㄚ [挺括]〈方 ***dialect***〉(衣服、纸张等)较硬而平整(of clothes, paper, etc) stiff and smooth; neat [一塌括子]〈方 ***dialect***〉一股脑儿,全部 all; entirely

⊖ kuò 见407页 see p407

苦 guā ㄍㄨㄚ [苦蒌](-lóu)同"栝楼" same as 栝楼

栝 guā ㄍㄨㄚ 就是圆柏。参看255页"桧"(guì)(i. e. 圆柏) Chinese juniper (*Juniperus chinensis*) (see 桧 on p255)

[栝楼](-lóu)多年生草本植物,爬蔓(wàn),开白花,果实卵圆形。块根和果实都可入药 Chinese trichosanthes (*Trichosanthes kirilowii*)

鸹 guā ㄍㄨㄚ [老鸹]乌鸦的俗称(popular name for 乌鸦) crow

䯄(騧) guā ㄍㄨㄚ 黑嘴的黄马 yellow horse with a black mouth

𫄨(緺) guā ㄍㄨㄚ ❶古代青紫色的绶带 purple-blue ribbon used in ancient China ❷比喻妇女盘结的发髻(of a woman) strand of hair

呱 ⊜ guǎ ㄍㄨㄚˇ [拉呱儿](lāguǎr)〈方 ***dialect***〉聊天 to chat

⊖ guā 见244页 see p244

⊜ gū 见238页 see p238

剐(剮) guǎ ㄍㄨㄚˇ ❶被尖锐的东西划破 to be cut; to be split: 把手~破了 *to have a cut on the hand* | 裤子上~了个口子。*There is a split in the trousers.* ❷封建时代一种残酷的死刑,把人的身体割成许多块 (a form of capital punishment in feudal times) to dismember a body

寡 guǎ ㄍㄨㄚˇ ❶少,缺少 few; scant: ~言 *reticent; taciturn* | 优柔~断 *irresolute and hesitant; indecisive* | 多~不等 *vary in number* ❷古代君主的自称(used by an emperor to call himself in ancient China) I: 称孤道~ *to call oneself king; to act like an absolute ruler* ❸妇女死了丈夫 widowed: ~妇 *widow*

卦 guà ㄍㄨㄚˋ 八卦,中国古代用来占卜的象征各种自然现象的八种符号,相传是伏羲氏所创 *Bagua*, the Eight Trigrams used to divine various natural phenomena in ancient China, which is said to be originated by *Fuxi* [变卦]㊥ ***figurative*** 已定的事情忽然改变(含贬义)(with derogatory sense) to go back on one's word; to break an agreement

诖 guà ㄍㄨㄚˋ 失误 fault; mistake [诖误] **1** 被牵连而受谴责或处分 to be punished for an implication: 为人~~ *to be implicated in trouble for sb else's mistake* **2** 旧时也指撤职,失官(in former times) being dismissed from office

G

挂(*掛、❷*罣) guà ㄍㄨㄚˋ ❶悬 to hang ([连] *doublet* 悬— to hang):红灯高～。*A red lantern is hanging high.* | ～图 *wall map* (or *chart*) ❷惦记 to be concerned about ([连] *doublet* 牵— to be concerned about):～念 *to worry about* | ～虑 *to worry about* | 记～ *to be concerned about* ❸登记 to register:～号 *to register* | ～失 *to report or declare the loss of sth* ❹量词 *quantifier*,多用于成串的东西 (usually used for a set or string of things):一～鞭 *a string of firecrackers* | 一～珠子 *a string of pearls*

褂 guà ㄍㄨㄚˋ (—子、—儿)上身的衣服 Chinese-style garment; gown:大～子(长衫) *gown* | 小～儿 *coat*

GUAI ㄍㄨㄞ

乖 guāi ㄍㄨㄞ ❶不顺,不和谐 abnormal; irregular ([连] *doublet* —僻 eccentric) ❷指小孩听话,懂事 (of child) well-behaved; obedient:宝宝很～,大人省事多了。*A well-behaved baby will save his parents a lot of trouble.* ❸机灵,伶俐 clever; smart; alert ([连] *doublet* —巧 clever; cute):这孩子嘴～。*The child is honey-tongued.*

掴(摑) guāi ㄍㄨㄞ guó ㄍㄨㄛˊ (又 also guó) 打耳光 to slap; to slap sb on the face

拐(❹*柺) guǎi ㄍㄨㄞˇ ❶转折 to turn:～过去就是大街。*Turn over the corner and you'll see the main street.* | ～弯抹角 *to proceed along a zigzag road; to talk in a roundabout way* | ～角 *corner; turning* ❷骗走人或财物 to abduct; to swindle:～骗 *to abduct; to swindle* | ～卖 *to abduct and sell* ❸腿脚有毛病,失去平衡,走路不稳 to limp:走道一瘸(qué)一～ *to walk with a limp; to limp along* ❹走路时帮助支持身体的棍子 crutch:～杖 *crutch* | ～棍 *walking stick* | 架～ *to walk on crutches*

夬 guài ㄍㄨㄞˋ 坚决,果断 resolute

怪(*恠) guài ㄍㄨㄞˋ ❶奇异,不平常 strange; odd; queer ([连] *doublet* 奇— strange):～事 *strange happening* | ～模～样 *odd-looking; peculiar* [引] *extension* 惊奇 to wonder at:大惊小～ *to make a fuss* ❷怪物,神话传说中的妖魔之类 (in mythology) monster; demon ([连] *doublet* 妖— monster) [喻] *figurative* 性情乖僻或形状异样的人 freak; eccentric ❸副词 *adverb*,很,非常 very; quite; rather:～好的天气 *unusually fine weather* | 这孩子～讨人喜欢的。*The child is really lovely.* ❹怨,责备 to blame:责～ *to blame* | ～罪 *to blame* | 这不能～他。*He is not to blame for it.* or *It isn't his fault.*

GUAN ㄍㄨㄢ

关（關、**閞）guān ㄍㄨㄢ ❶闭，合拢 to close; to shut：～门 *to shut the door*｜～上箱子 *to close the case* ㉡ ***extension*** 拘禁 to take into custody ❷古代在险要地方或国界设立的守卫处所 pass or guard post set up at strategic points or on the border in ancient China：～口 *strategic pass; checkpoint*｜山海～*Shanhaiguan Pass* ㉡ ***extension*** 征收出口、入口货税的机构 tax-collector's checkpoint; customs house：海～*customs house*｜～税 *customs duty; tariff* ❸重要的转折点，不易度过的一段时间 barrier; critical juncture：渡过难～ *to get over the difficulties; to pull through the crisis*｜紧要～头 *critical moment* ❹起转折关联作用的部分 joint; key part：～节(两骨连接的地方)(*of bones*) *joint*｜～键 *key* ❺牵连，连属 to involve; to concern：毫不相～*to have nothing to do with*｜无～紧要 *of no importance* [关系] **1** 事物之间的关涉牵连(between things) relation; relationship：这个电门和那盏灯没有～～。*This switch has nothing to do with that light*. **2** 人事的联系(between persons) relation; relationship：同志～～*relationship between comrades*｜亲戚～～*relationship between relatives* **3** 影响 influence; impact：这件事～～太大。*It matters a lot*.[关于]介词 ***preposition***，表示事物之间的关联 about; on; with regard to：～～这个问题 *in regard to this question*｜～～养蜂的书 *book on beekeeping* ❻旧指发给或支领(薪饷)to give out or draw (pay) in former times

观（觀）㊀ guān ㄍㄨㄢ ❶看 to look at; to watch; to observe (㊎ ***doublet*** 一看 to watch)：坐井～天 *to look at the sky from the bottom of a well — to take a narrow view of things*｜～摩 *to watch, inspect and learn from each other's work; to view and emulate*｜走马～花 *to look at flowers while riding on horseback — to gain a superficial understanding through cursory observation* [观察]仔细考察 to observe; to survey：细心～～一切客观现象 *to observe every objective phenomenon carefully* [观光]参观别国或别处的文物、建设等 to go sightseeing; to visit ❷看到的景象 sight; view (㊎ ***doublet*** 一瞻 sight; view)：奇～ *wonderful* (*or marvellous*) *spectacle*｜壮～ *grand sight* ❸对事物的认识，看法 outlook; view：乐～*optimism*｜人生～*outlook on life; philosophy*｜宇宙～*world view* [观点]从某一角度或立场出发形成的对事物的看法 viewpoint [观念] **1** 思想，理性认识 idea;

concept **2** 客观事物在意识中构成的形象 image in one's mind

㊁ guàn 见249页 see p249

纶(綸) ㊁ guān ㄍㄨㄢ 青丝带 blue silk ribbon [纶巾]古代配有青丝带的头巾。传说三国时诸葛亮平常戴这种头巾 blue-ribboned silk kerchief in ancient China (It is said that Zhuge Liang in the period of Three Kingdoms was used to wearing this kind of kerchief.)

㊀ lún 见474页 see p474

官 guān ㄍㄨㄢ ❶政府机关或军队中经过任命的、一定级别以上的公职人员 government official; officer ❷旧时称属于国家的(in former times) government-owned: ～办 *government-run* | ～款 *government money* [官话] **1** 旧时指通行于广大区域的北方话,特指北京话(northern dialect in former times) Mandarin **2** 官腔 official jargon; bureaucratic tone ❸器官,生物体上有特定机能的部分(of body) organ: 五～ *five sense organs* | 感～ *sense organ*

倌 guān ㄍㄨㄢ ❶农村中专管饲养某些家畜的人 herdsman; keeper of domestic animals: 牛～儿 *cowherd* ❷旧时称服杂役的人 hired hand: 堂～儿(茶、酒、饭馆的服务人员) *waiter*

棺 guān ㄍㄨㄢ 棺材,装殓死人的器物 coffin

冠 ㊀ guān ㄍㄨㄢ ❶帽子 hat: 衣～整齐 *to be neatly dressed* ❷(－子)鸟类头上的肉瘤或高出的羽毛 crest; comb: 鸡～子 *rooster's comb*

㊁ guàn 见250页 see p250

矜 ㊁ guān ㄍㄨㄢ 〈古 ***archaism***〉❶同"鳏" same as 鳏 ❷同"瘝" same as 瘝

㊀ jīn 见351页 see p351

㊂ qín 见607页 see p607

瘝 guān ㄍㄨㄢ 病,痛苦 illness; pain

鳏 guān ㄍㄨㄢ 鳏夫,无妻或丧妻的男人 widower; old wifeless man: ～寡孤独 *widowers, widows, orphans and the childless; those who have no kith and kin and cannot support themselves*

莞 ㊀ guǎn ㄍㄨㄢˇ [东莞]地名,在广东省 Dongguan, a place in Guangdong Province

㊁ wǎn 见775页 see p775

馆(*舘) guǎn ㄍㄨㄢˇ ❶招待宾客或旅客食宿的房舍 house to accommodate guests or tourists: 宾～ *guesthouse* | 旅～ *hotel; inn* ❷一个国家在另一个国家办理外交的人员常驻的处所 embassy; legation; consulate: 大使～ *embassy* | 领事～ *consulate* ❸(－子、－儿)某些服务性商店的名称(of service trades) shop: 照相～ *photo studio* | 理发～ *barbershop* | 饭～儿 *restaurant* ❹开展文化等活动的场所 place for cultural activities: 文化～ *cultural centre* | 体育～ *gymnasium* | 图书～ *library* | 博物～ *museum* ❺旧时指教学的地方(in former times) private school:家～ *family school* | 蒙～ *old-style private primary school*

琯 guǎn ㄍㄨㄢˇ 玉管,古代管乐器 *guan*, wind instrument made of jade in ancient China

管(*筦) guǎn ㄍㄨㄢˇ ❶吹奏的乐器 wind instrument:丝竹～弦 *traditional stringed and woodwind instruments* | ～乐器 *wind instrument* ❷(一子、一儿)圆筒形的东西 tube; pipe:～道 *pipeline* | 竹～儿 *bamboo pipe* | 无缝钢～ *seamless steel tube* | ～见(喻浅陋的见识) *my humble opinion; my limited understanding* ❸负责,经理 to be in charge of; to manage:红～家 *good housekeeper* | ～账 *to keep accounts* | ～伙食 *to be in charge of food* ㊀ **extension** **1** 干预,过问 to concern oneself with; to bother about; to mind:工作要大家～。*The work concerns everyone.* | 这事我们不能不～。*We have to do something about this matter.* **2** 负责供给 to provide:～吃～住 *to provide food and accommodation* | 生活用品都～ *to provide all daily necessities* ❹管教,约束 to discipline:～孩子 *to discipline children* | ～住自己的嘴,不说粗话。*Discipline yourself not to speak vulgar language.* [管制] **1** 监督,管理 to control:～～灯火 *to enforce a blackout* **2** 刑事处分的一种,对某些有罪行的人,由政府和群众监督教育,使能改过自新 to put a criminal, etc under surveillance [不管] ㊟ ***transfer*** 连词 ***conjunction*** 跟"无论"义相近(close to 无论) no matter what, how, etc; regardless of:～～多大困难,我们都能克服。*We can overcome any difficulties, however great they are.* ❺保证 to guarantee:～用 *to be effective* | 不好～换。*We guarantee to change it if it is not good.* | ～保有效 *to guarantee the effectiveness of sth* ❻介词 ***preposition***,把(与动词"叫"连用)(used together with the verb 叫) to be called:有的地区～玉米叫苞谷。*In some areas corn is called* baogu.

鳤 guǎn ㄍㄨㄢˇ 鱼名。体长筒形,银白色,鳞小。生活在我国南方淡水中(*Ochetobius elongatus*)

观(觀) ㊁ guàn ㄍㄨㄢˋ 道教的庙宇 Taoist temple

㊀ guān 见247页 see p247

贯 guàn ㄍㄨㄢˋ ❶连贯,穿通 to follow in a continuous line; to pass through:语气～注 *consistent in the manner of speaking* | 一直～串下去 *to run through* | 融会～通 *to achieve mastery through a comprehensive study of the subject* [贯彻]使全部实现 to carry out (*or* through):～～执行 *to carry out* | ～～党的政策和决议 *to carry out the Party's policies and decisions* [一贯]向来如

G

此，始终一致 consistently; all along：艰苦朴素是他的～～作风。*He consistently maintains a hard work and plain living style*. ❷旧时把方孔钱穿在绳子上，每一千个叫一贯(used in former times) *guan*, a string of 1,000 copper coins with square holes in the middle ❸原籍，出生地 birthplace; native place：籍～*birthplace*

掼 guàn ㄍㄨㄢˋ〈方 **dialect**〉掷，扔 to throw; to toss：往地下一～*to throw it to the ground*

惯 guàn ㄍㄨㄢˋ ❶习以为常的，积久成性的 to be accustomed to; to be in the habit of：～技 *customary tactic; old trick*｜～例 *convention*｜穿～了短装 *to be used to wearing a Chinese-style jacket and trousers* [惯性]物体没有受外力作用时保持原有的运动状态或静止状态，这种性质叫惯性 inertia ❷纵容，放任 to indulge; to spoil：～坏了脾气 *to become bad-tempered by being spoiled*｜娇生～养 *to be pampered (or coddled) since childhood*

冠 ㊁ guàn ㄍㄨㄢˋ ❶把帽子戴在头上 to put on a hat ❷超出众人，居第一位 to take the first place：勇～三军 *the bravest in the whole army* [冠军] ㊕ ***transfer*** 比赛的第一名 champion ❸在前面加上某种名号 to be crowned as：～以诗人的桂冠(guān) *to be crowned as poet laureate*

㊀ guān 见248页 see p248

涫 guàn ㄍㄨㄢˋ 沸 to boil：～汤 *to boil soup*

祼 guàn ㄍㄨㄢˋ 古代祭祀时把酒浇在地上的礼节(in ancient China) libation; spreading wine over the ground in worship

盥 guàn ㄍㄨㄢˋ 洗(手、脸) to wash (hands or face)：～洗室 *washroom; lavatory; bathroom*

灌 guàn ㄍㄨㄢˋ 浇，灌注 to water; to irrigate：引水～田 *to channel water to irrigate the fields*｜～一瓶水 *to fill a bottle with water; to pour water into a bottle*

[灌木]主茎不发达，丛生而矮小的树木，如茶树、酸枣树等 bush; shrub

瓘 guàn ㄍㄨㄢˋ 古玉器名 *guan*, an ancient jade article

鹳 guàn ㄍㄨㄢˋ 鸟名。羽毛灰色、白色或黑色，嘴长而直，形状像鹤。生活在江、湖、池、沼的近旁，捕食鱼、虾等 stork (*Ciconiiformes*)

罐(**鑵、*鑵) guàn ㄍㄨㄢˋ (一子、一儿)盛东西或汲水用的瓦器。泛指各种圆筒形的盛物器 jar; pot; tin：铁～儿 *iron jar*｜易拉～儿 *pop-top; pull-top* [罐头](一tou)指罐头食品，加工后装在密封罐子里的食品 tinned (*or* canned) food

GUANG ㄍㄨㄤ

光 guāng ㄍㄨㄤ ❶光线，照耀在物体上能使视觉看见物体的那种物质，如灯光、阳光等 light; ray [光明]亮 bright [喻] ***figurative*** 襟怀坦白，没有私心 honest and above board; selfless：心地～～ *openhearted* [光盘]用激光束记录和读取信息的圆盘形存储载体，可分为只读光盘和可刻录光盘 compact disk; CD [激光]一种由激光器产生的颜色很纯、能量高度集中并朝单一方向发射的光。广泛应用在工业、军事、医学、通讯、探测等方面 laser ❷光彩，荣誉 honour; glory：为国增～ *to bring honour to one's country* | ～荣之家 *honoured family* 敬辞 **polite**：～临 *presence* | ～顾 *patronage* ❸景物 scenery：春～ *spring scenery; view of spring* | 风～ *scenery* | 观～ *sightseeing* [光景] **1** 同"光❸"same as 光❸ **2** 生活的情况 living conditions：～～一年好似一年。*Living conditions are becoming better year by year.* ❹光滑，平滑 smooth; glossy：磨～ *to polish* | ～溜(liu) *smooth; slippery* ❺完了，一点不剩 used up; nothing left：把敌人消灭～ *to wipe out the enemy* ❻露着 bare：～头 *bare-headed* | ～膀子 *to be bare* (or *stripped*) *to the waist* ❼副词 **adverb**，单，只 only; alone：大家都走了，～剩下他一个人了。*All the others had left and he was the only one to stay behind.*

咣 guāng ㄍㄨㄤ 拟声词 ***onomatopoeia***，撞击或振动的声音 bang; crash：～的一声，门被关上了。*The door banged shut.*

洸 guāng ㄍㄨㄤ 见263页"浛"字条"浛洸"(hán—) see 浛洸 on p263

桄 ㊀ guāng ㄍㄨㄤ [桄榔](—láng)常绿乔木，大型羽状叶，生于茎顶。花序的汁可制糖，茎髓可制淀粉，叶柄的纤维可制绳 gomuti palm (*Arenga pinnata*)

㊁ guàng 见252页 see p252

胱 guāng ㄍㄨㄤ 见552页"膀"字条"膀胱"(páng—) see 膀胱 on p552

广(廣) ㊀ guǎng ㄍㄨㄤˇ ❶宽度 width：长五十米，～三十米 *50 metres in length and 30 metres in width* [广袤](—mào)东西叫广，南北叫袤，指土地的面积(Distance from east to west is called 广, from north to south 袤.) land area ❷宽，大 widespread; vast：～场 *square* | 我国地～人多。*Our country is a vast and densely populated area.* or *Our country is vast in area and dense in population.* [广泛]范围大，普遍 wide; broad; extensive：～～宣传 *to give* (or *accord*) *wide publicity to* | 意义～～ *to have far-reaching meaning* ❸多 numerous：大庭～众 *in front of a big crowd; in* *public* ❹扩大，扩充 to spread; to expand:～播 *to broadcast* | 推～先进经验 *to spread advanced experience* ❺姓 Guang, a surname

㊁ ān 见5页 see p5

犷（獷） guǎng ㄍㄨㄤˇ 粗野 rustic; rough; uncouth: 粗～*rustic; rough* | ～悍 *rough and ferocious*

桄 ㊀ guàng ㄍㄨㄤˋ ❶绕线的器具 reel ❷量词 ***quantifier***, 用于线(used for thread): 一～线 *a reel of thread*

㊁ guāng 见251页 see p251

逛 guàng ㄍㄨㄤˋ 闲游，游览 to stroll; to roam: ～公园 *to stroll in a park*

GUI ㄍㄨㄟ

G

归（歸） guī ㄍㄨㄟ ❶返回，回到本处 to return; to go back: ～家 *to return home* | ～国 *to return to one's country* ㊀ ***extension*** 还给 to give back; to return: 物～原主 *to return sth to its rightful owner* | ～本还原 *to return to the original state* ❷趋向 to converge: 殊途同～*All roads lead to Rome.* or *to reach the same goal by different means* | 众望所～*the centre of popular confidence; the expectation of the masses* ❸归并，合并 to merge into; to put together: 把书～在一起 *to put the books together* | 这两个机构～成一个 *to merge two organizations into one* | ～里包堆(总共) *in all; in total; altogether* [归纳] 由许多的事例概括出一般的原理 to sum up ❹由，属于 to be in sb's charge; to belong to: 这事～我办。*I'm in charge of it.* ❺珠算中称一位数的除法(on the abacus) division with a one-digit divisor: 九～*rules for doing division with a one-digit divisor on the abacus*

圭（❶ **珪） guī ㄍㄨㄟ ❶古代帝王、诸侯在举行典礼时拿的一种玉器，上圆(或剑头形)下方 *gui*, jade tablet with round (*or* pointed) top and square bases held by ancient emperors, dukes and princes on ceremonial occasions ❷古代测日影的器具 sundial [圭臬](—niè) 标准，法度 criterion; standard ❸古代容量单位名，一升的十万分之一 *gui*, an ancient unit of measurement of volume, equal to one 100,000th of a litre

邽 guī ㄍㄨㄟ [下邽] 地名，在陕西省渭南 Xiagui, a place in Weinan, Shaanxi Province

闺 guī ㄍㄨㄟ ❶上圆下方的小门 arched door ❷旧时指女子居住的内室(in former times) boudoir: 深～*innermost boudoir* [闺女] **1** 未出嫁的女子 girl; maiden **2** 女儿 daughter

硅 guī ㄍㄨㄟ 一种非金属元素，符号 Si，有褐色粉末、灰色晶体等形态。硅是一种极重要的半导体材料，能制成高效率的电子元件。硅酸盐在制造玻璃、水泥等工业上很重要。旧称"矽"(xī)(formerly called 矽) silicon; silicium (Si)

鲑 guī ㄍㄨㄟ 鱼名。身体大,略呈纺锤形,鳞细而圆,肉味美 salmon (*salmonidae*)

龟(龜) ㊀ guī ㄍㄨㄟ 爬行动物,种类很多。腹背都有硬甲,头尾和脚能缩入甲中,能耐饥渴,寿命很长。龟甲也叫龟板,可以入药。古人用龟甲占卜(迷信) tortoise; turtle:~卜 *tortoise-shell divination*|蓍(shī)~ (*tools used for divination*) *alpine yarrow and tortoise shell* [龟鉴][龟镜]用龟卜,用镜照,比喻可资借鉴的事例或道理 oracle inscription on tortoise shell and mirror — both can serve as an objective lesson or a warning

㊁ jūn 见378页 see p378

㊂ qiū 见614页 see p614

妫(嬀、**媯) guī ㄍㄨㄟ 妫河,水名,在北京市延庆 Guihe River, in Yanqing, Beijing

规 guī ㄍㄨㄟ ❶圆规,画圆形的仪器 compasses:两脚~ *dividers* ❷法则,章程 rule; regulation ([连] ***doublet*** — 则 rule; regulation):成~*set rules*|常~*convention; common practice; rule* [规格]产品质量的标准,如大小、轻重、精密度、性能等 specification; standard; norm:合~~*to be up to standard* [规矩](—ju) **1** 标准,法则 rule; custom:守~~*to observe the rules*|老~~*established rules* **2** 合标准,守法则 well-behaved; well-disciplined:~~老实 *well-behaved; well-disciplined* [规模] **1** 格局(多指计划、设备) (usually used to denote a plan or equipment) pattern; scale:略具~~*to be taking shape*|这座工厂~~宏大。*This factory has a large scale.* **2** 范围 scale; scope:大~~的经济建设 *economic construction on a large scale* ❸相劝 to admonish; to advise:~劝 *to admonish*|~勉 *to advise and encourage* ❹谋划 to plan:~定 *to stipulate*|~避(设法避开) *to evade; to avoid* [规划]较长期的大致计划 programme; plan:农业发展~~*programme of agricultural development*

鬶 guī ㄍㄨㄟ 古代陶制炊具,嘴像鸟喙,有把柄和三个空心的短足 *gui*, an ancient cooker made of clay with a beak-like spout, handles and three short hollow legs

皈 guī ㄍㄨㄟ [皈依]原指佛教的入教仪式,后泛指信仰佛教或参加其他宗教组织。也作"归依"(also written as 归依) originally used to denote ceremony of initiating sb as a Buddhist, now conversion to Buddhism or other religions in a broad sense

瑰(*瓌) guī ㄍㄨㄟ ❶一种像玉的石头 jade-like stone ❷奇特,珍奇 marvellous; rare:~丽 *mag-*

nificent | ～异 *fantastic* | ～宝 *treasure*

氿 ㊀ guǐ ㄍㄨㄟˇ 氿泉，从侧面喷出的泉 sideway gushing spring

㊁ jiǔ 见364页 see p364

宄 guǐ ㄍㄨㄟˇ 坏人 evildoer：奸～*evildoer*

轨 guǐ ㄍㄨㄟˇ ❶车辙 rut ❷轨道，一定的路线 path; roadway：火车～道 *railway* 特指铺设轨道的钢条 rail; track：钢～*steel rail* | 铁～*iron rail* | 铺～*to lay the rails* ㊗ ***figurative*** 应遵循的规则 course; rule：步入正～*to be on the right track* | ～外行动 *actions against law*

匦 guǐ ㄍㄨㄟˇ 箱子，匣子 case; box：票～*ballot box*

庋 guǐ ㄍㄨㄟˇ ❶放东西的架子 shelf ❷搁置 to keep; to preserve：～藏 *to preserve; to store up*

诡 guǐ ㄍㄨㄟˇ ❶欺诈，奸滑 deceitful; sly：～辩（无理强辩）*sophistry* | ～计多端 *to have a whole bag of tricks; to be very crafty* ❷怪异，出乎寻常 weird; uncanny：～秘 *secretive* | ～异 *strange; queer*

姽 guǐ ㄍㄨㄟˇ［姽婳］（— huà）形容女子娴静美好（of a woman）demure and pretty

鬼 guǐ ㄍㄨㄟˇ ❶迷信的人以为人死之后有灵魂，叫鬼 ghost：妖魔～怪 *evil forces* ❷阴险，不光明 stealthy; surreptitious：～话 *falsehood; lie* | ～胎（喻不可告人之事）*sinister design; evil plot* ❸机灵（多指小孩子）（of a child）clever; smart; quick：这孩子真～。*What a clever boy!* ❹对小孩儿的爱称 term of endearment for a child：小～*child* ❺对人蔑称或憎称（derogatory term for a person）：酒～*drunkard* | 吸血～*bloodsucker* ❻星宿名，二十八宿之一 *gui*, 23rd of the 28 constellations

癸 guǐ ㄍㄨㄟˇ 天干的第十位，用作顺序的第十 *gui*, last of the 10 Heavenly Stems; tenth

晷 guǐ ㄍㄨㄟˇ 日影 shadow of the sun ㊕ ***transfer*** 时间 time：日无暇～*with no time to spare; busy from morning to night*［日晷］按照日影测定时刻的仪器。也叫"日规"（also called 日规）sundial

簋 guǐ ㄍㄨㄟˇ 古代盛食物的器具，圆口，两耳 *gui*, an ancient food vessel with a round mouth and two handles

柜（**櫃**）㊀ guì ㄍㄨㄟˋ（—子）一种收藏东西用的器具，通常作长方形，有盖或有门 cupboard; cabinet：衣～*wardrobe* | 保险～*safe*

㊁ jǔ 见369页 see p369

炅 ㊁ guì ㄍㄨㄟˋ 姓 Gui, a surname

㊀ jiǒng 见363页 see p363

刿（**劌**）guì ㄍㄨㄟˋ 刺伤 to stab

刽（**劊**）guì ㄍㄨㄟˋ 砍断 to cut off; to chop off［刽子手］旧指执行斩刑的人（in former times）headsman; executioner [引] ***extension*** 杀害人民的人 slaughterer; butcher

桧(檜) ㊀ guì ㄍㄨㄟˋ 植物学上叫"圆柏"。常绿乔木,幼树的叶子针状,大树的叶子鳞片状,果实球形,木材桃红色,有香气,可供建筑及制造铅笔杆等(also called 圆柏 in botany) Chinese juniper (*Juniperus chinensis*)

㊁ huì 见299页 see p299

贵 guì ㄍㄨㄟˋ ❶价格高 expensive:这本书不～。*This book is not expensive.* | 钢比铁～。*Steel is more expensive than iron.* ❷旧指社会地位高(in former times) of high rank:～族 *noble man; aristocrat* | 达官～人 *high officials and important people; VIPs* 敬辞 ***polite***:～姓 *your surname, please* | ～处 *your place* | ～校 *your school* | ～宾 *honoured* (or *distinguished*) *guest* ❸特别好,价值高 valuable; precious ([连] ***doublet*** 宝－valuable | －重 precious):珍～的礼品 *precious gifts* | 宝～的意见 *valuable suggestions* ❹重视,崇尚 high valued:～精不～多 *to be valued for the quality, not for the quantity* | 这种见义勇为的精神是可～的。*The readiness to take up the cudgels for a just cause is valuable.*

桂 guì ㄍㄨㄟˋ ❶植物名 plant name **1** 肉桂,常绿乔木,花白色,树皮有香气,可入药,又可做香料 Chinese cinnamon (*Cinnamomum aromaticum*) **2** 月桂树,常绿乔木,花黄色,叶可做香料 laurel (*Laurus nobilis*) **3** 桂花树,又叫"木犀"。常绿小乔木或灌木,花白色或黄色,有特殊香气,供观赏,又可做香料(also called 木犀) sweet osmanthus (*Osmanthus fragrans*) ❷广西壮族自治区的别称 Gui, another name for the Guangxi Zhuang Autonomous Region

跪 guì ㄍㄨㄟˋ 屈膝,使膝盖着地 to kneel: ～下射击 *kneeling fire*

鳜 guì ㄍㄨㄟˋ 鳜鱼(也作"桂鱼"),鱼名。体侧扁,尾鳍呈扇形,口大鳞细,体青黄色,有黑色斑点。肉味鲜美。是淡水鱼类之一(also written as 桂鱼) mandarin fish (*Siniperca chuatsi*)

GUN ㄍㄨㄣ

衮 gǔn ㄍㄨㄣˇ 古代君王的礼服 ceremonial dress for royalty in ancient China: ～服 *emperor's ceremonial dress*

滚 gǔn ㄍㄨㄣˇ ❶水流翻腾(叠 ***reduplication***) (of water) to roll; to tumble: 白浪翻～ *white-crested waves rolling* | 大江～～东去。*The great river is rolling to the east.* [引] ***extension*** 水煮开(of water) to boil: 水～了。*The water is boiling.* ❷旋转着移动 to roll; to trundle:小球～来～去。*The small ball is rolling back and forth.* | ～铁环 *to roll a hoop* | 打～ *to*

G

roll about ❸走,离开(含斥责意)(speaking in an angry tone) to get away:～出去! *Get out of here!* ❹极,特 extremely:～烫 *burning hot*|～圆 *perfectly round*

磙 gǔn ㄍㄨㄣˇ (－子)用石头做的圆柱形的压、轧用的器具 stone roller

绲 gǔn ㄍㄨㄣˇ ❶织成的带子 ribbon ❷绳 string; cord ❸沿衣服等的边缘缝上布条、带子等 to trim; to hem:～边儿 *hem*

辊 gǔn ㄍㄨㄣˇ 机器上圆筒状能旋转的东西 roller:皮～花 *lap waste*|～轴 *roll shaft*

鲧(**鮌) gǔn ㄍㄨㄣˇ ❶古书上说的一种大鱼 *gun*, a kind of big fish mentioned in ancient Chinese texts ❷古人名,传说是夏禹的父亲 Gun, the father of Yu, the legendary King, who founded the Xia Dynasty

棍 gùn ㄍㄨㄣˋ ❶(－子、－儿)棒 stick; rod ❷称坏人 scoundrel; rascal:赌～ *gambler*|恶～*scoundrel; ruffian*

GUO ㄍㄨㄛ

过(過) ㊁ guō ㄍㄨㄛ 姓 Guo, a surname

㊀ guò 见258页 see p258

彍(彍) guō ㄍㄨㄛ 拉满弩弓 to draw a bow to the full

呙(咼) guō ㄍㄨㄛ 姓 Guo, a surname

埚(堝) guō ㄍㄨㄛ 见216页"坩"字条"坩埚"(gān－) see 坩埚 on p216

涡(渦) ㊁ guō ㄍㄨㄛ 涡河,水名,发源于河南省,流至安徽省注入淮河 Guohe River, originating from Henan Province and flowing into the Huaihe River in Anhui Province

㊀ wō 见791页 see p791

锅(鍋) guō ㄍㄨㄛ ❶烹煮食物的器具 pot; pan [锅炉] **1** 一种烧开水的设备(apparatus for heating water, especially a device providing hot water for a house) boiler **2** 使水变成蒸汽以供应工业或取暖需要的设备。也叫"汽锅"(also called 汽锅)(sealed vessel where water is converted to steam) boiler ❷(－儿)像锅的 pot-like:烟袋～ *bowl of a pipe*

郭 guō ㄍㄨㄛ 城外围着城的墙 outer wall of a city(㊥ ***doublet*** 城－ inner and outer city walls)

崞 guō ㄍㄨㄛ 崞县,地名,在山西省。现叫原平(now called 原平) Guoxian, a place in Shanxi Province

啯(嘓) guō ㄍㄨㄛ 拟声词 ***onomatopoeia***(叠 ***reduplication***), cackle; cluck; gurgle

蝈(蟈) guō ㄍㄨㄛ [蝈蝈儿](－guor)一种昆虫,身体绿色或褐色,翅短,腹大,雄的前翅根部有发声

器，能振翅发声。对植物有害 katydid (*Tettigoniidae*)

聒 guō ㄍㄨㄛ 声音嘈杂，使人厌烦 unpleasantly noisy：～耳 *strident; to grate on one's ears*｜～噪 *noisy; clamorous*

国（國、**囯） guó ㄍㄨㄛˊ ❶ 国家 country; state：保家卫～ *to protect our homes and defend our country; to guard our homes and our country*｜～内 *internal; domestic; home*｜祖～ *motherland* [国家] **1** 阶级统治和管理的工具，是统治阶级对被统治阶级实行专政的暴力组织，主要由军队、警察、法庭、监狱等组成。国家是阶级矛盾不可调和的产物和表现，它随着阶级的产生而产生，也将随着阶级的消灭而自行消亡 state **2** 一个独立的国家政权所领有的区域 country [国际主义] 各国无产阶级、劳动人民在民族解放的斗争中互相支持紧密团结在一起的思想 internationalism ❷ 属于本国的 national; of the state：～货 *domestic* (or *national*) *goods*｜～歌 *national anthem*

掴（摑） guó ㄍㄨㄛˊ (又 also guāi) 见246页(guāi) see (guāi) on p246

帼（幗） guó ㄍㄨㄛˊ 古代妇女包头的巾、帕 ancient woman's headdress：巾～英雄(女英雄) *heroine*

涸（漍） guó ㄍㄨㄛˊ [北涸] 地名，在江苏省江阴 Beiguo, a place in Jiangyin, Jiangsu Province

腘（膕） guó ㄍㄨㄛˊ 膝部的后面 back of the knee

虢 guó ㄍㄨㄛˊ 周代诸侯国名 Guo, a princedom in the Zhou Dynasty **1** 西虢，在今陕西省宝鸡东，后来迁到河南省陕县东南 the state of West Guo in the east of today's Baoji, Shaanxi Province before being moved to the southeastern Shanxian, Henan Province **2** 东虢，在今河南省郑州西北 the state of East Guo, located in the northwest of today's Zhengzhou, Henan Province

馘（**聝） guó ㄍㄨㄛˊ 古代战争中割取敌人的左耳以计数献功。也指割下的左耳 number of severed left ears of enemies as a measure of a fighter's merit in ancient wars, also the left ears cut off in this way

果（❶*菓） guǒ ㄍㄨㄛˇ ❶ (一子) 果实，某些植物花落后含有种子的部分 fruit：水～ *fruit*｜干～(如花生、栗子等) *dry fruit or nuts* (*such as peanut, chestnut, etc*) ❷ 结果，事情的结局或成效 result; consequence：成～ *achievement*｜恶～ *bad consequence*｜前因后～ *cause and effect* ❸ 果断，坚决 resolute; determined (㊥ **doublet** 一决 firm and resolute)：～敢 *resolute and daring*｜言必信，行必～ *trustworthy in word and resolute in action* ❹ 果然，确

G

实，真的 really; as expected：～不出所料 *just as expected* | 他～真来了吗？ *Did he really and truly come?*

馃 guǒ ㄍㄨㄛˇ（—子）一种油炸的面食 doughnut

蜾 guǒ ㄍㄨㄛˇ［蜾蠃］（—luǒ）蜂类的一种，常用泥土在墙上或树枝上做窝，捕捉螟蛉等小虫存在窝里，留做将来幼虫的食物。旧时误认蜾蠃养螟蛉为己子，所以有把抱养的孩子称为“螟蛉子”的说法（In former times, people wrongly thought that parasitic wasps took corn earworms as their own larvae, so they called an adopted child 螟蛉子）parasitic wasp

裹 guǒ ㄍㄨㄛˇ 包，缠 to wrap; to bind：～伤口 *to bind (or dress) a wound* | 用纸～上 *to wrap it up in paper* | ～足不前（喻停止不进行）*to hesitate to proceed* ㊕ ***figurative*** 卷在里头 to carry along：洪水～着泥沙。*The flood carried along mud and sand.*

椁（＊槨） guǒ ㄍㄨㄛˇ 棺材外面套的大棺材 outer coffin

过（過） ㊀ guò ㄍㄨㄛˋ ❶从这儿到那儿，从甲方到乙方 to cross; to transfer：～江 *to cross a river* | 没有～不去的河。*There is no river that cannot be crossed.* | ～户 *to transfer ownership; to change the name of the owner in a register* | ～账 *to transfer items (as from a daybook to a ledger)* ㊞ ***extension*** **1** 传 to conduct：～电 *to get an electric shock* **2** 交往 to associate：～从 *to associate*［过去］**1** 已经经历了的时间 past **2**（—qu）从这儿到那儿去 to go over ❷经过，度过 to pass or spend (time)：～冬 *to spend the winter; to winter* | ～节 *to celebrate a festival* | 日子越～越好。*Life is getting better and better.* ㊞ ***extension*** 使经过某种处理 to undergo; to go through：～秤 *to weigh (on the steelyard or scale)* | ～目 to go over | ～一～数 *to count* | 把菜～一～油 *to fry vegetables*［过年］**1** 度过新年 to spend the New Year **2**（—nian）明年，指说话时候以后的一个年头 next year ❸超出 to exceed **1** 数量(of quantity) more numerous than：～半数 *more than half* | ～了一百 *to exceed a hundred* **2** 程度 beyond what is allowed, necessary or advisable：～分(fèn) *to go too far* | ～火 *to go too far* | 未免太～。*This is going too far.* ❹超越 to surpass［过费］（—fei）〈方 ***dialect***〉**1** 花费过多 undue expense **2** 辜负 to let down［过逾］（—yu）过分 excessive：小心没～～。*You can't be too careful.* ❺（—儿）量词 ***quantifier***，次，回，遍 time：衣服洗了好几～儿。*The clothes have been washed several times.* ❻错误 fault; mistake（㊟ ***doublet*** —错 fault）：改～自

新 *to turn over a new leaf* | 知～必改。*You must correct your mistake when you are aware of it.* ❼(guo)放在动词后(used after a verb) **1** 助词 ***auxiliary***, 表示曾经或已经(used to express the completion of an action):看～*to have seen* | 听～*to have heard* | 用～了 *to have used* | 你见～他吗? *Have you ever seen him?* **2** 跟"来"、"去"连用,表示趋向(used together with 来 or 去 to express direction):拿～来 *to bring* | 转～去 *to turn round*

㊁ guō 见256页 see p256

H 厂

HA 厂Y

哈(❸**䶖) ㊀ hā 厂Y ❶张口呼气(with the mouth open) to breathe out [哈哈]拟声词 *onomatopoeia*,笑声(sound of laughing) ha-ha ❷叹词 *interjection*,表示得意或惊喜(叠 *reduplication*)(expressing self-pride or pleasant surprise) aha:~,我赢啦! *Aha, I've won*. ❸哈腰,稍微弯腰,表示礼貌 to bend one's back; to bow slightly to show courtesy

[哈喇](—la) **1** 含油的食物日子久了起了变化的味道 rancid **2** 杀死(元曲多用)(usually used in *Yuanqu*) to kill

[哈尼族]我国少数民族,参看附表(see the appendix) the Hani ethnic group, one of the ethnic minorities of China

[哈萨克族] **1** 我国少数民族,参看附表(see the appendix) the Kazak ethnic group, one of the ethnic minorities of China **2** 哈萨克斯坦的主要民族 Kazak, the main ethnic group in Kazakstan

㊁ hǎ 见260页 see p260

㊂ hà 见260页 see p260

铪 hā 厂Y 一种金属元素,符号Hf,银白色,熔点高,用于核反应堆控制棒等 hafnium (Hf)

虾(蝦) ㊁ há 厂Ý [虾蟆](—ma) 旧同"蛤蟆"(formerly same as 蛤蟆) frog; toad

㊀ xiā 见807页 see p807

蛤 ㊁ há 厂Ý [蛤蟆](—ma) 青蛙和癞蛤蟆的统称 general term for frog and toad

㊀ gé 见224页 see p224

哈 ㊁ hǎ 厂Y̌ 姓 Ha, a surname

[哈达](藏 *Tibetan*)一种长形薄绢,藏族和部分蒙古族人用以表示敬意或祝贺 *hada*, a long piece of silk presented to sb to show respect or congratulation by the Tibetans and some Mongolians

[哈巴狗](—ba—)一种个儿小腿短的狗。也叫"狮子狗"、"巴儿狗"。常用来比喻驯顺的奴才(also called 狮子狗 or 巴儿狗)(usually used as a metaphor for a lackey) pug; Pekinese

㊀ hā 见260页 see p260

㊂ hà 见260页 see p260

哈 ㊂ hà 厂Y̌ [哈什蚂](—shimǎ)蛙的一种,灰褐色,生活在阴湿的地方,主要产在我国东北各省。雌的腹内有脂肪状物质,叫哈什蚂油,中医用作补品 Chinese forest frog

H

(*Rana temporaria*)

㊀ hā 见260页 see p260

㊁ hǎ 见260页 see p260

HAI 厂历

咳 ㊁ hāi 厂历 ❶叹息 to sigh:～声叹气 *to heave a deep sigh* ❷叹词 ***interjection*** **1** 表示惋惜或后悔(used to express regret):～,我为什么这么糊涂! *Oh no, how stupid I was!* **2** 招呼人,提醒人注意(used to call sb or sb's attention):～,到这儿来。*Hey! Come here!*

㊀ ké 见389页 see p389

嗨 ㊀ hāi 厂历 叹词 ***interjection***,同"咳㊁❷" same as 咳㊁❷

㊁ hēi 见274页 see p274

还(還) ㊁ hái 厂历 副词 ***adverb*** ❶仍旧,依然 still; yet:你～是那样。*You are still the same as before.* | 这件事～没有做完。*It hasn't been finished yet.* ❷更 even more; still more:今天比昨天～热。*It is even hotter today than yesterday.* ❸再,又 also; too:另外～有一件事要做。*There is something else to do.* | 提高产量,～要保证质量。*Not only the quantity of the products should be increased, but the quality should be assured as well.* ❹尚,勉强过得去 passably; fairly:身体～好 *to be fairly well* | 工作进展得～不算慢。*The work is progressing fairly fast.* ❺尚且 even:他那么大年纪～这么干,咱们更应该加油干了。*He is still working so hard despite his old age, so we should work harder.* [还是](-shi) **1** 副词 ***adverb***,表示这么办比较好 had better:咱们～～出去吧。*We'd better go out.* **2** 连词 ***conjunction***,用在问句里表示选择(used in questions) or:是你去呢,～～他来? *Are you going or is he coming?* ❻表示对某件事物,没想到如此,而居然如此(used to express that sth unexpected has happened):他～真有办法。*He is really resourceful.*

㊀ huán 见290页 see p290

孩 hái 厂历 (-子、-儿)幼童 child ㊓ ***extension*** 子女 offspring; son and daughter:他有两个～子。*He has two children.* [孩提]指幼儿时期 early childhood; infancy

骸 hái 厂历 ❶骨头 bones of the body; skeleton (㊥ ***doublet*** 一骨 skeleton):尸～ *skeleton; dead body* ❷指身体 body:病～ *ailing body* | 残～ *remains*

胲 hǎi 厂历 有机化合物的一类,通式 R—NH—OH,是 NH_2OH 的烃基衍生物的统称 hydroxylamine

海 hǎi 厂历 ❶靠近大陆比洋小的水域 sea:黄～ *Huanghai Sea; Yellow Sea* | 渤～ *Bohai Sea* | ～岸 *seacoast; coast* ❷用于湖泊名称(hai, used in a

H

lake name)：青～ *Qinghai Lake*｜洱～ *Erhai Lake* ❸容量大的器皿 container of great capacity：墨～ *big basin-shaped inkstone* ❹比喻数量多的人或事物(used as a metaphor for a large number of people or things)：人～ *sea of people*｜文山会～ *piles of documents and multitudes of meetings* ❺巨大的 immense：～碗 *huge bowl*｜～量 *magnanimity*｜夸下～口 *to boast about; to talk big; to brag of*

[海报]文艺、体育演出的招贴 poster

醢 hǎi ㄏㄞˇ ❶古代用肉、鱼等制成的酱(in ancient China) minced fish or meat paste ❷古代的一种酷刑，把人杀死后剁成肉酱(a severe punishment in ancient China) to kill sb and slice into mince

亥 hài ㄏㄞˋ ❶地支的末一位 Hai, the last of 12 Earthly Branches ❷亥时，指晚上九点到十一点 period of the day from 9 pm to 11 pm

骇 hài ㄏㄞˋ 惊惧 to frighten; to shock：惊涛～浪(可怕的大浪) *terrifying waves*｜～人听闻 *shocking; horrifying*

氦 hài ㄏㄞˋ 一种化学元素，在通常条件下为气体，符号He，无色无臭，不易跟其他元素化合。很轻，可用来充入气球或电灯泡等 helium (He)

害 hài ㄏㄞˋ ❶有损的 harmful：～虫 *pest; vermin*｜～鸟 *harmful bird* ❷祸害，坏处，跟"利"相对(the opposite of 利) evil; harm：为民除～ *to rid the people of a scourge*｜喝酒过多对身体有～。*Excessive drinking is harmful to your health.* ❸灾害，灾患 calamity; disaster：虫～ *plague of an insect pest* ❹使受损伤 to do harm to：～人不浅 *to do people great harm*｜危～国家 *to do harm to the country* ❺发生疾病 to contract an illness：～病 *to fall ill; to suffer from a disease*｜～眼 *to suffer from eye trouble* ❻心理上发生不安的情绪 to feel uneasy：～羞 *to be shy*｜～臊 *to feel ashamed*｜～怕 *to be afraid*

〈古 **archaism**〉又同"曷"(hé) also same as 曷

嗐 hài ㄏㄞˋ 叹词 ***interjection***：～！想不到他病得这样重。*Oh, I didn't know he was so seriously ill.*

HAN ㄏㄢ

犴 ㊀ hān ㄏㄢ 就是驼鹿。也叫"堪达罕"(i. e. 驼鹿, also called 堪达罕) elk; moose (*Alces alces*)

㊁ àn 见7页 see p7

顸 hān ㄏㄢ 粗，圆柱形的东西直径大的 thick：这线太～。*This thread is too thick.*｜拿根～杠子来抬。*Fetch a thick stick to lift it.*

鼾 hān ㄏㄢ 熟睡时的鼻息声 snore：～声如雷 *thunderous snores*

蚶 hān ㄏㄢ （一子）俗叫“瓦垄子”。软体动物，贝壳厚，有突起的纵线像瓦垄，我国有几十种。生活在浅海泥沙中。肉味鲜美（popularly called 瓦垄子）ark clam（*Arcidae*）

酣 hān ㄏㄢ 酒喝得很畅快（to drink）to one's heart's content：～饮 *to carouse; to drink to one's heart's content* ⓘ **extension** 尽兴，痛快 to one's heart's content：～睡 *to sleep soundly*｜～战（长时间紧张地战斗）*hard-fought battle*

憨 hān ㄏㄢ ❶傻，痴呆 foolish; silly：～笑 *to simper* ❷朴实，天真 simple; naive：～直 *simple and straightforward*｜～态 *air of charming naivety* ［憨厚］朴实，厚道 simple and honest

邗 hán ㄏㄢˊ ［邗江］地名，在江苏省扬州 Hanjiang, a place in Yangzhou, Jiangsu Province

汗 ㊀ hán ㄏㄢˊ 指可汗。参看390页“可㊁”（see 可㊁ on p390）khan

㊀ hàn 见264页 see p264

邯 hán ㄏㄢˊ ［邯郸］（-dān）地名，在河北省 Handan, a place in Hebei Province

含 hán ㄏㄢˊ ❶嘴里放着东西，不吐出来也不吞下去 to keep（*or* hold）in the mouth：嘴里～着块糖 *to have a candy in the mouth* ⓘ **extension** 藏在眼眶里 to keep in the eyes：～着泪 *with tears in one's eyes* ❷带有某种意思、感情等，不完全表露出来 to nurse（*or* cherish）a certain idea or feeling：～怒 *with suppressed anger*｜～羞 *bashful*｜～笑 *with a smile* ❸里面存在着 to contain：～水分 *containing water or moisture*｜～养分 *containing nutrients* ［含糊］（*含胡）（-hu）**1** 不明确，不清晰 ambiguous; vague **2** 怯懦，畏缩，常跟“不”连用（usually used in collocation with 不）to show weakness or cowardice：绝不～～ *not to show any cowardice at all* **3** 不认真，马虎 careless; perfunctory：这事可不能～～。*This matter must be handled with meticulous care.*

浛 hán ㄏㄢˊ ［浛洸］（-guāng）地名，在广东省英德 Hanguang, a place in Yingde, Guangdong Province

晗 hán ㄏㄢˊ 天将明 before dawn

焓 hán ㄏㄢˊ 单位质量的物质所含的全部热能 enthalpy

函（*凾） hán ㄏㄢˊ ❶匣，套子 case; envelope：石～ *stone casket*｜镜～ *case for a mirror*｜全书共四～。*The whole work is in four cases.* ⓩ **transfer** 信件（古代寄信用木函）（wooden cases in which letters are posted in ancient China）letter：～件 *letters; correspondence*｜来～ *letter received*｜公～ *official letter*｜～授 *to teach by correspondence; to offer a correspondence* *course* ❷包容,包含 to contain; to include

涵 hán ㄏㄢˊ 包容,包含 to contain:包～ *to excuse; to forgive* | 海～ *generous forgiveness* | ～义 *meaning; implication* | ～养 *ability to control oneself; self-possession*

韩(韓) hán ㄏㄢˊ 战国国名,在现在河南省中部、山西省东南一带 Han, a state of the Warring States Period covering today's central Henan Province and southeastern Shanxi Province

寒 hán ㄏㄢˊ ❶冷 cold(㊀ **doublet** 一冷 cold):御～ *to keep out the cold* | 天～。*It is cold*.[寒噤]因受冷或受惊而发抖 to shiver from cold or fear [寒心] **1** 害怕,战栗 to be afraid; to be fearful **2** 灰心,痛心失望 to be bitterly disappointed [胆寒]害怕 to be terrified ❷穷困 poor:家里很贫～。*The family is poverty-stricken*. 谦辞 **humble**:～门 *my humble family* | ～舍 *my humble house*

罕 hǎn ㄏㄢˇ 稀少 rare(㊀ **doublet** 稀一rare):～见 *seldom seen* | ～闻 *rarely heard of* | ～物 *rare and valuable thing*

喊 hǎn ㄏㄢˇ 大声叫,呼 to shout; to call:～口号 *to shout slogans* | ～他一声 *to call him*

阚 ㊁ hǎn ㄏㄢˇ 虎叫声(of a tiger) roar

㊀ kàn 见384页 see p384

噉 hǎn ㄏㄢˇ 同"阚㊁"。(柳宗元文《黔之驴》用此字。)(used in Liu Zongyuan's essay *The Donkey of Qian*) same as 阚㊁

汉(漢) hàn ㄏㄢˋ ❶汉江,又称汉水,发源于陕西省南部,在湖北省武汉入长江(also called 汉水) Hanjiang River, rising in the south of Shaanxi Province and flowing into Changjiang River at Wuhan, Hubei Province [银汉]天河 Milky Way ❷朝代名 name of a dynasty **1** 汉高祖刘邦所建立(公元前 206—公元 220 年) Han Dynasty, founded by Liu Bang (206 BC – 220 AD) **2** 五代之一,刘知远所建立(公元 947—950 年),史称后汉 Later Han Dynasty (947 – 950), one of the Five Dynasties, founded by Liu Zhiyuan ❸(一子)男人,男子 man:老～ *old man* | 好～ *brave man* | 英雄～ *hero* ❹汉族,我国人数最多的民族 the Han ethnic group, the majority of the Chinese population [汉奸]出卖我们国家民族利益的败类 traitor to China

闬 hàn ㄏㄢˋ 〈古 **archaism**〉❶里巷门 gate to a lane ❷墙 wall

汗 ㊀ hàn ㄏㄢˋ 由身体的毛孔里排泄出来的液体 sweat; perspiration

㊁ hán 见263页 see p263

旱 hàn ㄏㄢˋ ❶长时间不下雨,缺雨,跟"涝"相对 (the opposite of 涝) drought: 防～ *to prevent drought* | 天～ *dry weather* ❷陆地,没有水的 land; dry land: ～路 *overland route* | ～田 *dry farmland* | ～稻 *dry rice; upland rice*

捍(*扞) hàn ㄏㄢˋ 保卫,抵御 to defend; to guard: ～卫祖国 *to safeguard one's motherland* | ～海堰(挡海潮的堤) *dike* [捍格]相抵触 to conflict; to contravene: ～～不入 *conflicting*

悍(*猂) hàn ㄏㄢˋ ❶勇敢 brave; bold: 强～ *intrepid; valiant* | 短小精～ (*of writing*) *short but effective; terse and forceful* ❷凶暴 fierce; ferocious (㊣ ***doublet*** 凶 — ferocious; fierce and tough): ～然不顾 *in gross defiance of*

焊(*銲、*釬) hàn ㄏㄢˋ 用熔化的金属或某些非金属把工件连接起来,或用熔化的金属修补金属器物 to weld; to solder: 电～ *electric welding* | 铜～ *brazing*

菡 hàn ㄏㄢˋ [菡萏](—dàn) 荷花的别称 another name for 荷花

颔 hàn ㄏㄢˋ ❶下巴颏 chin ❷点头 to nod: ～首 *to nod* | ～之而已 *to greet with a mere nod*

撖 hàn ㄏㄢˋ 姓 Han, a surname

撼 hàn ㄏㄢˋ 摇动 to shake: 震～天地 *to shake heaven and earth; to shake the world*

憾 hàn ㄏㄢˋ 悔恨,心中感到有所缺欠 to regret: ～事 *matter for regret* | 遗～ *regret*

翰 hàn ㄏㄢˋ 长而坚硬的羽毛,古代用来写字 (used as a writing brush in ancient China) quill ㊕ ***transfer*** **1** 毛笔 writing brush: ～墨 *writing, painting, or calligraphy* | 染～ *to dip a writing brush in Chinese ink* **2** 诗文,书信 writing; letter: 文～ *writing* | 华～ *your letter* | 书～ *writings and letters*

瀚 hàn ㄏㄢˋ 大 vast: 浩～(广大,众多) *vast*

HANG ㄏㄤ

夯(**硂) ㊀ hāng ㄏㄤ ❶砸地基的工具 ram ❷用夯砸 to ram: ～地 *to pound the earth*

㊁ bèn 见33页 see p33

行 ㊁ háng ㄏㄤˊ ❶行列,排 line; row: 单～ *single line; odd line* | 双～ *even row; double row* ❷职业 profession: 咱们是同～。*We are of the same profession.* [行家]精通某种事务的人 expert; specialist ❸某些营业性机构 business firm: 银～ *bank* | 车～ *car dealer's; bike dealer's* | 电料～ *electrical material and appliance firm* [行市](—shi)市场上商品的一般价格 quotation on the market ❹兄弟、姊妹长幼的次第 seniority among brothers and sisters: 排～ *seniority among brothers and sisters* | 您

～几？我～三。*Where do you come among your brothers and sisters? I'm the third.* ❺量词 ***quantifier***，用于成行的东西 (used for things in lines)：几～字 *a few lines of words*｜两～树 *two rows of trees*

㊀ xíng 见836页 see p836

绗 háng ㄏㄤˊ 做棉衣、棉褥等，粗粗缝，使布和棉花连在一起 to sew with long stitches

吭 ㊀ háng ㄏㄤˊ 喉咙，嗓子 throat：引～(拉长了嗓音)高歌 *to sing at the top of one's voice; to sing one's throat out*

㊁ kēng 见393页 see p393

迒 háng ㄏㄤˊ ❶野兽、车辆经过的痕迹 track ❷道路 path

杭 háng ㄏㄤˊ 杭州，地名，在浙江省 Hangzhou, a place in Zhejiang Province

航 háng ㄏㄤˊ 行船 to sail; to navigate：～海 *navigation* ㊀ ***extension*** 飞机等在空中飞行(of a plane, etc) to fly：～空 *aviation*

颃 háng ㄏㄤˊ 见829页"颉"字条"颉颃"(xié—) see 颉颃 on p829

沆 hàng ㄏㄤˋ 大水 vast expanse of water［沆瀣］(—xiè)夜间的水汽 night mist［沆瀣一气］㊉ ***figurative*** 气味相投的人勾结在一起 to wallow in the mire with sb; to act evilly in collusion with sb

巷 ㊁ hàng ㄏㄤˋ［巷道］采矿或探矿时挖的坑道(dug underground for mining or prospecting purposes) tunnel

㊀ xiàng 见821页 see p821

HAO ㄏㄠ

蒿 hāo ㄏㄠ 一类植物，种类很多，草本和灌木均有，用手揉时常有香味。有的可入药，如青蒿、茵陈蒿、艾等 wormwood

嚆 hāo ㄏㄠ 呼叫 to call; to shout［嚆矢］带响声的箭 whistling arrow ㊉ ***figurative*** 发生在先的事物，事物的开端 forerunner; beginning

薅 hāo ㄏㄠ 拔，除去 to pull; to get rid of：～草 *to pull up weeds; to weed*

号(號) ㊁ háo ㄏㄠˊ ❶大声呼喊 to howl; to yell(㊇ ***doublet*** 呼— to wail)［号叫］大声叫 to howl; to yell ❷大声哭 to wail：悲～ *to cry with sorrow*［号啕］［号咷］(—táo)大声哭喊 to cry loudly; to wail

㊀ hào 见268页 see p268

蚝(*蠔) háo ㄏㄠˊ 牡蛎(lì) oyster (*Ostrea*)：～油(用牡蛎肉制成的浓汁，供调味用) *oyster sauce*

毫 háo ㄏㄠˊ ❶长而尖细的毛 fine long hair：狼～笔 *writing brush made of weasel hair* ❷秤或戥子上的提绳 loop on a steelyard for hanging from the user's hand：头～ *the first loop*｜二～ *the second loop* ❸法定计量单位中十进分数单位词

头之一，表示 10^{-3}（符号 m）milli-(m) ❹计量单位名，10 丝是 1 毫，10 毫是 1 厘 *hao*, unit of measure, equal to 10 *si* and 0.1 *li* ❺〈方 **dialect**〉货币单位，角，毛 （unit of currency）*hao*, same as *jiao* or *mao* ❻数量极少，一点(used in the negative) in the least; at all: ～无诚意 *to have no sincerity at all* | ～不费力 *without the slightest effort*

嗥(*嘷) háo ㄏㄠˊ 野兽吼(hǒu)叫(of wild beasts) to howl: 虎啸熊～。*Tigers roar and bears howl.*

貉 ㊁ háo ㄏㄠˊ 同"貉㊀"，用于"貉子、貉绒"(used in 貉子 or 貉绒) same as 貉㊀

㊀ hé 见272页 see p272

豪 háo ㄏㄠˊ ❶具有杰出才能的人 person of extraordinary endowments (㊥ **doublet** —杰hero): 文～ *literary giant* | 英～ *hero; outstanding figure* [自豪]自己感到骄傲 proud: 我们以有这样的英勇战士而～～。*We are proud of such brave soldiers.* ❷气魄大，直爽痛快，没有拘束的 bold and unconstrained; forthright: ～放 *bold and unconstrained* | 性情～爽 *bold and uninhibited character* | ～迈的事业 *heroic cause; splendid undertaking* ❸强横的，有特殊势力的 despotic; rich and powerful: ～门 *rich and powerful family; rich and influential clan* | 土～劣绅 *local despots and evil gentry* | 巧取～夺 *to take away by force or trickery*

壕 háo ㄏㄠˊ 沟 trench: 战～ *trench*

嚎 háo ㄏㄠˊ 大声哭喊 to cry loudly; to wail [嚎啕][嚎咷]同"号啕" same as 号啕

濠 háo ㄏㄠˊ ❶护城河 moat ❷濠水，水名，在安徽省 Haoshui River, in Anhui Province

好 ㊀ hǎo ㄏㄠˇ ❶优点多的或使人满意的，跟"坏"相对(the opposite of 坏) good; nice: ～人 *good person* | ～汉 *brave person; hero* | ～马 *fine horse* | ～东西 *good thing* | ～事 *good deed; happy event* ㊊ **extension** 指生活幸福、身体健康或疾病消失 to get well: 您～哇！*How are you?* | 他的病完全～了。*He has completely recovered from his illness.* [好手]擅长某种技艺的人，能力强的人 expert; good hand; ace ❷友爱，和睦 friendly: 相～ *to be on intimate terms* | 我跟他～。*I'm on intimate terms with him.* | 友～ *friendly* ❸易于，便于 to be easy; to be convenient: 这件事情～办。*This can be easily done.* | 请你闪开点，我～过去。*Could you step aside for me, so I can get through?* ❹完，完成 to be ready: 我们的计划已经订～了。*Our plan has been made.* | 我穿～衣服就去。*I'll go as soon as I have my clothes on.* | 预备～了没有？*Are you ready?* ❺副

词 **adverb**，很，甚 very；quite：～冷 *so cold*｜～快 *so quick*｜～大的风。*What a strong wind!* [好不]副词 **adverb**，很 very：～～高兴 *very glad* ❻表示赞许、应允或结束等口气的词(used to express approval，agreement，ending，etc)：～，你真不愧是劳动英雄！*Well done，you deserve the title of a labour hero.*｜～，就照你的意见做吧！*Okay，let's do it according to your suggestion.*｜～，不要再讨论了！*All right，there's no need to discuss it any more!*

㊁ hào 见268页 see p268

郝 hǎo ㄏㄠˇ 姓 Hao，a surname

号(號) ㊀ hào ㄏㄠˋ ❶名称 name：国～ *title of a dynasty*｜别～ *alias*｜牌～ *name of a shop；trademark* ㊕ **transffer** 商店 shop；business house：本～ *this shop*｜分～ *branch of a firm* ❷记号，标志 mark；sign：暗～ *signal；secret signal*｜信～灯 *signal lamp*｜做记～ *to mark* ❸表示次第或等级(used to express order)：挂～ *to register*｜第一～ *number one*｜大～ *large size*｜中～ *medium size* [号码]代表事物次第的数目字 number [号外]报社报道重要消息临时印发的报纸(of edition) extra ❹指某种人(used to denote person of a given type)：病～ *patient*｜伤～ *the wounded* ❺量词 **quantifier**，用于人数(used for the number of people)：全队有几十～人。*There are dozens of people on the team.* ❻标上记号 to mark：把这件东西～上 *to make a mark on it* ❼号令，命令 order：发～施令 *to issue orders* [号召](—zhào)召唤(群众共同去做某一件事) to call (the masses to join forces to do sth)：坚决响应党的～～ *to respond to the Party's call resolutely* [口号]号召群众或表示纪念等的语句 slogan；watchword ❽军队或乐队里所用的西式喇叭 brass wind instrument：吹～ *to blow a bugle*｜～兵 *bugler；trumpeter* ❾用号吹出的表示一定意义的声音 bugle call：熄灯～ *lights-out bugle call；taps*｜冲锋～ *bugle call to charge*

㊁ háo 见266页 see p266

好 ㊁ hào ㄏㄠˋ 爱，喜欢 to love；to like(㊇ **doublet** 爱— to like；to be fond of)：～学 *to be fond of learning*｜～劳动 *to love labour*｜这孩子不～哭。*This child seldom cries.*

㊀ hǎo 见267页 see p267

昊 hào ㄏㄠˋ 广大的天 vast and boundless sky

滈 hào ㄏㄠˋ 水清 (of water) clear

耗 hào ㄏㄠˋ ❶减损，消费 to cost；to consume(㊇ **doublet** —费 to expend｜消— to consume)：消～品 *consumer goods*｜别～灯油了。*Stop wasting the lamp oil.* ❷拖延 to dawdle；to waste time：～时

间 *to waste time*｜别～着了，快去吧！*Stop dawdling and get going*. ❸音信，消息 news：噩(è)～(指亲近或敬爱的人死亡的消息)(*of the death of a person close or dear to one*) sad news

浩 hào ㄏㄠˋ 广大 vast(叠 ***reduplication***)(连 ***doublet*** 一大 very great; huge)：声势～大 *in great impetus*｜大队人马～～荡荡 *large contingents of troops*

皓(*皜、*暠) hào ㄏㄠˋ 洁白，明亮 white; bright：～齿 *white teeth*｜～首(白发，指老人) *hoary head; old man*｜～月当空 *bright moon hanging in the sky*

鄗 hào ㄏㄠˋ 古县名，在今河北省柏乡 Hao, an ancient county in today's Baixiang, Hebei Province

滈 hào ㄏㄠˋ 滈河，水名，在陕西省西安 Haohe River, in Xi'an, Shaanxi Province

镐 ㊀ hào ㄏㄠˋ 西周的国都，在今陕西省长安西北 Hao, capital of the Western Zhou Dynasty, in the northwest of today's Chang'an, Shaanxi Province

㊁ gǎo 见222页 see p222

皞 hào ㄏㄠˋ 明亮 bright

颢 hào ㄏㄠˋ 白的样子 white and shining

灏 hào ㄏㄠˋ 水势大(of the flow of water) great

HE ㄏㄜ

诃 hē ㄏㄜ 同"呵㊅❶" same as 呵㊅❶

［诃子］(—zǐ)常绿乔木，叶子、幼果(藏青果)、果实(诃子)、果核均可入药 chebulic myrobalan (*Terminalia chebula*)

呵 ㊅ hē ㄏㄜ ❶怒责 to scold (连 ***doublet*** 一斥 to scold sharply)：～禁 *to berate and ban* ❷呼气 to breathe out：～冻 *to breathe on one's hands to warm them*｜～气 *to breathe out* ［呵呵］拟声词 ***onomatopoeia***，笑声 sound of laughter; ha ha：笑～～ *to laugh heartily* ［呵护］爱护，保护 to take good care of ❸同"嗬"same as 嗬

㊀ ā 见1页 see p1

㊁ á 见1页 see p1

㊂ ǎ 见2页 see p2

㊃ à 见2页 see p2

㊄ a 见2页 see p2

喝(**欱) ㊀ hē ㄏㄜ 吸食液体饮料或流质食物，饮 to drink：～水 *to drink water*｜～酒 *to drink (alcohol)*｜～粥 *to have porridge*

㊁ hè 见273页 see p273

嗬 hē ㄏㄜ 叹词 ***interjection***，表示惊讶(used to express surprise) ah; oh：～，真不得了！*Ah, how terrible!*

蠚 hē ㄏㄜ 〈方 ***dialect***〉蜇(zhē)，刺 to sting

禾 hé ㄏㄜˊ ❶谷类植物的统称 general term for cereals

H

❷古代特指粟(谷子) especially millet in ancient China

和(❶❷❼*龢) ㊀ hé ㄏㄜˊ ❶相安,谐调 on good terms; harmonious: ～睦 *harmony* ㊁ ***extension*** 平静,不猛烈 calm; not severe: 温～ *mild* | 心平气～ *calm; in a placid mood* | 风～日暖 *with a gentle breeze and bright sun* [和平] **1** 没有战争的状态 peace: ～～环境 *peace time* **2** 温和,不猛烈 mild; not severe: 药性～～。*The medicine is mild.* [和气](－qi) 态度温和 gentle; kind: 他说话真～～。*He speaks so gently.* ❷平息争端 to settle a dispute: 讲～ *to make peace* | ～解 *to become reconciled* ❸数学上指两个或两个以上的数加起来的总数 sum: 2跟3的～是5。*2 and 3 is 5.* ❹连带 together with: ～盘托出(完全说出来) *to make a clean breast of everything* | ～衣而卧 *to sleep without undressing* ❺连词 ***conjunction***, 跟,同 and: 我～他都不同意。*Neither he nor I agree.* ❻介词 ***preposition***, 对,向 to: 你～孩子讲话要讲得通俗些。*When you speak to children, you should use simple words.* ❼姓 He, a surname

[和尚]佛教男性僧侣的通称 Buddhist monk

㊁ hè 见272页 see p272
㊂ huó 见303页 see p303
㊃ huò 见304页 see p304
㊄ hú 见282页 see p282

盉 hé ㄏㄜˊ 古代用来调和酒的器皿 *he*, vessel used to mix liquors in ancient China

合(❸閤) ㊀ hé ㄏㄜˊ ❶闭,对拢 to close; to shut: ～眼 *to close one's eyes* | ～抱 *to get one's arms around* | ～围(四面包围) *to surround* [合龙]修筑堤坝或桥梁时从两端施工,最后在中间接合 to close a dam [合口呼]u韵母和以u开头的韵母叫作"合口呼" the vowel u or a final beginning with u ❷聚,集 to join; to combine: ～力 *to join effort; to join forces* | ～办 *to operate (or run) jointly* | ～唱 *chorus* [合同]两方或多方为经营事业或在特定的工作中规定彼此权利和义务所订的共同遵守的条文 contract: 产销～～ *production and sales contract* [合作]同心协力做某事 to cooperate [合作社]根据互相合作的原则自愿建立起来的经济组织;按经营业务的不同,可以分为生产合作社、消费合作社、供销合作社、信用合作社等 cooperative ❸总共,全 total; whole: ～计 *total* | ～家 *whole (or entire) family* ❹不违背,一事物与另一事物相应或相符 to conform to; to suit: ～格 *qualified; up to the standard* | ～法 *legal; lawful; rightful* | ～理 *rational; reasonable; sensible* ㊁ ***extension*** 应该 ought to: 理～声明。*It is deemed appropriate to make a statement.* ❺计,折算 to be equal to; to add up to: 这件

衣服做成了～多少钱？*How much does it cost to make such a coat?*｜一米～多少市尺？*How many* chi *is a metre equal to?* or *How many* chi *are there in a metre?* ❻旧时乐谱记音符号的一个，相当于简谱中的低音"5̣" *he*, one of the notes of the scale in the ancient musical notation, corresponding to "5̣" in the numbered musical notation ❼姓 He, a surname

㊁ gě 见226页 see p226

"閤"又 gé 见224页"阁" (also gé) see 阁 on p224

郃 hé ㄏㄜˊ ［郃阳］地名，在陕西省。今作"合阳"（now written as 合阳）Heyang, a place in Shaanxi Province

饸 hé ㄏㄜˊ ［饸饹］(－le)一种条状食品，多用荞麦面轧(yà)成。有的地区叫"河漏"(also called 河漏 in some areas) *hele*, noodles made from buckwheat flour

盒 hé ㄏㄜˊ (－子、－儿)底盖相合的盛(chéng)东西的器物 box; case: 饭～儿 *lunch box*｜墨～儿 *ink box*

颌 ㊀ hé ㄏㄜˊ 构成口腔上部和下部的骨头和肌肉等组织叫作颌，上部的叫上颌，下部的叫下颌 jaw

㊁ gé 见224页 see p224

纥 ㊀ hé ㄏㄜˊ 见297页"回"字条"回纥" see 回纥 on p297

㊁ gē 见223页 see p223

龁 hé ㄏㄜˊ 咬 to bite

何 hé ㄏㄜˊ 代词 **pronoun**，表示疑问(used to express doubt) **1** 什么 what: ～人？*Who?*｜～事？*What?*｜为～？*Why?*｜有～困难？*What difficulty do you have?* **2** 为什么 why: ～不？*Why not?*｜～必如此。*Why act in this way?* **3** 怎样 how: ～如？*How about?*｜如～？*How about?* **4** 怎么 why; how: 他学习了好久，～至于一点进步也没有？*How can he make no progress at all after studying so long?* **5** 哪里 where: 欲～往？*Where are you going?*

〈古 ***archaism***〉又同"荷"(hè) also same as 荷

河 hé ㄏㄜˊ ❶水道的通称 river, general term for watercourse: 运～ *canal*｜淮～ *Huaihe River* ［河汉］银河，又叫"天河"。天空密布如带的星群 (also called 天河) Milky Way; galaxy ❷专指黄河，我国的第二大河，发源于青海省，流入渤海 Huanghe River (*or* Yellow River), the second longest river in China, rising in Qinghai Province and flowing into the Bohai Sea: ～西 *the west of the Huanghe River*｜～套 *the Great Bend of the Huanghe River*｜江淮～汉 *Changjiang-Huaihe Valley and Huanghe-Hanshui Valley*

荷 ㊀ hé ㄏㄜˊ 莲 lotus (*Nelumbo nucifera*)

㊁ hè 见273页 see p273

菏 hé ㄏㄜˊ ［菏泽］地名，在山东省 Heze, a place in

H

Shandong Province

劾 hé ㄏㄜˊ 揭发罪状 to expose sb's misdeeds or crimes(㊀ **doublet** 弹— to impeach)

阂 hé ㄏㄜˊ 阻隔不通 to cut off from：隔～ *estrangement; barrier*

核(❹*覈) ㊀ hé ㄏㄜˊ ❶果实中坚硬并包含果仁的部分 pit; stone ❷像核的东西 nucleus：菌～ *sclerotium*|细胞～ *cell nucleus* [核酸]存在于生物体中的有机化合物，是生命的基本物质之一，对生物的生长、遗传、变异等起决定作用 nucleic acid [核心]中心，主要部分 nucleus; core：领导～～ *core of leadership*|～～作用 *key role* [结核]传染病名，病原体是结核杆菌 tuberculosis ❸指原子核、核能、核武器等 atomic nucleus; nuclear energy; nuclear weapon：～潜艇 *nuclear-powered submarine*|～试验 *nuclear test*|～战争 *nuclear war* ❹仔细地对照、考察 to examine; to check：～算 *to assess*|～实 *to check*

㊁ hú 见283页 see p283

曷 hé ㄏㄜˊ 文言代词 **pronoun in classical Chinese**，表示疑问(used to express doubt) **1** 怎么 how **2** 何时 when

饸 ㊁ hé ㄏㄜˊ 馓子，一种油炸的面食 a kind of fried dough

㊀ ài 见5页 see p5

鹖 hé ㄏㄜˊ 古书上说的一种善斗的鸟 *he*, a kind of combative bird mentioned in ancient Chinese texts

鞨 hé ㄏㄜˊ 见515页"靺"字条"靺鞨"(mò—) see 靺鞨 on p515

盍(*盇) hé ㄏㄜˊ 何不 why not：～往观之？ *Why not go and have a look?*

阖 hé ㄏㄜˊ ❶全，总共 whole; total：～家 *whole family*|～城 *entire city* ❷关闭 to close; to shut：～户 *to close the door*|～口 *to shut one's mouth; to close the gap*

涸 hé ㄏㄜˊ 水干 dry up：～辙(水干了的车辙) *dry rut*

貉 ㊀ hé ㄏㄜˊ 野兽名。毛棕灰色，耳小，嘴尖，昼伏夜出，捕食虫类，皮很珍贵 raccoon dog (*Nyctereutes procyonoides*) [一丘之貉]㊀ **figurative** 彼此相似，没什么差别，指坏人 jackals of the same lair; (of bad people) much the same 〈古 **archaism**〉又同"貊"(mò) also same as 貊

㊁ háo 见267页 see p267

翮 hé ㄏㄜˊ ❶鸟翎的茎，翎管 quill; shaft of a feather ❷翅膀 wing：奋～高飞 *to flutter and soar high*

吓(嚇) ㊁ hè ㄏㄜˋ ❶恫吓，恐吓 to threaten; to intimidate ❷叹词 **interjection**，表示不满(used to express dissatisfaction) humph：～，怎么能这样呢！ *Humph, how could you do like that?*

㊀ xià 见810页 see p810

和 ㊁ hè ㄏㄜˋ 声音相应。特指依照别人所做诗词的题

材和体裁而写作 to join in the singing; to compose a poem in reply, using the same theme and rhyme scheme: ～诗 *to compose a poem in reply; a poem written in reply* | 唱～ *one singing a song and the others joining in the chorus; responsory*

㊀ hé 见270页 see p270

㊂ huó 见303页 see p303

㊃ huò 见304页 see p304

㊄ hú 见282页 see p282

贺 hè ㄏㄜˋ 庆祝，祝颂 to celebrate; to congratulate(㊟ ***doublet*** 庆一 to celebrate; to congratulate): ～年 *to extend New Year greetings* | ～喜 *to offer congratulations* | ～功 *to celebrate success* | ～电 *congratulatory telegram; message of congratulations*

荷 ㊁ hè ㄏㄜˋ ❶担，扛 to carry on one's shoulder: ～锄 *to carry a hoe on one's shoulder* [电荷]构成物质的许多基本粒子所带的电。有的带正电(如质子)，有的带负电(如电子)，习惯上也把物体所带的电叫电荷 electric charge; charge: 正～ *positive charge* | 负～ *negative charge* ❷承受恩惠(常用在书信里表示客气)(usually used in correspondence to express courtesy) grateful: 感～ *to feel sincerely grateful; to be thankful* | 为～ *to be appreciated*

㊀ hé 见271页 see p271

喝 ㊁ hè ㄏㄜˋ 大声喊叫 to shout loudly: ～令 *to shout a command* | 呼～ *to shout; to bawl* | 大～一声 *to give a loud cry; to shout loudly* [喝彩]大声叫好 to acclaim; to cheer

㊀ hē 见269页 see p269

褐 hè ㄏㄜˋ ❶粗布或粗布衣服 coarse cloth or clothing ❷黑黄色 dark brown

赫 hè ㄏㄜˋ ❶显明，盛大(叠 ***reduplication***) conspicuous; grand: 显～ *illustrious* | 声势～～ *to be powerful and influential* ❷频率单位名(符号Hz) hertz (Hz)

[赫哲族]我国少数民族，参看附表(see the appendix) the Hezhe ethnic group, one of the ethnic minorities of China

熇 hè ㄏㄜˋ [熇熇]烈火燃烧的样子(of blazing fire) flaming

翯 hè ㄏㄜˋ [翯翯]羽毛洁白润泽的样子(of feathers) shiningly white

鹤 hè ㄏㄜˋ 鸟名。有许多种，如丹顶鹤、白鹤、灰鹤、黑颈鹤等。颈、腿细长，翼大善飞，叫的声音很高，很清脆 crane (*Gruidae*)

壑 hè ㄏㄜˋ 山沟或大水坑 gully; big pool: 沟～ *gully; ravine* | 以邻为～ *to use neighbours' land as a drain; to shift one's troubles onto others*

HEI ㄏㄟ

黑 hēi ㄏㄟ ❶煤或墨那样的颜色，跟"白"相对(the opposite of 白) black: ～布 *black*

H

cloth｜～头发 *black hair* ❷暗，光线不充足 dark：天～了。*It's getting dark.*｜那间屋子太～。*That room is too dark.* ❸秘密的，隐蔽的 secret；shady：～话 *cant*｜～市 *black market* ❹恶毒 wicked；vicious：～心 *wicked heart；evil mind*

［黑客］（外 loanword）hacker **1** 精通电子计算机技术，善于发现网络系统缺陷的人 expert at programming and solving problems with a computer **2** 通过互联网非法侵入他人电子计算机系统进行破坏活动的人 person who illegally gains access to a computer system and tampers with information and the computer programme

嘿 ㊀ hēi ㄏㄟ 叹词 ***interjection*** **1** 表示惊异或赞叹（used to express surprise or acclamation）hey；why：～，这个真好！*Hey! How nice it is!*｜～，你倒有理啦！*Why, you think you are right!* **2** 表示招呼或提醒注意（used to greet or call attention）hey；why：～，老张，快走吧！*Hey, Old Zhang, hurry up!*｜～，你小心点，别滑倒！*Hey, mind your step. It's slippery.*

［嘿嘿］拟声词 ***onomatopoeia***，多指冷笑（usually used to denote sneering）ha ha

㊁ mò 见516页 see p516

镙 hēi ㄏㄟ 一种人造的放射性元素（符号 Hs）hassium (Hs)

嗨 ㊀ hēi ㄏㄟ 同"嘿㊀"same as 嘿㊀

㊁ hāi 见261页 see p261

HEN ㄏㄣ

痕 hén ㄏㄣˊ 痕迹，事物留下的印迹 mark；trace：水～ *water stain*｜泪～ *tear stain*｜伤～ *bruise；scar*

很 hěn ㄏㄣˇ 副词 ***adverb***，非常，表示程度高 very；very much：～好 *very good*｜好得～ *great；very good*

狠 hěn ㄏㄣˇ ❶凶恶，残忍 ruthless；relentless：心～ *cruel；merciless*｜～毒 *vicious；wicked* ㊕ ***transfer*** 勉强地抑制住难过的心情 to suppress one's sorrowful feelings；to make a painful effort：～着心送走了孩子 *to harden one's heart and send the child off* ❷严厉地（叠 ***reduplication***）severely；sternly：～～地打击敌人 *to deal the enemy a heavy blow*［狠命］拼命，用尽全力 to go all out：～～地跑 *to run for all one's worth* ❸全力 with full energy or strength：～抓科学研究 *to make great efforts to do scientific research* ❹同"很"same as 很

恨 hèn ㄏㄣˋ ❶怨，仇视 to hate；to resent（㊐ ***doublet*** 怨— to resent）：～入骨髓 *to hate sb to the marrow of one's bones — to hate intensely* ❷懊悔，令人懊悔或怨恨的事 regret；remorse：悔～ *remorse*｜遗～ *eternal regret；lasting remorse*

HENG ㄏㄥ

亨 hēng ㄏㄥ ❶通达,顺利 to go smoothly(㊟ ***doublet*** —通 to go smoothly):万事～通。*Everything is going smoothly.* ❷电感单位名亨利的简称 *short for* 亨利(符号 H),henry (H)

〈古 ***archaism***〉又同"烹"(pēng) also same as 烹

哼 ㊀ hēng ㄏㄥ ❶鼻子发出痛苦的声音 to groan:他病很重,却从不～一声。*He never groans though he is seriously ill.* ❷轻声随口地唱 to hum; to croon:他一面走一面～着歌。*He was humming a song as he walked along.*

㊁ hng 见276页 see p276

脝 hēng ㄏㄥ 见558页"膨"字条"膨脝"(péng—) see 膨脝 on p558

啈 hēng ㄏㄥ 叹词 ***interjection***,表示禁止的意思(used to express prohibition)

恒(*恆) héng ㄏㄥˊ ❶持久 lasting:～心 *perseverance* ❷经常的,普通的 usual; common:～言 *common saying*

姮 héng ㄏㄥˊ [姮娥]嫦娥 Heng'e, another name for Chang'e, the goddess of the moon

珩 héng ㄏㄥˊ 佩玉上面的横玉 top gem of a girdlependant

桁 héng ㄏㄥˊ 就是檩(i. e. 檩) purlin

鸻 héng ㄏㄥˊ 鸟名。种类很多,身体小,嘴短而直,只有前趾,没有后趾。多群居在海滨 plover (*Charadriidae*)

衡 héng ㄏㄥˊ ❶称东西轻重的器具 weighing apparatus ❷称量 to weigh:～其轻重 *to weigh; to measure* [衡量]**1** 称轻重 to weigh **2** 评定高低好坏 to measure; to judge:测验只是～～学习成绩的一种办法。*Testing is only one way of measuring one's learning.* ❸平,不倾斜 level; even:平～ *balance*|均～ *equilibrium* ❹古同"横" same as 横 in ancient Chinese

蘅 héng ㄏㄥˊ [杜蘅]多年生草本植物,开暗紫色的花。全草可入药。现作"杜衡"(now written as 杜衡) wild ginger (*Asarum forbesii*)

横 ㊀ héng ㄏㄥˊ ❶跟地面平行的,跟"竖"、"直"相对(the opposite of 竖 or 直) horizontal:～额 *horizontal inscribed board*|～梁 *crossbeam* ❷地理上指东西向的,跟"纵"相对(the opposite of 纵) in geography from east to west or from west to east:～渡太平洋 *to cross the Pacific* ❸从左到右或从右到左的,跟"竖"、"直"、"纵"相对(the opposite of 竖, 直 or 纵) from left to right or from right to left:～写 *to write sideways* ❹跟物体的长的一边垂直的,跟"竖"、"直"、

"纵"相对(the opposite of 竖，直 or 纵) at a right angle to the longer side of sth：～剖面 *cross-section* | 人行～道 *pedestrian crossing；zebra crossing* ❺使物体成横向 to place sth crosswise or horizontally：把扁担～过来。*Put the carrying pole crosswise.* ❻纵横杂乱 unrestrained；turbulent：蔓草～生 *overgrown with creepers* ❼不合情理的 unreasonably；willfully：～加阻拦 *to obstruct willfully* ❽汉字由左到右的笔形(一) horizontal stroke in a Chinese character (一)："王"字是三～一竖。王 *has three horizontal strokes and a vertical one.* [横竖]副词 **adverb**，反正，无论如何 in any case；anyway：～～我也要去。*I will go there anyway.*

㊁ hèng 见276页 see p276

横 ㊁ hèng ㄏㄥˋ ❶凶暴，不讲理 harsh and unreasonable (㊣ **doublet** 蛮— rude and unreasonable)：这个人说话很～。*This person speaks very harshly.* ❷意外的 unexpected：～财 *windfall；ill-gotten wealth* | ～事 *untoward accident；unlucky happening* | ～死 *to die a violent (or unnatural) death*

㊀ héng 见275页 see p275

HM ㄏㄇ

噷 hm ㄏㄇ 〔h 跟单纯的双唇鼻音拼合的音〕叹词 **interjection**，表示申斥或禁止 (used to express disapproval or reproach) humph：～，你还闹哇！*Humph，you are still making a scene!* | ～，你骗得了我！*Humph，how can you cheat me?*

HNG ㄏㄫ

哼 ㊁ hng ㄏㄫ 〔h 跟单纯的舌根鼻音拼合的音〕叹词 **interjection**，表示不满意或不信任 (used to express dissatisfaction or disbelief) humph：～，你信他的！*Humph! How can you believe him?*

㊀ hēng 见275页 see p275

HONG ㄏㄨㄥ

吽 hōng ㄏㄨㄥ 佛教咒语用字 hum，word used in Buddhist incantation

轰(轟、❸**揈) hōng ㄏㄨㄥ ❶拟声词 **onomatopoeia**，指雷鸣、炮击等发出的巨大声音 (of thunder or bombardment) bang；boom [轰动]同时引起许多人的注意 to cause a sensation：～～全国 *to make a sensation throughout the country* [轰轰烈烈]形容气魄雄伟，声势浩大 with vigour and vitality；on a grand and spectacular scale：职工们展开了～～～～的劳动竞赛。*The workers have launched a vigorous labour emulation.* ❷用大炮或炸弹破坏 to bombard (㊣ **doublet** —击 to shell)：～炸

to bomb | 炮～ *to bombard* ❸驱逐，赶走 to drive off; to shoo away：把猫～出去 *to shoo away the cat*

哄 ㊀ hōng ㄏㄨㄥ 好多人同时发声 to make hubbub or din：～传(chuán) *to circulate widely* | ～堂大笑 *with the whole room rocking with laughter*

㊁ hǒng 见278页 see p278

㊂ hòng 见278页 see p278

烘 hōng ㄏㄨㄥ 用火烤干或靠近火取暖 to dry or warm by the fire：衣裳湿了，～一～。*The clothes are wet. Dry them by the fire.* [烘托]用某种颜色衬托另外的颜色，或用某种事物衬托另外的事物，使在对比下，表现得更明显 to throw into sharp relief

訇 hōng ㄏㄨㄥ 形容声响很大 loud noise：～然 *with a loud noise* | ～的一声 *with a loud crash*

[阿訇]伊斯兰教主持教仪、讲授经典的人 imam

薨 hōng ㄏㄨㄥ 古代称诸侯或有爵位的大官的死(of dukes or high officials with titles of nobility in ancient China) to die; to pass away

弘 hóng ㄏㄨㄥˊ ❶大 great; grand：～愿 *great aspirations* ❷扩充，光大 to enlarge; to expand：恢～ *broad*

泓 hóng ㄏㄨㄥˊ 水深而广(of water) deep and broad

红 ㊀ hóng ㄏㄨㄥˊ ❶像鲜血那样的颜色 red [转] ***transfer*** **1** 喜庆 joyous：办～事 *to celebrate a happy event* **2** 革命的，觉悟高的 revolutionary; having a high level of political consciousness：～军 *Red Army* | ～色政权 *red political power* | 又～又专 *to be both red and expert; to be both politically conscious and professionally competent* **3** 象征顺利、成功 symbol of smoothness or success：开门～ *to make a good start; to get off to a good start* ❷指人受宠信 to find favour with sb：～人 *a favourite of sb in power* ❸红利 bonus; dividend：分～ *to draw dividends* ❹姓 Hong, a surname

㊁ gōng 见231页 see p231

荭 hóng ㄏㄨㄥˊ 荭草，一种供观赏的草本植物 prince's feather (*Amaranthus hypochondriacus*)

虹 ㊀ hóng ㄏㄨㄥˊ 雨后天空中出现的彩色圆弧，有红、橙、黄、绿、蓝、靛、紫七种颜色。是由大气中的小水珠经日光照射发生折射和反射作用而形成的。这种圆弧常出现两个，红色在外，紫色在内，颜色鲜艳的叫"虹"，也叫"正虹"；红色在内，紫色在外，颜色较淡的叫"霓"，也叫"副虹"rainbow

㊁ jiàng 见336页 see p336

鸿 hóng ㄏㄨㄥˊ ❶鸿雁，就是大雁(i. e. 大雁) swan goose (*Anser cygnoides*) [鸿毛] goose feather [喻] ***figurative*** 轻微 very light; insignificant：轻于～～ *to be lighter than a goose feather — to be entirely*

H

of no significance ❷大 great; grand:～儒 *erudite scholar* [鸿沟]楚汉(项羽和刘邦)分界的一条水 Honggou, a river that served as a boundary between the Chu and the Han armies headed by Xiang Yu and Liu Bang respectively during the Qin Dynasty ⊛ ***figurative*** 明显的界限 wide gap; chasm

闳 hóng ㄏㄨㄥˊ ❶里巷门 gate of a lane ❷宏大 great; grand

宏 hóng ㄏㄨㄥˊ 广大 broad; grand:～伟 *magnificent* | 气量宽～ *broad-minded* | 规模～大 *on a grand scale*

纮 hóng ㄏㄨㄥˊ 古代帽子(冠冕)上的系带 (in ancient China) lace on a hat

竑 hóng ㄏㄨㄥˊ 广大 broad

洪 hóng ㄏㄨㄥˊ ❶大 big; vast:～水 *flood* ❷大水 flood:山～ *mountain torrents* | ～峰 *flood peak; crest of a flood* | 溢～道 *spillway*

葓 hóng ㄏㄨㄥˊ 同"荭"(hóng) same as 荭

蕻 ㊁ hóng ㄏㄨㄥˊ [雪里蕻]一种像芥菜的菜,茎叶可以吃。也作"雪里红"(also written as 雪里红) potherb mustard (*Brassica juncea*)

㊀ hòng 见278页 see p278

黉(黌) hóng ㄏㄨㄥˊ 古代称学校 (in ancient China) school

哄 ㊁ hǒng ㄏㄨㄥˇ ❶说假话骗人 to fool(⊜ ***doublet*** 一骗 to cheat):你不要～我。*Don't try to fool me.* ❷用语言或行动使人欢喜 to coax:他很会～小孩儿。*He knows well how to handle children.*

㊀ hōng 见277页 see p277

㊂ hòng 见278页 see p278

讧 hòng ㄏㄨㄥˋ 乱,溃败 chaos; being utterly defeated:内～ *internal strife*

澒 hòng ㄏㄨㄥˋ [澒洞]弥漫无际 endlessly pervasive

哄(*閧) ㊂ hòng ㄏㄨㄥˋ 吵闹,搅扰 uproar; disturbance:一～而散 *to break up in an uproar* | 起～(故意吵闹扰乱) *to create a disturbance*

㊀ hōng 见277页 see p277

㊁ hǒng 见278页 see p278

蕻 ㊀ hòng ㄏㄨㄥˋ ❶茂盛 luxuriant ❷〈方 ***dialect***〉某些蔬菜的长茎 long stem of certain vegetables:菜～ *vegetable stems*

㊁ hóng 见278页 see p278

HOU ㄏㄡ

齁 hōu ㄏㄡ ❶鼻息声 snore ❷很,非常(多表示不满意) (usually used to express dissatisfaction) awfully; too:～咸 *awfully salty* | ～冷 *awfully cold* | ～麻烦的 *quite troublesome* ❸太甜或太咸的食物使喉咙不舒服 sickeningly sweet or salty:糖吃多了～人。*Too much sugar will make people sick.*

侯 ㊀ hóu ㄏㄡˊ ❶我国古代五等爵位(公、侯、伯、子、男)的第二等 marquis, the second of the five ranks of nobility (公,侯,伯,子 and 男) in ancient China: 封～ *to confer a title of nobility* ❷泛指达官贵人(in a broad sense) nobleman or high official: ～门 *noble family* ❸姓 Hou, a surname

㊁ hòu 见280页 see p280

喉 hóu ㄏㄡˊ 喉头,颈的前部和气管相通的部分,通常把咽喉混称"嗓子"或"喉咙"。larynx; throat(图见940页"脏"picture on p940)[白喉]一种急性传染病,病原体是白喉杆菌。症状是发热,喉痛,并生一层白色假膜 diphtheria

猴 hóu ㄏㄡˊ (一子、一儿)哺乳动物,种类很多。毛灰色或褐色,颜面和耳朵无毛,有尾巴,两颊有储存食物的颊囊 monkey (*Cercopithecoidea*)

瘊 hóu ㄏㄡˊ (一子)皮肤上长的无痛痒的小疙瘩 wart

篌 hóu ㄏㄡˊ 见394页"箜"字条"箜篌"(kōng—) see 箜篌 on p394

糇(*餱) hóu ㄏㄡˊ 〈古 ***archaism***〉干粮 solid food: ～粮 *solid food*

骺 hóu ㄏㄡˊ 骨骺,长形骨的两端 epiphysis

吼 hǒu ㄏㄡˇ 兽大声叫(of an animal) to roar; to howl: 牛～ *roar of an ox* | 狮子～ *roar of a lion* 也指人因愤怒而呼喊 (of angry people) to shout; to roar: 怒～ *to roar with rage*

后(❸❹後) hòu ㄏㄡˋ ❶上古称君王(in ancient China) monarch; sovereign: 商之先～(先王) *king of the Shang Dynasty* ❷皇后,帝王的妻子 queen; empress ❸跟"前"相对(the opposite of 前) **1** 指空间,在背面的,在反面的(of space) behind; back: ～门 *back door* | 村～ *behind the village* **2** 指时间,晚,未到的(of time) after; afterwards; later: ～天 *the day after tomorrow* | 日～ *in the future* | 先来～到 *in the order of arrival* **3** 指次序靠末尾的 (of order) last: ～排 *back row* | ～十名 *the last ten persons* [后备]准备以后使用的 reserve: ～～军 *reserves; reserve force* ❹后代,子孙 offspring: ～嗣 *descendants*

郈 hòu ㄏㄡˋ 姓 Hou, a surname

茩 hòu ㄏㄡˋ 见831页"薢"字条"薢茩"(xiè—) see 薢茩 on p831

垕 hòu ㄏㄡˋ [神垕]地名,在河南省禹州 Shenhou, a place in Yuzhou, Henan Province

逅 hòu ㄏㄡˋ 见831页"邂"字条"邂逅"(xiè—) see 邂逅 on p831

厚 hòu ㄏㄡˋ ❶扁平物体上下两个面的距离 thickness: 长宽～ *length, width and thickness* | 五厘米～的木板

plank 5cm thick | 下了三厘米～的雪。*The snow is 3cm deep.* ❷扁平物体上下两个面的距离较大的，跟“薄”相对（the opposite of 薄）thick：～纸 *thick paper* | ～棉袄 *heavy cotton-padded coat* ❸深，重，浓，大 deep; strong; large：～望 *high hopes; great expectations* | ～礼 *generous* (or *substantial*) *gifts* | ～情 *deep feeling* (or *affection*) | ～味 *strong flavour* | 深～的友谊 *profound friendship* ❹不刻薄（bó），待人好 kind; magnanimous：～道 *honest and kind* | 忠～ *honest and tolerant; sincere and kindhearted* ❺重视，注重 to favour; to stress：～今薄古 *to stress the present rather than the past* | ～此薄彼 *to favour one and discriminate against the other*

侯 ㊁ hòu ㄏㄡˋ ［闽侯］地名，在福建省 Minhou, a place in Fujian Province

㊀ hóu 见279页 see p279

候 hòu ㄏㄡˋ ❶等待 to wait（㊌ ***doublet*** 等— to wait）：～车室 *waiting room* | 你先在这儿～一～，他就来。*Please wait a moment. He'll be right here.* ❷看望 to visit; to see ㊟ ***transfer*** 问候，问好 to inquire after ❸观察，守候 to watch; to watch over［候人］古代称哨兵。也省称“候”（in ancient times, the term, or its short form 候，used for）sentry; guard ❹时节 time; season：时～ *time* | 气～ *climate* | 季～风 *monsoon* ［候鸟］随气候变化而迁移的鸟，像大雁、家燕都是 migratory bird ❺事物在变化中间的情状（of sth changing）state; condition：症～ *symptom* | 火～ *duration and degree of heating, cooking, smelting, etc; crucial moment*

堠 hòu ㄏㄡˋ 古代瞭望敌情的土堡（in ancient China）earthen watchtower for overseeing an enemy's situation

鲎（鱟） hòu ㄏㄡˋ ❶俗叫“鲎鱼”。节肢动物，生活在海中，全体黄褐色，剑状尾。肉可以吃（popularly called 鲎鱼）king crab ❷〈方 ***dialect***〉虹 rainbow

HU ㄏㄨ

乎 hū ㄏㄨ ❶文言助词 ***auxiliary in classical Chinese***，表示疑问、感叹等语气（used to express doubt, exclamation, etc）**1** 同白话的“吗”same as 吗 in the vernacular：天雨～？*Is it raining?* **2** 同白话的“呢”，表选择答复的疑问（used in an alternative）same as 呢 in the vernacular：然～？否～？*Yes or no?* or *Is it right or not?* **3** 同白话的“吧”，表推测和疑问（used to express supposition and doubt）same as 吧 in the vernacular：日食饮得无衰～？*Do you still have a good appetite?* **4** 同白话的“啊”same as 啊 in the vernacular：天～！*My* *heavens!* ❷于(放在动词或形容词后)(suffix of a verb or an adjective):异～寻常 *to be out of the ordinary*|合～情理 *to be reasonable*|不在～好看,在～实用。*Its worth lies not in the beautiful appearance but in the utilization.*

呼(*嘑) hū ㄏㄨ ❶喊 to shout; to cry out:高～万岁! *to shout 'Long live'!*|欢～ *to hail; to cheer* ❷唤,叫 to call:～之即来 *to be ready to come at one's beck and call*|～应(yìng)(彼此声气相通,互相照应) to echo; to work in concert with [呼声]代表群众希望和要求的言论 opinions and requirements of the masses [呼吁](－yù)大声疾呼地提出要求 to appeal; to call on ❸往外出气,跟"吸"相对(the opposite of 吸) to breathe out; to exhale:～吸机 *respirator* ❹拟声词(叠 ***redu-plication***) ***onomatopoeia***:风～～地吹。*The wind is whistling.*

轷 hū ㄏㄨ 姓 Hu, a surname

烀 hū ㄏㄨ 半蒸半煮,把食物弄熟 to stew-steam in shallow water:～白薯 *to stew-steam sweet potatoes*

滹 hū ㄏㄨ [滹沱河]水名,从山西省流入河北省 Hutuo River, flowing from Shanxi Province into Hebei Province

戏(戲、*戱) ㊁ hū ㄏㄨ 见793页"於"字条"於戏"(wū－) see 於戏 on p793

㊀ xì 见806页 see p806

昒 hū ㄏㄨ [昒昕](－xīn)[昒爽]天快亮的时候 time before dawn

曶 hū ㄏㄨ ❶疾速,转眼之间 rapidly; in a flash ❷古人名 *Hu*, name of an ancient person:～鼎(西周中期青铜器,作者名曶) *huding*, a bronzeware in the middle period of the Western Zhou Dynasty, made by a man named Hu

忽 hū ㄏㄨ ❶粗心,不注意 careless:～略 *to neglect; to overlook*|～视 *to ignore*|疏～ *carelessness* ❷副词 ***adverb***,忽然,突然地 suddenly:工作情绪不要～高～低。*Stabilize your working enthusiasm and prevent it from rising and falling frequently.* ❸计量单位名,10忽是1丝,10丝是1毫 *hu*, unit of measurement (10 *hu* is equal to 1 *si* and 10 *si* to 1 *hao*)

唿 hū ㄏㄨ [唿哨]同"呼哨"。参看661页"哨"字条"呼哨"same as 呼哨, see 呼哨 on p661

淴 hū ㄏㄨ [淴浴]〈方 ***dia-lect***〉洗澡 to bathe; to take a bath

惚 hū ㄏㄨ 见295页"恍"字条"恍惚"(huǎng－) see 恍惚 on p295

糊 ㊂ hū ㄏㄨ 涂抹或粘合使封闭起来 to plaster:用泥把墙缝～上 *to plaster up the*

cracks in the wall

㊀ hú 见283页 see p283

㊁ hù 见285页 see p285

囫 hú ㄏㄨˊ ［囫囵］（－lún）整个的，完整 whole：～～吞枣（喻不加分析地笼统接受）*to swallow a date whole — to lap up information without digesting it*

和 ㊄ hú ㄏㄨˊ 打麻将或斗纸牌用语，表示赢了（used in a game of mahjong or cards）to win

㊀ hé 见270页 see p270

㊁ hè 见272页 see p272

㊂ huó 见303页 see p303

㊃ huò 见304页 see p304

狐 hú ㄏㄨˊ 狐狸，野兽名。性狡猾多疑，遇见敌人时肛门放出臭气，乘机逃跑 fox（*Vulpes*）［狐媚］曲意逢迎，投人所好 to entice by flattery［狐肷］（－qiǎn）毛皮业上指狐狸腋下和腹部的毛皮 furs of a fox's chest, belly and armpits［狐疑］多疑 to show discredit

弧 hú ㄏㄨˊ ❶木弓 bow ❷圆周的一段 arc：～形 *arc*｜～线 *arc; curved line*

胡（❹鬍、❻*衚） hú ㄏㄨˊ ❶我国古代称北方和西方的少数民族（in ancient China）Hu, the ethnic minorities living in the north and west：～人 *member of a northern or western tribe in ancient China*｜～服 *Hu dress* 泛指外国或外族的（in a broad sense）from abroad or other ethnic groups：～椒 *pepper*［胡萝卜］（－luóbo）草本植物。根也叫胡萝卜，长圆锥形，肉质，有紫红、橘红等多种，是一种蔬菜 carrot（*Daucus carota*）［胡琴］（－qin）弦乐器，在竹弓上系马尾毛，放在两弦之间拉动发声 *huqin*, two stringed fiddle-like instrument ❷乱，无道理 recklessly; outrageously：～来 *to act recklessly*｜～闹 *to be mischievous; to make trouble*｜～说 *nonsense*｜说～话 *to talk nonsense* ❸文言代词 ***pronoun in classical Chinese***，表示疑问，为什么 why：～不归？*Why not return?* ❹（－子）胡须 beard; moustache; whiskers ❺古指兽类颔间下垂的肉（in ancient China）animal's flesh drooping from the chin ❻［胡同］（－tòng）巷 *hutong*; lane; alley

葫 hú ㄏㄨˊ ［葫芦］（－lu）一年生草本植物，爬蔓，夏天开白花。果实中间细，像大小两个球连在一起，可以做器皿或供观赏。还有一种瓢葫芦，也叫"匏"（páo），果实梨形，对半剖开，可做舀水的瓢 bottle gourd; calabash（*Lagenaria siceraria*）

猢 hú ㄏㄨˊ ［猢狲］（－sūn）猴的俗称。参看279页"猴"（see 猴 on p279）popular name for 猴

湖 hú ㄏㄨˊ 陆地上聚积的大水 lake：洞庭～ *Dongting Lake*｜太～ *Taihu Lake*［湖色］淡绿色 light green

瑚 hú ㄏㄨˊ 见652页"珊"字条"珊瑚"(shān—) see 珊瑚 on p652

煳 hú ㄏㄨˊ 烧得焦黑 burnt black:馒头烤~了。*The* mantuo *is charred*.

鹕 hú ㄏㄨˊ 见739页"鹈"字条"鹈鹕"(tí—) see 鹈鹕 on p739

蝴 hú ㄏㄨˊ [蝴蝶]见151页"蝶"(dié) (see 蝶 on p151) butterfly

糊(❷*餬) ㊀ hú ㄏㄨˊ ❶ 黏合,粘贴 to paste:拿纸~窗户 *to paste a sheet of paper over a window* | 裱(biǎo)~ *to paper* [糊涂](—tu)不清楚,不明事理 muddled; confused; bewildered ❷ 粥类 porridge [糊口]旧指勉强维持生活(in former times) to keep body and soul together; to eke out a living ❸ 同"煳" same as 煳

㊁ hù 见285页 see p285

㊂ hū 见281页 see p281

醐 hú ㄏㄨˊ 见740页"醍"字条"醍醐"(tí—) see 醍醐 on p740

壶(壺) hú ㄏㄨˊ 一种有把儿有嘴的容器,通常用来盛茶、酒等液体 kettle; pot:酒~ *wine pot* | 茶~ *teapot*

核 ㊁ hú ㄏㄨˊ (—儿)义同"核㊀❶❷",用于某些口语词,如杏核儿、煤核儿等 same as 核㊀❶❷ in meaning, used in certain colloquial collocations, such as 杏核儿,煤核儿, etc

㊀ hé 见272页 see p272

斛 hú ㄏㄨˊ 量器名。古时以十斗为斛,后来又以五斗为斛 *hu*, a measure used in ancient China with a capacity equal to 10 *dou*, and later to 5 *dou*

槲 hú ㄏㄨˊ 落叶乔木或灌木,花黄褐色,果实球形。叶子可以喂柞蚕,树皮可做染料,果壳可入药。木材坚实,可供建筑或制器具用 daimyo oak (*Quercus dentata*)

鹄 ㊀ hú ㄏㄨˊ 鸟名,也叫"天鹅",形状像鹅而较大,羽毛白色,飞得高而快,生活在海滨或湖边(also called 天鹅) swan (*Cygnus*):~立(静静地站着等候) *to stand and wait in silence*

㊁ gǔ 见242页 see p242

鹘 ㊀ hú ㄏㄨˊ 隼(sǔn) falcon (*Falconidae*)

㊁ gǔ 见241页 see p241

縠 hú ㄏㄨˊ 有皱纹的纱 crepe

觳 hú ㄏㄨˊ [觳觫](—sù)恐惧得发抖 to tremble with fear

虎 hǔ ㄏㄨˇ ❶ 老虎,野兽名。毛黄褐色,有条纹。性凶猛,能吃人和兽类 tiger (*Panthera tigris*) ㊗ *figurative* 威武,勇猛 brave; powerful:一员~将 *a valiant general* [虎口] **1** ㊗ *figurative* 危险境地 the jaws of death:~~余生 *to escape from a tiger's mouth — to have a narrow escape* **2** 手上拇

H

指和食指相交的地方 part of the hand between the thumb and the index finger ❷同"唬" same as 唬

唬 ㊀ hǔ ㄏㄨˇ 威吓(hè)或蒙混 to bluff：你别～人了。*Stop bluffing.*

㊁ xià 见810页 see p810

琥 hǔ ㄏㄨˇ［琥珀］(—pò)黄褐色透明体，是古代松柏树脂落入地下所成的化石。可做香料及装饰品 amber

浒 ㊀ hǔ ㄏㄨˇ 水边 waterside

㊁ xǔ 见845页 see p845

互 hù ㄏㄨˋ 互相，彼此 mutual; each other：～助 *to help each other*｜～致问候 *to extend greetings to each other*｜～为因果 *to interact as both cause and effect*［互动］彼此影响，互相推动 to interact：～～教学 *interactive teaching*｜实现企业和消费者之间的良性～～ *to realize a good interaction between enterprises and consumers*［互联网］由若干个计算机网络相互连接而成的网络 internet［互生］植物每节长出一个叶子，相间地各生在一边，叫"互生"alternate phyllotaxy

冱(**沍) hù ㄏㄨˋ 寒冷凝结 to freeze

枑 hù ㄏㄨˋ 见39页"梐"字条"梐枑"(bì—) see 梐枑 on p39

户 hù ㄏㄨˋ ❶一扇门 door [引] *extension* 门 door：夜不闭～。*Doors are not bolted at night.* ❷人家 family; household：千家万～ *thousands upon thousands of families*［户口］住户和人口 households and residents：报～～ *to register (or apply for) one's residence*｜～～簿 *household registration booklet* ❸门第 family status：门当～对 *to be well-matched in social and economic status* ❹户头 account：开～ *to open an account*｜账～ *account*

护(**護**) hù ㄏㄨˋ 保卫 to protect; to guard ([连] ***doublet*** 保— to protect)：爱～ *to take good care of*｜～路 *to patrol and guard a road* (or *railway*) [引] ***extension*** 袒护，包庇 to shield; to be partial to：～短 *to hide a shortcoming or fault*｜不要一味地～着他。*Don't be always partial to him.*［护士］医院里担任护理工作的人员 nurse［护照］**1** 外交主管机关发给本国公民进入另一国停留时用以证明身份的执照 passport **2** 旧时旅行或运货时所带的政府机关证明文件 certificate issued by a government agency for a trip or goods transport in former times

沪(**滬**) hù ㄏㄨˋ ❶沪渎，松江的下流，在今上海 Hudu, the lower reaches of the Songjiang River in today's Shanghai ❷上海的别称 *Hu*, another name for Shanghai：～剧 *Shanghai opera*｜～杭铁路 *Shanghai-Hangzhou Railway*

戽 hù ㄏㄨˋ ❶戽斗，灌田汲水用的旧式农具 bailing bucket, old farm tool for bailing water to irrigate fields ❷ 用戽斗汲水 to bail

扈 hù ㄏㄨˋ 随从 retinue (㊈ *doublet* 一从 retinue)

岵 hù ㄏㄨˋ 多草木的山 mountain covered with vegetation

怙 hù ㄏㄨˋ 依靠,仗恃 to rely on:～恶不悛(quān)(坚持作恶,不肯悔改) *to persist in evil-doings and not repent*

祜 hù ㄏㄨˋ 福 blessing; bliss

糊 ㊂ hù ㄏㄨˋ 像粥一样的食物 paste: 辣椒～ *chilli paste* [糊弄](—nong) **1** 敷衍,不认真做 to go through the motions; to be slipshod in work: 做事不应该～～。*No work should be done in a sloppy way*. **2** 蒙混,欺骗 to fool; to deceive: 你不要～～人。*Don't try to fool others*.

㊀ hú 见283页 see p283

㊁ hū 见281页 see p281

笏 hù ㄏㄨˋ 古代大臣上朝拿着的手板(in ancient China) tablet held before the chest by officials when received in audience by the emperor

瓠 hù ㄏㄨˋ [瓠瓜]一年生草本植物,爬蔓,夏开白花,果实长圆形,嫩时可吃。俗称"瓠子"(popularly called 瓠子) calabash gourd (*Lagenaria siceraria*)

鄠 hù ㄏㄨˋ 鄠县,在陕西省。今作"户县"(now written as 户县) Huxian County, in Shaanxi Province

鹱 hù ㄏㄨˋ 鸟名。身体大,嘴的尖端略呈钩状,趾间有蹼,会游泳和潜水,生活在海边,吃鱼类和软体动物等 shearwater (*Puffinus*)

HUA ㄏㄨㄚ

化 ㊁ huā ㄏㄨㄚ 同"花❼" same as 花❼

㊀ huà 见287页 see p287

华(華) ㊂ huā ㄏㄨㄚ 〈古 *archaism*〉同"花" same as 花

㊀ huá 见286页 see p286

㊁ huà 见288页 see p288

哗(嘩) ㊁ huā ㄏㄨㄚ 拟声词(叠 *reduplication*) ***onomatopoeia***: 水～～地流。*The water went gurgling on*.

㊀ huá 见287页 see p287

花 huā ㄏㄨㄚ ❶(一儿)种子植物的有性生殖器官,有各种的形状和颜色,一般花谢后结成果实 flower ㊀ ***extension*** 供观赏的植物 ornamental plant ❷(一儿)样子或形状像花的 anything resembling a flower: 雪～儿 *snowflakes* | 浪～ *sprays* | 火～儿 *sparks* | 葱～儿 *chopped green onion* | 印～ *printing; stamp* [天花]一种急性传染病,病原体是病毒,又叫"痘"或"痘疮",也省称"花"。结痂后留下的疤痕就是麻子(also called 痘 or 痘疮, and also 花 for short) smallpox [挂花]战士在战斗中受了伤(of a soldier) to be wounded in action

H

❸错杂的颜色或花样 multicoloured; variegated: ～布 *cotton print* | 头发～白 *grey-haired; with grey hair* | ～边 *decorative border; fancy lace* | 那只猫是～的。*That cat is spotted.* [花哨](— shao)颜色鲜艳,花样多,变化多 garish; full of flourishes; varied: 这块布真～～。*This piece of cloth is garish.* ❹混杂的,不单纯的 mixed; mingled: 粗粮细粮～搭着吃 *to diversify one's diet with coarse and fine grains* [花甲]天干地支配合用来纪年,从甲子起,六十年成一周,因称六十岁为花甲 (using items from the Heavenly Stems and the Earthly branches respectively to form 60 unique pairs to represent a cycle of 60 years, beginning with 甲子) sixty years of age ❺虚伪的、用来迷惑人的 showy; tricky: 耍～招 *to play a trick* | ～言巧语 *sweet words* ❻模糊不清 blurred; dim: ～眼 *presbyopia* | 眼～了。*The eyes blurred.* ❼用掉 to spend; to expend: ～钱 *to spend money* | ～一年工夫 *to spend a year's time* [花消](—xiao)费用。也作"花销"(also written as 花销) expense; cost

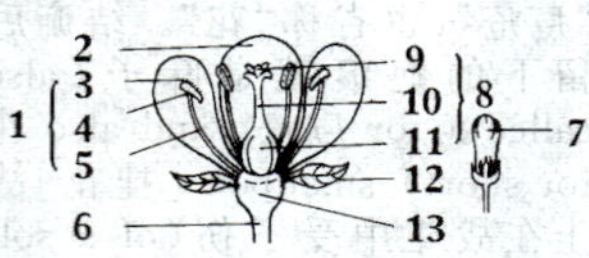

花 flower

1 雄蕊 stamen
2 花瓣 petal
3 花粉 pollen
4 花药 anther
5 花丝 filament
6 花梗 pedicel
7 花蕾 bud
8 雌蕊 pistil
9 柱头 stigma
10 花柱 style
11 子房 ovary
12 萼片 sepal
13 花托 receptacle

砉 ㊁ huā ㄏㄨㄚ 拟声词 ***onomatopoeia***,迅速动作的声音 whoosh; swish: 乌鸦～的一声飞了。*The crow whooshed away.*

㊀ xū 见843页 see p843

划(❶劃) ㊀ huá ㄏㄨㄚˊ ❶用刀或其他东西把别的东西分开或从上面擦过 to scratch; to cut the surface of: 把这个瓜用刀～开 *to cut the melon with a knife* | ～了一道口子 *to have a scratch* | ～火柴 *to strike a match* ❷用桨拨水使船行动 to paddle; to row: ～船 *to row a boat* [划子](— zi)用桨拨水行驶的小船 small rowboat ❸合算,按利益情况计较相宜不相宜 to be worth or not: ～不来 *not worth it*

㊁ huà 见288页 see p288

㊂ huai 见289页 see p289

华(華) ㊀ huá ㄏㄨㄚˊ ❶美丽有光彩的 magnificent; splendid(连 ***doublet*** 一丽 magnificent): ～灯 *colourfully decorated lanterns* | 光～ *brilliance; splendour* 敬辞 ***polite***: ～诞(生日) *birthday* | ～翰(书信) *your letter* ❷繁荣昌盛 prosperous: 繁～ *prosperous; thriving* ❸ 事物最好的部分

best part：精～ *essence; cream*｜英～ *outstanding persons or things* ❹指时光，岁月 time; years：韶～ *spring time; youth*｜似水年～。*Time passes like flowing water.* ❺（头发）花白（of hair）grizzled; grey：～发（fà）*grey hair* ❻指中华民族或中国 Chinese or China：～夏 *Huaxia, ancient name for China*｜～侨 *overseas Chinese*｜～北 *northern China*

㊁ huà 见288页 see p288

㊂ huā 见285页 see p285

哗（嘩、*譁）㊀ huá ㄏㄨㄚˊ 人多声杂，乱吵 noise; clamour（㊟ ***doublet*** 喧— hubbub）：全体大～。*All those present made an uproar.*｜～众取宠（在别人面前夸耀自己，骗取别人称赞）*to try to please the public with claptrap*

㊁ huā 见285页 see p285

骅（驊）huá ㄏㄨㄚˊ ［骅骝］（—liú）古代称赤色的骏马（in ancient China）red steed

铧（鏵）huá ㄏㄨㄚˊ 犁铧，安装在犁上用来破土的铁片 ploughshare

猾 huá ㄏㄨㄚˊ 狡猾，奸诈 cunning; crafty

滑 huá ㄏㄨㄚˊ ❶滑溜，光溜，不粗涩 slippery; smooth：下雪以后地很～。*The ground is very slippery after the snowfall.*｜桌面很光～。*The tabletop is very smooth.* ❷在光溜的物体表面上溜动 to slip; to slide：～了一跤 *to slip and fall*｜～雪 *to ski*｜～冰 *to skate* ［滑翔］航空上指借着大气浮力飘行 to glide：～～机 *glider* ❸狡诈，不诚实 cunning; dishonest：～头 *slyboots; slippery fellow*｜耍～ *to act in a slick way*｜这人很～。*This fellow is very cunning.*

［滑稽］（—ji）诙谐，使人发笑 funny; amusing：他说话很～～。*He speaks in a funny way.*

搳 huá ㄏㄨㄚˊ ［搳拳］饮酒时两人同时伸出手指并各说一个数，谁说的数目跟双方所伸手指的总数相符，谁就算赢，输的人喝酒。现作"划拳"（now written as 划拳）*huaquan*, a finger-guessing game played by two drinkers（The game requires them to extend a number of fingers and announce a number at the same time. The one whose announced number tallies with the sum of fingers extended by both sides is the winner, and the loser will take a drink）

化 ㊀ huà ㄏㄨㄚˋ ❶性质或形态改变 to change; to turn：～整为零 *to break up the whole into parts*（or *pieces*）｜变～ *to change; to alter*｜开～ *to become civilized*｜冰都～了。*The ice has melted.* ［化合］两种或两种以上的物质互相结合变成一种性质跟原来物质都不相同的新物质 chemical combination ［化石］埋藏在地下的古代生物的遗骸变成的石块，或带着古代生物遗迹的石块 fossil [化学]研究物质的结构、组成、性质、应用及其变化规律的科学 chemistry ❷使思想、行为等有所转变 to convert; to influence: 感～ *to convert; to influence* | 教～ *to train in good manners* | 潜移默～ *to influence imperceptibly* ❸指化学 chemistry: ～工 *chemical industry* | ～肥 *chemical fertilizer* ❹佛教道教徒募集财物(of a Buddhist monk or Taoist priest) to ask for alms: ～缘 *to beg alms* | ～斋(乞食) *to beg a meal* ❺词尾,放在名词或形容词后,表示转变成某种性质或状态 suffix, used after a noun or an adjective to express sth or sb is becoming or made to have that attribute: 革命～ *revolutionization* | 农业机械～ *agricultural mechanization* | 工业现代～ *industrial modernization* | 科学～ *scientization* | 绿～ *to afforest*

㊁ huā 见285页 see p285

华(華) ㊀ huà ㄏㄨㄚˋ ❶华山,五岳中的西岳,在陕西省华阴 Huashan Mountain (*or* Mount Hua; Mt. Huashan), the western mountain of the five sacred mountains, in Huayin, Shaanxi Province ❷姓 Hua, a surname

㊀ huá 见286页 see p286

㊂ huā 见285页 see p285

桦(樺) huà ㄏㄨㄚˋ 白桦树,落叶乔木,树皮白色,容易剥离,木材致密,可制器具 birch (*Betula*)

划(劃) ㊀ huà ㄏㄨㄚˋ ❶分开 to delimit; to differentiate: ～分区域 *to divide into regions* | ～清界限 *to make a clear distinction between; to make a clean break with* [划时代]由于出现了具有伟大意义的新事物,在历史上开辟一个新的时代 epoch-making ❷设计 to plan (㊟ **doublet** 计一 to plan | 筹一 to plan and prepare): 工作计～ *work plan* | 你去筹～筹～这件事。*Work out a plan for this, please.* [划一]使一致 to standardize: ～～制度 *to standardize the system*

㊁ huá 见286页 see p286

㊂ huai 见289页 see p289

画(畫) huà ㄏㄨㄚˋ ❶描画或写 to draw or write: ～画儿 *to draw a picture* | ～个圈 *to draw a circle* | ～十字 *to cross oneself; to make the sign of the cross* | ～押 *to make one's cross or mark; to sign* ❷(一儿)画成的作品 drawing; painting; picture (㊟ **doublet** 图一 picture): 一张～儿 *a picture* (or *drawing*) | 年～儿 *New Year picture* | 油～ *oil painting* ❸汉字的一笔叫一画 stroke of a Chinese character: "人"字是两～。*The character* 人 *is made up of two strokes.* | "天"字是四～。*The character* 天 *is made up of four strokes.* ❹同"划㊀" same as 划㊀

婳(嫿) huà ㄏㄨㄚˋ 见254页"姽"字条"姽婳"(guǐ—) see 姽婳 on p254

话 huà ㄏㄨㄚˋ ❶语言 word; remark; talk: 说～ *to speak* | 谈了几句～ *to have said a few words* [话剧]用平常口语和动作表演的戏剧 modern drama; stage play ❷说,谈 to speak or talk about: ～别 *to say a few words before departure* | 茶～ *chatter at a tea party* | ～旧 *to talk about old times* [话本]宋元时期民间艺人说唱故事的底本 script for story-telling in the Song and Yuan dynasties

HUAI ㄏㄨㄞ

怀(懷) huái ㄏㄨㄞˊ ❶思念 to miss; to think of(㊃ **doublet** 一念 to miss): ～友 *to think of a friend* | ～念伟大的祖国 *to miss one's great motherland* ❷包藏,心里存有 to keep in mind; to cherish: ～胎 *to be pregnant* | ～疑 *to doubt* | ～恨 *to nurse hatred* | 胸～壮志 *to harbour lofty ambitions* ❸胸前 chest; bosom: 把小孩抱在～里 *to carry a child in one's arms* ❹心意 mind: 无介于～ *not to mind* | 正中(zhòng)下～ *to one's wishes*

徊 huái ㄏㄨㄞˊ 见548页"徘"字条"徘徊"(pái—) see 徘徊 on p548

淮 huái ㄏㄨㄞˊ 淮河,源出河南省,流经安徽省,至江苏省注入洪泽湖 Huaihe River, rising in Henan Province, flowing through Anhui and Jiangsu provinces into the Hongze Lake

槐 huái ㄏㄨㄞˊ 槐树,落叶乔木,花黄白色。果实长荚形。木材可供建筑和制家具之用。花蕾可做黄色染料 Chinese scholar tree (*Styphnolobium japonicum*)

踝 huái ㄏㄨㄞˊ 踝子骨,脚腕两旁凸起的部分。(图见741页"体" picture ankle on p741)

耲 huái ㄏㄨㄞˊ 用耲耙翻土 to harrow [耲耙](—bà)翻土用的一种农具 harrow

坏(壞) huài ㄏㄨㄞˋ ❶跟"好"相对(the opposite of 好) bad: 坚决向～人～事作斗争 *to firmly struggle against evil-doers and evil deeds* ❷东西受了损伤,被毁 to break down(㊃ **doublet** 破— to destroy): 自行车～了。*The bike broke down.* ❸坏主意 evil idea: 使～ *to play a dirty trick* ❹放在动词或形容词后,表示程度深(used after a verb or an adjective to express a great degree) extremely; badly: 真把我忙～了。*I was extremely busy.* | 气～了 *to be beside oneself with rage*

划(劃) ㊂ huai · ㄏㄨㄞ 见15页"刮"字条"刮划"(bāi—) see 刮划 on p15
㊀ huà 见288页 see p288
㊁ huá 见286页 see p286

HUAN ㄏㄨㄢ

欢(歡、*懽、*讙、*驩)

huān ㄏㄨㄢ ❶快乐,高兴 happy; merry(㊀ **doublet** 一喜 joyful):～庆胜利 *to celebrate the victory*|～呼声经久不息。*There arose prolonged cheers.*|～天喜地 *overjoyed*|～迎贵宾 *to welcome distinguished guests* ❷活跃,起劲 vigorously; in full swing:孩子们真～。*The children are vigorous.*|机器转得很～。*The machine is running in full swing* (or *at full speed*). ㊀ **extension** 旺盛 exuberant:炉子里的火很～。*The fire in the stove is roaring.* ❸喜爱,也指所喜爱的人 liking; love:～心 *favour; love*|喜～ *to like; to love*|新～(新的相好) *new sweet heart*

獾(*貛) huān ㄏㄨㄢ 野兽名。毛灰色,头部有三条白色纵纹。毛可制笔,脂肪炼油可入药 badger (*Melinae*)

还(還) ㊀ huán ㄏㄨㄢ ❶回,归 to return; to restore:～家 *to return home*|～原(恢复原状) *to restore to the original state or shape* ❷回报 to give or do sth in return:～礼 *to return a salute; to give a gift in return*|～手 *to hit back*|以眼～眼,以牙～牙 *an eye for an eye and a tooth for a tooth; to answer blows with blows* ❸归还 to give back; to return(㊀ **doublet** 偿一 to repay):～钱 *to pay back the money* ❹姓 Huan, a surname

〈古 **archaism**〉又同"旋"(xuán) also same as 旋

㊁ hái 见261页 see p261

环(環) huán ㄏㄨㄢ ❶(一儿)圈形的东西 ring; hoop:连～ *chain of rings*|铁～ *iron hoop* ❷围绕 to surround; to encircle:～城马路 *ring road; beltway*|～视 *to look around* [环境]周围的一切事物 environment; surroundings:优美的～～ *beautiful environment* ❸指射击、射箭比赛中射中环靶的环数(target) ring, points scored in shooting or archery

郇 ㊁ huán ㄏㄨㄢ 姓 Huan, a surname

㊀ xún 见854页 see p854

洹 huán ㄏㄨㄢ 洹河,水名,在河南省安阳。也叫"安阳河"(also called 安阳河) Huanhe River, in Anyang, Henan Province

桓 huán ㄏㄨㄢ ❶古代立在驿站、官署等建筑物旁作为标志的木柱,后称华表(later called 华表) wooden columns erected by such buildings as post stations, government offices, etc, as signs in ancient China ❷姓 Huan, a surname

貆 huán ㄏㄨㄢ ❶幼小的貉 young racoon dog ❷豪猪 porcupine (*Hystricidae*)

萑 huán ㄏㄨㄢ 古书上指芦苇一类的植物(in ancient Chinese texts) common reed (*Phragmites australis*)

锾 huán ㄏㄨㄢ 古代重量单位,也是货币单位 *huan*, an ancient unit of both weight and currency

圜 ㊀ huán ㄏㄨㄢˊ 围绕 to surround

㊁ yuán 见927页 see p927

阛 huán ㄏㄨㄢˊ ［阛阓］(—huì)街市 street market

澴 huán ㄏㄨㄢˊ 澴水，水名，在湖北省东北部 Huanshui River, in the northeast of Hubei Province

寰 huán ㄏㄨㄢˊ 广大的地域 extensive region ［寰球］［寰宇］全世界。也作“环球”、“环宇”(also written as 环球 or 环宇) the earth; the whole world

嬛 huán ㄏㄨㄢˊ 见417页“嫏”字条“嫏嬛”(láng—) see 嫏嬛 on p417

缳 huán ㄏㄨㄢˊ ❶绳套 noose: 投～(自缢) *to hang oneself* ❷绞杀 hanging: ～首 *to hang (sb)*

鹮 huán ㄏㄨㄢˊ 鸟名。有朱鹮、白鹮、彩鹮等多种。嘴细长而向下弯曲，腿长。生活在水边 ibis (*Threskiornithinae*)

镮 huán ㄏㄨㄢˊ 圆形有孔可贯穿的东西 ring

鬟 huán ㄏㄨㄢˊ 古代妇女梳的环形的发结(fàjié) bun of hair (of an ancient woman) ［丫鬟］(yāhuan)［小鬟］旧称年轻的女仆 (former term for a young maid servant) maid

睆 huǎn ㄏㄨㄢˇ ❶明亮 bright ❷美好 fine; beautiful

缓 huǎn ㄏㄨㄢˇ ❶慢，跟“急”相对 (the opposite of 急) slow: 轻重～急 *in order of importance and urgency; order of priority* | ～步而行 *to walk slowly* | ～不济急。*Slow action cannot save a critical situation.* ❷延迟 to delay; to postpone: ～兵之计 *delaying tactics; stratagem to gain a respite* | ～刑 *probation* | ～两天再办 *to put it off for a couple of days* ［缓冲］把冲突的两方隔离开，使紧张的局势缓和 to buffer: ～～地带 *buffer zone* ［缓和］使紧张的情势转向平和 to ease off ❸苏醒，恢复 to come to; to revive: 病人昏过去又～了过来。*The patient came to himself again after fainting.* | 下过雨，花都～过来了。*The withered flowers revived after the rain.* | ～～气再往前走 *to take a short break before walking on*

幻 huàn ㄏㄨㄢˋ ❶空虚的，不真实的 unreal; imaginary: ～境 *fairyland; vision* | 打消一切～想 *to give up all illusions* ［幻灯］一种娱乐和教育用的器具。利用凸透镜和灯光把图片放大，映射在白幕上 slide projector ［幻灭］幻想或不真实的事受到现实的打击而消灭 to disillusion ❷奇异地变化 to change magically (㊟ **doublet** 变—to change irregularly): ～术(魔术) *magic; conjuring*

奂 huàn ㄏㄨㄢˋ ❶盛，多 abundant; plentiful ❷文采鲜明(of writing) brilliant

H

换 huàn ㄏㄨㄢˋ ❶给人东西同时从他那里取得别的东西 to exchange; to trade: 互～ *to exchange* | 交～条件 *conditions or prerequisites of exchange* ❷变换,更改 to change: ～衣服 *to change clothes* | ～汤不～药 *old wine in a new bottle; to change in form but not in content* ❸兑换(用证券换取现金或用一种货币换另一种货币) to convert (securities into cash or one currency into another)

唤 huàn ㄏㄨㄢˋ 呼叫,喊 to call out (㊌ **doublet** 呼一 to call): ～鸡 *to call the chickens* | ～狗 *to call the dog*

涣 huàn ㄏㄨㄢˋ 散开 to dissolve; to vanish: 士气～散 *to have a deflated morale* | ～然冰释 *to melt like ice; to disappear* [涣涣]水势盛大(of water) overflowing

焕 huàn ㄏㄨㄢˋ 光明 shining; glowing: ～然一新 *all fresh and new* [焕发]光彩外现的样子 shining; glowing: 精神～～ *full of vigour*

痪 huàn ㄏㄨㄢˋ [瘫痪]见727页"瘫"(see 瘫 on p727) paralysis; palsy

宦 huàn ㄏㄨㄢˋ 官 official (㊌ **doublet** 官一 official | 仕一 to take up an official career) [宦官]封建时代经过阉割在皇宫里伺候皇帝及其家族的男人。也叫"太监"(also called 太监) eunuch

浣(*澣) huàn ㄏㄨㄢˋ ❶洗 to wash: ～衣 *to wash clothes* | ～纱 *to rinse yarns* ❷旧称每月的上、中、下旬为上、中、下浣 former term for any of the three ten-day periods of a month

鲩(**鰀) huàn ㄏㄨㄢˋ 鲩鱼,鱼名。身体微绿色,鳍微黑色,生活在淡水中,是我国特产的重要鱼类之一。也叫"草鱼"(also called 草鱼) grass carp (*Ctenopharyngodon idella*)

患 huàn ㄏㄨㄢˋ ❶灾祸 disaster (㊌ **doublet** 一难 trials and tribulations; adversity | 灾一 calamity | 祸一 disaster): 有备无～。 *Preparedness averts peril.* | 防～未然。 *Nip the evil in the bud.* | 免除水～ *to be free from flood* | ～难之交 *friends in need* ❷忧虑 to worry: 不要～得～失。 *Don't worry about personal gains and losses.* ❸害病 to contract (a disease): ～病 *to fall ill* | ～脚气 *to suffer from beriberi*

漶 huàn ㄏㄨㄢˋ [漫漶]文字图像等磨灭、模糊(of scripts or pictures, etc) blurred

逭 huàn ㄏㄨㄢˋ 逃,避 to escape; to evade

豢 huàn ㄏㄨㄢˋ 喂养牲畜 to feed or keep (domestic animals) (㊌ **doublet** 一养 to feed; to keep)

擐 huàn ㄏㄨㄢˋ 穿 to wear; to put on: ～甲执兵 *to put on armours and take up weapons*

轘 huàn ㄏㄨㄢˋ 古代用车分裂人体的一种酷刑 (an

ancient form of execution) tearing the body apart with horse-drawn carts

HUANG ㄏㄨㄤ

肓 huāng ㄏㄨㄤ [膏肓]我国古代医学把心尖脂肪叫膏,心脏和膈之间叫肓,认为膏肓之间是药力达不到的地方(in classical Chinese medicine, the fat at the tip of the heart is called 膏, the section between the heart and the diaphragm is called 肓, and the place between 膏 and 肓 is considered untreatable) *gao huang*:病入～～(指病重到无法医治的地步) *The patient is beyond cure.*

荒 huāng ㄏㄨㄤ ❶庄稼没有收成或严重歉收 crop failure:饥～ *famine* | ～年 *famine year* | 备～ *to prepare against crop failure* ㊀ ***extension*** 严重缺乏 severe shortage; scarcity:煤～ *coal shortage* | 房～ *housing shortage* ❷长满野草或无人耕种 waste; uncultivated(㊟ ***doublet*** 一芜 to lie waste):～地 *wasteland* | 垦～ *to cultivate the wasteland* | 开～ *to open up the wasteland* ㊀ ***extension*** **1** 废弃 to discard:～废 *to neglect* **2** 荒凉,偏僻 desolate:～村 *deserted village* (or *hamlet*) | ～郊 *desolate outskirts; wilderness* [荒疏]久未练习而生疏 rusty; out of practice:学业还没～～ *not rusty in one's studies* ❸不合情理的,不正确的 unreasonable:～谬 *absurd* | ～诞 *fantastic* [荒唐] **1** 浮夸不实 absurd; ridiculous:这话真～～。*This remark is simply ridiculous.* **2** 行为放荡 dissipated; loose

塃 huāng ㄏㄨㄤ 〈方 ***dialect***〉开采出来的矿石 ore

慌 huāng ㄏㄨㄤ ❶慌张,急忙,忙乱 flurried; confused (㊟ ***doublet*** 一忙 in a rush):他做事太～。*He is too flurried in doing things.* | ～里～张 *in a flurry* ❷恐惧,不安 panicky:心里发～ *to feel panicky* | 惊～ *panic-stricken* ❸表示难忍受 to an unbearable degree:累得～ *to be tired out* | 闷(mèn)得～ *to be bored to death*

皇 huáng ㄏㄨㄤˊ ❶君主 monarch; emperor (㊟ ***doublet*** 一帝 emperor) ❷大(叠 ***reduplication***) grand; magnificent:～～巨著 *monumental work* ❸古同"遑"、"惶" same as 遑 or 惶 in ancient Chinese

凰 huáng ㄏㄨㄤˊ ❶凤凰。参看199页"凤"(fèng) (see 凤 on p199) phoenix ❷传说中指雌凤 (legendary) female phoenix

隍 huáng ㄏㄨㄤˊ 没有水的城壕 dry moat outside a city wall

喤 huáng ㄏㄨㄤˊ 拟声词(叠 ***reduplication***) ***onomatopoeia*** **1** 钟鼓声 sound of bells and drums **2** 小儿啼哭声 sound of a baby bawling

H

遑 huáng ㄏㄨㄤˊ ❶闲暇 leisure:不～(没有功夫) *to have no time* ❷匆忙(叠 ***reduplication***) in a hurry

徨 huáng ㄏㄨㄤˊ 见551页"彷"字条"彷徨"(páng—) see 彷徨 on p551

湟 huáng ㄏㄨㄤˊ 湟水,水名,在青海省 Huangshui River in Qinghai Province

惶 huáng ㄏㄨㄤˊ 恐惧 fear(㊎ ***doublet*** —恐 scared):人心～～ *People are in a state of widespread anxiety.*|～恐不安 *in a state of trepidation*

煌 huáng ㄏㄨㄤˊ 明亮(叠 ***reduplication***) bright:星火～～ *bright with sparks*|灯火辉～ *brightly lit*

锽 huáng ㄏㄨㄤˊ ❶古代的一种兵器 *huang*, a kind of ancient weapon ❷形容钟鼓声(叠 ***reduplication***) sound of bells and drums

H

蝗 huáng ㄏㄨㄤˊ 蝗虫,一种吃庄稼的害虫,常常成群飞翔。也叫"蚂蚱"(màzha)(also called 蚂蚱) locust (*Locusta*)

篁 huáng ㄏㄨㄤˊ 竹林 bamboo grove 泛指竹子(in a broad sense) bamboo

艎 huáng ㄏㄨㄤˊ 见915页"艅"字条"艅艎"(yú—) see 艅艎 on p915

鳇 huáng ㄏㄨㄤˊ 鳇鱼,鱼名。形状像鲟鱼,有五行硬鳞,嘴突出,半月形,两旁有扁平的须 kaluga (*Huso dauricus*)

黄 huáng ㄏㄨㄤˊ ❶像金子或向日葵花的颜色 yellow [黄色] **1** 黄的颜色 yellow **2** 指腐朽堕落的 decadent; pornographic:～～小说 *pornographic novel* ❷指黄河 Huanghe River; Yellow River:引～工程 *project to divert water from the Yellow River* ❸事情失败或计划不能实现 to fail; to be off:这件事～不了。*It will not end up with nothing definite.* ❹指黄帝,传说中的中国上古帝王 Huangdi, a legendary emperor in ancient China:炎～子孙 *the Chinese people*

潢 huáng ㄏㄨㄤˊ ❶积水池 pond; pool ❷染纸 to dye or colour paper [装潢]裱褙字画 to mount calligraphy and painting ㊁ ***extension*** 装饰货物的包装 packaging

璜 huáng ㄏㄨㄤˊ 半璧形的玉 semi-circular jade pendant

磺 huáng ㄏㄨㄤˊ 硫磺 sulphur:硝～ *nitre and sulphur*

鐄 huáng ㄏㄨㄤˊ ❶大钟 big bell ❷钟声 sound of bells ❸同"簧"same as 簧

癀 huáng ㄏㄨㄤˊ 癀病,牛马等家畜的炭疽(jū)病 anthrax

蟥 huáng ㄏㄨㄤˊ 见482页"蚂"字条"蚂蟥"(mǎ—) see 蚂蟥 on p482

簧 huáng ㄏㄨㄤˊ ❶乐器里用铜等制成的发声薄片 reed:笙～ *reed pipe*|～乐器

reed instruments ❷器物里有弹力的机件 spring：锁～ *lock spring*｜弹～ *spring*

恍（*怳）huǎng ㄏㄨㄤˇ ❶恍然，忽然 all of a sudden; suddenly：～然大悟 *to realize all of a sudden* ❷仿佛 to seem：～若置身其境 *as if to be personally on the scene*
［恍惚］（—hū）**1** 神志不清，精神不集中 in a trance; absent-minded：精神～～ *to be in a trance; to look absent-minded* **2**（看得、听得、记得）不真切，不清楚 dimly; faintly：我～～看见他了。*I faintly saw him.*

晃 ㊀ huǎng ㄏㄨㄤˇ ❶明亮（叠 ***reduplication***）bright：明～～的刺刀 *shining bayonet* ❷照耀 to dazzle：～眼（光线强烈刺激眼睛）*dazzling* ❸很快地闪过 to flash past：窗户上有个人影，一～就不见了。*A figure flashed past the window and disappeared.*
㊁ huàng 见295页 see p295

幌 huǎng ㄏㄨㄤˇ 帐幔，帘帷 heavy curtain［幌子］（—zi）商店、饭店等门外的招牌或标志物 bar sign; shop sign; signboard ㊗ ***figurative*** 为了进行某种活动所假借的名义 pretence

谎 huǎng ㄏㄨㄤˇ ❶谎话，不真实的话 lie：撒～ *to tell a lie* ㊋ ***extension*** 商贩要的虚价 deceptive price：要～ *to overcharge* ❷说谎话 to lie：～称 *to claim falsely*

晃（*㨪）㊁ huàng ㄏㄨㄤˋ 摇动，摆动 to shake; to sway（㊥ ***doublet*** 摇— to sway）：树枝来回～。*The twigs are swaying.*
㊀ huǎng 见295页 see p295

滉 huàng ㄏㄨㄤˋ［滉瀁］（—yǎng）形容水广大无边（of water）deep and wide

鰉 huàng ㄏㄨㄤˋ 用于人名。慕容鰉，东晋初年鲜卑族的首领（*huang*, used in a given name）Murong Huang, the chief of the Xianbei ethnic group in the early years of the Eastern Jin Dynasty

HUI ㄏㄨㄟ

灰 huī ㄏㄨㄟ ❶物体燃烧后剩下的粉末状的东西 ash：炉～ *ashes from a stove*｜烟～ *cigarette ashes*｜～肥 *ash manure*［青灰］一种含有杂质的石墨，青黑色，是建筑上常用的材料，也可做染料 graphite powder［石灰］一种建筑上常用的材料，俗叫"白灰"，又叫"生石灰"。是用石灰石烧成的，化学成分是氧化钙。生石灰遇水变成氢氧化钙，叫熟石灰（popularly called 白灰, and also called 生石灰）lime ❷灰尘 dust ❸灰色，黑白之间的颜色 grey ❹消沉，失望 disheartened; discouraged：心～意懒 *to feel disheartened; to be in the blues*｜～心丧气 *to lose heart*

诙 huī ㄏㄨㄟ 诙谐，说话有趣 humorous; jocular

H

咴 huī ㄏㄨㄟ [咴儿咴儿]拟声词 ***onomatopoeia***，马叫声 neigh; whinny

恢 huī ㄏㄨㄟ 大，宽广 vast; extensive (叠 ***reduplication***)(㊟ ***doublet*** 一弘 broad): ～～有余 *to have more than plenty of space* | 天网～～。*Justice has long arms.*

[恢复]回到原来的状态 to recover; to regain: ～～健康 *to recover one's health*

㧑(撝) huī ㄏㄨㄟ ❶指挥 to command ❷谦逊 modest: ～谦 *modest*

挥 huī ㄏㄨㄟ ❶舞动，摇摆 to wave; to wield: ～刀 *to brandish a sword* | ～手 *to wave one's hand* | 大笔一～ *with one stroke of the pen* [指挥] **1** 指导，调度 to command; to direct; to conduct **2** 指导、调度的人 commander; director; conductor: 工程总～～ *general director of a project* | 乐队～～ *conductor of an orchestra* ❷散出，甩出 to scatter; to disperse: ～金如土 *to spend money like dirt* (or *like water*); *to spend money recklessly* | ～汗如雨 *to shed perspiration like rain; to drip with sweat* [挥发]液体或某些固体在常温中变为气体而发散 to volatilize [挥霍](—huò)用钱浪费，随便花钱 to squander; to spend money freely

珲 ㊀ huī ㄏㄨㄟ 见5页"瑷"字条"瑷珲"(ài—) see 瑷珲 on p5

㊁ hún 见301页 see p301

晖 huī ㄏㄨㄟ ❶阳光 sunshine; sunlight: 春～ *spring sunlight* | 朝～ *glow of the rising sun* | 余～ *last rays of the setting sun* ❷同"辉"same as 辉

辉(*煇) huī ㄏㄨㄟ 闪射的光彩 brightness; splendour (㊟ ***doublet*** 光一 lustre; glow): 光～四射 *brilliant* [辉煌]光彩耀眼 brilliant: 金碧～～ *dazzling magnificent* ㊔ ***figurative*** 极其优良，出色 splendid; outstanding: ～～的成绩 *outstanding achievements* [辉映]光彩照耀 to shine ㊀ ***extension*** 事物互相对照 to reflect: 前后～～ (*objects in front and behind*) *reflecting each other's brilliance*

翚 huī ㄏㄨㄟ ❶飞 to fly ❷古书上指具有五彩羽毛的雉 (in ancient Chinese texts) pheasant of multicoloured plumage

袆(褘) huī ㄏㄨㄟ 古代王后穿的祭服 (in ancient China) mourning robe worn by a queen or an empress

㧑 huī ㄏㄨㄟ 撞击 to ram; to strike [喧㧑]轰响声 roar

麾 huī ㄏㄨㄟ 古代指挥用的旗子 (in ancient China) standard of a commander ㊀ ***extension*** 指挥 to command: ～军 *to command an army*

徽 huī ㄏㄨㄟ ❶标志 emblem; badge: 国～ *national emblem* | 校～ *national emblem* (or *badge*) ❷美好的 fine; glorious: ～号 *title of honour* ❸指

安徽省徽州 Huizhou in Anhui Province：～墨 *Huizhou inkstick*

隳 huī ㄏㄨㄟ 毁坏 to destroy; to ruin

回（❸迴、❸*廻、**囬）huí ㄏㄨㄟˊ ❶还，走向原来的地方 to return; to go back：～家 *to go back home; to go home*｜～国 *to return to one's motherland*｜～到原单位工作 *to return to one's original unit to work* ❷掉转 to turn round：～过身来 *to turn round* [回头] **1** 把头转向后方 to turn one's head; to turn round：～～观望 *to turn round and look* **2** 回归，返回 to come back; to return：一去不～～ *to go away and never return* **3** 等一会 later：～～再说吧。*Let's talk about it later.* **4** 改邪归正 to repent：现在～～还不晚。*It's not late to repent now.* ❸曲折，环绕，旋转 to circle; to wind：～形针 *paper clip*｜巡～ *to do or go the rounds* [回避] 避免，躲开 to evade; to avoid ❹答复，报答 to answer; to requite：～信 *to write back; letter in reply*｜～话 *to reply; reply*｜～敬 *to do or give in return* ❺量词 ***quantifier***，指事件的次数 time：两～ *two times; twice*｜他来过一～。*He has been here once.* ㊕ ***transfer*** 我国长篇小说分的章节（in Chinese novels）chapter：《红楼梦》一共一百二十～。*A Dream of Red Mansions has 120 chapters.*

[回纥]（—hé）唐代西北的民族。也叫"回鹘"（hú）（also called 回鹘）the Huihe ethnic group in the northwestern region in the Tang Dynasty

[回族] 我国少数民族，参看附表（see the appendix）the Hui ethnic group, one of the ethnic minorities of China

茴 huí ㄏㄨㄟˊ [茴香] **1** 小茴香，多年生草本植物，叶分裂像毛，花黄色，茎叶嫩时可吃。子实大如麦粒，可作香料，又可入药 fennel (*Foeniculum vulgare*) **2** 大茴香，常绿小乔木，叶长椭圆形，初夏开花，果实呈八角形，也叫八角茴香或大料，可作调料或入药（also called 八角茴香 or 大料）anise (*Pimpinella anisum*)

洄 huí ㄏㄨㄟˊ 水流回旋（of water）to whirl

蛔（*蚘）huí ㄏㄨㄟˊ 蛔虫，寄生在人或其他动物肠子里的一种蠕形寄生虫，像蚯蚓而没有环节。能损害人畜的健康 roundworm (*Ascaris lumbricoides*)

虺 huǐ ㄏㄨㄟˇ 古书上说的一种毒蛇（in ancient Chinese texts）a kind of poisonous snake

[虺虺]〈古 ***archaism***〉打雷的声音 peal of the thunder

悔 huǐ ㄏㄨㄟˇ 后悔，懊恼 to regret; to repent：～过 *to be repentant*｜～之已晚 *too late to repent now; no use regretting it now*

H

毁(❷*燬、❹*譭) huǐ ㄏㄨㄟˇ ❶破坏,损害 to destroy; to damage:这把椅子是谁～的? *Who has damaged this chair?*|这样做就～了个人前途 *to ruin one's future by doing this*[毁灭]彻底地消灭 to destroy; to exterminate:给敌人以～～性的打击 *to deal the enemy a crushing blow* ❷烧掉 to burn:烧～ *to burn down*|焚～ *to burn up* [引] ***extension*** 使不存在 to destroy:拆～ *to demolish*|炸～ *to blow up*|摧～ *to destroy*|销～ *to destroy*|捣～ *to smash up*|撕～ *to tear up* ❸〈方 ***dialect***〉把成件的旧东西改造成别的东西 to refashion; to make over:这两个小凳是一张旧桌子～的。*These two stools were made from an old table.* ❹诽谤,说别人的坏话 to slander; to defame([连] ***doublet*** 诋—to vilify|—谤 to slander)

卉 huì ㄏㄨㄟˋ 草的总称 general term for plants:花～ *flowers and plants*

汇(匯、❷❸彙、*滙) huì ㄏㄨㄟˋ ❶河流会合在一起(of rivers) to converge:～成巨流 *to converge into a mighty river* ❷会聚在一起的东西 collection; assemblage:总～ *collection*|词～ *vocabulary* ❸聚合 to collect; to gather together:～集 *to collect*|～印成书 *to have articles, pictures, etc collected and printed in a book form*[汇报]汇集情况向上级或群众报告 to report; to give an account of ❹由甲地把款项寄到乙地 to remit:～款 *to remit money; remittance*|～兑 *remittance* ❺指外汇 foreign exchange:出口创～ *to earn foreign currency by exports*|～市 *foreign exchange market*

会(會) ㊀ huì ㄏㄨㄟˋ ❶聚合,合拢,合在一起 to get together; to assemble:在哪儿～合? *Where shall we meet?*|就在这里～齐吧。*Let's assemble here.*|～审 *joint trial; joint check-up*|～话(对面说话) *conversation*[会师]从不同地方前进的军队,在某一个地方聚合在一起 to join forces ❷多数人的集合 gathering **1** 有一定目的的集会 meeting; party:纪念～ *commemoration meeting*|群众大～ *mass rally*|开个～ *to hold a meeting* **2** 指某些团体 association; society:工～ *trade union*|学生～ *student union* ❸城市(通常指行政中心) major city; capital:都(dū)～ *capital; metropolis*|省～ *provincial capital* ❹彼此见面 to meet; to see:～客 *to receive a guest*|～一～面 *to meet*|你～过他没有? *Have you ever met him?* ❺付钱 to pay:～账 *to pay a bill*|饭钱我～过了。*I have paid for the meal.* ❻理解,领悟,懂 to understand; to grasp:误～ *misunderstanding*|～意 *understanding*|领～ *to comprehend*

❼能 can **1** 表示懂得怎样做或有能力做 can：他～游泳。*He can swim*. **2** 可能 to be likely to：我想他不～不懂。*I think he is sure to understand*. **3** 能够 to be able to：我们的理想一定～实现。*Our ideals are sure to be realized*. **4** 善于 to be good at：能说～道 *to have an eloquent tongue* ❽机会，时机，事情变化的一个时间 chance；opportunity：适逢其～ *to be lucky to be there at the time*｜趁着这个机～ *to take advantage of this opportunity* ❾一定，应当 surely；should（㊀ ***doublet*** 一当 should）：长风破浪～有时。*There will be a day when you can display all your talents*. ❿恰好，正好 to happen：～天大雨，道不通。*It happened to rain heavily and the road was blocked*. ⓫（一儿）一小段时间 a moment；a short time：一～儿 *a moment*｜这～儿 *now*；*at this moment*｜那～儿 *then*；*at that moment*｜多～儿 *when*；*ever*｜用不了多大～儿。*It won't take long*.

㊁ kuài 见399页 see p399

荟（薈） huì ㄏㄨㄟˋ 草木繁多 (of grass and trees) luxuriant［荟萃］（一cuì）聚集 to gather together：人才～～ *gathering of talented people*

绘（繪） huì ㄏㄨㄟˋ 画，描画 to paint；to draw：～图 *to chart*｜～形～声 *vivid*；*lively*

桧（檜） ㊁ huì ㄏㄨㄟˋ 用于人名。秦桧，南宋奸臣（*huì*，used in a given name）Qin Hui，a treacherous court official in the Southern Song Dynasty

㊀ guì 见255页 see p255

烩（燴） huì ㄏㄨㄟˋ 加浓汁或多种食物混在一起烹煮 to braise；to cook various foods mixed together：～豆腐 *to braise tofu*｜～饭 *to cook rice with meat*，*vegetables and water*｜杂～ *mixed stew*；*hotchpotch*

讳（諱） huì ㄏㄨㄟˋ ❶避忌，有顾忌不敢说或不愿说 to avoid as taboo；to avoid saying：～疾忌医 *to conceal one's disease for fear of treatment*；*to refuse to face up to one's errors*｜直言不～ *to speak frankly*｜忌～ *taboo* ❷封建时代称死去的皇帝或尊长的名字（in feudal times）name for a deceased emperor or head of a family

诲 huì ㄏㄨㄟˋ 教导，劝说 to teach；to instruct（㊀ ***doublet*** 教一 instruction）：～人不倦 *to be tireless in teaching*；*to teach with tireless zeal*

晦 huì ㄏㄨㄟˋ ❶昏暗不明 dark；obscure［晦气］**1** 不顺利，倒霉 unlucky **2** 指人不顺利或生病时难看的气色 pale and gloomy look：一脸～～ *unhealthy look* ❷夜晚 night：风雨如～ *wind and rain sweeping across a gloomy sky* — *grim*

H

and grave situation ❸夏历每月的末一天 last day of a lunar month

恚 huì ㄏㄨㄟˋ 恨,怒 hate; resentment

贿 huì ㄏㄨㄟˋ ❶财物(现指用来买通别人的财物)(now used to denote bribe) property ❷贿赂,用财物买通别人 to bribe

彗(**篲) huì ㄏㄨㄟˋ (旧读 formerly suì) 扫帚(sàozhou) broom [彗星]俗叫"扫帚星"。拖有长光像扫帚的星体(popularly called 扫帚星) comet

蔧 huì ㄏㄨㄟˋ (旧读 formerly suì)王蔧,就是地肤,俗叫"扫帚菜"。一年生草本植物,夏天开花,黄绿色。嫩苗可以吃。老了可以做扫帚(i. e. 地肤, and popularly called 扫帚菜) summer cypress (*Kochia scoparia*)

槥 huì ㄏㄨㄟˋ 〈古 ***archaism***〉一种小棺材 a kind of small coffin

慧 huì ㄏㄨㄟˋ 聪明,有才智 clever; intelligent(㊀ ***doublet*** 智～ wisdom): ～眼 *insight; discernment* | 明～ *bright; intelligent* | 发挥工人的智～ *to bring the wisdom of the workers into play*

硊 huì ㄏㄨㄟˋ [石硊]地名,在安徽省芜湖 Shihui, a place in Wuhu, Anhui Province

秽(**穢**) huì ㄏㄨㄟˋ 肮脏 dirty: ～土 *rubbish* ㊉ ***figurative*** 丑恶的 ugly; abominable: ～行 *abominable behaviour*

翙(**翽**) huì ㄏㄨㄟˋ [翙翙]鸟飞的声音 sound of flying birds

惠 huì ㄏㄨㄟˋ 好处 favour; benefit: 恩～ *favour; patronage* | 实～ *real benefit* | 加～于人 *to bestow a favour on sb* ㊀ ***extension*** 给人好处 to benefit: 根据互～的原则,建立贸易关系 *to establish trade relations according to the principle of mutual benefit* 敬辞 ***polite***,用于对方对自己的行动(used in complimentary reference to the other party's action toward oneself): ～赠 *kind gift* | ～临 *your gracious presence*

僡 huì ㄏㄨㄟˋ 同"惠" same as 惠

蕙 huì ㄏㄨㄟˋ 蕙兰,多年生草本植物,开淡黄绿色花,气味很香 faber cymbidium, a species of orchid (*Cymbidium faberi*)

憓 huì ㄏㄨㄟˋ 同"惠" same as 惠

蟪 huì ㄏㄨㄟˋ [蟪蛄](—gū)一种蝉,比较小,青紫色。也叫"伏天儿"(also called 伏天儿) a kind of cicada

喙 huì ㄏㄨㄟˋ 嘴,特指鸟兽的嘴(used especially to denote beak of a bird or snout of an animal) mouth: 毋庸置～(不要插嘴) *to permit no interruption*

阓 huì ㄏㄨㄟˋ 见291页"阛"字条"阛阓"(huán—) see 阛

阓 on p291

溃 ㊁ huì ㄏㄨㄟˋ 疮溃(kuì)烂 festering：～脓 *suppuration*

㊀ kuì 见405页 see p405

缋 huì ㄏㄨㄟˋ 同"绘"(huì) same as 绘

殨 huì ㄏㄨㄟˋ 疮溃(kuì)烂 festering

HUN ㄏㄨㄣ

昏 hūn ㄏㄨㄣ ❶黄昏，天将黑的时候 dusk：晨～(早晚) *at dawn and dusk* ❷黑暗 dark (㊀ ***doublet*** 一暗 dim)：天～地暗 *a murky sky over the dark earth；dark all round*｜～暗不明 *dim and obscure* ❸神志不清楚，认识糊涂 confused；muddled：发～ *to feel giddy*｜病人整天～～沉沉的。*The patient is in a daze all day long*. ㊃ ***transfer*** 失去知觉 to lose consciousness：～迷 *coma*｜他～过去了。*He fainted*. ❹古同"婚" same as 婚 in ancient Chinese

阍 hūn ㄏㄨㄣ ❶宫门 palace gate ❷看(kān)门 to keep the door

惛 hūn ㄏㄨㄣ 糊涂 muddled

婚 hūn ㄏㄨㄣ 结婚，男女结为夫妇 to marry：已～ *married*｜未～ *unmarried*｜结～证 *marriage certificate* [婚姻]嫁娶，结婚的事 marriage：～～自主 *marriage of one's free will*

荤 hūn ㄏㄨㄣ ❶鸡鸭鱼肉等食物 meat or fish：～素 *meat and vegetables*｜～菜 *meat dish*｜不吃～ *to eat no meat；to be a vegetarian* ❷葱蒜等有特殊气味的菜 odorous vegetables, such as onion, garlic, etc：五～ *five kinds of pungent vegetables* ❸粗俗的，下流的 vulgar；filthy：～话 *obscene words*

浑 hún ㄏㄨㄣˊ ❶水不清，污浊 muddy；murky：～水坑 *muddy puddle* ❷骂人糊涂，不明事理(in scolding) muddle-headed；foolish：～人 *stupid person*｜～话 *nonsense* ❸全，满 whole；full：～身是汗 *to be sweating all over* ❹天然的 natural：～朴 *simple and natural*｜～厚 *simple and honest；simple and vigorous；deep and sonorous*

珲 ㊀ hún ㄏㄨㄣˊ [珲春]地名，在吉林省 Hunchun，a place in Jilin Province

㊁ huī 见296页 see p296

馄 hún ㄏㄨㄣˊ [馄饨](—tun)一种煮熟连汤吃的食品，用薄面片包上馅做成 wonton，a kind of dumpling

混 ㊁ hún ㄏㄨㄣˊ 同"浑❶❷" same as 浑❶❷

㊀ hùn 见302页 see p302

魂 hún ㄏㄨㄣˊ 迷信的人指能离开肉体而存在的精神 soul(㊀ ***doublet*** 一魄 soul)：～不附体 *beside oneself；greatly frightened* [灵魂]㊅ ***figurative*** **1** 指人的精神、思想 spirit：

H

教师是人类～～的工程师。*A teacher is an engineer of man's soul.* **2** 事物的最精粹、最主要的部分 essence

诨 hùn ㄏㄨㄣˋ 开玩笑的话 joke; jest: 打～ *to crack a joke* | ～名(外号) *nickname*

混 ㊀ hùn ㄏㄨㄣˋ ❶掺杂在一起 to mix; to blend: ～合物 *mixture* | ～杂 *to mix* | ～入 *to infiltrate* | ～充 *to pass oneself off as* | ～为一谈 *to confuse sth with sth else* ❷苟且度过 to muddle along: ～日子 *to muddle along* | 鬼～ *to fool about* ❸蒙混 to pass off as: ～过去了 *to have slipped through* | 鱼目～珠 *to pass off fish eyes as pearls — to pass off the sham as genuine* ❹胡乱 carelessly; thoughtlessly: ～乱 *confusion* | ～出主意 *to put forward thoughtless suggestions*

[混沌](—dùn) **1** 传说中指世界开辟前的状态 chaos; the primeval state of the universe according to Chinese legend **2** 糊涂,不清楚 muddle-headed

㊁ hún 见301页 see p301

溷(**图) hùn ㄏㄨㄣˋ ❶肮脏 dirty (㊣ ***doublet*** —浊 muddy) ❷厕所 toilet; lavatory ❸猪圈 pigsty

HUO ㄏㄨㄛ

耠 huō ㄏㄨㄛ ❶(—子)翻松土壤的农具 hoe ❷用耠子翻土,代替耕、锄或耩的工作 to hoe: ～地 *to hoe the earth* | ～个八九厘米深就够了。*It will do to hoe as deep as eight or nine centimetres.*

騞(**剨) huō ㄏㄨㄛ 用刀解剖东西的声音 sound of cutting things open with a knife

锪 huō ㄏㄨㄛ 一种金属加工方法。用专门的刀具对金属工件已有的孔进行加工,刮平端面或切出锥形、圆柱形凹坑 to ream

劐 huō ㄏㄨㄛ ❶用刀、剪的尖儿插入物体后顺势划开 to slit with the point of a knife or scissors: 用剪刀～开 *to slit with scissors* ❷同"耠❷" same as 耠❷

嚄 ㊀ huō ㄏㄨㄛ 叹词 ***interjection***,表示惊讶(used to express surprise) wow: ～,好大的水库! *Wow! What a big reservior!*

㊁ ǒ 见544页 see p544

豁 ㊀ huō ㄏㄨㄛ ❶残缺,裂开 to split; to crack: ～口 *breach* | ～了一个口子。*There was a split.* | ～唇 *harelip; harelipped person* [豁子](—zi)残缺的口子 chip; breach: 碗上有个～～。*The bowl has a chip in it.* | 城墙拆了一个～～。*There is a breach in the city wall.* ❷舍弃,狠心付出高代价 ready to give up; ready to pay a high price: ～出性命 *ready to give up one's life* | ～出几天时间 *ready to spend several days' time*

H

㊁ huò 见305页 see p305

攉 huō ㄏㄨㄛ 把堆在一起的东西铲起掀到另一处去 to shovel:～土 *to shovel earth*｜～煤机 *coal shovel*

和 ㊂ huó ㄏㄨㄛˊ 在粉状物中加水搅拌或揉弄使粘在一起 to mix powdered material with water:～面 *to make dough*｜～泥 *to mix earth with water*

㊀ hé 见270页 see p270

㊁ hè 见272页 see p272

㊃ huò 见304页 see p304

㊄ hú 见282页 see p282

活 huó ㄏㄨㄛˊ ❶生存,能生长,跟"死"相对(the opposite of 死) to live:鱼在水里才能～。*Fish can only live in water.*｜新栽的这棵树～了。*The newly planted tree is alive.* ㊕ ***figurative*** 逼真地 exactly; simple:～像一只老虎 *just like a tiger*｜神气～现 *very cocky; high and mighty* ❷不固定,可移动的 movable; flexible:～期存款 *current deposit*｜～页本 *loose-leaf notebook*｜～塞 *piston*｜～扣 *slipknot* [活泼]活跃自然,不呆板 lively; vivacious:孩子们很～～。*The children are very lively.* ❸(～儿)工作或生产品 work; product:做～ *to work*｜这～儿做得真好。*The work is well done.*

[活该]表示就应该这样,一点也不委屈 to serve sb right:～～如此 *to get what one deserves*

火 huǒ ㄏㄨㄛˇ ❶东西燃烧时所发的光和焰 fire ㊕ ***figurative*** 紧急 urgent:～速 *at top speed*｜～急 *urgent* ❷指枪炮弹药 firearms; ammunition:军～ *firearms and ammunition*｜～器 *firearm*｜开～ *to fire* [火药]炸药的一类,主要用作引燃药或发射药。是我国古代四大发明之一 gunpowder; powder [火线] **1** 两军交战枪炮子弹交接的地带 battle front:轻伤不下～～ *to remain at the battle front with minor wounds* **2** 从电源输送电的导线 live wire ❸红色的 red:～狐 *red fox*｜～鸡 *turkey* ❹古代军队的组织,十个人为一"火" *huo*, an ancient army unit, consisting of ten men ❺中医指引起发炎、红肿、烦躁等症状的病因(in traditional Chinese medicine) internal heat:上～ *to suffer from excessive internal heat*｜败～ *to relieve one's internal heat* ❻(～儿)怒气 anger; temper:好大的～儿! *What a temper!* ❼(～儿)发怒 to be angry:他～儿了。*He flared up.* ❽兴隆,旺盛 prosperous; thriving:生意很～。*Business is brisk.*

伙(❶-❺△夥) huǒ ㄏㄨㄛˇ ❶(～儿)伙计,同伴,一同做事的人 companion; partner:同～儿 *companion* [伙伴](*火伴)同伴,伴侣 partner ❷旧指店员(formerly used to denote a shop assistant):店～ *salesman; shop assistant* ❸合伙,结伴,联合起来 to combine; to join:～办 *to operate in partnership*｜～同 *to* *gang together* ❹由同伴组成的集体 partnership; company: 合～ *to work in partnership* | 入～ *to enter into partnership* ❺量词 ***quantifier***, 用于人群 group of people: 一～歹徒 *a band of scoundrels* | 十人一～ *in groups of ten* ❻伙食 mess; board; meals: ～补 *food allowance* | 起～ *to cook meals*

钬 huǒ ㄏㄨㄛˇ 一种金属元素, 符号 Ho, 银白色, 质软。可用于电化学研究 holmium (Ho)

漷 huǒ ㄏㄨㄛˇ [漷县] 地名, 在北京市通州 Huoxian, a place in Tongzhou, Beijing

夥 huǒ ㄏㄨㄛˇ ❶多 much; many: 获益甚～ *to gain a large profit* ❷同"伙❶—❺" same as 伙❶—❺

或 huò ㄏㄨㄛˋ ❶连词 ***conjunction***, 表示选择 or; either...or: 同意～反对 *for or against; pros and cons* ❷副词 ***adverb***, 也许 perhaps; maybe: 明晨～可抵达 *may arrive tomorrow morning* ❸文言代词 ***pronoun in classical Chinese***, 某人, 有人 somebody; someone: ～告之曰 *somebody told him that*

惑 huò ㄏㄨㄛˋ ❶疑惑, 不明白对与不对 to be puzzled; to be bewildered: 大～不解 *to be greatly puzzled* | 我很疑～。*I feel quite puzzled.* ❷使迷乱 to delude; to mislead ([连] ***doublet*** 迷— to puzzle): ～乱人心 *to confuse people's minds* | 谣言～众。*Wild rumours mislead the masses.*

和 [四] huò ㄏㄨㄛˋ ❶粉状或粒状物掺和在一起, 或加水搅拌 to mix; to mix powdered material with water: ～药 *to mix medicine* ❷量词 ***quantiffier***, 洗衣物换水的次数 number of rinses: 衣裳已经洗了两～。*The clothes have been rinsed twice.* ❸量词 ***quantifier***, 煎药加水的次数 number of decoctions: 头～药 *first decoction of herbs* | 二～药 *second decoction of herbs*

[一] hé 见270页 see p270
[二] hè 见272页 see p272
[三] huó 见303页 see p303
[五] hú 见282页 see p282

货 huò ㄏㄨㄛˋ ❶货物, 商品 goods; commodity: 进～ *to replenish one's stock* | 订～ *to order goods* [货郎] 卖零星商品的流动小贩 itinerant pedlar ❷钱币 money: 通～ *currency* [货币] 即钱币, 是充当一切商品的一般等价物的特殊商品, 可以购买任何别的商品 currency ❸卖 to sell ❹骂人时指人 (used to denote a person in cursing): 他不是个好～。*He is not a good person.* | 笨～ *fool* | 蠢～ *idiot*

获(獲、❷穫) huò ㄏㄨㄛˋ ❶得到, 取得 to get; to obtain: 俘～ *to capture* | 不～全胜, 决不收兵。*We will not withdraw our forces till complete victory.* [引] ***extension*** 能得到机会或空闲

H

can find an opportunity or spare time:不～面辞 *unable to find an opportunity to say good-bye to sb* ❷收割庄稼 to harvest; to reap [收获]割取成熟的农作物 to harvest ㊞ ***extension*** 所得到的成果 gains; results:这次学习有很大的～～。*We have learnt much from this study.*

祸(禍) huò ㄏㄨㄛˋ ❶灾殃,苦难(nàn),跟"福"相对(the opposite of 福) misfortune; disaster:大～临头。*Disaster is hanging over one's head.* or *Disaster is imminent.* | 闯～ *to get into trouble* ❷损害,使受灾殃 to harm; to injure:～国殃民 *to bring disaster to the country and the people*

嚯 huò ㄏㄨㄛˋ 迅速分裂的声音 fast tearing sound:动刀甚微,～然已解。*It was torn quickly as soon as the knife moved slightly.*

霍 huò ㄏㄨㄛˋ 迅速,快 quickly:～然病愈 *to recover from an illness quickly* [霍乱] 一种急性传染病,病原体是霍乱弧菌,多由不洁的食物传染,患者上吐下泻,手脚冰凉,重的几小时就死 cholera
[霍霍]拟声词 ***onomatopoeia***:磨刀～～ *sharpening the knife; threatening with war*

藿 huò ㄏㄨㄛˋ 藿香,多年生草本植物,茎叶香气很浓,可入药 *huo xiang*, wrinkled giant hyssop (*Agastache rugosa*)

嚯 huò ㄏㄨㄛˋ ❶叹词 ***interjection***,表示惊讶或赞叹(used to express surprise or admiration) oh; wow:～,几年不见,孩子长这么高了! *Wow! How tall the child has grown! I haven't seen him only for a few years.* ❷拟声词 ***onomatopoeia***:他～地站了起来。*He jumped to his feet all of a sudden.*

豁 ㊁ huò ㄏㄨㄛˋ ❶开通,敞亮 open; clear:～达 *generous and open-minded* | ～然开朗 *to come to understand; to be suddenly enlightened* ❷免除 to exempt(㊀ ***doublet*** —免 to exempt)

㊀ huō 见302页 see p302

镬 huò ㄏㄨㄛˋ ❶〈方 ***dialect***〉(一子)锅 pot; pan:～盖 *pot lid* ❷古代的大锅 ancient cauldron:鼎～(常用为残酷的刑具)(*usually used as instruments of torture*) *tripod and cauldron*

蠖 huò ㄏㄨㄛˋ 尺蠖,尺蠖蛾的幼虫,生长在树上,颜色像树皮,行动时身体一屈一伸地前进,是害虫 looper; inchworm

J ㄐ

JI ㄐㄧ

几(❷❸ 幾) ㊀ jī ㄐㄧ ❶(一儿)小或矮的桌子 small or low table:茶~儿 *tea table* | 条~ *long narrow table* ❷差一点,近乎 nearly; close to:~乎 *nearly; almost; close to* | ~为所害 *almost harmed by* | 迄今~四十年 *nearly 40 years up to now* ❸苗头 slight sign (*or* trace):知~其神乎 *to sense what is coming miraculously*

㊁ jǐ 见314页 see p314

讥(譏) jī ㄐㄧ 讽刺,挖苦 to ridicule; to mock (㊈***doublet***—讽 to ridicule):冷~热嘲 *burning satire and biting irony* | ~笑 *to mock*

叽(嘰) jī ㄐㄧ 拟声词(叠 ***reduplication***) ***onomatopoeia***:小鸟~~地叫。*Little birds are chirping.* [叽咕](—gu)小声说话 to whisper

饥(❷ 饑) jī ㄐㄧ ❶饿 hungry(㊈***doublet***—饿 hungry):~不择食 *A hungry person is not picky and choosy.* or *All food is delicious to the starving.* | ~寒交迫 *to suffer from hunger and cold; to be poverty-stricken* ❷庄稼收成不好或没有收成 famine; crop failure:~馑 *famine; crop failure*

玑(璣) jī ㄐㄧ ❶不圆的珍珠 pearl that is not quite round:珠~ *pearls* ❷古代测天文的仪器 ancient astronomical instrument:璇~ *armillary sphere*

机(機) jī ㄐㄧ ❶事物发生、变化的枢纽 turning or crucial point:生~ *new lease of life; gleam of hope* | 危~ *crisis* | 转~ *turning for the better* ㊊ ***extension*** **1** 对事情成败有重要关系的中心环节,有保密性质的事件 key link; sth to be kept hidden:军~ *military plan* (or *secret*) | ~密 *secret* | ~要 *confidential* **2** 机会,合宜的时候 chance; opportunity:随~应变 *to act according to circumstances* | 勿失良~。*Don't miss the golden opportunity.* or *Make hay while the sun shines.* | 好时~ *favourable opportunity* [机能]生物体器官的作用 function:~~障碍 *malfunction; functional obstruction* [机体][有机体]具有生活机能的物体,如动物和植物 organism [动机]引起行动的意识,行动前定下的愿望 motive:~~好,方法也对头,才会有好效果。*A good result can only be achieved when the*

J

motive is good and the method is right. ❷灵巧,能迅速适应事物的变化的 flexible; adaptable:～巧 *deft; adroit*｜～智 *quick-witted; resourceful*｜～警 *alert; sharp-witted* [机动] **1** 依照客观情况随时灵活行动 flexible:～～处理 *to handle sth flexibly*｜～～作战 *tactical flexibility; to conduct flexible operations* **2** 利用机器开动的 motor-driven:～～车 *motor vehicle* [机灵]聪明,头脑灵活 smart; intelligent ❸机器,由许多零件组成可以做功或有特殊作用的装置或设备 machine:织布～ *loom*｜发电～ *generator*｜收音～ *radio*｜拖拉～ *tractor* [机关] **1** 控制整个机器的关键部分 key part that controls a machine ㊀ ***extension*** 办理事务的组织 office; organ:行政～～ *administrative office* 军事～～ *military unit*｜～～工作 *office work* **2** 计谋 scheme; trick:～～算尽 *to use up all one's tricks; to be at the end of one's resources*｜识破～～ *to see through a trick* [机械] **1** 利用力学原理组成的各种装置,各种机器、杠杆、滑轮以及枪炮等都是机械 mechanism:～～化 *mechanization*｜～～工业 *machine-building industry* **2** 呆板,不灵活,按照一定的方式工作而没变化,不是辩证的 mechanical:～～地工作 *to work mechanically*｜～～唯物论 *mechanical materialism* [飞机]利用机器发动能在空中飞行的工具 aeroplane; plane [手机]手持式移动电话 mobile phone; cellular (*or* cell) phone

肌 jī ㄐㄧ 肌肉,人或动物体的组织之一,由许多肌纤维组成,具有收缩特性 muscle:心～ *cardiac muscle*｜平滑～ *smooth muscle*

矶(磯) jī ㄐㄧ 水边突出的岩石。多用于地名 (ji, usually used in a place name) projecting rock on the water front:采石～(在安徽省马鞍山市) *Caishiji (a place in Ma'anshan, Anhui Province)*｜燕子～(在江苏省南京) *Yanziji (a place in Nanjing, Jiangsu Province)*

击(擊) jī ㄐㄧ ❶打,敲打 to strike; to beat:～鼓 *to beat a drum*｜～柝(tuò)(敲梆子) *to beat a clapper* ❷攻打 to attack:迎头痛～ *to deal* (or *give*) *sb head-on blows; to make a frontal attack*｜游～ *guerrilla warfare* ❸碰 to touch:撞～ *to ram; to collide*｜肩摩毂(gǔ)～(喻来往人多拥挤) *shoulder to shoulder and heel after heel — very crowded* ㊀ ***extension*** 接触 to come into contact with:目～(亲眼看见) *to witness*

圾 jī ㄐㄧ 见409页“垃”字条“垃圾”(lā —) see 垃圾 on p409

芨 jī ㄐㄧ [白芨]多年生草本植物,叶长形。块茎可入药 hyacinth bletilla (*Bletilla striata*)

乩 jī ㄐㄧ［扶乩］旧时迷信的人占卜问疑 planchette writing, a superstitious practice in former times

鸡(鷄、*雞) jī ㄐㄧ 一种家禽，公鸡能报晓，母鸡能生蛋 chicken

奇 ㊀ jī ㄐㄧ ❶数目不成双的，跟"偶"相对(the opposite of 偶) odd：一、三、五、七、九是～数。*One, three, five, seven and nine are odd numbers.* ❷零数，余数 fractional amount; remainder：长八分有～ *eight-odd fen long*

㊁ qí 见584页 see p584

剞 jī ㄐㄧ［剞劂］(－jué) **1** 雕刻用的弯刀 graver **2** 雕版，刻书 engraving; block-print

犄 jī ㄐㄧ［犄角］**1** (－儿)物体的两个边沿相接处，棱角 corner：桌子～～儿 *corner of a table* **2** (－儿)角落 corner：墙～～儿 *corner of the walls* **3** (－jiao) 兽角 horn：牛～～ *ox horns*

畸 jī ㄐㄧ ❶不规则的，不正常的 irregular; abnormal：～形 *deformity; malformation* ❷零余的数目 fractional amount：～零 *odd lots* ❸偏 lopsided; unbalanced：～轻～重 *to attach too much weight to this and too little weight to that; to favour either one side or the other*

咭 jī ㄐㄧ 同"叽" same as 叽

唧 jī ㄐㄧ ❶用水射击 to spurt; to squirt：～筒 *pump*｜～他一身水。*Water squirted all over him.* ❷拟声词 ***onomatopoeia***，虫叫声(叠 ***reduplication***)(of insects) chirp［唧咕］(－gu)同"叽咕"same as 叽咕

积(積) jī ㄐㄧ ❶聚集 to accumulate：～少成多。*Many a little makes a mickle.* or *Many pebbles make a beach.*｜～年累月 *for many years; for months and years*｜～习 *deep-rooted habit*｜～劳 *constant overwork*［积淀］**1** 积累沉淀 to accumulate and settle **2** 积累沉淀下来的事物(多指文化、知识、经验等) accumulation［积极］向上的，进取的，跟"消极"相对 (the opposite of 消极) positive; active：工作～～ *to be active in work*｜～～分子 *activist* ❷乘积，乘法的得数 product

笄 jī ㄐㄧ 古代盘头发用的簪子 (used in a bun in ancient China) hairpin

屐 jī ㄐㄧ 木头鞋。泛指鞋 clogs; shoes in general

姬 jī ㄐㄧ ❶古代对妇女的美称 complimentary term for women in ancient China ❷旧时称妾(in former times) concubine ❸旧时称以歌舞为业的女子(in former times) professional female dancer or singer：歌～ *singing girl; sing-song girl*

基 jī ㄐㄧ ❶建筑物的根脚(of a building) base; foundation：地～ *foundation*｜墙～ *base of a wall* ㊙ ***figurative*** 根本的 basic; foundamental：～数

cardinal number｜～层组织 *primary organization*［基础］建筑物的根脚和柱石 foundation of a building [喻] ***figurative*** 事物的根基 basis：钢铁是工业的～～。*Steel is the foundation of industry.*［基金］fund **1** 国民经济中有特定用途的资金(saved or made available for a particular purpose) sum of money：消费～～ *consumption fund*｜生产～～ *production fund* **2** 为兴办或发展某一事业而集聚、储备的资金或专门拨款 any amount of money that is collected and kept for a particular purpose：教育～～ *education fund*｜福利～～ *welfare fund* ❷化学上，化合物的分子中所含的一部分原子被看作是一个单位时，叫作基(of chemistry) radical：烃(tīng)～ *hydroxyl*｜氨～ *amino-group* ❸根据 on the basis of；according to：～于上述理由 *on the basis of the above-mentioned reasons*

［基督］(外 **loanword**)基督教徒称耶稣，意为"救世主"Christ，the Saviour

［基督教］宗教名。公元1世纪犹太人耶稣所创。11世纪分为罗马教会(天主教)和希腊教会(东正教)两派；16世纪罗马教会又分为新教和旧教。现在一般称新教为基督教 Christianity

［基诺族］我国少数民族，参看附表(see the appendix) the Jino ethnic group，one of the ethnic minorities of China

［基因］(外 **loanword**)生物体中携带遗传信息的最小功能单位 gene

期(*朞) ㊁ jī ㄐㄧ〈古 ***archaism***〉一周年，一整月 one whole year (*or* month)：～年 *whole year*｜～月 *whole month*

㊀ qī 见580页 see p580

箕 jī ㄐㄧ ❶簸箕(bòji)，用竹篾、柳条或铁皮等制成的扬去糠麸或清除垃圾的器具 dustpan ❷不成圆形的指纹 loop of a fingerprint ❸星宿名，二十八宿之一 *Ji*，the 7th of the 28 constellations

赍(*齎、*賫) jī ㄐㄧ ❶怀抱着，带着 to cherish；to harbour：～志而殁(mò)(志未遂而死去) *to die with one's ambition unfulfilled*｜～恨 *to have a gnawing regret* ❷把东西送给别人 to give as a present

嵇 jī ㄐㄧ 姓 Ji，a surname

稽 ㊀ jī ㄐㄧ ❶停留 to delay：～留 *to delay*｜～迟 *to delay*｜不得～延时日。*This is not to be delayed.* ❷考核 to check；to examine ([连] ***doublet*** —核 to check；to examine)：～查 *to check*｜无～之谈 *unfounded talks；idle gossip* ❸计较，争论 to argue：反唇相～(反过来责问对方) *to retort；to answer back* ❹姓 Ji，a surname

㊁ qǐ 见588页 see p588

缉 ㊀ jī ㄐㄧ 搜捕，捉拿 to seize；to arrest：～私 *to seize smugglers* (*or smuggled*) *goods；to suppress smuggling*｜

J

通～ *to order the arrest of a criminal at large; to list sb as wanted*

㊁ qī 见581页 see p581

跻(躋) jī ㄐㄧ 登，上升 to ascend; to mount

齑(齏) jī ㄐㄧ ❶捣碎的姜、蒜、韭菜等(used as seasoning) finely chopped ginger, garlic, Chinese chives, etc ❷细，碎 fine; powdery: 化为～粉 *to reduce to fine powder; to pulverize*

畿 jī ㄐㄧ 古代称靠近国都的地方 ancient name for environs of a capital city: 京～ *capital city and its vicinity*

墼 jī ㄐㄧ 土坯 adobe [炭墼] 用炭末做成的块状物 charcoal briquette [土墼] 未烧的砖坯 adobe

激 jī ㄐㄧ ❶水冲击或急速浇淋(of water) to swash; to surge: ～起浪花(*of water*) *to break into spray* | 他被雨～病了。*He caught a chill after being drenched in the rain.* ㊀ ***extension*** 使发作，使人的感情冲动 to arouse; to excite: 刺～ *to excite; to stimulate* | 用话～他 *to stimulate him with remarks* [激昂](情绪、语调等)激动昂扬 excited and impassioned: 慷慨～～ *fervent and excited* ❷急剧的，强烈的 radical; fierce (㊟ ***doublet*** 一 烈 intense; sharp): ～变 *radical change* | ～战 *pitched battle*

羁(*覊) jī ㄐㄧ ❶马笼头 bridle; headstall ❷束缚 to control; to restrain: ～绊 *trammels; fetters* | ～押 *to detain; to take into custody* ❸停留 to stay: ～留 *to stay; to stop over* [羁旅] 寄居作客 to stay long in a strange place

及 jí ㄐㄧˊ ❶到 to reach **1** 从后头跟上 to catch up with: 来得～。*There is still time.* | 赶不～。*There's not enough time.* or *It's too late.* ㊀ ***extension*** 比得上 to match: 我不～他。*I can't match him.* **2** 达到 to come up to: 由表～里 *from the outside to the inside; from the surface to what lies behind* | 将～十载。*Nearly a decade has passed.* | ～格 *to pass; to pass a test* (or *an examination*) ❷趁着，乘 to be in time for: ～时 *timely; in time* | ～早 *before it is too late* ❸连词 ***conjunction***，和，跟(通常主要成分在前) and; as well as: 烟、酒～其他有刺激性的东西对于儿童的身体都是有害的。*Cigarettes, alcohol and other stimulants are harmful to children.* [以及] 连词 ***conjunction***，连接并列的词、词组，意义和"及❸"相同(same as 及❸) and; as well as: 花园里种着状元红、矢车菊、夹竹桃～～各色的花木。*There are various kinds of flowers and trees in the garden, such as pyracantha cornflowers, and oleanders.*

伋 jí ㄐㄧˊ 用于人名。孔伋，字子思，孔子的孙子(Ji,

used in a given name) Kong Ji, a grandson of Confucius, whose style name was Zisi

岌 jí ㄐㄧˊ ❶山高(of mountains) high; towering ❷危险 dangerous [岌岌] **1** 形容山高(of mountains) high; towering **2** 形容危险 dangerous: ～～可危 *in impending danger; to be placed in jeopardy*

汲 jí ㄐㄧˊ ❶从井里打水 to draw (water from a well): ～水 *to draw water from a well* [汲引] 旧时喻提拔人才 used as a metaphor for promotion of talented people in former times ❷(叠 ***reduplication***) 急切的样子 anxious: 不～～于富贵 *not to crave wealth and power*

级 jí ㄐㄧˊ ❶层,层次 step; tier: 那台阶有十多～。*That flight has a dozen or so steps.* | 七～浮屠(七层的塔) *seven-storeyed tower* ❷等次 level; rank: 高～ *senior* | 低～ *junior* | 初～ *elementary* | 上～ *superior* | 下～ *subordinate* ❸年级,学校编制的名称,学年的分段 grade: 同～不同班 *in different classes of the same grade* | 三年～ *grade three* | 高年～ *senior grade*

极(極) jí ㄐㄧˊ ❶顶端,最高点,尽头处 utmost point: 登峰造～ *to reach the apex of perfection; to have a very high level* ❷指地球的南北两端,磁体的两端或电路的正负两端 pole: 南～ *South Pole; Antarctic Pole* | 北～ *North Pole; Arctic Pole* | 阳～ *positive pole* | 阴～ *negative pole* [南极洲] 世界七大洲之一 Antarctic Continent, one of the 7 continents of the world ❸副词 ***adverb***,最,达到顶点 extremely: 大～了 *extremely big* | ～好 *extremely good* | 穷凶～恶 *extremely violent and wicked* ❹竭尽 to the utmost: ～力 *to do one's utmost; to spare no effort* | ～目 *to look as far as the eye can see*

笈 jí ㄐㄧˊ ❶书箱 book chest ❷书籍,典籍 book; ancient classics

吉 jí ㄐㄧˊ ❶幸福的,吉利的 lucky; auspicious (㊀ ***doublet*** 一祥 lucky | 一庆 auspicious occasion): ～日 *auspicious day* | ～期 *wedding day* ❷(外 ***loanword***)法定计量单位中十进倍数单位词头之一,表示 10^9(符号 G) giga- (G)

佶 jí ㄐㄧˊ 健壮 robust and sturdy

[佶屈][诘屈]曲折 complicated: ～～聱(áo)牙(文句拗口) *to be full of words that are difficult to pronounce*

诘 ㊁ jí ㄐㄧˊ [诘屈]同"佶屈"。参看311页"佶"(jí) (see 佶 on p311) same as 佶屈

㊀ jié 见346页 see p346

姞 jí ㄐㄧˊ 姓 Ji, a surname

即 jí ㄐㄧˊ ❶就是 that is; namely; i. e. : 番茄～西红

柿。*Fanqie*（*tomato*）*is Xihongshi*（*tomato*）. ❷当时或当地 present moment; prompted by the occasion:～日 *this*（or *that*）*very day*; *a short time from now*|～刻 *at once*; *immediately*|～席发表谈话 *to make an impromptu speech*|～景生情 *to be touched at what one sees* ❸副词 **adverb**，便，就 promptly; at once:胜利～在眼前。*Victory is coming in sight.*|用毕～行奉还 *to return sth immediately after using it* [即使]连词 **conjunction**，常和"也"字连用表示假设性让步(usually used in collocation with 也 to express suppositional concession) even if; even though:～～我们的工作取得了很大的成绩，也不能骄傲自满。*We should not get conceited and self-satisfied even if we have achieved much in our work.* ❹靠近 to approach:不～不离 *to be neither too close nor too distant* [即位]指封建统治者登上帝王的位子，做君主或诸侯 to ascend the throne

亟 ㊀ jí ㄐㄧˊ 副词 **adverb**，急切地 urgently; anxiously:～待解决 *to demand prompt solution*|缺点～应纠正。*The faults should be speedily put right.*

㊁ qì 见589页 see p589

殛 jí ㄐㄧˊ 杀死 to kill:雷～ *to be struck dead by lightning*

革 ㊁ jí ㄐㄧˊ 〈古 **archaism**〉(病)危急(of an illness) in a critical condition

㊀ gé 见224页 see p224

急 jí ㄐㄧˊ ❶焦躁 impatient; anxious(㊊ **doublet** 焦—anxious; worried):真～死人了。*I'm worried to death.*|不要着～。*There is no hurry.* or *Don't worry.* ㊊ **extension** 气恼，发怒 irritated; annoyed:没想到他～了。*I didn't expect him to get angry.* ❷匆促 hurried; hasty:～～忙忙 *in a hurry*|～就 *finished in haste*|～于完成任务 *to be eager to complete the task* ㊊ **extension** 迅速，又快又猛 fast; rapid and violent:水流得～。*The water flows swiftly.*|～病 *acute disease* ❸迫切，要紧 urgent; pressing:～事 *urgent matter*|不～之务 *not a pressing thing*; *matter of no great urgency*|～件 *urgent document*（or *dispatch*）㊊ **extension** 严重 critical:情况紧～ *emergency*|告～ *to appeal for emergency help*|病～乱投医(喻临事慌乱) *to turn to any doctor one can find in case of critical illness — to try anything when in a desperate situation* ❹对大家的事或别人的困难赶快帮助 to be eager to help those in need:～公好义 *zealous for the public interest*; *public-spirited*|～难(nàn) *to be eager to help those in danger*

J

疾 jí ㄐㄧˊ ❶病，身体不舒适 disease; illness（㊥ **doublet** 一病 disease）：目～ *eye trouble*｜积劳成～ *to fall ill from overwork* ㊀ **extension** 一般的痛苦 suffering：关心群众的～苦 *to be concerned about the distress of the masses* ❷恨 to hate：～恶如仇 *to hate evil as if it were one's enemy* ❸快，迅速，猛烈 fast; quick; violently：～走 *to go swiftly*｜～风知劲草。*The strong wind reveals the strength of the grass.* or *Only in time of crisis can one's moral stamina be best tested.*｜～言厉色（指发怒的样子）*hasty speech and angry looks* ❹疼痛 pain：痛心～首 *with bitter hatred; with great resentment*

蒺 jí ㄐㄧˊ ［蒺藜］(—li) **1** 一年生草本植物，茎横生在地面上，开小黄花。果实也叫蒺藜，有刺，可入药 puncture vine (*Tribulus terrestris*) **2** 像蒺藜的东西 things that are like puncture vine：铁～～ *caltrap*｜～～骨朵（旧时一种兵器）jiliguduo (*an ancient weapon consisting of a shaft and a caltrap-shaped hammerhead*)

嫉 jí ㄐㄧˊ 因别人比自己好而憎恨 jealous; envious（㊥ **doublet** 一妒 to be jealous of; to envy｜妒一 to be jealous of; to envy）：～才 *to be jealous of a talented person*｜他很羡慕你，但并不～妒你。*He admires you very much but he is not jealous.*

棘 jí ㄐㄧˊ ❶酸枣树，落叶灌木，开黄绿色小花，茎上多刺。果实小，味酸 sour jujube ❷针形的刺 thorn：～皮动物 *echinoderm*［棘手］刺手，扎手 thorny ㊙ **figurative** 事情难办 troublesome ❸指有刺的草木 thorny plants; brambles：披荆斩～ *to open a way by breaking through brambles and thorns; to clear obstacles from one's way*

集 jí ㄐㄧˊ ❶聚，会合，总合 to gather; to collect（㊥ **doublet** 聚一 to assemble）：～思广益 *to pool the collective wisdom*｜～会 *assembly; meeting; rally*｜～中 *to concentrate; to assemble*［集体］许多人合起来的有组织的总体 collectiveness：～～利益 *collective interests*｜～～所有制 *collective ownership* ❷会合许多著作编成的书 collection; anthology：诗～ *collection of poems*｜文～ *collected writings*｜选～ *selected works* ❸某些篇幅较长的著作或作品中相对独立的部分 volume; part：影片分上下～。*The film is in two parts.*｜十～电视纪录片 *ten-part television documentary* ❹定期交易的市场 market; fair：赶～ *to go to a country fair* ❺完成 to accomplish：大业未～。*The great undertaking has not been accomplished yet.*

J

楫(*檝) jí ㄐㄧˊ 划船用的桨 oar

辑 jí ㄐㄧˊ ❶聚集。特指聚集材料编书 to collect; to compile; to edit:～录 *to compile*|纂～ *to edit* ❷整套书籍、资料等按内容或发表次序分成的各个部分 part; volume; division:丛书第一～ *first part of a set of books* ❸和睦 harmonious:～睦 *harmonious*

戢 jí ㄐㄧˊ 收敛,收藏 to restrain; to put away:～翼 (*of a bird*) *to fold its wings* — *to go into retirement*|载～干戈(把兵器收藏起来) *to store up arms* ㊀ ***extension*** 止,停止 to stop:～怒 *to keep one's temper*

蕺 jí ㄐㄧˊ 蕺菜,也叫"鱼腥草"。多年生草本植物,茎上有节,花小而密。茎和叶有腥味,根可作蔬菜,全草可入药(also called 鱼腥草) cordate houttuynia (*Houttuynia cordata*)

嵴 jí ㄐㄧˊ 山脊 mountain (*or* hill) ridge

瘠 jí ㄐㄧˊ ❶瘦弱 thin and weak ❷土地不肥沃 barren; poor:～土 *barren land; sterile soil*|把贫～的土地变成良田 *to turn barren land into fertile farmland*

鹡 jí ㄐㄧˊ [鹡鸰](—líng)鸟名。头黑额白,背部黑色,腹部白色,尾巴较长,生活在水边,捕食小虫 wagtail (*Motacilla*)

踖 jí ㄐㄧˊ 小步行走 to take short steps; to walk with small paces

踖 jí ㄐㄧˊ 见111页"蹴"字条"蹴踖"(cù—) see 蹴踖 on p111

藉 ㊁ jí ㄐㄧˊ ❶践踏,凌辱 to tread on; to insult [狼藉] (*狼籍)乱七八糟 in disorder; in a mess:杯盘～～ *with wine cups and plates lying about in disorder after a feast*|声名～～ *to bring into disrepute; to have a bad name* ❷姓 Ji, a surname

㊀ jiè 见350页 see p350

籍 jí ㄐㄧˊ ❶书,书册 book(㊊ ***doublet*** 书— book):六～(六经) *the Six Classics*|古～ *ancient books* ❷登记隶属关系的簿册,隶属关系 register; membership:户～ *census register; household register*|国～ *nationality*|党～ *party membership*|学～ *school register*

[籍贯]自身出生或祖居的地方 place of one's birth; native place

几(幾) ㊀ jǐ ㄐㄧˇ ❶询问数量多少 how many:～个人? *How many people are there?*|来～天了? *How many days have you been here?*

[几何] **1** 多少 how many; how much **2** 几何学,研究点、线、面、体的性质、关系和计算方法的学科 geometry ❷表示不定的数目 a few; several; some:他才十～岁。*He is only in his* *teens*. | 所剩无～ *not much left*

㊁ jī 见306页 see p306

虮（蟣） jǐ ㄐㄧˇ（一子）虱子的卵 nit

麂 jǐ ㄐㄧˇ（一子）兽名。像鹿，比鹿小，毛黄黑色，雄的有很短的角 muntjac (*Muntiacus*)

己 jǐ ㄐㄧˇ ❶代词 ***pronoun***，自己，对人称本身 self; oneself：舍～为人 *to sacrifice oneself for others* | 身不由～ *not to be one's own master* ❷天干的第六位，用作顺序的第六 *Ji*, the 6th of the 10 Heavenly Stems; sixth

纪 ㊁ jǐ ㄐㄧˇ 姓 Ji, a surname

㊀ jì 见316页 see p316

鲯 jǐ ㄐㄧˇ 鱼名。身体侧扁，略呈椭圆形，头小，口小，生活在海底岩石间 girella (*Girella punctata*)

挤（擠） jǐ ㄐㄧˇ ❶用压力使排出 to squeeze; to press：～牛奶 *to milk* | ～牙膏 *to squeeze toothpaste from a tube* ❷互相推、拥 to jostle; to push against：人多～不过去。*There are too many people for us to push through.* | ～进会场 *to squeeze into the conference hall* ㊀ ***extension*** 排斥 to expel; to exclude（㊉ ***doublet*** 排一 to exclude）：互相排～ *each trying to exclude the other* ❸许多人、物很紧地挨着，不容易动转 to crowd; to pack：一间屋子住十来个人，太～了。*The room is too crowded for a dozen people to live in.*

济（濟） ㊁ jǐ ㄐㄧˇ 济水，古水名，发源于今河南省，流经山东省入渤海 Jishui River, an ancient river that originated in today's Henan Province and flowed through Shandong Province into the Bohai Sea [济南][济宁]地名，都在山东省 Jinan, Jining, places both in Shandong Province

[济济]众多 many; numerous：人才～～ *a galaxy of talented people*

㊀ jì 见318页 see p318

给 ㊁ jǐ ㄐㄧˇ ❶供应 to supply; to provide：自～自足 *self-sufficient* | 补～ *supplies* | ～养（军队中主副食、燃料，以及牲畜饲料等物资供应的统称）*provisions* ❷富裕，充足 ample; abundant：家～人足 *Each family is provided for and every person is well-fed and well-clothed.* or *All live in plenty.*

㊀ gěi 见227页 see p227

脊 jǐ ㄐㄧˇ ❶人或动物背中间的骨头 spine; backbone：～椎骨 *spine* | ～髓 *spinal cord* | ～梁 *backbone* ❷物体中间高起、形状像脊柱的部分 ridge：屋～ *ridge of a roof* | 山～ *mountain ridge*

掎 jǐ ㄐㄧˇ 拖住，牵制 to pin down

戟（**戟） jǐ ㄐㄧˇ 古兵器的一种，长杆头上附有月牙状的利刃 halberd

计 jì ㄐㄧˋ ❶核算 to count; to calculate（㊉ ***doublet*** 一算 to count）：不～其数 *countless*;

innumerable ❷测量或计算度数、时间等的仪器 meter; gauge：时～ *timer*; *timepiece*｜体温～ *thermometer* ❸主意，策略 idea; stratagem（㊥ ***doublet*** 一策 stratagem）：妙～ *brilliant scheme*｜百年大～ *programme benefiting future generations* ❹计划，打算 to make a plan; to intend：为工作方便～ *with a view to making work easier* [计较]（—jiào）**1** 打算，商量 to intend; to discuss：来，咱们～～一下。*Come on, let's discuss it.* **2** 争论，较量 to argue; to dispute：大家都没有和他～～。*None of us disputed with him.*

痣 jì ㄐㄧˋ 皮肤上生来就有的深色斑。现多写作"记"（now usually written as 记）birthmark

记 jì ㄐㄧˋ ❶记忆，把印象保持在脑子里 to remember; to bear in mind：～住这件事 *to bear this in mind*｜～性 *memory* ❷把事物写下来 to write down; to record：～录 *to take notes*｜～账 *to keep accounts*｜把这些事情都～在笔记本上。*Write down everything in the notebook.* [记者]报刊、电台、电视台、通讯社里做采访报道工作的人员 reporter; correspondent ❸记载事物的书册或文字 note; record：游～ *travel notes*｜日～ *diary*｜大事～ *chronicle of major events* ❹记号，标志 mark; sign：以红色为～ *marked by red*｜戳～ *stamp* ❺同"痣"same as 痣

纪 ㊀ jì ㄐㄧˋ ❶记载 to record：～事 *chronicle of events* [纪念]用事物或行动对人或事表示怀念 to commemorate [纪元]纪年的开始，如公历以传说的耶稣出生那一年为元年 era; epoch; beginning of an era (e.g. the Gregorian calendar adopted the birth year of Christ as its first year) ❷古时把十二年算作一纪 *ji*, twelve years' period in ancient China [世纪]一百年叫一世纪 century ❸制度，法度 discipline：军～ *military discipline*｜违法乱～ *to break laws and violate discipline* [纪律]集体生活里必须共同遵守的规则 discipline：遵守劳动～～ *to observe* (or *keep*) *labour discipline* ❹地质年代分级的第三级，在"代"之下 period, the third stage of geologic time divisions under 代：第四～ *the fourth period*｜侏罗～ *Jurassic Period*｜寒武～ *Cambrian Period*

㊁ jǐ 见315页 see p315

忌 jì ㄐㄧˋ ❶嫉妒，憎恨 to be jealous of; to envy：猜～ *to be jealously suspicious*｜～才 *to be jealous of talented people* ❷怕，畏惧 to fear; to dread：肆无～惮 *unscrupulous* [顾忌]有所顾虑，不敢大胆说话或行动 scruple：有话尽管说，不要有什么～～。*Don't hesitate to speak your mind.* ❸禁戒 to quit; to give up：～酒 *to give up alcohol*｜～口 *to avoid certain food*｜～食生冷 *to avoid cold and un-*

J

cooked food [忌讳] **1** 由于风俗、习惯的顾忌,言谈或动作有所隐避,日久成为禁戒 taboo **2** 对某些能产生不利后果的事力求避免 to avoid as a taboo

跽 jì ㄐㄧˋ 长跪,挺直上身两膝着地 to kneel with the upper part of the body erect

伎 jì ㄐㄧˋ ❶技巧,才能 skill; ability [伎俩](—liǎng)手段,花招 trick; intrigue ❷古代称以歌舞为业的女子 professional female singer or dancer in ancient China

技 jì ㄐㄧˋ 才能,手艺 ability; skill(㊟ ***doublet*** —艺 skill|—能 technical ability; skill):~巧 *technique; skill*|口~ *vocal mimicry* (or *imitation*)|~师 *technician*|一~之长(cháng) *proficiency in a particular field* [技术] **1** 进行物质资料生产所凭借的方法、能力或设备等 technology; technique:~~革新 *technological* (or *technical*) *innovation* **2** 专门的技能 skill:他打球的~~很高明。*He is very skillful at playing ball.*

芰 jì ㄐㄧˋ 古书上指菱(in ancient Chinese texts) water chestnut; water caltrop

妓 jì ㄐㄧˋ 妓女,以卖淫为生的女人 prostitute; whore

系(繫) ㊁ jì ㄐㄧˋ 结,扣 to tie; to button up:把鞋带~上 *to tie shoe laces*

㊀ xì 见806页 see p806

际(際) jì ㄐㄧˋ ❶交界或靠边的地方 border; edge:林~ *edge of woods*|水~ *waterside*|天~ *horizon*|春夏之~ *time between spring and summer* ❷彼此之间 between; among:国~ *international*|厂~竞赛 *interfactory contest* ❸时候 occasion; time:当祖国进行社会主义建设之~ *at the time when the motherland is implementing the socialist construction* ❹当,适逢其时 on the occasion of:~此盛会 *on the occasion of this grand gathering*

季 jì ㄐㄧˋ ❶兄弟排行,有时用伯、仲、叔、季做次序,季是最小的 fourth (*or* youngest) among brothers, the other three being 伯,仲 and 叔, from elder to younger:~弟 *the fourth* (or *the youngest*) *brother*|~父(小叔叔) *youngest uncle; uncle* ㊀ ***extension*** 末了 last:~世 *last phase of an age; last period of a dynasty*|~春(春季末一月) *last month of spring* ❷三个月为一季 season:一年分春、夏、秋、冬四~。*A year is divided into four seasons: spring, summer, autumn and winter.* ㊀ ***extension*** (—儿)一段时间 period of time:瓜~儿 *watermelon season*|淡~ *slack season*|雨~ *rainy season*

悸 jì ㄐㄧˋ 因害怕而心跳(of the heart) to beat (*or* throb) with terror:~栗(心惊肉跳) *to shake* (or *tremble*) *with fear*|惊~ *to palpitate with terror*|心有余~ *to have a*

lingering fear

剂(劑) jì ㄐㄧˋ ❶配合而成的药 pharmaceutical preparation:药～ *medicament; pharmaceutical preparation*|清凉～ *cooling ointment* [调剂](tiáo－) **1** 配制药物 to make up (*or* fill) a prescription **2** 适当调整 to adjust; to regulate ❷量词 ***quantifier***,用于水煎服的中药(of Chinese herbal medicine) dose:一～药 *a dose of decoction*

荠(薺) ㊀ jì ㄐㄧˋ 荠菜,二年生草本植物,花白色。茎叶嫩时可以吃 shepherd's purse (*Capsella bursa-pastoris*)

㊁ qí 见590页 see p590

济(濟) ㊀ jì ㄐㄧˋ ❶对困苦的人加以帮助 to aid; to relieve; to help:救～金 *relief fund*|～困扶危 *to assist the poor and help those in trouble* ❷补益 to be helpful; to benefit:无～于事 *in vain; useless* ❸渡,过河 to cross a river:同舟共～ *to be in the same boat —to share in trouble with someone*

㊁ jǐ 见315页 see p315

霁(霽) jì ㄐㄧˋ ❶雨、雪停止,天放晴 to clear up after rain or snow:雪初～。*The snow is over and the sky is clearing up.* ❷怒气消除 to calm down after being angry:色～ *to calm down after losing temper*

鲚(鱭) jì ㄐㄧˋ 鱼名。有刀鲚、凤鲚等多种。身体侧扁,无侧线,头小而尖,尾尖而细。生活在海洋中 anchovy (*Engraulidae*)

垍 jì ㄐㄧˋ 坚土 solid earth

洎 jì ㄐㄧˋ 到,及 up to:自古～今 *from ancient times up to the present*

迹(*跡、*蹟) jì ㄐㄧˋ 脚印 mark; footprint (㊥ ***doublet*** 踪－ trace):足～ *footmark; trace*|兽蹄鸟～ *animals' footprints and birds' traces* ㊀ ***extension*** **1** 物体遗留下的印痕 mark; trace (㊥ ***doublet*** 痕－ trace):～象 *sign* **2** 前人遗留下的事物(多指建筑、器物等) remains; ruins; vestige:古～ *historic site; place of historic interest*|陈～ *thing of the past*

既 jì ㄐㄧˋ ❶终了,尽 finished; over:言未～。*It's not yet the last word.* or *The speech isn't over yet.* [食既] 指日食、月食的食尽 the second contact of an eclipse ❷副词 ***adverb***,已经 already:霜露～降。*Frost and dew have already descended.*|～往不咎 *to forgive one's past misdeeds*|保持～有的荣誉 *to keep an acquired reputation* [既而] 副词 ***adverb***,后来,经过一段时间以后 afterwards; later:起初以为困难很多,～～看出这些困难都是可以克服的。*At first I thought there were many difficulties,* *but later on I found that all these difficulties could be overcome.* ❸连词 ***conjunction*** **1** 既然,后面常与"就"、"则"相应(usually used in collocation with 就 or 则) since; now that: ～要做,就要做好。*Now that you want to do that, do it well.* **2** 常跟"且"、"又"连用,表示两者并列(usually used in collocation with 且 or 又) both … and: ～高且大 *tall and big* | ～快又好 *both quickly and well done*

塈 jì ㄐㄧˋ ❶用泥涂屋顶 to spread plaster on the roof ❷休息 to rest ❸取 to take; to fetch

暨 jì ㄐㄧˋ 与,及,和 and

觊(覬) jì ㄐㄧˋ 希望,希图 to hope; to covet [觊觎](－yú)非分的希望或企图 to covet

继(繼) jì ㄐㄧˋ 连续,接着 to continue; to follow (㊇ ***doublet*** 一续 to continue): ～任 *to succeed to an office* | ～往开来 *to carry the past tradition forward and make new advances* | 前仆后～ *Behind the fallen is an endless column of successors.* [继承] **1** 接受遗产 to inherit **2** 继续前人的事业 to continue the work left by the deceased

偈 ㊀ jì ㄐㄧˋ 和尚唱的词句 words for chanting in Buddhist scripture

㊁ jié 见347页 see p347

徛 jì ㄐㄧˋ 〈方 ***dialect***〉站立 to stand

寄 jì ㄐㄧˋ ❶托付,寄托 to entrust; to deposit: ～放 *to leave in the care of sb; to leave with sb* | ～希望于未来 *to place hope on the future* ❷依靠,依附 to depend on; to attach oneself to: ～居 *to live away from home; to live temporarily with sb* | ～生 *parasitism* | ～宿 *to lodge at* (or *with*) ❸托人传送。特指由邮局传递 to send; to post: ～信 *to post* (or *mail*) *a letter* | ～钱 *to remit* (or *send*) *money* | ～包裹 *to send* (or *dispatch*) *a parcel by post*

祭 jì ㄐㄧˋ ❶对死者表示追悼、敬意 to hold a memorial ceremony for the deceased (㊇ ***doublet*** 一奠 to hold a memorial ceremony for the deceased): 公～烈士 *to hold a public memorial ceremony for martyrs* ❷供奉鬼神等 to offer sacrifices to gods and ghosts: ～神 *to offer sacrifices to gods* | ～天 *to offer sacrifices to Heaven*

穄 jì ㄐㄧˋ (－子)又叫"糜(méi)子"。一种谷物,跟黍子相似,但不黏(also called 糜子) broomcorn millet (*Panicum miliaceum*)

寂 jì ㄐㄧˋ 静,没有声音 quiet; silent(㊇ ***doublet*** 一静 quiet): ～然无声 *in complete silence* [寂寞](－mò)清静,孤独 solitary; lonely; lonesome

绩(❷*勣) jì ㄐㄧˋ ❶把麻搓(cuō)捻成线

J

或绳 to twist hemp into thread ❷功业,成果 achievement; accomplishment:成～ *achievement* | 战～ *military achievement* | 伟大的功～ *brilliant feats*

惎 jì ㄐㄧˋ ❶毒害 to poison ❷忌恨 to hate

蓟 jì ㄐㄧˋ 多年生草本植物,茎叶多刺,春天出芽,花紫色,可入药 thistle (*Circium japonicum*)

稷 jì ㄐㄧˋ ❶古代一种粮食作物,有的书说是黍属,有的书说是粟(谷子)(in ancient China) millet; grain crop ❷古代以稷为百谷之长,因此帝王奉祀为谷神 god of grains worshipped by emperors, as millet was the foremost of all cereals in ancient China [社稷] [转] *transfer* 古代指国家(in ancient China) state; country:执干戈以卫～～ *to take up arms to defend the state*

鲫 jì ㄐㄧˋ 鲫鱼,鱼名。形似鲤鱼,没有须,背脊隆起,生活在淡水中,肉可吃 goldfish (*Carassius auratus*)

髻 jì ㄐㄧˋ 梳在头顶或脑后的发结 hair bun:高～ *high hair bun*

冀 jì ㄐㄧˋ ❶希望 hope ❷河北省的别称 Ji, another name for Hebei Province

骥 jì ㄐㄧˋ 好马 fine horse:按图索～ *to look for a horse with the aid of its picture —to look for sth by following up a clue; to do things mechanically*

罽 jì ㄐㄧˋ 用毛做成的毡子一类的东西 felt

檵 jì ㄐㄧˋ 檵木,常绿灌木或小乔木,叶子椭圆形或卵圆形,花淡黄色,结蒴果,褐色。枝条和叶子可以提制栲胶,种子可以榨油。叶可入药 Chinese fringe flower (*Loropetalum chinense*)

JIA ㄐㄧㄚ

加 jiā ㄐㄧㄚ ❶增多,几种事物合起来 to add; to increase ([连] ***doublet*** 增—to increase; to add):～价 *to raise the price* | 三个数相～ *to add up three numbers* | 增～工资 *to increase one's salary* (or *wage*) [加法] 几个数求和的算法 addition [加工] 把原料制成成品或使粗制物品精良 to process; to refine [加油儿] [喻] ***figurative*** 努力,加劲儿 to step up efforts ❷施以某种动作 to carry out a certain action:希～注意。*Please pay attention.* | ～以保护 *to protect* ❸把本来没有的添上去 to put in; to add:～引号(" "或' ') *to put in quotation marks* (" " *or* ' ')

伽 ㊂ jiā ㄐㄧㄚ [伽倻](—yē) 伽倻琴,朝鲜族弦乐器 (traditional Korean zitherlike string instrument) gayageum [伽利略] 意大利天文学家、物理学家 Galileo, Italian astronomer and physicist

㊀ qié 见603页 see p603
㊁ gā 见212页 see p212

J

茄 ㊁ jiā ㄐㄧㄚ〈古 ***archaism***〉荷茎 stem of lotus

[雪茄]（外 ***loanword***）一种较粗较长用烟叶卷成的卷烟 cigar

㊀ qié 见604页 see p604

迦 jiā ㄐㄧㄚ 译音用字（used in transliteration）

珈 jiā ㄐㄧㄚ 古代妇女的一种首饰 *jia*, an ornament attached to a woman's hairpin in ancient China

枷 jiā ㄐㄧㄚ 旧时一种套在脖子上的刑具（in former times）cangue [枷锁][喻] ***figurative*** 束缚 bonds：砸碎封建～～ *to smash the feudal yoke*

痂 jiā ㄐㄧㄚ 伤口或疮口血液、淋巴液等凝结成的东西 scab

耞 jiā ㄐㄧㄚ 见437页"连"字条"连耞"（lián—）see 连耞 on p437

笳 jiā ㄐㄧㄚ 胡笳，我国古代北方民族的一种乐器，类似笛子 Tartar reed flute, a reed instrument used by northern tribes in ancient China

袈 jiā ㄐㄧㄚ [袈裟]（—shā）和尚披在外面的一种法衣 *kasaya*, long garment worn by a Buddhist monk

跏 jiā ㄐㄧㄚ [跏趺]（—fū）佛教徒的一种坐姿 cross-legged sitting posture of a Buddhist

嘉 jiā ㄐㄧㄚ ❶美好 good; fine：～宾 *honoured* (*or distinguished*) *guest* ❷赞美 to praise：～许 *to praise; to approve*｜精神可～。*The spirit deserves commendation.*

夹（夾）㊀ jiā ㄐㄧㄚ ❶从东西的两旁钳住 to pinch：书里～着一张纸。*There is a piece of paper between the leaves of the book.* [引] ***extension*** **1** 两旁有东西限制住 in between：～道 *passageway*｜两山～一水。*There is a river in between two mountains.* or *The river is sandwiched between two mountains.* **2** 从两面来的 from both sides：～攻 *to attack from two flanks* ❷胳膊向胁部用力，使腋下放着的东西不掉下 to carry sth under one's armpit：～着书包 *to carry a schoolbag under one's armpit* ❸掺杂 to mix; to mingle ([连] ***doublet*** —杂 to be mixed up with)：～七杂八 *to talk incoherently*｜～生 *half-cooked; half-baked* ❹（—子、—儿）夹东西的器具 clip; folder：文件～ *folder*｜皮～儿 *wallet*

㊁ jiá 见322页 see p322

㊂ gā 见212页 see p212

浃（浹）jiā ㄐㄧㄚ 湿透，遍及 to soak through; to spread all over：汗流～背 *streaming with sweat*

佳 jiā ㄐㄧㄚ 美，好的 good; fine：～音（好消息）*good news*｜～句 *beautiful line*｜～作 *fine piece of writing*

家 ㊀ jiā ㄐㄧㄚ ❶家庭，人家 family; household：勤俭持～ *to be industrious and thrifty in running a household; to manage one's household with*

industry and frugality｜张～有五口人。*There are five people in Zhang's family*. 谦辞 ***humble***，用于对别人称自己亲属中比自己年纪大或辈分高的 (used to address relatives older than oneself) my：～兄 *my brother*｜～父 *my father*［家常］家庭日常生活 daily life of a family：～～便饭 *ordinary home-cooked meal* — *common occurrence*｜叙～～ *to talk about daily life*［家畜］(—chù) 由人喂养的禽兽，如马、牛、羊、鸡、猪等 domestic animals; livestock［家伙］(—huo) **1** 一般的用具、工具 tool; utensil **2** 指武器 weapon **3** 指牲畜或人(轻视或玩笑) (used to denote domestic animals or men contemptuously or jokingly) guy; fellow［家具］家庭用具，主要指床、柜、桌、椅等 furniture［家什］(— shi) 用具，器物 tools; utensils; furniture：厨房里的～～擦洗得干干净净。*The kitchen utensils have been wiped clean*. ❷ 家庭的住所 home：回～ *to go home*｜这儿就是我的～。*Here is my home*. ❸指经营某种行业或有某种身份的人家 person or family engaged in a certain trade：农～ *farm household*｜酒～ *inn* ❹掌握某种专门学识或有丰富实践经验以及从事某种专门活动的人 specialist：科学～ *scientist*｜水稻专～ *rice expert*｜政治～ *statesman* ❺学术流派 school; school of thought：儒～ *Confucian school*｜道～ *Taoist school*｜百～争鸣。*Let a hundred schools of thought contend*. ❻指相对各方中的一方 one side; one party：上～ *previous player* (or *party*)｜下～ *next player* (or *party*) ❼(jiɑ) 词尾 ***suffix***，指一类的人(多按年龄或性别分) (used to denote a specific group of people, usually according to age or gender)：姑娘～*girls*｜孩子～ *kids* ❽量词 ***quantifier***：一～人家*a family*｜两～饭馆 *two restaurants* ❾姓 Jia, a surname

㊁ jie 见350页 see p350

傢 jiā ㄐㄧㄚ “家”的繁体字。用于“傢伙”、“傢具”、“傢什”。参看 321 页“家㊀❶” (used in 傢伙，傢具 and 傢什，see 家㊀❶ on p321) the original complex form of 家

镓 jiā ㄐㄧㄚ 一种金属元素，符号 Ga，银白色，质软。可制合金 gallium (Ga)

葭 jiā ㄐㄧㄚ 初生的芦苇 young reed［葭莩］(— fú) 苇子里的薄膜 membrane of a reed stem ⑩ ***figurative*** 关系疏远的亲戚 distant relative

豭 jiā ㄐㄧㄚ 公猪 boar

夹(夾、*裌、△*袷)

㊁ jiá ㄐㄧㄚˊ 两层的衣物 double-layered clothing：～裤 *lined trousers*｜～被 *lined quilt*

㊀ jiā 见321页 see p321

㊂ gā 见212页 see p212

“袷”又 qiā 见 590 页 also

qiā, see p590

郏(郟) jiá ㄐㄧㄚˊ 郏县,在河南省 Jiaxian County, in Henan Province

荚(莢) jiá ㄐㄧㄚˊ 豆类植物的长形的果实 pod:豆～(豆角) *bean pod* | 皂～ *Chinese honey locust* | 槐树～ *pod of a Chinese scholar tree*

铗(鋏) jiá ㄐㄧㄚˊ ❶冶铸用的钳 pincers; tongs ❷剑 sword ❸剑柄 hilt

颊(頰) jiá ㄐㄧㄚˊ 脸的两侧 cheek:两～绯红 *rosy cheeks* (图见758页"头" picture on p758)

蛱(蛺) jiá ㄐㄧㄚˊ [蛱蝶](—dié)蝴蝶的一类,翅有各种鲜艳的色斑。前足退化或短小,触角锤状 painted lady (*Vanessa cardui*)

恝 jiá ㄐㄧㄚˊ 无忧愁,淡然 indifferent; unconcerned [恝置]不在意,置之不理 to ignore; to neglect

戛(*戞) jiá ㄐㄧㄚˊ ❶打击 to knock; to tap ❷拟声词 ***onomatopoeia***:～然而止 *to come to an abrupt halt* [戛戛]形容困难 difficult:～～乎难哉。*How difficult it is!*

甲 jiǎ ㄐㄧㄚˇ ❶天干的第一位,用作顺序的第一 *Jia*, the 1st of the 10 Heavenly Stems; first ㊀ ***extension*** 居首位,超过所有其他的 to rank first:桂林山水～天下。*The mountains and waters of Guilin are the finest under heaven.* [甲子]我国纪日、纪年或计算岁数的一种方法,以十干和十二支顺序配合,六十组干支字轮一周叫一个甲子(a method of designating days, years or age in China, which combines the ten Heavenly Stems and twelve Earthly Branches to form 60 unique pairs to represent a cycle of 60 years) *jiazi*, a cycle of 60 years ❷古代军人打仗穿的护身衣服,用皮革或金属做成 armour:盔～ *armour* ❸动物身上有保护功能的硬壳 shell:龟～ *tortoise shell* | ～虫 *beetle* [甲骨文]我国商周时代刻在龟甲兽骨上的文字 inscriptions on tortoise shells or animal bones of the Shang and Zhou dynasties [甲鱼]鳖 soft-shelled turtle ❹手指或脚趾上的角质硬壳 nail:指～ *fingernail* ❺现代用金属做成有保护功用的装备 armour:装～汽车 *armoured vehicle* [甲板]轮船上分隔上下各层的板(多指最上面即船面的一层) deck ❻旧时户口的一种编制。参看25页"保❸"(see 保❸ on p25) *jia*, a former unit of civil administration

岬 jiǎ ㄐㄧㄚˇ ❶岬角,突入海中的尖形陆地。多用于地名(jia, usually used in a place name) cape; promontory:野柳～(在台湾省台北) *Yeliujia, a place in Taibei, Taiwan Province* ❷两山之间 space between two mountains

J

胛 jiǎ ㄐㄧㄚˇ 肩胛，肩膀后方的部位 shoulder blade［肩胛骨］肩胛上部左右两块三角形的扁平骨头 scapula（图见241页“骨” picture on p241）

钾 jiǎ ㄐㄧㄚˇ 一种金属元素，符号K，银白色，蜡状。钾的化合物用途很广，有的是重要的肥料 potassium（K）

蚆 jiǎ ㄐㄧㄚˇ 蚆虫，即甲虫，体壁比较坚硬的昆虫的通称，如金龟子、菜叶蚆等 beetle

贾 ㊀ jiǎ ㄐㄧㄚˇ ❶姓 Jia，a surname ❷古多用于人名 jia，usually used in a given name in ancient China

〈古 ***archaism***〉又同“价（價）”（jià）also same as 价（價）

㊁ gǔ 见241页 see p241

槚 jiǎ ㄐㄧㄚˇ ❶楸树的别名 another name for Chinese catalpa ❷茶树的古名 ancient name for tea tree

假（*叚） ㊀ jiǎ ㄐㄧㄚˇ ❶不真实的，不是本来的，跟“真”相对（the opposite of 真）false；fake：～头发 *wig*｜～话 *lie*［假如］［假使］连词 ***conjunction***，如果 if ❷借用，利用 to use the name of；to make use of（㊂ ***doublet*** 一借 in the name of）：～手于人 *to make sb else do the work for oneself*｜～公济私 *to promote one's private interests under the guise of serving the public* ❸据理推断，有待验证的 to suppose；to presume：～设 *to suppose*｜～说 *hypothesis*

㊁ jià 见325页 see p325

嘏 jiǎ ㄐㄧㄚˇ（又 also gǔ）见240页 gǔ see gǔ on p240

瘕 jiǎ ㄐㄧㄚˇ 肚子里结块的病 disease of having a lump in the abdomen

斝 jiǎ ㄐㄧㄚˇ 古代一种盛（chéng）酒的器皿 *jia*，an ancient wine vessel

价（價） ㊀ jià ㄐㄧㄚˋ 价钱，商品所值的钱数 price：～目 *price；market price*｜物～稳定。*Prices are stable.*｜减～ *to reduce the price*［价格］用货币表现出来的商品的价值 price［价值］**1** 政治经济学上指凝结在商品中的生产者的社会必要劳动 value **2** 通常指用途或重要性 worth；value：有～～ *to be of value*［原子价］化学上称能跟某元素一个原子直接或间接相化合或替代的氢原子数为这个元素的原子价。也省称“价”（also 价 for short）valence

㊁ jiè 见349页 see p349

㊂ jie 见350页 see p350

驾 jià ㄐㄧㄚˋ ❶把车套在牲口身上 to harness：～辕 *to pull a cart（or carriage）from between the shafts；to be harnessed in the shafts*｜～轻就熟（喻担任熟悉的事）*to drive a light carriage on a familiar road — to do a familiar job with ease* ❷古代车乘的总称（in ancient China）general term for vehicles 敬辞 ***polite***：劳～。*Excuse me.*｜大～光临 *your presence* ❸特指帝王的车，借指帝王 imperial carriage；em-

J

peror:～崩(帝王死去)(*of an emperor*) *to pass away*; *to die* ❹操纵,使开动 to operate; to drive:～飞机 *to pilot a plane* | ～驶员 *driver* [驾驭](-yù)驱使车马行进或停止 to drive ㉄ ***extension*** **1** 旧指对人员的管理和使用(in former times) personnel administration **2** 控制,支配 to control; to master

架 jià ㄐㄧㄚˋ ❶(-子、-儿)用作支承的东西 frame; shelf:书～儿 *bookshelf* | 葡萄～ *grape trellis*; *grape arbour* | 笔～儿 *pen-stand* | 房～子 *framework of a house* | 车～子 *bicycle rack* [担架]医院或军队中抬送病人、伤员的用具 stretcher ❷支承 to prop up **1** 支,搭起 to put up; to erect:把枪～住 *to mount a gun* | ～桥 *to build a bridge* **2** 搀扶 to support; to help:他受伤了,～着他走。*He is wounded. Please support him and help him along.* **3** 抵挡,禁(jīn)受 to fend off; to withstand:招～ *to fend off* | 这么重的负担,他～得住吗? *Can he withstand such a heavy burden?* ❸用强力把人劫走 to kidnap:绑～ *to kidnap* | 被几个人～走了 *to be kidnapped by several persons* ❹互相殴打或争吵的事 fight; quarrel:打了一～ *to have a fight* | 劝～ *to mediate between quarrelling parties* ❺量词 ***quantifier***,多用于有机械或有支柱的东西(usually used for things with machine or support):五～飞机 *five planes* | 一～机器 *a machine* | 一～葡萄 *a trellis of grapes* [架次]量词 ***quantifier***,一架飞机出动或出现一次叫一架次。如飞机出现三次,第一次五架,第二次十架,第三次十五架,共三十架次 sortie

假 ㊁ jià ㄐㄧㄚˋ 照规定或经过批准暂时离开工作、学习场所的时间 holiday; vacation; leave of absence:放～ *to have* (or *take*) *a vacation* | 寒～ *winter holidays* (or *vacation*) | ～期 *holidays* | 请～ *to ask for leave*

㊀ jiǎ 见324页 see p324

嫁 jià ㄐㄧㄚˋ ❶女子结婚(of a woman) to marry:出～(*of a woman*) *to marry* | ～娶 *marriage* [嫁接]把要繁殖的植物的芽或枝接在另一种植物上,以达到提早结果、增强抗性、提高品种质量等目的。所用的枝或芽叫接穗,被接的干叫砧(zhēn)木 to graft ❷把祸害、怨恨推到别人身上 to shift (*or* transfer) misfortune (*or* blame):～怨 *to put the blame on sb else* | ～祸于人 *to shift the blame on another person*

稼 jià ㄐㄧㄚˋ 种田 to sow [稼穑](-sè)种谷和收谷,农事的总称 sowing and reaping; farm work [庄稼]五谷,农作物 crops:种～～ *to plant crops*

JIAN ㄐㄧㄢ

戋(戔) jiān ㄐㄧㄢ 小,少(叠 ***reduplication***) small; little:所得～～ *to ob-*

J

tain but a little

溅(濺) ㊁ jiān ㄐㄧㄢ [溅溅]拟声词 ***onomatopoeia***,形容流水声 sound of flowing water

㊀ qiǎn 见595页 see p595

笺(箋、❷*牋、❷*椾) jiān ㄐㄧㄢ ❶注释 annotation ❷小幅的纸 small piece of paper:便～ *note pad* | 信～ *writing paper* [转] ***transfer*** 书信 letter:华～ *your letter*

溅(濺) ㊁ jiān ㄐㄧㄢ [溅溅]同"浅浅"(jiān —) same as 浅浅

㊀ jiàn 见332页 see p332

尖 jiān ㄐㄧㄢ ❶(～儿)物体锐利的末端或细小的部分 point; tip:笔～儿 *nib* | 刀～儿 *tip of a knife* | 针～儿 *pin point* | 塔～儿 *spire* [尖锐] **1** 刺耳的 shrill:～～的声音 *shrill sound* **2** 锋利的,深刻的 sharp; penetrating:～～的批评 *sharp criticism* **3** 激烈 intense:～～的思想斗争 *intense mental conflicts* | 矛盾～～化。*The contradictions intensified*. [打尖] **1** 掐去棉花等植物的尖 to top; to pinch the top of crops like cotton, etc **2** 旅途中休息饮食 to stop for refreshment while travelling ❷末端极细小 pointed; sharp:把铅笔削～了 *to sharpen a pencil* ❸感觉锐敏 (of sense) sharp; keen:眼～ *to have sharp eyes; to be sharp-eyed* | 耳朵～ *to have sharp ears; to be sharp-eared* ❹声音高而细(of voice) shrill; piercing:～声～气 *in a shrill voice* ❺出类拔萃的人或物品 best of its kind:～儿货 *goods of the best quality* | ～子生 *top student in a class*

奸(❸*姦) jiān ㄐㄧㄢ ❶虚伪,狡诈 false; wicked:～雄 *arch-careerist* | ～笑 *sinister smile* | 不藏～,不耍滑 *neither to hide treachery nor to act in a slick way* ❷叛国的人 traitor:汉～ *Chinese traitor* | 锄～ *to do away with traitors* [奸细]替敌人刺探消息的人 spy; enemy agent ❸男女发生不正当的性行为 illicit sexual relations:通～ *to commit adultery; to fornicate* | ～污 *to rape; to violate (sexually)*

歼(殲) jiān ㄐㄧㄢ 消灭 to annihilate; to wipe out([连] ***doublet*** 一灭 to annihilate):围～ *to surround and annihilate* | 全～入侵之敌 *to wipe out all the invading enemies*

坚(堅) jiān ㄐㄧㄢ ❶结实,硬,不容易破坏 solid; hard; firm([连] ***doublet*** 一固 firm):～不可破 *indestructible* | ～壁清野 *to strengthen the defences and clear the fields, and leave no provisions for the enemy* [引] ***extension*** 不动摇 firmly:～强 *firm; strong; staunch* | ～决 *firm; resolute* | ～持 *to persist in; to insist on* | ～守 *to hold one's ground; to stick to; to hold fast to* [中坚]骨干 backbone:～～分子 *back-*

bone element ❷坚固的东西或阵地 fortification; stronghold: 攻～战 *the attack against the heavily fortified positions* | 无～不摧 *to be capable of destroying any stronghold; to overrun all fortifications*

鲣(鰹) jiān ㄐㄧㄢ 鲣鱼，鱼名。身体呈纺锤形，大部分无鳞，腹白，背蓝黑 oceanic bonito; skipjack tuna (*Katsuwonus pelamis*)

间(*閒) ㊀ jiān ㄐㄧㄢ ❶中间，两段时间或两种事物相接的地方 between; among: 课～操 *setting-up exercises during the break between classes* | 彼此～有差别。*There are differences between them.* ❷在一定的地方、时间或人群的范围之内 within: 田～ *in the fields* | 晚～ *in the evening* | 人～ *in the world* ❸房间，屋子 room: 车～ *workshop* | 衣帽～ *cloakroom* | 卫生～ *toilet; washroom; restroom* ❹量词 ***quantifier***，用于房屋(used for a room): 一～房 *a room* | 广厦千～ *thousands of mansions*

㊁ jiàn 见331页 see p331

"閒"又 xián 见 812 页"闲" (also xián) see 闲 on p812

肩 jiān ㄐㄧㄢ ❶肩膀，脖子旁边胳膊上边的部分 shoulder (图见741页"体" picture on p741) ❷担负 to undertake; to shoulder: 身～重任 *to shoulder heavy responsibilities*

艰(艱) jiān ㄐㄧㄢ 困难 difficult; hard (㊟ ***doublet*** 一难 difficult; hard): ～辛 *hardship* | ～苦 *arduous; difficult* | 文字～深 *abstruse language* (or *writing*)

监(監) ㊀ jiān ㄐㄧㄢ ❶督察 to supervise; to inspect: ～察 *to supervise; to inspect* | ～工 *to supervise; supervisor* | ～考 *to invigilate; invigilator* ❷牢，狱 prison; jail (㊟ ***doublet*** 一牢 prison; jail | 一狱 prison; jail): 收～ *to imprison; to put into prison* | 坐～ *to be in prison* (or *jail*) [监禁]把犯罪的人收监，限制他的自由 to take into custody

㊁ jiàn 见333页 see p333

兼 jiān ㄐㄧㄢ ❶加倍，把两份并在一起 double; twice: ～旬(二十天) *20 days* | ～程(用加倍的速度赶路) *to travel at double speed* [兼并]并吞 to annex ❷所涉及的或所具有的不只一方面 concurrently; simultaneously: ～任 *to hold a concurrent post* | 德才～备 *to have both virtue and talent*

搛 jiān ㄐㄧㄢ 用筷子夹 to pick up with chopsticks: ～菜 *to pick up food with chopsticks*

蒹 jiān ㄐㄧㄢ 没长穗的芦苇 reed without spikes

缣 jiān ㄐㄧㄢ 细绢 fine silk

鹣 jiān ㄐㄧㄢ 鹣鹣，比翼鸟，古代传说中的一种鸟(in ancient legends) love birds flying in pairs

鲣 jiān ㄐㄧㄢ 鲣鱼，鱼名。一般两只眼都在身体的左侧或右侧，有眼的一面黄褐色，无眼的一面白色。主要产在我国南海地区，肉供食用 spiny-rayed flounder; big-mouthed flounder (*Psettodes erumei*)

菅 jiān ㄐㄧㄢ 多年生草本植物，叶子细长，根很坚韧，可做炊帚、刷子等 themeda (*Themeda villosa*) [草菅] ⑯ ***figurative*** 轻视 to belittle: ～～人命 *to treat human life as if it were not worth a straw; to act in utter disregard of human life*

渐 ⊜ jiān ㄐㄧㄢ ❶浸 to soak: ～染 *to be imperceptibly influenced* ❷流入 to flow into: 东～于海 *to flow east into the sea*

⊖ jiàn 见333页 see p333

犍 ⊖ jiān ㄐㄧㄢ 阉割过的公牛 bullock

⊜ qián 见595页 see p595

鞬 jiān ㄐㄧㄢ 马上盛弓箭的器具 quiver on a horse

湔 jiān ㄐㄧㄢ 洗 to wash

煎 jiān ㄐㄧㄢ ❶熬(áo) to simmer; to decoct: ～药 *to decoct medicinal herbs* ❷把食物放在少量的热油里弄熟 to fry in shallow oil: ～鱼 *to fry fish* | ～豆腐 *to fry bean curd* ❸量词 ***quantifier***, 熬中药的次数 decoction: 头～药 *first decoction* | 二～ *second decoction*

缄 jiān ㄐㄧㄢ 封，闭 to seal; to close: ～口 *to keep one's mouth shut; to say nothing* [缄默]闭口不言 to keep silent; to be reticent

瑊 jiān ㄐㄧㄢ [瑊石]一种像玉的美石 jade-like beautiful stone

鞯(韀) jiān ㄐㄧㄢ 垫马鞍的东西 saddle blanket: 鞍～ *saddle with a saddle blanket*

櫼 jiān ㄐㄧㄢ 木楔子(xiēzi) wooden wedge

囝 ⊖ jiǎn ㄐㄧㄢˇ 〈方 ***dialect***〉儿子 son

⊜ nān 见524页 see p524

拣(揀) jiǎn ㄐㄧㄢˇ ❶挑选 to choose; to select (㊀ ***doublet*** 挑— to pick and choose): ～好的交纳公粮 *to choose the best grain to deliver to the state* | 挑肥～瘦 *to pick the fat or choose the lean — to choose whatever is to one's own advantage; to pick and choose* ❷同"捡" same as 捡

枧 jiǎn ㄐㄧㄢˇ 〈方 ***dialect***〉肥皂 soap: 香～ *perfumed soap*

笕 jiǎn ㄐㄧㄢˇ 横安在屋檐或田间引水的长竹管 long bamboo pipe under the eaves or in the fields for channelling water

茧(繭、❶絸)** jiǎn ㄐㄧㄢˇ ❶(—子、—儿)某些昆虫的幼虫在变成蛹之前吐丝做成的壳。家蚕的茧是抽丝的原料 cocoon ❷同"趼" same as 趼

柬 jiǎn ㄐㄧㄢˇ 信件、名片、帖子等的泛称 general term for

letters, cards, notes, etc: 请～(请客的帖子) *invitation card*

俭(儉) jiǎn ㄐㄧㄢˇ 节省,不浪费 thrifty; frugal: ～朴 *thrifty and simple* | 省吃～用 *to be economical in daily spending* | 勤～办学 *to run a school industriously and frugally*

捡(撿) jiǎn ㄐㄧㄢˇ 拾取 to pick up; to collect: ～柴 *to gather firewood* | 把笔～起来 *to pick up the pen* | ～了一张画片 *to have picked up a picture*

检(檢) jiǎn ㄐㄧㄢˇ 查 to check up; to examine(㊀ ***doublet*** 一查 to check up): ～字 *to locate a word* | ～验 *to test; to examine* | ～阅 *to review* [检察]审查检举犯罪事实 procuratorial work [检点] **1** 仔细检查 to examine; to check **2** 注意约束(言行) to be cautious about what one says or does: 失于～～ *to be careless about one's words or conduct* [检举]告发坏人、坏事 to inform against an offender [检讨]对自己的思想、工作、生活等方面的缺点、错误进行检查 to make a self-criticism

硷(鹼、*鹻) jiǎn ㄐㄧㄢˇ 同"碱" same as 碱

睑(瞼) jiǎn ㄐㄧㄢˇ 眼睑,眼皮 eyelid(图见867页"眼" picture on p867)

趼 jiǎn ㄐㄧㄢˇ 手、脚上因摩擦而生的硬皮,也作"茧"(also written as 茧) callus: 老～ *callus*

减(*減) jiǎn ㄐㄧㄢˇ ❶由全体中去掉一部分 to subtract; to deduct: 三～二是一。*Three minus two is one.* | ～价 *to reduce the price* [减法]从一数去掉另一数的算法 subtraction ❷降低程度,衰退 to reduce; to decrease: ～肥 *to slim; to lose weight* | ～灾 *reduction of natural disasters* | ～色 *to lose lustre; to impair the excellence of* | 热情不～ *to be as zealous as ever*

碱(*城) jiǎn ㄐㄧㄢˇ ❶含有10个分子结晶水的碳酸钠,性滑,味涩 soda ❷化学上称能在水溶液中电离而生成氢氧离子(OH^-)的物质 alkali ❸被碱质侵蚀 alkalized: 好好的罐子,怎么～了? *Why is the perfectly good pot alkalized?* | 那堵墙全～了。*That wall has been alkalized.*

剪 jiǎn ㄐㄧㄢˇ ❶(一子)剪刀,一种铰东西的用具 scissors ❷像剪子的器具 scissor-shaped tool: 火～ *fire-tongs* | 夹～ *tongs* ❸用剪子铰 to cut with scissors; to clip: ～断 *to cut off* | ～开 *to cut open* [剪影]按人影或物体的轮廓剪成的图形 paper-cut silhouette ㊅ ***figurative*** 事物的一部分或概况 part; outline ❹除掉 to wipe out; to exterminate: ～灭 *to wipe out; to annihilate* | ～除 *to wipe out; to exterminate*

J

谫（**謭） jiǎn ㄐㄧㄢˇ 浅薄 shallow; superficial:学识～陋 *to have little learning*

翦 jiǎn ㄐㄧㄢˇ ❶同"剪"same as 剪 ❷姓 Jian, a surname

锏 ㊀ jiǎn ㄐㄧㄢˇ 古代的一种兵器,像鞭,四棱 (a kind of ancient weapon) mace

㊁ jiàn 见332页 see p332

裥 jiǎn ㄐㄧㄢˇ 衣服上打的褶子 pleat

简 jiǎn ㄐㄧㄢˇ ❶古时用来写字的竹板 bamboo slip, used for writing on in ancient China ㊕ ***transfer*** 书信 letters ❷简单,简化,跟"繁"相对(the opposite of 繁) simple; simplified:～写 *to write a Chinese character in its simplified form*｜删繁就～ *to simplify complicated material*｜精兵～政 *better staff and simpler administration* [简直]副词 ***adverb***,实在是,完全是 simply; at all:你若不提这件事,我～～想不起来了。*If you didn't mention it, I could not have recalled it at all*. ❸简选,选择人才 to select talented people:～拔 *to select and promote*

戬 jiǎn ㄐㄧㄢˇ ❶剪除,剪灭 to wipe out; to annihilate ❷尽 to the greatest extent:～谷(尽善) *to reach the acme of perfection* ❸福 bliss; blessedness

蹇 jiǎn ㄐㄧㄢˇ ❶跛,行走困难 crippled ❷迟钝,不顺利 slow; unlucky:～涩 *difficult; unlucky*｜～滞 *difficult; unlucky*｜命运多～ *bad lot* ❸指驽马,也指驴 inferior horse; donkey

謇 jiǎn ㄐㄧㄢˇ ❶口吃,言辞不顺畅 to stutter; to stammer ❷正直 upright

瀽 jiǎn ㄐㄧㄢˇ 泼(水),倾倒(液体) to sprinkle (water); to pour (liquid)

劗 jiǎn ㄐㄧㄢˇ 割断 to sever; to cut off

见(見) ㊀ jiàn ㄐㄧㄢˋ ❶看到 to see:眼～是实。*Seeing is believing*. ㊞ ***extension*** 接触,遇到 to meet with; to be exposed to:这种病怕～风。*Exposure to wind will make this kind of disease worse*.｜胶卷不能～光。*Films are not to be exposed to daylight*. [见习]学得专业知识的人初到工作岗位在现场中实习 to learn on the job; to be in the probation period:～～技术员 *technician on probation; probational technician* ❷看得出,显现出 to show evidence of; to appear to be:病已～好。*The patient is getting better*.｜～分晓 *to know the outcome* (or *result*)｜～效 *to be effective; to produce the desired result* ❸(文字等)出现在某处,可参考 to refer to; to see:～上 *to see above; vide supra*｜～下 *to see below; vide infra*｜～《史记·陈涉世家》*to refer to 'The Record of the Grand Historian: The Hereditary House of*

Duke Chenshe' ❹会见，会面 to meet：接～ *to grant an interview to*；*to receive*｜看望多年未～的老战友 *to call on an old-time comrade-in-arms that one has not met for years* ❺见解，对于事物的看法 view；opinion（㊟ ***doublet*** 一识 knowledge）：～地 *insight*｜远～ *foresight*｜不能固执己～。*One should not stubbornly stick to one's own views*. ❻助词 ***auxiliary*** **1** 用在动词前面表示被动（used before a verb to express passivity）：～笑 *to be laughed at*｜～疑 *to be suspected* **2** 用在动词前面表示对说话人怎么样（used before a verb to express the request that others would do sth for one）：～谅。*Please pardon me*.｜～告。*Please inform me*.｜～教。*Please instruct me*. ❼用在动词"听"、"看"、"闻"等字后，表示结果（used after a verb such as 听，看，闻，etc to express the result）：看～ *to see*｜听不～ *cannot hear* ❽姓 Jian，a surname

㊁ xiàn 见815页 see p815

舰（艦） jiàn ㄐㄧㄢˋ 军舰，战船 naval vessel；warship：～队 *fleet*；*naval force*｜巡洋～*cruiser*

件 jiàn ㄐㄧㄢˋ ❶量词 ***quantifier***，piece：一～事 *a matter*；*a thing*｜两～衣服 *two articles of clothing* ❷（一儿）指可以一一计算的事物 things that can be counted：零～儿 *spare part* ❸指文书等 document：文～ *document*｜来～ *received message*，*parcel*，*letter or document*

𡊅 jiàn ㄐㄧㄢˋ ❶斜着支撑（in a slanting way）to prop up：打～拨正（房屋倾斜，用柱子支起弄正）*to erect long logs to keep a dilapidated house from collapse*；*to support and right sth* ❷用土石挡水 to keep off water with earth and stone

间（*間） ㊁ jiàn ㄐㄧㄢˋ ❶（一儿）空隙 space or time in between：当～儿 *in the midst of* ㊞ ***extension*** 嫌隙，隔阂 grudge；enmity：亲密无～ *to be on intimate terms with each other* ❷不连接，隔开 to separate：～断 *to be disconnected*；*to be interrupted*｜～隔 *interval*｜黑白相～ *black alternating with white*；*black and white*｜晴～多云 *fine*（or *clear*）*with occasional clouds*［间或］副词 ***adverb***，偶尔 occasionally；now and then：他～～也来一两次。*He came here once a while*.［间接］通过第三者发生关系的（跟"直接"相对）（the opposite of 直接）indirect：～～经验 *indirect experience* ❸挑拨使人不和 to sow discord：离～ *to sow discord*｜反～计 *stratagem of sowing distrust among one's enemies*

㊀ jiān 见327页 see p327

"間"又 xián 见812页"闲"（also xián）see 闲 on p812

涧 jiàn ㄐㄧㄢˋ 夹在两山间的水沟 ravine

锏 ㊀ jiàn ㄐㄧㄢˋ 嵌在车轴上的铁，可以保护车轴并减少摩擦力 iron sleeve or collar on a wheel axle to reduce friction

㊁ jiǎn 见330页 see p330

饯（餞） jiàn ㄐㄧㄢˋ ❶饯行，饯别，设酒食送行 to give a farewell dinner ❷用蜜或糖浸渍（果品） to candy (fruit)：蜜～ *candied* (*or preserved*) *fruit*; *succade*

贱（賤） jiàn ㄐㄧㄢˋ ❶价钱低 cheap：这布真～。*This cloth is really cheap.* ❷指地位卑下 lowly; humble（㊟ **doublet** 卑— humble; lowly）：贫～ *poor and lowly* 谦辞 **humble**, my：～姓 *my surname*｜～恙 *my illness* ❸卑鄙 mean; base：下～ *base*

践（踐） jiàn ㄐㄧㄢˋ ❶踩，踏 to trample; to tread（㊟ **doublet** —踏 to tread on）［作践］(zuòjian) 糟蹋毁坏，浪费 to spoil; to waste：～～东西 *to spoil things* ❷履行，实行 to act or carry on：～约 *to keep a promise*｜～言 *to keep one's word*｜实～ *to practise*

溅（濺） ㊀ jiàn ㄐㄧㄢˋ 液体受冲激向四外飞射 to splash; to spatter：～了一脸水 *to be splashed with water all over the face*｜水花四～ *water spraying in all directions*

㊁ jiān 见326页 see p326

建 jiàn ㄐㄧㄢˋ 立，设立，成立 to establish; to found（㊟ **doublet** —立 to establish; to found）：八一～军节 *Army Day* (*August 1*)｜～都 *to found a capital*｜～筑铁路 *to build a railway*［建设］创立新事业或增加新的设施 to build; to construct：经济～～ *economic construction*｜文化～～ *cultural construction*［建议］向有关方面提出建设性的意见 to propose; to suggest

健 jiàn ㄐㄧㄢˋ ❶强壮，身体好 strong; healthy（㊟ **doublet** —康 healthy｜强— sturdy）：～儿 *valiant fighter*; *good athlete*｜保～ *health care*｜身体～康 *to be in good health*［健全］**1** 既无疾病又不残废 sound; healthy; perfect **2** 完备无缺欠或使完备 perfect or to perfect：制度很～～。*The system is sound.*｜～～组织 *to perfect the organization* ❷善于，对于某种事情精力旺盛 to be good at; to be strong in：～步 *to walk with vigorous strides*｜～谈 *talkative*｜～饭 *to have a good appetite*［健忘］容易忘，记忆力不强 forgetful; having a bad memory

楗 jiàn ㄐㄧㄢˋ 竖插在门闩上使门拨不开的木棍 vertical door bar (*or* door bolt)

毽 jiàn ㄐㄧㄢˋ（—子、—儿）一种用脚踢的玩具 shuttlecock

腱 jiàn ㄐㄧㄢˋ 肌腱，连接肌肉和骨骼的一种组织，白色，质地坚韧 tendon［腱子］人身上或牛、羊等小腿上特别发达的肌肉 shank

键 jiàn ㄐㄧㄢˋ ❶安在车轴头上管住车轮不脱离轴的铁棍。也叫"辖"(also called 辖) linchpin [关键][喻] ***figurative*** 事物的紧要部分,对于情势有决定作用的部分 key; crux ❷插在门上关锁门户的金属棍子 metal door bolt ❸某些乐器或机器上使用时按动的部分 key: ～盘 *keyboard*

踺 jiàn ㄐㄧㄢˋ 踺子(—zi),体操运动等的一种翻身动作(in gymnastics) somersault

荐(薦) jiàn ㄐㄧㄢˋ ❶推举,介绍 to recommend([连] ***doublet*** 举— to recommend|推— to recommend): ～人 *to recommend a person* ❷草 grass; straw 又指草席 straw mat

剑(劍、*劒) jiàn ㄐㄧㄢˋ 古代的一种兵器,长条形,两面有刃,安有短柄(in ancient China) sword; sabre

监(監) ㊁ jiàn ㄐㄧㄢˋ ❶帝王时代的官名或官府名 name of imperial office or officer: 太～ *eunuch*|国子～ *Imperial College*|钦天～(掌管天文历法的官府) *Division of Astronomy* ❷姓 Jian, a surname

㊀ jiān 见327页 see p327

槛(檻) ㊀ jiàn ㄐㄧㄢˋ ❶栏杆,栏板 banisters; balustrade ❷圈(juān)兽类的栅栏 sty; pen [槛车] **1** 运兽用的有栏杆的车 railed cart for transporting animals **2** 古代押运囚犯的车 carriage for transporting prisoners in ancient China

㊁ kǎn 见383页 see p383

鉴(鑒、*鑑) jiàn ㄐㄧㄢˋ ❶镜子 mirror [引] ***extension*** 可以作为警戒或引为教训的事 warning; lesson: 前车之覆,后车之～。*The overturned cart in front serves as a warning to the carts behind — one should take warning from another's mistake.*|引以为～ *to take warning from; to draw a lesson from* [鉴戒]可以使人警惕的事情 warning; lesson ❷照 to reflect; to mirror: 光可～人 *so shiny that it can serve as a mirror* ❸观看,审察 to inspect; to examine: ～定 *to appraise; appraisal*|～赏 *to appreciate*|～别真伪 *to discriminate the false from the genuine*|某某先生台～(书信用语) (*a form used after the name in the salutation of a business letter*) *Attention of Mr so-and-so; Dear Mr so-and-so* [鉴于]看到,觉察到 in view of; seeing that: ～～旧的工作方法不能适应需要,于是创造了新的工作方法。*Seeing that the old working method couldn't meet the requirements, they devised a new one.*

渐 ㊀ jiàn ㄐㄧㄢˋ 副词 ***adverb***, 慢慢地,一点一点地(叠 ***reduplication***) gradually: 循序～进 *to proceed in an orderly*

J

way and step by step | ～入佳境(*of a situation*) *to become better and better* | 他的病～～好了。*He is gradually getting over his illness.*

㊁ jiān 见328页 see p328

谏 jiàn ㄐㄧㄢˋ 旧时称规劝君主、尊长,使改正错误(in former times) to expostulate with one's monarch or superior

僭 jiàn ㄐㄧㄢˋ 超越本分,古时指地位在下的冒用在上的名义或器物等等 to overstep one's authority; to use illegally the title or articles designated for a superior in ancient China: ～越 *to overstep one's authority*; *to go beyond proper bounds*

箭 jiàn ㄐㄧㄢˋ 用弓发射到远处的兵器,用金属做头 arrow

JIANG ㄐㄧㄤ

江 jiāng ㄐㄧㄤ ❶大河的通称 river: 黑龙～ *Heilongjiang River* | 松花～ *Songhua River* ❷专指长江,我国最大的河流,发源于青海省,流入东海 Changjiang River (*or* Yangtze River), the longest river in China rising in Qinghai Province and flowing into the East China Sea

茳 jiāng ㄐㄧㄤ [茳芏](－dù) 多年生草本植物,茎三棱形,开绿褐色小花。茎可编席 *Cyperus malaccensis*

豇 jiāng ㄐㄧㄤ [豇豆]一年生草本植物,花淡青或紫色,果实为长荚,嫩荚和种子都可吃 cowpea (*Vigna unguiculata*)

将(將) ㊀ jiāng ㄐㄧㄤ ❶副词 ***adverb***,将要,快要 will; to be going to; to be about to: 天～明。*The day is breaking.* | 后日～返京 *will return to Beijing the day after tomorrow* [将来]未来 future: 我们的劳动是为了更美好的～～。*We work for a bright future.* ❷介词 ***preposition***,把 with; by means of; by: ～革命进行到底 *to carry the revolution through to the end* ❸下象棋时攻击对方的"将"或"帅"(in Chinese chess) to check: ～军(也比喻使人为难) *to check* 一 *to embarrass sb* ❹用言语刺激 to incite; to challenge: 别把他～急了。*Don't make him annoyed by goading him too much.* ❺带,领,扶助 to take; to support: ～雏 *to take along the child* | 扶～ *to support* [将军]对高级军官的称呼 general ❻保养 to take care of one's health: ～养 *to rest and recuperate* | ～息 *to rest; to recuperate* ❼〈方 ***dialect***〉兽类生子(of animals) to give birth; to breed: ～驹 *to foal* | ～小猪 *to give birth to a piglet* ❽助词 ***auxiliary***,用在动词和"出来"、"起来"、"上去"等的中间(used between a verb and its complements, such as 出来, 起来, 上去, etc): 走～出来 *to walk out* | 叫～起来 *to begin to shout* | 赶～上去 *to hurry to catch up* ❾姓 Jiang, a surname

J

[将就](—jiu)勉强适应,凑合 to make do with:~~着用 *to make do with*

㊁ jiàng 见336页 see p336

浆(漿) ㊀ jiāng ㄐㄧㄤ ❶比较浓的液体 thick liquid:纸~ *paper pulp* | 豆~ *soya-bean milk* | 泥~ *slurry* ❷用米汤或粉浆等浸润纱、布、衣服等物 to starch:~衣裳 *to starch clothes*

㊁ jiàng 见336页 see p336

鳉(鱂) jiāng ㄐㄧㄤ 鱼名。头扁平,腹部突出,口小。生活在淡水中 killifish (*Fundulus heterolitus*)

姜(❶薑) jiāng ㄐㄧㄤ ❶多年生草本植物,地下茎黄色,味辣,可供调味用,也可入药 ginger (*Zingiber officinale*) ❷姓 Jiang, a surname

僵(❶*殭) jiāng ㄐㄧㄤ ❶直挺挺,不灵活 stiff; rigid; numb:~尸 *corpse* | ~蚕 *inactive silkworm* | 手冻~了。*The hands were numb with cold.* ❷双方相持不下,两种意见不能调和 to deadlock:闹~了 *to get into an impasse* | ~局 *deadlock* | ~持不下 *to refuse to budge*

缰(*韁) jiāng ㄐㄧㄤ 缰绳,拴牲口的绳子 reins; halter:信马由~ *to ride with lax reins*

礓 jiāng ㄐㄧㄤ 砂礓,沙土中的不规则钙质硬块,可用作建筑材料 conglomerate [礓礤儿](—cār)台阶 steps

疆 jiāng ㄐㄧㄤ 边界,境界 boundary; border:~土 *territory* | ~域 *territory; domain* | 边~ *border area; frontier region* ㊞ ***extension*** 界限 limit; bound:万寿无~ *boundless longevity* [疆场](—chǎng)战场 battle field [疆埸](—yì)边界 border

讲(講) jiǎng ㄐㄧㄤˇ ❶说,谈 to speak; to say; to tell:~话 *to speak; to talk* | 他对你~了没有? *Has he told you that?* ❷解释 to explain; to interpret; to expound(㊥ ***doublet*** —解 to explain):~书 *to lecture; to explain a text* | 这个字有三个~法。*There are three explanations for this Chinese character.* [讲演][演讲]把观点或主张对听众说明 to give a speech (*or* lecture) [讲义]教师为讲课编写的教材 teaching materials; lecture sheets ❸谋求,顾到 to stress; to pay attention to; to be particular about:~卫生 *to pay attention to hygiene* [讲究](—jiu) **1** 讲求,注重 to stress; to pay attention to; to be particular about:~~质量 *to emphasize quality* **2** 精美 exquisite; superb:这房子盖得真~~。*The house was tastefully built.* **3** (—儿)一定的方法或道理,惯例 certain method or way; convention:写春联有写春联的~~儿。*There are conventions in writing Spring Festival couplets.* ❹商量 to discuss; to negotiate: ～价儿 *to bargain*

奖(奬) jiǎng ㄐㄧㄤˇ ❶劝勉,勉励 to encourage; to reward: ～励 *to encourage and reward* ❷称赞,表扬 to praise(㊀ ***doublet*** 夸一 to praise | 褒一 to praise and honour): ～状 *certificate of merit; citation* ❸为了鼓励或表扬而给予的荣誉或财物等 award; prize: 得～ *to win* (or *get*) *a prize* | 发～ *to award* (or *give*) *a prize* ❹指彩金 lottery prize: ～券 *lottery ticket* | 中～ *to win a prize in a lottery*

桨(槳) jiǎng ㄐㄧㄤˇ 划船的用具。常装置在船的两旁 oar

蒋(蔣) jiǎng ㄐㄧㄤˇ 姓 Jiang, a surname

耩 jiǎng ㄐㄧㄤˇ 用耧播种 to sow with a drill; to drill: ～地 *to drill a field* | ～棉花 *to drill cotton seeds*

膙 jiǎng ㄐㄧㄤˇ (一子)手、脚上因摩擦而生的硬皮,即趼(jiǎn) (i.e. 趼) callus

J

匠 jiàng ㄐㄧㄤˋ ❶有专门手艺的人 craftsman: 木～ *carpenter* | 瓦～ *bricklayer* | 能工巧～ *skilled craftsman* ❷灵巧,巧妙 ingenious: ～心 *ingenuity; craftsmanship* ❸指在某方面有很深造诣的人 master: 文学巨～ *literary giant*

降 ㊀ jiàng ㄐㄧㄤˋ ❶下落,落下 to fall; to drop; to go down(㊀ ***doublet*** 一落 to descend): ～雨 *rainfall* | 温度下～。*The temperature dropped.* | ～落伞 *parachute* ❷使下落 to lower; to reduce: ～级 *to demote* | ～格 *to degrade* | ～低物价 *to lower* (or *reduce*) *the price* ❸姓 Jiang, a surname

㊁ xiáng 见819页 see p819

洚 jiàng ㄐㄧㄤˋ 大水泛滥 to overflow; to inundate: ～水(洪水) *flood*

绛 jiàng ㄐㄧㄤˋ 赤色,深红 deep red; crimson

虹 ㊁ jiàng ㄐㄧㄤˋ 义同"虹"(hóng),限于单用 same meaning as 虹, used alone

㊀ hóng 见277页 see p277

将(將) ㊁jiàng ㄐㄧㄤˋ ❶军衔名。在校级之上 general [将领]较高级的军官 general; high-ranking officer ❷统率指挥 to command; to lead: ～兵 *to command troops*

㊀ jiāng 见334页 see p334

浆(漿) ㊁ jiàng ㄐㄧㄤˋ [浆糊](-hu)[浆子](-zi)同"糨糊"、"糨子"same as 糨糊 or 糨子

㊀ jiāng 见335页 see p335

酱(醬) jiàng ㄐㄧㄤˋ ❶用发酵后的豆、麦等做成的一种调味品,有黄酱、甜面酱、豆瓣酱等 thick sauce ❷用酱或酱油腌制 to pickle in soya sauce: 把萝卜～一～ *to pickle radish in soya sauce* ❸像酱的糊状食品 paste; jam: 芝麻～ *sesame butter* | 果子～ *jam* | 虾～ *shrimp paste*

弶 jiàng ㄐㄧㄤˋ ❶捕捉老鼠、鸟雀等的工具 trap; snare ❷

用弶捕捉 to catch in a trap; to trap

强(*強、*彊) ㊂ jiàng ㄐㄧㄤˋ ❶强(qiáng)硬不屈 obdurate; unyielding; unbending: 倔～ *unbending; obdurate* ❷固执己见,不服劝导 stubborn; obdurate: 你别～嘴。*Don't answer back.*

㊀ qiáng 见598页 see p598

㊁ qiǎng 见599页 see p599

犟(**勥) jiàng ㄐㄧㄤˋ 同"强㊂" same as 强㊂

糨(**糡) jiàng ㄐㄧㄤˋ 稠,浓 thick: 粥太～了。*The porridge is too thick.* [糨糊](—hu)[糨子](—zi)用面等做成的可以粘贴东西的物品 paste

JIAO ㄐㄧㄠ

艽 jiāo ㄐㄧㄠ [秦艽]草本植物,叶阔而长,花紫色,根可入药 large-leaf gentian (*Gentiana macrophylla*)

交 jiāo ㄐㄧㄠ ❶付托,付给 to turn over; to hand in; to deliver: 这事～给我办。*Leave it with me.* | 货已经～齐了。*All goods have been delivered.* [交代] **1** 把经手的事务移交给接替的人 to hand over; to transfer: ～～工作 *to hand over work to one's successor* **2** 把事情或意见向有关的人说明 to account for: 把事情～～清楚 *to account for it* ❷相连,接合 to meet; to join: ～界 *to have a common boundary* | 目不～睫(jié) *not to sleep a wink* | ～叉 *to cross; to intersect* ㊎ ***extension*** 相交处 meeting part: 春夏之～ *time when spring is changing into summer* ❸互相来往联系 to associate with: 结～ *to associate with* | ～朋友 *to make friends* | ～流经验 *to exchange experience* | ～换意见 *to exchange* (or *interchange*) *opinions* (or *views, ideas*) | 公平～易 *fair deal* | 打～道 *to have dealings with* [交际]人事往来接触 social intercourse; communication [交涉]互相商量解决彼此间相关的问题 to negotiate: 我去跟他～～一下儿。*I'll go and take up the matter with him.* | 那件事还没有～～好。*That matter hasn't been settled through negotiations yet.* [交通] **1** 各种运输和邮电事业的总称 general term for transportation and postal services; communications: ～～方便 *to have traffic facilities; to be well located* **2** 抗日战争和解放战争时期指通信联络工作,也指通信员(in the War of Resistance against Japan and the War of Liberation) communication; liaison; liaison man ❹交情,友谊 friendship: 我和他没有深～。*He and I are not very close friends.* | 一面之～ *limited* (or *passing, casual*) *acquaintance* ❺一齐,同时 together; simultaneously: 风雨～加 *rain ac-*

J

companied by winds|饥寒～迫 *to suffer hunger and cold* ❻同"跤"(jiāo) same as 跤

郊 jiāo ㄐㄧㄠ 城外 suburbs; outskirts:西～ *the western suburbs*|～游 *outing*

茭 jiāo ㄐㄧㄠ [茭白]经黑粉菌寄生后膨大的菰的嫩茎,可作蔬菜 wild rice stem

峧 jiāo ㄐㄧㄠ 地名用字 jiao, used in a place name:～头(在浙江省舟山) *Jiaotou (a place in Zhoushan, Zhejiang Province)*

姣 jiāo ㄐㄧㄠ 形容相貌美 beautiful; handsome

胶(膠) jiāo ㄐㄧㄠ ❶黏性物质,有用动物的皮、角等熬制成的,也有植物分泌的或人工合成的 glue; gum:鹿角～ *deerhorn glue*|鳔(biào)～ *isinglass*|桃～ *peach gum*|万能～ *all-purpose adhesive* ❷指橡胶 rubber:～鞋 *rubber overshoes; rubber-soled shoes*|～皮 *rubber* ❸有黏性像胶的 gluey; sticky:～泥 *clay* ❹黏着,黏合 to glue:～着状态 *deadlock; stalemate*|～柱鼓瑟(喻拘泥不知变通) *to play the* se *(25 stringed zither-like plucked instrument) with the pegs glued — to stick to the old ways in the face of changed circumstance; strait-laced*

鸡 jiāo ㄐㄧㄠ [鸡鹊](—jīng)古书上说的一种水鸟,腿长,头上有红毛冠(in ancient Chinese text) aquatic bird with long legs and red crest

蛟 jiāo ㄐㄧㄠ 蛟龙,古代传说中能发洪水的一种龙(in ancient legends) flood dragon

跤 jiāo ㄐㄧㄠ 跟头(tou) fall; tumble:跌了一～ *to have a fall*|摔～ *to fall*

鲛 jiāo ㄐㄧㄠ 鲨鱼。参看650页"鲨"(shā)(see 鲨 on p650) shark

浇(澆) jiāo ㄐㄧㄠ ❶灌溉 to irrigate; to water:～地 *to irrigate fields* ❷淋 to pour liquid on; to sprinkle water on:～了一身水 *to be drenched with water* ❸把液汁倒入模型 to cast:～版 *casting*|～铅字 *type casting* ❹刻薄 unkind; mean (㊟ ***doublet*** — 薄 mean)

娇(嬌) jiāo ㄐㄧㄠ ❶美好可爱 lovely; charming:～娆 *enchantingly beautiful* ❷爱怜过甚 to spoil; to pamper:～生惯养 *pampered since childhood*|小孩子别太～了。*Don't spoil children.* ❸娇气 delicate; squeamish

骄(驕) jiāo ㄐㄧㄠ ❶自满,自高自大 arrogant; conceited:戒～戒躁 *to guard against arrogance and impetuosity*|～兵必败。*An army puffed up with pride is bound to lose.* [骄傲] **1** 自高自大,看不起别人 arrogant; conceited:～～自满是一定要失败的。*Arrogance and complacency must lead to failure.* **2** 自豪 pride:这些伟大的成就是我们中国人民的光荣和～～。

These great achievements are our Chinese people's glory and pride. | 光荣的历史传统是值得我们～～的。*The glorious historical traditions are worthy of our pride.* ❷ 猛烈 intense：～阳似火 *scorching sun*

教 ⊜ jiāo ㄐㄧㄠ 传授 to teach; to instruct：～书 *to teach; to teach school* | 我～历史。*I teach history.* | 我～给你做。*I'll teach you how to do it.*

⊖ jiào 见342页 see p342

椒 jiāo ㄐㄧㄠ 植物名 plant name **1** 花椒，落叶灌木，果实红色，种子黑色，可供药用或调味 Chinese prickly ash (*Zanthoxylum bungeanum*) **2** 胡椒，常绿灌木，茎蔓生。种子味辛香，可供药用或调味 pepper (*Piper nigrum*) **3** 番椒，辣椒，秦椒，一年生草本植物，开白花。有的果实味辣，可做菜吃或供调味用 chili pepper (*Capsicum annuum*)

焦 jiāo ㄐㄧㄠ ❶火候过大或火力过猛，使东西烧成炭样 burnt; scorched; charred：饭烧～了。*The rice is burnt.* | 衣服烧～了。*The clothes are scorched.* | ～头烂额（喻十分狼狈）*badly battered; in a sorry plight* ❷ 焦炭 coke：煤～ *coking coal* | 炼～ *to coke* ❸酥，脆 crisp：麻花炸得真～。*The fried dough twist is very crisp.* ❹着急，烦躁 worried; anxious：心～ *worried* | ～急 *anxious* | 万分～灼 *deeply worried; extremely anxious* ❺能量、功、热等单位名焦耳的简称，符号 J (short for 焦耳) joule (J)

僬 jiāo ㄐㄧㄠ ［僬侥］(—yáo) 古代传说中的矮人 (in ancient legends) dwarf

蕉 jiāo ㄐㄧㄠ 植物名 plant name **1** 香蕉，又叫"甘蕉"。形状像芭蕉。果实长形，稍弯，果肉软而甜 (also called 甘蕉) banana **2** 见11页"芭"字条"芭蕉"(bā—) see 芭蕉 on p11

礁 jiāo ㄐㄧㄠ 在海里或江里的岩石 reef; rock：暗～ *submerged reef*

鹪 jiāo ㄐㄧㄠ ［鹪鹩］(—liáo) 鸟名。身体很小，头部浅棕色，有黄色眉纹，尾短，捕食小虫。也叫"巧妇鸟"(also called 巧妇鸟) wren (*Troglodytidae*)

矫（矯） ⊜ jiáo ㄐㄧㄠˊ ［矫情］(—qing)〈方 *dialect*〉指强词夺理 argumentative; quarrelsome; contentious：瞎～～ *to quibble unreasonably*

⊖ jiǎo 见340页 see p340

嚼 ⊖ jiáo ㄐㄧㄠˊ 用牙齿磨碎食物 to chew ［嚼舌］信口胡说，搬弄是非 to gossip; to blabber

⊜ jué 见377页 see p377

⊜ jiào 见343页 see p343

角 ⊖ jiǎo ㄐㄧㄠˇ ❶牛、羊、鹿等头上长出的坚硬的东西 horn; antler ［画角］古代军中吹的乐器 military bugle in ancient China ❷形状像角的 horn-shaped：菱～ *water caltrop; water chestnut* | 皂～

Chinese honey locust ❸几何学上称自一点引两条射线所成的形状 angle：直～ *right angle* | 锐～*acute angle* ❹(一儿)物体边沿相接的地方 corner：桌子～儿 *corner of a table* | 墙～儿 *corner of a wall* ❺突入海中的尖形的陆地。多用于地名(jiao, usually used in a place name) cape; promontory：成山～(在山东省荣成) *Chengshanjiao* ❻星宿名，二十八宿之一 jiao, the 1st of the 28 constellations ❼货币单位，一圆钱的十分之一 *jiao*, unit of currency in China, equal to one tenth of a *yuan* ❽量词 ***quantifier*** **1** 从整块划分成角形的 quarter; wedge-shaped section of a circular figure or thing：一～饼 *a quarter of a pancake* **2** 旧时指公文的件数(in former times) number of official documents：一～公文 *an official document*

㊁ jué 见375页 see p375

侥(僥、*儌) ㊀ jiǎo ㄐㄧㄠˇ [侥幸](*儌倖)由于偶然的原因获得利益或免去不幸 lucky; by luck：怀着～～心理 *with the idea of leaving things to chance* (or *trusting to luck*)

㊁ yáo 见874页 see p874

佼 jiǎo ㄐㄧㄠˇ 美好 beautiful; handsome

狡 jiǎo ㄐㄧㄠˇ 狡猾，诡诈 crafty; cunning

饺 jiǎo ㄐㄧㄠˇ (一子、一儿)包成半圆形的有馅的面食 *jiaozi* (*or* Chinese dumpling), crescent-shaped small wheat dough wrappings with meat and vegetable filling

绞 jiǎo ㄐㄧㄠˇ ❶拧，扭紧 to twist; to wring ❷用绳子把人勒死的一种酷刑 capital punishment of hanging by the neck ❸量词 ***quantifier***，用于纱、毛线等 skein; hank：一～毛线 *a skein of woollen yarn*

铰 jiǎo ㄐㄧㄠˇ ❶用剪刀剪 to cut with scissors：把绳子～开 *to cut the rope* ❷机械工业上的一种切削法 to bore with a reamer; to ream：～孔 *to ream a hole* | ～刀 *reamer*

皎 jiǎo ㄐㄧㄠˇ 洁白明亮(叠 ***reduplication***) clear and bright：～～白驹 *pure white foal* | ～洁的月亮 *bright and clear moon*

筊 jiǎo ㄐㄧㄠˇ 竹索 bamboo rope

挢(撟) jiǎo ㄐㄧㄠˇ ❶举，翘 to lift; to raise：舌～不下(形容惊讶得说不出话来) *to be too surprised to utter a word* ❷纠正 to correct; to rectify：～邪防非 *to correct irregularities and guard against wrong doings*

矫(矯) ㊀ jiǎo ㄐㄧㄠˇ ❶纠正，把弯曲的弄直 to correct; to straighten：～正 *to correct* | ～枉过正 *to overcorrect* | ～揉造作(喻故意做作) *to be artificial; to behave in an affected way* [矫情]故意违反常情，表示与众不同 to be de-

J

liberately unconventional; to pretend to be uncommon ❷假托 to pretend; to feign:～命 *to counterfeit an order; to feign an order from higher authority* ❸强健,勇武 strong; brave (㊣ **doublet** 一健 strong and vigorous):～捷 *vigorous and nimble* ❹古同"挢"same as 挢 in ancient Chinese

㊁ jiáo 见339页 see p339

脚(*腳) ㊀ jiǎo ㄐㄧㄠˇ ❶人和某些动物身体最下部接触地面的肢体 foot (图见741页"体"picture on p741) ❷最下部 base; the lowest part:山～ *foot of a hill (or mountain)*|墙～ *foot of a wall*

[脚本]剧本,表演戏剧或拍电影等所根据的底本 script; scenario

㊁ jué 见376页 see p376

搅(攪) jiǎo ㄐㄧㄠˇ ❶扰乱 to disturb; to upset (㊣ **doublet** 一扰 to disturb):～乱 *to disorder; to disturb*|不要胡～。*Don't create a disturbance.* ❷拌 to stir; to mix up:把锅～一～ *to give the pot a stir*|～匀了 *to mix thoroughly*

湫 ㊁ jiǎo ㄐㄧㄠˇ 低洼 low-lying [湫隘]低湿狭小 narrow, wet and low-lying

㊀ qiū 见615页 see p615

敫 jiǎo ㄐㄧㄠˇ 姓 Jiao, a surname

徼 ㊀ jiǎo ㄐㄧㄠˇ [徼倖]旧同"侥幸"same as 侥幸 in former times

㊁ jiào 见343页 see p343

缴 ㊀ jiǎo ㄐㄧㄠˇ ❶交纳,交出(多指履行义务或被迫 of an obligation or under compulsion) to pay; to hand over or in:～公粮 *to hand in grain tax*|～纳税款 *to pay tax* ❷迫使交出 to capture; to compel to hand over:～了敌人的械 *to have disarmed the enemy*

㊁ zhuó 见1008页 see p1008

剿(*勦) ㊀ jiǎo ㄐㄧㄠˇ 讨伐,消灭(to send armed forces) to suppress; to put down:～匪 *to suppress bandits*|围～ *to encircle and annihilate*

㊁ chāo 见79页 see p79

叫(*呌) jiào ㄐㄧㄠˋ ❶呼喊 to cry; to shout; to yell:大～一声 *to give a loud cry* ❷动物发出声音(of an animal) to make its characteristic cry:鸡～ *to crow* ❸称呼,称为 to call; to name:他～什么名字? *What's his name?*|这～机关枪。*This is called machine gun.* ❹召唤 to call; to ask for:～他明天来 *to ask him to come tomorrow*|请你把他～来。*Please ask him over.* ❺使,令 to make:这件事应该～他知道。*We should let him know about the matter.*|～人不容易懂 *to make sth difficult to understand* ❻介词 **preposition**,被(后面必须说出主动者)(used to introduce the doer of an action) by:敌人～我们打得落花流水。*The enemy was*

J

soundly defeated by us.

峤(嶠) ㊀ jiào ㄐㄧㄠˋ 山道 mountain path

㊁ qiáo 见601页 see p601

轿(轎) jiào ㄐㄧㄠˋ (一子)旧式交通工具,由人抬着走(a former vehicle) sedan; sedan chair

觉(覺) ㊁ jiào ㄐㄧㄠˋ 睡眠 sleep

㊀ jué 见375页 see p375

校 ㊁ jiào ㄐㄧㄠˋ ❶比较 to compare:~场(旧日演习武术的地方)(*in former times*) *drill ground* ❷订正 to check; to proofread:~订 *to check against the authoritative text*|~稿子 *to proofread manuscripts*

㊀ xiào 见826页 see p826

较 jiào ㄐㄧㄠˋ ❶比 to compare (㊟ ***doublet*** 比一 to compare):~量 *to have a contest*|两者相~,截然不同。*The two are completely different by comparison.*|斤斤计~ *to haggle over every ounce; to think about narrow personal gains and losses* ㊄ ***extension*** 副词 ***adverb***,对比着显得更进一层的 comparatively:中国应当对于人类有~大的贡献。*China should make greater contributions to mankind.*|成绩~好。*The result is comparatively good.* ❷明显 clear; obvious:彰明~著 *obvious; conspicuous*|两者~然不同。*The two are clearly different.*

教 ㊀ jiào ㄐㄧㄠˋ ❶指导,教诲 to teach; to instruct (㊟ ***doublet*** 一导 to instruct):施~ *to teach*|受~ *to be taught; to receive instruction*|指~ *to instruct; to give advice* [教育] **1** 教导和培养 to educate:~~干部 *to educate officials* **2** 教育事业。按一定要求培养人的事业,主要指各级学校的工作 education ❷使,令 to make:风能~船走。*Wind can move a boat.* ❸宗教 religion:佛~ *Buddhism*|道~ *Taoism*|~会 *the Church* [宗教]一种社会意识形态,是对客观世界的虚幻的反映,它提倡对超自然神灵的信仰和崇拜 religion [教条主义]主观主义的一种,不分析事物的变化、发展,不研究事物矛盾的特殊性,只是生搬硬套现成的原则、概念来处理问题 dogmatism; doctrinairism ❹姓 Jiao, a surname

㊁ jiāo 见339页 see p339

滘 jiào ㄐㄧㄠˋ 同"滘"。东滘,在广东省广州(same as 滘) Dongjiao, a place in Guangzhou, Guangdong Province

酵 jiào ㄐㄧㄠˋ 发酵,有机物由于某些真菌或酶而分解。能使有机物发酵的真菌叫酵母菌。有的地区把含酵母菌的面团叫"酵子" to ferment; to leaven

窖 jiào ㄐㄧㄠˋ ❶收藏东西的地洞 cellar (*or* pit) for storing things:地~ *cellar*|白菜~ *Chinese vegetable cellar* ❷把东西藏在窖里 to store sth in a cellar (*or* pit): ～萝卜 *to store radishes in a cellar*

滘 jiào ㄐㄧㄠˋ〈方 ***dialect***〉分支的河道。多用于地名 (jiao, usually used in a place name) tributary of a river: 双～(在广东省阳春) *Shuangjiao* (*a place in Yangchun, Guangdong Province*) | 沙～(在广东省顺德) *Shajiao* (*a place in Shunde, Guangdong Province*)

斠 jiào ㄐㄧㄠˋ ❶古时平斗斛的器具(used in ancient China) strickle ❷校订 to check against the authoritative text

覺 jiào ㄐㄧㄠˋ〈方 ***dialect***〉只要 if only; provided

嚼 jiào ㄐㄧㄠˋ 嚼,吃东西 to chew; to eat [噍类]尚生存的人 living human beings [倒噍]同"倒嚼"same as 倒嚼

醮 jiào ㄐㄧㄠˋ ❶古代婚娶时用酒祭神的礼 libation at an ancient wedding ceremony: 再～(再嫁)(*of a woman*) *to remarry* ❷道士设坛祭神 Taoist sacrificial ceremony: 打～ *to perform Taoist rites*

徼 ㊀ jiào ㄐㄧㄠˋ ❶边界 boundary ❷巡察 to patrol

㊁ jiǎo 见341页 see p341

藠 jiào ㄐㄧㄠˋ (－子、－头)就是薤(xiè) (i. e. 薤) Chinese onion (*Allium chinense*)

嚼 ㊂ jiào ㄐㄧㄠˋ [倒嚼](dǎo－)反刍 to ruminate; to chew the cud

㊀ jiáo 见339页 see p339

㊁ jué 见377页 see p377

爝 jiào ㄐㄧㄠˋ (又 also jué) 见377页 jué see jué on p377

JIE ㄐㄧㄝ

节(節) ㊁ jiē ㄐㄧㄝ [节骨眼儿](－gu－)〈方 ***dialect***〉喻 ***figurative*** 紧要的、能起决定作用的环节或时机 vital link; critical moment

㊀ jié 见345页 see p345

疖(癤) jiē ㄐㄧㄝ (－子)小疮 furuncle

阶(階、*堦) jiē ㄐㄧㄝ 台阶,建筑物中为了便于上下,用砖、石砌成的、分层的东西 steps; stairs (图见188页 picture on p188) [阶层]指在同一个阶级中因社会经济地位不同而分成的层次 stratum [阶段]事物发展的段落 stage; phase: 球赛已经进入最后～～。*The football match has entered the final stage.* [阶级]指人们在一定的社会生产体系中,由于所处的地位不同和对生产资料关系的不同而分成的集团 class [阶梯]台阶和梯子 flight of stairs; ladder 喻 ***figurative*** 升高的凭借或途径 stepping stone

皆 jiē ㄐㄧㄝ 副词 ***adverb***,全,都 all: ～大欢喜。*Everybody is happy.* | 人人～知 *known to all the people*

喈 jiē ㄐㄧㄝ (叠 ***reduplication***) ❶形容声音和谐(of sounds) harmonious: 鼓钟～～。*Bells and drums sounded harmoniously.* ❷鸟鸣声 chirp;

J

twitter：鸡鸣～～。*Cocks are crowing.*

湝 jiē ㄐㄧㄝ （叠 ***reduplication***）形容水流动的样子（of water）running；flowing：淮水～～。*The Huaihe River is flowing.*

楷 ㊁ jiē ㄐㄧㄝ 楷树，落叶乔木，果实长圆形，红色。木材可制器具。也叫"黄连木"（also called 黄连木）Chinese pistache（*Pistacia chinensis*）

㊀ kǎi 见382页 see p382

结 ㊁ jiē ㄐㄧㄝ 植物长果实 to bear fruit：树上～了许多苹果。*The tree has borne many apples.* [结实] **1** 植物长（zhǎng）果实 to bear fruit：开花～～ *to blossom and bear fruit* **2**（－shi）坚固耐用 solid；durable：这双鞋很～～。*This pair of shoes is durable.* **3**（－shi）健壮 strong；sturdy：他的身体很～～。*He is very strong.* [结巴]（－ba）**1** 口吃 to stammer；to stutter **2** 口吃的人 stammerer；stutterer

㊀ jié 见346页 see p346

秸（*稭） jiē ㄐㄧㄝ 某些农作物收割以后的茎 stalk of threshed grain；straw：麦～ *wheat straw*｜秫～ *sorghum stalk*｜豆～ *bean stalk*

接 jiē ㄐㄧㄝ ❶连接 to connect；to join；to link（㊥ ***doublet*** 一连 in a row；in succession）：～电线 *to connect electric wires*｜～纱头 *to join thrums* ❷继续，连续 to continue；to carry on：～着往下讲 *to go on speaking* ❸接替 to take over；to succeed：～好革命班 *to be worthy successors to the revolution* ❹接触，挨近 to come into contact with；to come close to：～洽 *to take up a matter with；to arrange business with*｜交头～耳 *to whisper to each other* ❺收，取 to receive；to take：～到一封信 *to receive a letter*｜～受群众的意见 *to take the advice of the public* ❻迎 to meet：～待宾客 *to receive guests*｜～家眷 *to meet one's family*｜到车站～朋友 *to go to the station to meet a friend* ❼托住，承受 to catch；to take hold of：～球 *to catch（or field）a ball*｜把包～住 *to catch the bag*

痎 jiē ㄐㄧㄝ 古书上说的一种疟疾（in ancient Chinese texts）malaria

揭 jiē ㄐㄧㄝ ❶把盖在上面的东西拿起或把粘合着的东西分开 to uncover；to tear off；to rip off：～锅盖 *to remove the pot lid*｜把这张膏药～下来 *to tear the plaster off* ❷使隐瞒的事物显露 to expose；to show up：～短 *to disclose one's shortcomings*｜～发 *to expose；to unmask*｜～露 *to unmask；to expose；to disclose*｜～穿敌人的阴谋 *to uncover the enemy's plot* ❸高举 to raise：～竿而起（指人民起义）*to raise the standard of revolt；to start an uprising*

嗟 jiē ㄐㄧㄝ 文言叹词 ***interjection in classical Chinese***：～乎 *oh*；*ah*

街 jiē ㄐㄧㄝ 两边有房屋的、比较宽阔的道路。通常指开设商店的地方 street；downtown street［街坊］（—fang）邻居 neighbour

孑 jié ㄐㄧㄝˊ 单独，孤单 lonely；all alone：～立 *lonely with no one to depend on*｜～然一身 *all alone in the world*

节（節） ㊀ jié ㄐㄧㄝˊ ❶（—儿）植物学上称茎上长叶的部位 node ❷（—儿）物体的分段或两段之间连接的地方 joint；knot：骨～ *joint*｜两～火车 *two railway carriages* ❸段落 division；section；part：季～ *season*｜时～ *season*；*time*｜章～ *chapter*［节气］我国历法把一年分为二十四段，每段的开始叫作一个节气，如立春、雨水等，共有二十四个节气。也省称"节"（also 节 for short）solar term ❹节日，纪念日或庆祝的日子 festival；holiday：五一国际劳动～ *May Day*｜春～ *Spring Festival* ❺礼度 courtesy：礼～ *courtesy*；*etiquette* ❻音调高低缓急的限度 certain pitch or rate：～奏 *rhythm*｜～拍 *metre*；*beat* ❼省减，限制 to economize；to save（㊥ ***doublet*** —省 to economize｜—约 to practise thrift）：～制 *to control*｜开源～流 *to broaden the sources of income and reduce expenditure*；*to increase income and decrease expenditure*｜～衣缩食 *to economize* (or *scrimp*) *on food and clothing*；*to practise frugality* ㊁ ***extension*** 扼要摘取 to abridge：～录 *to extract*；*to excerpt*｜～译 *abridged translation* ❽操守 moral integrity；chastity（㊥ ***doublet*** —操 moral integrity）：保持晚～ *to keep one's integrity in one's later years*｜守～（封建礼教称夫死不再嫁人）（*of a woman*）*to preserve chastity by not remarrying after the death of her husband or fiancé in feudal society* ❾事项 item：情～ *plot*｜细～ *details* ❿古代出使外国所持的凭证 certificate (*or* credentials) for an envoy in ancient China［使节］派到外国的外交官员 envoy ⓫航海速度单位名，每小时航行1海里的速度为1节（符号 kn）knot (kn)

㊁ jiē 见343页 see p343

讦 jié ㄐㄧㄝˊ 揭发别人的阴私 to expose sb's hidden misdeeds：攻～ *to expose sb's hidden misdeeds and attack him*

劫（*刦、*刧） jié ㄐㄧㄝˊ ❶强取，掠夺 to rob；to loot（㊥ ***doublet*** 抢— to rob）：趁火打～ *to loot a burning house*；*to profit from the misfortune of another* ❷威逼，胁迫 to coerce；to compel：～持 *to abduct*；*to hijack* ❸灾难 calamity；disaster：浩～ *great calamity*｜～数 *inexorable doom*；*predestined fate*

J

杰(*傑) jié ㄐㄧㄝˊ ❶才能出众的人 outstanding person(㊥ *doublet* 俊— outstanding talent):英雄豪～ *heroes and outstanding figures* ❷特异的,超过一般的 outstanding:～作 *masterpiece*|～出的人才 *outstanding talent*

桀 jié ㄐㄧㄝˊ ❶凶暴 ferocious ❷古人名,夏朝末代的君主,相传是暴君 Jie, the last ruler of the Xia Dynasty, traditionally considered a tyrant ❸古代指鸡栖的小木桩(in ancient China) wood pile on which chickens perch ❹古同"杰(傑)" same as 杰(傑) in ancient Chinese

劼 jié ㄐㄧㄝˊ ❶坚固 solid ❷谨慎 prudent ❸勤勉 hard-working; diligent

诘 ㊀ jié ㄐㄧㄝˊ 追问 to question closely; to interrogate:反～ *to counter with a question*|盘～ *to cross-examine; to interrogate*

㊁ jí 见311页 see p311

拮 jié ㄐㄧㄝˊ [拮据](—jū)经济境况不好,困窘 short of money; in straitened circumstances

洁(潔) jié ㄐㄧㄝˊ 干净 clean(㊥ *doublet* —净 clean):街道清～。*The streets are clean.*|～白 *spotless (or pure) white* ㊗ *figurative* 清白,不贪污 incorruptible:贞～ *chaste and undefiled*|廉～ *incorruptible*

结 ㊀ jié ㄐㄧㄝˊ ❶系(jì),绾(wǎn) to tie; to knot:～网 *to weave a net*|～绳 *to knot ropes*|张灯～彩 *to hang up lanterns and silk streamers; to decorate with lanterns and festoons* [结构] **1** 各组成部分的搭配和排列 structure; composition:文章的～～ *structure of an essay* **2** 建筑上指承重的部分(of building) structure; construction:钢筋混凝土～～ *reinforced concrete structure* [结舌]因害怕或理屈说不出话来 tongue-tied:问得他张口～～。*When asked, he was at a loss for words.* ❷(—子)用绳、线或布条等绾成的扣 knot:打～ *to knot*|活～ *slipknot* ❸聚,合 to congeal; to associate **1** 凝聚 to congeal:～冰 *to freeze*|～晶 *to crystallize* **2** 联合,发生关系 to associate:～婚 *to marry*|～交 *to associate with*|集会～社 *assembly and association* ❹收束,完了(liǎo) to settle; to finish:～账 *to settle accounts*|～局 *final result; outcome* [结论]对人或事物所下的总结性的论断 conclusion ❺一种保证负责的字据 written guarantee; affidavit:具～ *to have a written guarantee; to sign an undertaking*

㊁ jiē 见344页 see p344

桔(❷**櫂) ㊀ jié ㄐㄧㄝˊ ❶[桔梗](—gěng)多年生草本植物,花紫色,根可以入药 balloon flower (*Platycodon grandiflorus*)

❷[桔槔](—gāo)一种汲水的设备 well sweep

㊁ jú 见369页 see p369

袺 jié ㄐㄧㄝˊ 用衣襟兜东西 to hold sth in one's lap

颉 ㊀ jié ㄐㄧㄝˊ [仓颉]上古人名，传说是黄帝的史官，汉字的创造者 Cang Jie, an ancient person, legendary official historian of the Yellow Emperor and creator of Chinese characters

㊁ xié 见829页 see p829

鲒 jié ㄐㄧㄝˊ 古书上说的一种蚌(in ancient Chinese texts) clam [鲒埼](—qí)地名，在浙江省奉化 Jieqi, a place in Fenghua, Zhejiang Province

絜 jié ㄐㄧㄝˊ 同"洁"。多用于人名(jie, usually used in a given name) same as 洁

捷(*捷) jié ㄐㄧㄝˊ ❶战胜 to triumph over: 我军大～。*Our army gained a great victory.* |～报 *news of a victory; report of a success* ❷快，速 prompt; quick(㊨ ***doublet*** 敏— nimble): 动作敏～ *to be agile in movement* |～径(近路) *shortcut; royal road* |～足先登(比喻行动敏捷，先达到目的)。*The early bird gets the worm.* or *The fastest reaches the goal first.*

婕 jié ㄐㄧㄝˊ [婕妤](—yú)汉代宫中女官名 official title for an imperial concubine in the Han Dynasty

睫 jié ㄐㄧㄝˊ 睫毛，眼睑边缘上生的细毛。它的功用是防止尘埃等东西侵入眼内，又能遮蔽强烈的光线 eyelash: 目不交～ *not to sleep a wink*(图见866页"眼" picture on p866)

偈 ㊀ jié ㄐㄧㄝˊ ❶勇武 valiant ❷跑得快(of running) fast

㊁ jì 见319页 see p319

楬 jié ㄐㄧㄝˊ 用作标志的小木桩 small marking stake [楬櫫](—zhū)标明，揭示 to mark; to make public

碣 jié ㄐㄧㄝˊ 圆顶的石碑 stone tablet: 残碑断～ *remains of a stone tablet*

竭 jié ㄐㄧㄝˊ 尽，用尽 to exhaust; to use up: ～力 *to do one's utmost; to spare no effort* |～诚 *wholeheartedly; with all one's heart* |声嘶力～ *to be hoarse and exhausted* |取之不尽，用之不～ *inexhaustible and resourceful; unexhausted*

羯 jié ㄐㄧㄝˊ ❶公羊，特指骟过的 wether; gelded ram ❷我国古代北方的民族 Jie, an ancient ethnic group in the north of China

截 jié ㄐㄧㄝˊ ❶割断，弄断 to cut; to sever: ～开这根木料 *to sever this timber* |～长补短 *to cut off the length to make up for the shortage; to make up one's shortcomings by means of one's merits* [截然]分明地，显然地 sharply; distinctly: ～～不同 *entirely different* ❷(—子、—儿)量词 ***quantifier***, 段 section; chunk: 上半～儿

upper section | 一～儿木头 *a piece of wood* | 一～路 *a stretch of a road* ❸阻拦 to stop：～住他。*Stop him.* [截止]到期停止 to end; to close：～～报名 *to close the registration* | 到月底～～。*The closing date is by the end of the month.*

姐 jiě ㄐㄧㄝˇ ❶称同父母比自己年纪大的女子(叠 ***reduplication***) elder sister; sister ❷对比自己年纪大的同辈女性的称呼 elder female relative of the same generation in the clan：表～ *elder female cousin* (*on the maternal side*); *cousin*

毑 jiě ㄐㄧㄝˇ 见 3 页"娭"字条"娭毑"(āi—) see 娭毑 on p3

解(**鮮) ㊀ jiě ㄐㄧㄝˇ ❶剖开，分开 to separate; to divide (㊟ ***doublet*** 分— to decompose)：尸体～剖 *post-mortem examination; autopsy* | 难～难分 *hard to be separated; to be inextricably involved in a dispute* | 瓦～ *to disintegrate* ❷把束缚着、系(jì)着的东西打开 to untie; to undo：～扣 *to unbutton* | ～衣服 *to untie the clothes* [解放] **1** 推翻反动政权，使广大人民群众脱离压迫，获得自由 liberation **2** 解除束缚，得到自由或发展 to emancipate; to release; to unbind：～～生产力 *to release productive forces* ❸除去 to remove **1** 消除 to dispel：～恨 *to vent one's hatred* | ～渴 *to relieve* (or *quench*) *one's thirst* **2** 废除，停止 to relieve; to terminate：～职 *to dismiss from office; to relieve sb of his post* | ～约 *to break off an agreement; to cancel* (or *annul*) *a contract* ❹讲明白，分析说明 to explain; to interpret (㊟ ***doublet*** —释 to explain | 注— to annotate)：～答 *to answer; to explain* | ～劝 *to soothe; to mollify* ❺懂，明白 to understand; to comprehend：令人不～ *puzzling* | 通俗易～ *popular and easy to understand* ❻代数方程中未知数的值 solution ❼演算 to solve; to calculate：～方程 *to solve an equation* ❽解手儿，大小便 to relieve oneself：大～ *to defecate; to have a bowel movement; to go to stool* | 小～ *to urinate; to pass water*

㊁ jiè 见350页 see p350

㊂ xiè 见831页 see p831

槲 jiě ㄐㄧㄝˇ 槲树，一种木质像松的树 (tree whose wood is similar to a pine) Quercus dentata Thunb

介 jiè ㄐㄧㄝˋ ❶在两者中间 in between：～乎两者之间 *to be between the two* [介词]表示地点、时间、方向、方式等等关系的词，如"从、向、在、以、对、于"等 preposition [介绍]使两方发生关系 to introduce; to recommend：～～人 *introducer; go-between; referee* | ～～工作 *to recommend sb for a post* [介音]字音中在主要元音前的元音，普通话有 i、u 和 ü 三个介音 (any of the three vowels i, u

J

and ü used in compound vowels in the standard Chinese pronunciation) initial vowel ❷放在心里 to take to heart; to mind:不必～意 *need not take it to heart* ❸正直 upright:耿～ *honest and frank; upright* ❹甲 armour; shell **1** 古代军人穿的护身衣服 armour:～胄在身 *to be armoured* **2** 动物身上的甲壳 shell:～虫 *beetle* ❺量词 ***quantifier***,个(用于人)(used of a person) a; an:一～书生 *an intellectual* ❻旧戏曲脚本里表示情态动作的词(word used to express motion or action in old drama scripts):打～ *fighting*|饮酒～ *drinking*

价 ㊁ jiè ㄐㄧㄝˋ 旧时称派遣传送东西或传达事情的人(in former times) messenger; errand man

㊀ jià 见324页 see p324

㊂ jie 见350页 see p350

芥 ㊀ jiè ㄐㄧㄝˋ 芥菜,一年或二年生草本植物,开黄花,茎叶及块根可吃。种子味辛辣,研成细末,可调味 mustard (*Brassica juncea*)

㊁ gài 见214页 see p214

玠 jiè ㄐㄧㄝˋ 古代的一种礼器,即大圭(i. e. 大圭) elongated pointed tablet of jade held in the hands of ancient rulers on ceremonial occasions

界 jiè ㄐㄧㄝˋ ❶相交的地方 boundary; border:边～ *boundary*|～碑 *boundary monument* (or *tablet*)|国～ *national boundary*|省～ *provincial boundary* ❷范围 scope; range:眼～ *field of vision*|管～ *jurisdiction* 特指按职业或性别等所划的范围 circles:教育～ *educational circles*|科学～ *scientific circles*|妇女～ *women's circles* ❸生物分类中的最高一级单位,其下为"门"(the highest taxonomic rank, immediately above 'phylum', in biology) kingdom:动物～ *animal kingdom*|植物～ *plant kingdom* ❹地层系统分类的第二级,在"宇"之下、"系"(xì)之上,是在地质年代"代"的时间内形成的地层(second level in the division in stratigraphy, corresponding to 'era' in geochronology where below 'erathem' is 'system') erathem:古生～ *Palaeozoic Erathem*|中生～ *Mesozoic Erathem*|新生～ *Cenozoic Erathem*

疥 jiè ㄐㄧㄝˋ 疥疮,因疥虫寄生而引起的一种皮肤病,非常刺痒 scabies

蚧 jiè ㄐㄧㄝˋ 见224页"蛤"字条"蛤蚧"(gé—) see 蛤蚧 on p224

戒 jiè ㄐㄧㄝˋ ❶防备 to take precautions:～心 *vigilance; wariness*|～备森严 *heavily guarded* [戒严]非常时期在全国或一地所采取的增设警戒、限制交通等措施 to enforce martial law; to impose a curfew ❷警惕着不要做或不要犯 to guard against:～骄～躁 *to guard against conceit and rashness* ❸革除嗜好 to give up; to quit:～酒 *to give up drinking*|～烟 *to give up smoking* ❹佛教约束教徒的条规 Buddhist monastic discipline:五～ *the five commandments*|清规～律 *regulations and taboos*

诫 jiè ㄐㄧㄝˋ 警告,劝人警惕 to warn; to admonish:告～ *to admonish*

届(*屆) jiè ㄐㄧㄝˋ ❶到 to expire; to fall due:～时 *when the time comes; at the appointed time; on the occasion*|～期 *when the time comes; on the appointed date* ❷量词 ***quantifier***,次,期 session; class:第一～ *first session of*|上～ *last session of* [应届](yīng—)指本期的,用于毕业生 this year's graduates

借(❸❹△藉) jiè ㄐㄧㄝˋ ❶暂时使用别人的财物等 to borrow:～钱 *to borrow money*|～车 *to borrow a bicycle, a car, etc*|～用 *to borrow* [借光]请人让路或问事的客气话 Excuse me. ❷暂时把财物等给别人使用 to lend:～给他几块钱 *to lend him several yuan* ❸假托 to use as a pretext:～端 *to use as a pretext; to find an excuse*|～故 *to find (or invent) an excuse*|～口 *to use as an excuse; excuse*|～题发挥 *to make use of the subject under discussion to express one's own ideas; to seize on an incident to exaggerate matters* ❹凭借,依靠 to make use of; to rely on:～助 *to have the aid of; with the help of*

唶 jiè ㄐㄧㄝˋ 赞叹 to gasp in admiration

藉 ㊀ jiè ㄐㄧㄝˋ ❶垫在下面的东西 cushion; mat ❷垫衬 to pad:枕～ *lying on top of each other; lying in disorder* ❸同"借❸❹"same as 借❸❹

㊁ jí 见314页 see p314

解(**觧) ㊁ jiè ㄐㄧㄝˋ 指押送财物或犯人 to send under guard; to escort:～款 *transfer of fund*|起～ *to send a prisoner under escort* [解元]明、清两代称乡试考取第一名的人 a scholar who won the first place in provincial imperial examinations during the Ming and Qing dynasties

㊀ jiě 见348页 see p348

㊂ xiè 见831页 see p831

犗 jiè ㄐㄧㄝˋ 阉割过的牛 bullock

褯 jiè ㄐㄧㄝˋ (—子)婴儿的尿布 diaper

价(價) ㊂ jie ·ㄐㄧㄝ 词尾 ***suffix***:震天～响。*The sound is deafening.*|成天～闹 *to make a racket all day long*

㊀ jià 见324页 see p324

㊁ jiè 见349页 see p349

家 ㊁ jie ·ㄐㄧㄝ 词尾 ***suffix***:整天～ *all day long*|成年～ *all year long; throughout the whole year*

㊀ jiā 见321页 see p321

J

JIN ㄐㄧㄣ

巾 jīn ㄐㄧㄣ 擦东西或包裹、覆盖东西用的纺织品（used for wiping, wrapping or covering things）piece of cloth：手～ *towel*｜头～ *scarf*

斤（❶*觔）jīn ㄐㄧㄣ ❶市制重量单位，1斤是10两（旧制16两），合0.5千克（公斤）*jin*, unit of weight, equal to 10 *liang*（16 old *liang*）or 0.5 kilograms ❷古代砍伐树木的工具（in ancient China）axe; chopper

［斤斤］过分看重微小的利害 particular about trivial things：～～计较 *to haggle over every ounce; to be calculating and unwilling to make the smallest sacrifice*

今 jīn ㄐㄧㄣ 现在，跟"古"相对（the opposite of 古）now; present-day：～天 *today*｜～年 *this year*｜～昔 *present and past*｜从～以后 *from now on*

衿 jīn ㄐㄧㄣ ❶襟 front of a garment：青～（旧时念书人穿的衣服）*scholar's garment in former times* ❷系（jì）衣裳的带子 belt; girdle

矜 ㊀ jīn ㄐㄧㄣ ❶怜悯，怜惜 to pity; to sympathize with ❷自尊自大，自夸 to be self-important; to be conceited：自～其功 *to claim to have performed meritorious deeds* ❸慎重，拘谨 prudent; restrained：～持 *restrained; reserved*

㊁ guān 见248页 see p248

㊂ qín 见607页 see p607

金 jīn ㄐㄧㄣ ❶一种金属元素，符号Au，通称"金子"。黄赤色，质软，是一种贵重的金属（generally called 金子）gold; aurum（Au）[喻] ***figurative*** 尊贵，珍贵 valuable：～榜 *list of successful candidates in the final imperial examinations*｜～玉良言 *invaluable advice; precious words*｜～科玉律 *golden rule and precious precept; infallible laws* ❷金属，指金、银、铜、铁等，具有光泽、延展性，容易传热和导电 metal：五～ *hardware*｜合～ *alloy* ❸钱 money：现～ *cash*｜奖～ *bonus*｜基～ *fund*

津 jīn ㄐㄧㄣ ❶渡口，过江河的地方 ferry crossing; ford：问～（打听渡口，比喻探问）*to ask the way to the ford — to make inquiries* ［津梁］桥 bridge [喻] ***figurative*** 作引导用的事物 guide ❷口液，唾液 saliva：～液 *saliva* ［津津］形容有滋味，有趣味 tasty; interesting：～～有味 *with appetite; full of interest*｜～～乐道 *to indulge in elaborating; to take a delight in talking about* ❸滋润 moist; damp ［津贴］**1** 用财物补助 to grant allowance **2** 正式工资以外的补助费，也指供给制人员的生活零用钱 allowance ❹指天津 Tianjin

筋（*觔）jīn ㄐㄧㄣ ❶肌肉的旧称 former term for muscle ❷俗称皮下可

J

以看见的静脉管 popular name for veins that stand out under the skin ❸俗称肌腱或骨头上的韧带 popular name for a tendon or sinew：～骨 *muscles and bones*｜牛蹄～ *tendon of an ox hoof* ❹像筋的东西 anything resembling a tendon：钢～ *steel bar*｜铁～ *iron bar*

禁 ㊁ jīn ㄐㄧㄣ ❶禁受，受得住，耐（用） to bear; to stand：～得起考验 *to be able to stand trials*｜这种布～穿。*This kind of cloth is durable.* ❷忍耐 to contain oneself：他不～（忍不住）笑起来。*He couldn't help laughing.*

㊀ jìn 见356页 see p356

襟 jīn ㄐㄧㄣ 衣服胸前的部分 front of a garment：大～ *front of a Chinese garment*｜小～ *smaller piece on the right side of a Chinese garment*｜底～ *narrow piece of cloth under the front of a Chinese garment*｜对～ *Chinese-style jacket with buttons down the front*（图见882页“衣” picture on p882）［襟怀］胸怀 bosom; heart; breadth of mind［连襟］姐妹的丈夫间的关系，也省作“襟”（also 襟 for short） brothers-in-law whose wives are sisters：～兄 *husband of one's wife's elder sister*｜～弟 *husband of one's wife's younger sister*

仅（僅、**廑） ㊀ jǐn ㄐㄧㄣˇ 副词 ***adverb***，只（叠 ***reduplication***） only; merely：～～三个月就建成了 *to have been built in only three months; it only took three months to build (sth)*｜～写过两篇短文 *to have written only two short articles*｜这些意见～供参考。*These suggestions are for reference only.*

㊁ jìn 见353页 see p353

尽（儘） ㊀ jǐn ㄐㄧㄣˇ ❶极，最 furthest; extreme：～底下 *at the very bottom*｜～里头 *innermost*｜～先录用 *to employ or enroll sb first* ❷有多少用多少 to the greatest extent：～量 *to the best of one's ability; as far as possible*｜～着力气做 *to spare no effort in (doing sth)*［尽管］**1** 连词 ***conjunction***，纵然，即使 though; even if：～～他不接受这个意见，我还是要向他提。*Although he refused to accept this suggestion, I'll put it forward anyway.* **2** 只管，不必顾虑 to feel free to; not to hesitate to：有话～～说吧！*Don't hesitate to speak out what you want to say.* ❸放在最先 to give priority to：座位先～着请来的客人坐。*Let the guests invited take their seats first.*｜先～着旧衣服穿。*Wear the old clothes first.*

㊁ jìn 见354页 see p354

卺 jǐn ㄐㄧㄣˇ 瓢，古代结婚时用作酒器（in ancient China） nuptial wine cup［合卺］旧时夫妇成婚的一种仪式（in a former marriage ceremony） newlyweds

J

drinking wine in nuptial cups (made from a gourd split in two)

紧(緊) jǐn ㄐㄧㄣˇ ❶密切合拢，跟"松"相对 (the opposite of 松) tight：捆～ *to bundle up tightly* ㊊ ***extension*** 靠得极近 close; very near：～邻 *close neighbour; next-door neighbour* | ～靠着 *to keep close to* ❷物体受到几方面的拉力以后所呈现的紧张状态 taut; tight：鼓面绷得非常～。*The surface of the drum is stretched tight.* [紧张]不松弛，不缓和 nervous; tense：精神～～ *to be nervous* | 工作～～ *to have intense work* ❸使紧 to tighten：把弦～一～ *to tighten the string* | ～一～腰带 *to tighten one's belt* ❹事情密切接连着，时间急促没有空隙 urgent; pressing：功课很～。*The schoolwork is pressing.* | 抓～时间 *to make the best use of one's time; to lose no time in doing sth* ㊊ ***extension*** 因时间短促而加快 to quicken：～走 *to quicken one's steps* | 手～点就能多出活。*If we work quicker, we can get a lot more done.* ❺形势严重或关系重要 critical; crucial：～要关头 *critical moment* | 事情～急。*The matter is urgent.* ❻生活不宽裕 hard up; short of money：以前他家日子很～。*His family was hard pressed in the past.*

堇 jǐn ㄐㄧㄣˇ ❶堇菜，今多指紫花地丁，犁头草。多年生草本植物，春夏开紫花，果实椭圆形，全草可入药 violet (*Viola*) ❷紫堇，草本植物，夏天开淡紫红色花。全草味苦，可入药 corydalis (*Corydalis*)

谨 jǐn ㄐㄧㄣˇ ❶慎重，小心 careful; cautious(㊈ ***doublet*** 一慎 prudent)：～守规程 *to adhere to the rules strictly* ❷郑重，恭敬 solemnly; sincerely：～启 *yours respectfully* | ～向您表示祝贺。*I wish to extend my sincere congratulations to you.*

馑 jǐn ㄐㄧㄣˇ 荒年 famine year (㊈ ***doublet*** 饥一 famine)

瑾 jǐn ㄐㄧㄣˇ 美玉 beautiful jade

槿 jǐn ㄐㄧㄣˇ 木槿，落叶灌木，花有红、白、紫等颜色，茎的纤维可造纸，树皮和花可入药 rose of Sharon (*Hibiscus syriacus*)

锦 jǐn ㄐㄧㄣˇ ❶有彩色花纹的丝织品 brocade：～缎 *brocade and satin* | 蜀～ *Sichuan brocade* | ～上添花 *to add flowers to the brocade; to give an added grace to what is already beautiful* ❷鲜明美丽 bright and beautiful：～霞 *rose-tinted clouds* | ～鸡 *golden pheasant*

仅(僅) ㊁ jìn ㄐㄧㄣˋ 将近，几乎(多见于唐人诗文) (usually seen in the poems of Tang Dynasty) nearly; approximately：山城～百层。*The mountain city is nearly a hundred storeys in height.* | 士

J

卒～万人。*There are nearly 10,000 soldiers.*

㊁ jǐn 见352页 see p352

尽（盡） ㊀ jìn ㄐㄧㄣˋ ❶完毕 exhausted; finished：用～力气 *to use up one's strength*｜说不～的好处 *With more advantages than you can imagine* ㊔ **extension** 达到极端 to the utmost; to the limit：～善～美 *to reach the acme of perfection*｜～头 *end* [自尽]自杀 to commit suicide ❷全部用出 to use up; to exhaust：～心 *to put all one's heart and soul into*｜～力 *to do all one can*｜仁至义～ *to have done one's best to help sb; to be extremely magnanimous towards sb* ㊔ **extension** 竭力做到 to try one's best：～职 *to carry out duties* ❸都，全 all; entire：到会的～是战斗英雄。*All those who attended the meeting were combat heroes.*

㊁ jǐn 见352页 see p352

荩（藎） jìn ㄐㄧㄣˋ ❶荩草，一年生草本植物，茎很细，花灰绿色或带紫色，茎和叶可做黄色染料，纤维可做造纸原料 hispid arthraxon (*Arthraxon hispidus*) ❷忠诚 loyal; faithful：～臣 *loyal official*

浕（濜） jìn ㄐㄧㄣˋ 浕水，古水名，在湖北省枣阳。今称沙河 (now called 沙河) Jinshui River, an ancient river in Zaoyang, Hubei Province

赆（贐） jìn ㄐㄧㄣˋ 临别时赠的礼物 parting gift：～仪 *parting gift*

烬（燼） jìn ㄐㄧㄣˋ 物体燃烧后剩下的东西 ash; cinder (㊧ **doublet** 灰～ ashes)：化为灰～ *to turn to ashes*｜烛～ *candle ashes*

进（進） jìn ㄐㄧㄣˋ ❶向前、向上移动，跟"退"相对 (the opposite of 退) to advance; to move ahead：前～ *to advance*｜～军 *to march*｜更～一层 *to make progress and reach another level*｜～一步提高产品质量 *to further improve the quality of the product* [进步] **1** 向前发展，比原来好 to make progress; to improve：时代又～～了。*The times made progress again.* **2** 适合时代要求，对社会发展起促进作用的 progressive：思想很～～ *to have progressive ideas* [进化]事物由简单到复杂、由低级到高级的发展过程 evolution ❷入，往里面去 to enter; to go into：～工厂 *to enter the factory*｜～学校 *to enter the school* ❸收入或买入 to receive; to buy：～款 *income*｜～项 *income*｜～货 *to replenish one's stock* ❹旧式建筑房院前后的层次 any of several rows of houses in an old-style residential compound：这房子是两～院子。*This residence has a compound with two rows of houses.* ❺奉呈 to submit; to present：～献 *to submit; to present*

琎（璡） jìn ㄐㄧㄣˋ 一种像玉的石头 jade-like

stone

近 jìn ㄐㄧㄣˋ ❶跟"远"相对(the opposite of 远) **1** 距离短(of distance) near; close:路很～。*It's not far from here.* or *It's a short way.* |天津离北京很～。*Tianjin locates very near to Beijing.* **2** 现在以前不久的时间 a short time before:～几天 *recent days* |～来 *recently; lately* ❷亲密,关系密切 intimate; closely related:亲～ *intimate* |他们是～亲。*They are close relatives.* ❸接近,差别小,差不多 approaching; close to:相～ *approximate; near* |～似 *similar* |年～五十 *to be verging on 50; coming on to 50* ❹浅近 easy to understand; simple and obvious:言～旨远。*Some simple words carry a profound meaning.* or *Simple in language but profound in meaning.*

靳 jìn ㄐㄧㄣˋ〈古 ***archaism***〉吝惜,不肯给予 to be stingy

妗 jìn ㄐㄧㄣˋ ❶舅母 wife of one's mother's brother; aunt ❷(-子)妻兄、妻弟的妻子 wife of one's wife's brother:大～子 *wife of one's wife's elder brother* |小～子 *wife of one's wife's younger brother*

劲(勁) ㊀ jìn ㄐㄧㄣˋ (-儿) 力气,力量 strength; energy:有多大～使多大～ *to bring all one's strength into play* ㊁ ***extension*** **1** 效力,作用 force; effect:酒～儿上来了 *to begin to feel the wine's effect* |药～不够。*The efficacy of the medicine is inadequate.* **2** 精神、情绪、兴趣等 spirit; mood; interest:干活儿起～ *to work with vigour* |一股子～头儿 *to be full of drive* |一个～儿地做 *to work continuously* |老玩儿这个真没～。*It is boring to play this all the time.* **3** 指属性的程度(used to denote the degree of property):你瞧这块布这个白～儿。*Look, how white this piece of cloth is!* |咸～儿 *very salty* |香～儿 *how fragrant*

㊁ jìng 见361页 see p361

晋(*晉) jìn ㄐㄧㄣˋ ❶进,向前 to enter; to advance:～见 *to call on sb holding high office* |～级 *to rise in rank; to be promoted* ❷周代诸侯国名,在今山西省和河北省南部,河南省北部,陕西省东部 Jin, a princedom during the Zhou Dynasty, occupying parts of today's Southern Shanxi and Hebei provinces, Northern Henan Province and Eastern Shaanxi Province ❸山西省的别称 Jin, another name for Shanxi Province ❹朝代名 Jin, name of a dynasty **1** 晋武帝司马炎所建立(公元265—420年) the Jin Dynasty (265－420), founded by Sima Yan, Emperor Wu **2** 五代之一,石敬瑭所建立(公元936—947年),史称后晋 Later Jin Dynasty (936－947), one of the Five Dynasties, founded by Shi Jingtang

搢(**搢) jìn ㄐㄧㄣˋ 插 to insert [搢绅]同"缙绅"same as 缙绅

缙(**縉) jìn ㄐㄧㄣˋ 赤色的帛 red silk [缙绅]古代称官僚或做过官的人。也作"搢绅"(also written as 搢绅)(in ancient China) government official; retired government official

浸 jìn ㄐㄧㄣˋ ❶泡,使渗透 to soak; to steep; to immerse:～透 *to soak*|～入 *to immerse*|把种子放在水里～一～ *to soak the seeds in water* ❷逐渐 gradually:～渐 *gradually*|交往～密 *to get into closer contact gradually*

祲 jìn ㄐㄧㄣˋ 迷信的人称不祥之气(so called by superstitious people) sinister atmosphere

禁 ㊀ jìn ㄐㄧㄣˋ ❶不许,制止 to prohibit; to forbid; to ban:～止攀折花木。*There is ban on picking flowers.*|～赛 *to forbid sb from participating in a match* ❷法律或习惯上制止的事 what is forbidden by law or custom:入国问～ *to ask about taboos and bans upon entering a foreign country*|犯～ *to violate a ban* ❸拘押 to imprison; to detain:～闭 *confinement*|监～ *imprisonment* ❹旧时称皇帝居住的地方 royal residence in former times:～中 *central forbidden area*|紫～城 *Forbidden City* ㊀ ***extension*** 不能随便通行的地方 forbidden area:～地 *forbidden zone* ❺避忌 taboo:～忌 *taboo*

㊁ jīn 见352页 see p352

噤 jìn ㄐㄧㄣˋ 闭口,不作声 to keep silent:～若寒蝉 *to be as silent as the cicada in late autumn —to keep silent out of fear*

觐 jìn ㄐㄧㄣˋ 朝见君主或朝拜圣地 to present oneself before a monarch; to go on a pilgrimage:～见 *to present oneself before a monarch; to go to court*

殣 jìn ㄐㄧㄣˋ ❶掩埋 to bury ❷饿死 to starve to death

JING ㄐㄧㄥ

茎(莖) jīng ㄐㄧㄥ ❶常指植物的主干。它起支撑作用,又是养料和水分运输的通道。有些植物有地下茎,并且发生各种变态,作用是储藏养料和进行无性繁殖 stem; stalk ❷量词 ***quantifier***,用于长条形的东西(used for long and narrow things):数～小草 *a few blades of grass*|数～白发 *some white hairs*

泾(涇) jīng ㄐㄧㄥ 泾河,发源于宁夏回族自治区,流至陕西省入渭河 Jinghe River, originated in the Ningxia Hui Autonomous Region and flowing through Shaanxi Province into the Weihe River [泾渭分明]泾河水清,渭河水浊,两河汇流处清浊不混 as different as the waters of the Jinghe and the Weihe rivers — wholly different ⓨ *figurative* 两件事显然不同 to be entirely different

经(經) jīng ㄐㄧㄥ ❶经线，织布时拴在机上的竖纱，编织物的纵线 warp ❷地理学上假定的沿地球表面连接南北两极并与赤道垂直的线，从通过英国格林尼治天文台原址的经线起，以东称“东经”，以西称“西经”，各为 180° longitude ❸持久不变的，正常 constant; regular: ～常 *often* | 不～之谈 *absurd and groundless sayings; nonsense* ⓨ **extension** 指义理，法则 canon; norm: 离～叛道 *to deviate from the canon and stray into error; to be heretical* | 天～地义 *nature's law and earth's way; unalterable truth* ❹尊为典范的著作或宗教的典籍 classic; scripture: ～典 *classics; scriptures* | 佛～ *Buddhist scriptures* | 圣～ *Holy Bible; the Scriptures* | 古兰～ *the Koran* ❺治理，管理 to administer; to manage: ～商 *to engage in trade; to go into business* [经济] **1** 通常指一个国家的国民经济或国民经济的某一部门，例如工业、农业、商业、财政、金融等 economy **2** 指经济基础，即一定历史时期的社会生产关系。它是政治和意识形态等上层建筑的基础 economic base **3** 指国家或个人的收支状况 financial condition; income: ～～富裕 *rich; well-off; well-to-do* **4** 节约 economical; thrifty: 这样做不～～。*It is uneconomical to do so.* [经纪] **1** 经营管理 to manage: 善于～～ *to be good at managing* **2** 经纪人，为买卖双方撮(cuō)合并从中取得佣金的人 broker; agent [经理] **1** 经营 to handle; to manage: 他很会～～事业。*He knows well how to manage his business.* **2** 企业的主管人(of an enterprise) manager; director [经营] 计划，调度，管理 to manage; to operate ❻经受，禁(jīn)受 to stand; to bear; to endure: ～风雨，见世面 *to face the world and brave the storm; to see life and stand its test* ❼经过，通过 through; via; by way of: ～他一说我才明白。*From what he said it became clear to me.* | 久～考验 *long-tested; well steeled* | 途～上海 *to pass by Shanghai* [经验] 由实践得来的知识或技能 experience ❽在动词前，跟“曾”、“已”连用，表示动作的时间过去而且完成了(used in collocation with 曾 or 已 before a verb to denote the fulfilment of the action): 曾～说过 *to have said* | 他已～是个很得力的干部。*He has become a competent official.* ❾中医称人体内的脉络(of traditional Chinese medicine) arteries and veins: ～络 *main and collateral channels in the human body* ❿月经，妇女每月由阴部排出血液 menses: ～期 *menstrual period* | 停～ *amenorrhoea* ⓫缢死

to die by hanging: 自～ *to hang oneself*

京 jīng ㄐㄧㄥ ❶京城，国家的首都。特指我国首都北京 capital; Beijing: ～广铁路 *the Beijing-Guangzhou railway* | ～剧 *Beijing Opera; Peking Opera* ❷古代数目，指一千万 (ancient number) ten million

[京族] 1 我国少数民族，参看附表(see the appendix) the Jing ethnic group, one of the ethnic minorities of China 2 越南的主要民族 chief ethnic people in Vietnam

猄 jīng ㄐㄧㄥ [黄猄]鹿的一种 muntjac (*Muntiacus*)

惊(驚) jīng ㄐㄧㄥ ❶骡、马等因为害怕狂奔起来不受控制(of horses, mules, etc) to shy; to stampede: 马～了。*The horse shied.* | ～了车 *The horse drawing the cart was stampeded.* ❷害怕，精神受了刺激突然不安 to startle; to be frightened: 受～ *to be frightened* | 吃～ *to be surprised* | ～心动魄 *to be soul-stirring; to be profoundly moving* | 十分～慌 *panic-stricken* ❸出人意料的感觉 surprise: ～喜 *pleasant surprise* ❹惊动 to alarm: 打草～蛇 *to beat the grass and startle the snake; to act rashly and alert the enemy* [惊风]有痉挛症状的小儿病，通常分急性、慢性两种。也省称"惊"(also 惊 for short) infantile convulsions

鲸 jīng ㄐㄧㄥ 生长(zhǎng)在海里的哺乳类动物，形状像鱼，胎生，用肺呼吸，最大的种类可长达 30 米，小的只 1 米左右。俗叫"鲸鱼"(popularly called 鲸鱼) whale (*Cetacea*)

[鲸吞]吞并，常指强国对弱国的侵略行为 to swallow like a whale; to annex (territory)

荆 jīng ㄐㄧㄥ ❶落叶灌木，叶子有长柄，掌状分裂，花小，蓝紫色，枝条可用来编筐、篮等。古时用荆条做刑具 chaste tree (*Vitex agnus-castus*), its twigs being used as an instrument of punishment in ancient China: 负～请罪(向人认错) *to bear bramble twigs and ask for a flogging — to make a humble and heartfelt apology* [荆棘](－jí)泛指丛生多刺的灌木 thorny undergrowth ㊥ ***figurative*** 障碍和困难 obstacles and difficulties ❷春秋时楚国也称"荆"Jing, another name for the Chu State during the Warring States Period

菁 jīng ㄐㄧㄥ (叠 ***reduplication***)草木茂盛 lush; luxuriant [菁华]最精美的部分 essence; cream; quintessence

睛 jīng ㄐㄧㄥ 眼球，眼珠 eyeball: 目不转～ *to gaze fixedly* | 画龙点～ *to bring the painted dragon to life by putting in the pupils of the eyes — to add the finishing touches*

腈 jīng ㄐㄧㄥ 有机化合物的一类，通式 R—CN，无色的

J

液体或固体，有特殊的气味，遇酸或碱就分解 nitrile

鹊 jīng ㄐㄧㄥ 见338页"鸩"字条"鸩鹊"（jiāo—）see 鸩鹊 on p338

精 jīng ㄐㄧㄥ ❶细密的 fine; meticulous：～制 *refined*｜～选 *carefully chosen; choice*｜～打细算 *to make a careful and detailed calculation; to be very careful in reckoning* ❷聪明，思想周密 smart; shrewd：这孩子真～。*The child is very smart.*｜他是个～明强干的人。*He is a shrewd man.* ❸精华，物质中最纯粹的部分，提炼出来的东西 essence; extract：麦～ *malt extract*｜酒～ *alcohol*｜炭～ *charcoal products* [精神] **1** 即主观世界，包括思想、作风等，是客观世界的反映 spirit; mind：物质可以变成～～，～～可以变成物质。*Matter can be transformed into spirit, and spirit can be transformed into matter.* **2** 内容实质 essence; gist：文件～～ *gist of a document* **3**（—shen）指人表现出来的活力 vigour; vitality：他的～～很好。*He is very vigorous.*｜做事有～～ *to do sth with energy* ❹完美，最好 perfect; excellent：～美 *exquisite; delicate*｜～装 *hardcover; deluxe packing*｜～益求～ *to keep improving* [精彩]最出色的 brilliant; superb ❺精液，男子和雄性动物体内的生殖物质 sperm; semen ❻专一，深入 skilled; conversant; proficient：博而不～ *to have wide but not expert knowledge*｜～通 *to be proficient in; to master*｜他～于针灸。*He is well versed in acupuncture and moxibustion.* ❼很，极 very; extremely：～湿 *extremely wet*｜～瘦 *very thin*｜～光 *with nothing left; shiny* ❽迷信的人以为多年老物变成的妖怪 goblin; spirit; demon：妖～ *demon*｜狐狸～ *fox spirit —seductive woman*

鼱 jīng ㄐㄧㄥ 小鼠 shrew; shrewmouse

旌 jīng ㄐㄧㄥ ❶古代用羽毛装饰的旗子。又指普通的旗子 feather-decorated banner in ancient China; banner ❷表扬 to praise [旌表]指封建统治阶级对遵守封建礼教的人的表扬（of feudal rulers）to confer honours on those who conform to the feudal ethical codes

晶 jīng ㄐㄧㄥ 形容光亮（叠 ***reduplication***）shiny; glittering：～莹 *sparkling and crystal-clear*｜亮～～的 *glittering* [晶体]原子、离子、分子按一定的空间位置排列而成，且具有规则外形的固体 crystal [结晶] **1** 由液体或气体变成许多有一定形状的小颗粒的现象 crystallization **2** 由结晶现象生成的小颗粒 crystals [喻] ***figurative*** 成果 achievement：这本著作是他多年研究的～～。*This book is the result of his many years' research.* [水晶]矿物名。坚硬透明，种类很多，可制光学仪器等 crystal

J

粳(*杭、*稉) jīng ㄐㄧㄥ 粳稻，稻的一种，米粒短而粗 round-grained nonglutinous rice

兢 jīng ㄐㄧㄥ [兢兢]小心，谨慎 cautious：战战～～ *trembling with fear; gingerly* | ～～业业 *to be cautious and conscientious*

井 jǐng ㄐㄧㄥˇ ❶从地面向下挖成的能取出水的深洞，洞壁多砌上砖石 well ❷形状跟井相像的 sth in the shape of a well：天～ *small courtyard* | 盐～ *salt well* | 矿～ *mine; pit* ❸整齐，有秩序（叠 ***reduplication***）neat; orderly：～～有条 *arranged in regular and good order; in an orderly manner* | 秩序～然 *to be in good order* ❹星宿名，二十八宿之一 *jing*, the 22nd of the 28 constellations

阱(*穽) jǐng ㄐㄧㄥˇ 陷阱，捕野兽用的陷坑 trap; pitfall

肼 jǐng ㄐㄧㄥˇ 有机化合物的一类，是联氨（通式 $H_2N—NH_2$）及其烃基衍生物（通式 $R—NH—NH_2$）的统称 hydrazine

刭(剄) jǐng ㄐㄧㄥˇ 用刀割脖子 to cut the throat：自～ *to commit suicide by cutting one's throat*

颈(頸) ㊀ jǐng ㄐㄧㄥˇ 脖子，头和躯干相连接的部分 neck（图见741页"体"picture on p741）

㊁ gěng 见230页 see p230

景 jǐng ㄐㄧㄥˇ ❶风景，风光 view; scenery：良辰美～ *beautiful scene on a fine day* | ～致真好。*The scenery is lovely.* | ～色秀丽。*The landscape is beautiful.* ❷景象，情况 situation; condition：盛～ *grand occasion* | 晚～ *evening scene; circumstances in old age* | 幸福生活的远～ *prospect of a happy life* ❸戏剧、电影等中的场面和景物 scenery; setting：布～ *setting* | 内～ *indoor setting* | 外～ *outdoor scenery* ❹景仰，佩服，敬慕 to admire; to revere; to respect：～慕 *to esteem; to revere* ❺指日光 sunlight：春和～明。*In spring, the weather is mild and the scenery brilliant.*

[景颇族]我国少数民族，参看附表(see the appendix) the Jingpo ethnic group, one of the ethnic minorities of China

〈古 ***archaism***〉又同"影"(yǐng) also same as 影

憬 jǐng ㄐㄧㄥˇ 觉悟 to wake up to reality; to come to see the truth

璟 jǐng ㄐㄧㄥˇ 玉的光彩 lustre of jade

儆 jǐng ㄐㄧㄥˇ 使人警醒，不犯过错 to warn; to admonish：～戒 *to warn; to admonish* | 惩(chéng)一～百 *to punish one as a warning to one hundred*

警 jǐng ㄐㄧㄥˇ ❶注意可能发生的危险 to warn; to alarm:

～戒 *to guard* (or *warn*) *against*|～备 *to guard; to garrison*|～告(提醒人注意) *to warn; to caution* [警察]国家维持社会治安和秩序的武装力量，也指参加这种武装力量的成员。也省称"警"(also 警 for short) police：人民～～ *people's police*|民～ *people's policeman* ❷需要戒备的危险事件或消息 alarm; emergency：火～ *fire alarm*|告～ *to report an emergency; to give an alarm*|～报 *alarm; siren* ❸感觉敏锐 alert; vigilant：～觉 *vigilance; alertness*|～醒 *to sleep lightly*

劲(勁) ㊁ jìng ㄐㄧㄥˋ 坚强有力 strong; powerful：～旅 *strong contingent; powerful army*|～敌 *strong opponent*|刚～ *vigorous; sturdy*|疾风知～草。*The force of the wind tests the strength of the grass.* or *Strength of a character is tested in a crisis.*

㊀ jìn 见355页 see p355

径(徑、❶❸*逕) jìng ㄐㄧㄥˋ ❶小路 path; track：山～ *mountain track* ㊞ ***figurative*** 达到目的的方法 way; means：捷～ *shortcut*|门～ *access; way* [径赛]各种长短距离的赛跑和竞走项目比赛的总称 track events [径庭] ㊞ ***figurative*** 相差太远 quite different：大相～～ *entirely different* ❷直径，两端以圆周为界，通过圆心的线段或指它的长度 diameter：半～ *radius*|口～ *bore; calibre* ❸直截了当 directly; straight：～启者 *one who opens straightway*|～向有关单位联系 *to contact with the units concerned directly*

胫(脛、*踁) jìng ㄐㄧㄥˋ 小腿，从膝盖到脚跟的一段 shin [胫骨]小腿内侧的骨头 shin bone; tibia (图见241页"骨" picture on p241)

痉(痙) jìng ㄐㄧㄥˋ 痉挛(luán)，俗叫"抽筋"。肌肉收缩，手脚抽搐(chù)的现象，小孩子发高烧时常有这种症状(popularly called 抽筋) convulsion; spasm

净(*淨) jìng ㄐㄧㄥˋ ❶干净，清洁 clean：～水 *pure* (or *clean*) *water*|脸要洗～。*Wash your face clean.* ❷洗，使干净 to wash; to clean：～面 *to wash one's face*|～手 *to clean one's hands; to wash one's hands* ❸什么也没有，空，光 with nothing left：钱用～了。*The money has been used up.* ❹单纯，纯粹的 pure; net：～利 *net profit*|～重 *net weight* ❺副词 ***adverb*** **1** 单只，仅只 only; merely：～剩下棉花了。*Nothing but cotton is left over.* **2** 全(没有别的) all; nothing but：满地～是树叶。*There are nothing but leaves all over the ground.* ❻传统戏曲里称花脸 painted-face role in a traditional Chinese opera

J

静 jìng ㄐㄧㄥˋ ❶停止的，跟"动"相对(the opposite of 动) still; motionless: ～止 *static; motionless* | 风平浪～ *with gentle breeze and fine ripples; calm and tranquil* ❷没有声音 quiet; silent: 这个地方很清～。*This place is very quiet.* | 更(gēng)深夜～ *in the dead hours of the night; in the deep of night* | ～悄悄的 *very quiet*

倞 ㊀ jìng ㄐㄧㄥˋ 强，强劲 strong

㊁ liàng 见443页 see p443

竞(競) jìng ㄐㄧㄥˋ 比赛，互相争胜 to compete; to contest: ～走 *heel-and-toe walking* | ～渡 *to have a boat or swimming race* [竞赛] 互相比赛，争取优胜 contest; competition: 劳动～～ *labour emulation* [竞争] 为了自己或本集团的利益而跟人争胜 to compete

竟 jìng ㄐㄧㄥˋ ❶终了(liǎo)，完毕 to end; to finish: 读～ *to finish one's reading* | 继承先烈未～的事业 *to carry on the martyrs' unaccomplished cause* ㊂ ***extension*** **1** 到底，终于 in the end; finally: 有志者事～成。*Where there's a will, there's a way.* | 他的话毕～不错。*What he said is right after all.* **2** 整，从头到尾 whole; throughout: ～日 *the whole day; throughout the day* ❷副词 ***adverb***，居然，表示出乎意料 actually; unexpectedly: 这样巨大的工程，～在短短半年中就完成了。*To our surprise, such a great project was finished in only half a year.*

境 jìng ㄐㄧㄥˋ ❶疆界 border; boundary(㊃ ***doublet*** 边一 border; frontier): 国～ *national boundary* | 入～ *to enter a country; to cross the border* ❷地方，处所 place; area; land: 如入无人之～ *like entering unpopulated land; meeting with no resistance* ㊂ ***extension*** **1** 品行学业的程度 degree of one's moral conduct or studies: 学有进～ *to make progress in one's studies* **2** 环境，遭遇到的情况 situation; circumstances: 处～不同 *in different circumstances* | 事过～迁 *Events have passed and times have changed.*

獍 jìng ㄐㄧㄥˋ 古书上说的一种像虎豹的兽，生下来就吃生它的母兽(in ancient Chinese texts) *jing*, legendary animal similar to a tiger or a leopard that eats its own mother immediately after its birth

镜 jìng ㄐㄧㄥˋ ❶(一子)用来反映形象的器具，古代用铜磨制，现代用玻璃制成 mirror ❷利用光学原理特制的各种器具 lens: 显微～ *microscope* | 望远～ *telescope* | 眼～ *glasses; spectacles* | 凸透～ *convex lens* | 三棱～ *triangular prism*

婧 jìng ㄐㄧㄥˋ 女子有才能(of a woman) talented

靓 ㊀ jìng ㄐㄧㄥˋ 妆饰，打扮 to dress; to make up

J

㊁ liàng 见443页 see p443

靖 jìng ㄐㄧㄥˋ ❶安静，平安 quiet; peaceful ❷旧指平定，使秩序安定。参看715页"绥❶"(see 绥❶ on p715) (in former times) to pacify; to suppress

敬 jìng ㄐㄧㄥˋ ❶尊重，有礼貌地对待 to respect; to honour; to esteem(㊣ ***doublet*** 尊— to respect)：～客 *to treat one's guest with respect*｜～之以礼 *to extend a salute*｜～赠 *to offer a present respectfully*｜～献 *to present politely; to offer respectfully* ❷表示敬意的礼物 gift of respect：喜～ *gift offered on a happy occasion* ❸有礼貌地送上去 to offer politely：～酒 *to propose a toast*｜～茶 *to serve tea*

JIONG ㄐㄩㄥ

坰 jiōng ㄐㄩㄥ 离城市很远的郊野 open country; outermost suburb

扃 jiōng ㄐㄩㄥ 从外面关门的闩(shuān)、钩等 bolt, hook, etc for fastening a door from outside ㊕ ***transfer*** **1** 门 door **2** 上闩，关门 to bolt (*or* shut) a door

冏 jiǒng ㄐㄩㄥˇ ❶光 light ❷明亮 bright

迥 jiǒng ㄐㄩㄥˇ 远 remote; far away：～异(相差很远) *widely different* [迥然]显然，清清楚楚地 obviously; plainly：～～不同 *utterly different*

泂 jiǒng ㄐㄩㄥˇ 远 far away

絅(**褧) jiǒng ㄐㄩㄥˇ 古代称罩在外面的单衣(in ancient China) unlined outer garment

炯 jiǒng ㄐㄩㄥˇ 光明，明亮(叠 ***reduplication***) bright; shining：目光～～ *flashing eyes*

炅 ㊀ jiǒng ㄐㄩㄥˇ 火光 firelight

㊁ guì 见254页 see p254

煚 jiǒng ㄐㄩㄥˇ ❶火 fire ❷日光 sunlight

窘 jiǒng ㄐㄩㄥˇ ❶穷困 impoverished：生活很～ *to live a very hard life* ❷为难 awkward; embarrassed：这种场面让人觉得很～ *to be embarrassed by such an occasion* ❸使为难 to embarrass：你一言，我一语，～得他满脸通红。*He blushed with embarrassment as every tongue wagged at once.*

JIU ㄐㄧㄡ

纠 jiū ㄐㄧㄡ ❶缠绕 to entangle(㊣ ***doublet*** —缠 to get entangled)：～缠不清 *to be entangled in; to get involved* [纠纷]牵连不清的争执 dispute; issue ❷矫正 to correct; to rectify：～偏救弊 *to rectify deviations and remedy defects* [纠察]在群众活动中维持秩序 to maintain order at a public gathering [纠正]把有偏向的事情改正 to correct; to put right：～

～工作中的偏向 *to put right the deviation in one's work* ❸集合 to assemble; to gather together:～合众人(含贬义)(*derogatory*) *to band together a group of people*

赳 jiū ㄐㄧㄡ [赳赳]健壮威武的样子 valiant; gallant:雄～～ *valiant; gallant*

鸠 jiū ㄐㄧㄡ ❶鸽子一类的鸟，常见的有斑鸠、山鸠等 turtledove ❷聚集 to gather together:～聚 *to band together; to muster*

究 jiū ㄐㄧㄡ (旧读 formerly jiù)推求，追查 to study carefully; to probe into:～办 *to investigate and deal with*|追～ *to look into; to find out; to investigate*|推～ *to study; to examine*|必须深～ *must go into (a matter) seriously; must get to the bottom of (a matter)*[究竟]1 副词 ***adverb***,到底 actually; exactly:～～是怎么回事? *What's all this about exactly?* 2 结果 outcome; truth:大家都想知道个～～。*Everybody wants to know the whole story.* [终究]副词 ***adverb***,到底 eventually:问题～～会弄清楚的。*The problem will be cleared up in the end.*

阄(鬮) jiū ㄐㄧㄡ (～儿)抓阄时用的纸团等 lot [抓阄儿]为了赌胜负或决定事情而各自抓取做好记号的纸团等 to draw lots

揪 jiū ㄐㄧㄡ 用手抓住或拉住 to hold tight; to grab; to seize:赶快～住他。*Quick! Grab him!*|～断了绳子 *to snap a rope by stretching*|～下一块面 *to pluck off a piece of dough* [揪心]心里紧张，担忧 anxious; worried

啾 jiū ㄐㄧㄡ [啾啾]拟声词 ***onomatopoeia***,常指动物的细小的叫声 chirp

鬏 jiū ㄐㄧㄡ (～儿)头发盘成的结(of hair) bun

九 jiǔ ㄐㄧㄡˇ ❶数目字 nine [数九](shǔ—)从冬至日起始的八十一天，每九天作一单位，从"一九"数到"九九"81 days counted from Winter Solstice, or nine nine-days (meaning the nine equal divisions of the days), which are reckoned to be the coldest days of the year ❷表示多次或多数 many; numerous:～死一生 *nine chances to die and one chance to live — narrow escape from one's death*|～霄 *highest heavens*

氿 ㊀jiǔ ㄐㄧㄡˇ 湖名，在江苏省宜兴，分东氿、西氿 Jiu, a lake in Yixing, Jiangsu Province, including Dongjiu and Xijiu

㊁ guǐ 见254页 see p254

久 jiǔ ㄐㄧㄡˇ ❶时间长 long; for a long time:年深日～ *age-old; after a long lapse of time*|很～没有见面了 *to have not seen each other for a long time* ❷时间的长短 specified duration:你来了多～了? *How long have you been here?*

玖 jiǔ ㄐㄧㄡˇ ❶一种像玉的浅黑色石头 jade-like black stone ❷"九"字的大写 nine, capital form of 九

灸 jiǔ ㄐㄧㄡˇ 烧,多指用艾叶等烧灼或熏烤身体某一部分的治疗方法 moxibustion:针～ *acupuncture and moxibustion*

韭(*韮) jiǔ ㄐㄧㄡˇ 韭菜,多年生草本植物,丛生,叶细长而扁,开小白花。叶和花嫩时可以吃 Chinese chives (*Allium tuberosum*)

酒 jiǔ ㄐㄧㄡˇ 用高粱、米、麦或葡萄等发酵制成的含乙醇的饮料,有刺激性,多喝对身体害处很大 alcoholic drink; wine; liquor [酒精]用酒蒸馏制成的无色液体,化学上叫乙醇,工业和医药上用途很大 alcohol

旧(舊) jiù ㄐㄧㄡˋ ❶跟"新"相对(the opposite of 新) old 1 过去的,过时的 past; outdated; old: ～脑筋 *outdated ideas*｜～社会 *old society* 2 因经过长时间而变了样子 used; old; second-hand: 衣服～了。*The clothes are old.* ❷指交情,有交情的人 old friendship; old friend: 有～ *used to be friends*｜故～ *old friends*

臼 jiù ㄐㄧㄡˋ ❶舂米的器具,一般用石头制成,样子像盆 mortar ❷像臼的 mortar-shaped: ～齿 *molar*

桕 jiù ㄐㄧㄡˋ 乌桕树,落叶乔木,夏日开花,黄色。种子外面包着一层白色脂肪叫桕脂,可以制造蜡烛和肥皂。种子可以榨油。是我国特产植物的一种 Chinese tallow tree (*Sapium sebiferum*)

舅 jiù ㄐㄧㄡˋ ❶母亲的弟兄(叠 ***reduplication***) mother's brother; uncle ❷(一子)妻子的弟兄 wife's brother: 妻～ *wife's brother; brother-in-law*｜小～子 *wife's younger brother* ❸古代称丈夫的父亲(in ancient China) husband's father: ～姑(公婆) *husband's parents; parents-in-law*

咎 jiù ㄐㄧㄡˋ ❶过失,罪 fault; blame: ～由自取 *to have only oneself to blame; to bring the trouble on oneself* ❷怪罪,处分 to censure; to punish; to blame: 既往不～ *to let sb off for his past mistake; to forgive one's past misdeeds* ❸凶 ill luck; bad fortune: 休～(吉凶) *good luck and misfortune*

疚 jiù ㄐㄧㄡˋ 长期生病 to have a chronic (*or* lasting) illness ㊕ ***transfer*** 忧苦,心内痛苦 remorse: 负～ *to feel guilty*｜内～ *guilty conscience; compunction*

柩 jiù ㄐㄧㄡˋ 装着尸体的棺材 coffin with a corpse in it: 灵～ *coffin containing a corpse*

救(*捄) jiù ㄐㄧㄡˋ 帮助,使脱离困难或危险 to rescue; to save: ～济 *to relieve*｜～援 *to rescue*｜～命 *to save one's life; Help!*｜～火(帮助灭火) *to fight a fire; to try to put out a fire*｜～生圈

lifebuoy; life ring | 求～ *to ask sb to come to the rescue; to cry for help* ［救星］指帮助人脱离苦难的集体或个人 liberator; saviour

厩（*廄）jiù ㄐㄧㄡˋ 马棚，泛指牲口棚 stable; cattle-shed; pen：～肥 *barnyard manure*

就 jiù ㄐㄧㄡˋ ❶凑近，靠近 to come near; to approach：～着灯光看书 *to read by lamp light* ❷从事，开始进入 to undertake; to engage in：～学 *to go to school* | ～业 *to get a job; to find employment* ❸依照现有情况，趁着 to take advantage of：～近上学 *to go to a nearby school* | ～地解决 *to settle a problem on the spot* ❹随同着吃下去（of food, etc）to go with：炒鸡子～饭 *to have scrambled eggs to go with the rice* ❺完成 to accomplish; to make：造～人才 *to train competent personnel* ❻副词 ***adverb***，表示肯定语气（used to express affirmation）**1** 加强（used for emphasis）：这么一来～好办了。*At this rate, it will be easier.* **2** 在选择句中跟否定词相应（used in collocation with a negative in an alternative sentence）：不是你去，～是我去。*Either you or I will go.* ❼副词 ***adverb***，立刻，不用经过很多时间 at once; right away：他一来，我～走。*I'll go as soon as he comes.* | 他～要参军了。*He is going to join the army soon.* ❽连词 ***conjunction***，就是，即使，表示假定 even if：天～再冷我们也不怕。*We'll not be afraid even if it gets colder.* | 你～送来，我也不要。*Even if you send it here, I won't take it.* ❾副词 ***adverb***，单，只，偏偏 only; merely：他～爱看书。*He likes doing nothing but reading.* | 怎么～我不能去？*Why am I the only one who cannot go there?*

僦 jiù ㄐㄧㄡˋ 租赁 to rent; to hire; to lease：～屋 *to rent a room*

鹫 jiù ㄐㄧㄡˋ 一种猛禽。有的颈部无毛，食动物尸体，也捕食小动物。如秃鹫、兀鹫 vulture (*Accipitridae*)

JU ㄐㄩ

车（車）㊀ jū ㄐㄩ 象棋棋子的一种 chariot, one of the pieces in Chinese chess

㊁ chē 见80页 see p80

且 ㊁ jū ㄐㄩ 〈古 ***archaism***〉❶文言助词 ***auxiliary in classical Chinese***，相当于"啊"（equal to 啊）oh; ah：狂童之狂也～。*Oh, how crazy the young fool is.* ❷用于人名 ju, used in a given name

㊀ qiě 见604页 see p604

苴 jū ㄐㄩ 大麻的雌株，开花后能结果实 female plant of hemp

岨 jū ㄐㄩ 带土的石山 earthy stone hill

狙 jū ㄐㄩ 古书里指一种猴子 (in ancient Chinese texts) a kind of monkey

[狙击]乘人不备,突然出击 to snipe; to ambush

疽 jū ㄐㄩ 中医指一种毒疮(in traditional Chinese medicine) subcutaneous ulcer

趄 ㊁ jū ㄐㄩ 见1009页"越"字条"赵趄"(zī—) see 赵趄 on p1009

㊀ qiè 见605页 see p605

雎 jū ㄐㄩ 雎鸠,古书上说的一种鸟。也叫"王雎"(also called 王雎)(in ancient Chinese texts) turtledove

拘 jū ㄐㄩ ❶逮捕或扣押 to arrest; to detain:～票 *arrest warrant; capias*｜～留 *to detain; to hold in custody*｜～禁 *to detain; to take into custody* ❷限,限制 to restrict; to limit:～管 *to restrain; to restrict*｜不～多少 *no limit on quantity* ❸拘束,不变通 to restrain; to be inflexible:～谨 *overcautious; reserved*｜～泥成法 *to stick fast to established laws*

[拘挛] **1** (—luán)痉挛 to have cramps **2** (——儿,—juanr)蜷曲 to curl:手冻～～了。*The hands were frozen stiff.*

泃 jū ㄐㄩ 泃河,水名,发源于河北省东北部,流经北京市东部和天津市北部 Juhe River, originated in the northeastern part of Hebei Province, flowing through the eastern part of Beijing and the northern part of Tianjin

驹 jū ㄐㄩ ❶少壮的马 colt:千里～ *winged steed; thousand-li colt* ❷(—子)小马 foal:马～子 *foal of a horse* 又指小驴、骡等 young donkey, mule, etc.:驴～子 *foal of a donkey*

居 jū ㄐㄩ ❶住 to reside; to live:分～(*of a married couple*) *to live apart*｜久～乡间 *to live in the countryside for a long time* ❷住处 residence; house; home:新～ *new home*｜鲁迅故～ *Former Residence of Lu Xun* ❸站在,处于 to be in a certain position:～中 *to be placed in the middle*｜～间 *to mediate between two parties* ❹当,任 to assert; to claim:以前辈自～ *to claim to be a senior* ❺安放 to harbour:是何～心? *What are you up to?* ❻积蓄,储存 to store up; to lay by:奇货可～ *rare commodities worth hoarding; to corner the market*｜囤积～奇 *to store up goods and raise their prices* ❼停留 to stay put; to be at a standstill:岁月不～。*Time and tide wait for no man.* or *Time marches on.*

[居然]副词 ***adverb***,竟,出乎意外地 unexpectedly; to one's surprise:他～～来了。*To every one's surprise, he came.*

据 ㊁ jū ㄐㄩ 见346页"拮"字条"拮据"(jié—) see 拮据 on p346

㊀ jù 见371页 see p371

J

崌 jū ㄐㄩ 见432页"岍"字条"岍崌山"(lì— —) see 岍崌山 on p432

琚 jū ㄐㄩ 古人佩带的一种玉 ancient jade pendant

椐 jū ㄐㄩ 古书上说的一种树，枝节肿大，可以做拐杖(in ancient Chinese texts) a small tree with swelling knots that can be used to make walking sticks

腒 jū ㄐㄩ 干腌的鸟类肉 dried and preserved bird meat

锯 ⊜ jū ㄐㄩ 同"锔"(jū) same as 锔

⊖ jù 见372页 see p372

裾 jū ㄐㄩ 衣服的大襟 full front of a Chinese garment ㊀ *extension* 衣服的前后部分 full front and back of a Chinese garment

掬 jū ㄐㄩ 用两手捧 to hold with both hands：以手～水 *to scoop up water with both hands*｜笑容可～(形容笑得明显) *to be radiant with smiles; to grin from ear to ear*

鞠 jū ㄐㄩ ❶养育，抚养 to rear; to bring up ❷古代的一种皮球(in ancient China) a kind of a ball：蹴(cù)～(踢球) *to kick a ball*

[鞠躬]弯腰表示恭敬谨慎。现指弯身行礼 to bow

娵 jū ㄐㄩ [娵隅](—yú)古代南方少数民族称鱼为娵隅(used by ancient ethnic minorities of southern China) fish

锔 ⊜ jū ㄐㄩ 用锔子连合破裂的器物 to mend crockery with clamps：～盆 *to mend a basin with clamps*｜～缸 *to mend a jar with clamps*｜～锅 *to mend a pot with clamps*｜～碗儿的 *crockery mender* [锔子](—zi)用铜、铁等制成的扁平有钩的两脚钉，用来连合陶瓷等器物的裂缝 clamp

⊖ jú 见369页 see p369

鞫 jū ㄐㄩ ❶审问 to interrogate：～讯 *to make a judicial investigation*｜～审 *to examine and judge a case* ❷穷困 impoverished

局(❼❽*跼、❽*侷) jú ㄐㄩˊ ❶部分 part; portion：～部麻醉 *local anaesthesia* ❷机关及团体组织分工办事的单位 bureau; office：教育～ *bureau of education*｜公安～*public security bureau* ❸某些商店或办理某些业务的机构的名称 shop; functional office：书～ *bookshop; publishing house*｜邮电～ *post office* ❹棋盘 chess board ❺着棋的形势 development of a chess game ㊥ ***figurative*** 事情的形势、情况 situation; state of affairs：结～ *final result; outcome*｜大～ *overall situation*｜时～ *current political situation* [局面] **1** 一个时期内事情的状态 aspect; phase; situation：稳定的～～ *stable situation* **2**〈方 ***dialect***〉规模 scale; size; scope ❻量词 ***quantifier***，下棋或其他比赛一次叫一局 game; set; innings ❼弯曲 bending ❽拘束，拘谨 restrained; reserved [局促] **1** 狭小 narrow **2** 拘谨不自然 constrained; disconcerted：他

初到这里，感到有些～～。*Being a newcomer, he feels constrained*.［局蹐］(—jí)拘束不敢放纵 constrained

焗 jú ㄐㄩˊ〈方 ***dialect***〉一种烹饪方法，利用蒸气使密封容器中的食物变熟 to steam：盐～鸡 *salted and steamed chicken* ［焗油］一种染发、养发、护发方法。在头发上抹油后，用特制机具蒸气加热，待冷却后用清水冲洗干净 to treat hair with cream to make it soft and shiny or to dye the hair

锔 ㊀ jú ㄐㄩˊ 一种人造的放射性元素(符号 Cm) curium (Cm)

㊁ jū 见368页 see p368

桔 ㊁ jú ㄐㄩˊ "橘"俗作"桔" popular written form for 橘

㊀ jié 见346页 see p346

菊 jú ㄐㄩˊ 菊花，多年生草本植物，秋天开花，种类很多。有的花可入药，也可做饮料 chrysanthemum (*Chrysanthemum*)

湨 jú ㄐㄩˊ 湨河，水名，在河南省济源 Juhe River, in Jiyuan, Henan Province

鶪 jú ㄐㄩˊ 古书上说的一种鸟，就是伯劳，背灰褐色，尾长，上嘴钩曲，捕食鱼、虫、小鸟等，是一种益鸟 (a bird mentioned in ancient Chinese texts, i. e. 伯劳) shrike (*Laniidae*)

橘 jú ㄐㄩˊ 橘树，常绿乔木，初夏开花，白色。果实叫橘子，味甜酸，可以吃，果皮可入药 mandarin; mandarin orange (*Citrus reticulata*)

柜 ㊁ jǔ ㄐㄩˇ 柜柳，即枫杨，落叶乔木，羽状复叶，小叶长椭圆形，性耐湿、耐碱，可固沙，枝韧，可以编筐 Chinese wingnut; Chinese ash (*Pterocarya stenoptera*)

㊀ guì 见254页 see p254

矩(*榘) jǔ ㄐㄩˇ ❶画方形的工具 square：～尺(曲尺) *square*｜不以规～不能成方圆。*It is impossible to draw a circle or a square if one does not make use of compasses or a T square —rules and regulations must be adhered to in handling affairs*. ❷法则，规则 rules; regulations：循规蹈～ *to follow rules tamely*

咀 ㊀ jǔ ㄐㄩˇ 含在嘴里细细玩味 to chew：含英～华(喻读书吸取精华) *to study and relish the beauties of literature* ［咀嚼］(—jué)嚼(jiáo) to masticate; to chew ㊞ ***figurative*** 体味 to mull over; to ruminate

㊁ zuǐ 见1020页 see p1020

沮 ㊀ jǔ ㄐㄩˇ ❶阻止 to stop; to prevent ❷坏，败坏 to turn gloomy; to feel dejected［沮丧］(—sàng)失意，懊丧 dejected; depressed

㊁ jù 见371页 see p371

龃 jǔ ㄐㄩˇ［龃龉］(—yǔ)牙齿上下对不上 upper and lower teeth not meeting properly ㊞ ***figurative*** 意见不合 disagreement

莒 jǔ ㄐㄩˇ 周代诸侯国名，在今山东省莒南一带 Ju, a princedom in the Zhou Dynasty, in today's Junan, Shandong Province

筥(**簇) jǔ ㄐㄩˇ 圆形的竹筐 round bamboo basket

枸 ㊂ jǔ ㄐㄩˇ [枸橼](—yuán) 也叫"香橼",常绿乔木,初夏开花,白色。果实有香气,味很酸(also called 香橼) citron (*Citrus medica*)

㊀ gōu 见235页 see p235

㊁ gǒu 见236页 see p236

蒟 jǔ ㄐㄩˇ 植物名 plant name **1** 蒟蒻(ruò),多年生草本植物,开淡黄色花,外有紫色苞片。地下茎像球,有毒,可入药 konjak (*Amorphophallus konjak*) **2** 蒟酱,蔓生木本植物,夏天开花,绿色。果实像桑葚,可以吃 betel pepper (*Piper betle*)

举(舉、*擧) jǔ ㄐㄩˇ ❶向上抬,向上托 to lift; to raise; to hold up: ～手 *to raise one's hand* | 高～红旗 *to hold the red flag high* ㊀ ***extension*** **1** 动作行为 act; deed: ～止 *bearing; manner; mien* | 一～一动 *every act and every move* **2** 发起,兴起 to start: ～义 *to start a revolt* | ～事 *to stage an uprising* | ～办科普讲座 *to give popular science lectures* ❷提出 to cite; to enumerate: ～证 *to show evidence* | ～例说明 *to cite instances to illustrate* | ～出一件事实来 *to cite a fact* ❸推选,推荐 to elect; to choose: 大家～他做代表。*He was elected as the representative.* ❹全 whole; entire: ～国 *the whole nation* | ～世闻名 *world-famous* ❺举人的简称 short for 举人, a successful candidate in the imperial examination at the provincial level in the Ming and Qing dynasties: 中(zhòng)～ *to pass the imperial examination at the provincial level* | 武～ *imperial examination specializing in military knowledge and skill; one who passed the provincial imperial examination in military knowledge and skill*

榉(櫸) jǔ ㄐㄩˇ ❶榉,落叶乔木,和榆相近,木材耐水,可造船 zelkova ❷山毛榉,落叶乔木,春天开花,淡黄绿色。树皮有粗纹,像鳞片,木材很坚硬,可做枕木、家具等 beech (*Fagus*)

踽 jǔ ㄐㄩˇ [踽踽]形容独自走路孤零零的样子 to walk alone: ～～独行 *to walk alone*

巨(*鉅) jù ㄐㄩˋ 大 huge; tremendous; gigantic: ～浪 *huge waves* | ～型飞机 *giant plane* | ～款 *huge (or large) sum of money*

讵 jù ㄐㄩˋ 岂,怎(used to introduce a rhetorical question): ～料 *who could have expected* | ～知 *who could have expected*

拒 jù ㄐㄩˋ 抵挡,抵抗 to resist; to repel(㊟ ***doublet*** 抗— to resist): ～敌 *to resist the enemy* | ～捕 *to resist arrest* | ～腐蚀,永不沾 *to resist corruption and never to be contaminated by it* [拒绝]不接受 to refuse; to reject

苣 ㊀ jù ㄐㄩˋ 见791页“莴”字条“莴苣”(wōju) see 莴苣 on p791

㊁ qǔ 见619页 see p619

炬 jù ㄐㄩˋ 火把 torch：火～ *torch*

距 jù ㄐㄩˋ ❶距离，离开 to distance; to be away from：相～数里 *to be several* li *apart*｜～今已数年 *many years ago* ㊂ ***extension*** 两者相离的长度 distance：株～ *distance between two plants* ❷雄鸡爪后面突出像脚趾的部分 spur of a cock ❸古同“拒” same as 拒 in ancient Chinese

句 ㊀ jù ㄐㄩˋ (一子)由词和词组组成的能表示一个完整意思的话 sentence

㊁ gōu 见235页 see p235

具 jù ㄐㄩˋ ❶器具，器物 utensil; tool; implement：工～ *tool*｜家～ *furniture*｜文～ *stationery*｜农～ *farm tool* ❷备，备有 to possess; to have：～备 *to possess; to have*｜～有 *to possess; to have*｜略～规模 *to begin to take shape* [具体] **1** 明确，不抽象，不笼统 concrete; detailed：这个计划订得很～～。*The plan is made in great detail.* **2** 特定的 particular; specific：～～的人 *specific person*｜～～的工作 *specific job*

俱 jù ㄐㄩˋ (旧读 formerly jū) ❶全，都 all：父母～存。*Both parents are alive.*｜面面～到 *to be well considered in every respect; to pay attention to all sides; well-rounded* ❷偕同 accompanied by; together with [俱乐部]进行社会、政治、文艺、娱乐等活动的团体或场所 club

惧(懼) jù ㄐㄩˋ 害怕 to fear; to dread(㊇ ***doublet*** 恐一 to fear; to dread)：临危不～ *to face danger fearlessly*

犋 jù ㄐㄩˋ 畜力单位名，能拉动一辆车、一张犁、一张耙等的一头或几头牲口叫一犋，多指两头 *ju*, unit of animal power of one or more draft animals, strong enough to pull a cart, a plough, a harrow, etc

飓 jù ㄐㄩˋ 飓风，发生在大西洋西部和西印度群岛一带热带海洋上的风暴，风力常达12级以上，同时有暴雨 hurricane

沮 ㊁ jù ㄐㄩˋ [沮洳](一rù)低湿的地带 marsh; swamp

㊀ jǔ 见369页 see p369

倨 jù ㄐㄩˋ 傲慢 haughty; arrogant：前～后恭 *to treat with rudeness at first but afterwards with respect; to change from arrogance to humility*｜～傲 *haughty; arrogant*

剧(劇) jù ㄐㄩˋ ❶厉害，猛烈 acute; severe：～痛 *acute pain*｜病～ *seriously ill*｜争论得很～烈 *to have a hot debate* ❷戏剧，文艺的一种形式，作家把剧本编写出来，利用舞台由演员化装演出 drama; play

据(據) ㊀ jù ㄐㄩˋ ❶凭依，倚仗 to rely on; to depend on [据点]军队据以作战的地点 stronghold; strong point ❷介词 ***preposition***，依据 according to; on the ground of：～理力

争 *to argue strongly on just grounds; to fight for one's point of view* | ～我看问题不大。*In my opinion, there's hardly any problem.* ❸占 to occupy([连] ***doublet*** 占— to occupy):～守 *to defend; to guard* | ～为己有 *to appropriate; to seize by force* ❹可以用作证明的事物,凭证 evidence; certificate([连] ***doublet*** 凭— evidence | 证— evidence):收～ *receipt* | 字～ *written pledge* | 票～ *bill; receipt* | 真凭实～ *factual evidence* | 无凭无～ *without any evidence*

㊁ jū 见367页 see p367

锯 ㊀ jù ㄐㄩˋ ❶用薄钢片制成有尖齿可以拉(lá)开木、石等的器具 saw:拉～ *to work a two-handed saw* | 手～ *hand saw* | 电～ *electric saw* ❷用锯拉(lá) to saw:～木头 *to saw wood* | ～树 *to saw a tree*

㊁ jū 见368页 see p368

踞 jù ㄐㄩˋ ❶蹲或坐 to crouch; to squat; to sit:龙蟠(pán)虎～(形容地势险要) *coiling dragon and crouching tiger; formidable strategic point* | 箕～(古人席地坐着把两腿像八字形分开)(*of ancient people*) *to sit on the floor with legs stretched out in the form of* 八 ❷占据 to occupy:盘～ *to occupy*

聚 jù ㄐㄩˋ 会合,集合 to assemble; to gather([连] ***doublet*** —集 to assemble; to gather):大家～在一起谈话。*We gathered together and had a talk.* | ～少成多 *to increase bit by bit;* or *Many pebbles make a beach.* | 欢～ *to have a joyous gathering*

窭(窶) jù ㄐㄩˋ 贫穷 poor; impoverished

屦(屨) jù ㄐㄩˋ 古代的一种鞋,用麻、葛等制成 (in ancient China) straw sandals

遽 jù ㄐㄩˋ ❶急,仓猝 hurriedly; hastily:不敢～下断语 *dare not jump to a hasty conclusion* ❷遂,就 then

澽 jù ㄐㄩˋ 澽水,水名,在陕西省 Jushui River, in Shaanxi Province

醵 jù ㄐㄩˋ ❶凑钱喝酒 to pool money for a drink together ❷聚集,凑(指钱) to pool money:～资 *to pool funds*

JUAN ㄐㄩㄢ

捐 juān ㄐㄩㄢ ❶捐助或献出 to contribute; to donate:～钱 *to donate money* | ～棉衣 *to contribute cotton-padded clothes* | ～献 *to contribute; to donate* ❷赋税的一种 tax; levy:房～ *housing tax* | 车～ *tax paid by a vehicle owner* ❸舍弃 to abandon:为国～躯 *to sacrifice one's life for one's country*

涓 juān ㄐㄩㄢ 细小的流水 tiny stream [涓滴]极小量的水 tiny drop; dribble [喻] ***figurative*** 极少的,极微的 tiny:～～归公。*Every bit goes to the public treasury.*

娟 juān ㄐㄩㄢ 秀丽,美好 beautiful; graceful:～秀 *beautiful; graceful*

J

鹃 juān ㄐㄩㄢ 见162页"杜"字条"杜鹃"see 杜鹃 on p162

圈 ㊂ juān ㄐㄩㄢ 关闭起来，用栅栏等围起来 to enclose in a pen; to pen in：把小鸡～起来 *to pen up the chickens*

㊀ quān 见621页 see p621

㊁ juàn 见373页 see p373

朘 juān ㄐㄩㄢ 缩，减 to reduce; to cut down

镌（**鐫） juān ㄐㄩㄢ 雕刻 to engrave; to carve：～刻图章 *to engrave a seal*｜～碑 *to engrave a tablet*

蠲 juān ㄐㄩㄢ 免除 to remit; to exempt：～免 *to remit; to exempt*

卷（捲） ㊀ juǎn ㄐㄩㄢˇ ❶把东西弯转裹成圆筒形 to roll up; to curl：～行李 *to roll up one's bedding*｜～帘子 *to roll up the curtain* ❷一种大的力量把东西撮(cuō)起或裹住 to sweep along; to pull up; to carry along：风～着雨点劈面打来。*The wind blew the rain right into one's face.*｜～入旋涡(喻被牵连到不利的事件中) *to be drawn into a whirlpool — to be involved in some trouble* ❸(－儿)弯转裹成的筒形的东西 roll：烟～儿 *cigarette*｜行李～儿 *bedding roll*｜纸～儿 *paper roll* ❹(－儿)量词 ***quantifier***，用于成卷儿的东西 roll; spool; reel：一～胶布 *a roll of adhesive tape*｜两～纸 *two rolls of paper*

㊁ juàn 见373页 see p373

锩 juǎn ㄐㄩㄢˇ 刀剑卷刃(of the edge of a sword or knife) turned

卷 ㊁ juàn ㄐㄩㄢˋ ❶可以舒卷(juǎn)的书画 book; scroll：手～ *hand scroll*｜长～ *long scroll* ❷书籍的册本或篇章 volume：第一～ *the first volume*｜上～ *Volume One*｜～二 *Volume Two* ❸(－子、－儿)考试写答案的纸 examination paper：试～ *examination paper*｜交～ *to hand in an examination paper*｜历史～子 *history examination paper* ❹案卷，机关里分类汇存的档案、文件 file; dossier：～宗 *file; dossier*｜查一查底～ *to look through the files*

㊀ juǎn 见373页 see p373

倦 juàn ㄐㄩㄢˋ 疲乏，懈怠 tired; weary(㊟ ***doublet*** 疲－ tired; weary)：诲人不～ *to be tireless in teaching*｜厌～ *to be tired of*

圈 ㊁ juàn ㄐㄩㄢˋ 养家畜等的栅栏(of livestock) pen; sty：猪～ *pigsty; pig pen*｜羊～ *sheepfold; sheep pen*

㊀ quān 见621页 see p621

㊂ juān 见373页 see p373

桊 juàn ㄐㄩㄢˋ 穿在牛鼻上的小铁环或小木棍儿 small iron ring or wooden stick pierced through the nose of an ox：牛鼻～儿 *small iron ring* (or *wooden stick*) *pierced through the nose of an ox; ox nose ring* (or *stick*)

眷（❶*睠） juàn ㄐㄩㄢˋ ❶顾念，爱恋 to care for; to have tender feelings for：～恋过去 *to have tender feelings for the past* ❷亲属 relatives：～

属 *family dependants*; *one; one's family*|家～ *family dependants*; *one's family*|亲～ *relatives*

隽(*雋) ㊀ juàn ㄐㄩㄢˋ 肥肉 fat meat; fat [隽永](言论、文章)意味深长(of speech or essay) meaningful

㊁ jùn 见379页 see p379

狷(*獧) juàn ㄐㄩㄢˋ ❶胸襟狭窄,急躁 narrow-minded; impetuous: ～急 *impetuous* ❷耿直 upright

绢 juàn ㄐㄩㄢˋ 一种薄的丝织物 thin tough silk [手绢]手帕 handkerchief

罥 juàn ㄐㄩㄢˋ 挂 to hang; to put up

鄄 juàn ㄐㄩㄢˋ 鄄城,地名,在山东省 Juancheng, a place in Shandong Province

JUE ㄐㄩㄝ

屩(屫、*蹻) juē ㄐㄩㄝ 草鞋 straw sandals

"蹻"又 qiāo 见600页"跷"also qiāo, see 跷 on p600

撅(❶*噘) juē ㄐㄩㄝ ❶翘起 to stick up: ～嘴 *to pout one's lips*|～着尾巴 *to stick up the tail*|小辫ㄦ～着。*The pigtails are sticking up.* ❷折 to break; to snap: 把竿子～断了。*The pole was snapped in half.*

注 note:"噘"只用于"噘嘴" only used in 噘嘴

孓 jué ㄐㄩㄝ [孑孓](jié—)蚊子的幼虫 wriggler

决(*決) jué ㄐㄩㄝ ❶原意为疏导水流,后转为堤岸被水冲开口子 to dredge; (of dyke) to be breached: 堵塞～口 *to close up a breach* [决裂]破裂(指感情、关系、商谈等) to break with; to rupture: 谈判～～。*The negotiations have broken down.* ❷决定,拿定主意 to decide; to determine: ～心 *determination*; *resolution*|迟疑不～ *to be irresolute*; *to hesitate to make a decision* [决议]经过会议讨论决定的事项 resolution ㉃ ***extension*** 副词 ***adverb***,一定,必定 definitely; certainly: 他～不会失败。*He will never fail.* ❸决定最后胜负 to decide the final result: ～赛 *finals*|～战 *decisive battle* ❹执行死刑 to execute a person: 枪～ *to execute (a person) by shooting*

诀 jué ㄐㄩㄝ ❶诀窍,高明的方法 knack; know-how: 秘～ *secret of success*|妙～ *knack* ❷用事物的主要内容编成的顺口的便于记忆的词句 rhymed formula: 口～ *pithy formula in rhyme*|歌～ *formula put into verse* ❸辞别,多指不再相见的分别 to bid farewell; to part forever: 永～ *to part forever*; *to be parted by death*

抉 jué ㄐㄩㄝ 剔出 to pick out [抉择]挑选 to choose

駃 jué ㄐㄩㄝ [駃騠](—tí) **1** 驴骡,由公马和母驴交配所生 hinny **2** 古书上说的一种骏马

(in ancient Chinese texts) fine horse; steed

玦 jué ㄐㄩㄝ 环形有缺口的佩玉 penannular jade pendant

鴃 jué ㄐㄩㄝ 鸟名。即伯劳(i. e. 伯劳) shrike (*Laniidae*)

觖 jué ㄐㄩㄝ 不满 dissatisfied; discontented [觖望]因不满而怨恨 to be resentful due to dissatisfaction

角 ㊁ jué ㄐㄩㄝ ❶竞争,争胜 to compete; to contend: ～斗 *to wrestle* | ～逐 *to contend* | 口～(吵嘴) *to quarrel* ❷(一儿)演员,角色 actor (*or* actress); role: 主～ *leading role; main character* | 他演什么～儿? *What role does he play?* [角色](*脚色) **1** 戏曲演员按所扮演人物的性别和性格等分的类型。如京剧的"生、旦、净、丑"。也叫"行当"(also called 行当) the type of role **2** 戏剧或电影里演员所扮演的剧中人物 role; character ❸古代五音"宫、商、角、徵(zhǐ)、羽"之一 *jue*, one of the five ancient Chinese musical notes 宫, 商, 角, 徵 and 羽 ❹古代形状像爵的酒器 *jue*, ancient three-legged wine cup ❺姓 Jue, a surname

㊀ jiǎo 见339页 see p339

桷 jué ㄐㄩㄝ 方形的椽(chuán)子 square rafter

珏 jué ㄐㄩㄝ 合在一起的两块玉 two pieces of jade fitted together

觉(覺) ㊀ jué ㄐㄩㄝ ❶(人或动物的器官)对刺激的感受和辨别 to sense; to feel: 视～ *sight* | 听～ *sense of hearing* | 他～得这本书很好。*He thinks that this book is very good.* | 不知不～ *unconsciously* ❷睡醒,醒悟 to wake; to awake: 如梦初～ *as if just awakening from a dream; to be startled into attentiveness* | ～醒 *to awaken* | ～悟 *to come to realize; to become aware of*

㊁ jiào 见342页 see p342

绝 jué ㄐㄩㄝ ❶断 to cut (*or* break) off; to sever: ～望 *to despair; to have lost all hope* | 络绎不～ *to come one after another; to be in an endless procession* [绝句]我国旧体诗的一种,每首四句,每句五字或七字,有一定的平仄和押韵的限制 quatrain; Chinese old-style poem of four lines, each containing five to seven characters, with a strict tonal pattern and rhyme scheme ❷尽,穷尽 exhausted; used up: 气～ *to stop breathing; to die* | 法子都想～了。*All possible ways have been explored.* [绝境]没有希望、没有出路的情况 hopeless situation; impasse ❸极,极端的 extremely: ～妙 *extremely clever; excellent; perfect* | ～密 *top-secret; most confidential* ㊀ **extension** 精湛的,少有的 unique; superb: ～技 *unique* (*or consummate*) *skill* | 这幅画真叫～了。*This painting is really superb.* [绝顶] **1** 山的最高峰 peak; summit: 泰山～～

summit of Taishan Mountain **2** 副词 ***adverb***，极端，非常 extremely; utterly：～～巧妙 *extremely ingenious* ［绝对］**1** 副词 ***adverb***，一定，肯定 absolutely; definitely：～～可以胜利。*Victory can be definitely achieved.* | ～～能够办到。*It can absolutely be done.* **2** 无条件，无限制，不依存于任何事物的，跟"相对"相对(the opposite of 相对) absolute; unconditional; unlimited：物质世界的存在是～～的。*The existence of the physical world is absolute.* ❹副词 ***adverb***，一定，无论如何 absolutely; by no means; on any account：～不允许这样的事再次发生。*Such a thing will on no account be permitted to happen again.*

倔 ㊀ jué ㄐㄩㄝˊ 义同"倔㊁"，只用于"倔强"same meaning as 倔㊁, only used in 倔强 ［倔强］(－jiàng)(性情)刚强不屈，固执 stubborn; unyielding：性格～～ *to have a tenacious character*

㊁ juè 见377页 see p377

掘 jué ㄐㄩㄝˊ 挖，刨 to dig：～地 *to dig the ground* | 临渴～井 *to dig a well upon feeling thirsty —to start acting too late*

崛 jué ㄐㄩㄝˊ 高起，突起 to rise abruptly：～起 *to rise abruptly*

脚(*腳) ㊁ jué ㄐㄩㄝˊ (－儿)同"角㊁❷"same as 角㊁❷

㊀ jiǎo 见341页 see p341

厥 jué ㄐㄩㄝˊ ❶气闭，昏倒 to faint; to lose consciousness：晕～ *to faint; to get fainted* | 痰～ *coma due to blockage of respiratory system by profuse phlegm* ❷其，他的，那个的 his (*or* her); its; theirs：～父 *his or her father* | ～后 *after that*

劂 jué ㄐㄩㄝˊ 见308页"剞"字条"剞劂"(jī－) see 剞劂 on p308

蕨 jué ㄐㄩㄝˊ 多年生草本植物，野生，用孢(bāo)子繁殖。嫩叶可吃，地下茎可制淀粉 fern

獗 jué ㄐㄩㄝˊ 见76页"猖"字条"猖獗"(chāng－) see 猖獗 on p76

澽 jué ㄐㄩㄝˊ 澽水，水名，在湖北省随州，涢水支流 Jueshui River, a tributary of the Yunshui River in Suizhou, Hubei Province

橛 jué ㄐㄩㄝˊ (－子、－儿)小木桩 short wooden stake; wooden pin

镢 jué ㄐㄩㄝˊ 〈方 ***dialect***〉(～头)刨地用的农具 pick; pickaxe

蹶(**蹷) ㊀ jué ㄐㄩㄝˊ 跌倒 to fall ㊗ ***figurative*** 挫折，失败 setback; failure：一～不振 *to be unable to get up after a fall; to collapse after one setback*

㊁ juě 见377页 see p377

傕 jué ㄐㄩㄝˊ 用于人名，used in a given name 李傕，东汉末人 Li Jue, a person who lived towards the end of the Eastern Han Dynasty

谲 jué ㄐㄩㄝˊ 欺诈，玩弄手段 to cheat; to swindle：诡～ *treacherous; crafty; cunning*

鐍 jué ㄐㄩㄝˊ 箱子上安锁的环状物 ring on a trunk for installing a lock

噱 ㊀ jué ㄐㄩㄝˊ 大笑 to laugh loudly

㊁ xué 见852页 see p852

爵 jué ㄐㄩㄝˊ ❶古代的酒器 ancient wine vessel ❷爵位，君主国家贵族封号的等级 peerage：侯～ *marquis*｜封～ *to confer a title of nobility on sb*

嚼 ㊁ jué ㄐㄩㄝˊ 义同"嚼㊀"，用于书面语复合词 same meaning as 嚼㊀, used in written compounds：咀（jǔ）～ *to chew*

㊀ jiáo 见339页 see p339

㊂ jiào 见343页 see p343

爝 jué ㄐㄩㄝˊ jiào ㄐㄧㄠˋ（又 also jiào）火把 torch

矍 jué ㄐㄩㄝˊ ［矍铄］（—shuò）形容老年人精神好 (of the aged) hale and hearty

攫 jué ㄐㄩㄝˊ 用爪抓取 to grab with claws ㊞ ***extension*** 夺取 to seize; to grab（㊌ ***doublet*** —夺 to grab）

镢 jué ㄐㄩㄝˊ ❶（—头）刨土的工具 pick; pickaxe ❷用锄掘地 to dig the ground with a pick

蹶 ㊁ juě ㄐㄩㄝˇ ［尥蹶子］（liào— zi）骡马等跳起来用后腿向后踢 (of mules, horses, etc) to kick backwards with hind legs

㊀ jué 见376页 see p376

倔 ㊁ juè ㄐㄩㄝˋ 言语直，态度生硬 gruff; surly; blunt：那老头子真～。*The old man is rather surly.*

㊀ jué 见376页 see p376

JUN ㄐㄩㄣ

军 jūn ㄐㄩㄣ ❶武装部队 armed forces; army; troops：～队 *armed forces; the army*｜解放～ *People's Liberation Army*｜海～ *navy* ❷军队的编制单位，是师的上一级 army, military unit above a division ❸泛指有组织的集体 any organized collective：劳动大～ *labour army*

皲 jūn ㄐㄩㄣ 皮肤因寒冷或干燥而破裂。也作"龟"（jūn）(also written as 龟) (of skin) to chap

均 jūn ㄐㄩㄣ ❶平，匀（yún） equal; even（㊌ ***doublet*** —匀 even｜平— average）：～分 *to divide equally; to share out equally*｜平～数 *average*｜势～力敌 *to match each other in strength; to be evenly matched* ❷副词 ***adverb***，都（dōu），皆 all; without exception：老小～安。*All the family is safe and sound.*｜～已布置就绪。*Everything is ready.*

J

〈古 ***archaism***〉又同“韵”(yùn) also same as 韵

钧 jūn ㄐㄩㄣ ❶古代的重量单位,合三十斤 *jun*, ancient unit of weight, equal to 30 *jin*:千~一发(喻极其危险) *hundred weight hanging by a hair – in a most dangerous condition* ❷制陶器所用的转轮 potter's wheel:陶~(喻造就人才)(*metaphor*) *to train talent* ❸敬辞(对尊长或上级) ***polite*** (used to address one's elders or superiors) you; your: ~命 *your order* | ~安 *to wish you good health* | ~鉴 *your attention*

筠 ㊁ jūn ㄐㄩㄣ [筠连]地名,在四川省 Junlian, a place in Sichuan Province

㊀ yún 见932页 see p932

龟(龜) ㊂ jūn ㄐㄩㄣ 同“皲”same as 皲

㊀ guī 见253页 see p253

㊁ qiū 见614页 see p614

君 jūn ㄐㄩㄣ 封建时代指帝王、诸侯等(in feudal times) monarch; sovereign 敬辞 ***polite***, Mr.:张~ *Mr Zhang* [君子]古指有地位的人,后又指品行好的人 man of high rank; man of virtue; gentleman

莙 jūn ㄐㄩㄣ [莙荙菜](—dá—)菾(tián)菜的变种,也叫“厚皮菜”、“牛皮菜”。叶大,是常见的蔬菜(also called 厚皮菜 or 牛皮菜) spinach beet (*Beta vulgaris*)

鲪 jūn ㄐㄩㄣ 鱼名。体长,侧扁,口大而斜,尾鳍圆形。生活在海里 gopher rock cod (*Sebastodes*)

菌 ㊁ jūn ㄐㄩㄣ 低等生物名 name of lower organism **1** 真菌,不开花,没有茎和叶子,不含叶绿素,不能自己制造养料,营寄生生活,种类很多 fungus **2** 细菌,一大类单细胞的微生物,特指能使人生病的病原细菌 bacterium

㊀ jùn 见379页 see p379

麇 ㊀ jūn ㄐㄩㄣ 古书里指獐子(in ancient Chinese texts) river deer

㊁ qún 见626页 see p626

俊 jùn ㄐㄩㄣˋ ❶才智过人的 unusually talented:~杰 *person of outstanding talent; hero* | ~士 *outstanding personage* ❷容貌美丽 pretty; beautiful; handsome:那个小姑娘真~。*That little girl is really pretty*.

峻 jùn ㄐㄩㄣˋ 山高而陡(of mountains) high and steep:高山~岭 *high and steep mountains* 喻 ***figurative*** 严厉苛刻 harsh; severe:严刑~法 *severe penal codes*

馂 jùn ㄐㄩㄣˋ 吃剩下的食物 leftovers (of a meal)

浚(*濬) ㊀ jùn ㄐㄩㄣˋ 疏通,挖深 to dredge:~井 *to dredge a well* | ~河 *to dredge a river*

㊁ xùn 见856页 see p856

骏 jùn ㄐㄩㄣˋ 好马 fine horse; steed

焌 ㊁ jùn ㄐㄩㄣˋ 用火烧 to burn

㊁ qū 见618页 see p618

畯 jùn ㄐㄩㄣˋ 指西周管奴隶耕种的官 official in the Western Zhou Dynasty in charge of slaves' farming

竣 jùn ㄐㄩㄣˋ 事情完毕 to complete; to finish: ～事 *(of a task) to be concluded* | 大工告～ *to be accomplished*

郡 jùn ㄐㄩㄣˋ 古代行政区域，秦以前比县小，从秦朝起比县大 (in ancient China) prefecture, administrative division, smaller than a county before the Qin Dynasty and larger than a county after

捃 jùn ㄐㄩㄣˋ 拾取 to pick up: ～摭(zhí)(搜集) *to collect*

珺 jùn ㄐㄩㄣˋ 一种美玉 a kind of fine jade

隽(*雋) ㊁ jùn ㄐㄩㄣˋ 同"俊❶"same as 俊❶

㊀ juàn 见374页 see p374

菌 ㊀ jùn ㄐㄩㄣˋ 就是蕈(xùn)(i. e. 蕈) field mushroom (*Agaricus campestris*)

㊁ jūn 见378页 see p378

J

K ㄎ

KA ㄎㄚ

咖 ㊁ kā ㄎㄚ [咖啡](—fēi)(外 **loanword**)常绿灌木或小乔木,产在热带,花白色,果实红色,种子可制饮料。也指这种饮料 coffee (*Coffea*)

㊀ gā 见212页 see p212

喀 kā ㄎㄚ 拟声词 ***onomatopoeia***:~的一声,快门儿响了。*The shutter clicked.* [喀嚓](—chā)拟声词 ***onomatopoeia***,树枝等折断的声音 crack; snap

[喀斯特](外 **loanword**)可溶性岩石(石灰石、石膏等)受水侵蚀而形成的地貌,形状奇特,有洞穴,也有峭壁 karst

揢 kā ㄎㄚ 用刀子刮(with a knife) to scrape

卡 ㊀ kǎ ㄎㄚˇ (外 **loanword**) ❶卡车,载重的大汽车 truck; lorry: 十轮~ *ten-wheeled truck* ❷卡片,小的纸片(一般是比较硬的纸)card: 资料~ *reference card* | 贺年~ *New Year card* [绿卡]某些国家发给外国侨民的长期居留证的俗称 green card ❸卡路里,热量的非法定计量单位,1克纯水的温度升高1摄氏度所需的热量为1卡,合4.1868焦 calorie

[卡通](外 **loanword**) **1** 动画片 cartoon **2** 漫画 caricature

㊁ qiǎ 见591页 see p591

佧 kǎ ㄎㄚˇ [佧佤族](—Wǎ—)佤族的旧称 former term for 佤族

咔 kǎ ㄎㄚˇ [咔叽](—jī)(外 **loanword**)一种很厚的斜纹布 khaki

胩 kǎ ㄎㄚˇ 即异腈(jīng),有机化合物的一类,通式 R—NC,无色液体,有恶臭,剧毒,容易被酸分解(i. e. 异腈) carbylamine

咯 ㊀ kǎ ㄎㄚˇ 用力使东西从食道或气管里出来 to cough up: 把鱼刺~出来 *to cough up* (or *out*) *a fishbone* | ~血 *to cough up blood* | ~痰 *to cough up phlegm*; *to expectorate*

㊁ lo 见460页 see p460

㊂ gē 见223页 see p223

KAI ㄎㄞ

开(開) kāi ㄎㄞ ❶把关闭的东西打开 to open; to turn on: ~门 *to open a door* | ~抽屉 *to open a drawer* | ~口说话 *to start to talk* ㊉ ***extension*** **1** 收拢的东西放散 to unfold; to open out: ~花 *to blossom*; *to bloom* | ~颜(笑) *to smile* **2** 把整体的东西划分成部分的 to divide into: 三十二~本 *32 mo* **3** 凝结的东西融化 to thaw：～冻 *to thaw；to unfreeze*｜～河（河水化冻）（*of a frozen river*）*to thaw*［开刀］用刀割治 to perform an operation；to operate：这病得～～。*An operation is needed for this disease.*［开关］有控制作用的机关。通常指电门、电键 switch［开交］分解，脱离 to get free from：忙得不可～～ *to be up to one's neck in work；to be awfully busy*｜闹得不可～～ *to get into a hot dispute*［开口呼］不用 i、u、ü 开头的韵母（vowels not having i，u or ü as their beginning）❷通，使通 to open：想不～ *cannot straighten out one's thinking*｜～路先锋 *pathbreaker；pioneer*［开通］（—tong）思想不守旧，容易接受新事物 open-minded；enlightened ❸使显露出来 to open up；to exploit：～矿 *to open up*（or *out*）*a mine；to exploit a mine*｜～采石油 *to exploit*（or *recover*）*petroleum*［开发］使埋藏着的显露出来 to develop；to exploit ❹扩大，发展 to expand；to develop：～拓（tuò）*to pioneer；to open up；to develop*｜～源节流 *to open up the source and regulate the flow；to increase income and reduce expenditure*｜～展工作 *to go about one's work* ❺发动，操纵 to start；to operate：～车 *to drive a car*｜～炮 *to fire a cannon*｜～船 *to set sail*｜～动脑筋 *to use one's brains*（or *head*）［开火］指发生军事冲突 to open fire；to fire 喻 ***figurative*** 两方面冲突 conflict ❻起始 to begin；to start：～端 *beginning；start*｜～春 *beginning of spring；* or *Spring begins.*｜～学（*of a school*）*to start；*（*of a school term*）*to begin*｜～工（*of a factory，etc*）*to go into operation；*（*of construction，etc*）*to start*｜戏～演了。*The play has begun.* ❼设置，建立 to establish；to set up；to run：～医院 *to open a hospital*［开国］建立新的国家 to found a state ❽支付 to pay：～支 *to pay；expenses*｜～销 *to pay；expenses* ❾沸，滚 to boil：～水 *boiling water；boiled water*｜水～了。*The water is boiling.* ❿举行 to hold：～会 *to hold a meeting；to attend*（or *have*）*a meeting* ⓫写 to write out；to make out：～发票 *to make out an invoice*｜～药方 *to write out a prescription；to prescribe* ⓬放在动词后面，表示趋向或结果（used after a verb to express inclination or result）**1** 表示分开或扩展（used to express separation or spreading）：睁～眼 *to open one's eyes*｜张～嘴 *to open one's mouth*｜打～窗户 *to open the window*｜消息传～了。*The news has spread.* **2** 表示开始并继续下去（used to express beginning and continuing）：雨下～了。*It begins to rain.*｜唱～了 *to begin to sing* **3** 表示容下（used to express capacity）：屋子小，坐不～。*The room is* *not big enough to seat all the people*. ⑬(外 **loanword**)黄金的纯度单位(以二十四开为纯金) carat:十四~金 *14 carat gold* ⑭热力学温度单位名开尔文的简称 short for 开尔文(符号 K) Kelvin (K)

锎 kāi ㄎㄞ 一种人造的放射性元素(符号 Cf) californium (Cf)

揩 kāi ㄎㄞ 擦,抹 to wipe; to rub:~鼻涕 *to wipe away one's snivel; to wipe one's nose* | ~背 *to wipe one's back* | ~油(占便宜 piányi) *to get petty advantages at the expense of other people or the state*

剀(剴) kǎi ㄎㄞˇ [剀切](-qiè) **1** 符合事理 true and pertinent:~~中理 *to be true and pertinent* **2** 切实 earnest:~~教导 *to teach earnestly*

凯(凱) kǎi ㄎㄞˇ 军队得胜回来奏的乐曲 triumphant strains:~歌 *song of victory* (or *triumph*) | 奏~ *to win victory; to triumph* | ~旋(得胜回还) *to return in triumph*

垲(塏) kǎi ㄎㄞˇ 地势高而干燥 (of terrain) high and arid

闿(闓) kǎi ㄎㄞˇ 开 to open

恺(愷) kǎi ㄎㄞˇ 快乐,和乐 merry; joyful

铠(鎧) kǎi ㄎㄞˇ 铠甲,古代的战衣,上面缀有金属薄片,可以保护身体 armour

莰 kǎi ㄎㄞˇ 莰烷,有机化合物,分子式 $C_{10}H_{18}$,天然的尚未发现。它的重要衍生物莰酮,气味像樟脑 carane

楷 ㊀ kǎi ㄎㄞˇ ❶法式,模范 model; pattern (㊟ **doublet** 一模 model; example) ❷楷书,现在通行的一种汉字字体,是由隶书演变而来的(of Chinese calligraphy) regular script:小~ *regular script in small characters* | 正~ *regular script*

㊁ jiē 见344页 see p344

锴 kǎi ㄎㄞˇ 好铁。多用于人名(kai, usually used in a given name) iron of fine quality; quality iron

慨(❷*嘅) kǎi ㄎㄞˇ ❶愤激 indignant:愤~ *indignant* ❷感慨 to sigh with emotion:~叹 *to lament with sighs; to sigh with regret* ❸慷慨,不吝啬 generous:~允 *to consent readily; to promise kindly* | ~然相赠 *to give (as a present) generously*

忾(愾) kài ㄎㄞˋ 愤怒,恨 hatred:同仇敌~(大家一致痛恨敌人) *to share a bitter hatred of the enemy*

欬 kài ㄎㄞˋ 咳嗽 to cough

KAN ㄎㄢ

刊 kān ㄎㄢ ❶刻 to engrave:~石 *to engrave on a stone* | ~印 *to cut blocks and print; to compose and print* ㊟ **transfer**

排版印刷 to print:~行 *to print and publish* | 停~ *to stop* (or *suspend*) *publication* [刊物]报纸、杂志等出版物,也省称"刊"(also 刊 for short) publication: 周~ *weekly* | 月~ *monthly* ❷ 削除,修改 to delete; to correct: 不~之论(喻至理名言) *unalterable statement; statement for all times* | ~误表 *errata; corrigenda*

看 ㊁ kān ㄎㄢ 守护 to look after; to take care of: ~门 *to guard the entrance; to look after a house* | ~家 *to look after the house; to mind the house* | ~守 *to look after; to watch* ㊕ ***transfer*** 监视 to keep under surveillance; to keep an eye on: 把他~起来。*Keep him under surveillance.* [看护] **1** 护理 to nurse **2** 旧时称护士(in former times) nurse

㊀ kàn 见384页 see p384

勘 kān ㄎㄢ ❶ 校对,复看核定 to proofread; to collate (㊣ ***doublet*** 校— to collate): ~误 *to correct errors in printing* | ~正 *to proofread* ❷ 细查,审查 to investigate; to survey: ~探 *to explore* | ~验 *to inspect; to examine* | ~测 *to survey* | 实地~查 *on-the-spot survey*

堪 kān ㄎㄢ ❶ 可以,能,足以 may; can: ~以告慰 *can take as comfort* | 不~设想 *unimaginable; dreadful to contemplate* ❷ 忍受,能支持 to bear; to endure: 难~ *unbearable; embarrassed* | 狼狈不~ *in an extremely awkward position; in a sorry* (or *wretched*) *plight*

戡 kān ㄎㄢ 平定(叛乱) to suppress; to put down: ~乱 *to suppress a rebellion*

龛(龕) kān ㄎㄢ 供奉佛像、神位等的小阁子 niche; shrine

坎 kǎn ㄎㄢˇ ❶ 低陷不平的地方,坑穴 pit; hole ❷ 八卦之一,符号是"☵",代表水 *kan*, one of the Eight Trigrams in the shape of ☵ that represents water ❸ 同"槛㊁" same as 槛㊁ ❹ 发光强度单位名坎德拉的简称(符号 cd) candela (cd)

[坎坷](—kě) **1** 道路不平的样子 bumpy; rough **2** 比喻不得志 full of frustrations

砍 kǎn ㄎㄢˇ 用刀、斧等猛剁,用力劈 to cut; to chop; to hack: ~柴 *to cut firewood* | 把树枝~下来 *to cut off the branch*

莰 kǎn ㄎㄢˇ 莰烷,有机化合物,分子式 $C_{10}H_{18}$,白色晶体,有樟脑的香味 camphane

侃 kǎn ㄎㄢˇ 闲谈,聊天 to chat idly: 他真能~。*He is a real chatterbox.* or *He can really chew the rag* (or *fat*). | ~大山 *to chat idly*

[侃侃]理直气壮、从容不迫的样子 with assurance and composure: ~~而谈 *to talk with ease and confidence*

槛(檻) ㊁ kǎn ㄎㄢˇ 门槛,门限 threshold (图见188页 picture on p188)

㊀ jiàn 见333页 see p333

K

颇 kǎn ㄎㄢˇ [颇颔](—hàn)面黄肌瘦 famished-looking

看 ㊀ kàn ㄎㄢˋ ❶瞧，瞅 to look at; to see: ～书 *to read a book* | ～电影 *to see a film* ❷观察 to observe; to watch (㊣ **doublet** 察— to watch; to inspect): ～脉 *to take (or feel) sb's pulse* | ～透 *to see through* ㊂ **extension** 诊治(of a doctor) to treat: ～病 *to treat a patient; to see a doctor* | 大夫把我的病～好了。*The doctor cured my disease.* ❸访问，拜望 to visit; to call on (㊣ **doublet** —望 to visit): 到医院里去～病人 *to go to the hospital to see a patient* ❹看待，照应，对待 to regard; to look after; to treat: 另眼相～ *to regard sb with special respect* (or *concern*) | ～重 *to value; to regard as important* | 照～ *to look after* ❺想，以为 to think; to consider: 我～应该这么办。*I think it should be done this way.* ❻先试试以观察它的结果 to try and see: 问一声～ *to ask and see* | 做做～ *to have a try* ❼提防，小心 to mind; to look out: 别跑，～摔着。*Don't run, or you'll fall to the ground.*

㊁ kān 见383页 see p383

衎 kàn ㄎㄢˋ ❶快乐 merry; jovial ❷刚直 upright

崁 kàn ㄎㄢˋ [赤崁]地名，在台湾省 Chikan, a place in Taiwan Province

墈 kàn ㄎㄢˋ 〈方 **dialect**〉高的堤岸。多用于地名(kan, usually used in a place name) high embankment: ～上(在江西省乐平) *Kanshang (a place in Leping, Jiangxi Province)*

磡 kàn ㄎㄢˋ 山崖 cliff

阚 ㊀ kàn ㄎㄢˋ 姓 Kan, a surname

㊁ hǎn 见264页 see p264

瞰(*矙) kàn ㄎㄢˋ 望，俯视，向下看 to look down from; to overlook [鸟瞰] **1** 从高处向下看 to get a bird's-eye view **2** 事物的概括描写 bird's-eye view; general survey: 世界大势～～ *general survey of the world situation*

KANG ㄎㄤ

闶 ㊀ kāng ㄎㄤ [闶阆](—láng)〈方 **dialect**〉建筑物中空旷的部分。也叫"闶阆子"(also called 闶阆子) open space in a building

㊁ kàng 见385页 see p385

康 kāng ㄎㄤ ❶安宁 healthy; peaceful: 身体健～ *to be in good health; physical health* | ～乐 *peaceful and happy* ❷富裕，丰盛 affluent; abundant: ～年 *good year* | 小～ *comparatively well-off* ❸同"糠❷" same as 糠❷

[康庄]平坦通达的 broad and smooth: ～～大道 *broad (or main) road*

慷(**忼) kāng ㄎㄤ [慷慨](—kǎi) **1** 情绪激昂 fervent; vehement: ～

～陈词 *to present one's views vehemently; to express one's opinion excitedly* **2** 待人热诚，肯用财物帮助人 generous：他待人很～～。*He is very generous to others.*

槺 kāng ㄎㄤ 见417页"榔"字条"榔槺"(lángkang) see 榔槺 on p417

糠(*穅) kāng ㄎㄤ ❶从稻、麦等子实上脱下来的皮或壳 chaff; bran; husk ❷空，空虚 spongy：萝卜～了。*The radish has gone spongy.*

鱇 kāng ㄎㄤ 见6页"鮟"字条"鮟鱇"(ān—) see 鮟鱇 on p6

扛 ㊀ káng ㄎㄤˊ 用肩膀承担 to carry on the shoulder; to shoulder：～粮食 *to carry a bag of grain on one's shoulder* | ～着一杆枪 *to shoulder a gun; to have a gun on one's shoulder* | ～活(旧时指做长工)(*in former times*) *to work as a farm labourer*

㊁ gāng 见220页 see p220

亢 kàng ㄎㄤˋ ❶高 high ㊀ ***extension*** 高傲 haughty：不卑不～ *neither haughty nor humble* ❷过甚，极 excessive; extreme：～奋 *extremely excited* | ～旱 *severe drought* ❸星宿名，二十八宿之一 *kang*, 2nd of the 28 constellations

伉 kàng ㄎㄤˋ ❶对等，相称 matching; fit [伉俪](—lì)配偶，夫妇 married couple; husband and wife ❷正直 upright and outspoken：～直 *upright and unyielding*

抗 kàng ㄎㄤˋ ❶抵御 to resist; to combat; to fight (㊀ ***doublet*** 抵— to resist)：～战 *war of resistance against aggression; the War of Resistance Against Japan* (*1937—1945*) | ～旱 *to fight a drought* | ～涝 *to prevent waterlogging* ㊀ ***extension*** **1** 不妥协 not to compromise：～辩 *to contradict; to counterplea* **2** 拒绝，不接受 to refuse (㊀ ***doublet*** —拒 to defy)：～命 *to defy an order; to disobey* | ～粮 *to resist the grain levy* | ～税 *to refuse to pay taxes* [抗生素]动物、植物及微生物(细菌、霉菌等)所产生的对细菌等微生物具有抑制生长或杀灭作用的化学物质，如青霉素、链霉素等。旧称抗菌素(formerly called 抗菌素) antibiotics [抗议]声明不同意，同时谴责对方的行动 to protest; to remonstrate ❷匹敌，相当 to contend with; to be a match for：～衡(不相上下，抵得过) *to contend with; to match* | 分庭～礼(行平等的礼节，比喻势均力敌，也比喻相互对立) *to salute each other as equals; to stand up to sb as an equal; to make rival claims as an equal*

闶 ㊁ kàng ㄎㄤˋ 高大 tall and big; lofty

㊀ kāng 见384页 see p384

炕 kàng ㄎㄤˋ ❶北方用砖、坯等砌成的睡觉的台，下面

K

有洞，连通烟囱，可以烧火取暖 *kang*，heatable brick (*or* adobe) bed ❷〈方 ***dialect***〉烤 to bake (*or* dry) by the fire：把湿衣服放在火边～一～。Dry the wet clothes by the fire.

钪 kàng ㄎㄤˋ 一种金属元素，符号 Sc，银白色，常跟钆、铒等混合存在，产量很少 scandium (Sc)

KAO ㄎㄠ

尻 kāo ㄎㄠ 屁股 buttocks; bottom

考(❶—❸ *攷) kǎo ㄎㄠˇ ❶试验，测验 to give (*or* take) examination (*or* test) (㊣ ***doublet*** 一试 examination)：期～ *term examination* | ～语文 *to have a Chinese examination* (or *test*) ❷检查 to check; to inspect (㊣ ***doublet*** 一察 to inspect | 查一 to examine; to do research on)：～勤 *to check on work attendance; to keep attendance records* | ～绩 *to assess* (or *appraise*) *staff performance* [考验]通过具体行动、困难环境等来检验(是否坚定、正确)to test [考语]旧指考察成绩的评语(in former times) written comments on work (*or* performance) ❸推求，研究 to study; to investigate：～古 *to engage in archaeological studies; to do archaeology* | ～证 *textual criticism* (or *research*) [考虑]斟酌，思索 to consider; to think over：～～一下再决定 *to think over before making a decision* | ～～问题 *to think about the matter* [考究](—jiu) **1** 考查，研究 to investigate; to observe and study：～～问题 *to investigate a problem* **2** 讲究 to be meticulous (*or* fastidious) about; to pay attention to：衣着～～ *to be meticulous* (or *fastidious*) *about one's clothes* ❹老，年纪大 old; of an old age (㊣ ***doublet*** 寿一 long life; longevity) ❺原指父亲，后称已死的父亲 one's father (in original meaning); one's deceased father：如丧～妣 *to look as if one had lost one's parents; to look utterly wretched* | 先～ *my deceased father*

拷 kǎo ㄎㄠˇ 打 to flog; to beat; to torture (㊣ ***doublet*** 一打 to flog; to beat; to torture)：～问 *to interrogate with torture*

[拷贝](外 ***loanword***) **1** 复制 to copy **2** 复制本，电影方面指用拍摄成的电影底片洗印出来的胶片 copy

栲 kǎo ㄎㄠˇ 栲树，常绿乔木，木材坚硬，可做枕木及用于建筑等。树皮含鞣酸，可制栲胶，又可制染料 evergreen chinquapin (*Castanopsis*)

[栲栳](—lǎo)一种用竹子或柳条编的盛东西的器具。也叫"笆斗"(also called 笆斗) wicker basket

烤 kǎo ㄎㄠˇ ❶把东西放在火的周围使干或使熟 to bake;

K

to roast：～烟叶子 *flue-cured tobacco* | ～白薯 *to bake sweet potatoes* | ～箱 *oven; roaster* ❷向着火取暖 to warm oneself by a fire：～手 *to warm one's hands by a fire* | 围炉～火 *to warm oneself at the stove*

铐 kào ㄎㄠˋ ❶(－子)手铐子，束缚犯人手的刑具 handcuffs ❷用手铐束缚 to handcuff：把犯人～起来。*Handcuff the criminal.* or *Put handcuffs on the criminal.*

犒 kào ㄎㄠˋ 指用酒食或财物慰劳 to reward with food and drink：～劳 *to reward with food and drink* | ～赏 *to reward (a victorious army, etc) with bounties*

靠 kào ㄎㄠˋ ❶倚着，挨近 to lean against; to get near ([连] **doublet** 倚— to lean on)：～墙站着 *to stand against the wall* | 船～岸了。*The boat pulled in to the shore.* ❷依靠，依赖 to depend on; to rely on：要创造人类的幸福，全～我们自己。*It all depends on ourselves to bring about the happiness of the human race.* | ～劳动致富 *to get rich through sweat and toil* [靠山][喻] ***figurative*** 所依赖的人或集体 backer; backing ❸信赖 to trust：可～ *reliable; trustworthy* | ～得住 *reliable; trustworthy* [牢靠](－kao) **1** 稳固 reliable; firm; strong **2** 稳妥可信赖 dependable; reliable：这人做事最～～。*This person is the most reliable in handling affairs.*

KE ㄎㄜ

坷 ㊀ kē ㄎㄜ [坷垃](－la) 土块 clod
㊁ kě 见390页 see p390

苛 kē ㄎㄜ ❶苛刻，过分 harsh; excessive：～求 *to make excessive high demands; to be severely critical* | ～责 *to criticize severely* ❷苛细，繁重，使人难于忍受 overelaborate：～政 *tyrannical government* | ～捐杂税 *exorbitant taxes and miscellaneous levies*

珂 kē ㄎㄜ ❶玉名 jade-like stone ❷马笼头上的装饰 ornament on a bridle：玉～ *jade ornament on a bridle*
[珂罗版](外 **loanword**)印刷上用的一种照相版，把要复制的字、画的底片晒制在涂过感光胶层的玻璃片上而成 collotype

柯 kē ㄎㄜ ❶斧子的柄 axe-handle; helve ❷草木的枝茎 stalk; branch
[柯尔克孜族]我国少数民族，参看附表(see the appendix) the Kirgiz ethnic group, one of the ethnic minorities of China

轲 kē ㄎㄜ 用于人名。孟子，名轲，战国时人(Ke, used in a given name) Mencius, a man of the Warring States Period, whose given name is Ke

牁 kē ㄎㄜ [牂牁](zāng—) **1** 古水名 Zangke River, an ancient river **2** 古地名 Zangke, an ancient place

砢 kē ㄎㄜ 〈方 ***dialect***〉[砢碜](－chen)寒碜,难看 ugly; shabby

钶 kē ㄎㄜ 化学元素,铌(ní)的旧称(former term for 铌) columbium (Cb)

疴 kē ㄎㄜ (旧读 formerly ē) 病 illness:沉～(重病) *serious illness of long standing*|染～ *to contract an illness*

匼 kē ㄎㄜ 古代的一种头巾 (in ancient China) a kind of kerchief
[匼河]地名,在山西省芮城 Kehe, a place in Ruicheng, Shanxi Province

科 kē ㄎㄜ ❶分门别类用的名称 term of classification **1** 生物的分类单位之一,在"目"之下、"属"之上(one of the biological classifications which is under "order" and above "genus") family:狮子属于食肉类的猫～。*The lion belongs to the carnivorous cat family.*|槐树是豆～植物。*The Chinese scholar tree is a plant of the bean family.* **2** 机关内部组织划分的部门 administrative section:财务～ *finance section*|总务～ *general affairs section* **3** 学术或业务的类别 branch of academic or vocational study:文～ *humanities; liberal arts*|理～ *sciences*|内～ *internal medicine*|外～ *surgery*[科举]从隋唐到清代国家设立的分科考选文武官吏后备人员的制度 imperial civil examination system[科学]**1** 反映自然、社会、思维的客观规律的分科的知识体系 science **2** 合乎科学的 scientific:这种做法不～～。*It is not scientific to do it this way.* ❷法律条文 clause; law:～文 *legal articles*|犯～ *to violate the laws*|金～玉律 *golden rule and precious precept; infallible laws* ❸判定 to impose (a punishment); to sentence:～以徒刑 *to sentence; to pass a sentence*|～以罚金 *to impose a fine on sb; to fine* ❹古典戏剧里称演员的动作表情(in a classical Chinese opera) actor's actions and expressions:叹～ *sighing*|饮酒～ *drinking*

蝌 kē ㄎㄜ [蝌蚪](－dǒu)蛙或蟾蜍等的幼体,生活在水中,黑色,身体椭圆,有长尾。逐渐发育生出后脚、前脚,尾巴消失,最后变成蛙或蟾蜍 tadpole

棵 kē ㄎㄜ 量词 ***quantifier***,用于植物(used for a plant):一～树 *a tree*[棵儿]植物的大小(of a plant) size:这棵树～～很大。*This tree is quite big.*[青棵子]绿色庄稼、野草等 green crops, weeds, etc

稞 kē ㄎㄜ 青稞,麦的一种,产在西藏、青海等地,是藏族人民的主要食品糌粑(zānba)的原料 highland barley (*Hordeum vulgare*)

窠 kē ㄎㄜ 鸟兽的巢穴 nest; burrow[窠臼]㊗ ***figurative*** 文章或其他艺术品所依据的老套子(of writing or other artistic creation) set pattern

颗 kē ㄎㄜ 量词 ***quantifier***, 用于圆形或粒状的东西 (used for round or grain-like things):一～珠子 *a pearl* | 一～心 *a heart*

髁 kē ㄎㄜ 骨头上的突起，多长在骨头的两端 condyle

颏 kē ㄎㄜ 下巴颏儿，脸的最下部分，在两腮和嘴的下面 chin

搕 kē ㄎㄜ 敲，碰 to knock:～烟袋锅子 *to knock out a pipe*

榼 kē ㄎㄜ 古时盛酒的器皿 ancient wine vessel

磕 kē ㄎㄜ 碰撞在硬东西上 (against sth hard) to knock:～破了头 *to graze one's head* | 碗～掉一块。*The bowl has a chip in it.* | ～头(旧时的跪拜礼) *kowtow, former Chinese custom of kneeling and bowing in worship or submission*

瞌 kē ㄎㄜ [瞌睡]困倦想睡或进入半睡眠状态 sleepy; drowsy:打～～ *to drowse*

壳(殼) ㊀ ké ㄎㄜˊ (一儿) 坚硬的外皮 shell:核桃～儿 *walnut shell* | 鸡蛋～儿 *egg shell* | 贝～儿 *shell*

㊁ qiào 见602页 see p602

咳 ㊀ ké ㄎㄜˊ 咳嗽，呼吸器官受刺激而起一种反射作用，把吸入的气急急呼出，声带振动发声 to cough

㊁ hāi 见261页 see p261

揢 ké ㄎㄜˊ 〈方 ***dialect***〉❶卡(qiǎ)住 to get stuck; to wedge:抽屉～住了，拉不开。*The drawer is stuck. It won't open.* | 鞋小了～脚。*The shoes will pinch if they are too small.* ❷刁难 to create difficulties:～人 *to make things difficult for sb* | 你别拿这事来～我。*Don't try to baffle me with it.*

可 ㊀ kě ㄎㄜˇ ❶是，对，表示准许 to approve:许～ *to permit* | 认～ *to approve* | 不加～否 *to refuse to comment; to be noncommittal* [可以] **1** 表示允许(used to express permission) can; may; ok:～～，你去吧! *Ok, you may go.* **2** 适宜，能 can; may:现在～～穿棉衣了。*It's time to wear cotton-padded clothes.* | 马铃薯～～当饭吃。*Potatoes can serve as food.* **3** 过甚，程度深 terrible; awful:这几天冷得真～～。*It's awfully cold these days.* **4** 还好，差不多 not bad; passable:这篇文章还～～。*This article is not bad.* [小可] **1** 寻常 unimportant:非同～～ *no small matter* **2** 旧时谦称自己为小可(humble term in former times) I; me ❷能够 can; may:牢不～破的友谊 *unbreakable friendship* | ～大～小 *may be big or small* [可能]能够，有实现的条件 possible; probable:这个计划～～提前实现。*It's possible for the plan to be carried through ahead of schedule.* ❸值得，够得上(用在动词前)(used before a verb) to be worth:～怜 *pitiful; pitiable* |

K

～爱 *lovable; lovely* | ～恶(wù) *hateful; detestable* ❹ 适合 to fit; to suit: ～心 *satisfying; to one's liking* | 饭菜～口 *tasty (or delicious) food* [引] ***extension*** 尽(jǐn),就某种范围不加增减 to go as far as possible; to make do: ～着钱花 *to make do with the money* | ～着脑袋做帽子 *to make a hat according to the size of one's head* ❺ 连词 ***conjunction***,可是,但,却 but; yet; however: 大家很累(lèi),～都很愉快。*Everybody was very tired yet very happy.* ❻ 副词 ***adverb*** **1** 加强语气(used for emphasis) so; such: 这工具使着～得劲了。*This tool is just right.* | 他写字～快了。*He writes so fast.* | 这篇文章～写完了。*This article has been finished at last.* **2** 表示疑问(used to express doubt): 你～知道? *Do you really know it?* | 这话～是真的? *Is it true?* **3** 和"岂"字义近 close to 岂 in meaning: ～不是吗! *That's the way it is!* or *Exactly!* | ～不就糟了吗! *It's really in a mess!* **4** 大约 about: 年～三十许 *about 30 years of age* | 长～六米 *about six metres long* ❼ 义同"可以 2"same as 可以 2 in meaning: 根～食。*The root is edible.* ❽ 义同"可以 4"same as 可以 4 in meaning: 尚～ *passable; not bad*

㊁ kè 见390页 see p390

坷 ㊁ kě ㄎㄜˇ 见383页"坎"字条"坎坷"(kǎn—) see 坎坷 on p383

㊀ kē 见387页 see p387

岢 kě ㄎㄜˇ [岢岚](—lán) 地名,在山西省 Kelan, a place in Shanxi Province

渴 kě ㄎㄜˇ 口干想喝水 thirsty: 我～了。*I'm thirsty.* [喻] ***figurative*** 迫切地 yearningly; eagerly: ～望 *to yearn (or long) for*

可 ㊁ kè ㄎㄜˋ [可汗](—hán) 古代鲜卑、突厥、回纥、蒙古等族君主的称号 khan

㊀ kě 见389页 see p389

克 (❹❺△ 剋、❹❺* 尅) kè ㄎㄜˋ ❶能 can; to be able to: 不～分身 *cannot get away* | ～勤～俭 *to be industrious and frugal; to be both hard working and thrifty* ❷胜 to win a victory over: 我军～敌。*Our army has defeated the enemy.* [转] ***transfer*** 战胜而取得据点 to conquer; to capture: 攻无不～ *to be invincible* | 连～数城 *to conquer (or capture) one city after another* [克复]战胜而收回失地 to recapture; to recover ❸克服,制伏 to overcome; to restrain: ～己奉公 *to work selflessly for the public interest* | 以柔～刚 *to overcome the tough with the mild* ❹ 严格限定 to set a time limit: ～期 *to set a time limit; to set a date* | ～日完成 *to set a date for completion* ❺消化 to digest: ～食 *to help digestion* ❻(藏 **Tibetan**)容量单位,1克青稞约25市斤。也

是地积单位，播种1克种子的土地称为1克地，1克约合1市亩 *ke*, Tibetan unit of volume or dry measure, equal to about 25 *jin*, also Tibetan unit of land area, equal to about 1 *mu* ❼(外 **loanword**)质量的法定计量单位，一克等于一千克（公斤）的千分之一，旧称公分(formerly called 公分) gram, equal to one-thousandth of 1 kg

[克隆](外 **loanword**) **1** 生物体通过体细胞进行无性繁殖，复制出遗传性状完全相同的生命物质或生命体 to clone **2** 借指复制 to copy

“剋(尅)”又 kēi 见392页 also kēi, see p392

氪 kè ㄎㄜˋ 一种化学元素，在通常条件下为气体，符号Kr，无色、无味、无臭，不易跟其他元素化合 krypton (Kr)

刻 kè ㄎㄜˋ ❶雕，用刀子挖 to carve; to engrave (㊥ ***doublet*** 雕一 to carve; to engrave): ～图章 *to engrave a seal* [深刻]深入，对事理能进一层分析 deep; penetrating; profound: ～～地领会 *to understand profoundly* | 描写得很～～ *to make* (or *give*) *a profound description* ❷十五分钟为一刻(of an hour) quarter ❸时间 time; moment: 即～ *at once; immediately* | 顷～(时间极短) *in no time* ❹不厚道 unkind; harsh (㊥ ***doublet*** 一薄 harsh; unkind): 苛～ *harsh; overly strict* [刻苦]不怕难，肯吃苦 hardworking; assiduous: ～～用功 *to be hardworking* | 生活很～～ *to live a frugal life* ❺同“克❹”same as 克❹

恪 kè ㄎㄜˋ 恭敬，谨慎 scrupulous and respectful: ～遵 *to abide by scrupulously* | ～守 *to obey scrupulously*

客 kè ㄎㄜˋ ❶客人，跟“主”相对 guest (the opposite of 主)(㊥ ***doublet*** 宾一 guest): 来～了。*We've got a visitor.* | 招待～人 *to entertain guests* [客观] **1** 离开意识独立存在的，跟“主观”相对(the opposite of 主观) objective: 人类意识属于主观，物质世界属于～～。*Human consciousness belongs to the subjective, while the material world belongs to the objective.* **2** 依据外界事物而作观察的，没有成见的 impersonal; objective: 他看问题很～～。*He looks at things objectively.* [客家]古代移住闽、粤等地的中原人的后裔 Hakkas, descendants of people who migrated from the Central Plains to Fujian, Guangdong, etc in ancient China [客气]㊕ ***transfer*** 谦让，有礼貌 polite; courteous ❷出门在外的 to live (*or* settle) in a strange place: ～居 *to live away from home; to reside as a visitor; to stay in a strange land* | ～籍 *province into which a settler has moved; settler from another province* | ～商 *traveling trader* (or *merchant*) ❸指奔走他方，从事某种活动的人 person engaged in some particular pursuit requiring travelling and running around: 说～ *persuasive talker; lobbyist* | 侠～ *knight-errant* ❹旅客,顾客 passenger; customer: ～车 *bus; passenger train* | ～满 *to have a full house; to have no vacancy* | 乘～ *passenger*

[客岁]去年 last year

课 kè ㄎㄜˋ ❶功课,有计划的分段教学 class; lesson: 上～ *to attend* (or *give*) *a class* | 今天没～ *to have no class today* [课题]研究、讨论或急需解决的主要问题 topic (*or* question) for study (*or* discussion) ❷旧指教书 (in former times) to teach: ～徒 *to teach a student* | ～读 *to teach* ❸古赋税的一种 ancient tax ❹使交纳捐税 to levy; to collect; to impose: ～以重税 *to levy a heavy tax on sb* ❺旧指某些机关学校等行政上的单位 (in former times) division or subdivision of an administrative unit: 会计～ *accounting section* | 教务～ *office of academic affairs* ❻占卜的一种 divination session: 起～ *to divine*

骒 kè ㄎㄜˋ 雌,专指骡、马 (of a mule or horse) female

锞 kè ㄎㄜˋ (一子)小块的金锭或银锭 (of gold or silver) small ingot

缂 kè ㄎㄜˋ 缂丝(也作"刻丝"),我国特有的一种丝织的手工艺品。织纬线时,留下要补织图画的地方,然后用各种颜色的丝线补上,织出后好像是刻出的图画 (also written as 刻丝) *kesi* (*or* Cut Silk), a silk tapestry woven by using a unique Chinese traditional technique with the embroidery of cut designs

嗑 kè ㄎㄜˋ 上下门牙对咬有壳的或硬的东西 to crack sth between the teeth: ～瓜子 *to crack melon* (or *sunflower*) *seeds*

溘 kè ㄎㄜˋ 忽然 suddenly: ～逝(称人死亡) *to pass away suddenly; to die unexpectedly*

KEI ㄎㄟ

剋(*尅) ㊀ kēi ㄎㄟ 〈方 *dialect*〉❶打(人) to beat (sb) [剋架]打架 to come to blows; to fight ❷申斥 to scold: 狠狠地～了他一顿 *to give him a severe scolding*

㊁ kè 见390页"克" see 克 on p390

KEN ㄎㄣ

肯 kěn ㄎㄣˇ ❶许可,愿意 to agree; to be willing to: 他不～来。*He won't come over.* | 只要你～做就能成功。*If you are willing to do it, you can be successful.* | 首～(点头答应) *to nod approval; to approve* [肯定] **1** 正面承认 to affirm; to confirm: ～～成绩,指出缺点 *to affirm the achievements*

and point out the shortcomings **2** 确定不移 definitely; undoubtedly: 我们的计划～～能超额完成。*Our plan can be overfulfilled definitely.* ❷骨头上附着的肉 flesh attached to bone［肯綮］(—qìng) 筋骨结合的地方 bone joint［中肯］(zhòng—) ⓔ ***figurative*** 抓住重点，切中要害 pertinent; to the point: 说话～～ *to make pertinent remarks*

啃 kěn ㄎㄣˇ 用力从较硬的东西上一点一点地咬下来 to gnaw; to nibble: ～老玉米 *to nibble at corn on the cob*｜老鼠把抽屉～坏了。*The rats nibbled away the drawer.*

垦(墾) kěn ㄎㄣˇ ❶用力翻土 to cultivate land: ～地 *to cultivate* (or *plough*) *the soil* ❷开垦，开辟荒地 to reclaim wasteland: ～荒 *to reclaim wasteland; to open up virgin soil*｜～殖 *to reclaim and cultivate wasteland*

恳(懇) kěn ㄎㄣˇ 诚恳，真诚 sincerely; earnestly: ～求 *to implore; to entreat; to beseech*｜～托 *to make a sincere request; to entrust earnestly*｜～谈 *to talk sincerely; to have a heart-to-heart conversation*

龈 ⊜ kěn ㄎㄣˇ 同"啃"same as 啃

⊖ yín 见896页 see p896

掯 kèn ㄎㄣˋ 压迫，强迫，刁难 to press; to force; to make things difficult for sb: 勒～(lēi)～ *to make things difficult for sb*

裉(**褙) kèn ㄎㄣˋ 衣服腋下前后相连的部分 (of a jacket) seam under the armpit connecting the front and the back: 杀～(把裉缝上) *to sew up the seams under the armpits*｜抬～(称衣服从肩到腋下的宽度 *measurement of clothing from the shoulder to the armpit* (图见882页"衣"picture on p882)

KENG ㄎㄥ

坑(*阬) kēng ㄎㄥ ❶(—子、—儿) 洼下去的地方 pit; hole; hollow: 水～ *puddle*｜泥～ *mud pit* ❷把人活埋 to bury alive: ～杀 *to kill sb by burying him alive* ❸坑害，设计使人受到损失 to entrap; to cheat: ～人 *to cheat; to entrap* ❹地洞，地道 tunnel; pit: ～道 *gallery in a mine; tunnel*｜矿～ *pit*

吭 ⊜ kēng ㄎㄥ 出声，发言 to utter a sound or word: 不～声 *not to utter a sound*｜一声也不～ *not to say a word*

⊖ háng 见266页 see p266

硁(硜、**磬) kēng ㄎㄥ 拟声词 ***onomatopoeia***，敲打石头的声音 clangour; sound of striking stones

铿(鏗) kēng ㄎㄥ 拟声词 ***onomatopoeia***［铿锵］(—qiāng) 声音响亮而有节

K

奏(of sound) rhythmic and sonorous:～～悦耳 *sonorous and pleasant to the ear*

KONG ㄎㄨㄥ

空 ㊀ kōng ㄎㄨㄥ ❶里面没有东西或没有内容,不合实际的 empty; hollow; unrealistic:～房子 *empty house*|～碗 *empty bowl*|～话 *empty* (or *idle*) *talk*; *hollow words*|～想 *daydream*; *wishful thinking*|～谈 *empty* (or *idle*) *talk* [空洞]没有内容的 empty; hollow; devoid of substance:他说的话很～～。*His remarks are devoid of substance.* [空头]不发生作用的,有名无实的 nominal; phony:～～支票 *bad cheque*; *empty promise* [凭空]无根据 without foundation; groundless:～～捏造 *to make sth out of nothing*; *to fabricate* [真空]没有空气的空间 vacuum:～～管 *vacuum tube*|～～地带(战争时双方没有军队的地带) *no-man land* ❷无着落,无成效,无结果 in vain; for nothing:～跑了一趟 *to make a wasted trip*|～忙一阵 *to make fruitless efforts*; *to be busy for nothing*|落～ *to come to nothing*; *to fail*|扑了个～ *to fail to get what one wants* ❸天空 sky; air:～军 *air force*|航～ *aviation* [空间]一切物质存在和运动所占的地方 space [空气]包围在地球表面,充满空间的气体。是氮、氧和少量惰性气体及其他气体的混合物 air [喻] ***figurative*** 情势 atmosphere:～～紧张 *to have a tense atmosphere* ❹姓 Kong, a surname

㊁ kòng 见395页 see p395

崆 kōng ㄎㄨㄥ [崆峒](-tóng) **1** 山名,在甘肃省平凉 Kongtong Mountain, in Pingliang, Gansu Province **2** 岛名,在山东省烟台 Kongtong Island, in Yantai, Shandong Province

箜 kōng ㄎㄨㄥ [箜篌](-hóu)古代弦乐器,像瑟而比较小 *konghou*, an ancient plucked stringed instrument in China

孔 kǒng ㄎㄨㄥˇ ❶小洞,窟窿 hole; opening:鼻～*nostril*|针～ *pinhole* ❷很 very:需款～急 *to be in urgent demand for money* ❸通达 to lead to:交通～道 *transport* (or *traffic*) *junction*; *junction*

恐 kǒng ㄎㄨㄥˇ ❶害怕,心里慌张不安 to fear; to dread ([连] ***doublet*** —惧 fear|—怖 terror; horror):唯～完成不了任务 *to be afraid of not finishing the task* [恐吓](-hè)吓唬,威吓(hè) to threaten; to intimidate [恐慌] **1** 慌张害怕 scared; frightened **2** 危机,使人感觉不安的现象 panic:经济～～ *economic panic* ❷恐怕,表示疑虑不定或推测,有"或者"、"大概"的意思 perhaps; probably; maybe:～不可信。*I'm afraid it's untrustworthy.*|～

K

事出有因。*There is probably some reason for it.*

倥 kǒng ㄎㄨㄥˇ [倥偬](—zǒng) **1** 事情紧迫匆促 urgent; pressing **2** 穷困 impoverished

空 ㊁ kòng ㄎㄨㄥˋ ❶使空，腾出来 to leave empty or blank; to vacate: ～一个格 *to leave a space blank* | ～出一间房子 *to vacate a room* | 想法～出一些时间来 *to try to leave some time free* ❷闲着，没被利用的 vacant; unoccupied: ～房 *vacant room* | ～地 *unused land; space available* ❸(一儿)没被占用的时间或地方 unoccupied space or free time: 有～儿再来。*Come over again when you are free.* | 屋子里满得连一点儿～儿都没有。*The room is so fully occupied that there's no more space.* [空子](—zi) **1** 同"空㊁❸" same as 空㊁❸ **2** 可乘的机会 chance; opportunity: 钻～～ *to exploit an opportunity; to avail oneself of a loophole* ❹亏空，亏欠 to have a deficit; to be in debt

㊀ kōng 见394页 see p394

控 kòng ㄎㄨㄥˋ ❶告状，告发罪恶 to accuse; to charge (㊀ ***doublet*** —告 to accuse; to charge): 指～ *to accuse; to charge* | 被～ *to be accused of; to be charged with* [控诉] **1** 向法院起诉 to accuse **2** 当众诉说(坏人罪恶) to denounce; to condemn ❷节制，驾驭 to control; to dominate: 遥～ *remote control* [控制]支配，掌握，节制，调节 to control; to dominate ❸倒悬瓶、罐等，使其中的液体流净 to turn a bottle, a jar, etc, upside down to let the liquid inside trickle out

鞚 kòng ㄎㄨㄥˋ 带嚼子的马笼头 headstall

KOU ㄎㄡ

抠(摳) kōu ㄎㄡ ❶用手指或细小的东西挖 to dig out with a finger or sth pointed; to scratch: ～了个小洞 *to scratch out a small hole* | 把掉在砖缝里的豆粒～出来 *to dig out the beans from a crack between the bricks* ㊂ ***extension*** 向狭窄的方面深求 to study punctiliously; to delve into: ～字眼 *to pay too much attention to wording; to find fault with the choice of words* | 死～书本 *to delve mechanically into books* ❷雕刻(花纹) to carve ❸〈方 ***dialect***〉吝啬，小气 stingy; miserly: ～门儿 *stingy; miserly* | 这人真～。*He is a downright miser.*

眍(瞘) kōu ㄎㄡ [眍䁖](—lou)眼睛深陷 (of the eyes) to become (*or* be) sunken: ～～眼 *sunken eyes* | 他病了一场，眼睛都～～了。*His eyes were sunken after the illness.*

芤 kōu ㄎㄡ ❶古时葱的别名 (in ancient China) another name for scallion ❷芤脉，中医

称按起来中空无力的脉象，好像按葱管的感觉（in traditional Chinese medicine）hollow pulse

口 kǒu ㄎㄡˇ ❶嘴，人和动物吃东西的器官。有的也是发声器官的一部分。mouth（图见758页“头”picture on p758）［口舌］**1** 因说话引起的误会或纠纷 dispute（*or* misunderstanding）caused by what one says **2** 劝说、交涉或搬弄是非时说的话（of advice，negotiation or gossip）words：费尽～～ *to do a lot of talking* ［口吻］从语气间表现出来的意思 tone；note ❷容器通外面的部分（of a container）opening；mouth：缸～ *rim of a vat*｜碗～ *rim of a bowl*｜瓶～ *mouth of a bottle* ❸（－儿）出入通过的地方 entrance：门～ *doorway*；*gateway*｜胡同～儿 *entrance to an alley*｜河～ *estuary*｜海～ *seaport*｜关～ *pass* 特指长城的某些关口 some gateways of the Great Wall：～北 *the area north of the Great Wall*｜～蘑（*originally from the area north of the Great Wall*）*edible mushrooms*｜～马（*bred in the area north of the Great Wall*）*horse* ❹（－子、－儿）破裂的地方 opening；cut；hole：衣服撕了个～儿。*A hole was torn in the jacket.*｜伤～ *wound*｜决～ *to be breached*；*to burst* ❺锋刃 blade：刀还没有开～。*The knife hasn't its first edge yet.* ❻骡马等的年龄（骡马等的年龄可以由牙齿的多少和磨损的程度看出来）age of a draught animal：这匹马～还轻。*This horse is still young.*｜六岁～ *six years of age* ❼量词 ***quantifier*** **1** 用于人（used for people）：一家五～ *a family of five* **2** 用于牲畜（used for domestic animals）：一～猪 *a pig* **3** 用于器物（used for implements）：一～锅 *a pot*｜一～钟 *a bell*；*a clock*

叩 kòu ㄎㄡˋ ❶敲打 to knock；to tap：～门 *to knock at the door* ❷叩头（首），磕头，一种旧时代的礼节 kowtow，former Chinese custom of kneeling and bowing in worship or submission ❸询问，打听 to inquire；to ask：～问 *to make inquiries*

扣（❷ *釦）kòu ㄎㄡˋ ❶用圈、环等东西套住或拢住 to buckle；to button：把门～上 *to bolt up the door*｜把纽子～好 *to do up the buttons* ❷（－子、－儿）衣纽 button：衣～ *clothes button* ❸（－子、－儿）绳结 knot；loop：活～儿 *slipknot* ❹把器物口朝下放或覆盖东西 to place a container upside down；to cover with an inverted container：把碗～在桌上 *to place the bowl upside down on the table*｜用盆把鱼～上 *to cover the fish with a basin* ㊀ ***extension*** 使相合 to keep to the point：这句话～在题上了。*The words are relevant to the subject.* ❺扣留，关押 to detain；to take into custody：驾驶证被～了。*The driv-*

ing licence has been withdrawn.｜他被～了起来。*He was detained.* ❻从中减除 to deduct; to discount:九～(减到原数的百分之九十)*to give a 10 percent discount*｜七折八～(喻一再减除)*various deductions; at a great discount* [克扣]私行扣减,暗中剥削 to dock; to embezzle part of what should be issued to others:～～工资 *to dock sb's salary* ❼螺纹 screw thread:螺丝～ *screw thread*｜套～ *buckle* ㊀ ***extension*** 螺纹的一圈叫一扣(on a screw) one turn of the thread:拧上两～就行。*Driving in a screw in two twists will do.*

筘(**簆) kòu ㄎㄡˋ 织布机上的一种机件,经线从筘齿间通过,它的作用是把纬线推到织口 reed

寇 kòu ㄎㄡˋ ❶盗匪,侵略者 bandit; invader:敌～ *invading enemy* ❷敌人来侵略 to invade:～边 *to invade the border areas*

蔻 kòu ㄎㄡˋ [豆蔻]多年生草本植物,形似姜。种子暗棕色,有香味,可入药 cardamom (*Amomum*)

[豆蔻年华]指女子十三四岁的年龄(of a girl) age of 13 or 14

鷇 kòu ㄎㄡˋ 初生的小鸟 young bird; fledgling

KU ㄎㄨ

矻 kū ㄎㄨ [矻矻]努力、勤劳的样子 diligent; industrious

刳 kū ㄎㄨ 从中间破开再挖空 to hollow out:～木为舟 *to make a dugout canoe*

枯 kū ㄎㄨ 水分全没有了,干 dried up; withered (㊣ ***doublet*** 一干 dried up｜干一 withered):～树 *withered tree*｜～草 *withered grass*｜～井 *dry well* ㊙ ***figurative*** 肌肉干瘪(of muscle) dry and shrivelled:～瘦的手 *skinny hands* [枯燥]没趣味 dry and dull; uninteresting:～～乏味 *dry and dull*｜这种游戏太～～。*This kind of game is too dull.*

骷 kū ㄎㄨ [骷髅](—lóu)没有皮肉毛发的尸骨或头骨 skeleton

哭 kū ㄎㄨ 因痛苦悲哀等而流泪发声 to cry; to weep:痛～流涕 *to cry and shed bitter tears; to weep bitterly*｜～～啼啼 *to keep crying* (or *sobbing*)

圐(**啰) kū ㄎㄨ [圐圙](—lüè)(蒙 ***Mongolian***)围起来的草场。多用于地名(Kulüe, usually used in a place name) enclosed pasture:薛～～(在山西省山阴)*Xuekulüe* (*a place in Shanyin, Shanxi Province*)

窟 kū ㄎㄨ ❶洞穴 cave; hole:石～ *grotto; rock cave*｜狡兔三～。*A wily hare has three burrows—A crafty person has more than one hideout.* [窟窿](—long)孔,洞 hole; cavity ㊙ ***figurative*** 亏空,债务 deficit; debt:拉～～(借债) to

K

be in debt; to run into debt ❷某种人聚集的地方 den; lair: 贫民～*slum*|魔～ *den of monsters*

苦 kǔ ㄎㄨˇ ❶像胆汁或黄连的滋味,跟“甜”、“甘”相对 (the opposite of 甜 or 甘) bitter: ～胆 *gall bladder*|良药～口利于病。*Good medicine tastes bitter but it is effective.* [苦水] 味道不好的水,含硫酸钠、硫酸镁的水 bitter water: ～～井 *bitter water well* ㊗ ***figurative*** 藏在心里的苦楚 suffering; bitterness: 吐～～ *to pour out one's grievances* (or *suffering*) ❷感觉难受的,困苦的 painful; hard: ～境 *hard and painful circumstances; miserable plight*|～日子过去了。*Hard times are over.*|吃～耐劳 *to bear hardship and stand hard work* [苦主]被害人的家属 family of the victim in a murder case ❸为某种事物所苦 to suffer from; to be troubled by: ～夏 *to lose appetite and weight in summer*|从前他～于不识字。*He was handicapped by illiteracy in the past.* ❹有耐心地,尽力地 painstakingly; doing one's utmost: ～劝 *to advise* (or *exhort*) *earnestly*|～学 *to study hard*|～战 *to fight bitterly; to struggle* (or *work*) *hard*|～求 *to implore* ❺使受苦 to cause sb to suffer; to give sb a hard time: 这件事～了他。*This really gave him a hard time.*

K

库 kù ㄎㄨˋ ❶贮存东西的房屋或地方 warehouse; storehouse (㊀ ***doublet*** 仓— warehouse): 入～ *to put into storage*|水～ *reservoir* ❷电荷量单位名库仑的简称(符号 C) coulomb (C)

裤(*袴) kù ㄎㄨˋ 裤子 trousers (图见882页“衣”picture on p882)

绔 kù ㄎㄨˋ ❶同“裤”。古指套裤 same as 裤 (in ancient China) trouser legs worn over one's trousers ❷见774页“纨”字条“纨绔”(Wán—) see 纨绔 on p774

喾(嚳) kù ㄎㄨˋ 传说中上古帝王名 Ku, a legendary ruler of remote antiquity

酷 kù ㄎㄨˋ ❶残酷,暴虐、残忍到极点的 cruel; oppressive: ～刑 *torture; cruel punishment* ❷极,程度深 very; extremely: ～暑 *intense heat of summer*|～似 *to be the very image of; to resemble closely*|～爱 *to be very fond of*

KUA ㄎㄨㄚ

夸(誇) kuā ㄎㄨㄚ ❶说大话 to exaggerate; to overstate; to boast: ～口 *to boast; to talk big*|不要～大成就。*Don't exaggerate* (or *overstate*) *the achievements.*|～～其谈 *to indulge in exaggeration; to talk big* [夸张] 1 说得不切实际,说得过火 to exaggerate; to overstate **2** 一种修辞手法，用夸大的词句来形容事物 hyperbole ❷夸奖，用话奖励，赞扬 to praise：人人都～他进步快。*He is praised widely for his rapid progress.*

侉（**嗙）kuǎ ㄎㄨㄚˇ 口音与本地语音不同 with an accent other than the local one：他说话有点～。*He speaks with a slight accent.*

垮 kuǎ ㄎㄨㄚˇ 倒塌，坍塌 to collapse; to fall：房子被大水冲～了。*The house collapsed as the result of the flood.* ㊟ ***figurative*** 完全破坏 to break down：这件事让他搞～了。*He has caused the matter to fall through.*［垮台］崩溃瓦解 to collapse; to fall from power

挎 kuà ㄎㄨㄚˋ ❶胳膊弯起来挂着东西 to carry sth on the arm：他胳膊上～着篮子。*He carried a basket on his arm.* ❷把东西挂在肩头上或挂在腰里 to carry sth over one's shoulder or at one's side：肩上～着文件包 *to carry a briefcase on one's shoulder*

胯 kuà ㄎㄨㄚˋ 腰和大腿之间的部分 hip

跨 kuà ㄎㄨㄚˋ ❶抬起一条腿向前或旁边移动 to step; to stride：一步～过 *to stride over* (*or across*)｜～着大步 *to stride* ❷骑，两脚分在器物的两边坐着或立着 to sit (*or* stand) astride; to straddle：～在马上 *to sit astride a horse*｜小孩～着门槛。*The child is straddling the threshold.* ❸超越时间或地区之间的界限 to go beyond：～年度 *to straddle over the year; to go beyond the year*｜～两省 *to extend across two provinces* ❹附在旁边 attached to the side of sth：～院 *side courtyard*｜旁边～着一行(háng)小字。*A line of small characters is attached to the side.*

KUAI ㄎㄨㄞ

扻（**擓**）kuǎi ㄎㄨㄞˇ ❶搔，轻抓 to scratch：～痒痒 *to scratch an itch* ❷用胳膊挎着 to carry sth on one's arm：～着篮子 *to carry a basket on one's arm*

蒯 kuǎi ㄎㄨㄞˇ 蒯草，多年生草本植物，从生在水边，可织席 wool grass

会（**會**）㊁ kuài ㄎㄨㄞˋ 总计 to total［会计］**1** 管理和计算财务的工作 accounting **2** 管理和计算财务的人 accountant

㊀ huì 见298页 see p298

侩（**儈**）kuài ㄎㄨㄞˋ 旧指以拉拢买卖、从中取利为职业的人 (in former times) middleman; broker［市侩］唯利是图、庸俗可厌的人 sordid merchant

郐（**鄶**）kuài ㄎㄨㄞˋ 周代诸侯国名，在今河南省新密 Kuai, a princedom in the Zhou Dynasty, in today's

K

Xinmi, Henan Province: ～风 *folk songs of Kuai* | 自～以下(喻其余比较差的部分) *except so-and-so, none of them was worth a dime; those following are not worthy to be commented upon*

哙(噲) kuài ㄎㄨㄞˋ 咽下去 to swallow

狯(獪) kuài ㄎㄨㄞˋ 狡猾 cunning; sly: 狡～ *cunning; sly*

浍(澮) kuài ㄎㄨㄞˋ 田间水沟 field ditch

脍(膾) kuài ㄎㄨㄞˋ 细切的肉 finely sliced meat: ～炙人口(喻诗文等被人传诵) *to win universal praise; to enjoy great popularity*

鲙(鱠) kuài ㄎㄨㄞˋ 鲙鱼, 就是鳓(lè)鱼(i. e. 鳓鱼) Chinese herring

块(塊) kuài ㄎㄨㄞˋ ❶(一儿)成疙瘩或成团的东西 lump; piece: 糖～儿 *sugar lump* | 土～ *clod* | ～根 *root tuber* | ～茎 *stem tuber; tuber* ❷量词 ***quantifier***, piece; lump: 一～地 *a piece of land* | 一～钱 *one yuan* | 一～布 *a piece of cloth* | 一～肥皂 *a cake of soap*

快 kuài ㄎㄨㄞˋ ❶速度大, 跟"慢"相对(the opposite of 慢) fast; quick; rapid: ～车 *express train* (or *bus*) | 进步很～ *to make rapid progress* ❷赶紧, 从速 to hurry up; to make haste: ～上学吧! *Hurry away to school!* | ～回去吧! *Hurry back!* ❸副词 ***adverb***, 将, 就要, 接近 soon; to be about to: 天～亮了。*The day is breaking.* | 他～五十岁了。*He is going on 50.* | 我～毕业了。*I'll graduate soon.* ❹敏捷 quick-witted; nimble: 脑子～ *to have a quick mind; to be quick-witted* | 手疾眼～ *quick of eye and deft of hand; quick and sharp* ❺锐利 sharp; keen: 刀不～了, 该磨一磨。*The knife is no longer sharp. It needs sharpening.* | ～刀斩乱麻(喻办事爽利有决断) *to cut the Gordian knot* ❻爽快, 直截了当 straightforward; forthright: ～人～语 *straightforward talk from a straightforward man* | 心直口～ *open-hearted and outspoken; plain-spoken and straightforward* ❼高兴, 舒服 pleased; happy; gratified: ～乐 *happy; joyful* | ～活 *happy; merry; cheerful* | ～事 *pleasure; a joyful event* | 大～人心 *affording general satisfaction* | 身子不～ *to feel unwell*

筷 kuài ㄎㄨㄞˋ (一子)用竹、木、金属等制的夹饭菜或其他东西用的细棍儿 chopsticks

KUAN ㄎㄨㄢ

宽(寬) kuān ㄎㄨㄢ ❶阔大, 跟"窄"相对 wide; broad (㊟ ***doublet*** 一广 broad | 一阔 wide) (the opposite of 窄): 马路很～。*The road is very wide.* [宽绰](一

chuo) **1** 宽阔 spacious **2** 富裕 well-off ❷放宽,使松缓 to relax; to relieve: ～心 *to relieve sb's mind; to put sb's mind at rest* ㊀ ***extension*** **1** 解除,脱 to take off: 请～了大衣吧! *Take off your overcoat please!* **2** 延展 to extend: ～限几天 *to extend the deadline a few days; to give a few day's grace* **3** 宽大,不严 generous; lenient: ～容 *tolerant; lenient* | 从～处理 *to give lenient treatment* ❸物体横的方面的距离,长方形多指短的一边 width; breadth: 长方形的面积是长乘以～。*The area of a rectangle is its length multiplied by its width.* ❹宽裕,富裕 well-off: 手头不～ *to have little money to spare; to be in financial straits*

髋(髖) kuān ㄎㄨㄢ 髋骨,组成骨盆的大骨,左右各一,是由髂骨、坐骨、耻骨合成的。通称"胯骨"(commonly called 胯骨) hipbone

款(*欵) kuǎn ㄎㄨㄢˇ ❶法令、规定、条文里下分的项目(of an article in a legal document) section: 第几条第几～ *certain section in a certain article* ❷(一子)经费,钱财 sum of money; fund (㊥ ***doublet*** 一项 sum of money; fund): 存～ *to deposit; savings* | 拨～ *to allocate (or appropriate) money (or funds)* ❸器物上刻的字 characters inscribed on a utensil: 钟鼎～识(zhì) *inscriptions on ancient bronze objects* ㊀ ***extension*** (一儿)书画、信件头尾上的名字 name inscribed on a painting, a piece of calligraphy or a letter: 上～ *recipient's name* | 下～ *donor's name* | 落～(题写名字) *to sign one's name; signature* [款式] 格式,样子 pattern; style ❹诚恳 sincere: ～待 *to treat cordially; to entertain* | ～留 *to urge a guest to stay cordially* ❺敲打,叩 to knock; to tap: ～门 *to knock at the door* | ～关而入 *to knock at the door and enter* ❻缓,慢 slow; leisurely: ～步 *in leisurely steps* | 点水蜻蜓～～飞。*Dragonflies fly leisurely as they skim the water surface.*

窾 kuǎn ㄎㄨㄢˇ 空 empty

KUANG ㄎㄨㄤ

匡 kuāng ㄎㄨㄤ ❶纠正 to rectify; to correct: ～谬(miù) *to correct mistakes* | ～正 *to rectify* ❷救,帮助 to assist; to save: ～救 *to rescue; to relieve sb from evil* | ～助 *to help; to assist* ❸〈方 ***dialect***〉粗略计算,估算 to estimate roughly: ～算～算 *to estimate roughly*

劻 kuāng ㄎㄨㄤ [劻勷](－ráng)急促不安 anxious

诓 kuāng ㄎㄨㄤ 骗,欺骗 to deceive; to cheat; to hoax (㊥ ***doublet*** 一骗 to deceive; to cheat; to hoax): 别～人。*Don't try to deceive people.*

哐 kuāng ㄎㄨㄤ 拟声词 ***onomatopoeia***，撞击声 crash；bang：～啷（lāng）*crash；bang*｜～的一声脸盆掉在地上了。*The basin fell to the ground with a crash.*

洭 kuāng ㄎㄨㄤ 洭水，古水名，在今广东省 Kuangshui River，an ancient river in today's Guangdong Province

筐 kuāng ㄎㄨㄤ （－子、－儿）竹子或柳条等编的盛东西的器具 basket

狂 kuáng ㄎㄨㄤˊ ❶疯癫，精神失常 mad；crazy；insane（㊟ ***doublet*** 疯－ crazy｜癫－ insane）：～人 *madman*｜发～ *to go mad*（or *crazy*）❷任情地做，不用理智约束感情 unrestrainedly；wildly：～放不拘 *to behave wildly*｜～喜 *wild with joy*｜～欢 *revelry；carnival*［狂妄］极端自高自大 wildly arrogant；presumptuous ❸猛烈的，声势大的 violent；fierce：～风暴雨 *violent storm*｜～澜（大浪头）*raging*（or *huge*）*waves*｜～飙（急骤的大风）*hurricane*

诳 kuáng ㄎㄨㄤˊ 欺骗，瞒哄 to deceive；to cheat；to hoax：～语 *lie；falsehood*

夼 kuǎng ㄎㄨㄤˇ〈方 ***dialect***〉两山间的大沟。多用于地名（kuang，usually used in a place name）ravine：刘家～（在山东省烟台）*Liujiakuang*（*a place in Yantai，Shandong Province*）｜马草～（在山东省荣成）*Macaokuang*（*a place in Rongcheng，Shandong Province*）

邝（鄺）kuàng ㄎㄨㄤˋ 姓 Kuang，a surname

圹（壙）kuàng ㄎㄨㄤˋ ❶墓穴 open grave；coffin pit ❷旷野 open country［圹埌］（－làng）形容原野一望无际的样子（of open country）boundless

纩（纊）kuàng ㄎㄨㄤˋ 丝绵絮 silk floss（*or* wadding）

旷（曠）kuàng ㄎㄨㄤˋ ❶空阔 vast；spacious（㊟ ***doublet*** 空－ open and spacious）：～野 *wilderness；open country*｜地～人稀 *vast territory with a sparse population*［旷世］当代没有能够相比的 unparalleled（*or* matchless）in one's time；unique：～～功勋 *unique deeds* ❷心境阔大 free from worries and pettiness；relaxed：心～神怡 *carefree and happy*｜～达 *broad-minded；big-hearted* ❸荒废，耽搁 to neglect；to waste：～工 *to stay away from work without leave*｜～课 *to be absent from school without leave；to play truant；to stay away from school deliberately*｜～日持久 *to extend over days；to be prolonged*

矿（礦、*鑛）kuàng ㄎㄨㄤˋ（旧读 formerly gǒng）❶矿物，蕴藏在地层中的自然物质 mineral（*or* ore）deposit：铁～ *iron ore*｜煤～ *coal mine*｜油～ *oil deposit* ❷开采矿物的场所 mine：～井 *mine shaft；pit*｜～坑 *pit*｜下～

K

to go down into a mine

况（*況）kuàng ㄎㄨㄤˋ ❶情形 condition; situation：近～ *recent situation* ❷比，譬 to compare：以古～今 *to draw parallels from history* ❸文言连词 ***conjunction in classical Chinese***，表示更进一层 moreover; besides：～仓卒吐言，安能皆是？*Moreover, how can the words said in a hurry be always proper?*｜此事成人尚不能为，～幼童乎？*Even an adult cannot do this, let alone a child.*［况且］连词 ***conjunction***，表示更进一层 moreover; besides：这本书内容很好，～～也很便宜，买一本吧。*This book has very good substance and besides, it is very cheap; so buy it.*［何况］连词 ***conjunction***，表示反问(used in rhetorical questions) much less; let alone：小孩都能办到，～～我呢？*Even a child can do it, let alone me.*

贶 kuàng ㄎㄨㄤˋ 赐，赠 to give as a gift; to grant

框 kuàng ㄎㄨㄤˋ ❶门框，安门的架子 door frame（图见188页 picture on p188）❷(－子、－儿)镶在器物外围有撑架作用或保护作用的东西 frame：镜～儿 *mirror frame*｜眼镜～子 *rims of spectacles* ❸(－儿)周围的圈儿 circle ㊞ ***figurative*** 原有的范围，固有的格式 convention; set pattern：不要有～～儿。*Don't impose restrictions.* ❹加框 to draw a frame around：把这几个字～起来 *to frame these words* ❺限制，约束 to restrict; to restrain：不要～得太严，要有灵活性。*Don't make rigid restrictions; allow a certain latitude.*

眶 kuàng ㄎㄨㄤˋ（－子、－儿）眼的四周 eye socket; rim of the eye：眼～子发青 *to have livid rings round one's eyes*｜眼泪夺～而出。*Tears gushed from one's eyes.*

KUI ㄎㄨㄟ

亏（虧）kuī ㄎㄨㄟ ❶缺损，折(shé)耗 to lose; to have a deficit：月有盈～（圆和缺）。*The moon waxes and wanes.*｜气衰血～ *dual depletion of vital energy and blood*｜营业～本 *to lose money in business* ㊀ ***extension*** **1** 缺少，缺，欠 to be short of; to lack：功～一篑 *to fail to build a mound for want of one final basket of earth—to be just one step short of success*｜～秤 *to give short weight* (or *measure*); *to lose weight*｜理～ *to be in the wrong* **2** 损失 loss：吃～（受损失）*to suffer losses; to be at disadvantage*［亏空］(－kong) 所欠的钱物 debt; deficit：弥补～～ *to cover* (or *make up*) *a deficit* ❷亏负，对不起 to treat unfairly：～心 *to have a guilty conscience*｜人不～地，地不～人。*The land won't fail people as long as people don't fail the* *land*. ❸多亏,幸而 fortunately; thanks to:～了你提醒我,我才想起来。*I'd have forgotten about it if you hadn't reminded me*. ❹表示讥讽 (used to express irony):～你还学过算术,连这么简单的账都不会算。*You have studied arithmetic, so how come you can't even do simple accounts like this?*

刲 kuī ㄎㄨㄟ 割 to cut

岿(巋) kuī ㄎㄨㄟ 高大 towering; lofty:～然不动 *to stand one's ground steadfastly*

悝 kuī ㄎㄨㄟ 用于人名。李悝,战国时政治家 (Kui, used in a given name) Li Kui, a statesman of the Warring States Period

盔 kuī ㄎㄨㄟ ❶作战时用来保护头的帽子,多用金属制成 helmet:～甲 *suit of armour*|钢～ *steel helmet* ❷盆子一类的器皿 basin-like pottery container:瓦～ *earthen basin*

窥(*闚) kuī ㄎㄨㄟ 从小孔、缝隙或隐蔽处偷看 to peep; to spy:～探 *to spy upon; to pry into*|～伺 *to lie in wait for; to watch and wait*|～见真相 *to detect the truth*|管～蠡测(喻见识浅陋,看不清高深的道理) *to look at the sky through a bamboo tube and measure the sea with a calabash — to be restricted in vision and shallow in understanding*

奎 kuí ㄎㄨㄟ 星宿名,二十八宿之一 *kui*, the 15th of the 28 constellations

喹 kuí ㄎㄨㄟ [喹啉](— lín) 有机化合物,分子式 $C_6H_4(CH)_3N$,无色油状液体,有特殊臭味。工业上供制药和制染料 quinoline

蝰 kuí ㄎㄨㄟ 蝰蛇,一种毒蛇,生活在森林或草地里 viper (*Viperidae*)

逵 kuí ㄎㄨㄟ 通各方的道路 thoroughfare; road

馗 kuí ㄎㄨㄟ 同"逵" same as 逵

隗 ㊀ kuí ㄎㄨㄟ 姓 Kui, a surname

㊁ Wěi 见784页 see p784

魁 kuí ㄎㄨㄟ ❶为首的 chief; leading (㊥ **doublet** 一首 chief; head):罪～祸首 *chief criminal; arch-criminal* ❷大 tall and burly:身～力壮 *burly* [魁梧][魁伟]高大(指身体) big and tall ❸魁星,北斗七星中第一星。又第一星至第四星的总称 star at the tip of the bowl of the Big Dipper; general term for the four stars in the bowl

揆 kuí ㄎㄨㄟ ❶揆度(duó),揣测 to conjecture; to speculate:～情度理 *to consider and judge by common sense* ❷道理,准则 principle; criterion ❸掌管 to manage; to be in charge of:以～百事 *to be in charge of all things* ㊂ **extension** 旧称总揽政务的人,如宰

相、内阁总理等 former term for a person in charge of political affairs, such as a prime minister, etc:阁～ *premier*

葵 kuí ㄎㄨㄟˊ 植物名 plant name **1** 向日葵,一年生草本植物,花序盘状,花常向日。种子可吃,又可榨油 sunflower (*Helianthus annuus*) **2** 蒲葵,常绿乔木。叶可做蒲扇 Chinese fan palm (*Livistona chinensis*)

骙 kuí ㄎㄨㄟˊ [骙骙]形容马强壮(of a horse) strong

睽 kuí ㄎㄨㄟˊ 隔离 to separate; to part (㊥ **doublet** 一违 to separate; to part|一离 to leave each other; to part)

睽 kuí ㄎㄨㄟˊ ❶违背不合 to go against; to run contrary to ❷同"睽"same as 睽

[睽睽]张大眼睛注视 to stare; to gaze:众目～～ *all eyes gazing; in the full glare of publicity*

夔 kuí ㄎㄨㄟˊ ❶古代传说中一种奇异的动物,似龙,一足 *kui*, a dragon-like monopode animal in ancient legends ❷夔州,古地名,今重庆市奉节 Kuizhou, an ancient place in today's Fengjie, Chongqing

傀 kuǐ ㄎㄨㄟˇ[傀儡](—lěi)木偶戏里的木头人 puppet ㊥ **figurative** 徒有虚名,无自主权,受人操纵的人或组织 person or group whose actions are controlled by another:～～政府 *puppet government*

跬 kuǐ ㄎㄨㄟˇ 古代称半步,一只脚迈出的距离,相当于今天的一步 half a step in ancient China, equal to one step now:～步不离 *not to move even half a step from; to follow closely*

匮 kuì ㄎㄨㄟˋ 缺乏 deficient (㊥ **doublet** 一乏 short; deficient)〈古 **archaism**〉又同"柜"(guì) also same as 柜

蒉 kuì ㄎㄨㄟˋ 古时用草编的筐子 (in ancient China) straw basket

馈(*餽) kuì ㄎㄨㄟˋ 馈赠,赠送 to make a present of; to present a gift

溃 ㊀ kuì ㄎㄨㄟˋ ❶溃决,大水冲开堤岸 (of water) to burst a dyke (*or* dam) ❷散乱,垮台 to be defeated (*or* routed):～散 *to be defeated and dispersed*|敌军～败。*The enemy troops were defeated.*|～不成军 *to be utterly defeated* (or *routed*)|经济崩～ *economic collapse* [溃围]突破包围 to break through an encirclement ❸肌肉组织腐烂 to fester; to ulcerate:～烂 *to fester; to ulcerate* [溃疡](—yáng)黏膜或表皮坏死而形成的缺损 ulcer; canker

㊁ huì 见301页 see p301

愦 kuì ㄎㄨㄟˋ 昏乱,糊涂 muddle-headed; befuddled (㊥ **doublet** 昏一 muddle-headed; befuddled)

䙡 kuì ㄎㄨㄟˋ 〈方 **dialect**〉❶(一儿)用绳子、带子等拴成的结 knot:活～儿 *slipknot*|死～儿 *fast-knot* ❷拴,系(jì) to

K

tie; to fasten:～个襻儿 *to make (or tie) a knot*|把牲口～上 *to tie (or hitch) a draught animal (to sth)*

聩 kuì ㄎㄨㄟˋ 耳聋 deaf; hard of hearing:昏～(比喻不明事理) *decrepit and muddle-headed*|发聋振～(比喻用语言文字等方式唤醒愚昧麻木的人) *to rouse the deaf and awaken the unhearing — to enlighten the ignorant and the benighted*

篑 kuì ㄎㄨㄟˋ 古时盛土的筐子 (in ancient China) basket for holding earth:功亏一～ *to fail to build a mound for want of one final basket of soil — to be just one step short of success*

喟 kuì ㄎㄨㄟˋ 叹气 to sigh:感～ *to sigh with emotion*|～叹 *to sigh with deep emotion*

愧(*媿) kuì ㄎㄨㄟˋ 羞惭 ashamed; abashed ([连] **doublet** 惭～ ashamed; abashed):问心无～ *to have a good (or clear) conscience; to feel nothing to be ashamed of*|他真不～是劳动模范。*He is a worthy model worker.*

KUN ㄎㄨㄣ

坤(*堃) kūn ㄎㄨㄣ ❶八卦之一,符号是"☷",代表地 *kun*, one of the Eight Trigrams in the shape of ☷ that represents earth ❷称女性的 female; feminine:～鞋 *woman's shoes*|～车 *lady's (or woman's) bicycle*

注:"堃"多用于人名 note: 堃 usually used in a given name

昆(❹*崑) kūn ㄎㄨㄣ ❶众多 numerous [昆虫]节肢动物的一类,身体分头、胸、腹三部分,有三对足。蜂、蝶、蚤、蝗等都属昆虫类 insect ❷子孙,后嗣 offspring; progeny:后～ *descendants* ❸哥哥 elder brother:～弟 *brother*|～仲(*other people's*) *brothers* ❹[昆仑]山脉名,西起帕米尔高原,分三支向东分布 Kunlun Mountains

琨 kūn ㄎㄨㄣ 一种玉 a kind of jade

焜 kūn ㄎㄨㄣ 明亮 bright

鹍(**鵾) kūn ㄎㄨㄣ [鹍鸡]古书上说的一种像鹤的鸟(in ancient Chinese texts) crane-like bird

锟 kūn ㄎㄨㄣ [锟铻](—wú) 宝刀和宝剑名 name of a precious sword or a double-edged sword

醌 kūn ㄎㄨㄣ 一类有机化合物。含有两个双键的六元环状二酮(含两个羰基)结构。在维生素K和许多染料中有醌和它的衍生物 quinone

鲲 kūn ㄎㄨㄣ 传说中的一种大鱼 *kun*, an enormous legendary fish

裈 kūn ㄎㄨㄣ 古代称裤子为裈 ancient name for trousers

髡(**髠) kūn ㄎㄨㄣ 古代剃去头发的刑罚 ancient punishment of shaving a man's head

捆(*綑) kǔn ㄎㄨㄣˇ ❶用绳等缠紧、打结 to tie; to bind; to bundle up: 把行李～上 *to bundle up the luggage* ❷(一子、一儿)量词 ***quantifier***, 用于捆在一起的东西 bundle; bunch: 一～儿柴火 *a bundle of firewood* | 一～儿竹竿 *a bundle of bamboo poles* | 一～报纸 *a bundle of newspapers*

阃 kǔn ㄎㄨㄣˇ ❶门槛，门限 threshold ❷妇女居住的内室 woman's quarters; boudoir

悃 kǔn ㄎㄨㄣˇ 诚实，诚心 sincere

壸(壼) kǔn ㄎㄨㄣˇ 宫里面的路 path in a palace

困(❸❹睏) kùn ㄎㄨㄣˋ ❶陷在艰难痛苦里面 to be stranded; to be stricken: 为病所～ *to be afflicted with illness* ㊀ ***extension*** 包围住 to surround; to besiege: 把敌人～在城里 *to pin down the enemy in the city* ❷穷苦，艰难 difficult; poverty-stricken: ～难 *difficulty* | ～境 *difficult position; predicament* ❸疲乏，困倦 tired; sleepy: 孩子～了，该睡觉了。*The child is sleepy, and he should go to bed.* ❹〈方 ***dialect***〉睡 to sleep: ～觉 *to sleep*

KUO ㄎㄨㄛ

扩(擴) kuò ㄎㄨㄛˋ 放大，张大 to expand; to enlarge: ～音器 *loudspeaker; microphone; audio amplifier* | ～充机构 *to augment the organization* | ～大范围 *to extend (or widen) the scope*

括 ㊀ kuò ㄎㄨㄛˋ ❶扎，束 to tighten up; to contract: ～发(fà) *to tie up one's hair* | ～约肌(在肛门、尿道等靠近开口的地方，能收缩、扩张的肌肉) *sphincter* ❷包容 *to include* (㊟ ***doublet*** 包— to include): 总～ *to sum up*

㊁ guā 见245页 see p245

适 ㊁ kuò ㄎㄨㄛˋ 古同"适" same as 适 in ancient Chinese

㊀ shì 见685页 see p685

蛞 kuò ㄎㄨㄛˋ [蛞蝼](—lóu) 蝼蛄 mole cricket [蛞蝓](—yú)一种软体动物，身体像蜗牛，但没有壳，吃蔬菜或瓜果的叶子，对农作物有害 slug (*Limax*)

适 kuò ㄎㄨㄛˋ 疾速。多用于人名(*kuo*, usually used in a given name) fast

阔(*濶) kuò ㄎㄨㄛˋ ❶面积或范围宽广 wide; broad; vast (㊟ ***doublet*** 广— vast; wide): 广～天地 *vast world* | 高谈～论 *to talk bombastically; to indulge in loud and big talk* ㊀ ***extension*** 时间或距离长远 long in dis-

K

tance or time：～别 *to be long separated* ❷富裕的，称财产多生活奢侈的 wealthy；rich：～气 *luxurious；extravagant；lavish*｜～人 *rich* （or *wealthy*） *person；the rich*

廓 kuò ㄎㄨㄛˋ ❶物体的外缘 outline； contour：轮～ *outline；contour*｜耳～ *auricle；pinna* ❷空阔 wide；expansive：寥～ *vast；boundless* ❸扩大 to expand；to enlarge

［廓清］肃清，清除 to clarify；to clear away；to remove：～～道路上的障碍 *to clear away obstacles in the way*｜残匪已经～～。*The remaining bandits have been wiped out.*

K

L ㄌ

LA ㄌㄚ

垃 lā ㄌㄚ [垃圾](—jī)脏土或扔掉的破烂东西 garbage; rubbish; junk

拉 ㊀ lā ㄌㄚ ❶牵,扯,拽 to pull; to draw; to drag:~车 *to pull a cart* (or *carriage*)|把渔网~上来 *to draw up a fishing net* ㊊***extension*** **1** 使延长 to drag out; to draw out:~长声儿 *to drawl* **2** 拉拢,联络 to win over; to draw in:~关系 *to try to establish a relationship with sb; to cotton up to* [拉倒](—dǎo)算了,作罢 to forget about it; to let it be (*or* pass):他不来~~。*Let's forget about it if he doesn't come.* [拉杂]杂乱,没条理 rambling; jumbled; ill-organized ❷排泄粪便 to empty the bowels; to defecate:~屎 *to empty the bowels; to shit* ❸用车运 to transport by vehicle; to haul:~货 *to transport goods*|~肥料 *to transport fertilizer* ❹帮助 to give (*or* lend) a helping hand; to help:他有困难,应该~他一把 *We should give him a helping hand since he's in difficulty.* ❺牵累,牵扯 to drag in; to implicate:一人做事一人当,不要~上别人 *You should be responsible for your own actions and never implicate other people.* ❻使某些乐器发出声音 to play (a certain musical instrument):~小提琴 *to play the violin*|~二胡 *to play the erhu* ❼闲谈 to chat:~话 *to chat; to chitchat*|~家常 *to chat about trifles; to chitchat* ❽(la)放在某些动词后面,构成复合词。如:扒拉、趿拉、拨拉等(used after some verbs to form such compound words as 扒拉, 趿拉, 拨拉, etc)

[拉祜族](—hù—)我国少数民族,参看附表(see the appendix) the Lahu ethnic group, one of the ethnic minorities of China

[拉美]指拉丁美洲,美国以南的美洲地区 Latin America

㊁ lá 见410页 see p410

啦 ㊀ lā ㄌㄚ 拟声词 ***onomatopoeia***:呼~~ *flapping sound*|哇~乱叫 *to raise* (or *make*) *a hullabaloo; to cause an uproar*|叽哩呱~ *the sound of loud talk* (or *chatter*); *to talk noisily*

㊁ la 见411页 see p411

邋 lā ㄌㄚ [邋遢](—ta)不利落,不整洁 slovenly; sloppy; unkempt:他今天收拾得很整齐,不像过去那样~~了。

He's neatly-dressed today, not as slovenly as before.

旯 lá ㄌㄚˊ 见212页"旮"字条"旮旯"(gā—) see 旮旯 on p212

拉 ⊜lá ㄌㄚˊ 割,用刀把东西切开一道缝或切断 to slash; to slit; to cut:~了一个口子 *to get a cut*|~下一块肉 *to cut off a piece of meat*

⊖ lā 见409页 see p409

砬(**硦) lá ㄌㄚˊ 〈方 **dialect**〉砬子,大石块。多用于地名(la, usually used in a place name) big rock

剌 ⊜ lá ㄌㄚˊ 划破,割开 to slash; to slit; to cut; to gash 同"拉"(lá) same as 拉

⊖ là 见410页 see p410

喇 lǎ ㄌㄚˇ [喇叭](—ba) **1** 一种管乐器 trumpet or any similar brasswind instrument **2** 像喇叭的东西 loudspeaker; horn:汽车~~*horn* (*in a car*)|扩音~~*loudspeaker*

[喇嘛](—ma)(藏 **Tibetan**)蒙、藏佛教的僧侣,原义为"上人"(original meaning "superior") lama

剌 ⊖ là ㄌㄚˋ〈古 **archaism**〉违背常情、事理,乖张 perverse; disagreeable; brusque:乖~ *contrary to reason; perverse*|~谬 *to go against; to run counter to*

⊜ lá 见410页 see p410

瘌(**鬎) là ㄌㄚˋ [瘌痢](—lì)〈方 **dialect**〉秃疮,生在人头上的皮肤病 favus of the scalp

辣 là ㄌㄚˋ ❶姜、蒜、辣椒等的味道 peppery; hot; pungent ㊄ ***figurative*** 凶狠,刻毒 vicious; ruthless:毒~*sinister; diabolic; malignant*|心狠手~ *vicious and ruthless; extremely cruel and merciless* ❷辣味刺激(of smell or taste) to burn; to bite; to sting:~眼睛 *to make one's eyes sting*

落 ⊜ là ㄌㄚˋ 丢下,遗漏 to leave out; to be missing:丢三~四 *to leave this and that behind; to be always forgetting things*|~了一个字。*One word is missing.*|大家走得快,把他~下了。*He's left behind since everybody else walked so fast.* or *We went in a hurry and left him behind.*

⊖ luò 见478页 see p478

⊜ lào 见421页 see p421

腊(臘) ⊖ là ㄌㄚˋ ❶古代在夏历十二月举行的一种祭祀。*la*, an ancient practice of offering sacrifices to the gods in the 12th month of the lunar year ㊕***transfer*** 夏历十二月 the 12th lunar month:~八(夏历十二月初八)laba, *the 8th day of the 12th lunar month* (*on which, as a tradition, rice porridge with nuts and dried fruits is served*)|~肉(腊月或冬天腌制后风干或熏干的肉)(*made in the 12th lunar month or in winter*) *cured meat; bacon* ❷姓 La, a surname

⊜ xī 见801页 see p801

L

蜡(蠟) ㊀ là ㄌㄚˋ ❶动物、植物或矿物所产生的某些油质,具有可塑性,易熔化,不溶于水,如蜂蜡、白蜡、石蜡等 wax ❷蜡烛,用蜡或其他油脂制成的照明的东西,多为圆柱形,中心有捻,可以燃点 candle

㊁ zhà 见950页 see p950

镴 là ㄌㄚˋ 锡和铅的合金,可以焊接金属器物。也叫"白镴"或"锡镴"(also called 白镴 or 锡镴) solder

啦 ㊁ la・ㄌㄚ 助词 ***auxiliary***,"了"(le)"啊"(a)合音,作用大致和"了(le)❷"接近,但感情较为强烈(fusion of 了 and 啊, similar to 了, but with more stress):他已经来～。*He's already here.* |他早就走～。*He left a long time ago.*

㊀ lā 见409页 see p409

鞡 la・ㄌㄚ 见796页"靰"字条"靰鞡"(wù—)see 靰鞡 on p796

LAI ㄌㄞ

来(來) lái ㄌㄞˊ ❶由另一方面到这一方面,跟"去"、"往"相对(the opposite of 去 or 往) to come; to arrive:我～北京三年了。*I've been here in Beijing for three years.* |～信 *incoming letter; letter received* |～源 *source; origin* [来往]交际 contact; intercourse; dealing ❷表示时间的经过(used to express the passage of time) **1** 某一个时间以后 since; ever since:自古以～ *since ancient times; from time immemorial* |从～ *from past till present; always; at all times* |向～*always; all along* |这一年～他的进步很大。*He has made great progress this year.* **2** 现在以后 from now on; future:未～ *future* |～年(明年) *next year; the coming year* ❸表示约略估计的数目,将近或略超过某一数目(used to express an estimated number) approximately; about; or so:十～个 *about ten* |三米～长 *about three metres long* |五十～岁 *in one's fifties* ❹做某一动作(代替前面的动词)(used to substitute the preceding verb) to do:再～一个! *Encore!* |这样可～不得! *It won't do this way.* |我办不了,你～吧! *I cannot make it. You may have a try.* |我们打球,你～不～? *We're playing basketball. Will you join us?* ❺在动词前,表示要做某事(used before a verb to denote an intended action):我～问你。*Let me ask you.* |大家～想想办法。*Let's try to find a solution.* |我～念一遍吧! *Let me read it.* ❻在动词后,表示曾经做过(used after a verb to denote a past action):昨天开会你跟谁辩论～? *Whom did you argue with at yesterday's meeting?* |这话我哪儿说～? *How could I have said that?* [来着](—zhe)助词 ***auxiliary***,用于句尾,表示曾经发生过什

L

么事情(used at the end of a sentence to express sth has happened):刚才我们在这儿开会～～。*We were having a meeting here just now.*|我昨天上天津去～～。*I went to Tianjin yesterday.* ❼在动词后,表示动作的趋向(used after a verb to denote a movement towards the speaker):一只燕子飞过～。*A swallow is flying hither.*|大哥托人捎～了一封信。*Our eldest brother had someone bring a letter to us.*|拿～。*Bring it here.*|进～。*Come in.*|上～。*Come up.* or *Come upstairs.* ❽表示发生,出现(used to denote a happening or appearance):房屋失修,夏天一下暴雨,麻烦就～了。*The house is in bad repair. It will be in great trouble when the torrential rain comes in summer.*|问题～了。*Problems crop up.*|困难～了。*Difficulties have arisen.* ❾助词 ***auxiliary***,在数词"一"、"二"、"三"后,表示列举(used after 一, 二, 三 to denote enumeration):一～领导正确,二～自己努力,所以能胜利地完成任务。*For one thing, we had proper leadership; for another, we worked hard, hence we fulfilled the task successfully.* ❿助词 ***auxiliary***,诗歌中间用作衬字,或为了声音规律配合的音节(used as a syllable filler in ballads):正月里～是新春。*With the first lunar month comes the new year.*

莱(萊) lái ㄌㄞˊ 藜 lamb's-quarters (*Chenopodium album*)

[莱菔](—fú)萝卜 radish

崃(崍) lái ㄌㄞˊ 见613页"邛"字条"邛崃"(qióng—) see 邛崃 on p613

徕(徠) lái ㄌㄞˊ [招徕]把人招来 to solicit (customers or business); to attract:～～顾客 *to solicit (or appeal to) customers*

涞(淶) lái ㄌㄞˊ [涞水][涞源]地名,都在河北省 Laishui and Laiyuan, names of places both in Hebei Province

梾(棶) lái ㄌㄞˊ [梾木]落叶乔木,花黄白色,核果椭圆形。种子可榨油。木材坚硬、细致 Chinese dogwood (*Cornus kousa*)

铼(錸) lái ㄌㄞˊ 一种金属元素,符号 Re,可用来制电灯灯丝,化学上用作催化剂 rhenium (Re)

赉(賚) lài ㄌㄞˋ 赐,给 to grant; to bestow; to confer

睐(睞) lài ㄌㄞˋ ❶瞳人不正 squint ❷看,向旁边看 to look at; to glance:青～(指对人的喜欢或重视) *favour*

赖 lài ㄌㄞˋ ❶依赖,仗恃,倚靠 to depend; to rely:倚～ *to rely on; to depend on*|任务的提前完成有～于大家的共同努

力。*Only with our joint efforts can the task be fulfilled ahead of time.* ❷抵赖,不承认以前的事 to go back on one's word; to deny; to disavow:事实俱在,～是～不掉的。*Such being the facts, there's no use trying to deny them.* ❸诬赖,硬说别人有过错 to put the blame on (sb else); to shift the blame on (sb else):自己做错了,不能～别人。*If one has made mistakes by oneself, one should not try to shift the blame on someone else.* or *It's all your fault, so don't try to shift the blame on someone else.* ❹怪罪,责备 to blame:学习不进步只能～自己不努力。*You have only yourself to blame for making no progress in your studies.* ❺不好,劣,坏 no good; poor:今年庄稼长得真不～。*The crops are doing fine this year.* ❻留在某处不肯离开 to drag out one's stay (beyond what is necessary or welcome); to hang on where one does not belong:～着不走 *to hang on and refuse to leave*|每天～在家里,什么也不干 *to be at home everyday with nothing accomplished*

濑 lài ㄌㄞˋ 流得很急的水 swift current; rapids

癞 lài ㄌㄞˋ ❶癞病,即麻风 (i. e. 麻风) leprosy ❷像生了癞的 like favus of the scalp **1** 因生癣疥等皮肤病而毛发脱落的 loss of hair for favus of the scalp:～狗 *mangy dog*; *loathsome creature* **2** 表皮凹凸不平或有斑点的(of the outer skin) uneven or with freckles:～蛤蟆 *toad*|～瓜 *bitter gourd* (*Momordica charantia*)

籁 lài ㄌㄞˋ 古代的一种箫 lai, an ancient musical pipe ㊀ ***extension*** 孔穴里发出的声音,泛指声音 sound emitting from a hole; (in a broad sense) sound; noise:万～俱寂。*All is quiet and still.*

LAN ㄌㄢ

兰(蘭) lán ㄌㄢˊ 植物名。name of a plant **1** 兰花,常绿多年生草本植物,丛生,叶子细长,花味清香。有草兰、建兰等多种 orchid (*Orchidaceae*) **2** 兰草,多年生草本植物,叶子卵形,边缘有锯齿。有香气,秋末开花,可供观赏 fragrant thoroughwort (*Eupatorium fortunei*)

拦(攔) lán ㄌㄢˊ 遮拦,阻挡,阻止 to block; to bar; to hold back (㊥ ***doublet*** —挡 to block; to obstruct|阻— to bar the way; to stop; to block):～住他,不要让他进来。*Stop him. Don't let him in.*

栏(欄) lán ㄌㄢˊ ❶遮拦的东西 fence; railing; balustrade:木～ *wooden fence; paling*|花～ *railing with carved patterns* [栏杆]用竹、木、金属或石头等制成的遮拦物,也作"阑干"(also written as 阑干) railing; banisters;

L

balustrade:桥～～*railing of a bridge* ❷养家畜的圈(juàn) pen; shed; barn:牛～*cattle pen; cowshed* ❸书刊报章在每版或每页上用线条或空白分成的各个部分 column (in a newspaper or magazine):新闻～*news column*|广告～*advertisement* (or *ad*) *column*|每页分两～。*Each page has two columns.* ❹表格中分项的格子 column (of a form):前三～*first three columns*|备注～*remarks column* ❺专门用来张贴布告、报纸等的地方 board (for putting up notices or newspapers); billboard:报～*newspaper board*|宣传～*bulletin board*

岚 lán ㄌㄢˊ 山中的雾气 mountain haze (*or* mist)

婪 lán ㄌㄢˊ 贪爱财物 avaricious; greedy (㊀ ***doublet*** 贪— avaricious; greedy; rapacious):贪～成性 *to be avaricious by nature*

阑 lán ㄌㄢˊ ❶同"栏❶"same as 栏❶ [阑干] **1** 纵横交错,参差错落 crisscross; across:星斗～～(*the sky is*) *dotted with stars* **2** 同"栏杆" same as 栏杆 ❷同"拦"same as 拦 ❸尽,晚(of time) drawing to an end; late:夜～人静。*All is quiet in the dead of night.*
[阑珊]衰落,衰残 drawing to an end; waning
[阑入]进入不应进去的地方,混进 to enter a place that is forbidden to one; to trespass

谰 lán ㄌㄢˊ 抵赖,诬陷 to calumniate; to slander; to malign:驳斥侵略者的无耻～言 *to refute the invaders' audacious slander*

澜 lán ㄌㄢˊ 大波浪,波浪 billows; waves (㊀ ***doublet*** 波— huge waves; billows):力挽狂～*to exert one's utmost to stem a raging tide — to save a desperate situation*|推波助～*to make a stormy sea stormier; to add fuel to the flames*

斓 lán ㄌㄢˊ 见18页"斑"字条"斑斓"(bān—) see 斑斓 on p18

镧 lán ㄌㄢˊ 一种金属元素,符号 La,银白色,有延展性,在空气中燃烧发光。可制合金,又可做催化剂 lanthanum (La)

襕 lán ㄌㄢˊ 古代一种上下衣相连的服装 *lan*, an ancient Chinese costume with upper and lower garments connected together

蓝(藍) lán ㄌㄢˊ ❶蓼(liǎo)蓝,一年生草本植物,秋季开花,花落后结三棱形小果。从叶子提制的靛青可做染料,叶可入药 indigo plant (*Polygonum tinctorium*) ❷用靛青染成的颜色,像晴天天空那样的颜色 azure; blue [蓝本]著作所根据的原本 chief source of writing; original version of a book [蓝领]一般指从事生产、维修等体力劳动的工人 blue-collar worker

褴(襤) lán ㄌㄢˊ [褴褛](*蓝缕)(—lǚ)衣服破烂 ragged; shabby; tattered

篮(籃) lán ㄌㄢˊ (—子、—儿)用藤、竹、柳条等编的盛(chéng)东西的器具,上面有提梁 basket:菜~子 *vegetable basket; shopping basket*|网~*netting basket*

览(覽) lǎn ㄌㄢˇ 看,阅 to look at; to read (㊀ **doublet** 阅— to read):游~*to go sightseeing; to tour; to visit*|博~群书 *to read all kinds of books; to read widely*|一~表 *table; schedule; chart*

揽(攬、**擥) lǎn ㄌㄢˇ ❶把持 to grasp; to monopolize:大权独~*to arrogate all authority to oneself* ❷拉到自己这方面或自己身上来 to take on; to take upon oneself; to canvass:包~*to take on entirely; to undertake the whole thing*|~生意 *to canvass for business orders; to solicit business*|推功~过 *to owe one's achievements to others but take the blame on oneself* ❸搂,捆 to pull (*or* take) into one's arms; to fasten with a rope, etc:母亲把孩子~在怀里。*The mother clasped the child to her bosom.*|用绳子把柴火~上点儿。*Tie the firewood with a rope.*

缆(纜) lǎn ㄌㄢˇ ❶系船用的粗绳子或铁索 mooring rope; hawser; cable (㊀ **doublet**—绳 thick rope; cable):解~(开船)*to cast off; to cast loose* ㊁ **extension** 许多股绞成的粗绳 thick rope; cable:钢~*steel cable; wire rope* [电缆]用于电信或电力输送的导线,通常由一束相互绝缘的金属导线构成 power cable; cable ❷用绳子拴(船)to fasten (a boat) with a rope (*or* cable):~舟 *to moor a boat*

榄(欖) lǎn ㄌㄢˇ 见217页"橄"字条"橄榄"(gǎn—)see 橄榄 on p217

罱 lǎn ㄌㄢˇ ❶捕鱼或捞水草、河泥的工具 *lan*, a kind of rectangular net used for fishing, collecting water weeds, or dredging up river sludge, etc ❷用罱捞 to dredge up with *lan*:~河泥肥田 *to dredge up sludge from a river for fertilizer*

漤(**灠) lǎn ㄌㄢˇ ❶把柿子放在热水或石灰水里泡几天,去掉涩味 to soak a persimmon in hot water (*or* limewater) to take away its harsh, puckery taste ❷用盐腌(菜),除去生味 to cure (fresh vegetables) in salt

壈 lǎn ㄌㄢˇ [坎壈]困顿,不得志 in straits; full of frustrations; unsuccessful (in one's career)

懒(*嬾) lǎn ㄌㄢˇ ❶怠惰,不喜欢工作 lazy; indolent; slothful (㊀ **doublet**—惰 lazy; indolent):~汉 *lazybones; sluggard; idler*|好

吃～做要不得。*One must never be gluttonous and lazy.* [懒得](—de)不愿意,厌烦 not to feel like; to be tired of:我都～～说了。*I'm in no mood to talk about it.* ❷疲惫,困乏 sluggish; languid; listless:浑身发～ *to feel sluggish (or languid) all over*

烂(爛) làn ㄌㄢˋ ❶因过熟而变得松软 soft; pappy; mushy:稀粥～饭 *thin gruel and pulpy rice* | 蚕豆煮得真～。*How mushy the broad beans have been boiled!* [引]***extension*** 程度极深的 thoroughly; utterly:台词背得～熟 *to learn one's lines thoroughly (or off pat)* ❷东西腐坏 rot; fester; decay ([连]***doublet*** 腐— rot; decompose):桃和葡萄容易～。*Peaches and grapes are perishable.* [喻]***figurative*** 崩溃,败坏 corrupt; rotten:敌人一天天～下去,我们一天天好起来。*The enemy is deteriorating day by day, while we are getting better and better.* ❸破碎 worn-out; tattered ([连]***doublet*** 破— tattered; ragged; shabby):破铜～铁 *scrap iron and copper* | ～纸 *scrap paper* | 衣服穿～了。*The clothes are worn-out.* ❹头绪乱 messy; chaotic; disordered:～摊子 *shambles; awful mess*

[烂漫](*烂熳、*烂缦) **1** 色彩鲜明美丽 bright-coloured; brilliant:山花～～。*The mountain flowers are in full bloom.* **2** 坦率自然,毫不做作 unaffected; natural:天真～～ *innocent and naive; simple and unaffected*

滥(濫) làn ㄌㄢˋ ❶流水漫溢 to overflow; to flood; to inundate:解放前黄河时常泛～。*The Huanghe River often overflowed before 1949.* [滥觞](—shāng) [转]***transfer*** 事物的起源 origin; beginning ❷不加选择,不加节制 indiscriminate; without restraint; excessive:～交朋友 *to make friends indiscriminately and excessively* | ～用 *to abuse; to misuse; to use indiscriminately* | 宁缺毋～ *rather go without than have sth shoddy; to put quality before quantity* [引]***extension*** 浮泛不合实际 impractical; non-practical; hackneyed:陈词～调 *hackneyed and stereotyped expressions; stereotyped phrase*

LANG ㄌㄤ

啷 lāng ㄌㄤ 见129页"当"字条"当啷"(dāng—) see 当啷 on p129

郎 ㊀ láng ㄌㄤˊ ❶对年轻男子的称呼(term of address for a young man):～才女貌 *a talented man and a beautiful woman — perfect match* [引]***extension*** 对某种人的称呼(term of address for one's status):货～ *itinerant pedlar; migrant vendor* | 放牛～ *cowboy* ❷女子

称情人或丈夫(used by a woman in addressing her husband or lover) darling:情～*my love; lover*|～君 *my darling; husband* ❸古代官名 official title in ancient China:侍～*vice minister*［郎中］**1**〈方 ***dialect***〉医生 physician trained in herbal medicine; doctor **2** 古官名 official title in ancient China ❹姓 Lang, a surname

㊁ làng 见418页 see p418

廊 láng ㄌㄤˊ ❶(一子)走廊,有顶的过道 porch; corridor; veranda:游～*covered corridor; veranda*|长～*long corridor; gallery; arcade* ❷(一子)廊檐,房屋前檐伸出的部分,可避风雨,遮太阳 eaves of a veranda

嫏 láng ㄌㄤˊ ［嫏嬛］(一huán)即琅嬛,神话中天帝藏书的地方(i. e. 琅嬛)(in mythology) the library of the Lord of Heaven

榔 láng ㄌㄤˊ ［榔头］(一tou)锤子 hammer

［榔槺］(一kang)器物长(cháng)、大、笨重,用起来不方便 bulky; cumbersome; unwieldy

锒 láng ㄌㄤˊ ［锒头］旧同"榔头"same as 榔头 in former times

螂(*蜋) láng ㄌㄤˊ 见732页"螳"字条"螳螂"(táng一)、598页"蜣"字条"蜣螂"(qiāng一)、956页"蟑"字条"蟑螂"(zhāng一)、480页"蚂"字条"蚂螂"(mālang) see 螳螂 on p732, 蜣螂 on p598, 蟑螂 on p956, and 蚂螂 on p480

狼 láng ㄌㄤˊ 一种野兽,很像狗,嘴尖,耳直立,尾下垂,毛黄灰或黄褐色。性狡猾凶狠,昼伏夜出,能伤害人畜 wolf (*Canis lupus*)［狼狈］**1** 倒霉或受窘的样子 in a difficult position; in a tight corner:～～不堪 *in an extremely awkward situation; in dire straits* **2** 勾结起来(共同做坏事)to collude to do sth evil:～～为奸 *to act in collusion* (or *cahoots*) *with each other*［狼烟］古代报警的烽火,据说用狼粪燃烧 the smoke of wolves' dung burnt at border posts in ancient China to signal alarm [喻]***figurative*** 战火 flames of war; war:～～四起 *smoke of war rising from all sides; war alarms raised everywhere*

阆 ㊀láng ㄌㄤˊ 见384页"闶"字条"闶阆"(kāng一) see 闶阆 on p384

㊁ làng 见418页 see p418

琅(*瑯) láng ㄌㄤˊ ❶一种玉 a kind of jade［琅玕］(一gān)像珠子的美石 pearl-like stone［琅琅］拟声词 ***onomatopoeia***,金石相击的声音或响亮的读书声 tinkling (*or* jingling) sound or sound of reading aloud:书声～～*ringing sound of reading aloud* ❷洁白 spotlessly (*or* pure) white

锒 láng ㄌㄤˊ ［锒铛］(一dāng) **1** 铁锁链 iron chains **2** 形容金属撞击的声音

clanking (*or* clanging) sound

稂 láng ㄌㄤˊ 古书上指狼尾草(in ancient Chinese texts) Chinese pennisetum (*Pennisetum alopecuroides*)

朗 lǎng ㄌㄤˇ ❶明朗,明亮,光线充足 light; bright:晴～ *fine; sunny*|豁(huò)然开～*to be suddenly enlightened; to open up with a flash of understanding*|天～气清。*The sky is clear and the air is fresh.* ❷声音清楚、响亮(of voice) loud and clear:～诵 *to recite in elocution; to declaim*|～读 *to read aloud; to read loudly and clearly*

塱(**壆) lǎng ㄌㄤˇ [元塱]地名,在香港。今作"元朗"(now written as 元朗) Yuanlang (*or* Yuen Long), a place in Hong Kong

㮾 lǎng ㄌㄤˇ [㮾梨]地名,在湖南省长沙县 Langli, a place in Changsha County, Hunan Province

烺 lǎng ㄌㄤˇ 明朗 bright and clear

郎 ㊁làng ㄌㄤˋ [屎壳郎](—ke—)见598页"蜣"字条"蜣螂"(qiāngláng) see 蜣螂 on p598

㊀ láng 见416页 see p416

埌 làng ㄌㄤˋ 见402页"圹"字条"圹埌"(kuàng—) see 圹埌 on p402

莨 làng ㄌㄤˋ [莨菪](—dàng)多年生草本植物,开黄褐色微紫的花,全株有黏性腺毛,并有特殊臭味。有毒。根、茎、叶可入药(black) henbane (*Hyoscyamus niger*)

崀 làng ㄌㄤˋ [崀山]地名,在湖南省新宁 Langshan, a place in Xinning, Hunan Province

阆 ㊁làng ㄌㄤˋ [阆中]地名,在四川省 Langzhong, a place in Sichuan Province

㊀ láng 见417页 see p417

浪 làng ㄌㄤˋ ❶大波 wave; billow; breaker ([连] ***doublet*** 波一 wave):海～打在岩石上 *The sea waves crash against the rocks.* ❷像波浪起伏的东西 sth undulating like waves:声～ *clamour; din*|麦～*rippling wheat* ❸放纵 unrestrained; dissolute:～游 *to roam* (or *stroll*) *about aimlessly*|～费 *to waste; to squander; to be extravagant*

蒗 làng ㄌㄤˋ [宁蒗](níng—)彝族自治县,在云南省 Ninglang, Yi Autonomous County, in Yunnan Province

LAO ㄌㄠ

捞(撈) lāo ㄌㄠ ❶从液体里面取东西 to scoop up sth from liquid; to drag (*or* fish) for:～鱼 *to fish with a net; to net fish*|～面 *to strain noodles out of water*|打～*to take out of the water; to salvage* ❷用不正当的手段取得 to get by improper means; to wangle:～一把 *to reap handsome profit; to rake in*

profits

劳(勞) láo ㄌㄠˊ ❶劳动,人类创造物质或精神财富的活动 work; labour: 按～分配 *distribution according to work; to each according to his work* | 不～而获 *to reap without sowing; to profit by other people's toil* ❷疲劳,辛苦 fatigue; toil: 任～任怨 *to work hard and not be upset by any criticism; to bear the burden of office without complaint* ❸烦劳(polite term used when asking a favour of sb) to put sb to the trouble of [劳驾]请人帮助的客气话 excuse me; may I trouble you: ～～开门。*May I trouble you to open the door?* ❹慰劳,用言语或实物慰问 to bring gifts to, or send one's best wishes to, in recognition of services rendered; to reward: ～军 *to bring greetings and gifts to army units; to cheer up troops with gifts* ❺功勋 meritorious deed; service; exploit: 汗马之～ *distinctions won in battle; war exploits*

唠(嘮) ㊀ láo ㄌㄠˊ [唠叨](—dao)没完没了地说,絮叨 to be garrulous; to be talkative; to chatter: 人老了就爱～～。*As one grows old, one tends to be garrulous.*

㊁ lào 见421页 see p421

崂(嶗) láo ㄌㄠˊ 崂山,山名,在山东省青岛。也作"劳山"(also written as 劳山) Laoshan Mountain, in Qingdao, Shandong Province

铹(鐒) láo ㄌㄠˊ 一种人造的放射性元素(符号 Lr) lawrencium (Lr)

痨(癆) láo ㄌㄠˊ 痨病,中医指结核病,通常多指肺结核 consumptive disease; consumption; tuberculosis; TB

牢 láo ㄌㄠˊ ❶养牲畜的圈(juàn) animal enclosure; pen; fold: 亡羊补～(喻事后补救) *to mend the fold after a sheep is lost — Better late than never.* ㊗***transfer*** 古代称做祭品的牲畜(in ancient China) sacrificial animal; sacrifice: 太～(牛) *sacrificial ox* | 少～(羊) *sacrificial sheep* ❷监禁犯人的地方 prison; jail (㊌ ***doublet*** 监— prison; jail; cage): 坐～ *to be in jail; to be imprisoned* ❸结实,坚固 firm; fast; durable: ～不可破 *too strong to be broken; unbreakable; indestructible* | ～记党的教导 *to keep firmly in mind the Party's instructions*

[牢骚](—sao)烦闷不满的情绪 complaint; grumble; discontent: 发～～ *to grumble; to repine; to croak; to grouch*

醪 láo ㄌㄠˊ ❶浊酒 wine with dregs; undecanted wine [醪糟]江米酒 fermented glutinous rice; glutinous rice wine ❷醇(chún)酒 mellow wine

老 lǎo ㄌㄠˇ ❶年岁大,时间长 (of age) old; (of time) long **1** 跟"少"、"幼"相对(the opposite of 少, or 幼) old:～人 *old man or woman; the aged* 敬辞 ***polite***:吴～*revered old Wu*|范～*revered old Fan* **2** 陈旧的 old; dated; antiquated:～房子 *old house* **3** 经历长,有经验 seasoned; experienced; veteran:～手 *old hand; veteran*|～干部 *veteran cadre* **4** 跟"嫩"相对(the opposite of 嫩) overgrown; tough:～笋 *overgrown bamboo shoots*|菠菜～了。*The spinach is overgrown.*|～绿 *dark green* **5** 副词 ***adverb***,长久 for a long time; long:～没见面了 *haven't seen sb for a long time; long time no see* **6** 副词 ***adverb***,经常,总是 often; regularly; always:人家怎么～能提前完成任务呢? *Why can they always fulfil their tasks ahead of time?* **7** 原来的 original; former; same:～家 *old home; native place*|～脾气 *same old temperament*|～地方 *same old place* ❷副词 ***adverb***,极,很 extremely; very:～早 *very early*|～远 *very far away* ❸排行(háng)在末了的 last born; youngest:～儿子 *youngest son*|～妹子 *youngest sister* ❹词头 ***prefix*** **1** 加在称呼上(used before the address):～弟 *young man; young fellow*|～师 *teacher*|～张 *Lao Zhang* **2** 加在兄弟姊妹次序上(used to denote seniority between sisters and brothers):～大 *number one (in order of seniority); eldest child (in a family); the eldest*|～二 *number two; the second eldest* **3** 加在某些动植物名词上(used before names of some animals and plants):～虎 *tiger*|～鼠 *mouse; rat*|～玉米 *maize; corn*

佬 lǎo ㄌㄠˇ 成年男子(含轻视意 derogatory) man; guy; fellow:阔～*rich guy; moneybags*|乡巴～*country bumpkin; clodhopper*

荖 lǎo ㄌㄠˇ [荖浓溪]水名,在台湾省 Laonongxi River, in Taiwan Province

姥 ㊀ lǎo ㄌㄠˇ [姥姥][老老](—lao) **1** 外祖母(maternal) grandmother; (maternal) grandma **2** 旧时接生的女人(in former times) midwife

㊁ mǔ 见518页 see p518

栳 lǎo ㄌㄠˇ 见386页"栲"字条"栲栳"(kǎo—) see 栲栳 on p386

铑 lǎo ㄌㄠˇ 一种金属元素,符号 Rh,银白色,质地很坚硬,不受酸的侵蚀,用于制催化剂。铂铑合金可制热电偶 rhodium (Rh)

潦 ㊀ lǎo ㄌㄠˇ ❶雨水大 heavy rains ❷路上的流水,积水 running water or water puddles on the road

㊁ liáo 见445页 see p445

络 ㊁ lào ㄌㄠˋ 同"络㊀❶",用于一些口语词(used in some colloquial Chinese) same as 络㊀❶ [络子](—zi) **1** 用线绳结成的网状袋子 string bag **2** 绕线等的器具 spindle

㊀ luò 见478页 see p478

L

烙 ㊀ lào ㄌㄠˋ ❶用器物烫、熨 to brand; to iron: ～铁(tie) *flatiron; iron* | ～衣服 *to iron clothes* [烙印]在器物上烧成的做标记的印文 brand 喻 ***figurative*** 不易磨灭的痕迹 indelible mark; brand: 时代～～ *mark of the times* ❷放在器物上烤熟 to bake in a pan: ～饼 *to bake a round pancake*

㊁ luò 见478页 see p478

落 ㊂ lào ㄌㄠˋ 同"落㊀",用于一些口语词,如"落炕"、"落枕"等(used in some colloquial Chinese such as 落炕, 落枕) same as 落㊀

㊀ luò 见478页 see p478

㊂ là 见410页 see p410

酪 lào ㄌㄠˋ ❶用动物的乳汁做成的半凝固食品 junket: 奶～ *cheese* ❷用果实做的糊状食品 fruit jelly: 杏仁～ *almond jelly; apricot kernel cream* | 核桃～ *walnut cream (or paste)*

唠(嘮) ㊀ lào ㄌㄠˋ 〈方 ***dialect***〉说话,闲谈 to talk; to say; to chat: 来,咱们～一～。*Now, let's have a chat.*

㊁ láo 见419页 see p419

涝(澇) lào ㄌㄠˋ 雨水过多,被水淹,跟"旱"相对(the opposite of 旱) waterlogging: 防旱防～ *to take precautions against drought and waterlogging; to prevent both drought and waterlogging*

耢(耮) lào ㄌㄠˋ ❶用荆条等编成的一种农具,功用和耙(bà)相似。也叫"耱"(mò)、"盖"或"盖擦"(also called 耱, 盖 or 盖擦) *lao*, farm tool made from twigs of the chaste tree; leveller, similar to 耙 in use ❷用耢平整土地 to level land with a *lao*

嫪 lào ㄌㄠˋ 姓 Lao, a surname

LE ㄌㄜ

肋 ㊁ lē ㄌㄜ [肋脦](－de)(－te)(又 also lèi)衣裳肥大,不整洁(of clothes) sloppy and untidy: 瞧你穿得这个～～! *Look! How sloppy you are!*

㊀ lèi 见425页 see p425

仂 lè ㄌㄜˋ 〈古 ***archaism***〉余数 remainder

叻 lè ㄌㄜˋ [石叻]我国侨民称新加坡。也叫"叻埠"(also called 叻埠) Singapore, as referred to by overseas Chinese

泐 lè ㄌㄜˋ ❶石头被水冲击而成的纹理 veins in stones ❷同"勒㊀❹" same as 勒㊀❹: 手～(亲手写,旧时书信用语) (*term for letters in former times*) *to write in one's own hand*

竻 lè ㄌㄜˋ ❶竹根儿 bamboo root ❷一种竹子 a kind of bamboo

勒 ㊀ lè ㄌㄜˋ ❶套在牲畜头上带嚼子的笼头 headstall; halter ❷收住缰绳不使前进 to rein in: 悬崖～马 *to rein in at*

L

the brink of the precipice — to wake up to danger at the last moment ❸强制 to force; to compel; to coerce: ～令 *to compel (by legal authority)* | ～索 *to extort; to blackmail* ❹刻 to carve; to engrave; to inscribe: ～石 *to carve* (or *engrave*) *on a stone* | ～碑 *to carve* (or *inscribe*) *on a stone tablet*

㊁ lēi 见423页 see p423

簕 lè ㄌㄜˋ [簕竹]一种竹子 a kind of bamboo

鳓 lè ㄌㄜˋ 鳓鱼,又叫"鲙鱼"或"曹白鱼"。背青灰色,腹银白色(also called 鲙鱼 or 曹白鱼) Chinese herring

乐(樂) ㊀ lè ㄌㄜˋ ❶快乐,欢喜,快活 happy; cheerful; joyful: ～趣 *delight; pleasure; joy* | ～事 *pleasure; delight* | ～而忘返 *to enjoy oneself so much that one doesn't want to depart; to have a good time and forget all about going home* ❷乐于 to be glad to; to find pleasure in; to enjoy: ～此不疲 *to take delight in doing sth and never get tired of it; always enjoy it* [乐得]正好,正合心愿 readily take the opportunity to; to be happy to have the chance to; to be only too glad to: ～～这样做 *to be only too glad to do so* ❸(－子、－ㄦ)使人快乐的事情 pleasure; delight; fun: 取～ *to seek pleasure; to enjoy* (or *amuse*) *oneself; to make merry* | 逗～ㄦ *to try to make people laugh; to provoke laughter; to amuse* ❹笑 to laugh; to be amused: 可～ *funny; amusing* | 把一屋子人都逗～了。*Everyone in the room was greatly amused.* | 你～什么? *What are you laughing at?* ❺姓 Le, a surname

㊁ yuè 见929页 see p929

了 ㊁ le ·ㄌㄜ 助词 ***auxiliary*** ❶放在动词或形容词后,表示动作或变化已经完成 (used after verbs or adjectives to denote the completion of an action or a change): 买～一本书 *to have bought a book* | 水位低～两尺。*The waterline is two* chi *lower.* ❷用在句子末尾或句中停顿的地方,表示变化或出现新的情况(used at the end of a sentence or in the middle where there is a pause to express a happening or a new situation) **1** 指明已经出现或将要出现某种情况(used to denote that sth has happened or will happen): 下雨～。*It's raining.* | 明天就是星期日～。*It's Sunday tomorrow.* **2** 认识、想法、主张、行动等有变化(used to denote a change in knowledge, thoughts, stand or action): 我现在明白他的意思～。*I now understand what he means.* | 他今年暑假不回家～。*He won't go home this summer vacation.* | 我本来没打算去,后来还是去～。*I didn't intend to go at first, but later I went there anyway.* **3** 随假设的条件

转移(use to denote changing with the given condition):你早来一天就见着他～。*You could have seen him if you had come here one day earlier.* **4** 催促或劝止(used to urge or to persuade):走～,走～,不能再等～! *Let's go. We can't wait any longer.* |算～,不要老说这些事～! *That's enough! Talk no more about it.*

㊁ liǎo 见446页 see p446

饹 le·ㄌㄜ˙ 见271页"饸"字条"饸饹"(hé—)see 饸饹 on p271

LEI ㄌㄟ

勒 ㊁ lēi ㄌㄟ 用绳子等捆住或套住,再用力拉紧 to tie (*or* strap) sth tightly:～紧点,免得散(sǎn)了。*Fasten them tightly lest they should get loose.*

㊀ lè 见421页 see p421

累(縲) ㊂ léi ㄌㄟˊ ❶连缀或捆 to join together or tie up [累累]连续成串 clusters of; heaps of:果实～～*fruit growing in close clusters; fruit hanging heavy on the trees* [累赘](—zhui)多余的负担,麻烦 burdensome; cumbersome; troublesome:这事多～～. *What a troublesome matter!* ❷绳索 rope ❸缠绕 to bind; to wind

㊀ lěi 见424页 see p424

㊁ lèi 见425页 see p425

嫘 léi ㄌㄟˊ [嫘祖]人名,传说是黄帝的妃,发明了养蚕 Leizu, legendary wife of Yellow Emperor, who invented sericulture

缧 léi ㄌㄟˊ [缧绁](—xiè)捆绑犯人的绳索。借指牢狱 rope for binding prisoners; prison

雷 léi ㄌㄟˊ ❶云层放电时发出的强大声音 thunder:打～ *to thunder* |春～ *spring thunder* [雷霆]震耳的雷声 thunderclap; thunderbolt ㊗ ***figurative*** 怒气或威力 thunder-like power (*or* rage) great wrath:大发～～*to fly into a rage* (or *temper*)|～～万钧 *as powerful as a thunderbolt; powerful thun-derbolt* [雷同]打雷时,许多东西同时响应 to echo with thunder ㊗***figurative*** 随声附和,不该相同而相同 echoing what others have said ❷军事上用的爆炸武器 mine:地～(*land*) *mine*|鱼～*torpedo* [雷达](外 **loanword**)利用无线电波的反射原理制成的探测装置。广泛应用在军事、航空、航海、气象等方面 radar (radio detection and ranging)

擂 ㊀ léi ㄌㄟˊ ❶研磨 to grind; to pestle; to pound:～钵(研东西的钵)*mortar* ❷打 to hit; to beat:～鼓 *to beat a drum*|自吹自～(喻自我吹嘘) *to blow one's own trumpet* (*or horn*) — *to boast oneself; to boast smugly*

㊁ lèi 见425页 see p425

檑 léi ㄌㄟˊ 滚木,古代守城用的圆柱形的大木头,从城上推下打击攻城的人 rolling

logs

礌 léi ㄌㄟˊ 礌石，古代守城用的石头，从城上推下打击攻城的人(used by defenders of a besieged city) stone missiles; large stones

镭 léi ㄌㄟˊ 一种放射性元素，符号 Ra，银白色，有光泽，质软，能慢慢地蜕变成氦和氡，最后变成铅。医学上用镭来治癌症和皮肤病 radium (Ra)

羸 léi ㄌㄟˊ 瘦 thin; skinny; emaciated：身体～弱 *thin and weak; frail*

罍 léi ㄌㄟˊ 古代一种形状像壶的盛(chéng)酒的器具 ancient urn-shaped wine-vessel

耒 lěi ㄌㄟˇ 古代称犁上的木把(bà) wooden handle of an ancient plough［耒耜］(－sì)古代指耕地用的农具(in ancient China) plough-like farm tool

诔 lěi ㄌㄟˇ ❶古时叙述死者生平，表示哀悼的文章(in ancient China) funeral eulogy; elegy; dirge ❷做诔 to pronounce a eulogy over the dead

垒(壘) lěi ㄌㄟˇ ❶古代军中作防守用的墙壁 rampart：两军对～ *two armies confronting each other on the battlefield; two armies pitted against each other*｜深沟高～ *deep trenches and high ramparts; strong defence* ❷把砖、石等重叠砌起来 to build by piling up bricks, stones, etc.：～墙 *to build a wall*｜把井口～高一些 *to build the mouth of the well a bit higher*

累(❶纍) ㊀ lěi ㄌㄟˇ ❶重叠，堆积 to pile up; to accumulate; to gather：危如～卵 *as precarious as a pile of eggs; in imminent danger*｜积年～月 *month after month and year after year; for months and years*［累累］**1** 屡屡 again and again; many times **2** 形容累积得多 innumerable; countless：罪行～～ *to commit countless crimes; to have a long criminal history*［累进］照原数目多少而递增，如 2、4、8、16 等，原数越大，增加的数也越大 progression：～～率 *graduated rates*｜～～税 *progressive tax* ❷连累 to implicate; to involve：～及 *to implicate; to involve; to drag in*｜受～ *to get involved* (or *be implicated*) *on account of sb else*｜牵～ *to implicate; to involve* (*in trouble*)｜～你操心。*Sorry to get you involved in the trouble.* or *Sorry to cause you worry.*

㊁ lèi 见425页 see p425

㊂ léi 见423页 see p423

磊 lěi ㄌㄟˇ 石头多 heaps of stones; (of stones) innumerable

［磊落］心地光明坦白 open and upright

蕾 lěi ㄌㄟˇ 花骨朵，含苞未放的花 flower bud; bud：蓓～ *bud*｜花～ (*flower*) *bud*

儡 lěi ㄌㄟˇ 见405页"傀"字条"傀儡"(kuǐ－) see 傀儡 on p405

L

肋 ㊀ lèi ㄌㄟˋ 胸部的两旁 rib; costal region: 两～ *both sides of the chest* | ～骨 *rib; costa*

㊁ lē 见421页 see p421

泪(*淚) lèi ㄌㄟˋ 眼泪 tear; teardrop

类(類) lèi ㄌㄟˋ ❶种,好多相似事物的综合 kind; type; class (㊀**doublet** 种一kind; variety; category): 分～*to classify; to categorize* | ～型 *type; category; kind* | 以此～推 *to infer on the analogy of this; to deduce the rest from this* ❷类似,好像 to resemble; to be similar to: 画虎～犬 *to try to draw a tiger but end up with the likeness of a dog — to attempt sth overambitious and end in failure* ❸大率 generally; roughly: ～多如此。*It is generally the case.*

颣 lèi ㄌㄟˋ 缺点,毛病 defect; shortcoming; fault

累 ㊀ lèi ㄌㄟˋ ❶疲乏,过劳 tired; weary; fatigued: 我今天～了! *I'm tired today.* ❷使疲劳 to tire; to fatigue; to weary; to strain: 别～着他。*Don't get him worn out.*

㊀ lěi 见424页 see p424

㊂ léi 见423页 see p423

酹 lèi ㄌㄟˋ 把酒洒在地上表示祭奠 to pour a libation; to offer libation to

擂 ㊁ lèi ㄌㄟˋ 擂台,古时候比武的台子(in ancient China) platform for martial contests; arena: 摆～ *to set up a stage for contest and invite challengers; to take on challengers* (or *comers*) *one by one* | 打～ *to accept the challenge to join in a contest for supremacy in martial arts; to join in an open competition* (or *contest*)

㊀ léi 见423页 see p423

嘞 lei ·ㄌㄟ 助词 **auxiliary**, 跟"喽"(lou)相似 similar to the usage of 喽: 雨不下了,走～! *It has stopped raining. Let's go!*

LENG ㄌㄥ

塄 léng ㄌㄥˊ 田地边上的坡子。也叫"地塄"(also called 地塄) slope of an edge of a field

楞 léng ㄌㄥˊ 同"棱"same as 棱

崚 léng ㄌㄥˊ líng ㄌㄧㄥˊ (又 also líng) [崚嶒](—céng)形容山高(of mountains) high

棱(*稜) ㊀ léng ㄌㄥˊ (—子、—儿) ❶物体上不同方向的两个平面接连的部分 arris; edge: 见～见角 *angular* ❷物体表面上的条状突起部分 corrugation; ridge: 瓦～*rows of tiles on a roof* | 搓板的～儿 *ridges of a washboard*

㊁ líng 见455页 see p455

冷 lěng ㄌㄥˇ ❶温度低,跟"热"相对(the opposite of 热) cold; chilly (㊀**doublet** 寒

—cold; frigid)：昨天下了雪，今天真～。*It's really cold today for it snowed yesterday.* ❷寂静，不热闹 unfrequented; deserted; out-of-the-way：～清清 *cold and cheerless; quiet and deserted; desolate* | ～落 *unfrequented; desolate; deserted* ❸生僻，少见的 strange; rare; unpopular(㊀**doublet**—僻 rare; unfamiliar)：～字 *rarely used word; unfamiliar word* | ～货(不流行或不畅销的货物) *unpopular* (or *unattractive*) *goods; dull goods; unsalable goods* ❹不热情，不温和 cold in manner; frosty; icy：～脸子 *cold face* (or *expression*); *frosty look* | ～言～语 *sarcastic comments; ironical remarks* | ～酷无情 *unfeeling; cold-hearted; ruthless* [冷静]不感情用事 sober; calm; unruffled：头脑应该～～。*One should be cool-headed.* [冷笑]含有轻蔑、讥讽的笑 sarcastic smile (*or* grin); sneer ❺突然，意料以外的 unexpected; sudden; shot from hiding：～不防 *without warning; suddenly; unexpectedly* | ～枪 *gun shot from hiding; sniper's shot*

堎 lèng ㄌㄥˋ [长堎]地名，在江西省新建 Changleng, a place in Xinjian, Jiangxi Province

睖 lèng ㄌㄥˋ [睖睁](—zheng)眼睛发直，发愣 to stare blankly; to be in a daze; to be stupefied

愣 lèng ㄌㄥˋ ❶呆，失神 dumbfounded; stupefied; distracted：两眼发～ *to stare blankly* | 吓得他一～。*He was paralyzed with fear.* ❷鲁莽，说话做事不考虑对不对 rash; blunt; brusque：～头～脑 *rash; impetuous; reckless* | 他说话做事太～。*He speaks and acts too bluntly.* ㊀ **extension** 蛮，硬，不管行得通行不通 forcefully insist on sth without proof or basis; stubbornly; wilfully：～干 *to do things recklessly* (or *rashly*); *to persist in going one's own way whatever the cost* | 明知不对，他～那么说。*He knew it was wrong, but he still went ahead and said it.*

LI ㄌㄧ

哩 ㊂ li ㄌㄧ [哩哩啦啦]形容零零散散或断断续续的样子 scattered; sporadic; on and off：瓶子漏了，～～～～地洒了一地。*The bottle leaked and created a puddle on the floor.* | 雨～～～～下了一天。*It rained on and off all day.*

㊀ lǐ 见436页 see p436
㊁ lǐ 见430页 see p430

丽(麗) ㊁ lí ㄌㄧˊ [高丽] **1** 我国古族名，古国名。又称"高句(gōu)丽"(also called 高句丽) an ancient ethnic group and state in China **2** 朝鲜半岛历史上的王朝，即王

氏高丽(i. e. 王氏高丽) dynasty in the Korean Peninsula in history [丽水]地名,在浙江省 Lishui, a place in Zhejiang Province

㊀ lì 见434页 see p434

骊(驪) lí ㄌㄧˊ 纯黑色的马 pure black horse

鹂(鸝) lí ㄌㄧˊ [黄鹂]鸟名。羽毛黄色,从眼边到头后部有黑色斑纹。叫的声音很好听。也叫"黄莺" (also called 黄莺) oriole (*Oriolidae*)

鲡(鱺) lí ㄌㄧˊ 见485页"鳗"字条"鳗鲡" (mán—) see 鳗鲡 on p485

厘(*釐) lí ㄌㄧˊ ❶法定计量单位中十进分数单位词头之一,表示 10^{-2},符号 c (of measuring units) centi- (c) ❷计量单位名,10厘是1分 *li*, measuring unit, ten *li* is one *fen* **1** 市制长度,1厘约合0.333毫米 traditional unit for length, approximately equal to 0.333 mm **2** 市制地积,1厘约合6.667平方米 traditional unit for land area, approximately equal to 6.667m^2 **3** 市制重量,1厘合50毫克 traditional unit for weight, equal to 50 mg **4** 币制,10厘是1分 traditional unit for currency, equal to 0.1 *fen* ❸利率,年利率(lǜ)一厘按百分之一计,月利率一厘按千分之一计 traditional unit for interest, equal to 1% annual interest or 0.1% monthly interest ❹治理,整理 to put in order; to administer; to regulate: ～正 *to make corrections; to correct; to revise* | ～定 *to collate and stipulate* (*rules and regulations, etc*)

喱 lí ㄌㄧˊ 见212页"咖"字条"咖喱"(gā—) see 咖喱 on p212

狸 lí ㄌㄧˊ (—子)哺乳动物,又叫"山猫",毛棕黄色,有黑色斑纹。毛皮可制衣物(also called 山猫) leopard cat

离(離) lí ㄌㄧˊ ❶相距,隔开 off; away; from (㊟**doublet** 距—to be apart (or away) from; to be at a distance from):北京～天津一百多公里。*Beijing is more than a hundred kilometres from Tianjin.* | ～国庆节很近了。*National Day is drawing near.* or *It'll soon be National Day.* ❷离开,分开,分别 to leave; to part from; to be away from:～家 *to leave home; to depart* (or *be away*) *from home* | ～婚 *to divorce* | ～散 (*of relatives*) *to be dispersed; to be scattered about; to be separated from one another* [离间](—jiàn)从中挑拨,使人不团结 to sow discord; to play people off against each other; to drive a wedge between [离子]原子或原子团失去或得到电子后叫作离子。失去电子的带正电,叫作正离子或阳离子;得到电子的带负电,叫作负离子或阴离子 ion ❸

缺少 without; independent of: 发展工业～不了钢铁。*Industry cannot develop without steel.* ❹八卦之一，符号是"☲"，代表火 *li*, one of the Eight Trigrams, its form being ☲, representing fire

[离奇]奇怪的，出乎意料的 strange; odd; fantastic

蓠（蘺） lí ㄌㄧˊ [江蓠]红藻的一种，暗红色，分枝不规则。生在浅海湾中。可用来制造琼脂 Gracilaria confervoides

漓（❷灕） lí ㄌㄧˊ ❶见449页"淋"字条"淋漓"(lín—) see 淋漓 on p449 ❷漓江，水名，在广西壮族自治区桂林 Lijiang River, in Guilin, Guangxi Zhuang Autonomous Region

缡（**褵） lí ㄌㄧˊ 古时妇女的佩巾 (in ancient China) woman's veil: 结～（古时指女子出嫁）(*of a woman in ancient China*) *to get married*

篱（籬） lí ㄌㄧˊ 篱笆，用竹、苇、树枝等编成的障蔽物 hedge; fence: 竹～茅舍 *thatched cottage with bamboo fence; bamboo hedge and thatched hut*

醨 lí ㄌㄧˊ 味淡的酒 weak (*or* light) wine

梨（*棃） lí ㄌㄧˊ 梨树，落叶乔木，花五瓣，白色。果实叫梨 pear (*Pyrus*)

犁（*犂） lí ㄌㄧˊ ❶耕地的农具 plough ❷用犁耕 to work with a plough; to plough: 用新式犁～地 *to plough the fields with a new type of plough*

嫠 lí ㄌㄧˊ 寡妇 widow: ～妇 *widow*

黎 lí ㄌㄧˊ （又 also chí）见89页 chí see chí on p89

黎 lí ㄌㄧˊ 众 multitude; host: ～民 *the common people; the multitude; the populace* | ～庶 *the common people; the multitude*

[黎明]天刚亮的时候 dawn; daybreak

[黎族]我国少数民族，参看附表 (see the appendix) the Li ethnic group, one of the ethnic minorities of China

藜（❷*蔾） lí ㄌㄧˊ ❶一年生草本植物，开黄绿色花，嫩叶可吃。茎长(zhǎng)老了可以做拐杖 lamb's quarters (*Chenopodium album*) [藜藿]藜和藿都是野菜，泛指粗劣的食物 plain and coarse food ❷见313页"蒺"字条"蒺藜"(jíli) see 蒺藜 on p313

黧 lí ㄌㄧˊ 黑里带黄的颜色 dark and sallow

罹 lí ㄌㄧˊ ❶遭受灾难或不幸 to suffer from; to meet with: ～难(nàn) *to die in a disaster* (or *an accident*); *to be murdered* ❷忧患，苦难 suffering; hardship

蠡 ㊀ lí ㄌㄧˊ 贝壳做的瓢 calabash shell serving as a dipper; dipper: 以～测海(喻见识浅薄) *to measure the water in the sea with a calabash shell — to make an appraisal in the light of limited knowledge*

㊁ lǐ 见431页 see p431

劙 lí ㄌㄧˊ 割开 to pierce; to cut; to slash

礼(禮) lǐ ㄌㄧˇ ❶由一定社会的道德观念和风俗习惯形成的为大家共同遵行的仪节 ceremony; rite; ritual: 典～ *ceremony; celebration* | 婚～ *wedding ceremony; wedding* ❷表示尊敬的态度或动作 courtesy; etiquette; manners: 敬～ *to give a salute; to salute* | 有～貌 *to be courteous; to be polite* ㊞***extension*** 以礼相待 to treat with courtesy; to be courteous to: ～贤下士 (*of a ruler or a high minister*) *to treat worthy men with courtesy; to treat scholars and men of virtue with courtesy* ❸礼物,用来表示庆贺或敬意 gift; present: 五一献～ *gift for May Day* | 一份～ *a gift; a present* | 大～包 *generous present; big packet of gifts*

李 lǐ ㄌㄧˇ 李(子)树,落叶乔木,春天开花,花白色。果实叫李子,熟时黄色或紫红色,可吃 plum (*Prunus*)

里(❹❺裏、❹❺*裡) lǐ ㄌㄧˇ ❶市制长度单位,1里为150丈,合500米 *li*, a traditional unit of length, equal to 150 *zhang*, and equivalent to 500 metres ❷居住的地方 residence; dwelling place: 故～ *native place; hometown* | 返～ *to return to one's native place* (or *hometown*); *to return home* | 同～(现在指同乡) *fellow villager, townsman, or provincial* ❸街坊(古代五家为邻,五邻为里)(a *li* was made up of five *lin* while a *lin* was made up of five families in ancient China) neighbourhood: 邻～ *neighbourhood* | ～弄 *lanes and alleys; neighbourhood* ❹(一子、一儿)衣物的内层,跟"表"、"面"相对 (the opposite of 表 or 面) lining; inside (of clothing): 衣裳～儿 *lining of a garment* | 被～ *underneath side of a quilt* | 鞋～子 *shoe lining* | 箱子～儿 *lining of a box* (or *chest, case, etc*) ❺里面,内部,跟"外"相对 (the opposite of 外) inner; inside; in: 屋子～ *inside the room* | 手～ *in one's hands* | 碗～ *in one's bowl* | 箱子～面 *in* (or *inside*) *the suitcase* ㊞ ***extension*** 一定范围以内 within a certain limit (or place): 夜～ *at night; in the night* | 这～ *here* | 哪～ *where* [里手] **1** (一儿)靠里的一边,靠左边 (of a running vehicle or machine) left-hand side **2**〈方 ***dialect***〉内行 expert; old hand

俚 lǐ ㄌㄧˇ 民间的,通俗的 vulgar; rustic; unrefined: ～歌 *rustic* (or *folk*) *song* | ～语

L

slang

哩 ⊜ lǐ ㄌㄧˇ 也读作 yīnglǐ。英美制长度单位名，1 哩等于 5 280 呎，合 1 609 米。现写作"英里"（also yīnglǐ and now written as 英里）mile, a unit of length used in Britain and US, 1 mile equals 5280 feet, or 1609 metres

㊀ li 见436页 see p436

㊂ lī 见426页 see p426

浬 lǐ ㄌㄧˇ 也读作 hǎilǐ。计量海洋上距离的长度单位，1 浬合 1 852 米。现写作"海里"。符号 n mile，只用于航程（also pronounced hǎilǐ and now written as 海里）nautical (*or* sea) mile, a measure of distance at sea, 1 nautical mile equals 1 852 metres

娌 lǐ ㄌㄧˇ 见 990 页"妯"字条"妯娌"（zhóuli）see 妯娌 on p990

理 lǐ ㄌㄧˇ ❶物质组织的条纹 texture; grain (in wood, stone, skin, etc): 肌～ *skin texture* | 木～ *grain of wood; wood grain* ❷道理，事物的规律 reason; logic; truth: 讲～ *to listen to reason; to talk reasonably* | 合～ *conforming to reason; logical; reasonable* 特指自然科学 natural science: ～科 *science (as a field of study)* | ～学院 *college of science* [理论] **1** 人们从实践中概括出来又在实践中证明了的关于自然界和人类社会的规律性的系统的认识 theory; principle; doctrine: 基础～～ *basic theory* **2** 据理争论 to argue; to debate; to reason: 跟他～～一番 *to have a debate with him* [理念] 思想，观念。强调对目标、原则、方法等的认定和追求 idea; concept: 投资～～ *investment concept* | 营销～～ *marketing concept* [理性] 把握了事物内在联系的认识阶段，也指判断和推理的能力 rational faculty; reason ❸管理，办 to manage; to run; to administer: ～家 *to keep house; to manage family affairs* | 管～工厂 *to manage (or direct, supervise) a factory* ㊀***extension*** 整理，使整齐 to put in order; to tidy up: ～发 *to get a haircut; to go and have one's hair done; to go to the barber's (or hairdresser's)* | 把书～一～。*Put the books in order.* ❹对别人的言语行动表示态度 to pay attention to; to make a gesture or speak to; to acknowledge: 答～ *to acknowledge (sb's greeting, etc); to respond; to answer* | ～睬 *to pay attention to; to show interest in; to heed* | 置之不～ *to ignore; to pay no attention (or heed) to* [理会]（—huì）**1** 注意 to take notice of; to pay attention to: 这两天只顾开会，也没～～这件事。*I've been busy with a conference for the past two days and paid no attention to it.* **2** 领会 to understand; to comprehend: 这个意思大家都能～～。*Everybody can understand it.*

L

锂 lǐ ㄌㄧˇ 一种金属元素，符号Li，银白色，质软，是金属中比重最轻的，可制合金 lithium (Li)

鲤 lǐ ㄌㄧˇ 鲤鱼，生活在淡水中，体侧扁，嘴边有长短须各一对，肉可吃 carp (*Cyprinus carpio*)

逦（邐） lǐ ㄌㄧˇ 见887页"迤"字条"迤逦"(yǐ—) see 迤逦 on p887

澧 lǐ ㄌㄧˇ 澧水，水名，在湖南省北部，流入洞庭湖 Lishui River, in the north of Hunan Province, which flows into Dongting Lake

醴 lǐ ㄌㄧˇ 甜酒 sweet wine

鳢 lǐ ㄌㄧˇ 鱼名，又叫"黑鱼"。身体圆筒形，头扁，背鳍和臀鳍很长。生活在淡水底层，可以养殖，但性凶猛，对其他鱼类有危害(also called 黑鱼) northern snakehead (*Channa argus*)

蠡 ㊀ lǐ ㄌㄧˇ 蠡县，地名，在河北省 Lixian, a county in Hebei Province

㊁ lí 见429页 see p429

力 lì ㄌㄧˋ ❶力量，力气，动物筋肉的效能 physical strength：身强～壮(*of a person*) *strong; tough; sturdy* ㊞ ***extension*** **1** 身体器官的效能 power; strength; ability：目～ *vision; sight*|脑～*mental power; brains; intelligence* **2** 一切事物的效能 power; efficacy：电～*electric power*|药～*efficacy of a drug or medicine*|浮～*floating power; buoyancy*|说服～ *persuasive* (or *convincing*) *power; persuasion*|生产～ *productive forces; productivity* ❷用极大的力量，尽力 to do all one can; to make every effort; to exert oneself：～战 *to fight with all one's might; to fight gallantly*|据理～争 *to argue strongly on just grounds; to advance* (or *put forward*) *a strong argument* ❸改变物体运动状态的作用叫力。力有三个要素，即力的大小、方向和作用点 force

荔（*茘） lì ㄌㄧˋ ［荔枝］常绿乔木，果实也叫荔枝，外壳有疙瘩，果肉色白多汁，味甜美 litchi; lychee (*Litchi chinensis*)

历（歷、❹曆、❹*厤） lì ㄌㄧˋ ❶经历，经过 to go through; to undergo; to experience：～尽甘苦 *to have experienced all sweet and bitter; to go through hardships and difficulties*|～时十年 *to have lasted ten years* ❷经过了的 all previous (years, occasions, sessions, etc)：～年 *previous years; over the years*|～代 *successive* (or *past*) *dynasties*|～史 *history* ［历来］副词 ***adverb***，从来，一向 always; constantly; all through the ages：中国人民～～就是勤劳勇敢的。*The Chinese people have always been industrious and courageous.* ［历历］一个一个

很清楚的 distinctly; clearly:～～在目 *to come clearly into view; to leap up vividly before the eyes* ❸遍,逐一 covering all; one by one:～览 *to travel and see; to view during a tour*|～访名家 *to visit celebrities one by one* ❹历法,推算年、月、日和节气的方法 calendric system; calendar:阴～*lunar calendar*|阳～*solar calendar* ㊀**extension** 记录年、月、日、节气的书、表、册页 calendar:日～*calendar*|～书 *almanac*

坜(壢) lì ㄌㄧˋ 坑。多用于地名(li, usually used in a place name) hole; pit:中～(在台湾省)*Zhongli, a place in Taiwan Province*

苈(藶) lì ㄌㄧˋ 见751页"葶"字条"葶苈"(tíng—)see 葶苈 on p751

呖(嚦) lì ㄌㄧˋ [呖呖]拟声词 ***onomatopoeia***, warble of birds:～～莺声。*The orioles are warbling.*

屴(嶇) lì ㄌㄧˋ [屴崌山](—jū—)山名,在江西省乐平 Liju Mountain, in Leping, Jiangxi Province

沥(瀝) lì ㄌㄧˋ ❶液体一滴一滴地落下 to drip; to trickle:滴～*dripping of rain or water* [沥青]蒸馏煤焦油剩下的黑色物质,可用来铺路 pitch; asphalt; bitumen [呕心沥血]形容费尽心思 to shed one's heart's blood; to take infinite pains:为培养下一代～～～～*to take great pains in nurturing the younger generation* ❷液体渗出来的点滴 drop:余～*last drops; dregs; heeltap*

枥(櫪) lì ㄌㄧˋ 马槽 manger:老骥伏～,志在千里。*An old steed in the stable still aspires to gallop a thousand li — an old hero still cherishes high aspirations.*

疬(癧) lì ㄌㄧˋ 见477页"瘰"字条"瘰疬"(luǒ—)see 瘰疬 on p477

雳(靂) lì ㄌㄧˋ 见560页"霹"字条"霹雳"(pī—)see 霹雳 on p560

厉(厲) lì ㄌㄧˋ ❶严格,切实 strict; rigorous; rigid:～行节约 *to practise strict economy*|～禁 *to forbid (or prohibit, ban) strictly* ❷严厉,严肃 stern; severe; serious:正言～色 *in a grave tone and with a severe look* ❸凶猛 fierce; violent; ferocious [厉害][利害](—hai) **1** 凶猛 fierce; terrible; ferocious:老虎很～～。*Tigers are very fierce.* **2** 过甚,很 intense; severe; terrible:疼得～～*to have a severe pain*|闹得～～*to make a great fuss* ❹古同"砺"same as 砺 in ancient Chinese:秣马～兵 *to sharpen the weapons and feed the horses — to make preparations for war*

励(勵) lì ㄌㄧˋ 劝勉,奋勉 to encourage; to urge:～志 *to be determined to fulfil*

one's aspirations; to be bent on realizing one's aspirations | 奖～*to award; to reward*

砺(礪) lì ㄌㄧˋ ❶粗磨刀石 whetstone ❷磨(mó) to whet; to sharpen: 砥～*to temper; to encourage*

蛎(蠣) lì ㄌㄧˋ 牡(mǔ)蛎,一种软体动物,身体长卵圆形,有两面壳,生活在浅海泥沙中,肉味鲜美。壳烧成灰,可入药。也叫"蚝"(háo) (also called 蚝) oyster (*Ostreidae edulis*)

粝(糲) lì ㄌㄧˋ 粗糙的米 coarse grain; unpolished rice

疠(癘) lì ㄌㄧˋ ❶瘟疫 pestilence; plague ❷恶疮 sore; ulcer

立 lì ㄌㄧˋ ❶站 to stand: ～正 *to stand at attention* ⑤|**extension** 竖着,竖起来 to set or stand sth up; to make sth upright; to erect: ～柜 *clothes closet; wardrobe; hanging cupboard* | 把伞～在门后头。*Stand the umbrella behind the door.* [立场] **1** 认识和处理问题时所处的地位和所抱的态度 position; stand; standpoint **2** 特指阶级立场 class stand: ～～坚定 *to be steadfast in one's stand; to take a firm stand* [立方] **1** 六面都是正方形的形体 cube **2** 数学上称一数自乘三次 cube [立体]几何学上称有长、宽、厚的形体 solid ❷做出,定出 to set up; to establish **1** 建立,设立 to establish; to found; to set up: ～碑 *to set up* (or *erect, build*) *a monument* | 建～工厂 *to erect* (or *set up, build*) *a factory* **2** 建树 to make a contribution; to contribute: ～功 *to make contributions; to render meritorious service* **3** 制定 to draw up; to conclude: ～合同 *to conclude* (or *sign*) *a contract* **4** 决定 to make up one's mind; to make decisions: ～志 *to be resolved; to be determined* ❸存在,生存 to exist; to live; to grow: 自～*to stand on one's own feet; to earn one's own living; to support oneself* | 独～*independent; on one's own* ❹立刻,立时,马上,即刻 immediately; instantaneously; at once: ～奏奇效 *to produce immediate results; to feel the effect immediately* | 当机～断 *to make a prompt decision; to decide quickly*

莅(*蒞、*涖) lì ㄌㄧˋ 到 to arrive; to be present (⑥**doublet** 一临 to arrive; to be present): ～会 *to be present at a meeting*

粒 lì ㄌㄧˋ ❶(一儿)成颗的东西,细小的固体 grain; granule; pellet: 米～儿 *grains of rice* | 豆～儿 *beans* | 盐～儿 *grains of salt; salt grains* [粒子]构成物体的比原子核更简单的物质,包括电子、质子、中子、光子、介子、超子和各种反粒子等 particle ❷量词 ***quantifier***,多用于小的东西(usually

L

used for granular objects)：一～米 *a grain of rice*｜两～丸药 *two pills*｜三～子弹 *three bullets*

笠 lì ㄌㄧˋ 斗笠，用竹篾等编制的遮阳挡雨的帽子 large bamboo or straw hat for shielding sunlight and rain

吏 lì ㄌㄧˋ 旧时代的官员(in former times) official; mandarin：贪官污～*corrupt officials; venal officials*

丽(麗) ㊀ lì ㄌㄧˋ ❶好看，漂亮 beautiful; pretty：美～*beautiful; good-looking*｜秀～*beautiful; pretty; handsome*｜壮～*majestic; magnificent; glorious*｜富～*splendid; gorgeous*｜风和日～*The wind is mild and the sun is bright.* ❷附着 to attach oneself to; to depend on; to rely on (㊥**doublet** 附一 to attach oneself to; to depend on)

㊁ lí 见426页 see p426

郦(酈) lì ㄌㄧˋ 姓 Li, a surname

俪(儷) lì ㄌㄧˋ 相并的，对偶的 paired; parallel：～词 *form of literary writing marked by antithesis or complementarity*｜～句(对偶的文辞) *parallel sentences; couplet* ㊀**extension** 指属于夫妇的 of husband and wife：～影(夫妇的合影) *photograph of a couple; wedding picture*

利 lì ㄌㄧˋ ❶好处，跟"害"、"弊"相对(the opposite of 害 or 弊) advantage; benefit (㊥**doublet** 一益 interest; benefit)：这件事对人民有～。*It benefits the people.* or *It is good for the people.*｜个人～益服从集体～益。*The interests of the individual must be subordinated to those of the collective.* ❷使得到好处 to do good to; to benefit：毫不～己，专门～人 *to bring benefit* (*or do good*) *to other people without any thought of oneself; to be utterly devoted to others without any thought of self* [利用]发挥人或事物的作用，使其对自己方面有利 to make use of; to use; to utilize：废物～～*to make use of waste materials; to convert waste into useful materials*｜～～他的长处 *to take advantage of his merits*｜～～这个机会 *to take this opportunity* ❸顺利，与主观的愿望相合 favourable; smooth; convenient：吉～*good fortune; good luck*｜敌军屡战不～。*The enemy troops met with repeated setbacks.* ❹利息，贷款或储蓄所得的子金 interest：本～两清 *to have paid back both principal and interest; the capital and interest have been cleared up*｜放高～贷是违法的行为。*It's illegal to practise usury.* ❺利润 profit：暴～*sudden huge profits; exorbitant profits*｜薄～多销 *small profits and quick returns; small profits and good sales* ❻刀口快，针尖锐 sharp; keen:

～刃 *sharp knife* (or *sword*) | ～剑 *sharp sword* | ～口(喻善辩) *to have a glib* (or *sharp*) *tongue — to be able to argue effectively* [利害] **1** (—hài)利益和损害 advantages and disadvantages; gains and losses: 不计～～ *regardless of gains or losses* **2** (—hai)同"厉害" same as 厉害 [利落](—luo) [利索](—suo) **1** 爽快,敏捷 agile; nimble; dexterous: 他做事很～～。*He's very agile at his work.* **2** 整齐 neat; orderly: 东西收拾～～了。*Everything has been put in good order.*

俐 lì ㄌㄧˋ 见452页"伶"字条"伶俐"(líng—) see 伶俐 on p452

莉 lì ㄌㄧˋ 见514页"茉"字条"茉莉"(mòli) see 茉莉 on p514

猁 lì ㄌㄧˋ 见662页"猞"字条"猞猁"(shē—) see 猞猁 on p662

痢(❷ **鬁) lì ㄌㄧˋ ❶痢疾,传染病名,按病原体的不同,主要分成杆菌痢疾和阿米巴痢疾。症状是发烧、腹痛、粪便中有血液、脓或黏液。通常把粪便带血的叫赤痢,带脓或黏液的叫白痢 dysentery ❷见410页"瘌"字条"瘌痢"(là—) see 瘌痢 on p410

例 lì ㄌㄧˋ ❶(—子)可以做依据的事物 example; instance: 举一个～子 *to give* (or *take*) *an example; to cite an instance* | 史无前～ *without precedent in history; unprecedented; unparalleled* ❷规定,体例 rule; regulation: 条～ *regulations; rules; ordinances* | 发凡起～ *to initiate a rule; to write an introduction; to set* (or *give*) *an example to others* [例外]不按规定的,和一般情况不同的 exception: 全体参加,没有一个～～。*Everybody should attend the meeting. There is no exception.* | 遇到～～的事就得灵活处理。*We should be flexible in dealing with exceptions.* ❸合于某种条件的事例 case; instance: 病～ *case of illness; case* | 案～ *case* ❹按条例规定的,照成规进行的 regular; routine: ～会 *regular* (or *routine*) *meeting* | ～行公事 *routine; routine business; mere formality* (or *routine*)

戾 lì ㄌㄧˋ ❶罪过 crime; sin ❷乖张,不顺从 perverse; unreasonable: 乖～ *perverse; unreasonable; disagreeable* | 暴～ *ruthless and tyrannical; cruel and fierce* ❸〈古 **archaism**〉至 to come to; up to: 鸢(yuān)飞～天,鱼跃于渊。*The hawk soars in the heavens, and the fish dives in the deep.*

唳 lì ㄌㄧˋ 鸟鸣 cry of a bird: 鹤～ *cry of a crane*

隶(隸、*隷) lì ㄌㄧˋ ❶附属,属于 to be subordinate to; to be affiliated to (*or* with); to be under (㊀ ***doublet***—属 to be subordinate to; to be under the jurisdiction or command of):直～中央 *to be under the direct control of the central government* ❷封建时代的衙役 yamen runner:～卒 *government servants; yamen runner* ❸隶书,汉字的一种字体,相传是秦朝程邈所创 official script, an ancient style of calligraphy allegedly created by Cheng Miao in the Qin Dynasty ❹旧时地位低下而被奴役的人(in former times) person in servitude:奴～*slave*|仆～*servant*

栎(櫟) ㊀ lì ㄌㄧˋ 俗叫"柞(zuò)树"或"麻栎"。落叶乔木,花黄褐色,果实叫橡子或橡斗。木材坚硬,可制家具,供建筑用。树皮可鞣皮或做染料。叶子可喂柞蚕。另有一种栓皮栎,树皮质地轻软,富有弹性,是制造软木器物的主要原料(popularly called 柞树 or 麻栎) oak (*Quercus*)

㊁ yuè 见929页 see p929

轹(轢) lì ㄌㄧˋ 车轮碾轧 to crush with cartwheels; to run over ㊞ ***figurative*** 欺压 to bully; to oppress

砾(礫) lì ㄌㄧˋ 小石,碎石 gravel; shingle:砂～*gravel; grit*|瓦～*rubble; debris*

跞(躒) ㊀ lì ㄌㄧˋ 走,跨越 to walk about; to leap:骐骥一～,不能千里。*Even a fine horse cannot cover a thousand* li *in one leap.*

㊁ luò 见477页 see p477

鬲(**䰛) ㊀ lì ㄌㄧˋ 古代炊具,形状像鼎而足部中空 *li*, ancient cooking tripod with hollow legs

㊁ gé 见225页 see p225

栗(❷*慄) lì ㄌㄧˋ ❶栗(子)树,落叶乔木,果实叫栗子,果仁味甜,可以吃。木材坚实,供建筑和制器具用,树皮可供鞣皮及染色用,叶子可喂柞蚕 Chinese chestnut (*Castanea mollissima*) ❷发抖,因害怕或寒冷而肢体颤动 to tremble; to shudder:不寒而～*to shiver all over though not cold—to tremble with fear*

傈 lì ㄌㄧˋ [傈僳族](—sù—)我国少数民族,参看附表 (see the appendix) the Lisu ethnic group, one of the ethnic minorities of China

溧 lì ㄌㄧˋ [溧水][溧阳]地名,都在江苏省 Lishui and Liyang, names of places both in Jiangsu Province

篥 lì ㄌㄧˋ 见41页"觱"字条"觱篥"(bì—) see 觱篥 on p41

詈 lì ㄌㄧˋ 骂 to scold; to curse; to berate:～骂 *to scold; to abuse; to curse*

哩 ㊀ li ·ㄌㄧ 助词 ***auxiliary***, 同"呢㊁"same as 呢㊁

㊁ lǐ 见430页 see p430

㊂ lī 见426页 see p426

蜊 li ·ㄌㄧ 蛤蜊。参看224页"蛤"(gé)(see 蛤 on p224) clam

璃(*瓈) li ·ㄌㄧ 见53页"玻"字条"玻璃"

(bō—)、459页"琉"字条"琉璃"(liú—)see 玻璃 on p53 and 琉璃 on p459

LIA 㐅丨丫

俩(倆) ㊀ liǎ 㐅丨丫ˇ 两个(本字后面不能再用"个"字或其他量词)(this character should never be followed by 个 or other quantifiers) two:夫妇～*man and wife*|买～馒头 *to buy two* mantou

㊁ liǎng 见442页 see p442

LIAN 㐅丨ㄢ

奁(奩、*匳、*匲) lián 㐅丨ㄢˊ 女子梳妆用的镜匣 toilet case for women [妆奁]嫁妆 dowry; trousseau

连 lián 㐅丨ㄢˊ ❶相接,连续 to link; to join; to connect (㊂ ***doublet*** 一接 to join; to link):天～水,水～天。*The sky and the water seem to merge into each other.*|骨肉相～*as close as flesh and blood*|～成一片 *to join together*|接～不断 *in succession; uninterrupted*|～年 *in successive years; in consecutive years; for years running* [连词]连接词、词组或句子的词,如"和"、"或者"、"但是"等(used to connect words, phrases, clauses or sentences, such as 和, 或者, 但是, etc) conjunction [连枷][连耞](—jiā)打谷用的农具 flail [连忙]副词 ***adverb***,急忙 hastily; hurriedly; promptly:～～让坐 *to be eager to offer one's seat to sb* [连绵](*联绵)接续不断 continuous; unbroken; uninterrupted [连夜]当天夜里赶着(做某事)(to do sth) all through the night; the same night:～～赶造 *to run the production line all through the night* ❷带,加上 including (㊂ ***adverb*** 一带 incidentally; in passing):～说带笑 *talking and laughing*|～根拔 *to tear up by the roots; to uproot*|～我一共三个人。*There are three people, including me.* ❸介词 ***preposition***,就是,即使(后边常用"都"、"也"跟它相应)(used correlatively with 都 or 也) even:他从前～字都不认得,现在会写信了。*He can write letters now but he couldn't even read a word before.*|精耕细作,～荒地也能变成良田。*Intensive and meticulous farming can change even a wasteland into a fertile land.* ❹军队的编制单位,是排的上一级(military unit) company

莲 lián 㐅丨ㄢˊ 多年生草本植物,生浅水中。叶子大而圆,叫荷叶。花有粉红、白色两种。种子叫莲子,包在倒圆锥形的花托内,合称莲蓬。地下茎叫藕。种子和地下茎都可以吃。也叫"荷"、"芙蕖"(fúqú)或"菡萏"(hàndàn)(also called 荷, 芙蕖 or 菡萏) lotus (*Nelumbo nucifera*)

L

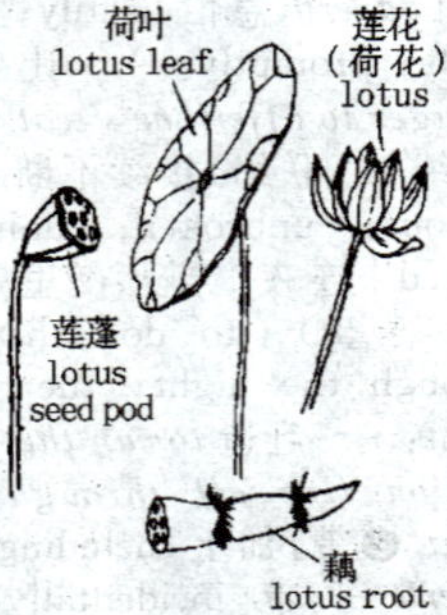

莲 lotus

涟 lián ㄌㄧㄢˊ ❶水面被风吹起的波纹 ripples：～漪(yī) ripples ❷泪流不止（叠 ***reduplication***）continuous flow of tears：泪～～ *tears flowing continuously* ［涟洏］（－ér）形容涕泪交流 weeping copiously

鲢 lián ㄌㄧㄢˊ 鲢鱼，又叫“白鲢”。鳞细，腹部色白，体侧扁，肉可以吃（also called 白鲢）silver carp（*Hypophthalmichthys molitrix*）

怜（憐） lián ㄌㄧㄢˊ ❶可怜，同情 to sympathize with；to pity：同病相～。*Fellow sufferers sympathize*（or *commiserate*）*with each other.*｜我们决不～惜坏人。*We should never take pity on evil people.* ❷爱 to love tenderly：爱～*to show*（or *have*）*tender affection for*

帘（❷簾） lián ㄌㄧㄢˊ （－子、－儿）❶旧时店铺做标志的旗帜 flag（*or* banner）used as a shop sign in former times ❷用布、竹、苇等做的遮蔽门窗的东西 curtain；(hanging) screen

联（聯） lián ㄌㄧㄢˊ ❶联结，结合 to ally oneself with；to unite；to combine：工农～盟 *alliance of workers and peasants；worker-peasant alliance*｜～席会议 *joint conference*（or *meeting*）［联络］接洽，彼此交接 to get in touch with；to come into contact with［联合国］1945年10月24日成立的国际组织。中国是创始国之一。总部设在美国纽约。联合国宪章规定，其主要宗旨为维护国际和平与安全，发展国际友好关系，促进经济文化等方面的国际合作 United Nations (UN) ❷（－儿）对联，对子 antithetical couplet：上～*the first line of a couplet*｜下～*the second*（or *complementary*）*of a couplet*｜挽～*elegiac couplet*｜春～*Spring Festival couplets*

廉 lián ㄌㄧㄢˊ ❶品行正，不贪污 honest and clean：～洁 *honest and clean；incorruptible*｜清～*honest and upright；fair and square；free from corruption* ❷便宜，价钱低 low in price；inexpensive；cheap（㊣ ***doublet*** 低－cheap；low）：～价 *cheap；low-priced；inexpensive* ❸察考，访查 to examine；to inspect：～得其情 *to know facts through investigation；to learn the truth after investigation；to examine and get to the bottom of something*

濂 lián ㄌㄧㄢˊ 濂江,水名,在江西省南部 Lianjiang River, in the south of Jiangxi Province

臁 lián ㄌㄧㄢˊ 小腿的两侧 two sides of the shank:~骨 *shank bones* | ~疮 *ulcer on the shank*

镰(*鎌) lián ㄌㄧㄢˊ 镰刀,收割谷物和割草的农具 sickle

蠊 lián ㄌㄧㄢˊ 见191页“蜚”字条“蜚蠊”(fěi—)see 蜚蠊 on p191

琏 liǎn ㄌㄧㄢˇ 古代宗庙盛黍稷的器皿 *lian*, vessel used to hold grain at an ancestral temple in ancient China

敛(斂) liǎn ㄌㄧㄢˇ ❶收拢,聚集 to hold back; to keep back; to collect (㊥ **doublet** 收— to restrain oneself; to pull in one's horns):~足(收住脚步,不往前进) *to check one's steps and not go forward; to hold back from going* | ~钱 *to raise money* ❷约束,检束 to keep within bounds; to restrain:~迹 *temporarily desist from one's evil ways; to go into hiding; to lie low*

脸(臉) liǎn ㄌㄧㄢˇ (—儿)面孔,头的前部,从额到下巴 face ㊊**extension** 1 物体的前部 front part of sth:鞋~儿 *front of a shoe; instep* | 门~儿 *facade of a shop; shop front* 2 体面,面子,颜面 face (㊥ **doublet** —面 face):有错就承认,别怕丢~。*Admit it whenever you make mistakes. Don't feel ashamed.*

裣(襝) liǎn ㄌㄧㄢˇ [裣衽](—rèn)旧时指妇女行礼(of a woman in former times) to greet by holding the lower corners of one's jacket

蔹(蘞) liǎn ㄌㄧㄢˇ 多年生蔓生草本植物,叶子多而细,有白蔹、赤蔹等 ampelopsis (*Ampelopsis*)

练(練) liàn ㄌㄧㄢˋ ❶白绢 white silk:江平如~。*The river lies as smooth as silk.* ❷把生丝煮熟,使柔软洁白 to boil and scour raw silk ❸练习,反复学习,多次地操作 to practise; to train; to drill:~兵 *to train troops; to drill soldiers* | ~本领 *to practise one's skill* ❹经验多,精熟 experienced; skilled; seasoned:~达 *experienced and worldly-wise* | 老~ *experienced; seasoned* | 熟~ *skilled; practised; proficient*

炼(煉、*鍊) liàn ㄌㄧㄢˋ ❶用火烧制 to temper (a metal) with fire; to smelt:~钢 *to make (or smelt) steel* | ~焦 *to make coke; to coke* ❷用心琢磨使精练 to weigh one's words; to seek the right phrase:~字 *to weigh one's words (while writing); to rack one's brains for the right word* | ~句 *to endeavour to find the best turn of phrase; to polish and repolish a sentence* ❸烹熬炮制 to refine:～乳 *condensed milk*

恋(戀) liàn ㄌㄧㄢˋ 想念不忘,不忍舍弃,不想分开 to long for; to feel attached to:留～ *to be reluctant to leave (a place); can't bear to part (from sb or sth)*|～～不舍 *to be reluctant to part from; to hate to see sb go* [恋爱]男女相爱 to love; to be in love; to have a courtship [恋栈]马舍不得离开马棚,喻贪恋禄位(of a horse) to be loath to leave its stable—(of an official) to be loath to give up his post

殓(殮) liàn ㄌㄧㄢˋ 装殓,把死人装入棺材里 to put a body into a coffin; to encoffin:入～ *to put a corpse in a coffin; to encoffin*|大～ *encoffining ceremony*

潋(瀲) liàn ㄌㄧㄢˋ [潋滟](—yàn)水波相连的样子 rippling; wavy; undulating

链(*鍊) liàn ㄌㄧㄢˋ ❶(—子、—儿)多指用金属环连套而成的索子 chain:表～ *watch chain*|铁～ *iron chain* ❷英美制长度单位,1链合20.1168米 chain, a unit for measuring distance, equal to 20.1168m

楝 liàn ㄌㄧㄢˋ 落叶乔木,花淡紫色,果实椭圆形,种子、树皮都可入药 chinaberry (*Melia azedarach*)

裢 lian ·ㄌㄧㄢ 见118页"褡"字条"褡裢"(dā—) see 褡裢 on p118

LIANG ㄌㄧㄤ

良 liáng ㄌㄧㄤˊ ❶好 good; fine (㊀**doublet** —好 good; well|优— fine; good; of high quality|善— good and honest; kind-hearted):～药 *good (or effective) medicine*|～田 *good (or fertile) farmland*|品质优～ *to be of fine quality; of the best quality*|消化不～ *indigestion; dyspepsia* ❷很 very; very much:～久 *a good while; a long time*|获益～多 *to benefit a great deal*

粮(糧) liáng ㄌㄧㄤˊ ❶可吃的谷类、豆类等 grain; food; provisions:食～ *foodgrain; grain; food*|杂～ *grains other than wheat and rice; coarse food grains* ❷作为农业税的粮食 grains in the form of an agricultural tax:交公～ *to deliver tax grain to the state*

踉 ㊀ liáng ㄌㄧㄤˊ [跳踉]跳跃 to jump; to leap
㊁ liàng 见443页 see p443

凉(*涼) ㊀ liáng ㄌㄧㄤˊ 温度低(若指天气,比"冷"的程度浅)(of weather, not as severe as cold) cool; cold; chilly:饭～了。*The food's gotten cold.*|立秋之后天气～了。*It gets cool after the Beginning of Autumn.* ㊞ ***figurative*** 灰心或失望 discouraged; disappointed:听到这消息,我心里就～了。*My heart*

sank at the news. [凉快](—kuai) **1** 清凉爽快 nice and cool; pleasantly cool **2** 乘凉 to cool oneself; to cool off: 到外头～～～～去。*Let's go out and cool off.*

㊁ liàng 见443页 see p443

椋 liáng ㄌㄧㄤˊ 椋子木，乔木，叶似柿叶，果实细圆形，生时青色，熟时黑色。木质坚硬 tatarian dogwood (*Cornus alba*)

辌 liáng ㄌㄧㄤˊ 见787页"辒"字条"辒辌"(wēn—) see 辒辌 on p787

梁(❶-❹ *樑) liáng ㄌㄧㄤˊ ❶房梁，架在墙上或柱子上支撑房顶的横木 roof beam: 上～*upper beam* (图见188页 picture on p188) ❷桥 bridge (㊟ ***doublet*** 桥 — bridge): 石～*stone bridge* | 开山挑土架桥～*to open up a mountain, move the soil and build a bridge* ❸(—子、—儿)器物上面便于提携的弓形物 curved handle: 茶壶～儿 *handle of a teapot* | 篮子的提～儿坏了。*The basket handle is broken.* ❹(—子、—儿)中间高起的部分 ridge: 山～ *mountain ridge; hill ridge* | 鼻～*bridge of the nose* ❺朝代名 dynasty name **1** 南朝之一，萧衍所建立(公元502—557年) Liang Dynasty (502—557), one of the Southern Dynasties, founded by Xiao Yan **2** 五代之一，朱温所建立(公元907—923年)，史称后梁 Later Liang Dynasty (907—923), one of the Five Dynasties, founded by Zhu Wen

粱 liáng ㄌㄧㄤˊ 粟的优良品种的统称 fine strain of millet [高粱]一年生草本植物，茎高，子实可供食用，又可以酿酒 *kaoliang*; Chinese sorghum

量 ㊀ liáng ㄌㄧㄤˊ ❶用器物计算东西的多少或长短 to measure: 用斗～米 *to mete out rice with a* dou *measure* | 用尺～布 *to measure cloth with a ruler* ❷估量 to appraise; to evaluate; to estimate: 思～(liang) *to turn over in one's mind; to consider* | 打～(liang) *to measure with the eye; to look up and down*

㊁ liàng 见444页 see p444

两(兩) liǎng ㄌㄧㄤˇ ❶数目，一般用于量词和"半、千、万、亿"前(usually used before a quantifier and before 半，千，万 or 亿) two: ～本书 *two books* | ～匹马 *two horses* | ～个月 *two months* | ～半 *two halves* | ～万 *twenty thousand* ["两"和"二"用法不全同。读数目字只用"二"不用"两"，如"一、二、三、四；二、四、六、八"。小数和分数只用"二"不用"两"，如"零点二(0.2)，三分之二，二分之一"。序数也只用"二"，如"第二，二哥"。在一般量词前，用"两"不用"二"。如："两个人用两种方法。""两条路通两个地方。"在传统的度量衡单位前，"两"和"二"一般都可用，用"二"为多("二两"不能说"两两")。新的度量衡单位前一般用"两"，如"两吨、两公

L

里”。在多位数中，百、十、个位用“二”不用“两”，如“二百二十二”。“千、万、亿”的前面，“两”和“二”一般都可用，但如“三万二千”、“两亿二千万”，“千”在“万、亿”后，以用“二”为常。][两 and 二 are not entirely identical in usage. In some cases, only 二, not 两, is used: in reading numbers, e. g. 一，二，三，四 and 二，四，六，八；in decimal fraction and fraction, e. g. 零点二(0. 2)，三分之二，二分之一；in ordinal number, e. g. 第二，二哥；before the common quantifiers, e. g. 两个人用两种方法 and 两条路通两个地方. Before the traditional unit of measurement, both 两 and 二 can be used, but 二 is used more frequently (二两 can never be spoken as 两两)；before the new unit of measurement, 两 is more popular, e. g. 两吨，两公里. In the multi-digit numbers, only 二 (not 两) is used in hundreds place, tens place and unit place, e. g. 二百二十二, while before 千，万 and 亿, both 二 and 两 can be used, but in 三万二千 and 两亿二千万, if 千 is after 万 or 亿, 二 is more popular] ❷ 双方 both (sides); either (side): ～便 *to be convenient to both; to make things easy for both* | ～可 *both will do; either will do; could go either way* | ～全 *to be satisfactory to both parties; to have regard for both sides; to take both aspects into consideration* | ～相情愿 *both parties being willing; mutual consent on both sides* ❸表示不定的数目(十以内的) a few; some (less than ten): 过～天再说吧。*Let's leave it for a couple of days.* | 他真有～下子。*He is really clever and capable.* ❹市制重量单位，1斤是10两(旧制1斤是16两)，1两合50克 *liang*, traditional unit of weight, 1 *jin* equal 10 *liang* (in former times, 1 *jin* equal to 16 *liang*), 1 *liang* equal to 50 grams

俩(倆) ㊀ liǎng ㄌㄧㄤˇ [伎俩](jì—)手段，花招 trick; intrigue; ruse

㊁ liǎ 见437页 see p437

唡(啢) liǎng ㄌㄧㄤˇ 也读作 yīngliǎng。英美制重量单位，常衡1唡是1磅的1/16，约合28. 35克。也写作“英两”。现用“盎司”(also pronounced as yīngliǎng and written as 英两, now 盎司 is used as a substitute) ounce, a unit of weight in the British and US system, equal to one-sixteenth of a pound, approximately 28. 35 grams

緉(緉) liǎng ㄌㄧㄤˇ 一双，古时计算鞋、袜的单位(in ancient China)(of shoes and socks) a pair of

魉(魎) liǎng ㄌㄧㄤˇ 见777页“魍”字条“魍魉”(wǎng—) see 魍魉 on p777

亮 liàng ㄌㄧㄤˋ ❶明，有光 bright; light: 天～了。

The day breaks. | 敞～ *bright and spacious* | 刀磨得真～。*How bright the knife is after it has been sharpened.* ❷(一儿)光线 light:屋里一点～儿也没有。*There is no light in the room at all.* ㊀**extension** 灯烛等照明物 light (of a lamp, candle, etc):拿个～儿来 *Bring a light.* ❸明摆出来 to show; to reveal; to lay open:～相 *to strike a pose on the stage; to make one's debut* | 把牌一～ *to show one's cards* | 有本事～几手。*Make a show of it if you can.* ❹明朗,清楚 enlightened; clear:你这一说,我心里头就～了。*I find what you say most enlightening.* | 打开窗子说～话 *to speak frankly; to talk in explicit terms* ❺声音响 loud and clear; clarion:洪～ *loud and clear; sonorous*

喨 liàng ㄌㄧㄤˋ [嘹喨]旧同"嘹亮"。参看445页"嘹"(liáo)(see 嘹 on p445) same as 嘹亮 in former times

倞 ㊀ liàng ㄌㄧㄤˋ 求索 to search for; to ask for; to request

㊁ jìng 见362页 see p362

凉(*涼) ㊁ liàng ㄌㄧㄤˋ 放一会儿,使温度降低 to make (or become) cool; to cool

㊀ liáng 见440页 see p440

谅 liàng ㄌㄧㄤˋ ❶原谅 to forgive; to excuse; to understand:体～(体察其情而加以原谅) *to show consideration and sympathy for; to make allowance for* | 敬希见～。*I sincerely hope you'll excuse me.* [谅解]由了解而消除意见 to understand; to make allowance for ❷信实 trustworthy; reliable:～哉斯言。*How trustworthy the words are!* ❸推想 I think; I suppose; I expect:～他不能来。*I don't think he will come.*

晾 liàng ㄌㄧㄤˋ ❶把衣物放在太阳下面晒或放在通风透气的地方使干 to dry in the air (or sun); to air; to sun:～衣服 *to hang clothes out to dry; to sun clothes* ❷冷落,不理睬 to ignore; to slight; to give the cold shoulder to:把他～在一边 *to give him the cold shoulder; to ignore him* ❸同"凉㊁"same as 凉㊁

悢 liàng ㄌㄧㄤˋ 悲伤,惆怅 sad; sorrowful:～然 *sorrowful; sad*

踉 ㊁ liàng ㄌㄧㄤˋ [踉跄](—qiàng)走路不稳 to stagger

㊀ liáng 见440页 see p440

辆(輛) liàng ㄌㄧㄤˋ 量词 ***quantifier***,用于车(used for vehicles):一～汽车 *a car; an automobile; a motor vehicle*

靓 ㊁ liàng ㄌㄧㄤˋ 〈方 ***dialect***〉漂亮,好看 beautiful; pretty; handsome:～女 *beautiful (or pretty) girl*

㊀ jìng 见362页 see p362

L

量 ⊜ liàng ㄌㄧㄤˋ ❶计算东西体积多少的器具的总称 general term for vessels used to measure volume [量词]表示事物或行动单位的词,如张、条、个、只、遍等 quantifier, word indicating a unit for things or actions, such as 张, 条, 个, 只 or 遍, etc ❷限度 capacity: 酒～*capacity for liquor; one's drinking capacity*|气～ *tolerance; forbearance*|饭～ *appetite*|胆～ *courage; guts; pluck* ❸数量,数的多少 quantity; amount; volume: 质～并重 *to lay equal stress on quality and quantity*|大～生产新式农具 *mass-production of new farm tools* [分量](fènliang) 重量 weight: 不够～～*to be short of measure*|称称～～*to weigh it* ❹估计,审度(duó) to estimate; to measure: ～力而行 *to do what one is capable of; to act according to one's capability*|～入为出 *to keep expenditure within the limits of income; to live within one's means*

⊖ liáng 见441页 see p441

LIAO ㄌㄧㄠ

撩 ⊖ liāo ㄌㄧㄠ ❶提,掀起 to raise or lift up (a part of sth which is hanging): ～起长衫 *to lift (or hold up) the hem of one's long gown*|把帘子～起来 *to lift (or raise) the curtain* ❷用手洒水 to sprinkle (with one's hand): 先～上点水再扫。*Sprinkle some water before you sweep the floor.*

⊜ liáo 见445页 see p445

蹽 liāo ㄌㄧㄠ〈方 **dialect**〉跑,走 to walk fast; to rush; to run: 他一气～了二里地。*He walked over two* li *at a stretch.*

辽(遼) liáo ㄌㄧㄠˊ ❶远 distant; faraway (㊥**doublet** 一远 distant; faraway; remote): ～阔 *vast; extensive* ❷朝代名。耶律阿保机建立(公元916—1125年) Liao Dynasty (916—1125), which was founded by Yelü Abaoji

疗(療) liáo ㄌㄧㄠˊ 医治 to treat; to cure (㊥**doublet** 医一 medical treatment|治一 to treat; to cure): ～病 *to treat a disease*|诊～*to make a diagnosis and give treatment* ㊗**figurative** 解除痛苦或困难 to relieve; to get rid of (misery or difficulty): ～饥 *to allay (or appease) one's hunger*|～贫 *to relieve the poor*

窌 liáo ㄌㄧㄠˊ 针灸穴位名 *liao*, an acupuncture point

聊 liáo ㄌㄧㄠˊ ❶姑且,略 merely; just; barely: ～以自慰 *just to console oneself; merely to find relief in sth*|～胜一筹 *slightly better; a notch (or cut) above*|～胜于无 *better than nothing; A little is better than none.* ❷依赖 to rely; to depend: 百无～赖 *to languish in boredom; not to know how to while away the time*|民不～生

(无法生活)。*The people have no means of livelihood.* [无聊] **1** 没有兴趣 bored; dull **2** 没有意义 senseless; silly; stupid ❸〈方 ***dialect***〉聊天,闲谈 to chat; to gab; to chew the fat: 别～啦,赶快干吧! *Stop gabbing and do your work quickly!*

僚 liáo ㄌㄧㄠˊ ❶官 official [官僚]指旧时各级政府里的官吏。现在把脱离人民群众,不深入实际工作的领导作风和工作作风叫官僚主义 official; bureaucrat ❷旧时指在一块做官的人(in former times) associate in office: 同～*colleague; fellow official* [僚机]空军编队中受长(zhǎng)机指挥作战的飞机(in a flying formation) wing plane

撩 ㊁ liáo ㄌㄧㄠˊ 挑弄,引逗 to tease; to provoke; to stir up: ～拨 *to tease; to incite; to provoke* | 景色～人。*The scenery is stimulating.*

㊀ liāo 见444页 see p444

嘹 liáo ㄌㄧㄠˊ [嘹亮](*嘹喨)声音响亮 resonant; loud and clear; clarion

獠 liáo ㄌㄧㄠˊ 面貌凶恶(of appearance) fierce; fiendish: ～面 *fierce appearance* [獠牙]露在嘴外面的长牙 long, sharp, protruding tooth; fang; snag tooth

潦 ㊁ liáo ㄌㄧㄠˊ [潦倒](—dǎo)颓丧,不得意 to be frustrated; to be down on one's luck: 穷困～～*to be poverty-stricken and downtrodden; to be (down) on one's uppers* [潦草]草率,不精细 hasty and careless; sloppy; slovenly: 工作不能～～。*One should never be slipshod in work.* | 字写得太～～。*The handwriting is illegible.*

㊀ lǎo 见420页 see p420

寮 liáo ㄌㄧㄠˊ 小屋 small house; hut: 竹～*bamboo hut* | 茶～*teahouse*

缭 liáo ㄌㄧㄠˊ ❶缠绕 entangled: ～乱 *in a tangle; confused* | 炊烟～绕 *smoke curling up from kitchen chimneys* ❷用针线缝缀 to sew with slanting stitches: ～缝(fèng) *to stitch up a seam; to seam* | ～贴边 *to stitch a hem; to hem*

燎 ㊀ liáo ㄌㄧㄠˊ 延烧(of fire) to spread; to burn: 星星之火,可以～原。*A single spark can start a prairie fire.*

㊁ liǎo 见446页 see p446

鹩 liáo ㄌㄧㄠˊ 见339页"鷦"字条"鷦鹩"(jiāo—)see 鷦鹩 on p339

寥 liáo ㄌㄧㄠˊ ❶稀疏 few; scanty; scarce (叠 ***reduplication***): ～若晨星 *as sparse as the morning stars; few and far between* | ～～无几 *very few; hardly any* ❷空旷,静寂 broad and empty; vast; silent: ～廓 *boundless; vast; infinite* | 寂～*deserted and lonely*

飂 ㊁ liáo ㄌㄧㄠˊ [飂戾](—lì) **1** 风声 sound of wind **2** 很快的样子 very fast; rapidly

L

㊁ liù 见460页 see p460

髎 liáo ㄌㄧㄠˊ 同"窌"(liáo) same as 窌

了(❶△瞭) ㊀ liǎo ㄌㄧㄠˇ ❶ 明白 to know clearly; to understand: 明～ *to understand; to know clearly* | 一目～然 *to be clear at a glance* | 不甚～～ *to be unclear about; to know little about* [了解]弄明白,懂得很清楚 to find out; to understand; to comprehend: ～～情况 *to understand (or find out) a situation* ❷完了,结束 to finish; to conclude; to end; to settle: 事情已经～了(le)。*The case has been settled.* | 话犹未～。*It seemed that he hadn't finished his talk.* | 不～～之 *to end up without a decision; to end up with no conclusion* | 没完没～ *endless; without end* | 不能敷衍～事。*Things shouldn't be done perfunctorily.* [了当]爽快 frank; straightforward; outright: 直截～～ *blunt; point-blank; straightforward* ❸在动词后,跟"不"、"得"连用,表示不可能或可能(used in conjunction with 不 or 得 after a verb to express possibility): 这本书我看不～。*I cannot read this book.* | 这事你办得～。*You can do this.* [了不得](—bude)表示不平常,严重 extraordinary; terrific; extreme: 他的本事真～～～。*He's got really terrific capabilities.* | ～～了,着了火了! *Good heavens! It's on fire!* | 疼得～～～。*It's awfully painful.* [了得](—de) **1** 有"能办、可以"的意思,多用于反诘语句中,表示不平常,严重(usually used in retort to denote seriousness) can: 这还～～! *How terrible!* or *How outrageous* (or *awful*)! **2** 能干,厉害 able; capable: 真～～。*Really smart!* or *How capable!*

㊁ le 见422页 see p422

"瞭"又 liào (also liào) 见447页 see p447

钌 ㊀ liǎo ㄌㄧㄠˇ 一种金属元素,符号 Ru,银灰色,质坚而脆。纯钌可以做装饰品,三氯化钌可以做防腐剂、催化剂 ruthenium (Ru)

㊁ liào 见446页 see p446

蓼 liǎo ㄌㄧㄠˇ 一年生或多年生草本植物,花白色或浅红色,生长在水边 knotweed (*Polygonum*)

燎 ㊁ liǎo ㄌㄧㄠˇ 挨近了火而烧焦 to singe; to char by fire: 把头发～了 *to have one's hair singed*

㊀ liáo 见445页 see p445

尥 liào ㄌㄧㄠˋ [尥蹶子](—juězi)骡马等跳起来用后腿向后踢(of mules, horses, etc) to give a backward kick

钌 ㊁ liào ㄌㄧㄠˋ [钌铞儿](—diàor)钉在门窗上可以把门窗扣住的东西 hasp and staple: 门～～～ *hasp and staple on a door*

㊀ liǎo 见446页 see p446

L

料 liào ㄌㄧㄠˋ ❶料想,估计,猜想 to suppose; to expect; to anticipate:预～ *to predict; to anticipate; to expect* | 不出所～ *as might have been expected; as expected* | 他～事～得很准。*He can foretell things with great accuracy.* ❷处理,照管 to manage; to take care of:～理 *to arrange; to manage; to take care of* | 照～ *to take care of; to look after* ❸(一子、一儿)材料,可供制造其他东西的物质 material; stuff:原～ *raw material* | 木～ *timber; lumber* | 衣裳～子 *material for making clothes; dress material* | 肥～ *fertilizer; manure* | 燃～ *fuel* ❹喂牲口用的谷物(grain) feed; forage; fodder:～豆儿 *soybeans, or black beans used as feed for livestock* | 草～ *forage; fodder* | 牲口得喂～才能肥。*The cattle is fattened by fodder.* ❺烧料,一种熔点较低的玻璃,用来制造器皿或手工艺品 imitation frosted glass (used to make utensils and handicrafts):～器 *glassware* ❻量词 ***quantifier***,中药配方全份叫一料(多用于配制丸药)(usually used for pills of traditional Chinese medicine) prescription

撂 liào ㄌㄧㄠˋ 放下,搁置 to put down; to leave behind; to shelve:把碗～在桌子上 *to put the bowl down on the table* | ～下工作不管 *to throw up the work; to abandon work*

廖 liào ㄌㄧㄠˋ 姓 Liao, a surname

瞭 ㊀ liào ㄌㄧㄠˋ 瞭望,远远地望 to watch from a height or a distance:你在远处～着点儿。*Keep a sharp lookout from a distance.* | ～望台 *observation (or lookout) tower*

㊁ liǎo 见446页"了"see 了 on p446

镣 liào ㄌㄧㄠˋ 脚镣,套在脚腕上使不能快走的刑具 fetters; shackles

LIE ㄌㄧㄝ

咧 ㊁ liē ㄌㄧㄝ [咧咧](—lie)〈方 ***dialect***〉**1** 乱说,乱讲 to speak carelessly; to make irresponsible remarks; to gossip:瞎～～ *to be blabbering* **2** 小孩儿哭(of children) to cry; to blubber:这孩子一～～起来就没完。*The child never stops crying once he gets started.*

㊀ liě 见447页 see p447

㊂ lie 见449页 see p449

咧 ㊀ liě ㄌㄧㄝˇ 嘴向旁边斜着张开 to stretch one's mouth from ear to ear; to grin:～嘴 *to stretch one's mouth wide; to grin* | ～着嘴笑 *to grin from ear to ear*

㊁ liē 见447页 see p447

㊂ lie 见449页 see p449

裂 ㊁ liě ㄌㄧㄝˇ〈方 ***dialect***〉东西的两部分向两旁分开(of two pieces joined together) to come apart; to part in the middle; to split or break open:衣服没扣好,～着怀。*His shirt was unbuttoned, exposing his chest.*

㊀ liè 见448页 see p448

列 liè ㄌㄧㄝˋ ❶行(háng)列,排成的行 row; file; rank:站在前～ *to stand in the front row* ❷陈列,排列,摆出 to set out; to arrange; to line up:姓名～后 *with the names listed behind*|～队 *to line up*|开～账目 *to draw up* (or *make out*) *a list of the account* ㉠***extension*** **1** 归类 to enter in a list; to list; to rank:～入甲等 *to be classified as first-rate; to be rated as class A* **2** 类 kind; sort; category:不在讨论之～*not among the subjects to be discussed* [列席]参加会议,而没有表决权 to attend (a meeting) without voting rights ❸众多,各 various; each and every:～国 *various countries, states, or kingdoms*|～位 *all of you; all the ladies and gentlemen present* ❹量词 ***quantifier***,用于成行列的事物(used for a series or row of things):一～火车 *a train*

冽 liè ㄌㄧㄝˋ 寒冷 cold; chilly (㊀***doublet*** 凛 — piercingly cold):北风凛～。*The north wind was blowing sharply* (or *icily*).

洌 liè ㄌㄧㄝˋ ❶水清(of water) clear ❷酒清(of wine or spirit) clear

烈 liè ㄌㄧㄝˋ ❶猛烈,厉害 strong; fierce; intense:～火 *fierce fire; raging* (or *intense*) *flames*|～日 *burning* (or *scorching*) *sun* ❷气势盛大 vigorous; grand(叠 ***reduplication***):轰轰～～*on a grand and spectacular scale; with vim and vigour; dynamic* ❸刚直,有高贵品格的,为正义、人民、国家而死难的 staunch; upright; dying for a just cause:刚～*fiery and forthright; upright and unyielding*|先～ *martyr*|～士 *martyr*

䴕 liè ㄌㄧㄝˋ 就是啄木鸟,嘴坚硬,舌细长,能啄食树中的虫,是一种益鸟 woodpecker (*Picidae*)

裂 ㊀ liè ㄌㄧㄝˋ 破开,开了缝(fèng) to split; to crack; to rend:～痕 *rift; crack; fissure*|～缝 *crack; rift; crevice*|手冻～了。*The hands are chapped by the cold.*|感情破～ *(of marriage, affections, relations, etc) to break up*|四分五～ *to fall apart; to be rent by disunity; to be all split up*

㊁ liě 见447页 see p447

趔 liè ㄌㄧㄝˋ [趔趄](—qie)身体歪斜,脚步不稳要摔倒的样子 to stagger; to reel; to stumble

劣 liè ㄌㄧㄝˋ ❶恶,不好,跟"优"相对(the opposite of 优) bad; inferior; of low quality (㊀ ***doublet*** 恶 — odious; abominable; disgusting):不分优～*to make no distinction between the good and the bad*|土豪～绅 *local tyrants and evil gentry*|品质恶～ *to be morally corrupt; unprincipled; base* ❷仅仅 merely; only

L

埒 liè ㄌㄧㄝˋ ❶矮墙 low wall ❷同等 equal; on a par with: 财力相～ *to be equal in financial resource*

捩 liè ㄌㄧㄝˋ 扭转 to twist; to turn: 转～点(转折点) *turning point*

猎(獵) liè ㄌㄧㄝˋ ❶打猎,捕捉禽兽 to hunt; to catch birds and beasts: 狩～ *hunting* | 渔～ *fishing and hunting* | ～人 *hunter; huntsman* | ～狗 *hunting dog; hound* ❷搜寻 to hunt; to seek: ～奇 *to hunt for novelty; to seek novelty*

躐 liè ㄌㄧㄝˋ ❶超越 to overstep; to go beyond; to skip over: ～等(越级) *to skip over the normal steps; not to follow the proper order* | ～进(不依照次序前进) *to advance by skipping necessary steps* ❷踩,践踏 to trample

鬣 liè ㄌㄧㄝˋ 兽类颈上的长毛 mane: 马～ *horse's mane*

咧 ㊂ lie ·ㄌㄧㄝ 〈方 **dialect**〉助词 **auxiliary**, 意思相当于"了"、"啦" similar in meaning to 了 or 啦: 好～ *OK!* or *All right!* | 他来～。*He's coming.* or *He comes.* or *Here he comes.*

㊀ liě 见447页 see p447

㊁ liē 见447页 see p447

LIN ㄌㄧㄣ

拎 līn ㄌㄧㄣ 〈方 **dialect**〉提 to carry; to lift; to hold: ～着一篮子菜 *to carry a basket of vegetables*

邻(鄰、*隣) lín ㄌㄧㄣˊ ❶住处接近的人家 neighbour: 东～ *neighbour living on the eastern side* | 四～(*surrounding*) *neighbours* ❷邻近,接近,附近 neighbouring; near; adjacent: ～国 *neighbouring country* | ～居 *neighbour* | ～舍 *neighbour* ❸古代五家为邻 *lin*, an administrative unit composed of five households in ancient China

林 lín ㄌㄧㄣˊ ❶长在土地上的许多树木或竹子 forest; woods; grove: 树～ *woods; grove* | 竹～ *bamboo grove* | 防护～ *shelter-forest* | ～立(像树林一样密集排列) *to stand in great numbers* (*like trees in a forest*) ㊃ ***figurative*** 聚集在一起的同类的人或事物 group of similar objects or persons: 民族之～ *great family of nationalities* | 著作之～ *numerous works* ❷林业 forestry: 农～牧副渔 *farming, forestry, animal husbandry, sideline production and fishery*

啉 lín ㄌㄧㄣˊ 见404页"喹"字条"喹啉"(kuí—) see 喹啉 on p404

淋 ㊀ lín ㄌㄧㄣˊ 浇 to pour; to sprinkle; to water: 花蔫了,～上点水吧。*The flowers are droopy. Sprinkle them with some water.*

[淋巴](外 ***loanword***) 即淋巴液,人身体里的一种无色透明液体,起血液和细胞之间的物质交换

作用 lymph
[淋漓](—lí)湿淋淋往下滴落 dripping wet; pouring; streaming:墨迹~~*full of ink marks*|大汗~~ *dripping with sweat; sweating all over* ㊕***transfer*** 畅达 free from inhibition; unrestrained:~~尽致 *vividly and incisively; thoroughly*|痛快~~ *to be impassioned and forceful*

㊁ lìn 见452页 see p452

琳 lín ㄌㄧㄣˊ 美玉 beautiful jade [琳琅](—láng) **1** 珠玉一类的东西 beautiful jade; gem:~~满目(喻优美的东西很多) *superb collection of beautiful things; feast for the eyes* **2** 玉撞击的声音 tinkling of jade pieces

霖 lín ㄌㄧㄣˊ 久下不停的雨 continuous heavy rain [甘霖]对农作物有益的雨 good rain after a long drought; timely rainfall ㊕ ***transfer*** 恩泽 bounties bestowed by a monarch or an official

临(臨) lín ㄌㄧㄣˊ ❶到,来 to arrive; to be present:喜事~门。*Great happiness descended upon the house.*|身~其境 *to be present on the scene* ㊀***extension*** 遭遇,碰到 to meet; to confront:~渴掘井 *not to dig a well until one is thirsty; to make no preparation until the last moment* [临时] **1** 到时候,当时 at the time when sth is needed or is expected to happen:事先有准备,~~就不会忙乱。*One will not be in a rush at the last moment if he gets everything ready in advance.* **2** 暂时,非经常的 temporarily; for the time being:你先~~代理一下。*You may act for him for the time being.*|~~会议 *provisional meeting* ❷挨着,靠近 to be near to; to be close to **1** 指地点,多指较高的靠近较低的(of a place) to overlook (the street, etc); to face; to confront:~河 *to face* (or *overlook, be close to*) *a river*|~街 *to overlook* (or *face, be close to*) *the street* **2** 指时间。将要,快要(of time) on the point of; just before; to be about to:~走 *just before leaving*|~别 *just before parting; at parting* [临床]医学上称医生给人诊治疾病 clinical [临盆]孕妇快要生小孩儿 to be giving birth to a child; to be confined ❸照着字、画模仿 to copy (a model of calligraphy or painting):~帖 *to practise calligraphy after a model*|~画 *to copy a painting*

粼 lín ㄌㄧㄣˊ [粼粼]形容水清澈(of water) clear; limpid:~~碧波 *clear, blue ripples*

嶙 lín ㄌㄧㄣˊ [嶙峋](—xún)山石一层层的重叠不平(of mountain rocks, cliffs, etc) jagged; rugged; craggy

遴 lín ㄌㄧㄣˊ 谨慎选择 to choose (*or* select) carefully (㊀ ***doublet*** —选 to select for a post; to select; to recruit): ～选人才 *to select qualified personnel; to select talented people*

〈古〉又同"吝"(lìn) also same as 吝

璘 lín ㄌㄧㄣˊ 玉的光彩 lustre of jade

辚 lín ㄌㄧㄣˊ [辚辚]拟声词 ***onomatopoeia***,形容车行走时的声音 sound made by a running cart, chariot, etc: 车～～,马萧萧 *chariots rattling and horses neighing*

磷(*燐、*粦) lín ㄌㄧㄣˊ 一种非金属元素,符号 P,常见的有两种:黄磷(也叫"白磷")和红磷。黄磷有毒,燃烧时生浓烟,可做军事上用的烟幕弹和燃烧弹。红磷无毒,可制安全火柴。磷是植物营养的重要成分之一 phosphorus (P) [磷火]夜间在野地里常见的青色火光,是磷化氢遇到空气燃烧而发的光。俗叫"鬼火"(popularly called 鬼火) phosphorescent light; will-o'-the-wisp; jack-o'-lantern

瞵 lín ㄌㄧㄣˊ 注视,瞪着眼睛看 to stare; to gaze: 鹰～鹗视 *to eye vigilantly; to look fiercely (at sth)*

鳞 lín ㄌㄧㄣˊ ❶鱼类、爬行动物等身体表面长的角质或骨质的小薄片(of fish, etc) scale [鳞爪](— zhǎo) scales and claws ㊃***figurative*** **1** 琐碎细小的事 small bits; scraps; fragments **2** 事情的一小部分 a small part of a matter; odd scraps ❷像鱼鳞的 like the scales of a fish; scale-like: ～茎 *bulb* | 芽～ *bud scale* | 遍体～伤(伤痕密得像鱼鳞似的) *to be covered with bruises (or injuries); to be a mass of bruises; to be black and blue all over*

麟(*麐) lín ㄌㄧㄣˊ 麒麟,古代传说中的一种动物,像鹿,比鹿大,有角(Chinese) unicorn: 凤毛～角(喻罕见而珍贵的东西) *phoenix feathers and unicorn horns — rarity of rarities*

凛(**凜) lǐn ㄌㄧㄣˇ ❶寒冷 cold; frigid (㊀ ***doublet*** —冽 piercingly or bitingly cold): 北风～冽。*The north wind was blowing sharply (or icily).* ❷严肃,严厉 strict; stern; severe (叠 ***reduplication***): 威风～～ *majestic-looking; of an awe-inspiring demeanor; with dignified bearing* | 大义～然 *to inspire awe by upholding justice; with stern righteousness* ❸同"懔" same as 懔

廪(**廩) lǐn ㄌㄧㄣˇ ❶粮仓 granary (㊀ ***doublet*** 仓—granary) ❷指粮食 grain

懔(**懍) lǐn ㄌㄧㄣˇ 畏惧 afraid; fearful;

L

apprehensive

檩（**檁）lǐn ㄌㄧㄣˇ 屋上托住椽子的横木 purlin（图见188页 picture on p188）

吝（*悋）lìn ㄌㄧㄣˋ 当用的财物舍不得用，过分爱惜 stingy; miserly; close-fisted（㊣ *doublet* 一 啬 stingy; niggardly; miserly）：～惜 *to grudge; to stint*｜他一点也不～啬。*He's not stingy at all.*

赁 lìn ㄌㄧㄣˋ 租 to rent; to hire; to lease（㊣ *doublet* 租—to rent; to lease; to hire）：～房 *to hire a house*｜～车 *to hire a car*｜出～ *to rent* (or *hire, let*) *out*

淋 ㊁ lìn ㄌㄧㄣˋ ❶过滤 to strain; to filter：～盐 *to strain salt*｜～硝 *to filter the nitre* ❷淋病，一种性病，病原体是淋病球菌，病人尿道红肿溃烂，重的尿里夹带脓血。也叫"白浊"（also called 白浊）gonorrhoea

㊀ lín 见449页 see p449

蔺 lìn ㄌㄧㄣˋ［马蔺］多年生草本植物，根茎粗，叶线形，花蓝紫色。叶坚韧，可系物，又可造纸。根可制刷子。有的地区叫"马兰"（also called 马兰 in some areas）Chinese small iris（*Iris lactea*）

躏 lìn ㄌㄧㄣˋ 见637页"蹂"字条"蹂躏"（róu—）see 蹂躏 on p637

膦 lìn ㄌㄧㄣˋ 磷化氢（PH_3）分子中的氢原子部分或全部被烃基取代而形成的有机化合物的总称 phosphine

LING ㄌㄧㄥ

〇 líng ㄌㄧㄥˊ 数的空位，用于数字中（used in numbers）zero：三～六号 *No. 306*（*number three-o-six*）｜一九七～年 *1970*（*nineteen seventy*）；*year of nineteen seventy*

伶 líng ㄌㄧㄥˊ 伶人，旧称以唱戏为职业的人（former term for）actor or actress（㊣ *doublet* 优—actor or actress）：坤（女的）～ *actress*｜名～ *famous actor* (or *actress*)

［伶仃］（*零丁）（—dīng）孤独 left all alone; lonely; solitary：孤苦～～ *orphaned and helpless; alone and uncared for*

［伶俐］（—lì）聪明，灵活 clever; bright; smart：很～～的孩子 *very clever child*｜～牙～齿（能说会道）*to have the gift of gab; to have a glib* (or *ready*) *tongue*

［伶俜］（—pīng）形容孤独 lonely; solitary; all alone

苓 líng ㄌㄧㄥˊ ❶指茯（fú）苓 fuling（*Poris cocos*）❷苓耳，古书上说的一种植物 *ling'er*, a plant mentioned in ancient Chinese texts

囹 líng ㄌㄧㄥˊ［囹圄］（*囹圉）（—yǔ）古代称监狱（in ancient China）jail; prison; gaol：身陷～～ *to be thrown into prison; to be jailed*

泠 líng ㄌㄧㄥˊ 清凉 cool and fresh：～风 *cool, fresh breeze*［泠泠］**1** 形容清凉 cool; chilly **2** 声音清越(of sound) clear and melodious

玲 líng ㄌㄧㄥˊ 形容玉碰击的声音(叠 ***reduplication***) tinkling of jade pieces：～～盈耳 *One's ears are filled with the tinkling of jade pieces.*［玲珑］(—lóng) **1** 金玉声 tinkling of metal or jade pieces **2** 器物细致精巧(of things) ingeniously and delicately made; exquisite; cute：小巧～～ *small and exquisite; cute* **3** 灵活敏捷(of people) nimble and smart：～～活泼 *clever and lively*

柃 líng ㄌㄧㄥˊ 柃木，常绿灌木或小乔木，花小，白色，叶椭圆形或披针形，浆果球形，枝叶可入药 eurya (*Eurya japonica*)

瓴 líng ㄌㄧㄥˊ 古代一种盛(chéng)水的瓶子 ancient water jar：高屋建～(从房顶上往下泻水，喻居高临下的形势) *to pour water off a steep roof — to sweep down irresistibly from a commanding height; to operate from a strategically advantageous position*

铃 líng ㄌㄧㄥˊ ❶(—儿)铃铛，用金属做成的响器 bell：摇～ *to ring a bell*｜车～儿 *bicycle bell*｜电～儿 *electric bell* ❷形状像铃的东西 bell-like (*or* bell-shaped) thing：杠～ *barbell*｜哑～ *dumbbell*

鸰 líng ㄌㄧㄥˊ 见314页"鹡"字条"鹡鸰"(jí—) see 鹡鸰 on p314

聆 líng ㄌㄧㄥˊ 听 to listen; to hear：～教(*used in letters*) *to hear your words of wisdom*

蛉 líng ㄌㄧㄥˊ ［白蛉］昆虫，比蚊子小，吸人、畜的血，能传染黑热病等。俗叫"白蛉子"(popularly called 白蛉子) sandfly (*Phlebotomus*)

笭 líng ㄌㄧㄥˊ ［笭箵］(—xīng) 打鱼时盛(chéng)鱼的竹器(used for holding fish while angling) bamboo basket; creel

翎 líng ㄌㄧㄥˊ 鸟翅和尾上的长羽毛 tail or wing feather; plume; quill：雁～ *wild goose feather*｜野鸡～ *pheasant plumes* (or *feathers*)

羚 líng ㄌㄧㄥˊ 羚羊，种类繁多，体形一般轻捷，四肢细长，蹄小而尖 antelope; gazelle

零 líng ㄌㄧㄥˊ ❶落 to drop; to fall **1** 植物凋谢(of grass, trees, flowers) to wither and fall (㊟***doublet*** —落 to wither and fall｜凋— to wither; to wilt) **2** 液体滴落(of rain, tears, etc) to fall; to drop：感激涕～ *to be moved to tears of gratitude; to shed tears of gratitude* ❷零头，放在整数后表示附有零数 fraction; odd lot; extra：一千挂～儿 *a thousand odd*｜一年～三天 *a year and three days* ❸部分的，细碎的，跟"整"相对(the opposite of 整) fractional; fragmentary;

part（㊣**doublet** 一碎 scrappy; fragmentary; piecemeal）：～件 *part; spare part; spares*｜～钱 *small change; pocket money*｜～用 *to spend money on minor purchases; pocket money*｜～活（零碎工作）*odd jobs; chores* ❹数学上把数字符号"0"读作零 zero（0）；nought ㊈**extension** 没有，无 zero; nought; nil：一减一得～*One minus one equals zero.* or *One minus one leaves nought* (or *zero*).｜他的计划等于～。*His plan amounts to nothing.* or *His plan is worthless.*｜～距离 *no distance*｜～污染 *no pollution* ❺温度表上的零度 zero (on a thermometer)：～下五度 *five degrees below zero; 5℃ below zero*

龄 líng ㄌㄧㄥˊ ❶岁数 age; years（㊣**doublet** 年一age）：高～*advanced age* ❷年数 length of time or service; duration：工～*length* (or *years*) *of service; standing*｜党～*party standing* ❸某些生物体发育过程中的不同阶段。如昆虫的幼虫第一次蜕皮前叫一龄虫 instar; stadium (life-stage between molts of an insect)

灵（靈） líng ㄌㄧㄥˊ ❶有效验 efficacious; effective（㊣**doublet** 一验 efficacious; effective）：这种药吃下去很～。*This medicine is very effective.* ❷聪明，机敏 quick; clever; nimble（㊣**doublet** 一敏 sensitive; keen; acute）：心～手巧 *quick-witted and nimble-fingered; clever and deft*｜耳朵很～ *to have sharp ears* ❸活动迅速，灵巧 quick; sensitive：这架机器最～。*This machine is most sensitive.* ❹旧时称神或关于神仙的（former usages）fairy; sprite; elf：神～*gods; deities; divinities* ❺灵魂，精神 soul; spirit; intelligence：在天之～*sb's soul in heaven*｜英～*spirit of the brave departed; spirit of a martyr*｜～感 *inspiration (for creative work)*｜～性 *intelligence; aptitude; wisdom* ❻属于死人的 of the deceased：～柩 *coffin*｜～床 *bier* ㊇**transfer** 装着死人的棺材 coffin; bier; hearse：移～*to move the hearse*

棂（欞、櫺）** líng ㄌㄧㄥˊ 窗棂（子），窗户上构成窗格子的木条或铁条（window）lattice; lattice-work

凌 líng ㄌㄧㄥˊ ❶冰 icicle：冰～*ice*｜黄河～汛 *the ice run of the Huanghe River*｜滴水成～ *water freezes as it drips; freezing cold* ❷欺凌，侵犯，欺压 to insult; to bully：～辱 *to insult; to humiliate*｜盛气～人 *with overweening airs; domineering; arrogant* ❸升，高出 to rise high; to tower aloft：～云 *to reach the clouds; to soar to the skies*｜～空而过 *to soar across the sky* ❹迫近 to approach; to draw close：～晨 *in the small hours; before dawn*

L

陵 líng ㄌㄧㄥˊ ❶大土山 hill; mound (㊟ *doublet* 丘— hills) [陵谷]高低地势的变动 change of mountains and valleys ㊗ *figurative* 世事变迁 vicissitude of life; great change in the world ❷高大的坟墓 tomb; mausoleum: 黄帝～ *Mausoleum of the Yellow Emperor* | 中山～ *Sun Yat-sen Mausoleum*

菱 líng ㄌㄧㄥˊ 一年生草本植物,生在池沼中,叶略呈三角形,叶柄有气囊,花白色。果实有硬壳,大都有角,叫菱或菱角,可吃 water caltrop (*Trapa natans*) [菱形]邻边相等的平行四边形 diamond; rhombus; lozenge

崚 líng ㄌㄧㄥˊ (又 also léng) 见425页 léng see léng on p425

淩 líng ㄌㄧㄥˊ 同"凌❷❸❹" same as 凌❷❸❹

绫 líng ㄌㄧㄥˊ (－子)一种很薄的丝织品,一面光,像缎子 damask silk: ～罗绸缎 *silks and satins*

棱(*稜) ㊁ líng ㄌㄧㄥˊ [穆棱]地名,在黑龙江省 Muling, a place in Heilongjiang Province

㊀ léng 见425页 see p425

祾 líng ㄌㄧㄥˊ 〈古 *archaism*〉福 good fortune; blessing

鲮 líng ㄌㄧㄥˊ 鲮鱼,又叫"土鲮鱼"。属鲤科鱼类,是我国华南淡水主要养殖对象之一,性怕冷(also called 土鲮鱼) Chinese mud carp; dace (*Cirrhinus chinensis*) [鲮鲤]哺乳动物的一种,就是穿山甲,全身有角质的鳞片,吃蚂蚁 pangolin

酃 líng ㄌㄧㄥˊ 旧县名,在今湖南省衡阳东。现叫炎陵县 Lingxian County, former name of Yanling county, located in the east of today's Hengyang, Hunan Province

醽 líng ㄌㄧㄥˊ [醽醁](－lù)古代的一种美酒 *linglu*, a kind of good (or mellow) wine in ancient China

令 ㊂ lǐng ㄌㄧㄥˇ (外 **loanword**) 量词 ***quantifier***, 原张的纸500张为1令 ream (500 sheets of paper)

㊀ lìng 见456页 see p456

岭(嶺) lǐng ㄌㄧㄥˇ 山脉 ridge (of a mountain); mountains: 五～ *The Five Ridges* (*across the borders between Hunan and Jiangxi on the one hand and Guangdong and Guangxi on the other*) | 秦～ *Qinling Mountains* | 翻山越～ *to cross over mountain after mountain; to tramp over hill and dale*

领 lǐng ㄌㄧㄥˇ ❶颈,脖子 neck: 引～而望 *to crane one's neck to see; to look forward to eagerly* ❷(－子、－儿)衣服围绕脖子的部分。collar; neckband(图见882页"衣"picture on p882) ㊂ ***extension*** 事物的纲要 outline; main point: 不得要～ *to fail to grasp the main*

points (or *essentials*) [领袖][转] *transfer* 国家、政治团体、群众组织等的高级领导人(of a country, political group, mass organization, etc) leader ❸带,引,率 to lead; to usher; to head ([连]*doublet* 带一 to lead; to guide | 率一 to lead; to head):～队 *to lead a group; leader of a group, sports team, etc* | ～头 *to take the lead; to be the first to do sth* ❹领有的,管辖的 to have jurisdiction over; to be in possession of; to be in sb's possession:～海 *territorial waters* (or *sea*) | ～空 *territorial sky* (or *air*); *territorial air space* [领土]一个国家所领有的陆地、领水(包括领海、河流湖泊等)和领空 territory ❺接受,取得 to receive; to accept; to take:～教 *to receive* (or *get*) *instructions* | ～款 *to receive funds; to draw money* ❻了解,明白 to understand; to comprehend; to grasp:～会(对别人的意思有所理解)*to understand; to comprehend; to grasp* | ～悟 *to comprehend; to grasp* ❼量词 ***quantifier*** **1** 用于衣服(used for clothes):一～青衫 *a black shirt* **2** 用于席、箔等(used for mats, foil, etc):一～席 *a mat* | 一～箔 *a reed* (or *sorghum stalk*) *screen*

另 lìng ㄌㄧㄥˋ 代词 ***pronoun***,另外,别的,此外 other; another; separate:～买一个 *to buy another one* | 那是～一件事。*That's another matter.*

令 ㊀ lìng ㄌㄧㄥˋ ❶上级对下级的指示 command; order; decree:明～规定 *explicit order; formal decree; public proclamation* | 遵守法～ *to abide by laws and decrees* ❷上级指示下级 to order; to command:～全体官兵遵照执行。*All the officers and soldiers should act in accordance.* ❸古代官名 ancient official title:县～*county magistrate* ❹使,使得 to cause; to make:～人起敬 *to command esteem; to merit respect; to be admirable* | ～人兴奋 *exciting* ❺时令,时节 season:月～*weather and phenology in a certain lunar month* | 夏～ *summertime; summer weather* ❻美好,善 good; excellent:～名 *good name* (or *reputation*) 敬辞 ***polite*** your:～兄 *your elder brother* | ～尊(称对方的父亲)*your father* ❼词之短小者叫令 brief song-poem; short lyric:调笑～ *teasing* ci-*poem* | 十六字～ *short* ci-*poem set to the tune of* shiliuziling; *16-character* ci-*poem*

㊁ lǐng 见455页 see p455

呤 lìng ㄌㄧㄥˋ 见568页"嘌"字条"嘌呤"(piào—) see 嘌呤 on p568

LIU ㄌㄧㄡ

溜 ㊀ liū ㄌㄧㄡ ❶滑行 to slide; to glide:～冰 *to*

skate | 从滑梯上～下来 *to slide down a slide* ㊀ ***extension*** 滑溜，平滑，无阻碍 smooth：这块石头很滑～。*This stone is very slippery.* ❷溜走，趁人不见走开 to sneak off; to slip away：一眼不见他就～了。*He sneaked off in an instant when I looked away.* ❸沿着，顺着 along：～边儿 *to keep to the edge (of a road, river, etc)* | ～着墙根儿走 *to walk along the foot of a wall* ❹同"熘" same as 熘

[溜达]（*蹓跶）散步，随便走走 to go for a walk; to stroll; to saunter

㊁ liù 见460页 see p460

熘 liū ㄌㄧㄡ 一种烹调法，跟炒相似，作料里掺淀粉，也作"溜"(also written as 溜) to sauté (with thick gravy); to quick-fry：～肉片 *meat slices sauté*

蹓 ㊀ liū ㄌㄧㄡ ❶滑行 to slide; to glide：～冰 *to skate* ❷悄悄走开 to sneak off; to slip away

㊁ liù 见460页 see p460

刘（劉）liú ㄌㄧㄡˊ ❶古代斧钺一类的兵器 (in ancient China) *liu*, a battle-axe-like weapon ❷杀，戮 to kill; to slaughter ❸姓 Liu, a surname

浏（瀏）liú ㄌㄧㄡˊ 清亮 clear; limpid

[浏览]泛泛地看 to glance over; to skim through; to browse

留 liú ㄌㄧㄡˊ ❶停止在某一个地方 to remain; to stay (㊀ ***doublet*** 停一 to stay for a time; to stop; to remain)：他～在天津了。*He stayed on in Tianjin.* | ～学(留居外国求学) *to study abroad* ㊀ ***extension*** 注意力放在上面 to pay attention to; to concentrate on sth：～心 *to be careful; to take care* | ～神 *to be careful; to take care* ❷不让别人离开 to ask sb to stay; to keep sb where he (*or* she) is：挽～*to persuade sb to stay on* | 他一定要走，我～不住他。*He was determined to leave so I had no way to keep him here.* | ～难(nàn)(故意和人为难) *to make things difficult for sb; to put obstacles in sb's way* ❸接受，收容 to accept; to take; to keep (㊀ ***doublet*** 收一 to undertake the care of; to take sb in)：把礼物～下 *to accept the gift* ❹保留 to keep; to reserve：～余地 *to give some leeway; to allow for unforeseen circumstances* | ～胡子 *to grow a beard (or moustache)* | 今天请给我～饭。*Please keep some food for me today.* ❺遗留 to leave behind; to leave：祖先给我们～下了丰富的文化遗产。*Our forefathers have left us a rich cultural heritage.*

馏 ㊀ liú ㄌㄧㄡˊ 蒸馏，加热使液体变成蒸气后再凝成纯净的液体 to distil

L

㊁ liù 见460页 see p460

骝 liú ㄌㄧㄡˊ 古书上指黑鬣黑尾巴的红马(in ancient Chinese texts) red horse with black mane and tail

榴 liú ㄌㄧㄡˊ 石榴,又叫"安石榴"。落叶灌木,一般开红花,果实球状,内有很多种子,种子上的肉可吃。根、皮可入药(also called 安石榴) pomegranate (*Punica granatum*)

飗 liú ㄌㄧㄡˊ [飗飗]微风吹动的样子(of a gentle breeze) blowing

镏 ㊀ liú ㄌㄧㄡˊ 我国特有的镀金法,把溶解在水银里的金子用刷子涂在器物表面作装饰,所镏的金层经久不退(typical Chinese way of gold-plating, i. e. applying the gold dissolved in mercury with a brush to the surfaces of articles as a gilding, which lasts long) to gild; to gold-plate

㊁ liù 见460页 see p460

鹠 liú ㄌㄧㄡˊ [鸺鹠](xiū—)鸟名。羽毛棕褐色,尾巴黑褐色,有横斑,外形跟猫头鹰相似。捕食鼠、兔等,对农业有益 collared owlet (*Glaucidium brodiei*)

瘤 liú ㄌㄧㄡˊ (—子)生物体的组织增殖生成的疙瘩,多由刺激或微生物寄生而引起 tumour

流 liú ㄌㄧㄡˊ ❶液体移动 to flow:水往低处～。*Water flows to the lowest level.*|～水不腐 *Running water does not get stale.*|～汗 *to perspire; to sweat*|～血 *to shed blood; to bleed* [流浪]生活无着,漂泊不定 to roam about; to wander; to lead a vagrant life [流利]说话、书写等灵活顺畅 fluent; smooth:他的钢笔字写得很～～。*He writes a good hand with a pen.*|他说一口～～的普通话。*He speaks fluent standard Chinese.* [流线型]前端圆,后端尖,略似水滴的形状。因空气或水等对流线型的物体阻力小,所以常用作汽车、汽艇等交通工具的外形 streamline ❷像水那样流动 moving from place to place; drifting; flowing:货币～通 *circulation of money*|空气的对～现象 *air convection* ㊀***extension*** **1** 移动不定 to drift; to move:～星 *meteor; shooting star* **2** 运转不停 rotating; ever-moving:～光 *flowing time and tide*|～年 *fleeting time* **3** 不知来路,意外地射来的 flying; stray:～矢 *stray arrow*|～弹 *stray bullet* **4** 传播或相沿下来 to spread; to circulate; to propagate:～行 *popular; prevalent; fashionable*|～传 *to spread; to circulate; to hand down* [流产]孕妇怀孕未满28周就产出胎儿(of a woman) to have a miscarriage; to abort; to miscarry ❸流动的东西 sth resembling a stream of water; current:河～*river*|电～ *electric current*|寒～ *cold current* (or *wave*)|气～ *air current; airflow; airstream* ❹趋

向坏的方面 to change for the worse; to degenerate:开会不要～于形式。*Conferences should not be a mere formality.*|放任自～ *to let things drift; laissez-faire* ❺品类 class; rate; grade **1** 派别 class; school:九～ *nine schools of thought* **2** 等级 grade; rate:第一～产品 *first-rate product* ❻旧时刑法的一种，把人送到荒远的地方去，充军(a punishment in former times) to banish; to send into exile:～放 *to banish; to send into exile*

琉 liú ㄌㄧㄡˊ [琉璃](—li)一种用铝和钠的硅酸化合物烧制成的釉料 coloured glaze:～～瓦 *glazed tile*

硫 liú ㄌㄧㄡˊ 一种非金属元素，符号S，通常叫"硫磺"。淡黄色，质硬而脆，不易传热和电。可用来制造硫酸、药物、杀虫剂等(commonly called 硫磺) sulphur (S)

旒 liú ㄌㄧㄡˊ ❶旗子上面的飘带 flowing ribbon attached to a flag; streamer ❷古代皇帝礼帽前后的玉串(in ancient China) jade pendants on the imperial crown

鎏 liú ㄌㄧㄡˊ ❶成色好的金子 fine gold ❷同"镏"(liú) same as 镏

镠 liú ㄌㄧㄡˊ 成色好的黄金 fine gold

柳 liǔ ㄌㄧㄡˇ ❶柳树，落叶乔木，枝细长下垂，叶狭长，春天开花，黄绿色。种子上有白色毛状物，成熟后随风飞散，叫柳絮。另有一种河柳，枝不下垂 willow (*Salix*) ❷星宿名，二十八宿之一 *Liu*, 24th of the 28 constellations

绺 liǔ ㄌㄧㄡˇ (一儿)量词 ***quantifier***，用于成束的理顺了的丝、线、须、发等(used for thread, beard, hair, etc) tuft; lock; skein:两～儿线 *two skeins of thread*|五～儿须 *five wisps of beard*|一～儿头发 *a lock (or tuft, wisp) of hair*

锍 liǔ ㄌㄧㄡˇ 有色金属冶炼过程中生产出的各种金属硫化物的互熔体 sulphonium; matte

六 ⊖ liù ㄌㄧㄡˋ ❶数目字 six ❷旧时乐谱记音符号的一个，相当于简谱的"5" note of the scale in former times, corresponding to 5 in numbered musical notation

㊁ lù 见467页 see p467

陆(陸) ㊁ liù ㄌㄧㄡˋ "六"的大写 six, capital form of 六

⊖ lù 见467页 see p467

碌(*磟) ㊁ liù ㄌㄧㄡˋ [碌碡](—zhou)农具名。圆柱形，用石头做成，用来轧脱谷粒或轧平场院 stone roller (for threshing grain, levelling a threshing floor, etc)

⊖ lù 见468页 see p468

遛 liù ㄌㄧㄡˋ ❶散步，慢慢走，随便走走 to saunter; to stroll ❷牵着牲畜或带着鸟慢慢走 to walk (an animal):～马 *to walk a horse*|～鸟 *to go for a walk with a cage of birds in*

L

a quiet place

馏 ㊀ liù ㄌㄧㄡˋ 把凉了的熟食品再蒸热 to heat up (cold food in a steamer):把馒头～～ *to heat up the cold* mantou

㊁ liú 见457页 see p457

溜(❷❸**霤) ㊁ liù ㄌㄧㄡˋ ❶急流 swift current:大～ *strong current*|今天河水～很大。*The river has a strong current today.* ❷顺房檐滴下来的水 rainwater from the roof:檐～ *rainwater from the eaves* ❸屋檐上安的接雨水用的长水槽 eaves gutter:水～ *eaves gutter* ❹(一儿)量词 ***quantifier***,用于成行(háng)列的事物 line; column; row:一～三间房 *a row of three rooms*

㊀ liū 见456页 see p456

镏 ㊁ liù ㄌㄧㄡˋ [镏子]〈方 ***dialect***〉戒指(finger) ring:金～～ *gold ring*

㊀ liú 见458页 see p458

蹓 ㊁ liù ㄌㄧㄡˋ 同"遛❶"same as 遛❶

㊀ liū 见457页 see p457

飂 ㊀ liù ㄌㄧㄡˋ 西风 west wind

㊁ liáo 见445页 see p445

鹨 liù ㄌㄧㄡˋ 鸟名。身体小,嘴细长,吃害虫,是益鸟 pipit (*Anthus*)

LO ㄌㄛ

咯 ㊁ lo·ㄌㄛ 助词 ***auxiliary***:那倒好～! *That would be much better!*

㊀ kǎ 见380页 see p380

㊂ gē 见223页 see p223

LONG ㄌㄨㄥ

龙(龍) lóng ㄌㄨㄥˊ ❶我国古代传说中的一种身体长(cháng)的、有鳞有角的动物。能走,能飞,能游泳。近代古生物学上指一些大小不等的有脚有尾的爬行动物 dragon:恐～ *dinosaur*|翼手～ *pterosaur* (*Pterodactyloidea*) [龙头]自来水管放水的出口 tap; faucet; cock ❷古代指帝王(in ancient China) dragon as the symbol of the emperor; emperor:真～天子 *son of Heaven — the emperor*|～体 *body of the emperor; emperor's health*|～颜 *face* (or *look*) *of the emperor; imperial countenance*|～袍 *imperial robe*|～床 *emperor's bed* ❸形状像龙的或有龙的图案的 anything shaped like a dragon or with the pattern of a dragon on it:～灯 *dragon lantern*|～舟 *dragon boat*

[龙钟]年老衰弱行动不灵便的样子 decrepit; senile

〈古 ***archaism***〉又同"垄"(lǒng) also same as 垄

茏(蘢) lóng ㄌㄨㄥˊ [茏葱][葱茏]草木茂盛的样子 verdant; luxuriantly green

咙(嚨) lóng ㄌㄨㄥˊ 喉咙,咽喉。参看279页"喉"(hóu)(see 喉 on p279)

throat

泷(瀧) ㊀ lóng ㄌㄨㄥˊ 急流的水 rapids [七里泷]地名,在浙江省桐庐 Qililong, a place in Tonglu, Zhejiang Province

㊁ shuāng 见 699 页 see p699

珑(瓏) lóng ㄌㄨㄥˊ 见 453 页"玲"字条"玲珑"(líng—)see 玲珑 on p453

栊(櫳) lóng ㄌㄨㄥˊ ❶窗户 window ❷养兽的栅栏 cage for beasts

昽(曨) lóng ㄌㄨㄥˊ 见 497 页"曚"字条"曚昽"(méng—)、756页"曈"字条"曈昽"(tóng—)see 曚昽 on p497 and 曈昽 on p756

胧(朧) lóng ㄌㄨㄥˊ 见 497 页"朦"字条"朦胧"(méng—)see 朦胧 on p497

砻(礱) lóng ㄌㄨㄥˊ ❶去掉稻壳的器具 rice huller ❷用砻去掉稻壳 to hull (rice):～谷舂米 *to hull grain and pound rice*

眬(矓) lóng ㄌㄨㄥˊ 见 497 页"蒙"字条"蒙眬"(méng—)see 蒙眬 on p497

聋(聾) lóng ㄌㄨㄥˊ 耳朵听不见声音,通常把听觉迟钝也叫聋 deaf; hard of hearing:他耳朵～了。*He is deaf.*

笼(籠) ㊀ lóng ㄌㄨㄥˊ ❶(一子、一儿)养鸟、虫的器具,用竹、木条或金属丝等编插而成 cage; coop:鸟～子 *birdcage*|鸡～ *chicken coop*|蝈蝈～ *katydid cage* ㊀***extension*** 旧时囚禁犯人的东西(in former times) wooden framework for confining prisoners; cage:囚～(*wooden*) *prisoner's cage*|牢～ *prison* ❷用竹、木等材料制成的有盖的蒸东西的器具 (food) steamer:蒸～ *food steamer*|～屉 *bamboo* (or *wooden*) *utensil for steaming food* (*composed of several tiers*); *food steamer*

㊁ lǒng 见462页 see p462

隆 lóng ㄌㄨㄥˊ ❶盛大,厚,程度深 grand; solemn; profound:～冬 *midwinter; depth of winter*|～寒 *severe* (or *intense*) *cold*|～重的典礼 *grand ceremony* ❷兴盛 prosperous; thriving (㊀***doublet*** —盛 abundant; prosperous; thriving|兴—prosperous; thriving; flourishing) ❸高 to swell; to bulge; to protrude:～起 *to swell; to bulge*

癃 lóng ㄌㄨㄥˊ ❶古书上指年老衰弱多病(in ancient Chinese texts) infirm; weak; sickly ❷癃闭,中医指小便不通的病 retention of urine; difficulty in urination

窿 lóng ㄌㄨㄥˊ 〈方 ***dialect***〉煤矿坑道(in a coal mine) gallery

优(儱) lǒng ㄌㄨㄥˇ [优侗](—tǒng)同"笼统" same as 笼统

陇(隴) lǒng ㄌㄨㄥˇ ❶陇山,山名,位于陕

西、甘肃两省交界的地方 Longshan Mountain, on the borderland between Shaanxi and Gansu ❷甘肃省的别称 Long, another name for Gansu Province:～海铁路 *Long-Hai Railway*

垅(壠) lǒng ㄌㄨㄥˇ 同"垄" same as 垄

拢(攏) lǒng ㄌㄨㄥˇ ❶凑起,总合 to add up; to sum up:～共 *altogether; all told; in all*|～总 *altogether; all told; in all* ❷靠近,船只靠岸 to draw near; to approach; to reach (㊟ ***doublet*** 靠— to draw close; to close up):～岸 *to approach the shore; to come alongside the shore*|拉～ *to draw over to one's side; to win over; to rope in*|他们俩总谈不～。*They can never talk to each other in a heart-to-heart way.* or *They can never agree with each other.* ❸收束使不松散 to hold (*or* gather) together; to keep close together:～紧 *to hold* (*sth*) *tight*|用绳子把柴火～住 *to tie the firewood together with a rope* ❹梳,用梳子整理头发 to comb (hair):～一～头发 *to comb* (or *tidy*) *the hair* ❺合上,聚拢 to bring together; to close:笑得嘴都合不～了 *to grin from ear to ear*

垄(壟) lǒng ㄌㄨㄥˇ ❶田地分界的埂子 raised path between fields ❷农作物的行(háng)或行与行间的空地 ridge (in a field):宽～密植 *close planting between broad ridges* ❸像田埂的东西 ridge-like thing:瓦～*rows of tiles on a roof; tile ridge* [垄断]操纵市场,把持权柄,独占利益 to monopolize

笼(籠) ㊁ lǒng ㄌㄨㄥˇ ❶遮盖,罩住 to envelop; to cover; to enclose:黑云～罩着天空。*The sky is enveloped in thick clouds.* [笼络]用手段拉拢人 to win sb over by any means; to draw over; to rope in:～～人心 *to win people's heart by meeting their felt needs, etc* ❷比较大的箱子 large box (*or* chest); trunk:箱～*boxes and baskets; trunks*

[笼统](—tǒng)概括而不分明,不具体 general; sweeping:话太～～了,不能表明确切的意思。*The words are too general to convey the exact meaning.*

㊀ lóng 见461页 see p461

弄(*衖) ㊁ lòng ㄌㄨㄥˋ 〈方 ***dialect***〉弄堂,小巷,小胡同 lane; alley; alleyway

㊀ nòng 见540页 see p540

㟖 lòng ㄌㄨㄥˋ (壮 ***Zhuang***)石山间的平地 small piece of flat land between stone hills

LOU ㄌㄡ

搂(摟) ㊁ lōu ㄌㄡ ❶用手或工具把东西聚集起来 to gather up; to rake together:～柴火 *to rake up*

twigs, dead leaves, etc (*for fuel*) ㊗ ***figurative*** 搜刮 to squeeze (money); to extort: ～钱 *to extort money* ❷向着自己的方向拨 to pull; to draw: ～枪机 *to pull a trigger*

㊀ lǒu 见463页 see p463

瞜(瞜) lōu ㄌㄡ 〈方 ***dialect***〉看 to look: 让我～一～。*Let me have a look.*

剅(**劅) lóu ㄌㄡˊ 〈方 ***dialect***〉堤坝下面的水口，水道 discharge or outlet tunnel under a dam or dyke; water course through a dyke: ～口 *mouth of a water course under a dyke* | ～嘴 *mouth of a water course under a dyke*

娄(婁) lóu ㄌㄡˊ ❶星宿名，二十八宿之一 *lou*, 16th of the 28 constellations ❷〈方 ***dialect***〉(某些瓜类)过熟而变质 (of melons) overripe and unfit to eat: 瓜～了。*The melon is overripe.* ❸姓 Lou, a surname

偻(僂) ㊁ lóu ㄌㄡˊ [偻啰](—luo)旧同"喽啰" same as 喽啰 in former times

㊀ lǚ 见470页 see p470

蒌(蔞) lóu ㄌㄡˊ [蒌蒿](—hāo)多年生草本植物，花淡黄色，可入药 beach wormwood (*Artemisia stelleriana*)

喽(嘍) ㊁ lóu ㄌㄡˊ [喽啰](*偻啰)(—luo)旧时称盗贼的部下，现在多比喻追随恶人的人 (in former times) rank and file of a band of outlaws; underling; lackey

㊀ lou 见464页 see p464

溇(漊) lóu ㄌㄡˊ 溇水，水名，在湖南省 Loushui River, in Hunan Province

楼(樓) lóu ㄌㄡˊ ❶两层以上的房屋 storeyed building; multi-storey house: ～房 *building of two or more storeys* | 大～ *mansion* ❷楼房的一层 storey; floor: 一～ (*British*) *ground floor*; (*American*) *first floor* | 三～ (*British*) *second floor*; (*American*) *third floor*

耧(耬) lóu ㄌㄡˊ 播种用的农具 animal-drawn seed plough; drill barrow; drill

蝼(螻) lóu ㄌㄡˊ 蝼蛄(gū)，又叫"喇喇蛄"、"土狗子"。一种对农作物有害的昆虫，褐色，有翅，前脚很强，能掘地，咬农作物的根 (also called 喇喇蛄 or 土狗子) mole cricket (*Gryllotalpa orientalis*)

髅(髏) lóu ㄌㄡˊ 见397页"骷"字条"骷髅"(kū—)、161页"髑"字条"髑髅"(dú—) see 骷髅 on p397 and 髑髅 on p161

搂(摟) ㊀ lǒu ㄌㄡˇ ❶两臂合抱，用手臂拢着 to hold in one's arms; to hug; to embrace (㊟***doublet*** 一抱 to hug; to embrace; to cuddle): 把孩子～在怀里 *to clasp the baby to one's breast* ❷量词 ***quantifier***:一～粗的大树 *a tree one arm-span around*

㊁ lōu 见462页 see p462

嵝(嶁) lǒu ㄌㄡˇ 见 236 页"岣"字条"岣嵝"(gǒu—)see 岣嵝 on p236

篓(簍) lǒu ㄌㄡˇ (～子、～儿)盛(chéng)东西的器具,用竹、荆条等编成 basket:字纸～儿 *wastepaper basket; wastebasket*|油～ *oil container (small-mouthed and big-bellied basket made of wicker chips or bamboo chips and lined with oil paper)*

陋 lòu ㄌㄡˋ ❶丑的,坏的,不文明的 plain; ugly:丑～ *ugly*|～规 *objectionable practices*|～习 *corrupt customs; bad habits* ❷狭小(of a dwelling)humble; mean:～室 *humble room*|～巷 *mean alley* ❸少,简略(of knowledge) scanty; limited; shallow:学识浅～*to be shallow in knowledge; to have meagre knowledge; to have little learning*|因～就简 *to make do with whatever is available*|孤～寡闻(见闻少) *ignorant and ill-informed*

镂(鏤) lòu ㄌㄡˋ 雕刻 to engrave; to carve:～花 *ornamental engraving*|～骨铭心(喻永远不忘) *to be engraved on the bones and imprinted on the heart — to be borne in mind or remembered forever with gratitude*

瘘(瘻、**瘺) lòu ㄌㄡˋ 瘘管,身体里面因发生病变而向外溃破所形成的管道,病灶里的分泌物可以由瘘管里流出来 fistula

漏 lòu ㄌㄡˋ ❶物体由孔缝透过或滴下 to leak; to trickle:水壶～了。*The kettle leaks.*|油箱～了。*The petrol tank is leaking.* [漏洞]做事的破绽,不周密的地方 flaw; hole; loophole:堵塞～～ *to stop up loopholes* [漏斗]灌注液体等到小口的器具里的用具 funnel; hopper ❷泄漏,泄露 to divulge; to leak; to let out:～了风声 *to divulge a secret; to leak* (or *let out*) *information*|走～消息 *to leak information; to let out a secret* ❸遗落 to be missing; to leave out by mistake:这一项可千万不能～掉。*Be sure not to leave out this item.* ❹漏壶,古代计时的器具,用铜制成。壶上下分好几层,上层底有小孔,可以滴水,层层下注,以底层蓄水多少计算时间 hourglass; water clock; clepsydra

露 ㊁ lòu ㄌㄡˋ 义同"露㊀❸",用于一些口语词语,如"露怯"、"露马脚"等(used in some colloquial expressions, e.g. 露怯(display one's ignorance),露马脚(give oneself away), etc) same meaning as 露㊀❸

㊀ lù 见469页 see p469

喽(嘍) ㊀ lou ·ㄌㄡ 助词 ***auxiliary***,意思相

当于“啦”equal to 啦：够～，别说～！*That's enough! Stop talking!*

㊁ lóu 见463页 see p463

LU ㄌㄨ

撸 lū ㄌㄨ 〈方 **dialect**〉❶捋(luō) to rub one's palm along (sth long); to strip with the hand：～袖子 *to push up* (or *roll up*) *one's sleeves*｜～树叶 *to strip a twig of its leaves* ❷撤职 to dismiss sb from his post：他的职务被～了。*He was dismissed from his post.* ❸责备，训斥 to scold; to take to task; to dress down：他被～了一顿。*He got a good scolding.*

噜 lū ㄌㄨ ［噜苏］(—su)〈方 **dialect**〉啰唆 wordy; long-winded; over-elaborate

卢(盧) lú ㄌㄨ 姓 Lu, a surname

［卢比］(外 **loanword**) 印度、巴基斯坦、尼泊尔、斯里兰卡等国的货币单位 rupee, a unit of currency in India, Pakistan, Nepal, Sri Lanka, etc

［卢布］(外 **loanword**) 俄罗斯等国的货币单位 rouble (*or* ruble), a unit of currency in Russia, etc

垆(壚、❷罏)** lú ㄌㄨ ❶黑色坚硬的土 black earth ❷旧时酒店里安放酒瓮的土台子。也指酒店(also used to denote wineshop) earthen stand for wine jars (in former times)

泸(瀘) lú ㄌㄨ ［泸州］地名，在四川省 Luzhou, a place in Sichuan Province

栌(櫨) lú ㄌㄨ ［黄栌］落叶小乔木，花黄绿色，叶子秋天变成红色。木材黄色，可制器具，也可做染料 smoke tree (*Cotinus coggygria*)

胪(臚) lú ㄌㄨ 陈列，陈述 to set out; to display; to state：～列 *to enumerate; to list*｜～情(陈述心情) *to state one's case*

鸬(鸕) lú ㄌㄨ ［鸬鹚］(—cí) 水鸟名，俗叫“鱼鹰”。羽毛黑色，闪绿光，能游泳，善于捕食鱼类，用树叶、海藻等筑巢。渔人常用来捕鱼 (popularly called 鱼鹰) cormorant (*Phalacrocorax*)

轳(鑪) lú ㄌㄨ 一种人造的放射性元素，(符号 Rf) rutherfordium (Rf)

颅(顱) lú ㄌㄨ 头的上部，包括头骨和脑，也指头(also used to denote head) cranium; skull：～骨 *cranial bones*

舻(艫) lú ㄌㄨ 见994页“舳”字条“舳舻”(zhú—) see 舳舻 on p994

鲈(鱸) lú ㄌㄨ 鲈鱼，鱼名。体侧扁，嘴大，鳞细，银灰色，背部和背鳍上有小黑斑。肉味鲜美 perch (*Perca*)

芦(蘆) lú ㄌㄨ 芦苇，苇子，多年生草本植

物,生在浅水里。茎中空,可造纸、编席等。根茎可入药 reed

庐(廬) lú ㄌㄨˊ 房舍 hut; cottage:茅~ *thatched cottage*

炉(爐、*鑪) lú ㄌㄨˊ (—子)取暖、做饭或冶炼用的设备 stove; oven; furnace:电~ *electric stove* (or *furnace*)|煤气~ *gas stove* (or *furnace, cooker*)|煤球~子 *briquettes stove*|炼钢~ *steel furnace*

卤(鹵、滷) lǔ ㄌㄨˇ ❶制盐时剩下的黑色汁液,是氯化镁、硫酸镁、溴化镁及氯化钠等的混合物,味苦有毒。也叫"苦汁"或"盐卤"(also called 苦汁 or 盐卤) bittern [卤砂]矿物名。化学成分为 NH_4Cl,常为皮壳状或粉块状结晶,无色或白色,间带红褐色,有玻璃光泽。在工业、农业和医药上都有广泛的用途。也作"硇砂",也叫"硇(náo)砂" (also written as 硇砂, also called 硇砂) sal (*or* natural) ammoniac; ammonium chloride [卤素]化学中统称氟、氯、溴、碘、砹等五种元素 halogen ❷浓汁 thick infusion; thick gravy:茶~ *strong tea* (*to be diluted before drinking*)|打~面 *noodles served with thick gravy* ❸用盐水、酱油等浓汁制作食品 to stew in salty water with spices or in soy sauce:~鸡 *to stew chickens in salty water with spices and soy sauce; potstewed chicken*|~煮豆腐 *pot-stewed beancurd*

硵(磠) lǔ ㄌㄨˇ [硵砂]同卤砂。参看466页"卤"(see 卤 on p466) same as 卤砂

虏(虜) lǔ ㄌㄨˇ ❶俘获 to take prisoner (㊣ *doublet* 俘— to capture; to take prisoner):~获甚众 *to capture a lot of enemy soldiers and weapons*|俘~敌军数万人 *to capture tens of thousands of enemy soldiers* ❷打仗时捉住的敌人 captive; prisoner of war (㊣ *doublet* 俘— captive; captured personnel):优待俘~ *to treat prisoners of war kindly*

掳(擄) lǔ ㄌㄨˇ 抢取 to carry off; to capture (㊣ *doublet* —掠 pillage; to loot):烧杀~掠 *burning, killing and looting*

鲁 lǔ ㄌㄨˇ ❶愚钝,莽撞 stupid; dull; rash:粗~ *rough; rude; boorish*|愚~ *dull-witted; stupid; uncouth* [鲁莽](*卤莽)仔细考虑事理,冒失 crude and rash; rash ❷周代诸侯国名,在今山东省南部一带 Lu, a princedom in the Zhou Dynasty, located in the south of today's Shandong Province ❸山东省的别称 Lu, another name for Shandong Province

橹(*樐、*艣、*艪) lǔ ㄌㄨˇ 拨水使船前进的器具 scull; sweep:摇~ *to scull*

镥 lǔ ㄌㄨˇ 一种金属元素,符号Lu,银白色,质软。可

用作催化剂等 lutetium (Lu)

六 ㊁ lù ㄌㄨˋ［六安］地名，在安徽省 Lu'an, a place in Anhui Province［六合］地名，在江苏省南京 Luhe, a place in Nanjing, Jiangsu Province

㊀ liù 见459页 see p459

甪（**冄） lù ㄌㄨˋ［甪直］地名，在江苏省苏州 Luzhi, a place in Suzhou, Jiangsu Province［甪里堰］地名，在浙江省海盐 Luliyan, a place in Haiyan, Zhejiang Province

陆（陸） ㊀ lù ㄌㄨˋ ❶陆地，高出水面的土地 land：登～ *to land; to disembark*｜～路 *land route*｜～军 *army; ground* (or *land*) *force* ❷姓 Lu, a surname

［陆离］形容色彩繁杂 varicoloured：光怪～～ *grotesque in shape and gaudy in colour*

［陆续］副词 **adverb**，接连不断 one after another; in succession：开会的人～～地到了。*People attending the conference arrived one after another.*

㊁ liù 见459页 see p459

录（録） lù ㄌㄨˋ ❶录制，记录，抄写，记载 to record; to write down; to copy：～像 *to videotape; to video*｜～音 *to tape-record* (*sound*); *to record; to tape*｜把这份公文～下来。*Copy the document.* ❷记载言行或事物的书刊 record; register; collection：语～*quotations*｜备忘～ *memorandum* (*book*)｜回忆～ *reminiscences; memoirs; recollections* ❸采取，任用 to choose; to employ; to hire：收～ *to employ; to include; to enter*｜～用 *to employ; to recruit; to take on the staff*｜～取 *to enroll; to recruit; to admit*

峚 lù ㄌㄨˋ（壮 *Zhuang*）土山间的平地 small piece of flat land between hillocks

渌 lù ㄌㄨˋ 渌水，水名，在湖南省株洲 Lushui River, in Zhuzhou, Hunan Province

逯 lù ㄌㄨˋ 姓 Lu, a surname

绿 ㊁ lù ㄌㄨˋ 义同"绿㊀" same meaning as 绿㊀［绿林］greenwood **1** 原指西汉末年聚集在湖北绿林山的农民起义军，后来泛指聚集山林、反抗封建统治者的人们 (originally used to denote the uprising of peasants in the Lulin Mountain in Hubei Province at the end of the Western Han Dynasty, later generally to denote any uprising against feudal rulers) **2** 旧指上山为匪、抢劫财物的集团 (formerly used to denote groups of outlaws or looters in mountains)［鸭绿江］水名。是中国和朝鲜两国的界河。源出吉林省东南中朝边境的白头山，西南流到辽宁省丹东入黄海 Yalu River, boundary river between China and Korea, originating from Baitou Mountain in Jilin Province and flowing southwestward through Dandong, Liaoning Province, to the Yellow Sea

㊁ lù 见472页 see p472

禄 lù ㄌㄨˋ 古代官吏的俸给(in ancient China) official's salary; emolument:高官厚～ *high position and handsome salary*

碌 ㊀ lù ㄌㄨˋ ❶平凡 commonplace; mediocre:庸～common and vulgar; mediocre [碌碌]平庸,无所作为 mediocre; commonplace:庸庸～～*mediocre and unambitious* ❷繁忙 busy:忙～*to be busy; to bustle about*

㊁ liù 见459页 see p459

盝 lù ㄌㄨˋ ❶古代的一种盒子 a kind of box in ancient China❷漉,过滤 to strain; to filter; to filtrate

箓(籙) lù ㄌㄨˋ ❶簿子,册子 booklet ❷符箓,道士画的驱使鬼神的符号,是一种迷信骗人的东西 Taoist talisman, magic figure or sign drawn by Taoist priests to invoke or expel spirits

醁 lù ㄌㄨˋ 见455页"醽"字条"醽醁"(líng－) see 醽醁 on p455

辂 lù ㄌㄨˋ ❶古代车辕上用来牵引车子的横木(in ancient China) horizontal bar on a cart shaft ❷古代的大车(in ancient China) cart

赂 lù ㄌㄨˋ ❶贿赂,用财物买通别人 to give costly presents; to bribe ❷财物,特指赠送的财物 property; (gift of) goods or money

鹿 lù ㄌㄨˋ 哺乳动物,反刍类,尾短,腿细长,毛黄褐色,有的有花斑,性情温驯,有的雄鹿有树枝状的角 deer (*Cervus*)

漉 lù ㄌㄨˋ 液体往下渗,过滤 to seep through; to filter:～网(*screen used in making paper*) *vat-net* | ～酒 *to filter wine* [漉漉]潮湿的样子 wet; dripping with sweat:湿～～ *moist; damp*

辘 lù ㄌㄨˋ [辘轳](－lu) **1** 安在井上绞起汲水斗的器具 well-pulley; windlass **2** 机械上的绞盘 winch; windlass; capstan

簏 lù ㄌㄨˋ 竹箱 bamboo chest (*or* trunk)

麓 lù ㄌㄨˋ 山脚下 foot of a hill or mountain:泰山之～ *foot of Taishan Mountain*

路 lù ㄌㄨˋ ❶道,往来通行的地方 road; path; way (㊀ ***doublet*** －途 road; way | －径 route; way | 道－ road; way; path):公～ *highway; road* | 水～ *waterway; water route* | 高架～ *overhead road* ㊀ ***extension*** 思想或行动的方向、途径 way; means:走社会主义道～ *to follow* (or *take*) *the socialist road* | 思～ *train of thoughts; line of thinking* | 生～ *means of livelihood* (or *subsistence*); *way out* ❷方面,地区 region; area; district:南～货 *southern products* | 外～货 *imported* (or *non-local*) *goods* ❸种类 sort; grade; class:两～货 *two different sorts of goods* |

L

他俩是一～人。*These two fellows are of the same sort.*

蕗 lù ㄌㄨˋ 甘草的别名 another name for liquorice (*Glycyrrhiza uralensis*)

潞 lù ㄌㄨˋ ❶潞水，水名，即今山西省的浊漳河 Lushui River, in Shanxi Province, now called Zhuozhang River ❷潞江，水名，即云南省的怒江 Lujiang River, in Yunnan Province, now called Nujiang River [潞西]地名，在云南省 Luxi, a place in Yunnan Province

璐 lù ㄌㄨˋ 美玉 beautiful (*or* fine) jade

鹭 lù ㄌㄨˋ 水鸟名。翼大尾短，颈和腿很长，常见的有白鹭、苍鹭、绿鹭等 egret; aigrette; heron (*Ardeidae*) [鹭鸶](— sī)就是白鹭，羽毛纯白色，顶有细长的白羽，捕食小鱼 little egret (*Egretta garzetta*)

露 ㊀ lù ㄌㄨˋ ❶露水，靠近地面的水蒸气因夜间遇冷凝结成的小水珠 dew ㊁***extension*** 露天，没有遮蔽，在屋外的 outside a house; in the open; outdoors: 风餐～宿 *to eat in the wind and sleep in the dew — to be exposed to inclement weather on a journey* | ～营 *to camp (out); to encamp; to bivouac* ❷用药料、果汁等制成的饮料 beverage distilled from flowers, fruit or leaves; drink mixed with fruit juice; syrup: 枇杷～ *loquat syrup* | 果子～ *fruit syrup* | 玫瑰～ *rose syrup* ❸显出来，现出来 to show; to reveal; to betray (㊃***doublet*** 显—to become visible; to appear; to reveal): ～骨 *thinly veiled; undisguised; barefaced* | 暴～思想 *to lay bare one's thoughts* | 揭～ *to expose; to unmask; to bring to light* | 不～面 *not to show oneself*

㊁ lòu 见464页 see p464

僇 lù ㄌㄨˋ ❶侮辱 insult; humiliate ❷同"戮" same as 戮

戮(❶*剹、❷*勠) lù ㄌㄨˋ ❶杀 to kill; to slay (㊃***doublet*** 杀—to massacre; to butcher) ❷并，合 to unite; to join; to combine [戮力]合力，并力 to make concerted efforts; to join forces (*or* hands): ～～同心 *to unite in a concerted effort; to make concerted efforts*

轳(轤) lu ·ㄌㄨ 见468页"辘"字条"辘轳"(lù—)see 辘轳 on p468

氇 lu ·ㄌㄨ 见578页"氆"字条"氆氇"(pǔ—)see 氆氇 on p578

LÜ ㄌㄩ

驴(驢) lǘ ㄌㄩˊ 一种家畜，像马，比马小，耳朵和脸都较长，能驮东西、拉车、供人骑乘 donkey; ass

闾 lǘ ㄌㄩˊ ❶里门，巷口的门 gate of (*or* entrance to) an alley ❷古代二十五家为一闾 *lü*, a neighbourhood of 25 families in ancient China

榈 lú ㄌㄩˊ 见51页"栟"字条"栟榈"(bīng—)、1015页"棕"字条"棕榈"(zōng—) see 栟榈 on p51 and 棕榈 on p1015

吕 lǚ ㄌㄩˇ 我国音乐十二律中的阴律,有六种,总称六吕 *lü*, any of the 6 even-numbered pitches (called 六吕) in the 12 standard pitches in ancient Chinese music

侣 lǚ ㄌㄩˇ 同伴 companion; associate (㊥***doublet*** 伴— companion; mate; partner):情～ *lover; sweetheart*

铝 lǚ ㄌㄩˇ 一种金属元素,符号Al,银白色,有光泽,质地坚韧而轻,有延展性。做日用器皿的铝通常叫钢精或钢种 aluminium (Al)

稆(**穭) lǚ ㄌㄩˇ 谷物等不种自生的,也作"旅"(also written as 旅) (of grains) naturally grown:～生 *naturally-grown; self-sown*

捋 ㊁ lǚ ㄌㄩˇ 用手指顺着抹过去,整理 to smooth out with the fingers; to stroke:～胡子 *to stroke one's beard*|～头发 *to stroke one's hair*

㊀ luō 见475页 see p475

旅 lǚ ㄌㄩˇ ❶出行,在外作客 to travel; to journey; to live away from home:～行 *to travel; to journey; to tour*|～馆 *inn; hotel*|～途 *journey; trip*|～居 *to live away from one's native place; to sojourn*|～客 *hotel guest; traveller; passenger*|～美华侨 *overseas Chinese residing in the US; Chinese living in the US* ❷军队的一种编制单位(military unit) brigade ❸指军队 troops; force:军～ *army; troops*|强兵劲～ *formidable force; strong army to be reckoned with* ❹共同 together; jointly:～进～退 *to advance and retreat together with somebody; to always follow the steps of others, forward or backward* ❺同"稆" same as 稆:～生 *naturally grown; self-sown*|～葵 *self-sown sunflower*

膂 lǚ ㄌㄩˇ 脊梁骨 backbone [膂力]体力 muscular (*or* physical) strength; brawn:～～过人 *possessing extraordinary muscular* (or *physical*) *strength*

偻(僂) ㊀ lǚ ㄌㄩˇ ❶脊背弯曲 hunchbacked; bent; crooked:伛(yǔ)～ *hunchbacked; humpbacked* ❷迅速 instantly; directly; immediately:不能～指(不能迅速指出来) *unable to point out straight away*

㊁ lóu 见463页 see p463

屡(屢) lǚ ㄌㄩˇ 副词 ***adverb***, 屡次,接连着,不止一次 time and again; repeatedly; frequently:～见不鲜 *common occurrence; nothing new*|～战～胜 *to be ever-victorious; to win* (or score) *one victory after another*

缕(縷) lǚ ㄌㄩˇ ❶线 thread:一丝一～ *a tiny bit* ❷一条一条地 detailed;

L

in detail：～述 *to state in detail; to give all the details* | ～析 *to make a detailed analysis* ❸量词 ***quantifier***，股 wisp; lock; strand：一～炊烟 *a wisp of smoke from the kitchen chimney* | 两～线 *two strands of thread*

褛(褸) lǚ ㄌㄩˇ 见 415 页"褴"字条"褴褛"(lán—) see 褴褛 on p415

履 lǚ ㄌㄩˇ ❶鞋 shoe：革～ *leather shoes* | 削足适～(喻不合理地迁就现有条件) *to cut the feet to fit the shoes — unreasonably conform to existing conditions* ❷踩在上面，走过 to tread on; to walk on：如～薄冰 *as if treading on thin ice; gingerly* ㉄ ***extension*** 履行，实行 to carry out; to implement; to fulfil：～约 *to fulfil one's promises; to keep an agreement, appointment, etc* | ～行合同 *to enforce (or execute, fulfil) a contract* [履历] **1** 个人的经历 personal record (of education and work experience); antecedents **2** 记载履历的文件 CV; résumé ❸脚步 footstep：步～轻盈 *to walk with a light step*

律 lǜ ㄌㄩˋ ❶法则，规章 law; statute; rule [律诗] 一种诗体，有一定的格律和字数，分五言、七言两种 *lüshi*, a classical Chinese poem of eight lines, each containing five or seven characters [规律] 事物之间的内在的必然的联系，也叫"法则"。它具有十分明显的重复性。它决定事物发展的必然趋向，是不以人的主观意志为转移的(also called 法则) law; regular pattern [一律] 同样，没有例外。same; alike; without exception ❷约束 to restrain; to keep under control：严于～己 *to be strict with oneself; to exercise strict self-discipline* ❸我国古代审定乐音高低的标准，把乐音分为六律(阳律)和六吕(阴律)，合称十二律 *lü*, a series of 12 standard musical pitches (also called 十二律) are divided into 六律(阳律) and 六台(阴律) and used, in ancient China, in classifying musical sounds

葎 lǜ ㄌㄩˋ 葎草，一年生草本植物，茎有倒钩刺，能缠绕他物，开黄绿色小花，全草和果实可入药 scandent hop (*Humulus scandens*)

虑(慮) lǜ ㄌㄩˋ ❶思考，寻思 to consider; to ponder; to think over：深思远～ *to think deeply and plan carefully* ❷担忧 to concern; to be anxious; to worry：忧～ *to be worried; to be anxious; to be concerned* | 过～ *to be over-anxious; to worry unnecessarily* [顾虑] 有所顾忌，担心，不肯或不敢行动 misgiving; apprehension; anxiety; worry

滤(濾) lǜ ㄌㄩˋ 使液体、气体经过纱布、木炭、沙子等物，除去其中所含的杂质、毒气而变纯净 to strain; to

L

filter

率 ⊜ lǜ ㄌㄩˋ 指两个相关的数在一定条件下的比值 rate; ratio; proportion：速～ *speed; rate* | 增长～ *rate of growth* (or *increase*); *growth rate* | 出勤～ *attendance rate; attendance*

⊖ shuài 见697页 see p697

绿 ⊖ lǜ ㄌㄩˋ 一般草和树叶的颜色，蓝和黄混合成的颜色 green：红花～叶 *red flowers and green leaves* | ～地 *greenery patches; greens (in a town or city); afforested land* [绿色]㊕***transfer*** 无公害、无污染的 not to be polluted：～～食品 *green food*

⊜ lù 见467页 see p467

氯 lǜ ㄌㄩˋ 一种化学元素，在通常条件下为气体，符号Cl，黄绿色，味臭，有毒，能损伤呼吸器官。可用来漂白、消毒 chlorine (Cl)

LUAN ㄌㄨㄢ

峦(巒) luán ㄌㄨㄢˊ ❶小而尖的山 low but steep and pointed hill ❷连着的山 mountains in a range：山～起伏 *The mountain ranges rise and fall.*

孪(孿) luán ㄌㄨㄢˊ 双生，一胎两个 twin：～生子 *twin children*

娈(孌) luán ㄌㄨㄢˊ 美好 pretty; beautiful; handsome

栾(欒) luán ㄌㄨㄢˊ 栾树，落叶乔木，夏天开花，黄色。叶可作青色染料。花可入药，又可作黄色染料。木材可制器具，种子可榨油 goldenrain tree (*Koelreuteria paniculata*)

挛(攣) luán ㄌㄨㄢˊ 手脚蜷曲不能伸开 contraction：痉～*convulsion; spasm*

鸾(鸞) luán ㄌㄨㄢˊ 传说中凤凰一类的鸟 fabulous bird related to the phoenix：～凤和鸣(喻夫妻和美) *to be blessed with conjugal felicity; to be a happy couple*

脔(臠) luán ㄌㄨㄢˊ 切成小块的肉 small slice of meat：～割(分割) *to slice up; to cut up; to carve up*

滦(灤) luán ㄌㄨㄢˊ 滦河，水名，在河北省东北部 Luanhe River, in northeast Hebei Province

銮(鑾) luán ㄌㄨㄢˊ 一种铃铛 a small tinkling bell

卵 luǎn ㄌㄨㄢˇ 动植物的雌性生殖细胞，特指动物的蛋 ovum; egg; spawn：鸟～*bird's egg* | 鸡～ *(hen's) eggs* | ～生 *oviparity*

乱(亂) luàn ㄌㄨㄢˋ ❶没有秩序 in disorder; in disarray; in a mess (㊟***doublet*** 纷—numerous and disorderly; helter-skelter; chaotic)：杂～ *mixed and disorderly; untidy; chaotic* | 这篇稿子写得太～。

The manuscript is too messy. ❷战争，武装骚扰 upheaval; rebellion; riot: 叛～ *armed rebellion; mutiny* | 兵～ *turmoil* (or *havoc*) *brought about by war* | 避～ *to flee from social upheaval; to seek refuge from war* ❸混淆(xiáo) to throw into disorder; to confuse; to mix up: 以假～真 *to mix the false with the true; to mix the spurious with the genuine* ❹任意，随便 indiscriminate; random; arbitrary: ～吃 *to eat indiscriminately* | ～跑 *to run all over the place; to dash about* ❺男女关系不正当 illicit sexual relations; promiscuous sexual behaviour: 淫～ (*sexually*) *promiscuous; licentious*

LÜE ㄌㄩㄝ

掠 lüè ㄌㄩㄝˋ ❶夺取 to plunder; to pillage; to sack (㊟ ***doublet*** 一夺 to plunder; to loot; to pillage): ～取 *to seize; to grab; to plunder* | ～人之美(把别人的好处说成是自己的) *to claim credit due to sb else* ❷轻轻擦过 to sweep (*or* brush) past; to graze; to skim over: 燕子～檐而过。*The swallows brushed past the eaves.*

略(*畧) lüè ㄌㄩㄝˋ ❶大致，简单，不详细 brief; sketchy: ～图 *sketch map; sketch* | ～表 *brief table* | ～知一二 *to have only a smattering of; to know only a little* | ～述大意 *to give a brief account* | 叙述过～。*The narration is too sketchy.* | 粗～地计算一下 *to make a rough calculation* ❷省去，简化 to omit; to delete; to leave out: ～去 *to leave out* | 从～ *to be omitted* ❸简要的叙述 brief account; summary; outline: 史～ *outline of history; brief history* | 要～ *outline; summary* ❹计谋 strategy; plan; scheme: 方～ *general plan; overall strategy* | 策～ *tactics; strategy* | 战～ *strategy* | 雄才大～ *great talent and bold vision; rare gifts and bold strategy* ❺抢，掠夺 to capture; to seize: 攻城～地 *to attack cities and seize territories*

锊 lüè ㄌㄩㄝˋ 古代重量单位，约合旧制六两 *lüe*, ancient unit of weight about 6 *liang*

圙(**啳) lüè ㄌㄩㄝˋ 见397页"圐"字条"圐圙"(kū—) see 圐圙 on p397

LUN ㄌㄨㄣ

抡(掄) ㊀ lūn ㄌㄨㄣ 手臂用力挥动 to brandish; to swing: ～刀 *to brandish a sword* | ～拳 *to shake one's fist*

㊁ lún 见474页 see p474

仑(侖、❷*崙) lún ㄌㄨㄣˊ ❶条理，伦次 logical sequence; coherence ❷见406页"昆"字条"昆仑" see 昆仑 on p406

伦(倫) lún ㄌㄨㄣˊ ❶辈,类 peer; match:无与～比 *incomparable; unparalleled; peerless* ❷条理,次序 logic; order:语无～次 *to speak incoherently* (or *illogically*); *to talk in a confused manner* ❸人伦,指人与人之间的关系,特指长幼尊卑之间的关系 human relations, esp as conceived by feudal ethics:天～之乐 *parental joys*|～常 *feudal order of importance or seniority in human relationships*

论(論) ㊁ lún ㄌㄨㄣˊ 论语,古书名,主要记载孔子及其门人的言行(ancient book which mainly recorded the words and deeds of Confucius and his disciples) *The Analects of Confucius; The Analects*

㊀ lùn 见475页 see p475

抡(掄) ㊁ lún ㄌㄨㄣˊ 选择,选拔 to choose; to select:～材 *to select men of ability*

㊀ lūn 见473页 see p473

囵(圇) lún ㄌㄨㄣˊ 见188页"囫"字条"囫囵"(hú—) see 囫囵 on p188

沦(淪) lún ㄌㄨㄣˊ ❶水上的波纹 ripple ❷沉没(mò),陷落 to sink; to fall; to be reduced to (㊈**doublet** —陷 to submerge; to be occupied by the enemy|沉— to sink into (vice, degradation, depravity, etc):～亡(*of a country*) *to be annexed* (or *subjugated*); *to perish*

纶(綸) ㊀ lún ㄌㄨㄣˊ ❶钓鱼用的线 fishing line:垂～*to go fishing; to go angling* ❷指某些合成纤维 synthetic fibre:锦～*polyamide fibre*|涤～ *polyester fibre*

㊁ guān 见248页 see p248

轮(輪) lún ㄌㄨㄣˊ ❶(—子、—儿)车轮,车轱辘 wheel:三～车 *tricycle; pedicab* ㊎**extension** 安在机器上能旋转并促使机器动作的东西 wheel:齿～儿 *toothed* (or *cog*) *wheel; gear*|飞～儿 *flywheel; free wheel* (*of a bicycle*)|偏心～儿 *eccentric wheel; eccentric* ❷像车轮的东西 sth resembling a wheel; disc; ring:日～ *sun disc; the sun*|年～ *annual* (or *growth*) *ring* [轮廓](—kuò) **1** 物体的外围 outline; profile; contour **2** 事情的大概情形 survey; general situation ❸轮船 steamer; steamship; steamboat:海～*seagoing* (or *oceangoing*) *vessel*|油～ *oil tanker* (or *carrier*); *tanker* ❹轮流,依照次第转 to take turns; to do by turns:～班 *in shifts; in relays; by turns*|～值 *to be on duty in turns*|这回～到我了。*It's my turn now.* ❺量词 **quantifier**,用于圆形物或循环的事物、动作(used for sth round-shaped or the movement that rotates):一～红日 *a red sun*|他比我大两～。*He is twenty-four years older than me.*

L

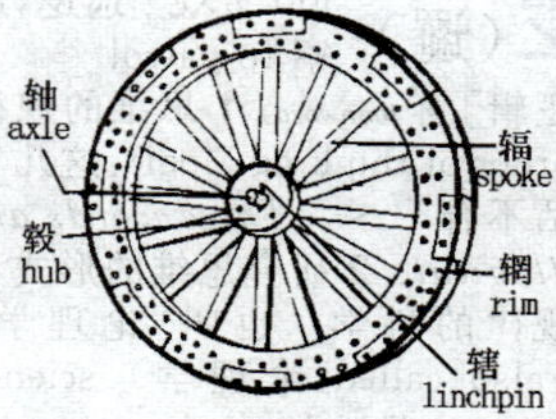

旧式车轮
an old-style wheel

论(論) ㊀ lùn ㄌㄨㄣˋ ❶ 分析、判断事物的道理 to discuss; to talk about; to discourse (㊀ *doublet* 评— to comment on; to discuss | 议— to comment; to talk; to discuss):不能一概而～ *not to be lumped together; must not generalize about sth* | 大家讨～一下吧! *Let's talk it over!* ❷ 分析、阐明事物道理的文章、理论和言论 dissertation; essay; theory; statement: 实践～ *on practice* | 唯物～ *materialism* | 社～ *editorial; leading article* | 舆～ *public opinion* ❸ 按照某种单位或类别说 by; in terms of: ～件 *by piece* | ～天 *by day* | 买西瓜～斤还是～个儿? *Is the watermelon sold by its weight, or by its size?* ❹ 衡量,评定 to decide on; to determine; to appraise: 按质～价 *to determine the price according to the quality* | ～功行赏 *to dispense rewards or honours according to merits; to award people according to their contributions*

㊁ lún 见474页 see p474

LUO ㄌㄨㄛ

捋 ㊀ luō ㄌㄨㄛ 用手握着东西,顺着东西移动 to rub one's palm along (sth long); to strip sth by closing the palm around it and running one's hand along the length: ～榆钱儿 *to strip an elm twig of its seeds* | ～虎须(喻冒险) *to stroke a tiger's whiskers — to do sth very daring*

㊁ lǚ 见470页 see p470

啰(囉) ㊂ luō ㄌㄨㄛ [啰唆][啰嗦](—suo) 1 说话絮絮叨叨 talkative; long-winded; wordy 2 办事使人感觉麻烦 overelaborate; fussy; troublesome

㊀ luó 见476页 see p476

㊁ luo 见479页 see p479

罗(羅) luó ㄌㄨㄛˊ ❶ 捕鸟的网 net for catching birds (㊀ *doublet* —网 net; trap):天～地网 *nets above and snares below; tight encirclement* ❷ 张网捕捉 to catch (birds) with a net: 门可～雀 *You can catch sparrows on the doorstep — visitors are few and far between.* [罗致]招请(人才) *to enlist the services of; to secure sb in one's employment* ❸ 散布,陈列 to display; to spread out; to set out: 星～棋布 *to spread out like stars in the sky or pieces on the chessboard; to be dotted with* | ～列事实 *to enumerate the facts* ❹

L

过滤流质或筛细粉末用的器具，用木或铁片做成圆框，蒙上粗绢或马尾网、铁丝网制成 sieve; sifter; screen ❺用罗筛东西 to sieve; to sift: ～面 *to sift flour* ❻轻软有稀孔的丝织品 silk gauze: ～衣 *garment of thin silk* | ～扇 *silk gauze fan* ❼(外 loanword) 量词 ***quantifier***, 十二打叫一罗 twelve dozen; gross ❽同"脶"(luó) same as 脶

[罗汉]梵语"阿罗汉"的省称，佛教对某种"得道者"的称呼 (short for 阿罗汉 in Buddhism, used to address someone who has achieved nirvana and freed himself from the bonds of desire) (Sanskrit) arhat

[罗盘]测定方向的仪器。把磁针装置在圆盘中央，盘上刻着度数和方位。是我国古代四大发明之一。也叫"罗盘针"(also called 罗盘针) compass

萝(蘿) luó ㄌㄨㄛˊ 莪蒿。通常指某些能爬蔓的植物 climbing plant; vine: 茑～ *cypress vine* | 女～ *usnea*

[萝卜](—bo)二年生草本植物，种类很多，块根也叫萝卜，可吃，种子可入药 radish (*Raphanus sativus*)

啰(囉) ㊀ luó ㄌㄨㄛˊ [啰唣](—zào)吵闹 to quarrel noisily; to make (*or* kick up) a row

㊁ luo 见479页 see p479

㊂ luō 见475页 see p475

逻(邏) luó ㄌㄨㄛˊ 巡逻，巡察 to patrol

[逻辑](外 loanword) **1** 思维的规律 order of thinking; logic: 这几句话不合～～。*These words are illogical*. **2** 研究思维的形式和规律的科学。也叫"论理学" (also called 论理学) science that studies the form and order of thinking; logic **3** 有时也用作"规律"的同义语 (sometimes used as a synonym for 规律) objective law; logic

猡(玀) luó ㄌㄨㄛˊ 〈方 ***dialect***〉猪猡，猪 pig; swine

椤(欏) luó ㄌㄨㄛˊ 见717页"桫"字条"桫椤"(suō—) see 桫椤 on p717

锣(鑼) luó ㄌㄨㄛˊ 一种打击乐器，形状像铜盘，用槌子敲打，发出声音 gong: ～鼓喧天 *The deafening sound of drums and gongs fills the air*.

箩(籮) luó ㄌㄨㄛˊ 用竹子编的底方上圆的器具 square-bottomed bamboo basket

觇(覼、**覶) luó ㄌㄨㄛˊ [觇缕](—lǚ)逐条详尽地陈述 to tell (*or* narrate) in detail

脶(腡) luó ㄌㄨㄛˊ 手指纹 fingerprint

骡(*贏) luó ㄌㄨㄛˊ (—子)一种家畜，是由驴、马交配而生的。鬃短，尾巴略扁，生命力强，一般没有生

育能力。可以驮(tuó)东西或拉车 mule

螺 luó ㄌㄨㄛˊ ❶一大类软体动物,有硬壳,壳上有旋纹 spiral shell; snail:～蛳 *spiral shell; snail*|田～ *river snail*|海～ *conch*|钉～ *oncomelania; snail* [螺丝]应用螺旋原理做成的使物体固定或把两个物体连接起来的东西,有螺钉和螺母 screw [螺旋] **1** 一种简单机械,圆柱体表面或物体孔眼里有像螺蛳壳纹理的螺纹 screw **2** 螺旋形的 spiral; helix:～～桨(*screw*) *propeller; screw* ❷同"脶"(luó) same as 脶

倮 luǒ ㄌㄨㄛˇ 同"裸"same as 裸

裸(*羸) luǒ ㄌㄨㄛˇ 光着身子 bare; naked; nude:～体 *naked; nude*|赤～～ *naked; to wear not a stitch of clothes* ㊀***extension*** 没有东西包着的 bare; exposed:～线(没有外皮的电线)*bare* (or *naked, open*) *wire*|～子植物 *gymnosperm* [裸机] **1** 没有加入通信网的手机、寻呼机 bare cell phone; bare pager; cell phone or pager not connected to a communications network **2** 没有安装操作系统和其他软件的计算机 bare computer; computer without an operating system and other software

蓏 luǒ ㄌㄨㄛˇ 古书上指瓜类植物的果实(in ancient Chinese texts) different kinds of melon

瘰 luǒ ㄌㄨㄛˇ [瘰疬](－lì)结核菌侵入淋巴结,发生核块的病,多在颈部。有些地区也叫"老鼠疮"(also called 老鼠疮 in some areas) scrofula

蠃 luǒ ㄌㄨㄛˇ 见258页"蜾"字条"蜾蠃"(guǒ－)see 蜾蠃 on p258

泺(濼) ㊀ luò ㄌㄨㄛˋ 泺水,古水名,在今山东省济南 Luoshui River, an ancient river, in today's Jinan, Shandong Province [泺口]地名,在山东省济南 Luokou, a place in Jinan, Shandong Province

㊁ pō 见573页 see p573

跞(躒) ㊁ luò ㄌㄨㄛˋ [卓跞][卓荦]卓绝 unsurpassed; outstanding; extraordinary:才华～～ *brilliant talents*

㊀ lì 见436页 see p436

荦(犖) luò ㄌㄨㄛˋ [荦荦]明显,分明 conspicuous; obvious; apparent:～～大端 *major items; salient points*

洛 luò ㄌㄨㄛˋ 洛河,水名 Luohe River **1** 在陕西省北部。也叫北洛河(also called 北洛河 River) Luohe River, in the north of Shaanxi Province **2** 发源于陕西省南部,流至河南省西部入黄河。古作"雒"(written as 雒 in ancient China) Luohe River, originating in the south of Shaanxi Province and flowing into the west of Henan Province and pouring into the

Huanghe River

骆 luò ㄌㄨㄛˋ ❶古书上指黑鬃的白马(in ancient Chinese texts) white horse with a black mane ❷姓 Luo, a surname

[骆驼](—tuo)哺乳动物,反刍类,身体高大,背上有肉峰。能耐饥渴,适于负重物在沙漠中远行。也叫"橐驼"(tuótuó),省称"驼"(also called 橐驼, 驼 for short) camel

络 ㊀ luò ㄌㄨㄛˋ ❶像网子那样的东西 sth resembling a net:脉～ *arteries and veins; veins (of a leaf, etc)* | 橘～ *tangerine pith* | 丝瓜～ *vegetable sponge; loofah* ❷用网状物兜住,笼罩 to hold sth in place with a net:用络(lào)子～住 *to hold sth in place with a net* ❸缠绕 to twine; to coil; to wind:～纱 *winding yarn; spooling* | ～线 *winding thread*

[络绎](—yì)连续不断 in an endless stream:参观的人～～不绝。*There's a continuous flow of visitors to the exhibition.*

㊁ lào 见420页 see p420

珞 luò ㄌㄨㄛˋ 见900页"瓔"字条"瓔珞"(yīng—) see 瓔珞 on p900

[珞巴族]我国少数民族,参看附表(see the appendix) the Lhoba ethnic group, one of the ethnic minorities of China

烙 ㊁ luò ㄌㄨㄛˋ 见553页"炮"字条"炮烙"(páo—) see 炮烙 on p553

㊀ lào 见421页 see p421

硌 ㊀ luò ㄌㄨㄛˋ 山上的大石 big rock (*or* boulder) on a mountain

㊁ gè 见227页 see p227

落 ㊀ luò ㄌㄨㄛˋ ❶掉下来,往下降 to fall; to descend; to drop:～泪 *to shed tears; to weep* | 飞机降～。*The plane is landing.* | 太阳～山了。*The sun has set.* ❷衰败 to decline; to come down; to deteriorate:没(mò)～ *to decline; to decay; to wane* | 破～户 *declined family* ❸遗留在后面 to lag behind; to fall behind:～后 *to fall behind; to lag behind; to be behind* | ～伍 *to fall behind; to lag behind; to drop out* (or *off*) | ～选 *to fail to be chosen* (or *elected*); *to lose an election* ❹停留 to stay; to settle; to remain:安家～户 *to make one's home* (or *take up residence*) *in a new place; to settle* | ～脚 *to stay (for a time); to stop over* | 小鸟在树上～着。*The little bird is perching in a tree.* ㉑ ***extension*** 留下 to stay; to leave behind:不～痕迹 *to leave no trace* ❺停留或聚居的地方 settlement; whereabouts:村～ *village; hamlet* | 下～ *whereabouts* | 着～ *outcome; assured source* [部落] **1** 由若干血缘相近的氏族结合成的集体 clan; tribe **2** 我国史书上多指少数民族(usually used to denote the ethnic groups in Chinese history records) ❻归属 to fall onto; to belong to; to rest with:今天

政权～在人民手里了 *Political power has passed into the hands of the people nowadays.* ㊀**extension** 得到 to get; to gain; to receive: ～不是 *to be blamed* | ～埋怨 *to be blamed* | ～了个好名誉 *to gain a good reputation* ❼古代指庆祝建筑物完工 (used to denote the completion of a building in ancient China): 新屋～成。*The new house has been completed.* ❽写下 to write down; to put down: ～款 *to write the names of the sender and the recipient on a painting, gift or letter; to inscribe names (on a gift, etc)* | ～账 *to make an entry in an account book; to enter sth in an account*

[落泊] (—bó) [落魄] (—pò) [落拓] (—tuò) **1** 潦倒失意 to be in dire straits; to be down and out **2** 豪迈,不拘束 untrammeled by convention; casual; unconventional

㊁ lào 见421页 see p421

㊂ là 见410页 see p410

摞 luò ㄌㄨㄛˋ ❶把东西重叠地往上放 to pile up; to stack up; to heap up: 把书～起来 *to pile up the books* ❷量词 **quantifier**, 用于重叠着放起来的东西 pile; stack: 一～砖 *a pile of bricks* | 一～碗 *a stack of bowls*

漯 ㊀ luò ㄌㄨㄛˋ [漯河] 地名, 在河南省 Luohe, a place in Henan Province

㊁ tà 见723页 see p723

雒 luò ㄌㄨㄛˋ 伊洛(伊河和洛河,水名,都在河南省)的"洛"字古作"雒"(Yihe River and Luohe River in Henan Province) 洛, in the phrase 伊洛, written as 雒 in ancient Chinese [雒南] 地名, 在陕西省。今作"洛南"(now written as 洛南) Luonan, a place in Shaanxi Province

啰(囉) luo ·ㄌㄨㄛ 见463页"偻"字条"偻啰"(lóu—) see 偻啰 on p463

啰(囉) ㊁ luo ·ㄌㄨㄛ ❶助词 **auxiliary**, 作用大致和"了(le)❷"一样 nearly the same as 了❷: 你去就成～。*OK, you go there.* ❷见463页"喽"字条"喽啰"(lóu—) see 喽啰 on p463

㊀ luó 见476页 see p476

㊂ luō 见475页 see p475

M ㄇ

M ㄇ

呒(嘸) ḿ ㄇ́ 〈方 ***dialect***〉没有 not to have; there is not; to be without

呣 ㊀ ḿ ㄇ́ 〔单纯的双唇鼻音〕[pure bilabial nasal] 叹词 ***interjection***,表示疑问(used to express doubt) eh: ～,你说什么? *Eh? What did you say?*

呣 ㊁ m̀ ㄇ̀ 叹词 ***interjection***,表示答应(used to express response):～,我知道了。*Um* (or *Uh-huh*), *I see*. or *Yeah, now I see*.

MA ㄇㄚ

孖 ㊁ mā ㄇㄚ 〈方 ***dialect***〉相连成对 twin; geminate

㊀ zī 见1008页 see p1008

妈 mā ㄇㄚ ❶称呼母亲(叠 ***reduplication***) ma; mom; mum ❷对女性长辈的称呼(term of address for a woman of the elder generation):大～ *aunt*|姑～ *aunt*

蚂 ㊂ mā ㄇㄚ [蚂螂](—lang)〈方 ***dialect***〉蜻蜓 dragonfly

㊀ mǎ 见482页 see p482

㊁ mà 见482页 see p482

抹 ㊂ mā ㄇㄚ ❶擦 to wipe; to mop:～桌子 *to wipe a table clean* ❷用手按着并向下移动 to put (*or* rub) sth down; to slip sth off:把帽子～下来 *to slip one's cap off*|～不下脸来(碍于脸面或情面) *to find it difficult to be strict with sb* (*for fear of hurting his feelings*)

㊀ mǒ 见514页 see p514

㊁ mò 见514页 see p514

摩 ㊁ mā ㄇㄚ [摩挲](—sa) 用手轻轻按着一下一下地移动 to smooth out with one's hand or palm; to stroke gently; to caress

㊀ mó 见513页 see p513

吗 ㊁ má ㄇㄚ́ 〈方 ***dialect***〉什么 what

㊀ ma 见482页 see p482

㊂ mǎ 见481页 see p481

麻(❶*蔴) má ㄇㄚ́ ❶草本植物,种类很多,有大麻、苎麻、苘(qǐng)麻、亚麻等等。茎皮纤维通常也叫麻,可以制绳索、织布 general term for hemp, ramie, etc [麻烦](—fan)由于事物杂乱,感到费手续、难办 troublesome; bothersome; inconvenient:这事真～～。*It is really a troublesome matter*. or *It's really a hard nut to crack*. [芝麻](*脂麻)(—ma)一种草本植物,茎秆

略成方形。种子有白的和黑的两种，所榨的油就是平常吃的香油 sesame（*Sesamum indicum*）❷像腿、臂被压后的那种不舒服的感觉 feeling pins and needles；tingling；numb：腿～了 *to have a tingling feeling in the legs*｜手发～ *to feel numb in one's hand* ❸感觉不灵或全部丧失 numb；insensible（㊣ **doublet** 一 木 numb）［麻痹］（*痲痹）**1** 身体的一部分因为神经系统的病变而发生知觉或运动的障碍 paralysis；palsy **2** 失去警惕性 to slacken one's vigilance；to drop one's guard：～～大意 *to be off guard；to be careless*［麻风］（*痳风）俗叫"癞病"，是一种慢性传染病。病原体是麻风杆菌。患者皮肤发生斑纹或结节，知觉丧失，毛发脱落，指节烂掉（popularly called 癞病）leprosy［麻醉］**1** 用药物或针刺使全身或局部暂时失去知觉 to anaesthetize **2** 使人思想认识模糊，不能明辨是非 to corrupt（sb's mind）；to poison；to enervate ❹表面粗糙 rough；rugged；coarse：这张纸一面光一面～。*This sheet of paper is smooth on one side and rough on the other.*［麻疹］（*痳疹）一种急性传染病，由滤过性病毒引起，儿童容易感染 measles；rubeola［麻子］（—zi）**1** 出天花留下的瘢痕 pockmarks **2** 脸上有麻子的人 person with a pockmarked face

痳 má ㄇㄚˊ［痳痹］、［痳风］、［痳疹］旧同"麻痹"、"麻风"、"麻疹"。参看480页"麻"（see 麻 on p480）same as 麻痹，麻风，or 麻疹 in former times

马（馬）mǎ ㄇㄚˇ 一种家畜，颈上有鬃，尾有长毛。供人骑或拉东西等 horse；steed［马脚］破绽（zhàn），漏洞 sth that gives the game away；clue；trace：露出～～来了 *to have betrayed oneself；to have given oneself away*［马力］功率（lǜ）的非法定计量单位，1马力等于每秒钟把75公斤重的物体提高到1米所做的功，约合735.499瓦 horsepower（h.p.），unit of power equal to 735.499w or the power needed to lift a 75kg weight by one metre per second［马上］副词 **adverb**，立刻 at once；immediately；straight away：我～～就到。*I'll be right there.*
［马达］（外 **loanword**）用电力或汽油发动的机器，特指电动机 motor
［马虎］（—hu）不认真 careless；casual；slipshod：这事可不能～～。*This matter cannot be handled casually.*

吗 ㊂ mǎ ㄇㄚˇ［吗啡］（—fēi）（外 **loanword**）用鸦片制成的有机化合物，白色粉末，味很苦。医药上用作镇痛剂 morphine
㊀ ma 见482页 see p482
㊁ má 见480页 see p480

犸 mǎ ㄇㄚˇ［猛犸］一种古脊椎动物，像现代的象，全身有长毛，已绝种。也叫"毛象"（also called 毛象）mammoth

(*Mammuthus*)

玛 mǎ ㄇㄚˇ [玛瑙](—nǎo)矿物名，主要成分是氧化硅，颜色美丽，质硬耐磨，可做轴承、研钵、装饰品等 agate

码 mǎ ㄇㄚˇ ❶(—子、—儿)代表数目的符号 sign or thing indicating number; numeral:苏州～子(〡、〢、〣、〤、〥等)(*numeric signs used in the Ming and Qing dynasties*) *Suzhou numerals*｜明～儿售货(在商品上标明价码出售) *to put goods on sale with the prices clearly marked; to sell goods at (clearly) marked prices* [乱码]计算机或通信系统中因某种原因而造成的混乱的、不能识别的字符 error (or confusion) codes ❷(—子)计算数目的用具，如砝码、筹码等 instrument used to indicate number, e.g. weight (used on a balance), chip, counter, etc ❸量词 ***quantifier***,用于一件事或一类的事(used for the same thing or the same kind):这是两～事。*These are two different things.* ❹〈外 **loanword**〉英美长度单位，1码等于3英尺，合0.9144米 yard (yd) ❺〈方 ***dialect***〉摞(luò)起，垒起 to pile up; to stack:～砖头 *to stack bricks*｜小孩儿～积木(*of a child*) *to stack building blocks* [码头]水边专供停船的地方 wharf; quay; pier ㊀ ***extension*** 临海、临河的城市 port city

蚂 ㊀ mǎ ㄇㄚˇ [蚂蟥](—huáng)"蛭"的俗称。参看982页"蛭"(zhì)(popular name for 蛭)(see 蛭 on p982) leech (*Hirudinea*) [蚂蚁](—yǐ)蚁。参看887页"蚁"(see 蚁 on p887) ant

㊁ mā 见480页 see p480

㊂ mà 见482页 see p482

祃 mà ㄇㄚˋ 古代行军时，在军队驻扎的地方举行的祭礼 sacrificial ceremonies held at an army garrison in ancient China

蚂 ㊂ mà ㄇㄚˋ [蚂蚱](—zha)蝗虫的俗称。参看294页"蝗"(huáng)(popular name for 蝗虫)(see 蝗 on p294) locust (*Acrididae*)

㊀ mǎ 见482页 see p482

㊁ mā 见480页 see p480

骂(*罵) mà ㄇㄚˋ ❶用粗野的话侮辱人 to abuse; to curse; to swear:不要～人。*No swearing, please!* ❷〈方 ***dialect***〉斥责 to chide; to reprove; to rebuke

么 ㊁ ma ·ㄇㄚ 同"吗㊀" same as 吗㊀

㊀ me 见491页 see p491

㊂ yāo 见873页 see p873

吗 ㊀ ma ·ㄇㄚ 助词 ***auxiliary*** **1** 表疑问，用在一般直陈句子末了(used at the end of a sentence to express doubt):你听明白了～? *Did you get what I said?* **2** 表有含蓄的语气，用在前半句末了(used at the end of the first part of a sentence to express an implicit tone):天要下雨～，我就坐车去。*If it rains, I'll go by bus.*

㊁ má 见480页 see p480

[三] mǎ 见481页 see p481

嘛 ma · ㄇㄚ 助词 ***auxiliary***,表示很明显,事理就是如此(有时有提示意)[(sometimes with a suggestive meaning) used to indicate that the reason is obvious]:有意见就提～。*Air your opinions if you have any.*|不会不要紧,边干边学～。*It doesn't matter if you don't know how to do it. Doing is learning.*

蟆 ma · ㄇㄚ 见260页"蛤"字条"蛤蟆"(há—) see 蛤蟆 on p260

MAI ㄇㄞ

埋 [一] mái ㄇㄞ 把东西放在坑里用土盖上 to cover up (with earth); to bury:掩～ *to bury*|～地雷 *to lay a landmine* [引] ***extension*** 隐藏,使不显露 to hide; to conceal:隐姓～名 *to conceal one's identity; to live in anonymity* [埋伏]在敌人将要经过的地方布置下军队,准备袭击 to lie in ambush; to ambush [埋没](— mò)使人才、功绩、作用等显露不出来 to neglect; to stifle; to hide:不要～～人才。*Don't keep the talented people from reaching their full potential.* [埋头][喻] ***figurative*** 专心,下功夫 to immerse oneself in; to concentrate on; to be engrossed in:～～苦干 *to immerse oneself in hard work; to work hard with concentrated attention*

[二] mán 见484页 see p484

霾 mái ㄇㄞ 阴霾,空气中因悬浮着大量的烟、尘等微粒而形成的混浊现象 haze

买(買) mǎi ㄇㄞ 拿钱换东西,跟"卖"相对(the opposite of 卖) to buy; to purchase ([连] ***doublet*** 购— to purchase; to buy):～戏票 *to buy a theatre ticket*|～了一头牛 *to have bought an ox* [引] ***extension*** 贿赂 to bribe:～通 *to bribe; to buy over* (or *off*) [买办] **1** 采购货物的人 purchasing agent; buyer **2** 殖民地、半殖民地国家里替外国资本家在本国市场上经管商业、银行业、工矿业、运输业等等的中间人和经纪人 comprador [买卖](— mai)生意,商业 purchase and sale; business; transaction:做～～ *to go into business* [引] ***extension*** 铺子(private) shop; store

荬(蕒) mǎi ㄇㄞ 见619页"苣"字条"苣荬菜"(qǔ——) see 苣荬菜 on p619

劢(勱) mài ㄇㄞ 努力 to make great efforts; to exert oneself; to try hard

迈(邁) mài ㄇㄞ ❶抬起腿来跨步 to step; to stride; to walk:～过去 *to step over*|～了一大步 *to take a large stride; to make great strides (towards sth)*|向前～进 *to advance forward with big strides* ❷老 advanced in years; old ([连] ***doublet*** 老—

M

aged; senile):年～ *old; aged* ❸(外 *loanword*)英里,用于机动车行驶速度(used to indicate the speed of a vehicle) mile:一小时走六十～ *to cover 60 miles per hour*

麦(麥) mài ㄇㄞˋ (一子)一年生或二年生草本植物,分大麦、小麦、燕麦等多种,子实磨面供食用。通常专指小麦 general term for barley, wheat, oats, etc, usually denoting wheat (*Triticum*)

唛(嘜) mài ㄇㄞˋ 译音用字。商标,进出口货物的包装上所做的标记 (used for transliteration) (shipping) mark

鿏 mài ㄇㄞˋ 一种人造的放射性元素(符号 Mt) meitnerium (Mt)

卖(賣) mài ㄇㄞˋ ❶拿东西换钱,跟"买"相对(the opposite of 买) to sell:～菜 *to sell vegetables* ⓘ ***extension*** 出卖 to betray:～国贼 *traitor (to one's country)* ❷尽量使出(力气) to do one's utmost; to spare (*or* stint) no effort:～力 *to exert all one's strength; to do all one can; to spare no effort*|～劲儿 *to exert all one's strength; to spare no effort* ❸卖弄,显示自己,表现自己 to show off; to vaunt; to flaunt:～功 *to boast about one's merit*|～乖 *to flaunt one's petty cleverness; to show off one's wits*|～弄才能 *to parade one's talent*

脉(*脈、*衇) ㊀ mài ㄇㄞˋ ❶分布在人和动物周身内的血管 arteries and veins:动～ *artery*|静～ *vein* ❷脉搏,动脉的跳动 pulse:诊～ *to feel the pulse* ❸像血管那样分布的东西 sth with a vein-like pattern; range; vein:山～ *mountain range (or chain)*|矿～ *mineral ore (or vein)*|叶～ *vein (in a leaf); leaf vein*

㊁ mò 见515页 see p515

霡 mài ㄇㄞˋ [霡霂](—mù)小雨 drizzle

MAN ㄇㄢ

颟(顢) mān ㄇㄢ [颟顸](—han) 1 不明事理 muddle-headed:糊涂～～ *muddle-headed* 2 漫不经心 scatterbrained; careless:那人太～～,做什么事都靠不住。*That chap is too muddle-headed and careless to do anything right.*

埋 ㊁ mán ㄇㄢˊ [埋怨](—yuan)因为事情不如意而对人或事物表示不满,责怪 to complain; to grumble:他自己不小心,还～～别人。*He blamed his own carelessness on others.*

㊀ mái 见483页 see p483

蛮(蠻) mán ㄇㄢˊ ❶粗野,不通情理 savage; rough; unreasonable (㊥ ***doublet*** 野— savage; barbarous; cruel):～横(hèng) *rude and*

unreasonable; arbitrary; peremptory | ～不讲理 *to be impervious to reason; to persist in being unreasonable* | 胡搅～缠 *to harass* (or *plague*) *sb with unreasonable demands; to pester sb endlessly* [引] ***extension*** 愣，强悍 reckless; rash; brute: ～劲不小 *to have great sheer masculine strength* | 只是～干 *only to act rashly* ❷我国古代称南方的民族 ancient name for ethnic groups in the south ❸〈方 ***dialect***〉副词 ***adverb***，很 quite; pretty; jolly: ～好 *quite* (or *pretty, jolly*) *good* | ～快 *pretty fast*

谩 ㊁ mán ㄇㄢˊ 欺骗，蒙蔽 to cheat; to deceive; to hoodwink

㊀ màn 见486页 see p486

蔓 ㊂ mán ㄇㄢˊ [蔓菁](—jing)芜菁，二年生草本植物，春天开花，黄色。叶大，块根扁圆形。块根也叫蔓菁，可以吃 turnip (*Brassica rapa*)

㊀ wàn 见776页 see p776

㊁ màn 见486页 see p486

馒 mán ㄇㄢˊ [馒头](—tou)一种用发面蒸成的食品，无馅 *mantou*, a kind of food made with leavened dough, without filling; steamed bun (*or* bread)

鳗 mán ㄇㄢˊ [鳗鲡](—lí)鱼名。身体前圆后扁，背部灰黑色，腹部白色带淡黄色。生活在淡水中，到海洋中产卵。也省称"鳗"(also 鳗 for short) Japanese eel (*Anguilla japonica*)

鬘 mán ㄇㄢˊ 形容头发美(of hair) beautiful

瞒(瞞) mán ㄇㄢˊ 隐瞒；隐藏实情，不让别人知道 to hide the truth from; to cover up; to conceal: 这事不必～他。*There is no need to keep him in the dark.*

满(滿) mǎn ㄇㄢˇ ❶全部充实，没有余地 full; filled; brimful: 会场里人都～了。*The assembly hall is filled to capacity.* | ～地都是绿油油的庄稼。*Stretching all around is a vast expanse of green crops.* | ～口答应 *to promise with readiness; to consent readily* [满意]愿望满足或符合自己的意见 satisfied; contented; gratified; pleased: 这样办，他很～～。*He is satisfied with the way it has been handled.* [满足] **1** 觉得够了 satisfied; gratified; contented: 他并不～～于现有的成绩。*He is not content with the present achievements.* **2** 使人觉得不缺什么了 to satisfy; to gratify; to meet: ～～人民的需要 *to satisfy* (or *meet*) *the needs of the people* [自满]不虚心，骄傲 self-conceited; complacent; smug ❷到了一定的限度 to expire; to complete; to reach the limit: 假期已～。*The holidays are over.* | ～了一年。*It has been one full year.* ❸(斟酒)使满 to fill (a cup with wine): ～上一杯 *to fill a cup* (*with wine*) ❹副词 ***adverb***，十分，完

M

全 completely; entirely; fully: 积极性～高 *with great initiative*｜～以为不错 *to take it for granted that it was well done*｜～不在乎 *do not mind at all; do not care in the least*

[满族]我国少数民族,参看附表 (see the appendix) the Manchu ethnic group, one of the ethnic minorities of China

螨(蟎) mǎn ㄇㄢˇ 蛛形动物的一类,体形微小,多数为圆形或卵形,头胸腹无明显分界,有足四对,下唇隐藏,无齿。有的危害人畜,传染疾病,并危害农作物 mite (*Acari*)

曼 màn ㄇㄢˋ ❶延长 prolonged; long-drawn-out: ～声而歌 *to drawl out a song* ❷柔美 graceful; gentle: 轻歌～舞 *to sing softly and dance gracefully*

谩 ㊀ màn ㄇㄢˋ 轻慢,没有礼貌 disrespectful; uncivil; rude: ～骂 *to hurl* (or *fling*) *abuses; to vilify*

㊁ mán 见485页 see p485

墁 màn ㄇㄢˋ 用砖或石块铺地面 to pave (*or* surface) a floor with bricks, stones, etc: 花砖～地 *to cover the floor with coloured tiles*

蔓 ㊁ màn ㄇㄢˋ 同"蔓㊀",多用于合成词,如蔓草、蔓延等 (usually used in compound words, such as 蔓草, 蔓延, etc) same as 蔓㊀ [蔓延]形容像蔓草一样地不断扩展滋生 to spread; to stretch; to extend

㊀ wàn 见776页 see p776

㊂ mán 见485页 see p485

幔 màn ㄇㄢˋ (一子)悬挂起来作遮挡用的布、绸子等 curtain; screen: 布～ *cotton curtain*｜窗～ *window curtain*

漫 màn ㄇㄢˋ ❶水过满,漾出来 to overflow; to run (*or* brim) over: 河水～出来了。*The river overflowed its banks.* ㊕ ***transfer*** 淹没 to flood; to inundate: 水不深,只～到脚面。*The water wasn't deep. It only came to just above my ankles.*｜大水～过房子了。*The flood has inundated the house.* ❷满,遍 all over the place; in all places; everywhere: ～山遍野 *all over the mountains and plains; across the countryside*｜大雾～天 *dense fog obscuring the sky* ❸没有限制,没有约束 without restraint (*or* purpose); casual; free: ～谈 *to have an informal discussion*｜～不经心 *careless; absent-minded*｜～无边际 *boundless; without limit*

[漫长]时间长或路程远 very long; endless; prolonged: ～～的岁月 *prolonged period of time*｜～～的道路 *long course*

[漫画]简单而夸大事物特征的绘画,多含有讽刺的意义 caricature; cartoon

慢 màn ㄇㄢˋ ❶迟缓,速度低,跟"快"相对(the opposite of 快) slow: ～车 *local train*｜～～地走 *to walk slowly*｜我的表～五分钟。*My watch is five minutes slow.* [慢条斯理]

迟缓，不慌忙 slowly; leisurely; unhurriedly ❷态度冷淡，不热情 cold and indifferent; supercilious; rude: 怠～ *to slight*; *to cold-shoulder*; *to neglect* | 傲～ *haughty*; *arrogant*; *impudent*

嫚 màn ㄇㄢˋ 侮辱，怠慢 to scorn; to despise; to humiliate

缦 màn ㄇㄢˋ 没有彩色花纹的丝织品 plain silk fabrics

熳 màn ㄇㄢˋ［烂熳］旧同"烂漫" same as 烂漫 in former times

镘 màn ㄇㄢˋ 抹(mò)墙用的工具 trowel

MANG ㄇㄤ

牤(**犆) māng ㄇㄤ 〈方 **dialect**〉牤牛，公牛 bull

邙 máng ㄇㄤˊ ［邙山］山名，在河南省西北部 Mangshan Mountain, in the northwest of Henan Province

芒 máng ㄇㄤˊ ❶禾本科植物子实壳上的细刺 awn; beard; arista ❷像芒的东西 awn-like things: 光～ *rays of light*; *brilliant rays* ❸多年生草本植物，秋天开花，黄褐色。叶细长有尖，可以造纸、编鞋 Chinese silvergrass (*Miscanthus sinensis*)

忙 máng ㄇㄤˊ ❶事情多，没空闲 busy; fully occupied: 工作～ *to be busy at work* | ～～碌碌 *bustling about*; *fully occupied*; *busy* ❷急 impatient; anxious; hasty (㊈ **doublet** 急～ in a hurry; in a rush; in haste): 不慌不～ *unhurried*; *calm*; *leisurely* | 先别～着下结论。*Don't jump to conclusions*. ❸急速地做 to hurry; to hasten; to make haste: 大家都～生产。*Everybody is busy with his work*.

杧 máng ㄇㄤˊ ［杧果］常绿乔木，果实也叫杧果，形状像腰子，果肉可吃。也作"芒果" (also written as 芒果) mango (*Mangifera indica*)

盲 máng ㄇㄤˊ 瞎，看不见东西 blind: ～人 *blind person*; *the blind* ［盲打］㊉ **figurative** 打字或录入用手敲键时，眼睛不看键盘 to touch-type ［盲道］在人行道或其他公共场所，为方便盲人行走用特制砖铺设的道路 blind track; sidewalk for the blind ㊉ **figurative** 对某种事物不能辨认的 ignorant; illiterate: 文～ *illiterate person*; *illiterate* | 色～ *achromatopsia*; *colour blindness* (or *blind*) | 扫～ *to eliminate* (or *wipe out*) *illiteracy* ［盲从］㊉ **figurative** 自己没有原则，没有见地，随着别人 to follow (*or* obey) blindly ［盲目］㊉ **figurative** 对事情认识不清楚 blind; unseeing; ignorant: ～～的行动是不会有好结果的。*Blind action won't bring about good results*.

氓 ㊁ máng ㄇㄤˊ ［流氓］原指无业游民，后来指品质恶劣，不务正业，为非作歹的坏人 (formerly a jobless riff-raff, later a ne'er-do-well with bad intent) rogue; hoodlum; hooligan

㊁ méng 见496页 see p496

茫 máng ㄇㄤˊ ❶对事理全无所知，找不到头绪 ignorant; unaware; in the dark: ～然无知 *to be completely in the dark* | ～无头绪 *not to know how to go about things; to have no clue whatever* ❷形容水势浩渺(of water) vast and indistinct; boundless [茫茫]面积大，看不清边沿 boundless and indistinct; vast: 大海～～ *vast sea* | 雾气～～ *thick pall of fog*

硭 máng ㄇㄤˊ [硭硝]现作"芒硝"。一种矿物，成分是硫酸钠，无色或白色晶体。医药上用作泻剂，工业上供制玻璃、造纸等(now written as 芒硝) mirabilite; Glauber's salt

铓 máng ㄇㄤˊ ❶刀、剑等的尖端 point of a knife ❷一种民间打击乐器，流行于云南省傣族和景颇族地区 *mang*, a percussion instrument (popular in the Dai and Jingpo ethnic areas in Yunnan Province)

駹 máng ㄇㄤˊ 毛色黑白相间的马 black-and-white horse

牻 máng ㄇㄤˊ 毛色黑白相间的牛 black-and-white cattle

莽 mǎng ㄇㄤˇ ❶密生的草 rank grass: 草～ *rank growth of grass* ❷粗鲁，冒失 rash; rude; crude: ～汉 *rude (or boorish) fellow; boor* | 这人太鲁～。*This fellow is too reckless.*

漭 mǎng ㄇㄤˇ [漭漭]形容水广阔无边 (of water) vast; boundless

蟒 mǎng ㄇㄤˇ 一种无毒的大蛇，背有黄褐色斑纹，腹白色，常生活在近水的森林里，捕食小禽兽 boa (*Boidae*); python (*Python*)

MAO ㄇㄠ

猫(*貓) ㊀ māo ㄇㄠ 一种家畜，面呈圆形，脚有利爪，善跳跃，会捉老鼠 cat (*Felis catus*)

㊁ máo 见489页 see p489

毛 máo ㄇㄠˊ ❶动植物的皮上所生的丝状物 hair; feather; down ❷像毛的东西 hair-like thing **1** 指谷物等 crops; vegetation: 不～(未开垦不长庄稼)之地 *land without vegetation; barren land* **2** 衣物等上长的霉菌 mildew; mould: 老没见太阳都长～了。*It has some mildew on it as it hasn't been exposed to the rays of the sun for a long time.* ❸粗糙，没有加工的 semifinished; coarse: ～坯 *semifinished product; blank* ❹不是纯净的 gross: ～重10吨 *gross weight 10 ton* | ～利 *gross profit* ❺小 little; small: ～孩子 *little child* | ～～雨 *drizzle; mizzle* ❻行动慌忙 careless; crude; rash: ～～腾腾(—maotēngtēng) *flurried and excited; flustered* | ～手～

脚 *careless* (*in handling things*); *brash and clumsy* ❼惊慌失措 panicky; scared; nervous: 把他吓～了。*He was frightened out of his wits*. ❽货币贬值(of currency) to devalue; to depreciate: 钱～了。*Money has gone down in value*. ❾角,一圆钱的十分之一 mao (=1/10 *yuan*)

[毛南族](—nán—)我国少数民族,参看附表(see the appendix) the Maonan ethnic group, one of the ethnic minorities of China

牦(*犛、*氂) máo ㄇㄠˊ [牦牛]一种牛,身体两旁和四肢外侧有长毛,尾毛很长。我国西藏出产,当地人民用来拉犁和驮运货物。肉和乳都可供食用 yak (*Bos grunniens*)

旄 máo ㄇㄠˊ 古代用牦(máo)牛尾装饰的旗子 ancient flag decorated with yak's tails 〈古 ***archaism***〉又同"耄"(mào) also same as 耄

酕 máo ㄇㄠˊ [酕醄](—táo)大醉的样子 as drunk as a fiddler; dead drunk; smashed

髦 máo ㄇㄠˊ 古代称幼儿垂在前额的短头发 (in ancient China) children's bangs [时髦]时兴的 fashionable; stylish; latest

矛 máo ㄇㄠˊ 古代兵器,在长柄的一端装有金属枪头(in ancient China) spear; lance; pike [矛盾]㊄ ***figurative*** **1** 言语或行为前后抵触,对立的事物互相排斥 contradictory; conflicting; opposing **2** 指事物内部各个对立面之间的互相依赖又互相排斥的关系 contradiction

茅 máo ㄇㄠˊ 茅草,多年生草本植物,有白茅、青茅等。可以覆盖屋顶或做绳 cogon grass (*Imperata cylindrica*)

蝥 máo ㄇㄠˊ [斑蝥]一种昆虫,腿细长,鞘翅上有黄黑色斑纹。可入药 Spanish fly (*Lytta vesicatoria*)

蟊 máo ㄇㄠˊ 吃苗根的害虫 insect that destroys the roots of seedlings [蟊贼]㊄ ***figurative*** 对人民有害的人 person harmful to the people

茆 máo ㄇㄠˊ 同"茅" same as 茅

猫(*貓) ㊁ máo ㄇㄠˊ [猫腰]弯腰 to arch the back (like a cat); to stoop down

㊀ māo 见488页 see p488

锚 máo ㄇㄠˊ 铁制的停船器具,用铁链连在船上,抛到水底,可以使船停稳 anchor

冇 mǎo ㄇㄠˇ 〈方 ***dialect***〉没有 do not have; there is not; to be without

卯 mǎo ㄇㄠˇ ❶地支的第四位 *Mao*, 4th of the 12 Earthly Branches ❷卯时,指早晨五点到七点 period of the day from 5 a.m. to 7 a.m. ❸(—子、—儿)器物接榫(sǔn)的地方凹入的部分 mortise: 对～眼 *to mortise* | 凿个～儿 *to cut* (*or chisel*) *a mortise*

峁 mǎo ㄇㄠˇ〈方 ***dialect***〉小山包 small hill：下了一道坡，又上一道～ *to go up hill and down dale*

泖 mǎo ㄇㄠˇ 水面平静的小湖 small calm lake［泖湖］古湖名，在今上海市松江西部 Maohu Lake, an ancient lake in the west of present Songjiang, Shanghai［泖桥］地名，在上海市 Maoqiao, a place in Shanghai

昴 mǎo ㄇㄠˇ 星宿名，二十八宿之一 *mao*, 18th of the 28 constellations

铆 mǎo ㄇㄠˇ 用钉子把金属物连在一起 to fasten with a rivet; to rivet：～钉 *rivet*｜～眼 *rivet hole*｜～接 *to rivet; rivet-joint*｜～工 *riveter*

芼 mào ㄇㄠˋ 拔取(菜、草) to pick; to pull up (grass, vegetables)

眊 mào ㄇㄠˋ 眼睛看不清楚 dim-sighted; blurred in eyesight

耄 mào ㄇㄠˋ 年老，八九十岁的年纪 octogenarian：～耋(dié)之年 *advanced in age*

茂 mào ㄇㄠˋ 茂盛(shèng)，草木旺盛 luxuriant; exuberant; flourishing：根深叶～ *to have deep roots and thick foliage* ㊥ ***figurative*** 丰富而美好 rich and exquisite; splendid：图文并～ *excellent in both pictures and language; to be well written and beautifully illustrated*｜声情并～ *(of a singer) to be remarkable for both voice and expression; to sing in a good voice and with much emotion*

冒 ㊀ mào ㄇㄠˋ ❶向外透，往上升 to emit; to send out (*or* up, forth); to give off：～泡 *to send up bubbles; to bubble*｜～烟 *(of smoke) to rise; (of a chimney, etc) to belch smoke*｜～火 *to burn with anger; to get angry; to flare up* ❷不顾(恶劣的环境或危险等) to risk; to brave; to be exposed to (hardships)：～雨 *to brave rains*｜～险 *to take a risk; to take chances; to brave dangers* ❸不加小心，鲁莽，冲撞 imprudently; recklessly; boldly：～昧 *to venture; to make bold; to take the liberty of*｜～犯 *to offend; to affront*［冒进］不顾具体条件，急于进行 prematurely advance; to advance rashly［冒失］鲁莽，轻率 rash; thoughtless; imprudent ❹用假的充当真的，假托 to falsify one's identity; to pass for：～牌 *to be an imitation; to counterfeit*｜～名 *to go under sb else's name; to assume another's name* ❺〈古 ***archaism***〉贪婪 to have an insatiable desire for; to be greedy for ❻姓 Mao, a surname

㊁ mò 见515页 see p515

帽 mào ㄇㄠˋ ❶帽子 headgear; hat; cap ❷(～儿)作用或形状像帽子的东西 cap-like cover for sth：螺丝～儿 *(screw) nut*｜～钉 *hatpeg*｜笔～儿 *cap of a pen, pencil or writ-*

ing brush

瑁 mào ㄇㄠˋ 见123页"玳"字条"玳瑁"(dài—) see 玳瑁 on p123

贸 mào ㄇㄠˋ ❶交换财物 to trade; to barter; to exchange:抱布～丝 *to trade cloth for silk* [贸易]商业活动 trade; commerce:国际～～ *international trade* ❷冒冒失失或轻率的样子(叠 ***reduplication***) rashly; hastily; without careful consideration:～然参加 *to join* (or *take part in*) *rashly*|～～然来 *to come hastily*

袤 mào ㄇㄠˋ 南北距离的长度 north-to-south length:广～数千里 *several thousand* li *in length and breadth*

瞀 mào ㄇㄠˋ ❶目眩,看不清楚 dizzy; dazzled ❷精神昏乱 confused; bewildered (㊀ ***doublet*** —乱 confused; delirious; muddled)

懋 mào ㄇㄠˋ ❶努力,勉励 to urge; to encourage ❷盛大 grand; majestic; splendid

鄚 mào ㄇㄠˋ (旧读 formerly mò)[鄚州]地名,在河北省任丘 Maozhou, a place in Renqiu, Hebei Province

貌(**皃) mào ㄇㄠˋ ❶相貌,长(zhǎng)相 looks; appearance (㊀ ***doublet*** 容— facial appearance; looks):不能以～取人。*Don't judge people by their appearances.* ❷外表,表面 appearance; exterior:～合神离(*of two persons or parties*) *to look concerted but differ at heart; to be apparently in harmony but essentially at variance*|～似强大 *to be outwardly strong; to be seemingly powerful* ㊕ ***transfer*** 样子 appearance; shape:工厂的全～ *complete view of the factory*|恢复原～ *to resume the original shape; to return to the original state* ❸古书注解里表示状态用的字,如"飘飘,飞貌"等(a word used in the notes of ancient Chinese texts to express a state, such as 飘飘,飞貌, etc)

ME ㄇㄜ

么(△麽) ㊀ me ·ㄇㄜ ❶词尾 ***suffix***:怎～ *how; what; why*|那～ *in that case* (or *way*); *so*|多～ *how; what*|这～ *so; such; this way; like this*|什～ *what* ❷助词 ***auxiliary***,表有含蓄的语气,用在前半句末了(used at the end of the first part of a sentence to express an implicit tone):不让你去～,你又要去。*When we didn't allow you to go there, you asked to go again.*

㊁ ma 见482页 see p482

㊂ yāo 见873页 see p873

"麽"又 mó 见512页 see p512

嚜 me ·ㄇㄜ 助词 ***auxiliary***,跟"嘛"的用法相同 same as 嘛 in usage

MEI ㄇㄟ

没 ㊀ méi ㄇㄟˊ ❶ **1** 没有,无 do not have; there is not (*or* no); to be without:他~哥哥。*He has no elder brother.*|我~那本书。*I don't have that book.* **2** 表示估量或比较,不够,不如 to be not so … as:他~(不够)一米八高。*He is less than 1.8 metres tall.*|汽车~(不如)飞机快。*The automobile isn't as fast as the plane.* ❷副词 ***adverb***,没有,不曾,未 to have not had; did not:他们~做完。*They haven't finished yet.*|衣服~干。*The clothes haven't dried.*

㊁ mò 见515页 see p515

玫 méi ㄇㄟˊ [玫瑰](—gui) 落叶灌木,枝上有刺。花有紫红色、白色等多种,香味很浓,可以做香料,花和根可入药 rose, rugosa rose (*Rosa rugosa*)

枚 méi ㄇㄟˊ ❶树干 stock; trunk:伐其条~ *to cut its twigs and fell its trunk* ❷古代士兵衔于口中以禁喧声的用具(in ancient China) gag:衔~疾走 *to run swiftly with the gag between one's teeth — to march swiftly* ❸量词 ***quantifier***,相当于"个"equal to 个:三~勋章 *three medals* [枚举]一件一件地举出来 to enumerate; to recount one by one:不胜~~ *so many as to defy enumeration; too numerous to be mentioned individually* (or *one by one*)

眉 méi ㄇㄟˊ ❶眉毛,眼上额下的毛 eyebrow; brow:~飞色舞 *with dancing eyebrows and radiant face-enraptured; exultant*|~开眼笑 *to be all smiles; to beam with joy* (图见758页"头" picture on p758) [眉目][喻] ***figurative*** 事情的头绪或事物的条理 prospect of a solution; sign of a positive outcome; sequence of ideas:有点~~了。*It is beginning to take shape.*|~~不清楚 (*of writing*) *not well organized* ❷书眉,书页上端的空白 top margin of a page:~批 *notes and commentary at the top of a page*

郿 méi ㄇㄟˊ 郿县,在陕西省。今作"眉县"(now written as 眉县) Meixian County, in Shaanxi Province

嵋 méi ㄇㄟˊ 见172页"峨"字条"峨嵋"(é—) see 峨嵋 on p172

猸 méi ㄇㄟˊ (—子)又叫"蟹獴"。哺乳动物,毛灰黄色,生活在水边,毛皮珍贵(also called 蟹獴) crab-eating mongoose (*Herpestes urva*)

湄 méi ㄇㄟˊ 河岸,水滨 river bank; waterside

楣 méi ㄇㄟˊ 门框上边的横木。lintel (of a door) (图见188页 picture on p188)

镅 méi ㄇㄟˊ 一种人造的放射性元素,符号 Am americium (Am)

鹛 méi ㄇㄟˊ 鸟名。通常指画眉,羽毛多为棕褐色,翅短,嘴尖,尾巴长,叫的声音好听 babbler (*Timaliidae*)

莓 méi ㄇㄟˊ 植物名。种类很多,常见的是草莓,开白花,结红色的果实,味酸甜 berry

梅(*楳、*槑) méi ㄇㄟˊ ❶落叶乔木,初春开花,有白、红等颜色,分五瓣,香味很浓。果实味酸 Chinese plum (*Prunus mume*) ❷梅花 Chinese plum flower; plum blossom ❸梅的果实 fruit of the Chinese plum tree; plum

脢 méi ㄇㄟˊ (一子)〈方 ***dialect***〉猪、牛等脊椎两旁的条状瘦肉,即里脊 loin; tenderloin

酶 méi ㄇㄟˊ 一大类有机化合物,对于生物化学变化起催化作用,发酵就是靠酶的作用 enzyme; ferment

霉(❷黴) méi ㄇㄟˊ ❶衣物、食品等受了潮热长霉菌 to become (*or* get) mildewed; to go mouldy: ～烂 *to mildew and rot* | 发～ *to become* (or *get*) *mildewed; to mildew* ❷霉菌,一类真菌,常寄生或腐生在食物或衣物的表面,呈细丝状,有分枝,没有叶绿素;有白霉、青霉等多种 mould; mildew

媒 méi ㄇㄟˊ 撮合男女婚事的人 matchmaker; go-between (㊟ ***doublet*** 一妁 shuò matchmaker; go-between) [媒介]使双方发生关系的人或物 medium; vehicle; intermedium: 蚊子是传染疟疾的～～。*The mosquito is the carrier of malaria.*

煤 méi ㄇㄟˊ ❶古代的植物压埋在地底下,在缺氧高压的条件下,年久变化成的黑色或黑褐色固体,成分以碳为主,是很重要的燃料和化工原料。也叫"煤炭"或"石炭" (also called 煤炭 or 石炭) coal [煤油]从石油中分馏出来的一种产品 kerosene; paraffin ❷〈方 ***dialect***〉(一子)烟气凝结的黑灰 soot: 锅～子 *soot on the bottom of a pan*

糜(**䵋) ㊁ méi ㄇㄟˊ (一子)就是穄。参看319页"穄"(jì) (i. e. 穄, see 穄 on p319) common millet (*Panicum miliaceum*)

㊀ mí 见500页 see p500

每 měi ㄇㄟˇ 代词 ***pronoun*** ❶指全体中的任何一个或一组 every; each: ～人 *everyone; each one* | ～回 *every time* | ～次 *every* (or *each*) *time* | ～三天 *every three days* | ～一分钱 *every penny* ❷指反复的动作中的任何一次或一组 on each occasion; each time: ～战必胜 *to be victorious in every battle; to be invincible* | ～逢十五日出版 *to be published on the 15th day of each month* [每每]副词 ***adverb***,常常 often

美 měi ㄇㄟˇ ❶好,善 beautiful; good; kind: ～德 *virtue; moral excellence; goodness* | ～意 *good intention;*

M

kindness|～貌 *good looks*|～景 *beautiful scenery* (or *landscape*)|尽善尽～ *perfectly good and beautiful; most beautiful and virtuous; perfect*|物～价廉 *good in quality and cheap in price; good and inexpensive* ❷赞美，称赞，以为好 to praise; to eulogize ❸使美、好看 to beautify; to prettify:～容 *to improve one's looks; to beautify one's appearance; to cosmeticize*|～发(*of men*) *to get a haircut*; (*of women*) *to go to the hairdresser's* ❹〈方 **dialect**〉得意，高兴 to be pleased with oneself; to feel smug:～滋滋的 *self-pleased; very pleased with oneself* ❺指美洲，包括北美洲和南美洲，世界七大洲中的两个洲 America ❻指美国 United States of America; America; US

镁 měi ㄇㄟˇ 一种金属元素，符号Mg，银白色，略有延展性，在湿空气中表面易生碱式碳酸镁薄膜而渐失金属光泽，燃烧时能发强光。镁与铝的合金可制飞机、飞船。硫酸镁可做泻药，俗叫泻盐 magnesium (Mg)

浼 měi ㄇㄟˇ ❶污染 to contaminate; to stain; to soil ❷恳托 to entrust

妹 mèi ㄇㄟˋ ❶(一子)称同父母比自己年纪小的女子(叠 **reduplication**) younger sister; sister ❷对比自己年纪小的同辈女性的称呼(younger female of the same generation):表～ cousin

昧 mèi ㄇㄟˋ ❶昏，糊涂，不明白 to have hazy notions; to be ignorant of:愚～ *ignorant; benighted*|蒙～ *ignorant; unenlightened*|冒～ *to venture; to make bold; to take the liberty of* ❷隐藏，隐瞒 to hide; to conceal:拾金不～ *not to pocket the money one happens to pick up*

寐 mèi ㄇㄟˋ 睡，睡着(zháo) to sleep:假～ *to catnap; to doze; to drowse*|夜不能～ *unable to sleep at night; cannot go to sleep at night*|梦～以求 *to long* (or *yearn*) *for sth day and night; to covet all the time*

魅(**鬽) mèi ㄇㄟˋ 传说中的鬼怪(in legends) evil spirit; demon; monster:鬼～ *ghosts and goblins; evil forces; bogey* [魅力]很能吸引人的力量 glamour; charm; fascination

袂 mèi ㄇㄟˋ 衣袖 sleeve:联～(结伴)赴津 *to go to Tianjin together* [分袂]离别 to part (from each other); to separate

媚 mèi ㄇㄟˋ ❶巴结，逢迎 to fawn on; to curry favour with; to flatter:献～ *to try to ingratiate oneself with; to curry favour with* ❷美好，可爱 charming; fascinating; enchanting:妩～ *charming; lovely; graceful*|春光明～ *bright spring*

MEN ㄇㄣ

闷 ㊀ mēn ㄇㄣ ❶因气压低或空气不流通而引起的不舒

服的感觉 stuffy; stifling:天气～热。*It's hot and stuffy.* | 这屋子矮,又没有窗子,太～了。*It's too stuffy in such a room with low ceilings and no windows.* ❷呆在屋里不出门 to shut oneself indoors:一个人总～在家里,心胸就不开阔了。*You won't be broad-minded if you always shut yourself at home.* ❸密闭 to cover tightly:茶刚泡上,～一会儿再喝。*The tea has just been made. It needs to draw* (or *steep*) *for a while.* ❹〈方 **dialect**〉声音不响亮 (of a sound) muffled; subdued:这人说话～声～气。*He spoke in a muffled voice.*

㊀ mèn 见495页 see p495

门(門) mén ㄇㄣˊ ❶(一儿)建筑物、车船等的出入口。又指安在出入口上能开关的装置 entrance; door; gate:防盗～ *burglar-proof door; anti-theft door* | ～镜 *peephole* (*in a door*) ㊙ ***figurative*** 门径,诀窍 way to do sth; knack:摸不着～儿 *cannot get the hang of sth* | 找窍～儿 *to try to find the key to a problem; to try to get the knack of doing sth* ❷(一儿)形状或作用像门的东西 valve; switch:电～ *electric switch* | 水～ *water valve* | 球～ *goal* ❸家族或家族的一支 branch of a family or clan; family:一～老小 *whole family* | 长(zhǎng)～长子 *eldest son of the eldest branch of a clan* ❹一般事物的分类 class; category; branch:分～别类 *to categorize; to divide* (or *put*) *into different categories* ❺生物的分类单位之一,在"界"之下、"纲"之上 phylum:被子植物～ *Magnoliophyta* | 脊索动物～ *Chordata* ❻学术思想或宗教的派别 (religious) sect; school (of thought):佛～ *Buddhism* | 儒～ *Confucianism* ❼量词 ***quantifier***:一～炮 *a cannon* | 一～功课 *a course of lessons*

[门巴族]我国少数民族,参看附表(see the appendix) the Menba (*or* Moinba, Monba, Menpa) ethnic group, one of the ethnic minorities of China

扪 mén ㄇㄣˊ 按,摸 to touch; to feel; to stroke:～心自问(反省) *to lay the hand on the heart and examine oneself* — *to examine one's own conscience*

钔 mén ㄇㄣˊ 一种人造的放射性元素(符号 Md) mendelevium (Md)

亹 mén ㄇㄣˊ [亹源]回族自治县,在青海省。今作"门源"(now written as 门源) Menyuan, a Hui autonomous county in Qinghai Province

闷 ㊀ mèn ㄇㄣˋ ❶心烦,不痛快 bored; depressed; dejected:～得慌 *to feel bored* | ～～不乐 *depressed; dejected; in low spirits* ❷密闭,不透气 tightly closed; sealed:～子车 *boxcar*

㊁ mēn 见494页 see p494

M

焖 mèn ㄇㄣˋ 盖紧锅盖,用微火把饭菜煮熟 to boil in a covered pot over a slow fire; to braise:～饭 *to cook rice over a slow fire*

懑(懣) mèn ㄇㄣˋ ❶烦闷 to feel vexed; to be depressed; to be out of sorts ❷愤慨,生气 angry; indignant:愤～ *depressed and discontented; resentful*

们 men ·ㄇㄣ 词尾 ***suffix***,表人的复数(used to form a plural number when added to a personal pronoun or a noun referring to a person):你～ *you*|咱～ *we; us*|他～ *they; them*|学生～ *students*|师徒～ *master and apprentice*

MENG ㄇㄥ

蒙(❶❷矇) ㊀ mēng ㄇㄥ ❶欺骗 to cheat; to deceive; to dupe (㊥ ***doublet*** 一骗 to deceive; to hoodwink; to cheat):别～人。*Stop kidding around!* or *No kidding!*|谁也～不住他。*He has never been fooled.* ❷胡乱猜测 to make a wild (*or* random) guess:这回叫你～对了。*You made a lucky guess this time.* ❸昏迷 unconscious; senseless:他被球打～了。*He was knocked senseless by a ball.*

㊁ méng 见497页 see p497

㊂ měng 见498页 see p498

氓(甿)** ㊀ méng ㄇㄥˊ 〈古 ***archaism***〉民(特指外来的)。也作"萌"(also written as 萌) common people (used specially for migrants from another place)

㊁ máng 见487页 see p487

虻(*蝱) méng ㄇㄥˊ 昆虫名。种类很多,身体灰黑色,翅透明。生活在野草丛里,雄的吸植物的汁液,雌的吸人、畜的血 horse-fly; *gad-fly* (*Tabanidae*)

萌 méng ㄇㄥˊ ❶植物的芽 sprout; bud; shoot ❷萌芽,植物生芽 to sprout; to bud; to shoot forth ㊀ ***extension*** 开始发生 to come into being; to arise:知者(有见识的人)见于未～。*The experienced can foresee the course of events.*|故态复～(多用于贬义)(*usually used in derogatory sense*) *to resume one's former manner; to relapse into one's old bad habits*

〈古 ***archaism***〉又同"氓"(méng) also same as 氓

盟 méng ㄇㄥˊ ❶旧时指宣誓缔约,现多指团体和团体、阶级和阶级或国和国的联合 alliance; coalition:工农联～ *worker-peasant alliance*|缔结友好同～互助条约 *to conclude a treaty of friendship, alliance and mutual aid* ❷发(誓) to take one's oath; to swear:～个誓 *to swear an oath* ❸内蒙古自治区的行政区划单位。包括若干旗、县、市(administrative division of the Inner Mongolian Autonomous Region, including prefectures, counties and cities) league

蒙(❹濛、❺曚、❻懞)

㊀ méng ㄇㄥˊ ❶没有知识，愚昧 ignorance：启～ *to enlighten* | 发～ *to teach a child to read and write* | ～昧 *ignorant; unenlightened* ❷覆盖 to cover; to wrap：～头盖脑 *to cover one's head* | ～上一张纸 *to cover with a piece of paper* [蒙蔽]隐瞒事实，欺骗 to deceive; to fool; to hoodwink ❸受 to receive; to suffer; to incur：～难(nàn) *(of a celebrity, etc) to encounter danger; to fall into the hands of the enemy* | 承～招待，感谢之至。*Thank you very much for your kind hospitality.* ❹形容雨点细小(叠 ***reduplication***) drizzly：～～细雨 *fine drizzle* [空蒙]形容景色迷茫 hazy; misty：山色～～。*The hills were shrouded in the mist.* ❺眼睛失明 to go blind [蒙眬]目不明 drowsy; half asleep; hazy：睡眼～～ *eyes heavy with sleep; drowsy* ❻朴实敦厚 simple and honest ❼姓 Meng, a surname

㊁ mēng 见496页 see p496

㊂ měng 见498页 see p498

幪 méng ㄇㄥˊ 见572页"帡"字条"帡幪"(píng—) see 帡幪 on p572

獴 méng ㄇㄥˊ (又 ***also*** měng) 见498页 měng see měng on p498

檬 méng ㄇㄥˊ 见538页"柠"字条"柠檬"(níng—) see 柠檬 on p538

曚 méng ㄇㄥˊ [曚昽](—lóng)日光不明(of daylight) dim

朦 méng ㄇㄥˊ [朦胧](—lóng) **1** 月光不明(of moonlight) dim; hazy **2** 不清楚，模糊 obscure; dim; hazy

鹲 méng ㄇㄥˊ 鸟名。体大，嘴大而直，灰色或白色，尾部有长羽毛，生活在热带海洋上，以鱼类为食 tropicbird (*Phaethontidae*)

礞 méng ㄇㄥˊ [礞石]岩石名，有青礞石和金礞石两种。可入药 chlorite schist

艨 méng ㄇㄥˊ [艨艟](—chōng)古代的一种战船 warship in ancient China

甍 méng ㄇㄥˊ 屋脊 ridge (of a roof)：碧瓦飞～ *green tiles and upturned ridge*

瞢 méng ㄇㄥˊ ❶日月昏暗无光(of daylight or moonlight) dim ❷目不明(of eyes) blurred; dim

勐 měng ㄇㄥˇ ❶勇敢 brave; courageous ❷云南省西双版纳傣族地区称小块的平地。多用于地名(*meng*, usually used in a place name in the Dai ethnic group area, Xishuangbanna, Yunnan Province) small piece of flat ground

猛 měng ㄇㄥˇ ❶气势壮，力量大 fierce; violent; strong：～虎 *fierce tiger* | 勇～ *coura-*

geous and powerful; *intrepid*; *valiant*|用力过～ *to use too much strength*; *to overexert oneself*|药力～ *strong efficacy of medicine*|火力～ *strong firepower* ❷忽然,突然 suddenly; abruptly:～然惊醒 *to wake up with a start*|～地跑了进来 *to run into all of a sudden*

锰 měng ㄇㄥˇ 一种金属元素,符号 Mn,银白色,有光泽,质硬而脆,在湿空气中氧化。锰与铁的合金叫锰钢,可做火车的车轮。二氧化锰可供瓷器和玻璃着色用。高锰酸钾可作杀菌剂 manganese (Mn)

蜢 měng ㄇㄥˇ 见950页"蚱"字条"蚱蜢"(zhà—) see 蚱蜢 on p950

艋 měng ㄇㄥˇ [舴艋](zé—)小船 small boat

蒙 ㊂ měng ㄇㄥˇ [蒙古族] **1** 我国少数民族,参看附表(see the appendix) the Mongolian (*or* Mongol) ethnic group, one of the ethnic minorities of China **2** 蒙古国的主要民族 the Mongols, majority ethnic group of Mongolia [内蒙古]我国少数民族自治区,1947年5月建立 Inner Mongolia, an autonomous ethnic minority region in China, founded in May, 1947

㊀ méng 见497页 see p497

㊁ mēng 见496页 see p496

獴 měng ㄇㄥˇ méng ㄇㄥˊ (又 *also* méng)哺乳动物的一类,身体长,脚短,嘴尖,耳朵小。捕食蛇、蟹等,如蛇獴、蟹獴 mongoose (*Herpestes*)

蠓 měng ㄇㄥˇ 蠓虫,昆虫名。比蚊子小,褐色或黑色,雌的吸人、畜的血,能传染疾病 midge; biting midge (*Ceratopogonidae*)

懵(**懜) měng ㄇㄥˇ [懵懂](—dǒng)糊涂,不明白事理 muddled; ignorant

孟 mèng ㄇㄥˋ ❶旧时兄弟姊妹排行(háng)有时用孟、仲、叔、季做次序,孟是老大(in former times) eldest among brothers and sisters:～兄 *eldest brother*|～孙 *eldest grandson* ❷指夏历一季中月份在开头的 first month of a season (of the Chinese lunar calendar):～春(春季第一月) *first month of spring*; *first lunar month*|～冬(冬季第一月) *first month of winter*; *tenth lunar month*

[孟浪]鲁莽,考虑不周到 rash; reckless; impetuous:此事不可～～。*It should not be done rashly*.

梦(夢) mèng ㄇㄥˋ ❶睡眠时体内体外各种刺激或残留在大脑里的外界刺激引起的影像活动 dream ❷做梦 to dream:～游 *to somnambulate*; *to sleepwalk*|～见 *to see in a dream*; *to dream about* ❸比喻虚幻 fancy; illusion:～想 *to dream of*; *to hope vainly*

MI ㄇㄧ

咪 mī ㄇㄧ 拟声词 ***onomatopoeia***,猫叫声(叠 ***redupli-***

cation) mew; meow; miaow

眯(*瞇) ㊁ mī ㄇㄧ ❶眼皮微微合拢 to narrow one's eyes:在床上～(合眼养神)一会儿 *to take a nap in bed; to close one's eyes in repose in bed* ❷眯缝 to narrow (one's eyes):～着眼笑 *to smile with half-closed eyes*|他～起眼睛看了半天。*He narrowed his eyes and gazed for a long while.*

㊀ mí 见499页 see p499

弥(彌、❹瀰) mí ㄇㄧˊ ❶满,遍 full; overflowing:～月(小孩儿满月) *completion of the first month after birth of a child*|～天大罪 *monstrous (or heinous, great) crime* ❷补,合 to cover; to fill; to complete (㊥ ***doublet*** 一补 to make up; to remedy; to make good) ❸更加 more; still (*or* even) more:～坚 *more strong-willed*|欲盖～彰 *the more one tries to hide, the more one is exposed; to try to cover up a misdeed, only to make it more conspicuous* ❹[弥漫](—màn) **1** 水满(of water) to overflow **2** 到处都是,充满 to spread all over the place; to permeate; to fill:硝烟～～ *to be enveloped in gun smoke*

祢(禰) mí ㄇㄧˊ (旧读 formerly nǐ)姓 Mi, a surname

猕(獼) mí ㄇㄧˊ [猕猴]哺乳动物,面部红色无毛,有颊囊,尾短,臀疣显著。产于亚洲南部和我国西南等地 macaque (*Macaca*); rhesus monkey (*Macaca mulatta*)

迷 mí ㄇㄧˊ ❶分辨不清,失去了辨别、判断的能力 to be confused; to be lost:～了路 *to lose one's way; to get lost* [迷彩]使人迷惑不易分辨的色彩 colours that confuse or mislead people; camouflage:～～服 *camouflage clothes; battle fatigues* [迷信]盲目地信仰和崇拜。特指信仰神仙鬼怪等 superstition; blind faith ❷醉心于某种事物,发生特殊的爱好(hào) to be fascinated by; to be crazy about; to be engrossed in:人～ *to be fascinated; to be enthralled; to be enchanted*|～恋 *to be infatuated with; to indulge in; to be addicted to* ❸沉醉于某种事物的人 fan; enthusiast; buff:棋～ *chess fiend (or fan)*|球～ (*ball game*) *fan*|戏～ *theatre fan; theatre-goer* ❹使人陶醉 to bewitch; to fascinate; to enchant:景色～人。*The scenery is of enchanting beauty.*

眯(*瞇) ㊀ mí ㄇㄧˊ 尘土入眼,不能睁开看东西(of dust, etc) to get into one's eye

㊁ mī 见499页 see p499

谜(**謎) mí ㄇㄧˊ 谜语,影射事物或文字的隐语 riddle; conundrum:灯～ *riddles written on lan-*

terns; lantern riddles｜～底 *answer* (or *solution*) *to a riddle* ㊞ ***figurative*** 还没有弄明白的或难以理解的事物 enigma; mystery; puzzle

醚 mí ㄇㄧˊ 有机化合物的一类，通式是 R—O—R′。乙醚是医药上常用的麻醉剂 ether

糜 ㊀ mí ㄇㄧˊ ❶粥 gruel; paste ❷糜烂，烂到难以收拾 rotten：～烂不堪 *rotten to the core* ❸浪费 to spend extravagantly; to waste：～财妨农 *Extravagance brings harm to farming*. ❹姓 Mi, a surname

㊁ méi 见493页 see p493

縻 mí ㄇㄧˊ ❶牛缰绳 reins of an ox ❷系(jì)，捆，拴 to tie; to fasten; to do up［羁縻］㊞ ***figurative*** 牵制，笼络 to keep (vassal states, etc) under control; to win sb over by hook (*or* by crook); draw over

靡 ㊀ mí ㄇㄧˊ 浪费 to spend extravagantly; to waste (㊣ ***doublet*** 奢— extravagant and wasteful)：不要～费钱财。*Don't waste money*.

㊁ mǐ 见500页 see p500

蘼 mí ㄇㄧˊ［蘼芜］(—wú)古书上指芎䓖(xiōng-qióng)的苗(in ancient Chinese texts) seedling or rhizome of *chuanxiong*

醾 mí ㄇㄧˊ［酴醾］(tú—)重(chóng)酿的酒 double-fermented wine

麋 mí ㄇㄧˊ 麋鹿，又叫"四不像"。头似马，身似驴，蹄似牛，角似鹿，全身灰褐色。是一种珍贵动物(also called 四不像) *milu*; David's deer (*Elaphurus davidianus*)

米 mǐ ㄇㄧˇ ❶谷类或其他植物子实去了壳的名称 shelled (*or* husked) seed：小～ *husked millet*｜花生～ *peanut seed* (or *kernel*); *shelled peanut* 特指去了壳的稻的子实 rice：买一袋～ *to buy a bag of rice*［虾米］去了壳的干虾肉，也指虾(also used to denote shrimp) dried, shelled shrimps ❷(外 ***loanword***)长度的法定计量单位(旧名公尺)，符号 m (formerly called 公尺) metre (m)

洣 mǐ ㄇㄧˇ 洣水，水名，在湖南省东南部 Mishui River, in southeast Hunan Province

脒 mǐ ㄇㄧˇ 有机化合物的一类，是含有 $\mathrm{HC}\begin{matrix} /\!\!/\mathrm{NH} \\ \diagdown\mathrm{NH_2} \end{matrix}$ 的化合物 amidine

敉 mǐ ㄇㄧˇ 安抚，安定 to soothe; to pacify; to placate

芈 mǐ ㄇㄧˇ ❶羊叫(of a sheep) to baa; to bleat ❷姓 Mi, a surname

弭 mǐ ㄇㄧˇ 止，息 to put an end to; to stop; to put down：水患消～。*The menace of floods has been eliminated*.

靡 ㊁ mǐ ㄇㄧˇ ❶无，没有 do not have; there is not; to

be without:～日不思 *not a day passes without one's thinking of sth or sb* ❷倒下 to fall:望风披～ *to bend to* (or *before*) *the wind* — *to scatter at the mere sight of the oncoming force*

㊁ mí 见500页 see p500

汨 mì ㄇㄧˋ [汨罗江]水名,在湖南省岳阳 Miluo River, in Yueyang, Hunan Province

觅(*覓) mì ㄇㄧˋ 找,寻求 to look for; to hunt for; seek (㊀ ***doublet*** 寻— to seek; to look for):～食(*of birds, beasts, etc*) *to look* (or *hunt*) *for food* | ～路 *to seek the way*

泌 ㊀ mì ㄇㄧˋ 分泌,从生物体里产生出某种物质 to secrete:～尿 *to urinate*

㊁ bì 见37页 see p37

宓 mì ㄇㄧˋ 安,静 tranquil; quiet

秘(*祕) ㊀ mì ㄇㄧˋ (旧读 formerly bì)不公开的,不让大家知道的 secret; mysterious; confidential (㊀ ***doublet*** —密 secret; confidential; clandestine):～方 *secret* (or *esoteric*) *recipe* | ～诀 *secret* (*to success*); *recipe* [秘书]掌管文书并协助负责人处理日常工作的人员 secretary [便秘]大便干燥、困难、次数少的症状 constipation

㊁ bì 见38页 see p38

密 mì ㄇㄧˋ ❶事物和事物之间距离短,空隙小,跟"稀"、"疏"相对(the opposite of 稀 or 疏) close; dense; thick (㊀ ***doublet*** 稠— dense; thick):小株～植 *to have small plants planted closely* | 我国沿海人口稠～。*The coastal areas in our country are densely populated.* | 枪声越来越～。*The gunfire was getting heavier and heavier.* ㊁ ***transfer*** 精致,细致 fine; precise; meticulous:精～ *precise; accurate* | 细～ *close; meticulous* ❷关系近,感情好 intimate; close; familiar (㊀ ***doublet*** 亲— close; intimate):～友 *close* (or *fast*) *friend; bosom friend* | 他们两个人很亲～。*The two of them are on intimate terms.* [密切]紧密,亲切 close; intimate; bosom:关系～～ *to be close with sb* | ～～地配合 *to act in close coordination with* ❸不公开 secret:～谋 *to conspire; to intrigue; to plot* | ～谈 *to have a secret* (or *confidential, private*) *talk; to talk behind closed doors* | ～码电报 *cipher telegram* ㊀ ***extension*** 秘密的事物 secret:保～ *to keep confidential; to maintain secrecy; to keep sth secret*

谧 mì ㄇㄧˋ 安静 quiet; tranquil; still (㊀ ***doublet*** 安— quiet; tranquil)

嘧 mì ㄇㄧˋ [嘧啶](—dìng)有机化合物,分子式 $C_4H_4N_2$,无色结晶,有刺激性气味,溶于水、乙醇和乙醚,供制化学药品 pyridine; pyrimidine

蜜 mì ㄇㄧˋ ❶蜂蜜,蜜蜂采取花的甜汁酿成的东西 hon-

M

ey [蜜饯]用蜜、糖浸渍果品。又指用蜜、糖浸渍的果品 to candy fruit; candied (*or* preserved) fruit ❷甜美 sweet; honeyed; luscious:甜言～语 *sweet words and honeyed phrases; sweet talk; fine-sounding words*

幂(＊冪) mì ㄇㄧˋ ❶覆盖东西的巾 cloth cover ❷覆盖,遮盖 to cover; to hood ❸表示一个数自乘若干次的形式叫幂。如 *t* 自乘 *n* 次的幂为 t^n power [乘幂]一个数自乘若干次的积数。也叫"乘方"。如 5 的 4 乘方又叫 5 的 4 乘幂或 5 的 4 次幂(also called 乘方) power product

蓂 ㊀ mì ㄇㄧˋ 见801页"菥"字条"菥蓂"(xī—) see 菥蓂 on p801

㊁ míng 见510页 see p510

MIAN ㄇㄧㄢ

眠 mián ㄇㄧㄢˊ ❶睡觉 to sleep (㊥ **doublet** 睡— to sleep):安～ *to sleep peacefully; to sleep in peace* | 失～ *to suffer from insomnia; insomnia* | 长～(指人死) *to have an eternal sleep; to be dead* ❷蚕在蜕皮时像睡眠那样不食不动 inactive state of the silkworm before it sheds its skin: 初～ *"first sleep", a period in which the newborn silkworm neither moves nor eats* | 蚕三～了。*The silkworms are inactive in the third stage of their life.* [冬眠]蜗牛、蛇、蛙、蝙蝠等动物到冬季不食不动。也叫"入蛰"(zhé) (also called 入蛰) hibernation

绵(＊緜) mián ㄇㄧㄢˊ ❶(—子)蚕丝结成的片或团,供絮衣被、装墨盒等用。也叫"丝绵"(also called 丝绵) silk floss ❷性质像丝绵的 with the quality of silk floss **1** 软弱,单薄 soft; thin; weak:～薄 *meagre strength; humble effort* **2** 延续不断 continuous; consecutive:～延(*of mountain ranges, land, etc*) *to be continuous; to stretch long and unbroken*

棉 mián ㄇㄧㄢˊ ❶草棉,一年生草本植物,叶掌状分裂,果实像桃。种子外有白色的絮,就是供纺织及絮衣被用的棉花。种子可以榨油 cotton plant (*Gossypium*) [木棉]落叶乔木,生在热带、亚热带,叶是掌状复叶。种子上有白色软毛,可以装枕褥等。木材可造船 kapok; bombax (*bombax malabaricus*) ❷棉花,草棉的棉絮 cotton:～衣 *cotton-padded coat* | ～线 *cotton thread; cotton*

丏 miǎn ㄇㄧㄢˇ 遮蔽,看不见 sheltered; covered; out of sight

沔 miǎn ㄇㄧㄢˇ 沔水,水名,汉江的上游河段,在陕西省南部 Mianshui River, the upper reaches of the Hanjiang River in the south of Shaanxi Province

免 miǎn ㄇㄧㄢˇ ❶去掉,除掉 to exempt; to dispense with; to remove from:～冠 *to take off one's hat; without a hat on; bareheaded*|～职 *to remove sb from office; to relieve sb of his post; to dismiss*|～费 *free (of charge); gratis* ❷避免 to avoid; to avert; to escape:～疫 *immunity (from disease)*|做好准备,以～临时抓瞎。*Get prepared in advance so as not to be in a rush at the last moment.* ❸勿,不可 to be not allowed; do not (do):闲人～进。*No admittance except on business. or Staff Only.*

勉 miǎn ㄇㄧㄢˇ ❶勉力,力量不够还尽力做 to exert oneself; to make an effort; to strive (*or* try) to do what is beyond one's power:～为其难(nán) *to try to do what is beyond one's power; to be obliged to undertake a difficult task* [勉强](-qiǎng) **1** 尽力 to manage with an effort; to do with difficulty:～～支持下去 *to hold out with an effort* **2** 刚刚地够,不充足 barely enough; inadequate; unconvincing:这种说法很～～(理由不充足)。*The argument is far-fetched (or unconvincing).*|勉勉强强及格 *to barely pass the examination* **3** 不是心甘情愿的 reluctant; grudging:～～答应 *to agree grudgingly* **4** 让人去做不愿做的事 to force sb to do sth unwillingly:不要～～他。*Don't force him to do it.* ❷勉励,使人努力 to encourage; to urge; to exhort:互～ *to encourage one another*|有则改之,无则加～。*Correct mistakes if you have made any and guard against them if you have not.*

娩 miǎn ㄇㄧㄢˇ 分娩,妇女生孩子 to give birth to a baby

冕 miǎn ㄇㄧㄢˇ 古代大(dà)夫以上的官戴的礼帽。后代专指帝王的礼帽 coronet; crown:加～ *to coronate*

鮸 miǎn ㄇㄧㄢˇ 鮸鱼,鱼名,又叫"鳘(mǐn)鱼"。身体长形而侧扁,棕褐色,生活在海中,肉可以吃(also called 鳘鱼) brown croaker (*Sciaenidae*)

勔 miǎn ㄇㄧㄢˇ 勉力,勤勉 diligent; industrious

湎 miǎn ㄇㄧㄢˇ 沉迷(多指喝酒) (usually used to denote drinking) to indulge in; to be given to

缅 miǎn ㄇㄧㄢˇ 遥远 remote; far back:～怀 *to cherish the memory of; to recall; to reminisce*|～想 *to think of (past events); to recall*

靦 ㊀ miǎn ㄇㄧㄢˇ [靦覥](-tiǎn)旧同"腼腆" same as 腼腆 in former times

㊁ tiǎn 见745页 see p745

腼 miǎn ㄇㄧㄢˇ [腼腆](-tiǎn)害羞,不敢见生人 shy; bashful; diffident:这孩子太～～。*The child is too shy.*

M

渑(澠) ㊀ miǎn ㄇㄧㄢˇ [渑池]地名,在河南省 Mianchi, a place in Henan Province

㊁ shéng 见672页 see p672

面(❽—⓫麵、❽—⓫*麪、❶—❼**靣) miàn ㄇㄧㄢˋ ❶面孔,脸,头的前部 face (㊥ **doublet** 脸一 face|颜一 face):~前 *in (the) face of; in front of; ahead of*|~带笑容 *to have (or wear) a smile on one's face* [面子](—zi) 1 体面 reputation; prestige; face:爱~~ *to be anxious to save face; to be concerned about face-saving*|丢~~ *to lose face* 2 情面 feelings; sensibilities:大公无私,不讲~~ *to be just and selfless and show no consideration for others' sensibilities* ❷用脸对着,向着 to face (a certain direction):背山~水 *with hills behind and a river* (or *lake*) *in front* ❸当面,直接接头的 face to face; personally; directly:~谈 *to speak (to sb) face to face; to have a face-to-face talk*|~议 *to negotiate face to face; to take up a matter with sb personally* ❹(—子、—儿)事物的外表,跟"里"相对(the opposite of 里) surface; face; right side:地~ *earth's surface; ground*|水~ *water surface; surface of a river, lake, sea, etc*|被~儿 *facing or outside cover of a quilt* ❺几何学上称线移动所生成的图形,有长有宽没有厚 surface:平~ *plane*|~积 *area* ❻方面,边,部 side; part; aspect:正~ *front; face; facade*|反~ *reverse side; wrong side; back*|上~ *above; upper; over*|下~ *below; under; beneath*|~~俱到 *to attend to every aspect of a matter; to be well considered in every aspect* ❼量词 **quantifier**:一~旗 *a flag*|一~镜子 *a mirror*|一~锣 *a gong* ❽粮食磨成的粉 flour:麦子~ *wheat flour*|小米~ *millet flour*|玉米~ *cornmeal; maize flour* 特指小麦磨成的粉 wheat flour ❾(—子、—儿)粉末 powder:药~儿 *medicinal powder*|粉笔~儿 *chalk powder* (or *dust*) ❿面条 noodles:挂~ *fine dried noodles; vermicelli*|炸酱~ *noodles served with fried soya paste*|方便~ *instant noodles*|一碗~ *a bowl of noodles* ⓫食物含纤维少而柔软(of food) soft and mealy:这种瓜很~。*This kind of melon is very soft and mealy.*

眄 miàn ㄇㄧㄢˋ 斜着眼睛看 to give a sidelong glance:顾~ *to turn round and look at; to look round*

MIAO ㄇㄧㄠ

喵 miāo ㄇㄧㄠ 拟声词 **onomatopoeia**,猫叫的声音 mew; miaow

苗 miáo ㄇㄧㄠˊ ❶（～儿）一般指幼小的植株 young plant; seedling: 麦～ *wheat seedling* | 树～ *tree seedling; sapling* [苗条]人的身材细长、好看（of a woman）slender; slim ❷（～儿）形状像苗的 sth resembling a young plant: 笤帚～儿 *broom spikes* | 火～儿 *tongue of flame; flame* [矿苗]矿藏露出地面的部分。也叫"露（lù）头"（also called 露头）outcropping; outcrop; crop ❸某些初生的饲养的动物 young of some animals: 鱼～ *fry* ❹子孙后代 offspring（㊟ **doublet** 一裔 progeny; descendants; offspring）❺疫苗，能使机体产生免疫力的微生物制剂 vaccine: 牛痘～（*bovine*）*vaccine*

[苗族]我国少数民族，参看附表（see the appendix）the Miao ethnic group, one of the ethnic minorities of China

描 miáo ㄇㄧㄠˊ 依照原样摹画或重复地画 to trace; to copy（㊟ **doublet** 一摹 to trace; to depict; to portray）: ～花 *to trace a flower* [描写]依照事物的情状，用语言或线条、颜色表现出来 to depict; to describe; to portray: 他很会～～景物。*He is skilful at describing the scenery.*

鹋 miáo ㄇㄧㄠˊ 见177页"鸸"字条"鸸鹋"（ér—）see 鸸鹋 on p177

瞄 miáo ㄇㄧㄠˊ 把视力集中在一点上，注意看 to concentrate one's gaze on; to take aim; to aim: 枪～得准 *to take good aim with the gun* | 眼光～向未来 *to fix*（or *cast, turn*）*one's gaze on the future* [瞄准]对准目标，使射出或扔出的东西能够命中 to take aim; to aim; to sight

杪 miǎo ㄇㄧㄠˇ 树枝的细梢 tip of a twig; top of a tree ㊕ **extension** 末尾 end（of a year, month or season）: 岁～ *end of the year; year-end* | 月～ *end*（or *close*）*of the month; month-end*

眇 miǎo ㄇㄧㄠˇ ❶瞎了一只眼睛。后也泛指瞎了眼睛 blind in one eye; blind ❷细小 tiny; fine; very small

秒 miǎo ㄇㄧㄠˇ ❶谷物种子壳上的芒 beard of grain; awn; arista ❷单位 unit: **1** 圆周的一分的六十分之一（of circumference）second **2** 经纬度的一分的六十分之一（of longitude or latitude）second **3** 时间的一分钟的六十分之一（of time）second

渺（❷* 淼）miǎo ㄇㄧㄠˇ ❶微小 tiny; insignificant; trivial: ～小 *tiny; negligible; insignificant* ❷水势辽远（of an expanse of water）vast: 浩～（*of water*）*stretching far into the distance; vast* [渺茫]离得太远看不清楚 distant and indistinct; remote and vague ㊗ **figurative** 看不见前途的或没有把握的 uncertain; indefinite: 这件事～～得

M

很。*This matter is still up in the air.*

注："淼"多用于人名 note: 淼 usually used in a given name

缈 miǎo ㄇㄧㄠˇ 见566页"缥"字条"缥缈"(piāo—) see 缥缈 on p566

藐 miǎo ㄇㄧㄠˇ 小 small; petty (㊣ **doublet** —小 tiny; negligible; insignificant): ~视 *to despise; to look down upon; to belittle*

邈 miǎo ㄇㄧㄠˇ 远 faraway; remote; distant

妙(*玅) miào ㄇㄧㄠˋ ❶美，好 wonderful; excellent; fine: ~品 *fine quality goods; fine work of art* | ~不可言 *too wonderful for words; wonderful beyond description* ❷奇巧，神奇 *ingenious; clever; subtle* (㊣ **doublet** 巧— ingenious; smart; clever): ~计 *excellent plan; clever ruse; brilliant idea* | ~诀 *clever way; ingenious method* | ~用 *ingenious application*

庙(廟) miào ㄇㄧㄠˋ ❶旧时供祖宗神位的地方 temple; shrine: 家~ *family shrine* ❷供神佛或历史上有名人物的地方 temple: 龙王~ *temple of the Dragon King (the God of Rain and Waters)* | 孔~ *Confucius Temple* ❸庙会，设在寺庙里或附近的集市 temple fair: 赶~ *to go to the temple fair*

缪 ㊀ miào ㄇㄧㄠˋ 姓 Miao, a surname

㊁ móu 见517页 see p517

㊂ miù 见511页 see p511

MIE ㄇㄧㄝ

乜 ㊁ miē ㄇㄧㄝ [乜斜](—xie) **1** 眼睛因困倦而眯成一条缝(of eyes) half-closed: ~~的睡眼 *eyes heavy with sleep* **2** 眼睛略眯而斜着看，多指不满意或看不起的神情(usually expressing an air of dissatisfaction or contempt) to squint; to look askance at

㊀ niè 见537页 see p537

咩(*哶) miē ㄇㄧㄝ 拟声词 ***onomatopoeia***，羊叫的声音 baa; bleat

灭(滅) miè ㄇㄧㄝˋ ❶火熄 (of fire) to go out (㊣ **doublet** 熄— to go out; to put out; to extinguish): ~火器 *fire extinguisher* | ~灯 *to put out the light* | 火~了。*The fire has gone out.* ❷完，尽，使不存在 to destroy; to exterminate; to wipe out (㊣ **doublet** 消— to perish; to eliminate; to exterminate): 消~敌人 *to annihilate* (or *wipe out*) *the enemy* | 功绩不会磨~。*The achievements are ineradicable.* or *The merits are unforgettable.* | 长自己的志气，~敌人的威风 *to boost one's own morale and deflate the arrogance of the enemy* ❸被水漫过 to submerge; to drown: ~顶 *to be drowned; to be swamped*

M

蔑(❸衊) miè ㄇㄧㄝˋ ❶无，没有 not; no; none：～以复加 *could not be surpassed; to reach the limit; in the extreme* ❷小 small; slight; petty：～视(看不起，轻视) *to despise; to scorn; to look down on* ❸涂染 to daub; to paint; to smear [诬蔑][污蔑]造谣毁坏别人的名誉 to slander; to smear; to vilify

篾 miè ㄇㄧㄝˋ (一子、一儿)劈成条的竹片 thin bamboo strip：竹～子 *thin bamboo strip* 泛指劈成条的芦苇、高粱等茎皮 rind (*or* skin) of reed or sorghum：苇～儿 *rind of reed*

蠛 miè ㄇㄧㄝˋ [蠛蠓](一měng) 古书上指蠓。参看498页"蠓"(in ancient Chinese texts) midge (see 蠓 on p498)

MIN ㄇㄧㄣ

民 mín ㄇㄧㄣˊ ❶人民 the people：为国为～ *for the state and the people* [民主] **1** 指人民有管理国家和自由发表意见的权利 democracy; democratic rights **2** 根据大多数群众意见处理问题的工作方式 democratic way of working：作风～～ *to have a democratic workstyle* | 既要有～～，又要有集中 *to need both democracy and centralism* [公民]在一国内有国籍，享受法律上规定的公民权利并履行公民的义务的人 citizen [国民]指具有某国国籍的人 people of a nation; national ❷指人或人群 person or group of people [民族]历史上形成的稳定的人群共同体，其特征是有共同语言、共同地域、共同经济生活和表现于共同文化上的共同心理素质 nation; nationality; ethnic group [居民]在一个地区内较长时期固定居住，并且取得正式户籍的人或人群 resident; inhabitant; dweller ❸民间的 among (*or* of) the people; popular; folk：～俗 *folk custom; folkways* | ～歌 *folk song* ❹指从事不同职业的人 person of a certain occupation：农～ *peasant; farmer* | 牧～ *herdsman* | 渔～ *fisherman* ❺非军事的 civilian; civil：～用 *for civil use; civil* | ～航 *civil aviation* ❻同"苠" same as 苠

苠 mín ㄇㄧㄣˊ 庄稼生长期较长，成熟期较晚，也作"民"(also written as 民)(of crop) to grow longer and ripen later：～穇子(cǎnzi) *late billion-dollar grass* | ～高粱 *late sorghum* | 黄谷子比白谷子～。*The yellow millet grows longer than the white millet.*

岷 mín ㄇㄧㄣˊ 岷山，山名，在四川省北部，绵延于川、甘两省边境 Minshan Mountain, in the north of Sichuan Province, bordering Sichuan and Gansu provinces

珉 mín ㄇㄧㄣˊ 像玉的石头 jade-like stone

缗 mín ㄇㄧㄣˊ ❶古代穿铜钱用的绳 string for stringing

M

up copper cash in ancient China ❷钓鱼用的绳 fishline

旻 mín ㄇㄧㄣˊ ❶天,天空 sky:～天 *heaven; sky*|苍～ *blue sky; heavens* ❷秋天 autumn

皿 mǐn ㄇㄧㄣˇ 器皿,盘、盂一类的东西 household utensils, including jars, plates, etc

闵 mǐn ㄇㄧㄣˇ 忧患(多指疾病死丧)(usually used to denote diseases or death) sorrow; worry; grief

悯 mǐn ㄇㄧㄣˇ ❶哀怜 to pity; to commiserate; to sympathize (㊀ ***doublet*** 怜— to pity; to take pity on; to have compassion for):其情可～。*His case deserves sympathy.* ❷忧愁。也作"愍"(also written as 愍) sorrow; grief

闽 mǐn ㄇㄧㄣˇ 福建省的别称 Min, another name for Fujian Province

抿 mǐn ㄇㄧㄣˇ ❶刷,抹 smooth (hair, etc) with a wet brush:～了～头发 *to give a few touches to one's hair (with a brush)* ❷收敛 to close lightly; to tuck; to furl:～着嘴笑 *to smile with closed lips*|水鸟一～翅,往水里一扎。*The water bird tucked its wings and dived into the water.* ㊁ ***extension*** 收敛嘴唇,少量沾取 to sip:他真不喝酒,连～都不～。*He has never had a drink, not even a sip.*

泯 mǐn ㄇㄧㄣˇ 消灭 to vanish; to die out (㊀ ***doublet*** —灭 to vanish; to die out; to disappear)

湣 mǐn ㄇㄧㄣˇ 古谥号用字 word used in some posthumous titles in ancient China

愍(**惛) mǐn ㄇㄧㄣˇ 同"悯"same as 悯

黾(**黽**) mǐn ㄇㄧㄣˇ [黾勉](—miǎn)努力,勉力 to exert oneself; to make efforts; to strive

敏 mǐn ㄇㄧㄣˇ ❶有智慧,反应迅速,灵活 acute; smart; quick (㊀ ***doublet*** —捷 quick; nimble; agile|灵— sensitive; keen; acute):～感 *sensitive; susceptible; responsive*|～锐 *sharp; acute; keen*|机～ *alert and resourceful; quick-witted*|敬谢不～(婉转表示不愿意做)(*to politely refuse to do something*) *to beg to be excused* ❷努力 diligent; industrious; earnest:～行不怠 *to make unremitting efforts at self-cultivation*

鳘 mǐn ㄇㄧㄣˇ 鳘鱼,就是鮸鱼(i. e. 鮸鱼) slate cod croaker (*Sciaenidae*)

MING ㄇㄧㄥ

名 míng ㄇㄧㄥˊ ❶(—儿)名字,人或事物的称谓 name:您给他起个～儿吧。*Please name the baby for us.* [名词]表示人、地、事、物的名称的词,如学生、北京、戏剧、桌子等 noun; substantive ❷叫出,说出 to express; to describe:无以～之

not to know what to call it; cannot describe it properly｜莫～其妙 *to be unable to make head or tail* (*of sth*); *cannot make anything of it* ❸名誉，声誉 fame; reputation; renown: 有～ *famous; well-known; celebrated*｜出～ (*to be*) *famous;* (*to be*) *well-known*｜不为～，不为利 *to seek neither fame nor gain* 引 ***extension*** 有声誉的，大家都知道的 famous; celebrated; well-known; noted: ～医 *well-known doctor; celebrated* (or *noted*) *physician*｜～将 *famous general; great soldier*｜～胜 *place famous for its scenery or historic relics; well-known scenic spot*｜～言 *well-known saying; celebrated dictum; famous remark*｜～产 *famous product* ❹量词 ***quantifier***，用于人(used for person): 学生四～ *four students*

茗 míng ㄇㄧㄥˊ ❶茶树的嫩芽 tender tea leaves ❷茶 tea: 香～ *scented tea*｜品～ *to sip tea* (*for judgement of its quality*); *to taste tea; to sample tea*

洺 míng ㄇㄧㄥˊ 洺河，水名，在河北省南部 Minghe River, in the south of Hebei Province

铭 míng ㄇㄧㄥˊ ❶刻在器物上记述生平、事业或警惕自己的文字 inscription: 墓志～ *inscription on the memorial tablet in front of a tomb; epitaph*｜座右～ *motto; maxim* ❷在器物上刻字 to engrave: ～诸肺腑(喻永记) *to be deeply engraved in one's mind* (or *memory*); *to be borne in mind — to be remembered forever*

明 míng ㄇㄧㄥˊ ❶亮，跟"暗"相对(the opposite of 暗) bright; brilliant; light: ～亮 *bright; well-lit; shining*｜天～了。*The day is dawning.*｜～晃晃的刺刀 *gleaming bayonets* ❷明白，清楚 clear; distinct; obvious: 说～ *to explain; to illustrate; to show*｜表～ *to make known; to make clear; to indicate*｜黑白分～ *black and white* (or *right and wrong*) *clearly distinguished; the line between right and wrong is clearly drawn*｜情况不～。*The situation is not clear.*｜～～是他搞的。*This is obviously his doing.* 转 ***transfer*** 懂得，了解 to understand; to realize; to know: 深～大义 *to be deeply conscious of what is righteous; to have a strong sense of justice* ❸公开，不秘密，不隐蔽，跟"暗"相对(the opposite of 暗) open; plain; overt: ～讲 *to speak frankly; to speak* (or *say*) *openly*｜有话～说 *to speak one's mind plainly; to lay the cards on the table*｜～码售货 *to sell goods at marked prices*｜～枪易躲，暗箭难防。*It is easy to dodge an open spear thrust but difficult to guard against an arrow shot from behind.* ❹视觉，眼力 sight: 失～ *to lose one's eyesight; to go blind* ❺

能够看清事物 sharp-eyed; clear-sighted:英～ *wise; brilliant; sagacious*|精～ *astute; shrewd; smart*|眼～手快 *quick of eye and deft of hand; sharp-eyed and deft-handed* ❻神明,迷信称神灵 gods; deities; divinities [明器][冥器]殉葬用的器物 funeral object; burial furnishings ❼次(指日或年) immediately following in time; next:～日 *tomorrow*|～年 *next year* ❽朝代名,明太祖朱元璋所建立(公元 1368—1644 年) Ming Dynasty (1368-1644), founded by Zhu Yuanzhang, Emperor Taizu

鸣 míng ㄇㄧㄥˊ ❶鸟兽或昆虫叫(of birds, animals or insects) to cry:鸟～ *singing* (or *chirping*) *of a bird*|驴～ *braying of an ass*|蝉～*chirring of a cicada* ❷发出声音,使发出声音 to make a sound; to ring; to sound:自～钟 *striking* (or *chime*) *clock*|孤掌难～ *One hand does not clap.* or *One hand does not tie a package — a person needs his companion's help.*|～炮 *to fire a gun* ❸表达,发表(情感、意见、主张) to express; to air; to voice:～谢 *to express one's thanks formally*|～不平 *to complain about wrongdoing; to cry out against an injustice*

冥 míng ㄇㄧㄥˊ ❶昏暗 dark; obscure; dim ㉄ ***extension*** 愚昧 dull; stupid; foolish:～顽不灵 *dull and stupid; impenetrably thickheaded* ❷深奥,深沉 deep; profound; abstruse:～思苦想 *to think long and hard; to rack* (or *cudgel*) *one's brains* ❸迷信的人称人死以后进入的世界 underworld; nether world

[冥蒙][溟濛](—méng)形容烟雾弥漫 hazy; misty

蓂 ㊀míng ㄇㄧㄥˊ [蓂荚](—jiá)传说中尧时的一种瑞草 *mingjia*, a kind of legendary lucky grass in Yao times

㊁ mì 见502页 see p502

溟 míng ㄇㄧㄥˊ 海 sea:北～有鱼。*There are fish in the North Sea.*

暝 míng ㄇㄧㄥˊ ❶日落,天黑 (of the sun) to set; (of the sky) to grow dark ❷黄昏 dusk; evening twilight

瞑 míng ㄇㄧㄥˊ 闭眼 to close (or shut) one's eyes:～目(多指人死时心中无牵挂) (*usually used to denote that one is content when dying*) *to close one's eyes in death; to die in peace*

螟 míng ㄇㄧㄥˊ 螟虫,螟蛾的幼虫,有许多种,如三化螟、二化螟、大螟、玉米螟等。危害农作物 snout moth's larva (*Pyralidae*)

[螟蛉](—líng)一种绿色小虫 corn earworm (*Helicoverpa zea*) ㊕ ***transfer*** 义子,抱养的孩子。也叫"螟蛉子"。参看 258 页"蜾"字条"蜾蠃"(guǒluǒ) adopted son (also called 螟蛉子)(see 蜾蠃 on p258)

酩 mǐng ㄇㄧㄥˇ ［酩 酊］（—dǐng）醉得迷迷糊糊的 to be dead drunk：～～大醉 *to be dead drunk; to be completely drunken; to be smashed*

命 mìng ㄇㄧㄥˋ ❶生命，动物、植物的生活能力，也就是跟矿物、水等所以有区别的地方 life：性～ *life*｜救～ *to save sb's life; Help!*｜拼～ *to risk one's life; to defy death; to exert one's utmost* ❷迷信的人认为生来就注定的贫富、寿数等 fate; lot; destiny：算～ *fortune-telling*｜～该如此。*As fate would have it.* or *It is predestined.* ❸上级指示下级 to order; to command（㊟ ***doublet*** —令 to order; to command）：～你前往 *to order you to go there*｜～大军火速前进 *to command the main forces to go forward at top speed* ❹上级对下级的指示 order; command：奉～ *to act under orders*｜遵～ *to obey one's command; to comply with one's wish*｜恭敬不如从～。*The best way of showing respect is to do as ordered.* ❺给予（名称等）to assign (a name, etc); to name：～名 *to give a name to; to name*｜～题 *to assign a topic; to set a question* ［命中］（—zhòng）射中或击中目标 to hit the target (*or* mark); to score a hit ❻指派，使用 to order; to assign：～驾 *to order one's carriage; to set out*｜～笔 *to take up one's pen; to set pen to paper*

MIU ㄇㄧㄡ

谬 miù ㄇㄧㄡˋ ❶错误的，不合情理的 wrong; false; erroneous：～论 *fallacy; false* (or *absurd*) *theory; wrong view*｜荒～ *absurd; preposterous* ❷差错 error; mistake：失之毫厘，～以千里。*An error, the breadth of a single hair, can lead you a thousand* li *astray — A miss is as good as a mile.*

缪 ㊂ miù ㄇㄧㄡˋ 见559页"纰"字条"纰缪"（pī—）see 纰缪 on p559

㊀ miào 见506页 see p506

㊁ móu 见517页 see p517

MO ㄇㄛ

摸 mō ㄇㄛ ❶用手接触或轻轻抚摩 to feel; to stroke; to touch：～小孩儿的头 *to stroke a child's head*｜～～多光滑。*Feel how smooth it is.* ❷用手探取 to feel for; to grope for; to fumble：～鱼 *to catch fish* (*as in a shallow pond*) *with one's hands*｜从口袋里～出一张钞票来 *to feel in one's pocket and take out a banknote; to fish out a banknote from one's pocket* ㊊ ***extension* 1** 揣测，试探 to try to find out; to feel out; to sound out：～底 *to try to find out the real intention* (or *situation*)｜我～准了他的脾气了。*I have* *got to know his temperament well.*｜～不清他是什么意思。*I couldn't fathom his intention.* **2** 在黑暗中行动，在认不清的道路上行走 to grope in the dark：～营 *to raid the enemy camp under cover of night; to launch a surprise attack on the enemy camp at night*｜～黑 *to grope one's way on a dark night*｜～了半夜才到家 *not to get home till midnight*［摸索］多方面探求、寻找 to try to find out; to search for：工作经验靠大家～～。*It's up to all of us to grope for experience.*

谟 mó ㄇㄛˊ 计谋，计划 plan：宏～ *grand plan; great project*

馍（*饝） mó ㄇㄛˊ 〈方 **dialect**〉面制食品，通常指馒头(叠 **reduplication**) (usually used to denote *mantou*) *mo*, a kind of steam cooked wheaten food; steamed bun (*or* bread)

嫫 mó ㄇㄛˊ ［嫫母］传说中的丑妇 Momu, an ugly woman in Chinese legend

摹 mó ㄇㄛˊ 仿效，照着样子做 to copy; to trace：临～ *to copy (a model of calligraphy or painting)*｜把这个字～下来。*Please copy this Chinese character.*

模 ㊀ mó ㄇㄛˊ ❶法式，规范 pattern; standard：楷～ *model; paragon; example*［模型］依照原物或计划中的事物(如建筑)的形式做成的物品 model ❷仿效 to imitate（㊟ **doublet** 一仿 to imitate; to model on; to copy)：儿童常～仿成人的举止动作。*Children often imitate adults' behaviours.* ❸模范 model：劳～ *model worker*｜英～ *heroes and model workers*

［模糊］(一hu)不分明，不清楚 blurred; indistinct; hazy

［模棱］(一léng)意见或语言含糊，不肯定 (of opinion or words) vague; indistinct：～～两可 *equivocal; ambiguous*

［模特儿］(外 **loanword**)写生、雕塑时的描摹对象或参考对象，有时也指某些示范表演者 model：时装～～～ *dress (or fashion) model*

㊁ mú 见518页 see p518

膜 mó ㄇㄛˊ ❶(一儿)动植物体内像薄皮的组织 membrane：肋～ *pleura*｜耳～ *eardrum; tympanum*｜苇～ *reed membrane* ❷(一儿)像膜的薄皮 film; thin coating：面～ *face pack; mask*｜塑料薄～儿 *plastic film (or sheeting)*

麽 ㊀ mó ㄇㄛˊ ［幺麽］(yāo一)微小 small; little; petty：～～小丑 *despicable (or insignificant) wretch*

㊁ me 见491页"么"see 么 on p491

嬷 mó ㄇㄛˊ ［嬷嬷］(一mo) **1** 旧时称奶妈为嬷嬷(in former times) wet nurse **2** 〈方 **dialect**〉称呼老年妇女(term of address for an elderly woman)

M

momo

摩 ㊀ mó ㄇㄛˊ ❶摩擦，蹭(cèng) to rub; to scrape: ～拳擦掌 *to rub one's fists and palms — to be eager to get into action* ❷抚摩，摸 to stroke; to touch; to caress: ～弄 *to stroke* | 按～ *to massage* [摩挲](— suō)用手抚摩 to stroke; to caress ❸研究切磋 to mull over; to study; to fathom [观摩]观察之后，加以研究，吸收别人的优点 to inspect and learn from each other's work; to view and emulate: ～～教学 *mutual learning among fellow teachers by observing each other's classes; demonstration lecture* ❹物质的量的单位摩尔的简称，符号 mol (short for 摩尔) mole (mol)

[摩托](外 *loanword*)用汽油、柴油等发动的机器 motor: ～～车 *motorcycle; motor bicycle; motorbike* | ～～艇 *motorboat* | ～～化部队 *motorized troops*

㊁ mā 见480页 see p480

磨 ㊀ mó ㄇㄛˊ ❶摩擦 to rub; to grind; to wear: ～刀 *to grind* (or *sharpen*) *a knife* | ～墨 *to rub an ink stick against an inkstone; to make ink for brush-writing* [磨合]新组装的机器经过一定时期的使用，把摩擦面上的加工痕迹磨光而变得更加密合(of machines) to grind in; to wear in; to break in [磨炼][磨练]锻炼，下工夫 to put oneself through the mill; to steel oneself; to temper oneself ❷阻碍，困难 hardship; torment (㊟ *doublet* —难 tribulation; hardship; suffering | 折— to cause physical or mental suffering; to torment; to torture): 好(hǎo)事多～。*The road to happiness is strewn with setbacks.* or *Success is a triumph over continual difficulties.* ㊀ ***extension*** 纠缠 to keep nagging; to plague; to pester: 小孩子～人。*The child keeps pestering.* or *The children pester.* ❸拖延，耗时间 to dawdle; to waste time: ～工夫 *to take time; to consume time; to be time-consuming* ❹逐渐消失，消灭 to obliterate; to die out; to sink into oblivion: 百世不～ *will endure for centuries* | 这是永不～灭的真理。*This is an indelible truth.* [消磨] **1** 使精力等逐渐消失 to wear down; to fritter away; to blunt: ～～志气 *to sap one's will* **2** 消耗 to while away; to idle away; to fool away: 大好光阴不能白白～～掉。*We must not idle away the golden time.*

㊁ mò 见516页 see p516

蘑 mó ㄇㄛˊ 蘑菇，食用蕈(xùn)类，如口蘑、松蘑 mushroom

魔 mó ㄇㄛˊ ❶迷信传说指害人性命、迷惑人的恶鬼 evil spirit; demon; monster: 妖～鬼怪 *demons and ghosts; monsters of every description* | 恶～ *demon; devil; evil spirit* [入魔]嗜好成癖，入迷 to be infatuated; to be spellbound; to be hypnotized: 他搞无线电搞得～～了。*He is infatuated with radio.* ❷不平常,奇异的 magic; mystic; occult: ～力 *magical power; magics; charm* | ～术 *magic; conjuring; sleight of hand*

劘 mó ㄇㄛˊ 切削 to cut

抹 ㊀ mǒ ㄇㄛˇ ❶涂 to apply; to smear; to plaster (㊀ **doublet** 涂— to daub; to smear; to paint): 伤口上～上点药 *to apply some medicine onto the wound* ❷揩,擦 to wipe; to clean off: ～眼泪 *to wipe one's eyes; to be weeping* | 一～一手黑。*His hand got black when he touched it.* ❸除去 to cross (*or* strike, blot) out: ～零儿(不计算尾数) *to delete the fractional amount; not to count the small change (in a payment)* | ～掉几个字 *to cross out a few words* [抹杀][抹煞]一概不计,勾销 to blot out; to obliterate; to write off: 一笔～～ *to blot out* (or *write off*) *at one stroke — to deny completely*

㊁ mò 见514页 see p514
㊂ mā 见480页 see p480

万 ㊁ mò ㄇㄛˋ [万俟](—qí) 复姓 Moqi, a compound surname

㊀ wàn 见776页 see p776

末 mò ㄇㄛˋ ❶杪,梢,尖端,跟"本"相对(the opposite of 本) tip; end; point: ～梢 *tip; end* | 本～倒置 *to take the branch for the root — to put the incidental before the fundamental* | 秋毫之～ *tip of an animal's or bird's autumn hair — sth so small that one can hardly see; minutest tittle* | 细枝～节(比喻事情不重要的部分) *minor* (or *petty*) *details; nonessentials* ❷最后,终了(liǎo),跟"始"相对(the opposite of 始) end; last stage; bottom (㊀ **doublet** —尾 end): 十二月三十一日是一年的最～一天。*December thirty-first is the last day of the year.* ❸(—子、—儿)碎屑 *powder; dust* (㊀ **doublet** 粉— powder): 粉笔～儿 *chalk dust* | 茶叶～儿 *broken tea leaves; tea dust* | 把药材研成～儿 *to grind* (or *pestle*) *medicinal herbs into powder* ❹传统戏曲里扮演中年男子的角色 role of a middle-aged man in traditional operas

抹 ㊁ mò ㄇㄛˋ 涂抹,泥(nì) to daub; to plaster: 他正在往墙上～石灰。*He is plastering the wall.*

㊀ mǒ 见514页 see p514
㊂ mā 见480页 see p480

茉 mò ㄇㄛˋ [茉莉](—li) **1** 常绿灌木,花白色,很香,常用来熏制茶叶 jasmine (*Jasminum*) **2** 紫茉莉,又叫"草茉莉"。一年生或多年生草本植物,花有红、白、黄、紫各色。胚乳粉质,可作化妆粉用(also called 草茉莉) four o'clock flower (*Mirabilis jalapa*)

沫 mò ㄇㄛˋ（一子、一儿）液体形成的许多细泡 foam; froth（㊀ ***doublet*** 泡一 foam; froth）：肥皂～儿 *soapsuds; lather* | 唾～（tuò-mo）*saliva; spittle*

妹 mò ㄇㄛˋ 古人名用字（used in a given name in ancient China）mo

秣 mò ㄇㄛˋ ❶牲口的饲料 fodder：粮～ *grain and fodder;（army）rations and forage* ❷喂牲口 to feed animals：～马厉兵（喂马、磨兵器）to feed the horses and sharpen the weapons — to make preparations for war

靺 mò ㄇㄛˋ［靺鞨］（一hé）我国古代东北方的民族 Mohe, an ethnic group living in northeast China in ancient times

没 ㊀ mò ㄇㄛˋ ❶隐在水中 to sink; to submerge：～入水中 *to submerge in water* ㊁ ***extension*** 隐藏 to hide; to disappear; to conceal：深山有猛虎出～。*The deep mountains are haunted by fierce tigers.*［没落］衰落，趋向灭亡 to decline; to wane; to decay：～～阶级 *declining class* ❷漫过，高过 to overflow; to rise beyond：水～了头顶。*The water rises above a man's head.* | 庄稼都长得～人了。*The crops are taller than a man.* ❸把财物扣下 to confiscate; to impound; to expropriate：～收赃款 *to confiscate illicit income* ❹终，尽 till the end; to the last：～世（指终身，一辈子）*all one's life; lifelong* ❺同"殁"same as 殁

㊁ méi 见492页 see p492

殁 mò ㄇㄛˋ 死。也作"没"（also written as 没）to die

陌 mò ㄇㄛˋ 田间的小路 footpath between fields（running east and west）（㊀ ***doublet*** 阡一 crisscross footpaths between fields）：～头杨柳 *roadside willows*［陌生］生疏，不熟悉 strange; unfamiliar

貊 mò ㄇㄛˋ 我国古代称东北方的民族 *mo*, an ancient Chinese term for the ethnic peoples of the northeast

冒 ㊁ mò ㄇㄛˋ［冒顿］（一dú）汉初匈奴的一个首领名 Modu, a chieftain of Xiongnu（*or* the Huns）in the early Han Dynasty

㊀ mào 见490页 see p490

脉（*脈、**衇）㊁ mò ㄇㄛˋ［脉脉］形容用眼神表达爱慕的情意 affectionate; loving; amorous：～～含情 *to beam with tenderness and love*

㊀ mài 见484页 see p484

莫 mò ㄇㄛˋ ❶不要 don't：闲人～入。*No admittance except on business.* or *Staff Only.* ❷没有，无 no one; none; nothing：～不欣喜。*Nobody was unhappy.* | ～大的光荣 *greatest honour*［莫非］副词 ***adverb***，难道 can it be that; is it possible that：～～是他回来了吗？*Is it possible that he's*

come back?［莫逆］朋友之间感情非常好 very friendly; intimate: ～～之交 *bosom* (or *sworn*) *friends*［莫须有］也许有吧。后用来表示凭空捏造 there may be; (later used to express) groundless; fabricated ❸不 no; not: 变化～测 *to change unpredictably; changeable*

［莫邪］(－yé)古宝剑名 Moye, an ancient double-edged sword

〈古 **archaism**〉又同"暮"(mù) also same as 暮

蓦 mò ㄇㄛˋ 突然,忽然 suddenly; unexpectedly; abruptly: 他～地站起来。*He stood up abruptly.*

漠 mò ㄇㄛˋ ❶地面为沙石覆盖,缺乏流水,气候干燥,植物稀少的地区 desert: 沙～ *desert*［广漠］广大看不到边际 vast and bare ❷冷淡地,不经心地 indifferently; unconcernedly: ～视 *to treat with indifference; to ignore* | ～不关心 *to be indifferent to; to remain indifferent* (or *unconcerned*)

寞 mò ㄇㄛˋ 寂静,清静 lonely; deserted; solitary (㊀ **doublet** 寂－ lonely; quiet; still): ～～ *quiet; deserted* | ～然 *lonely*

镆 mò ㄇㄛˋ［镆铘］(－yé) 同"莫邪" same as 莫邪

瘼 mò ㄇㄛˋ 病 disease; illness: 民～(人民的痛苦) *sufferings* (or *hardships*) *of the people*

貘 mò ㄇㄛˋ 哺乳类动物。像猪而略大,鼻子圆而长,能伸缩。产于热带,善游泳 tapir (*Tapirus*)

嘿 ㊁ mò ㄇㄛˋ 闭口不说话。同"默"(same as 默) silent; tacit

㊀ hēi 见274页 see p274

墨 mò ㄇㄛˋ ❶写字绘画用的黑色颜料 China (*or* Chinese) ink; ink stick: 一锭～ *an ink stick* | ～汁 *prepared Chinese ink* ❷写字、绘画或印刷用的各色颜料 pigment; ink: 红～ *red ink* | 蓝～ *blue ink* ❸名家写的字或画的画 handwriting or painting (by accomplished master): ～宝 *treasured scrolls of calligraphy or painting* ❹黑色或近于黑色的 black; pitch-dark: ～晶(黑色的水晶) *smoky quartz* | ～菊 *dark chrysanthemum* ❺贪墨,贪污 corruption; graft; embezzlement: ～吏 *corrupt officials* ❻古代的一种刑罚,在脸上刺刻涂墨 (a punishment in ancient China) tattooing the face with ink

默 mò ㄇㄛˋ 不说话,不出声(叠 **reduplication**) silent; tacit: 沉～ *silent* | ～～不语 *to remain silent* (or *speechless*); *without saying a word* | ～读 *to read silently* | ～写(凭记忆写出) *to write from memory* | ～认(心里承认) *to give tacit consent to; to approve tacitly; to acquiesce in*

磨 ㊁ mò ㄇㄛˋ ❶把粮食弄碎的工具 mill; millstones:

M

石～ *millstones* | 电～ *electric mill* ❷用磨把粮食弄碎 to grind; to mill:～豆腐 *to grind soya beans to make bean curd* | ～面 *to mill flour* ❸掉转 to turn round:小胡同不能～车。*The alley is too narrow for a car to turn round.*

㊀ mó 见513页 see p513

礳 mò ㄇㄛˋ [礳石渠]地名,在山西省阳城 Moshiqu, a place in Yangcheng, Shanxi Province

耱 mò ㄇㄛˋ 耢(lào) *mo*, a kind of farm tool used to level land

MOU ㄇㄡ

哞 mōu ㄇㄡ 拟声词 ***onomatopoeia***,牛叫的声音(sound made by an ox) moo; low; bellow

牟 ㊀ móu ㄇㄡˊ 贪取 to try to gain; to obtain; to seek: 投机商哄抬物价,借机～利。*The speculative businessmen boosted up the prices to gain private profit.*

㊁ mù 见519页 see p519

侔 móu ㄇㄡˊ 相等,齐 to equal; to match:超五帝,～三王 *to surpass the five emperors in virtue and equal the three kings in merits*

眸 móu ㄇㄡˊ (一子)眼中瞳人,泛指眼睛 pupil (of the eye); eye:凝～远望 *to gaze into the distance*

蛑 móu ㄇㄡˊ 见910页"蝤"字条"蝤蛑"(yóu—) see 蝤蛑 on p910

谋 móu ㄇㄡˊ ❶计划,计策,主意 plan; scheme; stratagem (㊇ ***doublet*** —略 astuteness and resourcefulness; strategy | 计— stratagem; scheme):有勇无～ *to have valour but lack strategy; to be brave but not resourceful* ❷设法寻求 to work for; to seek; to strive: ～职 *to seek employment; to try to find a job* | 为人民～幸福 *to work for the happiness of the people* ❸商议 to consult; to deliberate:不～而合 *to agree without prior (or previous) consultation; to happen to hold the same view*

缪 ㊁ móu ㄇㄡˊ [绸缪](chóu—) 1 修缮 to repair:未雨～～(喻事先做好准备) *to repair the house before it rains — to take preventive measures; to make hay while the sun shines* 2 缠绵 to be sentimentally attached:情意～～ *to be deeply in love; to be head over heels in love*

㊀ miào 见506页 see p506

㊂ miù 见511页 see p511

鍪 móu ㄇㄡˊ 古代的一种锅 *mou*, a kind of pot in ancient China [兜鍪]古代打仗时戴的盔 helmet (worn in ancient battles)

某 mǒu ㄇㄡˇ 代词 ***pronoun***,代替不明确指出的人、地、事、物等 certain; some: ～人

someone｜～国 *some country*｜～天 *some day*｜张～ *someone called Zhang*｜～～学校 *some school*

MU ㄇㄨ

毪 mú ㄇㄨˊ 毪子，西藏产的一种氆氇（pǔlu） woollen fabric made in Tibet

模 ㊀ mú ㄇㄨˊ （—儿）模子 mould; matrix; pattern: 字～儿（*type*） *matrix*｜铜～儿 *matrix; copper mould*［模子］（—zi）用压制或浇灌的方法制造物品的工具 mould; matrix; pattern［模样］形状，容貌 appearance; countenance; look

㊁ mó 见512页 see p512

母 mǔ ㄇㄨˇ ❶母亲，妈妈，娘 mother: ～系 *maternal; matrilineal*｜～性 *maternal instinct* ❷对女性长辈的称呼（term of address for one's female elders）：姑～ *father's sister; aunt*｜舅～ *wife of mother's brother; aunt*｜姨～（*married*）*maternal aunt; aunt* ❸雌性的 female（animal）：～鸡 *hen*｜这口猪是～的。*This is a sow.* ❹事物所从产生出来的 origin; parent: ～校 *one's old school; alma mater*｜～株 *female parent; maternal*（or *mother*）*plant*｜工作～机 *machine tool*｜失败为成功之～。*Failure is the mother of success.* ㊉ ***extension*** 一套东西中间可以包含其他部分的 nut: 子～环 *composite hoop; snap ring*｜子～扣 *snap fastener; press-stud; popper*｜螺丝～（*screw*）*nut*［母音］见924页"元"字条"元音"see 元音 on p924

拇 mǔ ㄇㄨˇ 拇指，手脚的大指 thumb; big toe

姆 mǔ ㄇㄨˇ 保姆，负责照管儿童或料理家务的女工（children's）nurse; housemaid; housekeeper

牳 mǔ ㄇㄨˇ 牛名 *mu*, ox name

牡 mǔ ㄇㄨˇ 雄性的鸟、兽，跟"牝"相对。又指植物的雄株（the opposite of 牝, also used to denote a male plant） male: ～麻 *male hemp*

亩（畆） mǔ ㄇㄨˇ 市制地积单位，1 亩是 10 分，约合 666.7 平方米 *mu*, a Chinese unit of area, one *mu* equal to 10 *fen*, approximately 666.7 square metres

姥 ㊀ mǔ ㄇㄨˇ 年老的妇人 old woman（*or* lady）

㊁ lǎo 见420页 see p420

木 mù ㄇㄨˋ ❶树木，树类植物的通称 tree: 乔～ *arbor; tree*｜灌～ *bush; shrub*［木本植物］具有木质茎的植物，如松柏等 xylophyta; woody plant ❷木头，供制造器物或建筑用的木料 timber; lumber; wood: ～材 *wood; timber; lumber*｜枣～ *jujube*（or *date*）*wood*｜杉～ *fir wood* ❸用木料制成的 made of wood; wooden: ～器 *wooden furniture*（or *articles*）｜～犁 *wooden plough* ❹棺材

coffin：棺～ *coffin*｜行将就～ *to be getting closer and closer to the coffin — to be near one's end* (or *death*) ❺感觉不灵敏，失去知觉 numb; wooden ([连] **doublet** 麻一 numb)：手脚麻～。*One's limbs have gone numb.*｜舌头发～。*The tongue has gone numb.*

沐 mù ㄇㄨˋ 洗头 to wash one's hair：栉(zhì)风～雨(喻奔波辛苦) *to be combed by the wind and washed by the rain — to travel* (or *work*) *in the open despite wind and rain* [沐浴] 洗澡 to have (or take) a bath

霂 mù ㄇㄨˋ 见484页"霡"字条"霡霂"(mài —) see 霡霂 on p484

目 mù ㄇㄨˋ ❶眼睛 eye：～瞪口呆 *to gape goggle-eyed and dumbstruck; to be flabbergasted; to be stupefied*｜～空一切(自高自大) *to consider everybody and everything beneath one's notice — to be extremely supercilious or arrogant* [目标] **1** 射击、攻击或寻求的对象 target; objective：对准～～射击 *to aim at the target and shoot*｜不要暴露～～。*Don't expose your position.* **2** 想达到的境地 goal; aim; objective：实现四个现代化是我们奋斗的～～。*Our goal is to realize the Four Modernizations.* [目前][目下]眼前，现在 at present; at the moment ❷看 to look; to regard; to see：一～了然 *to see clearly at a glance; to understand fully at a glance* ❸大项中再分的小项 item：大纲细～ *broad outline and specific items* ❹目录 catalogue; list：剧～ *list of plays* (or *operas*); *repertoire*｜书～ *booklist; title catalogue* ❺生物的分类单位之一，在"纲"之下、"科"之上 order：鸽形～ *Columbiformes*｜银耳～ *Tremellales* ❻计算围棋比赛输赢的单位(in *weiqi* or go) eye

苜 mù ㄇㄨˋ [苜蓿](— xu)多年生草本植物，叶子长圆形，花紫色，果实为荚果。可以喂牲口、做肥料 alfalfa; lucerne (*Medicago sativa*)

钼 mù ㄇㄨˋ 一种金属元素，符号Mo，银白色，在空气中不易变化。可与铝、铜、铁等制成合金。为电子工业重要材料 molybdenum (Mo)

仫 mù ㄇㄨˋ [仫佬族](— lǎo —)我国少数民族，参看附表(see the appendix) the Mulao (or Mulam) ethnic group, one of the ethnic minorities of China

牟 ㊁ mù ㄇㄨˋ [牟平]地名，在山东省烟台 Muping, a place in Yantai, Shandong Province

㊀ móu 见517页 see p517

牧 mù ㄇㄨˋ 放养牲口 to tend (sheep, cattle, etc); to herd：～羊 *to tend sheep*｜～童 *shepherd* (or *buffalo*) *boy; cowboy*｜～场 *grazing land; pastureland; pasture*｜畜～业 *animal husbandry; livestock*

M

husbandry (or *farming*)|游～ *to move about in search of pasture; to rove around as a nomad*[牧师]基督教的教士,管理教堂及礼拜等事务 priest; clergyman

募 mù ㄇㄨˋ 广泛征求 to raise; to collect; to enlist: ～捐 *to solicit contributions; to collect* (or *solicit*) *donations*|～了一笔款 *to have raised a fund*

墓 mù ㄇㄨˋ ❶埋死人的地方 grave; tomb; mausoleum (㊇ ***doublet*** 坟— grave; tomb): 公～ *cemetery*|烈士～ *tombs* (or *graves*) *of revolutionary martyrs; martyrs' cemetery* ❷与墓相关的 of the grave (*or* tomb): ～碑 *tombstone; gravestone*|～地 *graveyard; burial ground; cemetery*|～道 *path leading to a grave* (or *tomb*); *tomb passage*

幕 mù ㄇㄨˋ ❶帐。**1** 覆盖在上面的 tent; canopy (㊇ ***doublet*** 帐— tent) **2** 垂挂着的 curtain; screen: 银～ (*motion-picture*) *screen; projection screen*|开～ *rise of a curtain; opening*[黑幕]暗中作弊捣鬼的事情 inside story of a plot, shady deal, etc[内幕]内部的实际情形(多指隐秘的事) what goes on behind the scenes; inside story ❷古代将帅办公的地方 office of a commanding general in ancient China: ～府 (*in ancient China*) *office of a commanding general;* (*in Japan*) *shogun* ❸话剧或歌剧的较完整的段落 act (of a play): 独～剧 *one-act play; one-acter*

〈古 ***archaism***〉又同沙漠的"漠"(mò) also same as 漠 in 沙漠

暮 mù ㄇㄨˋ ❶傍晚,太阳落的时候 dusk; evening; sunset: 朝(zhāo)～ *morning and evening* [暮气]㊈ ***figurative*** 精神衰颓,不振作 lethargy; apathy; languor ❷晚,将尽 towards the end; late: ～春 *late spring* (*the third month of the lunar year*)|～年 *evening of one's life; declining years*|天寒岁～。*It gets cold as the year draws to its end.*

慕 mù ㄇㄨˋ ❶羡慕,仰慕 to admire; to envy: ～名 *to admire a person's reputation; out of admiration for a famous person* ❷思念 to long for; to yearn for: 思～ *to think of sb with respect; to admire*

睦 mù ㄇㄨˋ 和好,亲近 peaceful; harmonious (㊇ ***doublet*** 和— harmony; concord; amity): ～邻(同邻家或邻国和好相处) *good-neighbourliness*

穆 mù ㄇㄨˋ ❶温和 peaceful; serene ❷恭敬 respectful; reverent; solemn (㊇ ***doublet*** 肃— solemn and quiet; solemn and respectful) (叠 ***reduplication***)

N ㄋ

N ㄋ

唔 ㊂ ń ㄋ̀ (又 *also* ng) 同"嗯㊀"same as 嗯㊀
㊀ wú 见794页 see p794
㊁ ńg 见531页 see p531

嗯 ㊀ ń ㄋ̀ (又 *also* ng) 见531页 ńg see ńg on p531

嗯(**呃) ㊁ ň ㄋ̌ (又 *also* ňg) 见531页 ňg see ňg on p531

嗯(**叽) ㊂ ǹ ㄋ̀ (又 *also* ǹg) 见531页 ǹg see ǹg on p531

NA ㄋㄚ

那 ㊂ nā ㄋㄚ 姓 Na, a surname
㊀ nà 见522页 see p522
㊁ nèi 见530页 see p530

拿(*拏) ná ㄋㄚˊ ❶用手取,握在手里 to hold; to take (in one's hand): ～笔 *to hold a pen* | ～枪 *to hold a gun* | ～张纸来 *to fetch a piece of paper* | ～着镰刀割麦子 *to reap wheat with a sickle* ❷掌握,把握 to have a firm grasp of; to hold the reins of; to control: ～主意 *to make up one's mind; to make a decision; to decide* | 做好做不好,我可～不稳。*I am not sure whether I can do it well or not.* [拿手]擅长 to be good (*or* adept) at; to be skilled in: ～～好戏 *drama that an actor is good at; one's forte* (or *speciality*) | 做这样的事,他很～～。*He is very adept at this kind of job.* ❸拿捏,挟(xié)制 to corner; to bluff; to blackmail: 这样的事～不住人。*You cannot bluff me in such matters.* ❹侵蚀,侵害 to erode; to corrode; to destroy: 这块木头让药水～白了。*The chemical solution has bleached this piece of wood.* ❺逮捕,捉 to catch; to seize; to capture (㊈ **doublet** 捉 — to catch; to arrest; to collar): ～获 *to apprehend (a criminal); to capture; to nab* | 猫～老鼠。*Cats catch mice.* ❻介词 **preposition**, 把 (used to introduce the object of a following verbal phrase): 我～你当朋友看待。*I treat you as my friend.* ❼用(used to introduce the tool, material, method, etc for doing sth) by means of; with; in: ～这笔钱做身制服。*Use this sum of money for a uniform.*

镎 ná ㄋㄚˊ 一种放射性元素,符号 Np neptunium (Np)

哪 ㊀ nǎ ㄋㄚˇ 代词 ***pronoun*** **1** 表示疑问,后面跟量词或数量词,要求在所问范围中有所确定(used to express question, followed by a quantifier, seeking an affirmation within the scope in question) which; what; who: 你喜欢读～种书? *What kind of books do you like to read?* [哪儿][哪里]什么地方 where; somewhere; wherever: 你在～～住? *Where do you live?* |～～有困难,就到～～去。*Go and work where the challenge is the greatest.* ㊕ ***transfer*** 用于反问句(used in rhetorical questions):我～～知道?(我不知道) *How can I know?* |他～～笨啊?(他不笨)*Who says he is stupid?* |这项工作一个人～～能做好?(一个人做不好) *How can one person do the job well by himself?* **2** 表示反问(used to express a rhetorical question):没有耕耘,～有收获。*How can you reap without sowing?* or *No pains, no gains.*

㊁ něi 见529页 see p529

㊂ na 见523页 see p523

㊃ né 见529页 see p529

那 ㊀ nà ㄋㄚˋ 代词 ***pronoun***, 指较远的时间、地方或事物,跟"这"相对(the opposite of 这)(used to denote sth or sb farther away from the speaker) that:～时(*at*) *that time*; (*in*) *those days*; *then* |～里 *that place*; *there* |～个 *that one*; *that thing* (or *matter*) |～样 *like that*; *of that kind*; *such* |～些 *those* [那么](*那末)(—me)**1** 代词 ***pronoun***, 那样(used in place of sth or sb farther away from the speaker) that; so; of that kind: 就～～办吧。*Just do it that way.* 要不了～～多。*I don't need that much.* |～～个人 *person of that kind* |～～个脾气 *temper of that kind* — *bad temper* **2** 连词 ***conjunction***, 跟前面"如果"、"若是"等相应(used in combination with 如果, 若是, etc in the former clause) then; in that case; that being the case: 如果敌人不投降,～～就消灭他。*If the enemies do not surrender, we will annihilate them.*

㊁ nèi 见530页 see p530

㊂ nā 见521页 see p521

娜 ㊀ nà ㄋㄚˋ 用于人名 Na, used in a given name

㊁ nuó 见542页 see p542

呐 nà ㄋㄚˋ [呐喊]大声叫喊 to shout loudly; to cry out; to cheer: 摇旗～～ *to wave flags and shout battle cries; to beat* (or *bang*) *the drum for sb* (*to boost the morale of fighters*); *to give support to sb*

纳 nà ㄋㄚˋ ❶收入,放进 to receive; to let in; to admit: 出～ *cashier* (or *teller*) |吐故～新 *to get rid of the stale and take in the fresh*; *to exhale the old and inhale the new* ㊉ ***extension*** **1** 接受 to accept; to take: 采～建议 *to follow* (or *adopt*) *one's advice*; *to seize on*

N

a suggestion **2** 享受 to enjoy: ～凉 *to enjoy the cool air* (*in the open air* or *in the shade*) ❷ 缴付 to give (as a duty required by an authority); to hand in; to pay: ～税 *to pay duty* (or *taxes*) | 缴～公粮 *to deliver tax grain to the state* ❸ 补缀, 缝补, 现在多指密密地缝 to patch up; to sew close stitches (over): ～鞋底 *to stitch soles* (*of cloth shoes*) ❹ (外 **loanword**) 法定计量单位中十进分数单位词头之一, 表示 10^{-9} (符号 n) nano- (n)

[纳西族] 我国少数民族, 参看附表 (see the appendix) the Naxi ethnic group, one of the ethnic minorities of China

肭 nà ㄋㄚˋ 见772页"腽"字条"腽肭兽"(wà——) see 腽肭兽 on p772

钠 nà ㄋㄚˋ 一种金属元素, 符号 Na, 银白色, 质地软, 能使水分解放出氢, 平时要贮藏在煤油里。钠的化合物很多, 如食盐(氯化钠)、烧碱(氢氧化钠)、纯碱(碳酸钠)等 natrium (Na)

衲 nà ㄋㄚˋ ❶ 僧衣 *kasaya*, outer vestment worn by a Buddhist monk; cassock ㊕ ***transfer*** 僧人 Buddhist monk: 老～ *old Buddhist monk*; (*used by an old Buddhist monk to refer to himself*) *this old monk*; *I*; *me* ❷ 同"纳❸" same as 纳❸ to patch up: 百～衣 *heavily patched garment* (or *coat*); *kasaya*

捺 nà ㄋㄚˋ ❶用手按 to press; to push ❷(一儿)汉字从上向右斜下的笔画(㇏)(in Chinese character) right-falling stroke: "人"字是一撇一～。*The Chinese character* 人 *is composed of a left-falling stroke and a right-falling stroke.*

哪 ㊂ na ·ㄋㄚ 助词 ***auxiliary***, "啊"受到前一字韵母 n 收音的影响而发生的变音 (allophone of "ɑ" influenced by the acoustic final n before it): 同志们, 加油干～! *Comrades, work with added vigour!* or *Comrades, work hard!*

㊀ nǎ 见522页 see p522
㊁ něi 见529页 see p529
㊃ né 见529页 see p529

NAI ㄋㄞ

乃 (*迺、*廼) nǎi ㄋㄞˇ ❶文言代词 ***pronoun in classical Chinese***, 你, 你的 you; your: ～父 *your father* | ～兄 *your brother* ❷副词 ***adverb***, 才, 就 just; only then; only thus: 吾求之久矣, 今～得之。*I have long been seeking it, but I've just got it.* | 知己知彼, 胜～不殆。*Only when you know the enemy and know yourself can you win* (*the battle*) *with no danger of defeat.* ❸是, 就是 to be: 失败～成功之母。*Failure is the mother of success.*

[乃至] **1** 甚至 even: 全班～～全

校都行动起来了。*The whole class, and even the whole school, went into action* (or *became active*). **2** 以至于 to go so far as to; even to the extent that: 平日疏于管理，～～如此。*The day-to-day management is so lax that it results in such a situation.*

艿 nǎi ㄋㄞˇ [芋艿]就是芋头。也作"芋奶"(i. e. 芋头, also written as 芋奶) taro (*Colocasia esculenta*)

奶(*嬭) nǎi ㄋㄞˇ ❶乳房，哺乳的器官 breast ❷乳汁 milk: 牛～ *cow's milk* | ～油 *cream* | ～粉 *milk powder; powdered milk; dried* (or *dehydrated*) *milk* ❸用自己的乳汁喂孩子 to breastfeed; to nurse; to suckle: ～孩子 *to breastfeed a baby; to nurse a baby; to suckle a baby*

[奶奶] **1** 祖母(paternal) grandmother; grandma **2** 对老年妇人的尊称(polite form of address for an elderly woman): 老～～ *grandma; granny; grannie*

氖 nǎi ㄋㄞˇ 一种化学元素，在通常条件下为气体，符号Ne，无色无臭，不易与其他元素化合。真空管中放入少量的氖气，通过电流，能发出红色的光，可做霓虹灯 neon (Ne)

奈 nài ㄋㄞˋ 奈何，怎样，如何 can not but; what; how: 无～ *cannot but; unfortunately; but* | 怎～ *but; however* | 无～何(无可如何，没有办法可想) *cannot do anything about; to have no alternative* (or *choice*) *but; to be in a helpless situation*

柰 nài ㄋㄞˋ (一子)落叶小乔木，花白色，果小。可做苹果砧木 crab apple (*Malus asiatica*)

萘 nài ㄋㄞˋ 一种有机化合物，分子式 $C_{10}H_8$，无色晶体，有特殊气味，容易挥发。过去用的卫生球就是萘制成的，现已禁用 naphthalene

佴 ㊀ nài ㄋㄞˋ 姓 Nai, a surname

㊁ èr 见178页 see p178

耐 nài ㄋㄞˋ 受得住，禁(jīn)得起 to be able to bear (*or* endure); to withstand: ～劳 *to be able to endure hard work; to work tirelessly; to be industrious* | ～用 *durable; serviceable* | ～火砖 *refractory brick; firebrick* [耐心]不急躁，不厌烦 patient: ～～说服 *to persuade sb with patience*

鼐 nài ㄋㄞˋ 大鼎 big tripod; large caldron

褦 nài ㄋㄞˋ [褦襶](—dài)不晓事，不懂事 insensible; unreasonable

NAN ㄋㄢ

囝 ㊁ nān ㄋㄢ 〈方 **dialect**〉同"囡"same as 囡

㊀ jiǎn 见328页 see p328

囡 nān ㄋㄢ 〈方 **dialect**〉小孩儿 child; kid

男 nán ㄋㄢˊ ❶男子，男人 man; male: ～女平等 *equality between men and women; gender equality* | ～学生 *male student; boy student* ❷儿子 son; boy: 长(zhǎng)～ *eldest son* ❸我国古代五等爵位(公、侯、伯、子、男)的第五等 lowest of the five ranks of nobility in ancient China; baron: ～爵 *baron*

南 nán ㄋㄢˊ 方向，早晨面对太阳右手的一边，跟"北"相对(the opposite of 北) south: ～方 *south; areas south of the Changjiang* (or *Yangtze*) *River; southern China* | 指～针 *compass*

喃 nán ㄋㄢˊ [喃喃]小声叨唠 to murmur; to mutter; to mumble: ～～自语 *to murmur* (or *mutter*) *to oneself*

楠(*枬、*柟) nán ㄋㄢˊ 楠木，常绿乔木，木材坚固，是贵重的建筑材料。又可做船只、器物等 nanmu (*Phoebe nanmu*)

难(難) ㊀ nán ㄋㄢˊ ❶不容易 difficult; hard (㊥ **doublet** 艰— difficult; tough; arduous): ～事 *sth difficult to do; hard nut to crack* | ～题 *difficult* (or *thorny*) *problem; poser* | ～写 *hard to write* | ～产 *difficult delivery* (or *labour*); *dystocia*; (*of literary work, plan, etc*) *difficult to fulfil* (or *realize*); *slow in coming* | ～得 *hard to come by* (or *get*); *rare; seldom* ❷不大可能 hardly possible; uncertain; unlikely: ～免 *can hardly avoid; to be hard to avoid* | ～保 *can't say for sure that ...; there is no guarantee that ...; it is hard to say that ...* [难道]副词 **adverb**，加强反问语气(used in a rhetorical question for emphasis): 河水～～会倒流吗? *Rivers can never flow upstream, can they?* | 他们能完成任务，～～我们就不能吗? *If they can accomplish the task, why can't we?* ❸使人不好办 to put sb in a difficult position; to put sb on the spot; to corner: 这可真～住他了。*That really put him on the spot.* or *You've got him here.* or *This question really baffled him.* [难为](—wei) **1** 令人为难 to make it difficult (or hard) for sb; to embarrass; to bluff: 他不会跳舞，就别～～他了。*Since he can't dance, don't press* (or *force*) *him to.* **2** 亏得，表示感谢(used to express gratitude to sb for his assistance) it is generous of (sb); it is kind of (sb): 这么冷天～～你还来看我。*It is kind of you to come to see me in such cold weather.* | ～～你把机器修好了。*Thank you very much for having repaired the machine.* or *I am really grateful to you for having repaired the machine.* ❹不好 bad: ～听 *unpleasant to the ear; (of remarks) vulgar; (of things)*

disgraceful | ～看 *unpleasant to the eyes; unpleasant-looking; ugly*
〈古 **archaism**〉又同"傩"(nuó) also same as 傩
㊁ nàn 见526页 see p526

赧 nǎn ㄋㄢˇ 因羞惭而脸红 to flush (with shame); to blush: ～然 *shamefaced; blushing; flushing* | ～颜 *to be shamefaced; to blush; to flush*

腩 nǎn ㄋㄢˇ〈方 **dialect**〉牛胸腹部的松软肌肉 sirloin; tenderloin

蝻 nǎn ㄋㄢˇ (一子、一儿)仅有翅芽还没生成翅膀的蝗虫 nymph of a locust

难(難) ㊁ nàn ㄋㄢˋ ❶灾患,困苦 disaster; calamity; catastrophe (㊥ ***doublet*** 灾一 disaster; calamity; catastrophe | 患一 trials and tribulations; adversity; trouble): ～民 *refugee* | 遭～ *to meet with misfortune; to suffer disaster (or misfortune); to be killed in an accident* | 逃～ *to seek refuge (or safety) in flight; to flee from a calamity* ❷诘责 to blame; to reproach; to rebuke: 非～ *to blame; to condemn; to censure* | 责～ *to censure; to reproach; to blame*
㊀ nán 见525页 see p525

N

NANG ㄋㄤ

囊 ㊀ nāng ㄋㄤ [囊膪](一chuài) 见100页"膪"字条 see 膪 on p100
㊁ náng 见526页 see p526

囔 nāng ㄋㄤ [囔囔](一nang)小声说话 to whisper; to murmur; to mutter

囊 ㊁ náng ㄋㄤˊ 口袋 pocket; bag; sack: 探～取物(喻极容易) *as easy as taking sth out of one's pocket; as easy as winking* [囊括]全部包罗 to include (all); to embrace (all); to sweep: ～～四海 *to bring the whole country under one's rule* | ～～本次比赛全部金牌 *to win* (or *bag*) *all the gold medals of this event* (or *contest*)
㊀ nāng 见526页 see p526

馕 ㊁ náng ㄋㄤˊ (维 **Uygur**)一种烤制成的面饼 (staple food of the Uygur and Kazak ethnic groups) *nang*, flat baked cake made of flour
㊀ nǎng 见526页 see p526

曩 nǎng ㄋㄤˇ 从前的,过去的 former; past: ～日 *bygone days* | ～者(从前) *in the past; formerly; in former times*

攮 nǎng ㄋㄤˇ 用刀刺 (with a knife) to stab (*or* thrust): 用刺刀～死了敌人 *to stab an enemy to death with a bayonet* [攮子](一zi)短而尖的刀 dagger

馕 ㊀ nǎng ㄋㄤˇ 拼命地往嘴里塞食物 to cram food into one's mouth; to stuff
㊁ náng 见526页 see p526

齉(儴)** nàng ㄋㄤˋ 鼻子堵住,发音不清

snuffling; blocking: ～鼻儿 *speaking through the nose; snuffling; person who speaks with a twang*

NAO ㄋㄠ

孬 nāo ㄋㄠ〈方 **dialect**〉❶不好,坏 bad:人品～ *person of bad character* ❷怯懦,没有勇气 chicken-hearted; cowardly; craven:这人太～。*This guy is a coward indeed.*|～种 *chicken-hearted person; coward; caitiff*

呶 náo ㄋㄠ 喧哗(叠 **reduplication**) to talk noisily; to clamour:～～不休 *to talk on and on foolishly and tediously; to babble on; to gabble on*

挠(撓) náo ㄋㄠ ❶扰乱,搅 to disturb; to hinder; to obstruct:阻～ *to put a spoke in sb's wheel; to obstruct; to thwart* ❷弯屈 to bend; to give in; to yield:不屈不～(喻不屈服) *unbendable; unyielding; indomitable*|百折不～(喻有毅力) *to keep on fighting despite repeated setbacks; never to yield in spite of reverses* (or *frustrations*); *to be undaunted despite repeated failures* ❸搔,抓 to scratch:～痒痒 *to scratch an itch*

铙(鐃) náo ㄋㄠ ❶铜质圆形的打击乐器,比钹大 *nao*, a big cymbal ❷古代军中乐器,像铃铛,但没有中间的锤 *nao*, an ancient musical instrument used in the army, resembling a small tongueless bell

蛲(蟯) náo ㄋㄠ 蛲虫,大肠里的一种寄生虫,长约1厘米,白色线状,雌虫在夜里爬到肛门处产卵,多由手、水或食物传染 pinworm (*Enterobius vermicularis*)

侬(儂) náo ㄋㄠ 懊侬,痛悔 heartfelt regret; remorse

猱(**巙) náo ㄋㄠ 古山名,在今山东省临淄附近 Nao, an ancient mountain in vicinity of present-day Linzi, Shandong Province

硇(**硵、**碙) náo ㄋㄠ [硇砂]即卤砂。参看466页"卤(lǔ)"(see 卤 on p466)(i. e. 卤砂) ammonium chloride; sal ammoniac [硇洲]岛名,在广东省湛江东南海中 Naozhou, an island, in the sea to the southeast of Zhanjiang, Guangdong Province

猱 náo ㄋㄠ 古书上说的一种猴(in ancient Chinese texts) a kind of monkey

巙 náo ㄋㄠ 同"猱"。用于人名(Nao, used in a given name) same as 猱

垴 nǎo ㄋㄠ〈方 **dialect**〉山岗、丘陵较平的顶部。多用于地名(Nao, usually used in a place name) flat top of a hill (or hillock)

恼(惱) nǎo ㄋㄠ ❶发怒,愤恨 to get angry

N

(*or* irritated); to annoy; to resent:～羞成怒 *to fly into a shameful rage; to become* (or *turn*) *angry from embarrassment* | 你别～我。*Don't annoy me.* or *Don't irritate me.* or *Leave me alone.* ❷烦闷,苦闷 worried; upset; vexed (㊥ ***doublet*** 烦～ vexed; upset; annoyed | 苦～ vexed; worried; distressed)

脑(腦) nǎo ㄋㄠˇ ❶(～子) 人和高等动物神经系统的主要部分,在颅腔里,分大脑、小脑、中脑、间脑、延髓等部分,主管感觉和运动。人的脑子又是主管思想、记忆等心理活动的器官 brain; encephalon [脑筋][脑子] ㊕ ***transfer*** 指思考、记忆等能力 brain; mind; head: 开动～～。*Use your head* (or *brains*). ❷(～儿) 形状或颜色像脑子的东西 sth resembling a brain: 豆腐～儿 *jellied bean curd*

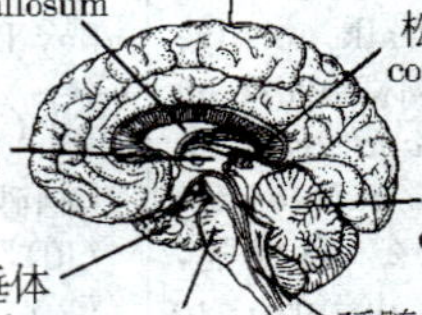

人的脑 Human Brain

瑙 nǎo ㄋㄠˇ 见482页"玛"字条"玛瑙"(mǎ—) see 玛瑙 on p482

闹(鬧) nào ㄋㄠˋ ❶不安静 not quiet **1** 人多声音杂 noisy; boisterous: ～市 *busy street; downtown area* **2** 喧哗,搅扰 to make a scene; to disturb; to clamour: 不要～了! *Don't clamour any more!* ㊀ ***extension*** 戏耍,耍笑 to crack (*or* make) jokes (at sb's expense); to tease: ～着玩儿 *to do sth for fun* ❷发生(疾病或灾害) to suffer from; to be affected by; to be troubled by: ～病 *to be taken ill* | ～嗓子 *to suffer from* (or *have*) *a sore throat* | ～水灾 *to be hit by floods; to suffer from floods* | ～蝗虫 *to be troubled by locusts; to suffer from a plague of locusts* ❸发泄,发作 to give vent to (one's anger, resentment, etc); to vent: ～情绪 *disgruntled* (*at sth or with sb*); *depressed; in a fit of a pique* | ～脾气 *venting one's anger; in*

N

a tantrum; in a fit of temper ❹搞,弄 to make; to go in for; to engage oneself in:~生产 *to go in for production; to be engaged in production*|~革命 *to carry out a revolution; to make a revolution*|把问题~清楚 *to find out the truth about sth; to get to the bottom of a matter*

淖 nào ㄋㄠˋ 烂泥 mud; mire
[淖尔](蒙 **Mongolian**) 湖泊 (Mongolian word for lake) nur; nor:达里~~(就是达里泊,在内蒙古自治区)(*i.e.* 达里泊) *Dalai Nur, a lake in Inner Mongolian Autonomous Region*|库库~~(就是青海湖)(*i.e.* 青海湖) *Kokonor, a lake in Qinghai Province*|罗布~~(就是罗布泊,在新疆维吾尔自治区)(*i.e* 罗布泊) *Lop Nur, a lake in Xinjiang Uygur Autonomous Region*

臑 nào ㄋㄠˋ 牲畜前肢的下半截 lower part of forelimbs of a domestic animal

NE ㄋㄜ

哪 ㊃ né ㄋㄜˊ [哪吒](—zhā) 神话里的神名 *Nezha*, a god in Chinese mythology
㊀ nǎ 见522页 see p522
㊁ něi 见529页 see p529
㊂ na 见523页 see p523

讷 nè ㄋㄜˋ 语言迟钝,不善讲话(of speech) slow

呢 ㊁ ne·ㄋㄜ 助词 ***auxiliary*** **1** 表示疑问(句中含有疑问词)(used at the end of a sentence to express a question):你到哪儿去~? *Where are you going?*|怎么办~? *What's to be done?* **2** 表示确定的语气(used to express affirmation):早着~。*It is still early.*|还没有来~。*(He) has not come yet.* **3** 表示动作正在进行(used to express continuation of action):他睡觉~。*He is sleeping.* **4** 用在句中表示略停一下(used in the midst of a sentence to express a pause):喜欢~,就买下;不喜欢~,就不买。*If you like it, buy it; if you don't, then you don't have to.*
㊀ ní 见531页 see p531

NEI ㄋㄟ

哪 ㊁ něi ㄋㄟˇ "哪"(nǎ)和"一"的合音,但指数量时不限于一(combined pronunciation of 哪 and 一, but used to denote one or more than one in number) which (ever); what (ever); who(ever):~个 *which (one)*|~些 *which (ones); who; what*|~年 *which year*|~几年 *which years*
㊀ nǎ 见522页 see p522
㊂ na 见523页 see p523
㊃ né 见529页 see p529

馁 něi ㄋㄟˇ ❶饥饿 hungry; famished:冻~ *cold and hungry* [喻] ***figurative*** 没有勇气

N

disheartened; discouraged; dispirited: 气～ *to lose heart; to be disheartened; to become dejected* (or *crestfallen*) | 胜不骄,败不～。*Don't be dazzled by success or discouraged by failure*. ❷古称鱼腐烂为馁(in ancient China)(of fish) putrid; rotten

内 nèi ㄋㄟˋ ❶里面,跟"外"相对(the opposite of 外) in; inside; interior: ～室 *inner* (or *interior*) *room; inner chamber; bedroom* | ～衣 *underwear; underclothes; undergarment* | ～科 *internal medicine; general medicine* | ～情 *inside information* (or *story*) | 国～ *internal; domestic; home* | 党～ *inside the party* [内行](－háng)对于某种事情有经验 expert; virtuoso; professional [内务] **1** 集体生活中室内的日常事务 daily routine chores in a dormitory: 整理～～ *to tidy up the barracks* (or *dormitories*) **2** 指国内事务(多指民政) internal affairs; domestic affairs: ～～部 *Ministry of Internal Affairs* ❷指妻子或妻子的亲属 one's wife or her relatives: ～人 *my wife* | ～兄 *wife's elder brother; elder brother-in-law* | ～侄 *son of one's wife's brother; wife's nephew*

〈古 **archaism**〉又同"纳"(nà) also same as 纳

那 ㊁ nèi ㄋㄟˋ "那"(nà)和"一"的合音,但指数量时不限于一(combined pronunciation of 那 and 一, but used to denote one or more than one in number): ～个 *that one; that* | ～些 *those* | ～年 *that year* | ～三年 *those three years*

㊀ nà 见522页 see p522

㊂ nā 见521页 see p521

NEN ㄋㄣ

恁 nèn ㄋㄣˋ 〈方 **dialect**〉代词 **pronoun** ❶那么 so; such; that: ～大 *that big* | ～高 *that tall* | 要不了～些。*Don't need that much*. ❷那 that; those: ～时 *at that time; then* | ～时节 *at that time; in those days*

嫩 nèn ㄋㄣˋ ❶初生而柔弱,娇嫩,跟"老"相对(the opposite of 老) tender; delicate: ～芽 *tender sprout; bud* | 肉皮～ *delicate skin* [引] **extension** **1** 经火力烧制的时间短(of food) underdone; tender; rare: 鸡蛋煮得～。*The egg is soft-boiled*. **2** 阅历浅,不老练 inexperienced; unsophisticated; green: 他担任主编还～了点儿。*He is too inexperienced to be the editor-in-chief*. ❷淡,浅(of colour) light; pale: ～黄 *light yellow* | ～绿 *light green; pale green*

NENG ㄋㄥ

能 néng ㄋㄥˊ ❶能力,才干,本事 ability; capability; competence: 各尽其～ *from each according to his ability;*

each doing his best | 他很有才～。*He is very talented*. [能耐] (— nai) 技能, 能力 skill; capability; ability ❷有才干的 capable; able: ～人 *capable person*; *talented person* | ～者多劳。*Able people are to do more work*. | ～手 *dab hand*; *expert*; *crackerjack* ❸能够, 胜任 to be able to; to be capable of; can: 他～耕地。*He is able to plough the field*. | ～完成任务 *to be able to fulfil the task* [能动] 自觉努力, 积极活动的 active; dynamic; self-motivated: 主观～～性 *subjective initiative*; *dynamism* | ～～地争取胜利 *to strive for victory by taking the initiative into one's own hands* ❹会 (表示可能性) can; to be able to: 他还～不去吗? *How can he possibly refuse to go?* ❺应, 该 should: 你不～这样不负责任。*You shouldn't be so irresponsible*. ❻能量, 度量物质运动的一种物理量 energy: 电～ *electric energy* | 原子～ *atomic energy* | 核～ *nuclear energy*

NG 兀

唔 ㊀ ńg 兀 ń ㄋ (又 *also* n) 同 "嗯㊀" same as 嗯㊀
㊁ wú 见 794 页 see p794
㊂ ń 见 521 页 see p521

嗯 ㊀ ńg 兀 ń ㄋ (又 *also* n) 叹词 ***interjection***, 表示疑问 (used to express a question): ～! 你说什么? *Eh, what did you say?*

嗯 (**咹) ㊁ ňg 兀 ň ㄋ (又 *also* ň) 叹词 ***interjection***, 表示不以为然或出乎意外 (used to express not taking sth serious or surprise): ～! 我看不一定是那么回事。*Well, I don't think so*. | ～! 你怎么还没去? *Hey, why haven't you gone yet?*

嗯 (**叽) ㊂ ǹg 兀 ǹ ㄋ (又 *also* ǹ) 叹词 ***interjection***, 表示答应 (used to express a positive response): ～, 就这么办吧。*Ok, just do it this way*.

NI ㄋ丨

妮 nī ㄋ丨 (一子、一儿) 女孩子 girlie; lassie

尼 ní ㄋ丨́ 梵语"比丘尼"的省称。佛教指出家修行的女子。通常叫"尼姑" (short for 比丘尼, popularly called 尼姑) Buddhist nun; nun

坭 ní ㄋ丨́ ❶同"泥" same as 泥 [红毛坭] 〈方 ***dialect***〉 水泥 cement ❷地名用字 (Ni, used in a place name): 白～ (在广东省佛山) *Baini, a place in Foshan, Guangdong Province*

呢 ㊀ ní ㄋ丨́ (一子) 一种毛织物 woollen fabric
[呢喃] (— nán) 形容燕子的叫声 (of swallows) twittering; chirruping; tweeting
㊁ ne 见 529 页 see p529

泥 ㊀ ní ㄋ丨́ ❶土和水合成的东西 mud; mire; silt ❷

像泥的东西 sth resembling mud:印～(印色) *red ink paste used for seals; ink pad; Chinese vermilion seal paste*|枣～ *jujube paste; date paste*|山药～ *mashed Chinese yam*

㊁ nì 见532页 see p532

怩 ní ㄋㄧˊ 见539页"忸"字条"忸怩"(niǔ—) see 忸怩 on p539

铌 ní ㄋㄧˊ 一种金属元素,符号Nb,钢灰色,主要用于制造耐高温的合金钢和电子管。旧称"钶"(kē)(formerly called 钶) niobium (Nb)

倪 ní ㄋㄧˊ 端,边际 limit; end; beginning [端倪]头绪 main thread of (complicated affair); clue; indication:已略有～～ *to have an inkling (of); to see an indication (of)*

猊 ní ㄋㄧˊ 见713页"狻"字条"狻猊"(suān—) see 狻猊 on p713

霓 ní ㄋㄧˊ 副虹。参看277页"虹"(see 虹 on p277) secondary rainbow [霓虹灯]在长形真空管里装氖、汞蒸气等气体,通电时产生各种颜色的光,这种灯叫霓虹灯。多用作广告或信号 neon lamp (*or* light); neon

鲵 ní ㄋㄧˊ 两栖动物,有大鲵和小鲵两种。大鲵俗叫"娃娃鱼",眼小,口大,四肢短,尾巴扁。生活在淡水中 salamander (*Caudata*)

麑 ní ㄋㄧˊ 小鹿 fawn

拟(擬) nǐ ㄋㄧˇ ❶打算 to plan; to intend:～往上海 *to intend (or plan) to go to Shanghai* ❷初步设计编制,起草 to work out; to draw up; to draft:～稿 *to make (or prepare) a draft; to draft*|～议 *proposal; recommendation*|～定计划 *to lay out (or draw up) a plan; to frame (or draft) a plan* ❸仿照 to imitate; to mimic; to simulate:～作 *work modelled after a certain author; imitation work* [拟声词]模拟事物声音的词,如"咚、砰、丁当、哐啷"等 onomatopoeia

你 nǐ ㄋㄧˇ 代词 ***pronoun***,指称对方 you

旎 nǐ ㄋㄧˇ 见888页"旖"字条"旖旎"(yǐ—) see 旖旎 on p888

泥 ㊁ nì ㄋㄧˋ ❶涂抹 to cover (*or* smear) with plaster; to plaster:～墙 *to cover the crevices in a wall with mud or plaster; to daub a wall with mud; to plaster a wall*|～炉子 *to coat a stove with plaster* ❷固执,死板 stubborn; obstinate; bigoted([连] ***doublet*** 拘— to cling to; to stick fast to; to rigidly adhere to)

㊀ ní 见531页 see p531

昵(*暱) nì ㄋㄧˋ 亲近 close; intimate([连] ***doublet*** 亲— intimate; attached; affectionate)

逆 nì ㄋㄧˋ ❶方向相反,跟"顺"相对(the opposite of 顺)

against; counter; adverse: ～风 *against the wind; in the teeth of the wind; upwind* | ～境 *unfavourable circumstances* (or *conditions*); *adverse circumstances* (or *conditions*); *adversity* | ～水行舟 *sailing against the current* | 倒行～施 *trying to put the clock back; going against the trend of the times; acting perversely* ❷抵触,不顺从 to go against; to disobey; to defy: 忠言～耳 *Honest exhortations may be unpleasant to the ear.* or *Good advice grates* (or *jars*) *on the ear.* or *Golden words offend the ear.* ❸背叛者或背叛者的 traitor; traitorous: ～产 *traitor's property* (or *estate*) ❹迎接 to meet; to greet; to welcome: ～战 *to rise to the challenge of an adversary; to accept challenge; to fight head-on* [转] ***transfer*** 预先 in advance; beforehand: ～料 *to foretell; to predict; to prognosticate*

匿 nì ㄋㄧˋ 隐藏,躲避 to conceal; to hide; to cache; to bury ([连] ***doublet*** 隐— to hide; to conceal; to lie low | 藏— to hide; to go into hiding; to conceal): ～名信 *anonymous letter*

睨 nì ㄋㄧˋ 斜着眼睛看 to look askance; to cast an oblique look; to squint: ～视 *to look askance; to cast an oblique look; to squint*

腻 nì ㄋㄧˋ ❶食物油脂过多 fatty; greasy; oily: 油～ *oily; greasy* | 肥～ *fatty and greasy* [细腻] **1** 光滑 fine and smooth; delicate **2** 细致 exquisite; superb; minute ❷腻烦,因过多而厌烦 to be tired of; to be fed up (*or* bored with); to loathe: 玩～了 *to have become tired of playing* (*sth*) | 听～了 *to have become bored with listening* (*to sth*) ❸积污,污垢 dirt; filth; grime: 尘～ *dirt; grime*

溺 ㊀ nì ㄋㄧˋ ❶淹没 to drown; to submerge; to inundate: ～死 *to be drowned* ❷沉迷不悟,过分 to be addicted to; to indulge in; to abandon (*or* give) oneself to: ～信 *to have blind faith in; to be a devout believer in* | ～爱 *to spoil; to dote on; to pamper*

㊁ niào 见536页 see p536

NIAN ㄋㄧㄢ

拈 niān ㄋㄧㄢ 用手指搓捏或拿东西 (with the thumb and one or two other fingers) to pick up; to pinch; to nip: ～须 *to finger* (or *pluck at*) *one's beard* | ～花 *to pick flowers* | ～阄(抓阄儿) *to draw lots*

蔫 niān ㄋㄧㄢ 植物因失去水分而萎缩 (of plants) withered; wilted; shrivelled (up): 花～了。*Flowers faded.* | 菜～了。*The vegetables have shrivelled up.* [引] ***extension*** 精神不振,不活泼 depressed; spiritless; listless

N

年（*秊） nián ㄋㄧㄢˊ ❶地球绕太阳一周的时间。现行历法规定平年365日，闰年366日 year ㊀ ***extension*** **1** 年节，一年的开始 New Year：过～ *to celebrate the New Year* (or *Spring Festival*)｜～画 *New Year picture*；*Spring Festival picture* **2** 时期 period (in history)；age；times：光绪～间 *during the reign of Emperor Guangxu of the Qing Dynasty*｜民国初～ *in the early years of the Republic of China* [年头儿]**1** 全年的时间 year：看看已是三个～～～。*Three years has passed.* **2** 时代 days；times：那～～～穷人可真苦哇。*What a miserable life the poor people lived in those days!* **3** 庄稼的收成 harvest：今年～～～真好，比去年多收一倍。*The harvest is good this year, the yield doubling that of last year.* ❷每年的 yearly；annual：～会 *annual meeting*｜～产量 *annual production*；*annual output* (or *yield*) ❸年纪，岁数 age（㊁ ***doublet*** 一龄 age｜一岁 age）：～老 *old*｜～轻 *young*；*youthful* ㊀ ***extension*** 人一生所经年岁的分期 period in one's life：青～ *youth*；*youthful days*；*young people*｜壮～ *in one's thirties or forties*；*meridian of life* ❹年景，年成，收成 harvest：丰～ *bumper harvest*；*year of abundance*；*good year*

粘 ㊁ nián ㄋㄧㄢˊ ❶同"黏" same as 黏 ❷姓 Nian，a surname

㊀ zhān 见952页 see p952

鲇 nián ㄋㄧㄢˊ 鲇鱼，鱼名。头大，口宽，尾侧扁，皮有黏质，无鳞，可吃 catfish (*Siluriformes*)

黏 nián ㄋㄧㄢˊ 像胶水或糨糊所具有的能使物体粘(zhān)合的性质 sticky；glutinous；viscid：～液 *mucus*｜这江米很～。*The polished glutinous rice is very sticky.*

鲶 nián ㄋㄧㄢˊ 同"鲇"same as 鲇

捻（*撚） niǎn ㄋㄧㄢˇ ❶用手指搓转(zhuàn) to twist with fingers：～线 *to twist a thread*｜～麻绳 *to make a rope by twisting hemp fibres* ❷(一子、一儿)用纸、布条等搓成的像线绳样的东西 sth made by twisting；wick；spill：纸～儿 *paper spill*｜药～儿 *slender roll of medicated paper or gauze (for insertion into wounds)*；*fuse*；*medicated wick*｜灯～儿 *lampwick*

辇 niǎn ㄋㄧㄢˇ (旧读 formerly liǎn)古时用人拉着走的车，后来多指皇帝、皇后坐的车 (in ancient China) man-drawn carriage；imperial carriage

撵 niǎn ㄋㄧㄢˇ ❶驱逐，赶走 to drive out；to oust；to banish：～走 *to drive away*；*to oust*；*to eject*｜～出去 *to drive out*；*to cast* (or *kick*) *out* ❷追赶 to catch up with；to chase：他～不

N

上我。*He can't catch up with me.*

碾 niǎn ㄋㄧㄢˇ ❶(一子)把东西轧碎或压平的器具 roller: 石～ *stone roller* | 汽～ *steam-roller* ❷轧(yà),滚压 to grind or husk with a roller; to crush: ～米 *to husk rice; to mill rice* | ～药 *to grind medical medicine*

蹍 niǎn ㄋㄧㄢˇ 〈方 **dialect**〉踩 to stamp; to tread; to step on

廿 niàn ㄋㄧㄢˋ 二十 twenty: ～四史(*official history of China up to the end of the Ming Dynasty authorized by Emperor Gaozong of the Qing Dynasty*) Twenty-Four Histories

念(❷*唸) niàn ㄋㄧㄢˋ ❶惦记,常常地想 to think of; to miss (㊈ **dialect** 惦— to keep thinking about; to be concerned about; to worry out): 思～ *to think of; to long for; to miss* | 想～ *to recall with longing; to miss; to yearn for* | 不～旧恶 *to forget past grudges; to discard old animosities* | 怀～革命先烈 *to cherish the memory of revolutionary martyrs* [念头](-tou)思想,想法 idea; thought; intention: 不该有这种～～。*You should not have such an idea.* ❷诵读 to read aloud; to read out; to declaim: ～书 *to read a text aloud* | ～诗 *to declaim a poem* ❸"廿"的大写 capital form of 廿

埝 niàn ㄋㄧㄢˋ 用土筑成的小堤或副堤 low bank between fields or shallow waters; boundary ridge; baulk

NIANG ㄋㄧㄤ

娘(*孃) niáng ㄋㄧㄤˊ ❶对年轻女子的称呼 young woman; girl: 渔～ *young fisherwoman* | 新～ *bride* [娘子] **1** 尊称青年或中年妇女(多见于早期白话)(usually used in early vernacular)(polite form of address for a young or middle-aged woman) madam **2** 旧称妻(former term) wife [姑娘](-niang) **1** 未婚女子的通称 girl; lass **2** 女儿 daughter ❷母亲 mother; mum; ma ❸称长(zhǎng)一辈或年长的已婚妇女(form of address for a married woman who is elderly or of the elder generation): 大～ *aunt* | 婶～ *wife of one's father's younger brother*

酿(釀) niàng ㄋㄧㄤˋ ❶利用发酵作用制造 to make (wine); to brew (beer); to ferment: ～酒 *to distil alcoholic drinks; to make wine; to brew beer* | ～造 *to distil (alcoholic drinks); to make (wine, vinegar, etc); to brew (beer)* ㊀ **extension** **1** 蜜蜂做蜜(of bees) to make honey: ～蜜 *to make honey* **2** 逐渐形成 to lead to; to result in; to brew: ～成水灾 *to cause floods* ❷指酒

N

wine：佳～ *vintage wine*；*good wine*

NIAO ㄋㄧㄠ

鸟（鳥） niǎo ㄋㄧㄠˇ 脊椎动物的一类，温血卵生，用肺呼吸，全身有羽毛，后肢能行走，一般前肢变为翅能飞 bird

茑 niǎo ㄋㄧㄠˇ 一种小灌木，茎能攀缘其他树木 birdvine and viscum［茑萝］一年生蔓草，开红色小花 cypress vine（*Ipomoea quamoclit*）

袅（*嫋、*嬝） niǎo ㄋㄧㄠˇ［袅袅］**1** 烟气缭绕上腾的样子（of smoke，etc）spiralling upwards；swirling upwards：炊烟～～。*The smoke is curling upwards from kitchen chimneys*. **2** 细长柔软的东西随风摆动的样子（of sth slender and delicate）waving in the wind；swaying：垂杨～～。*Weeping willows are swaying in the wind*. **3** 声音绵延不绝（of sound）lingering（long in the air）：余音～～。*The melody is still lingering in the air*.［袅娜］（—nuó）**1** 形容草木柔软细长（of grass，tree，etc）lithe and slender **2** 形容女子姿态美（of the figure of a woman）willowy；slender and delicate；lissome and graceful

嬲 niǎo ㄋㄧㄠˇ 戏弄，纠缠 to tease；to flirt with；to pester（*or* annoy）

尿 ㊀ niào ㄋㄧㄠˋ ❶小便，从肾脏滤出由尿道排泄出来的液体 urine；piss；pee ❷排泄小便 to make（*or* pass）water；to urinate；to piss

㊁ suī 见714页 see p714

脲 niào ㄋㄧㄠˋ 尿素，有机化合物，分子式$CO(NH_2)_2$，无色晶体。广泛用在塑料、药剂和农业等生产中 urea；carbamide

溺 ㊀ niào ㄋㄧㄠˋ 同"尿"same as 尿

㊀ nì 见533页 see p533

NIE ㄋㄧㄝ

捏（*揑） niē ㄋㄧㄝ ❶用拇指和其他手指夹住 to hold between the thumb and other fingers；to pinch：～着一粒豆 *to hold a bean*（or *pea*）*in one's fingers* ❷用手指把软的东西做成一定的形状 to knead with the fingers；to mould：～饺子 *to knead the wrappers when making* jiaozi；*to make* jiaozi｜～泥人儿 to make clay figurines ❸假造，虚构 to concoct；to fabricate；to cook up：～造 *to concoct*；*to fabricate*；*to make*（or *trump*）*up*｜～报 *to fake*（or *fabricate*）*a report*

苶 nié ㄋㄧㄝˊ 〈方 **dialect**〉疲倦，精神不振 lethargic；listless；languid：发～ *looking listless*｜～呆呆的 *in a state of lethargy*

N

乜 ㊀ niè ㄋㄧㄝˋ 姓 Nie, a surname
㊁ miē 见506页 see p506

陧 niè ㄋㄧㄝˋ 见796页"杌"字条"杌陧"(wù—) see 杌陧 on p796

涅 niè ㄋㄧㄝˋ ❶可做黑色染料的矾石 alunite ❷染黑 to dye sth black; to blacken:～齿 *to blacken the teeth* [涅白]不透明的白色 opaque white

聂(聶) niè ㄋㄧㄝˋ 姓 Nie, a surname

嗫(囁) niè ㄋㄧㄝˋ [嗫嚅](—rú)口动,吞吞吐吐,想说又停止 to speak haltingly; to hesitate in speech; to hem and haw

镊(鑷) niè ㄋㄧㄝˋ 镊子,夹取毛发、细刺及其他细小东西的器具 tweezers

颞(顳) niè ㄋㄧㄝˋ [颞颥](—rú)头颅两侧靠近耳朵上方的部分。也省称"颞"(also short for 颞) temple

蹑(躡) niè ㄋㄧㄝˋ ❶踩 to tread; to trample; to step on:～足其间(指参加到里面去)*to join* (*a profession*); *to follow* (*a trade*); *to associate with* (*a certain type of people*) [蹑手蹑脚]行动很轻的样子 to walk stealthily (*or* gingerly); to tiptoe; to sneak ❷追随 to follow; to track; to dog:～踪 *to follow the trail of*; *to track*; *to trace*

臬 niè ㄋㄧㄝˋ ❶箭靶子 target (for arrows) ❷古代测日影的标杆 gnomon ❸标准,法式 standard; criterion; norm:圭～ *criterion; standard*

嵲 niè ㄋㄧㄝˋ 见151页"嵽"字条"嵽嵲"(dié—) see 嵽嵲 on p151

镍 niè ㄋㄧㄝˋ 一种金属元素,符号 Ni,银白色,有光泽,有延展性。可用来制造器具、货币等,镀在其他金属上可以防止生锈,是制造不锈钢的重要原料 nickel (Ni)

啮(*齧、*嚙) niè ㄋㄧㄝˋ 咬 to gnaw; to nibble:虫咬鼠～ *to be bitten by pests and gnawed by mice*

孽(*孼) niè ㄋㄧㄝˋ 恶因,恶事 evil; sin; crime:造～ *to do evil*; *to commit a sin* | 罪～ *sin*; *crime*; *iniquity*

蘖(**櫱) niè ㄋㄧㄝˋ 树木砍去后又长出来的芽子 sprout; tiller:萌～ *to begin to sprout* (*or bud*) [分蘖]稻、麦等农作物的种子生出幼苗后在接近地面主茎的地方分枝 to sprout; to tiller

糵(**糱) niè ㄋㄧㄝˋ 酒曲 distiller's yeast; leaven (for making wine)

NIN ㄋㄧㄣ

您 nín ㄋㄧㄣˊ 代词 ***pronoun***,"你"的敬称(polite form of address for 你) you; thou

NING ㄋㄧㄥ

宁(寧、*甯) ㊀ níng ㄋㄧㄥˊ ❶安宁 peaceful; serene; tranquil [归宁]旧时女子出嫁后回娘家看望父母 (in former times)(of a married woman) to visit her parents; to pay a visit to her parents ❷使安宁 to pacify; to placate; to mollify:息事～人 *to patch up a quarrel and reconcile the parties concerned; to make concessions to avoid trouble* ❸江苏省南京的别称 Ning, another name for Nanjing, Jiangsu Province

㊁ nìng 见538页 see p538

拧(擰) ㊀ níng ㄋㄧㄥˊ 握住物体的两端向相反的方向用力 to twist; to wring: ～手巾 *to wring a towel*|～绳子 *to twist a rope*

㊁ nǐng 见538页 see p538

㊂ nìng 见539页 see p539

苧(薴) ㊀ níng ㄋㄧㄥˊ 有机化合物,分子式 $C_{10}H_{16}$,是一种有香味的液体。存在于柑橘类的果皮中,供制香料 limonene

㊁ zhù 见996页"苎"see 苎 on p996

咛(嚀) níng ㄋㄧㄥˊ 见152页"叮"字条"叮咛" see 叮咛 on p152

狞(獰) níng ㄋㄧㄥˊ 凶恶。参看971页"狰"字条"狰狞"(zhēng—) (see 狰狞 on p971) (of facial expression) ferocious; hideous

柠(檸) níng ㄋㄧㄥˊ [柠檬](—méng)常绿小乔木,产在热带、亚热带。果实也叫柠檬,椭圆形,两端尖,淡黄色,味酸,可制饮料 lemon (*Citrus limon*)

聍(聹) níng ㄋㄧㄥˊ [耵聍](dīng—)耳垢,耳屎 earwax; cerumen

凝 níng ㄋㄧㄥˊ ❶凝结,液体遇冷变成固体,气体因温度降低或压力增加变成液体 to condense; to congeal; to coagulate:油～住了。*The lard has already congealed.* ❷聚集,集中 to concentrate; to focus; to fix:～神 *with fixed (or concentrated) attention; attentively*|～视 *to fix (or focus) one's eyes on; to gaze fixedly; to stare*|独坐～思 *to be lost in thought while sitting alone*

拧(擰) ㊁ nǐng ㄋㄧㄥˇ ❶扭转,控制住东西的一部分而绞转(zhuàn) to screw; to twist; to wrench:～螺丝钉 *to turn a screw*|～墨水瓶盖 *to screw on (or off) the cap of an ink bottle* ❷〈方 **dialect**〉相反,不顺 to get wrong; to be at cross-purposes; to discord:我弄～了。*I got it the wrong way around.*|别让他俩闹～了。*Keep them from being discordant (or disagreeing) with each other.*

㊀ níng 见538页 see p538

㊂ nìng 见539页 see p539

宁(寧、*甯) ㊁ nìng ㄋㄧㄥˋ ❶宁可,表示比较后做出的选择,情愿 would rather; rather:～死不屈 *would rather die than yield (or submit); to prefer*

death to surrender | ～缺毋滥 *would rather go without than make do with a substandard substitute; would rather go without than have sth shoddy —to place quality above quantity* ❷姓 Ning, a surname

㊀ níng 见537页 see p537

拧(擰) ㊂ nìng ㄋㄧㄥˋ 倔强，别扭，不驯服 obstinate; pigheaded; stubborn: ～脾气 *willful disposition*

㊀ nǐng 见538页 see p538

㊁ níng 见538页 see p538

泞(濘) nìng ㄋㄧㄥˋ 烂泥 mud; slush; mire [泥泞]1 有烂泥难走 muddy; slushy; miry: 道路～～。*The road is muddy.* 2 淤积的烂泥 mud; slush; mire: 陷入～～ *to get bogged down in the mud*

佞 nìng ㄋㄧㄥˋ ❶有才智 wise; talented; intelligent: 不～(旧时的谦称)(*humble term in former times*) *your unintelligent servant —I; me* ❷善辩，巧言谄媚 witty; given to flattery; sycophantic: ～口 *eloquent tongue* | ～人(有口才而不正派的人) *sycophant; toady*

NIU ㄋㄧㄡ

妞 niū ㄋㄧㄡ (一儿)女孩子 girl

牛 niú ㄋㄧㄡˊ ❶哺乳动物，常见的有黄牛、水牛等家畜。力量大，能耕田、拉车。肉和奶可吃。角、皮、骨可做器物。野牛、野牦牛等为国家保护动物 cattle; ox; cow ❷星宿名，二十八宿之一 *niu*, the 9th of the 28 constellations

扭 niǔ ㄋㄧㄡˇ 转动一部分 to turn: ～过脸来 *to turn one's head around* | ～转身子 *to turn round; to turn on one's heel* ㊀ ***extension*** 1 走路时身体摇摆转动 to swing; to wriggle; to sway: ～秧歌 *to do a* yangge *dance* | 一～一～地走 *to walk with a rolling gait* 2 拧伤筋骨 to sprain; to strain; to wrench: ～了筋 *to get one's tendon wrenched* (or *sprained*) | ～了腰 *to have one's back sprained* 3 扳转，转变情势 to turn back; to change; to reverse: ～转局面 *to change the situation; to turn the tide* (or *tables*); *to reverse a trend*

狃 niǔ ㄋㄧㄡˇ 因袭，拘泥 to be bound (*or* constrained) by; to adhere rigidly to; to hold fast to: ～于习俗 *to be bound by custom* | ～于成见 *to be bound by prejudice; to be deeply prejudiced* (or *biased*)

忸 niǔ ㄋㄧㄡˇ [忸怩](—ní) 不好意思、不大方的样子 bashful; coy

纽 niǔ ㄋㄧㄡˇ ❶器物上可以提起或系挂的部分 button loop; handle; knob: 秤～ *lifting cord of a steelyard* | 印～ *seal top engraved in the likeness of animals, with a hole for a tassel; knob of a seal in animal shape* ❷(一子)纽扣，可以扣合衣物的球状物或片状

N

物 button ❸枢纽 key position; pivot; hub: ～带 *bond; tie; link*

杻 ㊁ niǔ ㄋㄧㄡˇ 古书上说的一种树 (in ancient Chinese texts) a kind of tree

㊀ chǒu 见95页 see p95

钮 niǔ ㄋㄧㄡˇ ❶器物上用手开关或调节的部件 knob; button: 按～ *push-button; button* | 旋～ *knob* ❷同"纽❷" same as 纽❷

拗(*抝) ㊂ niù ㄋㄧㄡˋ 固执, 不驯顺 obstinate; stubborn; bigoted: 执～ *stubborn; headstrong; mulish* | 脾气很～ *stubborn by nature; bullheaded*

㊀ ǎo 见9页 see p9

㊁ ào 见10页 see p10

NONG ㄋㄨㄥ

农(農、*辳) nóng ㄋㄨㄥˊ ❶种庄稼, 属于种庄稼的 farming; agricultural: 务～ *to go in for farming; to be engaged in farming* | ～业 *agriculture; farming* ❷农民 farmer; peasant: 菜～ *vegetable grower; market gardener; truck farmer* | 老～ *old farmer; old peasant; old farm hand* | 工～联盟 *alliance of workers and peasants; worker-peasant alliance*

侬(儂) nóng ㄋㄨㄥˊ 代词 ***pronoun*** ❶〈方 ***dialect***〉你 you ❷我(多见于旧诗文) (usually used in classical poetry) I; me

哝(噥) nóng ㄋㄨㄥˊ [哝哝](—nong) 小声说话 to whisper; to murmur; to mutter

浓(濃) nóng ㄋㄨㄥˊ ❶含某种成分多, 跟"淡"相对 (the opposite of 淡) concentrated; thick; dense: ～茶 *strong tea* | ～烟 *dense smoke* ❷深厚, 不淡薄 great; strong; deep: 兴趣正～ *having a great* (or *keen*) *interest* (*in sth*) | 感情～厚 *strong and deep feelings*

脓(膿) nóng ㄋㄨㄥˊ 化脓性炎症病变所形成的黄白色汁液, 是死亡的白细胞、细菌及脂肪等的混合物 pus

秾(穠) nóng ㄋㄨㄥˊ 花木繁盛 (of flowers, trees, etc) luxuriant; lush; gorgeously blooming

弄 ㊀ nòng ㄋㄨㄥˋ (旧读 formerly lòng) ❶拿着玩, 戏耍 to play with; to fool with; to fiddle with (㊣ ***doublet*** 玩— to play with; to dally with; to play (tricks, etc) | 戏— to make fun of; to play a prank on sb; to tease): 不要～火。*Don't play with fire.* ❷搞, 做 to get; to do; to make: ～好 *to get sth well done* | ～点水喝 *to get* (or *fetch*) *some water to drink* | ～饭 *to prepare a meal; to cook a meal* ❸搅扰 to disturb; to annoy; to upset: 这消息～得人心不安。*The news upsets everybody.* ❹耍, 炫耀 to play; to show off; to manipulate (*or* manoeuvre):～手段 *to play tricks* | 舞文～墨 *to play with words; to engage in phrase-mongering; to be fond of writing*

㊁ lòng 见462页 see p462

NOU ㄋㄡ

耨(**鎒) nòu ㄋㄡˋ ❶古代锄草的器具 (in ancient China) weeding hoe ❷锄草 to mow grass; to weed: 深耕易～ *deep ploughing and thorough weeding*

NU ㄋㄨ

奴 nú ㄋㄨˊ 旧社会中受剥削阶级压迫、剥削、役使的没有自由的人 bond servant; slave; serf: 农～ *serf* | 家～ *bond servant of a family* [奴隶]受奴隶主奴役而没有人身自由的人 slave [奴役]把人当作奴隶使用 to enslave [奴才] **1** 旧时婢仆对主人的自称(formerly used to denote oneself when addressing royalty or one's master) your humble slave **2** 指甘心供人驱使、帮助作恶的坏人 lackey; flunkey

孥 nú ㄋㄨˊ 儿子,或指妻和子 sons; wife and children: 妻～ (*one's*) *wife and children*

驽 nú ㄋㄨˊ 驽马,劣马,走不快的马 inferior (*or* mediocre) horse; nag; jade ㊗ ***figurative*** 愚钝无能 incapable; incompetent; dull: ～钝 *dull; stupid; dumb*

努(❷**呶) nǔ ㄋㄨˇ ❶尽量地使出(力量) to put forth (one's strength); to exert oneself; to make an effort: ～力 *to make efforts; to exert oneself; to strive* ❷突出 to pout; to bulge; to protrude: ～嘴 *to pout* (or *purse*) *one's lips* (*as a signal*) ❸〈方 ***dialect***〉因用力太过,身体内部受伤 to injure oneself through overexertion; to strain oneself: 箱子太重,你别扛,看～着。*Don't shoulder that heavy trunk, or you'll get a bad strain.*

弩 nǔ ㄋㄨˇ 一种利用机械力量射箭的弓 crossbow

砮 nǔ ㄋㄨˇ ❶可做箭镞的石头 stone that can be made into an arrowhead ❷石制箭头 stone arrowhead

胬 nǔ ㄋㄨˇ [胬肉]一种眼病,即翼状胬肉 pterygium

怒 nù ㄋㄨˋ ❶生气,气愤 anger; rage; fury; wrath: 发～ *to get angry; to fly into a rage; to flare up* | ～发(fà)冲冠(形容盛怒) *standing hair pushing up one's hat — extremely angry; bristling with anger; bursting with indignation* | ～容满面 *wearing a scowl (on one's face); flushed with anger* ❷气势盛 vigorous; flourishing: ～涛 *angry* (or *raging*) *billows; roaring* (or *violent*) *waves; turbulent wa-*

N

ters | ～潮 *angry* (or *raging*) *tide*; *surging tide*; *tidal bore* | 草木～生 *plants growing in profusion*; (*of place*) *overgrown with vegetation*

[怒族]我国少数民族，参看附表 (see the appendix) the Nu ethnic group, one of the ethnic minorities of China

NÜ ㄋㄩ

女 nǚ ㄋㄩˇ ❶女子，女人，妇女 woman; female: ～士 *lady* | ～工 *woman worker* | 男～平等 *equality between men and women*; *gender equality* ❷女儿 daughter: 一儿一～ *a son and a daughter* ❸星宿名，二十八宿之一 *nü*, the 10th of the 28 constellations

〈古 ***archaism***〉又同"汝"(rǔ) also same as 汝

钕 nǚ ㄋㄩˇ 一种金属元素，符号 Nd，银白色。用来制激光材料、催化剂等 neodymium (Nd)

恧 nǜ ㄋㄩˋ 惭愧 ashamed

衄(*衂、*䘐) nǜ ㄋㄩˋ 鼻衄，鼻子流血 nosebleed; epistaxis

朒 nǜ ㄋㄩˋ 亏缺，不足 to be deficient in; to lack

NUAN ㄋㄨㄢ

暖(*煖) nuǎn ㄋㄨㄢˇ 暖和(huo)，不冷 warm; cosy; snug (㊥ ***doublet*** 温— warm; mild): 风和日～ *with a warm breeze and clear skies* (or *full sunshine*); *warm and sunny with a mild breeze* ㊀ ***extension*** 使温和(huo) to warm (up); to heat: ～一～手 *to warm up one's hands*

NÜE ㄋㄩㄝ

疟(瘧) ㊀ nüè ㄋㄩㄝˋ 疟疾(ji)，又叫"疟子"(yàozi)。一种周期性发冷发烧的传染病。病原体是疟原虫，由疟蚊传染到人体血液中。发疟子，有的地区叫"打摆子" (also called 疟子, and to suffer malaria is called 打摆子 in some areas) malaria; ague

㊁ yào 见876页 see p876

虐 nüè ㄋㄩㄝˋ 残暴 cruel; brutal; ferocious (㊥ ***doublet*** 暴— brutal; tyrannical; despotic): ～待 *to maltreat*; *to abuse*; *to tyrannize*

NUO ㄋㄨㄛ

挪 nuó ㄋㄨㄛˊ 移动 to move; to shift; to appropriate: 把桌子～一～。*Move the table a little.* | ～用款项 *to misappropriate funds*; *to divert funds*; *to embezzle funds*

娜 ㊀ nuó ㄋㄨㄛˊ 见536页"袅"字条"袅娜"(niǎo—) see 袅娜 on p536

㊁ nà 见522页 see p522

傩(儺) nuó ㄋㄨㄛˊ 旧指驱逐瘟疫的迎神赛会

ancient festival to exorcize a devil causing a plague

诺 nuò ㄋㄨㄛˋ ❶答应的声音，表示同意（叠 ***reduplication***）（used to express agreement）yes；yeah：～～连声 *to keep saying yes；to eagerly agree* ❷应允 to promise；to assent；to consent：～言 *promise；pledge；word* | 慨～ *to generously* (or *kindly*) *agree；to magnanimously* (or *readily*) *consent*

喏 ㊀ nuò ㄋㄨㄛˋ ❶〈方 ***dialect***〉叹词 ***interjection***，表示让人注意自己所指示的事物（used to call attention to what one refers to）look；see：～，这不就是你的那把伞？*There! Isn't that your umbrella?* ❷同"诺"same as 诺

㊁ rě 见630页 see p630

锘 nuò ㄋㄨㄛˋ 一种人造的放射性元素（符号 No）nobelium (No)

搦 nuò ㄋㄨㄛˋ 握，持，拿着 to hold (in one's hand)：～管（执笔）*to wield the pen；to write*

懦 nuò ㄋㄨㄛˋ 怯懦，软弱无能 cowardly；weak；craven（㊈ ***doublet*** 一弱 cowardly；weak；craven）：～夫 *coward；weakling；craven*

糯（*稬、*穤）nuò ㄋㄨㄛˋ 糯稻，稻的一种，米富于黏性（unhusked）glutinous rice：～米 (*threshed and polished*) *glutinous rice*

O ㄛ

o ㄛ

噢 ō ㄛ 叹词 ***interjection***，表示了解（used to express realization）oh；oho；aha：～，就是他！*Oho，it's him！*｜～，我懂了。*Oh，I see.*［噢唷］［噢哟］（—yō）叹词 ***interjection***，表示惊异、痛苦（used to express surprise，suffering，etc）：～～，这么大的西瓜！*Oh，what a big watermelon！*｜～～，好痛！*Ouch！It hurts！*

哦 ㊀ ó ㄛ́ 叹词 ***interjection***，表示疑问、惊奇等（used to express doubt，surprise，etc）：～，是这样的吗？*Oh，is that so？*｜～，是那么一回事。*Oh，so that is？*

㊁ ò 见544页 see p544

㊂ é 见172页 see p172

嚄 ㊁ ǒ ㄛ̌ 叹词 ***interjection***，表示惊讶（used to express surprise）ah；oh：～，这是怎么搞的？*Hmm，how it comes to this？*

㊀ huō 见302页 see p302

哦 ㊁ ò ㄛ̀ 叹词 ***interjection***，表示领会、醒悟（used to express realization，understanding，etc）oh；ah；oho：～，我明白了。*Oh，I see.*

㊀ ó 见544页 see p544

㊂ é 见172页 see p172

ou ㄡ

区（區）㊁ ōu ㄡ 姓 Ou，a surname

㊀ qū 见616页 see p616

讴（謳）ōu ㄡ 歌唱 to sing［讴歌］歌颂，赞美 to sing the praises of；to pay tribute to；to eulogize

沤（漚）㊁ ōu ㄡ 水泡 water bubble；froth；foam：浮～ *bubbles gathering on the surface of water；froth；foam*

㊀ òu 见545页 see p545

瓯（甌）ōu ㄡ ❶小盆 bowl ❷杯 cup：茶～ *tea cup* ❸瓯江，水名，在浙江省南部 Oujiang River，in the south of Zhejiang Province ❹浙江省温州的别称 Ou，another name for Wenzhou，Zhejiang Province

欧（歐）ōu ㄡ ❶姓 Ou，a surname ❷指欧洲，世界七大洲之一 Europe，one of the seven continents in the world

殴（毆）ōu ㄡ 打人 to beat up；assault and battery（㊣ ***doublet*** 一打 to beat up；to hit；to strike）：～伤 *to beat and injure*

O

鸥(鷗) ōu ㄡ 水鸟名。羽毛多为白色，生活在湖海上，捕食鱼、螺等 gull (*Laridae*)

呕(嘔) ǒu ㄡˇ 吐(tù) to vomit; to retch; to throw up ([连] **doublet** —吐 to vomit; to throw up; to puke): ～血(xuè) *haematemesis; to spit blood* [作呕](zuò—)恶心，比喻非常厌恶(wù) to feel like vomiting; to feel nausea — to be disgusted at

偶 ǒu ㄡˇ ❶偶像，用木头或泥土等制成的人形 idol; image ❷双，对，成双或成对，跟"奇"(jī)相对(the opposite of 奇) even (number); in pairs: ～数 *even number* | 无独有～ *rare but not unique* [对偶]文字作品中音调谐和，意义相对，字数相等的语句，骈体文的基本形式 antithesis ❸偶然 by chance; accidental; fortuitous: ～发事件 *chance occurrence; freak accident; accident* [偶然]不经常，不是必然的 by chance; accidentally; occasionally: ～～去一次 *to go there occasionally* | 这些成就的取得绝不是～～的。*It is by no means accidental for us to have made these achievements.*

耦 ǒu ㄡˇ ❶两个人在一起耕地(of two persons) to plough side by side ❷同"偶❷" same as 偶❷

藕 ǒu ㄡˇ 莲的地下茎，肥大有节，中间有许多管状小孔，可以吃。(图见438页"莲") (picture on p438) lotus root [藕荷][藕合]淡紫色 pale pinkish purple; pale lavender-pink

沤(漚) ㊀ òu ㄡˋ 长时间地浸泡 to soak (*or* steep); to macerate; to ret: ～麻 *to ret flax* (or *hemp*)

㊁ ōu 见544页 see p544

怄(慪) òu ㄡˋ 故意惹人恼怒，或使人发笑，逗弄 to annoy; to irritate; to tease: 你别～人了。*Don't annoy me.* or *Stop annoying me.* | ～得他直冒火。*He is irritated into a rage.* [怄气]闹别扭，生闷气 to sulk: 不要～～。*Don't sulk!*

P 夂

PA 夂丫

趴 pā 夂丫 ❶肚子向下卧倒 to lie on one's stomach; to lie prone: ～下放枪 *to shoot (a rifle) from the prone position* ❷身体向前靠在东西上 to bend over; to lean on: ～在桌子上写字 *to bend over the desk to write*

啪 pā 夂丫 拟声词 ***onomatopoeia***,放枪、拍掌或东西撞击等的声音 the sound of shooting, clapping, or striking

葩 pā 夂丫花 flower: 奇～*extraordinarily beautiful flowers; exotic flowers; fabulous flowers*

扒 ㊀ pá 夂丫́ ❶用耙(pá)搂(lōu),聚拢 to gather (*or* collect) with a rake; to rake up: ～草 *to rake up hay* | ～土 *to rake the soil* ❷扒窃 to pick sb's pocket; to steal; to pinch: ～手(小偷) *pickpocket* ❸炖烂,煨烂 to stew; to braise: ～猪头 *to stew a hog's head*

㊁ bā 见11页 see p11

杷 pá 夂丫́ 见561页"枇"字条"枇杷"(pípa) see 枇杷 on p561

爬 pá 夂丫́ ❶手和脚一齐着地前行,虫类向前移动(of human beings, insects, reptiles, etc) to crawl; to worm one's way (into); to creep: ～行 *to crawl; to creep* | 小孩子会～了。*The baby can crawl now.* | 不要吃苍蝇～过的东西。*Don't eat anything that has been touched by flies.* [爬虫] 爬行动物的旧称,行走时多用腹面贴地,如龟、鳖、蛇等 former term for a reptile ❷攀登 to climb; to clamber; to shinny: ～山 *to climb a mountain; mountaineering* | ～树 *to climb a tree; to shinny up a tree* | 猴子～竿。*The monkey is climbing up a pole.*

钯 ㊁ pá 夂丫́ 同"耙"(pá) same as 耙

㊀ bǎ 见14页 see p14

耙 ㊁ pá 夂丫́ ❶(一子)聚拢谷物或平土地的用具 rake; harrow ❷用耙子聚拢谷物或平土地 to make smooth with a rake; to rake: ～地 *to rake the soil smooth*

㊀ bà 见14页 see p14

筢 pá 夂丫́ (一子)搂(lōu)柴草的竹制器具 bamboo rake

琶 pá 夂丫́ 见561页"琵"字条"琵琶"(pípa) see 琵琶 on p561

潖 pá 夂丫́ [潖江口]地名,在广东省清远 Pajiangkou, a

place in Qingyuan, Guangdong Province

掱 pá ㄆㄚˊ [掱手]从别人身上窃取财物的小偷儿。现作"扒手"(now written as 扒手)pickpocket

帕 pà ㄆㄚˋ ❶(一子)包头或擦手脸用的布或绸 handkerchief; scarf; kerchief:首～*kerchief* | 手～*handkerchief* ❷压强单位名帕斯卡的简称,符号Pa。天气预报中常用"百帕"(in weather forecast 百帕 is frequently used) pascal (Pa)

怕 pà ㄆㄚˋ ❶害怕 to be afraid of; to fear; to dread:老鼠～猫。*Rats are afraid of cats.* ❷恐怕,或许,表示疑虑或猜想 I'm afraid; I suppose; perhaps:他～不来了。*I'm afraid he won't come.* |～他别有用意。*Perhaps he has something else in his mind.*

PAI ㄆㄞ

拍 pāi ㄆㄞ ❶用手掌轻轻地打 to pat; to clap; to tap:～球 *to bounce a ball; to dribble a ball* |～手 *to clap one's hands* ㊀ ***extension*** (一子)乐曲的节奏 rhythm (㊟ ***doublet*** 节一 beat; time):这首歌每节有四～。*Each bar has four beats in this song.* ❷(一子、一儿)拍打东西的用具 bat; racket; swatter:蝇～儿 *fly swatter* | 球～子 *bat; racket* ❸拍马屁 to flatter; to fawn on; to toady:吹吹～～ *to stoop to boasting and flattery* ❹摄影 to take; to shoot:～照片 *to take a photo* ❺发 to send:～电报 *to send a telegraph; to telegraph* ❻(外 **loanword**)法定计量单位中十进倍数单位词头之一,表示 10^{15}(符号P) peta-(P)

俳 pái ㄆㄞˊ 古代指杂戏、滑稽戏,也指演这种戏的人(in ancient China) variety show; farce; actors who play a variety show (*or* farce) ㊕ ***transfer*** 诙谐,玩笑 comical; funny; humorous

排 ㊀ pái ㄆㄞˊ ❶摆成行(háng)列 to put in order; to line up; to align(㊟ ***doublet*** 一列 to put in order; to arrange; to align):～队 *to line up; to queue up* [排场](一chang)铺张的场面 display of splendour; ostentation and extravagance:不讲～～ *to be averse to ostentation and extravagance; not to go in for the grandiose* [排行](一háng)兄弟姊妹的长幼次序 order of birth; seniority among siblings ❷排成的行列 line; row:我坐在前～。*I sat in the front row.* ❸同"簰"same as 簰 ❹军队的编制单位,是班的上一级 platoon ❺量词 ***quantifier***,用于成行列的 line; row:一～椅子 *a row of chairs* ❻除去,推开 to remove; to exclude; to push (away):～水 *to drain water* |～山倒海(喻力量大) *to topple mountains and overturn seas — to have the momentum*

P

of an avalanche; with great power and influence; forceful (or *mighty*)|～难(nàn) *to help get rid of worries and overcome difficulties; to relieve sb of anxieties by helping him solve problems; to mediate disputes* [排泄]生物把体内的废物如汗、尿、屎等排出体外 to excrete; to defecate; to evacuate ❼排演,练习演戏 to rehearse:～戏 *to rehearse a play*|彩～*dress rehearsal*

㊁ pǎi 见548页 see p548

徘 pái ㄆㄞˊ [徘徊](—huái)来回地走 to walk up and down; to wander; to loiter:他在那里～～了很久。*He has wandered about there for a long time.* ㊗ ***figurative*** 犹疑不决 to hesitate; to waver; to vacillate:左右～～*to hesitate between two alternatives; to vacillate between two alternatives*

棑 pái ㄆㄞˊ 同"簰"same as 簰

牌 pái ㄆㄞˊ ❶(—子、—儿)用木板或其他材料做的标志或凭信物 board; sign; plate:招～*shop sign; signboard*|指路～*signpost*|存车～儿 *parking receipt* (or *ticket*) ㊞ ***extension*** 商标 brand; trade mark; make:解放～汽车 *Jiefang truck*[牌价]市场上用牌告方式公布的标准价格 list price; posted price [牌楼](—lou)用以装点或庆贺的建筑物 *pailou*, a decorated archway; ceremonial gateway ❷古代兵士战争时用来遮护身体的东西 shield:挡箭～*shield*|藤～*cane shield; rattan shield* ❸娱乐或赌博用的东西 cards; dominos; mahjong:扑克～*playing cards* ❹词或曲的曲调的名称 title of a *ci* or *qu*; tunes in poems or plays:词～*title of a* ci *tune*|曲～*title of a* qu *tune*

簰(**簿) pái ㄆㄞˊ 筏子,竹子或木材平摆着编扎成的交通工具,多用于江河上游水浅处。也指成捆的在水上漂浮、运送的木材或竹材。也作"排"、"棑"(also written as 排 or 棑) raft

迫(*廹) ㊁ pǎi ㄆㄞˇ [迫击炮]从炮口装弹,以曲射为主的火炮 trench mortar

㊀ pò 见574页 see p574

排 ㊁ pǎi ㄆㄞˇ [排子车]〈方 ***dialect***〉用人拉的搬运东西的一种车 handcart

㊀ pái 见547页 see p547

哌 pài ㄆㄞˋ [哌嗪](—qín)有机化合物,分子式 $\underline{NHCH_2CH_2NHCH_2CH_2}$,白色结晶,易溶于水。有溶解尿盐酸、驱除蛔虫等药理作用 piperazine

派 pài ㄆㄞˋ ❶水的支流(of a river) tributary ❷一个系统的分支(of a system) branch (㊟***doublet*** —系 faction; clique):流～*school*|～生 *to derive* ❸派别。政党和学术、宗教团体等内部因主张不同而形成的分支

school; faction; sect ❹作风,风度 style; bearing; manner and air:正～*upright; honest; decent*|气～*imposing bearing; imposing manner; dignified air* ❺分配,指定 to send; to assign; to distribute:分～*to assign; to distribute*|～人去办 *to send sb to do sth*

蒎 pài ㄆㄞˋ 有机化合物,分子式 $C_{10}H_{18}$,化学性质稳定,不易被无机酸和氧化剂分解 pinane

湃 pài ㄆㄞˋ 见558页"澎"字条"澎湃"(péng—) see 澎湃 on p558

PAN ㄆㄢ

番 ㊁ pān ㄆㄢ [番禺](—yú)地名,在广东省广州 Panyu, a place in Guangzhou, Guangdong Province

㊀ fān 见181页 see p181

潘 pān ㄆㄢ ❶淘米汁 water in which rice has been washed ❷姓 Pan, a surname

攀 pān ㄆㄢ ❶抓住别的东西向上爬 to climb; to clamber; to scale:～登 *to climb; to clamber; to scale*|～树 *to climb up a tree*|～岩 *rock climbing* ❷拉拢,拉扯 to involve; to implicate (㊎ **doublet** 一扯 to involve; to implicate):～谈 *to strike up a conversation; to engage in chitchat*|～亲道故 *to claim ties of blood or friendship*

爿 pán ㄆㄢˊ 〈方 ***dialect***〉❶劈开的成片的木柴 thin broad split bamboo; chopped wood ❷量词 ***quantifier***,用于商店等(used for shops, factories, etc):一～水果店 *a fruit shop*

胖 ㊁ pán ㄆㄢˊ 安泰舒适 peaceful and comfortable; easy and carefree; fit and happy:心广体～。*A carefree mind engenders health and happiness.*

㊀ pàng 见552页 see p552

盘(盤) pán ㄆㄢˊ ❶(—子、—儿)盛放物品的扁而浅的用具,多为圆形 tray; plate; dish:托～*tray*|茶～儿 *tea tray*|和～托出(喻全部说出) *to lay all the cards on the table — to reveal everything; to hold nothing back; to make a clean breast of everything* [通盘]全面 overall; all-round; comprehensive:～～打算 *comprehensive plan* ❷(—儿)形状像盘或有盘的功用的物品 sth in the shape, or with the function, of a plate or tray:脸～儿 *shape (or contour) of one's face; cast of one's face*|磨(mò)～*millstones*|棋～*chessboard*|算～*abacus* ❸回旋地绕 to coil; to twist; to wind:～香 *incense coil*|～杠子(在杠子上旋转运动) *to exercise on a horizontal bar; to do gymnastic movements on a horizontal bar*|把绳子～起来 *to coil up a rope*|～山公路 *winding moun-*

tain road | ～根错节 *twisted roots and gnarled branches; complicated relationship* [盘剥]利上加利地剥削 to exploit; to practice usury [盘旋]绕着圈地走或飞 to loop; to hover; to circle ❹垒,砌(炕、灶) to build; to construct: ～炕 *to build a kang* | ～灶 *to build a kitchen stove* ❺盘查,仔细查究 to check; to examine; to interrogate: ～账 *to check accounts; to audit* | ～货 *to take stock; to make an inventory of stock on hand* | ～问 *to question; to interrogate; to cross-examine* | ～算(细心打算) *to calculate; to figure; to plan* ❻(一儿)指市场上成交的价格 current price; market quotation: 开～儿 *to open quotation* | 收～儿 *to close quotation* | 平～儿 *to balance quotation* ❼量词 ***quantifier***: 一～机器 *a machine* | 一～磨(mò) *a set of millstones* | 一～棋 *a game of chess*

[盘费](—fei)[盘缠](—chan) 旅途上的费用 travel expenses; travel money

[盘桓](—huán)留恋在一个地方,逗留 to linger; to pace up and down

槃 pán ㄆㄢˊ 同"盘❶❸"same as 盘❶❸

磐 pán ㄆㄢˊ 大石头 huge rock; monolith; boulder: 安如～石 *as solid (or stable) as a rock*

磻 pán ㄆㄢˊ [磻溪]古水名,在今陕西省宝鸡东南 Panxi, an ancient river in the southeast of today's Baoji, Shaanxi Province

蟠 pán ㄆㄢˊ 屈曲,环绕 to coil; to curl: 虎踞龙～*coiling dragon and crouching tiger—(describing) formidable strategic point*

蹒(蹣) pán ㄆㄢˊ [蹒跚](*盘跚)(—shān) **1** 走路一瘸(qué)一拐 to limp; to hobble **2** 走路缓慢、摇摆 to stagger; to falter

判 pàn ㄆㄢˋ ❶分辨,断定 to distinguish; to judge (㊀ ***doublet*** 一断 to judge): ～别是非 *to distinguish between right and wrong; to tell right from wrong* [批判]分析、批驳错误的思想、观点和行为 to criticize: ～～腐朽的剥削阶级思想 *to criticize the decadent outlook of the exploiting class* ❷分开 to separate ㊟ ***transfer*** 截然不同 absolutely different: ～若两人 *to be a changed man; to be no longer one's former self* ❸判决,司法机关对案件的决定 to decide; to judge; to sentence: ～案 *to decide a case* | ～处徒刑 *to sentence sb to imprisonment*

泮 pàn ㄆㄢˋ ❶融解,分散 to dissolve; to melt; to thaw ❷泮池,旧时学宫前的水池 pond in front of a government school in former times

叛 pàn ㄆㄢˋ 背叛,叛离 to betray; to revolt; to rebel: ～国分子 *traitor*

P

畔 pàn ㄆㄢˋ ❶田地的界限 border of a field ㊀ ***extension*** 边 *side; bank*: 河～ *river bank; riverside* | 篱～ *foot of a fence* ❷古同"叛"same as 叛 in ancient Chinese

袢 pàn ㄆㄢˋ 同"襻"same as 襻

拚 ㊀ pàn ㄆㄢˋ 舍弃，豁出去 to go all out in doing sth: ～命 *to go all out in total disregard of danger to one's life; to defy death*

㊁ pīn 见568页 see p568

盼 pàn ㄆㄢˋ ❶盼望，想望 to hope for; to expect; to long for ❷看 to look (㊥ ***doublet*** 顾— to look around): 左顾右～ *to look right and left; to look around*

鋬 pàn ㄆㄢˋ 〈古 ***archaism***〉器物上的提梁 (of a utensil) handle

襻 pàn ㄆㄢˋ ❶(—儿)扣襻，扣住纽扣的套 loop for fastening a button; buttonhole ❷(—儿)功用或形状像襻的东西 anything in the shape, or with the function, of a button loop: 鞋～儿 *shoe strap* ❸扣住，使分开的东西连在一起 to fasten (with a rope, string, etc); to tie: ～上几针(缝住) *to mend with a few stitches*

PANG ㄆㄤ

乓 pāng ㄆㄤ 拟声词 ***onomatopoeia***: ～的一声 *pop; bang; slap*

雱 pāng ㄆㄤ 雪下得很大(of a snowfall) thick; heavy

滂 pāng ㄆㄤ 水涌出的样子 (of water) overflowing; pouring; gushing [滂湃](—pài)水势盛大(of the momentum of water) great; torrential [滂沱](—tuó)雨下得很大(of rain) pouring; torrential: 大雨～～。*The rain falls in torrents.* or *It's raining cats and dogs.* ㊄ ***figurative*** 泪流得很多 gushing; running: 涕泗～～ *with tears flowing down one's checks; drenched with tears and snivel*

膀(**髈) ㊁ pāng ㄆㄤ 浮肿 swollen: 他肾脏有病，脸有点～。*His face is swollen because he has some kidney trouble.*

㊀ bǎng 见21页 see p21

㊂ páng 见552页 see p552

彷(**徬) ㊀ páng ㄆㄤˊ [彷徨](*旁皇)(—huáng)游移不定，不知道往哪里走好 to walk up and down; to hesitate; to vacillate

㊁ fǎng 见188页 see p188

庞(龐、**龎) páng ㄆㄤˊ ❶大(指形体或数量)(of size or number) huge; massive; mammoth: 数字～大 *innumerable* | ～然大物 *behemoth; huge monster; colossus* ❷杂乱 disorderly; jumbled (㊥ ***doublet*** —杂 numerous and disorderly; in a cumbersome jumble) ❸面庞，脸盘 face

P

逄 páng ㄆㄤˊ 姓 Pang, a surname

旁 páng ㄆㄤˊ ❶旁边,左右两侧 side:～观 *to look on; to be an onlooker*|～若无人 *to act as if there were no one else present — to be self-assured or overweening; to disregard the people around*|两～都是大楼。*There are tall buildings on both sides.* ❷其他,另外 else; other:～人 *someone else*|～的话 *other words*

〈古 ***archaism***〉又同"傍"(bàng) also same as 傍

膀 ㊂ páng ㄆㄤˊ [膀胱](—guāng)俗叫"尿脬"(suīpāo)。暂存尿液的囊状体,在骨盆腔的前方。(图见940页"脏" picture on p940)(popularly called 尿脬) bladder

㊀ bǎng 见21页 see p21

㊁ pāng 见551页 see p551

磅 ㊁ páng ㄆㄤˊ [磅礴](—bó) **1** 广大无边际 boundless; vast; tremendous:大气～～*of great momentum; full of power and grandeur* **2** 扩展,充满 to fill; to permeate:正义之气,～～宇内。*The force of justice permeates the entire world.*

㊀ bàng 见22页 see p22

螃 páng ㄆㄤˊ [螃蟹](—xiè) 见831页"蟹" see 蟹 on p831

鳑 páng ㄆㄤˊ [鳑鲏](—pí) 鱼名。形状像鲫鱼,体长不足10厘米,生活在淡水中,卵产在蚌壳里 bitterling (*Rhodeus sericeus*)

嗙 pǎng ㄆㄤˇ 〈方 ***dialect***〉夸大,吹牛,信口开河 to blow one's own trumpet; to brag; to boast:你别听他瞎～。*Don't believe his stories.*|他一向是好(hào)胡吹乱～的。*He always likes to shoot his mouth off.*

耪 pǎng ㄆㄤˇ 用锄翻松地,锄 to hoe:～地 *to hoe the soil*

胖(**胮) ㊀ pàng ㄆㄤˋ 人体内含脂肪多,跟"瘦"相对(the opposite of 瘦) fat; stout; plump:他长得很～。*He is quite fat.*

㊁ pán 见549页 see p549

PAO ㄆㄠ

抛(**拋) pāo ㄆㄠ ❶扔,投 to cast; to throw; to toss:～球 *to toss a ball* [抛锚]把锚投入水底,使船停稳(of ships) to drop anchor; to cast anchor; to anchor ㊔ ***transfer*** **1** 汽车等因发生故障,中途停止(of vehicles) to break down **2** 进行中的事情因故停止(of ongoing projects) to stop midway; to be suspended [抛售]为争夺市场牟取利润,压价出卖大批商品 to sell (good, shares, etc) in large quantities (usually in the anticipation of, or in order to bring about, a fall in price); to dump; to undersell ❷舍弃 to cast aside; to discard; to desert (㊎ ***doublet*** —弃 to cast aside;

to discard; to desert)

泡 ㊁ pāo ㄆㄠ ❶(一儿)鼓起而松软的东西 sth puffy and soft: 豆腐～儿 *beancurd puff* ❷虚而松软,不坚硬 spongy; porous: 这块木料发～。*This piece of wood is rather porous.* ❸同"脬❷"same as 脬❷

㊀ pào 见554页 see p554

脬 pāo ㄆㄠ ❶尿(suī)脬,膀胱(pángguāng) bladder ❷量词 ***quantifier***,用于屎尿(used for excrement or urine): 一～屎 *a turd*

刨 ㊀ páo ㄆㄠˊ ❶挖掘 to dig; to excavate; to unearth: ～花生 *to dig (up) peanuts*|～坑 *to dig a hole; to dig a pit* ❷减,除去 excluding; not counting; minus: ～去他还有俩人。*There are two people, not counting him.*|十五天～去五天,只剩下十天了。*Fifteen minus five — there are only ten days left.*

㊁ bào 见26页 see p26

咆 páo ㄆㄠˊ [咆哮](-xiào)猛兽怒吼(of animals) to roar; to howl; to bellow ㊗ ***figurative*** 江河奔腾轰鸣或人暴怒叫喊(of rivers) to roar on; to roar with fury; to bellow: 黄河在～～。*The Huanghe (or Yellow) River is rumbling on.*|～～如雷 *roaring with fury; in a thundering rage*

狍(**麅) páo ㄆㄠˊ (一子)鹿一类的动物,毛夏季栗红色,冬季棕褐色,雄的有分枝状的角 roe deer (*Capreolus capreolus*)

庖 páo ㄆㄠˊ 庖厨,厨房 kitchen: ～人(古代称厨师)(*an ancient term for* 厨师) *cook* [庖代][代庖]㊕ ***transfer*** 替人处理事情或代做别人的工作 to act in sb else's place; to do sb else's job

炮 ㊀ páo ㄆㄠˊ 烧 to set fire to; to burn [炮烙](-luò,旧读 formerly -gé)[炮格]古代的一种酷刑 hot-bronze pillar, an instrument of torture, for cruel punishment in ancient China [炮制]用烘、炒等方法把原料加工制成中药 to prepare herbal Chinese medicine by roasting, parching or stir-frying it in a pan: 如法～～(喻照样做) *to prepare herbal medicine by the prescribed method — to follow a set pattern; to follow suit*

㊁ bāo 见23页 see p23

㊂ pào 见554页 see p554

袍 páo ㄆㄠˊ (一子、一儿)长衣 robe; gown; housecoat: 棉～儿 *cotton-padded gown*|～笏登场(登台演戏,比喻上台做官) *to dress up and go onstage — to take office; to assume an official post*

匏 páo ㄆㄠˊ 匏瓜,俗叫"瓢葫芦"。葫芦的一种,果实比葫芦大,对半剖开可以做水瓢(popularly called 瓢葫芦) bottle gourd (*Lagenaria siceraria*)

P

跑 ㊁ páo ㄆㄠˊ 走兽用脚刨地(of animals) to dig the ground with paws or hoofs; to paw the ground: ～槽(牲口刨槽根)(*of animals*) *to dig a trough* | 虎～泉(在杭州) *Hupao Spring* (or *Tiger-Dug Spring*) (*in Hangzhou*)

㊀ pǎo 见554页 see p554

跑 ㊀ pǎo ㄆㄠˇ ❶奔,两只脚或四条腿交互向前跃进 to run; to race; to gallop: 赛～ *to race* | ～步 *to run; to jog; to march at the double* ㊞ ***extension*** 很快地移动 to move quickly: 汽车在公路上飞～。*The car is running at a high speed on the highway.* ❷逃跑,逃走 to run away; to escape; to flee: 鸟儿关在笼里～不了。*The caged bird can't flee.* ㊥ ***figurative*** 漏出 to leak: ～电 *electricity leakage* | ～油 *oil leakage* ❸为某种事务而奔走 to run about doing sth; to run errands: ～外的 *traveling agent; salesman of a firm* | ～买卖 *to travel around doing business; to go from place to place buying or selling goods; to work as a commercial traveler* | ～材料 *to go about buying raw materials*

㊁ páo 见554页 see p554

奅 pào ㄆㄠˋ 虚大 large; big; puffy

泡 ㊀ pào ㄆㄠˋ ❶(一儿)气体在液体内使液体鼓起来形成的球状或半球状体 bubble; effervescence; fizz (㊟ ***doublet*** 一沫 bubbles; foam; froth): 冒～儿 *to rise in bubbles; to bubble* ❷(一儿)像泡一样的东西 sth shaped like a bubble: 脚上起了一个～。*He developed* (or *got*) *a blister on his foot.* | 电灯～儿 *electric bulb* ❸用液体浸物品 to sop; to soap; to steep: ～茶 *to make* (or *brew*) *tea* | ～饭 *cooked-rice soaked usually in hot water*

㊁ pāo 见553页 see p553

炮(*砲、*礮) ㊂ pào ㄆㄠˋ ❶武器的一类,有迫击炮、高射炮、火箭炮等 mortar; cannon; artillery ❷爆竹 firecracker: 鞭～ (*string of*) *firecrackers* | ～仗(zhang) *firecracker*

㊀ páo 见553页 see p553

㊁ bāo 见23页 see p23

疱(*皰) pào ㄆㄠˋ 皮肤上长的像水泡的小疙瘩。也作"泡"(also written as 泡) blister; bleb

PEI ㄆㄟ

呸 pēi ㄆㄟ 叹词 ***interjection***,表示斥责或唾弃 pah; bah; pooh: ～! 胡说八道。*Pooh! That's nonsense.*

胚 pēi ㄆㄟ 初期发育的生物体 embryo [胚胎]初期发育的动物体 embryo ㊥ ***figurative*** 事情的开始 beginning (*or* rudimentary) stage

衃 pēi ㄆㄟ 凝聚的血 coagulated (*or* curdled) blood

醅 pēi ㄆㄟ 没过滤的酒 unfiltered liquor

陪 péi ㄆㄟˊ 随同，在旁边做伴 to keep sb company; to accompany; to escort (㊥ ***doublet*** 一伴 to keep sb company; to accompany; to escort)：～同 *to go with; to accompany* | 我～你去。*I'll go with you.* | ～客人 *to keep one's visitor company; to show one's guest around a place* [陪衬]从旁衬托 to serve as a contrast or foil; to set off

培 péi ㄆㄟˊ 为保护植物或墙堤等，在根基部分加土 to bank up (with earth); to earth up [培养] **1** 训练教育 to train; to foster; to groom：～～干部 *to groom cadres* **2** 使繁殖 to cultivate; to culture：～～真菌 *to culture fungus* [培育]培养幼小的生物，使它发育成长 to cultivate; to foster; to breed：～～树苗 *to breed* (or *cultivate*) *saplings*

赔 péi ㄆㄟˊ ❶补还损失 to compensate; to pay for; to refund (㊥ ***doublet*** 一偿 to compensate; to pay for; to refund)：～款 *to pay money as compensation; to pay an indemnity* | ～礼(道歉) *to make a formal apology* | 照价～偿 *to compensate according to the cost* ❷亏损 to stand or incur a loss; to lose：～钱 *to sustain losses in business; to compensate for the loss or damage of property* | ～本 *to sustain losses in business*

锫 péi ㄆㄟˊ 一种人造的放射性元素(符号 Bk) berkelium (Bk)

裴 péi ㄆㄟˊ 姓 Pei, a surname

沛 pèi ㄆㄟˋ 盛(shèng)，大 abundant; copious; exuberant：精力充～ *full of energy; vigorous*

旆 pèi ㄆㄟˋ 旗子上镶的边。泛指旌旗 decorative edge on a flag; banners and flags (in general)

霈 pèi ㄆㄟˋ ❶大雨 heavy rain ❷雨多的样子 (of rain) rainy; heavy; torrential

帔 pèi ㄆㄟˋ 古代披在肩背上的服饰 short embroidered cape worn over a woman's shoulder in ancient China：凤冠霞～ *phoenix coronet and colorful embroidered cape — official female dress in ancient China*

佩 (❸ ＊＊珮) pèi ㄆㄟˋ ❶佩带，挂 to wear; to bear; to carry：～带勋章 *to wear a medal on one's chest* | 腰间～着一支手枪 *with a pistol in one's belt* ❷佩服，心悦诚服 to admire; to esteem; to revere：可敬可～ *worthy of respect and admiration* | 劳动模范人人～服。*Model workers are universally admired.* ❸古代衣带上佩带的玉饰 jade ornament worn as a pendant at the waist in ancient China：环～

P

round pendant

配 pèi ㄆㄟˋ ❶两性结合 to join in marriage **1** 男女结婚 to join in wedlock; to match in marriage:婚～*marriage* **2** 使牲畜交合 to mate; to breed:～种 *breeding*｜～猪 *to mate pigs* [配偶]指夫或妻 spouse ❷用适当的标准加以调和 to mix; to blend; to mingle:～颜色 *to blend colours*｜～药 *to concoct a medicine from medicinal herbs; to make up a prescription; to prepare a prescription* ❸有计划地分派,安排 to distribute according to plan; to apportion; to assign:分～*to distribute; to assign*｜～备人力 *to provide manpower* ❹流放 to exile; to banish:发～*to be on exile; to banish* ❺把缺少的补足 to find sth to fit or replace sth else:～零件 *to replace parts*｜～把钥匙 *to have a key made to fit a lock; to have a duplicate key cut*｜～一块玻璃 *to replace a piece of glass* [配套]把若干相关的事物组合成一整套 to form a complete set or system (by putting related things together) ❻衬托,陪衬 to match; to set off; to foil:红花～绿叶 *red flowers set off by green leaves*｜～角(jué) *supporting role; minor role; minor role actor* ❼够得上 to deserve; to be worthy of; to qualify:他～称为先进工作者。*He deserves to be a model worker.*

辔(轡) pèi ㄆㄟˋ 驾驭牲口的嚼子和缰绳 bridle:鞍～*saddle and bridle* [辔头]辔 bridle

PEN ㄆㄣ

喷 ㊀ pēn ㄆㄣ 散着射出 to spurt; to spray; to sprinkle:～壶 *sprinkling can*｜～泉 *fountain*｜～气式飞机 *jet plane*｜火山～火。*The volcano is spewing fire.* [喷嚏](—tì)嚏喷(tìpen)。参看743页"嚏"(see 嚏 on p743) sneeze

㊁ pèn 见556页 see p556

盆 pén ㄆㄣˊ (—子、—儿)盛放或洗涤东西的用具,通常是圆形,口大,底小,不太深 basin; tub; pot:花～*flower pot*｜脸～*washbasin* [盆地]被山或高地围绕着的平地 basin:四川～～*Sichuan Basin*｜塔里木～～*Tarim Basin*

湓 pén ㄆㄣˊ 湓水,水名,在江西省西北部 Penshui River, in the northwest of Jiangxi Province

喷 ㊁ pèn ㄆㄣˋ ❶香气扑鼻 savory; fragrant; aromatic:～鼻儿香 *very appetizing; extremely fragrant*｜香～～ *delicious; fragrant* ❷(—儿)蔬菜、鱼虾、瓜果等上市正盛的时期(of vegetables, melons, fruit, fish, etc) in season:西瓜～儿 *watermelon season*｜对虾正在～儿上。*Prawns are in season.* ❸(—儿)开花结实的次数或成熟收割的次数 numbers of times of flowering, fruit bearing, or harvesting: 头～棉花 *first cotton crop* | 二～棉花 *second cotton crop* | 麦子开头～花儿了。*The wheat is in its first flowering.* | 绿豆结二～角了。*The mung beans are putting out the second round of pods of the year.*

㊀ pēn 见556页 see p556

PENG ㄆㄥ

抨 pēng ㄆㄥ 抨击,攻击对方的短处 to criticize; to censure; to impeach

怦 pēng ㄆㄥ 形容心跳(叠 ***reduplication***)(of heart) pounding; thumping

砰 pēng ㄆㄥ 拟声词 ***onomatopoeia***:～的一声,枪响了。*The rifle went off with a bang.*

烹 pēng ㄆㄥ ❶煮 to cook in water; to boil; to brew: ～调(tiáo) *to cook* ❷一种做菜的方法,用热油略炒之后,再加入液体调味品,迅速搅拌 to fry quickly in hot oil and stir in sauce: ～对虾 *quick-fried prawns*

嘭 pēng ㄆㄥ 拟声词 ***onomatopoeia***(叠 ***reduplication***) bang: ～～的敲门声 *thumps on the door*

澎 ㊁ pēng ㄆㄥ 〈方 ***dialect***〉溅 to splash; to spatter; to splatter: ～了一身水 *to have been splashed all over with water*

㊀ péng 见558页 see p558

芃 péng ㄆㄥˊ [芃芃]形容草木茂盛(of plants) luxuriant; lush

朋 péng ㄆㄥˊ 彼此友好的人 friend(㊇ ***doublet*** 一友 friend): 亲～好友 *relatives and friends; kith and kin* | 宾～满座 *to have a roomful of guests*

堋 péng ㄆㄥˊ 我国战国时代科学家李冰在修建都江堰时所创造的一种分水堤 watershed dyke

棚 péng ㄆㄥˊ (一子、一儿)❶把席、布等搭架支张起来遮蔽风雨或日光的东西 canopy, awning, or shelter of reed mats, etc.: 天～ *overhead canopy* | 凉～ *mat awning; mat shelter* ❷简易的或临时性的建筑物 shed; shack; makeshift shelter: 牲口～ *livestock shed; stock barn* | 工～ *work shed* | 防震～ *temporary shelter for earthquake victims*

硼 péng ㄆㄥˊ 一种非金属元素,符号B,有结晶与非结晶两种形态。结晶硼是有光泽的灰色晶体,很坚硬;非结晶硼是暗棕色的粉末。用于制合金钢,也可用作原子反应堆的材料。硼酸可以做消毒防腐剂;硼砂是制造珐琅、玻璃等的原料 boron (B)

鹏 péng ㄆㄥˊ 传说中最大的鸟 legendary bird of the largest size; roc [鹏程]㊉ ***figurative*** 远大的前途 promising future; brilliant prospects

鬅 péng ㄆㄥˊ 头发松散(of hair) fluffy

彭 péng ㄆㄥˊ 姓 Peng, a surname

澎 ㊀ péng ㄆㄥˊ ［澎湃］(— pài)大浪相激 to surge; to billow

［澎湖］(— hú)我国岛屿,在台湾海峡东南部,与其附近岛屿共有 64 个,总称“澎湖群岛”(generally called 澎湖群岛) Penghu Islands

㊁ pēng 见557页 see p557

膨 péng ㄆㄥˊ 胀大 to expand; to swell; to inflate

［膨脝］(— hēng)肚子胀的样子 potbellied ［膨胀］(— zhàng)物体的体积或长度增加 to expand; to swell; to dilate: 空气遇热～～。*Air expands when heated*. ㊞ ***extension*** 数量增加 to inflate; to expand; to swell: 通货～～*inflation* (*of the currency*)

蟛 péng ㄆㄥˊ ［蟛蜞］(— qí)螃蟹的一种,身体小,生长在水边,对农作物有害 amphibious crab; brackish-water crab (*Brachyura*)

搒 ㊀ péng ㄆㄥˊ 用棍子或竹板子打 to flog with wood or bamboo stick

㊀ bàng 见22页 see p22

蓬 péng ㄆㄥˊ ❶飞蓬,多年生草本植物,开白花,叶子像柳叶,子实有毛 bitter fleabane (*Erigeron acer*) ❷散乱(叠 ***reduplication***) fluffy; dishevelled; shock-headed: ～头散发 *with dishevelled hair* | 乱～～的茅草 *fluffy weeds* ［蓬松］松散(指毛发或茅草)(of hair or grass) fluffy; puffy

［蓬勃］(— bó)旺盛 vigorous; flourish; thriving: ～～发展 *to develop vigorously; to grow vigorously* | 朝气～～ *full of vigour and vitality; full of youthful vitality*

篷 péng ㄆㄥˊ ❶张盖在上面,遮蔽日光、风、雨的东西,用竹篾、苇席、布等做成 awning; covering: 船～ *awning of a boat* ❷船帆 sail: 扯起～来 *to raise the sails; to hoist the sails*

捧 pěng ㄆㄥˇ ❶两手托着 to hold (*or* carry) in both hands: ～着一个坛子 *to hold a jar in both hands* ［捧腹］捧着肚子,形容大笑 to split (*or* burst) one's sides with laughter; to shake with laughter: 令人～～ *to set people roaring with laughter; to make people burst out laughing* ❷奉承或代人吹嘘 to flatter; to compliment; to praise: 用好话～他 *to flatter him* | ～场(chǎng) *to be a member of a claque* (*for an actor or actress*); *to give patronage to; to support an activity by being present* ❸量词 ***quantifier***, 用于两手能捧起的东西(used for what can be held in both hands): 一～花生 *a double handful of ground nuts* (*or peanuts*)

碰(*掽) pèng ㄆㄥˋ ❶撞击 to touch; to knock; to bump: ～杯(表示祝贺) *to*

clink glasses (*in a toast*) | ～破了皮。*His skin was bruised.* | ～钉子 *to meet with a rebuff; to run into snags; to suffer setbacks* | ～壁(喻事情做不通) *to bump against the wall — to meet with refusal; to be rebuffed; to suffer setbacks* ❷相遇 to meet; to come across; to run into:我在半路上～见他。*I met him mid-way upon the road.* ❸没有把握地试探 to have a try; to try one's luck; to take a chance:～一～机会 *to take a chance; to take a gamble*

PI ㄆ丨

丕 pī ㄆ丨 大 big; great; tremendous:～业 *great cause* | ～变 *great* (or *immense*) *change*

伾 pī ㄆ丨 [伾伾]有力的样子 strong; energetic; muscular

邳 pī ㄆ丨 [邳州]地名,在江苏省 Pizhou, a place in Jiangsu Province

坯 pī ㄆ丨 ❶没有烧过的砖瓦、陶器等。特指砌墙用的土坯 bricks, pieces of pottery, or cloisonne, etc, already in desired shapes but not yet fired in the kiln; adobe:打～ *to make an adobe* | 脱～ *to mould adobe blocks* | 土～墙 *adobe wall* ❷(一子、一儿)半制成品 semi-finished product:酱～子 *fermented soya paste before seasonings are added* | 面～儿 *cooked noodles without seasonings*

狉 pī ㄆ丨 [狉狉]野兽蠢动的样子(of beasts) roaming about:鹿豕～～。*Deer and boars are roaming in herds.*

批 pī ㄆ丨 ❶用手掌打 to slap ❷写上字句,判定是非、优劣、可否 to write instructions or comments (on a report from a subordinate):～示 *to write instructions or comments to show approval or disapproval* (*on a memo submitted by a subordinate*) | ～准 *to approve; to ratify; to sanction* | ～驳 *to criticize; to refute; to rebut* | ～改作文 *to correct compositions* ❸(一儿)附注的意见或注意之点 comments or instructions (of documents, etc):眉～(写在书头上的批) *notes and comments at the top of a page; notes and comments in the top margin* | 在文后加了一条小～儿 *to put a brief note at the end of an article* ❹批评,批判 to criticize; to refute:挨了一通～ *to have experienced a severe criticism* ❺量词 ***quantifier***:一～货 *a batch of goods* | 一～人 *a group of people* [批发]大宗发售货物 wholesale

纰 pī ㄆ丨 布帛、丝缕等破坏散开(of cloth, thread, etc) unravelled; unwoven; untwisted [纰漏]因疏忽而引起的错误 careless mistake; small error; slip [纰缪](一miù)错误 mistake; error

砒 pī ㄆ丨 ❶"砷"(shēn)的旧称 former name for 砷 ❷

砒霜，砷的氧化物，剧毒，可做杀虫剂 arsenic; arsenic trioxide

铍 pī ㄆㄧ 铍箭，古代箭的一种 (in ancient China) arrow

披 pī ㄆㄧ ❶覆盖在肩背上 to drape over one's shoulder; to wrap around one's shoulder: ～红 *to drape a band of red silk across one's shoulder (on a festive occasion as a mark of honour for meritorious services)* | ～着大衣 *to have an overcoat wrapped around one's shoulders; to drape an overcoat over one's shoulders* | ～星戴月(喻晚上赶路或劳动) *to go to work before dawn and come home when the moon is up — to work from before dawn till after dark; to travel or work outdoors by night* ❷打开 to open; to spread out; to unroll: ～襟 *to loosen one's jacket* | ～卷(juàn) *to open a book; to leaf through books* | ～肝沥胆(喻竭诚效忠) *to bare one's heart — to be loyal and faithful* [披露](—lù)发表 to publish [披靡](—mǐ)草木随风散倒(of trees and grass, etc) can't stand the force of wind; to be swept and bent down by the wind ⓨ ***figurative*** 敌军溃散(of the enemy) to be defeated and dispersed; to flee: 所向～～*to carry all before one; to sweep away all obstacles; to be invincible* ❸裂开 to split; to crack: 竹竿～了。*The bamboo stick has split.* | 指甲～了。*The fingernail cracked.* ❹劈开，劈去 to cleave; to hew: ～荆斩棘(喻开创事业的艰难) *to break through brambles and thorns — to hew one's way through difficulties*

劈 ㊀ pī ㄆㄧ ❶用刀斧等破开 to chop; to split; to cleave: ～木头 *to chop wood* ❷冲着，正对着 right against (one's face, etc): ～脸 *right against the face; right in the face* | 大雨～头浇下来。*The heavy rain poured down over our heads.* ❸雷电毁坏或击毙(of thunder) to strike: 大树让雷～了。*The big tree was struck by lightning.* ❹尖劈，物理学上两斜面合成的助力器械，刀、斧等都属于这一类 wedge

[劈啪]拟声词 ***onomatopoeia***, sound of crackling, clapping, etc

㊁ pǐ 见563页 see p563

噼 pī ㄆㄧ [噼啪]同"劈啪" same as 劈啪

霹 pī ㄆㄧ [霹雳](—lì)响声很大的雷，是云和地面之间强烈的雷电现象 thunderbolt; thunderclap

皮 pí ㄆㄧˊ ❶人和动植物体表面的一层组织 surface tissue of humans and organisms; skin: 牛～*cowhide* | 树～*bark* | 荞麦～*buckwheat husk* | 碰破了点儿～*to scrape off a bit of skin* ❷皮革 leather; hide: ～包 *leather handbag* | ～箱 *leather case* | ～鞋 *leather shoes* ❸表面 surface: 地～*earth's surface* |

P

水～儿 *surface of water* ❹包在外面的东西 cover; wrapper: 书～ *book cover* | 封～ *paper wrapping* ❺薄片状的东西(of some thin material) broad flat piece; sheet: 铅～*lead sheet* | 粉～*sheet jelly made from starch* | 海蜇～*jellyfish skin* ❻韧性大,不松脆 pliable; sticky; soft and soggy: ～糖 *chewy sticky candy made of sugar and starch* | 饼～了。*The cake has become soggy.* ❼顽皮,不老实,淘气 naughty; mischievous: 这孩子真～。*What a naughty boy!* ❽(外 **loanword**)法定计量单位中十进分数单位词头之一,表示 10^{-12}(符号 p) pico-(p)

陂 ㊁ pí ㄆㄧˊ [黄陂]地名,在湖北省武汉 Huangpi, a place in Wuhan, Hubei Province

㊀ bēi 见27页 see p27

㊂ pō 见573页 see p573

铍 pí ㄆㄧˊ 一种金属元素,符号 Be,钢灰色。合金质坚而轻,可用来制飞机机件。在原子能研究及制造 X 射线管中,都有重要用途 beryllium (Be)

疲 pí ㄆㄧˊ 身体感觉劳累 tired; weary; exhausted(㊣ ***doublet*** 一乏 tired; weary; exhausted | 一倦 tired and sleepy): 精～力尽 *completely exhausted; tired out* | ～于奔命 *to be kept constantly on the run* [疲癃](一lóng)衰老多病 old and infirm; aged and ailing [疲沓](*疲塌)(一ta)懈怠,不起劲 slack; negligent; sluggish: 消除工作中的～～现象 *to eliminate slackness at work*

鲏 pí ㄆㄧˊ 见552页"鳑"字条"鳑鲏"(páng一) see 鳑鲏 on p552

枇 pí ㄆㄧˊ [枇杷](一pa)常绿乔木,叶大,长椭圆形,有锯齿,开白花。果实也叫枇杷,圆球形,黄色,味甜。叶可入药 (also used to denote its fruit) loquat (*Eriobotrya japonica*)

毗(*毘) pí ㄆㄧˊ ❶辅佐 to assist; to aid ❷接连 to border on; to be adjacent to; to adjoin: ～连 *to border on; to be adjacent to; to adjoin* | ～邻 *to border on; to be adjacent to; to adjoin*

蚍 pí ㄆㄧˊ [蚍蜉](一fú)大蚂蚁 large ant

琵 pí ㄆㄧˊ [琵琶](一pa)弦乐器,用木做成,下部长圆形,上有长柄,有四根弦。是民间流行的乐器 *pipa*, a plucked string instrument with a fretted finger board

貔 pí ㄆㄧˊ 传说中的一种野兽,似熊 legendary bear-like wild animal [貔貅](一xiū)传说中的一种猛兽 *pixiu*, a legendary fierce animal ㊑ ***figurative*** 勇猛的军队 brave troops

郫 pí ㄆㄧˊ 郫县,地名,在四川省 Pixian County, a place in Sichuan Province

陴 pí ㄆㄧˊ 城墙上呈ꟷ⊓⊓形的矮墙 parapet wall; parapet

P

埤 pí ㄆㄧˊ 增加 to increase; to augment: ～益 *to increase greatly*

啤 pí ㄆㄧˊ [啤酒]用大麦作主要原料制成的酒 beer

脾 pí ㄆㄧˊ 脾脏,人和高等动物的内脏之一,人的脾在胃的左下侧,椭圆形,赤褐色,是个淋巴器官,也是血库。(图见940页“脏” picture on p940) spleen [脾气](—qi) **1** 性情 temperament; disposition; temper: ～～好 *good-tempered* **2** 容易激动的感情 bad temper; irritable disposition: 有～～ *to have a bad temper; to have an irritable nature* | 发～～ *to lose one's temper; to fly into a rage; to flare up* [脾胃] [喻] ***figurative*** 对事物的喜好 taste; temperament; inclination: 不合他的～～ *not to fit his temperament; to go against his propensity; not to suit his taste* | 两人～～相投。*They have similar likes and dislikes.* or *They appreciate the same thing.*

P

裨 ㊀ pí ㄆㄧˊ 副,辅佐的 assistant; secondary; subordinate ([连] ***doublet*** 偏— assistant; adjutant): ～将(*in ancient China*) *adjutant general*

㊁ bì 见39页 see p39

蜱 pí ㄆㄧˊ 蜘蛛一类的动物,体形扁平,种类很多,大部分以吸血为生,对人、畜及农作物有害 tick (*Ixodoidea*)

鼙 pí ㄆㄧˊ 古代军中用的一种鼓 small drum used in the army in ancient China: ～鼓(古代军队中用的小鼓) *war drum; battle drum*

罴(羆) pí ㄆㄧˊ 熊的一种,毛棕褐色,能爬树、游水。也叫“马熊”或“人熊”(also called 马熊 or 人熊) brown bear (*Ursus arctos*)

匹(❶*疋) pǐ ㄆㄧˇ ❶ 量词 ***quantifier*** **1** 用于骡、马等 (used for mules, horses, etc): 三～马 *three horses* **2** 用于整卷的布或绸缎等 (used for rolls of cloth or silk): 一～红布 *a bolt of red cloth* ❷ 相当,相敌,比得上 to be equal to; to be a match for; to rival [匹敌]彼此相等 to be well matched; to be equal to each other [匹配] **1** 婚配 to mate; to marry **2** (元器件等)配合 (of components, parts, etc) matching

苉 pǐ ㄆㄧˇ 一种有机化合物,分子式 $C_{22}H_{14}$,存在于煤焦油中 picene

庀 pǐ ㄆㄧˇ ❶ 具备 to possess; to be provided with ❷ 治理 to administer; to control

圮 pǐ ㄆㄧˇ 坍塌,倒塌 to collapse; to fall apart; to be in ruin

仳 pǐ ㄆㄧˇ [仳离]夫妻离散 (of husband and wife, especially for a husband to forsake his wife) to separate from each other; to part from each other; to divorce one's spouse

否 ⊜ pǐ ㄆㄧˇ ❶恶，坏 bad; evil：～极泰来(坏的到了尽头，好的就来了。否和泰都是《周易》六十四卦中的卦名，分别代表坏和好的事情) *When misfortune reaches its limit, good fortune is at hand.* or *Out of the depth of misfortune comes bliss.* or *Extreme adversity marks the beginning of fortune.* ❷贬斥 to censure; to condemn; to denounce：臧～人物(评论人物的优劣) *to pass judgement on a person; to make comments on the merits and demerits of a person; to remark on sb's strong and weak points*

⊖ fǒu 见200页 see p200

痞 pǐ ㄆㄧˇ ❶痞块，痞积，中医指肚子里可以摸得到的硬块 lump in the abdomen ❷流氓，无赖 scoundrel; hooligan; ruffian：地～*local ruffian*｜～棍 *ruffian; riffraff*

嚭(**噽) pǐ ㄆㄧˇ 大 big; large; huge

劈 ⊜ pǐ ㄆㄧˇ 分开 to cut; to chop; to split：～柴 *to chop firewood*｜～成两份儿 *to cut sth into two portions; to divide sth into halves*｜～一半给你 *to cut it and give you a half*

⊖ pī 见560页 see p560

擗 pǐ ㄆㄧˇ 分裂，使从原物体上分开 to break off：～棒子(玉米) *to break off ears of corn*

癖 pǐ ㄆㄧˇ 对事物的偏爱成为习惯 addiction; partiality; propensity：烟～*cigarette addiction*｜酒～*alcoholism; bibulosity*｜洁～*cleanliness; mysophobia*｜怪～*peculiarity; mannerism; foible*

屁 pì ㄆㄧˋ 从肛门排出的臭气 wind (from bowels); fart

媲 pì ㄆㄧˋ 并，比 to be equal to; to compare with：～美 *to compare favourably with; to match; to rival*

淠 pì ㄆㄧˋ 淠河，水名，在安徽省西部 Pihe River, in the west of Anhui Province

睥 pì ㄆㄧˋ bì ㄅㄧˋ (又 **also** bì) [睥睨](-nì)眼睛斜着看 to look at sb or sth out of the corner of one's eyes; to look sideways; to look askance ㊀ ***extension*** 看不起 to look disdainfully; to look scornfully：～～一切 *to consider everything beneath one's notice; to treat everything with disdain; to look superciliously at the whole world*

辟(❶❷❸闢) ⊜ pì ㄆㄧˋ ❶开辟，从无到有地开发建设 to open up (territory, land etc); to break (ground)：开天～地 *heaven was separated from earth — the beginning of creation of the world; genesis of history; dawn of history*｜在那里开～一片新园地 *to open up a new garden plot there* ❷驳斥，排除 to refute; to counter; to repudiate：～谣 *to refute a rumour*｜～邪说 *to refute heresies* ❸透

P

彻 penetrating; incisive: 精～ *profound* ❹法,法律 law [大辟]古代指死刑 capital punishment in ancient China

㊁ bì 见40页 see p40

僻 pì ㄆㄧˋ ❶偏僻,距离中心地区远的 out-of-the-way; secluded; isolated: ～静 *secluded; lonely; out-of-the-way* | 穷乡～壤 *poor and remote country; remote, backward place; remote hinterland* ❷不常见的 rare; uncommon: 冷～ *desolate; unfamiliar* | 生～字 *rare word* ❸性情古怪,不合群 eccentric; odd(㊀ **doublet** 乖一 eccentric; odd): 孤～ *unsociable and eccentric; unsociable and whimsical* | 怪～ *eccentric; peculiar; odd*

澼 pì ㄆㄧˋ 见572页"洴"字条"洴澼"(píng—) see 洴澼 on p572

甓 pì ㄆㄧˋ 砖 brick

䴙 pì ㄆㄧˋ [䴙䴘](—tī) 水鸟名。形状略像鸭而小,羽毛黄褐色 grebe (*Podicipedidae*)

譬 pì ㄆㄧˋ 打比方 to make an analogy; to give an example (*or* instance)(㊀ **doublet** 一喻 metaphor; simile; analogy): ～如游泳,不是光看看讲游泳术的书就会的。*Take swimming for example, one can't learn how to swim only by reading books on swimming.*

PIAN ㄆㄧㄢ

片 ㊁ piān ㄆㄧㄢ (一子、一儿) 同"片㊀❶",用于"相片儿、画片儿、唱片儿、电影片儿"等 same as 片㊀❶ and used in 相片儿, 画片儿, 唱片儿, 电影片儿, etc

㊀ piàn 见566页 see p566

扁 ㊁ piān ㄆㄧㄢ [扁舟]小船 small boat; skiff: 一叶～～ *a small boat*

㊀ biǎn 见43页 see p43

偏 piān ㄆㄧㄢ ❶歪,不在中间 inclined to one side; slanting; askew: 镜子挂～了。*The mirror is hanging askew.* | 太阳～西了。*The sun slanted to the west.* ㊂ **extension** 不全面,不正确 partial; prejudiced: ～于一端 *to be partial to one side; to favour one side* | ～听～信 *to heed and trust only one side; to listen only to one side* [偏差](—chā)工作上产生的过分或不及的差错 error; deviation; aberration: 掌握政策不出～～ *no aberration in policy-implementing* [偏向] **1** 不公正,袒护 to be partial to; to give unprincipled support or protection to; to show preference to **2** 执行政策不正确,不全面 erroneous tendency in policy-implementation; aberration; deviation: 纠正～～ *to correct a deviation* ❷副词 **adverb**,表示跟愿望、预料或一般情况不相同(叠 **reduplication**) showing perversity,

P

stubbornness, or ill luck:不让他干,他～干。*He simply would do it though he was not allowed.* |～～不凑巧 *as ill luck would have it; unfortunately; unexpectedly*

犏 piān ㄆㄧㄢ 犏牛,牦牛和黄牛杂交生的牛 dzo

篇 piān ㄆㄧㄢ ❶首尾完整的文章,一部书可以分开的大段落 article; essay; piece of writing:《孙子》十三～ *Sunzi's thirteen chapters on The Art of War* ❷(一儿)量词 ***quantifier*** **1** 用于文章(used for an article):一～论文 *a thesis* **2** 用于纸张、书页(一篇是两页)(used for paper, book leaves, etc, usually in two pages) sheet; leaf; piece [篇幅]文章的长短,书籍报刊篇页的数量(of a piece of writing) length; (of books, newspapers, magazines, etc) number of pages an article takes up

翩 piān ㄆㄧㄢ 很快地飞 to fly swiftly [翩翩]轻快地飞舞的样子 to dance (*or* flutter) lightly ㊍ ***figurative*** 风流潇洒 graceful; elegant; genteel:风度～～*to have an elegant manner; to behave with grace and ease*

[翩跹](—xiān)形容轻快地跳舞(to dance) lightly; trippingly

便 ㊁ pián ㄆㄧㄢˊ [便便]肚子肥大的样子 bulging; swelling; exceedingly paunchy:大腹～～ *potbellied; paunchy*

[便宜](—yi)物价较低 inexpensive; at a bargain price:这些花布都很～～。*The cotton prints are very cheap.* ㊊ ***extension*** 小利,私利 undeserved gain; unearned gain; petty advantage:不要占～～。*Don't try to gain extra advantage by unfair means.*(另 biànyí 见44页"便"biàn see also 便 biàn for biànyí on p44)

㊀ biàn 见44页 see p44

骈 pián ㄆㄧㄢˊ 两物并列成双的,对偶的 parallel; antithetical (㊟ ***doublet*** —俪 art of parallelism; ornate style of writing consisting of antithetical or parallel construction of Chinese characters):～句 *parallel sentences* [骈文]旧时的一种文体,文中用对偶的句子,讲究声韵和谐,词藻华丽(in former times) parallel prose; rhythmical prose characterized by parallelism and ornate language

胼 pián ㄆㄧㄢˊ [胼胝](—zhī)俗叫"膙(jiǎng)子"。手上、脚上因为劳动或运动被摩擦变硬了的皮肤(popularly called 膙子) callosity; callus; tylosis

蹁 pián ㄆㄧㄢˊ [蹁跹](—xiān)形容旋转舞动 whirling about (in dancing); twirling

谝 piǎn ㄆㄧㄢˇ 显示,夸耀 to show off:～能 *to show off one's abilities, skills, etc*

P

片 ㊀ piàn ㄆㄧㄢˋ ❶（一子、一儿）平而薄的物体 flat, thin piece; slice; flake: 明信～ *postcard* | 铁～子 *iron sheet* ❷切削成薄片 to cut into slices; to slice; to pare: ～肉片 *to slice meat* | 把豆腐干～一～ *to slice bean curds* ❸少，零星 a few; fragmentary: ～言（几句话）*brief words; a few words* | ～纸只字 *a short piece of writing; brief note; fragments of writing* | ～刻（短时间）*a short while; an instant; a moment* [片面]不全面，偏于一面的 incomplete; partial; one-sided: 观点～～ *biased view; lopsided view; one-sided view* | 不要～～看问题。*Don't take one-sided views on matters.* ❹指较大地区内划分的较小地区 section of a place; sub-area: 分～儿开会 *to hold district meetings* ❺量词 ***quantifier***，用于地面、水面、景色或成片的东西等 (used for land, water, scenery, or other things in the form of flat, thin piece): 一大～绿油油的庄稼 *a vast stretch of green crops* | 一～汪洋 *a wide expanse of ocean* | 两～儿药 *two tablets* | 一～好心 *with the best of intentions*

㊁ piān 见564页 see p564

骗 piàn ㄆㄧㄢˋ ❶欺蒙 to deceive; to cheat; to dupe（㊣ ***doublet*** 欺— to deceive; to cheat; to dupe）: ～人 *to deceive sb; to practice a deceit (or fraud) on sb* ❷用欺蒙的手段谋得 to get sth by fraud; to cheat (*or* swindle) sb of sth（㊣ ***doublet*** 诓— to deceive; to cheat; to hoax）: ～钱 *to get money by fraud; to defraud sb of his money; to swindle sb of his money* | ～取信任 *to gain sb's trust by fraudulent means* [骗子]（—zi）骗取财物的人 deceiver; fraud; swindler ❸侧身抬腿跨上 to swing onto; to jump onto: 一～腿上了车 *to swing onto the bicycle*

PIAO ㄆㄧㄠ

剽（❷ **慓）piāo ㄆㄧㄠ ❶抢劫，掠夺 to rob; to loot; to plunder（㊣ ***doublet*** —掠 to loot; to plunder）[剽窃]抄袭他人著作 to plagiarize; to lift; to crib ❷轻快而敏捷 nimble; swift: ～悍 *intrepid; quick and fierce*

漂 ㊀ piāo ㄆㄧㄠ 浮在液体上面不沉下去 to float; to drift: 树叶在水上～着。*Leaves are floating on the water.* [漂泊]（—bó）㊗ ***figurative*** 为了生活、职业而流浪奔走 to lead a wandering life; to drift aimlessly: ～～在外 *to wander away from home for a living*

㊁ piǎo 见567页 see p567

㊂ piào 见568页 see p568

缥 ㊀ piāo ㄆㄧㄠ [缥缈][飘渺]（—miǎo）形容隐隐约约，若有若无 dimly discernible; misty; elusive: 山在虚无～～间。*The mountain is dimly*

P

discernible.

㊁ piǎo 见567页 see p567

飘(飃、*飄) piāo ㄆㄧㄠ 随风飞动 to float in the air; to flutter; to waft:～雪花。*Snowflakes are falling.*|～起了炊烟。*Chimney smoke is rising.*|五星红旗迎风～扬。*The Five-star Red Flag is fluttering in the breege.*[飘零]花、树叶等坠落(of flowers, leaves, etc) to fade and fall; to whirl and scatter ㊎ ***figurative*** 无依无靠 to lead a wandering life; to drift alone; forsaken [飘摇](*飘飖)(—yáo)随风摆动 to sway; to toss in the wind:烟云～～上升。*Smoke and clouds are drifting up in the wind.*

薸 piāo ㄆㄧㄠ (又 ***also*** piáo) 见567页 piáo see piáo on p567

螵 piāo ㄆㄧㄠ [螵蛸](—xiāo)螳螂的卵块 egg capsule of a mantis

朴 ㊃ piáo ㄆㄧㄠˊ 姓 Piao, a surname

㊀ pò 见574页 see p574

㊁ pǔ 见577页 see p577

㊂ pō 见572页 see p572

嫖(**闞) piáo ㄆㄧㄠˊ 指玩弄妓女的堕落行为 to visit prostitutes; to go whoring; to wench

瓢 piáo ㄆㄧㄠˊ (—儿)舀(yǎo)水或取东西的用具,多用瓢葫芦或木头制成 gourd ladle; wooden dipper

薸 piáo ㄆㄧㄠˊ piāo ㄆㄧㄠ (又 ***also*** piāo)[大薸]多年生水草,叶子可以做猪饲料。也叫"水浮莲"(also called 水浮莲) duckweed (*Lemnoideae*)

莩 ㊁ piǎo ㄆㄧㄠˇ 同"殍" same as 殍

㊀ fú 见203页 see p203

殍 piǎo ㄆㄧㄠˇ 饿死的人。也作"莩"(also written as 莩) bodies of those who died from starvation

漂 ㊁ piǎo ㄆㄧㄠˇ ❶用水加药品使东西退去颜色或变白 to bleach:～白 *to bleach* ❷用水淘去杂质 to rinse:用水～一～*to rinse in water*|～朱砂 *to rinse cinnabar*

㊀ piāo 见566页 see p566

㊂ piào 见568页 see p568

缥 ㊀ piǎo ㄆㄧㄠˇ ❶青白色 light blue ❷青白色丝织品 light-blue silk fabric

㊁ piāo 见566页 see p566

瞟 piǎo ㄆㄧㄠˇ 斜着眼看一下 to look sidelong (*or* askance) at; to glance sideways at:～了他一眼 *to give him a sidelong glance*

票 piào ㄆㄧㄠˋ ❶(—子、—儿)钞票,纸币 bank note; bill; paper money ❷印的或写的凭证 printed slip as a certificate; ticket:车～*bus* (or *train*) *ticket*|股～*stock; share*|选～*vote; ballot* ❸称非职业的演戏 amateur performance:～友 *amateur performer*|玩儿～*to play a role in a performance as an amateur; to act* (or *perform*)

as a sideline ❹强盗抢来作抵押的人 person held for ransom by kidnappers; hostage: 绑～儿 *to kidnap* (*for ransom*)

嘌 piào ㄆㄧㄠˋ [嘌呤](—lìng) 有机化合物,分子式 $C_5H_4N_4$,无色结晶,易溶于水,在人体内嘌呤氧化而变成尿酸 purine

漂 ㊂ piào ㄆㄧㄠˋ [漂亮](—liang) 1 美,好看 handsome; beautiful; good-looking 2 出色 remarkable; brilliant; beautiful: 活儿干得很～～*well-done; to have done a beautiful* (or *good*) *job*

㊀ piāo 见566页 see p566

㊁ piǎo 见567页 see p567

骠 ㊀ piào ㄆㄧㄠˋ ❶勇猛 brave; valiant; intrepid: ～勇 *brave; gallant; valiant* ❷马快跑的样子(of horses) galloping [骠骑]古代将军的名号 title of a high-ranking general of cavalry in ancient China: ～～将军 *cavalry general*

㊁ biāo 见46页 see p46

P

PIE ㄆㄧㄝ

氕 piē ㄆㄧㄝ 氢的同位素之一,符号¹H,质量数 1,是氢的主要成分 protium(1H)

撇 ㊀ piē ㄆㄧㄝ ❶丢开,抛弃 to put aside; to cast aside; to discard: ～开 *to put aside; to leave aside; to bypass* | ～弃 *to give up; to abandon; to discard* [撇脱]〈方 **dialect**〉 1 简便 simple and plain; easy; convenient 2 爽快,洒脱 frank; candid; straightforward ❷由液体表面舀取 to skim (off): ～油 *to skim off fat*

㊁ piě 见568页 see p568

瞥 piē ㄆㄧㄝ 很快地大略看一下 to shoot a glance at; to catch a glimpse of; to dart a look at: 只是～了一眼 *just to dart a look at sth; just to cast a glimpse of sth*

苤 piě ㄆㄧㄝˇ [苤蓝](—lan)二年生草本植物,叶有长柄。茎扁球形,可吃 kohlrabi (*Brassica oleracea*)

撇 ㊁ piě ㄆㄧㄝˇ ❶平着向前扔 to throw; to fling; to cast: ～砖头 *to cast bricks* | ～球 *to throw a ball* ❷(—儿)汉字向左写的一种笔形(丿)left-falling stroke in a Chinese character: 八字先写一～儿。*Write a left-falling stroke first when writing the Chinese character* 八 ❸(—儿)像汉字的撇形的(of things) resembling the left-falling stroke: 两～儿胡子 *two strokes of a mustache; mustache resembling the Chinese character* 八

㊀ piē 见568页 see p568

镲 piě ㄆㄧㄝˇ [曹镲]地名,在江苏省东台 Caopie, a place in Dongtai, Jiangsu Province

PIN ㄆㄧㄣ

拚 ㊁ pīn ㄆㄧㄣ 同"拼" same as 拼

㊁ pàn 见551页 see p551

拼 pīn ㄆㄧㄣ ❶连合，凑合 to piece together; to put together; to join together (㊟ *doublet* 一凑 to put together; to piece together; to knock together): ～音 *to combine sounds into syllables; to phoneticize* | 东～西凑 *to knock together; to scrape together; to pinch and scrape* | 把两块板子～起来 *to join the two wooden boards together* ❷不顾一切地干，豁(huō)出去 to risk all (in doing sth); to exert one's utmost in work; to fight tooth and nail: ～命 *to do sth desperately* | ～到底 *to fight to the finish*

姘 pīn ㄆㄧㄣ 非夫妻而同居 to cohabit: ～夫 *illicit male lover of a woman*

玭 pín ㄆㄧㄣˊ 珍珠 pearl

贫 pín ㄆㄧㄣˊ ❶穷，收入少，生活困难，跟"富"相对(the opposite of 富) poor; needy; impoverished (㊟ *doublet* 一穷 poor; needy; impoverished): ～困 *poor; impoverished; destitute* | 清～(*usually of scholars in ancient China*) *to be poor; to be impoverished* ❷缺乏，不足 inadequate; deficient; poor: ～血 *anaemia* [贫乏]少，不丰富 deficient; scanty; poor: 经验～～ *to lack experience; to be deficient in experience* ❸絮烦可厌 garrulous; loquacious; talkative: 他的嘴太～。*He is too garrulous.*

频 pín ㄆㄧㄣˊ 屡次，连次 frequently; repeatedly (㊟ *doublet* 一繁 frequent; repeated | 一数 shuò frequent and successive) (叠 *reduplication*): ～～招手 *to wave one's hand repeatedly* | 捷报～传 *News of victory keeps pouring in.* [频率](一lǜ)在一定的时间或范围内事物重复出现的次数 frequency

蘋(蘋) pín ㄆㄧㄣˊ 多年生水生蕨类植物，茎横卧在浅水的泥中，四片小叶，像"田"字。也叫"田字草"(also called 田字草) four-leaf clover (*Marsilea quadrifolia*)

"蘋"又 píng 见571页"苹" (also pronounced píng) see 苹 on p571

颦 pín ㄆㄧㄣˊ 皱眉头 to frown; to knit one's brows [效颦]㊕ *transfer* 模仿他人而不得当 to imitate only to produce a ludicrous effect; to copy blindly; to play the ape

嫔(嬪) pín ㄆㄧㄣˊ 封建时代皇宫里的女官 woman attendant at court

品 pǐn ㄆㄧㄣˇ ❶物品，物件 article; product; commodity: ～名 *name of an article; description of a commodity* | 商～ *commodity; goods; merchandise* | 赠～ *gift; present* | 非卖～ *goods (or articles) not for sale* [品牌]产品的牌子。特指被社

P

会认同的体现标准化和品质优良的产品的牌子(especially for standardized and high-quality goods) brand ❷等级,种类 grade; class; rank:上～ *superior grade; top grade; highest grade* | 下～ *inferior grade; lowest grade* | 精～ *top-quality product; premium product; elaborate work* ❸性质 character; quality; disposition:人～ *moral character; personal character* | ～质 *character; quality; disposition* ❹体察出来好坏、优劣等 to taste sth with discrimination; to sample; to savour:～茶 *to sip tea and appraise its flavour and quality; to savour tea* | 我～出他的为人来了。*I came to appreciate his humanness.*

榀 pǐn ㄆㄧㄣˇ 量词 ***quantifier***, 房架一个叫一榀(of roof trusses) *pin*, roof truss

牝 pìn ㄆㄧㄣˋ 雌性的鸟兽,跟"牡"相对(the opposite of 牡) female bird or animal:～马 *female horse; mare* | ～鸡 *hen*

聘 pìn ㄆㄧㄣˋ ❶请人担任工作 to engage; to employ; to appoint:～书 *letter of appointment; contract of employment* | ～请 *to engage; to employ; to hire* ❷指女子出嫁(of girls) to get married; to be married off:行～ *to present a gift to consummate a betrothal* | 出～ *to get married*

PING ㄆㄧㄥ

乒 pīng ㄆㄧㄥ ❶拟声词 ***onomatopoeia***, ping, a short high-ringing sound ❷指乒乓球 ping-pong; table tennis:～队 *table tennis team* | ～坛 *table tennis circles* [乒乓](—pāng) **1** 拟声词 ***onomatopoeia***, rattling or clattering sound **2** 指乒乓球 ping-pong; table tennis

俜 pīng ㄆㄧㄥ [伶俜](líng—) 形容孤独 lonely; solitary

娉 pīng ㄆㄧㄥ [娉婷](—tíng) 形容女子姿态美好的样子(of a woman) slender and elegant; graceful and charming

平 píng ㄆㄧㄥˊ ❶不倾斜,无凹凸,像静止的水面那样 level; flat; even:～地 *flat* (or *level*) *ground* | 像水面一样～ *as smooth as water surface* | 把纸铺～了 *to smooth out the paper* ㊀ ***extension*** 均等 equal; just; fair:～分 *to divide equally* | 公～合理 *fair and reasonable* [平行] **1** 两个平面或在一个平面内的两条直线永远不相交 parallel:～～线 *parallel lines* | ～～面 *parallel planes* **2** 地位相等,互不隶属 of equal rank; on an equal footing; parallel:～～机关 *departments of equal rank; parallel departments* [天平]一种精确度高的称重量的器具。横杆两头各悬一小盘,称物时,一头放物品,一头放砝码 balance; scales ❷使平 to level; to make level:把地～一～ *to make* *the ground flat*; *to rake the soil smooth* ❸安定,安静 calm; quiet; tranquil: ～心静气 *calmly and patiently*; *dispassionately*|风～浪静 *calm and tranquil* ❹经常的,一般的 common; ordinary; usual: ～日 *ordinary days*|～淡无奇 *commonplace*; *pedestrian*; *prosaic* ❺平声,汉语四声之一。普通话的平声分阴平和阳平两类:阴平调子高而平,符号作"ˉ";阳平调子向高扬起,符号作"ˊ" level tone

评 píng ㄆㄧㄥˊ 议论或评判 to comment on; to review; to make remarks on(㊀ ***doublet*** 一论 to discuss; to comment on; to review|一议 to appraise sth through discussion; to comment and appraise): 书～ *book review*|～语 *comments*; *remarks*|～理 *to judge between right and wrong*; *to pass judgment on a matter*; *to reason things out*|～比 *to appraise through comparison*; *to compare and evaluate* [评价]对事物估定价值 to pass judgment on; to appraise; to evaluate: 客观～～ *to make an objective evaluation*|予以新的～～ *to appraise sth from a new viewpoint* [评介]评论介绍 to review and introduce (a new book, etc) [评判]判定胜负或优劣 to pass judgment on; to judge; to decide [评阅]阅览并评定(试卷、作品) to read and appraise; to read and grade [批评] 1 指出工作、思想、作风上的错误或缺点 to criticize; to censure: ～～与自我～～ *criticism and self-criticism*|～～了保守思想 *to have criticized conservative thinking* 2 评论 criticism: 文学～～ *literary criticism*

[评剧]戏曲的一种,流行于华北、东北等地区。也叫"评戏"(also called 评戏) *pingju*, a local opera popular in north and northeast China

坪 píng ㄆㄧㄥˊ 平坦的场地 level ground: 草～ *lawn*; *grass plot*|～坝 *level ground*; *stretch of flat*, *even land*

苹(蘋) píng ㄆㄧㄥˊ [苹果] 落叶乔木,叶椭圆形,有锯齿,开白花。果实也叫苹果,球形,红色、青色或黄色,味甜 apple tree; apple (*Malus domestica*)

"蘋"又 pín 见569页"蘋" (also pronounced pín) see 蘋 on p569

枰 píng ㄆㄧㄥˊ 棋盘 chessboard; checkerboard: 棋～ *chessboard*; *checkerboard*

萍 píng ㄆㄧㄥˊ 浮萍,在水面浮生的草,茎扁平像叶子,根垂在水里,有青萍、紫萍等 duckweed: ～踪(喻行踪不定) *to wander like drifting duckweed along uncertain tracks — to drift with great uncertainty*|～水相逢(喻偶然遇见) (*of strangers*) *to meet by chance like patches of drifting duckweed*

P

鲆 píng ㄆㄧㄥˊ 鱼的一类。体形侧扁，两眼都在身体的左侧，有眼的一侧灰褐色或深褐色，无眼的一侧白色，常见的有牙鲆、斑鲆等 left-eyed flounder (Bothidae)

凭(憑、*凴) píng ㄆㄧㄥˊ ❶靠着 to lean on; to prop oneself on; to support oneself on: ～栏 *to lean on a railing or balustrade* | ～几(jī) to lean on a small table ❷依靠，仗恃 to depend on; to rely on: 劳动人民～着双手创造世界。*The working people create the world with their labour.* | 光～武器不能打胜仗。*A war cannot be won with weapons alone.* ❸证据 evidence; proof (㊟ ***doublet*** —证 evidence; proof; voucher | —据 evidence; proof): 真～实据 *solid evidence; conclusive evidence; ironclad evidence* ❹介词 ***preposition***，根据 on the basis of; by virtue of: ～票入场 *Admission by ticket only.* | ～大家的意见作出决定。*The decision is made on the basis of everyone's opinions.* ❺连词 ***conjunction***，任凭，无论 no matter what (*or* how, where, etc): ～你怎么说，我也不信。*No matter what you say, I won't believe it.*

帡 píng ㄆㄧㄥˊ [帡幪](—méng)古代称覆盖用的东西，指帐幕等(in ancient time) covering

洴 píng ㄆㄧㄥˊ [洴澼](—pì)漂洗(丝绵) to rinse (silk wadding)

屏 ㊀ píng ㄆㄧㄥˊ ❶遮挡，遮挡物 screen; shield: ～藩 *screen and fence; surrounding territories; to shield* | ～蔽 *screen; shield* | ～风(挡风或阻隔视线用的家具) *screen* | 围～ *folding screen; multi-leaf screen* [屏障]像屏风那样遮挡着的东西(多指山岭、岛屿) things that give screen-like shelter and protection (such as mountains or islands, etc): 天然～～ *natural barrier; natural cover for defence* ❷字画的条幅，通常以四幅或八幅为一组 a set of scrolls of painting or calligraphy: 四扇～ *four-panel screen*

㊁ bǐng 见52页 see p52

瓶(*缾) píng ㄆㄧㄥˊ (—子、—儿)口小腹大的器皿，多为瓷或玻璃做成，通常用来盛液体 bottle; jar; flask: 酒～子 *wine bottle* | 花～儿 *vase* | 一～子油 *a bottle of oil*

艵 píng ㄆㄧㄥˊ 同"屏"(píng) same as 屏

PO ㄆㄛ

朴 ㊂ pō ㄆㄛ [朴刀]旧式武器，一种窄长有短把的刀 old-type sword with a long narrow blade and a short hilt

㊀ pò 见574页 see p574
㊁ pǔ 见577页 see p577
㊃ piáo 见567页 see p567

钋 pō ㄆㄛ 一种放射性元素，(符号 Po) polonium (Po)

陂 ⊜ pō ㄆㄛ [陂陀](—tuó) 不平坦 not smooth; uneven

㊀ bēi 见27页 see p27

⊜ pí 见561页 see p561

坡 pō ㄆㄛ (—子、—儿)倾斜的地方 slope: 山～*hillside* | 高～*high slope* | 上～*upward slope; to go up a slope* | 下～*downward slope; to go down a slope* [坡度]斜面与地平面所成的角度 degree of an incline; gradient; slope (grade)

颇 pō ㄆㄛ ❶偏，不正 inclined to one side; oblique; tilted: 偏～*partial; biased; unfair* ❷副词 ***adverb***，很，相当地 quite; rather; considerably: ～久 *quite a long time* | ～不易 *rather difficult*

泊 ⊜ pō ㄆㄛ 湖 lake: 湖～*lake* | 血～(一大摊血) *pool of blood* [梁山泊]古湖泊名，在今山东省西南部 Liangshan Lake, an ancient lake in the southwest of today's Shandong Province

㊀ bó 见55页 see p55

泺(濼) ⊜ pō ㄆㄛ 同"泊"(pō)，湖泊 (same as 泊) lake

㊀ luò 见477页 see p477

泼(潑) pō ㄆㄛ ❶猛力倒水使散开 to splash; to sprinkle; to spill: ～水 *to splash water; to sprinkle water* | ～街 *to sprinkle the street with water* ❷野蛮，不讲理 rude and unreasonable; shrewish; uncouth: 撒(sā)～*to act hysterically and refuse to see reason; to make a scene; to throw a tantrum* [泼辣]凶悍 rude and unreasonable; fierce and tough; shrewish [转] ***transfer*** 有魄力，不怕困难 bold and vigorous; daring and resolute: 他做事很～～。*He is bold and vigorous in handling affairs.*

钹(鏺) pō ㄆㄛ 〈方 ***dialect***〉❶用镰刀、钐(shàn)刀等抡开来割(草、谷物等) to cut (grass, crop, etc) with a sickle or chopper ❷一种镰刀 a kind of sickle

酦(醱) pō ㄆㄛ 再酿(酒) to remake (wine); to rebrew (beer)

婆 pó ㄆㄛˊ 年老的妇人 old woman(叠 ***reduplication***): 老太～*old woman* | 苦口～心 *(to admonish) earnestly and maternally* [引] ***extension*** **1** 丈夫的母亲(叠 ***reduplication***) husband's mother; mother-in-law **2** 祖母(叠 ***reduplication***) granny; grandma; grandmother [老婆] **1** (—子、—儿)年老的妇人 old woman **2** (—po)妻子 wife [婆娑](—suō)盘旋舞蹈的样子 whirling; dancing: ～～起舞 *to start dancing*

鄱 pó ㄆㄛˊ [鄱阳] **1** 湖名，在江西省北部 Poyang Lake, in the north of Jiangxi Province **2** 地名，在江西省。今作"波阳"(now written as 波阳) Po-

P

yang, a place in Jiangxi Province

皤 pó ㄆㄛˊ 形容白色 white: 白发～然 *white-haired*

繁 ㊀ pó ㄆㄛˊ 姓 Po, a surname

㊀ fán 见183页 see p183

叵 pǒ ㄆㄛˇ 不可 not; impossibly; improbably: ～信 *unbelievable*|居心～测 *to harbour dark designs; to nurse evil intentions; to have ulterior motives*

钷 pǒ ㄆㄛˇ 一种人造的放射性元素(符号 Pm) promethium (Pm)

笸 pǒ ㄆㄛˇ [笸箩](—luo)盛(chéng)谷物等的一种器具,用柳条或篾条编成 shallow basket made of wicker or bamboo strips

朴 ㊀ pò ㄆㄛˋ 朴树,落叶乔木,花淡黄色,果实黑色。木材供制家具 Chinese hackberry (*Celtis sinensis*) [厚朴] 落叶乔木,花大,白色,树皮可入药 Houpu magnolia (*Magnolia officinalis*)

㊁ pǔ 见577页 see p577

㊂ pō 见572页 see p572

㊃ piáo 见567页 see p567

迫(*廹) ㊀ pò ㄆㄛˋ ❶用强力压制,硬逼 to force; to compel; to press (㊟ **doublet** 逼— to force; to compel; to coerce): ～害 *to persecute; to oppress cruelly*|饥寒交～*to suffer hunger and cold; to live in hunger and cold; to be poverty-striken*|～使对方同意 *to force the other side to agree; to coerce the other side into an agreement* ❷急促 urgent; imminent; pressing (㊟ **doublet** 急— urgent; pressing; critical): ～切需要 *to be in urgent* (or *great*) *need of; to need sth with extreme* (or *great*) *urgency*|从容不～*calm and unhurried; in a leisurely manner; as cool as a cucumber*|～不及待 *unable to hold oneself back; too impatient to wait; itching to do sth* ❸接近 to approach; to go towards; to come near: ～近 *to approach; to get close; to draw near*

㊁ pǎi 见548页 see p548

珀 pò ㄆㄛˋ 见284页“琥”字条“琥珀”(hǔ—) see 琥珀 on p284

粕 pò ㄆㄛˋ 米渣滓 dregs (of grain) 参看941页“糟(zāo)❶[糟粕]”(see 糟❶ for [糟粕]on p941)

魄 ㊀ pò ㄆㄛˋ ❶迷信指依附形体而存在的精神 soul (㊟ **doublet** 魂— soul): 失魂落～*to be driven to distraction; to be panic-striken; to be scared out of one's wits* ❷精神,精力 vigour; spirit; energy: 气～ *boldness of vision; imposing manner*|体～健全 *sound physique; sound body*|做工作要有～力 *to show daring and determination in one's work; to be bold and resolute in one's work*

P

㊁ tuò 见770页 see p770
㊂ bó 见55页 see p55

破 pò ㄆㄛˋ ❶碎,不完整 broken; cracked; worn-out: 碗打～了。*The bowl is broken.*|衣服～了。*The clothes are worn out.*|手～了。*My hand got cut.*|牢不可～ *unbreakable; indestructible; impregnable* [破绽](—zhàn)衣服裂开 burst (*or* broken) seam ㊉ ***figurative*** 事情或说话的漏洞,矛盾 flaw; weak point; loophole: 他话里有～～。*There are flaws in his remarks.* ❷分裂 to split; to break; to cut (㊈ ***doublet*** —裂 to burst; to split; to break):势如～竹 *like splitting bamboo; like a hot knife cutting through butter; attacking with crushing* (or *irresistible*) *force*|一～两半 *to split* (or *break*) *in two* ㊀ ***extension*** 化整为零 to break a bank note into small notes; to give change for; to change: 一元的票子～成两张五角的 *to break* (or *change*) *a one*-yuan *note into two five*-jiao *notes* ❸使损坏 to destroy; to damage; to break down (㊈ ***doublet*** —坏 to destroy; to damage; to break down): ～釜沉舟 *to break the cauldrons and sink the boats* (*after crossing a river*)—*to cut off all means of retreat to show one's determination to press ahead; to burn one's bridges or boats; to cross the Rubicon* ㊉ ***figurative*** 破除,批判 to get rid of; to break with; to do away with: ～旧立新 *to abolish the old and build up the new*|不～不立 *There is no making without breaking.* ❹超出 to make an exception; to break: ～例 *to break a rule; to make an exception*|～格 *to break prescribed rules; to break a rule; to make an exception*|打～纪录 *to break a record*|突～定额 *to overfulfil a quota* ❺冲开,打败 to break through; to defeat (an enemy); to capture (a city, etc); to beat: ～阵 *to disrupt a battle array* (or *formation*)|大～敌军 *to defeat the enemy completely* ❻揭穿 to disclose; to reveal (*or* expose) the truth of; to lay bare: ～案 *to solve the case; to clear up a case*|说～ *to tell what sth really is; to puncture a fallacy; to expose a myth*|～除迷信 *to abolish all fetishes and superstitions; to banish all blind faith* ❼花费,耗费 to spend; to expend: ～费 *to spend money; to put to expense*|～工夫 *to take time; to require effort* [破产]企业或个人处于资不抵债的状态 bankruptcy ㊀ ***extension*** 丧失全部财产 to go bankrupt; to go broke; to become insolvent ㊉ ***figurative*** 失败,破灭 to come to naught; to fall through: 敌人的阴谋～～了。*The enemy's scheme fell through.* ❽表鄙视的形容词 poor; lousy; paltry:

～戏 *lousy play* | ～货 *spoiled goods* — *loose woman* | 这样的～差事谁也不愿意干。*Nobody likes to do such lousy work.*

桲 po ·ㄆㄛ 见787页"榅"字条"榅桲"(wēn—) see 榅桲 on p787

POU ㄆㄡ

剖 pōu ㄆㄡ ❶破开 to cut open; to rip open (㊟ ***doublet*** 解— to dissect): 把瓜～开 *to cut open the melon* [剖面]东西切开后现出的平面 section; profile: 横～～ *cross section* | 纵～～ *longitudinal section* ❷分析,分辨 to analyse; to examine; to dissect: ～析 *to analyse; to dissect* | ～明事理 *to analyse the whys and wherefores of a matter; to make an in-depth analysis*

抔 póu ㄆㄡˊ ❶用手捧东西 to hold with cupped hands: ～饮(两手捧起而饮) *to scoop up with cupped hands and drink* | ❷量词 ***quantifier***: 一～土(即一捧土) *a handful of earth*

裒 póu ㄆㄡˊ ❶聚 to gather; to collect ❷减少 to take out; to reduce: ～多益寡(减有余补不足) *to take from the fat to pad the lean; to cut off from the long to add to the short; to take from those who have too much and give those who have too little*

掊 pǒu ㄆㄡˇ 掊击,抨击 to attack; to lash out at; to blast

PU ㄆㄨ

仆 ㊀ pū ㄆㄨ 向前跌倒 to fall forward; to fall prostrate: 前～后继 *As those in front fall, those behind take up their position.* or *No sooner has one fallen than another steps into the breach.*

㊁ pú 见577页 see p577

扑(撲) pū ㄆㄨ ❶轻打,拍 to dab; to pat; to flap: ～粉 *to dab powder* | ～打 ～打衣服上的土 *to pat the dirt off one's clothes* ❷冲 to rush at; to attack; to catch: 向敌人猛～ *to attack the enemy violently* | 香气～鼻。*A fragrant smell greeted us.*

铺 ㊀ pū ㄆㄨ 把东西散开放置,平摆 to spread; to unfold: ～轨 *to lay a rail track* | 平～直叙(说话作文没有精彩处) *to tell in a simple, straightforward way; to speak or write in a flat* (or *monotonous*) *style* | 为实现共产主义社会～平道路 *to pave the way for the realization of communist society* [铺张]为了在形式上好看而多用人力物力 extravagant; ostentatious: 反对～～浪费 *to oppose extravagance and waste*

㊁ pù 见578页 see p578

噗 pū ㄆㄨ 拟声词 ***onomatopoeia*** [噗嗤](—chī) 拟声

词 ***onomatopoeia***,笑声或水、气挤出来的声音。也作"扑哧"(also written as 扑哧) sound of laughing, blowing air, or spurting water

潽 pū ㄆㄨ 液体沸腾溢出(of liquid) to boil over: 牛奶～了。*The milk is boiling over.*

仆(僕) ㊁ pú ㄆㄨˊ ❶被雇到家里做杂事、供役使的人 servant: ～人 *servant* | 女～ *maidservant* [仆从]旧时指跟随在身边的仆人(in former times) footman; retainer ㊗ ***figurative*** 受人控制并追随别人的 flunkey; henchman: ～～国 *vassal country* ❷旧时男子谦称自己 humble term for a man, used when he called himself in former times

㊀ pū 见576页 see p576

匍 pú ㄆㄨˊ [匍匐](－fú)爬,手足并行,也作"匍伏"(also written as 匍伏) to crawl; to creep: ～～前进 *to crawl forward*

葡 pú ㄆㄨˊ [葡萄](－tɑo)藤本植物,茎有卷须能缠绕他物,叶子像手掌。花小,黄绿色。果实也叫葡萄,圆形或椭圆形,可以吃,也可以酿酒 grape (*Vitis*)

莆 pú ㄆㄨˊ [莆田]地名,在福建省 Putian, a place in Fujian Province

脯 ㊁ pú ㄆㄨˊ (－子、－儿)胸脯,胸部 chest; breast: 挺着胸～子 *to throw* (*or puff*) *out one's chest*

㊀ fǔ 见207页 see p207

蒲 pú ㄆㄨˊ 香蒲,多年生草本植物,生于浅水或池沼中,叶长而尖,可以编席、蒲包和扇子。根茎、花粉、果穗可入药 cattail (*Typha latifolia*)

酺 pú ㄆㄨˊ 〈古 ***archaism***〉聚会饮酒 to meet and drink together

菩 pú ㄆㄨˊ [菩萨](－sà)梵语"菩提萨埵(duǒ)"的省称。佛教中指地位仅次于佛的人。泛指佛和某些神(short for 菩提萨埵 in Sanskrit) Bodhisattva; Buddha; deity

璞 pú ㄆㄨˊ 含玉的石头或没有雕琢过的玉石 uncut jade or stone containing jade: ～玉浑金(喻品质好) *uncut jade and unrefined gold — simple and pure character*

镤 pú ㄆㄨˊ 一种放射性元素,(符号 Pa) Protactinium (Pa)

濮 pú ㄆㄨˊ [濮阳]地名,在河南省 Puyang, a place in Henan Province

朴(樸) ㊁ pǔ ㄆㄨˇ 没有细加工的木料 unprocessed wood ㊗ ***figurative*** 朴实,朴素 simple; plain

㊀ pò 见574页 see p574
㊂ pō 见572页 see p572
㊃ piáo 见567页 see p567

埔 ㊀ pǔ ㄆㄨˇ [黄埔]地名,在广东省广州 Huangpu, a place in Guangzhou, Guangdong Province

㊁ bù 见60页 see p60

圃 pǔ ㄆㄨˇ 种植菜蔬、花草、瓜果的园子 plot of land for growing plants; garden:花～ *flower garden; flower nursery*

浦 pǔ ㄆㄨˇ 水边或河流入海的地区 water's edge; river mouth

溥 pǔ ㄆㄨˇ ❶广大 broad; immense; vast ❷普遍 common; universal

普 pǔ ㄆㄨˇ 普遍,全,全面 general; universal; common: ～天同庆 *The whole world joins in jubilation.* | ～查 *to make a general investigation* (or *survey*) [普及]传布和推广到各方面 to spread extensively; to popularize; to disseminate: ～～教育 *to make education universal; to popularize education* [普通]通常,一般 ordinary; common; average: ～～人 *average person* | ～～读物 *common reading material*

[普米族]我国少数民族,参看附表(see the appendix) the Pumi ethnic group, one of the ethnic minorities of China

谱 pǔ ㄆㄨˇ ❶依照事物的类别、系统编制的表册 register; record; chronicle: 年～ *chronicle* (*of sb's life*) | 家～ (记载家族世系的表册) *family tree; genealogical tree; pedigree* | 食～ *cookbook; recipe; menu* ❷记录音乐、棋局等的符号或图形 guide; music score; music: 歌～ *music of a song; music score for a song* | 乐(yuè)～ *music; music score* | 棋～ *chess manual* ❸编写歌谱 to set to music; to compose: ～曲 *to set to music; to compose a song* ❹(一儿)大致的准则,把握 sth to count on; a fair amount of confidence: 他做事有～儿。*He knows what he is doing.*

氆 pǔ ㄆㄨˇ [氆氇](一lu)(藏 ***Tibetan***)藏族地区出产的一种毛织品 woolen fabric produced in Tibet

镨 pǔ ㄆㄨˇ 一种金属元素,符号Pr,淡黄色。它的化合物多呈绿色,可作陶器的颜料 praseodymium (Pr)

蹼 pǔ ㄆㄨˇ 青蛙、乌龟、鸭子、水獭等动物脚趾中间的膜 web (that connects digits of ducks, frogs, etc)

铺(*舖) ㊁ pù ㄆㄨˋ ❶(一子、一儿)商店 shop; store: 饭～(*small*) *restaurant; eating house; eatery* | 杂货～ *grocery store* ❷床 bed (㊀ ***doublet*** 床一 bed; bunk): 上下～ *bunk beds; stored bed* | 临时搭～ *to make a makeshift bed* ❸旧时的驿站,现在用于地名(*pu*, now used in a place name) courier station in former times: 三十里～ *Sanshilipu*

㊀ pū 见576页 see p576

堡 ㊂ pù ㄆㄨˋ 地名用字 *pu*, used in a place name: 十里～ *Shilipu*

㊀ bǎo 见25页 see p25

P

㊂ bǔ 见59页 see p59

暴 ㊁ pù ㄆㄨˋ 晒，晒干。后作"曝"(pù)(later written as 曝) to bask; to sun; to dry in the sun

㊀ bào 见27页 see p27

瀑 ㊁ pù ㄆㄨˋ 瀑布，水从高山上陡直地流下来，远看好像垂挂着的白布 waterfall; cascade; cataract

㊀ bào 见27页 see p27

曝 ㊀ pù ㄆㄨˋ 晒 to expose to the sun：一～十寒（喻没有恒心）*to sun for one day and chill for ten days — to work hard for one day and do nothing for ten days; to work by fits and starts; to lack perseverance*

㊁ bào 见27页 see p27

P

Q ㄑ

QI ㄑㄧ

七 qī ㄑㄧ 数目字 seven

柒 qī ㄑㄧ “七”字的大写 seven, capital form of 七

沏 qī ㄑㄧ 用开水冲茶叶或其他东西(with boiling water) to infuse: ～茶 *to make tea; to infuse tea; to brew tea.*

妻 ㊀ qī ㄑㄧ (一子)男子的配偶,跟“夫”相对 (the opposite of 夫) wife

㊁ qì 见589页 see p589

凄(❶❸*淒、❷*悽) qī ㄑㄧ ❶寒凉 chilly; cold; freezing: ～风苦雨 *chilly wind and excessive rain — foul weather; wretched circumstances; sad plight.* ❷悲伤 sad; grieved; sorrowful (㊥ ***doublet*** — 惨 miserable; wretched) ❸冷落寂静 bleak and desolate: ～清 *chilly; bleak; cheerless* | ～凉 *desolate; bleak; dreary*

郪 qī ㄑㄧ 郪江,水名,在四川省东部,涪(fú)江支流 Qijiang River, tributary of the Fujiang River, in the east of Sichuan Province

萋 qī ㄑㄧ [萋萋]形容草生长得茂盛 (of grass) luxuriant; lush: 芳草～～ *luxuriant (or lush) growth of fragrant grass*

栖(*棲) ㊀ qī ㄑㄧ 鸟停留在树上 (of birds) to perch; to roost ㊇ ***extension*** 居住,停留 to dwell; to live; to stay: 两～ *amphibious* | ～身之处 *a shelter to stay in* [栖霞]地名,在山东省 Qixia, a place in Shandong Province

㊁ xī 见799页 see p799

桤(榿) qī ㄑㄧ 桤木,落叶乔木。木材轻软,可制器具。嫩枝叶可入药 alder (*Alnus cremastogyne*)

戚(❷*慼) qī ㄑㄧ ❶亲戚,因婚姻联成的关系 relative; kin ❷忧愁,悲哀 sorrow; grief: 休～相关 *to be bound by common interests; to share joys and sorrows; to share weal and woe* [戚戚]忧愁的样子 sad; distressed; anxious: 君子坦荡荡,小人常～～。*The gentleman is easy of mind, while the petty man is always full of anxiety.*

嘁 qī ㄑㄧ [嘁嘁]拟声词 ***onomatopoeia***: ～～喳喳(chāchā)地说话 to chatter; to babble; to jabber

期 ㊀ qī ㄑㄧ ❶规定的时间或一段时间 scheduled time; (of time) period: 定～举行 *to hold (a meeting, etc) at regu-*

lar intervals|分~付款 *to pay by instalments*|过~作废 *invalid after the expiry date*|如~完成任务 *to accomplish a task on schedule* ㊀ ***extension*** 刊物出版的号数 issue; number ❷约定时日 to appoint (time); to schedule:不~而遇 *to meet by chance* [期货交易]一种非现金、非现货的买卖。双方按约定的条件、时间交割货物、外汇或有价证券等 futures transaction ❸盼望,希望 to expect; to anticipate; to hope (㊀ ***doublet*** 一望 to expect; to anticipate; to hope):决不辜负大家的~望 *never to betray everybody's hope; never to let all of you down*|~待 *to look forward to; to expect; to anticipate*|~盼 *to hope; to expect; to look forward to*|以~得到良好的效果 *in the hope of getting good results*

㊁ jī 见309页 see p309

欺 qī ㄑㄧ ❶欺骗,蒙混 to deceive; to cheat; to dupe:自~~人 *to deceive oneself as well as others* [欺世盗名]欺骗世人,窃取名誉 to win fame by deceiving the public; to build up one's reputation by deceiving the public ❷欺负,压迫,侮辱 to bully; to intimidate; to take advantage of (㊀ ***doublet*** 一侮 to bully; to insult; to treat sb high-handedly):仗势~人 *to act as a bully under the protection of powerful connections; to use one's power to intimidate people; to take advantage of one's or sb else's power to bully people*

颀 qī ㄑㄧ [颀头]古时打鬼驱疫时用的假面具 mask worn by the impersonator of a god in rituals to drive away ghosts pestilence in ancient China

攲 qī ㄑㄧ 倾斜,歪向一边 to slant; to incline to one side:~侧 *to lean to one side; to incline to one side; to slant*|~倾 *to lean; to incline*

缉 ㊁ qī ㄑㄧ 一针对一针地缝 to sew in close and joint stitches:~鞋口 *to sew a shoe welt with close stitches*

㊀ jī 见309页 see p309

蹊 ㊁ qī ㄑㄧ [蹊跷](—qiāo)奇怪,跷蹊 strange; odd; suspicious

㊀ xī 见802页 see p802

漆 qī ㄑㄧ ❶各种黏液状涂料的统称。可分为天然漆和人造漆两大类 lacquer; paint [漆树]落叶乔木,用树皮里的黏汁制成的涂料就是漆 Chinese lacquer tree (*Toxicodendron vernicifluum*) ❷用漆涂 to paint; to cover with lacquer

㵴 qī ㄑㄧ 〈方 ***dialect***〉❶东西湿了之后要干未干 drying; almost dry:雨过了,太阳出来一晒,路上就渐渐~了。*When the sun comes through after rain, the road begins to dry.* ❷用沙土等吸收水分 to soak up water with sand or earth:地上有水,铺上点儿沙子

～一～。*Spread some sand over puddles in the road to soak up the water.*

亓 qí ㄑㄧˊ 姓 Qi, a surname

齐(齊) qí ㄑㄧˊ ❶整齐,东西一头平或排成一条直线 neat; even; uniform:庄稼长得很～。*The crops are growing evenly in height.*|队形整～*orderly queue; The people are in neat rows.*|纸叠得很～。*The paper is neatly folded.*[齐截](－jie)〈方 ***dialect***〉**1** 整齐 neat; even:字写得～～*to write a neat hand* **2** 全备 complete; all in readiness:东西都预备～～了。*Everything is made available.*[齐齿呼]i 韵母和以 i 开头的韵母 syllables with i as the final or a final beginning with i[看齐]站队的时候,以排头为准把队形排齐 to dress ㊥ ***figurative*** 争取与模范人物一样 to keep up with; to follow sb's example; to emulate:大家向劳动模范～～。*Everybody is emulating the model worker.* ❷达到,跟什么一般平 to reach the height of; to be on the same plane with; to be level with:河水～腰深。*The river is waist deep.* ❸同时,同样,一起 simultaneous; same; together:～心 *to be of one mind*|～声高唱 *to sing loudly in unison; to sing high in chorus*|百花～放,推陈出新 *to let a hundred flowers blossom and weed through the old to bring forth the new — a policy formulated in the early 1960's to develop theoretical art in socialist society*|一～用力 *to put forth one's strength simultaneously* ❹全,完全 complete; all in readiness; all present(㊜ ***doublet*** 一全 complete):材料都预备～了。*All the materials have been made available.*|代表都到～了。*All the representatives are present.* ❺周代诸侯国名,在今山东省北部、东部和河北省东南角 Qi, a princedom of the Zhou Dynasty, covering the north and east of today's Shandong Province and the southeast corner of today's Hebei Province ❻朝代名 name of dynasties **1** 南朝之一,萧道成所建立(公元 479—502 年)Southern Qi Dynasty (479 – 502 AD), established by Xiao Daocheng **2** 北朝之一,高洋所建立(公元 550—577 年),史称北齐(also called 北齐 in history) Northern Qi Dynasty (550 – 577 AD), established by Gao Yang

〈古 ***archaism***〉又同斋戒的"斋"(zhāi) also same as 斋 in 斋戒

脐(臍) qí ㄑㄧˊ ❶肚脐,胎儿肚子中间有一条管子,跟母体的胎盘连着,这个管子叫脐带,出生以后,脐带脱落的地方叫"脐"navel ❷螃蟹腹部下面的甲壳 abdomen of a crab:尖～ *V-shaped belly flap (in a male crab)*|团～ *round*

Q

belly flap (*in a female crab*)

蛴(蠐) qí ㄑㄧˊ [蛴螬](—cáo)金龟子的幼虫,约3厘米长,圆筒形,白色,身上有褐色毛,生活在土里,吃农作物的根和茎 grub

祁 qí ㄑㄧˊ 盛大 great; grand: ～寒(严寒,极冷) *severely cold*

圻 qí ㄑㄧˊ 地的边界 boundary 〈古 ***archaism***〉又同"垠"(yín) also same as 垠

祈 qí ㄑㄧˊ 向神求福 to pray (㊎ ***doublet*** —祷 to pray)。㊀ ***extension*** 请求 to beg; to request; to entreat: 敬～照准。*We respectfully ask you to grant our request.*

颀 qí ㄑㄧˊ 身子高(叠 ***reduplication***) (of stature) tall

蕲(蘄) qí ㄑㄧˊ ❶求 to beg; to beseech; to plead ❷地名用字 *qi*, used in a place name [蕲春]地名,在湖北省 Qichun, a place in Hubei Province

芪 qí ㄑㄧˊ 黄芪,多年生草本植物,茎横卧在地面上,开淡黄色的花,根入药 membranous milk vetch (*Astragalus membranaceus*)

祇 ㊀ qí ㄑㄧˊ 古代称地神(in ancient China) God of the Earth

㊁ zhǐ 见979页"只"see 只 on p979

岐 qí ㄑㄧˊ ❶岐山,山名,在陕西省宝鸡 Qishan Mountain, in Baoji, Shaanxi Province ❷同"歧" same as 歧

歧 qí ㄑㄧˊ ❶岔道,大路分出的小路(of roads) fork; branch: ～路亡羊 *to lose one's sheep at a fork in the road — to lose one's bearings when the situation is too complicated or changeable* [歧途]错误的道路 wrong road: 误入～～ *to go astray* ❷不相同,不一致 different; divergent: ～视 *to discriminate against* | ～义 *ambiguity*

跂 ㊀ qí ㄑㄧˊ 多生出的脚趾 extra toe

㊁ qì 见590页 see p590

其 qí ㄑㄧˊ ❶代词 ***pronoun*** **1** 他,他们 he; she; they: 不能任～自流 *cannot let things drift* | 劝～努力学习 *to persuade him to study hard* **2** 他的,他们的 his; her; their: 各得～所。*Each gets what he wants.* or *Each is in his or its place.* | 人尽～才,物尽～用 *to tap manpower and material resources to the full* ❷那,那个,那些 that; those; the: ～他 *other; else* | ～次 *next; then* | 本无～事。*Nothing of that sort has happened.* | ～中有个原因。*There is some reason for it.* [其实]实在的,事实上 in fact; as a matter of fact; actually: 他故意说不懂,～～他懂得。*He deliberately says that he doesn't understand it, but he does as a matter of fact.* ❸文

言助词 ***auxiliary in classical Chinese*** **1** 表示揣测、反诘(used to express a guess or retort)：岂～然乎？*Is this really the case?* | ～奈我何？*What can they do to me?* **2** 表示命令、劝勉(used to express an order or advice)：子～勉之！*Exert yourself to the uttermost!* ❹ 词尾 ***suffix***：极～快乐 *extremely happy* | 尤～伟大 *especially great*

萁 qí ㄑㄧˊ 〈方 ***dialect***〉豆茎 beanstalk

淇 qí ㄑㄧˊ 淇河，源出河南省林州，流入卫河 Qihe River, originating in Linzhou, Henan Province, and flowing into Weihe River

骐 qí ㄑㄧˊ 有青黑色纹理的马 black horse

琪 qí ㄑㄧˊ ❶一种玉 a kind of jade ❷珍异 rare：～花瑶草 *coralline flowers and jasper plants of fairy land; jade flowers of fairy land*

棋(*棊、*碁) qí ㄑㄧˊ 文娱用品名，有象棋、围棋等 chess or any board game, such as (Chinese) chess, *weiqi*, etc

祺 qí ㄑㄧˊ 吉祥，福气 good luck; blessing

綦 qí ㄑㄧˊ ❶青黑色 greenish black：～巾 *greenish black kerchief* ❷极 very, extremely：～难 *very difficult*

蜞 qí ㄑㄧˊ 见558页"蟛"字条"蟛蜞"(péng—) see 蟛蜞 on p558

旗(❶△*旂) qí ㄑㄧˊ ❶(一子、一儿)用布、纸、绸子或其他材料做成的标志，多半是长方形或方形 flag; banner：国～ *national flag* | 校～ *school flag* ❷清代满族的军队编制和户口编制，共分八旗。后又建立蒙古八旗、汉军八旗 Eight Banners, military and administrative organizations of the Manchu ethnic group in the Qing Dynasty; later Eight Banners were established among the Mongolian and Han ethnic groups. ㉄ ***extension*** 属于八旗的，特指属于满族的 of Eight Banners; of Manchu：～人 *Manchu* | ～袍 *mandarin gown*; Qipao; *cheongsam* (*straight, close-fitting silk dress with a high neck and slit skirt*) | ～装 *Manchu attire* ❸内蒙古自治区的行政区划单位，相当于县 banner, a county-level administrative division in the Inner Mongolia Autonomous Region

鲯 qí ㄑㄧˊ [鲯鳅]鱼名。黑褐色，体长而侧扁，头大眼小，生活在海洋中 dorado; dolphinfish (*Coryphaena hippurus*)

麒 qí ㄑㄧˊ [麒麟]见451页"麟"see 麟 on p451

奇 ㊀ qí ㄑㄧˊ ❶特殊的，稀罕，不常见的 special; strange; rare：～事 *strange affair; uncommon phenomenon* | ～闻 *sth*

unheard of; fantastic story | ～冷 *extremely cold* | ～丑 *very ugly* ⑧ **extension** 出人意料的，令人不测的 unexpected; unpredictable: ～兵 *army suddenly appearing from nowhere; troops moving swiftly and unexpectedly (to spring a surprise attack on the enemy)* | ～计 *unusually clever stratagem; ingenious ploy; surprising move* | ～袭 *surprise attack; raid* | 出～制胜 *to overwhelm the enemy by a surprise attack* ❷惊异，引以为奇 to astonish: 世人～之。*The people throughout the world are astonished at it.* ❸姓 Qi, a surname

㊁ jī 见308页 see p308

埼(**碕) qí ㄑㄧˊ 弯曲的岸 winding embankment; crooked bank; meandering coast

萕 qí ㄑㄧˊ ［萕莱主山］山名，在台湾省 the Peak of Mt. Qilai (*or* Mt. Cilai), in Taiwan Province

崎 qí ㄑㄧˊ ［崎岖］(－qū)形容山路不平 (of mountain path) rugged; uneven

骑 qí ㄑㄧˊ ❶跨坐在牲畜或其他东西上 to sit on the back of; to ride: ～马 *to ride a horse* | ～自行车 *to ride a bicycle* ⑧ **extension** 兼跨两边 to straddle: ～缝盖章 *to put a seal on the two halves of a voucher* ❷(旧读 formerly jì)骑兵，也泛指骑马的人(horseman in general) cavalry; cavalryman: 车～ *horse and carriage* | 轻～ *light cavalry* | 铁～ *strong cavalry; crack mounted soldiers* ❸骑的马 horse used to ride: 坐～ *saddle horse; one's mount*

琦 qí ㄑㄧˊ 美玉 fine jade ⑱ ***figurative*** 珍奇 rare

锜 qí ㄑㄧˊ ❶古代一种带三足的锅 a kind of ancient tripod cooker ❷古代的一种凿子 (in ancient China) a kind of ancient chisel

俟 ㊁ qí ㄑㄧˊ ［万俟］(mò－)复姓 Moqi, a compound surname

㊀ sì 见706页 see p706

耆 qí ㄑㄧˊ 年老，六十岁以上的人 (of a person) over sixty years old; very old: ～年 *old age; venerable age*

鳍 qí ㄑㄧˊ 鱼类和其他水生脊椎动物的运动器官，由薄膜、柔软分节的鳍条和坚硬不分节的鳍棘组成 fin

鬐 qí ㄑㄧˊ 马脖子上部的长毛。也叫"马鬃"、"马鬣" (also called 马鬃 or 马鬣) horse mane

旂 qí ㄑㄧˊ ❶古代指有铃铛的旗子 (in ancient China) flag attached with small bells ❷同"旗❶" same as 旗❶

畦 qí ㄑㄧˊ 田园中分成的小区 plot of land separated by ridges: 种一～菜 *to grow a bed of vegetables; to plant a plot of vegetables*

乞 qǐ ㄑㄧˇ 乞求，向人讨、要、求 to beg; to supplicate; to implore: ～怜 *to beg for pity (or mercy)* | ～恕 *to beg one's pardon; to ask sb for forgiveness* | ～食 *to beg for food; to beg for alms* | 行～ *to go begging*

芑 qǐ ㄑㄧˇ 古书上说的一种植物 (in ancient Chinese texts) glutinous rehmannia

屺 qǐ ㄑㄧˇ 没有草木的山 barren mountain

岂(豈) qǐ ㄑㄧˇ 副词 ***adverb***, 表示反诘 (used to introduce a rhetorical question) **1** 哪里，怎么 where; how: ～敢！*How dare!* | ～有此理？*Isn't it outrageous?* **2** 难道 (used for emphasis in a rhetorical question): ～非怪事？*It is strange, isn't it?*

〈古 ***archaism***〉又同"恺"、"凯"(kǎi) also same as 恺 or 凯

玘 qǐ ㄑㄧˇ 古代佩带的玉 (in ancient China) jade pendant

杞 qǐ ㄑㄧˇ ❶植物名 name of plants **1** 就是枸(gǒu)杞 (i. e. 枸杞) Chinese wolfberry (*Lycium chinense*) **2** 杞柳，落叶灌木，生在水边，枝条可以编箱、笼、筐、篮等物 purple willow (*Salix sinopurpurea*) ❷周代诸侯国名，在今河南省杞县 Qi, a princedom of the Zhou Dynasty, in today's Qixian County, Henan Province: ～人忧天(喻不必要的忧虑) *like the man of Qi who feared that the sky might fall — haunted by imaginary fears*

起 qǐ ㄑㄧˇ ❶由躺而坐或由坐而立等 to rise; to stand up: ～床 *to get up; to get out of bed; to rise* | ～立致敬 *to show reverence by standing up* ㉄ ***extension*** 离开原来的位置 to move; to remove **1** 移开，搬开 to move; to remove: ～身 *to set out; to leave; to stand up* | ～运 *to start shipment* **2** 拔出，取出 to pull out; to extract; to draw: ～钉子 *to pull out a nail; to remove a nail* | ～货 *to take goods (from a warehouse); to unload (from a ship); to debark* [起居]日常生活 daily life: ～～有恒 *to live a regular life* ❷由下向上升，由小往大里涨 to rise; to grow: 一～一落 *to go up and come down; to rise and fall* | ～劲 *with gusto; energetically; vigorously* | 面～了。*The flour has been leavened.* [起色]好转的形势，转机 improvement; favourable turn; pickup: 病有～～。*His (or Her) health has picked up.* ❸长出 to appear; to outgrow: ～燎泡 *to get blisters* | ～痱子 *to get prickly heat* ❹开始 to start; to begin: ～笔 *to start writing; first stroke of a Chinese character; first stroke of a Chinese character in a radical index* | ～点 *starting point* | 从今天～ *to start from* *today* [起码]最低限度,最低的 minimum; at least; rudimentary:~~要十天才能完工。*It takes at least ten days to complete the project.* ❺发生 to occur; to take place; to rise:~疑 *to become suspicious* | ~意(usually evil) *to hit upon an idea; to conceive a vicious design* | ~火 *to catch fire* | ~风 *The wind rises.* [起义]发动武装革命,也指脱离反革命集团投入革命阵营 revolt; insurrection; uprising ❻拟定 to draw up; to draft:~草 *to make a draft* ❼建造,建立 to build; to establish:~房子 *to put up a house* | 白手~家 *to build up one's fortune from scratch* ❽介词 ***preposition***,从 from:~南到北 *from south to north* | ~这里剪开 *to cut from here* ❾量词 ***quantifier*** **1** 批,群 batch; group:一~人走了,又来一~。*After a group of people left, another group came.* **2** 件,宗 case; instance:三~案件 *three cases* | 两~事故 *two accidents* ❿在动词后,表示动作的趋向、关涉等(used after a verb to express the tendency of an action or sb or sth involved in an action):抱~ *to hold up (in the arms)* | 拿~ *to take up* | 扛~大旗 *to carry a big flag on one's shoulder* | 提~精神 *to raise* (or *pluck*) *one's spirits; to brace oneself up* | 引~大家注意 *to attract* (or *draw*) *everyone's attention; to catch everyone's eye* | 想不~什么地方见过他。*I can't remember where I met him.* ⓫在动词后,跟"来"连用,表示动作开始(used after a verb in collocation with 来, to express the start of an action):大声念~来 *to start to read aloud* | 唱~歌来 *to begin to sing* ⓬在动词后,常跟"不"、"得"连用(used after a verb, usually in collocation with 不 or 得) **1** 表示胜任,能担得住 to stand; to afford:买不~ *can't afford it* | 经得~考验 *can stand the test* **2** 表示够格,达到某一种标准 up to a certain standard:看不~ *to look down upon; to scorn; to belittle* | 瞧得~ *to think highly of; to have a good opinion of; to value*

企 qǐ ㄑㄧˇ 踮着脚看,希望,盼望 to stand on tiptoe to get a better look at sth; to look forward to; to expect:~望 *to look forward to; to hope for* | ~待 *to look forward to; to expect* | ~盼 *to long for; to expect* [企图]图谋 to attempt; to seek to

[企业]从事生产、运输、贸易等经济活动的部门,如工厂、矿山、铁路、贸易公司等 enterprise; business

启(啓、*啟) qǐ ㄑㄧˇ ❶打开 to open:~封 *to unseal; to open an envelope, a wrapper, etc* | ~门 *to open the door* ㊂ ***extension*** 开导 to enlighten; to awaken; to inspire:~蒙(méng) *to impart*

rudimentary knowledge to beginners; to initiate [启发] 阐明事例,使对方因联想而领悟 to cite the example to elicit response and help sb see the point; to enlighten; to inspire: ～～教育 *heuristic education* | ～～他的政治觉悟 *to arouse his political awareness* [启示] 启发指点,使有所认识 enlightenment; inspiration; revelation ❷开始 to start; to initiate; to begin: ～用 *to start using; to employ* ❸陈述 to state; to inform: 敬～者 (*a set expression used at the beginning of a letter in ancient China*) *I beg to state; I wish to inform you* [启事] 向群众说明事情的文字,现在多登在报纸上 notice; announcement ❹书信 letter; missive; note: 书～ *letter; missive* | 小～ *brief note*

棨 qǐ ㄑㄧˇ 古时用木头做的一种通行证,略如戟形 (in ancient China) a halberd-like wooden pass [棨戟] 古时官吏出行的一种仪仗,用木头做成,状如戟 a halberd-like wooden object to certify an official's identity on an inspection tour

綮 qǐ ㄑㄧˇ 〈古 ***archaism***〉腓肠肌(小腿肚子) calf (of the leg)

绮 qǐ ㄑㄧˇ ❶有文彩的丝织品 figured woven silk material; damask: ～罗 *patterned silk fabrics; gorgeous silk fabrics* ❷美丽 beautiful; gorgeous; exquisite: ～丽 *beautiful; gorgeous; exquisite* | ～思 *beautiful thoughts* (*in literature*)

稽 ㊁ qǐ ㄑㄧˇ 稽首,古时跪下叩头的礼节 *kowtow*, an ancient etiquette to show reverence

㊀ jī 见309页 see p309

气(氣) qì ㄑㄧˋ ❶没有一定的形状、体积,能自由流动的物体 gas: 煤～ *coal gas; gas* | 蒸～ *vapour; steam* 特指空气 air: ～压 *atmospheric pressure; barometric pressure* | 给自行车打～ *to blow up a bike tyre; to inflate a bike tyre* ❷(－儿)气息,呼吸 breath: 没～了 *to stop breathing* | 上～不接下～ *breathless; to gasp for breath* ❸自然界寒、暖、阴、晴等等现象 weather: 天～ *weather* | 节～ *a day marking one of the 24 divisions of the solar year in the traditional Chinese calendar; solar term* ❹(－儿)鼻子闻到的味 smell; odour: 香～ *fragrance; sweet smell* | 臭～ *foul odour; stink* | 烟～ *smoke; fume; flue gas* ❺人的精神状态 mental state; spirit; morale: 勇～ *courage* | 朝～蓬勃 *vigorous; full of youthful vigour* [气势] 力量和形势 momentum; imposing manner; affecting grandness ❻作风,习气 airs; manner: 官～ *bureaucratic airs* | 俗～ *vulgar; in poor taste* | 骄娇二～ *self-conceited but fearful of hardship* ❼怒或使人发怒 to be angry; make angry; enrage:

他生～了。*He is angry.*|别～我了。*Stop annoying me.* ❽欺压 to bully; to insult: 受～ *to be bullied; to suffer wrong* ❾中医指能使人体器官正常发挥机能的原动力(in traditional Chinese medicine) *qi*; vital energy; energy of life; life force: ～血 qi *and blood; vital energy and the state of blood in the human body*|～虚 *deficiency of vital energy*|元～ *vigour; vitality; pneuma* ❿中医指某种症象(in traditional Chinese medicine) symptoms of diseases: 湿～ *eczema*|脚～ *beriberi*|痰～ *apoplexy*

汽 qì ㄑㄧˋ 蒸气,液体或固体变成的气体。特指水蒸气 vapour; steam: ～船 *steamboat; steamship*

讫 qì ㄑㄧˋ ❶完结,终了 settled; accomplished; completed: 收～ *cash received*|付～ *paid*|验～ *checked; examined* ❷截止 end: 起～ *the beginning and the end; alpha and omega*

迄 qì ㄑㄧˋ ❶到 up to; till: ～今未至。*He has not arrived up to now.* ❷始终 all along; so far: ～未成功。*We have not succeeded so far.*

汔 qì ㄑㄧˋ 庶几,差不多 almost; nearly; approximately

弃(*棄) qì ㄑㄧˋ 舍(shě)去,扔掉 to throw away; to discard; to abandon: 抛～ *to throw away; to discard*|遗～ *to desert; to abandon; to forsake*|～权 *to abstain from voting; to waive one's rights*|～置不顾 *to reject as unworthy of attention; to throw to the winds; to abandon*

妻 ㊁ qì ㄑㄧˋ 〈古 ***archaism***〉以女嫁人 to marry a girl to sb

㊀ qī 见580页 see p580

炁 qì ㄑㄧˋ 同"气"same as 气

泣 qì ㄑㄧˋ ❶无声或小声哭 to weep; to sob; to choke with sobs: ～不成声 *to sob too bitterly to speak* ❷眼泪 tears: ～下如雨。*Tears stream down one's cheeks.*

亟 ㊁ qì ㄑㄧˋ 屡次 repeatedly; time and again: ～来问讯 *to come repeatedly to ask for information*

㊀ jí 见312页 see p312

契(**栔) ㊀ qì ㄑㄧˋ ❶用刀雕刻 to engrave; to carve; to chisel ❷刻的文字 carved inscriptions: 书～ *carved characters* ❸契约,证明买卖、抵押、租赁等关系的合同、文书、字据 agreement; contract; deed: 地～ *title deed for land*|房～ *title deed for a house*|卖身～ *indenture by which one sells oneself or a member of one's family* ❹相合,情意相投 to agree; to get along well: 默～ *tacit agreement*|相～ *mutual understanding*|～友 *bosom friend*

[契丹]我国古代东北地区的一个民族,曾建立辽国 Qidan, (*or*

Khitan), an ethnic group in ancient northeast China who established the Liao Dynasty

㊁ xiè 见830页 see p830

碶 qì ㄑㄧˋ 用石头砌的水闸 (built with stones) water gate; stone dam; stone sluice

砌 qì ㄑㄧˋ 建筑时垒(lěi)砖石,用泥灰黏合 to build by laying bricks or stones with mortar:～墙 *to build a wall* | ～炕 *to build a* kang

跂 ㊁ qì ㄑㄧˋ 踮着脚站着 to stand on tiptoe:～望 *to look on tiptoe*

㊀ qí 见583页 see p583

葺 qì ㄑㄧˋ 用茅草覆盖房子 to thatch a roof:修～(修补)房屋 *to repair a house*

碛 qì ㄑㄧˋ 水中沙石 sand and gravel in water [沙碛]沙漠 desert

槭 qì ㄑㄧˋ 落叶小乔木,花黄绿色,叶子掌状分裂,秋季变成红色或黄色 maple (*Acer*)

器(**嚣) qì ㄑㄧˋ ❶用具的总称 general term for implements or apparatuses:武～ *weapon* | 容～ *container* [器官]生物体中具有某种独立生理机能的部分,如耳、眼、花、叶等,也省称"器"(also short for 器) organ:消化～ *digestive organs* | 生殖～ *reproductive organs; genitals* ❷人的度量、才干 tolerance; talent:～量 *tolerance; forbearance; magnanimity* | 成～ *to grow up to be a useful person; to become a useful person* ❸器重,看重,看得起 to think highly of; to value

憩(*憇) qì ㄑㄧˋ 休息 to rest; to take a rest:小～ *to take a short rest*

荠(薺) ㊁ qì ㄑㄧ˙ 见35页"荸"字条"荸荠"(bí—) see 荸荠 on p35

㊀ jì 见318页 see p318

QIA ㄑㄧㄚ

掐 qiā ㄑㄧㄚ ❶用手指用力夹,用指甲按或截断 to pinch; to nip ㊀ ***extension*** 割断,截去 to cut off; to nip off; to sever:～电线 *to cut off the wire* ❷用手的虎口及手指紧紧握住 to clutch; to grip:一把～住 *to grip sth with one's hand; to seize; to hold* ❸(—子、—儿)量词 ***quantifier***,拇指和食指或中指相对握着的数量(the amount of sth held between the thumb and the forefinger or middle finger) pinch; handful:一小～儿韭菜 *a small pinch of chives* | 一大～子青菜 *a big handful of green vegetables*

袷 ㊀ qiā ㄑㄧㄚ [袷袢](—pàn)(维 *Uygur*)维吾尔、塔吉克等民族所穿的对襟长袍 Uygur or Tajik robe buttoning down the front

㊁ jiá 见322页"夹" see 夹 on p322

葜 qiā ㄑㄧㄚ 见12页"菝"字条"菝葜"(bá—) see 菝葜 on p12

掐 qiá ㄑㄧㄚˊ 用两手掐住 to clutch (*or* grip) with both hands

卡 ㊀ qiǎ ㄑㄧㄚˇ ❶(一子)在交通要道设置的检查或收税的地方 checkpost; checkpoint: 关～ *tax office outpost; checkpost; toll-gate* ❷(一子)夹东西的器具 clip; clasp: 头发～子 *hair clip; hair pin* ❸夹在中间,堵塞 to get stuck; to wedge; to jam: 鱼刺～在嗓子里。*A fish bone got stuck in the throat.* | ～在里边拿不出来了。*It has got wedged inside and can't be pulled out.*

㊁ kǎ 见380页 see p380

洽 qià ㄑㄧㄚˋ ❶跟人联系,商量(事情) to arrange with; to consult; to discuss: 接～事情 *to contact sb for business arrangement* | 和他商～ *to arrange a discussion with him; to talk over (a matter) with him* ❷谐和 to be in harmony; to agree: 感情融～ *on very good terms; in perfect harmony in feeling*

恰 qià ㄑㄧㄚˋ ❶正巧,刚刚 just; exactly; precisely: ～巧 *by chance; coincidently* | ～到好处 *just right (for the purpose, occasion, etc); to a nicety* | ～如其分(fèn) *just right; appropriate; proper* | ～好他来了。*He came in the nick of time.* ❷合适,适当 proper; appropriate: 这里有几个字不～当。*There are a few inappropriate words here.*

髂 qià ㄑㄧㄚˋ 髂骨,腰部下面腹部两侧的骨,下缘与耻骨、坐骨联成髋(kuān)骨。ilium (图见241页"骨"picture on p241)

QIAN ㄑㄧㄢ

千(❸韆) qiān ㄑㄧㄢ ❶数目,十个一百 thousand ❷表示极多,常跟"万"、"百"连用(often used in collocation with 万 and 百) large numbers of; a great amount of; innumerable: ～言万语 *thousands and thousands of words; innumerable words* | ～军万马 *thousands upon thousands of horses and soldiers — mighty force; powerful army* | ～锤百炼 *thoroughly tempered; well-seasoned; much-steeled* [千万]副词 ***adverb***,务必 must; to make sure to; to be sure to: ～～不要铺张浪费。*Be sure not to be extravagant and wasteful.* ❸见614页"秋"字条"秋千"see 秋千 on p614 ❹法定计量单位中十进倍数单位词头之一,表示 10^3 (符号 k) kilo-(k)

仟 qiān ㄑㄧㄢ "千"字的大写 thousand, capital form of 千

阡 qiān ㄑㄧㄢ ❶田间的小路 footpath between fields, running north and south (㊄ ***doublet*** 一陌 mò crisscross footpaths between fields) ❷通往坟墓的道路 path leading to a grave

扦 qiān ㄑㄧㄢ ❶(一子、一儿)用金属或竹、木制成的像针的东西 needle-like piece of metal, bamboo, wood, etc ❷插,插进去 to insert; to stick in:～花 *to arrange flowers (in a vase, basket, etc)*|用针～住 *to fasten with a pin*

芊 qiān ㄑㄧㄢ 草木茂盛(叠 ***reduplication***)(of grass and trees) luxuriant; exuberant; flourishing:郁郁～～ *luxuriant; exuberant; flourishing* [芊绵][芊眠]草木茂密繁盛(of grass and trees) dense; thick; lush

迁(遷) qiān ㄑㄧㄢ ❶机关、住所等另换地点 to move; to relocate (㊀ ***doublet*** 一移 to move; to relocate):～都(dū) *to move the capital to another place*|～居 *to move (house); to change one's residence* [迁就]不坚持自己的意见,凑合别人 to accommodate oneself to; to yield to; to give in to:不能～～。*We can't accommodate ourselves to it.*|～～应该是有原则的。*We should accommodate ourselves to it according to the principle.* [迁延]拖延 to delay; to postpone; to defer:已经～～了一个多月了。*It has been delayed for more than a month.* ❷变动,改变 to change (㊀ ***doublet*** 变一 changes; vicissitude):事过境～。*Events have passed and the situation has changed.* or *Things change with the passage of time.*

瓩 qiānwǎ ㄑㄧㄢㄨㄚˇ 功率单位,1 瓩等于1 000瓦。现写作"千瓦"(now written as 千瓦) kilowatt (kw)

钎 qiān ㄑㄧㄢ (一子)一头尖的长钢棍,多用来在矿石上打洞 hammer drill; rock drill

岍 qiān ㄑㄧㄢ 岍山,山名,在陕西省宝鸡。今作"千山"(now written as 千山) Qianshan Mountain, in Baoji, Shaanxi Province

汧 qiān ㄑㄧㄢ [汧阳]地名,在陕西省。今作"千阳"(now written as 千阳) Qianyang, a place in Shaanxi Province

佥(僉) qiān ㄑㄧㄢ 〈古 ***archaism***〉全,都 all

签(簽、❸-❻籤) qiān ㄑㄧㄢ ❶亲自写上姓名或画上符号 to sign; to autograph:～名 *to sign one's name; to autograph*|请你～个字。*Please sign your name here.* ❷简要地写出(意见) to make brief comments (on a document, etc):～注 *to attach a slip of paper to a manuscript or book with reference materials; to write one's own opinions on a document before submitting it to a superior for examination and approval; to write comments or points for attention on a certificate, document, table, etc* ❸(一子、一儿)用竹木等物做成的细棍或片状物 bamboo slip; wood stick:牙～儿 *toothpick*|竹～儿

bamboo slip ❹(一儿)书册里作标志的纸片或其他物件上作标志的东西 tag; label: 书～ *bookmark* | 标～ *label; tag* | 浮～ *detachable note* (*usually stuck on the margin of a page*); *sticker* ❺粗粗地缝合起来 to fasten cloth or a seam with a loose basting stitch; to tack ❻旧时用于占卜或赌博的细长竹片或细棍(in former times) bamboo slip or tiny stick used for divination, gambling, etc

牵(牽) qiān ㄑㄧㄢ ❶拉,引领向前 to pull; to lead: ～着一条牛 *to lead a cow* | ～牲口 *to lead a draught animal* | 手～着手 *hand in hand* ❷连带,带累 to involve; to implicate; to entangle: 不要～扯别的问题。*Don't involve other matters.* or *Don't drag in other matters.* | 受～累 *to be tied down; to be encumbered; to be embroiled* | 互相～制 *to hold each other up; to encumber each other; to contain* (or *check*) *each other* [牵强](-qiǎng)硬拉硬扯,勉强,理由不足 forced (interpretation, etc); far-fetched; strained: 这话太～～。*These words are too far-fetched.* | ～～附会 *to stretch the meaning; to draw a forced analogy; to give a strained interpretation* ❸缠连 to be tied up: 意惹情～ *to be entangled in passion*

铅 ㊀ qiān ㄑㄧㄢ ❶一种金属元素,符号 Pb,银灰色,质地软,熔点低 lead; plumbum (Pb) [铅铁]指镀锌铁 zinc-plated iron; galvanized iron [铅字]印刷用的铅、锡、锑合金铸成的活字 type; letter ❷石墨 black lead: ～笔 *pencil*

㊁ yán 见865页 see p865

悭(慳) qiān ㄑㄧㄢ 吝啬 miserly; stingy; parsimonious ([连] ***doublet*** 一吝 miserly; stingy; parsimonious)

谦 qiān ㄑㄧㄢ 虚心,不自高自大 modest; unassuming: ～虚 *modest; self-effacing* | ～让 *to decline modestly* | 满招损,～受益。*The modest receive benefit, while the conceited reap failure.*

愆 qiān ㄑㄧㄢ ❶罪过,过失 transgression; fault: ～尤 *error; fault; sin* | 罪～ *guilt; offence; sin* ❷错过,耽误过去 to miss the deadline; to pass the time limit: ～期 *to pass the appointed time; to exceed the time limit; to delay*

鹐 qiān ㄑㄧㄢ 尖嘴的家禽或鸟啄东西(of birds with a sharp beak) to peck: 乌鸦把瓜～了。*The crow has pecked the melon.*

骞 qiān ㄑㄧㄢ 高举。多用于人名,如西汉有张骞(*qian*, usually used in a given name, e.g. Zhang Qian in the Western Han Dynasty) to hold high up

搴 qiān ㄑㄧㄢ ❶拔取 to pull out; to uproot: 斩将～旗 *to kill an enemy general and*

Q

pull down his flag ❷同"褰" same as 褰

褰 qiān ㄑㄧㄢ 把衣服提起来 to lift up (one's clothes, etc):～裳 *to lift up clothes*

荨(蕁、**蕁) ㊀ qián ㄑㄧㄢ [荨麻]多年生草本植物,茎叶生细毛,皮肤接触时会引起刺痛。茎皮纤维可以做纺织原料 nettle (*Urtica fissa*)

㊁ xún 见854页 see p854

钤 qián ㄑㄧㄢ ❶印章 seal; stamp [钤记]旧时印的一种(in former times) a kind of seal or stamp ❷盖印章 to affix a seal to; to stamp:～印 *to affix a seal to; to stamp*|～章 *official stamp*

黔 qián ㄑㄧㄢ ❶黑色 black:～首(古代称老百姓)(*in ancient China*) *common people* ❷贵州省的别称 Qian, another name for Guizhou Province

Q

前 qián ㄑㄧㄢ ❶跟"后"相对(the opposite of 后) **1** 指空间,人脸所向的一面,房屋等正门所向的一面,家具等靠外的一面(used to refer to space) front:在～面 *in front*|向～走 *to go ahead; to move forward*|天安门～ *in front of Tian'anmen*|楼～ *in front of the building*|床～ *before* (*or in front of*) *the bed* **2** 指时间,往日的,过去的(used to denote time) ago; before; past:～天 *the day before yesterday*|史无～例 *unprecedented in history; without parallel in history* **3** 指次序,靠头里的(used to denote order) front; first; top:～五名 *first five places* ❷向前行进 to move forward; to go ahead:勇往直～*to forge ahead dauntlessly; to advance bravely*|畏缩不～ *to hang back in fear; to hesitate to press forward; to recoil from* (*danger, a heavy task, etc*) ❸未来的(用于展望) prospect; future:～景 *prospect; future*|向～看 *to look towards the future; to look ahead*

虔 qián ㄑㄧㄢ 恭敬 pious; devout; sincere:～诚 *pious; devout; sincere*|～心 *pious; devout; sincere*

钱(錢) qián ㄑㄧㄢ ❶货币 currency; money:铜～ *copper coins* ㊙ ***extension*** 费用 expense:车～ *fare*|饭～ *money for a restaurant bill; money for food* ❷圆形像钱的东西 anything that resembles a coin in shape:纸～ *paper made to resemble money and burned as an offering to the dead; ghost money*|榆～儿 *elm tree seeds* ❸财物 wealth; riches:有～有势 *both rich and influential* ❹市制重量单位,一两的十分之一,合5克 *qian*, a unit of weight, equal to one-tenth *liang* or five grams

钳(**箝、❶**拑) qián ㄑㄧㄢ ❶用东西夹住 to hold with pincers; to grip with pincers; to clamp [钳制]用强力限制 to clamp down on; to pin down; to suppress ❷(一子)夹东西的用具 pliers; pincers; tongs: 老虎～ *pliers*

掮 qián ㄑㄧㄢˊ 用肩扛(káng)东西 to carry on the shoulder [掮客]〈方 ***dialect***〉指替买卖货物的双方介绍交易,从中取得佣钱的人 broker

乾 ㊀ qián ㄑㄧㄢˊ ❶八卦之一,符号是☰,代表天 *qian*, one of the Eight Trigrams ☰, representing heaven ❷乾县,在陕西省 Qianxian County, in Shaanxi Province

㊁ gān 见214页"干"see 干 on p214

犍 ㊁ qián ㄑㄧㄢˊ [犍为](—wéi)地名,在四川省 Qianwei, a place in Sichuan Province

㊀ jiān 见328页 see p328

潜(*濳) qián ㄑㄧㄢˊ ❶隐在水面下活动 to move about or exercise under water: ～水艇 *submarine* | 鱼～鸟飞。*Fish are swimming in the water and birds are flying in the sky*. ❷隐藏,隐蔽 to hide; to conceal: ～伏 *to hide; to lurk; to lie low* | ～藏 *to hide; to go into hiding* | ～力 *latent capacity; potentiality* [潜心]十分专心而深入 to devote oneself to; to work with great concentration: ～～研究 *to devote oneself to research; to concentrate on studies* ❸秘密地,不声张 secretly; stealthily; on the sly: ～行 *to move stealthily; to slink; to sneak* | ～逃 *to flee secretly; to abscond*

肷(**膁) qiǎn ㄑㄧㄢˇ 身体两旁肋骨和胯骨之间的部分(多指兽类的)(usually of animals) part between the ribs and the ilia: ～窝 *hip*

浅(淺) ㊀ qiǎn ㄑㄧㄢˇ ❶从表面到底或从外面到里面距离小,跟"深"相对(the opposite of 深) shallow: 这条河很～。*The river is very shallow*. | 这个院子太～。*There is little depth from the entrance of the yard to its rear*. ❷不久,时间短 not long in time: 年代～ *recent past* | 相处的日子还～。*They have not been together for long*. ❸程度不深的 not close; superficial; simple: ～见 *superficial view* | 阅历～ *to know little of the world; to have superficial knowledge of the world* | 交情～ *not to be on familiar terms* | 这篇文章很～。*This article is very simple*. | ～近的理论 *simple theories* ❹颜色淡薄(of colours) light: ～红 *light red* | ～绿 *light green*

㊁ jiān 见326页 see p326

遣 qiǎn ㄑㄧㄢˇ ❶派,差(chāi),打发 to send; to dispatch (㊟ ***doublet*** 派— to dispatch; to send | 差— to send sb on an errand or mission; to dispatch): 特～ *to send for a special purpose; to appoint for a*

special assignment | ～送 *to send back; to repatriate* ❷排解，发泄 to drive away; to dispel; to expel: ～闷(mèn) *to dispel boredom; to divert oneself from boredom; to seek relief from boredom* | 消～ *diversion; pastime*

谴 qiǎn ㄑㄧㄢˇ 责备 to blame; to reproach; to reprimand (㊟ ***doublet*** —责 to condemn; to censure; to denounce)

缱 qiǎn ㄑㄧㄢˇ [缱绻](-quǎn) 情意缠绵，感情好得离不开(of love between man and woman) to be deeply attached to each other; (of two persons) to be in such complete agreement so as to be unable to bear parting from each other

嗛 qiǎn ㄑㄧㄢˇ 就是颊囊。猴等嘴里两腮上暂时贮存食物的地方(i.e.颊囊) cheek pouch 〈古 ***archaism***〉又同"谦"(qiān)、"歉"(qiàn) also same as 谦 or 歉

Q

欠 qiàn ㄑㄧㄢˋ ❶借别人的财物还(hái)没归还(huán) to owe; to be behind with: 我～他十块钱。*I owe him ten* yuan. ❷缺乏，不够 to lack; to be short of; to be inadequate: 文章～通。*The article lacks coherence and logic.* | 身体～安 *to feel poorly; to be slightly indisposed; to be a bit under the weather* ❸身体稍稍向上移动 to raise slightly (part of one's body): ～身 *to rise slightly from one's seat; to raise oneself slightly* | ～脚 *to raise one's heels slightly; to stand on tiptoe* ❹哈欠(qian)，疲倦时张口出气 to yawn: ～伸 *to stretch oneself and yawn* | 打哈～ *to yawn*

芡 qiàn ㄑㄧㄢˋ ❶一年生水草，茎叶都有刺，开紫花。果实叫芡实，外皮有刺。种子的仁可以吃，可以制淀粉。也叫"鸡头"(also called 鸡头) gorgon plant (*Euryale ferox*) ❷烹饪时用淀粉调成的浓汁 starch used in cooking: 勾～ *to thicken a soup by means of starch* | 汤里加点～ *to add some starch to the soup to make it thicker; to put some starch in the soup*

嵌 qiàn ㄑㄧㄢˋ 把东西卡在空隙里 to inlay; to embed; to set: 镶～ *to inlay; to embed; to set* | ～入 *to inlay; to embed* | 匣子上～着象牙雕的花。*The box is inlaid with flowers carved out of ivory.*

纤(縴) ㊀ qiàn ㄑㄧㄢˋ 拉船的绳 rope for towing a boat; towrope; towline [纤手]给人介绍买卖产业的人 broker [拉纤] **1** 拉着纤绳使船前进 to track a boat; to tow a boat **2** 给人介绍买卖产业从中取利 to act as a broker (*or* middleman); to be a broker

㊁ xiān 见811页 see p811

茜(蒨)** ㊀ qiàn ㄑㄧㄢˋ ❶茜草，多年生蔓草，茎有刺毛，初秋开花，黄色。根红色，可做染料，也可入药

Chinese madder (*Rubia cordifolia*) ❷ 红色 alizarin red; crimson; red

㊁ xī 见799页 see p799

倩 qiàn ㄑㄧㄢˋ ❶ 美好 handsome; beautiful; attractive ❷ 请人代做 to ask sb to do sth on one's behalf: ～人代笔 *to ask sb to write on one's behalf*

堑 qiàn ㄑㄧㄢˋ 做防御用的壕沟 moat; chasm; ditch: 长江天～(喻险要) *natural moat of the Changjiang* (or *Yangtze*) *River; with the Yangtze River providing a natural barrier against attack* [喻] ***figurative*** 挫折 setback; reverse: 吃一～,长一智。*With every pitfall comes greater knowledge.*

椠 qiàn ㄑㄧㄢˋ ❶古代记事用的木板 wood block used in ancient China to record events ❷古书的雕版,版本 engraved edition of books: 古～ *ancient edition* | 宋～ *Song Dynasty wood-block edition*

慊 ㊀ qiàn ㄑㄧㄢˋ 不满,怨恨 to dissatisfy; to resent

㊁ qiè 见605页 see p605

歉 qiàn ㄑㄧㄢˋ ❶觉得对不住人 to feel apologetic: 抱～ *to be sorry; to feel apologetic* | 道～ *to make an apology; to apologize* | 深致～意 *to extend sincere apologies; to express profound regret* ❷收成不好 poor (harvest); crop failure: ～收 *crop failure; poor harvest* | ～年 *lean year; year of poor harvest*

QIANG ㄑㄧㄤ

抢(搶) ㊁ qiāng ㄑㄧㄤ 同"戗(qiāng)❶" same as 戗❶

㊀ qiǎng 见599页 see p599

呛(嗆) ㊀ qiāng ㄑㄧㄤ ❶水或食物进入气管而引起不适或咳嗽 to feel uncomfortable because food or water has entered one's windpipe; to choke: 喝水～着了 *to choke when drinking water* | 吃饭吃～了 *to choke over one's food* ❷〈方 **dialect**〉咳嗽 to cough

㊁ qiàng 见600页 see p600

玱(瑲) qiāng ㄑㄧㄤ 玉相击声 jingling sound of jade

枪(槍、*鎗) qiāng ㄑㄧㄤ ❶刺击用的长矛 spear: 长～ *long spear* | 红缨～ *red tasseled spear* ❷发射子弹的武器 rifle; gun; firearm: 手～ *pistol* | 机关～ *machine gun* ❸形状或性能像枪的器具 any appliance shaped or functioning like a gun: 焊～ *welding torch; (welding) blowpipe* | 水～ *nozzle; water gun; squirt gun*

戗(戧) ㊀ qiāng ㄑㄧㄤ ❶逆,反方向 towards the opposite direction: ～风 *against the wind* | ～水 *to go up the river* ❷(言语)冲突 verbal clash: 说～了。*Their argument ended in a row.*

Q

㊁ qiàng 见600页 see p600

羌 qiāng ㄑㄧㄤ 我国古代西部的民族 the Qiang ethnic group, one of the ancient ethnic minorities in western China [羌族]我国少数民族,参看附表(see the appendix) the Qiang ethnic group, one of ethnic minorities in China

蜣 qiāng ㄑㄧㄤ [蜣螂](-láng)俗叫"屎壳郎"(shǐkelàng)。昆虫,全身黑色,有光泽,会飞,吃粪、尿或动物的尸体(popularly called 屎壳郎) dung beetle (*Scarabaeidae*)

戕 qiāng ㄑㄧㄤ 杀害 to kill:自~ *to kill oneself; to commit suicide* [戕贼]伤害,损害 to harm; to injure; to undermine

斨 qiāng ㄑㄧㄤ 古代一种斧子 (in ancient China) an axe

腔 qiāng ㄑㄧㄤ ❶(-子)动物身体中空的部分 cavity:胸~ *thoracic cavity* | 口~ *oral cavity* ㉇ **extension** 器物中空的部分 hollow part in something:炉~ *furnace cavity* | 锅台~子 *belly of a kitchen stove* ❷(-儿)说话的语调,乐曲的调子 tone; tune; speech:开~(说话) *to start talking* | 南~北调 *(to speak) with a mixture of accents* | 离~走板 *to sing out of tune and go off key* | 梆子~ bangziqiang, *a general term for local operas in Shanxi, Shaanxi, Henan, Hebei, Shandong, etc, performed to the accompaniment of* bangzi [京腔]北京语音 Beijing accent:一口~~ *a pure Beijing dialect*

锖 qiāng ㄑㄧㄤ [锖色]某些矿物表面因氧化作用而形成的薄膜所呈现的色彩,常常不同于矿物固有的颜色 tarnish

锵(鏘) qiāng ㄑㄧㄤ 拟声词(叠 **reduplication**) **onomatopoeia**:锣声~~ *continuous clanging of gongs*

镪 ㊀ qiāng ㄑㄧㄤ [镪水]就是强酸(i. e. 强酸) strong acid:硝~~ *nitric acid*

㊁ qiǎng 见599页 see p599

强(*強、*彊) ㊀ qiáng ㄑㄧㄤˊ ❶健壮,有力,跟"弱"相对(the opposite of 弱) strong; powerful; mighty(㉆ **doublet** 一壮 strong; sturdy; robust | 一健 strong and healthy; sturdy; stout):~大 *big and powerful; powerful; formidable* | 身~力壮 *strong and healthy* ㉇ **extension** 有余 slightly more than; a little over; plus:四分之一~ *a little over one fourth* [强调]特别重视,用坚决的口气提出 to stress; to emphasize [强梁]强横不讲理 brutal and unreasonable; tyrannical; overbearing ❷程度高 to a high degree; of a high standard:责任心很~ *to have a strong sense of responsibility* ❸好 better (than); superior (to):要~ *to be eager to excel; to be anxious to outdo others* | 庄稼很~。*The crops are growing well.* | 他写的字

比你的～。*His handwriting is better than yours.* ❹使用强力 by force:～制 *to force; to compel; to coerce*|～占 *to occupy forcibly; to take by force; to seize*|～索财物 *to take possession of other people's property by force* ❺使强大或强壮 to strengthen; to enhance:～身之道 *the way to keep fit (by physical exercises or by taking tonics)*|富国～兵 *to enrich the country and strengthen the military* ❻姓 Qiang, a surname

㊁ qiǎng 见599页 see p599
㊂ jiàng 见337页 see p337

墙(墻、*牆) qiáng ㄑ丨尢 用砖石等砌成承架房顶或隔开内外的建筑物 wall (㊧ ***doublet*** —壁 wall):砖～ *brick wall*|城～ *city wall*|院～ *courtyard wall; wall surrounding a house*

蔷(薔) qiáng ㄑ丨尢 [蔷薇](—wēi)落叶灌木,茎上多刺,夏初开花,有红、黄、白等色,可制香料,也可入药 rose (*Rosa*)

嫱(嬙) qiáng ㄑ丨尢 古时宫廷里的女官名 woman court official in ancient China:妃～ *woman official in charge of imperial concubines*

樯(檣、*艢) qiáng ㄑ丨尢 帆船上挂风帆的桅杆 mast

抢(搶) ㊀ qiǎng ㄑ丨尢 ❶夺,硬拿 to rob; to loot; to snatch (㊧ ***doublet*** —夺 to snatch; to seize; to grab):～球 *to snatch the ball from (sb's hand or feet)*|～劫 *to rob; to loot; to plunder*|他把我的信～去了。*He snatched away my letter.* ❷赶快,赶紧,争先 to hurry; to rush:～着把活做了 *to vie with one another in getting the work done*|～修河堤 *to rush to repair the river bank* ❸刮,擦(去掉表面的一层) to scrape; to scratch:磨剪子～菜刀 *to sharpen scissors and kitchen knives*|摔了一跤,把肉皮～去一大块。*I got a scrape from a fall.*

㊁ qiāng 见597页 see p597

羟(羥) qiǎng ㄑ丨尢 羟基,就是氢氧基(—OH)(i. e. 氢氧基) hydroxyl (group)

强(*強、*彊) ㊁ qiǎng ㄑ丨尢 硬要,迫使 to try hard; to strive; to force:～迫 *to compel; to force; to coerce*|牵～ *forced; far-fetched; strained*|～词夺理 *to resort to sophistry; to reason fallaciously*|不能～人所难。*Don't try to make sb do what is beyond his power or against his will.*

㊀ qiáng 见598页 see p598
㊂ jiàng 见337页 see p337

镪 ㊀ qiǎng ㄑ丨尢 〈古 ***archaism***〉指成串的钱 string of copper coins [白镪]银子 silver

㊁ qiāng 见598页 see p598

襁(*繈) qiǎng ㄑ丨尢 [襁褓](—bǎo)包婴儿的被、毯等 quilt, blanket,

Q

etc used to wrap up a baby; swaddling clothes:在～～中 *to be in one's infancy*

呛(嗆) ㊁ qiàng ㄑㄧㄤˋ 有刺激性的气体使鼻子、嗓子等器官感到不舒服 to irritate (respiratory organs):烟～嗓子。*The smoke irritated my throat.*|辣椒味～得难受。*The smell of red pepper being fried is so irritating that it makes you uncomfortable.*

㊀ qiāng 见597页 see p597

戗(戧) ㊁ qiàng ㄑㄧㄤˋ 支持,支撑 to shore up; to prop; to buttress:墙要倒,拿杠子～住。*The wall is falling down; please prop it up with logs.*[够戗]形容十分厉害,很难支持 unbearable; terrible:他忙得真～～。*He has been terribly busy.*|他病得～～。*He is terribly ill.*

㊀ qiāng 见597页 see p597

炝(熗) qiàng ㄑㄧㄤˋ 烹饪法 way of cooking **1** 油锅热后,放主菜前先放入葱等急炒一下,使有香味 to quick-fry (chopped spring onion, etc) in hot oil (before putting in vegetables, etc); to flavour the dish; to quick-fry:～锅 *to fry sth quickly in hot oil to flavour a dish* **2** 把原料放在沸水中焯(chāo)一下,取出后再用香油等调料拌 to boil sth in boiling water for a while and then dress it with sesame oil, etc:～豆芽 *boiled and dressed bean sprouts*

跄(蹌、**蹡) qiàng ㄑㄧㄤˋ 见443页“踉”字条“踉跄”(liàng—) see 踉跄 on p443

QIAO ㄑㄧㄠ

悄 ㊁ qiāo ㄑㄧㄠ [悄悄]没有声音或声音很低 with as little noise as possible; quietly:静～～ *very quiet*|部队～～地出动。*The troops set out quietly.*

㊀ qiǎo 见602页 see p602

硗(磽) qiāo ㄑㄧㄠ 地坚硬不肥沃 (of soil) hard and infertile (㊟ ***doublet*** —薄 hard and infertile; barren; unproductive|—瘠 barren; infertile|—确 barren; unproductive):肥～ *fertile and barren*

跷(蹺、*蹻) qiāo ㄑㄧㄠ ❶脚向上抬 to lift up (a leg):～脚 *to stand on tiptoes*|～腿 *to lift up a leg* [高跷]踩着有踏脚装置的木棍表演的一种游艺 stilts ❷竖起大拇指 to hold up a thumb:～起大拇指称赞 *to hold up one's thumb in approval*

[跷蹊](—qi)奇怪,违反常理,让人怀疑 strange; fishy; suspicious:这事有点～～。*There is something fishy about it.* 也说“蹊跷”(qī—)(also called 蹊跷)

“蹻”(又 juē also juē)见374页“屩”see 屩 on p374

雀 ㊁ qiāo ㄑㄧㄠ 雀子,雀(què)斑 freckle

㊀ què 见625页 see p625

㊂ qiǎo 见602页 see p602

锹(*鍫) qiāo ㄑㄧㄠ 挖土或铲其他东西的器具 spade; shovel

劁 qiāo ㄑㄧㄠ 骟(shàn),割去牲畜的睾丸或卵巢 to geld; to castrate: ～猪 *to castrate a pig* | ～羊 *to geld a goat*

敲 qiāo ㄑㄧㄠ ❶打,击 to knock; to beat; to strike: ～锣 *to beat gongs* | ～边鼓(比喻从旁帮人说话) *to beat the drum on the side — to speak or act from the sidelines to assist sb* ❷敲竹杠,讹诈财物或抬高价格 to fleece; to blackmail

橇 qiāo ㄑㄧㄠ ❶古代在泥路上行走所乘的东西(in ancient China) equipment used for walking on a muddy road ❷在冰雪上滑行的工具 sledge; sled; sleigh

缲(**幧) ㊀qiāo ㄑㄧㄠ 做衣服边儿或带子时藏着针脚的缝法 to hem with invisible stitches: ～一根带子 *to hem a ribbon* | ～边 *to hem the edges*

㊁ sāo 见647页 see p647

乔(喬) qiáo ㄑㄧㄠ ❶高 tall [乔木]树干和树枝有明显区别的大树,如松、柏、杨、柳等 arbor; tree [乔迁]称人迁居的客气话(used for congratulations) to move into a new residence ❷做假,装 to disguise; to simulate; to dress up [乔装][乔妆]改变服装面貌,掩蔽身份 to deck oneself out as sb else: ～～打扮 *to masquerade; to disguise*

侨(僑) qiáo ㄑㄧㄠ ❶寄居在国外(从前也指寄居在外乡)(also to reside in a place other than one's hometown in former times) to live abroad; to reside in a foreign country: ～居 *to reside in a strange land* ❷寄居在祖国以外的人 person living abroad: 华～ *Chinese nationals living abroad; overseas Chinese*

荞(蕎、△*荍) qiáo ㄑㄧㄠ 荞麦,一年生草本植物,茎紫红色,叶子三角形,开小白花。子实黑色,磨成面粉供食用 buckwheat (*Fagopyrum esculentum*)

峤(嶠) ㊁ qiáo ㄑㄧㄠ 山尖而高(of a mountain) high and pointed

㊀ jiào 见342页 see p342

桥(橋) qiáo ㄑㄧㄠ 架在水上(或空中)便于通行的建筑物 bridge: 拱～ *arched bridge* | 天～ *platform bridge* | 独木～ *single-plank bridge* | 立交～ *flyover bridge; overpass* | 长江大～ *Changjiang River Bridge; Yangtze River Bridge*

硚(礄) qiáo ㄑㄧㄠ [硚口]地名,在湖北省武汉 Qiaokou, a place in Wuhan, Hubei Province

鞒(鞽) qiáo ㄑㄧㄠ 马鞍拱起的地方 arched

part of a saddle; pommel and cantle of a saddle

荍 qiáo ㄑㄧㄠˊ ❶即锦葵,二年或多年生草本植物,夏季开花,花紫色或白色,可供观赏(i. e. 锦葵) mallow; high mallow (*Malva sylvestris*) ❷同"荞"same as 荞

翘(翹) ㊀ qiáo ㄑㄧㄠˊ ❶举起,抬起,向上 to raise; to lift up:～首 *to lift up one's head (and look); to crane one's head*|～望 *to raise one's head to look at sth* ❷翘棱(leng),板状物体因由湿变干而弯曲不平 to become warped or bent:桌面～棱了。*The tabletop has become warped.*

㊁ qiào 见603页 see p603

谯 qiáo ㄑㄧㄠˊ 谯楼,古代城门上建筑的楼,可以瞭望(in ancient China) watchtower; drum tower

憔(*顦) qiáo ㄑㄧㄠˊ [憔悴](—cuì)黄瘦,脸色不好 wan and sallow; emaciated; haggard:面容～～ *looking wan and sallow*

樵 qiáo ㄑㄧㄠˊ ❶〈方 **dialect**〉柴 firewood ❷打柴 to gather firewood:～夫 *woodchopper; woodman*

瞧 qiáo ㄑㄧㄠˊ 看 to look; to see; to watch:～见 *to see; to notice; to catch sight of*|～得起 *to think highly of; to have high regard for; to look up to*|～不起 *to look down upon; to have little regard for; to despise*

巧 qiǎo ㄑㄧㄠˇ ❶技巧,技术 skill; technique; expertise ❷灵巧,灵敏,手的技能好 skillful; ingenious; deft:心灵手～ *clever and deft*|他很～。*His workmanship is excellent.* ❸虚浮不实(指话)(of words) cunning; deceitful; artful:花言～语 *honeyed words; fine-sounding words; deceitful talk* ❹恰好,正遇在某种机会上 luckily; opportunely; coincidentally:凑～ *luckily; fortunately*|碰～ *by chance; accidentally; by coincidence*|赶～ *to happen to*

悄 ㊀ qiǎo ㄑㄧㄠˇ ❶忧愁(叠 ***reduplication***) sad; worried; grieved:忧心～～ *to feel sad; to be worried* ❷寂静无声或声音很低 quiet; silent:～然无声 *silently; soundlessly; very quietly*|低声～语 *to speak in a low voice; to whisper*

㊁ qiāo 见600页 see p600

雀 ㊁ qiǎo ㄑㄧㄠˇ 义同"雀㊀",用于"家雀儿"等口语词(used colloquially as in 家雀儿, etc) same as 雀㊀

㊀ què 见625页 see p625

㊂ qiāo 见601页 see p601

愀 qiǎo ㄑㄧㄠˇ 脸色改变 to become stern or displeased:～然作色 *to turn stern*

壳(殼) ㊁ qiào ㄑㄧㄠˋ 坚硬的外皮 hard outer covering of sth; crust; shell:甲～ *crust; carapace; shell*|地～ *earth's crust*

㊁ ké 见389页 see p389

俏 qiào ㄑㄧㄠˋ ❶漂亮,相貌美好 pretty; smart-looking; good-looking:俊～ *pretty and charming* ❷货物的销路好 fast selling:～货 *highly salable goods; commodities in great demand; fast-selling goods* ❸〈方 **dialect**〉烹调时为增加滋味、色泽,加上少量的青蒜、香菜、木耳之类 to flavour (with); to season (with)

诮 qiào ㄑㄧㄠˋ 责备,讥讽 to blame; to ridicule; to deride:～责 *to blame; to reproach; to deride*|讥～ *to sneer at; to ridicule; to deride*

峭(*陗) qiào ㄑㄧㄠˋ 山又高又陡(of mountains) high and steep; abrupt; precipitous:～壁 *cliff; steep; precipice* 喻 **figurative** 严峻 severe; stern:～直 *upright and stern*

鞘 ㊀ qiào ㄑㄧㄠˋ 装刀、剑的套子 sheath; scabbard:刀～ *sheath; scabbard*

㊁ shāo 见660页 see p660

窍(竅) qiào ㄑㄧㄠˋ ❶窟窿,孔洞 hole; aperture; orifice:七～(耳、目、口、鼻) *seven orifices (of the head, i.e. the eyes, ears, nostrils and mouth)*|一～不通(喻一点也不懂) *to know nothing about; to have no knowledge of; to be completely ignorant of* ❷(一儿)事情的关键 key (to sth); trick; knack:诀～儿 *trick; knack*|～门儿 *key (to sth); trick; knack*

翘(翹、**蹺) ㊀ qiào ㄑㄧㄠˋ 一头向上仰起(of one end) to turn upwards; to bend upwards:板凳～起来了。*One end of the bench has turned upwards.*[翘尾巴] 喻 **figurative** 傲慢或自鸣得意 to stick one's tail up — to be cocky; to be haughty and snooty

㊁ qiáo 见602页 see p602

撬 qiào ㄑㄧㄠˋ 用棍、棒等拨、挑东西 to prize; to pry; to jimmy:把门～开 *to prize a door open*

QIE ㄑㄧㄝ

切 ㊀ qiē ㄑㄧㄝ ❶用刀从上往下割 to cut; to slice; to chop:～成片 *to cut into slices; to slice*|把瓜～开 *to cut open a melon; to slice up a melon*[切磋](一cuō) 喻 **figurative** 在业务、思想等方面互相研究讨论,取长补短 to learn from each other by exchanging views ❷几何学上直线与弧线或两个弧线相接于一点 tangency:～线 *tangent line*|～点 *tangent point; point of contact*|两圆相～。*The two circles are tangent.*

㊁ qiè 见604页 see p604

伽 ㊀ qié ㄑㄧㄝˊ [伽蓝]梵语"僧伽蓝摩"的省称,指僧众所住的园林,后指佛寺(short for 僧伽蓝摩 in Sanskrit) garden where monks live; Buddhist temple［伽南香］沉香，一种常绿乔木，木材重而坚硬，有香味，可入药 agalloch eaglewood（*Aquilaria sinensis*）

㊁ jiā 见320页 see p320

㊂ gā 见212页 see p212

茄 ㊀ qié ㄑㄧㄝˊ（－子）一年生草本植物，花紫色。果实也叫茄子，紫色，也有白色或绿色的，可以吃 eggplant；aubergine（*Solanum melongena*）［番茄］一年生草本植物，花黄色。果实也叫番茄，圆形，熟时红色或黄色，可以吃。也叫"西红柿"（also called 西红柿）tomato（*Solanum lycopersicum*）

㊁ jiā 见321页 see p321

且 ㊀ qiě ㄑㄧㄝˇ ❶连词 ***conjunction***，表示并列或进一层 and；both…and…；not only…but also：既高～大 *both tall and big* ❷连词 ***conjunction***，尚且，表示让步 even：死～不怕，还怕困难吗？*Even death holds no fear for us，let alone difficulties.* ❸副词 ***adverb***，表示暂时 for the time being；for the moment：～慢 *to wait a minute*｜～住 *to wait a moment；to hesitate* ❹文言副词 ***adverb of classical Chinese***，将要 nearly，almost：年～九十 *to be nearly ninety years old* ❺且……且……，表示两个动作同时进行 while；as：～走～说 *to talk while walking*｜～行～想 *to think while walking；to think while doing sth* ❻副词 ***adverb***，且……呢，表示经久 for a long time；for quite some time：这双鞋～穿呢。*This pair of shoes will last a long time.* ❼姓 Qie，a surname

㊁ jū 见366页 see p366

切 ㊁ qiè ㄑㄧㄝˋ ❶密合，贴近 to correspond to；to conform to；to be close to：～身利害 *one's immediate interests*｜不～实际 *not corresponding to reality；unrealistic*［切齿］咬牙表示痛恨 to grind（*or* gnash）one's teeth（in hatred）❷紧急 eager；keen；anxious：急～ *eager；impatient；urgent*｜迫～需要 *to be in urgent need of*｜回国心～ *to be anxious to return to one's native land* ❸切实，实在，着实 to make sure that；must；to have to：～记 *to keep firmly in mind；must always remember；to be sure to remember*｜～忌 *must guard against；to avoid by all means*｜言辞恳～ *to be sincere in what one says；to speak earnestly* ❹旧时汉语标音的一种方法，取上一字的声母与下一字的韵母和声调，拼成一个音，也叫"反切"。如"同"字是徒红切（also called 反切）traditional method of indicating the pronunciation of a Chinese character by using two other Chinese characters，the first having the same consonant as the given character and the second having the same vowel and tone，e. g. the pronunciation of 同 tóng is indicated as 徒红切，meaning a combination of the consonant t

from 徒 tú and the compound vowel óng from 红 hóng
[一切]所有的，全部 all; overall
㊁ qiē 见603页 see p603

窃(竊) qiè ㄑㄧㄝˋ ❶偷盗 to steal; to pilfer; to pinch: ～案 *case of theft; burglary* ㊞ ***metaphor*** 用不合法不合理的手段取得 to get sth in illegal and unreasonable ways and means; to plagiarize; to usurp: ～位 *to usurp a post* | ～国 *to usurp state power* ❷私自，暗中 secretly; furtively; stealthily: ～笑 *to laugh secretly; to laugh up one's sleeve* 旧谦辞 used in humble reference to oneself in former times: ～谓 *I would like to call* | ～以为 *in my humble opinion; I presume*

郄 qiè ㄑㄧㄝˋ 姓 Qie, a surname
〈古 ***archaism***〉又同"郤"(xì) also same as 郤

妾 qiè ㄑㄧㄝˋ ❶旧时男子在妻子以外娶的女子(in former times) concubine ❷谦辞 ***humble***，旧时女人自称 used by women in humble reference to themselves in former times

怯 qiè ㄑㄧㄝˋ ❶胆小，没勇气(㊀ ***doublet*** 一懦 timid and overcautious; weak and cowardly; chicken-hearted) timid; cowardly; nervous: 胆～ *timid; cowardly* | ～场 *to have stage fright* ❷〈方 ***dialect***〉俗气，见识不广，不合时宜 vulgar; superficial; outmoded: 露～ *to reveal one's inadequacies; to cut a poor figure* | 衣服的颜色有点～。*The colour of this dress is a bit tawdry.*

朅 qiè ㄑㄧㄝˋ ❶离去 to go; to leave ❷勇武 brave; courageous; valiant

挈 qiè ㄑㄧㄝˋ ❶用手提着 to lift: 提纲～领(喻简明扼要地把问题提示出来) *to grasp a net by the headrope (or to grasp a coat by the collar) — to concentrate on the main points; to bring out the essentials* ❷带，领 to take along: ～眷 *to take one's family along*

锲 qiè ㄑㄧㄝˋ 用刀子刻 to carve; to engrave; to chisel: ～金玉 *to carve gold and jade* | ～而不舍(喻有恒心，有毅力) *to keep on chiseling or chipping away — to stick to sth with persistence; to work with perseverance; to make unflagging efforts*

惬(愜、*悏) qiè ㄑㄧㄝˋ 满足，畅快 satisfied; content; carefree: ～意 *pleased; satisfied; gratified* | ～心 *pleased; satisfied; content* [惬当](－dàng) 恰当 proper; appropriate

箧(篋) qiè ㄑㄧㄝˋ 箱子一类的东西 small suitcase or container

趄 ㊀ qiè ㄑㄧㄝˋ 倾斜 slanting; inclined: ～着身子 *(of a person) leaning sideways*
㊁ jū 见367页 see p367

慊 ㊁ qiè ㄑㄧㄝˋ 满足，满意 contented; satisfied; gratified：不～（不满）*unsatisfied; discontented*

㊁ qiàn 见597页 see p597

QIN ㄑㄧㄣ

钦 qīn ㄑㄧㄣ ❶恭敬 to respect; to admire; to adore：～佩 *to admire; to esteem*｜～仰 *to revere; to venerate; to esteem* ❷封建时代指有关皇帝的（in feudal China）related to the emperor; imperial：～定 *authorized by the sovereign himself*｜～赐 *granted* （or *bestowed*） *by the emperor*｜～差（chāi）大臣 *imperial envoy; imperial commissioner*

嵚 qīn ㄑㄧㄣ ［嵚崟］（—yín）山高的样子（of a mountain）high; towering

侵 qīn ㄑㄧㄣ ❶侵犯，夺取别人的权利 to invade; to infringe on; to encroach upon：～害 *to encroach upon and damage; to infringe on and harm; to make inroads on*｜～吞 *to embezzle; to misappropriate; to defalcate*［侵略］侵犯别国领土、主权，掠夺别国财富，奴役别国人民，以及干涉别国内政等行动 to invade; to commit aggression (against)：我们热爱和平，反对～～。*We love peace and oppose aggression.* ❷渐近 approaching; drawing near：～晨 *toward daybreak; at the approach of dawn*

骎 qīn ㄑㄧㄣ ［骎骎］马跑得很快的样子（of horses）galloping ㊀ **extension** 急速，快速 speedily; apace：～～日上 *developing apace; forging ahead*

亲（親） ㊀ qīn ㄑㄧㄣ ❶亲属，有血统或夫妻关系的 related by blood; of blood relation; related by marriage：～人 *one's parents, spouse, children, etc; one's kinfolks; one's kith and kin*｜～兄弟 *blood brothers* 特指父母 parent：双～ *parents*｜养～ *foster parents* ❷婚姻 marriage; match：定～ *to be engaged to; to be betrothed to; to contract a marriage*｜～事 *marriage* ❸特指新妇 bride：娶～ *(of a man) to get married; to go to pick up his bride at her house* ❹亲戚，因婚姻联成的亲属关系 relatives by marriage; kin：姑表～ *relationship between the children of a brother and a sister; cousinship* ❺本身，自己的 in person; personally：～笔信 *personally handwritten letter; autograph letter; holograph letter*｜～眼见的。*He has seen it with his own eyes.*｜～手做的。*He has done it himself.* ❻感情好，关系密切 close; intimate; dear：他们很～密。*They are on very close terms.*｜兄弟相～。*Brothers are always on close terms.* ❼用嘴唇接触，表示喜爱 to kiss：他～了～孩子的小脸蛋。*He kissed the kid on the cheek.*

㊁ qìng 见612页 see p612

Q

衾 qīn ㄑㄧㄣ 被子 quilt：～枕 *quilt and pillow*

芹 qín ㄑㄧㄣˊ 芹菜，一年或二年生草本植物，夏天开花，白色，茎、叶可以吃 celery (*Apium graveolens*)

芩 qín ㄑㄧㄣˊ 植物名 name of plants **1** 古书上指芦苇一类的植物(in ancient Chinese texts) a kind of reed **2** 黄芩，多年生草本植物，开淡紫色花，根可入药 baikal skullcap (*Scutellaria baicalensis*)

矜(**穜) ㊂ qín ㄑㄧㄣˊ 〈古 ***archaism***〉矛柄 handle of a spear

㊀ jīn 见351页 see p351

㊁ guān 见248页 see p248

琴 qín ㄑㄧㄣˊ ❶古琴，一种弦乐器，用梧桐等木料做成，有五根弦，后来增加为七根 *qin*, a seven-stringed (early five-stringed) plucked musical instrument made of Chinese parasol wood, etc ❷某些乐器的统称，如风琴、钢琴、胡琴等 general term for certain musical instruments, such as organ, piano, *huqin*, etc

秦 qín ㄑㄧㄣˊ ❶周代诸侯国名，在今陕西省和甘肃省一带 Qin, a princedom of the Zhou Dynasty, covering today's Shaanxi Province and Gansu Province and nearby areas ❷朝代名。秦始皇嬴政所建立(公元前221—公元前206年)，建都咸阳(在今陕西省咸阳东)。秦是我国历史上第一个统一的中央集权的封建王朝 the Qin Dynasty (221 BC — 206 BC), established by Ying Zheng or Qinshihuang (first Emperor of the Qin Dynasty), with its capital in Xianyang (east of today's Xianyang in Shaanxi Province) ❸陕西省的别称 Qin, another name for Shaanxi Province

嗪 qín ㄑㄧㄣˊ 见548页"哌"字条"哌嗪"(pài—) see 哌嗪 on p548

溱 ㊁ qín ㄑㄧㄣˊ [溱潼](—tóng)地名，在江苏省泰州 Qintong, a place in Taizhou, Jiangsu Province

㊀ zhēn 见967页 see p967

螓 qín ㄑㄧㄣˊ 古书上说的一种昆虫，像蝉而较小(in ancient Chinese texts) a kind of cicada-like insect

覃 ㊁ qín ㄑㄧㄣˊ 姓 Qin, a surname

㊀ tán 见728页 see p728

禽 qín ㄑㄧㄣˊ ❶鸟类的总称 general name for birds：家～ *fowl; poultry*｜飞～ *birds; fowls of the air* ❷〈古 ***archaism***〉鸟兽的总称 general term for birds and animals ❸古同"擒" same as 擒 in ancient Chinese

擒 qín ㄑㄧㄣˊ 捕捉 to capture; to catch; to seize：～贼先～王。*To catch a gang of brigands, first catch their chieftain.*

噙 qín ㄑㄧㄣˊ 含在里面 to hold in the mouth or the eyes：

嘴里～了一口水 *with a mouthful of water* | 眼里～着眼泪 *eyes brimming with tears*

檎 qín ㄑㄧㄣˊ ［林檎］即花红。落叶小乔木，花粉红色，果实像苹果而小，可以吃 Chinese pear-leaved crabapple （*Malus asiatica*）

勤（❶**廑、❹*懃） qín ㄑㄧㄣˊ ❶做事尽力，不偷懒 hard working; diligent; industrious: ～快 *hard working; diligent; industrious* | ～劳 *hard working; diligent; assiduous* | ～学苦练 *to study diligently and train hard; to study assiduously and practice hard* ㊀ ***extension*** 经常，次数多 often; frequently; constantly: ～洗澡 *to take baths regularly* | 夏天雨～。*It often rains in summer.* | 房子要～打扫。*The house needs regular cleaning.* ❷按规定时间上班的工作（office, school, etc） attendance: 出～ *to attend class; to be at the work place; to show up for work* | 缺～ *to be absent （from school, workplace, duty etc）* | 考～ *to check on attendance; to keep attendance records* ［后勤］**1** 军事组织在后方担任兵工、军需供给、医疗、运输等的任务 rear service; logistics **2** 泛指总务工作 general affairs ❸勤务 work; duty; service: 内～ *office work* | 外～ *field work* ❹见895页"殷"字条"殷勤" see 殷勤 on p895

"廑"又 jǐn 见352页"仅"（also jǐn） see 仅 on p352

梫 qǐn ㄑㄧㄣˇ 古书上指肉桂。参看255页"桂"（see 桂 on p255） （in ancient Chinese texts） cinnamon tree; Chinese cinnamon tree; cassia-bark tree

锓 qǐn ㄑㄧㄣˇ 雕刻 to carve; to engrave; to etch: ～版 *carved block （for printing）*

寝（寢） qǐn ㄑㄧㄣˇ ❶睡觉 to sleep: 废～忘食（*so absorbed or occupied as*） *to forget about eating and sleeping;* （*so engrossed or absorbed as*） *to forget food and rest* ❷睡觉的地方 bedroom: 就～ *to go to bed* | 寿终正～ *to die in one's bed of a ripe old age; to die a natural death* ❸停止进行 to stop; to end: 事～。*The affair came to an end.* ❹面貌难看 ugly: 貌～ *ugly-looking*

吣（**吢、**唚） qìn ㄑㄧㄣˋ 猫狗呕吐（of cats or dogs） to vomit

沁 qìn ㄑㄧㄣˋ ❶渗入，浸润 to ooze; to seep; to exude: 香气～人心脾。*A sweet smell seeps into the heart.* ❷〈方 ***dialect***〉纳入水中 to put into the water ❸〈方 ***dialect***〉头向下垂 to lower （*or* droop） one's head: ～着头 *to droop one's head* ❹沁河，源出山西省沁源，东南流至河南省注入黄河 Qinhe River, originating in Qinyuan of Shanxi Province and flowing southeast into the Huanghe River in Henan Prov-

Q

ince

揿（*撳）qìn ㄑㄧㄣˋ〈方 ***dialect***〉用手按 to press; to push：～电铃 *to press a bell; to ring a bell.*

QING ㄑㄧㄥ

青 qīng ㄑㄧㄥ ❶颜色 colour **1** 绿色 green：～草 *green grass* **2** 蓝色 blue：～天 *blue sky* **3** 黑色 black：～布 *black cloth*｜～线 *black thread* ❷绿色的东西（多指绿苗、叶的庄稼、花草等）sth green：看（kān）～ *to keep watch over the ripening crops*｜～黄不接（陈粮已经吃完，新庄稼还没有成熟）。*The crop is still in the blade while the old stock has all been consumed.* or *The granary is nearly empty but the new crop is not yet ripe — temporary shortage of food, personnel, etc.* ❸青年 youth; young people：共～团 *Communist Youth League*｜老中～相结合 *combination of the old, the middle-aged and the young*

[青史]原指竹简上的记事，后指史书 events recorded on bamboo slips; annals of history：～～留名 *to have one's good name recorded in history; to be crowned with eternal glory*

圊 qīng ㄑㄧㄥ 厕所 latrine：～土 *human excrement; night soil*｜～肥 *barnyard manure*

清 qīng ㄑㄧㄥ ❶纯净透明，没有混杂的东西，跟"浊"相对（the opposite of 浊）pure; clear; unmixed：～水 *clear water; limpid water*｜天朗气～ *blue skies and clear air* ㊀ ***extension*** **1** 单纯地 unmixed; pure; unadulterated：～唱 *to sing opera arias without make-up; to sing without music accompaniment* **2** 安静 quiet; silent; still（㊥ ***doublet*** 一静 quiet; tranquil; serene）：～夜 *still night* ❷明白，不混乱 clear; distinct; explicit：分～ *to distinguish; to draw a clear distinction between*｜～楚 *clear; distinct; explicit*｜说不～ *can't explain sth clearly* ❸一点不留，净尽 to clear away; to clean up; to get rid of：～除 *to clear away; to clean up; to eliminate* ❹清除不纯成分以纯洁组织 to clear up; to clean up; to purge：～党 *to purge a political party; to carry out a party purge; to conduct a party purge* ❺查点（清楚）to count; to check：～仓 *to make an inventory of the storage; to give the warehouse a checkup* ❻公正廉明 impartial; honest; upright：～官 *honest and upright official; incorruptible and just official* ❼朝代名（公元1644—1911年）。公元1616年，女真族首领爱新觉罗·努尔哈赤建立后金。1636年国号改为清。1644年建都北京 the Qing Dynasty (1644 – 1911), founded by Aisin Gioro Nurhachi of the Nüzhen ethnic

Q

group, originally known as the Later Jin Dynasty, and changed to Qing in 1636. In 1644, the Qing made Beijing the capital.

蜻 qīng ㄑㄧㄥ [蜻蜓](—tíng) 昆虫名,俗叫"蚂螂"(mā-lang)。胸部有翅两对,腹部细长,常在水边捕食蚊子等小飞虫,是益虫(popularly called 蚂螂) dragonfly (*Anisoptera*)

鲭 qīng ㄑㄧㄥ 鱼类的一科,身体呈梭形,头尖口大。如鲐(tái)鱼就属于鲭科 Atlantic mackerel (*Scomber scombrus*)

轻(輕) qīng ㄑㄧㄥ ❶分量小,跟"重"相对 (the opposite of 重) of little weight; light:这块木头很~。*This piece of wood is very light*. [轻工业]制造生活资料的工业,如纺织工业、食品工业等 light industry ❷程度浅 small in degree:口~(味淡) *lightly-seasoned; not too salty* | ~伤不下火线 *not to leave the front line on account of minor wounds* ❸数量少 small in number or amount:年纪~ *to be young* | 他的工作很~。*His work load is very light*. ❹用力小 lightly; gently; softly:注意~放 *to handle with care* | 手~一点儿 *to handle gently* ❺认为没价值,不以为重要 to think sth unimportant; to belittle; to make light of:~视 *to look down on; to belittle; to despise* | ~敌 *to underestimate the strength of the enemy; to take the enemy lightly* | 人皆~之。*Everybody looks down upon him*. ❻随便,不庄重 random; casual; not serious:~薄(bó) *flirtatious; frivolous* | ~率(shuài) *thoughtless; rash; hasty* | ~举妄动 *to act blindly without careful consideration; to act impetuously; to take reckless action* [轻易](—yi)随便 rash; off-handed:他不~~下结论。*He doesn't draw a hasty conclusion*. or *He doesn't rush to a conclusion*.

[轻音乐]指轻松活泼、以抒情为主的乐曲,包括器乐曲、舞曲等 light music

氢(氫) qīng ㄑㄧㄥ 一种化学元素,在通常条件下为气体,符号H,是现在所知道的元素中最轻的,无色、无味、无臭,跟氧化合成水。工业上用途很广 hydrogen (H)

倾 qīng ㄑㄧㄥ ❶歪,斜 to slant; to incline; to lean (㊟ ***doublet*** 一斜 slanting; inclined; askew):身体稍向前~ *to bend slightly forward* ❷倾向,趋向 tendency; trend; inclination:~心(一心向往,爱慕) *to admire greatly; to adore; to fall in love* ❸倒塌 to collapse; to topple; to tumble:~颓 *to capsize; to overturn; to topple* [倾轧](—yà)互相排挤(in a political party or in the political world in general) to engage in factional strife; to jostle against each other; to squeeze people out of cliques in an organization ❹使器物反转或歪斜，倒(dào)出里面的东西 to overturn and pour out; to dump; to empty: ～盆大雨 *downpour; pouring rain; torrential rain* | ～箱倒箧 *to turn out all one's boxes and suitcases* ㊀ ***extension*** 尽数拿出，毫无保留 to do all one can; to use up all one's resources; to exhaust: ～吐(tǔ) *to say what is on one's mind without reservation; to pour forth* [倾销]一种以低于成本的价格大量抛售商品的不正当竞争手段 to sell at a low price; to dump

卿 qīng ㄑㄧㄥ ❶古时高级官名(in ancient China) title of senior official: 上～ *prime minister* | 三公九～ *three dukes and nine ministers* ❷古代用作称呼，君称臣，夫称妻或夫妻对称(in ancient China) term of address for a court official by an emperor; term of endearment used between husband and wife

勍 qíng ㄑㄧㄥˊ 强 powerful; strong: ～敌 *powerful enemy*

黥(**剠) qíng ㄑㄧㄥˊ 古代在犯人脸上刺刻涂墨的刑罚。也叫"墨刑"(also called 墨刑)(a punishment in ancient China) tattooing the face

情 qíng ㄑㄧㄥˊ ❶感情，情绪，外界事物所引起的爱、憎、愉快、不愉快、惧怕等的心理状态 feeling; sentiment; emotion ❷爱情 love; affection; comradery: 谈～说爱 *to talk love; to sweet-talk* ❸情面，情分 kindness; favour: 说～ *to plead for mercy for sb; to intercede for; to put in a good word for sb* | 求～ *to beg for leniency; to ask for a favour; to entreat sb for mercy* ❹状况 situation; condition; circumstances: 实～ *actual state of affairs; real situation; truth* | 真～ *real situation; actual circumstances* | 军～ *military situation* [情报]关于各种情况的报告(多带机密性质) information; intelligence [情况]事情在进行中的状况 situation; condition; circumstances: 报告大会～～ *a report on the conference* [情形]事物的情况和形势 state of affairs; situation; condition: 根据实际～～逐步解决 *to solve the problem step by step according to the actual situation*

晴 qíng ㄑㄧㄥˊ 天空中没有云或云量很少，跟"阴"相对(the opposite of 阴) clear; cloudless; fine: ～天 *clear day* | 天～了。*It is clearing up.*

赇 qíng ㄑㄧㄥˊ 承受财产等 to receive; to inherit; to succeed (㊁ ***doublet*** 一受 to receive; to inherit; to succeed)

氰 qíng ㄑㄧㄥˊ 一种碳与氮的化合物，分子式$(CN)_2$，无色气体，有杏仁味。剧毒，燃烧时发红紫色火焰 cyanogen

檠(**檄) qíng ㄑㄧㄥˊ ❶灯架。也指灯 lamp stand; light; lamp ❷矫正弓弩的器具 device for holding or setting a crossbow in position

擎 qíng ㄑㄧㄥˊ 向上托,举 to raise; to hold up; to lift up:~天柱 *one who shoulders heavy responsibility; pillar of state* (or *society*); *mainstay* | 众~易举。*With everybody lending a hand, it is easy to lift a load.* or *Many hands make light work.*

苘(**檾、**莔) qǐng ㄑㄧㄥˇ 苘麻,一年生草本植物,茎直立,开黄花,茎皮的纤维可以做绳子 Indian mallow; piemarker (*Abutilon theophrasti*)

顷 qǐng ㄑㄧㄥˇ ❶市制地积单位,1顷为100亩,相当于6.6667公顷,约合66 666.7平方米 *qing*, a unit of area equal to 100 *mu adding up to about* 6.6667 hectares or 66 666.7 *square meters* ❷短时间 short while; moment; instant:有~ *after a little while; soon after* | 俄~即去 *to disappear soon* | ~刻之间大雨倾盆。*It poured down in no time.* ㊀ **extension** 刚才,不久以前 just; just now:~闻 *I have just heard of it.* | ~接来信。*I have just received your letter.*

〈古 **archaism**〉又同"倾"(qīng) also same as 倾

庼(**廎) qǐng ㄑㄧㄥˇ 小厅堂 small hall

请 qǐng ㄑㄧㄥˇ ❶求 to ask; to request; to beg (㊃ **doublet** 一求 to ask; to request; to beg):~假 *to ask for leave; to ask for a leave of absence* | ~示 *to ask for* (or *request*) *instructions* 敬辞 **polite** (放在动词前面)(used before a verb) pleast:~坐。*Sit down, please.* | ~教 *to ask for advice; to consult* | ~问 *excuse me; please* | ~进来。*Come in, please.* ❷延聘,邀,约人来 to engage; to invite; to send for:~医生 *to send for a doctor* | ~专家作报告 *to invite an expert to deliver a speech*

謦 qǐng ㄑㄧㄥˇ 咳嗽 to cough [謦欬](一kài)指谈笑 to talk and laugh; to make a light conversation:亲聆~~ *to go in person to listen with reverence to sb's* (*often an elderly scholar's*) *talk*

庆(慶) qìng ㄑㄧㄥˋ ❶祝贺 to celebrate; to congratulate (㊃ **doublet** 一贺 to celebrate; to congratulate):~功大会 *victory celebration* | ~祝五一劳动节 *to celebrate the International Labour Day* ❷可祝贺的事 occasion for celebration:国~ *National Day* | 大~ *grand celebration*

亲(親) ㊁ qìng ㄑㄧㄥˋ [亲家]夫妻双方的父母彼此的关系或称呼 relationship or a form of address between parents-in-law

㊀ qīn 见606页 see p606

Q

箐 qìng ㄑㄧㄥˋ 〈方 ***dialect***〉山间的大竹林,泛指树木丛生的山谷 big bamboo grove in mountain valleys; wooded mountain valleys

綮 qìng ㄑㄧㄥˋ 相结合的地方。参看392页"肯❷[肯綮]"(see 肯❷ for 肯綮 on p392) joint in an animal body; juncture

磬 qìng ㄑㄧㄥˋ ❶古代打击乐器,用玉或石做成,悬在架上,形略如曲尺 *qing*, ancient percussion instrument made of jade or stone, hung on a shelf, shaped like a carpenter's square ❷和尚敲的铜铁铸的钵状物 Buddhist percussion instrument made of bronze and shaped like an alms bowl

罄 qìng ㄑㄧㄥˋ 器皿已空,尽,用尽 empty; used up; exhausted:告～ *to run out; to be exhausted*|售～ *to be all sold out*|～竹难书(诉说不完,多指罪恶) *One could find it difficult to record all the facts, esp crimes, even if one used up all the bamboo slips — to be too many to enumerate.*

QIONG ㄑㄩㄥ

邛 qióng ㄑㄩㄥˊ [邛崃](—lái)山名,在四川省。也叫"崃山"(also called 崃山) Qionglai Mountain, in Sichuan Province

筇 qióng ㄑㄩㄥˊ 古书上说的一种竹子,可以做手杖(in ancient Chinese texts) a kind of bamboo, which can be used to make walking sticks

穷(窮) qióng ㄑㄩㄥˊ ❶缺乏财物 poor; penniless; poverty-stricken (㊎ ***doublet*** 贫— poor):～人 *poor people*|他过去很～。*He used to be very poor.* ❷环境恶劣,没有出路 in trouble; without any way out:～愁 *poverty-stricken and full of worries*|～困 *poverty-stricken; impoverished; destitute* ❸达到极点 extremely; to the utmost; utterly:～凶极恶 *extremely brutal and vicious; incredibly ferocious and wicked; most barbarous* ❹尽,完 having an end or a limit:理屈辞～ *to fall silent on finding oneself bested in argument; to be unable to advance any further arguments to justify oneself; not to have a leg to stand on*|无～无尽 *endless; boundless*|日暮途～ *the sun is waning and the road is at an end — to approach the end of one's days; to head for doom* ❺推究到极限 thoroughly; exhaustedly; completely:～物之理 *to study the cause of sth thoroughly*

䓖(藭) qióng ㄑㄩㄥˊ 见840页"芎"字条"芎䓖"(xiōng—) see 芎䓖 on p840

茕(煢、**惸) qióng ㄑㄩㄥˊ ❶没有弟兄,孤独 without brothers; solitary; lonely ❷忧愁

sad; worried; depressed

穹 qióng ㄑㄩㄥˊ 高起成拱形的,隆起 vaulted; domed: ～苍(苍天) *dome of the sky*

琼(瓊) qióng ㄑㄩㄥˊ ❶美玉 fine jade ⓦ ***figurative*** 美好,精美 fine; exquisite: ～浆(美酒) *top-quality wine; nectar* ❷海南省的别称 Qiong, another name for Hainan Province

蛩 qióng ㄑㄩㄥˊ 〈古 ***archaism***〉❶蟋蟀 cricket ❷蝗虫 locust

跫 qióng ㄑㄩㄥˊ 形容脚踏地的声音(of footsteps) pattering: 足音～然 *approaching of footsteps; pattering of footsteps*

銎 qióng ㄑㄩㄥˊ 斧子上安柄的孔 hole in an axe for the handle

QIU ㄑㄧㄡ

丘(❸*坵) qiū ㄑㄧㄡ ❶土山 mound; hillock: 土～ *mound; hillock* | ～陵地带 *hilly area; hilly country* ❷坟墓 grave; tomb (㊟ ***doublet*** 一墓 grave; tomb) ❸〈方 ***dialect***〉量词 ***quantifier***,用于水田分隔开的块(used for plot of paddy field bordered by ridges): 一～五亩大的稻田 *a five-*mu *paddy field; a paddy field of five* mu ❹用砖石封闭有尸体的棺材,浮厝(cuò) to place a coffin in a temporary place and cover it with bricks and stones prior to burial

邱 qiū ㄑㄧㄡ ❶同"丘❶"same as 丘❶ ❷姓。古也作"丘"(also written as 丘 in ancient China) Qiu, a surname

蚯 qiū ㄑㄧㄡ [蚯蚓](— yǐn) 一种生长在土里的环节动物。它能翻松土壤,对农作物有益。也省称"蚓"(also short for 蚓) earthworm (*Oligochaeta*)

龟(龜) ㊂ qiū ㄑㄧㄡ [龟兹](— cí) 汉代西域国名,在今新疆维吾尔自治区库车一带 Qiuci, a state in the Western Region during the Han Dynasty, covering today's Kuche County and nearby areas of Xinjiang Uygur Autonomous Region

㊀ guī 见253页 see p253

㊁ jūn 见378页 see p378

秋(❺鞦、❶—❹*烁) qiū ㄑㄧㄡ ❶四季中的第三季 autumn; fall [三秋] **1** 指秋收、秋耕、秋播 autumn activities (harvesting, ploughing and sowing) **2** 指三年 three years ❷庄稼成熟的时期 harvest; harvest time: 麦～ *wheat harvest* ❸年 year: 千～万岁(*of sb*) *to live for centuries; to live long* ❹指某个时期(多指不好的)(usually troubled) period of time: 多事之～ *eventful period of time; troubled times* ❺[秋千](— qiān) 运动和游戏用具,架子上系(jì)两根长绳,绳端拴一块板,人在板上前后摆动 swing

萩 qiū ㄑㄧㄡ 古书上说的一种蒿类植物(in ancient Chinese texts) a wormwood-type plant

湫 ㊀ qiū ㄑㄧㄡ 水池 pond; pool [大龙湫]瀑布名,在浙江省北雁荡山 Dalongqiu, a waterfall, in the Northern Yandang Mountains, Zhejiang Province

㊁ jiǎo 见341页 see p341

楸 qiū ㄑㄧㄡ 楸树,落叶乔木,干高叶大,夏天开花,木材质地致密,耐湿,可造船,也可做器具 Chinese catalpa (*Catalpa bungei*)

鹙 qiū ㄑㄧㄡ 秃鹙,古书上说的一种水鸟,头颈上没有毛,性贪暴,好吃蛇(in ancient Chinese texts) bald crane

鳅 qiū ㄑㄧㄡ 泥鳅,一种鱼,口小,有须,体圆,尾侧扁,背青黑色,皮上有黏液,常钻在泥里,肉可吃 loach (*Misgurnus anguillicaudatus*)

鰌 qiū ㄑㄧㄡ 同"鳅" same as 鳅

鞧(**鞦) qiū ㄑㄧㄡ ❶后鞧,套车时拴在驾辕牲口屁股上的皮带子 leather strap used for harnessing a draught animal to a cart ❷〈方 ***dialect***〉收缩 to contract; to shrink: 大辕马～着屁股向后退。*The big shaft-horse pushed back on its haunches and backed up.*

仇 ㊁ qiú ㄑㄧㄡˊ 姓 Qiu, a surname

㊀ chóu 见94页 see p94

犰 qiú ㄑㄧㄡˊ [犰狳](－yú)一类哺乳动物,头尾、躯干及四肢都有鳞片,腹部无鳞片,有毛,穴居土中,吃杂食,产于南美洲等地 armadillo (*Dasypus*)

馗 qiú ㄑㄧㄡˊ 逼迫 to force; to compel; to coerce

囚 qiú ㄑㄧㄡˊ ❶拘禁 to imprison; to jail ❷被拘禁的人 prisoner; convict

泅 qiú ㄑㄧㄡˊ 游泳 to swim

求 qiú ㄑㄧㄡˊ ❶设法得到 to try to get; to strive for; to seek: 不～名,不～利 *to seek neither fame nor gain* | 供～相应 *balance between supply and demand; equilibrium of supply and demand* | ～学 *to pursue one's studies* | ～出百分比 *to work out the percentage* ❷恳请,乞助 to request; to beg; to solicit: ～教(jiào) *to ask for advice; to seek counsel* | ～人 *to ask for help*

俅 qiú ㄑㄧㄡˊ ❶恭顺的样子(叠 ***reduplication***) in a respectful and submissive manner; deferentially ❷俅人,我国少数民族"独龙族"的旧称 *qiuren*, former term for the Dulong ethnic group, one of the ethnic minorities of China

逑 qiú ㄑㄧㄡˊ 匹配,配偶 spouse; consort; life mate

球(❷*毬) qiú ㄑㄧㄡˊ (－儿) ❶圆形的立体物 anything shaped like a sphere: ～体 *sphere; spheroid*

❷指某些球形的体育用品 ball：足～ *football*｜乒乓～儿 *ping-pong*；*table tennis* ❸指地球，也泛指星体 earth；heavenly bodies：全～ *whole world*；*entire globe*｜北半～ *Northern Hemisphere*｜星～ *celestial body*；*heavenly body*｜月～ *moon*

赇 qiú ㄑㄧㄡˊ 贿赂 to bribe

裘 qiú ㄑㄧㄡˊ 皮衣 fur coat：集腋成～（比喻积少成多） *The finest fragments of fox fur, sewn together, will make a robe — many a little makes a mickle.*

虬（*虯） qiú ㄑㄧㄡˊ ❶虬龙，传说中的一种龙 a legendary Chinese dragon with horns ❷蜷曲的 coiled；curled；curly：～须 *curly beards* (or *moustaches*)｜～髯 *curly whiskers*

酋 qiú ㄑㄧㄡˊ ❶酋长，部落的首领 chief of a tribe ❷（盗匪、侵略者的）头子 chieftain (of bandits, aggressors, etc)：匪～ *bandit chief*｜敌～ *enemy chieftain*

遒 qiú ㄑㄧㄡˊ 强健，有力 strong；powerful；vigorous（㊀ ***doublet*** —劲 vigorous；powerful；sturdy｜—健 strong；vigorous）

蝤 ㊀ qiú ㄑㄧㄡˊ ［蝤蛴］（—qí）天牛的幼虫，身长足短，白色 longicorn's larva

㊁ yóu 见910页 see p910

巯（巰） qiú ㄑㄧㄡˊ 有机化合物中含硫和氢的基，通式为 —SH sulphydryl；mercapto

璆 qiú ㄑㄧㄡˊ 美玉 fine jade

糗 qiǔ ㄑㄧㄡˇ ❶干粮，炒米粉或炒面 solid food，such as parched rice flour or parched flour；rice flour；rice flour noodles ❷〈方 ***dialect***〉饭或面食粘（zhān）连成块状或糊状 (of rice or noodles) to stick together in a mass：面条儿～了。*The noodles stuck together in a lump.*

QU ㄑㄩ

区（區） ㊀ qū ㄑㄩ ❶分别 to distinguish；to differentiate；to discriminate（㊀ ***doublet*** —别 to distinguish；to differentiate；to discriminate｜—分 to distinguish；to differentiate；to discriminate） ❷地域 area；zone；region：工业～ *industrial area*｜开发～ *development zone*；*Open Economic Zone*｜自然保护～ *nature preservation zone*；*nature reserve* ❸行政区划单位，有跟省平行的自治区和比市低一级的市辖区等 region；district

［区区］小，细微 petty；trivial；trifling

㊁ ōu 见544页 see p544

岖（嶇） qū ㄑㄩ 见585页"崎"字条"崎岖"

(qí—) see 崎岖 on p585

驱(驅、*敺) qū ㄑㄩ ❶赶牲口 to drive; to spur; to goad (on): ~马前进 *to spur a horse on* ㊀ ***extension*** 赶走 to drive away; to expel; to exorcise (㊄ ***doublet*** 一逐 to drive out; to expel; to banish): ~逐出境 *to deport; to expel sb from a country; to banish sb from a country* [驱使]差遣,支使别人为自己奔走 to order about; to push around; to drive sb to do sth ❷快跑 to run quickly; to speed; to gallop (㊄ ***doublet*** 驰— to gallop; to do one's utmost in sb's service): 并驾齐~ *to run neck and neck; to keep abreast of each other*

躯(軀) qū ㄑㄩ 身体 human body (㊄ ***doublet*** 身— body; stature): 七尺之~ *body of seven* chi — *fully grown man* | 为国捐~ *to lay down (or sacrifice) one's life for one's country; to dedicate one's life to one's country*

曲(❹麴、❹△*麯) ㊀ qū ㄑㄩ ❶弯,跟"直"相对(the opposite of 直) bent; crooked; curved (㊄ ***doublet*** 弯— bent; crooked; curved): ~线 *curve* | ~径通幽 *A winding path leads to a secluded spot.* | 山间小路~~弯弯。*The footpaths in the mountains are tortuous.* ㊉ ***figurative*** 不公正,不合理 wrong; unjustifiable: ~解 *to misinterpret; to distort* | 是非~直 *rights and wrongs; truth and falsehood* ❷弯曲的地方 bend; curve; crook: 河~ *river bend* ❸偏僻的地方 remote area: 乡~ *out-of-the-way rural place; remote rural area* ❹酿酒或制酱时引起发酵的块状物,用某种霉菌和大麦、大豆、麸皮等制成 leaven; yeast: 酒~ *distiller's yeast* | 中~发酵饲料 *feed fermented by Chinese yeast* ❺姓 Qu, a surname

㊁ qǔ 见619页 see p619

"麯"又见618页"麹"also see 麹 on p618

蛐 qū ㄑㄩ ❶[蛐蛐儿](—qur) 蟋蟀 cricket (*Gryllidae*) ❷[蛐蟮](—shan) 蚯蚓 earthworm

诎 qū ㄑㄩ ❶短缩 to shorten; to curtail ❷嘴笨 to be slow of speech; to stutter; to stammer ❸屈服,折服 to yield (to); to submit (to); to succumb to

屈 qū ㄑㄩ ❶使弯曲,跟"伸"相对(the opposite of 伸) to bend; to crook: ~指可数 *can be counted on one's fingers — very few* [屈戌](—xū) [屈戌儿](—qur) 门窗箱柜等上面两个脚的小环儿,多用来挂锁、钉锦等 metal fastening for window, door, box, etc; hasp ❷低头,使屈服 to lower one's head; to submit; to yield: 宁死不~ *would rather die than submit (or surrender)* | 威武不

Q

能～ *can not be subdued by force; to be unyielding in the face of force* ❸委屈 grievance：受～ *to suffer wrong* [引] ***extension*** 冤枉 wrong; injustice; wrongful treatment ([连] ***doublet*** 冤— wrong; injustice; wrongful treatment)：叫～ *to complain of being wronged; to protest against an injustice*

胠 qū ㄑㄩ ❶从旁边撬开 to open from the side; to pry open：～箧(偷东西) *to pry open a trunk (to steal)* ❷腋下 armpit; axilla

祛 qū ㄑㄩ 除去，驱逐 to drive away; to dispel; to remove：～疑 *to remove sb's suspicion; to dispel sb's doubts* | ～暑 *to drive away summer heat* | ～痰剂 *expectorant*

袪 qū ㄑㄩ ❶袖口 sleeve cuff ❷同"祛"same as 祛

蛆 qū ㄑㄩ 苍蝇的幼虫，白色，身体柔软，有环节，多生在不洁净的地方 maggot

焌 ㊀ qū ㄑㄩ ❶把燃烧着的东西弄灭 to put out (*or* extinguish) a burning object ❷用不带火苗的火烧烫 to burn ❸烹饪法，在热锅里加油，油热后先放作料，然后放菜(of cooking method) to stir-fry vegetables as soon as condiments are mixed with the boiling oil：～锅儿 *to fry sth quickly in hot oil (to flavour a dish)*

㊁ jùn 见378页 see p378

黢 qū ㄑㄩ 形容黑 black; dark：～黑的头发 *coal-black hair; raven hair* | 屋子里黑～～的什么也看不见。*It is so pitch-dark in the room that you can see nothing.*

趋(**趨**) qū ㄑㄩ ❶快走 to hasten; to rush; to hurry along：～而迎之 *to hasten forward to meet sb* ❷情势向着某方面发展、进行 to incline towards; to tend to become; to head for：～势 *trend; tendency; inclination* | 大势所～ *as the trend of the times indicates; (according to) the prevailing trend* | 意见～于一致。*Their views are heading for consistency.* ❸鹅或蛇伸头咬人(of a goose or snake) to strike with its head to bite at people; to snap at

〈古 ***archaism***〉又同"促"(cù) also same as 促

麴(**麯**) qū ㄑㄩ ❶同"曲㊀❹"same as 曲㊀❹ ❷姓 Qu, a surname

劬 qú ㄑㄩˊ 劳累 fatigued; overworked ([连] ***doublet*** —劳 overworked; fatigued)

朐 qú ㄑㄩˊ [临朐]地名，在山东省 Linqu, a place in Shandong Province

鸲 qú ㄑㄩˊ 鸟名。身体小，尾巴长，嘴短而尖，羽毛美丽 crested myna (*Acridotheres cristatellus*) [鸲鹆](—yù) 鸟名，又叫"八哥儿"。全身黑色，头及背部微呈绿色光泽，能模仿人说话(also called 八哥儿)

myna

鼩 qú ㄑㄩˊ [鼱鼩]食虫动物，常被误认为鼠类。雄的有分泌芳香物质的腺体，生活在近水的地方，多数对农业有害。皮毛珍贵 shrew (*Soricidae*)

渠(❸**佢) qú ㄑㄩˊ ❶水道。特指人工开的河道，水沟 canal; channel; water course：沟～ *ditch; canal* | 水到～成 *Where water flows, a channel is formed.—When conditions are ripe, success is assured.* | 红旗～ *Red Flag Canal* ❷大 big; great：～帅 *commander in chief* | ～魁 *chieftain of an armed rebel group; enemy chief* ❸〈方 **dialect**〉他 he; him：不知～为何人。*I don't know who he is.*

蕖 qú ㄑㄩˊ [芙蕖](fú—)荷花的别名 another name for lotus

磲 qú ㄑㄩˊ 见81页"砗"字条"砗磲"(chē—) see 砗磲 on p81

璩 qú ㄑㄩˊ 〈古 **archaism**〉耳环 earrings

蘧 qú ㄑㄩˊ ❶[蘧麦]多年生草本植物，叶子对生，狭披针形，夏季开淡红或白花，可供观赏。全草入药。现作"瞿麦"(now written as 瞿麦) fringed pink ❷[蘧然]惊喜的样子 pleasantly surprised ❸姓 Qu, a surname

籧 qú ㄑㄩˊ [籧篨](—chú)古代指用竹子或苇子编的粗席(in ancient China) coarse mat of bamboo or reed

瞿 qú ㄑㄩˊ 姓 Qu, a surname

氍 qú ㄑㄩˊ [氍毹](—shū)毛织的地毯。古代演剧多在地毯上，因此又用氍毹代指舞台 wool carpet; stage; arena

臞 qú ㄑㄩˊ 同"癯"same as 癯

癯 qú ㄑㄩˊ 瘦 thin; lean; emaciated：清～ *lean; thin*

衢 qú ㄑㄩˊ 大路，四通八达的道路 main road; thoroughfare：通～ *broad avenue; thoroughfare*

蠼(**蠷) qú ㄑㄩˊ [蠼螋](—sōu)昆虫名。黑褐色，体扁平狭长，腹端有铗状尾须一对，生活在潮湿地方，危害家蚕等 earwig (*Dermaptera*)

曲 ⊜ qǔ ㄑㄩˇ(—子、—儿) ❶歌，能唱的文辞 song; tune; melody (㊥ **doublet** 歌—song)：戏～ *traditional opera* | 小～儿 *ballad; ditty* | 唱～儿 *to sing a song; to sing a tune* ❷歌的乐调(yuèdiào) music of a song：这支歌是他作的～。*The music of this song is composed by him.* ❸元代盛行的一种韵文体裁，可以入乐 *qu*, a type of verse, popular in the Yuan Dynasty, which can be set to music

⊖ qū 见617页 see p617

苣 ⊖ qǔ ㄑㄩˇ [苣荬菜](—mǎi—)多年生草本植物，花黄色。茎叶嫩时可以吃 endive (*Cichorium endivia*)

㊀ jù 见371页 see p371

取 qǔ ㄑㄩˇ ❶拿 to get; to fetch; to draw: ～书 *to fetch a book* | 到银行～款 *to go to the bank to draw money* [取消]废除,撤销 to cancel; to call off; to abolish ❷从中拿出合乎需要的 to pick out, select, or choose from a number of alternatives **1** 挑选 to choose; to select: 录～ *to enroll; to recruit; to matriculate* | ～个小名儿 *to choose an infant* (or *pet*) *name; to give an infant* (or *pet*) *name* | ～道天津 *by way of Tianjin; via Tianjin* **2** 寻求 to seek; to quest: ～暖 *to warm oneself* (*by a fire, etc*) | ～笑(开玩笑) *to laugh at; to make fun of; to ridicule* **3** 接受,采用 to accept; to adopt: 听～群众的意见 *to heed the opinions of the masses* | 吸～经验 *to extract experience* (*from*) ❸依照一定的根据或条件做 to do sth on a certain condition or according to a certain principle: ～决 *to depend on; to be decided by* | ～齐 *to make even; to even up*

娶 qǔ ㄑㄩˇ 把女子接过来成亲 to take a wife; to marry; to wed: ～妻 *to take a wife; to wive*

龋 qǔ ㄑㄩˇ [龋齿]因口腔不清洁,食物渣滓发酵,产生酸类,侵蚀牙齿的釉质而形成空洞。这样的牙齿叫作龋齿。俗叫"虫牙"或"虫吃牙"(popularly called 虫牙 or 虫吃牙) decayed tooth

去 qù ㄑㄩˋ ❶离开所在的地方到别处,由自己一方到另一方,跟"来"相对(the opposite of 来) to go: 我要～工厂。*I'm going to the factory.* | 马上就～ *to go at once; to go promptly* 给他～封信 *to send* (or *post*) *him a letter* | 已经～了一个电报。*A telegraph has been sent to him.* ❷距离,差别 distance; difference: 相～不远。*The two places are not far apart.* ❸已过的。特指刚过去的一年 previous; past; year just past: ～年 *last year* ❹除掉,减掉 to remove; to get rid of: ～皮 *to remove the peel* (or *skin*) | ～病 *to prevent* (or *cure*) *a disease* | 太长了,～一段。*It is too long; delete a paragraph.* ❺扮演(戏曲里的角色) to play a part (*or* role) ❻在动词后,表示趋向(used after a verb to express tendency): 上～ *to go up* | 进～ *to go into; to enter* ❼在动词后,表示持续(used after a verb to express continuity): 信步走～ *to walk on and on aimlessly* | 让他说～。*Let him say what he likes.* ❽去声,汉语四声之一。普通话去声的调子是下降的,符号作"ˋ" falling tone

阒 qù ㄑㄩˋ 形容寂静 quiet; still; silent: ～无一人。*It was dead still and not a soul was around.*

趣 qù ㄑㄩˋ ❶意向 interest; purport; inclination: 旨～ *purport; objective; intent* | 志～ *aspiration and interest; inclination* ❷兴味,使人感到愉快 interest; delight: 有～ *interesting* | ～味 *interest; delight* | ～事 *funny thing; interesting episode; amusing incident* | 讨没～(自寻不愉快、没意思) *to ask for a snub; to court a rebuff; to invite a cold shoulder*
〈古 **archaism**〉又同"促"(cù) also same as 促

觑(**覰、**覻) qù ㄑㄩˋ 看,窥探 to look; to peep at; to steal a glance at: 偷～ *to peep at; to steal a glance at* | 面面相～ *to look at each other in speechless despair* (or *in astonishment, in embarrassment*) [小觑]小看,轻视 to look down on; to belittle; to slight

QUAN ㄑㄩㄢ

悛 quān ㄑㄩㄢ 悔改 to repent; to be penitent; to make amends: 怙(hù)恶不～(坚持作恶,不肯悔改) *to persist in evil and refuse to repent*

圈 ㊀ quān ㄑㄩㄢ ❶(一子、一儿)环形,环形的东西 ring; circle: 画一个～儿 *to draw a circle* | 铁～ *iron ring* ㊂ **extension** 1 周,周遭 circuit; round; around: 跑了一～儿。*I have run a lap around the track.* | 兜了个大～子 *to go around in a big circle* 2 范围 scope; range: 这话说得出～儿了。*These words are beyond the topic.* ❷画环形 to draw a circle: ～个红圈作记号 *to mark with a red circle* ❸包围 to enclose; to encircle: 打一道墙把这块地～起来 *to build a wall and enclose this piece of land*
㊁ juàn 见373页 see p373
㊂ juān 见373页 see p373

棬 quān ㄑㄩㄢ 曲木制成的饮器 drinking vessel made of bended wood

权(權) quán ㄑㄩㄢˊ ❶权力,权柄,职责范围内支配和指挥的力量 power; authority: 政～ *political power; state power* | 有～处理这件事 *to be entitled to deal with this matter* ❷权利 right; droit; entitlement: 选举～ *right to vote; franchise* | 人～ *human rights* | 版～ *copyright* ❸势力,有利形势 advantageous (*or* favourable) position: 主动～ *initiative* | 制海～ *mastery of the sea; sea supremacy* ❹变通,不依常规 adaptability; expediency: ～且如此。*Let it be so for the moment.* ❺衡量,估计 to weigh; to measure; to consider: ～其轻重 *to weigh up one thing against another; to weigh the pros and cons* ❻〈古 **archaism**〉秤锤 steelyard weight; counterpoise

全 quán ㄑㄩㄢˊ ❶完备,齐备,完整,不缺少 all ready; complete (㊦ **doublet** 齐一 all

Q

ready; complete):百货公司的货很～。*The department store has a wide variety of goods.*｜这部书不～了。*This set of books is incomplete.* ❷整个,遍 all; while; entire:～国 *whole country; all over the country*｜～校 *whole school*｜～力以赴 *to spare no effort; to go all out; to do one's utmost* [全面]顾到各方面的,不片面 overall; comprehensive; all-sided:～～规划 *overall plan; comprehensive plan*｜看问题要～～*to view a problem in its entirety* (*or totality*) ❸保全,成全,使不受损伤 to keep from harm (*or* damage); to keep intact:两～其美 *to gratify both sides; to satisfy rival claims; to make the best of both worlds* ❹副词 **adverb**,都 all:代表们～来了。*The representatives are all here.*

佺 quán ㄑㄩㄢˊ 用于人名 *quan*, used in a given name

诠 quán ㄑㄩㄢˊ ❶解释 to explain; to expound; to annotate (㊥ **doublet** 一释 to explain; to expound; to annotate) ❷事物的理 reason; truth:真～ *truth*

荃 quán ㄑㄩㄢˊ 古书上说的一种香草(in ancient Chinese texts) an aromatic (*or* fragrant) plant

辁 quán ㄑㄩㄢˊ ❶古代指没有辐的小车轮(in ancient China) wheel without spokes ❷小,浅薄 shallow; superficial; limited:～才 *limited ability; superficial knowledge*

牷 quán ㄑㄩㄢˊ 古指供祭祀用的纯色毛的牛 cattle of pure colour (used as sacrifice in sacrificial rites in ancient China)

铨 quán ㄑㄩㄢˊ ❶衡量轻重 to weigh; to measure ❷旧时称量才授官,选拔官吏(in former times) to choose or select officials by qualification:～选 *to select and appoint officials according to rules and regulations* [铨叙]旧时称议定官吏的等级(in former times) to examine officials' credentials so as to fix their grades and ranks

痊 quán ㄑㄩㄢˊ 病好了,恢复健康 to recover from an illness (㊥ **doublet** 一愈 to recover from an illness)

筌 quán ㄑㄩㄢˊ 捕鱼的竹器 bamboo gear for fishing:得鱼忘～(喻达到目的后就忘了原来的凭借) *to forget the trap as soon as the fish is caught — to forget the means by which the end is attained; to forget the things or conditions which bring one success*

醛 quán ㄑㄩㄢˊ 有机化合物的一类,通式 R－CHO。醛类中的乙醛(CH_3—CHO),省称"醛"(short for 乙醛) aldehyde

泉 quán ㄑㄩㄢˊ ❶泉水 spring:清～*clear spring; crystal-*

clear spring | 甘～ *sweet spring water* ❷水源 mouth of a spring; source of underground water (㊟ ***doublet*** 一源 fountainhead; wellhead; wellspring) [黄泉] [九泉]称人死后所在的地方 nether world; nether regions; world of the dead ❸钱币的古称 former term for coin

鳈 quán ㄑㄩㄢˊ 鱼名。体长十几厘米,深棕色,有斑纹,口小,生活在淡水中,肉可吃 fat minnow (*Sarcocheilichthys lacustris*)

拳 quán ㄑㄩㄢˊ ❶(一头)屈指卷握起来的手 fist: 双手握～ *to clench one's fists* ❷拳术,一种徒手的武术 Chinese boxing: 打～ *to practise Chinese boxing* | 太极～ taijiquan; *shadowboxing* ❸肢体弯曲 to bend; to twist; to curl: ～起腿来 *to bend one's legs*

[拳拳]形容恳切 earnest; sincere: 情意～～ *sincere affection*

惓 quán ㄑㄩㄢˊ [惓惓]旧同"拳拳" same as 拳拳 in former times

蜷(**踡) quán ㄑㄩㄢˊ 身体弯曲 to bend; to curl (up); to huddle (up) [蜷局]蜷曲不伸展 to twist; to coil; to curl

鬈 quán ㄑㄩㄢˊ ❶头发美好 (of hair) beautiful; fine ❷头发卷曲(of hair) curly; wavy

颧 quán ㄑㄩㄢˊ 颧骨,眼睛下面、两腮上面突出的部分。(图见758页"头" picture on p758) cheekbone

犬 quǎn ㄑㄩㄢˇ 狗 dog [犬齿]门齿两旁的牙,上下各有两枚 canine tooth; cuspid

畎 quǎn ㄑㄩㄢˇ 田地中间的小沟 field ditch [畎亩]田间 field; farmland

绻 quǎn ㄑㄩㄢˇ 见596页"缱"字条"缱绻"(qiǎn—) see 缱绻 on p596

劝(勸) quàn ㄑㄩㄢˋ ❶劝说,讲明事理使人听从 to persuade; to advise; to urge: 规～ *to admonish; to expostulate; to exhort* | ～他不要喝酒 *to advise sb to refrain from drinking; to urge sb not to drink* ❷勉励 to encourage; to exhort (to do good) (㊟ ***doublet*** 一勉 to admonish and encourage): ～勉一番 *to give sb admonition and encouragement*

券 ㊀quàn ㄑㄩㄢˋ ❶票据或作凭证的纸片 certificate; ticket; voucher: 公债～ *public (or government) bonds* | 入场～ *admission ticket* ❷"拱券"的"券"(xuàn)的又音(also pronounced xuàn as in 拱券)

㊁ xuàn 见850页 see p850

QUE ㄑㄩㄝ

炔 quē ㄑㄩㄝ 炔烃(tīng),一类有机化合物,通式是 C_nH_{2n-2}。乙炔是烧焊及制作有机玻璃、聚氯乙烯、合成橡胶、合成纤维的重要原料 alkyne

Q

缺 quē ㄑㄩㄝ ❶短少,不够 to lack; to be short of; to be deficient in (㊀ ***doublet*** 一乏 to lack; to be short of; to be deficient in):东西准备齐全,什么也不～了。*We have got everything ready and need nothing more.* ❷残破 broken; dilapidated; incomplete (㊀ ***doublet*** 残一 incomplete; fragmentary; broken):～口 *breach; gap*|完整无～ *intact; complete* [缺点]工作或行为中不完美、不完备的地方 shortcoming; defect; fault [缺陷]残损或不圆满的地方 shortcoming; defect; flaw ❸该到未到 not to be present; to be absent: ～席 *not to be present; to be absent*|～勤 *to be absent from duty or work*|～考 *to be absent from exam; to miss an exam* ❹空额(指职位) unfilled position; vacancy; opening:补～*to fill a vacancy*

阙 ㊀ quē ㄑㄩㄝ ❶古代用作"缺"字(written as 缺 in ancient China) [阙如]空缺 to be wanting; to be deficient; yet to be provided: 尚付～～ *yet to be provided* [阙疑]有怀疑的事情暂时不下断语,留待查考 to leave a difficult question open; to reserve judgement for the time being ❷过错 fault; error; mistake: ～失 *mistake; fault* ❸ 姓 Que, a surname

㊁ què 见625页 see p625

瘸 qué ㄑㄩㄝˊ 腿脚有毛病,走路时身体不平衡 lame; gammy: 一～一拐 *to walk with a limp; to limp; to hobble*|他是摔～的。*He has gone lame after a fall.*

却(*卻) què ㄑㄩㄝˋ ❶退 to draw back; to retreat; to withdraw (㊀ ***doublet*** 退一 to fall back; to draw back; to retreat): 望而～步 *to shrink back at the sight of sth dangerous or difficult; to stand in awe*|打得敌人连夜退～。*The enemies were inflicted with such heavy casualties that they retreated under the cover of night.* ❷退还,不受 to refuse; to decline; to reject: 盛情难～ *It would be ungracious not to accept a kind offer.* ❸和"去"、"掉"用法相近(close to 去 or 掉 in usage) to lose; to get rid of; to remove: 失～力量 *to lose strength*|了～一件心事。*That's taken a load off my mind.* ❹副词 **adverb**,表示转折(used to express a transition) but; yet: 这个道理大家都明白,他～不知道。*We all understand it, but he does not.* or *Everyone except him understands it.*

埆 què ㄑㄩㄝˋ 土地不肥沃(of soil) infertile; sterile; barren

确(❶❷確、❶❷**塙、❶❷**碻) què ㄑㄩㄝˋ ❶真

实，实在 true; real; authentic（㊀ *doublet* 一实 true; authentic; exact）：千真万～ *absolutely true*｜正～ *correct; right*｜他～是进步很快。*He has really made rapid progress.*［确切］**1** 准确，恰当 definite; exact; precise **2** 真实可靠 true; reliable; dependable ❷坚固，固定 firm; rock-solid; steadfast：～定不移 *as solid as a rock*｜～保丰收 *to ensure a good harvest* ❸同"埆"same as 埆

悫（愨、**愨）què ㄑㄩㄝˋ 诚实，谨慎 honest; prudent

雀 ㊀ què ㄑㄩㄝˋ 鸟的一类，身体小，翅膀长，雌雄羽毛颜色多不相同，吃粮食粒和昆虫。特指麻雀，泛指小鸟 sparrow（*Passeridae*）; bird［雀斑］脸上密集的褐色斑点 freckle［雀盲］夜盲。也说"雀盲眼"（qiǎomangyǎn）（also called 雀盲眼）night blindness; nyctalopia［雀跃］㊗ *figurative* 高兴得像麻雀那样跳跃 to jump for joy; to leap for joy; to caper

㊁ qiāo 见601页 see p601

㊂ qiǎo 见602页 see p602

阕 què ㄑㄩㄝˋ ❶停止，终了 to end; to cease; to stop：乐～（奏乐终了）。*The music ended.* ❷量词 **quantifier**，用于词或歌曲 used for *ci* poems or songs

阙 ㊀ què ㄑㄩㄝˋ〈古 **archaism**〉❶皇宫门前面两边的楼 watchtower on either side of an imperial palace gate：宫～ *imperial palace* ❷墓道外所立的石牌坊 stone carvings erected in front of a tomb

㊁ quē 见624页 see p624

搉 què ㄑㄩㄝˋ ❶敲击 to knock; to strike; to beat ❷同"榷❷"same as 榷❷

榷（❷△*搉）què ㄑㄩㄝˋ ❶专利，专卖 monopoly ❷商讨 to discuss（㊀ **doublet** 商一 to discuss; to consult; to deliberate）

鹊 què ㄑㄩㄝˋ 喜鹊，鸟名。背黑褐色，肩、颈、腹等部白色，翅有大白斑，尾较长。常栖息于园林树木间 magpie（*Pica pica*）

QUN ㄑㄩㄣ

囷 qūn ㄑㄩㄣ 古代一种圆形的谷仓（in ancient China）a type of circular granary or barn

逡 qūn ㄑㄩㄣ 退 to yield; to shrink from; to retreat［逡巡］有所顾虑而徘徊或退却 to hang back; to hesitate; to shrink from

裙（*帬）qún ㄑㄩㄣˊ（一子、一儿）一种围在下身的服装 skirt：连衣～ *one-piece dress; dress*

群（*羣）qún ㄑㄩㄣˊ ❶聚集在一起的人或物（of people, things, animals, etc）crowd; cluster; flock：人～ *crowd*｜羊～（*of sheep*） *flock* | 楼～ (*of buildings*) *cluster* | 成～结队 *in crowds*; *in large numbers*; *in flocks* ㊀ **extension** 众多的 in large numbers; in groups: ～岛 *group of islands*; *archipelago* | ～山 *chain of mountains* (or *hills*); *continuous unbroken mountain range* | ～居 *to live in groups*; *to be gregarious* (or *social*) | ～集 *to crowd together*; *to assemble in large numbers*; *to gather in groups* | 博览～书 *to read extensively* (or *widely*); *to be well-read* ❷ 众人 large numbers of people; mass; multitude: ～策～力 *to pool the wisdom and efforts of the masses*; *to work with collective wisdom and efforts*; *to join hands to take concerted action* | ～起而攻之 *to rally together to attack sb or sth* ❸ 量词 **quantifier**, 用于成群的人或物 (used for a crowd of people or a large number of animals, etc): 一～娃娃 *a crowd of kids* | 一～牛 *a herd of cattle*

麇 (**麕) ㊁ qún ㄑㄩㄣˊ 成群 in large numbers; in groups; in flocks [麇集]许多人或物聚集在一起 to swarm; to assemble; to flock together

㊀ jūn 见378页 see p378

Q

R ㄖ

RAN ㄖㄢ

蚺 rán ㄖㄢˊ [蚺蛇]就是蟒蛇(i. e. 蟒蛇) python (*Python*)

髯 rán ㄖㄢˊ 两颊上的胡子。泛指胡子 whiskers; beard

然 rán ㄖㄢˊ ❶是,对 right; correct: 不以为～ *not to take seriously* ❷代词 ***pronoun***, 这样,如此 so; like that: 知其～,不知其所以～ *to know the hows but not the whys* [然后] 连词 ***conjunction***, 以后,这样以后(表示承接) (used to express an act that happens after certain act or under a certain condition) then; after that; afterward: 先通知他,～～再去请他。*Inform him of it first and then send sb to invite him.* [然则]连词 ***conjunction***, 既然这样,那么…… then; in that case; such being the case: ～～如之何而后可? *Then, what is to be done?* [然而]连词 ***conjunction***, 但是,可是(表示转折) (used to express transition of meaning) but; however; yet: 他虽然失败了多次,～～并不灰心。*He failed many times, but he didn't lose heart.* ❸词尾,表示状态(used as suffix to express a state): 突～ *sudden(ly); abrupt(ly); unexpected(ly)* | 忽～ *all of a sudden; unexpectedly* | 显～ *obviously* | 欣～ *gladly; happily; with pleasure* ❹古同"燃" same as 燃 in ancient Chinese

燃 rán ㄖㄢˊ ❶烧起火焰 to burn; to light; to kindle (㊇ ***doublet*** 一烧 to burn): ～料 *fuel* | 自～ *to self-ignite; to combust spontaneously* ❷引火点着(zháo) to set fire to; to light; to kindle: ～灯 *to light a lamp* | ～放花炮 *to set off fireworks and firecrackers*

冉(*冄) rǎn ㄖㄢˇ 姓 Ran, a surname [冉冉] 慢慢地 slowly; gradually: 红旗～～上升。*The red flag is being hoisted slowly.*

苒 rǎn ㄖㄢˇ [荏苒](rěn—) 时间不知不觉地过去(of time) to pass (*or* elapse) quickly (*or* imperceptibly); to slip by: 光阴～～。*Time slips by quickly.*

染 rǎn ㄖㄢˇ ❶把东西放在颜料里使着色 to dye; to colour: ～布 *to dye cloth* ❷感受疾病或沾上坏习惯 to catch (a disease); to acquire (*or* contract) (a bad habit): 传～ *to infect; to be contagious* | ～病 *to fall ill; to catch* (or *contract*) *an illness; to be infected*

with a disease | 一尘不～ *not to be soiled by a speck of dust — pure-hearted; to remain unaffected* [染指] ㊞ ***figurative*** 从中分取非分的利益 to take a share of what one is not entitled to; to reap undeserved profit from; to encroach upon

RANG ㄖㄤ

嚷 ㊁ rāng ㄖㄤ [嚷嚷] (— rang) to shout; to howl; to yell **1** 吵闹 to make a noise; to make an uproar: 大家别乱～～。*Don't yell!* or *Shut up!* **2** 声张 to make known; to make public: 这事先别～～出去。*Don't breathe a word about this.*

㊀ rǎng 见628页 see p628

勷 ráng ㄖㄤ 见401页"劻"字条"劻勷"(kuāng —) see 劻勷 on p401

蘘 ráng ㄖㄤ [蘘荷]多年生草本植物,花白色或淡黄色,结蒴果。根茎可入药 mioga ginger (*Zingiber mioga*)

禳 ráng ㄖㄤ 迷信的人祈祷消除灾殃(of superstition) to pray to exorcise evils

穰 ráng ㄖㄤ ❶ 禾茎,庄稼秆 grain stalks ❷丰盛(叠 ***reduplication***) (of harvest) rich; abundant: 五谷蕃熟,～～满家。*Food crops are ripe in abundance and the stores at home are filled with a bumper grain harvest.* ❸同"瓤" same as 瓤

瓤 ráng ㄖㄤ ❶(—子、—儿) 瓜、橘等内部包着种子的肉、瓣 flesh; pulp; pith: 西瓜～儿 *flesh of a watermelon* | 橘子～儿 *orange pulp* ㊞ ***extension*** 东西的内部 interior part of certain things: 秫秸～儿 *pith of grain stalks* | 信～儿 *letter inside an envelope* ❷〈方 ***dialect***〉身体软弱,技术差 (of health) weak; (of skills) bad: 病了一场,身子骨～了 *to be weak as an aftermath of an illness* | 你锄地的技术真不～。*You are not bad at hoeing.*

䘓 ráng ㄖㄤ 衣服脏 (of clothes) dirty

壤 rǎng ㄖㄤ ❶ 松软的土 soil [土壤] 农学上或地质学上指泥土 soil ❷地 earth: 天～之别 *as distinct as earth is from heaven; world of difference; poles apart*

攘 rǎng ㄖㄤ ❶ 侵夺 to seize; to grab; to snatch (㊥ ***doublet*** —夺 to seize; to grab; to usurp) ❷排斥 to exclude; to resist; to expel: ～除 *to get rid of; to cast* (or *weed*) *out; to reject* ❸ 窃取 to steal; to filch

[攘攘] 纷乱的样子 disorderly; chaotic; tumultuous

嚷 ㊀ rǎng ㄖㄤ 大声喊叫 to shout; to yell; to howl: 大～大叫 *to shout loudly* | 你别～了,大家都睡觉了。*Stop yelling! The others are sleeping.*

㊁ rāng 见628页 see p628

R

让(讓) ràng ㄖㄤˋ ❶不争，尽(jǐn)着旁人 to give precedence to others out of courtesy or thoughtfulness：～步 *to concede; to give ground* (or *way*); *to yield*｜谦～ *to decline (an offer) modestly* ㊀ ***extension*** **1** 请 to invite：把他～进屋里来 *to usher him into the room* **2** 避开 to make way; to make room：～开 *to get out of the way; to step aside*｜～路 *to make way for; to yield the right of way* ❷索取一定代价，把东西给人 to sell; to transfer; to convey：出～ *to sell*｜转～ *to transfer the ownership of; to make over* ❸许，使 to allow; to let：不～他来。*Don't allow him to come.*｜～他去取。*Let him fetch it.* ㊀ ***extension*** 任凭 to let sb do as he pleases; to allow sb to do at his discretion：～他闹去。*Let him do whatever he likes.* ❹介词 ***preposition***，被(used as a passive signifier) by：那个碗～他摔了。*That bowl was broken by him.*｜笔～他给弄坏了。*The pen was broken by him.*

RAO ㄖㄠ

荛(蕘) ráo ㄖㄠˊ 柴草 faggot; firewood

饶(饒) ráo ㄖㄠˊ ❶富足，多 rich; plentiful; abundant：物产丰～ *to be plentiful in products; to have a variety* (or *an abundance*) *of products*｜～舌(多话) *talkative; garrulous; loquacious* ❷添 to give sth extra; to throw in：～上一个 *to throw in one extra* ❸宽恕，免除处罚 to forgive; to spare; to pardon (㊁ ***doublet*** —恕 to forgive; to spare)：～了他吧。*Forgive him, please.* or *Spare him, please.*｜不能轻～ *can't let him off so easily* ❹〈方 ***dialect***〉尽管 although; despite; for all：～这么检查还有漏洞呢。*For all our efforts in the check up, there are still loopholes.*

娆(嬈) ㊀ ráo ㄖㄠˊ [妖娆][娇娆] 娇艳，美好 enchanting; fascinating; bewitching

㊁ rǎo 见629页 see p629

桡(橈) ráo ㄖㄠˊ 〈方 ***dialect***〉船桨 oar [桡骨] 前臂大指一侧的骨头。(图见241页"骨" picture on p241) radius

扰(擾) rǎo ㄖㄠˇ 扰乱，打搅 to trouble; to harass; to disturb (㊁ ***doublet*** 搅— to disturb; to annoy; to upset)

娆(嬈) ㊁ rǎo ㄖㄠˇ 烦扰，扰乱 tumult; perturbation

㊀ ráo 见629页 see p629

绕(繞、❷❸*遶) rào ㄖㄠˋ ❶缠 to wind; to coil：～线 *to wind thread* ㊀ ***extension*** 纠缠，弄迷糊 to confuse; to baffle; to befuddle：这句话一下子把他

R

～住了。*These words suddenly confused him.* ❷走弯曲、迂回的路 to make a detour; to bypass; to go round:～远 *to go the long way round* | ～过暗礁 *to bypass hidden reefs* | ～了一个大圈子 *to take a long circuitous route* ❸围着转 to go around; to circle; to revolve:鸟～着树飞。*Birds circle over the tree.* | 运动员～场一周。*The athletes took a spin around the arena.*

RE ㄖㄜ

喏 ㊀ rě ㄖㄜˇ 古代表示敬意的呼喊(used to express a reverence in ancient China) shout:唱～(旧小说中常用,对人作揖,同时出声致敬)(*usually used in novels in former times*) *to make a vocal response while bowing with folded hands held out before one*

㊁ nuò 见543页 see p543

惹 rě ㄖㄜˇ 招引,挑逗 to invite; to attract; to provoke:～事 *to invite trouble* | ～人注意 *to attract one's attention*

热(熱) rè ㄖㄜˋ ❶物理学上称能使物体的温度升高的那种能叫"热"heat ❷温度高,跟"冷"相对(the opposite of 冷) hot:炎～ *scorching; blazing* | 天～。*It is hot.* | ～水 *hot water* ❸使热,使温度升高 to heat; to warm (up):把菜～一～ *to heat up the dish* ❹情意深 warm; passionate; ardent:亲～ *affectionate; intimate* | ～情 *enthusiastic; ardent; zealous* | ～心 *enthusiastic; ardent; warmhearted* ❺衷心羡慕 envious; keen; eager:眼～ *to feel envious* ❻受人欢迎 popular; in great demand:～门儿 *popular; in great demand* | ～货 *popular commodities; goods in great demand* ❼指某种事物风行,形成热潮 craze; fever; fad:旅游～ *travel craze* | 集邮～ *stamp-collecting craze*

REN ㄖㄣ

人 rén ㄖㄣˊ ❶能制造工具并能使用工具进行劳动的高等动物。人是由古类人猿进化而成的 human being; people; humanity [人次]若干次人数的总和 person-time; man-time [人口] **1** 人的数目 population:～～普查 *population census* **2** 泛指人 person; people:拐卖～～ *to kidnap and sell people; to abduct and traffic in people* [人类]人的总称 mankind; humanity:造福～～ *to benefit humanity* [人事] **1** 事理人情 ways of the world:不懂～～ *to have no idea of the ways of the world* **2** 关于工作人员的录用、培养、调配、奖惩等工作 personnel matters:～～变动 *personnel changes* [人手]指参加某项工作的人 manpower; hands; staff:缺～～ *to be short*

R

of hands; to lack manpower; to be short-staffed | ～～齐全 *to be fully staffed; to have sufficient hands* ❷指某种人 person engaged in a particular activity：工～ *worker* | 客～ *guest* | 商～ *merchant; businessman* [当事人] **1** 诉讼中的原告、被告等 litigant; party engaged in a lawsuit, such as a prosecutor or defendant **2** 与法律事实有直接关系的人，如合同中的双方 person or party concerned ❸别人 other people; others：助～为乐 *to take pleasure (or delight) in helping people; to regard service to people as a source of joy* ❹指人的品质、性情 character：这位同志～不错。*This comrade is not bad.* or *This comrade is okay.* ㊀ ***extension*** 人格或面子 personality; reputation：丢～。*It is humiliating.* or *It is a shameful thing.* or *It is a disgrace.* ❺指人的身体 health：我今天～不大舒服。*I am not feeling very well today.*

壬 rén ㄖㄣˊ 天干的第九位，用作顺序的第九 *ren*, the 9th of the 10 Heavenly Stems; the 9th in order

任 ㊁ rén ㄖㄣˊ 姓 Ren, a surname

[任县][任丘] 地名，都在河北省 Renxian, Renqiu, both places in Hebei Province

㊀ rèn 见633页 see p633

仁 rén ㄖㄣˊ ❶同情、友爱 benevolence; kind-heartedness; humanity：～心 *kind-heartedness* | ～至义尽 *to do everything possible to help; to treat sb with the utmost decency and kindness; to be extremely magnanimous and tolerant* ❷敬辞 ***polite***，用于对对方的尊称(used in a respectful form of address for other than oneself)：～兄 *my respected elder brother; my dear friend* | ～弟 *my respected younger brother; my dear friend* ❸果核的最内部分 kernel; pit; stone：杏～儿 *apricot kernel*

[不仁] **1** 不仁慈，无仁德 not benevolent; heartless; malevolent：～～不义 *heartless; showing no benevolence; inhuman and unjust* **2** 手足痿痹，不能运动 numb as a result of flaccid paralysis：麻木～～ *insensitive; indifferent and apathetic* | 四体～～。*The limbs feel numb.*

忍 rěn ㄖㄣˇ ❶耐，把感觉或感情压住不表现出来 to bear; to endure; to tolerate (㊟ ***doublet*** 一耐 to endure)：～痛 *to endure pain; to bear pain* | ～受 *to bear; to endure; to stand* | 实在不能容～ *unbearable; beyond one's endurance* [忍俊不禁] (———jīn) 忍不住笑 can't help laughing; unable to keep a straight face ❷狠心，残酷 hardhearted; cruel (㊟ ***doublet*** 残一 cruel)：～心 *to be hardhearted enough (to do sth); to have the heart (to do sth)*

R

荏 rěn ㄖㄣˇ ❶就是白苏，一年生草本植物，叶有锯齿，开白色小花。种子可入药(i. e. 白苏) common perilla (*Perilla frutescens*) ❷软弱 weak; cowardly; timid: 色厉内～(外貌刚强，内心懦弱) *fierce of mien but faint of heart; ferocious in appearance but weak within*

稔 rěn ㄖㄣˇ ❶庄稼成熟 (of crops) to ripen ㊞ ***transfer*** 年 year: 凡五～ *five years in all* ❷熟悉 familiar; acquainted: ～知 *to know well; to be familiar with* | 素～ *to have known sb for a long time*

刃 rèn ㄖㄣˋ ❶(一儿)刀剑等锋利的部分 cutting edge of a knife; blade: 这刀～儿有缺口了。*The knife has broken edges.* ❷刀 knife: 手持利～ *with a sharp knife* (or *dagger*) *in hand* | 白～战 *bayonet fighting* (or *charge*); *hand-to-hand combat* ❸用刀杀 to kill with a knife (*or* sword): 若遇此贼，必手～之。*I will knife the thief with my own hand once I meet him.*

仞 rèn ㄖㄣˋ 古时以八尺或七尺为一仞 *ren*, an ancient unit of length, equal to seven or eight *chi*

纫 rèn ㄖㄣˋ ❶引线穿针 to thread a needle: ～针 *to thread a needle* ❷缝缀 to sew; to stitch: 缝～ *sewing; tailoring*

韧(韌、*靭) rèn ㄖㄣˋ 又柔软又结实，不易折断，跟"脆"相对 (the opposite of 脆) pliable but strong; likely to bend but not to crack; tough: ～性 *resilience; malleability; tenacity* | 坚～ *firm and tenacious; tough and tensile*

轫 rèn ㄖㄣˋ 支住车轮不让它转动的木头 log used to stop wheels [发轫] ㊞ ***figurative*** 事业开始 to commence an undertaking; to set (*or* start) the ball rolling: 根治黄河的伟大事业已经～～。*The great task to bring the Yellow River under permanent control has already been set afoot.*

牣 rèn ㄖㄣˋ 充满 full of; brimming with; imbued with (㊞ ***doublet*** 充一 filled to overflowing; overflowed with)

认(認) rèn ㄖㄣˋ ❶分辨，识别 to recognize; to identify; to distinguish (㊞ ***doublet*** 一识 to know): ～字 *to learn to read; to be able to read; to be literate* | ～明 *to clearly recognize* | ～不出 *can't recognize; can't identify* [认真]仔细，不马虎 careful; serious; earnest ❷承认，表示同意 to accept; to recognize: ～可 *to admit; to approve; to endorse* | ～错 *to admit a fault; to acknowledge a mistake; to make an apology* | 公～ *to be generally acknowledged; to be well established; to be universally accepted* | 否～ *to deny* ❸和没有关系的人建立某种关系 to enter into a certain kind of relationship with sb; to acknowledge; to accept: ～师 *to acknowledge sb as one's master; to apprentice oneself to sb* | ～干亲 *to take sb as one's nominally adoptive kinsman or kinswoman*

任 ㊀ rèn ㄖㄣˋ ❶相信,依赖 to believe; to trust; to rely on ([连] ***doublet*** 信— to trust; to have confidence in) ❷任命,使用,给予职务 to appoint; to assign sb to a post; to engage: ～用 *to appoint; to assign sb to a post; to employ sb as* ❸负担或担当 to assume; to hold; to undertake ([连] ***doublet*** 担— to assume the office of; to hold the post of): ～课 *to teach at a school; to give lessons* | 连选连～ *to be elected to a consecutive term of office* | ～劳～怨 *to work hard and never to feel upset by criticism; to stand the strain of labour and injustice; to bear the burden and blames of office willingly* ❹职务 office; official post: 到～ *to take office; to assume a post* | 接受重～ *to assume an important post* | 一身而二～ *a person holding two posts* ❺由着,听凭 to let; to allow; to give free rein to: ～意 *willfully; wantonly; arbitrarily* | ～性 *willful; self-willed; headstrong* | 放～ *to let alone; to connive (at sth)* | 不能～其自然发展 *can't let it run its own course* ❻连词 ***conjunction***, 不论 no matter (how, what, etc): ～谁说也不听。*No matter who tried to persuade him, he wouldn't listen.* | ～什么都不懂 *not to know anything; to be ignorant of anything* [转] ***extension*** 任何,无论什么 whatever; whoever: ～人皆知 *to be known to anyone*

㊁ rén 见631页 see p631

饪(*餁) rèn ㄖㄣˋ 烹饪,做饭做菜 to cook

妊(*姙) rèn ㄖㄣˋ 妊娠(shēn),怀孕 to be pregnant: ～妇 *woman in pregnancy*

纴(**紝) rèn ㄖㄣˋ〈古 ***archaism***〉❶织布帛的丝缕 silk and thread ❷纺织 to weave

衽(*袵) rèn ㄖㄣˋ〈古 ***archaism***〉❶衣襟 front of a Chinese gown ❷衽席,睡觉用的席子 sleeping mat

葚 ㊁ rèn ㄖㄣˋ [桑葚儿]桑树结的果实,用于口语(used colloquially) mulberry

㊀ shèn 见669页 see p669

RENG ㄖㄥ

扔 rēng ㄖㄥ ❶抛,投掷 to throw; to toss; to cast: ～球 *to throw a ball; to toss a ball* | ～砖 *to cast a brick* ❷丢弃,舍(shě)弃 to throw away; to cast aside: 把这些破烂东西～了吧。*Throw away the junk.*

R

仍 réng ㄖㄥˊ 副词 ***adverb***,仍然,依然,还,照旧 still; yet; as ever:～须努力 *still to need to make efforts*|他虽然有病,～不肯放下工作。*In spite of his illness, he won't put aside the work yet.*

礽 réng ㄖㄥˊ 福 happiness; blessing; good fortune

RI ㄖ

日 rì ㄖˋ ❶太阳 sun [日食](*日蚀)月亮运行到太阳和地球中间成直线的时候,遮住射到地球上的太阳光,这种现象叫作日食 solar eclipse ❷白天,跟"夜"相对(the opposite of 夜) day; daytime:～班 *day shift*|～场 *day show; daytime performance; matinee* ❸天,一昼夜 day:阳历平年一年三百六十五～。*There are 365 days in a common year according to the solar calendar.* [引] ***extension*** 某一天 particular day:纪念～ *commemoration day*|生～ *birthday* [日子](—zi) **1** 天 day; date:这些～～工作很忙。*I have been busy with my work these days.* **2** 指某一天 particular day:今天是过节的～～。*It is a festival today.* **3** 生活 life; livelihood:美好的～～万年长。*The happy life will last forever.* [工作日] 计算工作时间的单位。通常以八小时为一个工作日(unit of calculating work time, usually equal to 8 hours) workday; working day ❹一天天,每天 everyday; daily:～益强大 *to be getting stronger day by day*|～积月累 *to accumulate day by day and month by month*|～新月异 *to take a new look with each passing day; to change for the better day by day and month by month; to undergo changes day by day*|～理万机 *to be busy (or occupied) with a myriad of state affairs; to have numerous problems to attend to everyday* ❺时候 time:春～ *springtime*|往～ *bygone days; former days; past days*|来～方长 *There will be ample time.* or *There will be time for that.* ❻指日本国 Japan

RONG ㄖㄨㄥ

戎 róng ㄖㄨㄥˊ ❶武器 arms; weaponry ❷军队,军事 army; military affairs:从～ *to join the army; to enlist (in the army); to enter the service*|～装 *military uniform; martial attire; battle dress* ❸我国古代称西部的民族 the Rong ethnic group, one of the ancient ethnic minorities in western China

狨 róng ㄖㄨㄥˊ 古书上指金丝猴(in ancient Chinese texts) golden monkey

绒(*羢、*毧) róng ㄖㄨㄥˊ ❶柔软细小的毛 fine soft hair:～毛 *fine hair; down; villus*|驼～ *camel's hair*|鸭～被 *eiderdown;*

duck's down quilt ❷带绒毛的纺织品 fabric with a nap or pile：丝～ *velvet；velour*｜天鹅～ *velvet stuff；velvet*

茸 róng ㄖㄨㄥˊ ❶草初生纤细柔嫩的样子（of newly-grown grass）soft and fine；soft downy；smooth and thick：绿～～的草地 *carpet of green grass* ❷鹿茸，带细毛的才生出来的鹿角，可以入药（of a young stag）pilose antler

荣（榮）róng ㄖㄨㄥˊ ❶草木茂盛（of trees and plants）thriving；flourishing；luxuriant：欣欣向～ *full of life and vigour；thriving；flourishing* ㊀ ***extension*** 兴盛 prosperous；flourishing；thriving：繁～ *prosperous；booming；thriving* ❷光荣 honourable；glorious：～誉 *honour；credit*｜～军 *disabled soldier（honourably discharged from military service due to wounds）*

嵘（嶸）róng ㄖㄨㄥˊ 见971页"峥"字条"峥嵘"（zhēng—）see 峥嵘 on p971

蝾（蠑）róng ㄖㄨㄥˊ ［蝾螈］（—yuán）一种两栖动物，形状像蜥蜴 salamander；newt（*Caudata*）

容 róng ㄖㄨㄥˊ ❶容纳，包含，盛（chéng）to hold；to contain：～器 *container；vessel；receptacle*｜～量 *capacity*｜屋子小，～不下。*The room is too small to hold（so many people）.* ❷对人度量大，不计较 to tolerate；to bear；to forgive：～忍 *to tolerate；to put up with*｜大度～人 *to be magnanimous and tolerant* ❸让，允许 to allow；to permit；to let：～许 *permission*｜不～人说话 *not to allow others to explain；to allow no excuse*｜决不能～他这样做。*He can't be allowed to do things like that.* ❹相貌，仪表 looks；appearance（㊥ ***doublet*** 一貌 facial features；looks；appearance）：笑～满面 *to be all smiles；to have a broad smile on one's face；to be beaming with delight* ㊀ ***extension*** 样子 state of sth；appearance：军～ *soldier's discipline，appearance and bearing*｜市～ *appearance of a city* ❺或许，也许 maybe；perhaps；probably（㊥ ***doublet*** 一或 maybe；perhaps；probably）：～或有之。*That may be the case.*

蓉 róng ㄖㄨㄥˊ ❶用瓜果豆类等制成的粉状物，常用来做糕点馅儿 flour made from mashed fruit flesh or seeds：椰～ *mashed coconut kernel stuffing*｜莲～ *fine lotus mash*｜豆～ *fine bean mash（as stuffing）* ❷四川省成都的别称 Rong，another name for Chengdu，capital of Sichuan Province

溶 róng ㄖㄨㄥˊ 在水或其他液体中化开 to dissolve（㊥ ***doublet*** 一化 to dissolve）：樟脑～于酒精而不～于水。*Camphor dissolves in alcohol but not in water.*

R

瑢 róng ㄖㄨㄥˊ 见109页“玧”字条“玧瑢”(cōng—) see 玧瑢 on p109

榕 róng ㄖㄨㄥˊ ❶榕树，常绿乔木，树枝有气根，生长在热带和亚热带，木材可制器具 banyan (*Ficus benghalensis*) ❷福建省福州的别称 Rong, another name for Fuzhou, capital of Fujian Province

熔 róng ㄖㄨㄥˊ 固体受热到一定温度时变成液体 to melt; to fuse; to smelt (㊟ ***doublet*** 一化 to melt; to fuse): ～炼 *to temper; to smelt*

镕 róng ㄖㄨㄥˊ ❶铸造用的模型 mould (for casting metal) ㊞ ***figurative*** 陶冶(思想品质)(of one's thought and temperament) to mould ❷同“熔” same as 熔

R

融 róng ㄖㄨㄥˊ ❶固体受热变软或变为流体 to melt; to thaw (㊟ ***doublet*** 一化 to melt; to thaw; to run): 太阳一晒，雪就～了。*The snow will thaw as soon as the sun shines on it.* | 蜡烛遇热就要～化。*Wax will run when exposed to heat.* ❷融合，调和 to blend; to merge; to be in harmony: ～洽 *harmonious* | 水乳交～ *to be as well blended as water and milk — to be in perfect harmony* [融会贯通]参合多方面的道理而得到全面透彻的领悟 to master sth through comprehensive study; to achieve thorough understanding of a subject through mastery of all relevant material ❸流通 to circulate [金融]货币的流通，即汇兑、借贷、储蓄等经济活动的总称 finance; banking

冗(*宂) rǒng ㄖㄨㄥˇ ❶闲散的，多余无用的 redundant; superfluous; surplus: ～员 *redundant personnel; superfluous staff; surplus workers* | 文辞～长。*The essay is too wordy.* ❷繁忙，繁忙的事 busy; busy schedule; busy routine: ～务缠身 *to be tied up with daily chores of all sorts; to be weighed down by tons of trivia* | 拨～ *to find time from a busy schedule; to squeeze out some time from a busy schedule of routine trivialities* ❸繁琐 full of trivial details; overelaborate and tedious: ～杂 *miscellaneous; numerous and complicated*

氄(**毧) rǒng ㄖㄨㄥˇ 鸟兽细软的毛(of birds and animals) fine and soft hair or feathers

ROU ㄖㄡ

柔 róu ㄖㄡˊ ❶软，不硬 soft; supple; pliant (㊟ ***doublet*** 一软 soft; supple; pliant): ～枝 *soft twigs; pliant branches* | ～嫩 *tender; delicate* ❷柔和，跟“刚”相对(the opposite of 刚) gentle; mild; tender: 性情温～ *to be mild in disposition; to have a mild disposition* | 刚～相济 *to couple hardness with*

softness; to temper toughness with gentleness

揉 róu ㄖㄡˊ ❶回旋地按、抚摩 to rub and knead with hands; to massage; to caress: ~一~腿 *to massage one's legs* | 砂子到眼里可别~。*Don't rub your eyes if you have got sand in them.* ❷团弄 to knead; to roll: ~面 *to knead the dough* | ~馒头 *to knead the dough into* mantou ❸使东西弯曲 to bend: ~以为轮 *to bend a piece of wood into a wheel*

輮 róu ㄖㄡˊ ❶车轮的外周 rim of a wheel ❷使弯曲 to bend

煣 róu ㄖㄡˊ 用火烤木材使弯曲 to bend a piece of wood by the heat of a fire

糅 róu ㄖㄡˊ 混杂 to mix; to mingle: ~合 *to mix; to form a mixture; to blend* | 真伪杂~ *intermingling of the true and the false*

蹂 róu ㄖㄡˊ [蹂躏](-lìn)践踏,踩 to trample; to stamp ⑩ ***figurative*** 用暴力欺压、侮辱、侵害 to trample on; to violate; to ravage: 惨遭~~ *to be ruthlessly trampled on*

鞣 róu ㄖㄡˊ 制造皮革时,用栲胶、鱼油等使兽皮柔软 to tan: ~皮子 *to tan hides* | 这皮子~得不够熟。*The hide isn't properly tanned.*

肉 ròu ㄖㄡˋ ❶人或动物体内红色、柔软的物质。某些动物的肉可以吃 flesh; meat [肉搏]徒手或用短兵器搏斗 to fight hand-to-hand (*or* with short weapons): 跟敌人~~ *to engage the enemy in a hand-to-hand* (or *bayonet*) *fight* ❷果肉,果实中可以吃的部分 (of fruit) pulp; flesh; meat: 桂圆~ *longan pulp* ❸〈方 ***dialect***〉果实不脆,不酥 spongy; mushy; squashy: ~瓤西瓜 *watermelon of mushy flesh* (or *pulp*) ❹〈方 ***dialect***〉行动迟缓,性子慢 sluggish; slow-tempered; phlegmatic: 做事真~ *to be slow and phlegmatic in getting things done* | ~脾气 *phlegmatic temperament*

RU ㄖㄨ

如 rú ㄖㄨˊ ❶依照 according to; in conformity with: ~法炮(páo)制 *to concoct herbal medicine by a prescribed method —to follow a set pattern; to follow suit* | ~期完成 *to fulfill sth on schedule* ❷像,相似,同什么一样 like; as; as if: ~此 *so; such; like that* | 坚强~钢 *as strong as steel* | 整旧~新 *to repair sth old and make it as good as new; to restore sth to its original shape and appearance; to renovate* [如今]现在,现代 nowadays; now; today ❸及,比得上 to be as good as; can compare with; to measure up to: 我不~他。*I am not as good as he.* | 自以为不~ *to consider oneself inferior to sb* |

与其这样，不～那样。*It is better to do it that way than this way.* ❹到，往 to go to; to arrive at：纵（听任）舟之所～ *to let the boat drift without control* ❺连词 ***conjunction***，如果，假使 if; supposing：～不同意，可提意见。*If you disagree, you can put forward suggestions.* ❻词尾，表示状态（used as suffix to express a state）：空空～也。*Nothing whatsoever has been left there.*｜突～其来 *to arise unexpectedly; to come all of a sudden; to appear out of nowhere* ❼表示举例 for example; such as; like：在生产斗争中涌现了许多模范人物，～焦裕禄、王进喜等。*In the struggle for production, there emerged a lot of model figures, such as Jiao Yulu, Wang Jinxi, etc.*

茹 rú ㄖㄨˊ 吃 to eat：～素 *to eat vegetables and grain only; to be on a vegetarian diet*｜～毛饮血 *to eat uncooked game — to live a primitive life* ⓨ ***figurative*** 忍 to bear; to endure：～痛 *to bear pain*｜含辛～苦 *to endure all kinds of hardships*

铷 rú ㄖㄨˊ 一种金属元素，符号 Rb，银白色，质软而轻。是制造光电管的材料，铷的碘化物可供药用 rubidium (Rb)

儒 rú ㄖㄨˊ ❶旧时指读书的人（in former times）scholar; learned man：～生 *Confucian scholar; scholar; intellectual*｜腐～ *pedantic scholar* (or *intellectual*); *pedant* ❷儒家，春秋战国时代以孔子、孟子为代表的一个学派。提倡以仁为中心的道德观念，主张德治 Confucianism; Confucian school

薷 rú ㄖㄨˊ ［香薷］一年生草本植物，茎呈方形，紫色，叶子卵形，花粉红色，果实棕色。茎和叶可以提取芳香油 elsholtzia (*Elsholtzia*)

嚅 rú ㄖㄨˊ 见537页"嗫"字条"嗫嚅"（niè—）see 嗫嚅 on p537

濡 rú ㄖㄨˊ ❶沾湿，润泽 to immerse; to moisten; to dip in：～笔 *to dip a writing brush in Chinese ink — to write*｜耳～目染（喻听得多、看得多，无形中受到影响）*to be imperceptibly influenced by what one constantly sees and hears — to take in the impact of the circumstances* ❷停留，迟滞 to stay; to linger ❸容忍 to tolerate; to endure：～忍 *to tolerate*

孺 rú ㄖㄨˊ 小孩子，幼儿 child：～子 *child*｜妇～ *women and children*

襦 rú ㄖㄨˊ 短衣，短袄 short jacket; blouse

颥 rú ㄖㄨˊ 见537页"颞"字条"颞颥"（niè—）see 颞颥 on p537

蠕（*蝡）rú ㄖㄨˊ（旧读 formerly ruǎn）像蚯蚓那样慢慢地行动 to wriggle; to squirm：～动 *to wriggle; to squirm* ［蠕形动物］旧时动物

分类中的一大类。体长而柔软，如蛔虫、绦虫等（a category of animals in former times）vermes

汝 rǔ ㄖㄨˇ 文言代词 ***pronoun in classical Chinese***，你 you：～等 *you people*；*you*｜～将何往？*Where are you going?*

乳 rǔ ㄖㄨˇ ❶乳房，分泌奶汁的器官 breast；mamma；udder ❷乳房中分泌出来的白色奶汁 milk ❸像乳的东西 milk-like substance **1** 像乳汁的 milk-like：豆～ *soya bean milk* **2** 像乳头的 nipple-like：钟～（钟上可敲打的突出物）*projecting button on a bell to be struck* ❹生，繁殖 to breed；to give birth to；to multiply：孳（zī）～（*of mammals*）*to breed*；*to multiply*；*to propagate* ❺初生的，幼小的 newly-born；young；suckling：～燕 *young swallow*；*newly-hatched swallow*；*fledging swallow*｜～鸭 *young duck*；*newly-hatched duck*；*duckling*

辱 rǔ ㄖㄨˇ ❶羞耻 disgrace；dishonour；humiliation：奇耻大～ *galling shame and humiliation*；*deep humiliation*；*abyss of disgrace* ❷使受到羞耻 to insult；to humiliate；to disgrace：中国人民不可～。*The Chinese people can't be insulted*. ❸玷辱 to disgrace sb or sth；to insult：～命 *to disgrace*（or *fail*）*a mission* ❹谦辞 ***humble***：～承 *to receive*（*a favour*）*undeservingly*｜～蒙 *to be indebted*（*to sb for kindness*）；*to be honoured*

擩 rǔ ㄖㄨˇ〈方 ***dialect***〉插，塞 to insert；to stick into；to thrust：把棍子～在草堆里 *to stick a wooden rod into the haystack*

入 rù ㄖㄨˋ ❶跟"出"相对（the opposite of 出）**1** 从外面进到里面 to enter；to go in；to come in：～场 *to march into the arena*；*to enter*｜～夜 *as night falls*；*at nightfall*｜纳～轨道 *to channel*（or *bring*）*sth into the orbit*（*of*）；*to put sth on the right track* **2** 收进，进款 income：量～为出 *to live within one's income*；*to keep expenditure within the limits of income*｜～不敷出 *to spend more than one earns*；*to live beyond one's income* ❷参加 to join；to enroll；to enlist：～学 *to enroll in a school*｜～会 *to enroll as a member*；*to join a society*，*an association*，*etc* ❸合乎，合于 to suit；to conform to；to agree with：～时 *fashionable*；*stylish*；*in vogue*｜～情～理 *fair and just*；*fair and reasonable*；*perfectly logical and reasonable* ❹入声，古汉语四声之一。普通话没有入声。有的方言有入声，发音一般比较短促（in classical Chinese）entering tone

洳 rù ㄖㄨˋ 见 371 页"沮"字条"沮洳"（jù—）see 沮洳 on p371

蓐 rù ㄖㄨˋ 草席，草垫子 straw mat；straw mattress［坐

蓐]临产 to be confined in bed for recuperation after childbirth; confinement in childbirth; lying-in

溽 rù ㄖㄨˋ 湿 humid; damp: ～暑 *hot and humid summer; sweltering summer*

缛 rù ㄖㄨˋ 繁多，繁琐 elaborate; cumbersome: ～礼 *elaborate rules of etiquette* | 繁文～节 *cumbersome formalities; red tape*

褥 rù ㄖㄨˋ (一子)装着棉絮铺在床上的东西 cotton-padded mattress: 被～ *bedding; bedclothes*

RUAN ㄖㄨㄢ

阮 ruǎn ㄖㄨㄢˇ ❶一种弦乐器，四根弦。西晋阮咸善弹此乐器，故名阮咸，简称"阮"(short for 阮) *ruan*, a four-stringed plucked musical instrument, named after Ruan Xian, a poet of the Western Jin Dynasty ❷姓 Ruan, a surname

朊 ruǎn ㄖㄨㄢˇ 蛋白质的旧称 former term for 蛋白质

软(*輭) ruǎn ㄖㄨㄢˇ ❶柔，跟"硬"相对(the opposite of 硬) soft; pliable; supple (㊟ **doublet** 柔— soft; supple; pliable): 绸子比布～。*Silk is softer than cloth.* [软件] **1** 与计算机系统的运行有关的程序、文件、数据等的统称，是计算机系统的组成部分 software **2** 借指生产、科研、经营等过程中的人员素质、管理水平、服务质量等(used to denote the quality of personnel, management and service etc in production, scientific research, business operation, etc) ❷柔和 mild; gentle; soft: ～风 *soft (or gentle) breeze* | ～语 *soft words; gentle and sweet words* ❸懦弱 weak; feeble; effete (㊟ **doublet** —弱 weak; feeble; effete): ～弱无能 *weak and incompetent; weak and ineffectual* | 不要欺～怕硬。*Don't bully the weak and fear the strong.* ㊀ **extension 1** 容易被感动或动摇 easily moved; soft-hearted; apt to be influenced: 心～ *tender-hearted; soft-hearted; lenient* | 耳朵～ *credulous; easily influenced; susceptible to flattery* **2** 不用强硬的手段进行 gently; in soft words: ～磨(mó) *to use soft tactics* | ～求 *to ask for sth in soft words* ❹没有气力 weak; feeble: 两腿发～。*The two legs feel weak.* or *The two legs feel like jelly.* ❺质量差的，不高明的 poor (in quality, ability, etc): 工夫～ *inadequate (or incompetent) skill*

RUI ㄖㄨㄟ

蕤 ruí ㄖㄨㄟˊ 见779页"葳"字条"葳蕤"(wēi—) see 葳蕤 on p779

蕊(*蕋、*橤) ruǐ ㄖㄨㄟˇ 花蕊，种子植物有性生殖器官的一部分。

R

分雄蕊和雌蕊两种 stamen; pistil

芮 ruì ㄖㄨㄟˋ 周代诸侯国名，在今陕西省大荔东南 Rui, a princedom of the Zhou Dynasty, in the southeast of today's Dali, Shaanxi Province

汭 ruì ㄖㄨㄟˋ 河流会合的地方，河流弯曲的地方 river bend; place where two rivers converge

枘 ruì ㄖㄨㄟˋ〈古 ***archaism***〉榫(sǔn) tenon [枘凿](—záo)方枘圆凿，比喻意见不合 a square peg in a round hole — to be incompatible; to be at odds (*or* variance) with each other

蚋 ruì ㄖㄨㄟˋ 昆虫，略像蝇而较小，色黑，胸背隆起，吸人畜的血液，能传播疾病 buffalo gnat; blackfly (*Simuliidae*)

锐 ruì ㄖㄨㄟˋ ❶快或尖(指刀枪的锋刃)，跟"钝"相对 (the opposite of 钝)(of knives or spears) sharp; keen; pointed (㊀ ***doublet*** —利 sharp|尖— sharp):其锋甚～。*Its edge is very sharp.* or *It has a very keen edge.* ❷感觉灵敏(of senses) sharp; keen; acute:感觉敏～ *acute senses*|眼光～利 *to have a piercing eye; to have a keen eye* ❸锐气，勇往直前的气势 vigour; dash; drive:养精蓄～ *to recuperate and build one's energy; to nourish one's spirit and store up vigour — to conserve strength and store up energy* ❹骤，急剧 rapid; sudden; sharp:～减 *to decline sharply; to reduce drastically*|～增 *sharp increase*

瑞 ruì ㄖㄨㄟˋ 吉祥，好预兆 auspicious; propitious; lucky:～雪兆丰年。*A timely snow augurs a good harvest.* or *A timely snow bodes well for a year of abundance.* or *An auspicious snow foretells a bumper harvest.*

睿(*叡) ruì ㄖㄨㄟˋ 通达，看得深远 far-sighted; prescient; sagacious:聪明～智 *intelligent and far-sighted; wise and prescient*

RUN ㄖㄨㄣ

闰 rùn ㄖㄨㄣˋ 地球公转一周的时间为365天5时48分46秒。阳历把一年定为365天，所余的时间约每四年积累成一天，加在二月里。夏历把一年定为354天或355天，所余的时间约每三年积累成一个月，加在某一年里。这样的办法在历法上叫作闰 intercalary:～年 *leap year; intercalary year*|～月 *leap month; intercalary month*

润 rùn ㄖㄨㄣˋ ❶不干枯，湿燥适中 moist; damp; humid:湿～ *moist; damp; humid*|～泽 *moist; sleek* ❷加油或水，使不干枯 to moisten; to dampen; to lubricate:～肠 *to lubricate the intestines — to ease constipation*|～～嗓子 *to moisten one's throat* ❸细腻光滑 glossy;

R

sleek; smooth: 珠圆玉～ *round as pearls and smooth as jade-excellent singing* (or *polished writing*); *elegance and polish* | 他脸上很光～。*His face looks smooth*. ❹使有光彩,修饰 to polish; to embellish; to touch up (㊈ **doublet** 一饰 to polish; to embellish; to touch up): ～色 *to polish*; *to embellish*; *to touch up* ❺利益 benefit; profit; remuneration: 分～ *to divide profits*; *to share in the profit* | 利～ *profit*

RUO ㄖㄨㄛ

挼 ruó ㄖㄨㄛˊ ❶揉搓 to crumple; to knead; to rub: 把纸条～成团 *to crumple the scrip* (*up*) *into a ball* ❷皱缩 to crumple; to crease: 那张纸～了。*That sheet of paper is crumpled*.

若 ruò ㄖㄨㄛˋ ❶连词 **conjunction**, 若是,如果,假如 if: ～不努力学习,就要落后。*Unless you study hard, you will be left behind*. ❷如,像 as if; like; seem: 年相～ *to be about the same age* | ～有～无 *faintly discernible*; *intangible*; *vague* ❸文言代词 **pronoun in classical Chinese**, 你 you; your: ～辈 *you people*; *people like you*; *you*

[若干] (—gān) 代词 **pronoun**, 多少(问数量或指不定量) (used to ask about quantity or denote indefinite quantity) how many; how much; some

偌 ruò ㄖㄨㄛˋ 这么,那么 such; so: ～大年纪 *so old*; *so advanced in age* (or *years*)

婼 ruò ㄖㄨㄛˋ [婼羌] (—qiāng) 地名,在新疆维吾尔自治区。今作"若羌" (now written as 若羌) Ruoqiang, a place in Xinjiang Uygur Autonomous Region

箬 (*篛) ruò ㄖㄨㄛˋ ❶箬竹,竹子的一种,叶大而宽,可编竹笠,又可用来包粽子 indocalamus (*Indocalamus*) ❷箬竹的叶子 indocalamus leaf

弱 ruò ㄖㄨㄛˋ ❶力气小,势力差,跟"强"相对 (the opposite of 强) weak; feeble; fragile: 身体～ *physically weak*; *feeble in body* | ～小 *small and weak* | ～势群体 *weak group*; *disadvantaged group* ㊀ **extension** 不够,差一点 a little less than: 三分之二～ *a little less than two-thirds* ❷年纪小 young; little: 老～病残 *the old, weak, sick and disabled* ❸丧失(指人死) to die: 又～一个。*One more man is gone*.

蒻 ruò ㄖㄨㄛˋ 古书上指嫩的香蒲 (in ancient Chinese texts) young rush (*Typha japonica*)

爇 ruò ㄖㄨㄛˋ 点燃,焚烧 to light up; to burn

R

S ㄙ

SA ㄙㄚ

仨 sā ㄙㄚ 三个（本字后面不能再用"个"字或其他量词）(not to be followed by 个 or any other quantifier) three：他们哥儿～*they three pals*

撒 ㊀ sā ㄙㄚ ❶放，放开 to let go; to loosen; to cast：～网 *to cast a net*｜～手 *to let go one's hold; to release one's hold*｜～腿跑 *to break into a run; to take to one's heels*. ❷尽量施展或表现出来 to let oneself go; to throw off all restraints; to run wild：～娇 *to behave like a spoiled child; to play the pampered child*

［撒拉族］我国少数民族，参看附表(see the appendix) the Sala (*or* Salar) ethnic group, one of the ethnic minorities of China

㊁ sǎ 见 643 页 see p643

洒（灑） sǎ ㄙㄚˇ ❶把水散布在地上 to sprinkle; to spray：扫地先～些水。*Sprinkle some water on the ground before sweeping it.* ❷东西散落 to spill; to shed; to scatter：～了一地粮食。*Grain is spilled and scattered all over the ground.*

［洒家］指说话者自己（宋元时方言，用于男性）(dialect used by the male in the Song and Yuan dynasties) I; myself; me

［洒脱］（－tuo）言谈、举止自然，不拘束 free and easy; natural and unrestrained; unaffected：这个人很～～。*This person is a free spirit.*

靸 sǎ ㄙㄚˇ〈方 **dialect**〉把布鞋后帮踩在脚后跟下，穿（拖鞋）to wear cloth shoes with the backs turned in; to slip on slippers［靸鞋］**1** 一种草制的拖鞋 slippers made of straw **2** 一种鞋帮纳得很密，前面有皮脸的布鞋 a kind of cloth shoes with closely stitched uppers and leather insteps

撒 ㊁ sǎ ㄙㄚˇ ❶散播，散布 to scatter; to sprinkle; to spread：～种 *to scatter (or spread) seeds evenly in the field; to broadcast seeds* ❷散落，洒 to spill; to drop：小心点，别把汤～了。*Be careful. Don't spill the soup.*

㊀ sā 见 643 页 see p643

潵 sǎ ㄙㄚˇ 潵河，水名，在河北省迁西、兴隆一带 Sahe River, in the area of Qianxi and Xinglong, Hebei Province

卅 sà ㄙㄚˋ 三十 thirty

挲（㩬） sà ㄙㄚˋ 侧手击 to thrust at from the side; to make a flanking attack

S

脎 sà ㄙㄚˋ 有机化合物的一类,通式是

R—C═N—NHC_6H_5
　　|
R—C═N—NHC_6H_5

由同一个分子内的两个羰基和两个分子的苯肼缩合而成 osazone

飒 sà ㄙㄚˋ 形容风声(叠 ***reduplication***)(of wind) soughing; rustling:秋风～～。*The autumn wind is soughing.*[飒爽]豪迈而矫健 heroic and vigorous; valiant; of martial bearing:～～英姿 *of heroic and valiant bearing; mighty in spirit and heroic in bearing; bright and brave*

S

萨(薩) sà ㄙㄚˋ 姓 Sa, a surname

挲(*挱) ㊁ sa ·ㄙㄚ 见480页"摩"字条"摩挲"(mā—) see 摩挲 on p480

㊀ suō 见717页 see p717

㊂ sha 见651页 see p651

SAI ㄙㄞ

揌(**搋) sāi ㄙㄞ 同"塞㊀❶" same as 塞㊀❶

腮(*顋) sāi ㄙㄞ 面颊的下半部。也叫"腮帮子"(also called 腮帮子) cheek

鳃 sāi ㄙㄞ 鱼的呼吸器官,在头部两边 gill; branchia

塞 ㊀ sāi ㄙㄞ ❶堵,填入 to stop (up); to fill; to stuff:把窟窿～住 *to stop* (or *stuff*) *up the hole*|往书包里～了一本书 *to stuff a book into the school-bag* ❷(一子、一儿)堵住器物口的东西 stopper; plug:瓶子～儿 *bottle stopper*|软木～儿*cork*

㊁ sè 见648页 see p648

㊂ sài 见644页 see p644

噻 sāi ㄙㄞ [噻唑](—zuò)一种有机化合物,无色液体,容易挥发。供制药物和染料用 thiazole

塞 ㊂ sài ㄙㄞˋ 边界上的险要地方 stronghold of strategic importance:要～*fort; fortification; fortress*|～外 *area beyond the Great Wall*

㊀ sāi 见644页 see p644

㊁ sè 见648页 see p648

僿 sài ㄙㄞˋ 不诚恳 not sincere

赛 sài ㄙㄞˋ ❶比较好坏、强弱 to have a contest; to compete; to match:～跑 *to run a race; to race*|～歌会 *singing contest*|田径～*track and field events* ❷胜似 to be better than; to exceed; to surpass:一个～一个。*Each one is comparable to the other — they are equally good* ㊟ ***transfer*** 比得上 to be comparable to; to be as good as:～真的 *to be as good as the real one* ❸旧时举行祭典酬报神灵(in former times) to offer sacrifices to gods:～神 *to pay homage to gods; to worship gods*|～会 *religious festival with parades of idols,* *performers on stilts, floats, etc*

［赛璐玢］（— lùfēn）（外 **loanword**）玻璃纸的一种，可染成各种颜色，多用于包装 cellophane

［赛璐珞］（— lùluò）（外 **loanword**）一种化学工业制品，无色透明的固体，质轻，易燃，可制胶卷、玩具、日用品等 celluloid

SAN ㄙㄢ

三 sān ㄙㄢ ❶数目字 three ❷再三，多次 over and over again; repeatedly; time after time：～令五申 *to warn and issue an order time after time*｜～番五次 *over and over again; repeatedly; time and again*

叁（＊＊弎）sān ㄙㄢ “三”字的大写 three, capital form of 三

毵（毿）sān ㄙㄢ ［毵毵］毛发、枝条等细长的样子（of hair, twigs, etc）thin and long

伞（傘、❶＊繖）sǎn ㄙㄢ ❶挡雨或遮太阳的用具，可张可收 umbrella：雨～*umbrella* ❷像伞的东西 sth shaped like an umbrella：灯～*lamp shade*｜降落～*parachute*｜滑翔～*paraglider*

散 ㊁ sǎn ㄙㄢ ❶没有约束，松开 to be unrestrained; to become loose; to fall apart：披～着头发 *with one's hair hanging down loosely*｜绳子～了。*The ropes came loose.* 引 ***extension*** 分散（sàn）to disperse; to scatter：～居 *to live scattered*｜把队伍～开 *to disperse the troops* ［散漫］随随便便，不守纪律 undisciplined; slack; lax in discipline：自由～～*lax in discipline; slack*｜生活～～*to live a happy-go-lucky life; to lead a sloppy life* ［散文］文体的名称，对“韵文”而言，不用韵，字句不求整齐。现多指杂文、随笔、特写等文学作品（as compared with literary composition in rhyme）prose ❷零碎的 loose; scattered：～装 *unpackaged; in bulk; loose packed*｜零零～～*scattered* ❸药末（多用于中药名）（usually used in names of traditional Chinese medicine）medicine in powder form; medical powder：丸～膏丹 *pills, powders, ointment and boluses*｜健胃～*digestive powder*

㊀ sàn 见 645 页 see p645

馓 sǎn ㄙㄢ 馓子，一种油炸（zhá）食品 deep-fried dough twist

糁（糝）㊁ sǎn ㄙㄢ 〈方 ***dialect***〉米粒（指煮熟的）grains of cooked rice

㊀ shēn 见 666 页 see p666

散 ㊀ sàn ㄙㄢ ❶分开，由聚集而分离 to separate; to disperse; to break up：～会。*The meeting is over.* or *The meeting broke up.*｜云彩～了。*The clouds have dispersed.* ❷分布，分给 to give out; to distribute; to spread：～传单 *to*

S

give out handbills; to distribute leaflets|撒种(zhǒng)～粪 *to broadcast seeds and spread dung evenly in the field* ❸排遣 to drive away; to dispel; to dissipate: ～心 *to keep from worrying; to relieve one's boredom*|～闷 *to drive away one's cares; to divert oneself from illness and boredom* ❹〈方 ***dialect***〉解雇 to fire; to sack; to lay off: 过去资本家随便～工人。*In the past, capitalists laid off workers at will.*

㊁ sǎn 见 645 页 see p645

SANG ㄙㄤ

丧(喪、**丧) ㊀ sāng ㄙㄤ 跟死了人有关的事 funeral; mourning: ～事 *funeral affairs; funeral arrangements*|治～委员会 *funeral committee*

㊁ sàng 见 646 页 see p646

桑 sāng ㄙㄤ 落叶乔木，开黄绿色小花，叶子可以喂蚕。果实叫桑葚，味甜可吃。木材可以制器具，皮可以造纸 mulberry (*Morus*)

搡 sǎng ㄙㄤˇ 猛推 to push violently; to shove; to thrust: 用力一～，把他～一个跟头。*He was given a violent push and fell to the ground.*

嗓 sǎng ㄙㄤˇ ❶(一子)喉咙 throat; larynx ❷(一儿)发音器官的声带及发出的声音 voice: 哑～儿 *hoarse voice*

磉 sǎng ㄙㄤˇ 柱子底下的石礅 base of a pillar; pedestal

颡 sǎng ㄙㄤˇ 额，脑门子 forehead

丧(喪、**丧) ㊁ sàng ㄙㄤˋ 丢掉，失去 to lose; to forfeit (㊟ ***doublet*** 一失 to lose): ～命 *to lose one's life; to get killed; to meet one's death*|～失立场 *to depart from the correct stand*

[丧气] **1** 情绪低落 losing heart; depressed; crestfallen: 灰心～～ *to be utterly disheartened; to feel depressed* **2** (—qi)不吉利(迷信)，倒霉 having bad luck; ill-starred

㊀ sāng 见 646 页 see p646

SAO ㄙㄠ

搔 sāo ㄙㄠ 挠，用手指甲轻刮 to scratch: ～痒 *to scratch an itch; to scratch oneself to relieve itching; to scratch where it itches*

骚 sāo ㄙㄠ ❶扰乱，不安定 to disturb; to upset (㊟ ***doublet*** 一扰 to harass; to molest): ～动 *disturbance; tumult; commotion* ❷同"臊㊀" same as 臊㊀ ❸指屈原著的《离骚》*Li Sao* (or *Encountering Sorrow*), a poem by Qu Yuan in the 4th century BC [骚人]诗人 poet [骚体]文体名，因模仿屈原所作《离骚》的形式而得名 *Sao* style – poetry in imitation of the style of *Li Sao* [风骚] **1**

泛指文学 literature in general **2** 妇女举止轻佻 coquettish; flirtatious

缫 sāo ㄙㄠ 把蚕茧浸在滚水里抽丝 to soak cocoons in hot water and reel silk from them; to reel: ～丝 *to reel silk from cocoons; to reel* | ～车(缫丝用的器具) *reel machine; filature*

缲 ㊀ sāo ㄙㄠ 同"缫" same as 缫

㊁ qiāo 见 601 页 see p601

臊 ㊀ sāo ㄙㄠ 像尿那样难闻的气味 smell of urine; foul odour; stench: 尿～气 *foul smell of urine* | 狐～ *body odour; bromhidrosis*

㊁ sào 见 647 页 see p647

扫(掃) ㊀ sǎo ㄙㄠˇ ❶拿笤帚等除去尘土 to sweep; to clear away; to clean up: ～地 *to sweep the floor* ❷像扫一样的动作或作用 action or effect of sweeping **1** 消除 to wipe out; to eliminate; to get rid of: ～兴(xìng) *to dampen one's spirits; to spoil sb's happiness; to feel disappointed* | ～除文盲 *to eliminate (or eradicate) illiteracy* **2** 动作达到各方面 to move left and right quickly; to sweep across; to skim: ～射 *to strafe; to scan; to sweep* | 眼睛四下里一～ *to take a glance around (a place)* **3** 全,所有的 all; total: ～数归还 *all paid off*

㊁ sào 见 647 页 see p647

嫂 sǎo ㄙㄠˇ (一子)哥哥的妻子(叠 ***reduplication***) elder brother's wife; sister-in-law

扫(掃) ㊁ sào ㄙㄠˋ [扫帚] (—zhou)一种用竹枝等做的扫地用具(usually made of bamboo) broom

㊀ sǎo 见 647 页 see p647

埽 sào ㄙㄠˋ ❶河工上用的材料,以竹木为框架,用树枝、石子、土填实其中。做成柱形,用以堵水 fascine ❷用埽修成的堤坝或护堤 fascined bank

瘙 sào ㄙㄠˋ 皮肤发痒的病 pruritus

臊 ㊁ sào ㄙㄠˋ 害羞 shy; bashful; diffident: ～得脸通红 *to blush with shame; to be suffused with a blush of shame* | 不知羞～ *to have no sense of shame*

㊀ sāo 见 647 页 see p647

SE ㄙㄜ

色 ㊀ sè ㄙㄜˋ ❶颜色,由物体发射、反射的光通过视觉而产生的印象 colour: 日光有七～。*There are seven colours in sunlight.* | 红～ *red* ❷脸色,脸上表现出的神气、样子 look; countenance; expression: 和颜悦～ *with a kind and pleasant countenance; wearing a pleasing and gracious face; in a kindly and affable manner* | 喜形于～ *to be visibly pleased; to be radiant with joy; (of one's face) to light up with pleasure* ❸情景,景象 scene; view;

S

scenery:行～匆匆 *to set out on one's journey in a great hurry; to hit the road in haste* ❹种类 kind; sort; description: 各～用品 *all sorts of articles; articles of every description* | 货～齐全。*Goods of every description are available.* ❺成色,品质,质量 quality: 足～纹银 *silver of standard purity* | 这货成～很好。*These goods are of good quality.* ❻妇女容貌 woman's beautiful looks; feminine charms: 姿～(*of a woman*) *good looks* ❼情欲 sexual desire; erotism; lust: ～情 *sexy; pornographic; aphrodisiac*

㊁ shǎi 见 651 页 see p651

铯 sè ㄙㄜˋ 一种金属元素,符号 Cs,银白色,质软,在空气中很容易氧化。铯可做真空管中的去氧剂,化学上可做催化剂 caesium (Cs)

涩(澀、*濇) sè ㄙㄜˋ ❶不光滑,不滑溜 unsmooth; rough; hard-going: 轮轴发～,该上点油了。*The wheel axle doesn't work smoothly. It needs oiling.* ❷一种使舌头感到不滑润不好受的滋味 astringent; puckety: 这柿子很～。*This persimmon is puckety.* ❸文章难读难懂 difficult to understand; obscure: 文字艰～ *involved and obscure writing*

啬(嗇) sè ㄙㄜˋ 小气,当用的财物舍不得用 mean; stingy; miserly (㊀ ***doublet*** 吝～mean; stingy; miserly): 不浪费也不吝～ *to be neither lavish nor stingy*

穑(穡) sè ㄙㄜˋ 收割庄稼 to gather in crops; to harvest; to reap

瑟 sè ㄙㄜˋ 一种弦乐器 *se*, a kind of stringed plucked instrument [瑟瑟] **1** 形容轻微的声音(of wind) rustling: 秋风～～。*The autumn wind is rustling.* **2** 形容颤抖(of a person) shaking (*or* trembling): ～～发抖 *to be shaking (or trembling) all over*

塞 ㊂sè ㄙㄜˋ 同"塞㊀❶",用于某些合成词或成语中,如"闭塞、堵塞、阻塞、塞责、闭目塞听"等(usually used in compound words or idioms such as 闭塞,堵塞,阻塞,塞责,闭目塞听,etc) same as 塞㊀❶

㊀ sāi 见 644 页 see p644

㊁ sài 见 644 页 see p644

SEN ㄙㄣ

森 sēn ㄙㄣ 树木众多 full of trees; heavily wooded: ～林(大片生长的树木) *forest* [森森] 众多,深密 multitudinous; thick; dense: 林木～～ *dense cluster of towering trees* ㊃ ***figurative*** 气氛寂静可怕 silent and ghastly; gloomy and horrendous: 阴～～的 *gloomy and horrid; ghastly; gruesome* [森严] 整齐严肃,防备严密 solemn; stern; strict: 戒备～～ *heavily guarded; under close* *guard*

SENG ㄙㄥ

僧 sēng ㄙㄥ 梵语"僧伽"的省称。佛教指出家修行的男人(short for 僧伽 in Sanskrit) Buddhist monk; monk

SHA ㄕㄚ

杀(殺) shā ㄕㄚ ❶使人或动物失去生命 to kill; to slay; to slaughter:～敌立功 *to fight the enemy and do a deed of merit; to win glory on the battlefield; to serve with distinction in war*｜～虫药 *insecticide; pesticide; biocide*｜～鸡焉用牛刀。*Why kill a chicken with a butcher's cleaver?* or *There is no need to break a fly on the wheel.* ❷战斗 to go into battle; to fight:～出重(chóng)围 *to fight one's way out of a heavy encirclement* ❸消减 to reduce; to weaken; to abate:～价 *to force down the price; to slash the price*｜～暑气 *to reduce summer heat*｜拿别人～气 *to vent one's anger* (or *spleen*) *on others* ❹〈方 ***dialect***〉药物等刺激身体感觉疼痛 to sting; to smart:这药上在疮口上～得慌。*The medicine smarts when it is put on the open part of a sore.* ❺收束 to end; to wind up; to bring to a close:～尾 *to bring sth to an end; to wind up; to round off*｜～账 *to settle accounts; to close accounts* ❻勒紧,扣紧 to bind tightly; to tie (*or* strap) tightly; to fasten:～车(把车上装载的东西用绳勒紧) *to bind the goods in the truck tightly with a rope*｜～一～腰带 *to tighten one's belt* ❼在动词后,表示程度深(used after a verb to express degree) extremely; exceedingly:气～人 *to drive sb mad*｜笑～人 *to be ridiculous to the extreme*

刹 ㊀ shā ㄕㄚ 止住(车、机器等) to stop; to brake; to check:～车 *to put on the brakes; to step on the brake; to brake*

㊁ chà 见 71 页 see p71

铩(鎩) shā ㄕㄚ ❶古代一种长矛 *sha*, a kind of spear in ancient China ❷摧残,伤害 to wreck; to devastate; to injure:～羽之鸟(伤了翅膀的鸟,喻失意的人) *bird with injured wings — frustrated* (or *weakened*) *person*

杉 ㊁ shā ㄕㄚ 义同"杉㊀",用于"杉木、杉篙"等 same as 杉㊀, used in 杉木, 杉篙, etc

㊀ shān 见 652 页 see p652

沙 ㊀ shā ㄕㄚ ❶(一子)非常细碎的石粒 sand:～土 *sandy soil*｜～滩 *sandy beach; sand beach* ❷像沙子的 sand-like; granulated; powdered:蚕～(桑蚕的粪) *silkworm excrement; dung of silkworm*｜豆～ *bean paste*｜～瓤西瓜 *mushy watermelon* ❸声音不清脆不响

S

亮(of voice) hoarse; husky; raucous:～哑 *hoarse; husky; raucous* ❹姓 Sha, a surname

㊁ shà 见 650 页 see p650

莎 ㊀ shā ㄕㄚ 多用于人名、地名 sha, usually used in a given name or a place name [莎车]地名,在新疆维吾尔自治区 Shache, a place in the Xinjiang Uygur Autonomous Region

㊁ suō 见 717 页 see p717

痧 shā ㄕㄚ 中医病名,指霍乱、中暑、肠炎等急性病 (disease name in traditional Chinese medicine, used to denote acute diseases such as cholera, sunstroke, enteritis, etc):发～*to have a heatstroke* (or *sunstroke*)|绞肠～*dry cholera*

裟 shā ㄕㄚ 见 321 页"袈"字条"袈裟"(jiā—) see 袈裟 on p321

鲨 shā ㄕㄚ 鲨鱼,又叫"鲛"。生活在海洋中,种类很多,性凶猛,捕食其他鱼类。鳍可制成鱼翅,是珍贵的食品。肝可制鱼肝油。皮可以制革(also called 鲛) shark (*Selachimorpha*)

纱 shā ㄕㄚ ❶用棉花、麻等纺成的细缕,用它可以捻成线或织成布 yarn ❷经纬线稀疏或有小孔的织品 gauze; sheer:羽～*camlet; rayon* (or *luster*) *lining*|～布 *gauze* ㉧ ***extension*** 像纱布的 gauze-like:铁～*wire gauze; wire cloth*|塑料窗～*plastic gauze for screening windows*

砂 shā ㄕㄚ 同"沙㊀❶❷" same as 沙㊀❶❷

煞 ㊀ shā ㄕㄚ ❶同"杀❸❺❻❼"same as 杀❸❺❻❼ ❷同"刹㊀"same as 刹㊀

㊁ shà 见 651 页 see p651

啥 shá ㄕㄚˊ 〈方 ***dialect***〉代词 ***pronoun***,什么 what:你姓～? *What's your surname?*|他是～地方人? *Where is he from?*

傻(**儍) shǎ ㄕㄚˇ ❶愚蠢,糊涂 stupid; foolish; muddle-headed:说～话 *to talk rubbish*|吓～了 *to be struck dumb with fear; to be frightened out of one's wits; to be scared stiff* ❷死心眼 stubborn; bigoted; inflexible:这样好的事你都不干,真有点犯～。*It is stupid of you to have refused such a good offer.*

沙 ㊁ shà ㄕㄚˋ 经过摇动把东西里的杂物集中,以便清除 to sift; to sieve; to screen:把小米里的沙子～一～。*Sift the millet and sort out the sand.*

㊀ shā 见 649 页 see p649

唼 shà ㄕㄚˋ [唼喋](—zhá)形容鱼、鸟等吃东西的声音 sound made by fish, birds, etc when feeding

厦(*廈) ㊀ shà ㄕㄚˋ ❶大屋子 huge building; mansion:广～千万间 *thousands of mansions; thousands of huge buildings*|高楼大～*high-rise buildings and large mansions; high-rises* ❷房子后

面突出的部分 back veranda; porch:前廊后～*front and back verandas*

㊁ xià 见 810 页 see p810

嗄 ㊁ shà ㄕㄚˋ 嗓音嘶哑(of voice) hoarse

㊀ á 见 1 页 see p1

歃 shà ㄕㄚˋ 用嘴吸取 to suck

[歃血] 古人盟会时,嘴唇涂上牲畜的血,表示诚意(an ancient form of swearing an oath to express sincerity) to smear the blood of a sacrifice on the mouth

煞 ㊀ shà ㄕㄚˋ ❶极,很 extremely; very:～费苦心 *to take great pains; to make a painstaking effort; to rack one's brains*|脸色～白 *to look deathly* (or *ghastly*) *pale; to look pallid* ❷迷信的人指凶神 evil spirit; devil; goblin:～气 *evil spirit; ferocious look*|凶～*demon; fiend; devil*

㊁ shā 见 650 页 see p650

箑 shà ㄕㄚˋ 扇子 fan

霎 shà ㄕㄚˋ 小雨 light drizzle 也指轻微的风雨声 light sound of wind and rain

[霎时] 极短的时间,一会儿 in a very short time; in an instant; in a split second

挲(*挱) ㊂ sha ·ㄕㄚ 见 947 页"挓"字条"挓挲"(zhā—) see 挓挲 on p947

㊀ suō 见 717 页 see p717

㊁ sa 见 644 页 see p644

SHAI ㄕㄞ

筛(篩) shāi ㄕㄞ ❶(一子)用竹子等做成的一种有孔的器具,可以把细东西漏下去,粗的留下 sieve; sifter; screen ❷用筛子过东西 to sieve; to sift; to screen:～米 *to sift rice*|～煤 *to screen coal* ❸敲(锣) to beat (*or* strike) (a gong):～了三下锣。*The gong was beaten three times.*

[筛酒] **1** 斟酒 to pour (wine) **2** 把酒弄热 to warm up wine

酾(釃) shāi ㄕㄞ (又 *also* shī) 见 676 页 shī see shī on p676

色 ㊁ shǎi ㄕㄞˇ (一儿)同"色㊀",用于一些口语词(used colloquially) same as 色㊀:落(lào)～儿 *to fade in colour; to discolour*|掉～*to lose colour; to fade*|不变～儿 *not to change colour*

㊀ sè 见 647 页 see p647

晒(曬) shài ㄕㄞˋ 把东西放在太阳光下使它干燥,人或物在阳光下吸收光和热 to dry in the sun; to sun; to bask:～衣服 *to hang out the washing to dry in the sun; to air clothes*|～太阳 *to bask* (or *bathe*) *in the sun; to sun oneself; to sunbathe*

SHAN ㄕㄢ

山 shān ㄕㄢ ❶地面上由土石构成的高起的部分 hill;

S

mountain：深～ *remote mountains*｜～高水深 *high mountains and deep rivers — difficult journey*｜人～人海(喻人多) *huge crowds of people; oceans of people; multitude of people* ❷蚕蔟 bundle of straw, etc in which silkworms spin cocoons：蚕上～了。*The silkworms have gone into bushes to spin their cocoons*. ❸山墙，房屋两头的墙 gable：房～ *gable of a house*

舢 shān ㄕㄢ [舢板](*舢舨)一种小船。也叫"三板"(also called 三板) sampan

芟 shān ㄕㄢ 割草 to mow ㊀ ***extension*** 除去 to weed out; to get rid of; to eliminate

杉 ㊀shān ㄕㄢ 常绿乔木，树干高而直，叶子细小，呈针状，果实球形。木材供建筑和制器具用 China fir (*Cunninghamia lanceolata*)[水杉]落叶乔木，叶披针形。我国特产，是世界现存的稀有植物之一 metasequoia; dawn redwood (*Metasequoia glyptostroboides*)

㊁ shā 见 649 页 see p649

钐 ㊀ shān ㄕㄢ 一种金属元素，符号 Sm，银白色，有放射性。钐的氧化物是原子反应堆上陶瓷保护层的重要成分 samarium (Sm)

㊁ shàn 见 654 页 see p654

衫 shān ㄕㄢ 上衣，单褂 unlined upper garment：长～ *long gown*｜衬～ *shirt*

删(*刪) shān ㄕㄢ 除去，去掉文字中不妥当的部分 to delete; to leave out; to strike out：～改 *to prune out; to revise; to bowdlerize*｜～除 *to delete; to cross* (or *cut*) *out; to remove*｜这个字应～去。*This word should be deleted*.

姗 shān ㄕㄢ [姗姗]形容走路缓慢从容(of walking) leisurely; slowly：～～来迟 *to be slow in coming; to arrive late*

珊 shān ㄕㄢ [珊瑚]一种腔肠动物所分泌的石灰质的东西，形状像树枝，有红、白各色，可以做装饰品。这种腔肠动物叫"珊瑚虫"coral (calcareous substance secreted by coelenterate called 珊瑚虫)

栅(*柵) ㊀ shān ㄕㄢ [栅极]电子管靠阴极的一个电极 grid

㊁ zhà 见 950 页 see p950

跚 shān ㄕㄢ 见550页"蹒"字条"蹒跚"(pán－) see 蹒跚 on p550

苫 ㊀ shān ㄕㄢ 草帘子，草垫子 straw cover; straw mat：草～子 *straw mat* (or *cover*)

㊁ shàn 见 653 页 see p653

痁 shān ㄕㄢ 〈古 ***archaism***〉疟疾 malaria

埏 ㊀shān ㄕㄢ 用水和(huó)泥 to mix earth with water

㊁ yán 见 863 页 see p863

扇(❶❷**搧) ㊀ shān ㄕㄢ ❶摇动扇子或其他东西，使空气加速流动生风 to wave a fan; to fan：用扇子～ *to wave a fan; to fan*

oneself ❷用手掌打 to hit with hands；to box；to slap：～了他一耳光 *to give him a box on the ears；to slap him on the face* ❸同"煽❷"same as 煽❷

㊁ shàn 见 654 页 see p654

煽 shān ㄕㄢ ❶同"扇㊀❶" same as 扇㊀❶ ❷鼓动（别人做不应该做的事）to instigate；to incite；to stir up：～动 *to instigate；to foment；to provoke*｜～惑 *to agitate；to inflame；to incite*

潸（**潸）shān ㄕㄢ 流泪的样子 full of tears；tearful：不禁（jīn）～～ *can't hold back one's tears*｜～然泪下 *tears trickling（or streaming）down one's cheeks*

膻（*羶）shān ㄕㄢ 像羊肉的气味 smell of mutton：～气 *smell of mutton*｜～味儿 *odour of mutton*

闪 shǎn ㄕㄢˇ ❶天空的电光 lightning：打～ *to discharge a flash of lightning* ❷突然显现或忽明忽暗 to appear suddenly；to flash：灯光一～。*The light flashes.*｜～念 *sudden idea flashing across one's mind；flash of inspiration*｜山后～出一条小路来。*A tiny footpath suddenly appeared behind the mountain.*｜～得眼发花 *dizzily flashing* ❸光辉闪耀 to flash；to sparkle；to shine：～金光 *to emit golden rays of light*｜电～雷鸣。*The lightning flashes and the thunder roars.* ❹侧转身体躲避 to move quickly to one side；to duck；to dodge：～开 *to step aside；to get out of the way；to dodge* ❺因动作过猛，筋肉疼痛 to sprain；to strain；to twist：～了腰 *to have sprained one's back*

陕（陝）shǎn ㄕㄢˇ 陕西省，我国的一省 Shaanxi，a province in China

睐（**睒）shǎn ㄕㄢˇ 眨巴眼，眼睛很快地开闭 to wink；to blink；to twinkle：那飞机飞得很快，一～眼就不见了。*The plane flew so fast that it vanished in a wink.*

讪（❷**赸）shàn ㄕㄢˋ ❶讥笑 to mock；to scorn；to ridicule：～笑 *to mock；to deride；to scoff* ❷难为情的样子 embarrassed；discomfited；awkward：脸上发～ *to look embarrassed*｜他～～地走了。*He walked away in embarrassment.*［搭讪］为了想跟人接近或把尴尬的局面敷衍过去而找话说 to say sth to smooth over an embarrassing situation；to strike up a conversation

汕 shàn ㄕㄢˋ［汕头］地名，在广东省 Shantou，a place in Guangdong Province

疝 shàn ㄕㄢˋ 疝气，病名，种类很多，通常指阴囊胀大的病。也叫"小肠串气"（also called 小肠串气）hernia

苫 ㊁ shàn ㄕㄢˋ 用席、布等遮盖 to cover（with a straw

S

mat, tarpaulin, etc):拿席～上点 *to cover sth with a straw mat*

㊀ shān 见 652 页 see p652

钐 ㊁ shàn ㄕㄢˋ 抡开镰刀或钐镰割 to cut with a sickle (*or* scythe):～草 *to cut grass with a sickle*｜～麦 *to cut wheat with a sickle*［钐镰］［钐刀］一种把儿很长的大镰刀 big sickle with a long handle; scythe

㊀ shān 见 652 页 see p652

单(單) ㊂ shàn ㄕㄢˋ ❶姓 Shan, a surname ❷单县,在山东省 Shanxian County in Shandong Province

㊀ dān 见 125 页 see p125

㊁ chán 见 73 页 see p73

墠(壇) shàn ㄕㄢˋ 古代祭祀用的平地 level ground for holding sacrificial rituals in ancient times

掸(撣) ㊁ shàn ㄕㄢˋ ❶我国史书上对傣族的一种称呼(a term of address for the Dai ethnic group in Chinese history books) the Shan ethnic group ❷掸族,缅甸民族之一,大部分居住在掸邦 the Shan people, a Burmese people, mostly inhabiting in the Shan State of Myanmar［掸邦］缅甸自治邦之一 Shan State, one of the autonomous states in Myanmar

㊀ dǎn 见 127 页 see p127

禅(禪) ㊁ shàn ㄕㄢˋ 禅让,指古代帝王让位给别人,如尧让位给舜,舜让位给禹 to abdicate the throne in favour of another person, such as the Emperor Yao handing over the throne to Shun, and Shun to Yu

㊀ chán 见 73 页 see p73

剡 ㊁ shàn ㄕㄢˋ 剡溪,水名,在浙江省东北部 Shanxi River in the northeast of Zhejiang Province

㊀ yǎn 见 866 页 see p866

掞 shàn ㄕㄢˋ 发抒,铺张 to develop; to unfold

扇 ㊀ shàn ㄕㄢˋ ❶(一子)摇动生风取凉的用具 fan:折～ *folding fan*｜蒲～ *cattail-leaf fan*｜电～ *electric fan* ❷量词 ***quantifier***:一～门 *a door*｜两～窗户 *two windows*｜一～磨(mò) *a millstone*

㊁ shān 见 652 页 see p652

骟 shàn ㄕㄢˋ 割掉牲畜的睾丸或卵巢 to castrate (an animal); to geld (a male animal); to spay (a female animal):～马 *to geld a horse*｜～猪 *to castrate a pig*

镭 shàn ㄕㄢˋ 同"钐㊁" same as 钐㊁

善 shàn ㄕㄢˋ ❶善良,品质或言行好 good; benevolent; virtuous:心～*kind-hearted*｜～举 *charitable* (or *philanthropic*) *act; benevolent action*｜～事 *good deeds; charitable work; philanthropic act* ❷好的行为、品质,跟"恶"相对(the opposite of 恶) good; virtuous:行～*to do good deeds*｜劝～规过 *to advise people to do good and refrain from evil* ❸交好,和好 kind; friendly; amiable:友～*friendly*｜相～*to be friendly* *with each other* ⑤ **extension** 熟习 familiar：面～*to look familiar* ❹高明的，良好的 good；wise：～策 *good policy*；*wise policy* [善后]妥善地料理和解决事故、事件发生以后的问题 to handle the remaining problems (of an accident, war, etc) properly ❺长(cháng)于，能做好 to be good at；to be expert in；to be versed in：勇敢～战 *to be courageous and skillful in battle*；*to be valiant and well-versed in the art of war*｜～辞令(长于讲话) *to be good at speech*；*to be refined in speech* ⑤ **extension** 好好地 properly：～为说辞 *to put in a good word or two for sb* ❻爱，容易 to be apt to；to be liable to；to be likely to：～变 *to be apt to change*；*to be fickle*；*to be capricious*｜～疑 *to tend to doubt*；*to be doubtful*

鄯 shàn ㄕㄢˋ [鄯善] **1** 古代西域国名 Shanshan，a state of the Western Regions in ancient China **2** 地名，在新疆维吾尔自治区 Shanshan，a place in the Xinjiang Uygur Autonomous Region

墡 shàn ㄕㄢˋ 白色黏土 white clay

缮 shàn ㄕㄢˋ ❶修缮，修补，整治 to fix；to repair；to mend ❷抄写 to write out；to copy：～写 *to write out*；*to copy*

膳（*饍） shàn ㄕㄢˋ 饭食 meals；board：晚～*supper*｜～费 *board expenses*

镨 shàn ㄕㄢˋ 同"钐㊁"same as 钐㊁

鳝（*鱓） shàn ㄕㄢˋ 鳝鱼，鱼名。通常指黄鳝，形状像蛇，身体黄色有黑斑，肉可以吃 eel；yellow eel (*Anguillidae*)

擅 shàn ㄕㄢˋ ❶超越职权，独断独行 to do sth without the approval or prior consent of one's superior；to do sth on one's own authority；to act despotically：专～ *to usurp authority*；*to act presumptuously*｜～自处理 *to deal with sth without authorization* ❷专于某种学术或技能 to be good at；to be versed in；to be expert in：～长数学 *to be good at mathematics*

嬗 shàn ㄕㄢˋ 更替，变迁 to change；to transform；to evolve：～变 *to change*；*to evolve*；*to transmute*

赡 shàn ㄕㄢˋ ❶供给人财物 to support；to keep；to provide for：～养亲属 *to support one's family members* ❷富足，足够 abundant；sufficient

蟮 shan ·ㄕㄢ [蛐蟮](qū—) 蚯蚓 earthworm (*Pheretima*)

SHANG ㄕㄤ

伤（傷） shāng ㄕㄤ ❶身体受损坏的地方 wound；injury：腿上有块～。*There is a wound in his leg.*｜轻～不下火线 *not to leave the*

front line on account of minor wounds ❷损害 to injure; to wound; to hurt:～了筋骨。*He was injured in the sinews and bones.*|～脑筋(费思索) *knotty; troublesome; bothersome* ❸因某种致病因素而得病 to develop an illness:～风 *to catch* (or *have, get*) *a cold*|～寒 *typhoid fever; typhoid* ❹因过度而感到厌烦 to get sick of sth; to develop an aversion to sth:吃糖吃～了 *to get sick from eating too many candies* ❺妨碍 to be harmful; to hinder:无～大雅 *not to affect things as a whole; to involve no major principle* ❻悲哀 sad;distressed; grieved(㊀ ***doublet*** 悲— sad; sorrowful; mournful):～感 *sick at heart; sentiment al*|～心 *sad; grieved; broken-hearted* ❼得罪 to offend; to displease:～众 *to offend the public; to displease the public*|开口～人 *to offend the people with rude remarks; to use bad language to insult people*

汤(湯) ㊀shāng ㄕㄤ [汤汤]水流大而急(of water) vast and torrential:浩浩～～,横无际涯 *torrential and boundless*

㊁ tāng 见730页 see p730

殇(殤) shāng ㄕㄤ ❶还没到成年就死了 to die young ❷指战死者 person who dies in fighting (especially for his country):国～*national martyr*

觞(觴) shāng ㄕㄤ 古代喝酒用的器物(in ancient China) drinking vessel; wine cup; goblet:举～称贺 *to raise one's goblet to present compliments to sb; to propose a toast to sb*

商 shāng ㄕㄤ ❶商量,两个以上的人在一起计划,讨论 to discuss; to talk over; to consult:面～*to discuss with sb face-to-face; to consult personally*|有要事相～*to have sth important to discuss* ❷生意,买卖 business; trade; commerce:～业 *business; trade; commerce*|通～*to have trade* (or *commercial*) *relations* (*with*)|经～*to go into* (or *engage in, conduct*) *business* [商标]企业用来使自己的产品或服务与其他企业的产品或服务相区别的具有明显特征的标志。包括工业、商业或服务业商标等。商标经注册后受法律保护 brand; trademark [商品]为出卖而生产的产品 commodity; goods; merchandise ❸商人,做买卖的人 businessman; tradesman; merchant:布～*cloth dealer; cloth merchant*|富～*opulent dealer; rich merchant* ❹除法中的得数 quotient:八被二除～数是四。*The quotient is 4 if 8 is divided by 2.* ❺用某数做商 to use a number as quotient:二除八～四。*Two into eight goes four times.* or *Eight divided by two yields four.* ❻商朝,成汤所建立(公元前1600—

公元前1046年),盘庚迁殷后,又称殷朝(公元前1300—公元前1046年) Shang Dynasty (1600BC－1046BC), established by Cheng Tang, and called the Yin Dynasty (1300BC－1046BC) after Pan Geng moved the capital to Yin ❼古代五音"宫、商、角(jué)、徵(zhǐ)、羽"之一 *shang*, a note of the ancient Chinese five-note scale, corresponding to 2 in numbered musical notation ❽星宿名,二十八宿之一,就是心宿(i. e. 心宿) *shang*, the 15th of the 28 constellations

墒(**𤳙) shāng ㄕㄤ 田地里土壤的湿度 moisture in the soil:够～(*of soil*) *enough moisture* | 验～ *to examine the moisture* | 抢～ *to lose no time in sowing while there is sufficient soil moisture* | 保～ *to preserve soil moisture* | ～情 *soil moisture content*

熵 shāng ㄕㄤ 为了衡量热力体系中不能利用的热能,用温度除热能所得的商 entropy

上 shǎng ㄕㄤˇ "上声"(shàng —)的"上"的又音。见657页"上(shàng) ⓫"(another pronunciation for 上 in 上声) see 上(shàng) ⓫ on p657

垧 shǎng ㄕㄤˇ 量词 ***quantifier***,计算地亩的单位,各地不同。在东北一般合15亩 *shang*, a land measure, different from place to place, equal to 15 mu in most parts of northeast China

晌 shǎng ㄕㄤˇ ❶一天内的一段时间,一会儿 part of the day; period of time of the day; a while:工作了半～。*He has worked for a long while.* | 停了一～ *to have stopped for a while* ❷晌午(wu),正午 midday; noon:睡～觉 *to take a midday nap* | 歇～ *to take a midday rest* (or *nap*)

赏 shǎng ㄕㄤˇ ❶指地位高的人或长辈给地位低的人或晚辈财物 to grant (*or* bestow) a reward; to award (㊣ ***doublet*** 赏赐 to grant (*or* bestow) a reward; to award):～给他一匹马 *to award him a horse* ❷敬辞 ***polite***:～光(请对方接受自己的邀请) *to accept an invitation; to honour sb with one's presence* ❸奖励 reward:～罚分明 *to be fair and strict in meting out rewards and punishments; to be discriminating in one's rewards and punishments* ❹奖赏的东西 reward; award:领～ *to receive an award* | 悬～ *to offer a bounty; to post a reward* ❺玩赏,因爱好(hào)某种东西而观看 to feast one's eyes on; to enjoy; to admire:欣～ *to enjoy; to admire; to appreciate* | 鉴～ *to discriminate and appreciate; to appreciate* [赏识]认识到别人的才能或作品的价值而予以重视或赞扬 to recognize the worth of; to praise; to appreciate

上 shàng ㄕㄤˋ ❶位置在高处的,跟"下"相对(the oppo-

S

site of 下) upper; above; upward: 山~ *up on the mountain*; *mountain top* | ~面 *upper*; *above*; *over* 引 **extension** **1** 次序在前的 preceding (in order or time); previous: ~篇 *first section*; *first chapter* | ~卷 *first volume*; *volume I* | ~星期 *last week* **2** 等级高的(of grade) high; superior; top: ~等 *first-rate* (or *first-class*); *top-notch*; *superior* | ~级 *higher level*; *higher authority*; *superior* **3** 质量高的,好的(of quality) good; superior; top: ~策 *best policy*; *best thing to do*; *best way out* | ~等货 *high quality goods*; *goods of top quality* ❷由低处到高处 to go up; to mount; to get on: ~山 *to go up a hill*; *to climb* (*up*) *a mountain* | ~楼 *to go upstairs* 引 **extension** **1** 去,到 to go to; to leave for: 你~哪儿? *Where are you going?* | ~北京 *to leave for Beijing* | ~街去 *to go downtown* **2** 向前进 to go ahead; to forge ahead; to advance: 同志们快~啊! *Come on, comrades!* **3** 进呈 to present; to send in; to submit: ~书 *to submit a letter*; *to send in a memorial* | 谨~(*used after the signature in a formal letter*) *sincerely yours* ❸增加 to increase; to add **1** 添补 to fill; to replenish; to supply: ~水 *to add water to a steam engine, radiator* (*of an automobile*), *etc* | ~货 *to replenish stocks for sale* **2** 安装 to fix; to install; to fit: ~刺刀 *to fix a bayonet* | ~螺丝 *to set a screw*; *to fix a screw* **3** 涂上 to apply; to paint; to smear: ~颜色 *to apply colours*; *to colour* | ~药 *to apply medical liquid*; *to apply ointment* **4** 登载,记上 to put on record; to carry; to register: ~报 *printed in a newspaper*; *reported in a newspaper* | ~光荣榜 *to be on the honour roll* | ~账 *to make an entry on an account book*; *to enter sth in an account* ❹按规定时间进行某种活动 to be engaged in an activity at a fixed time: ~课(*of students*) *to attend class*; *to go to a class*; (*of teachers*) *to conduct a class* | ~班 *to go to work* ❺拧紧发条 to screw; to wind; to tighten: ~弦 *to wind up a clock* (*or toy, etc*); *to tighten the spring* | 表该~了。*It is time to wind the watch.* ❻放在名词后(used after a noun) **1** 表示在中间(to denote the inside of sth) in: 半路~ *in the midway*; *halfway* | 心~ *in one's mind* **2** 表示方面(to denote an aspect of sth) in: 领导~ *in the leadership* | 理论~ *in theory*; *theoretically* **3** 表示在某一物体的表面(to denote the surface of an object) on: 车~ *on the bus* | 墙~ *on the wall* | 桌子~ *on the table* **4** 表示在某一事物的范围内(to denote the scope of sth) at; in: 会~ *at the meeting* | 书~ *in the* *book* ❼在动词后，表示完成(used after a verb to express the completion of an action)：选～代表 *to have been elected as the representative* | 排～队 *to have stood in a queue* ❽在动词后(used after a verb) **1** 跟“来”、“去”连用，表示趋向(used together with 来 or 去 to express tendency)：骑～去 *to ride on* | 爬～来 *to climb up* **2** 表示要求达到的目标或已达到目标(to express the aim that has to be achieved or has been achieved)：锁～锁 *to lock the door; to lock up* | 沏～茶 *to infuse* (or *steep*) *tea* | 考～大学 *to get admitted to a college or university* ❾达到一定程度或数量 to reach (a certain amount or degree); to be as many or much as; to be up to：成千～万 *thousands of* ❿旧时乐谱记音符号的一个，相当于简谱的“1” *shang*, a note of the scale in the former Chinese music, corresponding to 1 in numbered notation ⓫(又 also pronounced shǎng)上声，汉语四声之一。普通话上声的调子是拐弯的，先降低再升高，符号作“ˇ”falling-rising tone, the third tone in modern standard Chinese pronunciation

尚 shàng ㄕㄤˋ ❶还(hái) still; yet：年纪～小 *still young* | ～不可知。*It is still unknown.* [尚且]连词 ***conjunction***，跟“何况”连用，表示进一层的意思(used together with 何况 to express a further situation)：你～～不行，何况是我。*You cannot manage it, let alone me.* | 细心～～难免出错，何况粗枝大叶。*Even carefulness cannot prevent you from making mistakes, to say nothing of carelessness.* ❷尊崇，注重 to esteem; to value; to set great store by：崇～ *to uphold; to advocate* [高尚]崇高 lofty; sublime; noble

绱(**鞝) shàng ㄕㄤˋ 把鞋帮、鞋底缝合成鞋 to stitch the sole to the upper; to sole a shoe：～鞋 *to sole a shoe; to stitch the sole to the upper*

裳 ㊁ shang ·ㄕㄤ [衣裳]衣服 clothes; clothing

㊀ cháng 见 77 页 see p77

SHAO ㄕㄠ

捎 shāo ㄕㄠ 捎带，顺便给别人带东西 to take sth to (or for) sb：～封信去 *to take a letter for sb*

梢 shāo ㄕㄠ (一儿)树枝的末端 thin end of a twig; tip：树～ *tip of a tree; treetop* ㊊ ***extension*** 末尾 end; tip：眉～ *tip of an eyebrow*

稍 ㊀ shāo ㄕㄠ 副词 ***adverb***，略微 a little; a bit; slightly(㊟ ***doublet*** 一微 slightly)：～有不同 *slightly different* | 请～等一下。*Please wait a moment.*

㊁ shào 见 661 页 see p661

蛸 ㊁ shāo ㄕㄠ 见 824 页“蠨”字条“蠨蛸”(xiāo—)

see 蟏蛸 on p824

㊀ xiāo 见 823 页 see p823

筲 shāo ㄕㄠ ❶一种竹器 a kind of bamboo utensil [筲箕](—jī)淘米用的竹器 bamboo utensil (for washing rice) ❷桶 pail made of bamboo strips or wood; bucket: 水～ *pail; bucket* | 一～水 *a pail* (or *bucket*) *of water*

艄 shāo ㄕㄠ ❶船尾 stern ❷舵 rudder; helm: 掌～ *to be at the helm; to take the helm* [艄公]掌舵的人,泛指船夫 helmsman; boatman

鞘 ㊁ shāo ㄕㄠ 鞭鞘,拴在鞭子头上的细皮条 whiplash [乌鞘岭]岭名,在甘肃省天祝 Wushaoling, a mountain, in Tianzhu, Gansu Province

㊀ qiào 见 603 页 see p603

烧(燒) shāo ㄕㄠ ❶使东西着火 to set fire to; to burn (㊟ **doublet** 燃— to burn; to flame; to kindle) ❷用火或发热的东西使物品受热起变化 to heat: ～水 *to heat up water* | ～砖 *to bake* (or *fire*) *bricks* | ～炭 *to make charcoal* ❸烹饪法的一种(of culinary art or cooking) to stew after frying; to fry after stewing: ～茄子 *stewed eggplant* ❹发烧,体温增高 to run a fever; to have a high temperature: 不～了。*There is no more fever.* ❺比正常体温高的体温 fever: ～退了。*The fever is down.* ❻施肥过多,使植物枯萎、死亡 to damage (or hurt) due to excessive application of manure

勺 sháo ㄕㄠˊ ❶(—子、—儿)—种有柄的可以舀(yǎo)取东西的器具 spoon; ladle; scoop: 饭～ *rice ladle; spoon* | 铁～ *iron spoon* ❷市制容量单位,一升的百分之一 *shao*, a unit of capacity, equal to one centilitre

芍 sháo ㄕㄠˊ [芍药](—yao)多年生草本植物,根可入药,花像牡丹,供观赏 Chinese peony (*Paeonia lactiflora*)

杓 ㊁ sháo ㄕㄠˊ 同"勺❶" same as 勺❶

㊀ biāo 见 45 页 see p45

苕 ㊁ sháo ㄕㄠˊ 〈方 **dialect**〉红苕,就是甘薯 sweet potato (*Ipomoea batatas*)

㊀ tiáo 见 747 页 see p747

韶 sháo ㄕㄠˊ ❶古代的乐曲名 *shao*, name of ancient music ❷美 beautiful; splendid: ～光 *beautiful time; beautiful springtime; glorious youth* | ～华(指青年时代) *youth*

少 ㊀ shǎo ㄕㄠˇ ❶跟"多"相对(the opposite of 多) **1** 数量小的 few; little: ～数服从多数。*The minority should be subordinate to the majority.* **2** 缺 scanty; short of; lacking (㊟ **doublet** 缺— to lack; to be short of): 文娱活动～不了他。*There won't be any recreational activity without him.* **3** 不经常的 seldom; rare; scarce: ～有 *seldom; rare; few and far between* | ～见 *seldom seen* ❷短

暂 a little while; a minute; a moment:～等 *to wait a moment*｜～待 *to wait a minute; to wait a little while* ❸丢,遗失 to lose; to miss:屋里～了东西。*Something is missing in the room.*

㊁ shào 见 661 页 see p661

少 ㊁ shào ㄕㄠˋ 年纪轻,跟"老"相对(the opposite of 老) young; youthful:～年人 *boys or girls in early teens; teenager; juvenile*｜～女 *young girl*｜男女老～*men and women, young and old*

㊀ shǎo 见 660 页 see p660

召 ㊁ shào ㄕㄠˋ ❶周朝国名,在陕西省凤翔一带 Shao, a state in the Zhou Dynasty, around today's Fengxiang in Shaanxi Province ❷姓 Shao, a surname

㊀ zhào 见 960 页 see p960

邵 shào ㄕㄠˋ 姓 Shao, a surname

劭(❷**卲) shào ㄕㄠˋ ❶劝勉 to advise and encourage; to admonish; to exhort ❷美好(of moral character) excellent; admirable; noble:年高德～*of venerable age and eminent virtue; old and admirable; venerable*

绍 shào ㄕㄠˋ 接续,继续 to carry on; to keep on; to continue

哨 shào ㄕㄠˋ ❶巡逻,侦察 to patrol; to reconnoitre:～探 *patrolman; scout* ❷警戒防守的岗位 sentry post; post:放～*to be on sentry duty; to be on patrol; to keep sentry*｜～兵 *guard; sentry; sentinel*｜观察～*observation post* ❸(－子、－儿)一种小笛 whistle:吹～集合 *to call together by blowing a whistle* [呼哨][唿哨]把手指放在嘴里吹出的高尖音 whistle:打～～*to give a whistle; to whistle* ❹鸟叫(of birds) to chirp; to warble

稍 ㊁ shào ㄕㄠˋ [稍息]军事或体操的口令,命令队伍从立正姿势变为休息的姿势(of military or exercise command) Stand at ease! *or* At ease!

㊀ shāo 见 659 页 see p659

潲 shào ㄕㄠˋ ❶雨点被风吹得斜洒(of rain) to fall slantwise; to slant in:雨往南～。*The rain is slanting south.* ㊞ ***extension*** 洒水 to spray; to sprinkle:马路上～些水。*Sprinkle some water on the road.* ❷〈方 ***dialect***〉泔水 swill; slops; wash:～水 *swill; slops; wash*｜猪～*slops* (or *swill*) *for swine; hogwash*

SHE ㄕㄜ

峚 shē ㄕㄜ 同"畲"。多用于地名(She, usually used in a place name) same as 畲

奢 shē ㄕㄜ ❶挥霍财物,过分享受 luxurious; extravagant; profligate(㊈ ***doublet*** 一侈 luxurious; extravagant;

wasteful)：～华 *luxurious; sumptuous; extravagant*｜～侈品 *luxury goods; luxuries; extravagance* ❷过分的 excessive; inordinate; extravagant: ～望 *extravagant hope; wild wish* (or *expectation*)

赊 shē ㄕㄜ ❶买卖货物时延期付款或延期收款 to buy or sell on credit:～账 *to buy or sell on credit; to have outstanding bills*｜～购 *to buy on credit* ❷远 far; distant; remote:江山蜀道～。*The journey to Sichuan is very long.* ❸古同"奢❶" same as 奢 in ancient Chinese

畲 shē ㄕㄜ [畲族]我国少数民族，参看附表(see the appendix) the She ethnic group, one of the ethnic minorities of China

畬 ㊀ shē ㄕㄜ 焚烧田地里的草木，用草木灰做肥料耕种 to burn grass and wood in the field and use the ash as fertilizer; to slash and burn

㊁ yú 见 915 页 see p915

猞 shē ㄕㄜ [猞猁](-lì)哺乳动物，像狸猫，毛多淡黄色，有黑斑，四肢粗长 lynx (*Felis lynx*)

舌 shé ㄕㄜˊ ❶舌头，人和动物嘴里辨别滋味、帮助咀嚼和发音的器官 tongue [舌锋]㊕ ***transfer*** 尖锐流利的话 sharp and smart words ❷像舌头的东西 sth shaped like a tongue:帽～*peak of a cap; visor*｜火～*tongue of flame* ❸铃或铎中的锤 clapper

折 ㊁ shé ㄕㄜˊ ❶断 to break; to snap:绳子～了。*The rope broke.*｜棍子～了。*The stick snapped.* ❷亏损 to lose money in business:～本 *to lose money in business* [折耗]亏耗，损失 damage and loss (to goods during transit, storage, etc):青菜～～太大。*There is too much damage and loss to green vegetables.* ❸姓 She, a surname

㊀ zhé 见 962 页 see p962

㊂ zhē 见 962 页 see p962

佘 shé ㄕㄜˊ 姓 She, a surname

蛇(*虵) ㊀ shé ㄕㄜˊ 爬行动物，俗叫"长虫"。身体细长，有鳞，没有四肢，种类很多，有的有毒，捕食蛙等小动物(popularly called 长虫) snake (*Serpentes*)

㊁ yí 见 885 页 see p885

阇 ㊁ shé ㄕㄜˊ [阇梨]梵语"阿阇梨"的省称。佛教指高僧，泛指僧(short for 阿阇梨 in Sanskrit) eminent monk; Buddhist monk; monk

㊀ dū 见 160 页 see p160

舍(捨) ㊀ shě ㄕㄜˇ ❶放弃，不要了 to give up; to discard; to abandon:～己为人 *to place the interest of others before one's own; to sacrifice one's own interest for the sake of others*｜～近求远 *to seek from afar what lies close at hand; to forgo what is close at hand and seek what is far*

afield; *to ignore sth right under one's eyes*, *yet try to seek what is far away* | 四～五入 *to round off*; *to the nearest whole number* ❷施舍 to give alms; to dispense charity: ～粥 *to give out porridge* | ～药 *to dispense medicine*.

㊀ shè 见 663 页 see p663

厍 shè ㄕㄜˋ 〈方 **dialect**〉村庄（多用于村庄名）(She, usually used in a village name) village

设 shè ㄕㄜˋ ❶布置，安置 to place; to set up; to establish: 办事处～在北京。*The branch office is in Beijing*. [设备]为某一目的而配置的建筑与器物等 equipment; installation; facilities: 这个工厂～～很完善。*This factory is well-equipped*. [设计]根据一定的目的要求预先制定方法、程序、图样等 to plan; to devise; to design ❷假定 given; supposing: ～x=a. *Given*: $x=a$ ❸假使 if; supposing; provided (㊥ **doublet** 一若 if; supposing; provided)

社 shè ㄕㄜˋ ❶古代指祭祀土地神的地方 (in ancient China) site of sacrifice to the god of land [社火]民间在节日扮演的各种杂戏 folk art performance given on a traditional or religious festival ❷指某些团体或机构 organization; agency; society: 合作～*cooperative*; *co-op* | 通讯～*news agency* | 集会结～(*freedom of*) *assembly and association* [社会] society **1** 指由一定的经济基础和上层建筑构成的整体 society; community; combination of the economic base and the superstructure: 封建～～*feudal society* | 社会主义～～*socialist society* **2** 指由于共同的物质条件和生活方式而联系起来的人群 society; group of people regarded as forming a single community on the basis of common material conditions and life style: 上层～～*high society*; *upper class* [社交]指社会上人与人的交际往来 social intercourse; social contact [社区]社会上有一定区域、人群、组织形式、生活服务设施等的居住区 community

舍 ㊀ shè ㄕㄜˋ ❶居住的房子 house: 旅～*hotel*; *hostel*; *inn* | 宿～*dormitory* ❷养家畜的圈 shed: 猪～*pigsty* | 牛～*cow shed* ❸古代行军三十里叫一舍 *she*, an ancient unit of distance equal to 30 *li*: 退避三～(喻对人让步) *to retreat ninety li* — *to give way to avoid conflict*; *to keep good distance from sb* ❹谦辞 **humble**, 用于对别人称自己的亲戚或年纪小辈分低的亲属 my: ～亲 *my relative* | ～弟 *my younger brother* | ～侄 *my nephew* ❺姓 She, a surname

㊁ shě 见 662 页 see p662

射 shè ㄕㄜˋ ❶放箭，用推力或弹(tán)力送出子弹等 to shoot; to fire; to eject: ～箭 *to*

S

shoot an arrow | 扫～*to strafe* | 高～炮 *anti-aircraft gun; anti-aircraft artillery; ack-ack gun* ❷液体受到压力迅速挤出 to discharge in a jet; to jet; to spout: 喷～*to spout; to spurt; to eject* | 注～*to inject* ❸放出光、热等 to send out (light, heat, etc); to emit: 反～*to reflect* | 光芒四～*to radiate brilliant light in all directions* ❹有所指 to allude to sb or sth; to insinuate; to hint at: 暗～*to insinuate; to allude to* | 影～*to insinuate; to allude to*

麝 shè ㄕㄜˋ 哺乳动物，又叫"香獐子"。有獠牙，没有角，雄的脐部有香腺，能分泌麝香 (also called 香獐子) *Siberian* musk deer (*Moschus moschiferus*)

涉 shè ㄕㄜˋ ❶趟(tāng)着水走，泛指渡水 to wade; to ford: 跋山～水 *to trek (or trudge) across mountains and rivers; to scale mountains and ford streams — to travel afar over difficult terrain* | 远～重洋 *to travel all the way from across the oceans; to travel across the oceans* ❷经历 to go through; to undergo; to experience: ～险 *to go through perils* | ～世 *to get along in the world; to make one's way in the world; to gain life experience* ❸牵连，关联 to involve; to implicate: 这件事牵～到很多方面。*The matter involves many aspects.* | 不要～及其他问题。*Don't touch upon other questions.*

赦 shè ㄕㄜˋ 免除刑罚 to remit (a punishment); to pardon; to absolve: 大～ *general pardon; amnesty* | ～罪 *to grant absolution; to absolve sb from guilt; to pardon*

摄(攝) shè ㄕㄜˋ ❶拿，取 to take; to absorb; to assimilate: ～影(照相) *to take a photo; to photo; to shoot* | ～像 *to make a video recording* | ～取养分 *to absorb nourishment* ❷保养 to conserve (one's health); to keep fit: 珍～(*used mostly in letters*) *to take good care of oneself* ❸代理(多指统治权) to act for: ～政 *to act as regent* | ～位 *to act as regent; to act for a legitimate ruler*

滠(灄) shè ㄕㄜˋ 滠水，水名，在湖北省 Sheshui River in Hubei Province

慑(懾、*慴) shè ㄕㄜˋ 恐惧，害怕 to fear; to dread: ～服 *to submit in fear; to succumb; to cow sb into submission* [威慑] 用武力或威势使对方感到恐惧 to terrorize with military force; to deter

歙 ㊁ shè ㄕㄜˋ 歙县，在安徽省 Shexian County in Anhui Province

㊀ xī 见 803 页 see p803

SHEI ㄕㄟ

谁 shéi ㄕㄟˊ shuí ㄕㄨㄟˊ (又 *also* shuí) 代词 ***pronoun*** ❶表

示疑问 who; whom:～来啦? *Who has come?* ❷任指,表示任何人,无论什么人 anyone; everyone; whoever:～都可以做。*Anyone can do it.*

SHEN ㄕㄣ

申 shēn ㄕㄣ ❶地支的第九位 *shen*, the 9th of the 12 Earthly Branches ❷申时,指下午三点到五点 period of the day from 3 pm to 5 pm ❸陈述,说明 to state; to explain; to expound:～请 *to apply for* | ～明理由 *to give one's reasons* | ～辩 *to explain* (*or defend*) *oneself*; *to plead* (*or argue*) *one's case*; *to justify oneself* | ～冤 *to appeal for redressing a wrong*; *to redress an injustice*; *to right a wrong* [申斥]斥责 to rebuke; to reprimand; to reprove ❹上海的别称 Shen, another name for Shanghai

伸 shēn ㄕㄣ ❶舒展开 to put out; to stretch; to extend:～手 *to put out* (*or extend*) *one's hand*; *to stretch out one's hand* (*as a sign of begging for sth*) | ～缩 *to stretch out and draw back*; *to lengthen and shorten*; *to expand and contract* ❷表白 to express; to explain; to vindicate:～冤 *to appeal for redressing an injustice*; *to right a wrong*

呻 shēn ㄕㄣ 吟诵 to recite; to chant; to intone [呻吟](－yín)哼哼,病痛时发出声音 to groan; to moan:无病～～ *to moan and groan without being ill*; *to make a fuss about an imaginary illness*; *to adopt a sentimental pose, lacking true feelings* (*in writing or speech*)

绅 shēn ㄕㄣ ❶古代士大夫束在腰间的大带子 (as worn by scholars and officials in ancient China) girdle; sash ❷绅士,旧称地方上有势力、有地位的人,一般是地主或退职官僚 (in former times) gentry; gentleman:乡～ *country gentleman*; *village gentleman*; *squire* | 土豪劣～ *local tyrants and evil gentry* | 开明士～ *enlightened gentry*

珅 shēn ㄕㄣ 一种玉 a kind of jade

砷 shēn ㄕㄣ 一种非金属元素,符号 As,旧称"砒"(pī)。有黄、灰、黑褐三种颜色,有金属光泽,质脆有毒。化合物可做杀菌剂和杀虫剂 (formerly called 砒) arsenium (As)

身 shēn ㄕㄣ ❶人、动物的躯体 body (㊀ ***doublet*** 一体 body; constitution; health | 一躯 body; stature):全～ *whole body* | 上～ *upper part of the body* | ～体健康 *to enjoy good health*; *to be healthy* | 人～自由 *personal freedom* ㊁ ***extension*** 物体的主要部分 main part of an object; body:船～ *hull of a ship*; *body of a ship* | 河～ *riverbed* | 树～ *trunk* (*of a tree*) [身子] 1 身体 health:～～不舒服 *not to feel well*; *to feel*

S

under the weather **2** 身孕 pregnancy：有了～～*to be pregnant* ❷指生命 life：以～殉职 *to die at one's post; to die in harness; to die a martyr on duty*｜舍～炸碉堡 *to sacrifice one's life to blow up the blockhouse of the enemy* ❸亲身，亲自，本人 oneself; personally; in person：～临其境 *to be personally on the scene — to experience personally; to be present on the scene*｜～体力行（亲身努力去做）*to practise earnestly what one advocates* (or *preaches*)｜以～作则 *to set an example with one's own conduct* ❹指人的地位 social position; status：～败名裂 *to lose all standing and reputation; to bring disgrace and ruin upon oneself; to be thoroughly discredited*［身份］［身分］(—fen) 在社会上及法律上的地位 status; position; capacity ❺(—儿)量词 **quantifier**，用于衣服 (of clothes) suit：我做了一～儿新衣服。*I have a new suit made for myself.*

诜 shēn ㄕㄣ ［诜诜］形容众多的样子 many; numerous

参（參、❷*葠、❷*蓡）

㊀ shēn ㄕㄣ ❶星宿名，二十八宿之一 *shen*, the 21st of the 28 constellations［参商］参和商都是二十八宿之一，两者不同时在天空出现 *shen* and *shang*, both of which are among the 28 constellations, but never appear in the sky at the same time ⑩ ***figurative* 1** 分离不得相见 (of family members or friends) to separate and never meet again **2** 不和睦 to be on bad terms; to be estranged and irreconcilable ❷人参，多年生草本植物。根肥大，略像人形，可入药 ginseng (*Panax ginseng*)

㊁ cān 见 64 页 see p64

㊂ cēn 见 68 页 see p68

糁（糝、**粈）㊀ shēn ㄕㄣ (—儿) 谷类制成的小渣 crushed grain：玉米～儿 *crushed corn*

㊁ sǎn 见 645 页 see p645

鲹（鰺） shēn ㄕㄣ 鱼名。身体侧扁，侧面呈卵圆形，鳞细，生活在海中 scad (*Carangidae*)

莘 ㊀ shēn ㄕㄣ ❶莘县，在山东省 Shenxian County in Shandong Province ❷姓 Shen, a surname

［莘莘］众多 numerous; a great many; multitudinous

㊁ xīn 见 832 页 see p832

娠 shēn ㄕㄣ 胎儿在母体中微动。泛指怀孕 (of foetus) to stir; to move slightly in its mother's womb; to be pregnant

深 shēn ㄕㄣ ❶从表面到底或从外面到里面距离大的，跟"浅"相对 (the opposite of 浅) deep：～水 *deep water*｜这条河很～。*The river is deep.*｜～山 *remote mountains*｜这个院子很～。*The courtyard is very*

spacious.[深浅] **1** 深度 depth **2** 说话的分寸 proper limits (for speech); sense of propriety:他说话不知道～～。*He often speaks thoughtlessly and without a sense of propriety*. ❷从表面到底的距离 depth:这口井两丈～。*The well is two* zhang *deep*. ❸久,时间长 long (in time); late:～秋 *late autumn*|～更半夜 *in the middle of the night; in the small hours of the night; far into the night*|年～日久 *over a long period of time; with the passage of time* ❹程度高的(used to express a high degree) great; deep:～信 *to be deeply convinced; to have a deep faith in; to believe firmly*|～知 *to know very well; to fully understand*|～谋远虑 *to think deeply and plan carefully; to be circumspect and far-sighted*|情谊很～*great friendship*|这本书内容太～。*The book is too difficult*.|讲理论应该～入浅出。*The profound theory should be explained in plain terms*. ❺颜色重(of colour) deep; dark; rich:～红 *deep red; dark red; crimson*|颜色太～。*The colour is too dark*.

燊 shēn ㄕㄣ 旺盛 flaming; ablaze; flourishing

什 ㊁ shén ㄕㄣˊ [什么](—me)代词 ***pronoun*** **1** 表示疑问(used in the interrogative) what; who:想～～? *What are you thinking about?*|～～人? *Who is it?* **2** 指不确定的或任何事物(used to denote sth indefinite or anything):我想吃点儿～～。*I'd like sth to eat*.|～～事都难不住他。*Nothing can befuddle him*. **3** 表示惊讶或不满(used to express surprise or discontent):～～!明天就走? *Really? Are you leaving tomorrow?*|这是～～破东西! *What a damned thing!*

㊀ shí 见676页 see p676

甚 ㊁ shén ㄕㄣˊ 同"什"(shén) same as 什

㊀ shèn 见669页 see p669

神 shén ㄕㄣˊ ❶迷信的人称天地万物的"创造者"和被他们崇拜的人死后的所谓精灵 god; deity; divinity:无～论 *atheism*|不信鬼～*to disbelieve in the existence of ghosts and gods* (or *supernatural beings*) [引] ***extension*** **1** 不平凡的,特别高超的 extraordinary; miraculous; supernatural:～力 *superhuman strength; extraordinary prowess*|～医 *miracle-working doctor; highly skilled doctor* **2** 不可思议的,特别稀奇的 magical; supernatural; miraculous ([连] ***doublet*** —秘 mysterious; mystical):这事真是越说越～了。*The more it is talked about, the more miraculous it becomes*. [神话]远古人们集体创作的神异故事 mythology; myth; fairy tale [喻] ***figurative*** 荒诞,夸张,不能实现的话 preposterous story [神通]特殊的手段或本领 magic power; remarkable

S

ability: 大显～～*to display one's prowess; to give full play to one's ability*|～～广大 *to have omnipotent magic power; to possess unusual powers; to be infinitely resourceful* ❷心力，心思，注意力 spirit; mind; attention: 劳～*to tax one's mind; to take trouble*|留～*to keep an eye out* (*for*); *to be careful; to take care*|看得出了～*to be lost in reading* (or *gazing at*)|聚精会～*to concentrate one's attention, thoughts, etc on; to fix* (or *focus*) *one's attention on* [神经]人和动物体内传达知觉和运动的组织 nerve ❸(～儿)神气，表情 expression; look; air: 你瞧他这个～儿。*Just look at the expression on his face.*|～色 *expression; look; air*

沈(❷❸瀋) ㊀ shěn ㄕㄣˇ ❶姓 Shen, a surname ❷汁 juice: 墨～未干。*The ink is still wet.* ❸[沈阳]地名，在辽宁省 Shenyang, a place in Liaoning Province

㊁ chén 见 82 页 see p82

审(審) shěn ㄕㄣˇ ❶详细，周密 careful; meticulous; circumspect: ～慎 *cautious; prudent; circumspect*|精～(*of writings, plans, opinions*) *precise and comprehensive; well-thought-out* ㊈ **extension** 仔细思考，反复分析、推究 to examine; to check up; to go over: ～查 *to examine; to check; to investigate*|～核 *to examine and verify; to check*|这份稿子～完了。*This manuscript* (or *draft*) *has been checked*. [审定]对文字著作、艺术创造、学术发明等详细考究、评定 to examine and approve; to examine and finalize [审计]专设机关对国家各级政府、金融机构、企业事业组织的财务收支情况进行监督、审查并提出意见 to audit ❷审问，讯问案件 to interrogate; to try: ～案 *to hold a court trial; to try a case*|～判 *to bring to trial; to put on trial; to try*|公～*to put sb on public trial; to stand public trial; to conduct a public trial* ❸知道，也作"谉"、"谂"(also written as 谉 or 谂) to know: 不～近况何如? *I wonder how everything is going on with you.* ❹的确，果然 indeed; really: ～如其言。*What he says is really true.*

谉(讅) shěn ㄕㄣˇ 同"审❸" same as 审❸

婶(嬸) shěn ㄕㄣˇ ❶(～子、～儿)叔叔的妻子(叠 **reduplication**) wife of one's father's younger brother; aunt ❷称呼与母亲辈分相同而年轻的已婚妇女(term of address for a married woman who is younger than one's mother but of the same generation) aunt; auntie: 张大～儿 *Elder Aunt Zhang*

哂 shěn ㄕㄣˇ 微笑 to smile: ～存 *to keep* (*gift, etc*) *kindly*|～纳 *to accept kindly*|聊博一～*just for your enter-*

tainment

矧 shěn ㄕㄣˇ 况，况且 moreover; besides; in addition

谂 shěn ㄕㄣˇ ❶同"审❸"same as 审❸ ❷劝告 to advise; to urge; to exhort

肾(腎) shèn ㄕㄣˋ 肾脏，俗叫"腰子"。人和动物的内脏之一，是滤出尿液的主要器官(popularly called 腰子) kidney

甚 ㊀ shèn ㄕㄣˋ ❶很，极 very; most; extremely：进步～快 *to make fast progress*｜他说得未免过～。*He somewhat stretched the truth*.［甚至］［甚至于］连词 ***conjunction***，表示更进一层 furthermore; (to go) so far as to; even to the extent that：不学习就会落后，～～会犯错误。*One who does not study will lag behind or even may make mistakes*.｜这件事扰乱了他的生活，～～～影响了他的工作。*Not only does this matter disturb his life, but it also interferes with his work*. ❷超过，胜过 more than：更有～者 *even better* (or *worse*)｜日～一日 *getting better* (or *worse*) *with each passing day* ❸〈方 ***dialect***〉代词 ***pronoun***，什么 what：要它做～？*What's the use of it?*｜姓～名谁？*What's your full name?*

㊁ shén 见 667 页 see p667

葚 ㊀ shèn ㄕㄣˋ［桑葚］桑树结的果实 mulberry (*Morus*)

㊁ rèn 见 633 页 see p633

椹 ㊁ shèn ㄕㄣˋ 同"葚"same as 葚

㊀ zhēn 见 968 页 see p968

胂 shèn ㄕㄣˋ 有机化合物的一类，通式 $RAsH_2$，是砷化氢分子中的氢被烃基替换后生成的化合物。胂类化合物大多有剧毒 arsine

渗(滲) shèn ㄕㄣˋ 液体慢慢地透入或漏出 to seep; to ooze; to leak：水～到土里去了。*Water has seeped into the earth*.｜天很热，汗～透了衣服。*It is so hot that our clothes are soaked with sweat*.

瘆(瘮) shèn ㄕㄣˋ 使人害怕 to horrify; to terrify; to petrify：～人 *to make one's flesh creep; horrifying*｜～得慌 *horrifying*

蜃 shèn ㄕㄣˋ 蛤蜊 clam［蜃景］由于不同密度的大气层对于光线的折射作用，把远处景物反映在天空或地面而形成的幻景，在沿海或沙漠地带有时能看到。古人误认为是大蜃吐气而成。也叫"海市蜃楼"(also called 海市蜃楼) mirage

慎 shèn ㄕㄣˋ 小心，加小心 careful; cautious; prudent (㊟ ***doublet*** 谨－careful; cautious; circumspect)：不～ *not careful; inadvertent*｜办事要～重 *to be discreet in doing things*｜谦虚谨～ *modest and circumspect*

SHENG ㄕㄥ

升(❸❹*昇、❹*陞) shēng ㄕㄥ ❶容积的法定计量

S

单位(市升与之相同),1 升等于 1 000 毫升 litre ❷量粮食的器具,容量为斗的十分之一 *sheng*, an instrument for measuring grain, equal to 0.1 *dou* ❸向上,高起 to rise; to ascend; to hoist:~旗 *to hoist a flag*|东方红,太阳~。*The East is red, (and) the sun has risen.* ❹提高 to elevate; to promote:~级 *to go up one grade (in school); to promote; to escalate*

生 shēng ㄕㄥ ❶出生,诞生 to be born; to come into being:~辰 *birthday*|孙中山~于公元 1866 年。*Sun Yat-sen was born in 1866.* ❷可以发育的物体在一定的条件下发展长大 to grow:种子~芽(*of seeds*)*to sprout*|~根 *to take* (or *strike*) *root; to root* ㉉ ***extension*** 发生,产生 to cause; to give rise to:~病 *to be ill; to get sick; to fall ill*|~疮 *to get* (or *develop*) *sores*|~事 *to create* (or *make*) *trouble; to foment disturbance* [生产] **1** 人们使用工具来创造各种生产资料和生活资料 to make; to produce; to manufacture **2** 生小孩儿 to give birth to a baby; to bear ❸活,跟"死"相对(the opposite of 死) to live; to exist:~老病死 *birth, old age, sickness and death — all the problems of one's life*|贪~怕死 *to cling to life cravenly instead of braving death; to crave for nothing but saving one's skin; to be mortally afraid of death*|苟且偷~*to live merely for the sake of living; to drag out an ignoble existence* ㉉ ***extension*** **1** 生计 life; livelihood:谋~*to make a living; to seek a livelihood*|营~*to make* (or *eke out*) *a living* **2** 生命 life:杀~*to take an animal's life; to kill living things*|丧~*to lose one's life; to get killed*|众~*all living creatures; all flesh* **3** 有生命力的 alive; living:~物 *living thing*|~龙活虎 *doughty as a dragon and lively as a tiger — brimming* (or *bursting*) *with energy; full of energy and spirits; full of vim and vigour* **4** 整个生活阶段 (all) one's life; life time; life span:平~*all one's life; one's whole life*|一~*all one's life; in one's lifetime* ❹使柴、煤等燃烧起来 to light:~火 *to light a fire; to make a fire*|~炉子 *to light a stove* ❺没有经过烧煮的或烧煮没有熟的 uncooked; raw; undercooked:夹~饭 *half cooked rice*|~肉 *raw meat*|不喝~水。*Don't drink unboiled water.* ❻植物果实没有成长到熟的程度 unripe; green:~瓜 *unripe melon* ❼不常见的,不熟悉的 unfamiliar; unacquainted; strange (㊈***doublet***—疏 unfamiliar; strange):陌~*strange; unfamiliar*|~人 *stranger*|~字 *new word; new Chinese character* ❽不熟练 unskillful:~手 *green hand* ❾没有经过炼制的 unprocessed;

raw; crude: ～皮子 *raw hide; untanned hide* | ～药 *crude drug; dried medicinal herbs* ❿生硬，硬，强（qiǎng） stiff; rigid; mechanical: ～拉硬拽 *to drag sb along against his will; to make a farfetched comparison; to stretch the meaning* | ～不承认 *to refuse to admit obstinately* ⓫表示程度深(used to express a greater degree) very; much: ～疼 *to be very painful; to ache badly* (or *intolerably*) | ～怕 *to be extremely afraid* ⓬指正在学习的人 pupil; student: 学～ *pupil; student* | 师～ *teachers and students* | 实习～ *trainee; intern* 旧时又指读书的人(in former times) intellectual; scholar: 书～ *scholar; intellectual* ⓭传统戏曲里扮演男子的一种角色 *sheng*, a male role in traditional Chinese opera: 老～ laosheng, *role of an older or middle-aged man* (*usually a scholar or an official*) | 小～ xiaosheng, *role of a young man* (*usually a scholar*) ⓮词尾 ***suffix***: 好～ *so; exceedingly; properly* | 怎～是好? *What's to be done?*

牲 shēng ㄕㄥ 牲口，普通指牛、马、驴、骡等家畜 domestic animal 古代特指供宴飨祭祀用的牛、羊、猪(in ancient China) animal sacrifice

胜 ㊁ shēng ㄕㄥ "肽"的旧称 former term for 肽

㊀ shèng 见 672 页 see p672

笙 shēng ㄕㄥ 管乐器，用若干根长短不同的簧管制成，用口吹奏 *sheng*, a multi-reed-pipe wind instrument

甥 shēng ㄕㄥ ❶外甥，姊妹的儿子 sister's son; nephew ❷〈方 ***dialect***〉外甥，称女儿的儿子 daughter's son; grandson

声(聲) shēng ㄕㄥ ❶声音，物体振动时所产生的能引起听觉的波 sound; voice: ～如洪钟 *to have a stentorian* (or *sonorous*) *voice* | 大～说话 *to speak in a loud voice* [声气]消息 information; message: 不通～～ *not to exchange information; not to be in contact with each other* ❷声母，字音开头的辅音，如"报(bào)告(gào)"、"丰(fēng)收(shōu)"里的 b、g、f、sh 都是声母 initial consonant of a Chinese syllable such as b, g, f and sh in bàogào or fēngshōu ❸声调(diào)，字音的高低升降。参看 149 页"调㊀❹"(see 调㊀❹ on p149) tone ❹说出来使人知道，扬言 to make known; to state; to declare: ～明 *to state; to declare; to announce* | ～讨 *to denounce; to condemn; to decry* | ～张 *to make public; to disclose* | ～东击西 *to make a feint to the east and attack in the west — to shoot at a pigeon and kill a crow; to look one way and row another; to take sb unawares* ❺名誉 fame; reputation: ～望 *reputation; prestige; popularity*

S

渑（澠） ㊀ shéng ㄕㄥˊ 古水名，在今山东省淄博一带 Sheng River, an ancient river around the area of today's Zibo, Shandong Province

㊁ miǎn 见 504 页 see p504

绳（繩） shéng ㄕㄥˊ ❶（一子）用两股以上的棉、麻纤维或棕、草等拧成的条状物 rope; cord; string［绳墨］木工取直用的器具 carpenter's line marker ㊘ ***figurative*** 规矩，法度 rules; rules and regulations ❷约束，制裁 to restrict; to restrain; to punish: ～之以法 *to punish sb in accordance with the law; to prosecute and punish according to law*

S

省 ㊀ shěng ㄕㄥˇ ❶行政区划单位，直属中央 province ❷节约，不费 to save; to economize; to be frugal: ～钱 *to save money; to be economical* | ～时间 *to save time* | ～事 *to save trouble; to simplify matters* ❸简略 to simplify（㊟ ***doublet*** —略 to omit; to leave out）: ～称 *abbreviated form of a name; abbreviation; short for* | ～写 *to write a Chinese character in simplified form; to simplify (a book for beginners, etc)*

㊁ xǐng 见 837 页 see p837

眚 shěng ㄕㄥˇ ❶眼睛生翳（yì）nebula in the eye; film; cataract ❷灾祸 adversity; disaster; calamity ❸过错 fault; mistake; error

圣（聖） shèng ㄕㄥˋ ❶最崇高的 holy; sacred: 革命～地 *sacred place of the revolution*［圣人］旧时称具有最高智慧和道德的人（in former times）wise man; saint; sage ❷称学问、技术有特殊成就的 master: ～手 *master (of certain skill)* | 诗～ *poet among poets; poet of genius; sage poet* | 棋～ *master chess player; champion chess* (or weiqi) *player* ❸封建时代尊称帝王 emperor (of feudal society): ～上 *emperor; Your Majesty; His* (or *Her*) *Majesty* | ～旨 *imperial edict*

胜（勝） ㊀ shèng ㄕㄥˋ ❶赢，胜利，跟"败"相对（the opposite of 败）to win; to triumph; to succeed: 打～仗 *to win a battle* | 得～ *to win* (or *score*) *a victory; to triumph; to succeed* ❷打败（对方）to defeat; to triumph over; to prevail over: 以少～多 *to defeat an enemy superior in number; to use a small force to defeat a large one* ❸超过 to surpass; to exceed; to be superior to: 今～于昔。*The present is superior to* (or *better than*) *the past.* | 一个～似一个。*One surpasses another.* ❹优美的 beautiful; wonderful; superb: ～地 *famous scenic spot* | ～景 *beautiful scenery; beautiful landscape; scenic beauty* ㊕ ***extension*** 优美的地方或境界 scenic spot; artistic conception: 名～

place famous for its scenery (or *historic relics*); *well-known scenic spot*; *point of tourist interest* | 引人入～ *fascinating*; *enchanting*; *enthralling* ❺(旧读 formerly shēng)能担任，能承受 can bear (*or* stand); to be equal (*or* up) to; to be competent at (*or* in): ～任 *to be equal to*; *to be competent at* (or *in*); *to be qualified for* | 不～其烦 *to be pestered* (or *bored*) *beyond endurance* ❻(旧读 formerly shēng) 尽 extremely; exhaustively: 不～感激 *to be extremely grateful*; *to be much obliged* | 不～枚举 *too numerous to mention individually* (or *one by one*); *so many as to defy enumeration*; *too many to list*

㊁ shēng 见 671 页 see p671

晟 shèng ㄕㄥˋ ❶光明 bright; light ❷旺盛，兴盛 prosperous; flourishing; vigorous

盛 ㊀ shèng ㄕㄥˋ ❶兴旺 flourishing; prosperous; exuberant: 旺～ *vigorous*; *exuberant*; *vibrant* | 茂～ *luxuriant*; *flourishing*; *exuberant* | 繁荣昌～ *thriving and prosperous* | 梅花～开。*The Chinese plum trees are in full bloom.* ❷炽烈 vigorous; energetic; aggressive: 年轻气～ *young and aggressive* | 火势很～。*The fire is raging.* ❸丰富，华美 rich; sumptuous: ～宴 *grand banquet*; *sumptuous dinner*; *luxurious feast* | ～装 *rich dress*; *splendid attire*; *Sunday best* ❹热烈，大规模的 grand; magnificent: ～会 *magnificent assembly*; *distinguished gathering*; *great meeting* | ～况 *grand occasion*; *spectacular affair* ❺深厚 deep; profound; profuse: ～意 *great kindness*; *generosity*; *magnanimity* | ～情 *great kindness*; *kind hospitality* ❻姓 Sheng, a surname

㊁ chéng 见 85 页 see p85

乘 ㊁ shèng ㄕㄥˋ ❶春秋时晋国的史书叫乘 historical records of the state of Jin during the Spring and Autumn Period; historical records: 史～ *historical records*; *annals of history* ❷量词 ***quantifier***，古代用于四匹马拉的兵车(in ancient China) war chariot drawn by four horses: 千～之国 *state with a thousand chariots*

㊀ chéng 见 87 页 see p87

剩(*賸) shèng ㄕㄥˋ 多余，余留下来 surplus; remnant; leftover (㊀ ***doublet*** — 余 surplus; remainder; residue): ～饭 *remains of a meal*; *leftovers* | ～货 *surplus wares* (or *goods*)

嵊 shèng ㄕㄥˋ [嵊州]地名，在浙江省 Shengzhou, a place in Zhejiang Province

SHI ㄕ

尸(❶*屍) shī ㄕ ❶尸首，死人的身体 dead body; corpse; carcass ❷

古代祭祀时代表死者受祭的人(in ancient China) person representing the spirit of the dead during the performance of the sacrificial rites ❸不做事情，空占职位 to hold (*or* occupy) a position without doing one's duty：～位 *to hold a post without doing anything*

鸤 shī ㄕ [鸤鸠](－jiū)古书上指布谷鸟(in ancient Chinese texts) cuckoo

失 shī ㄕ ❶丢 to lose (㊟ **doublet** 遗－ to lose)：～物招领 *to advertise for the owner of a lost article; lost-and-found*｜机不可～*can't afford to lose the opportunity; not to let the opportunity slip through one's fingers; now or never* ㊀ **extension 1** 违背 to break; to violate：～信 *to break one's promise; to go back on one's word*｜～约 *to fail to keep an appointment; to break an appointment* **2** 找不着 to get lost：～群之雁 *wild goose that has strayed from the flock*｜迷～*to lose one's way* ❷没有掌握住 to lose hold of; to let slip; to miss：～足 *to miss one's step; to slip; to go astray*｜～言 *to make a slip of tongue; to make an indiscreet remark*｜～火 *to catch fire; to be on fire* ❸没有达到目的 to fail to achieve one's ends：～意 *to be disappointed; to be frustrated*｜～望 *to lose heart; to lose hope; to despair*｜～策 *to be unwise (in devising tactics, etc); to misjudge; to miscalculate* [失败]计划或希望没能达到 to lose; to fail; to fizzle out ❹错误，疏忽 error; mistake; slip：千虑一～。*Even the wise are not always free from error.* ❺改变常态 to deviate from the normal; to become unusual (*or* abnormal)：～色 *to lose colour; to lose countenance; to turn pale*｜～声痛哭 *to lose control and cry out loud; to burst (or break) into tears*

师(師) shī ㄕ ❶老师，传授知识技能的人 teacher; master; tutor ㊀ **extension** 榜样 model; example; guide：前事不忘，后事之～。*Lessons learned from the past* (or *Past lessons if not forgotten*) *can guide one in the future.* [师傅]传授技艺的老师和对有实践经验的工人的尊称 master [律师]依法取得执业证书，为社会提供法律服务的专业人员 lawyer; attorney; counselor ❷由师徒关系而产生的 of one's master (*or* teacher)：～兄 *senior male fellow apprentice* (or *student*); *son of one's master* (or *teacher*) *older than oneself; father's male apprentice* (or *student*) *older than oneself* ❸对擅长某种技术的人的称呼 person skilled in a certain profession or trade：工程～*engineer*｜医～*qualified doctor; certified doctor*｜理发～*barber; hairdresser* ❹仿效

S

to follow; to imitate; to learn: ～法 *to model oneself after* (*a great master*); *to take as a model*; *to imitate* ❺军队 troops; army: 誓～ *to rally to pledge resolution before going to war*; *to take a solemn pledge at a mass rally*; *to take a mass pledge* | 百万雄～ *million bold* (or *powerful*) *warriors*; *mighty army of some million soldiers* ❻军队的编制单位，是团的上一级(of army unit) division

狮(獅) shī ㄕ 狮子(古书中也作"师子")，一种凶猛的野兽，毛黄褐色，雄的脖子上有长鬣，生活在有稀疏树林的热带草原地带，捕食其他动物。多产于非洲及印度西北部(also written as 师子 in ancient Chinese texts) lion (*Panthera leo*)

浉(溮) shī ㄕ 浉河，在河南省信阳，入淮河 Shihe River, in Xinyang, Henan Province, flowing into Huaihe River

䴓 shī ㄕ 鸟名。背青灰色，腹淡褐色，嘴长而尖，脚短爪强，捕食树林中的害虫 nuthatch (*Sitta*)

诗 shī ㄕ 一种文体，形式很多，多用韵，可以歌咏朗诵 poetry; poem; verse

虱(*蝨) shī ㄕ (一子)寄生在人、畜身上的一种昆虫，吸食血液，能传染疾病 louse (*Pediculus humanus*)

鲺 shī ㄕ 节肢动物，身体扁圆形，跟臭虫相似，头上有一对吸盘。寄生在鱼类身体的表面 carp louse; fish louse (*Argulus*)

絁 shī ㄕ 古时一种粗绸子(in ancient China) a kind of coarse silk fabric

施 shī ㄕ ❶实行 to put into practice; to carry out; to execute: ～工 *to carry out a construction of a project*; *to construct* | 无计可～ *to have exhausted one's whole bag of tricks — to be at a loss as to what to do*; *to have no card to play* | 倒行逆～ *to go against the trend of the times*; *to push a reactionary policy*; *to go against the wishes of the people* [施展]发挥能力 to put to good use; to give full play to; to display ❷用上，加上 to use; to apply: ～肥 *to apply fertilizer*; *to spread manure* | ～粉 *to apply powder*; *to powder* ❸给予 to bestow; to grant; to give: ～礼 *to bow*; *to salute* | ～恩 *to bestow favours on*; *to grant favours* (*to others*) ❹施舍，把财物送给穷人或出家人 to give alms to; to give sth in charity

湿(濕、*溼) shī ㄕ 沾了水或是含的水分多，跟"干"相对(the opposite of 干) wet; moist; damp: 地很～。*The ground is very wet.* | 手～了。*My hands are wet.*

S

蓍 shī ㄕ 蓍草,俗叫"蛐蜒草"或"锯齿草"。多年生草本植物,茎直立,花白色。可以入药,又供制香料(popularly called 蛐蜒草 or 锯齿草) alpine yarrow (*Achillea*)

釃(釃) shī ㄕ shāi ㄕㄞ (又 *also* shāi) ❶滤酒 to purify wine by a filter; to filtrate wine; to strain wine ❷斟酒 to pour wine ❸疏导河渠 to dredge a river or canal

嘘 ㊁ shī ㄕ 叹词 ***interjection***,表示反对、制止、驱逐等(used to express opposition, prevention, or dispersion of sb or sth) hush; shh

㊀ xū 见 845 页 see p845

S

十 shí ㄕˊ ❶数目 ten ❷表示达到顶点 topmost; highest:~足 *pure; sheer; full*|~分 *very; most; fully*|~全~美 *to be perfect in every way* (or *aspect*); *to be the acme of perfection; to be the paragon of excellence* ❸法定计量单位中十进倍数单位词头之一,表示 10^1(符号 da) deca- (da)

什 ㊀ shí ㄕˊ ❶同"十❶"(多用于分数或倍数)(usually used in fractions or multiples) same as 十❶:~一(十分之一) *one tenth*|~百(十倍或百倍) *tenfold; hundredfold* ❷各种的,杂样的 assorted; varied; miscellaneous:~物 *articles for daily use; odds and ends; sundries*|家~(家用杂物) *home utensils and furniture* [什锦]各种各样东西凑成的(多指食品) assorted; mixed:~~糖 *assorted* (or *mixed*) *candies; assorted sweets*|素~~*assorted vegetarian delights; assorted vegetable dish*

㊁ shén 见 667 页 see p667

石 ㊀ shí ㄕˊ ❶(一头)(tou) 构成地壳的坚硬物质,是由矿物集合而成的 stone; rock; pebble ❷用石制成的 of stone:~砚 *inkstone*|~磨 *millstones* ❸指石刻 stone inscription:金~ *inscription on ancient bronzes and stone tablets* ❹古代容量单位,一石合十斗 *shi*, a unit of capacity in ancient China, equal to ten *dou* ❺古代重量单位,一石合一百二十斤 *shi*, a unit of weight in ancient China, equal to one hundred and twenty *jin* ❻姓 Shi, a surname

㊁ dàn 见 127 页 see p127

炻 shí ㄕˊ [炻器]介于陶器和瓷器之间的陶瓷制品,如水缸、沙锅 ceramic product with qualities between porcelain and pottery, such as water vat, earthen pot, etc; stoneware

祏 shí ㄕˊ 古时宗庙中藏神主的石室 stone room used to hold a spirit tablet in the ancient ancestral temple or shrine of a ruling house

鼫 shí ㄕˊ 古书上指鼯(wú)鼠一类的动物(in ancient Chinese texts) animals like the flying squirrel

时(時、*旹) shí ㄕˊ ❶时间,一切物质不断变化或发展所经历的

过程 time ❷时间的一段 period of time **1** 比较长期的 times; days (⊜ ***doublet*** 一代 era; epoch; age): 古～*ancient times* | 唐～*the Tang Dynasty; the Tang era* | 盛极一～*to be in fashion* (or *vogue*) *for a time; to be all the rage at the moment; to prevail for a time* **2** 一年中的一季 season: 四～*four seasons* **3** 时辰,一昼夜的十二分之一 *shichen*, one of the 12 periods into which the day was divided in ancient China: 子～zishi, *the period of the day from 11 p. m. to 1 p. m.* **4** 小时,一昼夜的二十四分之一 hour **5** 时候 time: 平～*normal times; ordinary times; usual days* | 到～叫我一声。*Call me when time is up.* **6** 钟点 o'clock: 八～上班 *to go to work at 8 o'clock* [不时] **1** 不定时 any time; unexpected moment: ～～之需 *possible future needs* (or *want*); *unexpected want* **2** 常常 frequently; often; again and again: ～～照顾 *to look after frequently; to often take care of* ❸时机 opportune moment; opportunity; chance: 待～而动 *to wait for the right time to act* ❹规定的时间 specified (*or* scheduled) time: 准～起飞 *to take off at the scheduled time* ❺现在的,当时的 present; current: ～髦 *fashionable; stylish; in vogue* | ～事 *current events; current affairs* [时装]式样最新的服装,当代流行的服装 fashionable dress; latest fashion ❻时常,常常 (叠 ***reduplication***) often; frequently; again and again: 学而～习之 *to learn sth and review it every now and then; to review what you have learned frequently* | ～～发生困难。*Difficulties occurred frequently.* ❼有时候 sometimes; occasionally; now and then: 天气～阴～晴。*It is sometimes clear and sometimes cloudy.* | 身体～好～坏。*He has been ill off and on.*

埘(塒) shí ㄕˊ 古代称在墙壁上挖洞做成的鸡窝 (in ancient China) chicken roost built into a wall

鲥(鰣) shí ㄕˊ 鲥鱼,鱼名。背黑绿色,腹银白色,鳞下多脂肪。肉味鲜美 hilsa herring (*Tenualosa ilisha*); reeves shad

识(識) ⊖shí ㄕˊ ❶知道,认得,能辨别 to know; to recognize; to identify: ～货 *to be able to tell good from bad; to know what's what* | ～字 *to learn to read; to become literate* | ～别真假 *to distinguish between truth and falsehood; to tell the false from the genuine* ❷知识,所知道的道理 knowledge; learning; insight: 常～*common sense; general* (or *common*) *knowledge* | 知～(shi)丰富 *to have an encyclopedic knowledge; to be knowledgeable* (or *learned*) ❸见识,辨别是非的能力 insight;

S

judgement：卓～ *outstanding insight；judicious judgement；sagacity*

㊁ zhì 见 983 页 see p983

实（實、△*寔） shí 𠂆 ❶充满 solid；full：虚～*true or false —an actual situation*｜～心的铁球 *solid iron ball*｜～足年龄 *exact age* ❷真，真诚，跟"虚"相对（the opposite of 虚）true；real；sincere：～心～意 *honest and sincere；true and earnest；from the bottom of one's heart*｜～话～说 *to speak the plain truth；to call a spade a spade；to tell the truth*｜～事求是 *to seek truth from facts；to base oneself on the facts；to be practical and realistic* [实词]能够单独用来回答问题，有比较实在意义的词，如名词、动词等 notional word [实际]真实情况，也指实践 reality；practice：联系～～ *to integrate sth with practice；to apply sth to reality*（or *practice*）｜～～调查 *practical investigation* [实践] **1** 实行（自己的主张），履行（自己的诺言）to put into practice；to carry out；to implement **2** 人们改造自然和改造社会的有意识的活动 practice [实在] **1** 真，的确 indeed；really；in all conscience：～～好 *really good* **2**（—zai）不虚 real；true；practical：他的学问很～～。*He has a sound knowledge.*｜话说得挺～～*to talk straight* [老实]（—shi）诚实，不狡猾 honest；frank：～～人说～～话。*An honest person is honest in words.* ❸种子，果子 fruit；seed：开花结～*to blossom and bear fruit*

拾 shí 𠂆 ❶捡，从地下拿起来 to pick up（from the ground）；to gather；to collect：～麦子 *to glean stray ears of wheat；to glean wheat*｜～了一枝笔。*A pen has been picked up.* ❷"十"字的大写 ten，capital form of 十

[拾掇]（—duo）**1** 整理 to tidy up；to clean up；to put in order：把屋子～～一下 *to tidy up a room*｜把书架～～～～ *to put the books on the shelves in order；to sort out the books on the shelves* **2** 修理 to repair；to fix；to mend：～～钟表 *to repair watches and clocks*｜～～机器 *to fix a machine*｜～～房子 *to repair a house*

食 ㊀ shí 𠂆 ❶吃 to eat：～肉 *to eat meat* [食言]指失信 to break one's promise；to go back on one's word；to fall down on one's promise：决不～～。*Never break one's promise.* [食指]即示指，手的第二指 index finger；forefinger ㊙ ***figurative*** 家庭人口 number of people in a family：～～众多 *to have many mouths to feed；to have a large family to support* ❷吃的东西 food；meal：素～*vegetarian food*（or *diet*）｜零～*between-meal nibbles；snacks*｜面～*food made of wheat flour*｜丰衣足～*to have ample food* *and clothing; to be well-fed and well-clad* ❸日月亏缺或完全不见的现象 eclipse:日～*solar eclipse*|月～*lunar eclipse*|全～*total eclipse*

㊁ sì 见 706 页 see p706

蚀 shí ㄕˊ ❶损伤,亏缺 to damage; to lose; to erode:侵～*to erode* (or *corrode*); *to eat away; to encroach upon*|腐～*to erode; to corrode; to etch* ❷同"食❸"same as 食❸

湜 shí ㄕˊ 形容水清见底(叠 ***reduplication***)(of water) clear; transparent; limpid

寔 shí ㄕˊ ❶放置 to lay (up); to place ❷同"实" same as 实

史 shǐ ㄕˇ ❶历史,自然或社会以往发展的过程。也指记载历史的文字和研究历史的学科 history ❷古代掌管记载史事的官 officials in charge of historical records in ancient China

驶 shǐ ㄕˇ ❶车马快跑(of a vehicle, horse, etc) to go quickly; to speed; to gallop ❷驾驶,开动交通工具(多指有发动机的),使行动 to drive; to sail:驾～拖拉机 *to drive a tractor*|轮船～入港口。*The ship sailed into the port.*

矢 shǐ ㄕˇ ❶箭 arrow:有的(dì)放～*to shoot one's arrow at the target — to have a definite goal in view; to do sth with a definite purpose in mind* ❷发誓 to take an oath; to vow; to swear:～口抵赖 *to categorically deny one's guilt* (or *mistake*) ❸古同"屎"(in ancient China) same as 屎:遗～*to empty one's bowels; to defecate*

豕 shǐ ㄕˇ 猪 pig; hog; swine

使 shǐ ㄕˇ ❶用 to use; to employ; to exert:～劲 *to exert all one's strength; to exert oneself; to make efforts*|～拖拉机耕种 *to plough the fields with a tractor*|这支笔很好～。*This pen writes well.* ❷派,差(chāi)遣 to send; to have (sb do sth):支～*to order about; to boss about; to send away*|～人前往 *to send sb to go* ❸让,令,叫 to make; to cause; to enable:～人高兴 *to make one happy*|迫～敌人放下武器 *to force the enemy to lay down their arms* ❹假若,假使 if; supposing; provided ❺驻外国的外交长官 envoy; emissary; messenger:大～*ambassador*|公～*minister; envoy* [使命]奉命去完成的某种任务。泛指重大的任务 mission:历史～～*historic mission*|肩负着建设祖国的～～*to be entrusted with the mission to construct one's country*

始 shǐ ㄕˇ ❶开始,起头,最初,跟"末"相对(the opposite of 末) beginning; start:～祖 *first ancestor; earliest ancestor*|开～报告 *to start to deliver a speech*|自～至终 *from beginning to end; from start to finish*|原～社会 *primitive society*

S

［未始］未尝，本来没有（used before a negative to denote a mild affirmative）not；never：～～不可 *to have no strong reason not to do；may*（or *might*）*just as well；not impossible* ❷才 only when；not until：参观至下午五时～毕。*The visit did not end until 5 o'clock in the afternoon.*

屎 shǐ ㄕˇ 大便，粪 excrement；faeces；dung ⓘ ***extension*** 眼、耳所分泌的东西 secretion（from the eye，ear，etc）：眼～ *gum in the eyes*｜耳～*earwax*

士 shì ㄕˋ ❶古代介于卿大夫和庶民之间的一个阶层（in ancient China）social stratum between senior officials and the common people ❷古代指未婚的男子，泛指男子（in ancient China）unmarried man；bachelor；man：～女 *young men and women* ❸指读书人 scholar；intelligentsia：学～*scholar*｜～农工商 *scholars，farmers，artisans，and merchants* ❹对人的美称 commendable（*or* praiseworthy）person：志～*person of high ideals and integrity*｜壮～*brave*（or *heroic*）*man；hero；warrior*｜烈～*martyr* ❺军人的一级，在尉以下，也泛指军人 non-commissioned officer；soldier；armyman：上～（*of US army*）*staff sergeant*；（*of US navy*）*petty officer 1st class*；（*of US air force*）*technical sergeant*｜中～（*of US army*）*sergeant*；（*of US navy*）*petty officer 2nd class*；（*of US air force*）*staff sergeant*｜～气 *morale；spirit* ❻称某些专业人员 person trained in certain field：护～*nurse*｜助产～*midwife*

仕 shì ㄕˋ 旧称做官（in former times）to hold an official post；to be an official：出～*to assume an official post；to take up an official career*｜～途 *official career* ［仕女］**1** 宫女 maid in an imperial palace；maid of honour **2** 传统绘画中的美女 traditional Chinese painting of beautiful women

氏 ㊀ shì ㄕˋ ❶姓。古代姓和氏有区别，氏从姓分出，后来姓和氏不分了，姓、氏可以混用 family name；surname ［氏族］原始社会中由血统关系联系起来的人的集体，集体占有生产资料，集体生产，集体消费 clan ❷旧习惯对已婚的妇女，通常在夫姓后再加父姓，父姓后加"氏"，作为称呼（in former times）nee：张王～（夫姓张，父姓王）*Mrs Zhang，nee Wang* ❸后世对有影响的人的称呼 term of address for a famous person：神农～*Shen Nong*｜太史～*Sima Qian*｜摄～表 *Celsius thermometer*

㊁ zhī 见 976 页 see p976

舐 shì ㄕˋ 舔 to lick：老牛～犊（比喻人疼爱儿女）*A cow licks her calf — deep affection toward one's children；parental love*

示 shì ㄕˋ 表明，把事物拿出来或指出来使别人知道 to

show; to produce; to notify: ～众 *to expose publicly; to punish sb before the public* | ～威 *to hold a demonstration; to put on a show of force; to display one's strength* (or *prowess*) | 表～意见 *to air one's views* | ～范作用 *demonstration effect* | 以目～意 *to wink at sb; to tip sb the wink* [暗示]不正面说出自己的意见,用神气、手势等提示,或用不直接相关的语言表示 to drop a hint; to suggest; to intimate

胨 shì 户 有机化合物,溶于水,遇热不凝固,是食物蛋白和蛋白胨的中间产物 proteose

世(＊＊卋) shì 户 ❶一个时代 age; era; time: 近～*modern times* ❷一辈一辈相传的 from generation to generation; through generations: ～袭 *hereditary* | ～医 *doctor of traditional Chinese medicine with experience of medical practice for generations* ❸人的一生 life time; life: 一～为人 *one's lifelong conduct* ❹指从先辈起就有交往、友谊的 (of people who maintain good family relations): ～伯 *older friend of one's father* | ～兄 *son of father's friend, older than oneself; son of one's teacher; student of one's father* ❺世界,宇宙,全球 world; society: ～上 *in the world; on earth* | ～人 *common people; people at large*

贳 shì 户 ❶出赁,出借 to hire out; to let; to rent (out) ❷赊欠 to buy or sell on credit ❸宽纵,赦免 to pardon; to remit; to deal with leniently

市 shì 户 ❶做买卖或做买卖的地方 market: 开～ *to conduct* (or *make*) *the first transaction of a day's business; to open for business;* (*of a shop*) *to reopen after a cessation of business* | 菜～*food* (or *vegetable*) *market* | 牲口～*livestock market* [超市]超级市场的简称。一种任顾客自选商品的综合性零售商店 supermarket ❷买 to buy: ～恩 *to ingratiate oneself with sb; to curry favour with sb; to fawn on* | 沽酒～脯(fǔ) *to buy wine and dried meat* ❸卖 to sell: 转以～人 *to resell* (*sth*) *to sb* ❹人口密集的行政中心或工商业、文化发达的地方 city; municipality: 城～*town; city* | 都～*big city; metropolis* ❺行政区划单位,有直辖市和省(或自治区)辖市等 administrative units (i.e. cities directly under the jurisdiction of the State Council and those under the jurisdiction of provincial or autonomous region government): 北京～*city of Beijing; Beijing Municipality; Beijing* | 唐山～*city of Tangshan; Tangshan* ❻属于我国度量衡市用制的 (of unit) pertaining to the Chinese systems of weights and measures:

S

～尺 chi，*a unit of length*（*1/3 metre*）|～升 sheng，*a unit of dry measure for grain*（*1 litre*）|～斤 jin，*a unit of weight*（*1/2 kg*）

柿 shì 尸 柿树，落叶乔木，开黄白色花。果实叫柿子，可以吃。木材可以制器具 persimmon（*Diospyros*）

铈 shì 尸 一种金属元素，符号 Ce，铁灰色，质地软，有延展性，能导热，不易导电，可用来制造合金 cerium（Ce）

式 shì 尸 ❶物体外形的样子 type; style; fashion：新～ *new style* ［形式］事物的外表 form; mode; shape ❷特定的规格 form; pattern; model：格～ *form; pattern; format* | 程～ *form; pattern; formula* ❸仪式，典礼 ceremony; ritual; celebration：开幕～*opening ceremony; inaugural ceremony; inauguration* | 阅兵～*military review; military parade* ❹自然科学中表明某些规律的一组符号 formula：方程～*equation* | 分子～ *molecular formula* ［公式］依照科学上已经发现的法则定出来的可以通用于同类关系的基本格式 formula：代数～～*algebraic formula* | 经济学上的～～*formula in economics; economic formula*

试 shì 尸 ❶按照预定想法非正式地做 to try; to attempt：～用 *to try out; to be on probation* | ～一～看 *to try and see how it works; to have a try; to give sth a try* ❷考，测验 to test; to examine（㊈ ***doublet*** 考一 examination; test）：～题 *examination*（or *test*）*questions* | 口～ *oral examination; viva voce; viva*

拭 shì 尸 擦 to wipe（away）：～泪 *to wipe*（*away*）*one's tears* | ～目以待（形容殷切期待）*to wait and see; to wait expectantly*（*for sth to happen*）

轼 shì 尸 古代车厢前面用作扶手的横木（in ancient China）horizontal bar in the front of a carriage used as an armrest

弑 shì 尸 古时候指臣杀君、子杀父母等行为（in ancient China）to murder（one's sovereign or parent）：～君 *to murder one's sovereign; to commit regicide* | ～父 *to murder one's father; to commit patricide*

似 ㊁ shì 尸［似的］［是的］（-de）助词 ***auxiliary***，跟某种事物或情况相似 like...; as...as; as if：雪～～那么白 *as white as snow* | 瓢泼～～大雨 *raining cats and dogs; pouring rain; torrential rain*

㊀ sì 见 705 页 see p705

势（勢） shì 尸 ❶势力，权力，威力 power; force; influence：倚～欺人 *to take advantage of one's or somebody else's power to bully the people; to bully the people on the strength of one's powerful connections or position* ❷表现出来的情况，样子 appearance; posture; situation **1** 属于自然

界的 outward appearance of a natural object or phenomenon: 地～ *physical feature of a place; terrain; topography* | 山～险峻。*The mountain is high and precipitous.* **2** 属于动作的 about an action: 姿～ *posture; carriage; pose* | 手～ *gesture; sign* **3** 属于政治、军事或其他方面的 about politics, military affairs, or other fields: 时～ *current situations; prevailing circumstances* | 大～所趋 *trend of the times; general trend* | 乘～追击 *to take advantage of an opportunity to pursue sth* ❸雄性生殖器 male genitals: 去～ *to castrate; to emasculate*

事 shì 𠂆 ❶(一儿)事情,自然界和社会中的一切现象和活动 matter; thing; affair [事变] 突然发生的重大政治、军事性事件 incident; event; emergency: 七七～～ *July 7 Incident of 1937; Marco Polo Bridge Incident of 1937* [事态]形势或局面 state of affairs; situation: ～～严重。*The situation is serious.* ❷职业 occupation; job; work: 谋～ *to look for a job; to seek employment* | 他现在做什么～? *What's his job now?* or *What's his occupation now?* ❸关系或责任 involvement; responsibility: 你回去吧,没有你的～了。*You can go back. It has nothing to do with you now.* | 这件案子里还有他的～呢。*He is involved in this case.* ❹变故,事故 trouble; mishap: 出～ *to meet with a mishap; to have an accident* | 平安无～。*All is well.* [事故] 出于某种原因而发生的不幸事情,如工作中的死伤等 accident; mishap ❺做,治 to go in for; to be engaged in: 大～宣扬 *to launch a vigorous propaganda campaign; to publicize an event actively* | 不～生产 *not to go in for production* ❻旧指侍奉(in former times) to attend upon; to wait upon; to serve

侍 shì 𠂆 服侍,伺候,在旁边陪着 to wait upon; to attend upon; to serve: ～立 *to stand in attendance; to stand by respectfully* | 服～病人 *to nurse the sick*

峙 ㊁ shì 𠂆 [繁峙]地名,在山西省 Fanshi, a place in Shanxi Province

㊀ zhì 见 985 页 see p985

恃 shì 𠂆 依赖,仗着 to rely on; to depend on; to count on: 有～无恐 *to be unscrupulous in the knowledge of strong backing (from sb); to feel secure in the knowledge that one has sth to fall back upon*

饰 shì 𠂆 ❶修饰,装饰,装点得好看 to decorate; to adorn; to ornament: 油～门窗 *to paint doors and windows* [喻] ***figurative*** 假托,遮掩 to dress up; to cover up; to gloss over: ～辞 *excuse; pretext* | 文过～非 *to conceal mistakes and gloss*

over wrongs; to cover up one's errors; to explain away and whitewash mistakes ❷装饰用的东西 decoration; ornament: 首～ *head ornaments; jewels; jewellery* | 窗～ *window decorations* ❸装扮,扮演角色 to play the role of; to act (the part of); to impersonate

视(*眎) shì 户 ❶看 to look at; to view: 近～眼 *near-sightedness* | ～而不见 *to look but see not; to turn a blind eye to* ❷视察,观察 to inspect; to examine; to watch: 巡～一周 *to go on an inspection tour; to cast one's eyes around* | 监～*to keep watch on; to keep sb under surveillance* ❸看待 to look upon; to regard; to treat: 重～*to think highly of; to attach importance to; to lay stress on* | ～死如归 *to look upon death without flinching; to face death without fear; to meet one's death like a hero* | 一～同仁 *to treat equally without discrimination; to treat all alike* ❹活,生存 to live: 莫不欲长生久～。*No one doesn't like to live a long life.*

是 shì 户 ❶表示判断(used to express judgement): 他～工人。*He is a worker.* | 这朵花～红的。*This flower is red.* ❷表示存在(used to express existence): 满身～汗 *to be bathed in sweat* | 山上全～树。*The mountain is covered with trees.* ❸表示让步,先承认所说的,再转入正意(used to express concession): 东西旧～旧,可是还能用。*Old as it is, it can still be used.* | 话～说得很对,可是得(děi)认真去做。*What you have said is right, but you have got to do it seriously.* ❹表示适合(used to express fitness or suitability): 来的～时候。*You came at the right time.* or *You can't come at a better time.* | 放的～地方。*Things are put in their proper places.* ❺表示凡是,任何(used to denote each and everyone of the kind): ～重活儿他都抢着干。*He will vie with the others to do any difficult work.* ❻用于选择问句(used in an alternative question): 你～坐轮船～坐火车? *Would you like to go by steamboat or by train?* ❼加重语气(used for emphasis): ～谁告诉你的? *Who on earth told you so?* | 天气～冷。*It is cold indeed.* ❽对,合理,跟"非"相对(the opposite of 非) correct; right; true: 懂得～非 *to know what is right and what is wrong* | 他说的～。*What he said is right.* ㊁ ***extension*** 认为对 to consider right; to praise; to justify: ～其所是 *to justify what one considers correct* [是非]口舌,争执 quarrel; dispute; trouble: 挑拨～～*to foment discord; to stir up trouble* | 惹～～*to stir up trouble; to provoke trouble*

S

❾这，此 this；that：如～*like this*｜～日天气晴朗。*It was sunny that day.*［国是］国家大计 matter of vital importance to the state；affairs of national concern：共商～～*to confer with sb upon major affairs of state；to discuss state affairs together*

适（適） ㊀ shì ㄕ ❶切合，相合 suitable；proper；appropriate（㊟ ***doublet*** —合 to suit；to fit；to befit）：～宜 *suitable；proper；fit*｜～意 *agreeable；enjoyable；comfortable*｜～用 *to suit；to be applicable* ❷舒服 comfortable；well；at ease：稍觉不～*to feel a bit under the weather* ❸刚巧 just；right；opportune：～逢其会 *to happen to be present on the occasion；to turn up at the opportune moment* ❹刚才，方才 just now：～从何处来？*Where have you been just now?* ❺往，到 to go；to follow；to leave for：无所～从 *to be at a loss what to do；to be at a loss whom to turn to* ㊁ ***extension*** 旧指女子出嫁（of a girl in former times）to get married；to marry

㊁ kuò 见 407 页 see p407

室 shì ㄕ ❶屋子 house；room：～内 *indoor*｜教～*classroom* ㊁ ***extension*** **1** 妻子 wife：妻～*wife*｜继～*second wife (after the first one dies)* **2** 家，家族 family：皇～*royal family；imperial family*｜十～九空 *Nine houses out of ten are deserted — a scene of desolation (as in the aftermath of a plague or war).* ❷机关团体内的工作单位 administrative subdivision (of an agency，organization，institution，corporation，etc)；office：会计～*accounting room；accountant's office* ❸星宿名，二十八宿之一 *shi*，the 13th of the 28 constellations

逝 shì ㄕ ❶过去 to pass：光阴易～。*Time passes quickly.* or *Time flies.* ❷死，多用于表示对死者的敬意（usually used to express respect for the dead）to die；to pass away：～世 *to die；to pass away*｜不幸病～*to unfortunately die of illness*

誓 shì ㄕ ❶当众表示，决心依照说的话实行 to swear；to vow；to pledge：～为共产主义奋斗终身 *to pledge to devote one's whole life to communism* ❷表示决心的话 solemn promise；oath；vow：宣～*to take an oath；to make a vow* (or *a pledge*)

莳（蒔） shì ㄕ 移栽植物 to transplant：～秧 *to transplant rice seedlings*

释（釋） shì ㄕ ❶说明，解说 to explain；to expound；to elucidate（㊟ ***doublet*** 解—to explain；to expound；to elucidate｜注—to explain with notes；annotate）：解～字句 *to explain words and sentences*｜古诗浅～*explanations of an-*

cient poetry ❷消散 to clear up; to dispel:冰～(喻怀疑、误会等完全消除)(*of misgivings, misunderstandings, etc*) *to disappear; to vanish; to be dispelled*|～疑 *to dispel doubts; to explain difficult points* ❸放开,放下 to put down; to let go; to be relieved of:～放 *to release; to set free; to discharge*|手不～卷 *never to be seen without a book in one's hand — to be an avid reader; to be diligent* (or *studious*) *in one's studies*|如～重负 *as if relieved of a heavy load; to feel a sense of relief* ❹把坐监服刑的人释放 to set free; to release:保～*to release on bail; to bail*|开～*to release; to set free; to acquit* ❺佛教创始人"释迦牟尼"的省称,泛指关于佛教的(short for 释迦牟尼, the founder of Buddhism) of Buddhism:～氏(佛家) *Buddhist*|～子(和尚) *monk*|～教 *Buddhism*

谥(*諡) shì ㄕˋ 我国古代,在最高统治者或其他有地位的人死后,依其生前事迹给予的称号,如"武"帝、"哀"公等。也叫"谥号"(also called 谥号)(in ancient China) posthumous title (bestowed on a ruler, a nobleman, or an eminent official after his death for his achievement)

嗜 shì ㄕˋ 喜爱,爱好 to have a liking for; to take to; to be addicted to:～学 *to have a great liking for study*|～睡 *to be addicted to sleeping* [嗜好](—hào)对于某种东西特别爱好,爱好成癖 hobby; habit; addiction

筮 shì ㄕˋ 古代用蓍草占卦(迷信)(of superstition) to practise divination with yarrow stems

噬 shì ㄕˋ 咬 to bite:吞～*to swallow; to engulf; to gobble up*|～脐莫及(喻后悔无及)。*It is impossible for one to bite his own navel — it is late to repent.*

奭 shì ㄕˋ 盛大 grand; magnificent

襫 shì ㄕˋ 见 56 页"袯"字条"袯襫"(bó—) see 袯襫 under the entry of 袯 on p56

螫 ㊀ shì ㄕˋ 有毒腺的虫子刺人或牲畜 to sting

㊁ zhē 见 962 页 see p962

匙 ㊁ shi ·ㄕ 见 876 页"钥"字条"钥匙"(yào—) see 钥匙 under the entry of 钥 on p876

㊀ chí 见 89 页 see p89

殖 ㊁ shi ·ㄕ [骨殖](gǔ—)尸骨 skeleton (of a dead body)

㊀ zhí 见 978 页 see p978

SHOU ㄕㄡ

收(**収) shōu ㄕㄡ ❶接到,接受,跟"发"相对(the opposite of 发) to receive; to accept:～发 *to receive and dispatch*|～信 *to*

receive a letter | ～到 *to receive; to get; to achieve* | ～条 *receipt* | 接～物资 *to receive goods and materials* | 招～新生 *to enrol new students* | ～账(受款记账) *to enter into accounts; to charge to accounts* ❷藏或放置妥当 to put away; to put in a proper place; to store (up): 这是重要东西,要～好了。*This is very important. Put it in its proper place.* ❸割取成熟的农作物 to harvest; to gather in; to reap: 秋～ *autumn harvest* | ～麦子 *to harvest wheat* ❹获得(经济利益) to get; to obtain; to gain: ～益 *income; profit; earnings* | ～支相抵 *to strike a balance in revenue and expenditure; to make both ends meet* ❺招回 to call back; to recall: ～兵 *to recall (or withdraw) troops; to call off a battle* ❻聚,合拢 to close up; to heal: 疮～口了。*The sore is closing up.* ❼结束 to end; to stop; to conclude: ～尾 *to bring to a conclusion; to end; to wind up* | ～工 *to stop work for the day; to knock off; to pack up* | ～场 *to end; to stop; to wind up* ❽收心,收敛 to restrain; to control: 心似平原走马易放难～。*The mind is like a wild horse trotting on the plain — it is easy to let free but difficult to control; Once one becomes idle, it is difficult for him to concentrate on more serious things.* ❾逮捕拘禁 to take into custody; to arrest: ～监 *to put behind bars; to imprison*

熟 ㊀ shóu ㄕㄡˊ 义同"熟"(shú),用于口语(used colloquially) same as 熟(shú)

㊁ shú 见 692 页 see p692

手 shǒu ㄕㄡˇ ❶人体上肢前端拿东西的部分。(图见 741 页"体" picture on p741) hand [手足]㊞ ***figurative*** 兄弟 brothers ❷拿着 to have in one's hand; to hold: 人～一册。*A copy for each person.* ❸(一儿)技能、本领 skill: 有两～儿 *to have real skill; to know one's stuff* ❹亲手 personally; in person: ～书 *to write in one's own hand* | ～植 *to plant (a tree, etc) personally* ❺做某种事情或擅长某种技能的人 person skilled in sth; person good at sth: 选～ *contestant; player; competitor* | 生产能～ *skilled hand (or worker)* | 水～ *seaman; sailor* | 神枪～ *sharpshooter* ❻小巧易拿的 easy to carry; handy; portable: ～册 *handbook; manual*

[手段] 处理事情所用的方法 means; method; measure

守 shǒu ㄕㄡˇ ❶保持,卫护 to keep; to guard; to defend: ～城 *to defend a city* | 坚～阵地 *to hold fast to one's position; to hold one's ground* [墨守]㊕ ***transfer*** 依照老法子不肯改进 to stick to conventions and oppose change; to stay in a rut: ～～成规 *to stick*

S

to established practices; to follow conventionality ❷看守,看护 to keep watch; to watch over; to look after:～门 *to guard the gate; to keep the goal*|～着病人 *to look after a patient* ❸遵守,依照 to abide by; to observe; to follow:反对因循～旧 *to be against following a beaten track*|～时间 *to be punctual*|～纪律 *to observe discipline*|爱国～法 *to love one's motherland and observe the law* ❹靠近,依傍 close to; near; by the side of:～着水的地方,要多种稻子。*Plant more rice where there is water nearby.*

S

首 shǒu ㄕㄡˇ ❶头,脑袋 head:昂～ *to hold one's head high*|～饰 *head ornaments; jewellery* [首领]㊞ ***figurative*** 某些团体的领导人 head of an organization ❷领导人,带头的 leader; head; chief:～长 *senior officer; leading cadre* ❸第一,最高的 first; foremost; supreme:～要任务 *most important task*|～席代表 *chief delegate* (or *representative*) ❹最先,最早 first; initial:～次 *for the first time*|～创 *to originate; to initiate; to pioneer*|～播 *to broadcast* (or *telecast*) *for the first time* ❺出头告发 to come forward to denounce sb as a criminal; to bring charges against sb:自～ (*of a criminal*) *to surrender oneself; to give oneself up*|出～*to inform against sb* ❻量词 ***quantifier***,用于诗歌(used for poems or songs):一～诗 *a poem*

寿(壽) shòu ㄕㄡˋ ❶活得岁数大(of people) long life; longevity; old age:人～年丰 *people enjoying longevity and land yielding good harvests — people enjoying a happy and abundant life* ❷年岁,生命 age; life:长～ *long life; longevity*|～命 *lifespan; life; lifetime* ❸寿辰,生日 birthday:祝～*to congratulate (an elderly person) on his or her birthday; to offer birthday congratulations (to an elderly person)*|～礼 *birthday present* ❹装殓死人的 funerary; for burial:～材 (*prepared before one's death*) *coffin*|～衣 *shroud; graveclothes*

受 shòu ㄕㄡˋ ❶接纳,接受 to receive; to accept:～贿 *to take* (or *accept*) *bribes*|接～别人的意见 *to accept others' suggestions* ❷忍耐某种遭遇 to stand; to endure; to tolerate (㊟ ***doublet*** 忍— to stand; to bear; to tolerate):～不了 *cannot stand* (or *endure, bear*)|～罪 *to suffer hardships; to endure tortures* (or *rough conditions*)|忍～痛苦 *to endure sufferings* ❸遭到 to suffer; to sustain; to be subjected to:～批评 *to be criticized*|～害 *to be victimized; to be affected; to be afflicted*|～风 *to suffer from apoplexy*|～暑 *to suffer from* *heatstroke* (or *sunstroke*) ❹适合 to suit; to be pleasant to; to be agreeable to: 他这话倒是很～听。*His words sound pleasant.*

授 shòu ㄕㄡˋ ❶给,与 to award; to vest; to confer: ～旗 *to present* (*sb with*) *a flag*|～奖 *to award* (or *confer*) *a prize*|～意(把自己的意思告诉别人让别人照着办) *to incite* (or *get*) *sb to do sth* ❷传授 to teach; to instruct: ～课 *to give lessons; to give* (or *deliver*) *a lecture*

绶 shòu ㄕㄡˋ 一种丝质带子,古代常用来拴在印纽上 (in ancient China) silk ribbon attached to an official seal: ～带 *silk ribbon* (*attached to an official seal or medal*)|印～ *seal adorned with a silk ribbon*

狩 shòu ㄕㄡˋ 打猎,古代指冬天打猎 (in ancient China) (especially in winter) to hunt: ～猎 *to hunt*

售 shòu ㄕㄡˋ 卖 to sell: ～票 *to sell tickets*|零～ *to sell by* (or *at*) *retail; to retail*|销～ *to sell; to market* [引] **extension** 施展 to make (one's plan, trick, etc) work; to carry out (intrigues): 以～其奸 *to carry out one's evil design*

兽(獸) shòu ㄕㄡˋ ❶哺乳动物的通称。一般指有四条腿、全身生毛的哺乳动物,也指长鳞甲的穿山甲及在水中生活的鲸、海豚等 beast; animal ❷比喻野蛮,下流 beastly; bestial; brutal: ～欲 *animal desire; bestial lust*|～行 *brutal act; bestial behavior; brutality*

瘦 shòu ㄕㄡˋ ❶含脂肪少,跟"胖"、"肥"相对 (the opposite of 胖 or 肥) slim; thin; emaciated: ～肉 *lean meat*|身体很～ *to have a very thin figure* ❷衣服鞋袜等窄小 fitting too closely; tight: 这件衣裳穿着～了。*This dress is tight for me now.* ❸土地瘠薄 not fertile; poor; barren: ～田 *poor soil; infertile land* ❹笔画细 (of strokes in Chinese handwriting) thin: ～硬 *thin but powerful strokes of Chinese characters*|钟书体～。*The handwriting by the calligrapher Zhong You in the period of Three Kingdoms is in slim style.*|～金体 *style of Chinese calligraphy originated by the Emperor Huizong* (*Zhao Ji*) *of the Song Dynasty, featuring thin and sturdy strokes*

SHU ㄕㄨ

殳 shū ㄕㄨ 古代的一种兵器,用竹子做成,有棱无刃 (in ancient China) a kind of weapon made of bamboo, with ridges but no blade

书(書) shū ㄕㄨ ❶成本的著作 book ❷信 letter ([连] **doublet** 一信 letter): 家～ *letter from home*|～札 *letter*|来～已悉。*I have received*

S

your letter. ❸文件 official paper; document:证明～*certificate; testimonial* | 申请～*application* ❹写字 to write (㊀ **doublet** 一写 to write):～法 *calligraphy; penmanship; handwriting* ㊁ ***transfer*** 字体 style of calligraphy; script:楷～*regular script* | 隶～*official script*

抒 shū ㄕㄨ 抒发,尽量表达 to give voice to; to express; to convey:～情诗 *lyric poetry; lyrics* | 各～己见。*Each airs his own views*.

纾 shū ㄕㄨ 缓和,解除 to relieve; to alleviate; to remove:～难(nàn) *to relieve the distress of sb*

舒 shū ㄕㄨ ❶展开,伸展 to stretch; to spread; to unfold:～眉展眼 *to unknit the brows and stretch eyes — beaming with joy; cheerful* [舒服][舒坦]身心愉快 comfortable; pleasant ❷从容,缓慢 easy; leisurely

枢(樞) shū ㄕㄨ 门上的转轴 pivot; hub:户～不蠹 *A door hinge never gets worm-eaten — constant activity staves off decay*. [枢纽]重要的部分,事物相互联系的中心环节 key position; hub; pivot:运输的～～*traffic hub* [中枢]中心,中央 centre:神经～～*nerve centre*

叔 shū ㄕㄨ ❶兄弟排行,常用伯、仲、叔、季为次序,叔是老三 third among brothers ❷叔父,父亲的弟弟。又称跟父亲同辈而年纪较小的男子(叠 ***reduplication***) father's younger brother; uncle; term of address for a man who is younger than one's father but of the same generation:大～*father's younger brother*; (*polite form of address for a man of one's father's generation but younger than one's father*) *uncle* ❸(一子)丈夫的弟弟 husband's younger brother:小～子 *husband's younger brother; brother-in-law*

菽(**尗) shū ㄕㄨ 豆类的总称 general term for beans

淑 shū ㄕㄨ 善,美(of a woman) kind and gentle; graceful; fair:贤～(*of a woman*) *virtuous and kind; kind-hearted* | ～女 *fair maiden; virtuous woman; noble lady*

姝 shū ㄕㄨ 美丽,美好(of a woman) pretty; beautiful

殊 shū ㄕㄨ ❶不同 different:特～情况 *exceptional case* | ～途同归 *to reach the same goal by different routes* ❷特别突出 outstanding; special; remarkable:～荣 *special honour* | ～勋 *outstanding merit; distinguished service* ❸极,很 very; extremely:～佳 *very good* | ～可钦佩 *very admirable* ❹断,绝 to cut off; to break off; to sever [殊死] **1** 古代指斩首的死刑(in ancient China) death penalty of decapitation **2** 拼着性命 desperate; life-and-death:

～～战斗 *to fight a last-ditch battle; to fight to the bitter end*

倏(*倐、*儵) shū ㄕㄨ 极快地,忽然 swiftly; quickly; suddenly: ～忽 *swiftly; abruptly; quickly*|～尔而逝 *to disappear suddenly*

梳 shū ㄕㄨ ❶(一子)整理头发的用具。也叫"拢子"(also called 拢子) comb ❷用梳子整理头发 to comb one's hair: ～头 *to comb one's hair*

疏(❶-❹*踈) shū ㄕㄨ ❶去掉阻塞使畅通 to dredge (a river, etc) (㊀ **doublet** 一通 to dredge; to mediate between two parties): ～导 *to dredge; to relieve (traffic congestion)* ❷分散 to disperse; to scatter: ～散 *to evacuate; to disperse* ❸事物间距离大,空隙大,跟"密"相对(the opposite of 密) thin; sparse; scattered (㊀ **doublet** 稀一 thin; sparse; scattered): ～林 *thin (or sparse) woods*|～密不均 *of uneven density*|稀～的枪声 *scattered shots; sporadic gunfire* ㊀ **extension 1** 不亲密,关系远的(of family or social relations) distant: 亲～远近(*of relationship*) *close and distant*|他们一向很～远。*They have always been estranged from each other.* **2** 不细密,粗心 careless; negligent: ～神 *absent-minded; careless*|这人太～忽了。*This man is too careless.* ❹空虚 hollow; void; scanty: 志大才～ *to have lofty aspirations but inadequate talent* ❺粗 coarse; rough: ～食 *roughage; coarse food; coarse grain* ❻不熟悉 not familiar; unfamiliar: 生～ *unfamiliar; strange*|人生地～ *to be unfamiliar with the place and the people; to be a stranger in the land* ❼分条说明的文字 memorial: 上～ *to submit a memorial to the emperor*|奏～(封建时代臣下向皇帝陈述事情的文章) *memorial to the throne* ❽对古书旧有注文做的阐释 detailed annotation: 注～ *notes and commentaries*

蔬 shū ㄕㄨ 蔬菜,可以做菜的植物(多属草本)(usually of herb) vegetables; greens; greenstuff: ～食 *vegetarian meal; simple fare*

摅(攄) shū ㄕㄨ 发表或表示出来 to give voice to; to express: 各～己见 *Each airs his own views.*

输 shū ㄕㄨ ❶从一个地方运送到另一个地方 to transport; to transmit; to convey (㊀ **doublet** 运一 to transport; to convey): ～出 *to send out; to export; to output*|～血 *to transfuse blood* ❷送给,捐献 to contribute money; to donate: 捐～ *to donate*|～财助战 *to donate money for the war* ❸败,负 to lose; to be beaten; to suffer a defeat: ～了两个球 *to lose a ball game by two shots*

S

毹 shū ㄕㄨ 见 619 页"氍"字条"氍毹"(qú—) see 氍毹 on p619

秫 shú ㄕㄨˊ 黏高粱,可以做烧酒。有的地区就指高粱 *kaoliang*; (Chinese) sorghum: ~米 *husked sorghum* | ~秸(高粱秆) kaoliang *stalk*; *sorghum stalk*

孰 shú ㄕㄨˊ 代词 **pronoun** ❶谁 who: ~谓不可? *Who says it is impossible?* ❷什么 what: 是(这个)可忍,~不可忍? *If this can be tolerated, what can not?* ❸哪个 which; who: ~胜~负。*Who wins and who loses?*

S

塾 shú ㄕㄨˊ 旧时私人设立的教学的地方(in former times) private or family school: 私~ *old-style private school* | 村~ *old-style village school*

熟 ㊀ shú ㄕㄨˊ ❶食物烧煮到可吃的程度 cooked; done: 饭~了。*The rice is done.* | ~菜 *cooked food*; *prepared food* ❷成熟,植物的果实或种子长成 ripe: 麦子~了。*The wheat is ripe.* ❸程度深 deeply; profoundly; thoroughly: 深思~虑 *to ponder deeply* (*over sth*); *to give careful consideration* (*to sth*) | ~睡 *to sleep soundly* ❹习惯,常见,知道清楚 frequently seen or heard; familiar; well-acquainted: ~悉 *to know well*; *to be well acquainted* (*with*); *to be familiar* (*with*) | ~人 *acquaintance* | 这条路我~。*I am well acquainted with this route.* ❺熟练,做某种工作时间久了,精通而有经验 skilled; experienced; versed: ~手 *practised hand*; *old hand* | ~能生巧。*Skill comes from practice.* or *Practice makes perfect.* ❻经过加工或炼制的 processed; wrought: ~铁 *wrought iron* | ~皮子 *tanned hide*; *processed leather*

㊁ shóu 见 687 页 see p687

赎(贖) shú ㄕㄨˊ ❶用财物换回抵押品 to redeem; to ransom: ~当(dàng) *to redeem a pawned article*; *to redeem a pledge*; *to take sth out of pledge* | 把东西~回来 *to redeem a pledge* ❷用行动抵消、弥补罪过(旧时特指用财物减免刑罚) to atone for (a crime) with money and goods in former times; to atone for (a crime) through one's performance: 立功~罪 *to perform meritorious services to atone for one's crime*; *to make amends for one's crime by good deeds*

暑 shǔ ㄕㄨˇ 热 hot: 中(zhòng)~ *to get* (or *suffer*) *sunstroke* | ~天 *hottest days of the year*; *dog days*; *hot summer days*

署 shǔ ㄕㄨˇ ❶办公的处所 government office; office: 海关总~ *customs head office*; *customs bureau*; (*China*) *General Administration of Customs* ❷布置 to arrange; to make arrangements for: 部~ *to dispose*; *to deploy*; *to arrange*

❸签名,题字 to sign; to leave inscriptions on:签～*to sign; to subscribe; to endorse* | ～名 *to affix one's name to; to put one's signature to; to sign* ❹暂代 to stand proxy for; to act as deputy:～理 *to handle by proxy; to act as deputy*

薯(*藷) shǔ ㄕㄨˇ 植物名 name of plants **1** 甘薯,又叫"白薯"、"红薯"或"番薯"。草本植物,茎细长,块根可以吃(also called 白薯,红薯, or 番薯) sweet potato (*Ipomoea batatas*) **2** 马铃薯,又叫"土豆"或"山药蛋"。草本植物,块茎可以吃(also called 土豆 or 山药蛋) potato (*Solanum tuberosum*) [薯蓣](-yù) 又叫"山药"。草本植物,开白花,块根可以吃,也可入药(also called 山药) yam (*Dioscorea*)

曙 shǔ ㄕㄨˇ 天刚亮 daybreak; dawn:～色 *light of early dawn* | ～光 *first light of morning; sun's glow in the early morning; dawn sunshine*

黍 shǔ ㄕㄨˇ 一年生草本植物,子实叫黍子,碾成米叫黄米,性黏,可酿酒 millet (*Panicum miliaceum*) [蜀黍] 高粱 sorghum (*Sorghum bicolor*) [玉蜀黍] 一年生草本植物,也叫"玉米"、"棒子"或"包谷"。叶长而大,子实可做食粮(also called 玉米,棒子 or 包谷) corn (*Zea mays*)

属(屬) ㊀ shǔ ㄕㄨˇ ❶同一家族的 of the same family:家～*family members; (family) dependants* ❷类别 category:金～*metal* ❸生物的分类单位之一,在"科"之下、"种"之上(biology taxonomic group) genus:梨～*Pyus* | 狐～*Vulpes* ❹有管辖关系的 affiliated; subordinate (㊟ ***doublet*** 隶— to be subordinate to; to be under the jurisdiction of; to be affiliated to):直～*to be directly under; to be directly subordinate to; to be directly affiliated to* (or *with*) | ～局 *subordinate* (or *affiliated*) *bureaus; subordinate* (or *affiliated*) *departments* | ～员 *subordinates of a superior official; officials under a superior authority* ❺归类 to classify; to categorize:～于自然科学 *to be classified* (or *categorized*) *as natural science; to be under the heading of natural science* ❻为某人或某方所有 to be part of; to belong to:这本书～你。*This book is yours.* ❼是 be:查明～实 *to prove to be true* ❽用属相记生年(用干支纪年,十二支配合十二种动物,人生在哪年,就属哪种动物叫"属相") any of the 12 animals (representing the 12 Earthly Branches) used to symbolize the birth year of a person (as the year is named by a pair of Heavenly Stem and Earthly Branch) is called 属相:甲子、丙子等子年生的都～鼠。*The symbolic animal of those who* *were born in the year of* jiazi or bingzi *is mouse*.

㊁ zhǔ 见 996 页 see p996

蜀 shǔ ㄕㄨˇ ❶古国名 name of an ancient state **1** 周代诸侯国名，在今四川省成都一带 Shu, a princedom of the Zhou Dynasty, covering today's Chengdu, Sichuan Province and nearby areas **2** 蜀汉，三国之一，刘备所建立（公元 221—263 年），在今四川省，后来扩展到贵州省、云南省和陕西省汉中一带 the Kingdom of Shu Han (221—263), one of the Three Kingdoms, established by Liu Bei, in today's Sichuan Province, later extending to certain parts of Guizhou Province, Yunnan Province and the Hanzhong area of Shaanxi Province ❷四川省的别称 Shu, another name for Sichuan Province

鼠 shǔ ㄕㄨˇ 老鼠，哺乳动物，俗叫"耗子"。体小尾长，门齿发达，常咬衣物，又能传染疾病 (popularly called 耗子) mouse; rat (*Muridae*) [鼠疫] 一种急性传染病，又叫"黑死病"。病原体是鼠疫杆菌。消灭老鼠和预防注射是主要的预防方法 (also called 黑死病) plague

数(數) ㊀ shǔ ㄕㄨˇ ❶一个一个地计算 to count: ～一～ *to make* (or *take*) *a count* ㊂ ***extension*** 比较起来最突出 to be particularly conspicuous by comparison; to reckon as exceptionally good (bad, etc) by comparison: 就～他有本领。*He is considered as the most capable one among them*. ❷责备，列举过错 to enumerate (faults, etc); to blame; to scold: ～落(luo) *to scold sb by enumerating his wrongdoings; to reproach; to cite one example after another* | ～说 *to enumerate; to list; to rebuke*

㊁ shù 见 696 页 see p696

㊂ shuò 见 702 页 see p702

术(術) ㊀ shù ㄕㄨˋ ❶技艺 art; skill; technique: 武～ wushu; *kung fu; martial arts* | 技～ *technique; skill; expertise* | 美～ *fine arts* [术语] 学术和各种工艺上的专门用语 technical term; terminology ❷方法 method; trick; tactics: 战～ *(military) tactics* | 防御之～ *defence tactics*

㊁ zhú 见 993 页 see p993

述 shù ㄕㄨˋ 讲说，陈说 to state; to narrate; to relate (㊇ ***doublet*** 叙— to narrate; to recount; to relate | 陈— to state; to explain; to narrate): 口～ *to give an oral account; to recount orally*

沭 shù ㄕㄨˋ 沭河，发源于山东省，流至江苏省入新沂河 Shuhe River, originating in Shandong Province and flowing into the Xinyi River, Jiangsu Province

钵 shù ㄕㄨˋ ❶长针 long needle ❷刺 to prick ❸引导 to guide

戍 shù ㄕㄨˋ 军队防守 to defend; to garrison: 卫～ *to garrison* | ～边 *to garrison the frontier*

束 shù ㄕㄨˋ ❶捆住 to bind; to tie; to bundle up: ～发(fà) *to tie up one's hair; ceremony of capping a boy at the age of fifteen* | ～手～脚 *timid and hesitant; over-cautious* [束缚](—fù) 捆绑 to bind up; to tie ⓨ ***figurative*** 使受到限制 to fetter; to shackle; to stifle: 不要～～群众的创造性。*Don't stifle the creativity of the masses.* ❷成捆儿或成条的东西 bundle; beam: 花～*bouquet* | 光～*beam* ❸量词 ***quantifier***, 捆儿: 一～鲜花 *a bunch of flowers* ❹控制 to control; to restrain; to contain (㊟ ***doublet*** 约— to control; to restrain; to contain): 拘～*to restrain; constrained; to be ill at ease* | ～身自爱 *to treasure one's own good name and act within the bounds of propriety; to have scruples and not lower oneself*

树(樹) shù ㄕㄨˋ ❶木本植物的总称(general term for 木本植物) tree ❷种植,栽培 to plant; to cultivate ❸立,建立 to set up; to establish; to uphold (㊟ ***doublet*** —立 to set up; to establish; to build up): ～雄心,立壮志 *to have lofty ambitions; to aim high*

竖(竪、*豎) shù ㄕㄨˋ ❶直立 to set upright; to stand; to erect: 把棍子～起来 *to erect a stick* ❷上下的或前后的方向 vertical; upright; perpendicular: ～着写 *to write vertically downward from the top* | ～着挖道沟 *to excavate a ditch from the front to the rear* ❸直,汉字自上往下写的笔形(丨) vertical stroke (in Chinese character): 十字是一横一～。*The Chinese character 十 is composed of one horizontal stroke and one vertical stroke.* ❹竖子,古时指年轻仆人,也用于对人的一种蔑称(in ancient China) young servant; (***derogatory***) boy; chap

俞 ㊁ shù ㄕㄨˋ 同"腧"same as 腧

㊀ yú 见 916 页 see p916

腧 shù ㄕㄨˋ 腧穴,人体上的穴道 acupuncture point; acupoint: 肺～*acupuncture points for the lungs* | 胃～*acupuncture points for the stomach*

恕 shù ㄕㄨˋ 宽恕,原谅 to excuse; to forgive; to pardon: 饶～*to forgive; to pardon*

庶 shù ㄕㄨˋ ❶众多 numerous; multitudinous; myriad: ～民(旧指老百姓)(*in former times*) *the multitude; common people; plebeian* | 富～*rich and prosperous* ❷庶几(jī),将近,差不多 almost; nearly: ～乎可行。*It is quite feasible.* ❸宗法制度下指家庭的旁支 of (*or* by) the concubine (as distinguished from the wife): ～出 *to be born to* (or *of*) *a concubine*

裋 shù ㄕㄨˋ 古代仆役穿的一种衣服(in ancient China) coarse cotton clothes of a boy servant

数(數) ㊀ shù ㄕㄨˋ ❶数目,划分或计算出来的量 number; figure:基~ *cardinal number; base*|序~*ordinal number*|岁~*age*|次~*number of times; frequency*|人~太多,坐不下。*There are not enough seats for so many people.*[数词]表示数目的词,如一、九、千、万等 numeral ❷几,几个 several; a few:~次 *several times*|~日 *a few days*|~人 *a few people* ❸(迷信)劫数(of superstition) inexorable doom; fate; destiny:在~难逃。*It is impossible to escape one's doom.*

㊁ shǔ 见694页 see p694

㊂ shuò 见702页 see p702

墅 shù ㄕㄨˋ 别墅,住宅以外供游玩休养的园林房屋 villa

漱 shù ㄕㄨˋ ❶含水荡洗口腔 to rinse (the mouth); to gargle:~口 *to rinse one's mouth; to gargle* ❷洗涤,冲刷 to wash; to erode:悬泉瀑布,飞~其间。*The waterfall swiftly flows down.*

澍 shù ㄕㄨˋ 及时的雨 timely rain

SHUA ㄕㄨㄚ

刷 ㊀ shuā ㄕㄨㄚ ❶(一子、一儿)用成束的毛、棕等制成的清除东西或涂抹东西的用具 brush ❷用刷子或类似刷子的用具来清除或涂抹 to clean (*or* daub) with a brush; to paint; to scrub:~牙 *to brush* (or *clean*) *one's teeth*|~鞋 *to brush* (or *clean*) *one's shoes*|~锅 *to clean* (or *scour*) *a pot*|用石灰~墙 *to paint the wall with limewash; to whitewash a wall* ㊀ ***extension*** 淘汰(through election or competition) to eliminate; discharge; to remove:第一轮比赛就被~掉了。*He was eliminated in the first round of the competition.* ❸同"唰"same as 唰

㊁ shuà 见697页 see p697

唰 shuā ㄕㄨㄚ 拟声词 ***onomatopoeia***,形容迅速擦过去的声音 swishing; rustling:小雨~~地下起来了。*A light rain is falling with a swooshing sound.*

耍 shuǎ ㄕㄨㄚˇ ❶〈方 ***dialect***〉玩 to play(㊀ ***doublet*** 玩一 to play; to frolic; to amuse oneself):孩子们在院子里~。*The children are playing in the courtyard.* ❷玩弄,表演 to play with; to perform; to flourish:~猴 *to perform tricks with a monkey; to put on a monkey show*|~大刀 *to give a performance of broadsword; to flourish a broadsword* ❸戏弄 to make fun of; to play tricks on; to juggle:别~人。*Don't play tricks on others.* ❹弄,施展 to give full play to; to display; to show:~手艺 *to* *make a living as a craftsman* | ～威风 to vaunt *one's authority* (or *power*); *to flaunt one's seniority* (or *superiority*) | ～手腕(喻使用不正当的方法) *to resort to tricks; to use artifices*

刷 ㊁ shuà ㄕㄨㄚˋ [刷白]色白而略微发青 white; pale; ashen

㊀ shuā 见 696 页 see p696

SHUAI ㄕㄨㄞ

衰 ㊀ shuāi ㄕㄨㄞ 事物发展转向微弱 to decline; to wane (㊟ ***doublet*** 一微 to decline; to wane): ～败 *to decline; to wane; to be at a low ebb* | ～老 *old and feeble; senile; decrepit* | 神经～弱 *neurasthenia* [衰变]化学上指放射性元素放射出粒子后变成另一种元素 to decay; to disintegrate

㊁ cuī 见 112 页 see p112

摔(❹**踤) shuāi ㄕㄨㄞ ❶用力往下扔 to throw; to fling; to hurl: 把帽子往床上一～*to throw* (or *fling*) *one's cap onto the bed* ❷很快地掉下 to hurtle down; to plunge: 上树要小心,别～下来。*Be careful! Don't fall out of the tree.* ❸因掉下而毁坏 to cause to fall and break; to break: 把碗～了。*The bowl was broken.* ❹跌跤 to fall (or tumble) (after losing one's balance): 他～倒了。*He took a tumble.* | ～了一跤 *to have a fall; to stumble*

甩 shuǎi ㄕㄨㄞˇ ❶抡,扔 to swing; to fling; to throw: ～袖子 *to fling up one's sleeves; to wash one's hands of* (*work, matter, etc*) *to display* | ～手榴弹 *to fling* (or *throw*) *hand grenades* ❷抛开,抛弃 to leave sb behind; to throw off; to abandon: ～车 *to uncouple* (*some or all the railway coaches from the locomotive*) | 被～在后面 *to be left behind*

帅(帥) shuài ㄕㄨㄞˋ ❶军队中最高级的指挥官 commander-in-chief: 元～ *marshal;* (*in ancient China*) *supreme commander* | 统～*commander-in-chief; commander* ❷英俊,潇洒,漂亮 handsome; graceful; smart: 这个小伙儿很～。*What a handsome young man!* | 他的动作～极了。*His movements were graceful.* | 字写得～ *to write a beautiful hand*

率 ㊀ shuài ㄕㄨㄞˋ ❶带领,统领 to lead; to command; to head (㊟ ***doublet*** 一领 to lead; to command; to head): ～队 *to lead one's team* | ～师 *to lead one's troops* ❷轻易地,不细想,不慎重 rash; hasty; impetuous (㊟ ***doublet*** 轻一 rash; hasty; imprudent | 草一 careless; rash; perfunctory): 不要轻～地处理问题。*Don't be indiscreet in handling matters.* ❸爽直坦白 frank; straightfor-

S

ward; forthright (㊂ ***doublet*** 直一 frank; candid; straightforward) ❹大率,大概,大略 generally; usually:～皆如此。*This is usually the case.* ❺遵循 to follow; to obey; to conform to:～由旧章 *to act in accordance with established rules; to conform to conventions; to follow the established pattern* ❻模范 model; example:一方表～*model of some area; model from some walk of life* ❼同"帅❷"same as 帅❷

㊁ lǜ 见 472 页 see p472

蟀 shuài ㄕㄨㄞˋ 见 802页"蟋"字条"蟋蟀"(xī—) see 蟋蟀 on p802

S

SHUAN ㄕㄨㄢ

闩(**檂) shuān ㄕㄨㄢ ❶门闩,横插在门后使门推不开的棍子 door bolt; latch ❷用闩插上门 to fasten with a bolt (*or* latch):把门～上 *to bar* (or *bolt*) *the door*

拴 shuān ㄕㄨㄢ 用绳子系(jì)上 to tie; to bind; fasten:～马 *to tie* (or *hitch*) *a horse* (*to a tree, etc*)|～车 *to tie* (or *fasten*) *a cart* (or *carriage*) ㊥ ***figurative*** 被事物缠住而不能自由行动 to be bogged down; to be tied down:被琐事～住了 *to be tied* (or *bogged*) *down by trifles*|一项紧急任务又把几个老搭档～在一起了。*The old partners were bound together again by an urgent task.*

栓 shuān ㄕㄨㄢ ❶器物上可以开关的机件 bolt; plug:枪～*rifle bolt*|消火～*fire hydrant; fire-plug* ❷塞子或作用跟塞子相仿的东西 stopper; cork; sth resembling a stopper or cork:～塞 *embolism*|～剂 *suppository*|血～*thrombus*

涮 shuàn ㄕㄨㄢˋ ❶放在水中摆动,略微洗洗 to rinse; to wash:～～手 *to rinse one's hands*|把衣服～一～*to give clothes a rinse* ❷把水放在器物中摇动,冲洗 to rinse; to swill:～瓶子 *to rinse out the bottle; to swill out the bottle* ❸把肉片等在滚水里放一下就取出来(蘸作料吃) to scald (thin slices of meat, etc) in boiling water; to dip-boil; to instant-boil:～锅子 *to instant-boil slices of meat and vegetables in a chafing dish*|～羊肉 *instant-boiled mutton; dip-boiled mutton*

SHUANG ㄕㄨㄤ

双(雙、**雙) shuāng ㄕㄨㄤ ❶两个,一对 two; both; dual:～管齐下 *to paint a picture with a brush in each hand at the same time — to work along two lines at the same time; to do two things simultaneously*|取得～方同意 *to obtain mutual consent*
[双簧]曲艺的一种,一人蹲在后面说话,另一人在前面配合着做手势和表情 two-man comic show (with one man acting

in pantomime and the other hiding behind him doing the speaking); two-man act [双生儿]孪生子，一胎生的两个小孩 twins ❷量词 ***quantifier***，用于成对的东西 pair：一～鞋 *a pair of shoes* | 两～筷子 *two pairs of chopsticks* ❸偶数的 even：～数(二、四、六、八等，跟单数相对)(*the opposite of* 单数) *even numbers* (*such as* 2, 4, 6, 8) ❹加倍的 double; twofold：～份 *double portion* | ～料 *of reinforced material; extra quality*

泷(瀧) ㊀ shuāng ㄕㄨㄤ 泷水，水名，在广东省 Shuangshui River, Guangdong Province

㊁ lóng 见 461 页 see p461

霜 shuāng ㄕㄨㄤ ❶附着在地面或靠近地面的物体上的微细冰粒，是接近地面的水蒸气冷至零摄氏度以下凝结而成的 frost ㊟ ***figurative*** 白色 white; hoary：～鬓 *grey* (or *white*) *hair on the temples* ❷像霜的东西 frost-like powdery substance：柿～ *persimmon frost* | 盐～*salt frost* (or *icing*)

孀 shuāng ㄕㄨㄤ 寡妇，死了丈夫的妇人 widow：遗～ *widow* | ～居 *to live as a widow; to live in widowhood*

骦 shuāng ㄕㄨㄤ 见 711 页"骕"字条"骕骦"(sù—) see 骕骦 on p711

礵 shuāng ㄕㄨㄤ [北礵]岛名，在福建省霞浦 Beishuang Island in Xiapu, Fujian Province

鹴 shuāng ㄕㄨㄤ 见 711 页"鹔"字条"鹔鹴"(sù—) see 鹔鹴 on p711

爽 shuǎng ㄕㄨㄤˇ ❶明朗，清亮 bright; clear; fresh：秋高气～*clear sky and crisp air in autumn; clear and crisp autumn climate* | ～目 *pleasing* (or *pleasant*) *to the eye* ❷清凉，清洁 cool; fresh; clear：凉～*nice and cool; pleasantly* (or *comfortably*) *cool* | 清～ *fresh and cool* ❸痛快，率直 frank; straightforward; forthright：豪～*bold and unconstrained; unrestrained and frank; uninhibited and straightforward* | 直～ *forthright; frank; candid* | 这人很～快。*This man is very frank and straightforward.* [爽性]索性，干脆 might just as well：既然晚了，～～不去吧。*Since it is already late, we might just as well not go.* ❹舒适，畅快 feeling well; comfortable：身体不～*to feel unwell; to be under the weather* | 人逢喜事精神～。*Morale soars in happy times.* ❺不合，违背 to deviate：～约 *to break an appointment; to fail to keep an engagement* | 毫厘不～ *not to deviate the least bit; to free from the slightest error*

SHUI ㄕㄨㄟ

谁 shuí ㄕㄨㄟˊ (又 *also* shéi) 见 664 页 shéi see shéi on

p664

水 shuǐ ㄕㄨㄟˇ ❶一种无色无味无臭透明的液体,化学成分是 H_2O water ❷河流 river:湘～*Xiangshui River*|汉～*Hanshui River* ❸江、河、湖、海的通称(general term for 江,河,湖,海, etc) water:～陆交通 *land and water transport*|～旱码头 *water and land wharf*

[水平] **1** 静水的平面 surface of the still water — horizontal; level **2** 达到的程度 standard; level:文化～～*education level; cultural level* ❹汁液 juice; water; liquid:药～*liquid medicine; medical liquid*|橘子～*orange juice; orangeade* ❺额外附加的费用 extra cost; additional income:贴～*agio; premium* ❻衣服洗的次数 times of washing:这衣服不禁(jīn)穿,洗了两～就破了。*These clothes do not last; they have become wornout after two washings.*

[水族]我国少数民族,参看附表(see the appendix) the Shui ethnic group, one of the ethnic minorities of China

说 ㊁ shuì ㄕㄨㄟˋ 用话劝说别人,使他听从自己的意见 to try to persuade others to accept one's own view; to try to bring sb around (to sth);to try to lobby:游～*to go about selling an idea; to go around drumming up support; to lobby*

㊀ shuō 见 701 页 see p701

㊂ yuè 见 929 页 see p929

帨 shuì ㄕㄨㄟˋ 古代的佩巾,像现在的毛巾 ancient shawl that looks like today's towel

税 shuì ㄕㄨㄟˋ 国家向企业、集体或个人征收的作为财政收入的货币或实物 tax; duty; revenue:纳～*to pay taxes; to pay duty*|营业～*business tax; transactions tax; turnover tax*|个人所得～*personal income tax*

睡 shuì ㄕㄨㄟˋ 闭目安息,大脑皮质处于休息状态 to sleep(㊥ ***doublet*** —眠 to sleep):～着(zháo)了 *to have fallen asleep; to be asleep*|～午觉 *to take a nap after lunch; to take an afternoon nap*

SHUN ㄕㄨㄣ

吮 shǔn ㄕㄨㄣˇ 聚拢嘴唇来吸 to suck(㊥ ***doublet*** —吸 to suck):～乳 *to suck milk*

楯 ㊀ shǔn ㄕㄨㄣˇ 阑干 railings; banisters; balustrade

㊁ dùn 见 169 页 see p169

顺 shùn ㄕㄨㄣˋ ❶趋向同一个方向,跟"逆"相对(the opposite of 逆) in the same direction as; along with:～风 *to go with the wind; to follow the wind; to have a favourable* (or *tail*) *wind*|～水 *to go downstream; to go with the current* (or *tide*)|通～(*of writing*) *clear and coherent; smooth* ❷沿,循 along:～河边走 *to walk along the river* ㊞ ***extension*** 依次往上往下或依次往后 along; successively; in proper order:

～着楼梯(*to go*) *down or up the stairs*|～着台阶(*to go*) *up or down the flights*|～着坡 *along the slope*|遇雨～延 *to postpone in case of rain* ❸随，趁便 conveniently; in passing: ～手关门。*Close the door behind you.*|～口说出来 *to say* (or *mention*) *sth in passing; to speak out offhandedly; to slip from one's mouth* ❹整理，理顺 to arrange; to sort out; to straighten out: ～一～头发 *to smooth the hair*|文章太乱，得～一～。*The article is too messy. It needs polishing.* ❺服从，不违背 to obey; to yield to; to submit to: ～从 *to be obedient to; to yield to; to submit to*|归～*to cross over and pledge allegiance; to surrender to the enemy force* ❻适合，不别扭 to suit; to be agreeable to; to go well: ～心 *satisfactory; agreeable*|～眼 *pleasing to the eye; pleasant to look at*

瞬 shùn ㄕㄨㄣˋ 眼跳 (of one's eyes) to twitch

舜 shùn ㄕㄨㄣˋ 传说中上古帝王名 Shun, a legendary monarch in ancient China

瞬 shùn ㄕㄨㄣˋ 一眨(zhǎ)眼，转眼 wink; twinkling: ～息万变(喻极短时间内变化极多) *to undergo a myriad of changes in the twinkling of an eye — to change rapidly*|转～即逝 *to disappear* (or *vanish*) *in a wink*

SHUO ㄕㄨㄛ

说 ㊀ shuō ㄕㄨㄛ ❶用话来表达自己的意思 to speak; to talk; to say ❷说合，介绍 to introduce; to act as a matchmaker; to try to influence sb to do sth: ～亲 *to act as a matchmaker; to act as a go-between* ❸言论，主张 theory; doctrine; viewpoint: 学～ *theory; doctrine; teachings*|著书立～ *to write a book to expound a theory* (or *doctrine*); *to produce scholarly works* ❹责备 to scold; to criticize: 他挨～了。*He was scolded.*|～了他一顿。*He was given a good dressing-down* (or *talking-to*).

㊁ shuì 见 700 页 see p700

㊂ yuè 见 929 页 see p929

妁 shuò ㄕㄨㄛˋ 旧指媒人 (in former times) matchmaker; go-between

烁(爍) shuò ㄕㄨㄛˋ 光亮的样子 bright; brilliant; shining: 闪～ *to flicker; to twinkle; to glimmer*

铄(鑠) shuò ㄕㄨㄛˋ ❶熔化金属 to melt (metals, etc): ～金 *to make metals melt*|～石流金(喻天气极热) *to be hot enough to make rocks and metals melt — to be sweltering; to be extremely hot* ❷销毁，消损 to weaken; to destroy; to cripple ❸同"烁" same as 烁

S

朔 shuò ㄕㄨㄛˋ ❶夏历每月初一日 first day of the lunar month ❷北 north: ～风 *north wind* | ～方 *north*

搠 shuò ㄕㄨㄛˋ 扎,刺 to stab; to jab; to prick

蒴 shuò ㄕㄨㄛˋ 蒴果,果实的一种,由两个以上的心皮构成,成熟后自己裂开,内含许多种子,如芝麻、棉花、百合等的果实 capsule

槊 shuò ㄕㄨㄛˋ 长矛,古代的一种兵器 long spear, a kind of weapon in ancient China

硕 shuò ㄕㄨㄛˋ 大 big; large: ～果 *great fruit; great achievements* | ～大无朋(喻无比的大) *of unparalleled size; colossal; huge* [硕士]学位名,在学士之上,博士之下(of academic degree) master

数(數) ㊂ shuò ㄕㄨㄛˋ 屡次 frequently; repeatedly ([连] ***doublet*** 频— frequent and successive): ～见不鲜(xiān) *to be a frequent sight; to be a common occurrence; to be nothing new*
㊀ shù 见 696 页 see p696
㊁ shǔ 见 694 页 see p694

SI ㄙ

厶 sī ㄙ "私"的古字 ancient form of 私

私 sī ㄙ ❶个人的,跟"公"相对(the opposite of 公) personal; private: ～事 *private affairs* | ～信 *private letter; personal correspondence* [引] ***extension*** 为自己的 selfish; self-centred; egoistic: ～心 *selfish motives; selfishness* | 自～ *selfish; self-centred; egoistic* | 假公济～ *to exploit public office for personal gains* (or *ends*); *to promote one's own interests under the guise of serving the public; to seek one's own profit in public affairs* | 大公无～ *selfishless; unselfish; fair and just* ❷秘密而不公开,不合法 secret and illegal; illicit; unlawful: ～货 *smuggled goods; contraband (goods)* | ～自拿走了 *to take away without permission* ❸暗地里,偷偷地 secretly; stealthily; privately: ～语 *to speak in a low voice; to whisper*

司 sī ㄙ ❶主管,主持,经办 to take charge of; to manage; to operate: 各～其职 *Each attends* (or *discharges*) *his own duties*. or *Each manages his own affairs*. | ～令 *commander; commanding officer* | ～法 *administration of justice; judicature* ❷中央各部中所设立的分工办事的单位 department (under a ministry): 外交部礼宾～ *Protocol Department of the Ministry of Foreign Affairs* | ～长 *director of a department* (*in a ministry*)

丝(絲) sī ㄙ ❶蚕吐出的像线的东西,是织绸缎等的原料 silk [喻] ***figurative*** 细微,极少 tiny bit; least bit: 纹～不动 *absolutely still;*

perfectly motionless | 脸上没有一～笑容。*There is not a ghost* (or *trace*) *of a smile on his face*. ❷(一儿)像丝的东西 anything threadlike:铁～*iron wire* | 萝卜～儿 *radish shreds* ❸计量单位名,10 忽是 1 丝,10 丝是 1 毫 *si*, a unit of measure, equal to 10 *hu* or 0.1 *hao* [丝毫]㊃ ***figurative*** 极少,极小,一点(多和否定词连用)(usually used together with negatives) slightest amount or degree; least bit; at all:～～不错 *not to err by a hair's breadth*; *to tally in every detail*; *to be perfectly right*

咝(嘶) sī ㄙ 拟声词 ***onomatopoeia***,形容枪弹等很快地在空中飞过的声音(叠 ***reduplication***)(of shells or bullets) to whistle; to hiss:子弹～～地从身旁飞过。*The bullets whistled past* (*us*).

鸶(鷥) sī ㄙ 见 469 页"鹭"字条"鹭鸶"(lù—) see 鹭鸶 on p469

思 sī ㄙ ❶想,考虑,动脑筋 to think; to consider; to ponder:事要三～ *to think thrice before you act*; *to think carefully before doing anything* | 不假～索(*to respond*) *without thinking*; *without hesitation* | ～前想后 *to think over again and again*; *to ponder* (*over*) *deeply* [思维]在表象、概念的基础上进行分析、综合、判断、推理等认识活动的过程 thought; thinking [思想] **1** 即理性认识。正确的思想来自社会实践,是经过由实践到认识,由认识到实践多次的反复而形成的 thinking; thought **2** 某一阶级或某一政党所持的一定的观点、概念、观念的体系 ideology:工人阶级的～～ *thought* (or *ideology*) *of the working class* **3** 思考 to think; to consider; to deliberate **4** 想法,念头 idea; intention; thought ❷想念,挂念 to miss; to long for; to be concerned with (*or* about):相～ *yearning between lovers*; *lovesickness* | ～家心切 *to ache for home*; *to feel desperately homesick* | ～念战友 *to miss one's comrades-in-arms* ❸思路,想法 train of thought; thinking; reasoning:文～ *thread of ideas in writing*; *train of thought in writing* | 构～ *to work out the plot of a literary work* (or *the composition of a painting*); *to conceive*; *to construct*

偲 ㊀ sī ㄙ [偲偲]互相切磋,互相督促 to learn from each other by exchanging views; to urge and encourage each other
㊁ cāi 见 62 页 see p62

缌 sī ㄙ 细的麻布 fine linen (*or* flax)

飔 sī ㄙ 凉风 cool wind

罳 sī ㄙ 见 203 页"罘"字条"罘罳"(fú—) see 罘罳 on p203

锶 sī ㄙ 一种金属元素,符号 Sr,银白色晶体。硝酸锶

可制红色烟火。溴化锶是健胃剂。乳酸锶可治抽风 strontium (Sr)

虒 sī ㄙ [虒亭]地名，在山西省襄垣 Siting, a place in Xiangyuan, Shanxi Province

斯 sī ㄙ ❶文言代词 ***pronoun in classical Chinese***，这，这个，这里 this; here：～人 *this (kind of) person*｜～时 (*at*) *this moment* (or *time*)｜生于～，长于～。*This is where I was born and brought up.* ❷乃，就 then; thus：有备～可以无患矣。*If you are fully prepared, you will have nothing to worry about.*

厮(*廝) sī ㄙ ❶旧时对服杂役的男子的蔑称(in former times)(***derogatory***) male servant：小～*page boy; page* ⑭ ***transfer*** 对人轻慢的称呼(宋以来的小说中常用)(used in the novels since the Song Dynasty) (***derogatory***) guy; fellow：这～*this guy*｜那～*that guy* ❷互相 mutual; with each other; together：～守 *to stay together with; to stay with each other; to rely on each other*｜～打 *to exchange blows; to come to blows; to tussle*｜～混(hùn) *to hang out with; to chum around with; to fool about* (*with*)

澌 sī ㄙ 随水流动的冰 floating ice; ice floe

撕 sī ㄙ 扯开，用手使分开 to tear; to rip; to rend：把布～成两块 *to tear the cloth into two pieces*

嘶 sī ㄙ ❶马叫(of a horse) to neigh：人喊马～*people shouting and horses neighing* ❷声音哑 hoarse; husky：～哑 *hoarse; husky*｜声～力竭 *to be exhausted from shouting; to shout oneself hoarse; to yell oneself blue in the face*

澌 sī ㄙ 尽 totally; completely：～灭 *to disappear totally; to vanish completely; to extinguish*

蛳(螄) sī ㄙ [螺蛳](luó—)螺的通称 general term for spiral-shelled molluscs

死 sǐ ㄙˇ ❶生物失去生命，跟"活"相对(the opposite of 活) to die; to decease; to expire (㊀ ***doublet*** 一亡 death; doom) ㊁ ***extension*** **1** 不顾性命，拼死 to the death; desperately：～守 *to defend to the death; to make a last-ditch defence*｜～战 *to fight to the death* **2** 至死，表示坚决 adamantly; unyieldingly：～不认账 *to stubbornly refuse to acknowledge a debt; to stubbornly refuse to admit what one has said or done* **3** 表示达到极点 extremely; to death：乐～了 *to be dying of laughing*｜笑～人 *extremely funny* ❷不可调和的 irreconcilable; implacable; deadly：～敌 *implacable enemy* (or *foe*); *deadly* (or *sworn*) *enemy* ❸不活动，不灵活 stagnant; fixed; inflexible:

S

～水 *stagnant water; unfree water*｜～心眼 *as obstinate as a mule; stubborn*｜把门钉～了。*The door has been nailed fast*. [死机]使用计算机时因程序错误等原因，显示屏上图像静止不动，无法继续操作(of a computer) to crash; to go down ⑮ ***transfer*** 不通的 impassable; blocked; closed: ～胡同 *dead end; blind alley; impasse*｜把洞堵～了。*The hole has been stopped up*.

巳(**巳) sì ㄙˋ ❶地支的第六位 *si*, the 6th of 12 Earthly Branches ❷巳时，指上午九点到十一点 period of the day from 9 a.m. to 11 a.m.

汜 sì ㄙˋ 汜河，水名，在河南省郑州 Sihe River in Zhengzhou, Henan Province

祀(*禩) sì ㄙˋ ❶祭祀 to offer sacrifices to the gods or spirits of the dead ❷〈古 ***archaism***〉殷代人指年 (used in the Yin Dynasty) year: 十有三～*thirteen years*

四 sì ㄙˋ ❶数目字 four ❷旧时乐谱记音符号的一个，相当于简谱中的低音"6̣"(in former times) *si*, a note of the scale, corresponding to 6̣ in numbered musical notation

泗 sì ㄙˋ ❶鼻涕 nasal mucus; snivel: 涕～(眼泪和鼻涕) *tears and snivel* ❷泗河，水名，在山东省济宁 Sihe River in Jining, Shandong Province

驷 sì ㄙˋ 古代同驾一辆车的四匹马，或者套着四匹马的车(in ancient China) team of four horses harnessed to a chariot; chariot drawn by a team of four horses: 一言既出，～马难追(喻话说出后无法再收回) *Words once uttered cannot be taken back even by a team of four horses — what is said can't be unsaid*. or *A word spoken can never been taken back*.

寺 sì ㄙˋ ❶古代官署名(in ancient China) government house; government office: 太常～ *Ministry of Ceremonies and Worship* (*one of the nine courts under the central government and foremost in prestige among them*) ❷寺院，佛教出家人居住的地方 temple [清真寺]伊斯兰教徒礼拜的地方 mosque

似 ㊀ sì ㄙˋ ❶像，相类 to look like; to be similar to; to resemble (㊟ ***doublet*** 类— to be similar to; to be analogous to): 相～*to resemble; to be similar to; to be alike*｜～是而非 *seeming to be right* (or *reasonable*) *but not so in fact; specious* ❷副词 ***adverb***，似乎，好像，表示不确定 seemingly; apparently: ～应再行研究。*It seems that it needs further discussing*.｜这个建议～欠妥当。*I am afraid your suggestion is not appropriate*. ❸表示比较，

有超过的意思(used to denote comparison) than:一个高～一个。*One is comparatively high to another.*|人民生活一天好～一天。*People's lives are getting better day by day.*

㊁ shì 见 682 页 see p682

姒 sì ㄙˋ 古代称丈夫的嫂子(in ancient China) wife of husband's elder brother:娣～(妯娌) *wives of brothers; sisters-in-law*

兕 sì ㄙˋ 古书上指雌的犀牛(in ancient Chinese texts) female rhinoceros

伺 ㊀ sì ㄙˋ 守候,观察 to keep watch; to await; to spy on:～敌 *to keep watch on the enemy*|～隙进击敌人 *to wait for an opportunity to attack the enemy*

㊁ cì 见 108 页 see p108

饲 sì ㄙˋ 喂养 to feed; to raise; to rear:～鸡 *to raise chickens*|～蚕 *to raise silkworms* [饲料]喂家畜或家禽的食物 forage; fodder; feed

觇 sì ㄙˋ 窥视 to peep (at); to peek (at)

笥 sì ㄙˋ 盛饭或盛衣物的方形竹器 *si*, rectangular bamboo-plaited container for food or clothes

嗣 sì ㄙˋ ❶接续,继承 to succeed; to inherit; to continue:～位 *to succeed to the throne* ❷子孙 heir; descendant; offspring:后～*heir; descendant; offspring*

俟(*竢) ㊀ sì ㄙˋ 等待 to wait:～机 *to wait for an opportunity*|～该书出版后即寄去。*The book will be sent out as soon as it is published.*

㊁ qí 见 585 页 see p585

涘 sì ㄙˋ 水边 water front; water margin

食 ㊁ sì ㄙˋ 拿东西给人吃 to offer food to; to feed

㊀ shí 见 678 页 see p678

耜(**梠) sì ㄙˋ ❶古代的一种农具 *si*, a kind of farm tool in ancient China ❷古代跟犁上的铧相似的东西 sth resembling a ploughshare in ancient China

肆 sì ㄙˋ ❶不顾一切,任意去做 to be wanton; to unbridle oneself; to indulge oneself:～无忌惮 *to be reckless and unbridled; to be unscrupulous; to be audacious and unprincipled*|～意妄为 *to act recklessly; to do sth wantonly* ❷旧时指铺子,商店(in former times) shop:茶坊酒～*teahouses and wineshops* ❸"四"字的大写 four, capital form of 四

SONG ㄙㄨㄥ

忪 ㊀ sōng ㄙㄨㄥ 见 835 页"惺"字条"惺忪"(xīng—) see 惺忪 on p835

㊁ zhōng 见 987 页 see p987

松(❷-❺鬆) sōng ㄙㄨㄥ ❶常绿乔木,种类很多,叶子针形,木材用途

很广 pine (*Pinus*) ❷松散，不紧密，不靠拢，跟"紧"相对(the opposite of 紧) not tight; slack: 捆得太～。*They were loosely* (or *slackly*) *bound up*. | 土质～。*The soil is loose* (or *porous*). ❸宽，不紧张，不严格 lax; slack; loose: 规矩太～。*The regulations are too lax*. | 决不～懈。*Never slack off*. ❹放开，使松散 to loosen; to slacken; to untie: ～手 *to loosen one's grip; to let go* | ～绑 *to untie* (*a person*); *to relax restrictions* | ～一～马肚带 *to slacken the girth of a horse* ❺用瘦肉做成的茸毛或碎末形的食品 dried meat floss; dried minced meat: 肉～*dried minced meat*

凇 sōng ㄙㄨㄥ [雾凇]寒冷天水汽在树枝上结成的冰花。通称树挂(commonly called 树挂) rime

菘 sōng ㄙㄨㄥ 〈方 ***dialect***〉菘菜，即白菜，二年生草本植物，开黄花，叶可以吃(i. e. 白菜) Chinese cabbage (*Brassica pekinensis*)

淞 sōng ㄙㄨㄥ 吴淞江，发源于太湖，到上海市与黄浦江汇合流入长江 Wusong River, originating in the Taihu Lake, joining the Huangpu River in Shanghai, and flowing into the Changjiang River

嵩(**崧) sōng ㄙㄨㄥ ❶嵩山，又叫"嵩高"。五岳中的中岳，在河南省登封北(also called 嵩高) Song Mountain (*or* Mount Song), the Central Sacred Mountain of Five Sacred Mountains, to the north of Dengfeng, Henan Province ❷高(of mountains) lofty; high

扨(摗) sǒng ㄙㄨㄥˇ ❶挺立 to stand upright and erect; to straighten ❷〈方 ***dialect***〉推 to push

怂(慫) sǒng ㄙㄨㄥˇ 惊惧 alarmed and panicky; frightened; terrified

[怂恿](－yǒng)鼓动别人去做 to instigate; to incite; to foment

耸(聳) sǒng ㄙㄨㄥˇ ❶高起，直立 towering; high; lofty: 高～*to stand tall and erect; to tower* | ～立 *to tower aloft; to rise high* ❷耸动，惊动 to shock; to horrify; to terrify: ～人听闻(故意说夸大或吓人的话使人震惊) *to deliberately exaggerate so as to create sensation — sensational*

悚 sǒng ㄙㄨㄥˇ 害怕，恐惧 fearful; horrified; terrified: 毛骨～然 *with one's hair standing on end — absolutely terrified*

竦 sǒng ㄙㄨㄥˇ ❶恭敬，肃敬 respectful; deferential ❷同"悚"same as 悚

讼 sòng ㄙㄨㄥˋ ❶在法庭争辩是非曲直，打官司 to bring a case to court; to go to law (*or* court); to take into court: 诉～*lawsuit; litigation; accusation* | ～事 *lawsuit; litigation*

S

❷争辩是非 to debate; to argue; to contend: 聚～纷纭 *There is a welter of conflicting opinions over an issue.* or *People argue back and forth about an issue without reaching an agreement* (or *consensus*).

颂 sòng ㄙㄨㄥˋ ❶颂扬,赞扬别人的好处 to praise; to extol; to eulogize: 歌～*to extol; to eulogize; to laud* ❷祝颂,祝愿 to express good wishes: 敬～时绥 *Wish you peace and quiet.* or *All the best.* ❸古代祭祀时用的舞曲 (in ancient China) dance music played on the sacrificial occasions: 周～*sacrificial dance music of the Zhou Dynasty* | 鲁～*sacrificial dance music of the Lu princedom* ❹以颂扬为内容的文章或诗歌 ode; eulogy; paean

宋 sòng ㄙㄨㄥˋ ❶周代诸侯国名,在今河南省商丘一带 Song, a princedom of the Zhou Dynasty, covering today's Shangqiu, Henan Province and nearby areas ❷朝代名 name of a dynasty **1** 南朝之一,刘裕所建立(公元 420—479 年) Song Dynasty (420 – 479), founded by Liu Yu **2** 宋太祖赵匡胤所建立(公元 960—1279 年) Song Dynasty (960 – 1279), founded by Zhao Kuangyin ❸指宋刊本或宋体字 song typeface; books of the Song Dynasty: 影～ *photomechanical copies of the works of the Song Dynasty* | 老～ *Song typeface* | 仿～ *imitation Song-script typeface*

送 sòng ㄙㄨㄥˋ ❶把东西从甲地运到乙地 to send; to deliver; to carry: ～信 *to deliver letters* | ～公粮 *to deliver tax grain; to hand in tax grain* ❷赠给 to give as present; to offer; to give: 他～了我一支钢笔。*He gave me a pen.* ❸送行,陪伴人到某一地点 to see sb off (*or* out); to accompany; to escort: ～孩子上学去 *to take a child to school* | 把客人～到门口 *to see a guest to the door; to walk a guest to the gate* | 开欢～会 *to hold a farewell party; to hold a send-off meeting* ❹丢掉,丧失 to lose; to waste: ～命 *to lose one's life; to get killed; to meet* (or *go to*) *one's fate* | 断～*to lose* (or *forfeit*) (*one's life, future, etc*); *to ruin* | 葬～*to ruin; to wreck; to forfeit*

诵 sòng ㄙㄨㄥˋ ❶用有高低抑扬的腔调念 to read aloud; to chant; to declaim: 朗～ *to read aloud with expression; to recite; to declaim* | ～诗 *to declaim* (or *recite*) *a poem* ❷背诵,凭记忆读出 to recite: 熟读成～ *to read sth again and again until one can recite it; to learn by rote* ❸称述,述说 to state; to recount; to narrate: 传～*to be on everybody's lips; to be widely read*

SOU ㄙㄡ

鄋 sōu ㄙㄡ [鄋瞒]春秋时小国,也称"长狄"。在今山东省济南北。一说在今山东省高青(also called 长狄) Souman, a small ancient state in the Spring and Autumn Period, located to the north of today's Jinan, Shandong Province, but also believed to be located in today's Gaoqing, Shandong Province

搜(❶*蒐) sōu ㄙㄡ ❶寻求,寻找 to look for; to seek; to explore: ～集 *to collect; to gather; to solicit* | ～罗 *to collect; to gather; to recruit* | ～救 *to search for and rescue* ❷搜索检查 to search; to ransack; to rummage: ～身 *to search sb; to make a body search; to frisk*

嗖 sōu ㄙㄡ 拟声词 ***onomatopoeia***,形容迅速通过的声音 to whiz; to whistle; to whoosh:汽车～的一声过去了。*A car whooshed by.* | 子弹～～地飞过。*Bullets whizzed past.*

馊 sōu ㄙㄡ 食物等因受潮热引起质变而发出酸臭味(of food) to turn sour (*or* tart); to smell (*or* spoil); to go rotten: 饭～了。*The food has begun to smell.* or *The food has spoiled.*

廋 sōu ㄙㄡ 隐藏,藏匿 to hide; to conceal

溲 sōu ㄙㄡ ❶排泄大小便。特指排泄小便 to excrete stools and urine; (especially) to urinate ❷浸,泡 to soak; to immerse; to dip

飕 sōu ㄙㄡ ❶风吹(使变干或变冷) to dry (*or* cool) sth by wind: 洗的衣服被风～干了。*The breeze dried the washing.* ❷同"嗖" same as 嗖

锼 sōu ㄙㄡ 镂刻,用钢丝锯挖刻木头 to engrave; to carve:椅背的花是～出来的。*The patterns on the back of the chair are engraved.*

螋 sōu ㄙㄡ 见 619 页"蠼"字条"蠼螋"(qú—) see 蠼螋 on p619

艘 sōu ㄙㄡ 量词 ***quantifier***,用于船只(of a boat or ship):大船五～ *five ships of great bulk* | 军舰十～ *ten warships* (or *naval vessels*)

叟 sǒu ㄙㄡˇ 老头儿 old man: 童～无欺 *Neither the old nor the young shall be cheated — to be absolutely honest* (or *fair*).

瞍 sǒu ㄙㄡˇ ❶眼睛没有瞳人 pupilless ❷瞎子 blind person

嗾 sǒu ㄙㄡˇ ❶指使狗时发出的声音 whistling sound made as a signal to a dog ❷教唆指使 to instigate; to abet: ～使 *to instigate* (*others to do evil things*); *to incite; to abet*

擞(擻) ㊁sǒu ㄙㄡˇ [抖擞](dǒu—)振作,振奋 to enliven; to rouse; to invigorate: ～～精神 *to summon* (or *pluck*) *up one's spirits; to*

S

cheer (or *brace*) *up*; *to pull oneself together*|精神～～*full of energy*; *full of beans*; *in high spirits*

㊁ sòu 见 710 页 see p710

薮(藪) sǒu ㄙㄡˇ ❶生长着很多草的湖泽 lake overgrown with grass ❷人或物聚集的地方 gathering place of people or things; den; haunt:渊～*gathering place of people or things*; *den*; *haunt*

嗽 sòu ㄙㄡˋ 咳嗽。参看 389 页"咳㊀"(see 咳㊀ on p389) to cough

擞(擻) ㊀ sòu ㄙㄡˋ 用通条插到火炉里,把灰抖掉 to poke the ashes off a stove fire; to rake:把炉子～一～。*Give the stove a poking* (or *raking*).

㊁ sǒu 见 709 页 see p709

SU ㄙㄨ

苏(蘇、❺嚕、❷*甦) sū ㄙㄨ ❶植物名 name of plants **1** 紫苏,一年生草本植物,叶紫黑色,花紫色,叶和种子可入药 perilla (*Perilla frutescens*) **2** 白苏,一年生草本植物,茎方形,花白色,种子可以入药 common perilla ❷假死后再活过来 to revive; to come to life; to regain consciousness:～醒 *to regain consciousness*; *to come round*; *to revive*|死而复～*to come back to life* ❸指江苏或江苏苏州 short for Jiangsu Province, or Suzhou in Jiangsu Province:～剧(*of one of the local operas in Jiangsu Province*) *Suzhou opera*|～绣 *Suzhou embroidery* ❹(外 **loan-word**) 苏维埃,前苏联国家权力机关。我国第二次国内革命战争时期曾把工农民主政权也叫苏维埃 Soviet (governing councils of former Soviet Union; workers' and peasants' political power established during China's Second Revolutionary Civil War):～区 *Soviet area* ❺见 465 页"噜"字条"噜苏"(lū —) see 噜苏 on p465

酥 sū ㄙㄨ ❶酪,用牛羊奶凝成的薄皮制成的食物 butter ❷松脆,多指食物(usually of food) crisp; short; flaky:～糖 *crunchy candy* ❸含油多而松脆的点心 shortbread; shortcake; short pastry:桃～*walnut kernel shortbread* ❹软弱无力 weak; feeble; limp:～软 *limp*; *soft*; *languid*

稣 sū ㄙㄨ 同"苏❷"same as 苏❷

窣 sū ㄙㄨ 见 802 页"窸"字条"窸窣"(xī —) see 窸窣 on p802

俗 sú ㄙㄨˊ ❶风俗,社会上长期形成的风气、习惯等 custom; practice; convention:移风易～*to transform established traditions*; *to change prevailing customs and habits* ❷大众化的,最通行的,习见的 popular; common; current:～

语 *common* (or *popular*) *saying; folk adage* | 通～读物 *books for mass consumption* (or *general readership*); *popular literature; popular reader* ❸趣味低，不高雅 vulgar; boorish：～不可耐 *unbearably vulgar; helplessly boorish; in extreme poor taste* | 这张画儿画得太～。*This drawing is in rather poor taste.* [庸俗]肤浅的，鄙俗的 vulgar; philistine; low ❹指没出家的人，区别于出家的佛教徒等 secular person; layman：僧～ *monks and laymen; clerical and secular people; clergy and laity*

夙 sù ㄙㄨˋ ❶早 early (in the morning)：～兴夜寐(早起晚睡) *to rise early and retire late — to work hard day and night; to be very industrious* ❷一向有的，旧有的 long-standing; old; of yore：～愿 *long-cherished wish* | ～志 *long-cherished ambition*

诉(*愬) sù ㄙㄨˋ ❶叙说 to tell; to narrate; to relate：告～ *to tell; to inform; to let know* | ～苦 *to vent one's grievances; to pour out one's woes; to air one's sufferings* ❷控告 to accuse; to sue; to charge：～讼 *lawsuit; litigation; accusation* | 起～ *to bring a suit* (or *an action*) *against sb; to initiate legal proceedings against sb; to sue* (or *prosecute*) | 上～ *to appeal* (*to a higher court*) | 控～ *to accuse; to indict; to denounce* [公诉]追诉犯罪的一种方式。检察机关代表国家为追究被告人的刑事责任而向法院提起的诉讼 public prosecution [投诉]公民或单位认为其合法权益遭受侵犯，向有关部门请求依法处理 to complain

肃(肅) sù ㄙㄨˋ ❶恭敬 respectful：～立 *to stand in solemn silence; to rise as a mark of respect* | ～然起敬 *to be filled with deep veneration; to feel deep reverence* (*for*) ❷严正，认真 solemn; serious：严～ *serious; solemn; earnest* | ～穆 *solemn and quiet; solemn and respectful; grave* [肃清]清除 to eliminate; to get rid of; to clean up：～～流毒 *to eliminate poisonous influences; to liquidate pernicious influences* | ～～土匪 *to exterminate banditry*

骕(驌) sù ㄙㄨˋ [骕骦](— shuāng)古书上说的一种良马(in ancient Chinese texts) a kind of fine horse

鹔(鸛) sù ㄙㄨˋ [鹔鹴](— shuāng)古书上说的一种水鸟(in ancient Chinese texts) a kind of water bird

素 sù ㄙㄨˋ ❶本色，白色 white：～服(*usually as a sign of mourning*) *white clothing* | ～丝 *white silk* ㊀ ***extension*** 颜色单纯，不艳丽 plain; simple; quiet：这块布很～净。*This piece of cloth is very plain and neat.* ❷本来的 native; orig-

S

inal：～质 *nature；quality；diathesis*｜～性 *one's nature；one's disposition*（or *temperament*）㊀ ***extension*** 事物的基本成分 basic element or constituent：色～*pigment*｜毒～*toxin；poison*｜因～*factor；element* ❸蔬菜类的食品（对荤菜说）（as opposed to 荤菜）vegetable；vegetarian food：～食 *vegetarian food；vegetarian meal*｜吃～*to be a vegetarian；to be on a vegetarian diet* ❹平素，向来 usually；habitually；always：～日 *usually；ordinarily；generally*｜～不相识 *never having met；not being acquainted* ❺古代指洁白的生绢（in ancient China）white silk fabric：尺～（用绸子写的信）*one-foot-long white silk scroll — a letter written on white silk*

嗉（❶**膆）sù ㄙㄨˋ ❶（一子）嗉囊，鸟类食管下储存食物的地方（of a bird）crop；jowl：鸡～子 *crop of a hen*（or *chicken*）❷（一子）装酒的小壶 wine jar（or flask）

愫 sù ㄙㄨˋ 情愫，真实的心情 true feelings；innermost feelings；sincerity

速 sù ㄙㄨˋ ❶快 fast；rapid；quick（㊟ ***doublet*** 迅一 speedy；swift；prompt）：～成 *achieving by quick methods；accelerated；crash*｜～冻 *to quick-freeze；to snap-freeze*｜火～*at top speed；post-haste*［速度］运动的物体在单位时间内所通过的距离 velocity；speed；rate［速记］用便于速写的符号记录口语 to write down in shorthand（*or* stenography）❷邀请 to invite：不～之客 *uninvited*（or *unexpected*）*guest；gatecrasher；chance*（or *unwelcome*）*visitor*

涑 sù ㄙㄨˋ 涑水河，水名，在山西省西南部 Sushui River in the southeast of Shanxi Province

觫 sù ㄙㄨˋ 见 283 页“觳”字条“觳觫”（hú—）see 觳觫 on p283

宿 ㊀ sù ㄙㄨˋ ❶住，过夜，夜里睡觉 to put up for the night；to lodge for the night；to stay overnight：住～*to stay；to put up；to accommodate*｜～舍 *dormitory；hostel；living quarters* ❷年老的，长久从事某种工作的 old；experienced；veteran：～将（经历多，老练的指挥官）*experienced military commander；veteran general* ❸平素，素有的 long-standing；long-running；always：～愿得偿 *to realize one's long-cherished wish* ❹姓 Su，a surname

㊁ xiǔ 见 842 页 see p842

㊂ xiù 见 843 页 see p843

缩 ㊁ sù ㄙㄨˋ［缩砂密］多年生草本植物，种子可入药，叫砂仁（its seed，used as medicine，called 砂仁）black cardamom seed（*Amomum xanthioides*）

㊀ suō 见 718 页 see p718

蹜 sù ㄙㄨˋ［蹜蹜］小步快走 to walk briskly in small

steps; to trot

粟 sù ㄙㄨˋ 谷子,一年生草本植物,花小而密集,子实去皮后就是小米。旧时泛称谷类(generally used to denote cereals in former times) millet (*Setaria*)

傈 sù ㄙㄨˋ 见436页"傈"字条"傈僳族"(lì——) see 傈僳族 on p436

谡 sù ㄙㄨˋ 起,起来 to rise; to stand up

塑 sù ㄙㄨˋ 用泥土等做成人物的形象 sculpture; statue; model:~像 *statue* | 泥~木雕 *like a statue carved of wood or moulded from clay—as wooden as a dummy; as motionless and useless as a statue* [塑料]具有可塑性的高分子化合物的统称,种类很多,用途很广 plastic

溯(*泝、*遡) sù ㄙㄨˋ 逆着水流的方向走 to go against the stream; to go up stream:~河而上 *to go up a river* (or *stream*); *to go upstream* ㊣ ***extension*** 追求根源或回想 to trace back; to recall; to recollect:推本~源 *to trace the origin; to get to the root of the problem; to ascertain the cause* | 回~ *to recall; to recollect; to look back upon* | 追~ *to trace back to; to date from; to date back to*

蔌 sù ㄙㄨˋ 菜肴,野菜 vegetable:山肴野~ *mountain food and wild vegetables; game and edible wild herbs* (*as food*)

簌 sù ㄙㄨˋ [簌簌] **1** 拟声词 ***onomatopoeia***, rustling:忽然听见芦苇里~~地响。*Suddenly there came rustling sounds from the reed marshes.* **2** 纷纷落下的样子 streaming (*or* coursing) down profusely:泪珠~~地往下落。*Tears are streaming* (or *coursing*) *down his* (or *her*) *cheeks.*

SUAN ㄙㄨㄢ

狻 suān ㄙㄨㄢ [狻猊](—ní) 传说中的一种猛兽(in legend) a kind of fierce animal

痠 suān ㄙㄨㄢ 同"酸❸"same as 酸❸

酸 suān ㄙㄨㄢ ❶化学上称能在水溶液中产生氢离子(H^+)的物质,分无机酸、有机酸两大类 acid:盐~*hydrochloric acid; muriatic acid* | 硝~*hydrogen nitrate; nitric acid* | 醋~*acetic acid* [酸雨]含酸性物质超过一定数量的雨、雪、雾、雹等。能腐蚀建筑物外部,损害植物,污染水源 acid rain; acid precipitation ❷像醋的气味或味道 sour; tart; vinegary:~菜 *pickled Chinese cabbage; Chinese sauerkraut; pickled vegetables* | 这个梨真~。*This pear is really sour.* ❸微痛无力 aching; prickling; tingling:腰~腿痛 *to have an aching back and legs* | 腰有点儿发~ *to have a tingle in the waist* ❹悲痛,伤

S

心 sick at heart; grieved; distressed: 心～ *to feel sick at heart; to feel sad* | 十分悲～ *very sad and bitter; deeply grieved and depressed* ❺旧时讥讽人的迂腐(in former times) pedantic; hidebound; priggish: ～秀才 *priggish pedant; impractical old scholar; hidebound scholar* [寒酸]指文人的贫苦或不大方的样子(of a poor scholar) miserable and shabby; too simple to be decent

蒜 suàn ㄙㄨㄢˋ 大蒜,多年生草本植物,开白花。地下茎通常分瓣,味辣,可供调味用 garlic (*Allium sativum*)

筭 suàn ㄙㄨㄢˋ ❶计算用的筹码 chip ❷同"算" same as 算

算(**祘) suàn ㄙㄨㄢˋ ❶核计,计数 to calculate; to compute; to reckon: ～～多少钱 *to reckon costs; to tot* (or *add*) *up costs* | ～账 *to reckon up bills* (or *accounts*); *to balance the books; to make out bills* ❷打算,计划 to plan; to project; to programme: 失～ *to miscalculate; to misjudge* ㊀ ***extension*** 推测 to think; to suppose; to reckon: 我～着他今天该来。*I think he will come today.* ❸作为,当作 to regard as; to count as; to take for: 这个～我的。*I may take this as mine.* or *This may count as mine.* ㊀ ***extension*** 算数,承认 to count; to carry weight: 不能说了不～。*You can't go back on your promise.* ❹作罢,不再提起 come, come; let it be; let it pass: ～了,不要再啰唆了。*Come, come, let it go at that.* or *That's enough! Forget it.* ❺总算 at long last; in the end; finally: 今天～把问题弄清楚了。*I have at last gained a clear understanding of the problem.*

SUI ㄙㄨㄟ

尿 ㊀ suī ㄙㄨㄟ 小便,从尿道排泄出来的液体 urine [尿脬](—pāo)膀胱 bladder

㊁ niào 见 536 页 see p536

虽(雖) suī ㄙㄨㄟ 连词 ***conjunction***, 虽然,用在上半句,表示"即使"、"纵然"的意思,下半句多有"可是"、"但是"相应 although; even if; despite the fact that: 为人民而死,～死犹生。*Those who died for the people will be immortal in spirit — honoured though dead.* | 工作～忙,可是学习决不能放松。*Never slacken off in studies, although you are very busy at work.*

荽 suī ㄙㄨㄟ [胡荽]芫荽(yánsui),俗叫"香菜"(popularly called 香菜) coriander (*Coriandrum sativum*)

眭 suī ㄙㄨㄟ ❶〈古 ***archaism***〉目光深注 to gaze thoughtfully at ❷姓 Sui, a surname

睢 suī ㄙㄨㄟ 睢县,在河南省 Suixian County in Henan

Province

濉 suī ㄙㄨㄟ 濉河，水名，在安徽省北部 Suihe River in northern Anhui Province

绥 suí ㄙㄨㄟ ❶安抚 to placate; to pacify; to appease:～靖 *to placate; to pacify; to appease* ❷平安 peaceful:顺颂台～(书信用语)(*used at the end of a letter*) *I avail myself of this opportunity to express my kind regards.*

隋 suí ㄙㄨㄟ 朝代名，隋文帝杨坚所建立(公元 581—618 年) the Sui Dynasty (581—618AD), founded by Yang Jian

随(隨) suí ㄙㄨㄟ ❶跟着 to follow:～说～记 *to take down notes while talking*｜我～着大家一起走。*I will go along with all of you.* [随即]副词 **adverb**，立刻 soon after that; immediately; presently ❷顺从，任凭，由 to let sb do as he likes; to do at one's convenience; to do at one's discretion:～意 *as one pleases; at will; at random*｜～他的便。*Let him do whatever he wishes.* [随和](—he)和气而不固执己见 amiable; obliging; easygoing ❸顺便，就着 along with; in passing:～手关门。*Close the door behind you.* ❹〈方 **dialect**〉像 to look like; to take after; to resemble:他长(zhǎng)得～他父亲。*He takes after his father.*

遂 ㊀ suí ㄙㄨㄟ 义同"遂㊀❶"，用于"半身不遂"(身体一侧发生瘫痪) same as 遂㊀❶ and used in 半身不遂

㊁ suì 见 716 页 see p716

髓 suǐ ㄙㄨㄟ ❶骨髓，骨头里的像脂肪样的东西 marrow:敲骨吸～(喻残酷地剥削) *to break the bones and suck the marrow — cruel, bloodsucking exploitation* [精髓]事物精要的部分 marrow; quintessence ❷像髓的东西 sth like marrow:脑～ *brains*

岁(歲、*嵗、**亗) suì ㄙㄨㄟ ❶计算年龄的单位，一年为一岁 year (of age):三～的孩子 *three-year-old child* ❷年 year:去～*last year*｜～月 *years* ❸年成 year's harvest; year for crops:歉～*lean year*｜富～*good year; year of bumper harvest*

谇 suì ㄙㄨㄟ ❶责骂 to scold; to berate ❷问 to bring (*or* call) sb to account; to interrogate ❸直言规劝 to persuade bluntly; to counsel; to exhort

碎 suì ㄙㄨㄟ ❶完整的东西破坏成零片零块 broken pieces:粉～*to shatter to pieces; to smash; to crush*｜碗打～了。*The bowl was broken into pieces.* ❷零星，不完整 broken; fragmentary; scattered:～布 *oddments of cloth; rags*｜事情琐～*trivial matters; trifles* ❸说话唠叨 garrulous; gabby; loquacious:嘴～ *garrulous; gabby; loquacious*

S

祟 suì ㄙㄨㄟˋ 迷信说法指鬼神带给人的灾祸 disaster brought by spirits [鬼祟]行为不光明,常说"鬼鬼祟祟"(usually used in 鬼鬼祟祟) hole-and-corner; furtive; sneaky:行动～～ *to act furtively; to sneak* [作祟]暗中捣鬼 to make mischief; to cause trouble; to exercise evil influence:从中～～*to create difficulties for sb*

遂 ㊀ suì ㄙㄨㄟˋ ❶顺,如意 to gratify; to satisfy; to fulfil:～心 *after one's own heart; to one's liking; satisfied* | ～愿 *to have one's wish fulfilled; to achieve what one wishes; to be satisfied* (or *gratified*) ❷成功,实现 to complete; to succeed:未～ *to fail to accomplish; to abort* | 所谋不～ *to fail in an attempt* ❸于是,就 then; thereupon; hence:服药后腹痛～止。*His stomachache stopped after he took the medicine.*

㊁ suí 见 715 页 see p715

隧 suì ㄙㄨㄟˋ 隧道,凿通山石或在地下挖沟所成的通路 tunnel

燧 suì ㄙㄨㄟˋ ❶上古取火的器具(in remote past) flint, a tool used to make fire ❷古代告警的烽火(in ancient China) fire lit on a hilltop as a signal; beacon fire

邃 suì ㄙㄨㄟˋ 深远 deep; remote; profound **1** 指空间 of space (㊣ ***doublet*** 深— deep; remote) **2** 指时间 of time:～古 *remote antiquity* **3** 指程度 of degree:精～*profound*

襚 suì ㄙㄨㄟˋ 古代指赠死者的衣被,也指赠生者的衣物 (in ancient China) clothes and quilt given to the dead; clothes given to the living

繸 suì ㄙㄨㄟˋ 收丝,即缫丝 (i. e. 缫丝) silk reeling; reeling; filature

穗(❷**繐) suì ㄙㄨㄟˋ ❶(—儿)谷类植物聚生在一起的花或果实 ear of grain; spike:高粱～儿 *ear of kaoliang; spike of Chinese sorghum* | 麦～儿 *ear of wheat; spike of wheat* ❷(—子、—儿)用丝线、布条或纸条等结扎成的装饰品 tassel; fringe:大红旗上挂着金黄的～子。*The large red flag is fringed with golden tassels.* ❸广东省广州的别称 Sui, another name for Guangzhou, Guangdong Province

SUN ㄙㄨㄣ

孙(孫) sūn ㄙㄨㄣ ❶(—子)儿子的儿子 grandson [子孙]后代 descendants; offspring; posterity ❷孙子以后的各代 generations below that of the grandchildren:玄～ *great-great grandson* ❸跟孙子同辈的亲属 relatives of grandchildren's generation:外～ *daughter's son; grandson* | 侄～*brother's grandson; grand nephew* ❹植物再生的 second growth of plants：稻～*new rice shoots grown from the old stalk*｜～竹 *new shoots of bamboo from the old stump*

〈古 ***archaism***〉又同"逊"(xùn) also same as 逊

荪(蓀) sūn ㄙㄨㄣ 古书上说的一种香草(in ancient Chinese texts) an aromatic grass

狲(猻) sūn ㄙㄨㄣ 见282页"猢"字条"猢狲"(hú—) see 猢狲 on p282

飧(*飱) sūn ㄙㄨㄣ 晚饭 evening meal; supper

损 sǔn ㄙㄨㄣˇ ❶减少 to decrease; to diminish; to lose：～益 *to increase and decrease; profit and loss; gains and losses*｜增～*to increase and decrease*［损失］丧失财物、名誉等 to lose：避免意外～～*to avoid unexpected losses* ❷损坏，伤害 to damage; to harm; to injure：破～*damaged; broken; torn*｜完好无～*intact; undamaged; unimpaired*｜～伤 *to hurt; to harm; to injure*｜～人利己 *to harm others in order to benefit oneself; to benefit oneself at the expense of others* ❸用刻薄话挖苦人 to ridicule; to satirize; to mock：别～人啦！*Don't make a mockery of others!* ❹刻薄，毒辣 sarcastic; mean; caustic：说话不要太～。*Don't be so sarcastic in speaking.*｜这法子真～。*This is a dirty trick.*

笋(*筍) sǔn ㄙㄨㄣˇ 竹子初从土里长出的嫩芽，可以做菜吃 bamboo shoot ㊀ ***extension*** 幼嫩 tender; young：～鸡 *young* (or *pring*) *chicken; broiler*

隼 sǔn ㄙㄨㄣˇ 一类凶猛的鸟，又叫"鹘"(hú)。一般为灰褐色，捕食鼠、兔及鸟(also called 鹘) falcon

榫 sǔn ㄙㄨㄣˇ (一子、一儿、一头)器物两部分利用凹凸相接的凸出的部分 tenon

SUO ㄙㄨㄛ

莎 ㊀ suō ㄙㄨㄛ 莎草，多年生草本植物，茎三棱形，开黄褐色小花。地下的块茎叫香附子，可入药 nutgrass flatsedge (*Cyperus rotundus*)

㊁ shā 见650页 see p650

娑 suō ㄙㄨㄛ 见573页"婆"字条"婆娑"(pó—) see 婆娑 on p573

桫 suō ㄙㄨㄛ ［桫椤］(—luó) 蕨类植物，木本，茎高而直，叶片大，羽状分裂 spinulose tree fern (*Cyathea spinulosa*)

挲(*抄) ㊀ suō ㄙㄨㄛ 见513页"摩"字条"摩挲"(mó—) see 摩挲 on p513

㊁ sa 见644页 see p644

㊂ sha 见651页 see p651

唆 suō ㄙㄨㄛ 调唆，挑动别人去做坏事 to instigate; to abet; to incite：～使 *to instigate; to foment; to abet*｜～讼

S

to stir up litigation | 受人调～ *to be instigated by somebody*

梭 suō ㄙㄨㄛ （一子）织布时牵引纬线（横线）的工具，两头尖，中间粗，像枣核形 shuttle

睃 suō ㄙㄨㄛ 斜着眼睛看 to look askance (*or* obliquely) at; to cast a sidelong glance at

羧 suō ㄙㄨㄛ 羧基，有机化合物中含碳、氧、氢（—COOH）的基 carboxyl

蓑（*簑） suō ㄙㄨㄛ 蓑衣，用草或棕毛制成的雨衣 straw (*or* palm-bark) rain cape

嗍 suō ㄙㄨㄛ 用唇舌裹食，吮吸 to suck

趖 suō ㄙㄨㄛ 〈方 **dialect**〉移动 to move; to shift：日头～西。*The sun is moving westward.*

缩 ㊀ suō ㄙㄨㄛ ❶向后退 to draw back; to withdraw; to recoil：不要畏～。*Don't shrink back.* | 遇到困难决不退～。*Never retreat before difficulties.* ❷由大变小，由长变短，由多变少 to become smaller, shorter, or less; to contract; to shrink：热胀冷～ *to expand with heat and contract with cold* | ～了半尺。*It has shrunk half a* chi. | ～短战线 *to shorten the battle line; to narrow the scope of activity* | 节衣～食 *to economize on food and clothing; to lead a frugal life* | 紧～开支 *to cut down one's expenses; to retrench one's expenditure; to curtail outlay* [缩影]比喻可以代表同一类型的具体而微的人或事物 epitome; miniature; microcosm

㊁ sù 见 712 页 see p712

所（**听） suǒ ㄙㄨㄛˇ ❶处所，地方 place; location; site：住～ *dwelling place; residence; domicile* | 各得其～ *Each is in his or its proper place.* or *Each has a role to play.* or *Each gets what he wants.* ❷机关或其他办事的地方 office; bureau; institute：研究～ *research institute* | 派出～ *local police station; police substation; precinct station* | 诊疗～ *clinic; dispensary* ❸明代驻兵防边的地点，因大小不同有千户所、百户所。现在多用于地名（*suo*, place of garrison during the Ming Dynasty, the bigger one called 千户所, and the smaller one called 百户所, now usually used in a place name）：海阳～（在山东省乳山） *Haiyangsuo* (*in Shandong Province*) ❹量词 ***quantifier***，用于房屋（of houses）：两～房子 *two houses* ❺助词 ***auxiliary***，放在动词前，代表接受动作的事物（used before a verb to denote the object of an action） **1** 动词后不再用表事物的词（with no words used after the verb to denote a thing）：耳～闻，目～见 *what one sees and hears* | 我们对人民要有～贡献。*We should make some contribu-*

tions to the people. | 各尽～能，按劳分配 *from each according to his ability and to each according to his work — the socialist principle of distribution* **2** 动词后再用"者"或"的"字代表事物[also used with 者 or 的 (which appears directly after a verb) to denote a thing]：吾家～寡有者 *something that we lack* | 这是我们～反对的。*This is what we are against.* **3** 动词后再用表事物的词 (also used with after a verb a word denoting something)：他～提的意见 *opinions put forward by him* ❻ 助词 ***auxiliary***，放在动词前，跟前面"为"字相应，表示被动的意思 (used before a verb and cooperated with the previous word 为 to express a passive meaning)：为人～笑 *to be laughed at by others* [所以] **1** 连词 ***conjunction***，表因果关系，常跟"因为"相应 (used to express effect, and, in most cases, coupled with 因为) so; therefore; the reason why：他有要紧的事，～～不能等你了。*He has something urgent to do, so he can't wait for you any more.* | 他～～进步得这样快，是因为他能刻苦努力学习。*The reason why he has made such rapid progress is that he studies very hard.* **2** 用来 to use：～～自责者严，～～责人者宽。*People who apply rules to themselves are stricter with themselves than those who apply rules to others.*

索 suǒ ㄙㄨㄛˇ ❶ (一子) 大绳子 (thick) rope：麻～ *hempen rope* | 船～ *ship's hawser* | 铁～桥 *chain bridge* ❷ 搜寻，寻求 to look for; to search; to seek (㊣ ***doublet*** 搜一 to look for; to search; to seek)：按图～骥 *to look for a steed with the aid of its picture — to try to locate sth by following a clue; to deal with (or handle) a matter in a mechanical way* | 遍～不得 *to search high and low in vain* [索引] 把书籍或报刊里边的要项摘出来，分类或按字形、字音依次排列，标明页数，以便查检的资料 index ❸ 讨取，要 to demand; to ask (for)：～钱 *to ask for (or demand) money; to extort (or extract) money (from sb)* | ～价 *to ask a price; to charge* | ～赔 *to claim indemnity; to claim compensation against; to claim for damages* ❹ 尽，空 exhausted; void; empty：～然无味 *dull; insipid; dry* ❺ 单独 all alone; all by oneself; solitary：离群～居 *to live all alone; to live in solitude (or seclusion); to live the life of a hermit (or recluse)*

[索性] 副词 ***adverb***，直截了当，干脆 simply; just; might as well：～～走了 *to go away simply*

唢 suǒ ㄙㄨㄛˇ [唢呐] (一 nà) 管乐器，形状像喇叭 *suona*

S

horn; a Chinese wood wind instrument shaped like a trumpet

琐 suǒ ㄙㄨㄛˇ ❶形容玉声(of jade) tinkling ❷细小,零碎 tiny; petty; trivial (㊀ ***doublet*** 一碎 petty; trivial; trifling):~事 *trifles; trivial* (or *trifling*) *matter; trivia* (or *trivialities*)|繁~*loaded down with trivial details; complicated and overloaded*|这些事很~碎。*These matters are very trivial.* ❸卑微 lowly; humble:猥~(*of appearance, deportment, etc*) *wretched; uncouth; boorish*

锁 suǒ ㄙㄨㄛˇ ❶加在门、箱等上面使人不能随便打开的器具 lock:门上上~*to fix a lock on the door* ❷用锁关住 to fasten with a lock; to lock (up):把门~上 *to lock the door*|拿锁~上箱子 *to fasten the case with a lock* ❸链子 chain:枷~*yoke; fetters; shackles*|~镣 *fetters; shackles* ❹一种缝纫法,多用在衣物边沿上,针脚很密,线斜交或钩连 lockstitch:~扣眼 *to do a lockstitch on a buttonhole*|~边 *to lockstitch a border*

嗦 suo ·ㄙㄨㄛ 见169页"哆"字条"哆嗦"(duō—)、475页"啰"字条"啰唆"(luō—) see 哆嗦 on p169 and 啰唆 on p475

S

T 去

TA 去Y

他 tā 去Y 代词 ***pronoun*** ❶ 称你、我以外的第三人,一般指男性,有时泛指,不分性别 he; him ❷ 别的 other; another: ～人 *other people; anther person; others* | ～乡 *place away from hometown; alien land* [其他][其它]别的 other; another; else ❸ 虚指(used between a verb and a numeral as a form word): 睡～一觉。*Go and have a sleep.* | 干～一场。*Just do it.* ❹ 指另外的地方 other place; another place; somewhere else: 久已～往 *to have long left for somewhere else*

她 tā 去Y 代词 ***pronoun***, 称你、我以外的女性第三人。出于敬慕,也用以代称祖国、国旗、党旗等事物 she; her

它(*牠) tā 去Y 代词 ***pronoun***, 他,专指事物 it [其它]同"其他"same as 其他

铊 ㊀ tā 去Y 一种金属元素,符号 Tl,银白色,质柔软。铊的化合物有毒 thallium (Tl)

㊁ tuó 见 769 页 see p769

趿 tā 去Y 趿拉(lɑ),穿鞋只套上脚的前半部 to wear shoes with the backs turned in; to shuffle about with the backs of one's shoes trodden down; to wear shoes as slippers: ～拉着一双旧布鞋 *to shuffle about in a pair of old cloth shoes with their backs turned in; to wear a pair of old cloth shoes with their backs turned in* | ～拉着木板鞋 *to shuffle about in wooden slippers; to wear wooden slippers* [趿拉儿](—lɑr)拖鞋,只能套着脚的前半部没有后帮的鞋 slippers

塌 tā 去Y ❶ 倒(dǎo),下陷 to collapse; to fall in; to sink: 墙～了 | 。*The wall collapsed.* 房顶子～了。*The roof caved in.* | 人瘦得两腮都～下去了。*She* (or *He*) *is so thin that her* (or *his*) *cheeks have sunk in.* ❷ 下垂 to hang down; to droop: 这棵花晒得～秧了。*This flower drooped* (or *wilted*) *in the sun.* ❸ 安定,镇定 to calm down; to settle down; to ease: ～下心来 *to settle down* (*to work, etc*)

溻 tā 去Y 出汗把衣服、被褥等弄湿(of clothes, bedding, etc) to become soaked (*or* drenched) with sweat; (of sweat) to soak (clothes, bedding, etc): 天太热,我的衣服都～了。*It's so sweltering that my clothes have been soaked in*

sweat.

褟 tā ㄊㄚ 〈方 *dialect*〉在衣物上缝缀花边 to hem (*or* sew) (with lace): ～一道绦(tāo)子 *to hem* (or *sew*) *with a lace; to trim sth with a silk ribbon* [汗褟儿]贴身衬衣 Chinese-style singlet (*or* vest); undershirt

踏 ㊀ tā ㄊㄚ [踏实](-shi) **1** 切实,不浮躁 steady and sure; steadfast; solid: 他工作很～～。*He is steadfast in his work.* **2** (情绪)安定,安稳 free from anxiety; having peace of mind; feeling at ease: 事情办完就～～了。*Only after I've got my job done shall I feel at ease.*

㊁ tà 见 722 页 see p722

塔 tǎ ㄊㄚˇ ❶佛教特有的建筑物 Buddhist pagoda; pagoda ❷像塔形的建筑物 pagoda-shaped building; tower: 水～ *water tower* | 灯～ *lighthouse; beacon* | 纪念～ *memorial tower*

[塔吉克族] **1** 我国少数民族,参看附表(see the appendix) Tajik ethnic group, one of the ethnic minorities of China **2** 塔吉克斯坦的主要民族 main ethnic group in Tajikistan

[塔塔尔族] 我国少数民族,参看附表(see the appendix) Tatars ethnic group, one of the ethnic minorities of China

溚 tǎ ㄊㄚˇ (外 *loanword*)"焦油"的旧称。用煤或木材制得的一种黏稠液体,颜色黑褐,是化学工业上的重要原料,通常用作涂料,有煤焦油和木焦油两种(former term for 焦油) tar

獭 tǎ ㄊㄚˇ 水獭,一种生活在水边的兽,能游泳,捕鱼为食。皮毛棕色。另有旱獭,生活在陆地上 otter (*Lutrinae*)

鳎 tǎ ㄊㄚˇ 鱼名,又叫"鳎目鱼"。种类很多,体形似舌头,两眼都在身体的一侧,有眼的一侧褐色。侧卧在海底泥沙中(also called 鳎目鱼) sole (*Soleidae*)

拓(*搨) ㊁ tà ㄊㄚˋ 在刻铸文字、图像的器物上,蒙一层纸,捶打后使凹凸分明,涂上墨,显出文字、图像来 to make rubbings from (inscriptions, pictures, etc on stone tablets or bronze vessels)

㊀ tuò 见 770 页 see p770

沓 ㊀ tà ㄊㄚˋ 多,重复 numerous; crowded and repeated: 杂～ *numerous and disorderly* | 纷至～来 *to come one after another; to come thick and fast; to keep pouring in*

㊁ dá 见 119 页 see p119

踏 ㊀ tà ㄊㄚˋ 用脚踩 to step on; to tread; to stamp: 大～步地前进 *to stride forward; to advance in strides* ㊀ ***extension*** 亲自到现场去 to go to the spot (to make an investigation or survey): ～看 *to go to the spot to make an investigation; to make an onsite survey; to conduct a field survey* | ～勘 *to make a field survey* (*of a railway line, construction site, etc*)

㊁ tā 见 722 页 see p722

佻(**𠍫**) tà ㄊㄚˋ 见 745 页"佻"字条"佻佻"(tiāo—) see 佻佻 on p745

挞(**撻**) tà ㄊㄚˋ 打,用鞭、棍等打人 to flog; to whip: 鞭~ *to flog; to lash; to castigate*

闼(**闥**) tà ㄊㄚˋ 门,小门 door; small door; wicket: 排~直入(推开门就进去) *to push the door open and go straight in*

汰(**澾**) tà ㄊㄚˋ 滑 slippery; smooth

嗒 ㊀ tà ㄊㄚˋ 失意的样子 frustrated: ~丧 *depressed; dejected; despondent* | ~然若失 *mournful and dejected; deeply despondent*

㊁ dā 见 118 页 see p118

遝 tà ㄊㄚˋ 相及 close to one another [杂遝] 行人很多,拥挤纷乱。现作"杂沓" (of pedestrians) numerous and disorderly; crowded and disorderly

阘 tà ㄊㄚˋ [阘茸](—róng)无能,卑贱 incompetent; mean and low

榻 tà ㄊㄚˋ 狭长而低的床 long, narrow and low bed; couch [下榻] 寄居,住宿 to stay (*or* lodge) (at a place during a trip)

蹋 tà ㄊㄚˋ ❶踏,踩 to tread; to stamp; to trample ❷踢 to kick

漯 ㊀ tà ㄊㄚˋ 漯河,古水名,在今山东省 Tahe River, an ancient river in today's Shandong Province

㊁ luò 见 479 页 see p479

遢 ta ·ㄊㄚ 见 409 页"邋"字条"邋遢"(lā—) see 邋遢 on p409

TAI ㄊㄞ

台 ㊁ tāi ㄊㄞ [天台] 山名,在浙江省东部 Tiantai, a mountain in the east of Zhejiang Province

㊀ tái 见 723 页 see p723

苔 ㊁ tāi ㄊㄞ [舌苔] 舌头上面的垢腻,是由衰死的上皮细胞和黏液等形成的,观察它的颜色可以帮助诊断病症 tongue coating; tongue fur

㊀ tái 见 724 页 see p724

胎 tāi ㄊㄞ ❶人或其他哺乳动物母体内的幼体 foetus; embryo: 怀~ *to become* (or *be*) *pregnant; to conceive* | ~儿 *foetus; embryo* | ~生 *viviparity* ㊀ ***extension*** 事的开始,根源 beginning; source; root: 祸~ *cause of future trouble; breeder of future trouble; bane* ❷器物的粗坯或衬在内部的东西 (in the making of china, cloisonné, etc) roughcast; padding; wadding: 这个帽子是软~儿的。*This is a soft-padded hat.* | 泥~ *clay roughcast* | 铜~(塑像、做漆器等用) *bronze roughcast* ❸轮胎 tyre: 内~ *inner tube* | 外~ *tyre*

台(❶❸❻**臺**、❹**檯**、❺**颱**)

㊀ tái ㄊㄞˊ ❶高平的建筑物

T

platform; stage; terrace: 戏～ *stage*|讲～*platform; rostrum*|主席～*platform; rostrum*|楼阁亭～*pavilions and towers* ㊀ ***extension*** **1** (一儿)像台的东西 sth resembling a platform: 井～ *well platform; wellhead*|窗～儿 *windowsill* **2** 器物的座子 stand; support: 灯～*lamp-stand*|蜡～*candlestick* ❷敬辞 ***polite***, you; your: ～鉴(*used right after the salutation on an old-fashioned letter*) *attention of...; please read my letter*|～启(*used after the name of addressee on an envelope*) *for your information*|兄～*you* ❸量词 ***quantifier***: 唱一～戏 *to put on a play; to perform an opera*|一～机器 *a machine* ❹桌子,案子 desk; table: 写字～(*writing*) *desk*|柜～*counter; bar* ❺台风,发生在太平洋西部热带海洋上的一种极猛烈的风暴,中心附近风力达 12 级以上,同时有暴雨 typhoon ❻台湾省的简称 Tai, short for 台湾省

㊁ tāi 见 723 页 see p723

邰 tái ㄊㄞˊ 姓 Tai, a surname

抬(**擡) tái ㄊㄞˊ ❶举,提高 to raise; to lift: ～手 *to raise one's hand*|～脚 *to lift one's foot*|～起头来 *to raise one's head* ㊀ ***extension*** 使上升 to force up; to lift; to raise: ～价 *to force up prices of goods; to lift prices of commodities* [抬头] **1** (一儿)信函上另起一行或空格书写,表示尊敬 to begin a new line as a sign of respect when mentioning the addressee in letters, formal documents, etc **2** 发票、收据上写的户头(on receipts, bills, etc) name of the buyer, payer or receiver, or space for filling in such a name ❷共同用手或肩搬运东西(of two or more persons) to carry; to move: 一个人搬不动两个人～。*Let two carry it if one person cannot.*|把桌子～过来。*Carry* (or *Move*) *the desk over here.* [抬杠] ㊃ ***figurative*** 争辩 to argue for the sake of arguing; to wrangle; to bicker

苔 ㊀ tái ㄊㄞˊ 隐花植物的一类,根、茎、叶的区别不明显,绿色,常贴在阴湿的地方生长 liverwort; moss; lichen

㊁ tāi 见 723 页 see p723

骀 tái ㄊㄞˊ 劣马 inferior horse; broken-down nag [驽骀] (nú—) 劣马 jade; nag ㊃ ***figurative*** 庸才 mediocre person; philistine

炱 tái ㄊㄞˊ 烟气凝积而成的黑灰,俗叫"烟子"或"煤子"(popularly called 烟子 or 煤子) soot: 煤～*coal soot*|松～(松烟) *pine soot*

跆 tái ㄊㄞˊ 用脚踩踏 to tread; to stamp [跆拳道] 一种拳脚并用的搏击运动 tae kwon do

鲐 tái ㄊㄞˊ 鲐鱼,鱼名,俗叫"鲐巴鱼"。生活在海水中,身体呈纺锤形,背青蓝色,

腹淡黄色，肉可以吃（popularly called 鲐巴鱼）chub mackerel (*Scomber japonicus*)

薹 tái ㄊㄞˊ ❶多年生草本植物，生在水田里，茎扁三棱形，叶扁平而长，可制蓑衣等 sedge (*Cyperaceae*) ❷韭菜、油菜、蒜等蔬菜长出的花莛 bolt of leek, rape, garlic, etc

太 tài ㄊㄞˋ ❶副词 **adverb**，过于 over; too; excessively: ～长 *too long* | ～热 *too hot* ❷副词 **adverb**，极端，最 extremely; most: ～好 *extremely good; best* | 人民的事业～伟大了。*The cause of the people is really great.* [太古] 最古的时代 remote antiquity [太平] 平安无事 peaceful and tranquil ❸对大两辈的尊长的称呼所加的字 great-; grand-: ～老伯 *granduncle* ❹高，大 highest; greatest: ～空 *outer space* | ～学 *Imperial College — the highest institution of learning in ancient China, situated in the capital city* [太阳] **1** 银河系的恒星之一，是太阳系的中心天体 sun **2** 人头上眉梢后低凹的部分。也叫"太阳穴"（also called 太阳穴）temple ❺（外 **loanword**）法定计量单位中十进倍数单位词头之一，表示 10^{12}（符号 T）tera-(T)

汰 tài ㄊㄞˋ 淘汰，除去没有用的成分 to discard; to eliminate; to remove: 优胜劣～ *survival of the fittest*

态（態） tài ㄊㄞˋ 形状，样子 form; appearance (㊀ **doublet** 形 — form; shape; morphology | 状 — state; situation; condition | 姿 — posture; carriage; attitude): 丑～ *ugly (or ludicrous) performance; buffoonery* | 变～ *deformation; anomaly* ㊁**extension** 情况 state of affairs; situation: 事～扩大。*The situation becomes more serious.* [态度] **1** 指人的举止动作 manner; bearing; demeanour: ～～大方 *to have an easy manner; to be natural and poised* **2** 对于事情采取的立场或看法 attitude; approach; position: ～～鲜明 *clear-cut stand* | 表明～～ *to make one's attitude clear*

肽 tài ㄊㄞˋ 一种有机化合物，由氨基酸脱水而成，含有羧基和氨基，是一种两性化合物。旧称"胜"(shēng)（former term for 胜）peptide

钛 tài ㄊㄞˋ 一种金属元素，符号 Ti，银灰色，质硬而轻，熔点高。钛合金强度高且耐腐蚀，可用于飞机工业和航海工业 titanium (Ti)

酞 tài ㄊㄞˋ 有机化合物的一类，是由一个分子的邻苯二酸酐与两个分子的酚经缩合作用而生成的产物。酚酞就属于酞类 phthalein

泰 tài ㄊㄞˋ ❶平安，安定 safe, stable and peaceful: 国～民丰。*The country enjoys prosperity and the people live in peace.* | ～然处之 *to take sth calmly; to bear sth with equanimity; to act with composure*

T

❷极 most; extreme:～西(旧指欧洲 *formerly used to denote Europe*) *the West*; *the Occident*
[泰山]五岳中的东岳,在山东省中部 Taishan Mountain, the East Sacred Mountain, situated in the middle of Shandong Province [转] ***transfer*** 称岳父 wife's father; father-in-law

TAN ㄊㄢ

坍 tān ㄊㄢ 崖岸、建筑物或堆起的东西倒塌,从基部崩坏 to collapse; to fall in; to tumble ([连] ***doublet*** 一塌 to collapse; to fall in; to tumble):墙～了。*The wall collapsed.*

贪 tān ㄊㄢ ❶贪图,求多,不知足 to have an insatiable desire for; to be greedy for; to covet:～玩 *to be crazy about play*; *to be excessively fond of play* | ～便(pián)宜 *to be keen on getting things on the cheap*; *to covet small advantages* | ～得无厌 *inordinately greedy*; *insatiably avaricious* ❷爱财 to covet; to practise graft; to embezzle:～财 *to be greedy for money*; *to covet wealth* | ～墨 *corruption*; *graft*; *embezzlement* [贪污]利用职权非法地取得财物 to embezzle; to practise graft; to defalcate

怹 tān ㄊㄢ 〈方 ***dialect***〉"他"的敬称 respectful term of address for 他

啴(嘽) ㊀tān ㄊㄢ [啴啴]形容牲畜喘息的样子(of draught animals) panting; gasping for breath

㊁ chǎn 见75页 see p75

摊(攤) tān ㄊㄢ ❶摆开,展开 to spread out; to unfold; to unroll:～场(cháng)(把庄稼晾在场上) *to spread harvested grain on a threshing ground*; *to ted grain* | 把问题～到桌上来 *to put the problems on the table (and thrash them out)* [引] ***extension*** 烹饪法,把糊状物放在锅上使成薄片 to fry batter in a thin layer:～鸡蛋 *to make an omelet* | ～煎饼 *to make a pancake* ❷(一子、一儿)摆在地上或用席、板摆设的售货处 vendor's stand; booth; stall:水果～儿 *fruit stall* (or *stand*) ❸量词 ***quantifier***,用于摊开的糊状物(used for paste or thick liquid, that is spread out):一～泥 *a mud puddle* ❹分担财物 to take a share in; to share; to apportion:～派 *to apportion*; *to share out* | 每人～五元。*Each person is required to contribute 5 yuan.* ❺遇到,碰上 to befall; to happen to:他一向爱躲清静,这件事偏偏让他～上了。*He has been seeking peacefulness, but it just happened to him.*

滩(灘) tān ㄊㄢ ❶河海边淤积成的平地或水中的沙洲 beach; sands:～地 *beach land*; *floodland*; *floodplain* ❷水浅多石而水流很急的地方 shoal:险～ *dangerous*

shoals
[滩簧]流行于江苏省南部、浙江省北部的一种说唱艺术 *tanhuang*, a form of storytelling in rhymes popular in southern Jiangsu Province and northern Zhejiang Province

瘫(癱) tān ㄊㄢ 瘫痪(huàn),神经机能发生障碍,肢体不能活动 paralysis; palsy

坛(❶❷壇、❸罈、❸*壜、❸*罎) tán ㄊㄢ ❶古代举行祭祀、誓师等大典用的土、石等筑的高台 altar:天~*Temple of Heaven*|先农~*Xiannong Temple* ㊀ ***extension*** 指文艺界、体育界或舆论阵地(of sports, literary, etc) circles; world; arena:文~*literary circles* (*or world, arena*)|乒~*table tennis circles*|论~*forum; tribune* ❷用土堆成的平台,多在上面种花 raised plot of land, usually for planting flowers, etc; terrace:花~*flower bed* ❸(一子)一种口小肚大的陶器 earthen jar; jug

昙(曇) tán ㄊㄢ 云彩密布,多云 cloudy; overcast
[昙花]灌木状常绿植物,小枝扁平,花大,白色,开的时间很短。后常用"昙花一现"比喻事物一出现很快就消失(昙花一现 to last as briefly as the broad-leaved epiphyllum — ephemeral) broad-leaved epiphyllum (*Epiphyllum oxypetalum*)

倓 tán ㄊㄢ 安然不疑。多用于人名(*tan*, usually used in a given name) calm; tranquil; peaceful

郯 tán ㄊㄢ [郯城]地名,在山东省 Tancheng, a place in Shandong Province

谈 tán ㄊㄢ ❶说,对话 to talk; to speak; to discuss:面~*to have a face-to-face talk; to discuss face-to-face; to speak* (*to sb*) *face-to-face*|请你来~一~。*I ask you to come here to have a talk.*|~天(闲谈) *to chat* ❷言论 speech; remark:无稽之~*unfounded statement; sheer nonsense*

锬 tán ㄊㄢ 长矛 lance; spear

痰 tán ㄊㄢ 气管或支气管黏膜分泌的黏液 phlegm; sputum

弹(彈) ㊀ tán ㄊㄢ ❶被其他手指压住的手指用力伸开 to flick; to flip:用手指~他一下 *to flick him with one's fingers*|把帽子上的土~下去 *to flick the dust off one's hat* ❷使弦振动 to play; to pluck:~弦子 *to play the* xianzi, *a three-stringed plucked musical instrument*|~琵琶 *to play the* pipa, *a plucked string instrument with a fretted fingerboard*|~棉花 *to fluff cotton* (*with a bow*) [弹词]曲艺的一种,流行于南方各省,有说有唱,用三弦、琵琶等伴奏 *tan-*

ci, a form of storytelling to the accompaniment of stringed plucked musical instruments, popular in southern provinces of China ❸利用一个物体的弹性把另一个物体放射出去 to shoot (with a catapult, etc); to catapult; to send forth: ～射 *to shoot off; to launch; to eject* [弹性] 物体因受外力暂变形状,外力一去即恢复原状的性质 elasticity ㊀ ***extension*** 事物的伸缩性 flexibility ❹指检举违法失职的官吏 to impeach (㊈ ***doublet*** 一劾 to impeach)

㊁ dàn 见 128 页 see p128

覃 ㊀ tán ㄊㄢˊ ❶深 deep: ～思 *deep in thought* ❷延伸 to extend; to spread on: 葛之～兮。*The kudzu vine is very long*. ❸姓 Tan, a surname

㊁ qín 见 607 页 see p607

谭 tán ㄊㄢˊ ❶同"谈"same as 谈 ❷姓 Tan, a surname

潭 tán ㄊㄢˊ 深水池,深水坑 deep pool; pond: 清～*limpid pool* | 泥～*mire; morass; quagmire* ㊀ ***extension*** 深 deep: ～渊 *deep pool; abyss*

嘾 tán ㄊㄢˊ 〈方 ***dialect***〉坑,水塘。多用于地名(*tan*, usually used in a place name) pit; pool

澹 ㊁ tán ㄊㄢˊ [澹台](－tái)复姓 Tantai, a two-character surname

㊀ dàn 见 129 页 see p129

檀 tán ㄊㄢˊ 植物名 name of plants **1** 檀香,常绿乔木,产在热带及亚热带。木材坚硬,有香气,可制器物及香料,又可入药(white) sandalwood (*Santalum album*) **2** 紫檀,常绿乔木,产在热带及亚热带。木质坚硬,可做器具 padauk; red sandalwood; rosewood (*Pterocarpus indicus*) **3** 黄檀,落叶乔木,果实豆荚状,木质坚硬 yellow sandalwood **4** 青檀,落叶乔木,果实有翅,木质坚硬 wingceltis (*Pteroceltis tatarinowii*)

忐 tǎn ㄊㄢˇ [忐忑](－tè)心神不定 mentally disturbed; perturbed; fidgety: ～～不安 *uneasy; restless; fidgety*

坦 tǎn ㄊㄢˇ ❶平坦,宽而平 smooth; flat; broad and level: ～途 *smooth road; level road* ❷心地平静 calm; composed; collected: ～然 *unperturbed; to have no misgivings; composed* [坦白] **1** 直爽,没有私隐 frank; straightforward; candid: 襟怀～～ *frank; straightforward; candid* **2** 如实地说出(自己的错误或罪行) to confess; to own up

钽 tǎn ㄊㄢˇ 一种金属元素,符号 Ta,钢灰色,可用于航天工业及核工业,还可以做电解电容。碳化钽熔点高,极坚硬,可制切削刀具 tantalum (Ta)

袒 tǎn ㄊㄢˇ ❶脱去上衣,露出身体的一部分 to be stripped to the waist; to leave (the upper part of the body) uncovered; to bare: ～胸露臂

to bare one's neck and shoulders; to be décolleté ❷袒护,不公正地维护一方面 to give unfair preference to; to be partial to:左~*to be partial to*|偏~*to give unprincipled protection to; to be partial to; to have a bias in favour of*

菼 tǎn ㄊㄢˇ 古书上指荻(in ancient Chinese texts) amur silver grass (*Miscanthus sacchariflorus*)

毯 tǎn ㄊㄢˇ (一子)厚实有毛绒的织品 blanket; rug; carpet:地~*carpet; rug*|毛~*woolen blanket*

黮 tǎn ㄊㄢˇ 深黑色 jet-black; pitch-black

叹(嘆、*歎) tàn ㄊㄢˋ ❶吟咏 to recite with a cadence; to chant; to intone:一唱三~*When one sings, three others intone.* —(*of poems and articles*) *beautiful and emotionally appealing* ❷因忧闷悲痛而呼出长气 sigh:~了一口气 *to heave a sigh*|仰天长~*to look up to heaven and sigh heavily* ❸因高兴而发出长声 to exclaim in admiration; to acclaim:欢喜赞~*delighted and gasping in admiration*|~为观止 *to acclaim sth as the acme of perfection; to acclaim sth to be the best* [叹词]表示喜、怒、哀、乐各种情感以及应答、招呼的词,如"嗯、喂、哎呀"等 interjection; exclamation

炭 tàn ㄊㄢˋ ❶木炭,把木材和空气隔绝,加高热烧成的一种黑色燃料。燃烧时无烟 charcoal ❷像炭的东西 charcoal-like thing:山楂~*hawthorn charcoal* ❸煤炭,石炭,煤 coal:阳泉大~*Yangquan coal*

碳 tàn ㄊㄢˋ 一种非金属元素,符号C,无臭无味的固体。无定形碳有焦炭、木炭等,晶体碳有金刚石和石墨。碳是构成有机物的主要成分。炼铁需要焦炭。在工业上和医药上,碳和它的化合物用途极广 carbon (C) [碳水化合物]有机化学中,分子式可以用$C_m(H_2O)_n$表示的一类化合物,像糖类和淀粉等都是。旧称"醣"(former term for 醣) carbohydrate

探 tàn ㄊㄢˋ ❶寻求,探索 to seek; to explore:~源 *to trace to the source; to get to the root of the matter* ❷探测 to explore; to probe; to prospect:~矿 *to conduct a mineral exploration; to go prospecting (for)* ❸侦察,暗中考察 to scout; to spy on; to pry into:~案子 *to investigate a case*|~听消息 *to try to find out about the situation; to inquire about sb* (or *sth*); *to fish for information* ❹试探 to try to find out; to sound out:先~一~口气 *to sound out sb's attitude first* ❺做侦察工作的人 scout; detective; spy:密~*secret agent; spy* ❻探望,访问 to visit; to call on:~亲 *to go home to visit one's family; to go to*

T

visit one's relatives | ～视病人 *to visit a patient* ❼(头或上体)伸出 to stretch forward; to crane: ～出头来 *to crane one's neck; to pop one's head* | 车行时不要～身车外。*Don't lean out of the window while the bus is moving.*

TANG 去尢

汤(湯) ㊀ tāng 去尢 ❶热水 hot water; boiling water: 赴～蹈火 *to go through fire and water — to defy all difficulties and dangers* ❷煮东西的汁液 water in which sth has been boiled: 米～ *rice soup* | ～药 *decoction of medicinal ingredients* ❸烹调后汁特别多的副食 soup; broth: 白菜～ *Chinese cabbage soup* ❹姓 Tang, a surname

㊁shāng 见 656 页 see p656

铴(鐋) tāng 去尢 铴锣,小铜锣 small brass gong

耥 tāng 去尢 tǎng 去尢ˇ(又 *also* tǎng)用耥耙弄平田地、清除杂草 to weed and level the soil (in a paddy field) with a harrow [耥耙](—bà)清除杂草、弄平田地的农具 paddy-field harrow

趟(*蹚、*踼) ㊀ tāng 去尢 ❶从有水、草的地方走过去 to walk through water (*or* grasses); to wade; to ford: 他～着水过去了。*He waded across the river.* ❷用犁、锄等把土翻开,把草锄去 to turn the soil and dig up weeds with a plough, a hoe, etc: ～地 *to turn the soil and weed; to plough the fields*

㊁ tàng 见 733 页 see p733

嘡 tāng 去尢 拟声词 ***onomatopoeia***, clang; to clang: ～的一声,锣响了。*The gong sounded with a clang.*

镗 ㊀ tāng 去尢 拟声词 ***onomatopoeia***,钟鼓或敲锣的声音(of a drum, a gong, etc) clang

㊁ táng 见 732 页 see p732

羰 tāng 去尢 羰基,有机化合物中含碳和氧的基(=CO)。旧称"碳氧基"(formerly called 碳氧基) carbonyl

唐 táng 去尢ˊ ❶夸大,虚夸 exaggerative; boastful; bombastic: 荒～之言 *absurd words; fantastic words* | ～大无验 *sheer bragging; braggadocio* ❷空,徒然 for nothing; in vain: ～捐(白费) *to come to nothing; to be in vain* ❸朝代名 name of a dynasty **1** 唐高祖李渊所建立(公元 618—907 年) the Tang Dynasty (618—907), established by Li Yuan **2** 五代之一,李存勖所建立(公元 923—936 年),史称后唐 Later Tang Dynasty(923—936), one of the five dynasties, founded by Li Cunxu

[唐突] 冲撞,冒犯 to offend; to blaspheme; to profane

鄌 táng 去尢ˊ [鄌郚](—wú)地名,在山东省昌乐 Tang-wu, a place in Changle, Shandong Province

塘 táng ㄊㄤˊ ❶堤岸,堤防 dyke; embankment:河～ *river embankment* | 海～*seawall* ❷水池 pond; pool (㊀ ***doublet*** 池— pool; pond):荷～ *lotus pond* | 苇～*reed pond* ❸浴池 bathing pool:洗澡～ *bath-house*; *public baths*; *public bathing house*

搪 táng ㄊㄤˊ ❶挡,抵拒 to ward off; to fend off; to keep out:～饥 *to stave off hunger* ❷支吾 to prevaricate; to evade; to shirk:～差事(敷衍了事) *to do one's work perfunctorily*; *to perform one's duty perfunctorily*; *to dillydally on one's work* [搪塞](—sè)敷衍塞(sè)责 to prevaricate; to do sth perfunctorily:做事情要认真,不要～～。*Be serious in doing things. Don't be perfunctory.* ❸用泥土或涂料抹上或涂上 to spread (clay, paint, etc) over; to daub; to plaster:～炉子 *to line a stove with clay* [搪瓷]用石英、长石等制成的一种像釉子的物质涂在金属器物上,经过烧制形成的薄层,可防锈又可作装饰 enamel ❹加工切削机器零件的钻孔 boring:～床 *boring machine*; *boring lathe*; *borer*

溏 táng ㄊㄤˊ 泥浆 mud; slurry ㊀ ***extension*** 不凝结半流动的 half congealed; semi-fluid; viscous:～心鸡蛋 *soft-boiled egg*; *soft-fried egg*

瑭 táng ㄊㄤˊ 古书上指一种玉 (in ancient Chinese texts) a kind of jade

螗 táng ㄊㄤˊ 古书上指蝉(in ancient Chinese texts) a kind of cicada

糖(❷**醣) táng ㄊㄤˊ ❶从甘蔗、甜菜、米、麦等提制出来的甜的东西 sugar ❷碳水化合物 carbohydrate

赯 táng ㄊㄤˊ 赤色(指人的脸)(of one's complexion) red:紫～脸 *dark red cheeks*; *purple brown face* (or *complexion*); *cheeks with a deep tan*

堂 táng ㄊㄤˊ ❶正房,高大的屋子 main room of a house; tall and big house:～屋(*of a one-storey Chinese traditional house consisting of several rooms in a row*) *central room*; (*in a courtyard, usually facing south*) *principal rooms* | 礼～ *auditorium*; *assembly hall* [令堂]对对方母亲的尊称(respectful term of address for the other's mother) your mother ❷专供某种用途的房屋 room (*or* hall) for special purpose:课～ *classroom*; *schoolroom* ❸过去官吏审案办事的地方 courtroom in *yamen*; court of justice (*or* law):大～ *courtroom in a* yamen *in ancient China*; *magistrate's courtroom* | 过～(*in ancient China*) *to stand trial in a court* ❹表示同

祖父的亲属关系(used to denote the relationship between cousins, etc) with the same paternal grandfather or great-grandfather:～兄弟 *male cousins on the paternal side*|～姐妹 *female cousins on the paternal side*

[堂皇] 盛大,大方 grand; stately:冠冕～～ *high-sounding; high-toned*|富丽～～ *beautiful and imposing; magnificent; sumptuous*

[堂堂]仪容端正,有威严 dignified; imposing; impressive:相貌～～ *to have a dignified appearance; to have a majestic bearing*

棠 táng ㄊㄤˊ 植物名 name of plants **1** 棠梨树,就是"杜树"(i. e. 杜树) birchleaf pear (*Pyrus betulaefolia*) **2** 海棠树,落叶小乔木,春天开花。果实叫海棠,可以吃 Chinese flowering crabapple; cherry-apple tree (*Malus spectabilis*)

樘 táng ㄊㄤˊ ❶门框或窗框 frame (of a door or window):门～ *door frame*|窗～ *window frame* ❷量词 ***quantifier***,用于一套门(窗)框和门(窗)扇(used of doors or windows with their frames):一～玻璃门 *a pair of glass doors*

膛 táng ㄊㄤˊ ❶体腔 chest; thorax:胸～ *chest*|开～ *to open the chest* ❷(一儿)器物中空的部分 enclosed space inside sth; chamber; cavity:炉～ *chamber of a stove*|枪～ *bore of a gun; chamber*

镗 ㊁ táng ㄊㄤˊ 同"搪❹" same as 搪❹

㊀ tāng 见 730 页 see p730

螳 táng ㄊㄤˊ 螳螂 mantis:～臂当(dāng)车(喻做事不自量力必然失败) *mantis raising its forelegs to try to stop a chariot — to overrate oneself and try to hold back an overwhelming superior force* [螳螂]俗叫"刀螂"。一种食虫性昆虫,前脚很发达,好像镰刀,头为三角形,触角呈丝状(popularly called 刀螂) mantis; mantid (*Mantodea*)

帑 tǎng ㄊㄤˇ 古时指收藏钱财的府库和府库里的钱财(in ancient China) state treasury; funds in the state treasury

〈古 ***archaism***〉又同"孥"(nú) also same as 孥

倘(**儻) ㊀ tǎng ㄊㄤˇ 连词 ***conjunction***,假使,如果 if; supposing; in case:～若 *if; supposing; in case*|～能努力,定可成功。*If you work hard, you are bound to succeed.*

㊁ cháng 见 77 页 see p77

淌 tǎng ㄊㄤˇ 流 to drip; to trickle; to shed:～眼泪 *to shed tears*|汗珠直往下～。*Sweat was dripping from his face.*

惝 tǎng ㄊㄤˇ chǎng ㄔㄤˇ (又 *also* chǎng) 失意 disappointed; frustrated

耥 tǎng ㄊㄤˇ (又 *also* tāng) 见 730 页 tāng see p730

躺 tǎng ㄊㄤˇ 身体横倒，也指车辆、器具等倒在地上 to place oneself at rest in a flat, horizontal (*or* recumbent) position; to recline; (of vehicle, object, etc) to lie flat on the ground: ～在床上 *to lie in bed* | 一棵大树～在路上。*A tall tree lies on the road.*

傥(儻) tǎng ㄊㄤˇ ❶同"倘㊀" same as 倘㊀ ❷见742页"倜"字条"倜傥"(tì—) see 倜傥 on p742

镋(钂) tǎng ㄊㄤˇ 古代一种兵器，跟叉相似 *tang*, a fork-like weapon in ancient China

烫(燙) tàng ㄊㄤˋ ❶温度高，皮肤接触温度高的物体感觉疼痛 to scald; to burn: 开水很～。*The boiling water is extremely hot.* | ～手 *to scald* (or *burn*) *the hand* | 小心～着！*Be careful not to get yourself scalded.* ❷用热的物体使另外的物体起变化 to heat up; to warm; to iron: ～酒(使热) *to heat wine* | ～衣服(使平) *to iron clothes; to press clothes* ❸烫头发 to get a permanent wave; to perm; to have one's hair permed: 电～ *to have one's hair permed with electric hair rollers*

趟 ㊁ tàng ㄊㄤˋ 量词 ***quantifier*** **1** 来往的次数(used for a trip) time: 他来了一～。*He has been here once.* | 这～火车去上海。*This train is bound for Shanghai.* **2** (一儿)用于成行的东西(used for sth in a row or rows): 屋里摆着两～桌子。*Two rows of tables stand in the room.* | 用线把这件衣服缝上一～。*Sew a line of stitches in the dress.*

㊀ tāng 见730页 see p730

TAO ㄊㄠ

叨 ㊀ tāo ㄊㄠ 承受 to be favoured with; to get the benefit of; to receive: ～光 *to be much obliged to you* | ～教(jiào) *to have the benefit of your instruction; to thank you for your advice* [叨扰]谢人款待的话 Thank you for your hospitality.

㊁ dāo 见132页 see p132

涛(濤) tāo ㄊㄠ 大波浪 great waves; billows (㊟ ***doublet*** 波— great waves; billows)

焘(燾) tāo ㄊㄠ (又 *also* dào)见134页 dào，多用于人名(tao, usually used in a given name) see dào on p134

绦(縧、*絛、*縚) tāo ㄊㄠ (一子)用丝线编织成的花边或扁平的带子，可以装饰衣物 silk ribbon; silk braid [绦虫] 寄生在人或家畜、家禽、鱼等动物体内的虫子，身体长而扁，像绦子，由节片组成 tapeworm (*Taenia*)

掏(*搯) tāo ㄊㄠ ❶挖 to dig (a hole, etc); to hollow out: 在墙上～一个洞

to make a hole in the wall ❷伸进去取 to take out; to draw out; to pull out:把口袋里的钱～出来 *to take money out of one's pocket* | ～麻雀 *to take the young sparrow out of its nest*

滔 tāo ㄊㄠ 漫,充满 inundant; flooding:波浪～天 (*with*) *waves billowing* | 罪恶～天 *monstrous crimes* [滔滔] **1** 大水漫流 torrential; surging:海水～～ *seawater surging* **2** 连续不断 constant; continuous:～～不绝 *to speak unceasingly; to pour out words in a steady flow* | 议论～～ *comments tumbling out in a flood*

韬(韜、**弢) tāo ㄊㄠ ❶弓或剑的套子 sheath; bow case [韬略]指六韬、三略,古代的兵书 (used to denote two ancient Chinese books on the art of war) *Six Strategies and Three Tactics* [转] ***transfer*** 战斗用兵的计谋 military strategy ❷隐藏,隐蔽(多指才能) (usually used to denote one's talent) to hide; to conceal:～晦 *to conceal one's true features or intentions; to refrain from revealing one's ambitions and put others off the track*

饕 tāo ㄊㄠ [饕餮](—tiè)古代传说中的一种凶恶的兽,古代铜器上多刻它的头部形状作装饰 *taotie*, a legendary ferocious animal, the image of whose head was often engraved on brass utensils as ornaments in ancient China [喻] ***figurative*** **1** 凶恶的人 ferocious person **2** 贪吃的人 voracious eater; glutton; gourmand

逃(**迯) táo ㄊㄠˊ ❶逃跑,逃走 to run away; to escape; to flee:追歼～敌 *to pursue and wipe out the fleeing enemy* ❷逃避,避开 to dodge; to evade; to escape:～荒 *to flee from famine; to get away from a famine-stricken area* | ～难 *to flee from a calamity; to seek refuge* (or *safety*) *in flight*

洮 táo ㄊㄠˊ 洮河,水名,在甘肃省南部 Taohe River in the south of Gansu Province

桃 táo ㄊㄠˊ ❶桃树,落叶乔木,春天开花,白色或红色,果实叫桃子或桃ㄦ,可以吃 peach (*Prunus persica*) ❷(—ㄦ)形状像桃子的东西 sth resembling a peach:棉～ㄦ *cotton boll* ❸核桃 walnut:～仁 *walnut kernel* | ～酥 *walnut shortbread*

桃 táo ㄊㄠˊ [桃黍]〈方 ***dialect***〉高粱 sorghum (*Sorghum bicolor*)

陶 ㊀ táo ㄊㄠˊ ❶用黏土烧制的器物 pottery; earthenware [陶土]烧制陶器的黏土 potter's clay; pottery clay; kaolin ❷制造陶器 to make pottery; to mould:～铸(*of potters and blacksmiths*) *to mould and form* (*utensils*); *to cast* | ～冶(制陶器和炼金属,喻造就良好的品格、情操等) *to make*

pottery and smelt metal — to shape (or *mould*) *a person's character*, *etc* ❸陶然,快乐的样子 contented; happy; joyful: ～醉 *to be intoxicated* (*with success, happiness, etc*); *to revel in* ❹姓 Tao, a surname

㊁ yáo 见 874 页 see p874

萄 táo ㄊㄠˊ 指葡萄 grape: ～糖 *grape sugar; glucose*

啕(**咷) táo ㄊㄠˊ 见 267 页"号"字条"号啕"(háo—) see 号啕 on p267

淘 táo ㄊㄠˊ ❶洗去杂质 to wash in a pan (or basket) to get rid of gravel, sand, etc: ～米 *to wash rice* | ～金 *to wash for gold; to pan for gold* [淘汰]去坏的留好的,去不合适的留合适的 to eliminate (sb) through election (*or* competition); knock out (*or* off): 自然～～ *natural selection* ❷消除泥沙、渣滓等,挖浚 to clean out; to dredge: ～井 *to dredge a well* | ～缸 *to clean a vat* ❸淘气,顽皮 mischievous; naughty: 这孩子真～。*The boy is really naughty.*

绹 táo ㄊㄠˊ ❶绳索 rope ❷〈方 ***dialect***〉用绳索捆 to bind with a rope

醄 táo ㄊㄠˊ 见 489 页"酕"字条"酕醄"(máo—) see 酕醄 on p489

梼(檮) táo ㄊㄠˊ [梼杌](—wù) **1** 古代传说中的恶兽,恶人(in ancient China) legendary fierce beast; ferocious person **2** 春秋时楚史名 name for the history of the Chu State in the Spring and Autumn Period

鼗 táo ㄊㄠˊ 长柄的摇鼓,俗叫"拨浪鼓"(popularly called 拨浪鼓) drum-shaped rattle; rattle drum

讨 tǎo ㄊㄠˇ ❶查究,处治 to investigate and ascertain; to punish; to penalize ㊕ ***transfer*** 征伐,发动攻击 to go on a punitive expedition against; to launch an attack on; to send armed forces to suppress: 南征北～ *to fight south and north* [声讨]宣布罪行而加以抨击 to denounce; to condemn ❷研究,推求 to study; to discuss: 仔细研～ *to deliberate, to study and discuss seriously* [讨论]就某一问题交换意见或进行辩论 to discuss; to talk over ❸索取 to ask for; to demand: ～债 *to demand payment of a debt; to ask for payment of a debt* ❹求,请求 to beg for; to ask for: ～饶 *to beg for mercy; to ask for forgiveness* | ～教(jiào) *to ask for advice* ❺招惹 to incur; to court; to invite: ～厌 *disagreeable; disgusting; repugnant* | ～人欢喜 *likable; cute*

䅦 tǎo ㄊㄠˇ [䅦黍]〈方 ***dialect***〉高粱 sorghum

套 tào ㄊㄠˋ ❶(—子、—儿)罩在外面的东西 cover; sheath; case: 褥～ *mattress cover; bed tick* | 外～儿 *overcoat* | 手

T

～儿 *gloves* | 书～*slipcover for a book* [河套]地域名，被黄河三面环绕，在内蒙古自治区和宁夏回族自治区境内 Hetao, a region at the Great Bend of the Huanghe River across the Inner Mongolia and Ningxia autonomous regions ❷加罩 to cover with; to slip over; to encase in:～鞋 *overshoes; rubbers; galoshes* | ～上一件毛背心 *to put on a woollen vest; to slip on a woolen vest* ❸(～子、～儿)装在衣物里的棉絮 cotton padding (*or* wadding); batting:被～*cotton padding of a quilt* | 袄～*padded lining of a jacket of traditional Chinese style* | 棉花～子 *cotton wadding* ❹量词 ***quantifier***，同类事物合成的一组(used for series or sets of things) set; suit; suite: 一～制服 *a uniform suit* | 一～茶具 *a tea set* ❺模拟，照做 to model on; to copy; to imitate: 这是从那篇文章上～下来的。*This is copied from another article.* or *This was written in imitation of another article.* or *This is modelled on that piece of writing.* [套语] **1** 客套话，如"劳驾、借光、慢走、留步"等 polite formulas **2** 行文、说话中的一些不解决实际问题的俗套子 stereotyped expressions ❻(～儿)用绳子等做成的环 knot; loop; noose: 双～结 *double knot* | 用绳子做个活～儿 *to make a slip knot with a rope* | 牲口～*harness for a draught animal* | 大车～*cart harness* [圈套]陷害人的诡计 snare; trap; ploy:他不小心，上了～～。*He fell into a trap because of his carelessness.* | 那是敌人的～～。*That's the enemy's ploy.* ❼用套拴系 to hitch up (a draught animal to a cart); to harness (a draught animal):～车(把车上的套拴在牲口身上) *to harness a draught animal to a cart* ㊀ ***extension*** 用计骗取 to coax a secret out of sb; to pump sb about sth; to sound out:用话～他 *to coax the secret out of him* | ～出他的话来 *to trick him into telling the truth* ❽互相衔接或重叠 to overlap; to interlink; to interlock:～耕 *to make deep furrows by tilling the soil with two ploughs, one following the other* | ～种 *to interplant* ❾拉拢，表示亲近 to try to win (sb's friendship, flavour, etc):～交情 *to try to get in good relationship with sb; to try to establish friendship with sb* | ～近乎 *to try to form ties with sb; to cotton up to*

TE ㄊㄜ

忑 tè ㄊㄜ 见728页"忐"字条"忐忑"(tǎn—) see 忐忑 on p728

忒 ㊀ tè ㄊㄜ 差错 mistake; error: 差～*error; blunder*
㊁ tuī 见 764 页 see p764

铽 tè ㄊㄜˋ 一种金属元素，符号 Tb，银灰色。可用于制荧光物质及元件 terbium (Tb)

特 tè ㄊㄜˋ ❶特殊，不平常的，超出一般的 special; unusual; extraordinary: ～色 *distinctive feature; distinctive quality; characteristic* | ～效 *specially good effect; special efficacy* | ～产 *special* (or *unique*) *local product; speciality* [特别] **1** 特殊，与众不同 special; uncommon; distinctive: 样式很～～。*This fashion is very distinctive.* **2** 副词 ***adverb***，尤其 especially; particularly; extraordinarily: ～～聪明 *extraordinarily clever; very clever* | ～～是数学学得好 *to be especially good at mathematics* [特务] **1** 军队中指担任警卫、通讯、运输等特殊任务的 special task (*or* duties): ～～连 *special task company* **2** (—wu) 经过特殊训练，从事刺探情报、颠覆、破坏等活动的人 special (*or* secret) agent; spy ❷专，单一 for a special purpose; specially: ～为 *for a special purpose; specially* | ～设 *ad hoc* | 我～意来看你。*I specially come to see you.* ❸只，但 only, but: 不～此也。*This is not the only case.*

慝 tè ㄊㄜˋ 奸邪，罪恶 evil; wickedness; viciousness: 隐～(别人不知道的罪恶) *to conceal vice* (or *evil*)

膩 te ·ㄊㄜ (又) 见 421 页"肋"字条"肋膩"(lēde) see 肋膩 on p421

TENG ㄊㄥ

熥 tēng ㄊㄥ 把熟的食物蒸热 to heat up by steaming (*or* baking): ～馒头 *to heat mantou*

鼟 tēng ㄊㄥ 拟声词 ***onomatopoeia***，敲鼓声 rolls of drums; rub-a-dub

疼 téng ㄊㄥˊ ❶人、动物因病、刺激或创伤而引起的难受的感觉 to ache; to hurt; to be in pain (㊀ ***doublet*** —痛 to ache; to hurt; to be in pain): 肚子～ *to have a stomachache* | 腿摔～了。*My leg hurts from the fall.* ❷喜爱，爱惜 to love dearly; to be fond of; to dote on: 他奶奶最～他。*His granny dotes on him.*

腾 téng ㄊㄥˊ ❶奔跑，跳跃 to gallop; to jump; to prance (㊀ ***doublet*** 奔— to gallop; to surge forward): 万马奔～ *ten thousand horses galloping ahead — all going full steam ahead* | 万众欢～ *Millions of people rejoice.* ❷上升 to rise; to soar: ～空 *to rise high into the air; to rise to the sky; to soar* | ～云驾雾 *to mount the clouds and ride the mist — to speed across the sky; to feel giddy* (or *dizzy*) [腾腾] 形容气势旺盛 steaming; seething: 雾气～～ *hazy with mist; mist-laden* | 热气～～ *steaming hot; piping hot* ❸空出来，挪移 to make room; to vacate: ～出两间房来 *to vacate two rooms* | ～不出空来 *cannot set aside time* ❹(teng)词尾(在动词后,表示动作的反复连续)(used after a verb to express repetition or continuity of an action) suffix: 倒～ *to do sth over and over again* | 翻～ *to turn sth over and over* | 折(zhē)～ *to turn from side to side; to cause physical* (or *mental*) *suffering* | 闹～ *clamorous; noisy*

誊(謄) téng ㄊㄥˊ 照原稿抄写 to transcribe; to copy out: ～清 *to make a fair* (or *clean*) *copy of* | 这稿子太乱,要～一遍。*This draft is too messy. It must be recopied.*

滕 téng ㄊㄥˊ 周代诸侯国名,在今山东省滕州 Teng, a princedom of the Zhou Dynasty, in today's Tengzhou, Shandong Province

螣 téng ㄊㄥˊ 螣蛇,古书上说的一种能飞的蛇(in ancient Chinese texts) a kind of snake that can fly

縢 téng ㄊㄥˊ ❶封闭,约束 to seal off; to restrain ❷绳子 rope

藤(*籐) téng ㄊㄥˊ ❶植物名 name of plants **1** 紫藤,藤本植物,花紫色。俗叫"藤萝"(popularly called 藤萝) Chinese wisteria (*Wisteria sinensis*) **2** 白藤,常绿木本植物。茎细长,柔软而坚韧,可以编篮、椅、箱等用具。俗叫"藤子"(popularly called 藤子) rattan (*Calameae*) **3** 藤黄,常绿乔木,果实圆形。树脂可做黄色颜料,但有毒,不能染食品 garcinia ❷蔓 vine: 葡萄～ *grape vine* | 顺～摸瓜 *to follow the vine to get the melon — to track sth* (or *sb*) *down by following clues*

䲢 téng ㄊㄥˊ 䲢鱼,鱼名。身体青灰色,有褐色网状斑纹,头大眼小,下颌突出,有一个或两个背鳍。常栖息在海底。可食 stargazer (*Uranoscopidae*)

TI ㄊㄧ

体(體) ㊁ tī ㄊㄧ [体己] [梯己](—ji) **1** 家庭成员个人积蓄的财物 private savings (of a family member) **2** 亲近的 close; intimate; confidential: ～～话 *words said in confidence*

㊀ tǐ 见741页 see p741

剔 tī ㄊㄧ ❶把肉从骨头上刮下来 to clean a bone with a pointed instrument; to pick meat from bones: ～骨肉 *meat with bones removed* | 把肉～得干干净净 *to pick the bones clean* ㊞ **extension** 从缝隙或孔洞里往外挑(tiǎo)拨东西 to pick (as from a crack or fissure): ～牙 *to pick one's teeth* | ～指甲 *to clean the fingernails; to pick dirt from one's fingernails* ❷把不好的挑(tiāo)出来 to pick out and throw away; to reject; to get rid of (㊂ *extension* —除 to pick out and throw away; to reject; to get rid of): 把有伤的果子～出去 *to pick out the scarred fruits* | ～庄(旧指挑出有缺点的货品廉价出卖)(*in former times*) *to pick out soiled* (*or substandard*) *goods and sell them at reduced prices*

踢 tī ㄊㄧ 用脚触击 to kick; to play: ～球 *to kick a ball*; *to play football* | ～毽子 *to kick the shuttlecock* | 一脚～开 *to kick away*

梯 tī ㄊㄧ ❶(一子)登高用的器具或设备 ladder; steps; stairs: 楼～ *staircase*; *stairs* | 软～ *rope ladder* ❷像梯子的 shaped like a ladder; terraced: ～形 *trapezium* [梯田]在山坡上开辟的一层一层的田地 terraced fields ❸作用跟梯子相似的设备 apparatus with the same function as stairs: 电～ *lift*; *elevator*; *escalator*

锑 tī ㄊㄧ 有机化合物,锑化氢的特称。有剧毒(special term for 锑化氢) stibine

锑 tī ㄊㄧ 一种金属元素,符号 Sb,银白色,有光泽,质硬而脆。锑、铅和锡的合金可制印刷用的铅字。锑化铟是一种重要的半导体材料 stibium (Sb)

鹈 tī ㄊㄧ 见 564 页"䴙"字条"䴙䴘"(pì—) see 䴙䴘 on p564

荑 ㊀ tí ㄊㄧˊ ❶草木初生的叶芽 (of grass) sprout; shoot ❷稗子一类的草 tare

㊁ yí 见 884 页 see p884

绨 ㊀ tí ㄊㄧˊ 光滑厚实的丝织品 thick silk fabrics

㊁ tì 见 742 页 see p742

鹈 tí ㄊㄧˊ [鹈鹕](—hú)水鸟名,俗叫"淘河"或"塘鹅"。体大嘴长,嘴下有皮囊可以伸缩,捕食鱼类(popularly called 淘河 or 塘鹅) pelican (*Pelecanidae*)

提 ㊀ tí ㄊㄧˊ ❶垂手拿着(有环、柄或绳套的东西) to carry in one's hand with the arm down: ～着一壶水 *to carry a kettle of water in one's hand* | ～着一个篮子 *to carry a basket in one's hand* | ～心吊胆(喻害怕) *to have one's heart in one's mouth* — *to be in constant fear* | ～纲挈(qiè)领(喻扼要) *to grasp a net by the head rope* (*or to grasp a coat by the collar*) — *to concentrate on the main points* ❷使事物由低往高、由后往前移动 to lift; to advance: ～升 *to hoist*; *to elevate*; *to promote* | ～高 *to raise*; *to heighten*; *to improve* | ～前 *to shift to an earlier date*; *to move up* (*a date*); *to advance* | ～早 *to shift to an earlier time*; *to be earlier than planned* (*or expected*); *to do sth in advance* ❸舀取油、酒等液体的工具 dipper; ladle: 油～ *oil dipper* | 醋～ *vinegar dipper* ❹说

T

起,举出 to mention; to bring up; to put forward:经他一～,大家都想起来了。*Everyone remembered it as soon as he mentioned the matter.*|～意见 *to raise one's opinion; to offer a suggestion*|～供材料 *to provide materials* [提倡]说明某种事物的优点,鼓励大家使用或实行 to advocate; to promote; to encourage:要～～顾全大局 *to encourage the spirit of taking the interests of the whole into account* [提醒]从旁促使别人注意或指点别人 to call attention to; to remind; to alert:幸亏你～～,不然我就忘了。*But for your reminding, I would have forgotten it.* [提议]说出意见,供人讨论或采纳 to propose; to suggest; to move ❺取出 to draw; to withdraw; to extract (㊟ ***doublet*** —取 to draw; to pick up; to extract):把款～出来 *to draw* (or *withdraw*) *money from a bank*|～单(提取货物的凭单) *bill of lading* ❻汉字的一种笔形(㇀),即"挑"(tiǎo) rising stroke in Chinese character ❼姓 Ti, a surname

㊁ dī 见 139 页 see p139

騠 tí ㄊㄧˊ 见 374 页"駃"字条"駃騠"(jué—) see 駃騠 on p374

缇 tí ㄊㄧˊ 橘红色 orange red

题 tí ㄊㄧˊ ❶古指额头(in ancient Chinese) forehead:雕～*pattern engraved on the forehead* ❷题目,写作或讲演内容的总名目 subject; title; topic:命～*to set a question; to assign a topic* (or *subject*)|出～*to set an examination paper; to set a topic; to set a theme* (or *subject*)|难～(喻不容易做的事情) *difficult* (or *thorny*) *problem*|离～太远 *to stray far from the point* (or *subject*) ㊂ ***extension*** 练习或考试时要求解答的问题 question; problem:试～ *test* (or *examination*) *questions*|算～ *arithmetical questions; mathematical exercises; computational problems*|几何～*geometry questions*|问答～*essay questions* [题材]写作内容的主要材料 subject matter; theme ❸写上,签署 to write; to inscribe; to sign:～名 *to inscribe one's name; to autograph*|～字 *to write; to inscribe*|～词 *to write words of encouragement, appreciation or commemoration*

醍 tí ㄊㄧˊ [醍醐](—hú)精制的奶酪 finest cream

鳀 tí ㄊㄧˊ 鱼名。体长 10 厘米—13 厘米,银灰色,侧扁,腹部呈圆柱形,眼和口都大。生活在海中 anchovy (*Engraulidae*)

啼(*嗁) tí ㄊㄧˊ ❶哭,出声地哭 to weep aloud; to cry (㊟ ***doublet*** —哭 to cry; to wail):悲～ *to sob with grief; to cry sorrowfully*|

用不着哭哭～～。*There's no use keeping weeping and wailing.* ❷某些鸟兽叫(of certain birds and animals) to crow; to caw:鸡～。*Cocks crow.*|猿～。*Apes jabber.*

蹄(*蹏) tí ㄊㄧˊ (一子、一儿)马、牛、羊等生在趾端的角质保护物。又指有角质保护物的脚 hoof; foot of such animals with hoofs:马不停～。*The horse never stops running — is running without a moment's respite.*

体(體) ㊀ tǐ ㄊㄧˇ ❶人、动物的全身(of human or animal) body(㊣ ***doublet*** 身～ body):～重(*body*) *weight*|～温(身体的温度)(*body*) *temperature* ㊊ ***extension*** 身体的一部分 part of the body:四～ *limbs; arms and legs*|上～*upper part of the body*|肢～ *limbs; limbs and trunk* [体面](—mian) **1** 身份 dignity; prestige; face **2** 光彩,光荣 honourable; creditable **3** 好看 good-looking; handsome [体育]指锻炼身体增强体质的教育 physical culture; physical training; physical education:～～课 *physical education* (*PE*)|发展～～运动,增强人民体质 *to promote physical culture and build up people's health* ❷事物的本身或全部 thing per se; whole:物～ *object*|全～ *all; whole; entire*|个～ *individual*|～积 *volume* ❸形式,规格 style; form:字～ *form of written* (or *printed*) *character; style of calligraphy*|得～(合宜) *appropriate* ❹作品的体裁 genre; style; form:文～ *style of writing; literary form; genre*|骚～ Sao *style — poetry in the style of* Li Sao|骈～*ornate style of writing characterized by parallelism and rhythmical arrangement; parallel style*|

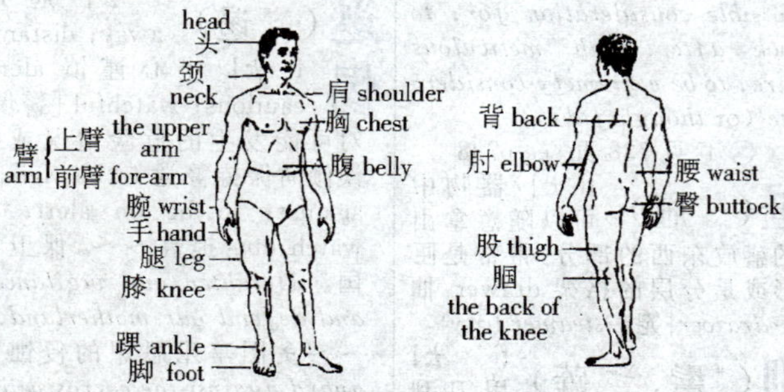

人 体
human body

古～*ancient style* (*of poetry*) —*a form of pre-Tang poetry, usually having four to seven characters per line* ❺亲身,设身处地 to do (*or* experience) sth personally; to put oneself in another's position: ～验 *to learn through personal experience; to learn through practice; to experience* | ～味 *to savour; to appreciate* | ～谅 *to show understanding and sympathy for; to make allowances; to give sympathetic consideration to* [体会]领会,个人的理解 to know (*or* learn) from experience; to understand; to realize: 我～～到你的意思。*I have realized what you mean.* | 对这个文件,我的～～还很肤浅。*My understanding of this document is very superficial.* [体贴]揣度别人的处境和心情,给予关心、照顾 to show consideration for; to give care to; to be considerate: ～～入微 *to show every possible consideration for; to look after with meticulous care; to be extremely considerate* (or *thoughtful*)

㊁ tī 见 738 页 see p738

屉(**屜) tì ㄊㄧˋ 器物中可以随意拿出的盛放东西的部分,常常是匣形或是分层的格架 drawer: 抽～*drawer* | 笼～*steamer tray*

剃(*鬀、△*薙) tì ㄊㄧˋ 用刀刮去毛发 to shave: ～头 *to have one's head shaved; to have one's hair cut; to have a hair-cut* | ～光 *to have one's head shaved clean — to score no points in a game*

涕 tì ㄊㄧˋ ❶眼泪 tears ❷鼻涕,鼻子里分泌的液体 mucus of the nose; snivel

悌 tì ㄊㄧˋ 指弟弟敬爱哥哥 love and respect for one's elder brother: 孝～*filial piety and fraternal love*

绨 ㊁ tì ㄊㄧˋ 比绸子厚实、粗糙的纺织品,用丝做经,棉线做纬 silk and cotton fabric

㊀ tí 见 739 页 see p739

俶 ㊁ tì ㄊㄧˋ [俶傥](—tǎng) 同"倜傥"same as 倜傥

㊀ chù 见 99 页 see p99

倜 tì ㄊㄧˋ [倜傥](—tǎng)洒脱,不拘束(of manner) free and easy; unrestrained; unconventional: 风流～～*unrestrained and overflowing with talent; unconventional and romantic*

逖(**逷) tì ㄊㄧˋ 远 far away; distant

惕 tì ㄊㄧˋ 小心谨慎 alert; cautious; watchful [警惕]对可能发生的危险情况或错误倾向保持警觉 to be vigilant against; to be on alert; to watch out: 提高～～,保卫祖国。*Heighten our vigilance, and defend our motherland.* | ～～贪图享乐思想的侵蚀 *to guard against the corrosive influence of the idea of seeking pleasure*

禢 ㊁ tì ㄊㄧˋ 婴儿的包被 swaddling clothes

㊀ xī 见 803 页 see p803

替 tì ㄊㄧˋ ❶代,代理 to take the place of; to replace; to substitute for ([连] ***doublet*** 一代 to take the place of; to replace; to substitute for | 代一 to take the place of; to replace; to supersede):～班 *to take sb else's place (in a work shift)* | 我～你洗衣服。*Let me do the washing for you.* ❷介词 ***preposition***,为(wèi),给 for:大家都～他高兴。*Everybody feels happy for him.* ❸衰废 declining; falling; waning:兴～*rising and falling (of dynasty)* | 隆～*rising and falling (of power); ups and downs*

殢(殢) tì ㄊㄧˋ ❶困倦 sleepy ❷滞留 to be held up; to be detained ❸困扰,纠缠 to be perplexed and pestered

薙 tì ㄊㄧˋ ❶除去野草 to remove weeds; to weed ❷同"剃"same as 剃

嚏 tì ㄊㄧˋ [嚏喷](—pen)因鼻黏膜受刺激而引起的一种猛烈带声的喷气现象。也叫"喷嚏"(pēn—)(also called 喷嚏) to sneeze

趯 tì ㄊㄧˋ ❶跳跃 to jump; to leap ❷汉字一种笔形(亅),今称"钩"(now called 钩) upward hook stroke in Chinese calligraphy

TIAN ㄊㄧㄢ

天 tiān ㄊㄧㄢ ❶在地面以上的高空 sky; heaven; firmament [喻] ***figurative*** **1** 在上的 overhead:～头(书页上部空白部分) *top* (or *upper*) *margin of a page* | ～桥(架在空中的高桥,桥下可以通行) *platform bridge; overpass; overhead walkway* **2** 最,极 most; extreme; best:～好,也只能是这样。*It is at best just like this.* [天文]日月星辰等天体在宇宙间分布、运行等现象 astronomy ❷自然的,天生的 natural; inborn; innate:～生 *inborn; innate; inherent* | ～性 *natural instinct; nature* | ～险 *natural barrier* (or *obstacle*) | ～然 *natural* ❸日,一昼夜,或专指昼间 day; daytime:今～*today* | 一整～*a whole day* | 白～黑夜工作忙 *to work day and night* [引] ***extension*** 一日之内的某一段时间 period of time in a day:～不早了。*It waxes late.* ❹气候 climate:～冷。*It is cold.* | 阴～*cloudy sky; overcast sky* [天气] **1** 冷、热、阴、晴等现象 weather:～～好。*It is a fine day.* | ～～要变。*It is going to spoil itself.* **2** 时间 time of (the day):～～不早了。*It is getting late.* ❺季节,时节 season:春～*spring* | 热～*hot days; hot season* ❻迷信的人指神佛仙人或他们所住的地方 God; heaven; paradise:～堂 *heaven;*

paradise|老～爷 *God; Heavenly Father* [天子]古代指统治天下的帝王 Son of Heaven — the emperor

添 tiān ㄊㄧㄢ 增加 to add; to get (*or* give) more; to increase (㊇ ***doublet*** 增— to add; to increase):再～几台机器。*Get several more machines.*|锦上～花 *to add flowers to the brocade — to make what is good still better*

黇 tiān ㄊㄧㄢ [黇鹿]鹿的一种,角的上部扁平或呈掌状,尾略长,性温顺 fallow deer (*Dama dama*)

田 tián ㄊㄧㄢˊ ❶种植农作物的土地(cultivated) land; farmland; field:水～*irrigated field*|稻～*paddy field; paddy*|种～*to till the land; to cultivate the soil; to farm* ㊁ ***extension*** 和农业有关的 related to farming:～家 *farming family; farm house* [田地] **1** 同"田" same as 田 **2** 地步,境遇(多指坏的) wretched situation; plight:怎么弄到这步～～了? *How come he got into such a sorry plight?* [田赛]田径运动中各种跳跃、投掷项目比赛的总称 field event ❷指可供开采的蕴藏矿物的地带 area with a workable mineral deposit; field:煤～*coal field*|油～*oil field*|气～*gas field* ❸同"畋" same as 畋

佃 ㊀ tián ㄊㄧㄢˊ 佃作,耕种田地 to till (*or* cultivate) (the field)

㊁ diàn 见 147 页 see p147

畋 tián ㄊㄧㄢˊ 打猎 to go hunting

畑 tián ㄊㄧㄢˊ (外 **loanword**)日本人姓名用字 Chinese character used in the name of a Japanese

钿 ㊀ tián ㄊㄧㄢˊ 〈方 ***dialect***〉钱,硬币 money; coin:铜～*copper coin*|洋～*silver dollar*

㊁ diàn 见 147 页 see p147

恬 tián ㄊㄧㄢˊ 安静 quiet; tranquil; peaceful (㊇ ***doublet*** — 静 quiet; tranquil; peaceful) ㊁ ***extension*** 安然,坦然,不在乎 not to care at all; to remain unperturbed; to be indifferent:～不知耻 *to be lost to all sense of shame; to have no sense of shame; not to feel ashamed at all*|～不为怪 *not to wonder in the least; not to be surprised at all; not to be disturbed*

甜 tián ㄊㄧㄢˊ 像糖或蜜的滋味,跟"苦"相对(the opposite of 苦) sweet; honeyed ㊃ ***figurative*** 使人感觉舒服的 comfortable; pleasing:～言蜜语 *sweet words and honeyed phrases; sweet talk*|睡得真～。*He slept soundly* (or *sweetly*).

湉 tián ㄊㄧㄢˊ [湉湉]形容水面平静(of a river) calm; quiet

菾 tián ㄊㄧㄢˊ [菾菜]二年生草本植物,开黄绿色花,叶可吃,根可制糖。现作"甜菜"

(now written as 甜菜) beet (*Beta vulgaris*)

填 tián ㄊㄧㄢˊ ❶把空缺的地方塞满或补满 to fill; to stuff: ～平洼地 *to fill a depression* ❷填写,在空白表格上按照项目写 to write; to fill in; to fill out: ～志愿书 *to fill in an application form* | ～表 *to fill in a form*

阗 tián ㄊㄧㄢˊ 充满 to be filled with; to be full of: 喧～ *bustling and crowded*

[和阗]地名,在新疆维吾尔自治区。今作"和田"(now written as 和田) Hetian, a place in the Xinjiang Uygur Autonomous Region

忝 tiǎn ㄊㄧㄢˇ 辱没 to bring disgrace to sb or sth; to be unworthy of the honour; to have the honour (though not worthy of it) 谦辞 ***humble***: ～属知己 *to have the honour to be counted among your bosom friends though unworthy of it* | ～列门墙 *to have the honour to be a student of sb's (or yours)*

舔 tiǎn ㄊㄧㄢˇ 用舌头接触东西或取东西 to lick; to lap

殄 tiǎn ㄊㄧㄢˇ 尽,绝 to extirpate; to exterminate: 暴～天物(任意糟蹋东西) *to waste nature's produce (such as grain) mindlessly; to squander natural resources*

惧 tiǎn ㄊㄧㄢˇ 惭愧 ashamed

觍 tiǎn ㄊㄧㄢˇ ❶形容惭愧 ashamed: ～颜 *shamefaced; ashamed* ❷厚着脸皮 to brazen: ～着脸(不知羞) *to brazen it out* ❸见 503 页"觍"字条"觍觍"(miǎn—) see 觍觍 on p503

腆 tiǎn ㄊㄧㄢˇ ❶丰厚 rich; sumptuous; plentiful ❷胸部或腹部挺起 to protrude; to bulge; to thrust out: ～胸脯 *to stick out one's chest* | ～着个大肚子 *to bulge one's belly* ❸见 503 页"腼"字条"腼腆"(miǎn—) see 腼腆 on p503

觍 ㊁ tiǎn ㄊㄧㄢˇ ❶同"觍" same as 觍 ❷〈古 ***archaism***〉形容人脸的样子 facial; faced: ～然人面 *to take on a shamefaced look*

㊀ miǎn 见 503 页 see p503

掭 tiàn ㄊㄧㄢˋ 用毛笔蘸墨汁在砚台上弄均匀 to dip (the brush) in ink and shape (it) properly against the inkstone: ～笔 *to bring the writing-brush to a fine point when preparing to write*

TIAO ㄊㄧㄠ

佻 tiāo ㄊㄧㄠ 轻薄,不庄重 frivolous; skittish; giddy

[佻㑊](—tà)轻佻 frivolous; loose; flippant

挑 ㊀ tiāo ㄊㄧㄠ ❶用肩担着 to carry on the shoulder with a pole; to shoulder: ～水 *to carry water with a shoulder pole* | 别人～一担,他～两担。 *While the others finished carrying loads on a shoulder pole*

to the destination once, he did the same twice. ❷(～子、～儿)挑、担的东西 carrying pole with its load(s); load(s) carried on a shoulder pole: 挑着空～子 *to carry empty baskets, etc on a shoulder pole* ❸(～儿)量词 ***quantifier***, (used for loads carried on a shoulder pole): 一～儿水 *two buckets of water on a shoulder pole* | 两～儿粪 *two shoulder poles loaded with baskets of dung on their ends* ❹选,拣 to choose; to select; to pick (㊥ ***doublet*** 一 选 to choose; to select; to pick (out) | 一 拣 to pick; to pick and choose): ～好的送给他 *to select the best for him* | ～错 *to find faults; to pick flaws; to find mistakes* | ～毛病 *to find fault (with); to pick holes (in)* [挑剔]严格地拣选,把不合规格的除去 to select and eliminate the ones that are not up to the standard ㊕ ***transfer*** 故意找错 to nit-pick; to be particular; to be captious

㊁ tiǎo 见 748 页 see p748

祧 tiāo ㄊㄧㄠ 古代称远祖的庙 former term for the temple of keeping the memorial tablets for remote ancestors 在封建宗法制度中指承继先代(in the feudal patriarchal clan system) to be (*or* become) heir to: 承～ *to be adopted as heir (to one's paternal uncle who has no son)*

条(條) tiáo ㄊㄧㄠˊ ❶(～子、～儿)植物的细长枝 twig: 柳～儿 *willow twig; wicker* | 荆～ *twig of the chaste tree* ❷(～子、～儿)狭长的东西 long narrow piece; strip; slip: 面～儿 *noodles* | 布～儿 *strip (of cloth)* | 纸～儿 *slip (of paper)* ❸细长的形状 long and slender in pattern (*or* shape); stripe; streak: ～纹 *stripe; streak* | 花～儿布 *striped cloth* | ～绒 *corduroy* ❹项目,分项目的 item; article: 宪法第一～ *first article of the constitution* | ～例 *regulations; rules; ordinances* [条件] **1** 双方规定应遵守的事项 terms; requirement; prerequisite **2** 事物产生或存在的因素 conditions; terms; factors: 自然～～ *natural conditions* | 有利～～ *favourable conditions; favourable factors* | 一切事物都依着～～、地点和时间起变化。*Everything changes along with different circumstances, times or places.* [条约]国与国之间关于权利义务等约定的条文 treaty; pact; covenant ❺条理,秩序,层次 order: 井井有～ *in perfect order; shipshape; well-organized* | 有～不紊 *in apple-pie order; methodical; systematic* ❻量词 ***quantifier*** **1** 用于长形的东西(used for sth long): 一～河 *a river* | 两～大街 *two streets* | 三～绳 *three ropes* | 四～鱼 *four fish* | 两～

腿 *two legs* **2** 用于分项目的事物(used for sth that can be listed item by item):这一版上有五～新闻。*There are five pieces* (or *items*) *of news on this page*.

鲦(鰷) tiáo ㄊㄧㄠˊ 鱼名。身体小,侧线紧贴腹部,银白色,生活在淡水中 sharpbelly (*Hemiculter leucisculus*)

苕 ㊀ tiáo ㄊㄧㄠˊ ❶古书上指凌霄花,也叫"紫葳"。落叶藤本植物,开红花(also called 紫葳)(in ancient Chinese texts) Chinese trumpet creeper (*Campsis grandiflora*) ❷苕子,一年生草本植物,花紫色。可以做绿肥 vetch (*Vicia sativa*) ❸苇子的花 flowers of reed

㊁ sháo 见 660 页 see p660

岧 tiáo ㄊㄧㄠˊ [岧峣](-yáo)山高(of mountains) high; lofty; towering

迢 tiáo ㄊㄧㄠˊ 远(叠 **reduplication**) far away; distant; remote:千里～～ *from thousands of li away; from afar; (to come) all the way from*

笤 tiáo ㄊㄧㄠˊ [笤帚](-zhou)扫除尘土的用具,用脱去子粒的高粱穗、黍子穗或棕等做成 small broom; whisk broom

龆 tiáo ㄊㄧㄠˊ 儿童换牙(of children) to shed milk teeth; to grow permanent teeth:～年(童年) *early childhood (about seven or eight)*

髫 tiáo ㄊㄧㄠˊ 古时小孩子头上扎起来的下垂的短发(in ancient China) child's hanging hair:垂～ *child's hanging hair*|～年(指幼年) *childhood*

调 ㊀ tiáo ㄊㄧㄠˊ ❶配合均匀 to mix; to adjust; to suit well:～色 *to mix* (or *blend*) *colours*|～味 *to flavour*|风～雨顺 *with timely wind and rain; favourable weather for crops* ㊂ **extension** 使和谐 to mediate; to reconcile:～解 *to mediate; to reconcile; to make peace*|～整 *to adjust; to regulate; to revise* [调剂] **1** 配药 to make up (*or* fill) a prescription **2** (-ji)调(diào)配,使均匀 to adjust; to regulate:组与组之间人力可以互相～～。*It is allowed to redistribute manpower among groups*. [调停]使争端平息 to mediate; to arbitrate ❷挑拨;挑逗 to tease; to provoke; to tantalize (㊃ **doublet** 一唆 to incite; to instigate; to abet):～嘴弄舌 *to gossip; to tittle-tattle; to tell tales*|～笑 *to make fun of; to poke fun at; to tease*|～戏 *to take liberties with (a woman); to trifle with (a woman); to dally*

[调皮]好开玩笑,顽皮 naughty; mischievous

㊁ diào 见 149 页 see p149

蜩 tiáo ㄊㄧㄠˊ 古书上指蝉(in ancient Chinese texts) cicada

蓨 tiáo ㄊㄧㄠˊ 即羊蹄草,多年生草本植物,叶子椭圆形,初夏开花。根茎叶浸出的汁液,可防治棉蚜、红蜘蛛、菜青虫等(i. e. 羊蹄草) Sowthistle Tasselflower Herb (*Emilia sonchifolia*)

挑 ㊁ tiǎo ㄊㄧㄠˇ ❶用竿子等把东西举起或支起 to pick (*or* hold) up with a pole (*or* stick); to lift up (*or* raise) with a pole (*or* stick):～起帘子来 *to raise the curtain*|把旗子～起来 *to hoist the flag* ❷用条状物或有尖的东西拨开或弄出 to poke; to pick; to prick:把火～开 *to poke a fire*|～了～灯心 *to pick the wick of an oil lamp*|～刺 *to pick out a splinter (as from one's finger)* ❸一种刺绣方法(in embroidery) to cross-stitch:～花 *cross-stitch work* ❹拨弄,引动 to stir up; to instigate; to foment (㊣ ***doublet*** —拨 to incite; to instigate; to sow dissention):～衅 *provoke*|～拨是非 *to stir up trouble; to foment discord* [挑战] **1** 激怒敌人出来打仗 to throw down the gauntlet; to challenge to battle **2** 鼓动对方和自己竞赛 to challenge to a contest:两个作业队互相～～。*The two work teams challenged each other to a contest.* ❺汉字由下斜着向上写的笔形(㇀) rising stroke in Chinese character

㊀ tiāo 见 745 页 see p745

朓 tiǎo ㄊㄧㄠˇ 古代称夏历月底月亮在西方出现。多用于人名(tiao, now usually used in a given name)(in ancient China) appearance of the moon in the west at the end of a lunar month

窕 tiǎo ㄊㄧㄠˇ 见 876 页"窈"字条"窈窕"(yǎo—) see 窈窕 on p876

眺 tiào ㄊㄧㄠˋ 眺望,往远处看 to look into the distance from a high place:登高远～ *to ascend a height to enjoy a distant view*

跳 tiào ㄊㄧㄠˋ ❶蹦,跃,两脚离地全身向上或向前 to jump; to leap; to spring (㊣ ***doublet*** —跃 to jump; to leap; to bound):～高 *high jump*|～远 *long jump; broad jump*|～绳 *rope skipping* ㊀ ***extension*** 越过 to make omissions; to skip (over); to jump over:这一课书～过去不学 *to skip over this text* [跳板] **1** 一头搭在车、船上的长板,便于上下 gangplank ㊀ ***extension*** 通路 gangway **2** 供游泳跳水的长板 springboard; diving board ❷一起一伏地动 to move up and down; to beat; to pulsate:心～(*of heart*) *to beat; to palpitate*|眼～(*of eyelid*) *to twitch*

粜(糶) tiào ㄊㄧㄠˋ 卖粮食 to sell (grain)

TIE ㄊㄧㄝ

帖 ㊂ tiē ㄊㄧㄝ ❶妥适 proper; appropriate:妥～ *proper; appropriate*|安～ *to feel at ease; to be free from*

anxiety; to set one's heart at rest ❷顺从，驯服 obedient; submissive: ～伏 *docile and obedient; submissive*|俯首～耳（含贬义 ***derogatory***）*to be docile and obedient; to be servile; to be submissive*

㊀ tiè 见750页 see p750

㊁ tiě 见749页 see p749

怗 tiē ㄊㄧㄝ 平定；安宁 to pacify; to quell; to suppress

贴 tiē ㄊㄧㄝ ❶粘(zhān)，把一种薄片状的东西粘在另一种东西上 to paste; to stick; to glue（㊇ ***doublet*** 粘— to paste; to stick; to glue）：～布告 *to put up a bulletin* (or *notice*)|～邮票 *to stick a stamp* (*on an envelope*) ❷靠近，紧挨 to cling to; to press (or nestle) closely to; to snuggle up to: ～身衣服 *underwear; underclothes; underclothing*|～着墙走 *to walk along the wall* [贴切]密合，恰当，确切(of words) apt; appropriate; proper ❸添补，补助 to help (out) financially; to subsidize（㊇ ***doublet*** —补 to subsidize）：煤～*coal allowance*|每月～给他一些钱 *to give him a monthly allowance* ❹适合，妥当 proper; appropriate 同"帖㊁❶" same as "帖㊁❶" ❺量词 ***quantifier***，用于膏药(used for medicated plaster) piece

萜 tiē ㄊㄧㄝ 有机化合物的一类，通式为$(C_5H_8)_n$，多为有香味的液体 terpene

帖 ㊁ tiě ㄊㄧㄝˇ ❶(～儿)便条 note; card: 字～儿 *brief note* ❷(～子)邀请客人的纸片 invitation: 请～*invitation*|喜～*wedding invitation* ❸旧时写着生辰八字等内容的纸片(in former times) card on which are written the hour, date, month and year of one's birth (traditionally used for betrothal, etc); age card: 庚～*age card*|换～*to exchange age cards*

㊀ tiè 见750页 see p750

㊂ tiē 见748页 see p748

铁(鐵、**銕) tiě ㄊㄧㄝˇ 一种金属元素，符号Fe，纯铁灰白色，有金属光泽，富延展性，在潮湿空气中易生锈。工业上的用途极大，可以炼钢，可以制造各种器械、用具 iron; ferrum (Fe) ㊕ ***figurative*** **1** 坚硬 hard as iron: ～蚕豆 *hard roasted broad bean*|～拳 *iron fist* **2** 意志坚定 strong (*or* firm) as iron: ～人 *iron man*|～姑娘队 *iron girl team* **3** 确定不移 ironclad; indisputable; unalterable: ～的纪律 *ironclad discipline*|～案如山 *ironclad case* **4** 残暴或精锐 violent; cruel; crack: ～蹄 *iron heel — cruel oppression of the people; tyrannical rule*|～骑 *armoured horses; strong cavalry; crack mounted soldiers* **5** 借指兵器 arms; weapon: 手无寸～ *completely unarmed; bare-handed; empty handed*

T

帖 ㊀ tiè ㄊㄧㄝˋ 学习写字时模仿的样本 book containing models of handwriting (*or* painting) for learners to copy：碑～(*usually used as a model for calligraphy*) *rubbings from stone inscriptions; stone rubbing; book of rubbings (from stone inscriptions)*｜字～*book of models of calligraphy; calligraphy models; copybook for calligraphy*

㊁ tiě 见 749 页 see p749

㊂ tiē 见 748 页 see p748

餮 tiè ㄊㄧㄝˋ 见 734 页"饕"字条"饕餮"(tāo—) see 饕餮 on p734

TING ㄊㄧㄥ

厅(廳) tīng ㄊㄧㄥ ❶聚会或招待客人用的大房间 hall：客～*living room; drawing room; parlour*｜餐～*dining hall; restaurant* ❷政府机关的办事单位 government department; office：办公～*administrative department; general office*

汀 tīng ㄊㄧㄥ 水边平地，小洲 low, level land by the waterside; spit of land [汀线]海岸被海水侵蚀而成的线状的痕迹 line track (of seashore)

听(聽) tīng ㄊㄧㄥ ❶用耳朵接受声音 to listen; to hear：～广播 *to listen to the broadcast*｜你～～外面有什么响声。*Listen! There is some sound outside.* ❷顺从，接受意见 to obey; to listen to; to accept：行动～指挥 *to act at the command*｜我告诉他了，他不～。*I told him, but he wouldn't listen.* ❸(旧读 formerly tìng)任凭，随 to let be (*or* do)：～其自然 *to let things take their own course; to let nature take its course; to let matters slide*｜～便 *to do as one pleases; to do whatever one likes*｜～凭你怎么办。*It's up to you what to do.* ❹治理，判断 to administer; to hear (a case); to judge：～政(指封建帝王临朝处理政事)(*of a monarch or regent*) *to hold court; to administer affairs of state* ❺(外 **loanword**)马口铁筒 tin; can：一～烟 *a tin of cigarettes*｜一～煤油 *a tin of kerosene*｜一～饼干 *a can of biscuits*

烃(烴) tīng ㄊㄧㄥ 碳氢化合物的总称 general term for hydrocarbon

桯 tīng ㄊㄧㄥ ❶锥子等中间的杆子 shaft of an awl：锥～子 *shaft of an awl* ❷古代放在床前的小桌子(in ancient China) small bedside table

鞓 tīng ㄊㄧㄥ 皮革制的腰带 leather waist belt(*or* sash)

廷 tíng ㄊㄧㄥˊ 朝廷，封建时代君主受朝问政的地方 court of a feudal ruler; royal (*or* imperial) court [宫廷] **1** 帝王的住所 imperial palace **2** 由帝王及其大臣构成的统治集团 ruling clique composed of an emperor and his ministers; royal court

莛 tíng ㄊㄧㄥˊ (一儿)草本植物的茎 stem of a herb:麦～儿 *stalks of wheat* | 油菜～儿 *stems of rape*

庭 tíng ㄊㄧㄥˊ ❶正房前的院子 front courtyard; front yard:前～*front courtyard* [家庭]以婚姻和血统关系为基础的社会单位,包括父母、子女和其他共同生活的亲属 family; household ❷厅堂 hall:大～广众 *before a big crowd; on a public occasion* ❸法庭,审判案件的处所或机构 law court:开～*to open a court session; to hold a court; to call the court to order (for interrogation and hearing)* | ～长 *president of a law court* (or *tribunal*); *presiding judge*

蜓 tíng ㄊㄧㄥˊ 见 610 页"蜻"字条"蜻蜓"(qīng—)、866 页"蝘"字条"蝘蜓"(yǎn—) see 蜻蜓 on p610 or 蝘蜓 on p866

霆 tíng ㄊㄧㄥˊ 劈雷,霹雳 thunderbolt

亭 tíng ㄊㄧㄥˊ ❶(一子)有顶无墙,供休息用的建筑物,多建筑在路旁或花园里 pavilion; gazebo ⑤ **extension** 建筑得比较简单的小房子 stall; kiosk; booth:书～*bookstall* | 邮～*postal kiosk* ❷适中,均匀 well-proportioned; well-balanced:调配得很～匀 *well-proportioned; well-balanced*

[亭亭] **1** 形容高耸 tall and erect; upright **2** 美好 gracefully slim; gracefully erect:～～玉立(*of a girl*) *to stand gracefully tall and erect; to be tall, slim and graceful*; (*of a tree, etc*) *to be tall and straight* 也作"婷婷"(also written as 婷婷)

[亭午] 正午,中午 midday; noon

停 tíng ㄊㄧㄥˊ ❶止住,中止不动 to stop; to cease; to halt (㊟ **doublet** 一顿 to halt; to pause | 一止 to stop; to cease; to end):一辆汽车～在门口。*A car is parked in front of the gate.* | 钟～了。*The clock stopped.* ❷停留 to stop over; to stay:我去天津,在北京～了两天。*I stopped over in Beijing for two days on my way to Tianjin.* ❸妥当 appropriate; proper; suitable:～妥 *well arranged; all set; in order* [停当](—dang) 齐备,完毕 ready; settled ❹(一儿)总数分成几份,其中一份叫一停儿 part (of a total); portion:三～儿中的两～儿 *two out of three* | 十～儿有九～儿是好的。*Nine out of ten are good.*

葶 tíng ㄊㄧㄥˊ [葶苈](—lì)一年生草本植物,开黄色小花,种子黑褐色,可入药 bog yellowcress; marsh cress (*Rorippa palustris*)

渟 tíng ㄊㄧㄥˊ 水停止不动(of water) to stagnate:渊～*deep stagnant water*

婷 tíng ㄊㄧㄥˊ (叠 **reduplication**)美好 graceful

町 ㊀ tǐng ㄊㄧㄥˇ〈古 ***archaism***〉❶田界 raised path between farm fields; balk ❷田地 farmland; field

㊁ dīng 见 152 页 see p152

侹 tǐng ㄊㄧㄥˇ 平直 level and straight

挺 tǐng ㄊㄧㄥˇ ❶笔直 straight; erect; upright: 笔～(*standing*) *straight as a ramrod*; *bolt straight* | ～进(勇往直前)(*of troops*) *to drive on boldly*; *to thrust into*; *to press forward* | 直～～地躺着不动 *to lie still and stiff* [挺拔] **1** 直立而高耸 tall and straight; erect; towering **2** 坚强有力 forceful; powerful; vigorous: 笔力～～(*in handwriting or drawing*) *forceful strokes* ❷撑直或凸出 to straighten up (physically); to stick out; to protrude: ～起腰来 *to straighten one's back*; *to straighten up* | ～胸抬头 *to stick out one's chest and hold up one's head* | ～身而出 *to step forward bravely*; *to rise courageously*; *to come out boldly* ㊕ ***transfer*** 勉强支撑 to endure; to hold out; to stand: 他虽然受了伤,硬～着不下火线。*Though wounded, he still held out and refused to leave the front line.* ❸副词 ***adverb***, 很 very; rather; quite: ～好 *pretty* (or *rather*) *good* | ～和气 *very kind* (or *amiable*) | ～爱学习 *to be keen on study* | 这花～香。*This flower has a very sweet smell.* ❹量词 ***quantifier***, 用于机枪 (used for machine guns): 一～机关枪 *a machine gun*

珽 tǐng ㄊㄧㄥˇ 玉笏(hù) jade tablet

梃 ㊀ tǐng ㄊㄧㄥˇ 棍棒 stick; club; cudgel

㊁ tìng 见 752 页 see p752

铤 tǐng ㄊㄧㄥˇ 快走的样子 (walking) quickly: ～而走险(指走投无路而采取冒险行动) *to risk danger in desperation*; *to make a reckless move*; *to rush headlong into danger*

颋 tǐng ㄊㄧㄥˇ 正直,直 upright; straight

艇 tǐng ㄊㄧㄥˇ 轻便的小船 (light) boat; skiff: 游～ *yacht*; *pleasure boat* | 汽～ *steamboat*; *motorboat*; *power boat* [潜艇]可以在水下潜行的舰艇。也称"潜水艇" (also called 潜水艇) submarine

梃 ㊁ tìng ㄊㄧㄥˋ ❶梃猪,杀猪后,在猪腿上割一个口子,用铁棍贴着腿皮往里捅(to cut a hole in one of the legs of a pig after slaughtering it and poke an iron rod along the skin before blowing air into the space between the flesh and the skin so as to separate them and pump up the skin for cleansing) to poke a hole in the slain pig ❷梃猪用的铁棍(used for poking a hole in the slain pig) iron rod

㊀ tǐng 见 752 页 see p752

TONG ㄊㄨㄥ

通 ㊀ tōng ㄊㄨㄥ ❶没有阻碍,可以穿过,能够达到 open; through: ～行 *to pass through; to go through* | 条条大路～北京。*All roads lead to Beijing.* | 四～八达 *to extend in all directions; to be accessible from all directions* | ～车 *to be open to traffic* | ～风 *to let air* (or *wind*) *through; to ventilate; to aerate* ㊂ ***extension*** **1** 顺,指文章合语法,合事理 grammatical; coherent; logical **2** 彻底明了(liǎo),懂得 to know; to understand fully; to comprehend: 精～业务 *conversant with one's profession* | 他～三国文字。*He knows three languages.* **3** 四通八达的,不闭塞的 extending in all directions; accessible: ～都大邑 *large city; metropolitan city; metropolis* [通过] **1** 穿过去,走过去 to pass (through); to cross; to traverse: 火车～～南京长江大桥。*The train crossed the Nanjing Changjiang Bridge.* **2** 介词 ***preposition***,经过 by means of; through; by: ～～学习提高了认识 *to improve one's understanding through study* **3** (提案)经过讨论大家同意 to adopt; to pass; to carry: ～～一项议案 *to pass* (or *carry*) *a motion* [通货]在社会经济活动中作为流通手段的货币 current money; currency: ～～膨胀 *inflation* (*of currency*) [通融]破例迁就 to stretch rules (*or* get around regulations) to accommodate sb; to make an exception in sb's favour ㊂ ***extension*** 适当互助,以有易无 to accommodate sb with (a short-term loan, etc): 新式农具不够,大家～～着用。*We have to share the new-type farm tools because there are not enough.* ❷传达 to communicate; to notify; to inform: ～报 *to circulate a notice; to report; to notify* | ～告 *to give public notice; to announce* (*in a circular, etc*) | ～信 *to communicate by letter; to correspond* [通知] **1** 传达使知道 to notify; to inform: ～～他一声 *to notify him* **2** 传达事项的文件 notice; circular; notification: 发～～*to send out* (or *dispatch*) *a notice* | 开会～～*meeting notice* ❸往来交接 to communicate; to exchange: ～商 *to have commercial relations with; to establish trade relations with* | 互～情报 *to exchange information* ❹普遍,全 common; all: ～病 *common mistake; prevalent problem* | ～共 *in all; altogether* | ～盘计划 *overall* (or *comprehensive*) *plan* | ～力合作 *to make a concerted effort; to give fully cooperation to; to pitch in for sth together* [通俗]浅显的,适合于一般文化程度的 common; popular: ～～读物 *popular literature* ❺姓 Tong, a surname

㊁ tòng 见 756 页 see p756

嗵 tōng ㄊㄨㄥ 拟声词 ***onomatopoeia***, to thump; to thud: 心～～地跳。*The heart is thumping.*

樋 tōng ㄊㄨㄥ 树名 name of a tree

恫 tōng ㄊㄨㄥ 病痛 pain: ～瘝(guān)在抱(把人民的疾苦放在心里) *to show extreme concern over the people's hardships*

仝 tóng ㄊㄨㄥˊ ❶同"同" same as 同 ❷姓 Tong, a surname

砼 tóng ㄊㄨㄥˊ 混凝土 concrete

同(△*仝) ㊀tóng ㄊㄨㄥˊ ❶一样,没有差异 same; similar; identical: ～等 *equal; of the same class, rank, or status; on an equal basis* (or *footing*)|～岁 *of the same age*|～感 *same feeling* (or *impression*)|大～小异 *alike except for minor differences; very much the same* [同化] 1 生物体将从食物中摄取的养料转化成自身细胞的成分并储存能量 to intussuscept 2 使不同的事物变成相同或相近的事物 to assimilate [同情] 对于别人的遭遇在感情上发生共鸣 to sympathize with; to show sympathy for; to feel compassion for: 我们～～并支持一切反殖民主义的斗争。*We sympathize with and support all the anti-colonial struggles.* [同时] 1 在同一个时候 at the same time; simultaneously; in the meantime 2 表示进一层,并且 moreover; besides; furthermore: 修好淮河可以防止水灾,～～还可以防止旱灾。*In addition to preventing flood, to harness the Huaihe River can also relieve drought.* [同志] 一般指志同道合的人,为共同的理想、事业而奋斗的人。特指同一个政党的成员(especially used to denote members of the same party) comrade ❷跟……相同 to be the same as; to be alike; to be similar to: ～上 *same as above; ditto; idem*|～前 *same as the previous; ibidem*|"仝"～"同"。仝 *is the same as* 同. ❸副词 ***adverb***, 共同,一起 together; jointly: ～居 *to live together; to cohabit*|～吃～住～劳动。*They not only live under the same roof and eat at the same table, but also work together.*|一路～行 *to go together all the way* ❹介词 ***preposition***, 跟 like; as: 他～哥哥一样勤奋。*He is as diligent as his elder brother.*|～坏人作斗争 *to fight against the bad persons; to struggle against evildoers* ❺连词 ***conjunction***, 和 and; together with: 我～你都去。*I will go with you together.*

㊁ tòng 见 756 页 see p756

侗 ㊁ tóng ㄊㄨㄥˊ 旧指童蒙无知(in former times) (of children) ignorant

㊀ dòng 见 156 页 see p156

㊂ tǒng 见 756 页 see p756

垌 ㊁ tóng ㄊㄨㄥˊ ［垌冢］（— zhǒng）地名，在湖北省汉川 Tongzhong, a place in Hanchuan, Hubei Province

㊀ dòng 见 156 页 see p156

茼 tóng ㄊㄨㄥˊ ［茼蒿］（— hāo）一年生或二年生草本植物，花黄色或白色，茎叶嫩时可吃 crown daisy (*Chrysanthemum coronarium*)

峒 ㊁ tóng ㄊㄨㄥˊ 见 394 页"崆"字条"崆峒"（kōng—） see 崆峒 on p394

㊀ dòng 见 157 页 see p157

桐 tóng ㄊㄨㄥˊ 植物名 name of plants **1** 泡（pāo）桐，落叶乔木，开白色或紫色花，生长快，是较好的固沙防风树木。木材可做琴、船、箱等物 paulownia (*Paulownia*) **2** 油桐，又叫"桐油树"，落叶乔木，花白色，有红色斑点，果实近球形，顶端尖。种子榨的油叫桐油，可做涂料（also called 桐油树） tung tree (*Vernicia fordii*) **3** 梧桐 phoenix tree; Chinese parasol (tree) (*Firmiana simplex*)

烔 tóng ㄊㄨㄥˊ ［烔炀镇］（— yáng—）地名，在安徽省巢湖 Tongyangzhen, a place in Chaohu, Anhui Province

铜 tóng ㄊㄨㄥˊ 一种金属元素，符号 Cu，淡紫红色，有金属光泽，富延展性，是热和电的良导体。在湿空气中易生铜绿，遇醋起化学作用生乙酸铜，有毒。铜可制各种合金、电业器材、器皿、机械等 copper; cuprum (Cu)

酮 tóng ㄊㄨㄥˊ 有机化合物的一类，通式 R—CO—R′ 酮类中的丙酮是工业上常用的溶剂 ketone

鲖 tóng ㄊㄨㄥˊ ［鲖城］地名，在安徽省临泉 Tongcheng, a place in Linquan, Anhui Province

佟 tóng ㄊㄨㄥˊ 姓 Tong, a surname

峂 tóng ㄊㄨㄥˊ ［峂峪］地名，在北京市海淀 Tongyu, a place in Haidian, Beijing

彤 tóng ㄊㄨㄥˊ 红色 red

童 tóng ㄊㄨㄥˊ ❶儿童，小孩子 child：～谣 *children's folk rhyme; nursery rhyme* ㊀ ***extension*** **1** 未长成的，幼 young：～牛（没有生角的小牛） *hornless calf* **2** 未结婚的 unmarried; virgin：～男 *virgin boy* | ～女 *virgin girl* **3** 秃的 bare; bald; barren：～山（没有草木的山） *bare hill* ［童话］专给儿童编写的故事 children's story; nursery story; fairy tales ❷旧时指未成年的男仆 (in former times) boy servant：家～ *boy servant*

僮 ㊁ tóng ㄊㄨㄥˊ ❶封建时代受役使的未成年的人 (in feudal China) boy servant：书～ *boy servant of a scholar* ❷古同"童❶" same as 童❶ in ancient Chinese

㊀ zhuàng 见 1003 页 see

T

p1003

潼 tóng ㄊㄨㄥˊ ［潼关］地名，在陕西省 Tongguan, a place in Shaanxi Province

橦 tóng ㄊㄨㄥˊ 古书上指木棉树（in ancient Chinese texts）silk cotton tree; kapok tree

曈 tóng ㄊㄨㄥˊ ［曈昽］（—lóng）天将亮的样子（because of the rising sun）turning bright;（of daybreak）twilight

瞳 tóng ㄊㄨㄥˊ 瞳孔，眼球中央的小孔，可以随着光线的强弱缩小或扩大。俗叫"瞳人"。（图见 867 页"眼" picture on p867）（popularly called 瞳人）pupil

侗 ㊂ tǒng ㄊㄨㄥˇ ［侊侗］（lǒng—）同"笼统" same as 笼统

㊀ dòng 见 156 页 see p156

㊁ tóng 见 754 页 see p754

筒（*筩） tǒng ㄊㄨㄥˇ 粗大的竹管 thick bamboo tube ㊄ **extension** 1 较粗的中空而高的器物 thick tube-shaped object：烟～（tong）*chimney; funnel; stovepipe* | 邮～*mailbox; pillar box; postbox* | 笔～*brush pot; pen container; pencil vase* 2（一儿）衣服等的筒状部分 tube-shaped part of clothing, etc：袖～*sleeve* | 袜～*leg of a stocking* | 靴～*leg of a boot*

统 tǒng ㄊㄨㄥˇ ❶总括，总起来 all; wholly; together：～率 *to command; to lead* | ～一 *to unite; to unify; to integrate* | ～筹 *to plan as a whole; to make overall plans* ❷事物的连续关系 continuum of interrelated things; interrelated system（㊃ **doublet** 系 — system）：血～*blood relationship; bloodline* | 传～*tradition; heritage*

捅（**通） tǒng ㄊㄨㄥˇ 戳、刺、碰 to poke; to stab; to nudge：把窗户～破了 *to poke a hole in the window* | ～马蜂窝（喻惹祸）*to stir up a hornet's nest — to ask for trouble* ㊅ **figurative** 揭露 to disclose; to expose; to lay bare：把问题全～出来了 *to lay bare all the problems*

桶 tǒng ㄊㄨㄥˇ 盛水或其他东西的器具，深度较大 bucket; pail; tank：水～*water bucket*（or *pail*）| 煤油～*kerosene tank*（or *drum*）［皮桶子］做皮衣用的成件的毛皮 fur lining

同（*衕） ㊁ tòng ㄊㄨㄥˋ ［胡同］巷，较窄的街道 lane; alley

㊀ tóng 见 754 页 see p754

恸（慟） tòng ㄊㄨㄥˋ ❶极悲哀 deep sorrow; grief; agony ❷指痛哭 to cry out loud; to weep bitterly; to wail

通 ㊁ tòng ㄊㄨㄥˋ 量词 **quantifier**：打了三～鼓 *to beat the drum three times* | 说了一～ *to give sb a good scolding; to give sb a talking to*

㊀ tōng 见 753 页 see p753

痛 tòng ㄊㄨㄥˋ ❶疼 pain; ache; hurt (㊟ **doublet** 疼—ache; pain; hurt): 头～ *headache* | 不～不痒 *to scratch only the surface; to be perfunctory; to be superficial* | ～定思～ *to recall a painful experience (as a reminder or warning); to draw a lesson from a bitter experience; to bring home a painful lesson* [痛苦] 身体或精神感到非常难受 pain; suffering; agony ❷悲伤 sadness; sorrow; grief (㊟ **doublet** 悲—grief; sorrow | 哀—grief; sorrow): ～心 *pained; distressed; grieved* ❸极,尽情地,深切地,彻底地 extremely; deeply; thoroughly: ～恨 *to hate bitterly; to detest utterly* | ～饮 *to drink one's fill; to drink to one's heart's content* | ～惜 *to regret deeply; to deplore; to feel remorse for* | ～改前非 *to repent thoroughly of one's misdeeds and turn a new leaf; to mend one's ways sincerely; to rectify one's errors thoroughly* [痛快] (—kuai) **1** 爽快,爽利 frank and direct; forthright; straightforward: 他是个～～人。*He is a straightforward man.* **2** 尽情,舒畅,高兴 happy; delighted; to one's great satisfaction: 这活干得真～～。*The job is simply and quickly done.* | 看他的样子好像有点不～～。*He looks somewhat unhappy.*

TOU ㄊㄡ

偷(❸*婾) tōu ㄊㄡ ❶窃取,趁人不知道拿人东西据为己有 to steal; to pilfer; to pinch [小偷(儿)] 偷东西的人 thief; pilferer; burglar ❷行动瞒着人(叠 **reduplication**) secretly; stealthily; on the sly: ～看 *to steal a glance at; to look secretly; to peep* | ～拍 *to take a photo without permission* | ～～地走了 *to sneak away* | ～懒(趁人不知道少做事) *to loaf on the job; to be indolent at work* ❸苟且 to drift along; to seek temporary ease; to muddle along: ～安 *to seek temporary ease* | ～生 *to drag out an ignorable existence* ❹抽出(时间) to find (time); to take (time) off: ～空(kòng) *to take time off (from work to do sth else); to snatch a moment* | ～闲 *to steal (or snatch) a moment of leisure; to spare a few minutes from work (to do sth else); to loaf on the job*

鍮 tōu ㄊㄡ 黄铜 brass

头(頭) tóu ㄊㄡˊ ❶脑袋,人身体的最上部分或动物身体的最前的部分 head (㊟ **doublet** —颅 head) ㊕ **transfer** 头发 hair: 他不想留～了。*He wants to have his hair cut.* [头脑] **1** 脑筋,思想 head; brains; mind: 他～～清楚。*He has a clear mind.* | 不要被胜利

冲昏～～。*Don't get carried away by success.* **2** 要领，门路 main threads (of sth complicated); clue：这事我摸不着～～。*I can't make head or tail of it.* ❷（一儿）事情的起点或终点 beginning; end：开～儿 *beginning*｜从～儿说起 *to tell from the very beginning*｜什么时候才是个～儿呀！*When will it be over?* ❸物体的顶端 top; tip; end：山～*hilltop*｜笔～*tip of a pen*; *pen nib* (转)***extension***（一儿）物品的残余部分 remnant; leftover; end：烟卷～儿 *cigarette end* (or *butt*)｜蜡～儿 *candle end* (or *stump*)｜布～儿 *leftover of a bolt of cloth*; *odd bits of cloth*; *scraps of cloth* [头绪]条理，处理事物的门径 main threads (of sth complicated); clue：我找不出～～来。*I cannot straighten things out.* or *I am unable to get things into shape.* ❹以前，在前面的 previous; last; in front：～两年 *the first two years*｜我在～里走。*I walk in front.* ❺次序在最前，第一 first; number one：～等 *first-class*; *first-rate*｜～号 *size one*; *number one*｜～班 *first shift* ❻接近，临 right before; prior to：～睡觉最好洗洗脚。*You'd better wash your feet before going to bed.* ❼（一子、一儿）首领（多指坏的）(usually derogatory) chief; head; boss：特务～子 *master spy*｜流氓～子 *head of a gang* ❽（一儿）方面 side; aspect：他们两个

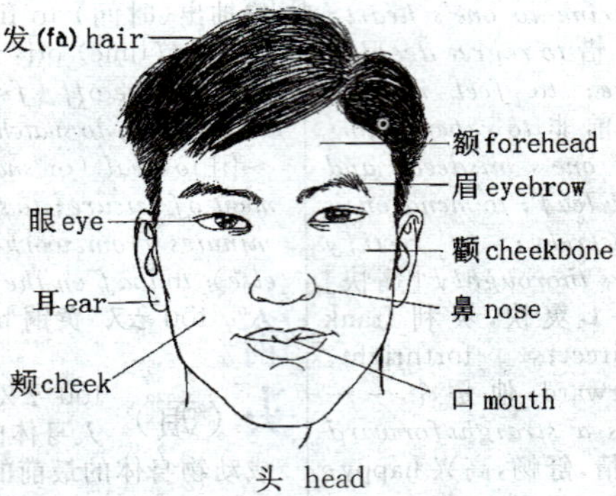

头 head

是一～儿的。*They two are on the same side.* ❾量词 ***quantifier*** **1** 用于牛驴等牲畜(used for certain domestic animals)：一～牛 *a head of cattle*; *an ox*｜两～驴 *two donkeys* **2** 用于像头的物体(used for head-shaped objects)：两～蒜 *two bulbs of garlic* ❿表示约计、不定数量的词 about; around; approximately：三～五百 *approximately 300 or 500*｜十～八块 *about 8 or 10 yuan* ⓫(tou)名词词尾 ***noun suffix*** **1** 放在名词性语素后(used after a nominal root)：木～*wood*｜石～*stone*｜拳～*fist* **2** 放在形容词性语素后(used after an adjectival root)：甜～儿 *sweetish taste; benefit*｜苦～儿 *bitter taste; suffering; hardship* **3** 放在动词性语素后(used after a verbal root)：有听～儿 *to be worth listening*｜没个看～儿 *not to be worth seeing or reading* ⓬(tou)方位词词尾 ***suffix of a locality***：前～*front*｜上～*above*｜外～*outside*

投 tóu ㄊㄡˊ ❶抛，掷，扔(多指有目标的)(usually toward a goal) to throw; to cast; to fling：～石 *to throw* (or *fling*) *a stone*｜～入江中 *to throw* (or *cast*) *sth into a river* ㊀ ***extension*** 跳进去 to jump into; to plunge into：～河 *to plunge into a river to drown oneself*｜～井 *to jump into a well to drown oneself; to commit suicide by jumping into a well*｜～火 *to throw oneself into the fire*［投票］选举或表决的一种方法。把自己的意见写在票上，投进票箱 to cast a vote; to cast a ballot; to ballot［投资］把资金应用在生产等事业上 to invest ❷投射 to cast; to project：影子～在窗户上。*A shadow is projected on the window.* ❸走向，进入 to go to; to enter; to join：～宿 *to put up for the night; to stop over for the night; to seek temporary lodging*｜弃暗～明 *to forsake darkness for light—to leave the reactionary camp and cross over the side of progress; to break away from the reactionaries and side with the people*｜～入新战斗 *to plunge into a new battle*［投奔］(－bèn)归向，前去依靠 to go to (a friend *or* place) for shelter (*or* help)：～～亲友 *to go to one's relatives and friends for help; to seek refuge with one's relatives and friends*｜～～祖国 *to go back one's motherland for shelter* ❹寄，递送 to send; to deliver; to dispatch (㊅ ***doublet*** 一递 to deliver)：～书寄信 *to send* (or *deliver*) *a letter*｜～稿 *to submit a piece of writing for publication; to contribute* (*to a newspaper or magazine*) ❺合 to agree with **1** 相合 to agree with; to fit in with; to be congenial to：情～意合 *to find each other congenial; to be in agreement in opinion and feelings; to find mutual affection and agreement* **2** 迎合 to cater to：～其所好(hào) *to cater to one's likes* (or *tastes*)［投机］**1** 意见相合 agreeable; congenial：他俩一见就很～～。*They felt congenial to each other at first sight.* **2** 利用时机，谋取私利 to speculate; to profiteer; to seek private gain by hook or crook：

～～取巧 *to seek every chance to gain advantage by trickery; to be opportunistic* | ～～分子 *opportunist; careerist* ❻临近，在……以前 approaching; before: ～明 *before dawn* | ～暮 *towards dusk*

骰 tóu ㄊㄡˊ 骰子，一般叫"色(shǎi)子"，游戏用具或赌具(generally called 色子) dice

钭 tǒu ㄊㄡˇ dǒu ㄉㄡˇ (又 *also* dǒu) 姓 Tou, a surname

敨 tǒu ㄊㄡˇ 〈方 **dialect**〉❶把包着或卷着的东西打开 to spread out; to unfold; to open up ❷抖搂(尘土等) to shake off (dust, etc)

透 tòu ㄊㄡˋ ❶穿通，通过 to pass through; to penetrate: 钉～了。*It has been nailed through.* | 这块厚纸扎不～。*This thick paper can't be pierced through.* | ～光 *to be pervious to light; to be photic; to be transparent* | ～气 *to aerate; to ventilate* | ～过现象看本质 *to see through the appearance to get the essence of the matter* ㊀ **extension** **1** 很通达，极明白 thoroughly; in a penetrating way; clearly: 话说得十分～彻。*It has been thoroughly explained.* | 理讲～了。*The reasons have been driven home.* **2** 泄漏 to let out; to disclose; to leak: ～露(lù)风声 *to disclose (or leak) information* **3** 暗地里告诉 to tell secretly; to inform on the sly: ～个信儿 *to tip sb off* [透支]支款超过存款的数目 to overdraw; to make an overdraft ❷极度 extremely; exceedingly: 恨～了 *to hate bitterly; to hate sb's guts* ❸显露 to show; to appear; to look: 他～着很老实。*He has an honest look.* | 这朵花白里～红。*The flower is white tinged with red.* ❹达到饱满的、充分的程度 to the saturation point; to the extreme: 雨下～了。*There was a drenching rain.*

TU ㄊㄨ

凸 tū ㄊㄨ 高出，跟"凹"(āo)相对(the opposite of 凹) protruding; raised; bulgy: ～出 *protruding; projecting; bulgy* | ～透镜 *convex lens*

秃 tū ㄊㄨ ❶没有头发 hairless; bald: ～顶 *to get bald; to be bald* ❷(树木)没有枝叶，(山)没有树木 bare; barren; naked: ～树 *bare (or naked) tree* | 山是～的。*The mountain is barren.* ❸羽毛等脱落，物体失去尖端 bare; unpointed; blunt: ～尾巴鸡 *bare-tailed chicken* | ～针 *unpointed needle; blunt needle* ❹表示不圆满，不周全 incomplete; unsatisfactory: 这篇文章写得有点～。*This article seems incomplete.*

突 tū ㄊㄨ ❶忽然 suddenly; abruptly; unexpectedly: ～变 *sudden change* | ～发 *to erupt; to burst (or break) out* [突击]战斗中出其不意地攻击敌人的要害 to make a sudden and violent attack; to assault ㊟ ***figurative*** 集中力量在较短的时间内完成某种紧急的任务 to make a concentrated effort to finish an urgent task in a short time: ～～队 *shock brigade; shock team; commando unit* | ～～工作 *to do a rush job* [突然]急速而出乎意外 suddenly; abruptly; unexpectedly: ～～事件 *eventuality; contingency* | 来得很～～*to arrive unexpectedly* | ～～停止 *to stop all of a sudden; to come to an abrupt stop; to stop short* ❷超出,冲破 to exceed; to surpass; to break through: 这是个～出的例子。*This is a striking example.* | ～破过去的纪录 *to break a record* | ～围 *to break through an encirclement* ❸古时灶旁的出烟口,相当于今天的烟筒 opening for letting out smoke from a fire beside a kitchen range in ancient China; chimney: 灶～*chimney* | 曲～徙薪(喻防患未然) *to bend the chimney and remove the firewood (to prevent a possible fire) — to take precautions against any possible danger*

葖 tū ㄊㄨ 见 239 页"菁"字条"菁葖"(gū—) see 菁葖 on p239

图(圖) tú ㄊㄨˊ ❶用绘画表现出来的形象 picture; diagram; chart: ～画 *picture; drawing; painting* | 地～*map* | 蓝～*blueprint* | 插～*figure; illustration; plate* [图解]画图或列表解释事物 diagram; figure; graph ❷画 to draw; to paint: 画影～形 *to draw the likenesses of a criminal at large for posting in various places; to draw sb's picture* ❸计谋,计划 scheme; plan; intention: 良～*good intentions* | 宏～*great plan; great prospect* ❹谋取,希望得到 to strike a blow for; to seek; to desire (㊟ ***doublet*** —谋 to plot; to scheme; to conspire): 唯利是～*to seek profit exclusively; to be intent on nothing but profit; to desire profit above all else*

[图腾](外 **loanword**)原始社会的人用动物、植物或其他自然物作为其氏族血统的标志,并把它当作祖先来崇拜,这种被崇拜的对象叫图腾 totem

荼 tú ㄊㄨˊ ❶古书上说的一种苦菜(in ancient Chinese texts) bitter edible plant [荼毒] ㊟ ***figurative*** 毒害 to afflict with great suffering; to torment ❷古书上指茅草的白花 (in ancient Chinese texts) white flowers of reeds: 如火如～*like wildfire — growing vigorously*

途 tú ㄊㄨˊ 道路 way; path; road (㊟ ***doublet*** —径 way; path; channel | 道—road | 路—journey; way; road | —程 road; way; course): 坦～*level (or smooth) road; easy path* | 道听～说 *hearsay; rumour; gossip* | 半～而废 *to give up*

T

halfway; to leave sth unfinished [前途] ㊃ ***figurative*** 未来的境地,发展的前景 prospects; future [用途] 用处 use

涂(塗、❺**凃) tú ㄊㄨˊ ❶使颜色、油漆等附着(zhuó)在物体上 to spread; to apply; to smear: ~上一层油 *to apply a coat of oil* ❷用笔等抹上或抹去 to scribble; to scrawl; to smear: ~写 *to scribble; to scrawl* |不要在书上乱~乱画。*Don't scrawl on the book.* |写错了可以~掉。*These wrongly written words can be blotted out.* |~改 *to change; to alter; to modify* [涂鸦] 比喻书法拙劣或胡乱写作 poor handwriting; scrawl; graffito ❸泥泞 mud; mire; slush [涂炭] ㊃ ***figurative*** mud and ashes **1** 极为困苦 utter misery; severe suffering **2** 肮脏污浊 dirty; muddy ❹同"途" same as 途 ❺姓 Tu, a surname

酴 tú ㄊㄨˊ ❶酒曲 distiller's yeast ❷酴酒,重(chóng)酿的酒 double-fermented wine

徒 tú ㄊㄨˊ ❶步行(不用车、马)(to go) on foot: ~行 *to go on foot; to walk* ❷空 bare; empty: ~手 *bare-handed; unarmed* ㊁ ***extension*** 徒然,白白地 in vain; futile: ~劳往返 *to hurry back and forth for nothing; to make a trip in vain; to make a futile journey* |~劳无益 *to work in vain; to make a futile effort* ❸只,仅仅 merely; only: ~托空言 *to make an empty promise; to pay lip service to* |不~无益,反而有害 *not only useless, but to the contrary harmful* ❹徒弟 apprentice; pupil; disciple: 学~ *apprentice* ❺同一派系或信仰同一宗教的人 believer; follower; clique member: 教~ *believer; follower of a religion; disciple* ❻人(今多指坏人) (now usually used to denote a bad person) person; fellow: 匪~ *bandit* |不法之~ *lawbreaker* ❼徒刑,剥夺犯人自由的刑罚,分有期徒刑和无期徒刑两种 punishment whereby criminals are deprived of their freedom for set term or life; imprisonment; sentence

菟 ㊀ tú ㄊㄨˊ [於菟](wū—) 〈古 ***archaism***〉老虎的别称 *wutu*, another name for 老虎

㊁ tù 见 763 页 see p763

屠 tú ㄊㄨˊ ❶宰杀牲畜 to slaughter (animals for food); to butcher (㊇ ***doublet*** —宰 to slaughter; to butcher): ~狗 *to butcher a dog* |~户 *butcher* ❷残杀人 to massacre; to slaughter; to butcher: ~杀 *to massacre; to slaughter; to butcher* |~城 *to massacre the inhabitants of a captured city; to kill all the residents of a conquered city*

腯 tú ㄊㄨˊ 肥(指猪) (of a pig) fat

土 tǔ ㄊㄨˇ ❶地面上的沙、泥等混合物 soil; earth; dirt

(㊟ ***doublet*** 一 壤 soil)：沙～ *sandy soil* | 黏 ～ *clay* | ～ 山 *earthen hill* ❷ 土 地 land; ground; territory：国～*territory; land of a country* | 领～*territory; domain* ❸本地的 local; native; indigenous：～产 *native product; local produce* | ～话 *local dialect* ❹指民间生产的，出自民间的 home-made; indigenous; local：～布 *handwoven* (or *homespun*) *cloth* | ～专家 *self-taught expert; local expert; native expert* ❺不开通，不时兴 unrefined; unenlightened; rustic：～里～气 *cloddish; rustic; countrified* | ～头～脑 *countrified; rustic; unsophisticated*

[土家族] 我国少数民族，参看附表（see the appendix） the Tujia ethnic group, one of the ethnic minorities of China

[土族] 我国少数民族，参看附表（see the appendix ） the Tu ethnic group, one of the ethnic minorities of China

吐 ㊀ tǔ ㄊㄨˇ 使东西从嘴里出来 to spit：不要随地～痰。*No spitting.* ㊥ ***extension*** **1** 说出 to say; to tell; to pour out：～露(lù)实情 *to tell the truth; to unbosom oneself* | 坚不～实 *steadfast in determination not to tell the truth* **2** 露出，放出 to emit; to send out; to put forth：高粱～穗了。*The sorghum is earing up.* | 蚕～丝。*Silkworms spin silk.*

㊁ tù 见 763 页 see p763

钍 tǔ ㄊㄨˇ 一种放射性元素，符号 Th，银灰色，质地柔软，可作为原子能工业的核燃料 thorium (Th)

吐 ㊁ tù ㄊㄨˋ 消化道或呼吸道里的东西从嘴里涌出 to vomit; to throw up; to retch (㊟ ***doublet*** 呕 一 to vomit; to throw up; to spew)：上～下泻 *to throw up on top and have loose bowels below — to suffer from both vomiting and diarrhea; to vomit and have loose bowels* | ～血 *to spit blood; to have haematemesis* ㊕ ***figurative*** 退还(侵吞的财物) to give up unwillingly; to disgorge; to cough up：～出赃款 *to disgorge sb's illicit money; to return the bribes*

㊀ tǔ 见 763 页 see p763

兔(*兎) tù ㄊㄨˋ (～子、～儿)哺乳动物，耳长，尾短，上唇中间裂开，后腿较长，跑得快 rabbit; hare *Leporidae*

堍 tù ㄊㄨˋ 桥两头靠近平地的地方 ramp of a bridge：桥～*end of a bridge*

菟 ㊀ tù ㄊㄨˋ 植物名 name of plants **1** 菟丝子，寄生的蔓草，茎细长，常缠绕在别的植物上，对农作物有害。秋初开小花，子实可入药 Chinese dodder (*Cuscuta chinensis*) **2** 菟葵，多年生草本植物，花淡紫红色，多生在山地树丛里 hellebore (*Helleborus*)

㊁ tú 见 762 页 see p762

TUAN ㄊㄨㄢ

湍 tuān ㄊㄨㄢ 急流的水 rushing water; rapids; torrent

团（團、❷糰） tuán ㄊㄨㄢˊ ❶圆形（叠 **reduplication**）round; circular: ～扇 *round fan* | 雌蟹是～脐的。*Female crabs have round abdomens.* ❷（一子、一儿）成球形的东西 sth shaped like a ball: 饭～儿 *rice ball* | 菜～子 *cornmeal dumpling with vegetable stuffing* ㊀ **extension** 量词 **quantifier**，用于成团的东西或抽象的事物（used for sth ball-shaped or abstract）: 一～线 *a ball of thread* | 两～废纸 *two rolls* (or *balls*) *of waste paper* | 一～和气 *a prevailing mood of harmony; situation of unconditional peace* | 一～糟 *a precious mess* ❸会合在一起 to congregate; to assemble; to conglomerate: ～聚 *to reunite* | ～圆 *reunion of* (*family members*) [团结]为了实现共同理想或完成共同任务而联合或结合 to unite; to rally: ～～起来，争取胜利 *to unite to fight for victory* ❹工作或活动的集体组织（for work or activities） collective; group: 文工～ *art troupe* | 代表～ *delegation; deputation; mission* [团体]有共同目的、志趣的人结合在一起的集体 group; organization; society: 工会、妇女联合会都是人民～～。*Both the Labour Union and the Women's Federation are organizations of the people.* ❺在我国特指共产主义青年团 Communist Youth League of China ❻军队的编制单位，是营的上一级（army unit） regiment

抟（摶） tuán ㄊㄨㄢˊ 把东西揉弄成球形 to roll sth into a ball; to roll: ～饭团子 *to make rice balls* | ～泥球 *to roll the clay into a ball* | ～纸团 *to roll the paper into a ball*

疃 tuǎn ㄊㄨㄢˇ ❶禽兽践踏的地方 path trodden down by animals or birds; track ❷村庄，屯。多用于地名（tuan, usually used in a place name） village

彖 tuàn ㄊㄨㄢˋ 论断，推断 to judge; to infer: ～凶吉 *to judge ill or good luck* [彖辞]《易经》中总括一卦含义的言辞 writings on the implication of divinatory symbols in *The Book of Changes*

TUI ㄊㄨㄟ

忒 ㊁ tuī ㄊㄨㄟ〈方 **dialect**〉副词 **adverb**，太 too; awful: 风～大。*The wind is too strong.* | 路～滑。*The road is awfully slippery.*

㊀ tè 见736页 see p736

推 tuī ㄊㄨㄟ ❶用力使物体顺着用力的方向移动 to push; to shove; to thrust: ～车 *to push a cart* | ～了他一把 *to*

give him a push | ～磨 *to turn* (or *push*) *a millstone* ㊀ ***extension*** 使工具向前移动进行工作 to mow; to plane; to pare: 用刨子～光 *to smoothen with a plane* | ～头(理发) *to cut sb's hair* (*with clippers*) [推敲] ㊁ ***transfer*** 斟酌文章字句 to weigh (one's words); to deliberate: 仔细～～ *to weigh* (*one's words, etc*) *carefully* | 一字费～～。*A word in writing needs careful deliberation.* ❷使事情开展 to push forward; to promote; to advance: ～广 *to popularize; to spread; to extend* | ～销 *to promote the sales* (*of goods*); *to sell; to market* | ～动 *to push forward; to promote; to propel* ❸进一步想，由已知推断其余 to infer; to deduce: ～求 *to find out; to enquire into; to explore* | ～测 *to infer; to conjecture; to guess* | ～理 *to infer; to reason; to ratiocinate* | ～算 *to calculate; to estimate; to reckon* | 类～ *to reason by analogy; to analogize* ❹辞让，脱卸 to decline; to shirk **1** 辞退，让给 to decline; to yield; to give: ～辞 *to decline; to refuse; to turn down* | ～让 *to decline* (*a position, favour, etc*) *out of modesty; to submit* (or *yield*) *to sb as a token of deference* **2** 脱卸责任，托辞 to push away; to shift; to shirk: ～诿 *to shift* (or *shirk*) (*blame, responsibility, etc*) *onto others; to pass the buck* | ～三阻四 *to make all sorts of excuses; to decline with all sorts of excuses; to give the runaround* | ～病不来 *to refuse to come on the pretext of illness* ❺往后挪动(时间) to put off; to delay; to postpone: 再往后～几天 *to postpone for a few days* ❻举荐，选举 to elect; to choose: 公～一个人做代表 *to recommend by general acclaim a person as the representative* ❼指出某人某物的优点 to praise highly (for); to hold in esteem (for): ～许(称赞) *to praise; to have a high regard for; to hold in esteem* | ～重(重视、钦佩) *to have a high regard for; to think highly of; to hold in esteem* | ～崇 *to praise highly; to hold in esteem; to extol*

颓(*穨) tuí ㄊㄨㄟˊ ❶崩坏，倒塌 collapsed; ruined; dilapidated: ～垣断壁 *crumbling walls and dilapidated houses — a devastated* (or *desolate*) *scene* [颓废] **1** 建筑物倒坏 dilapidated; ruined **2** 精神委靡不振 decadent; dispirited; dissipated ❷败坏 degenerate; dissipate; corrupt: ～风败俗 *degenerate practices and depraved customs* [颓唐] 精神不振，情绪低落 dejected; dispirited; disconsolate

魋 tuí ㄊㄨㄟˊ 古书上说的一种兽，像小熊 (in ancient Chinese texts) *tui*, a kind of animal, resembling a young bear

腿 tuǐ ㄊㄨㄟˇ ❶人和动物用来支持身体和行走的部分 leg:大～*thigh*|前～*foreleg*|后～*hind leg* (图见741页"体"picture on p741)[火腿]用盐腌制的猪腿 ham ❷(一儿)器物上像腿的部分 leg-shaped support:桌子～儿 *leg of a table*|凳子～儿 *leg of a stool*

退 tuì ㄊㄨㄟˋ ❶向后移动或使之向后移动,跟"进"相对(the opposite of 进) to move backwards; to back up; to retreat: ～兵 *to withdraw troops; to retreat*|败～*to retreat* (or *evacuate*) *in defeat; to lose the field; to lose one's ground*|敌人已经～了。*The enemy has retreated.*[退步] **1** 逐渐向下,落后 to fall or lag behind; to retrogress:工作积极,学习努力,才能不～～。*Only if you work vigorously and study hard will you not lag behind.* **2** 后退的余地 room for maneuver; leeway:话没有说死,留了～～*to leave some leeway in speaking* [退化]生物体的某一或某些器官在进化过程中,全然消失或部分残留而成为痕迹器官的现象。例如人的阑尾是退化器官 to degenerate; to retrograde; to retrogress ❷离开,辞去 to leave; to quit; to withdraw from:～席 *to leave a meeting* (or *banquet*); *to walk out*|～职 *to resign* (or *be discharged*) *from office; to quit; to leave office* ❸送还,不接受,撤销 to return; to give back; to retract:～货 *to return goods* (or *merchandise*)|～票 *to return a ticket; to get a refund for a ticket; to cancel a reservation*|～钱 *to refund; to reimburse*|～婚 *to break off an engagement* ❹减退,下降 to go down; to recede; to ebb:～色 *to discolour; to fade*|～烧 *to bring down* (or *allay*) *a fever*; (*of a person's temperature*) *to come down*

煺(**焞、**㨾) tuì ㄊㄨㄟˋ 已宰杀的猪、鸡等用滚水烫后去掉毛(of a pig, or chicken, etc) to scald in order to remove hairs or feathers

褪 ㊀ tuì ㄊㄨㄟˋ 脱落,脱去 to take off (clothes); to shed (feathers, hairs, etc):兔子正～毛 *The rabbits are shedding their hair.*[褪色]退色,颜色变淡或消失 to discolour; to fade

㊁ tùn 见767页 see p767

蜕 tuì ㄊㄨㄟˋ ❶蛇、蝉等脱下来的皮 exuviae; slough ❷蛇、蝉等动物脱皮 to exuviate; to slough off [蜕化]㊕ ***transfer*** 变质,腐化堕落 to degenerate

TUN ㄊㄨㄣ

吞 tūn ㄊㄨㄣ 不经咀嚼,整个咽到肚子里 to swallow; to devour; to gulp down:囫囵～枣 *to swallow a date whole — to lap up information without digesting it; to read with-*

out understanding | 狼～虎咽 *to wolf down; to gorge; to gobble up* ㊀ *extension* **1** 忍受不发作出来 to hold back; to forbear; to endure: 忍气～声(不敢作声) *to swallow an insult in meek submission; to stifle one's indignation; to submit to threat unwillingly* **2** 兼并,侵占 to take (illegal) possession of; to seize; to annex: ～没 *to embezzle; to misappropriate; to engulf* | ～并 *to seize; to annex; to take over*

暾 tūn ㄊㄨㄣ 刚出来的太阳 newly-risen sun: 朝～ *early morning sun*

黗 tūn ㄊㄨㄣ 黄色 yellow

屯 ㊀ tún ㄊㄨㄣˊ ❶聚集,储存 to collect; to gather; to store (*or* hoard) up: ～粮 *to store* (or *hoard*) *up grain* ㊀ *extension* (军队)驻扎 to station (*or* quarter) (troops): ～兵 *to station* (or *quarter*) *troops* ❷(一子、一儿)村庄 village: 皇姑～ *Huanggu Village*

㊁ zhūn 见 1004 页 see p1004

囤 ㊁ tún ㄊㄨㄣˊ 囤积,积存,存储货物、粮食 to store (*or* hoard) up: ～货 *to store up goods*

㊀ dùn 见 168 页 see p168

饨 tún ㄊㄨㄣˊ 见 301 页"馄"字条"馄饨"(húntun) see 馄饨 on p301

鲀 tún ㄊㄨㄣˊ 河豚,鱼名。种类很多,头圆形,口小,一般血液和内脏有剧毒 globefish; puffer; balloonfish (*Tetraodontidae*)

豚 tún ㄊㄨㄣˊ 小猪,也泛指猪 suckling pig; pig

臀 tún ㄊㄨㄣˊ 屁股 buttock; hip; rump: ～部 *buttocks* (图见 741 页"体" picture on p741)

氽 tǔn ㄊㄨㄣˇ 〈方 *dialect*〉 ❶漂浮 to float; to drift: 木头在水上～。*The wood is floating on the water.* ❷用油炸 to deep-fry: 油～花生米 *deep-fried peanuts*

褪 ㊀ tùn ㄊㄨㄣˋ 使穿着、套着的东西脱离 to slip out of sth: 把袖子～下来。*Slip your arms out of your sleeves (of your coat, shirt etc).* | 狗～了套跑了。*The dog broke loose from the leash and ran away.* ㊀ *extension* 向内移动而藏起来 to hide in one's sleeves, etc: 把手～在袖子里 *to keep one's hands in one's sleeves* | 袖子里～着一封信 *to hide a letter in one's sleeve*

㊁ tuì 见 766 页 see p766

TUO ㄊㄨㄛ

托(❹—❻*託) tuō ㄊㄨㄛ ❶用手掌向上承受着东西 to hold (up) in the palm; to support from under with the hand or palm: ～着枪 *supporting a gun in the palm* ❷衬,垫 to serve as a foil or contrast; set off: 烘云～月 *to paint clouds to set off the* *moon*—*to provide a foil to set off a character or incident* (*as in literary work*) ❸(～儿)承托器物的东西 sth serving as a support:茶～儿 *saucer*|花～儿 *flower receptacle; torus* ❹寄,暂放 to trust; to entrust:～儿所 *nursery; kindergarten; child-care centre* ❺请别人代办 to ask; to trust; to entrust (㊀ ***doublet*** 委～ to entrust; to trust):～你买本书。*Please buy a book for me.* ❻推托,借故推诿或躲闪 to give as a pretext; to plead:～病 *pleading illness; on the pretext of illness*|～故 *to give a pretext; to take* (*or find*) *an excuse.* ❼压强的非法定计量单位,1托合133.322帕 torr, a non-legal unit of measurement for pressure, equal to 133.322 pascal

饦 tuō ㄊㄨㄛ 见56页"馎"字条"馎饦"(bó—) see 馎饦 on p56

拖(*拕) tuō ㄊㄨㄛ ❶牵引,拉,拽 to pull; to tug; to drag:～车 *trailer*|～泥带水(喻做事不爽利) *messy; sloppy; slovenly*|～拉机 *tractor* ❷拖延,拉长时间 to drag on; to delay; to postpone:这件事应赶快结束,不能再～。*This should be settled as soon as possible. It can't be put off any longer.*

脱(❸**侻) tuō ㄊㄨㄛ ❶离开,落掉 to leave; to shed; to come off:～节 *to come apart; to be disjointed; to be out of line*|～逃 *to run away; to escape; to flee*|走～ *to go away; to get away*|～皮 *to slough off* (or *shed*) *skin; to exuviate; to peel* ㊕ ***transfer*** 遗漏(文字) to miss out (words); to omit; to elide:～误 *omissions and errors* (*in writing*)|这中间～去了几个字。*Several Chinese characters are missing here.* [脱离]断绝关系,离开 to break away from; to cut oneself off from; to divorce from:一刻也不～～群众。*Never isolate ourselves from the masses.* ❷取下,去掉 to take off; to cast off:～衣裳 *to take off one's clothes; to undress*|～帽 *to take off one's hat* (*in respect*) ❸[通脱]放达,不拘小节 not bothering about trifles; not punctilious; flexible and unconventional

驮 ㊀ tuó ㄊㄨㄛˊ 用背(多指牲口)负载人或物(of draught animals) to carry (*or* bear) on the back:那匹马～着两袋粮食。*That horse is carrying two sacks of grain.*

㊁ duò 见171页 see p171

佗 tuó ㄊㄨㄛˊ 负荷 to carry or bear on the back [华佗]三国时名医 Hua Tuo, a famous doctor in the period of the Three Kingdoms

陀 tuó ㄊㄨㄛˊ 山冈 low hill; hillock [陀螺](—luó) **1** 一种儿童玩具,呈圆锥形,用绳绕上后抽拉或用鞭子抽打,可以在地上旋转 top **2** 陀螺仪的简称,测量运动物体角速度和角位移的装置。用于飞机、舰船等的控制(short for 陀螺仪) gyroscope; gyro

坨 tuó ㄊㄨㄛˊ ❶(一子、一儿)成块或成堆的东西 lump; heap: 泥~子 *lump of mud; clod* ❷面食煮熟后黏结在一起(of cooked food made of flour) to stick: 饺子~了。*The* jiaozi (*or Chinese dumplings*) *stuck together in a lump.* ❸露天盐堆 salt mound in the open air

沱 tuó ㄊㄨㄛˊ ❶〈方 **dialect**〉可以停放船的水湾。多用于地名(tuo, usually used in a place name) small bay in a river (where ships or boats can berth) ❷沱江,长江的支流,在四川省东部 Tuojiang River, a tributary of Changjiang River in the east of Sichuan Province

驼 tuó ㄊㄨㄛˊ ❶骆驼 camel ❷身体向前曲,背脊突起 hunchbacked; humpbacked: ~背 *hunchbacked; humpbacked* | 背都~了。*He has a hunchback.* or *His back is hunched.*

柁 ㊀ tuó ㄊㄨㄛˊ 房柁,房架前后两个柱子之间的大横梁 girder

㊁ duò 见 171 页 see p171

砣 tuó ㄊㄨㄛˊ ❶秤锤 movable or sliding weight of a balance or steelyard ❷碾砣,碾子上的磙子 stone roller

铊 ㊁ tuó ㄊㄨㄛˊ 同"砣❶" same as 砣❶

㊀ tā 见 721 页 see p721

鸵 tuó ㄊㄨㄛˊ 鸵鸟,现在鸟类中最大的鸟,颈长,翅膀小,不能飞,走得很快,生活在沙漠中。毛可做装饰品 ostrich (*Struthio camelus*)

酡 tuó ㄊㄨㄛˊ 喝了酒,脸上发红(of one's face) flushed with drink: ~颜 *complexion flushed with drink*

跎 tuó ㄊㄨㄛˊ 见 115 页"蹉"字条"蹉跎"(cuō—) see 蹉跎 on p115

鼧 tuó ㄊㄨㄛˊ [鼧鼥](—bá)就是旱獭,俗叫"土拨鼠"。毛灰黄色,耳短,爪能掘地,毛皮可以做皮衣(i. e. 旱獭, and popularly called 土拨鼠) marmot (*Marmota*)

橐(**槖) tuó ㄊㄨㄛˊ 一种口袋 a kind of bag

[橐驼] 骆驼 camel

鼍(鼉) tuó ㄊㄨㄛˊ 鼍龙,即扬子鳄,俗叫"猪婆龙"。爬行动物,是鳄的一种(i. e. 扬子鳄, and popularly called 猪婆龙) Chinese alligator (*Alligator sinensis*)

妥 tuǒ ㄊㄨㄛˇ ❶适当,合适 appropriate; proper; suitable (㊥ **doublet** —当 appropriate; proper; suitable): 已经商量~了。*The negotiation is done properly.* | ~为保存 *to look after carefully; to take a good care of; to be under lock and key* | 这样做不~当。*It is not appropriate to do so.* [妥协]在发生争执或斗争时,一方

让步或双方让步 to come to terms; to compromise; to split the difference: 在原则性问题上决不能～～。*One should never compromise on principles*. ❷齐备,完毕 ready; settled; finished: 事已办～。*All is set*.

庹 tuǒ ㄊㄨㄛˇ 成人两臂左右伸直的长度(约5尺)(about 5 *chi* or 1.7 metres) arm span; arm spread

椭(橢) tuǒ ㄊㄨㄛˇ 椭圆,长圆形。把一个圆柱体或正圆锥体斜着用一个平面截开,所成的截口就是椭圆形 ellipse; oval

拓 ㊀ tuò ㄊㄨㄛˋ ❶开辟,扩充 to open up; to develop; to expand ❷姓 Tuo, a surname ❸见478页"落"字条"落拓"(luò—) see 落拓 on p478

㊁ tà 见722页 see p722

柝(**橐) tuò ㄊㄨㄛˋ〈古 ***archaism***〉打更用的梆子 watchman's clapper or knocker

跅 tuò ㄊㄨㄛˋ [跅弛](—chí) 放荡 dissolute; dissipated

萚(蘀) tuò ㄊㄨㄛˋ 草木脱落的皮或叶 fallen bark or leaves

箨(籜) tuò ㄊㄨㄛˋ 竹笋上一片一片的皮 sheaths of bamboo shoots

唾 tuò ㄊㄨㄛˋ ❶唾沫,唾液,口腔里分泌的液体,有帮助消化和杀菌等作用 saliva; spittle ❷啐,从嘴里吐(tǔ)出来 to spit; to expectorate: ～手可得(喻容易得到) *to be as easy as spit on one's own hand — to get or win sth with extreme ease; to be extremely easy to obtain* | ～弃(轻视、鄙弃) *to show one's contempt by spitting; to spurn; to conspue*

魄 ㊂ tuò ㄊㄨㄛˋ "落魄"(luòpò)的"魄"的又音 another pronunciation for 魄 in 落魄(luòpò)

㊀ pò 见574页 see p574

㊁ bó 见55页 see p55

W ㄨ

WA ㄨㄚ

挖(**窊) wā ㄨㄚ 掘,掏 to dig; to excavate:~个坑 *to dig a hole*|~战壕 *to dig a trench*
[挖苦](—ku)用尖刻的话讥笑人 to be sarcastic; to be ironical:你别~~人。*Don't be sarcastic.*

哇 ㊀ wā ㄨㄚ 拟声词 ***onomatopoeia*** (used to indicate sound of crying or vomiting):哭得~~的 *to cry out bitterly*|~的一声吐了一地 *to vomit everything that one has eaten with a burst*
㊁ wa 见 772 页 see p772

洼(窪) wā ㄨㄚ ❶(—儿)凹陷的地方 depression:水~儿 *waterlogged depression*|这里有个~儿。*Here is a depression.* ❷低凹,深陷 low-lying; depressed:~地 *low-lying land*|这地太~。*This land is too depressed.*|眼眶~进去 *sunken eyes*

蛙 wā ㄨㄚ 两栖动物,种类很多,卵孵化后为蝌蚪,逐渐变化成蛙。青蛙是常见的一种,捕食害虫,对农作物有益 frog (*Anura*)

娲(媧) wā ㄨㄚ [女娲]神话中的女神,传说她曾经炼五色石补天 *Nüwa*, the goddess in Chinese mythology who patched up the sky with multihued stones

娃 wá ㄨㄚˊ ❶(—子、—儿)小孩子 baby; child:女~儿 *girl*|胖~~ *chubby child* ❷旧称美女(in former times) belle:娇~ *pretty young girl* ❸〈方 ***dialect***〉某些幼小的动物 newborn animal:猪~ *piglet*|鸡~ *chick*

瓦 ㊀ wǎ ㄨㄚˇ ❶用陶土烧成的 earthen:~盆 *earthen basin*|~器 *earthenware* ❷用陶土烧成的覆盖房顶的东西 tile:~房 *tile-roofed house* [瓦解] ㊕ ***figurative*** 溃散 to disintegrate; to collapse:土崩~~ *to fall apart* ❸(外 **loanword**)功率单位名瓦特的简称,符号 W (short for 瓦特) watt (W)
㊁ wà 见 771 页 see p771

佤 wǎ ㄨㄚˇ [佤族]我国少数民族,参看附表(see the appendix) the Wa ethnic group, one of the ethnic minorities of China

瓦 ㊁ wà ㄨㄚˋ 盖(瓦) to tile (a roof):~瓦(wǎ) *to tile the roof* [瓦刀]瓦工用来砍断砖瓦并涂抹泥灰的工具 bricklayer's trowel
㊀ wǎ 见 771 页 see p771

W

袜(襪、*韤) wà ㄨㄚˋ(—子)穿在脚上、不直接着(zháo)地的东西，一般用布、纱线等制成 socks; stockings; hose

腽 wà ㄨㄚˋ [腽肭兽](—nàshòu)就是海狗。海里的一种哺乳动物，毛皮很美。阴茎和睾丸叫腽肭脐，可入药 (i. e. 海狗) fur seal; ursine seal

哇 ㊁ wa ·ㄨㄚ 助词 ***auxiliary***(前面紧挨着的音一定是 u、ao、ou 等结尾的) (used after such a word ending phonetically in u, ao, ou, etc):你别哭～。*Don't cry, please.* | 多好～! *How wonderful!* | 快走～。*Come on, please.*

㊀ wā 见 771 页 see p771

WAI ㄨㄞ

歪 wāi ㄨㄞ ❶不正，偏斜 off-centre; askew; inclined: ～着头 *with one's head tilted to one side* | 这张画挂～了。*This picture is tilted.* [歪曲] 故意颠倒是非 to distort; to misrepresent: ～～事实 *to distort the facts* ❷不正当的，不正派的 devious; crooked: ～门邪道 *crooked means; dishonest practices* | ～风 *evil wind; unhealthy trend*

㖞(喎) wāi ㄨㄞ 嘴歪 (of the mouth) awry: 口眼～斜 *awry-mouthed and cockeyed*

崴(❷**踒) ㊀ wǎi ㄨㄞˇ ❶〈方 ***dialect***〉(—子)山、水弯曲处。多用于地名 (wai, usually used in a place name) bend in a river or mountain range: 三道～子(在吉林省靖宇) *Sandaowaizi, a place in Jingyu, Jilin Province* ❷(脚)扭伤 (of a foot) to be sprained; to be twisted ❸山路不平 bumpy mountain footpath

㊁ wēi 见 779 页 see p779

外 wài ㄨㄞˋ ❶跟"内"、"里"相对 (the opposite of 内 or 里) out; outside: 国～ *abroad* | ～伤 *injury; wound; trauma* [外行](—háng)对某种业务不通晓，缺乏经验 layman; nonprofessional ❷不是自己这方面的 other (than one's own): ～国 *foreign country* | ～乡 *another part of the country; some other place* | ～人 *outsider; person from some other place* ❸指外国 foreign: 对～贸易 *foreign trade* | 古今中～ *past and present, Chinese and foreign; in modern or ancient times, in China or elsewhere* | ～宾 *foreign guest* (or *visitor*) ❹关系疏远的 not closely related: 这里没～人。*There is no outsider here.* | 不要见～。*Don't stand on ceremony, please.* or *Make yourself at home.* ❺称母亲、姐妹或女儿方面的亲戚 relatives of one's mother, sister or daughter: ～祖母 *maternal grandmother* | ～甥 *sister's son;*

nephew | ～孙 *daughter's son; grand-son* ❻(除此)另外,以外 besides; moreover: ～加 *extra; in addition* | 此～ *besides* ❼非正式的 unofficial: ～号 *nick-name* | ～史 *unofficial history; anecdotal account* ❽旧时戏曲角色名,多演老年男子 *wai*, a role for old men in Chinese traditional opera

WAN ㄨㄢ

弯(彎) wān ㄨㄢ ❶屈曲不直,使屈曲 curve; to curve (㊀ **doublet** 一曲 winding; meandering; zigzag): ～路 *winding road; tortuous path* | ～腰 *to bend one's waist* ❷(一子、一儿)曲折的部分 bend; turn; curve: 转～抹角 *to be full of twists and turns; to beat about the bush* | 这根竹竿有个～儿。*There is a bend in the bamboo pole.* ❸拉(弓) to pull (a bow): ～弓 *to pull a bow*

塆(壪) wān ㄨㄢ 山沟里的小块平地。多用于地名(wan, usually used in a place name) a small piece of flat land in a mountain valley

湾(灣) wān ㄨㄢ ❶水流弯曲的地方 bend of a stream: 汾河～*Fenhe River bend* ❷海湾,海洋伸入陆地的部分 gulf; bay: 胶州～ *Jiaozhou Bay* | 港～*harbour* ❸使船停住 to moor; to cast anchor: 把船～在那边。*Moor the boat over there.*

剜 wān ㄨㄢ 用刀挖,挖去 to gouge out (with a knife): ～肉补疮(喻只顾眼前,不惜用有害的方法来救急) *to cut out good flesh to patch up an ulcer — to resort to a remedy worse than the ailment; to adopt a stopgap measure at the expense of long-term interests*

帵 wān ㄨㄢ 〈方 **dialect**〉(一子)裁衣服剩下的大片材料 large piece of cloth remaining after a garment has been cut out, especially the remaining piece after cutting out the armpit of a Chinese-style garment

蜿 wān ㄨㄢ [蜿蜒](一yán) 蛇爬行的样子(of a snake) to wriggle; to twist ㊁ **extension** 弯弯曲曲 serpentine; to meander; to wind: 一条～～的小路 *a serpentine lane*

豌 wān ㄨㄢ [豌豆]一年或二年生草本植物,开白花,种子和嫩茎、叶都可吃 pea (*Pisum sativum*)

丸 wán ㄨㄢˊ ❶(一子、一儿)小而圆的东西 ball; pellet: 弹～*pellet* | 药～儿 *pill* | 肉～子 *meatball* ❷专指丸药 pill: ～散膏丹(*of traditional Chinese medicine*) *pills, powder and plaster* ❸量词 **quantifier**, 用于丸药(used for pills or boluses)

芄 wán ㄨㄢˊ 芄兰,多年生蔓(màn)草。叶对生,心脏形。花白色,有紫红色斑点。

茎、叶和种子可入药 butterfly weed

汍 wán ㄨㄢˊ [汍澜](—lán) 流泪的样子 weeping

纨 wán ㄨㄢˊ 细绢,很细的丝织品 fine silk fabrics; thin silk [纨绔](—kù)古代贵族子弟的华美衣着(zhuó) silk clothes worn by the children of noble families in ancient China: ～～子弟(指专讲吃喝玩乐的子弟) *playboy; dandy; beau*

W

完 wán ㄨㄢˊ ❶齐全 complete; integral; intact (㊄ **doublet** 一整 complete; integral; intact): ～美无缺 *perfect*|准备得很～善 *to be well prepared* ❷尽,没有了 to use up; to run out: 用～了 *to run out (of sth)*|卖～了(*of a shop*) *to sell out*|事情做～了 *to finish doing sth* ❸做成,了结 to be finished; to be over: ～成任务 *to carry out a task*|～工 *to finish the work*|～婚(*of a man*) *to get married* ❹交纳 to pay (tax): ～粮 *to finish delivering grain as tax in kind*|～税 *to pay tax*

玩(❸-❺*翫) wán ㄨㄢˊ ❶(—儿)游戏,做某种游戏 to play; to have fun (㊄ **doublet** 一耍 to play; to have fun): 出去～。*Go out and enjoy yourself.* or *Play outdoors.*|～皮球 *to enjoy playing ball* [玩弄] **1** 摆弄着玩 to play with; to toy with: 不要～～火柴。*Don't play with matches.* **2** 耍弄 to resort to (tricks, etc); to employ: ～～手段 *to resort to crafty manoeuvres; to play tricks* [玩笑]玩耍嬉笑,也指这样的行动或言语 to joke (with sb); joke: 开～～ *to be kidding; to crack a joke* [玩意儿] **1** 玩具 toy **2** 〈方 ***dialect***〉指杂技、曲艺,如魔术、大鼓等 acrobatics and folk art forms such as magic, *dagu*, etc **3** 指东西、事物 thing; creature ❷(—儿)耍弄,使用 to play; to use: ～花招儿 *to play tricks; to resort to crafty manoeuvres* ❸观赏 to enjoy; to appreciate: 游～ *to stroll about; to go sightseeing*|～物丧志 *to sap one's aspiration by seeking pleasure* ❹可供观赏、把玩的东西 object for appreciation: 古～ *curio; antique* ❺轻视,用不严肃的态度来对待 to trifle with; to treat lightly (㊄ **doublet** 一忽 to neglect): ～世不恭 *to be cynical; to live in defiance of conventions*|～视 *to trifle with* (❸—❺旧读 formerly wàn)

顽 wán ㄨㄢˊ ❶愚蠢无知 stupid; foolish: ～钝 *dull and obtuse; thickheaded*|愚～ *ignorant and stubborn* ❷固执,不容易变化 stubborn; persistent: ～梗 *pigheaded; bullheaded*|～癣 *stubborn dermatophytosis* [顽固] **1** 思想保守,不愿意接受新鲜事物 obstinate; to be conservative and unwilling to accept new things **2** 坚持自己的错误观点或做法,不加改变 diehard; to refuse to change one's stand or correct one's mistake [顽强]坚强,不屈服 tenacious; indomitable:～～地工作着 *to be tenacious at one's work* | 他很～～,并没被困难吓倒。*He is a tenacious man who has never been overwhelmed by difficulties.* ❸顽皮,小孩淘气 naughty; mischievous:～童 *naughty child* ❹同"玩❶❷"same as 玩❶❷

烷 wán ㄨㄢˊ 烷烃(tīng),一类有机化合物,通式是C_nH_{2n+2}。烷系化合物是构成石油的主要成分 alkane

宛 wǎn ㄨㄢˇ ❶曲折 winding; tortuous [宛转] 1 辗转(of a body) to toss and turn restlessly; to pass through many hands or places 2 同"婉转" same as 婉转 ❷宛然,仿佛 as if:音容～在 *as if the person were still around*

菀 wǎn ㄨㄢˇ ❶紫菀,多年生草本植物,叶子椭圆状披针形,花蓝紫色。根和根茎可入药 aster (*Aster tataricus*) ❷茂盛的样子 exuberant; luxuriant

惋 wǎn ㄨㄢˇ 叹惜 to sigh with regret; to bewail:～惜 *to feel sorry for; to sympathize*

婉 wǎn ㄨㄢˇ ❶和顺,温和 gentle; meek:～言 *gentle remarks; tactful persuasion* | 委～ *indirect; tactful* [婉转][宛转]说话温和而曲折,但不失本意(of rhetoric) tactful and indirect but retaining the meaning one wants to express:措词～～ *tactful choice of words* ❷美好 graceful; elegant

琬 wǎn ㄨㄢˇ 美玉 fine jade [琬圭]上端浑圆、没有棱角的圭 round-topped jade sceptre

碗(*盌、*椀) wǎn ㄨㄢˇ ❶盛(chéng)饮食的器皿 bowl ❷(一子、一儿)像碗的东西 bowl-like vessel or object:橡～子 *acorn* | 轴～儿 *axle-bowl*

畹 wǎn ㄨㄢˇ 古代称三十亩为一畹 *wan*, unit of land measurement in ancient China, equivalent to 30 *mu*

[畹町](—dīng)地名,在云南省瑞丽 Wanding, a place in Ruili, Yunnan Province

莞 ㊀ wǎn ㄨㄢˇ [莞尔]微笑的样子 smile

㊁ guǎn 见 248 页 see p248

脘 wǎn ㄨㄢˇ 胃脘,中医指胃的内部 gastral cavity

皖 wǎn ㄨㄢˇ 安徽省的别称 Wan, another name for Anhui Province

挽(❸*輓) wǎn ㄨㄢˇ ❶拉 to draw; to pull:～弓 *to draw a bow* | 手～着手 *arm in arm; hand in hand* ❷设法使局势好转或恢复原状 to reverse; to retrieve:～救 *to save; to rescue* | 力～狂澜 *to do one's utmost to stem a raging tide; to make vigorous efforts to turn the tables; to try one's best to save a desperate situation* ❸追悼死人 to lament; to elegize the deceased:～歌 *dirge* | ～联 *elegiac coup-*

let ❹同"绾"same as 绾

晚 wǎn ㄨㄢˇ ❶太阳落了的时候 evening：从早到～ *from morning till night*｜吃～饭 *to have supper*｜开～会 *to have an evening party* 引 ***extension*** 夜间 night：昨天～上没睡好。*I didn't sleep well last night.* ❷时间靠后的，比合适的时间居后 late；belated：～年（老年）*old age；one's later* (or *remaining*) *years*｜～秋 *late autumn*｜来～了 *to be late*｜赶快努力还不～。*It's not too late to make your effort right now.* ❸后来的 later：～辈 *the younger generation；juniors* ❹晚辈对长辈的自称 your humble；yours humbly

绾 wǎn ㄨㄢˇ ❶把长条形的东西盘绕起来打成结 to wind up and tie a narrow strip into a knot：～结 *to coil up into a knot*｜～个扣 *to tie a knot-like button*｜把头发～起来 *to tie up one's hair into a bun* ❷卷 to roll up：～起袖子 *to roll up one's sleeves*

万（萬）㊀ wàn ㄨㄢˋ ❶数目，十个一千（numeral）ten thousand 喻 ***figurative*** 多 large number of：～物 *everything on earth*｜气象～千 *majestic scene in all its variety；spectacular；majestic*｜～能胶 *all-purpose glue*［万岁］千秋万代永远存在（祝颂语）（good wishes）long live...：人民～～！*Long live our people!*｜祖国～～！*Long live our motherland!*［万一］转 ***transfer*** 意外，意外地 in case；if by any chance：以防～～ *to be ready for all eventualities；just in case*｜～～失败 *in case of failure* ❷极，很，绝对 absolutely；under all circumstances：～难 *beyond the bonds of possibility；all kinds of difficulties*｜～全 *foolproof；completely safe*｜～不得已 *as a last resort* ❸姓 Wan，a surname

㊁ mò 见 514 页 see p514

腕 wàn ㄨㄢˋ 胳膊下端跟手掌相连的部分。（图见 741 页"体"picture on p741）wrist

蔓 ㊀ wàn ㄨㄢˋ（一儿）细长能缠绕的茎 tendrilled vine：瓜～儿 *melon vine*｜扁豆爬～儿了。*The haricot bean plant has developed tendrils.*

㊁ màn 见 486 页 see p486

㊂ mán 见 485 页 see p485

WANG ㄨㄤ

尪（**尫）wāng ㄨㄤ ❶胫、脊或胸部弯曲的病 bent calves，back or chest ❷瘦弱 emaciated

汪 wāng ㄨㄤ ❶深广 deep and vast：～洋大海 *boundless sea* ❷液体聚集在一个地方（of liquid）to pool：地上～着水。*Puddles of water pooled on the ground.*［汪汪］**1** 充满水或眼泪的样子（of water or tears）brimming：水～～ *brimming with water*｜泪～～ *brimming eyes* **2** 拟声词 ***onomato-***

poeia，狗叫声 yap; bow-wow; bark ❸量词 ***quantifier***：一～水 *a puddle of water*

亡 ㊀ wáng ㄨㄤˊ ❶逃 to flee; to escape; to run away（㊟***doublet*** 逃一to go into exile; to flee from home)：～命 *to flee for life; to seek refuge*｜流～*to go into exile* ㊡ ***extension*** 失去 to lose：～羊补牢（喻事后补救）*to mend the fold after the sheep is lost — better late than never*｜唇～齿寒（喻利害相关）。*The teeth will be exposed to the cold once the lips are gone — to share a common lot.* ❷死 to die（㊟ ***doublet*** 死一death)：伤～很少 *to suffer light casualties* ㊡ ***extension*** 死去的 deceased：～弟 *deceased younger brother* ❸灭 to perish（㊟ ***doublet*** 灭一to become extinct)：～国 *to subjugate a nation; to let a nation perish*

㊁ wú 见 794 页 see p794

王 ㊀ wáng ㄨㄤˊ ❶古代指帝王或最高的爵位（the highest rank of nobility in ancient China）king; monarch ❷一族或一类中的首领 chieftain; ringleader; chief：兽～ *king of animals*｜蜂～ *queen bee*｜花中之～*queen of flowers* ❸大，辈分高 senior; grand：～父（祖父）*grandfather*｜～母（祖母）*grandmother* ❹姓 Wang, a surname

㊁ wàng 见 778 页 see p778

网（網） wǎng ㄨㄤˇ ❶用绳线等结成的捕鱼捉鸟的器具 net：渔～ *fishing net* [网罗]搜求，设法招致 to enlist; to recruit：～～人才 *to enlist talented people; to scout for talent* ❷用网捕捉 to catch with a net; to net：～鱼 *to net a fish*｜～鸟 *to net birds* ❸像网的东西 sth net-like：～兜儿 *string bag*｜铁丝～ *wire netting; wire meshes* ❹像网样的组织或系统 network：通信～ *telecommunications network*｜宣传～*publicity network* [网站]单位或个人在互联网上的虚拟站点，一般由一个主页和许多网页构成 website [上网]操作计算机进入互联网，在网上进行信息浏览、检索查询等 to log on (*or* in) [因特网]全球最大的互联网，由美国的阿帕网发展演变而成 Internet

罔 wǎng ㄨㄤˇ ❶蒙蔽，诬 to deceive：欺～ *to hoodwink* ❷无，没有 no; not：置若～闻（放在一边不管，好像没听见一样）*to turn a deaf ear to*

惘 wǎng ㄨㄤˇ 不得意 to feel frustrated（㊟ ***doublet*** 怅一melancholy)：～然 *frustrated; disappointed*

辋 wǎng ㄨㄤˇ 车轮外周的框子。（图见 475 页"轮" picture on p475）wheel rim (of a cart)

魍 wǎng ㄨㄤˇ [魍魉]（—liǎng）传说山林中的一种怪物 demons and monsters

枉 wǎng ㄨㄤˇ ❶曲，不直 crooked：矫～过正 *to straighten the crooked to excess*; *to overcorrect* ❷使歪曲 to twist; to pervert：～法 *to pervert* (or *bend*) *the law* ❸受屈，冤屈 to be treated unjustly; to be wronged（㊟ **doublet** 冤— to wrong; to treat unjustly | 屈— to be wronged; to be framed up）❹徒然，白白地 in vain; to no avail：～然 *in vain* | ～费心机 *to rack one's brains in vain*

往 wǎng ㄨㄤˇ ❶去，到 to go：～返 *to and fro* | 此车开～上海。*This train is bound for Shanghai.* ❷过去 past; previous（㊟ **doublet** —昔 in the past; in the former times）：～年 *before*; *former years* | ～事 *past events* ❸介词 ***preposition***，朝，向 towards; to：～东走 *to go east* | ～前看 *to look ahead*

［往往］副词 ***adverb***，常常 often; frequently：这些小事情～～被人忽略。*These trifles are often neglected.*

王 ㊁ wàng ㄨㄤˋ ❶统一天下 to reign over (a kingdom)：以德行仁者～。*One can reign over a country only by moral integrity and benevolence.* ❷统治 to govern; to rule：～此大邦 *to rule the big country*

㊀ wáng 见 777 页 see p777

旺 wàng ㄨㄤˋ 盛，兴盛 flourishing; prosperous：（㊟ **doublet** —盛 exuberant; vigorous | 兴— burgeoning; flourishing）：火很～*roaring fire*; *raging flames* | ～季 *peak period*; *busy season*

望 wàng ㄨㄤˋ ❶看，往远处看 to look (*or* gaze) into the distance：登高远～*to ascend a height to enjoy a distant view* | ～尘莫及 *so far behind that one can only see the dust of the rider ahead*; *too far behind to catch up* ❷探访问候 to pay a visit; to call on（㊟ **doublet** 看— to call on; to pay a visit）：拜～*to call on* ❸希图，盼 to expect; to look forward to（㊟ **doublet** 盼— to hope for; to long for; to expect | 希— to hope; to wish; to expect）：～子成龙 *to long to see one's son succeed in life*; *to hope one's son will have a bright future* | 喜出～外 *to be overjoyed*; *to be pleasantly surprised* | 丰收有～。*Prospects are good for a rich harvest.* ❹怨恨，责怪 hatred; hate ❺名望，声誉 reputation; fame; prestige：德高～重 *to enjoy moral eminence and high esteem*; *to be of good moral standing and undisputed reputation* | 威～*prestige* ❻夏历每月十五日 fifteenth day of a lunar month ❼介词 ***preposition***，向 to; toward：～东走 *to go eastwards*; *to go east* | ～上瞧 *to look upwards*; *to look up*

妄 wàng ㄨㄤˋ 乱，荒诞不合理 absurd; ridiculous; preposterous：～动 *rash* (or *reckless*) *action*; *ill-considered move* | ～想 *vain hope*; *futile attempt* | 勿～言。*Don't talk nonsense.*

忘 wàng ㄨㄤˋ 忘记，不记得，遗漏 to forget; to escape one's memory：别～了拿书。*Don't forget to take the books with you.* | 喝水不～掘井人。*When you drink water from the well, don't ever forget the well digger.*

WEI ㄨㄟ

危 wēi ㄨㄟ ❶不安全，跟"安"相对(the opposite of 安) danger; hazard; peril (㊀ ***doublet***—险 danger)：转～为安 *to pass from danger to safety*; *to turn danger into safety*; *to pull through a crisis* [危言]使人惊奇的话 alarmist talk：～～耸听 *to exaggerate things just to scare people* [临危]将死，面临生命危险 dying; facing death ❷损害 to harm; to endanger (㊀ ***doublet*** —害 to harm; to endanger)：～及家国 *to endanger both one's family and one's country* ❸高的，陡的 high; precipitous：～楼 *tall building* ❹端正 upright; proper：正襟～坐 *to straighten one's clothes and sit properly*; *to sit in state* ❺星宿名，二十八宿之一 *wei*, the 12th of the 28 constellations

委 ㊀ wēi ㄨㄟ [委蛇](—yí) **1** 敷衍，应付 to be perfunctory; to go through the motions：虚与～～ *to deal with sb courteously but without sincerity*; *to pretend politeness and compliance* **2** 同"逶迤" same as 逶迤

㊁ wěi 见 783 页 see p783

逶 wēi ㄨㄟ [逶迤](—yí) 道路、河道等弯曲而长 (of road, river, etc) long and serpentine; meandering：山路～～ *winding mountain paths*

巍 wēi ㄨㄟ 高大(叠 ***reduplication***) towering; lofty：～峨 *lofty* | ～～高山 *towering mountains*

威 wēi ㄨㄟ ❶使人敬畏的气魄 awe-inspiring：示～游行 *demonstration*; *parade*; *march* | ～力 *power* | ～望 *prestige* | 权～ *authority*; *authoritativeness* ❷凭借力量或势力 by force; by power：～胁 *to threaten* | ～逼 *to compel* (or *threaten*) *by force*

葳 wēi ㄨㄟ [葳蕤](—ruí) 草木茂盛的样子 (of foliage) luxuriant; lush

崴 ㊀ wēi ㄨㄟ [崴嵬](—wéi) 山高的样子 (of a mountain) lofty; towering

㊁ wǎi 见 772 页 see p772

偎 wēi ㄨㄟ 紧挨着，亲密地靠着 to snuggle up to; to nestle; to lean close to：小孩儿～在母亲的怀里。*The child nestles in his mother's arms.*

隈 wēi ㄨㄟ 山、水等弯曲的地方 mountain recess; river bend

煨 wēi ㄨㄟ ❶在带火的灰里把东西烧熟 to roast in hot cinders (*or* coals):～白薯 *to roast sweet potatoes in hot cinders* ❷用微火慢慢地煮 to cook over a slow fire; to stew; to simmer:～鸡 *to stew chicken*|～肉 *to stew meat*

鳂 wēi ㄨㄟ 鱼名。身体多为红色,眼大,口大而斜。生活在热带海洋 squirrelfish (*Holocentridae*)

W

微 wēi ㄨㄟ ❶小,细小 minute; tiny; little (㊧ ***doublet*** 细— slight; fine; subtle): 防～杜渐 *to check for erroneous ideas or faults at the outset so as to stop their development; to nip (an evil) in the bud* ❷轻微,稍 a little; slight (㊧ ***doublet*** 稍— a little; slightly) (叠 ***reduplication***):～感不适 *to feel a bit out of sorts*|～～一笑 *to give a faint smile* ❸衰落,低下 decline:衰～ *decline; wane* ❹精深,精妙 profound; abstruse:～妙 *delicate; subtle* ❺法定计量单位中十进分数单位词头之一,表示 10^{-6}(符号 μ) micro-(μ)

溦 wēi ㄨㄟ 小雨 drizzle

薇 wēi ㄨㄟ 一年生或二年生草本植物。花紫红色,是优良饲料,可入药。也叫"巢菜"或"野豌豆"(also called 巢菜 or 野豌豆) common vetch

韦(韋) wéi ㄨㄟˊ 熟皮子,去毛加工鞣制的兽皮 leather

违(違) wéi ㄨㄟˊ ❶背,反,不遵守 to violate; to disobey (㊧ ***doublet*** —背 to go against; to infringe|—反 to violate; to transgress; to break):～法 *to break* (or *violate*) *the law; to be illegal*|～章 *to break rules and regulations*|阳奉阴～*to agree in public but oppose in private; to feign compliance* ❷不见面,离别 to be separated; to leave:久～*to have not seen sb for ages*

围(圍) wéi ㄨㄟˊ ❶环绕,四周拦挡起来 to enclose; to surround; to encircle:～巾 *scarf; muffler*|～墙 *enclosure; enclosing wall*|包～敌人 *to encircle the enemy* ❷四周 around; circumference:四～都是山 *skirted by mountains*|这块地方周～有多大? *What is the size of this area?* ❸(一子)圈起来作拦阻或遮挡的东西 (enclosure used for defensive purpose or used as curtains) defensive wall; curtain:土～子 *fortified village*|床～子 *bed-curtain* ❹量词 ***quantifier***,两只手的拇指和食指合拢起来的长度 (length of the circle formed by both hands with thumbs and index fingers) hand span:腰大十～ *waist of ten hand spans* 又指两只胳膊合拢起来的长度(length of the circle formed by a person's two arms joining at the hands) arm span:树大十～ *a tree of ten* *arm spans in circumference*

帏(幃) wéi ㄨㄟˊ ❶帐子，幔幕 curtain; bed curtain ❷古代佩带的香囊(in ancient China) perfume pouch

闱(闈) wéi ㄨㄟˊ ❶古代宫室的旁门 side gate of an ancient palace：宫～(宫殿里边) *living quarters of a palace* ❷科举时代称考场 imperial examination site：秋～ *autumn (imperial) examination*｜入～ *to enter the imperial examination hall; to be selected as a candidate*

涠(潿) wéi ㄨㄟˊ [涠洲]岛名，在广西壮族自治区北海市南部海域 Weizhou, an island to the south of Beihai, the Guangxi Zhuang Autonomous Region

为(爲、**為) ㊀ wéi ㄨㄟˊ ❶做，行 to do; to act：事在人～。*It all depends on human effort.*｜所作所～ *what one has done; one's behaviour* (or *conduct*) ㊀ **extension** 作为，作事的能力 capability：年轻有～ *young and promising* ❷做，当 to act as; to serve as：他被选～人大代表。*He was elected deputy to the National People's Congress.*｜拜他～师 *to acknowledge him as teacher* ❸成为，变成 to become; to turn：一分～二。*A whole divides into two.* or *Everything tends to divide into two.*｜高岸～谷，深谷～陵。*High banks become valleys and deep valleys become hills.* or *The world is changing all the time.* ❹是 to be; to mean; to make：十二个～一打。*Twelve makes one dozen.* ❺介词 **preposition**，被 by：～人所笑 *to be laughed at (by others)* ❻助词 **auxiliary**，常跟"何"相应，表疑问(often used with 何 in a rhetorical question)：何以家～? *What need have I of a home?* ❼附于单音形容词后，表程度、范围(used after certain single-character adjectives to indicate degree or scope)：大～增色 *to add much beauty to*｜广～传播 *to be widely spread* ❽附于表程度的单音副词后，加强语气(used after certain single-character adverbs to strengthen the tone)：极～重要 *extremely important*｜尤～出色 *particularly outstanding*

㊁ wèi 见 784 页 see p784

沩(潙、**溈) wéi ㄨㄟˊ 沩水，水名，在湖南省长沙 Weishui River in Changsha, Hunan Province

圩 ㊀ wéi ㄨㄟˊ ❶低洼地区周围防水的堤 dyke; embankment ❷有圩围住的地区 dyke-enclosed area：～田 *polder; dyked low-lying paddy fields*｜盐～ *salt pond surrounded with dykes* ❸(－子)围绕村落四周的障碍物，也作"围子"(also written as 围子) village defensive wall：土～子 *fortified village*｜树～子 *thickly grown thorns sur-*

rounding village (or *houses*)

㊁ xū 见 843 页 see p843

桅 wéi ㄨㄟˊ 桅杆，船上挂帆的杆子 mast

硙(磑) ㊀wéi ㄨㄟˊ [硙硙] 形容很高的样子 very high

㊁ wèi 见 786 页 see p786

唯 wéi ㄨㄟˊ ❶同"惟❶" same as 惟❶ ❷文言叹词 ***interjection in classical Chinese***，表示答应 yes [唯唯诺诺] 形容一味顺从别人的意见 obsequious

帷 wéi ㄨㄟˊ (一子) 围在四周的帐幕 curtain：车～子 *vehicle curtain* | 运筹～幄 *to plan strategies within a command tent; to devise strategies and make decisions*

惟 wéi ㄨㄟˊ ❶单单，只 only; solely; alone：～有他因病不能去。*He is the only one who could not go there because of his illness.* | ～恐落后 *for fear that one should lag behind* ❷但是 but：雨虽止，～路途仍甚泥泞。*The rain has stopped but the road is still very muddy.* ❸文言助词 ***auxiliary in classical Chinese***，用在年、月、日之前 (used before year, month or day)：～二月既望 *on the 16th of the 2nd lunar month* ❹思，想。"思惟"通常写作"思维"(思惟 often written as 思维) thinking; thought

维 wéi ㄨㄟˊ ❶连接 to tie up; to hold together (㊟ ***doublet*** 一系 to hold together; to keep up; to maintain) [维护] 保全，保护 to protect; to uphold [维持] 设法使继续存在 to maintain; to keep ❷文言助词 ***auxiliary in classical Chinese***：～妙～肖 *remarkably true to life; vivid*

[维吾尔族] 我国少数民族，参看附表 (see the appendix) the Uygur ethnic group, one of the ethnic minorities of China

潍 wéi ㄨㄟˊ 潍河，水名，在山东省潍坊 Weihe River in Weifang, Shandong Province

嵬 wéi ㄨㄟˊ 高大耸立 towering; rising up high

伟(偉) wěi ㄨㄟˇ 大 great (㊟ ***doublet*** 一大 great)：身体魁～ *tall and strong; tall and sturdily built* | ～大的祖国 *great motherland* | ～人 (对人民有大功绩的人) *great man; great personage*

苇(葦) wěi ㄨㄟˇ (一子) 芦苇。参看 465 页"芦"(see 芦 on p465) reed

纬(緯) wěi ㄨㄟˇ ❶纬线，织布时用梭穿织的横纱，编织物的横线 weft; woof ❷地理学上假定的沿地球表面跟赤道平行的线，从赤道起，向北称"北纬"，向南称"南纬"，到南北极各 90° latitude ❸指纬书 (东汉神学迷信附会儒家经义的一类书) Wei Books, a category of books on Confucian doctrines misinterpreted by theology and superstition in the Eastern Han Dynasty

玮（瑋） wěi ㄨㄟˇ 玉名 a kind of fine jade

炜（煒） wěi ㄨㄟˇ 光明 bright

韡（韡） wěi ㄨㄟˇ（叠 ***reduplication***）盛，光明 bright; magnificent

韪（韙） wěi ㄨㄟˇ 是，对（常和否定词连用）(often used with a negative) right; yes：冒天下之大不～ *to risk everyone's condemnation; to dare do what the whole world considers to be wrong*

伪（僞、**偽） wěi ㄨㄟˇ ❶假，不真实 false; fake：去～存真 *to eliminate the false and retain the true*｜～造 *to fabricate*｜～装 *to pretend; to disguise* ❷不合法的(of a regime) illegal：～政府 *puppet government*

尾 ㊀ wěi ㄨㄟˇ ❶（一巴）鸟、兽、虫、鱼等身体末端突出的部分 tail：猪～巴 *pigtail* [交尾]动物交配(of animals) mating ❷末端 rear：排～*at the end in order* ❸尾随，在后面跟 to follow; to tail behind：～其后 *to follow at sb's heels* ❹量词 ***quantifier***，用于鱼(used for fish) ❺星宿名，二十八宿之一 *wei*, the 6th of the 28 constellations

㊁ yǐ 见 887 页 see p887

娓 wěi ㄨㄟˇ [娓娓]形容谈论不倦或说话动听 to speak tirelessly or pleasantly：～～动听 *nice to listen to; very pleasant to the ear*

委 ㊀ wěi ㄨㄟˇ ❶任，派，把事交给人办 to appoint; to entrust (㊦ ***doublet*** 一任 to appoint)：～以重任 *to assign an important task to sb* ❷抛弃，舍弃 to discard; to cast aside (㊦ ***doublet*** 一弃 to discard)：～之于地 *to throw sth on the ground* ❸推诿 to shift ❹曲折，婉转 indirect; roundabout：话说得很～婉 *to speak tactfully* [委屈](一qu)含冤受屈或心里苦闷 to feel wronged (*or* aggrieved)：心里有～～，又不肯说。*He would not like to pour out his grievances though he felt wronged.* ❺末，尾 end：原～*the whole story; all the details* ❻确实 certain; for sure：～系实情。*It's indeed true.*｜～实不错。*It is good indeed.* ❼委员或委员会的简称(short for 委员 or 委员会)：编～*(a member of) compilation board; (a member of) editorial board*｜体～*committee of physical culture*｜市～*municipal Party committee*

[委靡][萎靡](一mǐ)颓丧，不振作 listless; lethargic; dispirited：精神～～*dispirited; dejected; in low spirits*

㊁ wēi 见 779 页 see p779

诿 wěi ㄨㄟˇ 推托，推卸 to put blame on sb else; to shirk：互相推～*to shift responsibilities onto each other; to put the blame on each other*

萎 wěi ㄨㄟˇ 干枯衰落 to wilt：枯～ *to wither*｜～谢 *to*

W

wilt; to fade | 气～*deflated* [萎缩] **1** 体积缩小,表面变皱 to wither; to shrivel **2** 衰退 to shrink; to sag; to decline:经济～～。*The economy is sagging a bit.*

痿 wěi ㄨㄟˇ 身体某部分萎缩或丧失机能的病 illness caused by decline or loss of function of a certain body part; paralysis; flaccid paralysis

洧 wěi ㄨㄟˇ [洧川]地名,在河南省尉氏 Weichuan, a place in Weishi, Henan Province

痏 wěi ㄨㄟˇ ❶瘢痕 scar ❷伤口 cut; wound

鲔 wěi ㄨㄟˇ ❶古书上指鲟(xún)鱼(in ancient Chinese texts) sturgeon (*Acipenseridae*) ❷鱼的一类,纺锤形,背蓝黑色,生活在大洋中 yaito tuna (*Euthynnus yaito*)

隗 ㊀ wěi ㄨㄟˇ 姓 Wei, a surname

㊁ kuí 见 404 页 see p404

頠 wěi ㄨㄟˇ 安静 quiet

猥 wěi ㄨㄟˇ ❶鄙陋,下流 salacious; obscene: ～辞 *obscene words; dirty language* [猥亵](－xiè) **1** 淫秽,下流 lewd; obscene: 言辞～～ *to speak wantonly* **2** 做下流的动作 to act indecently: ～～妇女 *to harass a woman* ❷杂,多 many; mixed: ～杂 *miscellaneous*

卫(衛、**衞) wèi ㄨㄟˋ ❶保护,防护 to defend; to protect (㊐ **doublet** 保—to defend; to protect): 保家～国 *to protect our homes and defend our country* | 自～*self-defence* [卫生]保护身体的健康,预防疾病 good for one's health; hygienic sanitary: 个人～～*personal hygiene* | 环境～～*environmental sanitation* (or *hygiene*) ❷防护人员 guard: 警～ *guard; bodyguard* | 后～*rear guard; defender; linebacker* ❸文言指驴(in classical Chinese) donkey: 策双～来迎 *to drive two donkeys to meet sb* ❹明代驻兵的地点 location for the stationing of troops in the Ming Dynasty: ～所 *troop-station* ❺周代诸侯国名,在今河南省北部和河北省南部一带 Wei, a princedom of the Zhou Dynasty, situated in the northern part of today's Henan Province and the southern part of today's Hebei Province

为(爲、**為) ㊁ wèi ㄨㄟˋ ❶介词 **preposition**, 替,给 for: ～人民服务 *to serve the people* ❷介词 **preposition**, 表目的(可以和"了"连用)(also used together with 了) for the purpose of; for the sake of: ～早日实现四化而斗争。*Struggle for an early realization of the four modernizations.* | ～了美好的明天而努力。*Strive for a beautiful tomorrow.* ❸介词 **preposition**, 对,向 to: 且～诸

君言之。*Now, let me inform everybody about it.* ❹帮助,卫护 to help; to defend

㊀ wéi 见 781 页 see p781

未 wèi ㄨㄟˋ ❶地支的第八位 *wei*, the 8th of the 12 Earthly Branches ❷未时,指下午一点到三点 *weishi*, period of the day from 1 pm to 3 pm ❸副词 ***adverb***,表示否定 negative **1** 不 no; not:~知可否 *not to know whether it can be done or not* **2** 没有,不曾 not yet:~成年 *not yet of age; under age*|此人~来。*This person didn't come.* ❹放在句末,表示疑问(used at the end of a sentence to express doubt):君知其意~? *Do you know what he really means?*

味 wèi ㄨㄟˋ ❶(一儿)味道,滋味,舌头尝东西所得到的感觉 taste; flavour:五~ *the five flavours (sweet, sour, bitter, pungent and salty); all sorts of flavours*|带甜~儿 *to taste sweet* [口味] ㊑ ***figurative*** 对事物的喜好 one's taste (*or* liking):这件事正合他的~~。*It is just to his liking* (or *taste*). ❷(一儿)气味,鼻子闻东西所得到的感觉 smell; scent; odour:香~儿 *sweet smell; fragrance; perfume*|臭~儿 *offensive* (or *foul*) *smell; stench* ❸(一儿)意味,情趣 interest; delight:趣~ *interest; delight; liking*|意~深长 *of profound significance* ❹体会,研究 to distinguish the flavour of; to reflect on:细~其言 *to ponder what he said*|必须细细体~,才能懂得其中的道理。*One has to savour it in order to understand it.* ❺量词 ***quantifier***,用于中药的种类(used for ingredients of a traditional Chinese medicine prescription):这个方子一共七~药。*This prescription specifies seven medicinal herbs.*

位 wèi ㄨㄟˋ ❶位置,所在的地方 place; location:座~ *seat* ❷职位,地位 position; rank; status ❸特指皇位 throne:即~ *to accede to; to be enthroned*|在~ *to be on the throne; to reign*|篡~ *to usurp the throne* ❹一个数中,每个数码所占的位置 place; figure; digit:个~ *single digit; unit's place*|十~ *two digit number; ten's place* ❺量词 ***quantifier***,用于人(含敬意)(used in deferential reference to people):诸~同志 *every comrade; everybody*|三~客人 *three guests*

畏 wèi ㄨㄟˋ ❶怕 to fear; to dread (㊥ ***doublet*** —惧 fear; dread):大无~的精神 *dauntless spirit*|~首~尾 *to be full of misgivings; to be overcautious* ❷敬佩 to admire:后生可~。*The young are to be regarded with awe.*

喂 (❷❸*餵、❷❸*餧) wèi ㄨㄟˋ ❶叹词 ***interjection***,打招呼时用(used in greetings) hi; hello; hey:~,是谁? *Hey,*

W

W

who is it? | ～，快来呀！*Hi, come over here right now!* ❷把食物送进人嘴里 to put food into the mouth of a person：～小孩儿 *to feed a child* ❸给动物东西吃 to feed an animal：～牲口 *to feed cattle; to feed draught animals* [转] ***transfer*** 畜（xù）养 to raise; to feed; to keep：～鸡 *to raise chicken* | ～猪 *to raise pigs*

碨 wèi ㄨㄟˋ〈方 ***dialect***〉石磨（mò）millstone

硙（磑） ㊁ wèi ㄨㄟˋ 同"碨" same as 碨
㊀ wéi 见782页 see p782

胃 wèi ㄨㄟˋ ❶胃脏，人和某些动物消化器官的一部分，能分泌胃液、消化食物。（图见940页"脏"picture on p940）stomach ❷星宿名，二十八宿之一 *wei*, the 17th of the 28 constellations

谓 wèi ㄨㄟˋ ❶告诉 to say：人～予曰。*Someone told me.* ❷称，叫作 to call; to name：称～ *title; appellation* | 何～人工呼吸法？*What is artificial respiration?* [所谓] 所说的 what is called; so called：～～分析，就是分析事物的矛盾 *Analysis means to analyse the inherent contradictions of things.* [无谓] 没意义，说不出道理 meaningless; pointless; senseless：这种争论太～～了。*This argument is really meaningless.*

猬（*蝟） wèi ㄨㄟˋ 刺猬，哺乳动物，身上长着硬刺，嘴很尖，昼伏夜出，捕食昆虫和小动物等 hedgehog (*Erinaceinae*)

渭 wèi ㄨㄟˋ 渭河，发源于甘肃省，横贯陕西省入黄河 Weihe River, rising in Gansu Province and traversing Shaanxi Province where it empties into the Huanghe (*or* Yellow) River

尉 ㊀ wèi ㄨㄟˋ ❶古官名 ancient official title：太～ *imperial minister in charge of military affairs* ❷军衔名 military rank：上～ *captain; lieutenant*
[尉氏] 地名，在河南省 Weishi, a place in Henan Province
㊁ yù 见922页 see p922

蔚 ㊀ wèi ㄨㄟˋ ❶草木茂盛 luxuriant [引] ***extension*** 盛大 grand：～为大观 *to present a splendid sight; to afford a magnificent view* [蔚蓝] 晴天天空的颜色 azure; sky blue：～～的天空 *bright blue sky* ❷文采华美 colourful：云蒸霞～ *the rise of colourful clouds*
㊁ yù 见922页 see p922

慰 wèi ㄨㄟˋ ❶使人心里安适 to console; to soothe; to comfort：安～ *to comfort; to console* | ～问伤员 *to express sympathy and solicitude for the wounded* | ～劳前方战士 *to bring gifts to the soldiers at the front* [慰藉]（-jiè）安慰，抚慰 consolation; comfort ❷心安 to be relieved：欣～ *gratified; satisfied; pleased* | 甚～

greatly relieved

鳚 wèi ㄨㄟˋ 鱼名。体小，侧扁，无鳞，身体前端有侧线。生活在近海 blenny (*Blenniidae*)

遗 ㊁ wèi ㄨㄟˋ 赠与 to offer as a gift; to make a present of sth:～之千金 *to present sb with a generous gift of money*

㊀ yí 见 885 页 see p885

魏 wèi ㄨㄟˋ ❶古国名 Wei, a princedom in ancient China **1** 战国国名，在今河南省北部，山西省西南部一带 Wei, one of the Warring States covering today's northern Henan Province and southwestern Shanxi Province and nearby areas **2** 三国之一，曹丕所建立(公元 220—265 年)，在今黄河流域甘肃省以下各省和湖北、安徽、江苏三省北部和辽宁省南部 Wei (220 — 265), one of the Three Kingdoms, established by Cao Pi and situated in the provinces along today's Yellow River Valley east to Gansu, the northern part of Hubei, Anhui, and Jiangsu provinces, and southern Liaoning Province ❷北魏，北朝之一，拓跋珪所建立(公元 386—534 年) Northern Wei (386 — 534), one of the Northern Dynasties, established by Tuo Bagui

WEN ㄨㄣ

温 wēn ㄨㄣ ❶不冷不热 warm; lukewarm (㊦ ***doublet*** —暖 warm)：～水 *lukewarm (or warm) water* [温饱] 衣食充足 to dress warmly and eat one's fill; to have adequate food and clothing ❷温度，冷热的程度 temperature：气～ *atmospheric temperature* | 低～ *low temperature* | 体～ *body temperature* ❸性情柔和 gentle; tender; mild (㊦ ***doublet*** —柔 gentle and soft | —和 kindly; gentle; mild) ❹使东西热 to warm up：～酒 *to warm up wine (or liquor)* ❺复习 to review：～课 *to review one's lessons* | ～故知新 *to learn the new while restudying the old; to gain new knowledge by reviewing old; to recall the past helps one understand the present* ❻中医指温热病(in traditional Chinese medicine) seasonal febrile diseases：春～ *spring fever* | 冬～ *winter fever* ❼同"瘟" same as 瘟

榅 wēn ㄨㄣ [榅桲] (—po) 落叶灌木或小乔木，叶椭圆形，背面密生绒毛，花淡红色或白色。果实也叫榅桲，有香气，味酸，可制蜜饯 quince (*Cydonia oblonga*)

辒 wēn ㄨㄣ [辒辌] (—liáng) 古代可以卧的车，也用作丧车 *Wenliang*, an ancient sleeping carriage, also used for mourning purposes

瘟 wēn ㄨㄣ 瘟疫，流行性急性传染病 acute contagious disease：～病 *seasonal febrile diseases* | 猪～ *swine fever; hog cholera*

蕰 wēn ㄨㄣ [蕰草]〈方 *dialect*〉指水中生长的杂草，可作肥料 water weeds

鳁 wēn ㄨㄣ [鳁鲸] 哺乳动物，外形像鱼，生活在海洋中，体长 15 米—16 米，背黑色，腹部白色，头上有喷水孔，无牙齿，有鲸须，背鳍小 sei whale (*Balaenoptera borealis*)

文 wén ㄨㄣˊ ❶事物错综所成的纹理或形象 certain complex natural phenomena：天～ *astronomy* | 地～ *geography* ❷刺画花纹 tattoo：断发～身 *to have one's hair cut and one's body tattooed* ❸文字，记录语言的符号 characters; script; written language：甲骨～ *oracle bone inscriptions* | 外～ *foreign language* | 扫除～盲 *to wipe out illiteracy* [文献]有历史价值或参考价值的图书资料 document; literature [文学]用语言、文字表现出来的艺术作品，如诗歌、小说、散文、戏曲等 literature, such as poem, novel, prose, drama, etc [文言]以古汉语为基础的书面语，跟"白话"相对，也省称"文"(the opposite of 白话, also 文 for short) classical Chinese [文章]用文字写成的有条理的篇章，也省称"文"(also 文 for short) essay; article; writings：作～ *composition* | 古～ *writings in classical Chinese* ❹旧时指礼节仪式(in former times) rite; ritual：虚～ *mere formality* | 繁～缛节 *red tape; excessive formalities* [文化] culture **1** 人类在社会历史发展过程中所创造的物质财富和精神财富的总和，特指精神财富，如哲学、科学、教育、文学、艺术等 civilization; culture (sum total of the material wealth and cultural wealth created by man in the course of the historical development of society, cultural wealth in particular, such as philosophy, science, education, literature, arts, etc) **2** 考古学用语，指同一个历史时期的不依分布地点为转移的遗迹、遗物的综合体。同样的工具、用具，同样的制作技术等，是同一种文化的特征，如仰韶文化等(of archaeology) ancient culture (comprehensive body of sites and ruins left behind, which are independent of their locations in a given historical period, the identical tools, implements and manufacturing skills being the characteristics of the same culture, as the *Yangshao* culture, etc) **3** 语文、科学等知识 education; schooling; literacy：～～水平高 *of high educational level; highly educated* | 学～～ *to learn to read and write* [文明]社会发展到较高阶段表现出来的状态 civilization：中国是世界～～发达最早的国家之一。*China is one of the earliest civilized countries in the world.* [文物]过去遗留下来的在文化发展史上有价值的建筑、碑刻、器物等 cultural (*or* historical) relic ❺外表，容态

appearance; looks: ～质彬彬 *suave; urbane; quiet and scholarly* ❻指关于知识分子的，非军事的 intellectual; non-military; civilian: ～人 *man of letters; scholar* | ～臣武将 *civil and military officials; ministers and generals* [转] **transfer** 柔和 mild; soft; refined: ～雅 *refined; cultured; elegant* | ～绉绉 *genteel* [文火]不猛烈的火 slow fire; cooking fire ❼量词 **quantifier**, 用于旧时的铜钱 *wen*, unit of copper cash in old times: 一～钱 *one* wen *cash* | 一～不值 *not worth a penny; worthless* ❽(旧读 formerly wèn)文饰，掩饰 to conceal; to hide: ～过饰非 *to gloss over one's faults; to cover up one's errors*

纹 ㊀ wén ㄨㄣˊ 条纹 lines; veins; grain ([连] **doublet** 一理 veins; grain): 水～ *water wave; ripple* | 指～ *fingerprint* | 这木头～理很好看。*The grain of the wood is very beautiful.*

㊁ wèn 见 790 页 see p790

炆 wén ㄨㄣˊ 〈方 **dialect**〉用微火焖食物 to stew; to cook food over a slow fire

蚊 wén ㄨㄣˊ (一子)昆虫名。种类很多，幼虫叫孑孓，生活在水里。雌的吸人畜的血液，雄的吸植物汁液。蚊能传染疟疾、流行性乙型脑炎等 mosquito (*Culicidae*)

雯 wén ㄨㄣˊ 成花纹的云彩 patterned cloud

闻 wén ㄨㄣˊ ❶听见 to hear: 耳～不如目见。*Seeing is believing.* ❷听见的事情，消息 news; story: 新～ *news* | 奇～ *strange news; fantastic story* ❸(旧读 formerly wèn)出名，有名望 well-known; famous: ～人 *famous person; celebrity* ❹名声 reputation: 令～ *good name; reputation* | 丑～ *scandal* ❺用鼻子嗅气味 to smell: 你～～这是什么味? *Smell this and see what it is.* | 我～见香味了。*I smell something sweet.*

阌 wén ㄨㄣˊ [阌乡]地名，在河南省灵宝 Wenxiang, a place in Lingbao, Henan Province

刎 wěn ㄨㄣˇ 割脖子 to cut one's throat: 自～ *to cut one's own throat; to commit suicide by cutting one's own throat*

吻(*脗) wěn ㄨㄣˇ ❶嘴唇 lips: 接～ *to kiss* [吻合]相合 to be identical; to fit perfectly ❷用嘴唇接触表示喜爱 to touch by the lips; to kiss ❸动物的嘴 animal's mouth

抆 wěn ㄨㄣˇ 擦 to wipe: ～泪 *to wipe one's tears*

紊 wěn ㄨㄣˇ (旧读 formerly wèn)乱 disorderly; confused ([连] **doublet** 一乱 disorder; chaos; confusion): 有条不～ *orderly; in an orderly way*

W

稳(穩) wěn ㄨㄣˇ ❶稳当，安定，固定 steady; staid; firm：站～ *to stand firm*｜～步前进 *to advance steadily; to make steady progress* ⊜喻 ***figurative*** 沉着，不轻浮 steady; sedate：～重 *steady; staid; sedate* ❷使稳定 to stabilize; to calm：～住局势 *to stabilize the situation* ❸准确，可靠 sure; certain：十拿九～ *almost certain; 90 per cent sure*

W

问 wèn ㄨㄣˋ ❶有不知道或不明白的请人解答 to ask; to inquire：到～事处去～一～ *to ask at the Information Desk* [问题] **1** 要求回答或解释的题目 question **2** 尚待解决或弄不明白的事 problem; issue ❷慰问 to express sympathy and solicitude for; to extend one's regards to：～候 *to send one's regards to; to say hello to* ❸审讯，追究 to interrogate; to examine：～口供 *to interrogate someone* ㊀引 ***extension*** 问罪，惩办 to denounce; to condemn：胁从不～。*Those reluctant followers are not to be condemned.* ❹管，干预 to concern oneself with; to bother about; to participate in sth：概不过～ *to wash one's hands of the whole matter*

汶 wèn ㄨㄣˋ 汶河，水名，在山东省 Wenhe River in Shandong Province

纹 ㊁ wèn ㄨㄣˋ 同"璺"same as 璺

㊀ wén 见 789 页 see p789

揾 wèn ㄨㄣˋ ❶用手指按住 to press with fingers ❷擦 to wipe

璺 wèn ㄨㄣˋ 器物上的裂痕(in implement, glassware or earthenware, etc) crack：这个碗有一道～。*The bowl has a crack in it.*｜打破沙锅～(谐"问")到底(*punning on the likeness of* 璺 *and* 问) *to insist on getting to the bottom of a matter; to inquire persistently*

WENG ㄨㄥ

翁 wēng ㄨㄥ ❶老头儿 old man：渔～ *old fisherman*｜老～ *old man* ❷父亲 father ❸丈夫的父亲或妻子的父亲 father-in-law：～姑(公婆) *husband's parents*｜～婿 *father-in-law and son-in-law*

嗡 wēng ㄨㄥ 拟声词 ***onomatopoeia*** (叠 ***reduplication***) to buzz：飞机～～响。*A plane is buzzing overhead.*｜蜜蜂～～地飞。*Bees are buzzing all around.*

滃 ㊀ wēng ㄨㄥ 滃江，水名，在广东省北部 Wengjiang River in northern Guangdong Province

㊁ wěng 见 791 页 see p791

鹟 wēng ㄨㄥ 鸟名。身体小，嘴稍扁平，吃害虫，是益鸟 flycatcher (*Muscicapidae*)

鞥 wēng ㄨㄥ 〈方 ***dialect***〉靴鞥(yào) boot leg; leg of a boot

蓊 wěng ㄨㄥˇ 形容草木茂盛 (of vegetation) lush; luxuriant: ～郁 *lush; luxuriant* | ～茸 *luxuriant and downy*

滃 ㊀ wěng ㄨㄥˇ ❶形容水盛 (of water or spring) gush; abundance of water ❷形容云起 rise of clouds; cloudy

㊁ wēng 见 790 页 see p790

瓮(*甕) wèng ㄨㄥˋ 一种盛水、酒等的陶器 urn; earthen jar [瓮城]围绕在城门外的小城 barbican entrance to a city; enceinte of a city gate

蕹 wèng ㄨㄥˋ 蕹菜，俗叫"空心菜"。一年生草本植物，茎中空，叶心脏形，叶柄长，花白色，漏斗状。嫩茎叶可做菜吃 (popularly called 空心菜) water spinach (*Ipomoea aquatica*)

齆 wèng ㄨㄥˋ 鼻子堵塞不通气 stuffy nose

WO ㄨㄛ

挝(撾) ㊁ wō ㄨㄛ [老挝] 国名，在中南半岛 Laos, a country in Southeast Asia

㊀ zhuā 见 999 页 see p999

莴(萵) wō ㄨㄛ [莴苣] (—ju)一年或二年生草本植物，叶多长形，花黄色，分叶用和茎用两种。叶用的叫莴苣菜或生菜，茎用的叫莴笋 lettuce (*Lactuca sativa*)

涡(渦) ㊀ wō ㄨㄛ 旋涡，水流旋转形成中间低洼的地方 whirlpool; eddy: 卷入旋～(喻被牵入纠纷里) *to be drawn into a whirlpool —to be involved in a dispute*

㊁ guō 见 256 页 see p256

窝(窩) wō ㄨㄛ ❶(—儿) 禽兽或其他动物的巢穴 nest; lair: 鸡～ *hencoop; chicken roost* | 马蜂～ *hornet's nest* | 狼～ *wolf lair* ㊄ ***figurative*** 人的安身处，人或物所占的位置 one's home; place occupied by a person or an object: 安乐～ *snug retreat; cosy nest; den* | 挪个～儿 *to move to another place* ❷藏匿犯法的人或东西 to harbour (*or* shelter) a lawbreaker or illegal things: ～贼 *to harbour a thief* | ～赃 *to store* (or *stash*) *loot* | ～藏 *to harbour; to shelter* ❸坏人聚集之处 place where evildoers get together; lair: 贼～ *thieves' den* ❹(—儿)洼陷的地方 hollow place: 酒～儿 *dimple* ❺弄弯 to bend: 把铁丝～个圆圈 *to bend the wire into a hoop* ❻郁积不得发作或发挥 to hold in: ～火 *to be filled with anger* | ～心 *to be depressed* [窝工] 因调配不好，工作人员没有充分发挥作用 enforced idleness due to poor organization, etc; hold-up in work ❼量词 ***quantifier***: 一～小猪 *a litter of piglets*

蜗(蝸) wō ㄨㄛ 蜗牛，一类软体动物，有螺旋形扁圆的硬壳，头部有两对触角。吃嫩叶，对农作物有害 snail [蜗居] ㊄ ***figurative*** 窄小

的住所 humble abode

倭 wō ㄨㄛ 古代称日本(in ancient Chinese) Japan

踒 wō ㄨㄛ (手、脚等)猛折而筋骨受伤 to sprain (*or* strain) one's sinew or bone:手～了 *to sprain one's hand*

喔 wō ㄨㄛ 拟声词 ***onomatopoeia***,形容鸡叫声 cock's crow

W

我 wǒ ㄨㄛˇ 代词 ***pronoun***,自称,自己 I (my; myself; me); we (our; ourselves; us):～国 *our country* | 自～批评 *self-criticism* | 忘～精神 *selflessness*

肟 wò ㄨㄛˋ 有机化合物的一类,通式是 $\genfrac{}{}{0pt}{}{R}{R'}{>}C = NOH$。是羟胺($NH_2OH$)与醛或酮缩合而成的化合物 oxime

沃 wò ㄨㄛˋ ❶土地肥 fertile; rich ([连] ***doublet*** 肥— fertile):～土 *fertile soil* | ～野 *fertile land* ❷灌溉,浇 to irrigate

卧(**卧) wò ㄨㄛˋ ❶睡倒,躺或趴 to lie:仰～*to lie supine; to lie on the back* | ～倒 *to lie down* | ～病 *to be confined to bed* ❷有关睡觉的 for sleeping:～室 *bedroom* | ～铺 *sleeping berth* ❸趴伏(指动物)(of animal or bird) to crouch; to sit:鸡～在窝里。*The chickens were in the coop.* | 猫～在炉子旁边。*The cat crouched at the side of the stove.*

偓 wò ㄨㄛˋ 用于人名。偓佺(quán),古代传说中的仙人(wo, used in a name of a person) Wo Quan, legendary immortal

握 wò ㄨㄛˋ 攥(zuàn),手指弯曲合拢来拿 to hold; to grasp:～手 *to shake hands (with sb)*

幄 wò ㄨㄛˋ 帐幕 tent:帷～*army tent*

渥 wò ㄨㄛˋ ❶沾湿,沾润 wet; moisten ❷厚,重 strong; rich:优～(优厚) *munificent; favourable; generous*

龌 wò ㄨㄛˋ [龌龊](—chuò)肮脏,不干净 dirty; filthy [喻] ***figurative*** 人的品质恶劣 mean; base

涴 wò ㄨㄛˋ 〈方 ***dialect***〉弄脏,泥、油等沾在衣服、器物上 to make dirty; to stain oil or mud on clothes or utensils

硪 wò ㄨㄛˋ (—子)一种砸地基的工具 *wo*, a kind of tool used to ram earth for a foundation

斡 wò ㄨㄛˋ 转,旋 to revolve; to spin; to rotate [斡旋] [喻] ***figurative*** 居中调停,把弄僵了的局面扭转过来 to mediate:从中～～ *to mediate between the two parties*

WU ㄨ

乌(烏) ㊀ wū ㄨ ❶乌鸦,鸟名,俗叫"老鸹"(gua)或"老鸦"(popularly called 老鸹 or 老鸦) crow [乌

合] ㊉ ***figurative*** 无组织地聚集disorderly gathering：～～之众 *disorderly band; motley crowd; rabble* ❷ 黑色 black; dark：～云 *dark clouds* | ～木 *ebony* ❸〈古 ***archaism***〉表示疑问，哪，何 what; how：～足道哉？*What's there worth mentioning about it?* ❹姓 Wu, a surname

[乌呼]同"呜呼"same as 呜呼

[乌孜别克族] 我国少数民族，参看附表（see the appendix）the Uzbek (or Ozbek) ethnic group, one of the ethnic minorities of China

㊁ wù 见 797 页 see p797

邬(鄔) wū ㄨ 姓 Wu, a surname

呜(嗚) wū ㄨ 拟声词 ***onomatopoeia***（叠 ***reduplication***）toot; hoot; zoom：工厂汽笛～～地叫。*The factory kept sounding its whistle.*

[呜呼]文言叹词 ***interjection in classical Chinese***，旧时祭文常用"呜呼"表示叹息，后借指死亡（formerly in funeral orations）alas; alack; (now) to be dead; to die：一命～～*to die*

钨(鎢) wū ㄨ 一种金属元素，符号 W，灰黑色，质硬而脆，熔点很高，可以拉成很细的丝。钨丝可以做电灯泡中的细丝。钢里面加入少量的钨合成钨钢，可以制造机器、钢甲等 wolfram (W); tungsten

圬(**杇) wū ㄨ ❶泥瓦工人用的抹(mǒ)子(for plastering) trowel ❷抹(mò)墙 to plaster

污(*汚、*汙) wū ㄨ ❶肮脏 dirty（㊀ ***doublet*** 一秽 filthy; foul）：～泥 *mud; mire; sludge* ㊉ ***figurative*** 不廉洁 corrupt：贪～*to corrupt; to embezzle* ❷弄脏 to defile; to smear：玷～*to stain* | ～染 *to pollute; to contaminate*

[污辱]用无理的言行给人以难堪 to humiliate; to affront; to insult

巫 wū ㄨ 专以祈祷求神骗取财物的人 witch; wizard

诬 wū ㄨ 硬说别人做了某种坏事 to accuse falsely; to slander（㊀ ***doublet*** 一赖 to accuse sb without any evidence; to falsely incriminate）：～告 *to accuse sb falsely of committing a crime; to bring a false charge against* | ～蔑 *to slander; to vilify* | ～陷 *to frame a case against; to frame sb*

於 ㊂ wū ㄨ 文言叹词 ***interjection in classical Chinese***

[於乎][於戏]（－hū）同"呜呼" same as 呜呼

[於菟]（－tú）〈古 ***archaism***〉老虎的别称 another name for 老虎

㊀ yú 见 915 页 see p915

㊁ yū 见 913 页 see p913

屋 wū ㄨ ❶房 house（㊀ ***doublet*** 房一 house）㊊ ***extension***〈方 ***dialect***〉家 home ❷房间 room：他住在东房的北～。*He lives in the northern room of the east wing.*

W

恶(惡) [四] wū ㄨ 〈古 ***archaism***〉 ❶ 同"乌❸"same as 乌❸ ❷叹词 ***interjection***,表示惊讶(used to express surprise) oh:～,是何言也! *Oh! What a remark it is!*

[一] è 见 173 页 see p173
[二] wù 见 798 页 see p798
[三] ě 见 173 页 see p173

亡 [二] wú ㄨˊ 古同"无"same as 无 in ancient Chinese

[一] wáng 见 777 页 see p777

无(無) wú ㄨˊ ❶没有,跟"有"相对(the opposite of 有) nothing; without: ～产阶级 *proletariat* | 从～到有 *to grow out of nothing; to start from scratch* ❷ 不 no; not: ～须乎这样 *not necessary to be so* | ～妨试试。*(You) may have a try as well.* or *There is no harm to have a try.* [无非] 不过是,不外如此 nothing but; no more than; simply: 他批评你,～～是想帮助你进步。*He criticized you simply because he wanted to help you make progress.* [无论] 连词 ***conjunction***,不拘,不管,常跟"都"连用(usually used in collocation with 都) regardless of; no matter what (whether, when, where, how, etc): ～～是谁都要遵守纪律。*Everyone is to observe discipline no matter who he or she is.*

芜(蕪) wú ㄨˊ 长满乱草 overgrown with weeds ([连] ***doublet*** 荒一 to lie waste): ～城 *deserted city* [喻] ***figurative*** 杂乱 mixed and disorderly: ～杂 *mixed and disorderly; confusing* | ～词 *superfluous words; redundant words*

毋 wú ㄨˊ 副词 ***adverb***,不要,不可以 no; not: 宁缺～滥 *to be better to leave a vacancy unfilled than to give it to an incompetent; to rather go without than have sth shoddy; to place quality above quantity*

吾 wú ㄨˊ 文言代词 ***pronoun in classical Chinese***,我,我的 I; me; my (we, us, our)

郚 wú ㄨˊ 见 730 页"鄌"字条"鄌郚"(táng—) see 鄌郚 on p730

唔 [一] wú ㄨˊ 见 881 页"咿"字条"咿唔"(yī—) see 咿唔 on p881

[二] ńg 见 531 页 see p531
[三] ń 见 521 页 see p521

浯 wú ㄨˊ 浯河,水名,在山东省东部 Wuhe River in the east of Shandong Province

梧 wú ㄨˊ 梧桐,落叶乔木,树干很直,木质坚韧 Chinese parasol (tree); phoenix tree (*Firmiana simplex*)

铻 wú ㄨˊ 见 406 页"锟"字条"锟铻"(kūn—) see 锟铻 on p406

鼯 wú ㄨˊ 鼯鼠,哺乳动物,尾巴很长,前后肢之间有薄膜,能从树上滑翔下来,住在树洞中,昼伏夜出 flying squirrel

吴 wú ㄨˊ ❶古国名 Wu, a princedom of ancient China **1** 周代诸侯国名,在今江苏

省南部和浙江省北部，后来扩展到淮河下游一带 Wu, a princedom of the Zhou Dynasty, in today's southern part of Jiangsu Province and northern part of Zhejiang Province and later extending to the lower reaches of the Huaihe River **2** 三国之一，孙权所建立（公元 222—280 年），在今长江中下游和东南沿海一带 Wu (222—280), one of the Three Kingdoms, established by Sun Quan in the middle and lower reaches of the Yangtze River and part of the southeastern coastal area ❷指江苏省南部和浙江省北部一带 Wu, an area comprising southern Jiangsu and northern Zhejiang

蜈 wú ㄨˊ ［蜈蚣］（— gong）节肢动物，由许多环节构成，每节有脚一对，头部的脚像钩子，能分泌毒液，捕食小虫，可入药 centipede (*Chilopoda*)

鹀 wú ㄨˊ 鸟名。大小和形状似麻雀。雄鸟羽毛颜色较鲜艳。吃种子和昆虫 little bunting (*Emberiza pusilla*)

五 wǔ ㄨˇ ❶数目字 (numeral) five ❷旧时乐谱记音符号的一个，相当于简谱的"6" *wu*, note of the scale of Chinese traditional music, corresponding to '6' (la) in numbered musical notation

伍 wǔ ㄨˇ ❶古代军队的编制，五个人为一伍 *wu*, basic five-man army unit in ancient China ㊀ ***extension*** 军队 army: 入～ *to join the army* ❷一伙 company: 相与为～ *to keep company with sb* ❸"五"字的大写 five, capital form of 五

午 wǔ ㄨˇ ❶地支的第七位 *wu*, 7th of the 12 Earthly Branches ❷午时，指白天十一点到一点 noon; time from 11 am to 1 pm: ～饭 *midday meal; lunch* 特指白天十二点 noon; at 12 o'clock; at noon: ～前 *in the morning; before noon* | 下～一点开会。*The meeting begins at 1 o'clock in the afternoon.* ［午夜］半夜 midnight

仵 wǔ ㄨˇ ❶仵作，旧时官署检验死伤的人员 (in former times) coroner ❷姓 Wu, a surname

迕 wǔ ㄨˇ ❶相遇 to meet; to encounter ❷逆，违背 to go against: 违～ *to run counter to; to be against; to be defiant to*

忤 wǔ ㄨˇ 逆，不顺从 disobedient: ～逆 *unfilial; disobedient (to parents)*

庑（廡） wǔ ㄨˇ 古代堂下周围的屋子 side room or building in a traditional compound house; wing

沅（潕、**瀩） wǔ ㄨˇ 沅水，水名，在湖南省 Wushui River in Hunan Province

怃（憮） wǔ ㄨˇ 怃然，失意的样子 frustrated; disappointed

妩（嫵、**娬） wǔ ㄨˇ ［妩媚］（女子）

W

姿态美好(of a woman) charming; lovely

武 wǔ ㄨˇ ❶关于军事或技击的 about military affairs or martial arts: ～装 *armed forces; arms; military equipment* | ～器 *weapons* | ～术 *wushu; martial arts* ❷勇猛 brave and powerful; fierce; valiant: 英～ *gallant; brave; valiant* [武断]只凭主观判断 to make an arbitrary decision; to make a subjective assertion: 你这种看法太～～。*Your viewpoint is too arbitrary.* ❸半步 half a footstep: 行不数～ *within a few footsteps away; not far away*

鹉 wǔ ㄨˇ 见 900 页"鹦"字条"鹦鹉"(yīng—) see 鹦鹉 on p900

侮 wǔ ㄨˇ 欺负,轻慢 to insult; to bully (㊀ **doublet** —辱 to insult; to subject sb to indignity; to humiliate | 欺— to bully): 中国人民是不可～的。*The Chinese people are not to be bullied.* | 抵御外～ *to resist foreign aggression*

捂(**摀) wǔ ㄨˇ 严密地遮盖住或封闭起来 to seal; to cover: 用手～着嘴 *to cover one's mouth with one's hand* | 放在罐子里～起来免得走味儿。*Seal it in a jar so as not to lose its flavour.*

牾 wǔ ㄨˇ 抵触,冲突,不顺从 to violate; to go against; to be disobedient: 抵～ *to contradict*

舞 wǔ ㄨˇ ❶按一定的节奏转动身体表演各种姿势 to dance: 手～足蹈 *to gesticulate merrily with hands and feet; to wave one's arms and stamp one's feet in joy* | ～剑 *to perform swordplay* | 秧歌～ yangge *dance;* yangko [鼓舞]激励,使人奋发振作 to inspire; to encourage; to stimulate: ～～群众的热情 *to inspire the masses; to rouse the enthusiasm of the masses* ❷要弄 to play with: ～弊 *fraudulent practice; malpractice; embezzlement* | ～文弄墨 *to engage in phrase-mongering; to juggle with words*

兀 wù ㄨˋ ❶高而上平 high and flat ❷高耸特出 rising to a height; towering: 突～ *lofty; towering* ❸元曲中用为发语词(used at the beginning of a sentence in *Yuan* drama)

阢 wù ㄨˋ [阢陧](—niè)同"杌陧"same as 杌陧

杌 wù ㄨˋ 杌凳,较矮的凳子 small stool

[杌陧](—niè)(局势、心情等)不安 restless; unstable; uneasy

靰 wù ㄨˋ [靰鞡](—la)东北地区冬天穿的一种用皮革做的鞋,里面垫着靰鞡草。也作"乌拉"(also written as 乌拉) *wula*, leather boots lined with wula sedge and worn in winter in Northeast China

勿 wù ㄨˋ 副词 **adverb**,别,不要 do not; don't: 请～动手! *No touching!* | 闻声～惊。

Don't be frightened on hearing the sound.

芴 wù ㄨˋ ❶诸葛菜，一年生草本植物，产于我国北部和中部，可供观赏，也可当作蔬菜食用 Chinese violet cress (*Orychophragmus violaceus*) ❷有机化合物，化学式 $C_{13}H_{10}$。白色片状晶体，存在于煤焦油中。用来制染料、杀虫剂和药物等 fluorene

物 wù ㄨˋ ❶东西 thing; matter; substance: ～价(*commodity*) *price* | 万～*all things; everything on earth* | 新事～ *new things* [物流]产品从供应地到接受地的流动转移。一般经过包装、运输、存储、养护、流通加工、信息处理等环节 logistics ㊀ ***extension*** 具体内容 content; essence; substance: 言之有～ *speech with substance; to speak convincingly* [物色]寻求(合适的人选或东西) to look for; to seek out; to choose [物质] **1** 独立于人们意识之外，能为人们的意识所反映的客观存在 matter; substance; objects being independent of the consciousness of man: ～～不灭 *conservation of matter* | ～～是可以被认识的。*Matter can be known.* **2** 指金钱，供吃、穿、用的东西等 material; money; means of subsistence ❷"我"以外的人或环境，多指众人 outside world as distinct from oneself; people other than oneself: ～望所归 *to enjoy popular confidence* | 待人接～ *way one gets along with people*

乌(烏) ㊁ wù ㄨˋ [乌拉] (—la) 同"靰鞡" same as 靰鞡

㊀ wū 见 792 页 see p792

坞(塢、*隖) wù ㄨˋ ❶小障蔽物，防卫用的小堡 small castle; fort ❷四面高中间凹下的地方 depressed place: 山～ *col; pass; saddle* | 花～ *sunken flower bed* [船坞]在水边建筑的停船或修造船只的地方 dock; shipyard

戊 wù ㄨˋ 天干的第五位，用作顺序的第五 *wu*, the 5th of the 10 Heavenly Stems; the fifth

务(務) wù ㄨˋ ❶事情 affair; business (㊈ ***doublet*** 事— business; affair): 任～*task; mission* | 公～*official business* | 医～工作者 *medical worker* ❷从事，致力 to be engaged in; to devote one's efforts to: ～农 *to be engaged in farming; to be a farmer* ❸追求 to seek; to go after: 不要好(hào)高～远。*Do not aim too high.* or *Don't bite off more than you can chew.* ❹务必，必须，一定 must; to be sure to: ～请准时出席。*Please be sure to be present on time.* | 你～必去一趟。*You must go there yourself.*

雾(霧) wù ㄨˋ ❶接近地面的水蒸气，遇冷凝结后飘浮在空气中的小水点 fog ❷像雾的东西 fine spray of water: 喷～器 *sprayer; atomizer*

误（**悮） wù ㄨˋ ❶ 错 mistake; error（㊟ *doublet* 错—mistake; error）：～解 *to misread; to misunderstand*｜讹～*error* ❷耽误，耽搁 to miss; to delay; to hinder：～事 *to hold things up; to bungle matters*｜火车～点。*The train is behind the schedule.*｜生产学习两不～。*Neither production nor study suffers.* ❸因自己做错而使人受害 to harm; to damage：～人子弟 *to mislead the younger generation; to lead young people astray* ❹不是故意而做错事 by mistake; by accident：～伤 *to injure sb unintentionally* (or *by accident*)｜～入歧途 *to go astray*

恶（惡） ㊂ wù ㄨˋ 讨厌，憎恨 to loathe; to dislike; to hate：可～ *detestable; repulsive; abhorrent*｜深～痛绝 *to cherish intense hatred for; to detest*

㊀ è 见 173 页 see p173

㊁ ě 见 173 页 see p173

㊃ wū 见 794 页 see p794

悟 wù ㄨˋ 理解，明白，觉醒 to realize; to awaken（㊟ **doublet** 醒—to wake up to reality; to come to see the truth）：～出这个道理来 *to come to realize the truth*｜恍然大～*to be suddenly enlightened; to suddenly see the light* ［觉悟］**1** 由迷惑而明白 awareness; consciousness **2** 指政治认识 political consciousness：提高～～ *to raise one's consciousness*

晤 wù ㄨˋ 遇，见面 to meet; to interview; to see：～面 *to meet; to see*｜～谈 *to have a face-to-face talk; to have a talk; to interview*｜会～*to meet*

焐 wù ㄨˋ 用热的东西接触凉的东西，使它变暖 to warm up; to warm sth cold with a hot object：用热水袋～一～手 *to warm one's hands with a hot-water bag*

痦（**痂） wù ㄨˋ ［痦子］突起的痣 naevus; mole

寤 wù ㄨˋ 睡醒 to wake up

婺 wù ㄨˋ 婺水，古水名，在江西省东北部 Wushui River, an ancient river in the northeast of Jiangxi Province

骛 wù ㄨˋ ❶ 乱跑 to run about; to move freely and quickly ❷同"务❸" same as 务❸

鹜 wù ㄨˋ 鸭子 duck：趋之若～（像鸭子一样成群地跑过去，比喻很多人争着去，含贬义）（**derogatory**） *to go for sth like a flock of ducks — to scramble for sth*

鋈 wù ㄨˋ ❶白色金属 copper-nickel alloy; white copper ❷镀 plating; gilding

X ㄒ

XI ㄒㄧ

夕 xī ㄒㄧ ❶日落的时候 sundown; sunset; dusk:朝(zhāo)～ *morning and evening; from morning till night; daily*|～照 *sunset glow; evening glow* ❷夜 evening; night:前～*eve; evening of the previous day*|风雨之～*stormy night*

汐 xī ㄒㄧ 夜间的海潮 night tide

矽 xī ㄒㄧ 硅(guī)的旧称 former term for 硅

穸 xī ㄒㄧ [窀穸](zhūn—) 墓穴 grave; tomb

兮 xī ㄒㄧ 文言助词 ***auxiliary in classical Chinese***,相当于现代的"啊"或"呀"(akin to 啊 or 呀 in modern Chinese):大风起～云飞扬。*The high wind rises, and the clouds scud.*

西 xī ㄒㄧ ❶方向,太阳落的一边,跟"东"相对(the opposite of 东) west:由～往东 *from west to east*|～房 *western room*|～南角上 *at the south-west corner* ❷事物的样式或方法属于西方(多指欧、美两洲)的 Western:～餐 *Western(-style) food*|～服 *Western-style clothes; Western suit*

茜 ㊁ xī ㄒㄧ 多用于人名(人名中也有读 qiàn 的)(also pronounced qiàn in some names) xi, usually used in a given name

㊀ qiàn 见 596 页 see p596

恓 xī ㄒㄧ [恓惶](—huáng) 惊慌烦恼的样子 scared; vexed; troubled

栖 ㊁ xī ㄒㄧ [栖栖] 忙碌不安定的样子 unsettled; restless

㊀ qī 见 580 页 see p580

氙 xī ㄒㄧ "氙"(xiān)的旧称 former term for 氙

牺(犧) xī ㄒㄧ 古代指用作祭品的毛色纯一的牲畜 beast of a uniform colour for sacrifice in ancient China; sacrifice:～牛 *sacrificial ox* [牺牲] 古代为祭祀宰杀的牲畜 beast slaughtered for sacrifice; sacrifice ㊍ ***figurative*** **1** 为人民、为正义事业而献出自己的生命 to give one's life for; to die a martyr's death; to lay down one's life **2** 泛指为某种目的舍弃权利或利益等 to sacrifice; to give up; to do sth at the expense of

硒 xī ㄒㄧ 一种非金属元素,符号 Se,灰色晶体或红色粉末,导电能力随光的照射强度的增减而改变。硒可用来制半导体晶体管和光电管等,又供玻璃等着色用 selenium (Se)

舾 xī ㄒㄧ 船舶装备品 ship equipment [舾装] **1** 船舶装置和舱室设备如锚、舵、缆、桅樯、救生设备、航行仪器、管路、电路等的总称 fittings of a ship **2** 船体下水后,装备上述设备和刷油漆等项工作的总称 (of ships) outfitting work

粞 xī ㄒㄧ 碎米 broken rice: 糠~*broken chaff*

吸 xī ㄒㄧ ❶从口或鼻把气体引入体内,跟"呼"相对 (the opposite of 呼) to inhale; to breathe in: ~气 *to inhale* | ~烟 *to smoke (a cigarette); smoking* ❷引取 to absorb; to suck up: 棉花能~水。*Cotton can absorb water.* | ~墨纸 *blotting paper* | ~铁石 *magnet* | ~尘器 *vacuum cleaner* [吸收] 摄取,采纳 to absorb; to assimilate; to draw: 植物由根~~养分。*Plants assimilate nutrients through their roots.* | ~~先进经验 *to draw on advanced experience*

希 xī ㄒㄧ ❶少 rare: 物以~为贵。*A thing is valued in proportion to its rarity.* ❷盼望 to hope; to expect (㊟ ***doublet*** 一望 to hope): ~准时出席。*It is hoped that you will be present on time.* | ~早日归来。*I hope you will return earlier.*

郗 xī ㄒㄧ (旧读 formerly chī) 姓 Xi, a surname

唏 xī ㄒㄧ 叹息 to sign [唏嘘] 同"欷歔" same as 欷歔

浠 xī ㄒㄧ 浠河,水名,在湖北省黄冈 Xihe River in Huanggang, Hubei Province

晞 xī ㄒㄧ ❶干,干燥 dry: 晨露未~。*The morning dew is yet to dry — it is still early morning.* ❷破晓,天亮 first light of day; daybreak: 东方未~。*The first rays of the sun are yet to break the eastern horizon — it is before daybreak.*

欷 xī ㄒㄧ [欷歔] (—xū) 抽搭,哭泣后不自主地急促呼吸 to sob

烯 xī ㄒㄧ 烯烃(tīng),一类有机化合物,通式是 C_nH_{2n},如乙烯 alkene

稀 xī ㄒㄧ ❶事物中间距离远、空隙大,跟"密"相对 (the opposite of 密) sparse; scattered (㊟ ***doublet*** 一疏 few and scattered): 棉花种得太~了不好。*It is not good to grow cotton sparsely.* | ~客 *rare visitor* [稀松] **1** 懒散,松懈 sloppy; lax **2** 差劲 not good; badly **3** 平常,不关紧要 unimportant; trivial ❷浓度小,含水分多的 watery; thin (㊟ ***doublet*** 一薄 rare; thin): ~饭 *gruel; watery porridge* | ~硫酸 *dilute sulphuric acid* | ~泥 *thin mud; slime* | ~释 *to dilute* ❸少 few; rare; scarce (㊟ ***doublet*** 一少 few; rare; scarce | 一罕 rare; uncommon): ~有金属 *rare metal*

豨 xī ㄒㄧ 古书上指猪 (in ancient Chinese texts)

swine; pig
[豨莶](—xiān)豨莶草,一年生草本植物,茎上有灰白毛,花黄色。全草入药 common St. Pauls-wort (*Siegesbeckia orientalis*)

昔 xī ㄒㄧ 从前 past; former: ～日 *former days; bygone days* | 今～ *present and past; today and yesterday*

惜 xī ㄒㄧ ❶爱惜,重视,不随便丢弃 to value; to cherish: ～阴(爱惜时间) *to value every bit of time* | ～墨如金 *to regard one's ink as if it were gold — to be extremely prudent about one's writing, calligraphy, or painting* [怜惜]爱惜,同情 to show compassion and concern for; to take pity on; to have pity for ❷ 舍不得 to grudge; to stint ([连] **doublet** 吝— to grudge): ～别 *to be reluctant to part; to hate to see sb go* | 不～牺牲 *even at the cost of one's life* | ～指失掌(喻因小失大) *to try to save a finger only to lose the whole hand — to try to save a little only to lose a lot* ❸可惜,感到遗憾 to regret; to feel sorry for: ～未成功。*What a Shame it failed!*

腊 ㊁ xī ㄒㄧ 干肉 dried meat
㊀ là 见 410 页 see p410

析 xī ㄒㄧ 分开 to divide; to separate: 条分缕～ *to make meticulous analysis* | 分崩离～ *to fall to pieces* [引] **extension** 解释 to explain: ～疑 *to resolve a doubt; to clear up a doubtful point* | 分～ *to analyse*

菥 xī ㄒㄧ [菥蓂](—mì)又名"遏蓝菜"。一年生草本植物,叶匙形,花白色,果实扁圆形。叶可作蔬菜,种子可榨油。全草可入药(also called 遏蓝菜) Boor's Mustard; Dish Mustard; Field Pennycress; Wild Cress (*Thlaspi arvense*)

淅 xī ㄒㄧ 淘米 to wash rice
[淅沥](—lì)拟声词 ***onomatopoeia***,轻微的风雨声或落叶声等(sound of light rain, breeze, falling leaves, etc) rustle; patter

晰(*皙) xī ㄒㄧ 明白,清楚 clear; distinct: 看得清～ *to see clearly* | 十分明～ *quite clear*

皙 xī ㄒㄧ 人的皮肤白 light-complexioned; fair-skinned: 白～ *light-complexioned; fair*

蜥 xī ㄒㄧ [蜥蜴](—yì)一类爬行动物,俗叫"四脚蛇"。身上有细鳞,尾巴很长,脚上有钩爪,生活在草丛里(popularly called 四脚蛇) lizard

肸 xī ㄒㄧ 用于人名。羊舌肸,春秋时晋国大夫(xi, used in a given name) Yang Shexi, a high official of the state of Jin during the Spring and Autumn period

饻 xī ㄒㄧ 老解放区一种计算工资的单位,一饻等于几种实物价格的总和 *xi*, unit of wages in former liberated areas during the Liberation War of China, one *xi* equal to the total price of a number of goods

息 xī ㄒㄧ ❶呼吸时进出的气 breath：鼻～*breath*｜喘～*to pant*; *to gasp* ❷停止，歇 to cease; to stop：～怒。*Don't be angry.*｜经久不～*prolonged*; *enduring*｜按时作～*to keep to the timetable* ❸消息 news; information：信～*information* ❹利钱 interest：年～*annual interest* ❺儿女 children：子～*one's children* ❻繁殖，滋生 to breed; to multiply：生～*to subsist*; *to live*｜蕃～*to proliferate*; *to multiply quickly*

熄 xī ㄒㄧ 火灭，使灭 to extinguish (a fire); to put out (a light)：炉火已～。*The fire in the stove went out.*｜～灯 *to turn off the light* (or *lamp*)

螅 xī ㄒㄧ ［水螅］一种腔肠动物，身体圆筒形，上端有小触手，附着(zhuó)在池沼、水沟中的水草上 hydra (*Hydra*)

奚 xī ㄒㄧ ❶古代指奴隶(in ancient China) slave ❷文言代词 **pronoun in classical Chinese**，表示疑问(used to express doubt) **1** 为什么 why：～不去也？*Why not go?* **2** 什么 what：子将～先？*What to do first?* **3** 何处 where：水～自至？*Where does the water come from?*

［奚落］讥诮，嘲笑 to taunt; to jeer (*or* scoff) at

傒 xī ㄒㄧ ［傒倖］(－xìng) 烦恼，焦躁 annoyance; vexation

徯 xī ㄒㄧ ❶等待 to wait ❷同"蹊"same as 蹊

溪(*谿) xī ㄒㄧ 山里的小河沟 mountain stream (*or* brook)

［溪卡］(－kǎ) 西藏民主改革以前官府、寺院和贵族的庄园(of officials, monks and nobles in Tibet before the democratic reform) manor

蹊 ㊀ xī ㄒㄧ 小路 footpath; narrow road (㊟ ***doublet*** －径 path; way)

㊁ qī 见 581 页 see p581

鸂 xī ㄒㄧ ［鸂鶒］(－chì) 古书上指像鸳鸯的一种水鸟 *xichi*, a kind of water bird akin to the mandarin duck and drake in ancient Chinese texts

鼷 xī ㄒㄧ ［鼷鼠］小家鼠 mouse (*Mus musculus*)

悉 xī ㄒㄧ ❶知道 to know; to learn; to be informed of：获～*to get to know*; *to learn of*｜熟～此事 *to be familiar with it* ❷尽，全 all; entire：～心 *wholehearted*; *devoted*｜～数捐献 *to contribute all that one has*｜～听尊便。*Do as you like.*

窸 xī ㄒㄧ ［窸窣］(－sū) 拟声词 ***onomatopoeia***，细小的摩擦声(succession of slight, soft sounds of friction) rustle

蟋 xī ㄒㄧ ［蟋蟀］(－shuài) 北方俗叫"蛐蛐儿"。一类有害的昆虫，身体黑褐色，雄的好斗，两翅摩擦能发声(popularly called 蛐蛐儿 in the north of China) cricket (*Gryllidae*)

翕 xī ㄒㄧ ❶合 to fold; to close：～动(*as of lips, etc*) *to open and close*｜～张 *to*

open and close alternately ❷和顺 affable; agreeable

［翕忽］迅速的样子 rapidly; fleetly

噏 xī ㄒㄧ 同"吸"same as 吸

歙 ㊀ xī ㄒㄧ 吸气 to breathe; to inhale

㊁ shè 见 664 页 see p664

犀 xī ㄒㄧ ❶犀牛，哺乳动物，形状略似牛，全身几乎没有毛，皮粗厚多皱纹。角生在鼻子上，印度一带产的只有一只角，非洲产的有两只角，前后排列。角坚硬 rhinoceros (*Rhinocerotidae*) ❷坚固 firm: ～利(锐利) *keen; sharp; trenchant*

［木犀］(－xi) 桂花 sweet-scented osmanthus (*Osmanthus fragrans*)

樨 xī ㄒㄧ［木樨］同"木犀"，即桂花(i. e. 桂花) same as 木犀

锡 xī ㄒㄧ ❶一种金属元素，符号 Sn，银白色，有光泽，质软，富延展性，在空气中不易起变化 stannum (Sn) ❷赏赐 to grant; to bestow a reward

［锡伯族］(－bó－)我国少数民族，参看附表(see the appendix) the Xibe ethnic group, one of the ethnic minorities of China

裼 ㊀ xī ㄒㄧ 敞开或脱去上衣，露出身体的一部分 to unbutton or divest one's upper garment to expose a part of the body (㊟ **doublet** 袒－ to strip to the waist)

㊁ tì 见 743 页 see p743

熙 xī ㄒㄧ ❶光明 bright; sunny ❷和乐(叠 **reduplication**) merry; cheerful: 众人～～。*Everyone is happy and contented.* ❸古同"嬉"same as 嬉 in ancient Chinese

［熙攘］(－rǎng) 形容人来人往，非常热闹 bustling with activity: 熙熙攘攘 *bustling with activity; with people bustling about*

僖 xī ㄒㄧ 快乐 happy and joyous

嘻 xī ㄒㄧ 喜笑的样子或声音(叠 **reduplication**) sound of merry laughter: 笑～～*grinning*｜～皮笑脸 *grinning cheekily; smiling and grimacing*

嬉 xī ㄒㄧ 游戏，玩耍 to play; to have fun

熹 xī ㄒㄧ 光明 brightness［熹微］日光微明(of morning sunlight) dim; pale

嶲 xī ㄒㄧ［越嶲］地名，在四川省。今作"越西"(now written as 越西) Yuexi, a place in Sichuan Province

膝 xī ㄒㄧ 大腿和小腿相连的关节的前部。(图见 741 页"体" picture on p741) knee

羲 xī ㄒㄧ 姓 Xi, a surname

曦 xī ㄒㄧ 阳光(usually of early morning) sunlight: 晨～*morning glow; first rays of the morning sun*

爔 xī ㄒㄧ 同"曦"same as 曦

醯 xī ㄒㄧ ❶醋 vinegar ❷酰(xiān)的旧称 former term for 酰

巇 xī ㄒㄧ [险巇]形容山险(of a mountain path) dangerous ㊀ ***extension*** 道路艰难(of a road) difficult

X

习(習) xí ㄒㄧˊ ❶学过后再温熟,反复地学使熟练 to review; to practise:自~(*of students*) *to study by oneself in scheduled time*|复~ *to review*|~字 *to practise penmanship; to do exercises in calligraphy*|~作 *to do exercises in composition, painting, etc* ❷对某事熟悉 to be familiar with:~兵(熟于军事) *to be well versed in military affairs* ㊀ ***extension*** 常常地 often; frequently:~见(*of things*) *commonly seen; common*|~闻 *frequently heard of* ❸习惯,长期重复地做,逐渐养成的不自觉的行为 habit:积~*old habit*|铲除不良~气 *to get rid of the bad habit*|恶~*bad habit*

嶍 xí ㄒㄧˊ [嶍峨](-é)山名,在云南省玉溪 Xi'e Mountain in Yuxi, Yunnan Province

鳛 xí ㄒㄧˊ ❶古书上指泥鳅(in ancient Chinese texts) loach (*Cobitidae*) ❷鳛水,地名,在贵州省。今作"习水"(now written as 习水) Xishui, a place in Guizhou Province

席(❶*蓆) xí ㄒㄧˊ ❶(-子、-儿)用草或苇子等编成的东西,通常用来铺(pū)床或炕 mat ❷座位 seat:出~(到场) *to be present*|缺~(不到场) *to be absent*|入~*to be seated* ❸特指议会中的席位,表示当选的人数(in parliament, indicating number of people elected) seats ❹酒席,成桌的饭菜 banquet; feast:摆了两桌~*to lay out two tables for a banquet*

觋 xí ㄒㄧˊ 男巫 wizard; sorcerer

袭(襲) xí ㄒㄧˊ ❶袭击,趁敌人不备给以攻击 to raid; to assault:夜~*night raid*|空~*air raid* ❷照样做,照样继续下去 to copy; to imitate; to carry on as before:因~ *to follow* (*old customs, rules, methods, etc*); *to copy*|沿~*to carry on as before; to continue; to follow*|世~*hereditary* ❸量词 ***quantifier***,用于成套的衣服(used for counting suits of clothing):衣一~*a suit of clothes*

媳 xí ㄒㄧˊ 儿媳,儿子的妻子 daughter-in-law; son's wife [媳妇]儿子的妻子 daughter-in-law; son's wife [媳妇儿](-fur) **1** 妻子 wife:兄弟~~~ *one's brother's wife; sister-in-law* **2** 已婚的年轻妇女 married young woman

隰 xí ㄒㄧˊ ❶低湿的地方 low-lying marshy land; swamp ❷新开垦的田地 newly reclaimed land

檄 xí ㄒㄧˊ 檄文,古代用于征召或声讨等的文书(in

ancient China) official summons to arms; official proclamation (denouncing a usurper, traitor, etc)

洗 ㊀ xǐ ㄒㄧˇ ❶用水去掉污垢 to wash (㊇ ***doublet*** 一涤 to wash): ～衣服 *to wash clothes; to do one's laundry* | ～脸 *to wash one's face* [洗礼] **1** 基督教接受人入教时所举行的一种仪式 baptism **2** 指经受的锻炼和考验 to go through a severe test: 战斗的～～ *test of war* [洗手] 比喻盗贼等不再偷抢(of a thief, bandit, etc) to mend one's ways; to stop doing evil and reform oneself ❷清除干净 to clear away; to eliminate: 清～ *to clean; to eliminate* ❸冲洗,照相的显影定影 to develop (a film): ～相片 *to have photos printed* ❹洗雪 to redress (a wrong); to wipe out (a disgrace): ～冤 *to redress a grievance* ❺如水洗一样抢光,杀光 to kill and loot; to sack: ～城 *to sack a city and massacre its inhabitants* | ～劫一空(*of a house, city, etc*) *to be plundered of all its valuables* ❻掺和整理 to shuffle (cards, etc): ～牌 *to shuffle cards* (or *dominoes*)

㊁ xiǎn 见 814 页 see p814

铣 ㊀ xǐ ㄒㄧˇ 用一种能旋转的多刃刀具切削金属工件 milling: ～床 *milling machine* | ～刀 *milling cutter* (or *tool*)

㊁ xiǎn 见 814 页 see p814

枲 xǐ ㄒㄧˇ 大麻的雄株,只开花,不结果实 male nettle-hemp

玺(璽) xǐ ㄒㄧˇ 印,自秦朝以后专指皇帝的印 imperial (*or* royal) seal

徙 xǐ ㄒㄧˇ 迁移 to move (from one place to another) (㊇ ***doublet*** 迁一 migration)

蓰 xǐ ㄒㄧˇ 五倍 fivefold: 倍～(数倍) *several times; several-fold*

屣 xǐ ㄒㄧˇ 鞋 shoes; slippers; sandals

喜 xǐ ㄒㄧˇ ❶高兴,快乐 happy; delighted; pleased (㊇ ***doublet*** 一欢 to like; to love | 欢一 happy; delighted; joyful): ～出望外 *to be overjoyed* ❷可庆贺的,特指关于结婚的(especially a wedding) happy event: 要节约办～事。*Be economical in the celebration of happy events.* ❸妇女怀孕叫"有喜" to be in the family way; to be pregnant ❹爱好 to be fond of; to like: ～闻乐见 *to love to see and hear; appealing* ❺适于 to be suitable for; to have an inclination for: 海带～荤。*Kelp is best cooked with meat.* | 植物一般都～光。*Plants generally have an inclination for light.*

禧 xǐ ㄒㄧˇ ❶(旧读 formerly xī) 福,吉祥 happiness; auspiciousness ❷喜庆 happy event: 新～ *new year greetings; happy new year*

𬭳 xǐ ㄒㄧˇ 一种人造的放射性元素(符号 Sg) Seaborgium (Sg)

螅 xǐ ㄒㄧˇ 螅子(也作“喜子”),又叫“喜蛛”或“蟏蛸”。一种长腿的小蜘蛛(also written as 喜子 and also called 喜蛛 or 蟏蛸) elongated cob-web-weaver, spider with extra-long legs

葸 xǐ ㄒㄧˇ 害怕,畏惧 dread; fear; to be afraid:畏~不前 *to recoil in fear; to be too scared to press forward*

戏(戲、*戯) ㊀ xì ㄒㄧˋ ❶玩耍 play; game; sport:集体游~ *group game; team sport*|不要当作儿~。*Don't regard it as a trifling matter.* ❷嘲弄,开玩笑 to make fun of; to joke with: ~言 *joke* ❸戏剧,也指杂技 drama; opera; acrobatics:看~ *to see an opera*|唱~ *to sing in an opera; to be an actor*|听~ *to go to the theatre; to see an opera*|马~ *circus*|皮影~ *shadow play; shadow puppet*

㊁ hū 见 281 页 see p281

饩(餼) xì ㄒㄧˋ ❶古代祭祀或馈赠用的牲畜 livestock offered as a sacrifice or used as a gift in ancient China ❷赠送(谷物、饲料、牲畜等) to give as a gift (such as grain, forage, livestock, etc)

系(❸❺係、❸❹❻繫) ㊀ xì ㄒㄧˋ ❶有连属关系的 system; series:~统 *system*|一~列的事实 *a series of facts*|水~ *river system*|世~ *genealogy* ❷高等学校中按学科分的教学单位 (of an institution of higher learning) department:中文~ *Chinese Department*|化学~ *Department of Chemistry* ❸关联 to relate to; to rely on:干~ *implication; responsibility* ❹联结,拴 to tie; to fasten:~马 *to tether a horse* ㊀ ***extension*** 牵挂 to be concerned (*or* anxious) about:~念 *to be concerned about* [联系] 联络,接头 to get in touch with; to connect with: 时常和他~~ *to often keep in touch with him* ❺是 to be:确~实情。*It is indeed the truth.* ❻把人或东西捆住往上提或向下送 to tie up and carry; to fasten and pull up (*or* lower down):从房上把东西~下来 *to fasten it and lower it down from the roof* ❼地层系统分类的第三级,在“界”之下,是在地质年代“纪”的时间内形成的地层 system; third-level division of the earth's strata:第四~ *Quaternary system*|侏罗~ *Jurassic system*|寒武~ *Cambrian system*

㊁ jì 见 317 页 see p317

屃(**屭) xì ㄒㄧˋ 见 40 页“赑”字条“赑屃”(bì—) see 赑屃 on p40

细 xì ㄒㄧˋ ❶跟“粗”相对(the opposite of 粗) **1** 颗粒小的 fine; in small particles:~沙 *fine sand*|~末 *powder* **2** 长条东西直径小的 thin; slender:~竹竿 *thin bamboo pole*|~铅丝 *fine lead wire* **3** 工料精致的

exquisite; delicate: 江西～瓷 *fine porcelain from Jiangxi Province* | 这块布真～。*The cloth is exquisitely woven.* **4** 声音小(of sound, voice) soft; low: 嗓音～ *soft voice* **5** 周密 meticulous; detailed: 胆大心～ *brave but not reckless; bold but cautious* | 精打～算 *careful calculation and strict budgeting* | 深耕～作 *deep ploughing and careful cultivation; intensive farming* ❷俭朴 frugal; thrifty: 他过日子很～。*He lives a frugal life.* ❸细小的,不重要的 trivial; slight; petty: ～节 *minute detail*

肹 xì ㄒㄧˋ 怒视 to glare at; to glower at: 瞋目～之 *to stare at sb angrily*

咥 ㊀ xì ㄒㄧˋ 大笑 to laugh
㊁ dié 见151页 see p151

郤 xì ㄒㄧˋ ❶同"隙"same as 隙 ❷姓 Xi, a surname

绤 xì ㄒㄧˋ 粗葛布 coarse cloth

阋(鬩) xì ㄒㄧˋ 争吵 to quarrel; to brawl [阋墙]弟兄们在家里互相争吵 to quarrel inside the walls; to quarrel within the family ㊕ ***figurative*** 内部不和 internal discord

舄 xì ㄒㄧˋ ❶鞋 shoes ❷同"潟"same as 潟

潟 xì ㄒㄧˋ 咸水浸渍的土地 salinized land: ～卤(盐碱地) *saline-alkali land*

隙 xì ㄒㄧˋ ❶裂缝 crack; chink; crevice: 墙～ *crack in a wall* | 门～ *crack in a door* ㊕ ***figurative*** **1** 感情上的裂痕 discord; rift; grudge: 嫌～ *ill will; enmity* **2** 空(kòng)子,机会 loophole; opportunity: 乘～ *to exploit a loophole* ❷空(kòng),没有东西的 open; unoccupied: ～地 *open land; unoccupied place*

禊 xì ㄒㄧˋ 古代春秋两季在水边举行的除去所谓不祥的祭祀 waterside ritual held in spring and autumn in ancient China to get rid of bad or evil omen

滃 xì ㄒㄧˋ 水急流的声音 sound of surging torrents

XIA ㄒㄧㄚ

呷 xiā ㄒㄧㄚ 小口儿地喝 to sip; to take a sip of: ～茶 *to take a sip of tea* | ～一口酒 *to take a sip of wine*

虾(蝦) ㊀ xiā ㄒㄧㄚ 节肢动物,身上有壳,腹部有很多环节。生活在水里,种类很多,可以吃 shrimp (*Caridea*)
㊁ há 见260页 see p260

瞎 xiā ㄒㄧㄚ ❶眼睛看不见东西 blind; sightless; visionless ❷胡乱,没来由 groundlessly; foolishly; to no purpose: ～忙 *to be busy to no purpose* | ～说八道 *to talk nonsense; to talk rubbish* ❸〈方 ***dialect***〉乱 to become tangled: 把线弄～了。*The thread has got tangled up.* ❹〈方 ***dialect***〉农作

物子粒不饱满(of grain) not plump; blighted:～穗 *shrunken ear of grain* | ～高粱 *blight sorghum*

匣 xiá ㄒㄧㄚˊ (一子、一儿)收藏东西的器具,通常指小型的,有盖可以开合 small box (*or* case) with a lid[话匣子] **1** 留声机的俗称 popular name for a gramophone **2** 指话多的人(含讽刺义) chatterbox

狎 xiá ㄒㄧㄚˊ 亲近而态度不庄重 frivolous:～昵 *to be improperly familiar; to be intimate in a frivolous way* | ～侮 *to behave frivolously; to give an affront*

柙 xiá ㄒㄧㄚˊ 关猛兽的木笼。也指押解犯人的囚笼或囚车 cage for wild beasts; prisoner's cage

侠(俠) xiá ㄒㄧㄚˊ 旧称依仗个人力量帮助被欺侮者的人或行为(in former times) knight-errantry; person or his acts in being ready to help the weak with his own strength:武～ *chivalrous man* | ～客 *person adept in martial arts and given to chivalrous conduct* | ～义 *having a strong sense of justice and ready to help the weak; having a lofty sense of honour and gallantry; chivalrous* | ～骨 *chivalrous frame of mind* | ～肝义胆 *chivalrous deeds and fearless spirit; chivalrous and fearless*

峡(峽) xiá ㄒㄧㄚˊ 两山夹水的地方 gorge:三～ *Three Gorges of the Changjiang* (or *Yangtze*) *River* [地峡] 海洋中连接两块陆地的狭窄陆地 isthmus:马来半岛有克拉～～。*The Isthmus of Kra lies in the Malay Peninsula.* [海峡] 两块陆地之间连接两片海洋的狭窄水道 strait; channel; gullet:台湾～～ *the Taiwan Strait*

狭(狹、*陿) xiá ㄒㄧㄚˊ 窄,不宽阔 narrow (㊀ **doublet** 一窄 narrow; cramped | 一隘 narrow; narrow and limited; parochial):地方太～。*The place is too confined.* | ～隘的地方保护主义 *parochial protectionism* | ～路相逢(指仇敌相遇)(*of adversaries*) *to meet face to face on a narrow path — in an unavoidable confrontation*

硖(硤) xiá ㄒㄧㄚˊ [硖石] 地名,在浙江省海宁 Xiashi, a place in Haining, Zhejiang Province

遐 xiá ㄒㄧㄚˊ ❶ 远 distant; far:～迩(远近) *far and near; far and wide* | ～方 *distant place* | ～想 *reverie; daydream* ❷ 长久 lasting; long:～龄(高龄) *venerated age; advanced age*

瑕 xiá ㄒㄧㄚˊ 玉上面的斑点 flaw in a piece of jade ㊇ ***figurative*** 缺点 shortcoming; weakness (㊀ **doublet** 一疵 flaw; defect):～瑜互见 *to have defects as well as merits; to have both strong points and*

weak points | 纯洁无～ *pure and flawless*

暇 xiá ㄒㄧㄚˊ 空(kòng)闲,没有事的时候 free time; leisure:得～ *to have free time* | 无～ *to be too busy (with work)* | 自顾不～(连自己都顾不过来) *to be too busy to look after oneself*

霞 xiá ㄒㄧㄚˊ 因受日光斜照而呈现红、橙、黄等颜色的云 morning or evening glow; rosy clouds:朝(zhāo)～ *rosy sunrise; glow of sunrise; sunrise clouds* | 晚～ *sunset glow; evening glow*

辖(❶＊＊鎋、❶＊＊舝) xiá ㄒㄧㄚˊ ❶大车轴头上穿着的小铁棍,可使轮不脱落。(图见475页"轮"picture on p475) linchpin ❷管理 to govern; to have jurisdiction over (㊥ *doublet* 管— to govern; to have jurisdiction over):直～ *directly under the jurisdiction of* | 统～ *under unified command*

黠 xiá ㄒㄧㄚˊ 聪明而狡猾 crafty; cunning:狡～ *crafty; cunning; sly* | 慧～ *intelligent and crafty; smart and cunning*

下 xià ㄒㄧㄚˋ ❶位置在低处的,跟"上"相对(the opposite of 上) down:～面 *down* | 楼～ *downstairs* | 山～ *submontane; at the foot of a mountain* ㊞ *extension* **1** 次序靠后的 next; latter; later:～篇 *next chapter* | ～卷 *next volume* | ～月 *next month* **2** 级别低的 lower; inferior:～级服从上级。*The lower level is subordinate to the higher level*. 谦辞 ***humble***:正中(zhòng)～怀 *to be just what one wants; to one's liking* **3** 质量低的 low in grade:～品 *of the lowest quality; inferior* | ～策 *bad plan; unwise move* ❷由高处到低处 to go down (*or* downward):～山 *to go down the hill* | ～楼 *to go downstairs* ㊞ ***extension*** **1** 进去 to go into:～狱 *to throw (sb) into prison; to imprison* | ～水 *to enter the water* **2** 离开 to leave:～班 *to come off work* | ～课 *to finish class* **3** 往……去 to go to:～乡 *to go to the countryside* | ～江南 *to go down to the south of the lower reaches of the Changjiang* (or *Yangtze*) *River* **4** 投送,颁布 to issue; to deliver:～书 *to deliver a letter* | ～令 *to give orders; to order* **5** 向下面 downward:～达 *to transmit* (or *release*) *to lower levels* | 权力～放 *devolution of power* **6** 降落 to fall:～雨 *raining* | ～雪 *snowing* ❸方面,方位 side; position:两～里都同意。*The two sides reached agreement*. | 向四～一看 *to look around* ❹减除 to remove **1** 卸掉 to take away:～货 *to unload* **2** 除去 to get rid of:～火 *to reduce inflammation* (*or* internal heat) | ～泥 to clean o*ff the mud* ❺用 to use; to apply:～工夫 *to make an effort* ❻攻克,攻陷 to capture;

to take: 连～数城 *to seize several cities at one sweep* | 攻～*to capture; to seize* ❼退让 to give in; to yield: 各不相～。*Neither side would give in* (or *yield*). ❽用在名词后(used after a noun) **1** 表示在里面(used to indicate sth inside): 言～*with the implication* | 意～*in the mind; in the heart* | 都～(京城之内) *in the capital* (*of a country*) **2** 表示当某个时节(used to indicate a particular time or season): 年～*during the Spring Festival* | 节～*during a holiday* (*or festival*) ❾用在动词后(used after a verb) **1** 表示关系(used to indicate the relationship of): 培养(之)～*fostered by* | 指导(之)～*instructed by; guided by* | 鼓舞～*inspired by* **2** 表示动作的完成或结果(used to indicate completion or result of an action): 打～基础 *to lay a foundation* | 准备～材料 *to get materials ready* **3** 跟"来"、"去"连用表示趋向或继续(used together with 来 or 去 to indicate tendency or continuation): 滑～去 *to slip down* | 慢慢停～来 *to stop slowly* | 念～去 *to keep on reading* ❿(一子、一儿)量词 ***quantifier***, 指动作的次数(used to indicate repeated action) time: 打十～*to strike ten times* | 把轮子转两～子 *to rotate the wheel a few times* ⓫(动物)生产(of animals) to give birth to; to lay: 猫～小猫了。*The cat gave birth to a litter of kittens.* | 鸡～蛋。*A hen lays eggs.* ⓬少于(某数)(used in the negative) less than (a certain number): 不～三百人 *no less than three hundred people*

吓(嚇) ㊀ xià ㄒㄧㄚˋ 使害怕 to frighten; to terrify; to scare: 困难～不倒英雄汉。*Difficulties cannot scare heroes.* [吓唬](-hu)使人害怕,威胁 to frighten; to scare; to intimidate: 你别～～人。*Don't try to frighten me.*

㊁ hè 见 272 页 see p272

夏 xià ㄒㄧㄚˋ ❶四季中的第二季,气候最热 summer ❷华夏,中国的古名 Huaxia, ancient name for China ❸夏朝,传说是禹(一说启)建立的(约公元前 2070—公元前 1600 年) Xia Dynasty (2070 BC – 1600 BC), founded by King Yu (*or* Qi, according to another theory) [夏历]农历,旧历,这种历法的基本部分是夏朝创始的 traditional Chinese calendar; lunar calendar

厦(*廈) ㊀ xià ㄒㄧㄚˋ [厦门] 地名,在福建省 Xiamen (*or* Amoy), a place in Fujian Province

㊁ shà 见 650 页 see p650

唬 ㊁ xià ㄒㄧㄚˋ 同"吓"same as 吓

㊀ hǔ 见 284 页 see p284

罅 xià ㄒㄧㄚˋ 裂缝 crack; chink; rift

XIAN ㄒㄧㄢ

仙（*僊） xiān ㄒㄧㄢ 神话中称有特殊能力，可以长生不死的人 celestial being; immortal; fairy

氙 xiān ㄒㄧㄢ 一种化学元素，在通常条件下为气体，符号 Xe，无色无臭无味，不易跟其他元素化合。空气中只含有极少量的氙。把氙装入真空管中通电，能发蓝色的光 xenon (Xe)

籼（*秈） xiān ㄒㄧㄢ 籼稻，水稻的一种，米粒细而长 long-grained non-glutinous rice; indica rice

先 xiān ㄒㄧㄢ ❶时间在前的，次序在前的（in time or in order） early; earlier：占～ *to take the lead; to get ahead of* | 首～ *first of all* | 抢～一步 *one-up* | 争～恐后 *to try to be the first and fear to lag behind; to fall over each other to do sth* ［先进］水平高，成绩好，走在前头，值得推广和学习的 advanced ［先生］（－sheng）**1** 老师 teacher **2** 对一般人的敬称 mister (Mr); gentleman; sir **3** 称医生 doctor ［先天］人或某些动物的胚胎时期 congenital; inborn; inbred：～～不足 *to be congenitally deficient; to suffer from an inherent deficiency* ❷祖先，上代 ancestor; elder generation：～人 *ancestors; forefathers* | ～辈 *elder generation; forefathers* ❸对死去的人的尊称 deceased; the late：革命～烈 *revolutionary martyr*

酰 xiān ㄒㄧㄢ 酰基，通式可以用 R·CO—表示的原子团 acyl

纤（纖） ㊁ xiān ㄒㄧㄢ 细小 fine; minute ［纤尘］细小的灰尘 fine dust：～～不染 *without a speck of dust; to be not soiled by a particle of dust; to be spotlessly clean* ［纤维］细长像丝的物质。一般分成两大类：天然纤维，如棉、麻、羊毛、石棉等；合成纤维是用高分子化合物制成的，如锦纶、维尼纶等 fibre; staple ［光纤］光导纤维。一种能够传导光信号的纤维状光学材料 optical fibre; fibre-optic

㊀ qiàn 见 596 页 see p596

跹（蹮） xiān ㄒㄧㄢ 见 565 页“蹁”字条“蹁跹”（pián—） see 蹁跹 on p565

忺 xiān ㄒㄧㄢ 高兴，适意 happy; pleased

掀 xiān ㄒㄧㄢ 揭起，打开 to lift (a cover); to open up：～锅盖 *to take the pot's lid off* | ～帘子 *to lift the curtain (or screen)* ㊀ **extension** 发动，兴起 to set off (movement, campaign, etc)：～起生产热潮 *to set off a fervour of production*

锨（**杴、**鍁） xiān ㄒㄧㄢ 铲东西用的一种工具，用钢铁或木头制成板状的头，后面安把儿 shovel; spade：木～ *wooden shovel* | 铁～ *shovel*

祆 xiān ㄒㄧㄢ [祆教]拜火教，公元前6世纪波斯人琐罗亚斯德所创立，崇拜火，南北朝时传入我国 Zoroastrianism; Mazdaism

莶(薟) xiān ㄒㄧㄢ 见800页"豨"字条"豨莶"(xī—) see 豨莶 on p800

铦 xiān ㄒㄧㄢ ❶古代一种兵器 *xian*, an ancient weapon ❷锋利 sharp

鲜 ㊀ xiān ㄒㄧㄢ ❶新的，不陈的，不干枯的 fresh; new (㊟ **doublet** 新— fresh; new): ～果 *fresh fruit* | ～花 *fresh flowers* | ～肉 *fresh meat* | ～血 *blood* ❷滋味美好 delicious: 这汤真～。*This soup tastes great*. ❸有光彩的 bright-coloured: ～红的旗帜 *bright red flag* | 颜色十分～艳。*The colour is quite bright*. ❹新鲜的食物 delicacy: 尝～*to have a taste of a delicacy* ❺姓 Xian, a surname [鲜卑族](—bēi—)我国古代北方民族 the Xianbei (*or* Sienpi) ethnic group, an ancient ethnic minority in north China

㊁ xiǎn 见815页 see p815

暹 xiān ㄒㄧㄢ [暹罗]泰国的旧称 Siam, former name for Thailand

闲(❶❷❸*閒) xián ㄒㄧㄢ ❶没有事情做 not busy; idle; unoccupied (㊟ **doublet** —暇 free time; leisure): 没有～工夫 *to be busy; to have no free time* ㊞ **extension** 放着，不使用 not in use; unoccupied; lying idle: ～房 *vacant house* (*or room*) | 机器别～着。*Don't let the machine stand idle*. ❷没有事情做的时候 spare (*or* free) time: 农～*slack farming season* | 忙里偷～*to steal a moment of leisure from a busy schedule* ❸与正事无关的 having nothing to do with official business: ～谈 *to have a chat* | ～人免进 *No admittance except on business*. or *Admittance to staff only*. or *Staff Only* [闲话]与正事无关的话，背后不负责的议论 to gossip: 讲别人的～～*to gossip* ❹栅栏 railings; fence ❺防御 defence: 防～*to defend and guard*

"閒"又 jiān 见327页"间"；又 jiàn 见331页"间" also jiān see 间 on p327; also jiàn, see 间 on p331

娴(*嫺) xián ㄒㄧㄢ ❶熟练 adept; skilled (㊟ **doublet** —熟 adept; skilled): ～于辞令 *to be eloquent in speech* | 技术～熟 *skillful* ❷文雅 refined; elegant: ～静 *gentle and refined* | ～雅 *refined; elegant*

痫(癇) xián ㄒㄧㄢ 癫痫，俗叫"羊痫风"或"羊角风"。一种时犯时愈的暂时性大脑机能紊乱的病症。病发时突然昏倒，口吐泡沫，手足痉挛(formerly called 羊痫风 or 羊角风) epilepsy

鹇(鷳) xián ㄒㄧㄢˊ 白鹇,鸟名。尾巴长,雄的背为白色,有黑纹,腹部黑蓝色,雌的全身棕绿色 silver pheasant (*Lophura nycthemera*)

贤(賢) xián ㄒㄧㄢˊ ❶有道德的,有才能的或有道德的有才能的人 worthy person; able and virtuous person:～明 *wise and able; sagacious*|选～与能 *to recommend and appoint virtuous and able people to office* ❷敬辞 **polite**,用于平辈或晚辈(used in addressing people of the same or of a younger generation):～弟 *my worthy brother*|～侄 *my worthy nephew*

弦(*絃) xián ㄒㄧㄢˊ ❶弓上发箭的绳状物 bowstring ❷月亮半圆 crescent:上～*the first quarter (of the moon)*|下～*the last quarter (of the moon)* ❸数学名词 term in mathematics **1** 连接圆周上任意两点的线段 chord; straight line segment joining any two points on a circumference **2** 直角三角形中对着直角的边 hypotenuse; longer side of a right triangle, located opposite the right angle ❹(一儿)乐器上发声的线 string of a musical instrument [弦子](—zi)[三弦] 弦乐器 *xianzi* or *sanxian*, three-stringed plucked instrument ❺钟表等的发条 spring (of a watch, etc):表～断了。*The spring of the watch is broken.*

舷 xián ㄒㄧㄢˊ 船、飞机等的左右两侧 side of a ship or aircraft; board

挦(撏) xián ㄒㄧㄢˊ 扯,拔(毛发) to pull out (hair); to pluck:～鸡毛 *to pluck chicken feathers; to pluck a chicken*

咸(❷鹹) xián ㄒㄧㄢˊ ❶全,都 all:少长～集。*The young and old all get together.*|～知其不可。*Everybody knows that it should not be done.* ❷像盐的味道,含盐分多的,跟"淡"相对(the opposite of 淡) salted; salty

涎 xián ㄒㄧㄢˊ 口水 saliva:流～*to slaver*|垂～三尺(喻羡慕,想得到) *to have one's saliva hanging three feet long — to drool over*

衔(❷*啣) xián ㄒㄧㄢˊ ❶马嚼子 bit; snaffle ❷用嘴含,用嘴叼 to hold in the mouth:燕子～泥 *swallows carrying bits of earth in their bills* ㊀ ***extension*** **1** 心里怀着 to cherish; to harbour; to bear:～恨 *to nurse hatred; to harbour resentment; to bear a grudge* **2** 奉,接受 to accept (instructions or orders):～命 *to be authorized to do sth; to carry out an order* [衔接] 互相连接 to connect; to link ❸(一儿)职务和级别的名号 rank; title:职～*post and rank*|军～*military rank*

嫌 xián ㄒㄧㄢˊ ❶嫌疑，可疑之点 suspicion：避～ *to avoid suspicion* ❷厌恶（wù），不满意 to dislike；to loathe；to complain：讨人～ *to be a nuisance；to get disliked*｜这种布很结实，就是～太厚。*This kind of cloth is durable，only it is too thick.* ❸怨恨 ill will；resentment；enmity：前～ *previous resentment*｜夙无仇～ *without any old grudge；to have no long-standing enmity*

狝（獮） xiǎn ㄒㄧㄢˇ 古代指秋天打猎（in ancient China）autumn hunting

冼 xiǎn ㄒㄧㄢˇ 姓 Xian，a surname

洗 ㊁ xiǎn ㄒㄧㄢˇ 同"冼"same as 冼

㊀ xǐ 见 805 页 see p805

铣 ㊀ xiǎn ㄒㄧㄢˇ 有光泽的金属 bright metal［铣铁］铸铁，生铁，质脆，适于铸造器物 cast iron

㊁ xǐ 见 805 页 see p805

筅（**筅） xiǎn ㄒㄧㄢˇ〈方 *dialect*〉筅帚，炊帚，用竹子等做成的刷锅、碗的用具（usually made of bamboo）pot-scouring brush

跣 xiǎn ㄒㄧㄢˇ 光着脚 barefooted：～足 *with bare feet；barefoot；barefooted*

显（顯） xiǎn ㄒㄧㄢˇ ❶露在外面容易看出来 apparent；obvious；evident：～而易见 *obviously；as plain as daylight；as clear as day*｜这个道理是很～然的。*The truth is obvious.* ❷表现，露出 to show；to display；to reveal：～示 *to show；to display；to demonstrate*｜～微镜 *microscope*｜没有高山，不～平地。*The flatland is not flat without the comparison to high mountains.* ❸有名声、地位、权势的 illustrious and influential：～贵 *of high position；influential；high officials*（*in former times*）｜～宦 *ranking*（or *high*）*officials* ❹敬辞 ***polite***（称先人）（of the deceased）deceased；late：～考 *my late father*｜～妣 *my late mother*

险（險） xiǎn ㄒㄧㄢˇ ❶可能遭受的灾难 danger；peril；risk（㊇ ***doublet*** 危—danger；peril；risk）：冒～ *to risk；to take a risk*｜保～ *to insure；insurance*｜脱～ *to escape from danger*（or *risk*）❷可能发生灾难的 dangerous；perilous；risky：～症 *dangerous illness*（or *disease*）｜～境 *dangerous situation；perilous plight*｜好～。*How dangerous it is.* ❸要隘，不易通过的地方 place difficult of access：天～ *natural barrier* ❹存心狠毒 sinister；vicious：阴～ *sinister*｜～诈 *sinister and sly* ❺几乎，差一点 by a hair's breadth；almost；nearly：～遭不幸 *to have a narrow escape；to come within an ace of death*｜～些掉在河里 *to nearly fall into the river*

猃（獫、**玁） xiǎn ㄒㄧㄢˇ 古指长

(cháng)嘴的狗(in ancient China) dog with a long snout or muzzle
[猃狁](—yǔn)我国古代北方的民族,战国后称匈奴(also called Xiongnu or Huns after the Warring States Period) the Xianyun ethnic group, an ancient ethnic minority in the northern part of China

蚬 xiǎn ㄒㄧㄢˇ 一种软体动物,介壳形状像心脏,有环状纹。生在淡水软泥里。肉可吃,壳可入药 Asian clam; Corbicula (*Corbicula*)

鲜(*尟、*尠) ㊁ xiǎn ㄒㄧㄢˇ 少 little; rare: ~见 *rarely seen* | ~有 *rare; rarely available*
㊀ xiān 见 812 页 see p812

藓 xiǎn ㄒㄧㄢˇ 隐花植物的一类,茎叶很小,没有真根,生在阴湿的地方 moss (*Bryophyta*)

燹 xiǎn ㄒㄧㄢˇ 火,野火 wild fires [兵燹]指战乱所造成的焚烧毁坏等灾害 ravages of war

櫶 xiǎn ㄒㄧㄢˇ 常绿乔木,叶呈椭圆卵形,花白色,果实椭圆形,木材坚实细致,是我国珍贵的树种。也叫"蚬木"(also called 蚬木) linden (*Burretiodendron hsienmu*)

见(見) ㊁ xiàn ㄒㄧㄢˋ 同"现❶"same as 现❶
㊀ jiàn 见 330 页 see p330

苋 xiàn ㄒㄧㄢˋ 苋菜,一年生草本植物,开绿白色小花,茎叶都可以吃 three-coloured amaranth (*Amaranthus tricolor*)

岘 xiàn ㄒㄧㄢˋ 岘山,山名,在湖北省 Xianshan Mountain in Hubei Province

现 xiàn ㄒㄧㄢˋ ❶显露 to show; to reveal; to appear: 出~ *to appear; to arise; to emerge* | ~了原形 *to show one's true colours* [现象] 事物的表面状态 appearance (of things); phenomenon [实现] 成为事实或使成为事实 to come true; to realize; to carry out: 又一个五年计划~~了。*Another five-year plan has been carried out.* | ~~理想 *to fulfill one's aim* (or *ideal*) ❷现在,目前 now; at present: ~况 *current* (or *present*) *situation; status quo* | ~代化工业 *modern industry* ㊀ ***extension*** 当时 as the occasion arises; impromptu; extempore: ~趸~卖 *to sell sth immediately after it is bought* | ~成的 *ready-made* ❸实有的,当时就有的 on hand; ready; available: ~金 *cash* | ~钱买~货 *to buy merchandise on hand with ready money*

县(縣) xiàn ㄒㄧㄢˋ 行政区划单位,由直辖市、地级市、自治州等领导 county
〈古 ***archaism***〉又同"悬"(xuán) also same as 悬

限 xiàn ㄒㄧㄢˋ ❶指定的范围 limit; bounds: 给你三天~。*You have a three-day time limit.* ❷限制(范围) to limit; to restrict: ~三天完工 *to ful-*

fill it within three days｜作文不～字数。*The number of words in the composition is not limited.*［限制］规定范围，不许超过 to place (*or* impose) restrictions on; to restrict; to confine ❸〈古 ***archaism***〉门槛 threshold：门～*threshold*｜户～*threshold*

线(綫、△*線) xiàn ㄒㄧㄢˋ ❶用丝、金属、棉或麻等制成的细长的东西 thread; string; wire：棉～*cotton thread*｜电～*electric wire*｜毛～*wool* ⊛ ***figurative*** 细小的 a tiny amount：一～希望 *a ray of hope*［线索］⊛ ***figurative*** 事物发展的脉络或据以解决问题的头绪 clue; lead; thread：那件事情有了～～。*We have found some clues to that matter.* ❷几何学上指只有长度而无宽度和厚度的图形 line：直～*straight line*｜曲～*curve* ❸像线的东西 sth shaped like a line：光～*light; (light) ray*｜紫外～*ultraviolet light*｜航～*airline; air route; shipping line*｜京广～*Beijing-Guangzhou Railway*｜战～*battle line; front*｜生命～*lifeline* ❹边缘交界处 demarcation line; boundary; dividing line：防～*defence line*｜国境～*boundary line of a country; frontier*

宪(憲) xiàn ㄒㄧㄢˋ ❶法令 statute：～章 *charter* ❷指宪法 constitutional：立～*constitutionalism*［宪法］国家的根本法。具有最高的法律效力，是其他立法工作的根据。通常规定一个国家的社会制度、国家制度、国家机构和公民的基本权利和义务等 constitution

陷 xiàn ㄒㄧㄢˋ ❶掉进，坠入，沉下 to get stuck (*or* bogged) down; to sink into：～到泥里去了 *to get stuck in the mud*｜地～下去了。*The ground subsided.*［陷阱］为捉野兽或敌人而挖的坑 pitfall; trap ⊛ ***figurative*** 害人的阴谋 trap; snare ❷凹进 to sink; to cave in：两眼深～。*The eyes become sunken.* ❸设计害人 to frame up：～害 *to frame up; to make a false charge against*｜诬～*to make a false charge against* ❹被攻破，被占领 (of a town, etc) to be captured (*or* taken); to fall：失～*to fall*｜～落 *to be taken; to be captured* ❺缺点 defect; deficiency：缺～*defect; deficiency; shortcoming*

馅 xiàn ㄒㄧㄢˋ (－子、－儿)包在面食、点心等食品里面的肉、菜、糖等东西 filling; stuffing：饺子～儿 *stuffing for* jiaozi

羡 xiàn ㄒㄧㄢˋ ❶羡慕，因喜爱而希望得到 to admire; to envy; to covet ❷多余的 redundant; spare; superfluous：～余 *superfluity*

缐(線) xiàn ㄒㄧㄢˋ ❶旧同"线"formerly same as 线 ❷姓 Xian, a surname

腺 xiàn ㄒㄧㄢˋ 生物体内由腺细胞组成的能分泌某些化学

物质的组织 gland：汗～*sweat gland*｜泪～*lachrymal*｜蜜～*nectary*

锼 xiàn ㄒㄧㄢˋ 金属线 metal wire

献(獻) xiàn ㄒㄧㄢˋ 恭敬庄严地送给 to offer; to present; to donate：～花 *to present flowers* (or *bouquets*)｜～礼 *to present a gift*; *to offer a present*｜把青春～给祖国 *to dedicate one's youthful years to the motherland* ㉠ ***extension*** 表现出来 to show; to put on; to display：～技 *to display one's skill*｜～殷勤 *to court*; *to ingratiate oneself to*

霰 xiàn ㄒㄧㄢˋ 水蒸气在高空中遇到冷空气凝结成的小冰粒，在下雪花以前往往先下霰 graupel

XIANG ㄒㄧㄤ

乡(鄉) xiāng ㄒㄧㄤ ❶城市外的区域 country; countryside; village：他下～了。*He has gone to the countryside.*｜城～交流 *exchange between urban and rural areas* ❷自己生长的地方或祖籍 native place; home village (*or* town); birthplace：故～*native place*; *birthplace*｜还～*to return to one's native place*｜同～*person from the same place*; *fellow villager*; *townsman*｜背井离～*to leave one's native place* [老乡] 生长在同一地方的人 fellow-townsman; fellow-villager ❸行政区划单位，由县或区等领导 township, rural administrative unit under county or district

芗(薌) xiāng ㄒㄧㄤ ❶古书上指用以调味的香草 (in ancient Chinese texts) fragrant herb ❷同“香”same as 香

相 ㊀ xiāng ㄒㄧㄤ ❶交互，动作由双方来 each other; one another; mutually (㊥ ***doublet*** 互一 each other)：～助 *to come to sb's help*; *to aid*｜～亲～爱 *to be affectionate to each other*; *to love each other*｜言行～符 *to suit one's actions to one's words*; *the deeds match* (or *square with*) *the words* ㉠ ***extension*** 动作由一方来而有一定对象的，常加在动词前面(usually used before a verb to indicate an action one does to the other)：～信 *to believe*; *to trust*; *to be convinced*｜好言～劝 *to offer well-meant advice* [相当] **1** 对等，等于 to match; to correspond to; to be equal to：年纪～～*about the same age*; *well matched in age* **2** 副词 ***adverb***，有一定程度的 quite; fairly; rather：这首诗写得～～好。*The poem is rather well-written.* [相对] 依靠一定条件而存在，随着一定条件而变化的，跟“绝对”相对 (the opposite of 绝对) comparatively; relatively ❷看 to see and evaluate in person：～中 *to take a fancy to*; *to settle on*｜左～右

看 *to take a very critical look at*

㊁ xiàng 见 821 页 see p821

厢(*廂) xiāng ㄒㄧㄤ ❶厢房，在正房前面两旁的房屋(usually of a one-storeyed house) wing; wing-room：东～房 *eastern wing* | 西～ *western wing* ㊂ **extension** 边，方面 side：这～*this side* | 两～*both sides* ❷靠近城的地区 vicinity outside of a city gate：城～*city proper and area outside its gates* | 关～*neighbourhood outside a city gate* ❸包厢，戏院里特设的单间座位 theatre box ❹车厢，车里容纳人或东西的地方 compartment; railroad car

湘 xiāng ㄒㄧㄤ ❶湘江，源出广西壮族自治区，流至湖南省入洞庭湖 Xiangjiang River, originating in Guangxi and flowing into Dongting Lake in Hunan Province ❷湖南省的别称 Xiang, another name for Hunan Province

缃 xiāng ㄒㄧㄤ 浅黄色 light yellow

箱 xiāng ㄒㄧㄤ ❶(一子)收藏衣物的方形器具，通常是上面有盖扣住 box; chest; trunk ❷像箱子的东西 anything in the shape of a box：信～*mail box* | 风～*bellows* ❸同"厢❹"same as 厢❹

香 xiāng ㄒㄧㄤ ❶气味好闻，跟"臭"相对(the opposite of 臭) fragrant; aromatic; scented：～花 *fragrant flowers* ㊃ **figurative** 1 舒服 comfortable：睡得～*to have a sound sleep* | 吃得真～*to have a very good appetite* 2 受欢迎 vogue; popular; welcome：这种货物在农村～得很。*This kind of goods is in vogue in the countryside.* ❷味道好 savoury; appetizing; delicious：饭～。*The food is appetizing.* ❸称一些天然有香味的东西 perfume or spice：檀～*sandalwood* 特指用香料做成的细条(used specially to indicate a slender stick made of fragrant materials) incense; joss stick：线～*slender stick of incense* | 蚊～*mosquito-repellent incense; mosquito coil incense*

襄 xiāng ㄒㄧㄤ 帮助 to assist; to help：～办 *to help manage; to act as assistant* (or *deputy*) | ～理(*in banks, enterprises, etc*) *assistant manager*

骧 xiāng ㄒㄧㄤ 马抬着头快跑 (of horses) to gallop; to prance

瓖 xiāng ㄒㄧㄤ 同"镶"same as 镶

镶 xiāng ㄒㄧㄤ 把东西嵌进去或在外围加边 to inlay; to edge; to border：～牙 *to put in a false tooth; to insert an artificial tooth* | 在衣服上～一道红边 *to edge the dress with red lace; to lace the dress with a red thread* | 金～玉嵌 *inlaid with gold and jade*

详 xiáng ㄒㄧㄤˊ ❶细密，完备 detailed; minute (㊄ **doublet** 一细 detailed)：～谈 *to talk*

in detail; to go into details | ～解 *detailed explanation* | 不知～情 *to know nothing about the details* ❷清楚地知道 to know clearly: 内容不～ *its content unknown* ❸说明，细说 to explain in detail; to elaborate: 余容再～ *detailed explanation coming up later; to elaborate on the matter next time* | 内～ *see inside; name and address of the sender enclosed* ❹(仪态)从容稳重 (of manner) calmly and sedately: 神态安～ *to appear calm and composed* | 举止～雅 *to carry oneself with ease; to deport oneself gracefully*

庠 xiáng ㄒㄧㄤˊ 庠序，古代的乡学，也泛指学校 (in ancient China) country school; school

祥 xiáng ㄒㄧㄤˊ ❶吉利 auspicious; propitious; lucky ([连] **doublet** 吉～ auspicious; propitious; lucky): ～瑞 *auspicious sign; propitious omen* | 不～ *ominous; inauspicious; unlucky* [转] ***transfer*** 和善，友善 kind; gentle; benign: 慈～ *kindly* | 神情～和 *to wear a benign expression* ❷指吉凶的预兆(迷信) (of superstition) omen

降 ㊁ xiáng ㄒㄧㄤˊ ❶投降，归顺 to surrender: 宁死不～ *to rather die than surrender* ❷降服，使驯服 to subdue; to tame; to vanquish: ～龙伏虎 *to subdue the dragon and tame the tiger — to overcome powerful adversaries*

㊀ jiàng 见 336 页 see p336

翔 xiáng ㄒㄧㄤˊ 盘旋地飞而不扇动翅膀 to hover (*or* circle) in the air: 滑～ *to glide*

[翔实][详实] 详细而确实 full and accurate; detailed and thorough

享 xiǎng ㄒㄧㄤˇ 享受，受用 to enjoy: ～福 *to enjoy a happy life; to be in clover; to live in ease and comfort* | 久～盛誉 *to enjoy a high reputation for ages; to be prestigious for a long time* | 资源共～ *resources sharing*

响(響) xiǎng ㄒㄧㄤˇ ❶(～儿)声音 sound; noise: 听不见～儿了。*No sound could be heard.* ❷发出声音 to make a sound; to ring: 大炮～了。*The cannon fired.* | 钟～了。*The bell rang.* | 一声不～ *not to utter a sound; not to say a word* ❸响亮，声音高，声音大 loud; noisy; sonorous: 这个铃真～。*The bell rings resoundingly.* | 声音～亮。*The voice is loud and clear.* ❹回声 echo: 如～斯应(喻反应的迅速) *as if it were the echo of a sound — to be prompt in response* [响应] (-yìng) 回声相应 to echo correspondingly [喻] ***figurative*** 用言语、行动表示赞同 (to speak or take actions to show one's agreement and support to a call or proposal) to respond; to answer: ～～祖国的号召 *to answer the call of* *one's motherland*

饷(* 饟) xiǎng ㄒㄧㄤˇ ❶过去指军警的薪给(jǐ)(for soldiers, policemen, etc in former times) pay:领～ *to get one's pay* | 关～ *pay* (*of soldiers*) ❷用酒食等款待 to entertain with food and drink

蚃(蠁) xiǎng ㄒㄧㄤˇ 知声虫。也叫"地蛹"(also called 地蛹) injurious insect like leafhopper

飨(饗) xiǎng ㄒㄧㄤˇ ❶用酒食款待 to entertain with food and drink; to fete:以～读者(喻满足读者的需要) *to cater to the readers — to meet the needs of readers* ❷同"享"same as 享

想 xiǎng ㄒㄧㄤˇ ❶动脑筋,思索 to think; to ponder:我～出一个办法来了。*I've got an idea.* ⑤ ***extension*** **1** 推测,认为 to suppose; to consider; to think:我～他不会来了。*I don't think he will come.* | 我～这么做才好。*I think this is the best way to do it.* **2** 希望,打算 to hope; to want; would like to:他～去学习。*He wants to go to study.* | 要～学习好,就得努力。*You have to work hard if you want to study well.* ❷怀念,惦记 to miss; to remember with longing:～家 *to be homesick; to miss one's family* | 时常～着前方的战士 *to miss the soldiers fighting at the front now and again*

鲞(** 鯗) xiǎng ㄒㄧㄤˇ 剖开晾干的鱼 dried fish

向(❶❹❻ 嚮、❻ * 曏) xiàng ㄒㄧㄤˋ ❶对着,朝着 to face; to turn towards:这间房子～东。*This house faces east.* [向导] 引路的人 guide ❷介词 ***preposition***,表示动作的方向(used to indicate the direction of an action):～前看 *to look ahead* | ～雷锋同志学习。*Learn from Comrade Lei Feng.* ❸方向 direction:我转(zhuǎn)～(认错了方向)了。*I've got lost.* or *I have taken the wrong direction.* ⑤ ***extension*** 意志所趋 one's will:志～ *ideal; ambition* | 意～ *intention; purpose; will* ❹近,临 approaching; near; close to:～晚 *towards evening; at dusk* | ～晓雨停。*The rain stopped shortly before dawn.* ❺偏袒,袒护 to be partial to; to side with; to favour:偏～ *to be partial to; to side with* ❻从前 former:～日 *in former days; formerly* | ～者 *before; formerly; in the past* ⑤ ***extension*** 从开始到现在 from the beginning up to now:本处～无此人。*There's never been such a person here.* [向来][一向] 副词 ***adverb***,从来,从很早到现在 always; all along; invariably:他～～不喝酒。*He never drinks.*

项 xiàng ㄒㄧㄤˋ ❶颈的后部(of the neck) nape ❷事物的种类或条目 items：事～ *item; point; matter*｜～目 *item; project*｜义～ *items (in a dictionary entry arranged according to their meanings)*｜强～ *strong point* [转] ***transfer*** 钱，经费 sum of money ([连] ***doublet*** 款— sum of money; fund)：用～ *items of expenditure*｜进～ *items of income*｜欠～ *items of debt* ❸量词 ***quantifier***，用于分项目的事物(used for itemized things)：两～任务 *two assignments; two missions*｜三大纪律八～注意 *Three Main Rules of Discipline and Eight Points for Attention* ❹代数中不用加号、减号连接的单式，如 $4a^2b$，ax^3 (in algebra) unitary value, variable, unit and integer without plus or minus signs as connectors, e.g. $4a^2b$, ax^3

巷 ㊀ xiàng ㄒㄧㄤˋ 较窄的街道 lane; alley：大街小～ *streets and lanes*

㊁ hàng 见 266 页 see p266

相 ㊁ xiàng ㄒㄧㄤˋ ❶(一儿)样子，容貌 looks; appearance ([连] ***doublet***—貌 looks; appearance)：长(zhǎng)得很喜～(xiang) *to have features suggestive of good fortune*｜狼狈～ *flustered look*｜照～ *to have a picture taken; to take photos (or pictures)* ❷察看 to estimate (*or* decide) the quality of sth by observing its appearance：～马 *to observe and examine a horse to judge its worth*｜～机行事 *to do as one sees fit; to act flexibly in the light of the specific situation*｜人不可以貌～。*One cannot be judged by his appearance.* ❸辅助，也指辅佐的人，古代特指最高级的官(also used to indicate an assistant, or an official with the highest rank in ancient China) to assist：宰～ *prime minister* ❹姓 Xiang, a surname

[相声](—sheng)曲艺的一种，以说、学、逗、唱，引人发笑为特色，盛行于华北地区 *xiangsheng*, crosstalk (*or* comic dialogue) popular in Northern China

㊀ xiāng 见 817 页 see p817

象 xiàng ㄒㄧㄤˋ ❶哺乳动物，多产在印度、非洲等热带地方。鼻子圆筒形，可以伸卷。多有一对特长的门牙，突出唇外 elephant (*Elephantidae*) ❷形状，样子 shape; image; appearance ([连] ***doublet*** 形— image; form; figure)：景～ *scenery*｜万～更新。*All things take on a new look.* [象征]用具体的东西表现事物的某种意义，例如鸽子象征和平 to symbolize

像 xiàng ㄒㄧㄤˋ ❶相似 to be like; to resemble：他很～他母亲。*He looks quite like his mother.* [好像]似乎，仿佛 to look as if; to seem：我～～见过他。*It seems as if I have seen him before.* ❷比照人物做成的图形 portrait; picture：画

X

～portrait | 塑～statue ❸比如，比方 such as：～这样的事是值得注意的。*Such things as this deserve our attention.*

橡 xiàng ㄒㄧㄤˋ ❶橡树，就是栎树(i. e. 栎树) oak [橡子] 橡树的果实 acorn; nut of the oak tree ❷橡胶树，原产巴西，我国南方也有，树的乳状汁液可制橡胶 rubber tree; gum tree [橡胶] 用橡胶树一类植物的乳汁制成的胶质。用途很广 rubber [橡皮] **1** 经过硫化的橡胶 vulcanized rubber **2** 能擦去铅笔等痕迹的橡胶制品 eraser; rubber

蟓 xiàng ㄒㄧㄤˋ "蚕"的古名 name for 蚕 in ancient China

XIAO ㄒㄧㄠ

肖 ㊁ xiāo ㄒㄧㄠ "萧"(姓)俗作"肖"(popular written form for 萧) Xiao, a surname

㊀ xiào 见 825 页 see p825

削 ㊀ xiāo ㄒㄧㄠ 用刀平着或斜着去掉外面的一层 to peel：～铅笔 *to sharpen a pencil* | 把梨皮～掉 *to peel a pear*

㊁ xuē 见 851 页 see p851

逍 xiāo ㄒㄧㄠ [逍遥] (—yáo) 自由自在，无拘无束 free and unfettered; carefree：～～自在 *to be at peace with the world and oneself; to be leisurely and carefree*

消 xiāo ㄒㄧㄠ ❶溶化，散失 to vanish; to melt; to disappear：冰～。*The ice melts.* | 烟～火灭。*The fire has gone and the smoke has cleared.* [消化] 胃肠等器官把食物变成可以吸收的养料 to digest [喻] ***figurative*** 理解、吸收所学的知识 to understand and absorb (knowledge and learning) ❷灭掉，除去 to eliminate; to wipe out ([连] ***doublet*** —灭 to eliminate; to wipe out)：～毒 *to disinfect; to sterilize* | ～炎 *to diminish* (or *allay*) *inflammation* | ～灭敌人 *to wipe out the enemy* [消费] 为了满足生产、生活的需要而消耗物质财富 to consume [消极] 起反面作用的，不求进取的，跟"积极"相对 (the opposite of 积极) inactive; passive; negative：～～因素 *negative factor* | ～～态度 (*to take a*) *passive attitude* [消息] 音信，新闻 information; news ❸消遣，把时间度过去 to pass time in a leisurely way; to idle away (the time)：～夜 *to have a midnight snack* | ～夏 *to spend summer in a leisurely way* ❹〈方 ***dialect***〉需要 to need; to require; to take：不～说。*It goes without saying.*

宵 xiāo ㄒㄧㄠ 夜 night：通～ *all* (or *whole*) *night; throughout the night* [元宵] **1** 元宵节，夏历正月十五日晚上 Lantern Festival; night of the 15th of the first lunar month **2** 一种江米(糯米)面做成的球形有馅食品，多在元宵节吃 *yuanxiao*, stuffed sweet, round dumplings made of glutinous rice flour specially prepared for the Lantern Festival

绡 xiāo ㄒㄧㄠ 生丝。又指用生丝织的东西 raw silk; raw-silk fabric

硝 xiāo ㄒㄧㄠ ❶矿物名 name of mineral **1** 硝石,一种无色或白色晶体,成分是硝酸钾或硝酸钠,是氮肥的主要原料 nitre; saltpeter **2** 芒硝,一种无色透明的晶体,成分是硫酸钠,可做泻剂和制取钠 mirabilite ❷用芒硝加黄米面等处理毛皮,使皮板儿柔软 to tan; to taw:~一块皮子 *to tan a hide*

销 xiāo ㄒㄧㄠ ❶熔化金属 to melt (metal) [销毁] 毁灭,常指烧掉 to destroy by melting or burning ❷去掉 to cancel; to annul:~假(jià) *to report back after leave of absence* | 报~ *to submit a list of expended articles; to scrap; to discard* | 撤~ *to cancel; to revoke; to rescind* ❸卖出(货物) to sell:一天~了不少的货 *to sell quite a lot of goods within one day* | 供~合作社 *supply and marketing cooperative* | 脱~ *to run out of supplies* ❹开支,花费 to spend; to expend:花~ *expenses* | 开~ *expense; expenditure* ❺(一子)机器上像钉子的零件 pin; peg; dowel [插销] **1** 连通电路的一种装置 plug:电灯~~ *electric light plug* **2** 关锁门窗的一种装置 bolt ❻把机器上的销子或门窗上的插销推上 to pin; to bolt

蛸 ㊀ xiāo ㄒㄧㄠ [螵蛸] (piāo—) 螳螂的卵块 egg capsule of a mantis

㊁ shāo 见 659 页 see p659

霄 xiāo ㄒㄧㄠ ❶云 clouds (㊤ ***doublet*** 云—clouds) ❷天空 sky; heaven:重(chóng)~ *heaven of heavens; sky of skies* | 九~ *highest heavens* | ~壤(喻相去很远) *heaven and earth — to be far apart*

魈 xiāo ㄒㄧㄠ [山魈] **1** 猴的一种,尾巴很短,脸蓝色,鼻子红色,嘴上有白须,全身毛黑褐色,腹部白色。多群居,吃小鸟、野鼠等 mandrill (*Mandrillus sphinx*) **2** 传说中山里的鬼怪 legendary one-legged mountain spirit

枭(梟) xiāo ㄒㄧㄠ ❶即鸮 (i. e. 鸮) owl (*Strigiformes*) ❷勇健(常有不驯顺的意思) fierce and brave; valiant:~将 *brave general* | ~雄 *fierce and ambitious person; man with outstanding wisdom and valour* ❸魁首,首领 chief; head; ringleader:毒~ *drug-trafficking kingpin; drug lord (or king)* ❹〈古 ***archaism***〉悬挂(砍下的人头) to hang (a person's chopped-off head) for public display:~首 *to cut off a person's head and hang it up* | ~示 *to hang sb's head as a warning to others*

枵 xiāo ㄒㄧㄠ ❶空虚 empty; hollow:~腹从公 *to attend to official duties on an empty stomach; to work without pay* ❷布的丝缕稀而薄(of cloth) thin and loosely woven:~薄

thin

鸮 xiāo ㄒㄧㄠ 猫头鹰一类的鸟 owl (*Strigiformes*)

哓(嘵) xiāo ㄒㄧㄠ [哓哓] 因为害怕而乱嚷乱叫的声音(of bird's call in fear) twitter

X

骁(驍) xiāo ㄒㄧㄠ ❶好马 good horse ❷勇健 brave; valiant ([连] ***doublet*** 一勇 brave; valiant): ～将 *valiant general*

虓 xiāo ㄒㄧㄠ 猛虎怒吼(of a tiger) to roar

猇 xiāo ㄒㄧㄠ 同"虓"same as 虓

萧(蕭) xiāo ㄒㄧㄠ 冷落、没有生气的样子 desolate; dreary: ～然 *desolate* | ～瑟 *bleak* | ～索 *bleak and chilly; desolate* [萧条]寂寞冷落 desolate; bleak [喻] ***figurative*** 不兴旺 slump; depression

[萧萧] 拟声词 ***onomatopoeia***,马叫声或风声 sound of a neighing horse or a whistling wind; whinny and neigh

潇(瀟) xiāo ㄒㄧㄠ 水清而深(of water) deep and clear [潇洒](—sǎ) 行动举止自然大方,不呆板,不拘束 (of a person's appearance, demeanour, carriage, etc) natural and elegant; free and unconventional

蟏(蠨) xiāo ㄒㄧㄠ [蟏蛸](—shāo)蟢子。参看806页"蟢"(see 蟢 on p806) elongated cobweb-weaver

箫(簫) xiāo ㄒㄧㄠ 管乐器。古代的"排箫"是许多管子排在一起的,后世用一根管子做成,竖着吹的叫"洞箫" *xiao*, a vertical bamboo flute, the ancient 排箫 made from several bamboo pipes and the present day vertical bamboo flute called 洞箫

翛 xiāo ㄒㄧㄠ 〈古 ***archaism***〉 无拘无束,自由自在 free and unconstrained: ～然 *free and unconstrained*

[翛翛] 羽毛败坏的样子(of feathers) ruined or spoiled

嚣 xiāo ㄒㄧㄠ 喧哗 clamour; hubbub; din: 叫～*clamour* [嚣张]放肆,邪恶势力上升 rampant; audacious; aggressive: 气焰～～ *to behave with unbearable insolence; arrogance*

洨 xiáo ㄒㄧㄠˊ 洨河,水名,在河北省西南部 Xiaohe River in the southwest of Hebei Province

崤 xiáo ㄒㄧㄠˊ 崤山,山名,在河南省西部。也叫"崤陵"(also called 崤陵) Xiaoshan Mountain in the west of Henan Province

淆(*殽) xiáo ㄒㄧㄠˊ 混淆,错杂,混乱 to confuse; to mix: 混～不清 *confused and unclear*

小 xiǎo ㄒㄧㄠˇ ❶跟"大"相对(the opposite of 大) **1** 面积少的,体积占空间少的,容量少的 small; little; petty: ～山 *small hill* | 地方～ *small area* **2** 数量少的 of small quantity: 数

目～*small sum*｜一～半 *small part of; less than a half* **3** 程度浅的 low in degree：学问～ *with little schooling*｜～学 *primary school; elementary school* **4** 声音低的 low in voice：～声说话 *to speak in a low voice* **5** 年幼，排行最末的 younger; last in seniority among brothers and sisters：他比你～。*He is younger than you.*｜他是我的～弟弟。*He is my youngest brother.* **6** 年幼的人 the young：一家老～ *the whole family, young and old* **7** 谦辞 **humble**：～弟 *I; me*｜～店 *my shop* [小看] 轻视，看不起 to look down upon; to underestimate：别～～人。*Don't look down upon others.* or *Don't belittle others.* [小说] 描写人物故事的一种文学作品 fiction; novel ❷时间短 for a short while; for a little time：～坐 *to sit for a while*｜～住 *short stay; to stay for a few days* ❸稍微 a little; a bit; slightly：牛刀～试 *master hand's first small display; needless waste of energy* ❹略微少于，将近 a little less than; nearly：这里离石家庄有～三百里。*Shijiazhuang is nearly 300* li *from here.*

晓（曉） xiǎo ㄒㄧㄠˇ ❶天刚亮的时候 dawn; daybreak：～行夜宿 *to start off at dawn and lodge for the night; to travel by day and rest by night*｜鸡鸣报～ *the crow of a rooster heralding the break of dawn* ❷晓得，知道，懂得 to know; to understand：家喻户～ *to be widely known; to be known to every household* ❸使人知道 to let sb know; to tell：～以利害 *to tell sb clearly the advantages and disadvantages; to warn sb of the possible consequences*

筱（**篠） xiǎo ㄒㄧㄠˇ ❶小竹子 little slender bamboo ❷同"小"，多用于人名（xiao, usually used in a given name）same as 小

孝 xiào ㄒㄧㄠˋ ❶指尊敬、奉养父母 filial ❷指居丧的礼俗 conventional mourning rites for a deceased elder member of one's family：守～ *to be in mourning* ❸丧服 mourning clothes：戴～ *to wear mourning for a parent or relative; to be in mourning*

哮 xiào ㄒㄧㄠˋ 吼叫 to roar：咆～ *to bluster; to rave; to roar* [哮喘] 呼吸急促困难的症状 asthma

肖 ㊀ xiào ㄒㄧㄠˋ 像，相似 to resemble; to be like：子～其父。*The son is the very image of his father.* [肖像] 画像，相片 portrait; picture

㊁ xiāo 见 822 页 see p822

笑（*咲） xiào ㄒㄧㄠˋ ❶露出愉快的表情，发出欢喜的声音 to smile; to laugh：逗～ *to amuse; to tickle*｜眉开眼～ *to be all smiles; to beam with joy*｜啼～皆非 *not to*

know whether to laugh or cry; to find sth both laughable and irritating [笑话](—huɑ) **1** (——儿)能使人发笑的话或事 joke; jest **2** 轻视,讥讽 to laugh at; to deride: 别～～人。*Don't laugh at the others.* ❷讥笑,嘲笑 to sneer at; to mock: 见～*to be laughed at* | 耻～*to mock; to sneer at* | 别嘲～人。*Don't make fun of me.* or *Don't laugh at me.*

校 ㊀ xiào ㄒㄧㄠˋ ❶学校 school ❷军衔名,在尉和将之间 field officer, military officer of a rank between junior officers and generals

㊁ jiào 见 342 页 see p342

效(❶*倣、❸*効) xiào ㄒㄧㄠˋ ❶模仿 to imitate (㊀ *doublet* —法 to follow the example of; to imitate; to follow in the footsteps | 仿— to imitate; to copy; to be modelled after): 上行下～。*The subordinates imitate the superiors.* ❷效验,功用,成果 effect: 这药吃了很见～。*This medicine produces a very good effect.* | ～果良好 *to produce good results* | 无～ *invalid; to be of no effect* [效率] **1** 物理学上指有用的功在总功中所占的百分比 ratio of useful work to the total work performed in physics **2** 单位时间内所完成的工作量 efficiency: 生产～～ *production efficiency* | 工作～～ *working efficiency* ❸尽,献出 to devote (one's energy or life) to; to render (a service): ～力 *to serve; to render a service to* | ～劳 *to work for; to serve*

啸(嘯) xiào ㄒㄧㄠˋ ❶撮口作声,打口哨(of a person) to make a long and ringing sound; to whistle: 长～一声,山鸣谷应。*A long and loud whistle in the mountain echoes in the valley.* ❷动物拉长声音叫(of birds or animals) to scream; to roar; to howl: 虎～ *roar of a tiger* | 猿～ *scream of an ape* ❸自然界发出的或飞机、子弹等飞掠而过的声音 (the sound of nature or a speeding object, e. g. bullet, airplane, etc) whizz; buzz; hiss: 海～ *tsunami; seismic sea wave* | 子弹尖～着掠过头上。*Bullets whistled overhead.* | 飞机尖～着飞向高空。*A plane whizzed into the sky.*

斅(斆) xiào ㄒㄧㄠˋ 教导,使觉悟 to instruct; to teach; to enlighten

XIE ㄒㄧㄝ

些 xiē ㄒㄧㄝ ❶量词 ***quantifier***,表示不定的数量(used to indicate an indefinite quantity) some: 有～工人。*There are some workers.* | 炉子里要添～煤。*Put some more coal into the stove.* | 看～书。*Do some reading.* | 长(zhǎng)～见识 *to gain some experience; to widen one's knowledge* ❷跟"好"、

"这么"连用表示很多(used with 好 or 这么 to indicate quite a lot or so many):好～人 *quite a lot of people*|这么～天 *so many days*|制造出这么～个机器 *to turn out so many machines* ❸用在形容词后表示比较的程度(used after an adjective as a modifier of degree):病轻～了 *to feel a little better*|学习认真～,了解就深刻～。*The more attentively you study, the better you will understand.* [些微] 略微 slightly; a little; a bit

揳 xiē ㄒㄧㄝ 捶,打。特指把钉、橛等捶打到其他东西里面去 to drive (a wedge, nail, etc) into sth:在墙上～钉子 *to drive a nail into the wall*|把桌子～一～*to wedge the table up and make it steady*

楔 xiē ㄒㄧㄝ (一儿)填充器物的空隙使其牢固的木橛、木片等 wedge; peg:这个板凳腿活动了,加个～儿吧。*The stool is rickety. Drive a wedge into it.* [楔子](—zi) **1** 义同"楔"same as 楔 **2** 杂剧里加在第一折前头或插在两折之间的小段,小说的引子 prologue or interlude (in a poetic drama set to music); prologue (in some novels)

歇 xiē ㄒㄧㄝ ❶休息 to have a rest:坐下～一会儿。*Please sit down and rest for a while.* ❷停止 to stop (working, etc); to knock off:～工 *to quit* (or *stop*) *working*; (*of an enterprise*) *to close down*|～业 (*as of a shop*) *to go out of business* [歇枝] 果树在一定年限内停止结果或结果很少(*of fruit trees*) *to bear less fruit; to have a lean year* ❸〈方 ***dialect***〉很短的一段时间,一会儿 a little while; a very short period:过了一～*after a while*

[歇斯底里](外 **loanword**)即癔(yì)病(i. e. 癔病) hysteria ⑩ ***figurative*** 情绪激动,举止失常 to be unnaturally excited (*or* emotional)

蝎(*蠍) xiē ㄒㄧㄝ (一子) 一种节肢动物,卵胎生。下腮长成钳子的样子,胸脚四对,后腹狭长,末端有毒钩,用来防敌和捕虫,干制后可入药 scorpion (*Scorpiones*)

叶 ⊜ xié ㄒㄧㄝˊ 和洽,合 to be in harmony; to be in accord:～韵 *rhyme*

⊖ yè 见 879 页 see p879

协(協) xié ㄒㄧㄝˊ ❶共同合作,辅助 to cooperate; to assist:～商问题 *to negotiate; to talk things over*|～办 *to cooperate in doing sth; to assist*|～查 *to help to investigate; to assist in an investigation* [协会] 为促进某种共同事业的发展而组成的群众团体 association; society:对外友好～～*association for friendship with foreign countries* ❷调和,和谐 harmony; concord; coordination:～调 *to coordinate*|～和 *to harmonize*

X

胁(脅、*脇) xié ㄒㄧㄝˊ ❶从腋下到腰的部分 flank; side of the human body from the armpit to the waist: ～下 *under the armpit* ❷逼迫恐吓(hè) to coerce; to force: 威～ *to intimidate* | ～制 *to hold under duress; to abduct* [胁从] 被胁迫而随从别人做坏事 to be an accomplice under duress ❸收敛 to restrain oneself: ～肩谄笑(谄媚人的丑态) *to cringe and smile obsequiously; to behave in a servile manner; to bow and scrape*

邪 ㊀ xié ㄒㄧㄝˊ ❶不正当 evil; heretical; wicked: 歪风～气 *unhealthy trends and noxious influences* | 改～归正 *to give up evil and return to good* ㊀ ***extension*** 奇怪,不正常 irregular; abnormal: ～门 *strange; odd; abnormal* | 一股～劲 *a perverse touch* ❷中医指引起疾病的环境因素(of traditional Chinese medicine) unhealthy environmental influence that causes disease: 风～ *pathogenic factor of wind; chilly draught (as a cause of disease)* | 寒～ *disease caused by catching cold* ㊕ ***transfer*** 迷信的人指鬼神给予的灾祸(of superstition) disaster brought down by a ghost (*or* spirit): 驱～ *to exorcise evil spirits*

㊁ yé 见 877 页 see p877

挟(挾) xié ㄒㄧㄝˊ ❶夹在胳膊底下 to hold sth under the arm: ～山跨海逞英雄 *to jump over the sea with a mountain under one's arm — to parade onesely as a hero by doing sth impressive* ❷倚仗势力或抓住人的弱点强迫使服从 to coerce; to compel; to use one's power or take advantage of sb's weakness to enforce obedience: 要(yāo)～ *to coerce; to put pressure on (sb)* | ～制 *to take advantage of sb's weakness to enforce obedience; to force sb to do one's bidding* ❸心里怀着(怨恨等) to bear; to harbour (resentment, etc): ～嫌 *to harbour resentment* | ～恨 *to bear a grudge*

斜 xié ㄒㄧㄝˊ 不正,跟平面或直线既不平行也不垂直的 oblique; slanting; askew: ～坡 *slope* | 纸裁～了。*The paper has been cut on the slant.* | ～对过 *opposite slightly to the right or left; cater-cornered from*

偕 xié ㄒㄧㄝˊ (旧读 formerly jiē) 共同,在一块 together with; accompanied by; in the company of: ～老(*of husband and wife*) *to live together to a ripe old age; to grow old together* | ～行 *to go in the company of sb* | ～同贵宾参观 *to accompany foreign guests on a visit*

谐 xié ㄒㄧㄝˊ ❶和,配合得适当 in harmony; in accord (㊃ ***doublet*** 和一 in harmony; in accord): 音调和～。*The tone is harmonious.* ❷诙谐,滑

稽 humorous：～谈 *humorous talk*｜亦庄亦～ *both solemn and humorous*

絜 xié ㄒㄧㄝˊ 量度物体周围的长度 to measure the girth of sth

〈古 ***archaism***〉又同"洁"(jié) also same as 洁

颉 ㊁ xié ㄒㄧㄝˊ ❶鸟往上飞(of birds) to fly upwards [颉颃](－háng) **1** 鸟向上向下飞(of birds) to fly up and down **2** 不相上下 to be equally matched; to rival each other：他的书法与名家相～～。*His calligraphy is equally matched with famous experts'.* [转] ***transfer*** 对抗 antagonism：～～作用 *antagonistic effect* ❷姓 Xie, a surname

㊀ jié 见 347 页 see p347

撷 xié ㄒㄧㄝˊ ❶摘下，取下 to pick; to pluck ❷用衣襟兜东西 to hold things with the front of one's clothes

缬 xié ㄒㄧㄝˊ 有花纹的丝织品 patterned silk fabric

携(*攜、*擕) xié ㄒㄧㄝˊ 带 to carry; to take along ([连] ***doublet*** 一带 to carry; to take along)：～眷 *to bring one's wife and children along*｜～带武器 *to carry weapons with oneself* [携手] 手拉着手 hand in hand [喻] ***figurative*** 合作 to cooperate; to be jointly engaged in sth

鞋(*鞵) xié ㄒㄧㄝˊ 穿在脚上走路时着地的东西 shoes：皮～ *leather shoes*｜拖～ *slippers*｜旅游～ *sneakers*

勰 xié ㄒㄧㄝˊ 和谐，协调 harmonious 多用于人名。刘勰，南朝人(xie, usually used in a given name) Liu Xie, a person in the Southern Dynasties

写(寫) xiě ㄒㄧㄝˇ ❶用笔在纸或其他东西上做字 to write：～字 *to write*｜～对联 *to write couplets* ❷写作 writing：～诗 *to compose a poem*｜～文章 *to write an article* ❸描写 to describe：～景 *to describe the scenery*｜～情 *to write one's emotions* ❹绘画 to paint：～生 *to paint* (or *sketch*) *from nature*

血 ㊁ xiě ㄒㄧㄝˇ 义同"血㊀"，用于口语。多单用，如"流了点儿血"。也用于口语常用词，如"鸡血"、"血块子"[used only in colloquial Chinese, and, in most cases, not employed to form a compound word, e. g. 流了点儿血 (to bleed a little blood) except for everyday verbal expression, e. g. 鸡血 (chicken blood), 血块子(lumps of blood)] same as 血㊀

㊀ xuè 见 853 页 see p853

灺(**炧) xiè ㄒㄧㄝˋ 蜡烛烧剩下的部分 the stump of a burnt candle

泄(*洩) xiè ㄒㄧㄝˋ ❶液体、气体排出 to let out (a fluid or gas); to discharge; to release：～洪道 *flood-relief channel*; *flood-*

way ⓟ *figurative* 丧失希望、勇气 to lose hope; to feel discouraged: ～气 *to lose heart; to feel discouraged; to be disheartened* | ～劲 *to lose heart; to lose confidence; to slacken one's efforts* ❷透露 to let out; to leak (news, secrets, etc): ～漏秘密 *to leak a secret* | ～底(泄露内幕) *to reveal what it is at the bottom of sth* ❸发泄 to give vent to: ～恨 *to give vent to one's pent-up resentment* | ～私愤 *to give vent to one's personal spite*

绁(*紲) xiè ㄒㄧㄝˋ ❶绳索 rope; cord ❷系，拴 to fasten; to tie

渫 xiè ㄒㄧㄝˋ ❶除去 to get rid of; to remove ❷泄，疏通 to dredge; to discharge

泻(瀉) xiè ㄒㄧㄝˋ ❶液体很快地流下 to flow swiftly; to rush down; to pour out: 一～千里(*of a river*) *to rush down a thousand* li — *to flow powerfully* ❷拉稀屎 to have loose bowels; to have diarrhoea: ～肚 *to have loose bowels; to have diarrhoea*

契(**偰) ㊁ xiè ㄒㄧㄝˋ 商朝的祖先，传说是舜的臣 Xie, ancestor of the Shang Dynasty and minister of the legendary King Shun

㊀ qì 见 589 页 see p589

卨(离、**禼) xiè ㄒㄧㄝˋ 用于人名。万俟卨(mòqí—)，宋朝人 (xie, used in a given name) Moqi Xie, a person in the Song Dynasty

卸 xiè ㄒㄧㄝˋ ❶把东西去掉或拿下来 to unload; to remove; to discharge: ～货 *to unload* (or *discharge*) *a cargo* | ～车 *to unload a truck* (or *a car, etc*) | 大拆大～ *to disassemble completely* (*a machine, etc*) ❷解除 to lay down; to shirk: ～责 *to shirk one's responsibility* | ～任 *to be relieved of one's office* | 推～ *to shirk; to evade; to shift blame*

屑 xiè ㄒㄧㄝˋ 碎末 bits; scraps; crumbs: 煤～(*coal*) *slack* | 竹头木～ *bamboo ends and wood shavings* [琐屑]细小的事情 trifling; trivial

[不屑]认为事物轻微而不肯做或不接受 to disdain to do; to scorn: 他～～于做这件事。*He disdains to do it.*

榍 xiè ㄒㄧㄝˋ [榍石]一种矿物，多呈褐色或绿色，有光泽，是提炼钛的原料 titanite; sphene

械 xiè ㄒㄧㄝˋ ❶器物，家伙 apparatus; tool; instrument: 机～*machine; machinery* | 器～ *apparatus; appliance; instrument* ❷武器 arms; weapon: 缴～*to lay down the arms* | ～斗 *to fight with weapons* ❸刑具 fetters; shackles

亵(褻) xiè ㄒㄧㄝˋ ❶轻慢，亲近而不庄重 to treat with irreverence; to be disrespectful: ～渎 *to blas-*

pheme; to profane ❷指贴身的衣服 underwear：～衣 *underclothes; underwear* ❸淫秽 obscene; indecent：猥～ *licentious; obscene; to act indecently*

谢 xiè ㄒㄧㄝˋ ❶表示感激(叠 ***reduplication***) to thank：～～你！ *Thank you!* ❷道歉或认错 to make an apology; to excuse oneself：～罪 *to apologize for an offence* ❸辞去，拒绝 to decline：～绝参观 *not open to visitors* ❹凋落，衰退 to wither; to fade：花～了。*The flowers withered.* | 新陈代～ *to supersede the old by the new; metabolism*

塮 xiè ㄒㄧㄝˋ〈方 ***dialect***〉猪羊等家畜圈里积下的粪便 dung from pigs, sheep and other domestic animals in their pens

榭 xiè ㄒㄧㄝˋ 台上的屋子 pavilion or house on a terrace：水～ *pavilion by the waterside; waterside pavilion*

解 ㊂ xiè ㄒㄧㄝˋ ❶明白，懂得 to understand; to see：～不开这个理 *to be unable to see the point* ❷姓 Xie, a surname ❸解县，旧县名，在山西省 Xiexian County, former name of a county in Shanxi Province

㊀ jiě 见 348 页 see p348

㊁ jiè 见 350 页 see p350

蘚 xiè ㄒㄧㄝˋ［蘚茩］(—hòu) 菱 water chestnut

獬 xiè ㄒㄧㄝˋ［獬豸］(—zhì) 传说中的异兽名 *xiezhi*, a legendary beast in ancient China which could tell right from wrong and use its horn to butt an evildoer whenever there is a fight

邂 xiè ㄒㄧㄝˋ［邂逅］(—hòu) 没约会而遇到 to meet unexpectedly; to meet by chance; to run into sb

廨 xiè ㄒㄧㄝˋ 古代通称官署 (general term used in ancient China) government office：官～ *office for officials* | 公～ *government office*

澥 xiè ㄒㄧㄝˋ ❶糊状物或胶状物由稠变稀 (of paste, glue, etc) to become thinner; to thin down：糨糊～了。*The paste has become thinner.* ❷加水使糊状物或胶状物变稀 to add water to dilute a paste or glue：粥太稠，加点儿水～一～。*The porridge is too thick. Add some water to make it thinner.* ❸渤澥，古代海的别称，也指渤海(also for Bohai Sea) *Boxie*, another name for sea in ancient China

懈 xiè ㄒㄧㄝˋ 松懈，不紧张 to slack; to lax (㊟ ***doublet*** 一怠 to slack; to sluggish)：始终不～ *doggedly; persistently; perseveringly*

蟹(*蠏) xiè ㄒㄧㄝˋ 螃蟹，节肢动物，种类很多，水陆两栖，全身有甲壳。前面的一对脚长(zhǎng)成钳状，叫螯。横着走。腹部分节，俗叫脐，雄的尖脐，雌的团脐 crab (*Brachyura*)

薤 xiè ㄒㄧㄝˋ 多年生草本植物，叶细长，开紫色小花。鳞茎和嫩叶可以吃。也叫"藠头(jiàotou)"(also called 藠头) Chinese onion (*Allium chinense*)

瀣 xiè ㄒㄧㄝˋ 见 266 页"沆"字条"沆瀣"(hàng—) see 沆瀣 on p266

X

燮 xiè ㄒㄧㄝˋ 谐和，调和 to harmonize; to regulate

躞 xiè ㄒㄧㄝˋ 见 151 页"蹀"字条"蹀躞"(dié—) see 蹀躞 on p151

XIN ㄒㄧㄣ

心 xīn ㄒㄧㄣ ❶心脏，人和高等动物体内推动血液循环的器官。(图见 940 页"脏"picture on p940) heart [心腹] [喻] *figurative* **1** 最要紧的 vital: ～～之患 *disease in one's vital organs—danger from within; serious hidden trouble* (or *danger*) **2** 亲信的人 trusted subordinate; reliable agent [心胸] [喻] *figurative* 气量 mind; tolerance: ～～宽大 *broad-minded; unprejudiced* ❷习惯上也指思想器官和思想感情等 (also used customarily to indicate the heart, the mind, feeling, intention, etc): ～思 *thought; idea* | ～得 *what one has gained from work, study, etc* | 用～ *to concentrate one's mind on* | ～情 *frame* (or *state*) *of mind; mood* | 开～(快乐) *happy* | 伤～ *sad* | 谈～ *to have a heart-to-heart talk* | 全～全意 *whole-heartedly; with all one's heart; heart and soul* [心理] **1** 思想、感情、感觉等活动过程的总称 mentality; psychology **2** 想法，思想情况 idea; thought: 这是一般人的～～。*This is the way ordinary people feel about it.* [小心] 留神，谨慎 to look out; to be careful (*or* cautious): ～～火烛(谨慎防火)! *Mind the fire!* | 一路多加～～。*Be more cautious all the way.* ❸中央，在中间的地位或部分 centre; core: 掌～ *center of the palm; sphere of control* | 江～ *middle of a river* | 圆～ *center of a circle* [中心] **1** 心❸ centre; core; heart **2** 主要部分 main; chief; body: 政治～～ *political centre* | 文化～～ *cultural centre* | ～～任务 *main task* | ～～环节 *key link* ❹星宿名，二十八宿之一。也叫"商"(also called 商) *xin*, the 5th of the 28 constellations

芯 ㊀ xīn ㄒㄧㄣ 去皮的灯心草 rush pith: 灯～ *wick* (*of a lamp*)

㊁ xìn 见 834 页 see p834

辛 xīn ㄒㄧㄣ ❶辣 hot (in taste, flavour, etc) ❷劳苦，艰难 hard; laborious: ～勤 *industrious; hardworking* ❸悲伤 sad; suffering: ～酸 *sad; bitter; miserable* ❹天干的第八位，用作顺序的第八 *xin*, the 8th of the 10 Heavenly Stems; the eighth

莘 ㊀ xīn ㄒㄧㄣ 古指细辛。一种草本植物，花暗紫色，根细，有辣味，可入药(i. e. 细辛 in ancient Chinese) Herba Asari (*Aristolochiaceae*)

［莘庄］地名，在上海市 Xinzhuang, a place in Shanghai

㊀ shēn 见 666 页 see p666

锌 xīn ㄒㄧㄣ 一种金属元素，符号 Zn，旧称"亚铅"，蓝白色，质脆。可制锌版，涂在铁上可防生锈。氧化锌(俗叫"锌白")是一种重要的白色颜料 (formerly called 亚铅 and its oxide popularly called 锌白) zinc (Zn)

新 xīn ㄒㄧㄣ ❶跟"旧"相对 (the opposite of 旧) **1** 刚有的或刚经验到的 new:～办法 *new method*｜万象更～。*Everything looks fresh and gay.* or *Everything takes on a new look.*｜～事物 *new things* **2** 没有用过的 unused; brand new:～笔 *new pen*｜～房子 *new house* **3** 性质上改变得更好的，使变成新的 new; to make anew; to renew:～社会 *new society*｜～文艺 *new art and literature*｜粉刷一～ *to look brand new after being whitewashed; newly whitewashed* ［自新］改掉以往的过错，使思想行为向好的方面发展 to turn over a new leaf; to make a fresh start; to begin life anew ❷新近，刚才 recently; newly:这枝钢笔是我～买的。*This is my newly bought fountain pen.*｜他是～来的。*He is a newcomer.* ❸称结婚时的人或物 newly-married; bridal:～郎 *bridegroom*｜～房 *bridal chamber*

薪 xīn ㄒㄧㄣ 柴火 firewood; faggot:杯水车～ *trying to put out a burning cartload of faggots with a cup of water — action falling far short of the need; utterly inadequate measure; drop in the bucket* ［薪水］［薪金］工资 salary; pay; wages

忻 xīn ㄒㄧㄣ ❶同"欣" same as 欣 ❷忻州，地名，在山西省 Xinzhou, a place in Shanxi Province

昕 xīn ㄒㄧㄣ 太阳将要出来的时候 dawn; time when the sun is about to rise

欣 xīn ㄒㄧㄣ 快乐，喜欢 glad; happy; joyful:欢～鼓舞 *to be filled with exultation; jubilant*｜～然前往 *to go with pleasure* ［欣赏］用喜爱的心情来领会其中的意味 to appreciate; to enjoy; to admire ［欣欣］**1** 高兴的样子 joyful; glad; happy:～～然有喜色 *to wear a joyful expression* **2** 草木生机旺盛的样子 thriving; flourishing:～～向荣 *thriving; flourishing; prosperous*

訢 xīn ㄒㄧㄣ 同"欣" same as 欣

焮 xīn ㄒㄧㄣ xìn ㄒㄧㄣˋ (又 *also* xìn) 烧，灼 burning

歆 xīn ㄒㄧㄣ 喜爱，羡慕 to admire:～羡 *to admire*

馨 xīn ㄒㄧㄣ 散布很远的香气 strong and pervasive fragrance:～香 *fragrance*｜芳～ *aroma; fragrance*

鑫 xīn ㄒㄧㄣ 财富兴盛。商店字号、人名常用的字(*xin*, usually used in a given name or a name of a shop) prosperous; making a good profit

镡 xín ㄒㄧㄣˊ ❶古代剑柄的顶端部分 top part of an ancient sword hilt ❷古代兵器,似剑而小 *xin*, an ancient weapon similar to a sword, but smaller

囟(**顖) xìn ㄒㄧㄣˋ 囟门,囟脑门,又叫"顶门"。婴儿头顶骨未合缝的地方(also called 顶门) fontanelle (of a baby's skull)

芯 ㊁ xìn ㄒㄧㄣˋ ❶(一子)装在器物中心的捻子或消息儿,如蜡烛的捻子、爆竹的引线等 fuse (as in a firecracker); wick (as in a candle) ❷(一子)蛇的舌头 the forked tongue of a snake

㊀ xīn 见832页 see p832

信 xìn ㄒㄧㄣˋ ❶诚实,不欺骗 honesty; trust: ~用 *trustworthiness; credit* | 失~ *to break faith* ❷信任,不怀疑,认为可靠 to believe; to trust: ~赖 *to trust; to have faith in* | 这话我不~。*I don't believe it.* ㊕ ***transfer*** 信仰,崇奉 to believe in; to profess faith in: ~徒 *religious follower; believer* ❸(一儿)消息 message; information; word: 报~ *to notify; to inform* | 喜~儿 *good news* [信号] 传达消息、命令、报告等的记号 signal: 放~~枪 *to fire a signal pistol* ❹函件 letter; mail (㊈ ***doublet*** 书一 letter): 给他写封~。*Write to him.* ❺随便 at will; at random; casually: ~步 *to walk in a leisurely and aimless manner; to stroll; to roam* | ~口开河(随便乱说) *to talk off the top of one's head; to speak irresponsibly* ❻信石,砒霜 arsenic ❼同"芯㊁" same as 芯㊁ 〈古 ***archaism***〉又同"伸"(shēn) also same as 伸

衅(釁) xìn ㄒㄧㄣˋ ❶古代用牲畜的血涂器物的缝隙(in ancient China) to put animal blood in the cracks of an object: ~钟 *to brush animal blood on a bell* | ~鼓 *to brush animal blood on a drum* ❷缝隙,争端 quarrel; dispute: 挑~ *to provoke a quarrel* | 寻~ *to seek a pretext for quarrel (or fight)*

焮 xìn ㄒㄧㄣˋ (又 *also* xīn) 见833页 xīn see xīn on p833

XING ㄒㄧㄥ

兴(興) ㊀ xīng ㄒㄧㄥ ❶举办,发动 to begin; to start; to found: ~工 *to commence work; to begin building; to start construction* | ~利除弊 *to promote what is beneficial and get rid of what is harmful* | ~修水利 *to undertake water conservancy projects* ❷起来 to get up; to rise: 夙~夜寐(早起晚睡) *to rise early and retire late* | 闻风~起 *to spring* to action upon hearing the news ❸旺盛 prosperous; flourishing; thriving (㊊ **doublet** 一盛 prosperous | 一旺 flourishing; thriving) [兴奋] 精神振作或激动 excited ❹流行,盛行 to become popular: 时~ *in vogue; fashionable; popular* ❺准许 (usually used in the negative) to permit; to allow: 不~胡闹。*Don't make trouble.* ❻〈方 **dialect**〉或许 probably; maybe; perhaps: 他~来,~不来。*He may or may not come.* ❼姓 Xing, a surname

㊁ xìng 见 838 页 see p838

星 xīng ㄒㄧㄥ ❶天空中发光的或反射光的天体,如太阳、地球、北斗星等。通常指夜间天空中闪烁发光的天体 star; any heavenly body: 人造地球卫~ *man-made satellite* | ~罗棋布 *scattered all over (like stars in the sky or pieces on a chessboard)* | 月明~稀。*The moon is bright and the stars are few.* or *Few stars are seen when the moon shines brightly.* ㊕ **figurative** 称有名的演员、运动员等 famous performer or athlete; star: 明~ *star* | 球~ *ball-game star* | 歌~ *singing star* ❷(一子、一儿)细碎或细小的东西 bit; piece; particle: ~火燎原。*A single spark can start a prairie fire.* | 火~儿 *spark* | 唾沫~子 *spray of saliva* ❸星宿名,二十八宿之一 *xing*, the 25th of the 28 constellations

猩 xīng ㄒㄧㄥ 猩猩,哺乳动物,形状略似人,毛赤褐色或黑色,前肢长,无尾。吃野果。产于苏门答腊等地 orangutan (*Pongo pygmaeus*) [猩红热] 一种急性传染病,病原体是一种溶血性链球菌,症状是头痛、寒热、发红疹,口部周围苍白,舌如草莓。小儿容易感染 scarlet fever; scarlatina

惺 xīng ㄒㄧㄥ 醒悟 to realize; to come to the senses; to be awake to the truth [惺惺] **1** 清醒,聪明 clear-headed; awake **2** 聪明的人 intelligent person; wise man: ~~惜~~(喻指同类的人互相怜惜)。*The wise appreciate one another.* or *Intelligent people like intelligence in others.* or (*of people of similar disposition, ability or circumstances*) *to like each other and sympathize with each other* [假惺惺] 虚情假意的样子 hypocritically

[惺松] (*惺忪) **1** 苏醒 to revive; to come to; to regain consciousness **2** 刚睡醒尚未清醒 (of eyes) not yet fully open (as on waking up)

腥 xīng ㄒㄧㄥ ❶腥气,像鱼的气味 having the smell of fish, seafood, etc: 血~ *reeking of blood; bloody* | ~膻 (shān) *the smell of fish, mutton, etc* ❷鱼、肉一类的食品 raw meat or fish: 荤~ *dishes of meat or fish*

骍 xīng ㄒㄧㄥ 赤色的马或牛 reddish horse (or ox)

箵 xīng ㄒㄧㄥ 见 453 页“笭”字条“笭箵”(líng—) see 笭箵 on p453

刑 xíng ㄒㄧㄥˊ ❶刑罚,对犯人各种处罚的总称 punishment; penalty; sentence: 死～ *death sentence* (or *penalty*); *capital punishment* | 徒～ *imprisonment* | 缓～ *temporary suspension of a sentence; reprieve; probation* ❷特指对犯人的体罚,如拷打、折磨等 torture; corporal punishment: 受～ *to be tortured* | 动～ *to put* (*sb*) *to torture*

邢 xíng ㄒㄧㄥˊ 姓 Xing, a surname

形 xíng ㄒㄧㄥˊ ❶样子 form; shape: 三角～ *triangle* | 地～ *topography; terrain* | ～式 *form; shape; structure* | ～象 *image; form; figure* [形成] 逐渐发展成为(某种事物、状况或局面等) to form; to take shape; to come into being: 爱护公物已～～一种风气。*Taking good care of public property has become a common practice.* [形势] **1** 地理上指地势的高低,山、水的样子 terrain; topographical features **2** 事物发展的状况 situation; development of things: 国际～～ *international situation* ❷体,实体 body; entity: ～体 *figure; body* | 无～ *invisible; intangible; nonphysical* | ～影不离 *inseparable as body and shadow; always together* ❸表现 to appear; to express: 喜怒不～于色 *not to show joy or anger on one's face* [形容] **1** 面容 look; appearance; countenance: ～～枯槁 *wan-looking; haggard* **2** 对事物的样子、性质加以描述 to describe [形容词] 表示事物的特征、性质、状态的词,如大、小、好、坏、快、慢等 adjective ❹对照,比较 to contrast; to compare: 相～之下 *by comparison; as compared with* | 相～见绌(chù) *to prove inferior by comparison; to be outshone*

型 xíng ㄒㄧㄥˊ ❶铸造器物用的模子 mould ❷样式 model; type: 新～ *new type* | 小～汽车 *minicar*

钘 xíng ㄒㄧㄥˊ 古代盛酒器。又用于人名(*xing*, also used in a given name) ancient wine vessel

硎 xíng ㄒㄧㄥˊ ❶磨刀石 whetstone; grinding stone ❷磨制 to grind; to polish

铏 xíng ㄒㄧㄥˊ 古代盛羹的器具 *xing*, an ancient vessel for thick soup

行 ㊀ xíng ㄒㄧㄥˊ ❶走 to go; to walk; to travel: 日～千里 *to travel one thousand* li *a day* | 步～ *to go on foot* [行书] 汉字的一种字体,形体和笔势介于草书和楷书之间(of Chinese calligraphy) running script (*or* hand) ㊀ ***extension*** 出外时用的(of things) for travelling: ～装 *luggage; outfit for a journey* | ～箧(qiè) *traveling box* [行李](—*li*)出外时所带的包裹、箱子等 luggage; baggage [行头] (—tou) 演戏时穿戴的衣物 actor's costumes and paraphernalia [一行] 一组(指同行的人) a group (travelling together) ❷ 流通,传递 to be current; to circulate: ～销 *to be on sale* | 通～全国 *to be applicable throughout the country* | 发～报刊、书籍 *to issue newspapers, magazines and book* ❸流动性的,临时性的 temporary; makeshift: ～灶 *makeshift* (or *portable*) *cooking stove* | ～商 *itinerant trader; traveling merchant; pedlar* | ～营 *field headquarters* ❹ 进行(used before a two-character verb to express the performance of the action): 另～通知 *to be notified separately; till further notice* | 即～查处 *to investigate and deal with accordingly at once* ❺实做,办 to do; to perform; to carry out: ～礼 *to salute* | 举～ *to hold (a meeting, a ceremony, etc)* | 实～ *to carry out; to put into action* ❻(旧读 formerly xìng) 足以表明品质的举止行动 behaviour; conduct: 言～ *words and deeds* | 品～ *behaviour; conduct* | 德～ *moral conduct* (or *integrity*) | 操～ (*usually of students*) *behaviour* (or *conduct*) | 罪～ *crime; guilt* ❼ 可以 to be all right; will do: 不学习不～。*It's no good to stop learning.* ❽能干 capable; competent: 你真～! *How capable you are!* ❾将要 will; shall; to be going to: ～将毕业 *will graduate soon* ❿乐府和古诗的一种体裁 *xing*, a form of *Yuefu* and ancient poetry ⓫ 姓 Xing, a surname

㊁ háng 见 265 页 see p265

饧(餳) xíng ㄒㄧㄥˊ ❶糖稀 treacle; molasses ❷糖块、面团等变软(of candy, dough, etc) to become sticky and soft: 刚和(huó)好的面～一会儿好擀。*Wait till the kneaded dough becomes soft and sticky before you flatten it with a rolling pin.* ❸精神不振,眼睛半睁半闭(of eyes) drowsy; sleepy: 眼睛发～。*The eyes are sleepy.*

陉(陘) xíng ㄒㄧㄥˊ 山脉中断的地方 mountain pass; defile

荥(滎) ㊀ xíng ㄒㄧㄥˊ [荥阳] 地名,在河南省 Xingyang, a place in Henan Province

㊁ yíng 见 900 页 see p900

省 ㊁ xǐng ㄒㄧㄥˇ ❶检查自己 to examine oneself critically: 反～ *retrospection; self-examination* ❷ 知觉 to become conscious: 不～人事 *to lose consciousness* ❸省悟,觉悟 to be aware of; to realize: 猛～前非 *to realize one's fault suddenly* ❹看望,问候(父母、尊长) to visit (one's parents or elders): ～亲 *to pay a visit to one's parents or elders (living in another place)*

㊀ shěng 见 672 页 see

p672

醒 xǐng ㄒㄧㄥˇ ❶睡完或还没睡着(zháo) to be awake; to wake up ❷头脑由迷糊而清楚 to become conscious; to realize; to be clear in mind (㊟ **doublet** —悟 to come to realize; to wake up to reality): 清~*clear-headed*|惊~*to wake up with a start* [醒目][醒眼] 鲜明,清楚,引人注意的(of written words or pictures) to catch the eye; to attract attention; to be striking to the eye: 这一行字印得很~~。*This line of printed words is very eye-catching.* ❸酒醉之后恢复常态(after being drunk) to regain consciousness; to sober up: 水果可以~酒。*Fruits will help to sober up.*

擤(**揞) xǐng ㄒㄧㄥˇ 捏住鼻子,用气排出鼻涕 to blow (one's nose): ~鼻涕 *to blow one's nose*

兴(興) ㊁ xìng ㄒㄧㄥˋ 兴趣,对事物喜爱的情绪 interest; mood or desire to do sth: 游~*interest in travelling*|助~*to add to amusement; to make things more lively*|~高采烈 *in high spirits; excited* [高兴] 愉快,喜欢 pleased; delighted

㊀ xīng 见834页 see p834

杏 xìng ㄒㄧㄥˋ 杏树,落叶乔木,春天开花,白色或淡红色。果实叫杏儿或杏子,酸甜,可吃。核中的仁叫杏仁,甜的可吃,苦的供药用 apricot tree (*Prunus armeniaca*)

幸(❺*倖) xìng ㄒㄧㄥˋ ❶意外地得到成功或免去灾害 lucky; fortunate: ~免于难(nàn) *to survive a disaster; to escape death by sheer chance* [幸亏][幸而] 副词 **adverb**,多亏 fortunately; luckily: ~~你来了。*Luckily you've come.* ❷幸福,幸运 happiness; good luck: 荣~*to be honoured* ❸高兴 to be happy: 庆~*to rejoice*|欣~*to be glad and thankful* ❹希望 to hope: ~勿推却。*I hope that you will not decline my offer.* ❺旧指宠爱(in former times) favour: 宠~*to make a pet of sb*|得~*to win sb's favour* ❻旧指封建帝王到达某地(of a monarch) to come; to arrive: 巡~*imperial tour of inspection*

悻 xìng ㄒㄧㄥˋ [悻悻]怨恨,怒 angry; resentful: ~~而去 *to go away angrily; to leave in a huff*

婞 xìng ㄒㄧㄥˋ 倔强,固执 stubborn

性 xìng ㄒㄧㄥˋ ❶性质,人或事物的本身所具有的能力、作用等 nature; property; quality: 碱~*alkalinity; basicity*|弹(tán)~*elasticity; resilience*|向日~*heliotropism*|药~*properties of a medicine*|斗争~*fighting spirit; militancy* [性命] 生命 life [性子](—zi) 脾气 temper: 他的~~很急。*He is a hot-tempered person.* [个性][性格] 个人的思想、行

动上的特点 individuality; personality; temperament ❷男女或雌雄的特质 sex; gender: ～别 *gender; sex; sexual distinction* | 男～*male; masculine* | 女～ *female; feminine* | ～器官 *sexual organs; genitals* | ～教育 *sex education* ❸在思想、感情等方面的表现(noun-or adjective-forming suffix denoting an abstract quality): 党～*party spirit* | 组织纪律～*sense of organizational discipline*

姓 xìng ㄒㄧㄥˋ 表明家族系统的字 surname: ～名 *name*

荇(**莕) xìng ㄒㄧㄥˋ 荇菜,水生植物,叶浮在水面上,夏天开花,黄色,可入药 floating heart (*Nymphoides peltatum*)

XIONG ㄒㄩㄥ

凶(❸-❺ *兇) xiōng ㄒㄩㄥ ❶不幸的,与"吉"相对(the opposite of 吉) inauspicious; ominous: ～事(丧事) *unlucky event* (*death, burial, etc*) | 吉～*good or ill luck* ❷庄稼收成不好 famine; crop failure: ～年 *year of crop failure* (or *famine*) ❸恶,暴 vicious; fierce; brutal (㊀ ***doublet*** 一恶 fierce; ferocious; inhuman | 一暴 fierce and brutal; malignant; ruthless): ～狠 *fierce and malicious* | 穷～极恶 *extremely vicious and brutal; ferocious; fierce* ❹关于杀伤的 relating to violence or murder: ～手 *murderer; killer; assassin* | 行～ *to commit physical assault* (or *murder*); *to do violence* ❺厉害,过甚 terrible; fearful: 你闹得太～了。*What a terrible row you made!* | 雨来得很～。*The rain came down with a vengeance.*

匈 xiōng ㄒㄩㄥ 古同"胸" same as 胸 in ancient Chinese

[匈奴] 我国古代北方的民族 Xiongnu (*or* Huns), ancient nomadic people living in north China

讻(**訩) xiōng ㄒㄩㄥ 争辩 to argue; to quarrel [讻讻]喧扰,纷扰 turbulent; tumultuous

汹(*洶) xiōng ㄒㄩㄥ 水向上翻腾 water rushing upward [汹汹] **1** 形容水声或争吵声 sound of roaring waves or quarreling **2** 形容声势很大 violent; truculent: 来势～～ *to come threateningly towards; to break in violently*

[汹涌](—yǒng)水势很大,向上涌 surging; turbulent: 波涛～～*turbulent waves*

胸(*胷) xiōng ㄒㄩㄥ 胸膛,身体前面颈下腹上的部分。(图见741页"体" picture on p741) chest; breast; thorax[胸襟] ㊃ ***figurative*** 气量,抱负 mind; breadth of mind; tolerance

兄 xiōng ㄒㄩㄥ 哥哥 elder brother: ～嫂 *elder brother*

and his wife 敬辞 ***polite***：老～ *buddy; brother; man*｜仁～*my dear friend*｜某某～（*courteous form of address between male friends*）*brother so-and-so*［兄弟］**1** 兄和弟的统称 brothers; younger and elder brothers：～～三人 *three brothers* ㊀ ***extension*** 有亲密关系的 with close relationship：～～国家 *fraternal country* **2**（— di）弟弟 younger brother

芎 xiōng ㄒㄩㄥ［芎䓖］（— qióng）多年生草本植物，叶子像芹菜，秋天开花，白色，全草有香气，地下茎可入药。也叫"川芎"(also called 川芎) chuanxiong rhizome（*Ligusticum wallichii*）

雄 xióng ㄒㄩㄥˊ ❶公的，阳性的，跟"雌"相对（the opposite of 雌）male：～鸡 *cock; rooster*｜～蕊 *stamen* ❷强有力的 mighty; powerful; forceful：～师 *powerful army; mighty army*｜～辩 *convincing argument; eloquent speech* ❸宏伟，有气魄的 grand; imposing：～心 *great ambitions; lofty aspirations*｜～伟 *grand; imposing and great* ❹强有力的人或国家 person or state having great power and influence：英～*hero; heroine*｜两～不并立。*Two great powers cannot coexist.*｜战国七～*seven rival states of the Warring States Period*（*475 BC－221 BC*）

熊 xióng ㄒㄩㄥˊ ❶哺乳动物，种类很多，体大，尾短，能直立行走，也能攀登树木 bear（*Ursidae*）［熊猫］也叫"大熊猫"、"猫熊"。哺乳动物，体肥胖，形状像熊而略小，尾短，眼周、耳、前后肢和肩部黑色，其余均为白色。毛密而有光泽，耐寒。喜食竹叶、竹笋。生活在我国西南地区，是我国特有的珍贵动物（also called 大熊猫 or 猫熊）panda（*Ailuropoda melanoleuca*）❷〈方 ***dialect***〉斥责 to rebuke; to upbraid; to scold：～了他一顿 *to give him a scolding* ❸〈方 ***dialect***〉怯懦，没有能力 coward; timid; impotent：这人真～，一上场就败了下来。*The guy was really a good-for-nothing, for he was defeated as soon as he entered on the scene.*

［熊熊］形容火势旺盛 flaming; ablaze; raging

诇 xiòng ㄒㄩㄥˋ 刺探 to reconnoitre; to scout; to pry

敻 xiòng ㄒㄩㄥˋ 远，辽阔 far; remote; vast：～古（*in*）*remote antiquity*

XIU ㄒㄧㄡ

休 xiū ㄒㄧㄡ ❶歇息 to rest：～假（*of students, workers, etc*）*to have*（or *take, go on*）*a holiday or vacation*;（*of soldiers, personnel working abroad, etc*）*to be on leave of absence*｜～养 *to recuperate; to convalesce* ❷停止 to cease; to give up; to stop：～业 *to suspend business; to be closed down*｜

～学 *to suspend one's schooling* (*without losing one's status as a student*) | ～会 *to adjourn; to close a session or a meeting for a time* | 争论不～ *to argue endlessly* ㊀ ***extension*** 完结(多指失败或死亡) to be finished (usually indicating failure or death) ❸旧社会丈夫把妻子赶回母家,断绝夫妻关系(in the old society) to divorce one's wife and send her home: ～书 *letter by a husband unilaterally announcing his decision to divorce his wife* | ～妻 *to divorce and send one's wife away* ❹副词 ***adverb***,不要,别 don't: ～想 *don't think* (or *imagine*) *that it is possible; to stop dreaming* | ～要这样性急。*Don't be so impatient.* ❺吉庆,美善 good fortune; rejoicing: ～咎(吉凶) *good and ill luck; weal and woe* | ～戚(喜和忧)相关 *to share joys and sorrows*

咻 xiū ㄒㄧㄡ 吵,乱说话 to make a din

[咻咻]拟声词 ***onomatopoeia*** **1** 形容喘气的声音 sound of heavy breathing **2** 形容某些动物的叫声 sound made by certain birds or animals: 小鸭～～地叫着。*The ducklings are cheeping.*

庥 xiū ㄒㄧㄡ 庇荫,保护 to protect; to shelter; to shield

鸺 xiū ㄒㄧㄡ 见 88 页"鸱"字条"鸱鸺"(chī—)、458 页"鹠"字条"鸺鹠"(—liú) see 鸱鸺 on p88; see 鸺鹠 on p458

貅 xiū ㄒㄧㄡ 见 561 页"貔"字条"貔貅"(pí—) see 貔貅 on p561

髹(**髤) xiū ㄒㄧㄡ 把漆涂在器物上 to coat sth with lacquer

修(△*脩) xiū ㄒㄧㄡ ❶使完美或恢复完美 to embellish; to decorate; to repair: ～饰 *to embellish; to decorate; to adorn* | ～理 *to repair; to mend* | ～辞 *rhetoric* | ～车 *to repair a vehicle* ❷建造 to build; to construct: ～铁道 *to build a railway* | ～桥 *to build a bridge* ❸著作,撰写 to write; to compile: ～书 *to compile a book; to write a letter* | ～史 *to compile* (or *write*) *history* ❹钻研学习,研究 to study; to learn: ～业 *to study at school* | 自～ *self-study* ❺长(cháng) long; slender; tall and thin(㊁ ***doublet*** —长 long; tall and thin; slender): 茂林～竹 *thick forest and tall bamboo*

脩 xiū ㄒㄧㄡ ❶干肉 dried meat [束脩]一束干肉 a bundle of dried meat ㊕ ***transfer*** 旧时指送给老师的薪金(in former times) tuition fee ❷同"修" same as 修

羞 xiū ㄒㄧㄡ ❶感到耻辱 to feel ashamed (㊁ ***doublet*** —耻 shame): ～与为伍 *to feel ashamed to be seen with sb or in sb's company* ❷难为情,害臊 shy; bashful: 害～ *to feel bashful; to feel shy* | ～得脸通红 *to blush with shame* ㊀ ***extension***

使难为情 to make sb feel ashamed or embarrassed：你别～我。*Don't make me feel embarrassed.* ❸同"馐"same as 馐

馐 xiū ㄒㄧㄡ 美味的食品，也作"羞"(also written as 羞) delicacy; dainty：珍～*rare delicacies*

X

朽 xiǔ ㄒㄧㄡˇ ❶腐烂，多指木头(usually of wood) rotten; decayed(㊎ **doublet** 腐一 rotten)：～木 *rotten wood* (or *tree*)[不朽](精神、功业等)不磨灭(of spirit, feat, etc) immortal：永垂～～ *to be immortal; to live forever; eternal glory to* ❷衰老 aged; senile：老～*old and useless*

宿 ㊂ xiǔ ㄒㄧㄡˇ 夜 night：住了一～*to stay for one night*｜谈了半～*to chat till midnight*

㊀ sù 见712页 see p712

㊂ xiù 见843页 see p843

滫 xiǔ ㄒㄧㄡˇ 泔水 hogwash; slops; swill

秀 xiù ㄒㄧㄡˋ ❶植物吐穗开花，多指庄稼(usually of grain crops, etc) to put forth flowers or ears：高粱～穗了。*The sorghum has been putting forth ears.*｜六月六看谷～。*The 6th day of the 6th lunar month sees millet putting forth ears.* ❷特别优异的 excellent(㊎ **doublet** 优一 excellent)：～异 *outstanding*｜～挺 *straight and graceful* [秀才](—cai) 封建时代科举初考合格的人。泛指书生 *xiucai*, one who passed the imperial examination at the county level in the Ming and Qing dynasties; (in a broad sense) scholar; skillful writer ❸聪明，灵巧 clever; intelligent：内～*clever without showing it; one's inner wisdom; inwardly smart*｜心～*bright without seemingly so* ❹美丽 beautiful(㊎ **doublet** 一丽 beautiful)：眉清目～*fine eyebrows and beautiful eyes*｜山明水～*beautiful mountains and limpid waters*｜祖国的河山分外～美。*The scenery of our motherland is extremely beautiful.* [秀气](—qi) 1 清秀 elegant：小姑娘很～～。*The little girl is elegant.* 2 (器物)灵巧轻便(of article of use) handy; exquisite：这个东西做得很～～。*This is exquisitely made.*

绣(*繡) xiù ㄒㄧㄡˋ ❶用丝线等在绸、布上缀成花纹或文字 to embroider：～花 *to embroider; to do embroidery*｜～字 *to embroider Chinese characters* ❷绣成的物品 embroidery：湘～*Hunan embroidery*｜苏～*Suzhou embroidery*

琇 xiù ㄒㄧㄡˋ 像玉的石头 jade-like stone

锈(*鏽) xiù ㄒㄧㄡˋ ❶金属表面所生的氧化物 rust：铁～*rust*｜铜～*copper rust; verdigris*｜这把刀子长(zhǎng)～了。*The knife is rusty.* ❷生锈 to become rusty：门上的锁～住了。*The lock of*

the door is rusty and cannot be opened.

岫 xiù ㄒㄧㄡˋ ❶山洞 cave; cavern ❷山 mountain peak; mountain

袖 xiù ㄒㄧㄡˋ ❶(一子、一儿)衣服套在胳膊上的部分。(图见 882 页"衣"picture on p882) sleeve [袖珍]小型的 pocket; pocket-size: ～～字典 *pocket dictionary* | ～～收录机 *pocket radio recorder* ❷藏在袖子里 to tuck (*or* hide) inside the sleeve: ～着手 *hands tucked deep in the sleeves* | ～手旁观 *to stand by indifferently; to look on with folded arms*

臭 ㊁ xiù ㄒㄧㄡˋ ❶气味 odour; smell: 空气是无色无～的。*Air is colourless and odourless.* ❷同"嗅"same as 嗅

㊀ chòu 见 95 页 see p95

嗅 xiù ㄒㄧㄡˋ 闻,用鼻子辨别气味 to smell; to scent; to sniff by nose: ～觉 *sense of smell*

溴 xiù ㄒㄧㄡˋ 一种非金属元素,符号 Br,赤褐色的液体,性质很毒,能侵蚀皮肤和黏膜。可制染料、照相底版、镇静剂等 bromine (Br)

宿 ㊂ xiù ㄒㄧㄡˋ 我国古代的天文学家把天上某些星的集合体叫作宿 ancient Chinese astronomical term for constellation: 星～ *constellation* | 二十八～ *28 constellations*

㊀ sù 见 712 页 see p712

㊁ xiǔ 见 842 页 see p842

XU ㄒㄩ

圩 ㊁ xū ㄒㄩ 闽粤等地区称集市。古书里作"虚"(written as 虚 in ancient Chinese texts) country fair in Fujian, Guangdong, etc

㊀ wéi 见 781 页 see p781

吁 ㊀ xū ㄒㄩ ❶叹息 to sigh: 长～短叹 *to sigh and groan; to moan and groan; to sigh* ❷文言叹词 ***interjection in classical Chinese***, 表示惊疑 (used to express surprise or amazement) why; oh: ～,是何言欤! *Oh, what do you mean?*

㊁ yù 见 919 页 see p919

盱 xū ㄒㄩ 睁开眼向上看 to look up with eyes wide open [盱眙](—yí) 地名,在江苏省 Xuyi, a place in Jiangsu Province

戌 xū ㄒㄩ ❶地支的第十一位 *xu*, 11th of the 12 Earthly Branches ❷戌时,指晚上七点到九点 time of the day from 7 p.m. to 9 p.m.

砉 ㊀ xū ㄒㄩ 皮骨相离声 sound of tearing the skin from the bone

㊁ huā 见 286 页 see p286

须(❸❹鬚) xū ㄒㄩ ❶必须,必得(děi),应当 must; have to: 这事～亲自动手。*This must be done by oneself.* | 务～注意。*Be sure to be careful!* | 必～努力。*You have to work hard.* ❷等待 to wait ❸胡子 beard; mustache

X

(㊥ ***doublet*** 胡— beard; mustache) ❹像胡须的东西 beard-like; mustache-like: 触~ *cirrus; vibrissa; palp* | 花~ *pistil; stamen; tassel* | ~根 *fibrous root*

[须臾](—yú)片刻,一会儿 moment; instant

媭 xū ㄒㄩ 古代楚国人对姐姐的称呼(term of address among people of the state of Chu in ancient China) elder sister

胥 xū ㄒㄩ ❶古代的小官(in ancient China) petty official: ~吏 *petty official* [钞胥] 管誊写的小吏 petty official responsible for transcription ㊦ ***transfer*** 代人抄写书的人 person writing books or letters for others ❷全,都 all; each and every: 民~然矣。*All the people are right.* | 万事~备。*Everything is ready.*

谞 xū ㄒㄩ ❶才智 wisdom; talent ❷谋划 to scheme; to plan

顼 xū ㄒㄩ 见 1000 页"颛"字条"颛顼"(zhuān—) see 颛顼 on p1000

虚 xū ㄒㄩ ❶空 empty; void (㊥ ***doublet*** 空— empty; void): 弹不~发。*Not a single bullet missed its target.* | 座无~席。*All the seats have been occupied.* [虚心] 不自满,不骄傲 open-minded; modest: ~~使人进步,骄傲使人落后。*Modesty helps one to go forward, whereas conceit makes one lag behind.* ❷不真实的,跟"实"相对(the opposite of 实) not real; false: ~名 *false reputation; undeserved reputation* | ~荣 *vanity* | ~张声势 *to make an empty show of strength; bluff and bluster* [虚词] 意义比较抽象,有帮助造句作用的词(跟"实词"相对),如介词、连词等(the opposite of 实词) function word, word that cannot make a sentence alone, but has abstract meaning and helps to make a sentence such as prepositions, conjunctions, etc ❸心里怯懦 diffident; timid: 做贼心~ *to have a guilty conscience* ❹衰弱 weak: 身体~弱 *in poor health* | 他身子太~了。*He is very weak physically.* ❺徒然,白白地 in vain: ~度年华 *to live vainly through one's prime; to waste one's glorious youth* | 不~此行。*The visit is fruitful.* ❻指政治思想、方针、政策等方面的道理 general or guiding principle; theory: 务~ *to discuss principles or ideological guidelines* | 以~带实。*Let correct guidelines guide practical work.* ❼星宿名,二十八宿之一 *xu*, 11th of the 28 constellations

墟 xū ㄒㄩ ❶有人住过而现在已经荒废的地方 ruins: 废~ *ruins* | 殷~ *ruins of the Imperial Palace of the Yin Dynasty* [墟里][墟落] 村落 village; hamlet ❷〈方 ***dialect***〉集市,同"圩㊁"(same as 圩㊁)

country fair

嘘 ㊀ xū ㄒㄩ ❶从嘴里慢慢地吐气，呵气 to breathe out slowly ❷叹气 to sigh：仰天而～ *staring up at the sky and sighing helplessly* ❸火或汽的热力熏炙（of cooking fire, steam, etc）to scald; to burn：小心别～着手。*Be careful not to scald your hand.*｜把馒头放在锅里～一～。*Put* mantou *into the pot and put it on the fire for a while.*

［嘘唏］同"歔欷"same as 歔欷

㊁ shī 见 676 页 see p676

歔 xū ㄒㄩ ［歔欷］（—xī）哭泣时抽噎 to sob

欻 ㊁ xū ㄒㄩ 忽然 suddenly; all of a sudden：风雨～至。*A storm came up suddenly.*

㊀ chuā 见 99 页 see p99

需 xū ㄒㄩ ❶需要，必得用 to need; to require：～款 *required money*｜按～分配 *to distribute according to need* ❷必用的财物 necessaries; goods in need：军～ *military supplies*

繻 xū ㄒㄩ ❶彩色的丝织品 coloured silk fabric ❷古代一种用帛制的通行证 permit made of silk in ancient China

黢 xū ㄒㄩ 暗 dark; dim：黑～～ *dark; pitch-dark*

徐 xú ㄒㄩˊ 缓，慢慢地（叠 ***reduplication***）slowly; gently：～步 *to walk slowly* (*or leisurely*)｜清风～来。*A refreshing breeze was blowing gently.*｜火车～～开动了。*The train started to move slowly.*

许 xǔ ㄒㄩˇ ❶应允，认可 to permit; to allow（㊟ ***doublet*** 允—to permit; to allow｜准—to permit; to allow）：特～ *specially permitted*｜不～ *must not; do not allow; to prohibit* ㊀ ***extension*** 承认其优点 to praise：赞～ *to praise; to approve of*｜推～ *to praise; to approve*｜～为佳作 *to praise sth as an excellent piece of work* ❷预先答应给予 to promise：我～给他一本书。*I promised to give him a book.*｜以身～国 *to dedicate oneself to one's nation; to pledge to serve one's country* ❸或者，可能 maybe; perhaps：也～ *maybe; perhaps*｜或～ *maybe; perhaps*｜他下午也～来。*He may come this afternoon.* ❹处，地方 place：先生不知何～人也。*Where are you from, sir?* ❺表示约数（used to express rough estimate）：少～（少量）*a little*｜年三十～（三十岁左右）*about thirty years old* ❻这样 such：如～ *such as*

［许多］**1** 这样多，这么多 so many; so much **2** 很多 a lot of; many ［许久］**1** 时间这么长 so long a time **2** 时间很长 for a long time

浒 ㊁ xǔ ㄒㄩˇ ［浒墅关］地名，在江苏省苏州 Xushuguan, a place in Suzhou, Jiangsu Province ［浒浦］地名，在江苏省常熟 Xupu, a place in Changshu, Jiangsu Province

㊀ hǔ 见 284 页 see p284

诩 xǔ ㄒㄩˇ 说大话，夸张 to brag; to boast: 自～ *to brag; to boast*

栩 xǔ ㄒㄩˇ ［栩栩］形容生动的样子 vivid; lively: ～～如生 *lifelike; to the life*

姁 xǔ ㄒㄩˇ （叠 ***reduplication***）安乐，和悦 peaceful and happy; gentle; mild

湑 ㊀ xǔ ㄒㄩˇ ❶滤过的酒 filtered alcoholic drink [引] ***extension*** 清 clear ❷茂盛 luxuriant

㊁ xù 见 847 页 see p847

糈 xǔ ㄒㄩˇ ❶粮食 grains ❷古代祭神用的精米 husked rice offered as sacrifice to gods or ancestors in ancient China

醑 xǔ ㄒㄩˇ ❶美酒 mellow wine; fine wine ❷醑剂（挥发性药物的醇溶液）的简称（short for 醑剂）spirit; essence: 樟脑～ *camphor spirit* | 氯仿～ *chloroform*

旭 xù ㄒㄩˋ 光明，早晨太阳才出来的样子 brilliance of the rising sun［旭日］才出来的太阳 rising sun

序 xù ㄒㄩˋ ❶次第 order; sequence（[连] ***doublet*** 次— order; sequence）: 顺～ *order; sequence* | 工～ *working procedure* | 前后有～ *in perfect order* ❷排列次第 to arrange in order: ～齿（按年龄排次序）*order of seniority* ❸在正式内容之前的 introductory; initial: ～文 *preface* | ～曲 *overture; prelude* | ～幕 *prologue* 特指序文 used especially to indicate preface: 写一篇～ *to write a preface* ❹庠序，古代的学校 school in ancient China

叙（*敘、*敍） xù ㄒㄩˋ ❶述说 to talk; to chat（[连] ***doublet*** —述 to narrate; to recount）: ～旧（*of relatives and friends*）*to talk about the old days; to reminisce about the past* | ～家常 *to chitchat* ❷记述 to narrate; to recount; to relate: ～事 *to narrate (in writing)* | 记～ *to record and narrate; to narrate* ❸同"序❶❷❸" same as 序❶❷❸

溆 xù ㄒㄩˋ 水边 waterside［溆浦］地名，在湖南省 Xupu, a place in Hunan Province

洫 xù ㄒㄩˋ 田间的水道、沟渠 water course in a field; ditch

恤（*卹、*賉） xù ㄒㄩˋ ❶对别人表同情，怜悯 to pity; to sympathize: 体～ *to understand and sympathize; to show concern (or solicitude) for* ❷救济 to give relief; to compensate: ～金 *pension for a person disabled while on duty; pension for the dependants of a person who died while on duty* | 抚～ *to comfort and compensate a disabled person or a bereaved family* ❸忧虑 worry; misgiving; anxiety

畜 ㊀ xù ㄒㄩˋ 饲养 to raise (domestic animals): ～产

livestock (or *animal*) *product* | ～牧业 *animal husbandry; livestock husbandry* (or *farming*)

㊁ chù 见 99 页 see p99

蓄 xù ㄒㄩˋ 积聚,储藏 to store up; to save up (㊟ **doublet** 储—to save up):～财 *to store up wealth* ㊂ **extension** **1** 保存 to store; to preserve:～电池 *storage battery* | ～洪 *to store flood water* | 养精～锐 *to conserve strenth and store up energy* **2** 心里存着 to cherish; to entertain (ideas); to harbour: ～意已久 *long premeditated*

酗 xù ㄒㄩˋ 撒酒疯 to be roaring drunk; to be drunk and disorderly:～酒(没有节制地喝酒) *to indulge in excessive drinking*

勖(*勗) xù ㄒㄩˋ 勉励 to encourage; to prompt (㊟ **doublet**—勉 to encourage; to prompt)

绪 xù ㄒㄩˋ ❶丝的头 end of a silk thread ㊃ **figurative** 开端 beginning:千头万～ *tens of thousands of loose ends; (of things) complicated and difficult to unravel; many complications* [绪论]著作开头叙述内容要点的部分(of a book) introduction; introductory remarks of an academic writing ❷前人留下的事业 task; cause; undertaking:续未竟之～ *to carry on an unfinished mission; to take up where another has left off* ❸指心情、思想等 mental or emotional state:思～ *feeling; thinking* | 情～ *mood* ❹残余 remnant:～余 *surplus; remainder*

续(續) xù ㄒㄩˋ ❶连接,接下去 to continue; to go on (㊟ **doublet** 继—to continue):～假(jià) *to extend one's leave of absence* | ～编 *continuation of a book; sequence* | ～家谱 *to extend family tree* (or *genealogy*) ❷在原有的上面再加 to add; supply more:把茶～上 *to add more tea* | 炉子该～煤了。*The stove needs more coal.* or *More coal is to be added in the stove.*

[手续]办事的程序 formalities; procedure

絮 xù ㄒㄩˋ ❶棉絮,棉花的纤维 cotton wadding; cotton fibre:被～ *wadding for a quilt* | 吐～ *opening of bolls* ❷像棉絮的东西 sth resembling cotton:柳～ *willow catkins* | 芦～ *reed catkins* ❸在衣物里铺棉花(as with cotton) to wad; to pad:～被子 *to wad a quilt with cotton* | ～棉袄 *to line* (or *wad*) *one's clothes with cotton* ❹连续重复,惹人厌烦 long-winded; garrulous:～烦 *to be tired; to be bored* [絮叨](—dɑo)说话啰唆(of talking) repetitive; garrulous

溆 ㊁ xù ㄒㄩˋ 溆水河,水名,在陕西省汉中 Xushui River in Hanzhong, Shaanxi Province

㊀ xǔ 见 846 页 see p846

婿(*壻) xù ㄒㄩˋ ❶夫婿，丈夫 husband ❷女婿，女儿的丈夫 son-in-law; one's daughter's husband

煦(**昫) xù ㄒㄩˋ 温暖 warm; balmy: 春风和～。*Spring breeze is warm and gentle.*

蓿 xu ·ㄒㄩ 见519页"苜"字条"苜蓿"(mù—) see 苜蓿 on p519

XUAN ㄒㄩㄢ

轩 xuān ㄒㄩㄢ ❶古代的一种有围棚而前顶较高的车 *xuan*, a high-fronted, curtained carriage in ancient China [轩昂] **1** 高扬，高举 to hold high; to uplift **2** 气度不凡 dignified; imposing: 气宇～～ *dignified bearing; imposing manner* (or *appearance*) [轩轾](—zhì)车前高后低叫轩，前低后高叫轾(high-fronted carriage called 轩 and low-fronted carriage called 轾) ㊟ ***figurative*** 高低优劣 high or low; good or bad: 不分～～ *to be equal; to be hard to tell who or which is superior* ❷有窗的长廊或小室 small room or veranda with windows

宣 xuān ㄒㄩㄢ ❶发表，公开说出 to declare; to proclaim; to announce: ～誓 *to take a vow; to swear an oath; to make a pledge* | 心照不～ *to have a tacit understanding; to be understood but not expressed* [宣传]说明讲解，使大家相信并跟着行动 to publicize; to give publicity to: 热情～～好人好事 *to give publicity to good people and good deeds in a big way* ❷疏通 to give vent to: ～泄 *to drain* (or *lead*) *off* (*liquids*); *to give vent to one's pent-up feelings* ❸指宣纸，安徽省宣城等地产的一种高级纸张，吸墨均匀，能长期存放 *xuan* paper, quality paper made in Xuancheng, Anhui Province, absorbing ink evenly, and good for long preservation: 生～ shengxuan *paper, a kind of rigid* xuan *paper* | 虎皮～ hupixuan *paper, a kind of* xuan *paper with coloured light stripes; red, yellow or green* xuan *paper with faint stripes*

揎 xuān ㄒㄩㄢ 捋(luō)起袖子露出胳膊 to roll up the sleeves and bare the arms: ～拳捋袖 *to roll up the sleeves and raise the fists; to get ready to fight*

萱(*蘐) xuān ㄒㄩㄢ 萱草，多年生草本植物，叶细长，花红黄色 daylily (*Hemerocallis*)

喧(*諠) xuān ㄒㄩㄢ 大声说话，声音大而杂乱 talking noisily (㊟ ***doublet*** —哗 confused noise; hubbub; uproar): ～闹 *noise and excitement; bustle; racket* | 锣鼓～天 *deafening sound of gongs and drums*

瑄 xuān ㄒㄩㄢ 古代祭天用的璧 jade of sacrificial offering to heaven in ancient China

暄 xuān ㄒㄩㄢ ❶太阳的温暖 warm and sunny [寒暄] ㊕ *transfer* 见面时谈天气冷暖之类的应酬话 informal greetings：彼此～～了几句 *to exchange some informal greetings with each other* ❷松散，松软 fluffy; soft：～土 *soft soil* | 馒头又大又～。Mantou *is big and fluffy.*

煊 xuān ㄒㄩㄢ 同"暄❶"same as 暄❶

谖 xuān ㄒㄩㄢ ❶欺诈，欺骗 to deceive; to cheat; to swindle ❷忘记 to forget

儇 xuān ㄒㄩㄢ 轻薄而有点儿小聪明 frivolous and cunning

翾 xuān ㄒㄩㄢ 飞翔 to fly; to take wing; to hover

禤 xuān ㄒㄩㄢ 姓 Xuan, a surname

玄 xuán ㄒㄩㄢˊ ❶深奥不容易理解的 profound; abstruse：～理 *profound theory; theory of a philosophical sect of the Wei and Jin dynasties* | ～妙 *mysterious; abstruse* ❷虚伪，不真实，不可靠 unreliable; incredible：那话太～了，不能信。*That is too fantastic to believe.* or *That is a pretty tall story.* [玄虚] **1** 不真实 untrue **2** 欺骗的手段 deceitful trick：故弄～～ *to make a mystery of things; to turn simple things into mysteries on purpose* ❸黑色 black; dark：～狐 *black fox* | ～青(深黑色) *deep black*

痃 xuán ㄒㄩㄢˊ [横痃]由下疳引起的腹股沟淋巴结肿胀、发炎的症状 bubo; swelling of a lymph node in the groin caused by chancres; venereal disease

悬(懸) xuán ㄒㄩㄢˊ ❶挂，吊在空中 to hang; to dangle in the air：～灯结彩 *to be festooned with lanterns and colourful streamers* ㊗ ***figurative*** 没有着落，没有结束 unsolved; unsettled：～案 *unsettled law case* | 那件事还～着呢。*That remains unsolved.* [悬念] **1** 挂念 to be concerned about **2** 欣赏戏剧、电影或其他文艺作品时，对故事发展和人物命运的关切心情 suspense ❷凭空设想 to imagine; to assume; to conceive：～拟 *to fabricate; to make up* | ～揣 *to guess; to speculate* ❸距离远 distance; far apart：～隔 *to be far apart; to be separated by a great distance* | ～殊 *great disparity; wide gap* ❹〈方 ***dialect***〉危险 dangerous：真～！差点儿掉下去。*How dangerous! I just missed falling into it by a sheer chance.*

旋 ㊀ xuán ㄒㄩㄢˊ ❶旋转，转动 to revolve; to circle; to spin：螺～ *spiral* | 回～ *to circle; to go round and round* ❷回，归 to return; to come back：～里 *to return to one's hometown; to return home* | 凯～ *to return in*

X

X

triumph ❸不久 soon; quickly: ～即离去 *to leave soon* ❹姓 Xuan, a surname

㊁ xuǎn 见 850 页 see p850

漩 xuán ㄒㄩㄢˊ (一儿)水流旋转的圆窝 whirlpool; eddy

璇(*璿) xuán ㄒㄩㄢˊ 美玉 fine jade [璇玑](—jī) 古代天文仪器 armillary sphere; astronomical instrument in ancient China

选(選) xuǎn ㄒㄩㄢˇ ❶挑拣,择 to choose; to select; to pick (㊟ ***doublet*** 挑— to choose; to select; to pick out | —择 to select): ～种(zhǒng) *seed selection* [选举] 多数人推举认为合适的人担任代表或负责人 to vote; to elect: ～～代表 *to elect sb as a representative* ❷被选中了的人或物 those who are selected or chosen: 人～ *candidate* ❸被选出来编在一起的作品 selections; anthology: 文～ *anthology of essays* | 诗～ *selected poems*

晅 xuǎn ㄒㄩㄢˇ ❶日光 sunlight; daylight ❷光明 bright; brilliant ❸晒干 to dry up in the sun

烜 xuǎn ㄒㄩㄢˇ ❶火盛 ablaze ❷光明 bright [烜赫]声威昭著 of great renown and influence; prestigious and influential ❸晒干 to dry up in the sun

癣 xuǎn ㄒㄩㄢˇ 由真菌引起的皮肤病,有头癣、体癣、甲癣(灰指甲)等多种,患处常发痒 tinea; ringworm

券 ㊁ xuàn ㄒㄩㄢˋ 拱券,门窗、桥梁等建筑成弧形的部分 arch

㊀ quàn 见 623 页 see p623

泫 xuàn ㄒㄩㄢˋ 水珠下滴(of water) to drip; to trickle: ～然流涕 *tears trickling down the cheeks*

炫(❷**衒) xuàn ㄒㄩㄢˋ ❶光明照耀 dazzle: ～目 *glaring; dazzling* ❷夸耀 to show off [炫耀] **1** 照耀 to shine; to illuminate **2** 夸耀 to show off

眩 xuàn ㄒㄩㄢˋ ❶眼睛昏花看不清楚(of vision) dizzy; giddy; vertiginous: 头晕目～ *to feel dizzy* ❷迷惑,迷乱 puzzled; bewildered: ～于名利 *to lose one's self-control over the prospect of fame and wealth; to be obsessed with a desire for fame and wealth*

铉 xuàn ㄒㄩㄢˋ 横贯鼎耳以扛(gāng)鼎的器具 hook-like instrument to carry an ancient tripod by its ears

绚 xuàn ㄒㄩㄢˋ 有文彩的,色彩华丽 gorgeous; colourful; resplendent: ～烂 *splendid; gorgeous; brilliant* | ～丽 *bright and beautiful; a riot of colour*

旋(❸❹鏇) ㊁ xuàn ㄒㄩㄢˋ ❶旋转的 revolving; rolling; rotary: ～风 *cyclone; tornado; vortex* ❷临时(做) at the time when sth is needed; at the last moment: ～吃～做 *to cook for immediate*

service; to cook when one needs to eat ❸(～子)温酒的器具 metal hot-water container for warming wine (especially liquor) ❹用车床或刀子转(zhuàn)着圈地削 to cut sth by turning on a lathe; to peel circularly with a knife:用车床～零件 *to lathe a part* [旋床]把金属或木料切削成圆形或球形的机器。也叫"车床"(also called 车床) turning lathe

㊀ xuán 见 849 页 see p849

碹 xuàn ㄒㄩㄢˋ 同"碹"same as 碹

渲 xuàn ㄒㄩㄢˋ 中国画的一种画法,把水墨淋在纸上再擦得浓淡适宜 Chinese painting style to wash (a piece of drawing paper) with watercolours [渲染]用水墨或淡的色彩涂抹画面 to add washes of ink or pale colours to a Chinese painting; to apply colours to a drawing ⑩ ***figurative*** 夸大地形容 to exaggerate; to pile it on; to play up

楦(*楥) xuàn ㄒㄩㄢˋ ❶(～子、～头)做鞋用的模型 shoe last ❷拿东西把物体中空的部分填满使物体鼓起来 to fill up (*or* stuff) with padding:用鞋楦子～鞋 *to fit a last into a shoe*|把这个猫皮～起来 *to stuff the cat skin with padding*

碹 xuàn ㄒㄩㄢˋ ❶桥梁、涵洞等工程建筑的弧形部分。也作"券(xuàn)"(also written as 券) arch of a bridge, culvert or other engineering projects ❷用砖、石等筑成弧形 arch built of brick, stone, etc

XUE ㄒㄩㄝ

削 ㊁ xuē ㄒㄩㄝ 义同"削㊀",用于一些复合词(used in compound words) same as 削㊀:～除 *to cut off*|～减 *to cut down; to reduce*|～弱 *to weaken; to die down*|剥～*to exploit*

㊀ xiāo 见 822 页 see p822

靴(*鞾) xuē ㄒㄩㄝ (～子)有长筒的鞋 boots:马～*riding boots*|皮～*leather boots*|雨～*rain boots*

薛 xuē ㄒㄩㄝ 周代诸侯国名,在今山东省滕州、薛城一带 Xue, a princedom of the Zhou Dynasty, situated in today's Teng-zhou and Xuecheng, Shandong Province

穴 xué ㄒㄩㄝˊ ❶窟窿,洞 cave; cavern; grotto:不入虎～,焉得虎子? *How can you catch tiger cubs without entering the tiger's lair; nothing ventured, nothing gained.* or *A faint heart never conquers.*|～居野处 *to dwell in caves in the wilds; to lead a primitive life* ❷墓穴 coffin pit; grave:坟地里有五个～。*There are five coffin pits in the graveyard.* ❸穴位,人体或某些动物体可以进行针灸的部位,多为神经末梢密集或较粗的神经纤维经过的地方,也叫"穴道"(al-

X

so called 穴道）acupuncture point：太阳～*temple*

茓 xué ㄒㄩㄝˊ（一子）做囤用的狭而长的席，通常是用秫秸篾或芦苇编成的。也作"踅"（also written as 踅）matting；long and narrow matting woven of sorghum stalks or reed，used to make grain silos

岤（嶨）xué ㄒㄩㄝˊ［岤口］地名，在浙江省文成 Xuekou， a place in Wencheng，Zhejiang Province

学（學、**斈）xué ㄒㄩㄝˊ ❶学习 to learn；to study：活到老，～到老 *never too old to learn*；*to learn as long as one lives*［学生］1 在校学习的人 student；pupil 2 向前辈学习的人 disciple；follower 3 对前辈谦称自己 self-depreciating address before one's elder generation［学徒］在工厂或商店里学习技能的人 apprentice ❷模仿 to imitate；to mimic；to copy：他～赵体字，～得很像。*He is imitating the Zhao style of calligraphy and he does it well.* ❸学问，学到的知识 learning；knowledge；scholarship：饱～*erudite*；*learned*｜博～多能 *of great learning and versatility*［学士］1 学位名，在硕士之下 bachelor；bachelor's degree 2 古代官名 *xueshi*，an ancient official position［学术］比较专门而有系统的学问 learning；science ❹分门别类的有系统的知识 subject of study；branch of learning：哲～*philosophy*｜物理～*physics*｜语言～*linguistics* ❺学校 school：中～*middle school*｜大～*university*｜上～*to go to school*

鸴（鷽）xué ㄒㄩㄝˊ 鸟名。小型鸣禽，体形似雀，头部黑色，背青灰色。吃昆虫、果实等 oriental bullfinch（*Pyrrhula*）

踅 xué ㄒㄩㄝˊ ❶折回，旋转 to walk to and fro；to turn back：～来～去 *to hang*（*or wander*）*about*｜这群鸟飞向东去又～回来落在树上了。*The flock of birds flew eastward and then turned back again to settle in the tree.*［踅摸］（—mo）〈方 **dialect**〉寻找 to look for；to seek：到处～～旧书 *to look for old books everywhere* ❷同"茓"same as 茓

噱 ㊁ xué ㄒㄩㄝˊ 〈方 **dialect**〉笑 to laugh：发～*to make one laugh*［噱头］逗笑的话或举动 words to amuse；act meant to excite laughter

㊀ jué 见 377 页 see p377

雪 xuě ㄒㄩㄝˇ ❶冷天天空落下的白色结晶体，是空气中的水蒸气冷至零摄氏度以下凝结而成的 snow：～花 *snowflake*｜冰天～地 *world of ice and snow*；*icy landscape* ❷洗去，除去 to wipe out（a humiliation）；to avenge（a wrong）：～耻 *to avenge an insult*；*to wipe out a humiliation*｜～恨 *to wreak vengeance*；*to avenge*

鳕 xuě ㄒㄩㄝˇ 鳕鱼，鱼名，又叫"大头鱼"。下颌有一条须，肝脏含有大量的维生素A和D，是制鱼肝油的重要原料(also called 大头鱼) cod (*Gadus*)

血 ㊀ xuè ㄒㄩㄝˋ ❶血液，人或高等动物体内的一种红色液体(由红细胞、白细胞、血小板和血浆组成)，周身循环，分配养分给各组织，同时把废物带到排泄器官内 blood：～压 *blood pressure* | ～泊(pō) *pool of blood* | 出～ *to bleed* ❷同一祖先的 related by blood：～统 *blood relationship*；*blood lineage* | ～族 *blood relation* ❸比喻刚强热烈 staunch；unyielding：～性 *courageous and upright* (读xuè时用于复音词及成语。如"贫血"、"呕心沥血"等。) (when used in polysyllabic words or idioms, it is pronounced as xuè, such as in 贫血 and 呕心沥血)

㊁ xiě 见829页 see p829

谑 xuè ㄒㄩㄝˋ 开玩笑 to crack a joke；to banter；to tease：戏～ *to make fun of* | 谐～ *humorous joke*；*wisecrack*；*pleasantries*

XUN ㄒㄩㄣ

勋(*勳) xūn ㄒㄩㄣ ❶特殊功劳 merit；meritorious service；achievement (㊥ ***doublet*** 功一 merit；achievement)：～章 *medal*；*decoration* | 屡建奇～ *to perform one meritorious service after another* ❷勋章 medal；decoration：授～ *to confer titles (or medals)*

埙(*壎) xūn ㄒㄩㄣ 古代用陶土烧制的一种吹奏乐器 *xun*，egg-shaped ancient wind instrument made of pottery，with one to six holes

熏(❶*燻) ㊀ xūn ㄒㄩㄣ ❶气味或烟气接触物品 to expose to smoke or fumes；to fumigate：～豆腐 *smoked tofu* | ～肉 *smoked meat* | 把墙～黑了。*The wall was blackened by smoke.* | 用茉莉花～茶叶 *to flavour (or scent) tea with jasmine* ❷气味刺激人 to stink：臭气～人 *to be horribly stinking* ❸和暖 pleasantly warm；genial；mild：～风 *warm southerly breeze*

㊁ xùn 见856页 see p856

薰 xūn ㄒㄩㄣ ❶薰草，古书上说的一种香草 a kind of fragrant grass in ancient Chinese texts ㊀ ***extension*** 花草的香气 smell of fragrant grass ❷同"熏㊀❶" same as 熏㊀❶

獯 xūn ㄒㄩㄣ [獯鬻](-yù) 我国古代北方民族，战国后称匈奴(also called 匈奴 after the Warring States Period) Xunyu，ancient nomadic people living in north China

曛 xūn ㄒㄩㄣ 日没(mò)时的余光 last glow of the setting sun：～黄(黄昏) *nightfall*；*dusk*

X

醺 xūn ㄒㄩㄣ 醉 drunk [醺醺] 醉的样子 to get drunk:喝得醉～～的 *heavily drunk; dead drunk; as drunk as a fiddler*

窨 ⊖ xūn ㄒㄩㄣ 同"熏",用于窨茶叶。把茉莉花等放在茶叶中,使茶叶染上花的香味(same as 熏, used only in the phrase 窨茶叶, with the meaning of putting jasmine flowers into tea leaves for fragrance)

⊜ yìn 见 899 页 see p899

旬 xún ㄒㄩㄣˊ ❶十天叫一旬,一个月有三旬,分称上旬、中旬、下旬 period of ten days (for instance, a month made up of three 旬 — the first ten days, the middle ten days, and the last ten days) ❷指十岁 ten years in a person's age:三～上下年纪 *about thirty years old* | 年过六～*over sixty years old*

郇 ⊖ xún ㄒㄩㄣˊ ❶周代诸侯国名,在今山西省临猗西南 Xun, a princedom of the Zhou Dynasty, situated to the southwest of today's Linyi, Shanxi Province ❷姓 Xun, a surname

⊜ huán 见 290 页 see p290

询 xún ㄒㄩㄣˊ 问,征求意见 to ask; to enquire (㊣ ***doublet*** —问 to ask; to enquire):探～*to look over; to examine; to scout* | 查～*to enquire about*

荀 xún ㄒㄩㄣˊ 姓 Xun, a surname

峋 xún ㄒㄩㄣˊ 见 450 页"嶙"字条"嶙峋"(lín—) see 嶙峋 on p450

洵 xún ㄒㄩㄣˊ 诚然,实在 truly; indeed; to be sure:～属可敬 *truly respectable*

恂 xún ㄒㄩㄣˊ ❶诚信,信实 faithful; respectful and submissive ❷恐惧 dread; afraid

珣 xún ㄒㄩㄣˊ 一种玉 *xun*, a kind of jade

栒 xún ㄒㄩㄣˊ [栒邑] 地名,在陕西省。今作"旬邑" (now written as 旬邑) Xunyi, a place in Shaanxi Province

寻(尋) xún ㄒㄩㄣˊ ❶找,搜求 to look for; to search; to seek (㊣ ***doublet*** —找 to seek; to pursue; to look for | —觅 to look for; to search; to seek):～人 *to look for sb* | ～求真理 *to seek truth* [寻思](— si) 想,考虑 to think; to consider; to ponder [寻死] 自杀或企图自杀 to commit suicide; to try to commit suicide; to attempt suicide ❷古代的长度单位,八尺为寻 *xun*, measure of length, equal to 8 *chi* [寻常] ㊟ ***transfer*** 平常,素常 common; ordinary:这不是～～的事情。*This is not ordinary.*

荨(蕁) ⊜ xún ㄒㄩㄣˊ [荨麻疹] 一种过敏性皮疹,俗叫"风疹疙瘩"(popularly called 风疹疙瘩) nettle-rash; urticaria

⊖ qián 见 594 页 see p594

哻(噚) xún ㄒㄩㄣˊ 也读作 yīngxún。英美制计量水深的单位,1 哻是 6 英尺,合 1.828 米。现写作"英寻"(also pronounced yīngxún and now written as 英寻) fathom

浔(潯) xún ㄒㄩㄣˊ ❶水边 waterside: 江～ *riverside* ❷江西省九江市的别称 Xun, another name for Jiujiang, a city in Jiangxi Province

鲟(鱘、**鱏) xún ㄒㄩㄣˊ 鲟鱼,鱼名。身体呈纺锤形,背部和腹部有大片硬鳞,其余各部无鳞,为珍稀动物 sturgeon (*Acipenseridae*)

纠(紃) xún ㄒㄩㄣˊ 圆绦子 silk ribbon; silk braid

巡(*廵) xún ㄒㄩㄣˊ ❶往来查看 to patrol; to make one's rounds: ～夜 *to go on night patrol* | ～哨 (*of a small security detachment*) *to go on patrol* [巡回]按一定路线到各处 to go the rounds; to tour; to make a circuit of: ～～医疗队 *mobile medical team* | ～～演出 *performing tour* ❷量词 ***quantifier***,遍(用于给全座斟酒) round of drinks (served to all present):酒过三～。*The wine* (*or liquor*) *has gone round three times.*

循 xún ㄒㄩㄣˊ 遵守,依照 to follow; to abide by: ～规蹈矩 *to observe rules and follow orders docilely; to follow accepted customs and practices; to conform to convention* | ～序渐进 *to follow in order and advance step by step; to proceed in an orderly and gradual way* | 有所遵～ *to have sth to go by* [循环]周而复始地运动 to circulate; to cycle: 血液～～ *blood circulation* | ～～演出 *circulating show*

训 xùn ㄒㄩㄣˋ ❶教导,教诲 to lecture; to teach; to train: 接受教～ *to learn a lesson* | ～练 *to train; to drill* ❷可以作为法则的话 instruction; admonition: 遗～ *teachings of the deceased* | 不足为～ *not fit to serve as a model* ❸解释词的意义 explanation of a word; interpretation of a text: ～诂 *explanations of words in ancient books; gloss; textual exegesis*

驯 xùn ㄒㄩㄣˋ 驯服,顺从,服从人的指使 tame and docile: ～顺 *tame and docile; submissive* | ～良 *tractable; docile; tame and gentle* | ～马 *to tame a horse* | ～养野兽 *to raise and train wild animals*

讯 xùn ㄒㄩㄣˋ ❶问。特指法庭中的审问 to interrogate; to question: 审～ *to interrogate* ❷消息,音信 information; message; dispatch: 通～ *communication* | 新华社～ *dispatch from Xinhua News Agency*

汛 xùn ㄒㄩㄣˋ 江河定期的涨水 seasonal flood: 防～ *flood control* | 秋～ *autumn flood* | 桃

花～*spring flood*

迅 xùn ㄒㄩㄣˋ 快 fast; swift (㊀ ***doublet*** 一 速 fast; swift): ～跑 *to run fast* | ～猛 *swift and violent* | ～雷不及掩耳 *sudden; as sudden as lightening; sudden peal of thunder leaves no time for covering ears*

徇(*狥) xùn ㄒㄩㄣˋ ❶依从,曲从 to give in to; to submit to; to comply with: ～私舞弊 *to play favouritism and commit irregularities* ❷同"殉❶"same as 殉❶

殉 xùn ㄒㄩㄣˋ ❶为达到某种目的而牺牲性命 to sacrifice one's life for: ～国(为国捐躯) *to die for one's motherland; to give one's life for one's country* | ～难(nàn) *to die for (a just cause); to die a martyr; to martyrize* ❷古代逼迫活人陪着死人埋葬,也指用偶人或器物随葬 to force people to be buried alive with the dead in ancient China, and also referring to the carved figures or things that were buried with the dead: ～葬 *to be buried alive with the dead*

逊(遜) xùn ㄒㄩㄣˋ ❶退避,退让 to abdicate; to yield: ～位(让出帝王的位子) *to abdicate (one's throne)* ❷谦让,恭顺 unassuming; modest: 出言不～ *to utter imprudent remarks* ❸不及,差 inferior to: 稍～一筹 *to be a shade or cut inferior; to be slightly inferior*

浚(*濬) ㊁ xùn ㄒㄩㄣˋ 浚县,在河南省 Xunxian County in Henan Province

㊀ jùn 见 378 页 see p378

巽 xùn ㄒㄩㄣˋ 八卦之一,符号是☴。代表风 *xun*, one part of the Eight Trigrams, with the sign ☴ representing the wind

噀(**潠) xùn ㄒㄩㄣˋ 喷水 to spout water

熏 ㊁ xùn ㄒㄩㄣˋ 〈方 ***dialect***〉(煤气)使人窒息中毒 to be poisoned or suffocated by coal gas: 炉子安上烟筒,就不至于～着了。*Install a chimney over the stove, and you won't be suffocated by coal gas.*

㊀ xūn 见 853 页 see p853

蕈 xùn ㄒㄩㄣˋ 生长在树林里或草地上的某些菌类,形状略像伞,种类很多,无毒的可以吃 gill fungus (*Agaricaceae*): 松～ *pine mushroom* | 香～ xiangxun; *champignon*

Y Ⅰ

YA ⅠY

丫(❶*椏、❶*枒) yā ⅠY ❶上端分杈的东西 crotch; bifurcation; fork: ~杈 *crotch; fork; branch* | 树~巴 *crotch; fork* ❷[丫头](—tou) ㊕ ***transfer*** **1** 女孩子 girl **2** 旧时称供人役使的女孩子(in former times) maid-servant

压(壓) ㊀ yā ⅠY ❶从上面加重力 to press; to weigh down: ~住 *to keep under control* | ~碎 *to crush (into pieces)* ㊀ ***extension*** 搁置不动 to shelve; to pigeonhole: 积~资金 *to let funds lie idle* ❷用威力制服,镇服 to suppress; to subdue: 镇~ *to repress; to quell* | ~制 *to stifle; to oppress* ㊀ ***extension*** 胜过,超过 to surpass; to outdo: ~倒一切 *overriding; overwhelming* | 技~群芳 *to have incomparable skill; to be unmatched in skill* ❸抑制,控制 to restrain; to control: ~咳嗽 *to repress a cough; to ease the cough* | ~住气 *to hold one's breath; to control oneself; to repress one's anger* | ~不住火 *cannot control one's anger; to lose control of one's temper; to fail to hold back one's anger* ❹逼近 to approach: ~境 *to bear down on the border; to press on to the border* | 太阳~树梢。*The sun is touching the treetops.* ❺赌博时在某一门上下注 to stake

㊁ yà 见 860 页 see p860

呀 ㊀ yā ⅠY ❶叹词 ***interjection***,表示惊疑(used to express surprise and bewilderment) ah; oh: ~,这怎么办! *Oh! What shall we do?* ❷拟声词 ***onomatopoeia***: 门~的一声开了。*The door creaked open.*

㊁ ya 见 861 页 see p861

鸦(*鴉) yā ⅠY 乌鸦,鸟名,种类很多,身体黑色,嘴大,翼长 crow: ~雀无声(喻寂静)。*Silence reigns and not a crow or sparrow can be heard — in perfect silence; in complete silence.*

[鸦片](—piàn) 俗叫"大烟"。由罂粟的果实提制出来的一种毒品,内含吗啡等,能镇痛安眠,医药上可作麻醉药。久用成瘾,为害很大(popularly called 大烟) opium

押 yā ⅠY ❶在文书契约上所签的名字或所画的符号 signature; mark made on a document or contract: 画~ *to sign; to make one's cross; to make one's mark* | 签~ *to sign*

an official document; to put one's seal on an official document ❷把财物交给人作担保 to mortgage：～金 *cash deposit; cash pledge* ❸拘留 to detain：看～ *to keep sb in custody; to hold sb in detention* | ～起来 *to take sb into custody* ❹跟随看管 to escort：～车 *to escort a vehicle in transportation* | ～运货物 *to transport goods under escort*

鸭 yā ㄧㄚ (一子)水鸟名。通常指家鸭，嘴扁腿短，趾间有蹼，善游泳，不能高飞 duck (*Anatidae*)

垭(埡) yā ㄧㄚ yà ㄧㄚˋ (又 *also* yà)〈方 ***dialect***〉两山之间的狭窄地方。多用于地名(ya, usually used in a place name) mountain pass：黄桷(jué)～(在重庆市) *Huangjueya, a place in Chongqing*

哑(啞) ㊀ yā ㄧㄚ 同"呀"(yā) same as 呀 [哑哑]拟声词 ***onomatopoeia***，乌鸦叫声或小儿学语声 cawing; babbling

㊁ yǎ 见 859 页 see p859

牙 yá ㄧㄚˊ ❶牙齿，人和动物嘴里咀嚼食物的器官 tooth ❷(一子)像牙齿形状的东西 tooth-shaped thing：抽屉～子 *serrated edge of a drawer* ❸旧社会介绍买卖从中取利的人 broker; middleman (㊈ ***doublet*** 一侩 broker; middleman)：～行(háng) *middleman; brokerage*

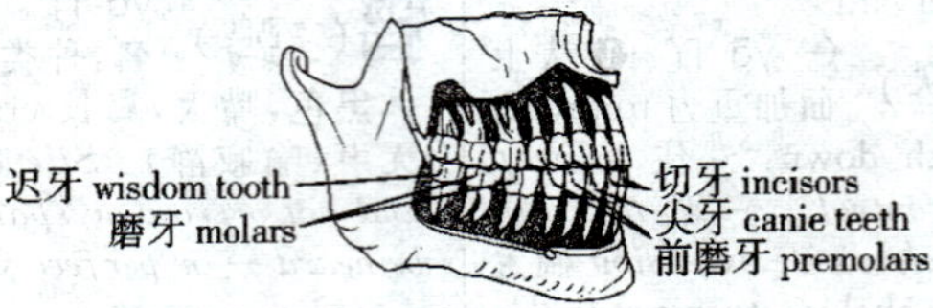

人的牙 human teeth

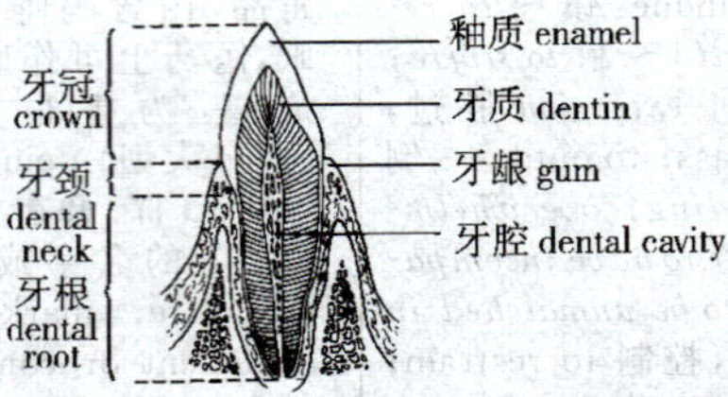

牙的纵切面结构 construction of the vertical section of the tooth

伢 yá ㄧㄚˊ 〈方 ***dialect***〉(—子、—儿)小孩子 child; kid

芽 yá ㄧㄚˊ ❶(—儿)植物的幼体,可以发育成茎、叶或花的那一部分 bud; sprout; shoot: 豆~儿 *bean sprouts* 麦子发~儿了。*The wheat is sprouting.* | ~茶 *tender tea leaves* [萌芽] [喻] ***figurative*** 事情的开端 rudiment; germ ❷像芽的东西 sprout-shaped thing: 肉~ *granulation tissue* | 银~(银矿苗) *the outcrop of a silver mine*

岈 yá ㄧㄚˊ 见 70 页"嵖"字条"嵖岈山"(chá — —) see 嵖岈山 on p70

玡(**琊) yá ㄧㄚˊ [琅玡](láng—) **1** 山名,在安徽省滁州 Langya Mountain in Chuzhou, Anhui Province **2** 山名,在山东省胶南 Langya Mountain in Jiaonan, Shandong Province

钘 yá ㄧㄚˊ 化学元素,镓的旧称 former term for 镓

蚜 yá ㄧㄚˊ 蚜虫,俗叫"腻虫"。能分泌一种甜液,所以又叫"蜜虫"。绿色,也有棕色带紫红色的。生在豆类、棉花、菜类、稻、麦等的幼苗上,吸食嫩芽的汁液,害处很大(also called 蜜虫; popularly called 腻虫) aphid; aphis (*Aphidoidea*)

崖(**崕、**厓) yá ㄧㄚˊ (旧读 formerly yái)高地或山石陡立的侧面 precipice; cliff; crag: 山~*cliff; crag* | 悬~勒马(喻到了危险的地步赶紧回头) *to rein in at the brink of the precipice — to refrain in face of imminent danger*

涯 yá ㄧㄚˊ 水边 waterside; shore; bank [引] ***extension*** 边际,极限 margin; limit: 天~海角 *ends of the earth; remotest corners of the earth* | 一望无~*as far as one can see; interminable*

睚 yá ㄧㄚˊ 眼角 canthus; corner of the eye [睚眦](—zì)发怒瞪眼 angry stare [引] ***extension*** 小的怨恨 petty grievance; grudge: ~~必报 *to seek revenge for petty grievance — to be utterly narrow-minded and revengeful*

衙 yá ㄧㄚˊ 衙门,旧时指官署 *yamen*; government office in former times: 官~ *government office*

哑(啞) ㊀ yǎ ㄧㄚˇ ❶由于生理缺陷或疾病而不能说话 dumb; mute: 聋~ *deaf-and-dumb* | ~口无言(喻无话可说) *to be rendered speechless* [哑巴](—ba) **1** 同"哑❶" same as 哑❶ **2** 指不能说话的人 dumb person; mute ❷嗓子干涩发音困难或不清楚 hoarse; husky: 嗓子喊~了 *to shout oneself hoarse* ❸无声的 soundless; silent: ~剧 *mime; dumb show* | ~铃(一种运动器械) *dumb-bell* ❹(旧读 formerly è)笑声 sound of laughing; laugh; laughter: ~然失笑(不由自主地笑出声来) *to be*

Y

unable to stifle a laugh; *cannot help laughing*

㊁ yā 见 858 页 see p858

痖(瘂) yǎ ㄧㄚˇ 同"哑"(yǎ) same as 哑

雅 yǎ ㄧㄚˇ ❶正规的，标准的 standard; formal: ～声(指诗歌) *standard poetic style* | ～言 *earnest advice* ❷高尚不俗，美好大方 elegant; refined; graceful: ～致 *tasteful* | ～观 *refined*; *graceful* ❸敬辞 ***polite***: ～鉴 *for your perusal* | ～教(jiào) *your esteemed opinion*; *your excellent advice* ❹平素，素来 usually; often: ～善鼓琴 *usually good at playing the zither* ❺极，甚 extremely; very: ～以为美 *to consider something very beautiful* | ～不欲为 *to have no intention to do it actually* ❻交往 acquaintance: 无一日之～ *not to have the pleasure of knowing sb* ❼周代朝廷上的乐歌，《诗经》中诗篇的一类，分为大雅和小雅 (court hymns of the Zhou Dynasty, one of the three genres of verse in *The Book of Songs*, divided into major odes and minor odes) odes

轧 ㊀ yà ㄧㄚˋ ❶圆轴或轮子等压在东西上面转 to roll; to run over: 把马路～平了 *to roll the road flat* | ～棉花 *to gin cotton* | ～花机 *cotton gin* ❷排挤 to oust; to push out; to give sb the elbow: 倾～ *to engage in internal strife* ❸姓 Ya, a surname

㊁ zhá 见 948 页 see p948

㊂ gá 见 212 页 see p212

亚(亞) yà ㄧㄚˋ ❶次，次一等的 second; inferior: ～军 *second place*; *runner-up* | ～热带 *subtropics*; *semitropics* ❷指亚洲，世界七大洲之一 Asia

垭(埡) yà ㄧㄚˋ (又 ***also*** yā) 见 858 页 yā see yā on p858

挜(掗) yà ㄧㄚˋ 〈方 ***dialect***〉硬把东西送给或卖给别人 to force sb to take or buy sth

娅(婭) yà ㄧㄚˋ 连襟 husband of one's sister

氩(氬) yà ㄧㄚˋ 一种化学元素，在通常条件下为气体，符号 Ar，无色无臭，不易跟其他元素化合。可用来放入电灯泡或真空管中 argon (Ar)

压(壓) ㊁ yà ㄧㄚˋ [压根儿] 副词 ***adverb***，根本，从来(多用于否定句) (usually used in negative sentences) at all; altogether: 我～～～没去过那个地方。*I've never been there.*

㊀ yā 见 857 页 see p857

讶 yà ㄧㄚˋ 惊奇，奇怪 surprised: 十分惊～ *astonished*

迓 yà ㄧㄚˋ 迎接 to welcome; to greet (㊜ ***doublet*** 迎一 to welcome; to greet): ～之于门 *to meet sb at the door* | 未曾迎～ *sorry for not meeting you at the gate*

砑 yà ㄧㄚˋ 碾压 to roll; to press［砑光］用卵形或弧形的石块碾压或摩擦皮革、布帛等使紧实而光亮 to calender

揠 yà ㄧㄚˋ 拔 to pull up; to tug upward:～苗助长(zhǎng)(喻欲求速成反而做坏) *to help seedlings grow by pulling them upward — to spoil things by excessive enthusiasm; Haste makes waste.* or *More haste, less speed.*

猰(**貏) yà ㄧㄚˋ［猰貐］(—yǔ) 古代传说中的一种凶兽(in ancient legend) fierce beast

呀 ㊁ ya ·ㄧㄚ 助词 ***auxiliary***,"啊"受前一字韵母 a、e、i、o、ü 收音的影响而发生的变音(variant of 啊 used after a Chinese character ending phonetically with a,e,i,o or ü):大家快来～! *All of you, come here at once!* | 你怎么不学一学～? *Why don't you try to learn it?* | 这个瓜～,甜得很! *This melon is, indeed, very sweet.*

㊀ yā 见 857 页 see p857

YAN ㄧㄢ

咽 ㊀ yān ㄧㄢ 咽头,食物和气体的共同通道,位于鼻腔、口腔和喉腔的后方,通常混称咽喉(generally called 咽喉) pharynx

㊁ yàn 见 867 页 see p867

㊂ yè 见 880 页 see p880

胭(*臙) yān ㄧㄢ［胭脂］(—zhi) 一种红色颜料,化妆用品 rouge

烟(*煙、❺❻*菸) yān ㄧㄢ ❶(—儿)物质燃烧时所产生的混有残余颗粒的气体 smoke:冒～ *to belch; (of smoke) to rise* | ～筒 *chimney*［烟火］**1** 道教指熟食 cooked food in Taoism:不食人间～～(现喻脱离现实) *not to eat cooked food — to escape from real life* **2** 在火药中掺上锶、钡等金属盐类制成的一种燃放的东西,燃烧时发出灿烂的火花或呈现种种景物,供人观赏 fireworks［烟幕弹］能放出大量烟雾的炸弹,供军事上做掩护用 smoke-bomb; smoke-grenade ㊍ ***figurative*** 用来掩盖真相或本意的言论或行为 smoke-screen ❷(—子)烟气中间杂有碳素的微细颗粒,这些颗粒附着在其他物体上凝结成的黑灰 soot:松～ *pine soot* | 锅～子 *pan soot* ❸像烟的东西 smoke-like thing:过眼云～ *as transient as fleeting clouds* | ～霞 *mists and clouds* ❹烟气刺激(眼睛)(of eyes) to be irritated by smoke:一屋子烟,～眼睛。*A roomful of smoke irritates one's eyes.* ❺烟草,一年生草本植物,叶大有茸毛,可以制香烟和农业上的杀虫剂等 tobacco (*Nicotiana*) ❻烟草制成品 tobacco (product):香～ *cigarette* | 旱～ *tobacco (smoked in a long-stemmed Chinese pipe)* | 请勿吸～ *No smoking!*

Y

❼指鸦片 opium：～土 *raw opium; crude opium*

恹(懨、**懕) yān ㄧㄢ [恹恹]有病而衰弱无力、精神不振的样子 weak and weary through illness; run-down

殷 ㊁ yān ㄧㄢ 黑红色 dark-red; blackish red：～红 *blackish red; dark red* | 朱～ *dark-red*

㊀ yīn 见 895 页 see p895

焉 yān ㄧㄢ 〈古 ***archaism***〉❶跟介词"于"加代词"是"相当(equal to preposition 于 plus pronoun 是)：心不在～ *absent-minded* | 罪莫大～。*There is no greater crime than this.* ❷乃,才 then; not … unless：必知疾之所自起,～能攻之。*Only by knowing the cause of the trouble can we deal with it.* ❸表示疑问,怎么,哪儿(used to express interrogation) how; where：～能如此？*How can it be like this?* | 其子～往？*Where has his son gone?* ❹助词 ***auxiliary***：因以为号～。*It serves as a signal.* | 有厚望～。*There are great expectations.*

鄢 yān ㄧㄢ [鄢陵]地名,在河南省 Yanling, a place in Henan Province

嫣 yān ㄧㄢ 美好,鲜艳 beautiful; bright：～然一笑 *to give a bewitching (or winsome) smile* | 姹紫～红 *beautiful flowers with a blaze of colours*

阏 yān ㄧㄢ [阏氏](－zhī)汉代匈奴称君主的正妻(in Han Dynasty) term of address for the wife of a Hun (Xiongnu) chief

崦 yān ㄧㄢ [崦嵫](－zī) **1** 山名,在甘肃省 Yanzi Mountain in Gansu Province **2** 古代指太阳落山的地方(in ancient China) where the sun sets：日薄～～。*The sun is setting below the horizon.*

阉 yān ㄧㄢ ❶阉割,割去生殖腺 to castrate; to spay; to neuter：～鸡 *capon* | ～猪 *hog; barrow* ❷封建时代的宦官,太监(in feudal times) eunuch

淹(❶**湮、❶△**渰) yān ㄧㄢ ❶浸没(mò) to flood; to submerge; to inundate：被水～了 *to be inundated* ❷皮肤被汗液浸渍(of skin) tingling from sweat ❸广 broad; wide：～博 *extensive*

"渰"又 yǎn 见 866 页 see p866

腌(*醃) ㊀ yān ㄧㄢ 用盐等浸渍食品 to pickle; to salt：～肉 *to salt (down) meat; salted meat* | ～咸菜 *to pickle vegetables*

㊁ ā 见 1 页 see p1

湮 ㊀ yān ㄧㄢ 埋没 to fall into oblivion; to sink into obscurity (㊀连 ***doublet*** －没 to submerge; to inundate)：有的古迹已经～没了。*Some of the historic sites are buried in oblivion.*

㊁ yīn 见 896 页 see p896

燕 ㊁ yān ㄧㄢ ❶周代诸侯国名，在今河北省北部和辽宁省南部 Yan, a princedom of the Zhou Dynasty, situated in today's northern Hebei Province and southern Liaoning Province ❷姓 Yan, a surname

㊀ yàn 见 869 页 see p869

延 yán ㄧㄢˊ ❶引长 to prolong; to extend: ～长 *to prolong; to extend; to lengthen* | ～年 *to prolong life; to enjoy longevity* | 蔓(màn)～ *to spread; to trail* ❷展缓，推迟 to postpone; to delay: ～期 *to defer; to put off* | 遇雨顺～ *to postpone in case of rain* | 迟～ *to delay; to retard* ❸引进，请 to engage; to invite: ～师 *to engage a teacher* | ～聘 *to engage; to employ; to hire* | ～医 *to send for a doctor*

埏 ㊁ yán ㄧㄢˊ ❶大地的边沿 edge of the earth ❷墓道 tomb passage; path leading to a grave

㊀ shān 见 652 页 see p652

蜒 yán ㄧㄢˊ 见 910 页"蚰"字条"蚰蜒"(yóuyan)、773 页"蜿"字条"蜿蜒"(wān—) see 蚰蜒 on p910, 蜿蜒 on p773

筵 yán ㄧㄢˊ ❶竹席 bamboo mat ❷酒席 banquet; feast: 喜～ *wedding banquet; wedding feast*

闫 yán ㄧㄢˊ 姓 Yan, a surname

芫 ㊁ yán ㄧㄢˊ [芫荽](—sui) 俗叫"香菜"，又叫"胡荽"(—suī)。一年生或二年生草本植物，花白色。果实球形，有香气，可以制药和香料。茎、叶可以吃(popularly called 香菜 and also called 胡荽) coriander; cilantro (*Coriandrum sativum*)

㊀ yuán 见 924 页 see p924

严(嚴) yán ㄧㄢˊ ❶紧密，没有空隙 tight: 把罐子盖～了 *to cover the pot tight* | 房上的草都长(zhǎng)～了。*The grass on the roof grows densely.* ❷认真，不放松 strict; rigorous: 规矩～ *rigorous rules; strict discipline* | ～厉 *stern; severe* | ～格 *strict; rigid* | ～办 *to deal with severely; to punish with severity* ㊕ ***transfer*** 指父亲 father: 家～ *my father* [严肃]郑重，庄重 serious; solemn: 态度很～～ *serious manners* ❸厉害的，高度的 severe; serious: ～冬 *severe winter* | ～寒 *frigid* [严重]紧急，重大 serious; grave; critical: 事态～～。*The situation is grave.* | ～～的错误 *serious mistake*

言 yán ㄧㄢˊ ❶话 speech; word (㊦ ***doublet*** 语— language): 发～ *to make a speech; to deliver a speech; to give a speech* | 格～ *motto; maxim; adage* | 名～ *well-known saying; famous remark* | 谣～ *rumour; hearsay* | 有～在先 *to make it clearly understood be-*

Y

forehand; to make a verbal contract beforehand|一～为定。*That's settled then.* or *Once something is said, it must be kept.*|一～以蔽之 *to sum up in a word; in short; in brief* ❷说 to speak; to say (㊀ ***doublet*** 一语 to speak):知无不～*to say all one knows* ❸汉语的字 Chinese character:五～诗 *pentasyllabic poem; Chinese poem with five-character lines*|七～绝句 *heptasyllabic quatrain; Chinese poem with seven-character lines*|洋洋万～*to run to ten thousand words; to be very copious*

阽 yán ㄧㄢˊ (又 ***also*** diàn) 见 147 页 diàn see diàn on p147

妍 yán ㄧㄢˊ 美丽 beautiful:百花争～。*The flowers are blooming in full beauty.* or *All the flowers are in full bloom.*

研 yán ㄧㄢˊ ❶细磨 to grind; to pestle:～药 *to grind medicine*|～墨 *to rub an inkstick on an inkslab (to prepare ink for painting or writing with a brush)* ❷研究,深入地探求 to study; to research:钻～*to study intensively; to do exhaustive research*|～求 *to study carefully*

〈古 ***archaism***〉又同"砚"(yàn) also same as 砚

岩(*巖、❶*嵒) yán ㄧㄢˊ ❶高峻的山崖 cliff; crag ❷岩石,构成地壳的石头 rack; stone:沉积～*sedimentary rock*|火成～*igneous rock*

炎 yán ㄧㄢˊ ❶热 scorching; burning hot (㊀ ***doublet*** 一热 scorching; blazing):～夏 *blazing summer; broiling summer*|～暑 *hot summer; scorching summer*|～凉 *snobbery* ❷炎症,身体的某部位发生红、肿、热、痛、痒的现象 inflammation:发～*inflamed*|脑～*encephalitis; brain fever*|皮～*dermatitis* ❸指炎帝,传说中的我国上古帝王 Emperor Yan, legendary ruler of remote antiquity in Chinese history:～黄子孙 *descendants of Emperor Yan and Huang — Chinese people*

沿 yán ㄧㄢˊ ❶顺着(道路、江河的边)along (the road or the river bank):～路 *along the road*|～江 *along the river*|铁路～线 *along the railway* ❷按照以往的规矩、式样等 to follow a convention or a pattern:～袭 *to follow*|积习相～*to be handed down from deep-rooted habits* [沿革]事物发展和变化的历程 evolution ❸(一儿)边 brim; rim; edge (㊀ ***doublet*** 边一edge):炕～儿 *edge of a* kang|缸～儿 *edge of a vat*|盆～儿 *brim of a basin*|河～儿 *bank of a river*|井～儿 *edge of a well* ❹在衣服等物的边上再加一条边 to trim; to hem; to border:～鞋口 *to trim the top of a shoe*|～个边 *to put a hem*

铅 ㊁ yán ㄧㄢˊ［铅山］地名，在江西省 Yanshan, a place in Jiangxi Province

㊀ qiān 见 593 页 see p593

盐（鹽）yán ㄧㄢˊ ❶食盐，又叫“咸盐”。化学成分是氯化钠，有海盐、池盐、井盐、岩盐等(also called 咸盐) salt ❷盐类，化学上指酸类中的氢根被金属元素置换而成的化合物 salt

阎 yán ㄧㄢˊ ❶里巷的门 gate of a lane ❷姓 Yan, a surname

颜 yán ㄧㄢˊ ❶颜面，脸面 face; countenance：无～见人 *to have no face to appear in public; to feel too ashamed to see anyone*｜喜笑～开 *to beam with pleasure; to be radiant with joy* ❷颜色，色彩 colour：～料 *pigment; paints*｜五～六色 *multicoloured; colourful*

檐（*簷）yán ㄧㄢˊ ❶(一儿)房顶伸出的边沿 eaves：房～儿 *eaves*｜前～ *front eaves* ❷(一儿)覆盖物的边沿或伸出部分 brim; edge：帽～儿 *brim of a hat*

奄 yǎn ㄧㄢˇ ❶覆盖 to cover ❷忽然，突然 suddenly：～忽 *suddenly; all of a sudden*

［奄奄］气息微弱 feeble breath：～～一息(快断气) *to be about to breathe one's last; to be dying*

〈古 ***archaism***〉又同“阉”(yān) also same as 阉

掩（**揜）yǎn ㄧㄢˇ ❶遮蔽，遮盖 to cover; to hide ([连] ***doublet*** 一盖 to cover; to conceal｜遮一 to hide; to obscure)：～鼻 *to hold one's nose*｜不～饰自己的错误 *not to cover up one's mistakes*

［掩护］**1** 用炮火等压住敌方火力，或利用自然条件的掩蔽，以便进行军事上的活动 to cover **2** 采取某种方式暗中保护 to screen; to shield ❷关，合 to shut; to close：把门～上 *to shut the door*｜～卷 *to close a book* ❸门窗箱柜等关闭时夹住东西 to nip; to pinch：关门～住手了。*The door pinched my finger as it shut.* ❹乘其不备(进行袭击) to attack by surprise：～杀 *to make a surprise attack*｜～取 *to capture by surprise*

罨 yǎn ㄧㄢˇ ❶覆盖，掩盖 to cover：冷～法 *cold compress*｜热～法(医疗的方法) *hot compress* ❷捕鱼或捕鸟的网 fishing net; bird-net

兖 yǎn ㄧㄢˇ［兖州］地名，在山东省 Yanzhou, a place in Shandong Province

龑（龔）yǎn ㄧㄢˇ 人名，五代时南汉刘龑为自己名字造的字(yan, used in a given name) Chinese character coined by Liu Yan of the Southern Han of the Five Dynasties as his own given name

俨（儼）yǎn ㄧㄢˇ 恭敬，庄严 dignified; solemn [转] ***transfer*** 很像真的，活像 just like; just as：～如白昼 *as*

bright as day [俨然] **1** 庄严 dignified; solemn: 望之～～ *to look dignified* **2** 整齐 neatly arranged: 屋舍～～。*The houses stand in neat order.* **3** 很像真的 very much alike: 这孩子说起话来～～是个大人。*The child speaks just like a grown-up.*

衍 yǎn 丨ㄢˇ ❶延长,展开 to extend; to spread: 推～*to elaborate; to develop; to popularize* ❷多余的(指文字) redundant; superfluous: ～文(书籍中因缮写、刻版、排版错误而多出来的字句) *redundancy due to copying; printing* (*or type-setting*) *mistakes*

弇 yǎn 丨ㄢˇ 覆盖,遮蔽 to cover

渰 ㊀ yǎn 丨ㄢˇ 云兴起的样子 (of clouds) piling up; rising up

㊁ yān 见 862 页"淹"see 淹 on p862

剡 ㊀ yǎn 丨ㄢˇ〈古 ***archaism***〉❶尖,锐利 sharp; pointed ❷削,刮 to scrape; to peel

㊁ shàn 见 654 页 see p654

琰 yǎn 丨ㄢˇ 美玉 fine jade

扊 yǎn 丨ㄢˇ [扊扅](－yí) 门闩 door bolt; door bar

厣(**厴**) yǎn 丨ㄢˇ 螺类介壳口圆片状的盖。蟹腹下面的薄壳有时也称"厣" operculum; lid covering the belly of a crab

魇(**魘**) yǎn 丨ㄢˇ 做可怕的梦,梦中觉得有什么东西压住不能动弹(tan) to have a nightmare

黡(**黶**) yǎn 丨ㄢˇ 黑色的痣 black mole

郾 yǎn 丨ㄢˇ [郾城]地名,在河南省 Yancheng, a place in Henan Province

偃 yǎn 丨ㄢˇ ❶仰面倒下,放倒 to fall on one's back: ～卧 *to lie on one's back* | ～旗息鼓 *to lower the flags and silence the drums — to call off the army maneuvers; to cease* (*or stop*) *all military activities* ❷停止 to stop; to cease: ～武修文 *to desist from military activities and engage in civil affairs; to beat swords into ploughshares*

蝘 yǎn 丨ㄢˇ 古书上指蝉一类的昆虫 (in ancient Chinese texts) cicada and similar insects

[蝘蜓](－tíng) 古书上指壁虎 (in ancient Chinese texts) gecko (*Gekkonidae*)

眼 yǎn 丨ㄢˇ ❶眼睛,视觉器官 eye [眼光]见识,对事物的看法 insight; vision: 把～～放远点 *to see things in a broader perspective* ❷(－儿)孔洞,窟窿 hole; aperture: 炮～ *porthole; embrasure* | 耳朵～儿 *external opening of the ear* | 针～儿 *eye of a needle* ❸(－儿)关节,要点 salient point; key point: 节骨～儿 *critical juncture; critical moment* | 字～ *wording; diction* ❹戏曲中的节拍 unaccented beat in traditional Chinese operas: 一板三～ *one accented beat*

and three unaccented beats

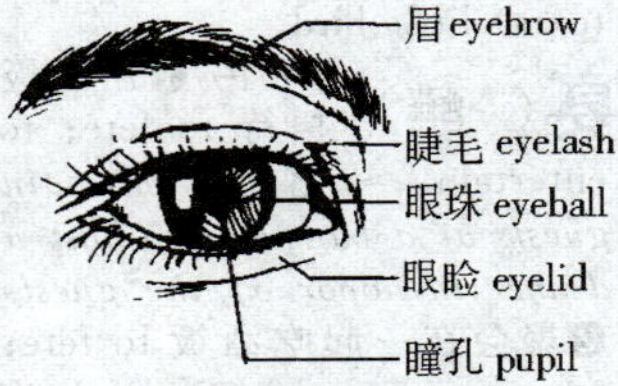

人的眼睛 human eye

演 yǎn ㄧㄢˇ ❶把技艺当众表现出来 to act; to perform; to play:～剧 *to act in a play; to put on a play*|～奏 *to play a musical instrument; to perform (a piece of music) on a musical instrument*|～唱 *to sing in a performance* ❷根据一件事理推广、发挥 to elaborate:～说 *to deliver a speech*|～义 *fictionalized history; historical novel* [演绎]由普遍到特殊的推演过程 deduction ❸演习,依照一定程式练习 to manoeuvre; to drill; to exercise:～武 *to practise* wushu; *to practise traditional martial arts*|～算习题 *to do sums* ❹不断变化 to develop; to evolve:～变 *to evolve*|～进 *evolution; gradual progress*|～化 *to evolve; to develop*

缜 yǎn ㄧㄢˇ 延长 to prolong; to extend

巘(巘) yǎn ㄧㄢˇ〈古 ***archaism***〉山峰,山顶 peak; summit:绝～(极高的山顶) *summit*

甗 yǎn ㄧㄢˇ 古代蒸煮用的炊具,陶制或青铜制(in ancient China) earthen or bronze utensils for steaming or boiling food

鼹(*鼴) yǎn ㄧㄢˇ 鼹鼠,俗叫"地排(pǎi)子"。一种哺乳动物,毛黑褐色,眼小,趾有钩爪,善掘土,生活在土中(popularly called 地排子) mole (*Talpidae*)

厌(厭) yàn ㄧㄢˋ ❶嫌恶,憎恶 to detest; to abominate (连 ***doublet*** 一恶 to abhor; to loathe):讨～*to hate; to dislike*|～弃 *to detest and reject* ❷满足 satisfied; satiated:贪得无～*to have insatiable greed; to be insatiably avaricious*

餍(饜) yàn ㄧㄢˋ 吃饱 to have enough food (引) ***extension*** 满足 to satisfy

砚 yàn ㄧㄢˋ [砚口]地名,在浙江省富阳 Yankou, a place in Fuyang, Zhejiang Province

砚 yàn ㄧㄢˋ 砚台,写毛笔字研墨用的文具 inkstone

咽(*嚥) ㊂ yàn ㄧㄢˋ 使嘴里的食物等通过咽喉到食道里去 to swallow:细嚼慢～*to chew carefully and swallow slowly*|狼吞虎～*to gobble up; to wolf down* [咽气]人死时断气 to breathe one's last; to die

㊀ yān 见 861 页 see p861

㊁ yè 见 880 页 see p880

唁 yàn ㄧㄢˋ 吊丧,对遭遇丧事的人表示慰问 to express condolences (连 ***doublet*** 吊一 to extend condolences):～电(吊

丧的电报）*telegram of condolence*

彦 yàn ㄧㄢˋ 古指有才学、德行的人（in ancient China）man of intelligence and virtue

谚 yàn ㄧㄢˋ 谚语，社会上流传的固定语句，用简单通俗的话反映出某种经验和道理 proverb; saying; adage：农～ *farmer's proverb; farmer's saying*｜古～*ancient saying*

艳（艷、**豔、*豓）yàn ㄧㄢˋ ❶鲜艳，色彩鲜明 gorgeous; colourful：～丽 *gorgeous; bright-coloured*｜～阳天 *bright spring day; bright sunny skies* ❷旧时指关于爱情方面的（in former times）of love, erotic affairs：～情 *amorous; erotic*｜～史 *love*（or *amorous*）*story*

［艳羡］非常羡慕 to admire; to envy

滟（灩、**灎）yàn ㄧㄢˋ［滟滪堆］（—yùduī）长江瞿塘峡口的巨石，为便利长江航运，1958 年将它炸除 Yanyudui, a mammoth monolith lying at the entrance to the Qutang Gorge of the Changjiang（*or* Yangtze）River, which was demolished in 1958 to dredge and straighten the navigation lane

晏 yàn ㄧㄢˋ ❶晚，迟 late：～起 *to get up late* ❷同"宴❹" same as 宴❹

鷃（**鴳）yàn ㄧㄢˋ 鷃雀（què），古书中说的小鸟（in ancient Chinese texts）little bird

宴（*醼）yàn ㄧㄢˋ ❶用酒饭招待 to fete; to entertain：～客 *to entertain guests at a banquet; to host a dinner in honor of the guests* ❷聚会在一起吃酒饭 to fete; to entertain：～会 *feast; banquet* ❸酒席 feast; banquet：设～ *to give*（or *hold; serve*）*a banquet* ❹安乐 ease and comfort：～安鸩（zhèn）毒（贪图享受等于喝毒酒自杀）。*Living at leisure is like drinking poisoned wine.*

堰 yàn ㄧㄢˋ 挡水的低坝 weir; dam; barrage：塘～ *small reservoir in a hilly area*｜围～ *coffer-dam*

验（驗、*騐）yàn ㄧㄢˋ ❶检查，察看 to examine; to check; to inspect：～血 *blood test*｜～收 *to check upon delivery; to check before acceptance* ❷有效果 effective：屡试屡～ *to prove effective in every test*

雁（*鴈）yàn ㄧㄢˋ 大雁，鸟名。多指鸿雁，羽毛褐色，腹部白色，嘴扁平，腿短，群居在水边，飞时排列成行。是候鸟 wild goose（*Anser cygnoides*）

赝（*贗）yàn ㄧㄢˋ 假的，伪造的 fake; counterfeit; spurious：～品 *fake; counterfeit*

焰（*燄）yàn ㄧㄢˋ 火苗 flame; blaze：火

～*blaze; fire*［气焰］气势 arrogance; bluster：～～万丈 *swollen with arrogance*

焱 yàn ㄧㄢˋ 火焰 flame; blaze; fire

酽（釅）yàn ㄧㄢˋ 浓，味厚 thick; strong：这碗茶太～。*This tea tastes too strong*.

谳（讞）yàn ㄧㄢˋ 审判定罪 to sentence：定～*to reach a verdict; to pronounce a sentence; to pass sentence* (*on sb*)

燕（❶*鷰）㊀ yàn ㄧㄢˋ ❶（一子）鸟名。翅膀很长，尾巴像张开的剪刀，背部黑色，肚皮白色，常在人家屋内或屋檐下用泥做巢居住，捕食昆虫。是候鸟 swallow (*Hirundinidae*) ❷古书里有时用作"宴"(used as 宴 in some ancient Chinese texts)：～居 *to lead a happy and easy life*｜～好 *family harmony; connubial bliss*｜～乐 *ease and comfort; music played at a court banquet*

㊁ yān 见 863 页 see p863

谳 yàn ㄧㄢˋ ❶相聚叙谈 to fete and chat ❷同"宴❶❷❸" same as 宴❶❷❸

YANG ㄧㄤ

央 yāng ㄧㄤ ❶中心 center; core：大厅中～*center of the hall* ❷恳求 to implore; to entreat; to beg (㊥ *doublet* —求 to plead; to implore)：只好～人去找 *to have to implore sb to look for sth* (or *sb*)｜～告了半天，他还是不去。*He refused to go although I begged him for a long time*. ❸尽，完了 to terminate; to end：夜未～ *The night is not yet spent*.

泱 yāng ㄧㄤ 深广，弘大（叠 ***reduplication***）vast; grand：河水～～*vast expanse of water*｜～～大国 *great country*

殃 yāng ㄧㄤ ❶祸害 calamity; disaster; misfortune (㊥ ***doublet*** 灾— disaster)：遭～*to suffer disaster*｜城门失火，～及池鱼（喻牵连受害）。*When the city wall gate caught fire, the disaster extended even to the fish in the moat — to involve the innocent in a disturbance*. ❷损害 to bring disaster to：祸国～民 *to bring calamity to the country and the people*

鸯 yāng ㄧㄤ 见 923 页"鸳"字条"鸳鸯"(yuān—) see 鸳鸯 on p923

秧 yāng ㄧㄤ ❶（一儿）植物的幼苗 seedling; sprout：树～儿 *sapling*｜茄子～*eggplant seedling* 特指稻苗 rice seedling：插～ *to transplant rice seedlings*［秧歌］(—ge)我国民间歌舞的一种 *yangge*, a popular folk dance of China ❷某些植物的茎 vine; stem：瓜～*melon vine*｜豆～*bean vine* ❸（一子）某些初生的小动物 young (of some new-born animals)：鱼～子 *minnow; fry*｜猪～子 *piglet* ❹〈方 ***dialect***〉栽植，畜

养 to plant; to raise:～几棵树 *to plant some trees* | 他～了一池鱼。*He raises a pond of fish.*

鞅 ㊀ yāng 丨尢 古代用马拉车时套在马颈上的皮子(in ancient China) martingale

㊁ yàng 见 872 页 see p872

扬(揚、❷*颺、❶-❸*敭) yáng 丨尢 ❶高举,向上 to raise; to hoist:～帆 *to hoist the sails* | ～手 *to wave one's hand* | 趾高气～(骄傲的样子) *to hold one's head high* [扬弃]事物在发展过程中,一面把积极因素提升到更高阶段,一面把消极因素抛弃 to sublate; to develop the useful and discard the useless [扬扬]得意的样子 complacent [扬汤止沸(fèi)]比喻办法不彻底 ineffectual remedy; to try to stop water from boiling by scooping it up and pouring it back ❷在空中飘动 to float; to flutter:飘～ *to wave; to flutter* | 飞～ *to flutter; to fly* ❸向上播撒 to throw up and scatter:～场(cháng) *to winnow* ㊂ ***extension*** 传布 to spread; to make known(㊣ ***doublet*** 宣— to propagate; to publicize):～名 *to make a name for oneself* | 赞～ *to praise; to commend; to acclaim* | 颂～ *to extol; to eulogize; to laud*

[扬长而去]大模大样地离去 to stalk away; to stride off; to swagger off

玚(瑒) yáng 丨尢 玉名 *yang*, a kind of jade

杨(楊) yáng 丨尢 杨树,落叶乔木,有白杨、大叶杨、小叶杨等多种,有的木材可做器物 poplar (*Populus*)

旸(暘) yáng 丨尢 ❶太阳出来 sunrise ❷晴天 fine day

炀(煬) yáng 丨尢 ❶熔化金属 to smelt ❷火旺(of fire) roaring; blazing

钖(鍚) yáng 丨尢 古代马额上的一种装饰(in ancient China) ornament on the forehead of a horse

疡(瘍) yáng 丨尢 ❶疮 sore ❷溃烂 to fester; to ulcerate:胃溃～ *gastric ulcer*

羊 yáng 丨尢 哺乳动物。常见的有山羊、绵羊等家畜。毛、皮、骨、角都可作工业上的原料,肉和乳供食用。黄羊、藏羚羊等为国家保护动物 sheep; goat

〈古 ***archaism***〉又同"祥"(xiáng) also same as 祥

佯 yáng 丨尢 假装 to pretend; to feign; to sham:～攻 *to feign an attack; to make a feint* | ～作不知 *to feign ignorance*

垟 yáng 丨尢 〈方 ***dialect***〉田地。多用于地名(yang, usually used in a place name) field:翁～(在浙江省乐清) *Wengyang, a place in Yueqing, Zhejiang Province*

徉 yáng ㄧㄤˊ 见 77 页“徜”字条“徜徉”(cháng—) see 徜徉 on p77

洋 yáng ㄧㄤˊ ❶比海更大的水域 ocean:海～*ocean*|太平～*the Pacific Ocean* ❷广大,多(叠 ***reduplication***) vast; multitudinous:～溢 *brimming over with*|～～大观 *spectacular; grandiose* ❸外国的 foreign:～为中用 *to make foreign things serve China; to adapt foreign things to Chinese use* ❹现代化的 modern:土～结合 *to combine indigenous methods with foreign ones; to use both traditional and modern methods* ❺洋钱,银元 silver dollar

烊 ㊀ yáng ㄧㄤˊ 熔化金属 to smelt ㊂ ***extension*** 〈方 ***dialect***〉溶化 to melt; to dissolve:糖～了。*The sweets have got dissolved.*

㊁ yàng 见 873 页 see p873

蛘 yáng ㄧㄤˊ 〈方 ***dialect***〉生在米里的一种小黑甲虫 rice weevil

阳(陽) yáng ㄧㄤˊ ❶明亮 bright ❷跟“阴”相对(the opposite of 阴) **1** 阳性,男性的 masculine; male **2** 太阳 sun:～历 *solar calendar*|～光 *sunlight; sunshine* **3** 带正电的 positive:～电 *positive charge; positive electricity*|～极 *anode; positive electrode* **4** 山的南面,水的北面(多用于地名) (yang, usually used in a place name) south of a hill or north of a river:衡～(地名,在湖南省衡山之南) *Hengyang, a place in the south of Hengshan Mountain in Hunan Province*|洛～(地名,在河南省洛河之北) *Luoyang, a place in the north of Luohe River in Henan Province* **5** 外露的,明显的 open; overt; obvious:～沟 *ditch; open drain*|～奉阴违 *to overtly agree but covertly oppose; to comply in public but undermine in private* **6** 凸出的 convex; in relief:～文图章 *seal in relief; relief seal* **7** 关于活人的(迷信) (of superstition) of this world; of this life:～间 *this world* ❸男性生殖器 male genitals ❹古同“佯”same as 佯 in ancient Chinese

仰 yǎng ㄧㄤˇ ❶脸向上,跟“俯”相对(the opposite of 俯) to face upward:～起头来 *to raise one's head*|～天大笑 *to face the sky and laugh sardonically*|人～马翻 *men and horses thrown off their feet* ❷敬慕 to admire; to revere:久～。*have long been looking forward to meeting you.*|信～*belief*|敬～*to revere; to venerate* ❸依赖 to rely on; to depend on (㊈ ***doublet*** —赖 to rely on):～人鼻息(喻依赖人,看人的脸色行事) *to be at sb's beck and call* ❹旧时公文用语,上行文中用在“恳、祈、请”等之前,表示尊敬;下行文中表命令,如“仰即遵照”(指示下属机关遵照公文内容办事)[used before 恳, 祈 or 请 in former times in submitting official documents to a superior to show respect, and in transmitting orders or requests to a subordinate such as 仰即遵照 (we hope that you will act in accordance at once)]

养(養) yǎng ㄧㄤˇ ❶抚育,供给生活品 to rear; to support (㊎ *doublet* 一育 to nurture): ～家 *to rear one's family; to support one's family*｜抚～子女 *to bring up children* ❷饲养(动物),培植(花草) to raise; to cultivate; to grow: ～鸡 *to raise chickens*｜～鱼 *to raise fish*｜～花 *to cultivate flowers* ❸生育 to give birth to: ～了个儿子 *to give birth to a boy* ❹(非血亲)抚养的 foster; adoptive; adopted: ～女 *fosterdaughter; adopted daughter*｜～父 *foster father* ❺使身心得到滋补和休息 to nourish; to recuperate: ～精神 *to nourish; to recuperate*｜～精蓄锐 *to conserve strength and store up energy; to get up steam*｜～病 *to recuperate; to convalesce*｜休～ *to recuperate* ㊀ **extension** 保护修补 to maintain: ～路 *to maintain a road* (*or railway*) ❻培养 to develop; to cultivate: 他～成了劳动习惯。*He is used to working.* ❼(品德学业等)良好的积累 refinement; cultivation: 修～ *refinement; cultivation*｜涵～ *self-restraint; self-possession*｜教～ *cultivation*｜学～ *scholarship and cultivation* ❽扶持,帮助 to support; to help: 以农～牧,以牧促农。*Foster animal husbandry by agriculture, and promote agriculture with animal husbandry.*

氧 yǎng ㄧㄤˇ 一种化学元素,在通常条件下为气体,符号O,无色、无味、无臭,比空气重。能帮助燃烧,是动植物呼吸所必需的气体 oxygen (O)

痒(癢) yǎng ㄧㄤˇ 皮肤或黏膜受刺激需要抓挠的一种感觉(叠 ***reduplication***) itch; tickle: 蚊子咬得身上直～～。*The mosquito bites itched me all over.*｜痛～相关 *to share a common lot* [技痒] 极想把自己的技能显出来 to itch to display one's skill

瀁 yǎng ㄧㄤˇ 见295页"滉"字条"滉瀁"(huàng—) see 滉瀁 on p295

怏 yàng ㄧㄤˋ 不服气,不满意 displeased; disgruntled: ～～不乐 *morose; disgruntled*｜～然不悦 *displeased; discontented*

鞅 ㊁ yàng ㄧㄤˋ 牛鞅,牛拉东西时架在脖子上的器具 yoke

㊀ yāng 见870页 see p870

样(樣) yàng ㄧㄤˋ ❶(一子、一儿)形状 shape; form: 模～ *appearance; look*｜这～ *such; so*｜不像～儿 *unpresentable* ❷(一儿)量词 ***quantifier***,种类 kind; type: 两～儿菜 *two dishes*｜四～儿果品 *four kinds of fruit*｜～～儿都行

capable of doing everything ❸(—子、—儿)做标准的东西 model; pattern: ～品 *sample; specimen* | 货～ *sample (goods)* | ～本 *sample (book)*

恙 yàng ㄧㄤˋ 病 ailment; illness: 偶染微～ *to be indisposed* | 安然无～(没受损伤或没发生意外) *safe and sound*

烊 ㊁ yàng ㄧㄤˋ [打烊]〈方 ***dialect***〉商店晚上关门停止营业(of shops, stores, etc) to close for the night

㊀ yáng 见 871 页 see p871

羕 yàng ㄧㄤˋ 形容水长(cháng) (of river) long

漾 yàng ㄧㄤˋ ❶水面微微动荡 rippling ❷液体溢出来 to overflow; to brim over: ～奶 *to throw up milk* | ～酸水 *to throw up gastric acid* | 汤太满都～出来了。*The soup in the bowl is so full as to overflow.*

YAO ㄧㄠ

么 ㊂ yāo ㄧㄠ 同"幺"same as 幺

㊀ me 见 491 页 see p491

㊁ ma 见 482 页 see p482

幺 yāo ㄧㄠ ❶〈方 ***dialect***〉小，排行最末的 youngest: ～叔 *youngest uncle* | ～妹 *youngest sister* | ～儿 *youngest son* ❷数目"一"的另一个说法(用于电话号码等)(another term for the numeral "one", usually used in reading telephone number, etc) one

吆(**吆) yāo ㄧㄠ [吆喝](—he)喊叫，用于叫卖东西、赶牲口等(used to call for peddling or to urge on animals) to cry out; to yell; to hawk

夭(❷*殀) yāo ㄧㄠ ❶茂盛(叠 ***reduplication***) luxuriant; exuberant: 桃之～～ *The beach trees are in full blossom* ❷未成年的人死去 to die young: ～亡 *to die young* | ～折 *to die young*

妖 yāo ㄧㄠ ❶神话、传说中称有妖术而害人的东西 goblin; demon: ～魔鬼怪 *evil spirits; demons and ghosts* ㉄ ***extension*** 邪恶，荒诞，迷惑人的 evil and bewitching; evil and fraudulent: ～术 *witchcraft; sorcery* | ～风 *evil wind; noxious trend* | ～言惑众 *to spread fallacies to deceive people* ❷装束、神态不正派 seductive: ～里～气 *seductive and bewitching; enticing* ❸媚，艳丽 charming; enchanting: ～娆 *bewitching; enchanting; fascinating*

约 ㊁ yāo ㄧㄠ 用秤称 to weigh: 你～～有多重? *See how much you weigh.*

㊀ yuē 见 928 页 see p928

要 ㊁ yāo ㄧㄠ ❶求 to demand; to ask [要求]提出具体事项，希望实现 to demand; to require: ～～大家认真学习 *to call upon everyone to study diligently* | ～～入党 *to apply for admission to the Party* ❷强求，有所仗恃而强

硬要求 to coerce; to force: ～挟(xié) *to coerce; to threaten* ❸古同"邀"、"腰"same as 邀 or 腰 in ancient Chinese ❹姓 Yao, a surname

㊁ yào 见 876 页 see p876

腰 yāo ㄧㄠ ❶胯上胁下的部分,在身体的中部。(图见 741 页"体"picture on p741) waist [腰子]肾脏 kidney ❷裤、裙等围在腰上的部分 waist (of garment): 裤～*waist* ❸事物的中段,中间 middle: 山～*halfway up a mountain* ❹中间狭小像腰部的地势 waist-shaped topography: 土～*isthmus* | 海～*strait*

邀 yāo ㄧㄠ ❶约请 to invite: ～他来谈谈 *to ask him for a talk* | 特～代表 *specially invited representative* ❷求得 to solicit; to seek: ～赏 *to seek rewards* | ～准 *to ask permission; to seek permission* ❸阻留 to intercept: 中途～截 *to intercept; to waylay*

爻 yáo ㄧㄠ (旧读 formerly xiáo)组成八卦中每一个卦的长短横道,如"—"、"--" solid and broken lines, i. e. — and --, which are used to form each of the Eight Trigrams

肴(*餚) yáo ㄧㄠ (旧读 formerly xiáo) 做熟的鱼肉等 meat or fish dishes: 佳～*delicacies* | 酒～*wine and dishes*

尧(堯) yáo ㄧㄠ 传说中上古帝王名 Yao, legendary sageking in remote antiquity

侥(僥) ㊁ yáo ㄧㄠ 见 339 页"僬"字条"僬侥"(jiāo—) see 僬侥 on p339

㊀ jiǎo 见 340 页 see p340

峣(嶢) yáo ㄧㄠ [岧峣](tiáo—)山高(of mountains) high and steep; lofty

垚 yáo ㄧㄠ 高 high; lofty 多用于人名 yao, usually used in a given name

轺 yáo ㄧㄠ 轺车,古代的一种轻便的小马车(in ancient China) light horse-drawn carriage

姚 yáo ㄧㄠ 姓 Yao, a surname

珧 yáo ㄧㄠ 江珧,又叫"玉珧"。一种生活在海里的软体动物,壳三角形,肉柱叫江珧柱,干制后又称干贝,是珍贵的海味品(also called 玉珧) pen shell

铫 ㊁ yáo ㄧㄠ ❶古代一种大锄(in ancient China) big hoe ❷姓 Yao, a surname

㊀ diào 见 150 页 see p150

陶 ㊁ yáo ㄧㄠ [皋陶](gāo—)传说中上古人名 Gaoyao, a legendary person in remote antiquity

㊀ táo 见 734 页 see p734

窑(*窯、*窰) yáo ㄧㄠ ❶烧砖、瓦、陶瓷等物的建筑物 kiln ❷为采煤而凿的洞 pit: 煤～*coal pit* ❸窑洞,在土坡上特为住人挖成的洞 cave dwelling ❹(一子)

旧指妓院(in former times) brothel

谣 yáo ㄧㄠˊ ❶歌谣,随口唱出、没有伴奏的韵语 ballad; rhyme:民～ *folkrhyme; ballads*|童～*children's rhymes* ❷谣言,凭空捏造的不可信的话 rumour; hearsay:造～ *to start a rumour*|辟～*to refute a rumour*

摇 yáo ㄧㄠˊ 摆动 to rock; to shake(㊀ ***doublet*** 一摆 to wave; to wag|一晃 to sway):～头 *to shake one's head*|～船 *to row a boat* [摇曳](-yè) 摇摆动荡 to flicker; to sway [动摇]变动,不坚定 to vacillate:思想～～ *to have a wavering mind*

徭(**傜) yáo ㄧㄠˊ 徭役,古时统治者强制人民承担的无偿劳动(in ancient China) corvee

遥 yáo ㄧㄠˊ 远 remote; far (叠 ***reduplication***)(㊀ ***doublet*** 一远 distant; far):～望 *to look into the distance*|路～知马力。*Distance tests a horse's strength — time measures a person's heart.*|～～相对 *to stand far apart facing each other* [遥感]利用现代电子、光学仪器远距离探测、识别研究对象 remote sensing [遥控]通过有线或无线装置控制一定距离以外的机器、仪器、武器、家用电器等 remote control; telecontrol

瑶 yáo ㄧㄠˊ 美玉 fine jade ㊕ ***figurative*** 美好 fine; precious:～函 *your letter* [瑶族]我国少数民族,参看附表(see the appendix) the Yao ethnic group, one of the ethnic minorities of China

飖 yáo ㄧㄠˊ [飘飖]旧同"飘摇"。参看567页"飘"(piāo)(formerly same as 飘摇) see 飘 on p567

繇 ㊂ yáo ㄧㄠˊ 同"徭"same as 徭

㊀ yóu 见910页 see p910

㊁ zhòu 见992页 see p992

鳐 yáo ㄧㄠˊ 鱼名。身体扁平,略呈圆形或菱形,有的种类有一对能发电的器官,生活在海中 skate; ray (*Batoidea*)

杳 yǎo ㄧㄠˇ 无影无声 voiceless and traceless:～无音信 *to disappear without a trace* or *There has been no news whatsoever.* or *No news has been received for a long time.*|音容已～。*The voice and face of my love are no longer there.*

咬(*齩、**鱙) yǎo ㄧㄠˇ ❶上下牙对住,压碎或夹住东西 to bite; to gnaw; to snap at:～了一口馒头 *to take a bite of* mantou ❷钳子等夹住或螺丝齿轮等卡住(of pliers, gears) to grip; to bite:螺丝勚(yì)了,～不住扣。*The nut is worn out and can't be screwed.* ❸受责问或审讯时拉扯上不相关的人 to incriminate another person when interrogated; to implicate:不许乱～好人。*Don't implicate the* *innocent*. ❹狗叫 to bark：鸡叫狗。～ *Cocks crow and dogs bark*. ❺读字音 to pronounce; to articulate; to enunciate：这个字我～不准。*I am not sure about the pronunciation of this word*.

舀 yǎo ㄧㄠˇ 用瓢、勺等取东西（多指流质）to ladle out; to spoon up：～水 *to scoop up water* | ～汤 *to ladle out soup* [舀子]（—zi）舀取液体的器具 dipper; ladle; scoop

窅 yǎo ㄧㄠˇ 眼睛眍进去（of eyes）sunken [喻] ***figurative*** 深远 profound

窈 yǎo ㄧㄠˇ ❶深远 profound ❷昏暗 dim ❸美好 graceful; fine [窈窕]（—tiǎo）**1** 形容女子文静而美好（of a lady）gentle and graceful **2**（宫室、山水）深远曲折（of a palace, landscape）secluded

疟（瘧） ㊁ yào ㄧㄠˋ 疟子，疟（nüè）疾 malaria; ague

㊀ nüè 见 542 页 see p542

药（藥） yào ㄧㄠˋ ❶可以治病的东西 medicine; drug ❷有一定作用的化学物品 certain chemicals：火～ *gunpowder* | 焊～ *welding agent or flux* | 杀虫～ *insecticide; pesticide* ❸用药物医治 to cure with medicine：不可救～ *incurable* ❹毒死 to kill with poison：～老鼠 *to kill rats with poison*

要 ㊀ yào ㄧㄠˋ ❶索取，希望得到 to want; to desire：我～这一本书。*I want this book*. [引] ***extension*** 作为己有，保留 to keep sth as one's own; to retain; to reserve：这东西他还～呢。*He still wants to keep it*. [要强]好胜心强，不愿落后 to be eager to excel; to be anxious to outdo ❷重大，值得重视的 important; essential：～事 *important matter* | ～点 *gist* [要紧][紧要]急切重要 urgent; crucial ❸重大的值得重视的东西 essentials：纲～ *outlines; sketches* | 提～ *synopsis* ❹应该，必须 must; should; have to：～努力学习。*We should study hard*. ❺将要，将 be going to; to be about to：我们～去学习了。*We're going to study*. ❻连词 ***conjunction***，要是，若，如果 if; suppose; in case：明天～下雨，我就不去了。*If it rains tomorrow, I shall not go*. | 他～来了，你就交给他。*Please give it to him if he comes*. ❼请求，叫 to ask; to request：他～我给他买本书。*He asks me to buy him a book*.

㊁ yāo 见 873 页 see p873

钥（鑰） ㊁ yào ㄧㄠˋ [钥匙]（—shi）开锁的东西 key

㊀ yuè 见 929 页 see p929

靿 yào ㄧㄠˋ 靴筒、袜筒 leg of a boot or stocking：高～靴子 *boots; Wellington boots*

鹞 yào ㄧㄠˋ（—子）鹞鹰，一种凶猛的鸟，样子像鹰，比鹰小，背灰褐色，腹白色，捕食鼠、兔和小鸟 sparrowhawk; harrier (*Accipitridae*)[纸鹞]风筝 kite

曜 yào 㠯 ❶照耀 to shine; to illuminate ❷日、月、星都称“曜”,一个星期的七天用日、月、火、水、木、金、土七个星名排列,因此星期几也叫什么“曜日”,如“日曜日”是星期日,“土曜日”是星期六。As the seven days in a week are respectively related to the seven luminaries, namely Sun, Moon, Mars, Mercury, Jupiter, Venus and Saturn which are translated as 曜, the day in a week is called 曜日 luminary day, e. g. 日曜日 for Sunday, 土曜日 for Saturday.

耀(*燿) yào 㠯 ❶光线强烈地照射 to shine; to illuminate (㊀ **doublet** 照一 to illuminate):~眼 *dazzling* ❷显扬,显示出来 to flaunt; to vaunt:~武扬威 *to make a big show of one's strength* ❸光荣 honour; glory:荣~ *honour; credit*

YE 㠯

耶 ㊀ yē 㠯 用于译音,如耶路撒冷 a word used in transliteration, e. g. Jerusalem is transliterated as 耶路撒冷

㊁ yé 见 878 页 see p878

倻 yē 㠯 [伽倻琴](jiā——)朝鲜族弦乐器 plucked and stringed Korean musical instrument used by the Korean ethnic group

椰 yē 㠯 椰子树,常绿乔木,产在热带,树干(gàn)很高。果实叫椰子,中有汁,可做饮料。果肉可以吃,也可榨油,果皮纤维可结网。树干可做建筑材料 coconut palm; coconut tree; coco (*Cocos nucifera*)

[枣椰]也叫“海枣”。常绿乔木,果实叫椰枣,味甜。产于伊拉克等地(also called 海枣) date palm

掖 ㊀ yē 㠯 把东西塞在衣袋或夹缝里 to tuck sth in the pocket or to thrust sth in between the crack:把钱~在兜里 *to tuck money into the pocket* | 把书~在书包里 *to tuck books into the satchel*

㊁ yè 见 880 页 see p880

暍 yē 㠯 中暑,伤暑 heatstroke; sunstroke

噎 yē 㠯 食物堵住食道 to choke:吃得太快,~住了 *to be chocked up from eating too fast* | 因~废食(喻因为偶然出毛病而停止正常的活动) *to stop eating for fear of choking — to refrain from doing something necessary for fear of a slight risk* ㊕ **figurative** 用话顶撞人,使对方说不出话来 to render sb speechless by saying sth blunt; to choke off:别~人。*Don't choke me off by it!*

邪 ㊁ yé 㠯 ❶见 516 页“莫”字条“莫邪” see 莫邪 on p516 ❷古同“耶㊁❶”same as 耶㊁❶ in ancient Chinese

㊀ xié 见 828 页 see p828

Y

铘 yé ㄧㄝˊ 见 516 页“镆”字条“镆铘”(mò—) see 镆铘 on p516

爷(爺) yé ㄧㄝˊ ❶父亲 father:～娘 *father and mother* ❷祖父(叠 ***reduplication***) paternal grandfather:～～奶奶 *paternal grandfather and grandmother* ❸对长辈或年长男子的敬称 respectful address for an elderly man; grandpa:张大～(ye) *Grandpa Zhang*|李～*Uncle Li* ❹旧时对官僚、财主等的称呼(form of address for an official or rich man in former times) sir; master; lord:老～*master; lord*|少～*young master* ❺迷信的人对神的称呼(form of address for god by superstitious people) god:土地～*God of Land; village god*|财神～*God of Wealth*

耶 ㊀ yé ㄧㄝˊ〈古 ***archaism***〉❶助词 ***auxiliary***,表示疑问(used to express doubt):是～非～? *Yes or no?* ❷同“爷” same as 爷

㊁ yē 见 877 页 see p877

揶 yé ㄧㄝˊ [揶揄](—yú) 耍笑,嘲弄 to ridicule; to deride

也 yě ㄧㄝˇ ❶副词 ***adverb*** **1** 表示同样、并行等意义 also; too; as well:你去,我～去。*If you go, I'll go too.*|～好,～不好。*It may be good or bad.* **2** 跟“再”、“一点”、“连”等连用表示语气的加强(多用在否定句里)(usually used in collocation with 再,一点,连, etc for emphasis in negative sentences):再～不敢闹了 *dare not make any more trouble*|这话一点～不错。*What you said is absolutely right.*|连一个人影～没找到。*Not even a single person was found there.* **3**(跟前文的“虽然、即使”连用)表示转折或让步(used in collocation with 虽然, 即使 to express transition or concession):我虽然没仔细读过这本书,～略知内容梗概。*I have a rough idea of the book though I haven't read it carefully.*|即使天下雨,我～要出门。*I'll go out even if it rains.* **4** 表示委婉语气(used to soften up the tone):我看～只好如此了。*I'm afraid we'll have to let it go at that.*|节目倒～不错。*The programme can be numbered among the good.* ❷文言助词 ***auxiliary in classical Chinese*** **1** 用在句末,表示判断语气(used at the end of a sentence to express judgement):环滁皆山～。*Chuzhou is surrounded with mountains.* **2** 表示疑问或感叹语气(used to express doubt or exclamation):何～? *What?*|何为不去～? *Why don't you go?*|是何言～? *What do you mean?* **3** 用在句中,表示停顿(used in the middle of a sentence to denote pause):向～不怒而今～怒,何也? *He has never got into a rage before, but why today?*

冶 yě ㄧㄝˇ ❶熔炼(金属) to smelt:～炼 *to smelt* | ～金 *metallurgy* ❷装饰、打扮得过分艳丽(含贬义)(derogatory) seductively dressed (*or* made up):～容 *seductive appearance* | 妖～*seductive; coquettish*

野(*埜) yě ㄧㄝˇ ❶郊外,村外 open country; wildland:～营 *camp; bivouac* | ～地 *wilderness* [野战军]适应广大区域机动作战的正规军 field army [分野]划分的范围,界限 to divide; dividing line ❷指不当政的地位 not being in power:朝～*the court and the commonality; the government and the populace* | 下～*to relinquish power; to retire from office* | 在～*to be not in power; to be out of office* ❸不讲情理,没有礼貌,蛮横 rude; rough:撒～*to behave rudely* | 粗～*boorish* ❹不驯顺,狂妄非分 wild; untamed:狼子～心(狂妄狠毒的用心) *a wolf cub with a savage heart — wolf-hearted; full of wild ambitions* ❺不受约束或难于约束 unrestrained; unruly:～性 *wild nature* | 这孩子心都玩～了。*The child was so crazy about playing that he became wild and couldn't concentrate on studying.* ❻不是人所驯养或培植的(动物或植物)(of plant or animal) not cultivated or domesticated; wild:～兽 *beast; wild animal* | ～草 *weed*

业(業) yè ㄧㄝˋ ❶事业,事情,所从事的工作 cause; enterprise **1** 国民经济中的部门 sector in national economy:农～*agriculture* | 工～*industry* | 渔～*fishery* | 交通事～*transport* **2** 职业,工作岗位 occupation; post; position:就～*employment* **3** 学业,学习的功课 course of study; course:毕～*to graduate* ❷从事某种工作 to engage in:～农 *to engage in farming* | ～商 *to be in business; to engage in commerce* ❸产业,财产 estate; property:～主 *proprietor; owner* ❹已经 already(㊂ **doublet** 一 已 already):～经公布 *to have already been announced* ❺梵语"羯磨"的意译,有造作之义。佛教称人的行为、言语、思念为业,分别叫作身业、口业、意业,合称三业,有善恶之分,一般均指恶业(In Buddhism, deed, speech and ideology are called, i. e. 身业, 口业, 意业; the three 业 may be good or evil, yet it generally denotes evil.) translation of karma from Sanskrit, meaning doings

邺(鄴) yè ㄧㄝˋ 古地名,在今河北省临漳西,河南省安阳北 Ye, an ancient place to the west of present Linzhang, Hebei Province, and to the north of present Anyang, Henan Province

叶(葉) ㊀ yè ㄧㄝˋ ❶(一子、一儿)植物的营养器官之一,多呈片状、绿色,长

在茎上 leaf; foliage: 树～*tree leaves* | 菜～*vegetable leaves* ❷像叶子的 leaf-shaped thing: 铜～*copper leaf sheet* | 铁～*iron leaf sheet* ❸同"页"same as 页 ❹较长时期的分段 part of a historical period: 20 世纪中～*middle of the 20th century; mid-1900s* ❺姓 Ye, a surname

㊁ xié 见 827 页 see p827

页(頁、**篥) yè ㄧㄝˋ ❶篇,张(指书、画、纸等) leaf; sheet; page: 活～*loose-leaf* [网页]可以在互联网上进行信息查询的信息页 web page [主页]可以在互联网上进行信息查询的起始网页 home page ❷量词 ***quantifier***, 我国旧指书本中的一张纸,现多指书本一张纸的一面(in former China) a leaf of a book, (now) a page of a book

曳(**拽) yè ㄧㄝˋ 拖,拉,牵引 to drag; to haul; to tug: ～光弹 *tracer bullet* | 弃甲～兵 *to throw away armour and trail weapons — to flee hurry-scurry*

拽 ㊂ yè ㄧㄝˋ 同"曳"same as 曳

㊀ zhuài 见 999 页 see p999

㊁ zhuāi 见 999 页 see p999

夜(*亱) yè ㄧㄝˋ 从天黑到天亮的一段时间,跟"日"、"昼"相对(the opposite of 日 or 昼) night: 日日～～*day and night* | 白天黑～*all day round; day and night* | 昼～不停 *round the clock; day and night*

掖 ㊀ yè ㄧㄝˋ ❶用手扶着别人的胳膊 to support sb by the arm [奖掖]奖励,提拔 to reward and promote ❷掖县,旧县名,今莱州,在山东省 Yexian County, former county in today's Laizhou, Shandong Province

㊁ yē 见 877 页 see p877

液 yè ㄧㄝˋ 液体,能流动、有一定体积而没有一定形状的物质 liquid; fluid: 血～*blood* | 溶～*solution* [液晶]一种同时具有液体的流动性和晶体的光学特性的有机化合物,在现代的仪器、设备中应用广泛 liquid crystal

腋 yè ㄧㄝˋ ❶夹(gā)肢窝,上肢同肩膀相连处靠里凹入的部分 armpit; axilla ❷其他生物体上跟腋类似的部分 axil: ～芽 *axillary bud*

咽 ㊂ yè ㄧㄝˋ 呜咽,哽咽,悲哀得说不出话来 to sob; to choke with sobs

㊀ yān 见 861 页 see p861

㊁ yàn 见 867 页 see p867

晔(曄) yè ㄧㄝˋ 同"烨"same as 烨

烨(燁、*爗) yè ㄧㄝˋ 火光很盛的样子 (of flames) blazing; roaring

谒 yè ㄧㄝˋ 拜见 to call on: ～见 *to pay a formal visit to; to have an audience with* | 拜～*to pay a formal visit; to call on to show respects*

馌 yè ㄧㄝˋ 往田里送饭 to send a meal to the field

靥(靨) yè ㄧㄝˋ 酒窝儿,嘴两旁的小圆窝儿 dimple:脸上露出笑～。*Her cheeks dimpled as she smiled.*

YI ㄧ

一 yī ㄧ ❶数目字,最小的正整数 one, the smallest positive integer ❷纯,专 pure; concentrated:～心～意 *wholeheartedly* [一定] **1** 特定 given; certain; particular:～～的政治路线 *certain political line* **2** 相当的 proper; fair; due:取得～～的成绩 *to have made due achievements* **3** 副词 ***adverb***,必定 certainly; surely:～～按期完成 *to be sure to finish in time* ❸满,全 whole; all; throughout:～屋子人 *a roomful of people* | ～冬 *throughout the winter* | ～生 *all one's life* ❹相同 same:～样 *the same; alike* | 大小不～*different in size* ❺另外的 another:番茄～名西红柿。Fanqie (*Tomato*) *is also known as* xihongshi *in Chinese*. ❻放在重叠的动词中间,表示稍微,轻微(used in the middle of a reduplicated verb) a little; slightly:看～看 *to have a look* | 听～听 *to listen for a while* ❼与"就"呼应(used in collocation with 就) **1** 表示两事时间紧接 no sooner ... than; as soon as:天～亮他就起来。*He got up as soon as the day broke.* **2** 表示每逢 whenever; every time; the moment:～想起祖国建设的突飞猛进,就觉着自己的努力太不够了。*Whenever I think of the giant progress of our motherland, I feel that I haven't done my share yet.* ❽起加强语气的作用(used for emphasis):～至于此 *should have come to such an extent* | ～何怒 *How angry he was!* | ～何悲 *How sorrowful he was!* ❾旧时乐谱记音符号的一个,相当于简谱中的低音"7" *yi*, note in the traditional Chinese musical scale in former times, equal to 7 in numbered musical notation

伊 yī ㄧ ❶代词 ***pronoun***,彼,他,她 that; he; she ❷文言助词 ***auxiliary in classical Chinese***:下车～始 *as soon as one alights from his official carriage — on arrival at a new post*

[伊斯兰教]宗教名。公元7世纪初阿拉伯人穆罕默德所创(founded by an Arab named Mohammed in the early 7th century) Islam; Islamism; Muslim religion

咿(*吚) yī ㄧ [咿呀](—yā) 拟声词 ***onomatopoeia***,小孩子学话的声音,摇桨的声音 babbling; prattling; (of oars) creaking; squeaking [咿唔](—wú)拟声词 ***onomatopoeia***,读书的声音 burbling; sound of reading aloud

洢 yī ㄧ ❶洢水,水名,在湖南省益阳,资水支流 Yishui River, the branch of the Zishui

River, located in Yiyang, Hunan Province ❷古水名,即今伊河,在河南省洛阳 ancient name for today's Yihe River in Luoyang, Henan Province

衣 ㊀ yī丨 ❶衣服(fu),衣裳(shang) clothes; garment; dress ❷披在或包在物体外面的东西 coating; covering:炮～ *gun cover* | 糖～炮弹 *sugar-coated bullet* ❸姓 Yi, a surname

㊁ yì 见 889 页 see p889

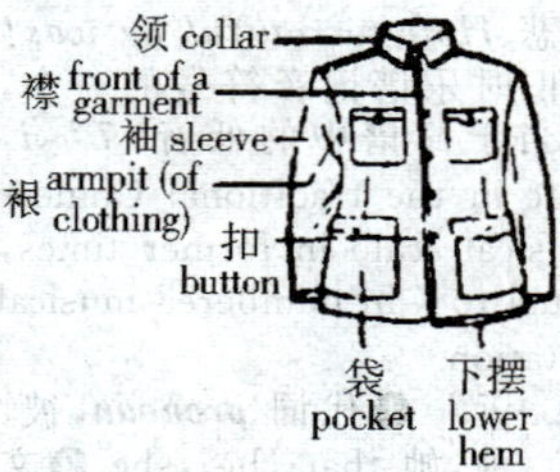

上衣 upper outer garment

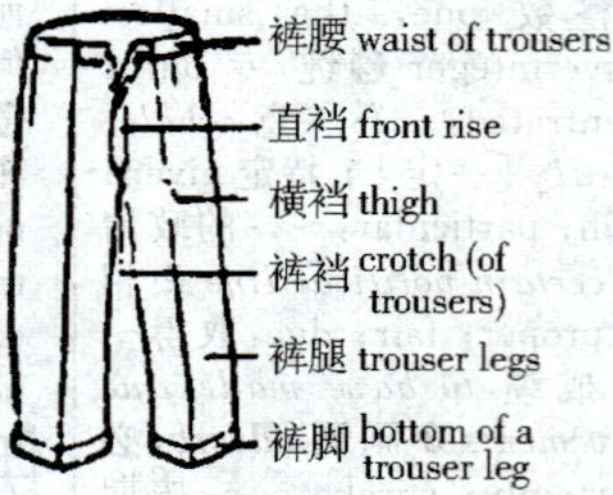

裤子 trousers

依 yī丨 ❶靠,仰赖 to rely on; to depend on (㊤ **doublet** 一靠 to rely on; to count on):相～为命 *to rely on each other for survival* | ～靠群众 *to rely on the masses* ❷介词 ***preposition***,按照 according to (㊤ ***doublet*** 一照 in the light of):～次前进 *to proceed in order* | ～我看,你最好不去。*In my point of view, you'd better not go.* ❸顺从,答应 to comply with; to yield to:不～不饶 *uncompromising*

[依依] **1** 形容留恋,不忍分离 reluctant to part:～～不舍 *to be reluctant to part; cannot bear to leave* **2** 柔软的东西摇动的样子 swaying:杨柳～～ *The willow twigs are swaying in the gentle breeze.*

铱 yī丨 一种金属元素,符号 Ir,银白色,熔点高,质硬而脆。合金可做坩埚、自来水笔尖等 iridium (Ir)

医(**醫**、**毉) yī丨 ❶医生,治病的人 doctor:中～*doctor of traditional Chinese medicine* | 西～*doctor of Western medicine* | 军～*military doctor; medical officer; military surgeon* ❷医学,增进健康、预防和治疗疾病的科学 medical science:中～ *traditional Chinese medicine* | 西～*Western medicine* | 学～*to study medicine* ❸治病 to treat; to cure (㊤ ***doublet*** 一疗 to treat | 一治 to cure):有病早～*to get timely medical treat-*

ment when one is ill｜～疗器械 *medical apparatus and instruments*

鹥 yī ㄧ 古书上指鸥(in ancient Chinese texts) gull

緊 yī ㄧ 文言助词 ***auxiliary in classical Chinese***,惟 only; alone:～我独无。*Only I have none!*

祎(禕) yī ㄧ 美好。多用于人名(yi, usually used in a given name) fine

猗 yī ㄧ 文言助词 ***auxiliary of classical Chinese***,用如"兮"equal to 兮:河水清且涟～。*The river is clear and rippling.*

椅 ㊁ yī ㄧ 又叫"山桐子"。落叶乔木,夏天开花,黄色,结小红果,木材可以制器物(also called 山桐子) idesia (*Idesia polycarpa*)

㊀ yǐ 见 888 页 see p888

漪 yī ㄧ 水波纹 ripple:清～ *clear ripples*｜～澜 *ripples and waves*

揖 yī ㄧ 拱手礼 to bow with hands clasped: 作～ *to make a slight bow with hands clasped*

壹(弌)** yī ㄧ "一"字的大写 one, capital form of the Chinese numeral 一

噫 yī ㄧ 文言叹词 ***interjection in classical Chinese*** [噫嘻](xī) 文言叹词 ***interjection in classical Chinese***,表示悲痛或叹息(used to express sorrow or sigh) alas

黟 yī ㄧ 黟县,在安徽省 Yixian County in Anhui Province

匜 yí ㄧˊ 〈古 ***archaism***〉❶一种洗手用的器具(utensil for washing one's hands) basin ❷一种盛(chéng)酒的器具 wine vessel

仪(儀) yí ㄧˊ ❶人的容貌、举止 appearance and behaviour:～表 *appearance; bearing*｜～容 *appearance; looks*｜威～ *dignified bearing; impressive manner* ❷仪式,按程序进行的礼节 ceremony; rite; ritual:司～*emcee; master of ceremony* ❸礼物 present; gift:贺～*gift as a token of congratulation*｜谢～ *gift in token of gratitude* ❹仪器,供测量、绘图、实验等用的有一定准则的器具 apparatus; instrument:浑天～ *armillary sphere; celestial globe*｜地动～ *seismograph*

圯 yí ㄧˊ 桥 bridge

夷 yí ㄧˊ ❶我国古代称东部的民族 general term for eastern ethnic groups in ancient China ❷旧指外国或外国的(in former times) foreign; foreign countries ❸平 to smooth **1** 平安 safe:化险为～*to turn danger into safety; to come out safely from danger* **2** 平坦 level ❹弄平 to raze:～为平地 *to raze to the ground; to level to the ground* ㊀ ***extension*** 消灭 to wipe out:～灭 *to extermi-*

nate; to wipe out

荑 ㊀ yí ㄧˊ 割去田地里的野草 to cut weeds in the field ㊁ tí 见 739 页 see p739

咦 yí ㄧˊ 叹词 ***interjection***，表示惊讶（used to express surprise) well; why:～！这是怎么回事？*Well, what's all this about?*

姨 yí ㄧˊ ❶姨母，母亲的姊妹 aunt; mother's sister ❷（一子）妻的姊妹 wife's sister:大～子 *wife's elder sister* | 小～子 *wife's younger sister*

胰 yí ㄧˊ 胰腺，人和动物的腺体之一，能分泌胰液，帮助消化，还分泌一种激素（胰岛素），起调节糖类代谢作用。旧称"膵(cuì)脏"(former term for 膵脏) pancreas [胰子]肥皂 soap:香～～ *toilet soap; perfumed soap* | 药～～ *medicated soap*

痍 yí ㄧˊ 伤，创伤 wound; trauma:疮～满目（喻到处是灾祸景象）。*A scene of devastation meets the eye everywhere.*

沂 yí ㄧˊ 沂河，源出山东省，至江苏省入海 Yihe River, originating in Shandong Province and running through Jiangsu Province into the sea

诒 yí ㄧˊ 传给 to hand down; to leave behind:～训 *teaching of the deceased*

饴 yí ㄧˊ ❶糖浆，糖稀 maltose:甘之如～ *to enjoy (pain, grief or hardship) as if it were malt sugar* ❷饴糖，一种糖果 maltose; malt sugar:高粱～ *sorghum candy*

怡 yí ㄧˊ 和悦，愉快 happy; cheerful; joyful:心旷神～ *refreshing; pleasant; carefree and joyous; relaxed and happy* | ～然自得 *happy and contented*

贻 yí ㄧˊ ❶赠给 to present ❷遗留 to bequeath; to leave behind:～害 *to leave a legacy of trouble* | ～笑大方 *to make a laughing stock of oneself before experts; to incur the ridicule of experts*

眙 yí ㄧˊ 见 843 页"盱"字条"盱眙"(xū—) see 盱眙 on p843

迤(**迆) ㊁ yí ㄧˊ 见 779 页"逶"字条"逶迤"(wēi—) see 逶迤 on p779
㊀ yǐ 见 887 页 see p887

椸(**箷) yí ㄧˊ 衣架 coat hanger; clothes stand; clothes rack

宜 yí ㄧˊ ❶适合，适当 suitable; appropriate (㊟ ***doublet*** 适— appropriate):你做这样的工作很相～。*It's very suitable for you to do such work.* ❷应该，应当 should; ought to:不～如此。*It shouldn't be like this.* | 不～操之过急。*It shouldn't be done in haste.* ❸当然，无怪 of course; no wonder:～其无往而不利也！*No wonder they'll meet with suc-*

cess wherever they go.

扅 yí ㄧˊ 见 866 页"扊"字条"扊扅"(yǎn—) see 扊扅 on p866

移(*迻) yí ㄧˊ ❶挪动 to move; to remove; to shift (㊀ ***doublet*** 迁— to remove; to shift; to migrate):～植 *to transplant*|愚公～山 *The Foolish Old Man removed the mountains — dogged perseverance.*|转～阵地 *to shift position* [移录]抄录,过录 to copy [移译]翻译 to translate ❷改变,变动 to change; to alter:～风易俗 *to change prevailing habits and customs; to transform social traditions*|坚定不～ *unswerving; unflinching*

簃 yí ㄧˊ 楼阁旁边的小屋 small hut beside a storeyed building

宧 yí ㄧˊ 古代称屋子里的东北角 (in ancient China) northeastern corner of a room

颐 yí ㄧˊ ❶面颊,腮 cheek:解～(开颜而笑) *to smile* ❷休养,保养 to nourish; to recuperate:～神 *to nourish the spirit*|～养天年 *to take good care of oneself so as to enjoy one's natural span of life*

蛇 ㊁ yí ㄧˊ 见 779 页"委"字条"委蛇"(wēi—) see 委蛇 on p779

㊀ shé 见 662 页 see p662

遗 ㊀ yí ㄧˊ ❶丢失 to lose (㊀ ***doublet*** —失 to lose):～失钢笔一枝 *to have lost a pen* ❷漏掉 to omit; to leave out (㊀ ***doublet*** —漏 to omit):～忘 *to forget* ❸丢失的东西,漏掉的部分 sth lost; missing part:路不拾～。*No one pockets anything left on the road.*|补～ *addendum; supplement* ❹余,留 to leave behind:不～余力 *to spare no effort*|～憾 *regret; pity* 特指死人留下的 to bequeath:～嘱 *testament; will*|～像 *portrait* (or *photo*) *of the deceased* [遗传]生物体的构造和生理机能由上一代传给下一代 inheritance; heredity ❺不自觉地排泄粪便或精液 involuntary discharge of urine or semen:～尿 *enuresis*|～精 *nocturnal emission*

㊁ wèi 见 787 页 see p787

疑 yí ㄧˊ ❶不信,因不信而猜度(duó) to doubt; to disbelieve (㊀ ***doublet*** —惑 doubtful; perplexed; puzzled):可～ *suspicious*|半信半～ *half-believing and half-doubting; not quite convinced*|～不能决 *to be hesitant to decide*|你不必～心。*You needn't be suspicious.* ❷不能解决的,不能断定的 doubtful; uncertain:～问 *question; query*|～案 *disputed case; doubtful case*|～义 *doubt; doubtful point*|存～(对怀疑的问题暂不做决定) *to leave a question open*

嶷 yí ㄧˊ [九嶷]山名,在湖南省宁远 Jiuyi Mountain in Ningyuan, Hunan Province

彝(**彜) yí ㄧˊ ❶古代盛酒的器具。又古代宗庙常用的祭器的总称 ancient wine vessel; also general term for sacrificial utensils used in an ancient ancestral temple:～器 *sacrificial ware* | 鼎～*ancient Chinese vessel with three legs* ❷常,常规,法度 regular practice:～训 *regular doctrine* | ～宪 *constant constitution*

[彝族]我国少数民族,参看附表(see the appendix) the Yi ethnic group, one of the ethnic minorities of China

乙 yǐ ㄧˇ ❶天干的第二位 *yi*, 2nd of the 10 Heavenly Stems 用作顺序的第二 second ❷旧时乐谱记音符号的一个,相当于简谱的"7" *yi*, note in the traditional Chinese musical scale in former times, equal to 7 in numbered musical notation ❸画乙字形的符号,作用有二 two functions of the mark 乙: **1** 古时没有标点符号,遇有大的段落用墨笔勾一个∠符号,形似乙字 to separate long paragraphs since there were no punctuation marks in ancient China **2** 遇有颠倒、遗漏的文字用∠符号改正过来或把遗漏的字勾进去 to correct the inverted word order or to show where something is to be inserted in the sentence

钇 yǐ ㄧˇ 一种金属元素,符号Y,暗灰色,有金属光泽。可制特种玻璃和合金 yttrium (Y)

已 yǐ ㄧˇ ❶止,罢了 to stop; to cease; to end:学不可以～。*Live and learn.* | 如此而～。*That's what it all adds up to.* or *That's all.* ❷已经,已然,表过去 already:时间～过。*Time has already passed.* ❸后来,过了一会儿,不多时 thereafter; afterwards:～忽不见。*Well, it disappeared afterwards.* ❹太,过 too:其细～甚 *in great detail* ❺古同"以❸" same as 以❸ in ancient Chinese:～上 *above; more than* | ～下 *below; and less* | 自汉～后 *since the Han Dynasty*

以 yǐ ㄧˇ ❶介词 ***preposition*** **1** 用,拿,把,将 with; by:～少胜多 *to defeat the opponent superior in number* | 晓之～利害 *to warn somebody of the possible consequences* | ～身作则 *to set an example for others; to set a good example with one's own conduct* | ～理论为行动的指南 *to guide one's action with theory* | ～劳动为光荣 *to take pride in labour; to glory in labour* [以为]心里想,认为 to think; to believe; to consider:意～～未足。*It's not enough in my view.* | 我～～应该这样做。*I think it should be done this way.* **2** 依,顺,按照 according to:众人～次就座。*All the people sat down in order.* | ～时启闭 *to open and close according to schedule* **3** 因,由于 because of:不～失败

自馁,不～成功自满。*Never lose heart in failure nor feel conceited in success.* **4** 在,于(指时日)(of time) at; on:中华人民共和国～1949年10月1日宣告成立。*The People's Republic of China was proclaimed to be founded on October 1, 1949.* ❷连词 ***conjunction*** **1** 表示目的关系 in order to; so as to:大力发展生产,～提高人民生活水平。*Production is to be boosted greatly so as to improve the people's living standard.* **2** 表示并列关系,跟"而"用法相同 and; as well as:其责己也重～周,其待人也轻～约。*They were strict with themselves but lenient to others.* ❸放在方位词前表明时间、地位、方向或数量的界限(used before words of locality to denote the limit of time, place, direction or number):水平～上 *above the standard* | 五岭～南,古称百粤。*The area to the south of the Five Ridges was called* Baiyue *in ancient China.* | 十天～后交货。*Goods should be delivered in ten days.* | 三日～内完成任务。*The task is expected to be fulfilled within three days.*

苡 yǐ ㄧˇ 见893页"薏"字条"薏苡"(yì—) see 薏苡 on p893

尾 ㊁ yǐ ㄧˇ (一儿) ❶马尾(wěi)上的长毛 hairs on a horsetail:马～罗 *sieve with a fabric woven from horsetail hairs* ❷蟋蟀等尾部的针状物 spikelets on a cricket's tail:三～儿(雌蟋蟀) *three-spikelet cricket (female cricket)*

㊀ wěi 见783页 see p783

矣 yǐ ㄧˇ 文言助词 ***auxiliary in classical Chinese*** **1** 直陈语气,与"了㊁❷"相当(used in a declarative sentence with the same function as 了㊁❷):艰难险阻,备尝之～。*Nearly all the hardships and dangers have been experienced.* **2** 感叹语气(used in an exclamatory sentence):大～哉 *How great!* **3** 命令语气(used in an imperative sentence):往～,毋多言! *Go and don't say anything more!*

苢 yǐ ㄧˇ 见203页"芣"字条"芣苢"(fú—) see 芣苢 on p203

迤(**迆) ㊀ yǐ ㄧˇ ❶地势斜着延长 to extend obliquely ❷延伸,向(专指方向地位) to go (*or* extend) towards:天安门～东(向东一带) *to the east of Tian'an Men*

[迤逦](—lǐ) 曲折连绵 winding; tortuous; meandering:沿着蜿蜒的山势～～而行 *to meander along the winding mountain path*

㊁ yí 见884页 see p884

酏 yǐ ㄧˇ 酏剂,含有糖和挥发油或另含有主要药物的酒精溶液的制剂 elixir

蚁(蟻、**螘) yǐ ㄧˇ 蚂蚁,昆虫名。多在地下做窝成群住着,

种类很多 ant (*Formicidae*)

舣(艤、**檥) yǐ 停船靠岸 to pull a boat in to shore; to moor a boat on the shore

倚 yǐ ❶靠着 to lean on (*or* against); to rest on (*or* against): ～门 *to lean against the door* ❷仗恃 to rely on; to count on: ～势欺人 *to take advantage of one's or sb else's power to bully people* ❸偏,歪 biased; partial: 不偏不～ *impartial*

椅 ㊀ yǐ (—子)有靠背的坐具 chair

㊁ yī 见 883 页 see p883

旖 yǐ [旖旎] (—nǐ) 柔和美丽 charming and gentle; enchanting: 风光～～ *What an enchanting scenery!*

踦 yǐ 抵住 to prop up; to sustain

扆 yǐ 古代一种屏风 (in ancient China) a kind of screen

乂 yì 治理,安定 to administer; to govern; to stabilize

刈 yì 割 (草或谷类) to mow; to cut down: ～除杂草 *to root out weeds*

艾 ㊁ yì 治理 to govern; to bring under control [自怨自艾]本义是悔恨自己的错误,自己改正。现在只指悔恨 (original meaning) to be remorseful of one's mistakes and make self-correction; (now) full of repentance; remorseful; reproachful

㊀ ài 见 4 页 see p4

弋 yì 用带着绳子的箭来射鸟 to shoot a bird with a retrievable arrow with a string attached to it: ～凫与雁 *to shoot wild ducks and wild geese with retrievable arrows*

杙 yì 小木桩 small wood stake

亿(億) yì 数目,一万万。旧时也指十万 (a hundred thousand in former times) a hundred million

忆(憶) yì ❶回想,想念 to recall; to recollect: 回～ *to recall; to recollect* | ～苦思甜 *to recall past sorrow and savour present joys* | ～故人 *to think of an old friend* ❷记得 to remember: 记～力 *memory*

义(義) yì ❶公正合宜的道理或举动 justice; righteousness (㊟ ***doublet*** 正— justice; righteousness): 见～勇为 *to be ready to take up the cudgels for a just cause; to have the courage to do what is right* | ～不容辞 *duty-bound* ㊀ ***extension*** 指合乎正义或公益的 just; righteous: ～举 *righteous act undertaken for the public good; righteous deed* [义务] **1** 应尽的责任 duty; obligation **2** 不受报酬的 voluntary: ～～劳动 *voluntary labour* ❷感情的联系 feeling; friendly feeling or affection involved in human ties or relationship：朋友的情～*friendship* ❸意义，意思，人对事物认识到的内容 meaning；significance：定～*definition*｜字～*word meaning*｜歧～*ambiguity* ❹指认作亲属的 adoptive；adopted：～父 *adoptive father*；*foster father*｜～子 *adopted son*；*foster son* ㊀ ***extension*** 人工制造的（人体的部分）（of a certain part of the body）artificial；false：～齿（镶上的牙）*false tooth*；*denture*｜～肢（配上的上肢或下肢）*artificial limb*；*prosthesis*

议（議） yì ❶表明意见的言论 opinion；view（㊂ ***doublet*** 一论 comment）：提～*proposal*｜建～*suggestion*；*proposition*；*advice*｜无异～*no objection* ❷商议，讨论 to discuss：会～*meeting*；*conference*｜～定 *to decide after negotiation*；*to agree on*

艺（藝） yì ❶才能，技能 technique； skill（㊂ ***doublet*** 技一 skill；technique）：手～*craftsmanship*｜～高人胆大 *Boldness of execution stems from superb skill*.［艺术］**1** 用形象来反映现实但比现实更有典型性的社会意识形态，包括音乐、舞蹈、美术、雕塑、文学、曲艺、戏剧、电影等 art **2** 指富有创造性的方式、方法 skill；art；craft：领导～～*art of leadership* ❷限度 limit：贪贿无～*to be insatiably greedy for bribes*

呓（囈、**讛） yì 梦话 somniloquy：梦～*somniloquy*｜～语 *ravings*

仡 ㊁ yì［仡仡］❶强壮勇敢 strong and brave ❷高大 tall

㊀ gē 见 223 页 see p223

屹 yì 山势高耸 high and steep；lofty ㊃ ***figurative*** 坚定不可动摇 firm and unshakable：～立 *to stand erect*｜～然不动 *to stand firm and erect*

亦 yì 副词 ***adverb***，也（表示同样），也是 too；also；as well as：反之～然 *and vice versa*｜～步～趋（喻自己没有主张，跟着别人走）*to ape sb at every step — to imitate sb else in every move without one's own ideas*

弈 yì ❶古代称围棋 ancient name for *weiqi*，a game played with black and white pieces on a board of 361 intersections ❷下棋 to play chess：对～（*of two people*）*to play chess*

奕 yì ❶大 grand；great ❷美丽 beautiful［奕奕］精神焕发的样子 radiating power and vitality；radiant：神采～～*with glowing health and radiating vigour*

衣 ㊁ yì 穿 to wear；to clothe：～布衣 *to wear cotton clothes*｜解衣（yī）～我。*He doffed his own garment to clothe me*.

㊀ yī 见 882 页 see p882

裔 yì 丨 ❶后裔,后代子孙 descendants; posterity ❷边,边远的地方 distant land; remote region:四～*borderlands; frontiers*

异(*異) yì 丨 ❶不同的 different:没有～议 *no objection*|～口同声 *in one voice; in unison* ❷分开 to separate; to depart:离～*to divorce*|分居～爨(cuàn)(*of brothers*) *to divide up the family property to live apart and have separate kitchens* ❸另外的,别的 other; another:～日 *some other day; future days*|～地 *other place; foreign land* ❹特别的 extraordinary:～味 *peculiar smell; unusual odour*|奇才～能 *extraordinary talents and abilities* ❺奇怪 surprised:惊～*amazed*|深以为～*to be greatly surprised*

抑 yì 丨 ❶压,压制 to restrain; to repress; to curb; to suppress:～制 *to check; to curb; to repress*|～扬 *to rise and fall; to modulate*|～强扶弱 *to restrain the strong and support the weak* [抑郁]忧闷 depressed; gloomy; dejected ❷文言连词 ***conjunction in classical Chinese*** **1** 表选择,还是 or:求之欤,～与之欤? *To get it, or to offer it?* **2** 表转折,只是 but **3** 表递进,而且 moreover:非惟天时,～亦人谋也。*It's not only a matter of opportunity but also a matter of human efforts.*

邑 yì 丨 ❶都城,城市 town; city; metropolis:通都大～*large city; metropolis* ❷县 county

挹 yì 丨 ❶舀,把液体盛出来 to scoop up; to ladle out the liquid [挹注] ⑩ ***figurative*** 从有余的地方取出来,以补不足 to draw from one to make good the deficits of another ❷拉 to pull

浥 yì 丨 沾湿 to moisten

悒 yì 丨 愁闷,不安(叠 ***reduplication***) sad; worried:～～不乐 *depressed; gloomy*

佚 yì 丨 同"逸❷❸"same as 逸❷❸

泆 yì 丨 ❶放纵 indulgent ❷同"溢"same as 溢

轶 yì 丨 ❶超过 to excel:～群(比一般的强)(*better than the average people*) *to excel all others*|～材(突出的才干) *outstanding talent* ❷散失 lost:～事(史书没有记载的事)(*story that is not kept in history books*) *anecdote*

昳 ⊜ yì 丨 [昳丽]美丽 beautiful:形貌～～*beautiful; pretty*

⊖ dié 见150页 see p150

役 yì 丨 ❶战事 battle; campaign:淮海战～*Huaihai Campaign* ❷指需要出劳力的事 labour; service:劳～*forced labour; corvee* ❸服兵役 military service:现～*active service; active duty*|预备～*re-*

serve service; *reserve duty* ❹使唤 to work; to use (㊥ **doublet** 一使 to work; to use): 奴～*to enslave* ❺旧日称被役使的人(in former times) servant: 杂～*odd-job man*; *man doing odd-jobs*

疫 yì 丨 瘟疫,流行性急性传染病的总称(general term for epidemic diseases) pestilence: ～情 *epidemic situation* | 防～*epidemic prevention* | 鼠～*bubonic plague*

毅 yì 丨 果决,志向坚定而不动摇 resolute; steadfast: 刚～*resolute*; *steadfast* | ～力 *willpower* | ～然决然 *resolutely*; *determinedly*

译(譯) yì 丨 把一种语言文字依照原义改变成另一种语言文字 to translate; to interpret: 翻～*to translate* | ～文 *translated text*; *translation*

峄(嶧) yì 丨 峄县,旧县名,在山东省。1960年撤销,划归枣庄市 Yixian County, former county in Shandong Province, which was canceled and incorporated into Zaozhuang City in 1960

怿(懌) yì 丨 欢喜 pleased; happy

驿(驛) yì 丨 旧日传递政府文书的人中途休息的地方(in former times) post station and rest stop for those who delivered official documents: ～站 *courier station*; *post house*

绎(繹) yì 丨 寻究,理出头绪 to unravel; to sort out: 寻～*to unravel*; *to inquire into* | 演～*deduction*

易 yì 丨 ❶容易,不费力 easy: 通俗～懂 *easy to understand* | 轻而～举 *very easy*; *as easy as ABC* ❷平和 amiable: 平～近人 *amiable and easy of approach* ❸改变 to change: 移风～俗 *to change prevailing habits and customs*; *to transform social traditions* ❹交易,交换 to exchange: 以物～物 *to barter* ❺轻视 to despise ❻芟治草木 to clear away woods and weeds: ～其田畴 *to hoe up weeds in fields*

埸 yì 丨 ❶田界 field boundary ❷边境 boundary: 疆～*frontier*; *border*

蜴 yì 丨 见801页"蜥"字条"蜥蜴"(xī—) see 蜥蜴 on p801

佾 yì 丨 古时乐舞的行列(in ancient China) dancing troupe

诣 yì 丨 到。特指到尊长那里去(to pay a visit to a respectable elder person) to go to: ～前请教 *to call on sb for advice* [造诣]学问或技术所达到的程度 attainments: 他对于医学～～很深。*He has great attainments in medicine*.

猘 yì 丨 [林猘]就是猞猁(shēlì)(i.e. 猞猁) lynx

羿 yì 丨 后羿,传说是夏代有穷国的君主,善于射箭 Hou Yi, legendary king and

master archer of the Youqiong State in the Xia Dynasty

翊 yì 丨 辅佐,帮助 to assist: ～戴(辅佐拥戴) *to assist and support*

翌 yì 丨 明天,明年 next day; next year: ～日 *next day* | ～年 *next year* | ～晨 *next morning*

翳 yì 丨 ❶遮盖 to screen; to conceal: 树林荫～ *shaded by dense foliage* ❷(一子)眼角膜上所生障蔽视线的白斑 slight corneal opacity; nebula

翼 yì 丨 ❶翅膀或像翅膀的东西 wing; wing-shaped thing: 鸟～ *bird's wings* | 蝉～ *cicada's wings* | 机～ *wings of an airplane* ❷左右两侧中的一侧 flank: 侧～ *flank* | 左～ *left flank* | 右～ *right flank* ❸帮助,辅佐 to aid; to assist ❹星宿名,二十八宿之一 *yi*, the 27th of the 28 constellations

益 yì 丨 ❶增加 to increase: 进～ *progress; improvement* | 延年～寿 *to prolong one's life* ❷利,有好处的 benefit; profit (㊀ **doublet** 利一 benefit): ～处 *advantage; benefit* | ～虫 *beneficial insect* | 良师～友 *good teacher and helpful friend* ❸更 all the more; even more: 日～壮大 *to be (getting) stronger day by day* | 多多～善。*The more, the better.*

嗌 ㊁ yì 丨 咽喉 throat
㊀ ài 见5页 see p5

溢 yì 丨 ❶充满而流出来 to overflow; to spill; to brim over: 河水四～。*The river overflowed (its bank).* | ～美(喻过分夸奖) *exaggerated praise; excessive praise* ㊊ ***extension*** 超出 to exceed: ～出此数 *to exceed the number* ❷古同"镒" same as 镒 in ancient Chinese

缢 yì 丨 用绳子勒死 to strangle; to hang: ～杀 *to strangle to death* | 自～ *to hang oneself*

镒 yì 丨 古代重量单位,合古代的二十两,一说是二十四两 *yi*, ancient measurement of weight, equal to 20 or 24 traditional taels

鹢 yì 丨 ❶水鸟名 *yi*, name of an aquatic bird ❷船头画有鹢的船,后泛指船 ship with an image of a *yi* on the bow, later generally used to denote boats

螠 yì 丨 无脊椎动物,雌雄异体,身体呈圆筒状,不分节,有少数刚毛,生活在海底泥沙中 echiuroid

谊 yì 丨 交情 friendship: 友～ *friendship* | 深情厚～ *profound friendship*

勚 yì 丨 ❶劳苦 toil ❷器物逐渐磨损,失去棱角、锋芒等 worn; dull; blunt: 螺丝扣～了。*The thread of the screw was worn.*

逸 yì 丨 ❶跑,逃跑 to escape; to flee ❷散失 lost (㊀ **doublet** 亡一 lost): ～书(已经散失的古书) *ancient books no longer extant* ❸安闲,安乐

leisure; ease ([连] ***doublet*** 安—leisure): 不能一劳永～。*We can't get it done once and for all.* | 劳～结合 *to alternate work with rest and recreation* ❹超过一般 to excel: ～群绝伦 *to excel all others*

意 yì ❶意思,心思 meaning; idea; thought: 来～ *purpose in coming* | 词不达～。*The words fail to convey the meaning.* [意见]见解,对事物的看法 view; opinion ❷心愿,愿望 wish; desire: 中(zhòng)～*to one's taste; to one's liking* | 任～*at will; at random* | 好～ *kindness; good intention* ❸料想 to expect; to anticipate: ～外 *unexpected; unforeseen* | 出其不～*to take sb by surprise; to catch sb unawares*

薏 yì [薏苡](-yǐ) 多年生草本植物,茎叶略似高粱,果实椭圆形,坚硬而光滑,种仁白色,叫薏仁米,可以吃,又可入药 Job's tears; tear grass (*Coix lacryma-jobi*)

臆(**肊) yì ❶胸 chest: 胸～(心里的话或想法) *thoughts or feelings deep in one's heart* ❷主观的,缺乏客观证据的 subjective: ～见 *subjective view* | ～说 *assumption; supposition* | ～造 *to fabricate; to concoct; to invent* | ～测 *to surmise; to conjecture; to guess* | ～断 *to assume; to speculate*

镱 yì 一种金属元素,符号Yb,银白色,质软。用来制特种合金,也用作激光材料等 ytterbium (Yb)

癔 yì [癔病]一种神经官能症,患者发病时喜怒无常,感觉过敏,严重时手足或全身痉挛,说胡话,可出现似昏迷状态。此病多由心理上剧烈的矛盾所引起。也叫"歇斯底里"(also called 歇斯底里) hysteria

肄 yì 学习 to study: ～业(指没有毕业或尚未毕业) (*used to denote one having not finished his education or having not graduated*) *to study in school or at college*

埶 yì 种植 to grow: 树～五谷 *to cultivate all food crops* | ～菊 *to grow chrysanthemums*

廙 yì 恭敬 respect; reverence

瘗(瘞) yì 掩埋,埋葬 to bury

鹝 yì 古书中说的一种水鸟 (in ancient Chinese texts) legendary aquatic bird

熠 yì 光耀,鲜明(叠 ***reduplication***) brilliant; bright: 光彩～～*brilliant splendour*

殪 yì ❶死 to die; to perish ❷杀死 to kill

懿 yì 美,好(多指德、行) virtuous; exemplary: ～行 *exemplary conduct* | ～德 *moral excellence; admirable virtue*

劓 yì 古代的一种割掉鼻子的酷刑(in ancient China) savage punishment of cutting off the nose

Y

燚 yì ㄧˋ 人名用字 yi, used in a given name

YIN ㄧㄣ

因 yīn ㄧㄣ ❶原因,缘故,事物发生前已具备的条件 cause; reason:事出有～。*There's good reason for it.* or *It's by no means accidental.* | 内～ *internal factor; internal cause* | 外～ *external factor; external cause* ❷介词 ***preposition***,因为,由于 on account of; because of; as a result of:会议～故改期。*The meeting has been put off for some reason.* | ～病缺席 *to be absent on sick leave* ❸连词 ***conjunction***,连接分句,表示因果关系 because; since; as; for:～雾气太重,高速路暂时关闭。*The expressway is blocked off temporarily because the fog is too heavy.* [因为]连词 ***conjunction***,表示因果关系 because:～～今天下雨,我没有出门。*I stayed indoors because it rained today.* ❹沿袭 to follow (㊥ ***doublet*** — 袭 to follow):陈陈相～*to follow a set routine* [因循] **1** 守旧,不改变 to follow the old routine:～～守旧 *to follow the beaten track; to follow the old routine* | ～～成规 *to follow the established practice* **2** 拖沓(tà) to procrastinate:～～误事 *to procrastinate until it's too late* ❺凭借,根据 in accordance with:～势利导 *to guide action adroitly according to circumstances* | ～陋就简 *to make do with whatever is available* | ～地制宜 *to suit measures to local conditions*

茵 yīn ㄧㄣ 古代车子上的席、垫 mattress or cushion in ancient carriages ㊀ ***extension*** 铺(pū)的东西 mattress:～褥 *mattress* | 绿草如～。*Green grass looks like a velvet carpet.*

洇 yīn ㄧㄣ 液体接触纸张等向周围渗透散开(of liquid) to spread and sink in (on paper):这种纸写起来有些～。*Ink runs on this paper.*

姻(*婣) yīn ㄧㄣ ❶婚姻 marriage:联～*to form a matrimonial alliance; to be related by marriage* | ～缘 *predestined marriage* ❷姻亲,由婚姻关系而结成的亲戚。古代专指婿家(family of son-in-law in ancient China) affinity; relation by marriage

骃 yīn ㄧㄣ 浅黑带白色的杂毛马 horse with light-black and white hairs

氤 yīn ㄧㄣ [氤氲](—yūn)烟云弥漫(of smoke, mist, etc) dense; thick; enshrouding

铟 yīn ㄧㄣ 一种金属元素,符号 In,银白色,能拉成细丝。可做低熔点的合金 indium (In)

裀 yīn ㄧㄣ ❶夹衣服 lined clothes ❷垫子,褥子 mattress; cotton-padded mattress

阴(陰、*隂) yīn ㄧㄣ ❶黑暗 dark ❷云彩遮住太阳或月、星 cloudy; overcast:天～了。*It's a bit cloudy.* ❸跟"阳"相对(the opposite of 阳) **1** 阴性,女性的 negative; feminine **2** 太阴,月亮 moon:～历 *lunar calendar* **3** 带负电的 negative:～电 *negative electricity*｜～极 *cathode; negative electrode* **4** 水的南面,山的北面(多用于地名)(*yin*, usually used in a place name) south of a river or north of a hill:江～(地名,在江苏省长江之南) *Jiangyin, a place south of the Changjiang* (or *Yangtze*) *River in Jiangsu Province*｜蒙～(地名,在山东省蒙山之北) *Mengyin, a place north of Mengshan in Shandong Province* **5** 暗,不露出来的 hidden; covert:～沟 *sewer; culvert* **6** 凹下的 in intaglio:～文图章 *seal in intaglio; intaglio seal* **7** 关于人死后的或鬼魂的(迷信)(superstition) of the nether world or of ghosts:～宅 *graveyard; tomb*｜～间 *nether world; Hades* ❹(—儿)光线被东西遮住所成的影 shade:树～儿 *tree shade*｜背～ *in the shade* ❺背面 backside:碑～ *the back of a stone tablet* ❻诡诈,不光明 sinister; treacherous:～谋诡计 *conspiracy; schemes and intrigues* [阴险]表面和善而内心险恶 insidious; sinister; treacherous ❼生殖器 private parts

音 yīn ㄧㄣ ❶声 sound (㊀ ***doublet*** 声— sound):口～ *accent*｜扩～器 *loudspeaker* ❷消息 news:佳～ *good news*｜～信 *message; mail; news*

喑(*瘖) yīn ㄧㄣ ❶哑,不能说话 mute; dumb:～哑 *mute; dumb* ❷沉默不语,又指动物不鸣叫 silent; mute:～默 *silent*｜万马齐～。*Ten thousand horses stand mute.* or *All fall mute.*

愔 yīn ㄧㄣ [愔愔] **1** 形容安静和悦 tranquil and harmonious **2** 形容沉默寡言 reticent; reserved

殷(❷*慇) ㊀ yīn ㄧㄣ ❶深厚,丰盛 abundant; rich:情意甚～ *to show great affection*｜～切的期望 *ardent expectations* [殷实]富足,富裕 substantial; well-to-do; well-off:家道～～ *well-off family* ❷[殷勤]周到,尽心 solicitous:做事很～～ *to be very attentive in one's job*｜～～招待 *to entertain solicitously; to show solicitous hospitality* ❸殷朝,商朝的后期,由盘庚起称殷(公元前1300—公元前1046年) Yin Dynasty, the latter part of the Shang Dynasty, starting from Pan Geng (1300BC—1046BC) ❹姓 Yin, a surname

㊁ yān 见 862 页 see p862

溵 yīn ㄧㄣ [溵溜](—liù)地名,在天津市蓟县 Yinliu, a place in Jixian County, Tianjin

Y

堙（*陻） yīn ㄧㄣ ❶堵塞 to block up ❷土山 mound

闉 yīn ㄧㄣ ❶古代城门外的曲城（in ancient China）enclosure for defence outside a city gate ❷堵塞 to block up

湮 ㊁ yīn ㄧㄣ 同"洇"same as 洇

㊀ yān 见 862 页 see p862

禋 yīn ㄧㄣ ❶古祭祀名，指祭天 name of an ancient ceremony of offering sacrifices to Heaven ❷泛指祭祀 offering sacrifices to deities or ancestors

吟（*唫） yín ㄧㄣˊ ❶唱，声调抑扬地念 to chant; to recite：～诗 *to recite a poem; to chant a poem* ❷诗歌的一种 song, a type of classical poetry：梁甫～*Song of Liang Fu* ❸呻吟，叹息 to groan; to moan

垠 yín ㄧㄣˊ 边，岸，界限 boundary; limit：一望无～的麦田 *a boundless stretch of wheat field*

银 yín ㄧㄣˊ ❶一种金属元素，符号 Ag，白色有光泽。质柔软，富延展性，是热和电的良导体，在空气中不易氧化。可以制货币、器皿、电器设备、感光材料等 argentum (Ag) ❷（一子）旧时用银铸成块的一种货币（in former times）silver-ingot currency［银行］办理存款、放款、汇兑等业务的机构 bank ❸像银的颜色 silver-coloured：～白色 *silvery white*｜～燕（喻白色的飞机）*silver swallow — silvery-white plane*｜～河（天河）*Milky Way; Galaxy*

龈 ㊀ yín ㄧㄣˊ 牙龈，牙床子，牙根上的肉 gum

㊁ kěn 见 393 页 see p393

狺 yín ㄧㄣˊ［狺狺］狗叫的声音 yap; bark

訚 yín ㄧㄣˊ（叠 ***reduplication***）和颜悦色地进行辩论 to argue genially

崟（**崯） yín ㄧㄣˊ 见 606 页"嵚"字条"嵚崟"（qīn—）see 嵚崟 on p606

淫（❷*婬） yín ㄧㄣˊ ❶过多，过甚 excessive; extreme：～威 *abuse of power; despotic power*｜～雨 *excessive rain* ❷在男女关系上态度或行为不正当的 licentious ❸放纵 wanton; lecherous：骄奢～逸 *extravagant and dissipated* ❹迷惑，使昏乱 confused：富贵不能～*to be immune to the temptation of wealth and high rank; not to be corrupted by power and riches*

霪 yín ㄧㄣˊ［霪雨］连绵不断下得过量的雨。现作"淫雨"（now written as 淫雨）excessive and continuous rain

寅 yín ㄧㄣˊ ❶地支的第三位 *yin*, the 3rd of the 12 Earthly Branches ❷寅时，指夜里三点到五点 the period from 3am to 5am

夤 yín ㄧㄣˊ ❶深 deep：～夜 *in the depth of night; at the dead of night* ❷恭敬 respect; reverence

[夤缘]攀缘上升 to climb up 喻 *figurative* 拉拢关系，向上巴结 to curry favour with

龂 yín ㄧㄣˊ ❶同"龈"(yín) same as 龈 ❷(叠 *reduplication*)争辩的样子 arguing

鄞 yín ㄧㄣˊ 鄞州，在浙江省宁波 Yinzhou, a place in Ningbo, Zhejiang Province

蟫 yín ㄧㄣˊ 古书上指衣鱼，一种咬衣服、书籍的小虫。也叫"蠹鱼"(also called 蠹鱼)(in ancient Chinese texts) silverfish

嚚 yín ㄧㄣˊ ❶愚蠢而顽固 stupid and stubborn ❷奸诈 fraudulent; crafty

尹 yǐn ㄧㄣˇ 旧时官名 ancient official title: 令～ *county magistrate* | 府～ *prefectural magistrate* | 道～ *provincial magistrate*

引 yǐn ㄧㄣˇ ❶领，招来 to lead; to guide; to draw (连 *doublet* 一导 to lead; to guide): ～路 *to guide; to lead the way* | ～火 *to ignite; to light* | 抛砖～玉 *to cast a brick in order to get a jade — to give a few commonplace remarks by way of introduction so that others may come up with valuable opinions; to break the ice* 引 *extension* 古时文体名，跟"序"差不多 ancient literary style, similar to 序 (introduction) [引子](—zi) **1** 乐曲、戏剧开始的一段 prelude; introduction **2** 中医称主药以外的副药 added ingredient to enhance the efficacy of a dose of herbal medicine in traditional Chinese medicine: 这剂药用姜做～～。*Ginger is an added ingredient to the medicine.* ❷拉，伸 to pull; to stretch: ～弓 *to draw a bow* | ～领(伸脖子) *to crane one's neck; to stretch one's neck* [引申]字、词由原义产生他义 to extend the meaning of a word or a phrase ❸用来做证据、凭借或理由 to quote; to cite: ～书 *to cite from a book* | ～证 *to cite as evidence* | ～以为荣 *to regard as an honour* ❹诱发，惹 to cause; to induce: 一句俏皮话，～得大家哄堂大笑。*His witty remark gave rise to a burst of laughter.* ❺退却 to leave: ～退 *to resign; to quit office* | ～避 *to resign one's position to avoid suspicion or implicity* ❻市制长度单位，1引是10丈 *yin*, a traditional unit of length, where one *yin* equals ten *zhang* ❼古代柩车的绳索 ropes or cords on ancient hearse: 发～(出殡) *to start a funeral procession*

吲 yǐn ㄧㄣˇ [吲哚](—duǒ)有机化合物，分子式 C_8H_7N，无色或淡黄色，片状结晶，溶于热水、醇、醚。供制香料和化学试剂 indole

蚓 yǐn ㄧㄣˇ 指蚯(qiū)蚓 earthworm (*Pheretima*) 参看614页"蚯"字条"蚯蚓"see 蚯蚓 on p614

饮 ㊀ yǐn ㄧㄣˇ ❶喝 to drink: ～水思源 *Think of the*

source when drinking water — *to bear in mind the source of one's happiness; never to forget where one's happiness comes from* ❷可喝的东西 drink; beverage; anything to drink:冷～*cold drink* ❸含忍 to harbour:～恨 *to harbour a grievance; to nurse a grievance*

㊁ yìn 见 898 页 see p898

隐(隱) yǐn ㄧㄣˇ ❶藏匿,不显露 to screen; to hide(㊇ **doublet** 一藏 to hide; to conceal):～蔽 *to take cover; to take shelter*|～痛 *secret anguish*|～患 *hidden trouble; hidden danger* ❷指隐秘的事 secret; privacy:难言之～*something embarrassing to mention; skeleton in the cupboard*

瘾(癮) yǐn ㄧㄣˇ 特别深的嗜好(shìhào) addiction:烟～*addiction to tobacco* or *smoking*|看书看上～啦 *to be particularly fond of reading; to become addicted to reading*

绾 yǐn ㄧㄣˇ 〈方 **dialect**〉绗(háng) to sew with long stitches; to baste:～棉袄 *to sew the cotton-padded clothes with long stitches*|中间～一行 *to sew with long stitches in the middle*

印 yìn ㄧㄣˋ ❶图章,戳记 seal; stamp:盖～*to affix a seal; to stamp a seal*|钢～*steel seal; embossing seal*|～信 *official seal*|～把(bà)子(也比喻政权) *seal of authority* — *power* ❷(一子、一儿)痕迹 trace; mark; vestige:脚～儿 *footprint*|烙～*brand* ❸留下痕迹。特指把文字或图画等留在纸上或器物上(especially characters or pictures left on the paper or wares) to leave marks; to print:～书 *to print books*|翻～*to reprint*|排～*to typeset and print* [印刷]把文字图画等制成版,加油墨印在纸上,可以连续印出很多的复制品。印刷术是我国古代四大发明之一 printing, one of the four great inventions of ancient China [印象]外界事物反映在头脑中所留下的形象 impression ❹合 to tally; to conform:～证(互相证明) *to confirm; to corroborate; to verify*|心心相～*to be kindred spirits; to have mutual affinity*

茚 yìn ㄧㄣˋ 有机化合物,分子式C_9H_8,无色液体,容易产生聚合反应。是制造合成树脂的原料 indene

鮣 yìn ㄧㄣˋ 鮣鱼,鱼名。身体细长,圆柱形,头小,前半身扁平,背上有吸盘,可以吸在大鱼或船底上。生活在海洋中,肉可以吃 remora; sharksucker; suckerfish (*Echeneidae*)

饮 ㊁ yìn ㄧㄣˋ 给牲畜水喝 to water (an animal):～马 *to water a horse*|～牛 *to water a cow*

㊀ yǐn 见 897 页 see p897

荫(蔭、❷❸*廕) yìn ㄧㄣˋ ❶不见日光,又凉又潮 sunless; dank; damp and chilly:这屋子很～。

The room is too damp and chilly. ❷封建时代帝王给功臣的子孙读书或做官的特权 official rank or privilege of education granted by an emperor to sb as a recognition of the meritorious service of his ancestors：封妻～子（*of an emperor*）*to confer titles of honour on an official's wife and hereditary ranks on his descendants.* ❸保佑，庇护 to shelter；to protect

胤 yìn ㄧㄣˋ 后代 offspring；posterity；descendant

窨 ㊀ yìn ㄧㄣˋ 地窨子，地下室 cell；cellar；basement

㊁ xūn 见 854 页 see p854

憖（憗） yìn ㄧㄣˋ〈古 ***archaism***〉❶宁愿 prefer；would rather ❷损伤 to injure；to hurt

［憖憖］谨慎的样子 cautious；circumspect

YING ㄧㄥ

应（應） ㊀ yīng ㄧㄥ ❶该，当 should；ought to（㊟ ***doublet*** —当 should；ought to｜—该 should；ought to）：～有尽有 *to have everything one expects to find* ❷答应，应承 to answer；to respond；to promise（㊟ ***doublet*** —许 to agree；to promise｜—允 to assent；to consent；to approve）：我喊他喊不～。*I called him，but he gave no response.*｜～他十天之内完工 *to promise him to finish the work within ten days* ❸姓 Ying，a surname

㊁ yìng 见 902 页 see p902

英 yīng ㄧㄥ ❶花 flower；blossom：落～ *fallen petals* ❷才能出众 outstanding；prominent：～俊 *eminently talented；handsome* 又指才能出众的人 outstanding person：群～大会 *gathering of heroes*

［英明］有远见卓识 wise；brilliant ［英雄］**1** 为人民利益英勇斗争而有功绩的人 hero **2** 英武过人的人 hero ❸指英国 Britain

瑛 yīng ㄧㄥ ❶似玉的美石 jade-like stone ❷玉的光彩 luster of jade

莺（鶯、*鸎） yīng ㄧㄥ 鸟名。身体小，褐色，嘴短而尖，叫的声音清脆。吃昆虫，是益鸟 warbler（*Acanthizinae*）［黄莺］即黄鹂（lí） oriole（*Oriolus*）

婴 yīng ㄧㄥ ❶婴儿，才生下来的小孩ル infant；new-born baby ❷触，缠绕 to harass；to entangle：～疾（得病）*to contract a disease；to fall ill*

撄 yīng ㄧㄥ ❶接触，触犯 to offend；to irritate：～其锋 *to blunt the thrust*｜～怒 *to incur sb's displeasure* ❷扰乱，纠缠 to ruffle；to harass

嘤 yīng ㄧㄥ 拟声词 ***onomatopoeia***，鸟叫的声音（叠 ***reduplication***）chirp；trill

缨 yīng ㄧㄥ ❶（—子、—ル）用线、绳等做的装饰品 tassel：帽～子 *cap tassels*｜红～枪

red-tasselled spear ❷（～子、～儿）像缨的东西 tassel-shaped thing：萝卜～子 *radish leaves*｜芥菜～儿 *mustard leaves* ❸带子，绳子 ribbon；rope：长～ *long ribbon*

璎 yīng 丨ㄥ 似玉的美石 jade-like stone［璎珞］（－luò）古代一种用珠玉穿成的戴在颈项上的装饰品 ancient pearl and jade necklace

樱 yīng 丨ㄥ 樱花，落叶乔木，开鲜艳的淡红花。木材坚硬致密，可做器具 oriental cherry（*Prunus serrulata*）［樱桃］樱桃树，樱的变种，开淡红或白色的小花。果实也叫樱桃，成熟时为红色，可以吃 cherry（*Prunus*）

鹦 yīng 丨ㄥ ［鹦鹉］（－wǔ）鸟名，也叫"鹦哥"。羽毛颜色美丽，嘴弯似鹰，舌圆而柔软，能模仿人说话的声音。产在热带、亚热带（also called 鹦哥）parrot（*Psittaciformes*）

罂（*甖） yīng 丨ㄥ 大腹小口的瓶子 small-mouthed and big-bellied container；jar［罂粟］二年生草本植物，花有红、紫、白等色。果实球形，未成熟时有白浆，是制鸦片的原料 opium poppy（*Papaver somniferum*）

膺 yīng 丨ㄥ ❶胸 breast；chest：义愤填～ *to be filled with righteous indignation* ❷承受，当 to bear；to take：～选 *to be elected；to be selected*｜荣～劳动英雄称号 *to be honoured with the title of labour hero* ❸伐，打击 to crusade；to smite：～惩 *to send a punitive expedition against*

鹰 yīng 丨ㄥ 鸟名。嘴弯曲而锐，四趾有钩爪。性猛，食肉。种类很多，常见的有苍鹰、鸢（yuān）等 eagle；hawk（*Accipitridae*）

迎 yíng 丨ㄥˊ ❶迎接，接 to meet；to receive：欢～ *to welcome；to greet*［迎合］为了讨好，使自己的言行符合别人的心意 to cater to；to pander to ❷向着 towards；against：～面 *head-on；in one's face；directly*｜～头赶上 *to try hard to catch up（with sb）*.

茔（塋） yíng 丨ㄥˊ 坟墓，坟地 tomb；grave：～地 *graveyard；cemetery*

荥（滎） ㊁ yíng 丨ㄥˊ ［荥经］地名，在四川省 Yingjing，a place in Sichuan Province

㊀ xíng 见 837 页 see p837

荧（熒） yíng 丨ㄥˊ ❶微弱的光亮 glimmering；shimmering［荧光］物理学上称某些物质受光或其他射线照射时所发出的可见光 fluorescence：～～屏 *fluorescent screen；screen*｜～～灯 *fluorescent lamp* ❷眼光迷乱 dazzled［荧惑］迷惑 to bewilder；to perplex

莹（瑩） yíng 丨ㄥˊ ❶光洁像玉的石头 bright and smooth jade-like stone ❷光洁，透明 lustrous and transparent：晶～ *sparkling and*

crystal-clear

萤(螢) yíng ㄧㄥˊ 萤火虫，一种能发光的昆虫，黄褐色，尾部有发光器 firefly (*Luciola terminalis*); glowworm; *lightning bug Lampyridae*

营(營) yíng ㄧㄥˊ ❶军队驻扎的地方 camp; barracks：军～*military camp*; *barracks*|安～扎寨 *to encamp*|露(lù)～*to camp (out)*; *to bivouac* ❷军队的编制单位，是连的上一级 battalion ❸筹划管理 to run; to operate (㊟ **doublet** 经～ to run; to manage)：～业 *to do business*|～造防风林 *to plant windbreak forests* ❹谋求 to seek; to strive for：～生 *to earn a living*; *to make a living*|～救 *to rescue*; *to save* [营养] 1 生物由食物内吸取养料或通过光合作用制造养料供养身体 nutrition; nourishment 2 养分，养料 nutrient：番茄、豆腐富于～～。*Tomatoes and tofu are rich in nutrients*.

萦(縈) yíng ㄧㄥˊ 缠绕 to entangle：～怀(挂心) *to occupy one's mind*; *to linger in one's mind*|琐事～身 *to be preoccupied with trivialities*

滢(瀠) yíng ㄧㄥˊ [滢湾]地名，在湖南省长沙 Yingwan, a place in Changsha, Hunan Province

蓥(鎣) yíng ㄧㄥˊ [华蓥]山名，在四川省东南和重庆市交界处 Huaying Mountain, located between the southeast part of Sichuan Province and Chongqing City

滢(瀅) yíng ㄧㄥˊ 清澈 crystal-clear

瑩(瑩) yíng ㄧㄥˊ 用于人名 ying, used in a given name

潆(瀠) yíng ㄧㄥˊ [潆洄]水流回旋 swirling

盈 yíng ㄧㄥˊ ❶充满 to be filled with：恶贯满～*to be replete with vices*; *to face retribution for a life of crime*|热泪～眶 *one's eyes brimming with tears* ❷多余 surplus (㊟ **doublet** —余 surplus)：～利 *profit*

楹 yíng ㄧㄥˊ ❶堂屋前部的柱子 principal pillar or column of a hall：～联 *couplet written on scrolls and hung on the pillars of a hall* ❷量词 **quantifier**，旧时房屋一间叫一楹 *ying*, a unit of measurement for rooms in former times and one room is counted as one *ying*

蝇(蠅) yíng ㄧㄥˊ (—子)苍蝇，幼虫叫蛆。能传染痢疾等疾病，害处很大 fly; housefly(*Musca domestica*)

嬴 yíng ㄧㄥˊ 姓 Ying, a surname

瀛 yíng ㄧㄥˊ 大海 sea; ocean：～寰(五洲四海) *the whole world*

籝(**籯) yíng ㄧㄥˊ ❶箱笼之类的器具

container such as a box or basket ❷筷笼子 chopstick container

赢 yíng ㄧㄥˊ ❶余利,赚钱 to make profit; to make money ❷胜 to win; to beat; to defeat:那个篮球队～了。*That basketball team won the game.*|～了三个球 *to win by three goals* ㊀ ***extension*** 因成功获得 to gain on account of success: ～得全场欢呼喝(hè)彩 *to win the acclamation of the whole audience*

郢 yǐng ㄧㄥˇ 郢都,楚国的都城,在今湖北省荆州 Yingdu, capital of the Chu State of the Warring States Period, located in today's Jingzhou, Hubei Province

颍 yǐng ㄧㄥˇ 颍河,发源于河南省登封,东南流至安徽省注入淮河 Yinghe River, originating from Dengfeng, Henan Province, and running southeastward through Anhui Province into the Huaihe River

颖 yǐng ㄧㄥˇ ❶禾的末端。植物学上指某些禾本科植物小穗基部的苞片 glume ❷东西末端的尖锐部分 tip; point:短～羊毫笔 *short-tipped writing brush*|锥处囊中,～脱而出 *The point of an awl in a bag will stick out through it.* ㊃ ***figurative*** 才能出众 outstanding:聪～ *clever*|～悟 *clever; bright* [新颖]新奇,与一般的不同 novel; original:花样～～*novel pattern (or design)*

影 yǐng ㄧㄥˇ ❶(一子、一儿)物体挡住光线时所形成的四周有光中间无光的形象 shadow ㊃ ***figurative*** 不真切的形象或印象 indistinct image; vague impression; vague memory:这件事在我脑子里没有一点～子了。*I have not the slightest idea of it.* [影壁]门内或门外作为遮挡视线或装饰用的短墙 screen wall [影响]一件事物对其他事物发生作用,也指所发生的作用 influence; affect; effect ❷描摹 to trace; to copy: ～宋本 *facsimile edition of a Song-Dynasty text* ❸形象,图像 image; picture:摄～*to photograph; to take pictures*|造～ *radiography*|留～ *to have a picture taken (as a memento)*|剪～ *papercut silhouette* [影印]用照相方法制版印刷 photolithoprint; photomechanical; photo-offset ❹指电影 motion picture; movie; film:～评 *film review; theatre review*

瘿 yǐng ㄧㄥˇ ❶生在脖子上的一种囊状的瘤子。多指甲状腺肿 goitre ❷虫瘿的简称,受害虫侵害植物组织发生变化而形成的瘤状物(short for 虫瘿) gall

应(應) ㊀ yìng ㄧㄥˋ ❶回答或随声相和 to answer; to respond; to echo:～声虫 *yes-man; echo*|山鸣谷～。*A sound produced at the mountaintop echoes in the deep valley —(of people) to find each other very congenial.*|呼～*to*

echo [反应] 1 化学上指物质发生化学变化,产生性质和成分与原来不同的新物质。也叫"化学反应"(also called 化学反应)(in chemistry) reaction 2 人及动植物有机体受到刺激而发生的活动和变化(of human organism and other living things) reaction 3 回响,反响 response; reaction ❷应付,对待 to deal with; to cope with: ~战 *to meet an enemy attack; to accept the challenge*|随机~变 *to play to the score; flexible*|~接不暇(*of scenes*) *to be more than one's eye's can take in — to have more visitors or business than one can attend to; to have one's hand full all the time* [供应]供给 to supply; to provide; to furnish ❸适合,配合 to suit (㊣ ***doublet*** 适— to suit): ~时 *seasonal; at a fixed time; at once*|得心~手 *serviceable; handy; to have everything under one's perfect control* ❹接受,答应 to accept; to agree: ~承 *to consent; to agree; to promise*|~征 *to be recruited; to be enlisted*|~邀 *on invitation to; at sb's invitation*|有求必~ *to respond to every plea; to grant whatever is requested*

㊀ yīng 见 899 页 see p899

映 yìng 动 照射而显出 to reflect; to mirror: 影子倒~在水里。*The shadow is mirrored in the water.*|放~电影 *to show a film*|夕阳把湖水~得通红。*The lake is crimsoned in the sunset.* [反映]反照 to reflect; to mirror ㊞ ***extension*** 1 把客观事物的实质表现出来 to reflect; to mirror: 文艺作品要~~现实生活。*Literature and art should reflect real life.* 2 向上级转达 to report; to make known: 及时~~群众的意见 *to report the view of the masses promptly*

硬 yìng 形 ❶物体组织紧密,性质坚固,跟"软"相对(the opposite of 软) hard; stiff: ~煤 *hard coal; anthracite*|~木 *hard wood* [硬件] 1 构成计算机的各个元件、部件和固定装置。是计算机系统的组成部分 hardware 2 借指生产、科研、经营等过程中的机器设备、物质材料等 mechanical equipment, material, etc ❷刚强有力 strong: 欺软怕~ *to bully the weak and fear the strong* ㊞ ***extension*** 1 坚强,不屈服 firm; unyielding (㊣ ***doublet*** 强— firm): ~汉子 *tough guy*|态度很~ *with a stiff attitude* 2 强横(hèng) forcibly; with effort: ~抢 *to take away by force*|生拉~拽 *to drag sb along against his will; far-fetched* ❸固执(多指不顾实际的) obstinately: ~不承认 *to deny obstinately*|他干(gàn)不了~干(gàn)。*He insisted on doing it in spite of his incapability.* ❹能力强,质量好 able (person); good (quality): ~手 *good hand; skilled hand*|货~

goods of high quality ❺勉强 to manage to do：这苦日子，他～熬过来了。*He barely managed to survive the hard times.*

媵 yìng ㄧㄥˋ〈古 ***archaism***〉❶陪送出嫁 to accompany a bride to her new home ❷随嫁的人 maid escorting a bride to her new home ❸妾 concubine

YO ㄧㄛ

呦 ㊀ yō ㄧㄛ 同"唷"same as 唷

㊁ yo 见 904 页 see p904

唷 yō ㄧㄛ 叹词 ***interjection***，表示惊讶或疑问(used to express surprise or query)：～，这是怎么了？*Gee, what happened?*

哟 ㊁ yo ·ㄧㄛ 助词 ***auxiliary*** 1 用在句末或句中停顿处(used at the end or in the middle of a sentence where there is a pause)：大家齐用力～！*Come on, everybody!* | 话剧～，京戏～，他都很喜欢。*Well, stage play or Beijing opera, he likes them all.* 2 歌词中作衬字(used as a syllable filler in a song)：呼儿嗨～！*Hu-er-hei-yo!*

㊀ yō 见 904 页 see p904

YONG ㄩㄥ

佣(傭) ㊀ yōng ㄩㄥ ❶被人雇用 employed; hired：～工 *hired labourer; servant* ❷受雇用的人 servant：女～*woman servant; maid*

㊁ yòng 见 907 页 see p907

拥(擁) yōng ㄩㄥ ❶抱 to embrace; to hug (㊟ ***doublet*** 一抱 to embrace; to hug) ❷围着 to gather around; to wrap around：～被而眠 *to sleep in a wrapped quilt* | 前呼后～*with attendants crowding round; with a large retinue* ❸拥护 to uphold; to endorse：一致～戴 *to enjoy universal support* | ～军优属 *(of civilians) to support the army and give preferential treatment to the families of revolutionary soldiers and martyrs* [拥护]忠诚爱戴，竭力支持 to uphold; to endorse：～～改革开放 *to uphold the reform and opening policy* ❹聚到一块儿 to crowd; to throng：～挤 *crowded; packed; congested* | 一～而入 *to pile in; to swarm in* ❺持有 to have：～有 *to own; to possess* | ～兵百万 *to have a million warriors*

痈(癰) yōng ㄩㄥ 一种毒疮，多生在脖子上或背部，常表现为大片块状化脓性炎症，表面疮口很多，疼痛异常 carbuncle

邕 yōng ㄩㄥ ❶邕江，水名，在广西壮族自治区 Yongjiang River in the Guangxi Zhuang Autonomous Region ❷广西壮族自治区南宁的别称 Yong, another name for Nanning, a city in the Guangxi Zhuang Autonomous Region

滃 yōng ㄩㄥ 滃水，水名，在江西省 Yongshui River in Jiangxi Province

庸 yōng ㄩㄥ ❶平常，不高明的 commonplace; mediocre ([连] **doublet** 平一 commonplace; mediocre)：～言 *commonplace*｜～俗 *vulgar; philistine; low* ❷用 need：毋～讳言。*There is no need for reticence.* ❸岂，怎么 how; in what way：～可弃乎？*How could this possibly be relinquished?*

鄘 yōng ㄩㄥ 周代诸侯国名，在今河南省卫辉一带 Yong, a princedom of the Zhou Dynasty, covering today's Weihui and nearby areas, Henan Province

墉(**牗) yōng ㄩㄥ ❶城墙 city wall ❷高墙 high wall

慵 yōng ㄩㄥ 困倦，懒 lethargic; languid

镛 yōng ㄩㄥ 大钟，古时的一种乐器 large bell, ancient musical instrument

鳙 yōng ㄩㄥ 鳙鱼，鱼名。生活在淡水中，头很大。也叫"胖头鱼"(also called 胖头鱼) variegated carp; bighead carp (*Hypophthalmichthys nobilis*)

雍(*雝) yōng ㄩㄥ 和谐 harmonious

[雍容]文雅大方，从容不迫的样子 graceful and poised; elegant and poised

壅 yōng ㄩㄥ ❶堵塞(sè) to block; to obstruct ([连] **doublet** 一塞 congested; clogged)：水道～塞。*The waterway is clogged.* ❷把土或肥料培在植物根上 to heap soil or fertilizer over and around the roots (of plants and trees)

臃 yōng ㄩㄥ [臃肿](一zhǒng)过于肥胖，以致动作不灵便 swollen; bloated [喻] **figurative** 1 衣服穿得太多 cumbersomely dressed 2 机构太庞大，妨碍工作 overstaffed

饔 yōng ㄩㄥ ❶熟食 cooked food ❷早饭 breakfast

喁 ㊀ yóng ㄩㄥˊ 鱼口向上，露出水面(of fish) sticking its mouth out of the water [喁喁][喻] **figurative** 众人景仰归向的样子(of everyone) looking up to sb

㊁ yú 见916页 see p916

颙 yóng ㄩㄥˊ ❶大头 big head [引] **extension** 大 big; large ❷仰慕 to admire; to look up to：～望 *to look up to*

永 yǒng ㄩㄥˇ ❶长 long：江之～矣。*How long the river is!* ❷长久，久远 perpetual; eternal ([连] **doublet** 一久 permanent; everlasting｜一远 forever; eternally)：～不掉队 *never to fall behind*｜～远牢记历史的教训 *to keep the historical lessons forever in mind*

咏(*詠) yǒng ㄩㄥˇ ❶声调抑扬地念，唱 to chant; to intone; to recite ([连] **doublet** 歌一 to sing; to chant｜吟一 to chant; to intone; to recite) ❷用诗词等来叙述 to express in poetic form：～梅 *ode to the plum blossom*｜～雪 *ode to the snow*

泳 yǒng ㄩㄥˇ 在水里游动 to swim（㊟ ***doublet*** 游— to swim）：仰～ *backstroke*｜蛙～ *breaststroke*

甬 yǒng ㄩㄥˇ 浙江省宁波的别称 Yong，another name for Ningbo，Zhejiang Province

［甬道］**1** 院落中用砖石砌成的路。也叫"甬路"（also called 甬路）brick-paved or stone-paved path in a courtyard **2** 走廊，过道 corridor；hallway；passage

俑 yǒng ㄩㄥˇ 古时殉葬用的木制或陶制的偶人（in ancient China）tomb figure，wooden or earthen human figurine buried with the dead

勇 yǒng ㄩㄥˇ ❶有胆量，敢干（gàn）brave；courageous：～敢 *dauntless；intrepid*｜英～ *valiant*｜很有～气 *to be full of courage；to be of great valour*｜奋～前进 *to advance valiantly* ㊇ ***extension*** 不畏避，不推诿 to be brave in；to be bold in：～于承认错误 *to have the courage to admit one's mistakes* ❷清朝称战争时期临时招募，不在平时编制之内的兵 temporary recruits in times of war during the Qing Dynasty：散兵游～ *stragglers and disbanded soldiers*

涌（＊湧）yǒng ㄩㄥˇ ❶水或云气冒出 to gush；to pour；to surge：～泉 *fountain*｜泪如泉～ *tears welling up in one's eyes*｜风起云～ *winds rising and clouds gathering；to surge forward* ❷像水涌般地出现 to surge；to pour：许多人从里面～出来。*Crowds poured out.*｜往事～上心头。*Memories of the past rushed through my mind.*

恿（＊慂）yǒng ㄩㄥˇ 见707页"怂"字条"怂恿"（sǒng—）see 怂恿 on p707

蛹 yǒng ㄩㄥˇ 某些昆虫从幼虫过渡到成虫时的一种形态，在这个期间，不食不动，外皮变厚，身体缩短 pupa：蚕～ *silkworm chrysalis*

踊（踴）yǒng ㄩㄥˇ 跳，跳跃 to leap；to jump

［踊跃］**1** 跳跃 to leap；to jump：～～欢呼 *to leap and cheer* **2** 争先恐后 to vie with each other：～～发言 *to take the floor eagerly*

鲬 yǒng ㄩㄥˇ 鱼名。身体长形，扁而平，黄褐色，有黑色斑点，无鳔。生活在海洋中 flathead（*Platycephalus*）

用 yòng ㄩㄥˋ ❶使用，使人、物发挥其功能 to use；to utilize；to apply：～电 *to use electricity*｜～拖拉机耕田 *to plough the field with a tractor*｜不同的矛盾要～不同的方法来解决。*Different disputes require different approaches.*｜公～电话 *public telephone*｜～笔写字 *to write with a pen* ❷进饭食 to eat；to drink：～茶 *to drink some tea*｜～饭 *to have a meal* ❸费用，花

费的钱财 expense; outlay:家～*family expenses; housekeeping money*|零～*pocket money* ❹物质使用的效果 use; utility; usefulness (㊟ **doublet** 功— function; use|效— effectiveness; usefulness):有～之材 *talent* ❺需要(多用于否定或反问)(usually used in negative sentences or rhetorical questions) need; have to:不～说 *needless to say*|还～你操心吗? *Is there anything for you to worry about?* ❻因 hence; therefore:～此 *hence; therefore*|～特函达。*Hence this letter.*

佣 ㊁ yòng ㄩㄥˋ 佣金,佣钱,买卖东西时给介绍人的钱 commission; brokerage

㊀ yōng 见 904 页 see p904

YOU ㄧㄡ

优(優) yōu ㄧㄡ ❶美好的,跟"劣"相对(the opposite of 劣) excellent; superior:～等 *first-rate; excellent; high-class*|品质～良 *of fine quality* ❷充足,宽裕 abundant; well-to-do:生活～裕 *to lead an affluent (or abundant) life* ❸优待 to give preferential treatment:拥军～属(*of civilians*) *to support the army and give preferential treatment to the families of revolutionary soldiers and martyrs* ❹古代指演剧的人(in ancient China) actor; actress (㊟ **doublet** 俳— comedian; comedienne|—伶 actor; actress)

[优柔] **1** 从容 leisurely **2** 犹豫不决 hesitant:～～寡断 *indecisive; irresolute*

忧(憂) yōu ㄧㄡ ❶发愁 to worry about (㊟ **doublet** —愁 worried):杞人～天(喻过虑) *A man of the Qi feared that the sky might fall—to entertain groundless anxiety; to be over-anxious.* ❷使人忧愁的事 anxiety; concern:高枕无～*to sit back and relax; to sleep in peace without any anxiety*

攸 yōu ㄧㄡ 所 concerning:责有～归 *Responsibility rests where it falls.*|性命～关(*matter*) *of life and death*

悠 yōu ㄧㄡ ❶长久 remote (㊟ **doublet** —久 time-honoured; long):历史～久 *long history* [悠悠] **1** 闲适,自由自在 leisurely:白云～～*floating clouds* **2** 忧郁 gloomy:～～我思。*Heavy is my heart.* **3** 长久,遥远 long; remote:～～岁月 *long-standing years* ❷闲适,闲散 leisurely:～闲 *leisurely and carefree*|～然 *leisurely and carefree* ❸在空中摆动 to swing; to sway:站在秋千上来回～*to sway back and forth on the swing* ❹稳住,控制 to take it easy:～着点劲 *to take it easy*

呦 yōu ㄧㄡ 叹词 **interjection**,表示惊异(used to express surprise):～,你怎么也来了? *Hey! Fancy seeing you here!*|

～，碗怎么破了！*Oops! The bowl is broken!*

［呦呦］鹿叫声（cry of deer）bleating：～～鹿鸣 *Deer are bleating out.*

幽 yōu 汉 ❶形容地方很僻静、光线暗 dim; gloomy; secluded：～谷 *deep and secluded valley*｜～林 *dense forest*｜～室 *dim room; gloomy room* ㊀ **extension** 隐藏，不公开的 secret; hidden：～居 *to lead a solitary life*｜～会 *tryst; rendezvous* ❷使人感觉沉静、安闲的 tranquil; serene：～香 *delicate fragrance*｜～美 *serene beauty*｜～雅 *serene and graceful* ❸幽禁，把人关起来不让跟外人接触 to incarcerate; to imprison ❹指阴间 nether world：～灵 *ghost; spirit; spectre*｜～明（阳间）永隔。*The dead and the living are worlds apart.* or *The worlds of the living and the dead are forever separate.* ❺幽州，古地名，相当于今河北省北部和辽宁省南部 Youzhou, an ancient place, comprising the northern part of today's Hebei Province and the southern part of today's Liaoning Province：～燕（yān）*Youyan*

［幽默］（外 **loanword**）有趣或可笑而意味深长 humour：～～画 *humourous painting*

麀 yōu 汉 古书上指母鹿（in ancient Chinese texts）female deer; doe

耰 yōu 汉 ❶古代弄碎土块使田地平坦的农具（in ancient China）rake ❷用耰使土覆盖种子 to rake, to turn up the soil with a rake to cover the seeds

尤（**尢）yóu 汉 ❶特异的，突出的 remarkable; outstanding; conspicuous：拔其～ *to select and promote those of outstanding ability* ❷尤其，更，格外 particularly; especially：～甚 *increasingly; more so*｜～妙 *even better; all the better* ❸过失 fault; mistake：勿效～（不要学着做坏事）*to shun bad examples* ❹怨恨，归咎 to have a grudge against; to lay the blame on：怨天～人 *to blame everyone and everything but not oneself*

犹（猶）yóu 汉 ❶如同 just as; like：虽死～生 *to live in the hearts of the people even though one is dead*｜战士的意志～如钢铁。*The soldiers' willpower is as strong as iron and steel.* ❷还（hái），尚且 still; even：记忆～新 *to remain fresh in one's memory*｜话～未了。*There's still more to say.*｜困兽～斗。*A cornered beast would still fight.*

［犹豫］（—yù）迟疑不决 hesitant; irresolute

疣（**肬）yóu 汉 一种皮肤病，俗叫"瘊子"。病原体是一种病毒，症状是皮肤上出现黄褐色的小疙瘩，不痛也不痒（popularly called 瘊子）wart［赘疣］喻多余而无用的东西 wart; anything superfluous and useless

莸（蕕）yóu ㄧㄡˊ ❶古书上说的一种有臭味的草（in ancient Chinese texts）stinking grass：薰～不同器（喻好人和坏人搞不到一起）。*Fragrant herbs and stinking weeds cannot be put in the same vessel — the good can never mix with the bad.* ❷落叶小灌木，花蓝色，供观赏 common bluebeard（*Caryopteris incana*）

鱿 yóu ㄧㄡˊ 鱿鱼，又叫"柔鱼"，"枪乌贼"的俗称。生活在海洋中的一种软体动物，头像乌贼，尾端呈菱形，体白色，有淡褐色斑点。肉可吃（also called 柔鱼 and popularly called 枪乌贼）squid; calamary

由 yóu ㄧㄡˊ ❶经过 via; by; through：必～之路 *the way one must follow; the only road*｜观其所～ *to observe the road he follows; to mark his motives* ❷原因 reason; cause（㊀ **doublet** 原— cause）：情～ *hows and whys; ins and outs*｜理～ *reason; ground* ❸顺随，听从 to be up to sb; to rest with sb：～着性子 *to do as one pleases; to do at will*｜～不得自己 *not to be up to oneself; to be beyond one's control* ❹介词 ***preposition*** **1** 自，从 from：～哪儿来？*Where are you from?*｜～上到下 *from top to bottom* **2** 凭借 by means of; according to：～此可知 *thus it can be seen* **3** 归（某人去做）（to be done）by：这事～你安排。*You are to handle the whole business.*［由于］**1** 介词 ***preposition***，表示原因 because of; on account of：这项任务～～大家的努力才圆满完成了。*Thanks to the collective efforts, the project has been completed.* **2** 连词 ***conjunction***，跟"所以"、"因而"等呼应，表示因果关系（used in collocation with 所以 or 因而 to express cause and effect）since; because; as; for：～～天气炎热，因而用电量猛增。*The consumption of electricity has been increasing drastically since the weather is too hot.*

邮（郵）yóu ㄧㄡˊ ❶邮递，由国家专设的机构传递信件 to post; to mail：～信 *to post a letter* ❷有关邮务的 postal：～票 *stamp; postage stamp*｜～费 *postage fee*｜～局 *post office*

油 yóu ㄧㄡˊ ❶动植物体内所含的脂肪物质 oil; fat; grease：猪～ *lard*｜花生～ *peanut oil* ❷各种碳氢化合物的混合物，一般不溶于水，容易燃烧 petroleum：煤～ *kerosene*｜汽～ *gasoline* ❸用油涂抹 to paint; to varnish：用桐油一～就好了。*Paint it with tung oil, and it will be OK.* ❹被油弄脏 to be stained with oil or grease：衣服～了一大片。*The dress has got a big oil stain on it.* ❺狡猾

slippery（㊂ *doublet* 一滑 slick; oily）:～腔滑调 *glib; unctuous*｜这个人太～。*He's too slippery.*

[油然] **1** 充盛地 densely; profusely: 天～～作云，沛然下雨。*Clouds were gathering, and rain was falling heavily.* **2**（思想感情）自然而然地产生 spontaneously: 敬慕之情～～而生。*Admiration is welling up in his heart.*

柚 ㊀ yóu ㄧㄡˊ [柚木] 落叶乔木，叶大，对生，花白色或蓝色。木材坚硬耐久，用来造船、车等 teakwood; teak (*Tectona grandis*)

㊁ yòu 见 913 页 see p913

铀 yóu ㄧㄡˊ 一种放射性元素，符号 U，银白色，质地坚硬，能蜕变。把铀熔合在钢中做成铀钢，非常坚硬，可以制造机器。铀是产生原子能的重要元素 uranium (U)

蚰 yóu ㄧㄡˊ [蚰蜒]（一yan）像蜈蚣，比蜈蚣略小，体短而稍扁，足细长，触角长，多栖息阴湿处 common house centipede (*Scutigera coleoptrata*)

鲉 yóu ㄧㄡˊ 鱼名。体侧扁，头部有许多棘状突起，生活在海洋中 scorpionfish (*Scorpaenidae*)

莜 yóu ㄧㄡˊ [莜麦] 一年生草本植物，花绿色，叶细长。茎叶可做牧草，子实可以吃。也作"油麦"(also written as 油麦) naked oat (*Avena nuda*)

游（❷❹❺*遊）yóu ㄧㄡˊ ❶人或动物在水里行动 to swim（㊂ *doublet* 一泳 to swim）:～水 *to swim*｜～鱼可数。*Swimming fish can be clearly seen.* ❷不固定 roving; unsettled: ～资 *idle fund*｜～牧 *nomadism*｜～击战 *guerrilla war* [游移] 主意不定 vacillant; vacillating; hesitant ❸河流的一段 reach (of a river): 上～ *upper reaches*｜下～ *lower reaches* ❹游逛，观赏 to saunter; to stroll: ～玩 *to go sightseeing*｜～人 *visitor; tourist*｜～园 *to visit a park or garden; to attend a celebration in a park*｜旅～ *to travel*｜春～ *spring outing* ❺交游，交往 to associate with ❻同"圝"(yóu) same as 圝

蝣 yóu ㄧㄡˊ 见 204 页"蜉"字条"蜉蝣"(fú—) see 蜉蝣 on p204

輶 yóu ㄧㄡˊ ❶古代一种轻便的车（in ancient China）light carriage ❷轻 light

猷 yóu ㄧㄡˊ 计谋，打算 plan; scheme: 鸿～（宏伟的计划）*grand plan; great plan*

蝤 ㊁ yóu ㄧㄡˊ [蝤蛑]（一móu）又叫"梭子蟹"。生活在海里的一种螃蟹，甲壳略呈梭形，肉可以吃（also called 梭子蟹）swimming crab

㊀ qiú 见 616 页 see p616

繇 ㊁ yóu ㄧㄡˊ 古书里同"由❹1.2."same as 由❹1.2. in ancient Chinese texts

㊀ yáo 见 875 页 see p875

㊂ zhòu 见 992 页 see p992

囮 yóu ㄧㄡˊ (一子)捕鸟时用来引诱同类鸟的鸟,也作"游"(also written as 游) decoy:鸟～子 *bird decoy*

友 yǒu ㄧㄡˇ ❶朋友 friend:好～ *good friend* | 战～*comrade-in-arms* | 网～*net friend; web friend* ⓘ**extension** 有友好关系的 friendly:～军 *friendly troops; friendly forces* | ～邦 *friendly nation; friendly country* ❷相好,互相亲爱 to be on affectionate terms:～爱 *friendly affection; fraternal love* | ～好往来 *friendly contacts; friendly exchanges*

有 ㊀ yǒu ㄧㄡˇ ❶跟"无"相对(the opposite of 无) **1** 表所属 to have; to possess:他～一本书。*He has a book.* | 我没～时间。*I have no time.* **2** 表存在 there be:那里～十来个人。*There are about ten people over there.* | ～困难。*There are difficulties.* | ～办法。*There is a solution.* | ～意见 *to have a different opinion* **3** 表示发生或出现(used to denote occurrence):～病了 *to be ill* | 形势～了新的发展。*There are new developments in the situation.* **4** 表示估量或比较(used to denote estimate or comparison):水～一丈多深。*The water is about more than one* zhang *deep.* | 他～他哥哥那么高了。*He is about the same height as his elder brother.* **5** 表示大,多(used to denote greatness):～学问 *learned* | ～经验 *experienced* [有的是]有很多,多得很 to have plenty of; there's no lack of; to be in abundance ❷用在某些动词前面表示客气(used before some verbs in polite formulae):～劳。*Thanks for the trouble.* or *May I trouble you ...?* | ～请 *to invite sb to come in* ❸跟"某"相近(similar to 某):～一天晚上 *one night* | ～人不赞成。*Some people don't agree.* ❹用在"人、时候、地方"前面,表示一部分(used before 人,时候 or 地方 to indicate a part):～人性子急,～人性子慢。*Some people are impetuous; others are mild.* ❺古汉语词头(used before the names of certain dynasties in classical Chinese):～夏 *the Xia Dynasty* | ～周 *the Zhou Dynasty*

㊁ yòu 见 913 页 see p913

铕 yǒu ㄧㄡˇ 一种金属元素,符号 Eu。可制彩色显像管中的荧光粉 europium (Eu)

酉 yǒu ㄧㄡˇ ❶地支的第十位 *you*, the 10th of the 12 Earthly Branches ❷酉时,指下午五点到七点 the period from 5 pm to 7 pm

卣 yǒu ㄧㄡˇ 古代一种盛酒的器皿(in ancient China) wine vessel

羑 yǒu ㄧㄡˇ [羑里]古地名,在今河南省汤阴 Youli, an ancient place, now in Tangyin, Henan Province

莠 yǒu ㄧㄡˇ (一子)狗尾草,一年生草本植物,样子很像

Y

谷子 green bristlegrass [喻] ***figurative*** 品质坏的，不好的人(of people) bad; vicious: 良～不齐。*There are weeds among seedlings — the good and the bad are intermingled.* or *There are bad as well as good people in the group.*

牖 yǒu [汉] 窗户 window

黝 yǒu [汉] 黑色 dark; swarthy: 一张～黑的脸 *a swarthy face*

又 yòu [汉] 副词 ***adverb*** ❶重复，连续，指相同的 again: 他～立功了。*He rendered meritorious services again.* | 今天～下雨了。*It rained again today.* ❷表示加重语气，更进一层 furthermore: 他～不傻。*Besides, he's not silly at all.* | 你～不是不会。*It isn't that you don't know how to do it.* ❸表示平列关系 and; not only… but also: ～高～大 *tall and big* | ～多～快 *more as well as faster* | ～好～省 *not only good but also economical* | 我～高兴，～着急。*I am both happy and worried.* ❹再加上，还有 and: 十～五年 *fifteen years* | 一～二分之一 *one and a half* ❺表示某种范围之外另有补充 in addition to: 穿上了棉袄～加了一件皮背心 *to put on a leather waistcoat in addition to a cotton-padded coat* ❻表示转折 but: 刚还想说什么，可～把它忘了。*I had something to say but don't have the slightest idea about it now.*

右 yòu [汉] ❶面向南时靠西的一边，跟"左"相对(the opposite of 左) right: ～手 *right hand; to the right* | ～边 *right side; on the right* [转] ***transfer*** 西方(以面向南为准)(when facing south) west: 江～ *west of a river; to the west of a river* | 山～ *west of a mountain* ❷政治思想上属于保守的或反动的 conservative; reactionary: ～倾 *Right deviation* ❸古以右为上，品质等级高的称右 superior in quality and grade in ancient China: 无出其～ *second to none; matchless; unparalleled* ❹崇尚，重视 to worship; to emphasize: ～文 *to lay stress on culture and learning; to value cultural and educational undertakings* ❺古同"佑" same as 佑 in ancient Chinese

佑 yòu [汉] 辅助，保护 to assist; to bless: ～助 *to aid; to help* | ～护 *to protect; to bless* | 庇～ *to bless*

祐 yòu [汉] 保祐，迷信的人指神帮助 to bless

幼 yòu [汉] ❶年纪小，初出生的，跟"老"相对(the opposite of 老) young; new-born: ～儿 *infant; child* | ～虫 *larva* | ～苗 *seedling* [幼稚]年纪小的 young [喻] ***figurative*** 知识见解浅薄、缺乏经验的 childish; puerile; naive: 思想～～ *naive; innocent* ❷小孩ル children; the young: 扶老携～ *to hold the old by the arm and the young by*

the hand — to help the aged and the young｜～有所养 *to take care of the young*

蚴 yòu ㄧㄡˋ 绦虫、血吸虫等的幼体 larva of a tapeworm; cercaria of schistosome: 毛～ *miracidium*｜尾～*cercaria*

有 ㊁ yòu ㄧㄡˋ 古同"又❹" same as 又❹ in ancient Chinese

㊀ yǒu 见 911 页 see p911

侑 yòu ㄧㄡˋ 在筵席旁助兴，劝人吃喝 to press sb to eat or drink: ～食 *to press sb to eat*

囿 yòu ㄧㄡˋ ❶养动物的园子 animal farm; enclosure; park: 鹿～ *deer farm; deer park* ❷局限，被限制 to be limited; to be hampered; to be constrained: ～于成见 *to be blinded by prejudice*

宥 yòu ㄧㄡˋ ❶宽容，饶恕，原谅 to excuse; to pardon; to forgive: ～我。*Excuse me.*｜请原～。*Pardon me.* ❷帮助 *to help*

狖 yòu ㄧㄡˋ 古书上说的一种猴 (in ancient Chinese texts) a kind of monkey

柚 ㊁ yòu ㄧㄡˋ 常绿乔木，种类很多。果实叫柚子，也叫文旦，比橘子大，多汁，味酸甜 pomelo (*Citrus maxima*)

㊀ yóu 见 910 页 see p910

釉 yòu ㄧㄡˋ (～子)以石英、长石、硼砂、黏土等为原料制成的东西，涂在瓷器、陶器外面，烧制后发出玻璃光泽，可增加陶瓷的机械强度和绝缘性能 glaze

鼬 yòu ㄧㄡˋ [黄鼬]哺乳动物，俗叫"黄鼠狼"。毛黄褐色，遇见敌人能由肛门附近分泌臭气自卫，常捕食田鼠(popularly called 黄鼠狼) weasel (*Mustela sibirica*)

诱 yòu ㄧㄡˋ (旧读 formerly yǒu) ❶劝导，教导 to guide; to direct; to induce: 循循善～*to guide patiently and systematically; to give guidance in a painstaking and systematic fashion* ❷引诱，使用手段引人 to lure; to seduce; to entice: ～敌 *to lure the enemy*｜利～*to lure by promise of gain*

YU ㄩ

迂 yū ㄩ ❶曲折，绕远 winding; tortuous; roundabout; circuitous: ～回前进 *to proceed in a circuitous route* ❷言行、见解陈旧不合时宜 impractical; unpractical (㊂ ***doublet*** — 腐 pedantic; trite): ～论 *impractical argument; unrealistic statement*｜～见 *impractical opinion; absurd view*

纡 yū ㄩ ❶弯曲，绕弯 winding; tortuous ❷〈古 ***archaism***〉系，结 to tie; to bind: ～金佩紫(指地位显贵) *to wear gold ornaments and a purple gown — to hold distinguished social position*

於 ㊁ yū ㄩ 姓 Yu, a surname

㊀ yú 见 915 页 see p915

㊂ wū 见 793 页 see p793

淤 yū ㄩ ❶水里泥沙沉积 to silt up:～了好些泥 *to be choked with silt* ❷河沟中沉积的泥沙 silt; ooze; sludge:河～ *river mud; alluvium; sludge*|沟～ *drainage silt* ❸同"瘀" same as 瘀

瘀 yū ㄩ 血液凝滞 stasis:～血 *blood stasis*

于 yú ㄩˊ ❶介词 ***preposition*** **1** 在 in; at:写～北京 *to be written in Beijing*|生～1949年 *to be born in 1949* **2** 对于,对 to:～人民有益 *to be beneficial to the people*|忠～祖国 *to be faithful to one's country*|勇～负责 *to dare to shoulder the responsibility* **3** 给 to:勿诿过～人。*Don't shift the blame onto others.*|光荣归～党。*Glory is credited to the Party.*|取之于民,用之～民。*What is taken from the people is to be used for the people.* **4** 自,由 from; out of:出～自愿 *of one's own free will; of one's own accord*|取之～民,用之于民。*What is taken from the people is to be used for the people.* **5** 向 to:问道～盲 *to ask a blind man about the way — the blind leads the blind; to seek advice from one who can offer none* **6** 在形容词后,表示比较,跟"过"的意思相同(used after an adjective to indicate comparison, with the same meaning as 过) than:霜叶红～二月花。*The frost-beaten leaves appear redder than the spring flowers.*|人民的利益高～一切。*The interest of the people is above everything else.* **7** 在动词后,表示被动(used after a verb to indicate a passive voice) by:见笑～大方 *to be laughed at by experts* [于是]连词 ***conjunction***,表示两件事前后紧接 hence; then; so:他听完报告,～～就回去了。*He went home after the lecture.* ❷姓 Yu, a surname

盂 yú ㄩˊ 一种盛液体的器皿 liquid vessel:痰～*spittoon*|漱口～*mouth cleansing cup*

竽 yú ㄩˊ 古代管乐器,像现在的笙(in ancient China) *yu*, wind instrument like the modern *sheng*, but a little bigger than it [滥竽充数]一个不会吹竽的人混在乐队里充数 to pass oneself off as one of the players in an ensemble [喻] ***figurative*** 没有真本领,占着工作岗位 to hold a post without adequate qualifications; simply to make up the number

与(與) ㊂ yú ㄩˊ 同"欤" same as 欤

㊀ yǔ 见 917 页 see p917

㊁ yù 见 919 页 see p919

玙(璵) yú ㄩˊ 玙璠(fán),美玉。也说"璠玙"(also called 璠玙) fine jade

欤(歟) yú ㄩˊ 文言助词 ***auxiliary in classical Chinese*** ❶表示疑问语气(used to express interrogative tone):在齐～?在鲁～? *In the Qi State or in the Lu State?*

❷表示感叹语气(used to express exclamatory tone):论者之言,一似管窥虎～! *Indeed, the speaker's argument was as one-sided as looking at a tiger through a bamboo tube!*

予 ㊀ yú ㄩˊ 文言代词 ***pronoun in classical Chinese***,我 I; me

㊁ yǔ 见 918 页 see p918

妤 yú ㄩˊ 见 347 页"婕"字条"婕妤"(jié—) see 婕妤 on p347

余(❶-❸餘) yú ㄩˊ ❶剩下来的,多出来的 surplus; spare (㊀ ***doublet*** 剩一 surplus):～粮 *surplus grain*|～兴(xìng) *lingering interest*|业～*spare time*|不遗～力 *to spare no effort; to do one's utmost* ❷十、百、千等整数或度量单位后面的零头 more than; over; odd:十～人 *more than ten people*|三百～米 *over 300 metres*|两吨～*two tons plus* ❸后 after:兴奋之～,高歌一曲 *to sing heartily at the moment of one's excitement* ❹文言代词 ***pronoun in classical Chinese***,我 I; me

馀(餘) yú ㄩˊ 同"余❶❷❸"。("餘"简化为"余",用"余"意义可能混淆时,用"馀"。如文言句"馀年无多"。)(馀 has now a simplified written form of 余, but the character 馀 is still used when 余 and 馀 might be confused in meaning, e.g. 馀年无多 I've only a few years left in my life.) same as 余❶❷❸

狳 yú ㄩˊ 见 615 页"犰"字条"犰狳"(qiú—) see 犰狳 on p615

畲 ㊀ yú ㄩˊ 开垦过两年的地 land that has been cultivated for two years

㊁ shē 见 662 页 see p662

艅 yú ㄩˊ [艅艎](—huáng) 古代一种大船(in ancient China) a kind of big boat

臾 yú ㄩˊ [须臾]片刻,一会儿 moment; instant

谀 yú ㄩˊ 谄媚,奉承 to flatter; to fawn on; to toady to:～辞 *flattery; adulatory words*

萸 yú ㄩˊ 见 992 页"茱"字条"茱萸"(zhū—) see 茱萸 on p992

腴 yú ㄩˊ ❶肥,胖 fat; plump:丰～ *fat; plump* ❷肥沃 fertile:土地膏～*fertile land*

鱼(魚) yú ㄩˊ 脊椎动物的一类,生活在水中,通常体侧扁,大都有鳞和鳍,用鳃呼吸,体温随外界温度而变化,种类很多。大部分可供食用或制造鱼胶 fish

渔 yú ㄩˊ ❶捕鱼 fishing; fishery:～船 *fishing boat*|～业 *fishery; fishing industry* ❷谋取不应得的东西 to take sth one is not entitled to:～利 *to reap unfair gains; to profit at others' expenses*

於 ㊀ yú ㄩˊ 同"于❶" same as 于❶

㊁ yū 见 913 页 see p913
㊂ wū 见 793 页 see p793

禺 yú ㄩˊ ❶古书上说的一种猴 (in ancient Chinese texts) a kind of monkey ❷见 549 页"番"字条"番禺"(pān —) see 番禺 on p549

隅 yú ㄩˊ ❶角落 corner; nook: 城～ *corner of a city wall* [隅反] ㊗ ***figurative*** 因此知彼,能够类推,举一反三 to know sth else by analogy [向隅] 对着屋子的一个角落,喻得不到机会而失望 to face a corner of the room — to feel disappointed for lack of opportunity ❷靠边的地方 edge; outlying place: 海～ *seaboard; coast*

喁 ㊁ yú ㄩˊ [喁喁] 形容低声细语 murmur: ～～私语 *to whisper*
㊀ yóng 见 905 页 see p905

嵎 yú ㄩˊ ❶山弯曲的地方 mountain recess ❷同"隅" same as 隅

愚 yú ㄩˊ ❶傻,笨 stupid; silly (㊀ ***doublet*** 一蠢 foolish; stupid): ～人 *fool* | ～昧无知 *ignorant* ㊁ ***extension*** 使愚蠢 to fool ❷谦辞 ***humble***: ～见 *in my humble opinion* ❸愚弄,欺骗 to deceive; to dupe: 为人所～ *to be deceived*

髃 yú ㄩˊ 肩髃,针灸穴位名 *jianyu*, an acupuncture point in the front part of the shoulder

舁 yú ㄩˊ 〈古 ***archaism***〉共同抬东西 (of two or more people) to carry together

俞 ㊀ yú ㄩˊ ❶文言叹词 ***interjection in classical Chinese***,表示允许 to permit; to allow ❷姓 Yu, a surname
㊁ shù 见 695 页 see p695

揄 yú ㄩˊ 拉,引 to draw [揄扬] 称赞 to praise

嵛 yú ㄩˊ [昆嵛] 山名,在山东省东部 Kunyu Mountain in the east of Shandong Province

逾 (❶ *踰) yú ㄩˊ ❶越过,超过 to exceed; to surpass: ～期 *overdue* ❷更,越发 even more: ～甚 *even more*

渝 yú ㄩˊ ❶变(多指感情或态度) (usually used to denote feeling or attitude) to change; to alter: 始终不～ *to stick to one's ideal* ❷重庆市的别称 Yu, another name for Chongqing: 成～铁路 *railway from Chengdu to Chongqing, Chengdu-Chongqing Railway*

愉 yú ㄩˊ 喜欢,快乐 joyful; cheerful (㊀ ***doublet*** 一快 happy; delighted): 轻松～快 *happy and relaxed* | ～悦 *cheerful; delighted*

瑜 yú ㄩˊ ❶美玉 fine jade ❷玉石的光彩 luster of jade ㊗ ***figurative*** 优点 virtue: 瑕(xiá)不掩～。*One flaw cannot obscure the splendour of the jade — the defects cannot obscure the virtues.*

榆 yú ㄩˊ 榆树，落叶乔木，三四月开小花。果实外面有膜质的翅，叫榆荚或榆钱。木材坚固，可以制器物 elm (*Elmus*)

覦 yú ㄩˊ 见 319 页"覬"字条"覬覦"(jì—) see 覬覦 on p319

窬(❷*踰) yú ㄩˊ ❶门边小洞 small hole beside the gate ❷从墙上爬过去 to climb over a wall：穿～之盗(穿墙和爬墙的贼) *burglar; thief who breaks through or climbs over a wall*

蝓 yú ㄩˊ 见 407 页"蛞"字条"蛞蝓"(kuò—) see 蛞蝓 on p407

娱 yú ㄩˊ 快乐或使人快乐 to entertain; to amuse (㊟ **doublet** —乐 amusement; recreation)：文～活动 *recreational activities*｜自～*to amuse oneself*

虞 yú ㄩˊ ❶预料 to suppose; to expect：以备不～*to be prepared against any contingency or eventuality* ❷忧虑 anxiety; worry; fear：无～*no worries* ❸欺骗 to cheat; to deceive; to fool：尔～我诈(互相欺骗) *each trying to cheat or outwit the other* ❹周代诸侯国名，在今山西省平陆东北 *Yu*, a princedom of the Zhou Dynasty, situated to the northeast of today's Pinglu, Shanxi Province

雩 yú ㄩˊ 古代求雨的一种祭祀(in ancient China) sacrificial rite to pray for rain

輿 yú ㄩˊ ❶车中载人载物的部分 part of a carriage for passengers and goods ❷车 cart; carriage; chariot：舍～登舟 *to change from carriage to boat* [肩輿]轿子 sedan chair ❸众人 public：～论 *public opinion* [輿情]群众的意见和态度 public sentiments：洞察～～*to have a keen insight into public sentiments* ❹地，疆域 area; territory：～地 *territory; land; earth*｜方～*land; earth*｜～图 *map*

歔 yú ㄩˊ 同"渔❶"same as 渔❶

与(與) ㊀ yǔ ㄩˇ ❶介词 ***preposition***，跟 with; against：～疾病作斗争 *to fight disease*｜～虎谋皮 *to ask a tiger for its skin — to request sb to act against his own interests* ❷连词 ***conjunction***，和 and：批评～自我批评 *criticism and self-criticism*｜父亲～母亲都来。*Both my father and mother will come here.* ❸给 to give; to offer; to grant：赠～*to grant*｜交～本人 *to give to the person concerned*｜～人方便 *to do others a favor* ❹交往，交好 to get along with; to be on good terms with：此人易～。*This person is easy to get along with.*｜相～*to be on good terms with*｜～国(相交好的国家) *friendly nation; allied state* ❺赞助 to help; to support：～人为善(原指赞助人学

好，后多指善意助人）(*originally used to indicate helping others learn from good examples*) *to help others with good intention*

［与其］连词 ***conjunction***，常跟"宁"、"宁可"、"不如"、"不若"等连用，表示比较(usually used in collocation with 宁，宁可，不如 or 不若 for comparison) rather than; better than：～～坐车，不如坐船。*It's better to go by ship than by bus.*

㊁ yù 见 919 页 see p919

㊂ yú 见 914 页 see p914

屿(嶼) yǔ ㄩˇ（旧读 formerly xù）小岛 small island; islet（㊇ ***doublet*** 岛— island）

予 ㊀ yǔ ㄩˇ 给予 to grant; to bestow; to award：授～奖状 *to award a certificate of merit* | ～以协助 *to give assistance to* | ～以处分 *to impose a punishment; to mete out a punishment*

㊁ yú 见 915 页 see p915

伛(傴) yǔ ㄩˇ 驼背 hunchbacked; humpbacked：～人 *hunchback; humpback* | ～偻(lǚ) *hunchbacked; humpbacked*

宇 yǔ ㄩˇ ❶屋檐 eaves ㊈ ***extension*** 房屋 house：庙～ *temple* ［眉宇］㊉ ***transfer*** 仪表，风度 bearing; mien; manners ❷上下四方，所有的空间 space; universe; world：～内 *in the world* ［宇宙］**1** 同"宇❷" same as 宇❷ **2** 指所有的空间和时间 universe; cosmos ❸地层系统分类的最高一级，在"界"之上，是在地质年代"宙"的时间内形成的地层 eonothem, the highest-level division of geologic time, as corresponding to "eon"：显生～ *Phanerozoic Eonothem* | 元古～ *Proterozoic Eonothem* | 太古～ *Archaean Eonothem*

羽 yǔ ㄩˇ ❶羽毛，鸟的毛 feather; plume：～翼 *wing* ㊈ ***extension*** 翅膀 wing：振～高飞 *to flap the wings and soar high* ❷古代五音"宫、商、角、徵(zhǐ)、羽"之一 *yu*, a note of the ancient Chinese five-tone scale, corresponding to *la*

雨 ㊀ yǔ ㄩˇ 空气中的水蒸气上升到天空中遇冷凝成云，再遇冷聚集成大水点落下来就是雨 rain

㊁ yù 见 920 页 see p920

俣 yǔ ㄩˇ 大 big

禹 yǔ ㄩˇ 传说中的古代部落联盟首领，曾治平洪水 Yu, legendary chief of an ancient tribe union who successfully harnessed a major flood

瑀 yǔ ㄩˇ 像玉的石头 jade-like stone

语 ㊀ yǔ ㄩˇ ❶话 words（㊇ ***doublet*** —言 language; tongue)：成～ *idiom* | ～文 *language and literature* | 外国～ *foreign language* ❷谚语或古语 proverb; old saying：～云 *as the saying goes* ❸代替语言的

动作或方式 nonlinguistic means of communication：手～ *dactylology; sign language* | 旗～ *semaphore; flag signal* ❹说 to speak; to say：不言不～*not to utter a single word* | 默默不～*to keep silence; to speak nothing*

㊁ yù 见 921 页 see p921

圄 yǔ ㄩˇ 见 452 页"图"字条"图圄"(líng—) see 图圄 on p452

敔 yǔ ㄩˇ 古代一种打击乐器，击敔使演奏停止 *yu*, an ancient percussion musical instrument, struck for ending a performance

龉 yǔ ㄩˇ 见 369 页"龃"字条"龃龉"(jǔ—) see 龃龉 on p369

圉 yǔ ㄩˇ 养马的地方 stable 也指养马的人 stableman; stableboy

庾 yǔ ㄩˇ ❶露天的谷仓 open-air granary［大庾岭］山名，在江西、广东两省交界的地方 Dayuling, a mountain at the juncture of Jiangxi Province and Guangdong Province ❷姓 Yu, a surname

瘐 yǔ ㄩˇ 瘐死，旧时称囚犯因受刑、冻饿、生病而死在监狱里(in former times) to die of torture, cold, hunger or illness in jail

貐(**貐) yǔ ㄩˇ 见 861 页"猰"字条"猰貐"(yà—) see 猰貐 on p861

窳 yǔ ㄩˇ 恶劣，坏 corrupt; bad：～劣(*of quality*) *inferior* | ～败(败坏) *corrupt; rotten; decayed*

与(與) ㊂ yù ㄩˋ 参与，参加 to take part in; to participate in：～会 *to attend a conference* | ～闻此事(参与并且得知此事的内情) *to have a participant's knowledge of the matter; to be in the know*

㊀ yǔ 见 917 页 see p917

㊁ yú 见 914 页 see p914

玉 yù ㄩˋ ❶矿物的一种，质细而坚硬，有光泽，略透明，可雕琢成簪环等装饰品 jade ❷喻洁白或美丽 pure; beautiful：～颜 *fair complexion* | 亭亭～立 *slim and graceful; tall and erect* ❸敬辞 **polite**：～言 *your valuable words* | ～体 *your health* | 敬候～音。*I'm looking forward to hearing from you.*

钰 yù ㄩˋ 宝物 treasure

驭 yù ㄩˋ ❶驾驭(车马) to drive (a carriage)：～车 *to drive a carriage* | ～马 *to ride a horse* | ～手 *driver of a chariot; soldier in charge of pack animals* ❷统率，控制 to command; to control：～下无方 *to have no good way to control a subordinate—to lack the ability to do sth*

芋 yù ㄩˋ 芋头，多年生草本植物，叶子略呈卵形，地下茎可以吃 taro (*Colocasia esculenta*)

吁(籲) ㊂ yù ㄩˋ 为某种要求而呼喊 to appeal; to plead：～请 *to*

implore; to petition | 大声呼～ *to utter fervent speeches of appeal*

㊀ xū 见 843 页 see p843

聿 yù ㄩˋ 文言助词 ***auxiliary in classical Chinese***，用在一句话的开头(used at the beginning of a sentence) then; and then

谷 ㊁ yù ㄩˋ [吐谷浑](tǔ—hún)我国古代西部民族名 the Tuyuhun ethnic group, one of the western ethnic groups in ancient China

㊀ gǔ 见 240 页 see p240

峪 yù ㄩˋ 山谷 valley; ravine; hollow

浴 yù ㄩˋ 洗澡 bath: ～室 *bathroom* | 沐～*to bathe; to take a bath*

欲(❶ *慾) yù ㄩˋ ❶欲望，想得到某种东西或想达到某种目的的要求 desire; yearning; longing: 食～ *appetite* | 求知～ *thirst for knowledge* ❷想要，希望 to want; to wish: ～盖弥彰(想要掩饰反而弄得更显明了)。*The more one tries to hide, the more one is exposed.* or *The more concealed, the more conspicuous.* ❸需要 need: 胆～大而心～细。*The bolder one is, the more prudent one should be.* ❹将要，在动词前，表示动作就要开始(used before a verb) to be set to; to be about to: 摇摇～坠 *tottering; to be on the verge of collapse* | 山雨～来风满楼。*The rising wind sweeping through the tower heralds a rising storm in the mountains.* or *The rising wind forebodes the coming storm.*

鹆 yù ㄩˋ 见 618 页"鸲"字条"鸲鹆"(qú—) see 鸲鹆 on p618

裕 yù ㄩˋ ❶丰富，宽绰 abundant; affluent: 生活富～ *well-to-do life* | 家里很宽～ *well-off family* | 时间不充～。*There isn't enough time.* ❷使富足 to enrich: 富国～民 *to enrich the country and its people*

[裕固族]我国少数民族，参看附表(see the appendix) the Yugu ethnic group, one of the ethnic minorities of China

饫 yù ㄩˋ 饱 to have eaten one's fill; to be full

妪(嫗) yù ㄩˋ 年老的女人 old lady; old woman

雨 ㊁ yù ㄩˋ 下(雨雪)(of rain or snow) to fall: ～雪 *to snow*

㊀ yǔ 见 918 页 see p918

郁(❶❷ 鬱) yù ㄩˋ ❶草木茂盛(叠 ***reduplication***) lush; luxuriant: ～～葱葱 *lush and verdant* ❷忧愁，愁闷 gloomy; depressed (㊀ ***doublet*** 忧— melancholy)(叠 ***reduplication***): ～～不乐 *depressed; gloomy* ❸有文采(叠 ***reduplication***) elegant; refined: 文采～～ *overflowing with literary elegance* ❹形容香气浓 rich fragrance: 馥(fù)～ *sweet-scented*

育 yù ㄩˋ ❶生养 to give birth to; to bear (㊥ *doublet* 生— to bear; to produce): 生儿～女 *to bear children; to have children* | 积极提倡计划生～ *to promote the policy of birth control* ❷养活 to rear; to raise; to bring up: ～婴 *to raise a baby* | ～蚕 *to raise silkworms* | ～林 *afforestation* ❸教育 to educate: 德～ *moral education* | 智～ *intellectual education* | 体～ *physical education*

堉 yù ㄩˋ〈古 *archaism*〉肥沃的土地 fertile farmland

淯 yù ㄩˋ 淯河, 水名, 在河南省栾川 Yuhe River in Luanchuan, Henan Province

昱 yù ㄩˋ ❶日光 sunlight; sunshine ❷光明 brightness

煜 yù ㄩˋ 照耀 to illuminate; to shine

狱(獄) yù ㄩˋ ❶监禁罪犯的地方 prison; jail (㊥ *doublet* 监— prison; jail) ❷官司, 罪案 lawsuit; case: 冤～ *unjust imprisonment; unjust verdict* | 文字～ *literary inquisition; imprisonment or persecution of an author on account of literary offence to rulers*

语 ㊀ yù ㄩˋ 告诉 to tell; to inform: 不以～人 *to keep sth unimformed from others*

㊁ yǔ 见 918 页 see p918

彧 yù ㄩˋ 有文采 of literary elegance

域 yù ㄩˋ ❶在一定疆界内的地方 territory: ～外 *outside the country; extraterritorial* ❷泛指某种范围 domain; sphere; range: 音～ *range of notes; compass of voice*

阈 yù ㄩˋ ❶门槛 threshold; doorsill ❷界限 limit; boundary: 视～ *visual threshold*

棫 yù ㄩˋ 古书上说的一种树 (in ancient Chinese texts) a kind of tree

蜮(**魊) yù ㄩˋ 传说中一种害人的动物 legendary animal to harm people: 鬼～ (喻阴险的人) *evil spirit; demon — the sinister*

预 yù ㄩˋ ❶预先, 事前 in advance; beforehand: ～备 *to prepare; to get ready* | ～见 *to predict; to foresee; to foretell* | ～防 *to prevent; to take precautions against; to guard against* | ～约 *to make an appointment* ❷加入到里面去 to take part in: 干～ *to interfere*

蓣 yù ㄩˋ 见 693 页"薯"字条"薯蓣"(shǔ—) see 薯蓣 on p693

滪 yù ㄩˋ 见 868 页"滟"字条"滟滪堆"(yàn——) see 滟滪堆 on p868

豫 yù ㄩˋ ❶欢喜, 快乐 pleased; delighted: 面有不～之色。*He looks displeased.* ❷同"预❶" same as 预❶ ❸安闲, 舒适 ease; comfortable: 忧劳兴国, 逸～亡身。*Care and diligence make a country prosperous while overindulgence spells ruin.* ❹河南省的别称 Yu, another name for Henan

谕 yù ㄩˋ ❶告诉，使人知道（旧指上级对下级或长辈对晚辈）(of superiors or seniors) to instruct; to decree; to enjoin: 面～ *face-to-face* (*or direct*) *order*; *personal order* | 手～ *hand-written directive* | 上～ *imperial edict* ❷〈古 ***archaism***〉同“喻” same as 喻

喻 yù ㄩˋ ❶比方 analogy; figure of speech (㊀ ***doublet*** 比— analogy; metaphor; simile): 我给你打个比～。*Let me show you an example.* ❷明白，了解 to understand; to know: 不言而～ *to be self-evident*; *it goes without saying* | 家～户晓 *household word*; *household name*; *known to all* ❸说明，使人了解 to explain; to make clear: ～之以理 *to expostulate with sb*; *to reason with sb*

愈(❸*瘉、❸*癒) yù ㄩˋ ❶更，越 more: ～来～好 *better and better* | ～甚 *even more* ❷贤，好 to surpass; to be better: 孰～(哪个好)? *Which is better?* ❸病好了 to heal; to recover (㊀ ***doublet*** 痊— to recover): 病～ *to recover from an illness*

尉 ㊁ yù ㄩˋ [尉迟]复姓 Yuchi, a two-character surname [尉犁]地名，在新疆维吾尔自治区 Yuli, a place in the Xinjiang Uygur Autonomous Region

㊀ wèi 见 786 页 see p786

蔚 ㊁ yù ㄩˋ ❶蔚县，在河北省 Yuxian County, in Hebei Province ❷姓 Yu, a surname

㊀ wèi 见 786 页 see p786

熨 ㊁ yù ㄩˋ [熨帖][熨贴](—tiē) **1** 妥帖舒服 comfortable; appropriate; fitting **2**〈方 ***dialect***〉(事情)完全办妥 settled; well-done

㊀ yùn 见 934 页 see p934

遇 yù ㄩˋ ❶相逢，会面，碰到 to meet; to encounter: ～雨 *to be caught in the rain* | 百年不～ *not to be seen in a hundred years*; *not likely to happen once in a century* | 不期而～ *to come across*; *to run into*; *unexpected encounter* ❷机会 opportunity; chance: 际～ *favourable turns in life*; *spells of good fortune* | 佳～ *favourable turns in life*; *spells of good fortune* ❸对待，款待 to treat; to entertain: 可善～之。*He deserves a good entertainment.* or *You'd better give him a good treatment.*

寓(*庽) yù ㄩˋ ❶居住 to reside; to inhabit; to live: ～所 *residence* | 暂～友人家 *to stay temporarily in a friend's home* ❷住的地方 residence; dwelling; abode: 张～ *Zhang's residence* | 公～ *flat*; *apartment* ❸寄托，含蓄在内 to imply: ～言 *fable*; *allegory* | ～意深刻 *to carry a profound moral*; *to be pregnant with meaning* [寓目]过目，看 to look over; to go through

御(❹禦) yù ㄩˋ ❶驾驶(车马) to drive (a

carriage)：～车 *to drive a carriage*｜～者(赶车的人) *carriage driver* ❷称与皇帝有关的 imperial：～用 *for the use of the emperor; to be employed by the emperor* ❸封建社会指上级对下级的管理，使用(of a superior in feudal society) to administer; to rule; to reign over：～下 *to administer one's subordinates* ❹抵挡 to resist; to defend; to ward off：防～ *to defend*｜～敌 *to resist an enemy*｜～寒 *to keep out the cold*

矞 yù ㄩˋ 矞云，象征祥瑞的彩云 auspicious colourful clouds

潏 yù ㄩˋ 水涌出(of water) to gush; to surge

遹 yù ㄩˋ 遵循。多用于人名(yu, usually used in a given name) to follow; to observe

燏 yù ㄩˋ 火光。多用于人名(yu, usually used in a given name) blaze; flame

鹬 yù ㄩˋ 鸟名。羽毛茶褐色，嘴、腿都很长，趾间无蹼，常在水边或田野中捕吃小鱼、小虫和贝类 sandpiper (*Scolopacidae*) [鹬蚌相争，渔翁得利]喻两败俱伤，便宜了第三者。When the snipe and the clam grapple, the fisherman profits — it's the third party that benefits from the tussle.

誉(譽) yù ㄩˋ ❶名誉，名声 reputation; fame：荣～ *honour* 特指好的名声(especially used to denote good reputation)：～满中外 *to attain international renown; to enjoy a reputation all over the world* ❷称赞 to praise; to commend; to extol (㊇ ***doublet*** 称一 to extol; to eulogize; to acclaim)：～不绝口 *to shower praise on sb*

毓 yù ㄩˋ 同"育"。多用于人名(yu, usually used in a given name) same as 育

燠 yù ㄩˋ 暖，热 warm; hot：～热(闷热) *sultry; sweltering*｜寒～失时 *unseasonably cold and hot; unseasonable weather*

鬻 yù ㄩˋ 卖 to sell; to vend：～文为生 *to make a living by writing*｜卖官～爵 *to sell ranks and titles*

YUAN ㄩㄢ

鸢 yuān ㄩㄢ 鸟名，即老鹰。身体褐色，常捕食蛇、鼠、兔等 kite; hawk [纸鸢]风筝 kite

眢 yuān ㄩㄢ 眼睛枯陷，失明(of eyes) wizened and blind ㊀ ***extension*** 干枯 dried-up：～井 *dry well*

鸳 yuān ㄩㄢ [鸳鸯](—yāng) 水鸟名。羽毛颜色美丽，形状像凫(fú)，但比凫小，雌雄常在一起 mandarin duck (*Aix galericulata*) 文学上用来比喻夫妻(used to denote an affectionate couple in Chinese literature)

鹓 yuān ㄩㄢ [鹓鶵](—chú) 古代传说中的一种像凤凰

的鸟(in ancient Chinese texts) legendary bird like the phoenix

篼 yuān ㄩㄢ 篼箕,用竹篾等编成的盛东西的器具 woven bamboo basket

冤(*寃) yuān ㄩㄢ ❶冤枉,屈枉 wrong; injustice; grievance:鸣～*to air grievances*|伸～*to redress an injustice; to right a wrong* ❷仇恨 hatred; enmity ([连] ***doublet*** —仇 enmity; rancour):～家 *enemy; foe*|～孽 *enmity and sin* ❸欺骗 to fool; to kid:不许～人。*Don't kid me!* or *No kidding!* ❹上当,不合算 not worthwhile:白跑一趟,真～。*What a bad luck, nothing came of my trip.*

渊(淵) yuān ㄩㄢ 深水,潭 abyss; deep pool:鱼跃于～。*Fish are springing up to the surface of the deep pool.* [喻] ***figurative*** 深 deep:～博(学识深而广) *erudite*

蜎 yuān ㄩㄢ 古书上指孑孓(in ancient Chinese texts) wriggler; wiggler

元 yuán ㄩㄢˊ ❶开始,第一 first; initial; primary ([连] ***doublet*** —始 beginning; genesis):～旦 *New Year's Day*|～月 *January; the first lunar month*|～年 *first year (of an era or of an emperor's reign)* [元素]在化学上,具有相同核电荷数的同一类原子的总称。现在已知的元素有 112 种 element [元音]发音的时候,从肺里出来的气使声带颤动,在口腔的通路上不受阻碍而发出的声音,也叫"母音"。拼音字母 a、o、u 等都是元音(also called 母音) vowel ❷为首的 chief; principal:～首 *head of state*|～帅 *marshal*|～勋 *hero of great distinction; a man of great merit* ❸构成一个整体的 unit; component:单～*unit*|～件 *part* ❹朝代名(公元 1271—1368 年)。公元 1206 年,蒙古孛儿只斤·铁木真称成吉思汗。1271 年,国号改为元。1279 年灭南宋。the Yuan Dynasty (1271－1368). In 1206, the Mongolian Temujin proclaimed himself to be Chenghis Khan. The dynasty was named Yuan in 1271. Later in 1279, the Yuan destroyed the Southern Song Dynasty. ❺同"圆❹" same as 圆❹

芫 ㊀ yuán ㄩㄢˊ 芫花,落叶灌木,开紫色小花,有毒,花蕾可入药 lilac daphne (*Daphne genkwa*)

㊁ yán 见 863 页 see p863

园(園) yuán ㄩㄢˊ ❶(—子、—儿)种植菜蔬花果的地方 garden; plot; plantation [园地] **1** 菜园、花园、果园等的统称 general term for vegetable plots, gardens and orchards **2** 比喻活动的范围 scope for activity:艺术～～ *field of activities for arts; art field* ❷(—儿)供人游玩或娱乐的地方 park; garden:公～ *park*|动物～ *zoo; zoological garden*

沅 yuán ㄩㄢˊ 沅江，发源于贵州省，东北流至湖南省注入洞庭湖 Yuanjiang River, originating in Guizhou Province and running northeastward through Hunan Province into the Dongting Lake

鼋(黿) yuán ㄩㄢˊ 即鳖 (i. e. 鳖) Asian giant softshell turtle (*Pelochelys bibroni*)

员 ㊀ yuán ㄩㄢˊ ❶指工作或学习的人 people engaged in some field of work or study: 学～*student*｜演～*actor; actress* ❷指团体组织中的成员 member: 党～*Party member; member of the Chinese Communist Party*｜团～*League member; member of the Communist Youth League of China*｜会～(*of an organization*) *member* ❸量词 ***quantifier***，用于武将等(used to describe a military officer): 一～大将 *a valiant general* ❹周围 vicinity: 幅～(指疆域) *width and vicinity — area of national territory*

㊁ yún 见 932 页 see p932

㊂ yùn 见 933 页 see p933

圆 yuán ㄩㄢˊ ❶圆形，从它的中心点到周边任何一点的距离都相等 circle ❷像球的形状 ball-shaped: 滚～*rotund; tubby*｜滴溜儿～ *perfectly round* ❸完备，周全 tactful; satisfactory: 结果很～满 *satisfactory result* ㊀ ***extension*** 使之周全(多指掩饰矛盾)(usually used to denote covering up contradictions) to make plausible: 自～其说 *to make one's statement consistent; to justify oneself*｜～谎 *to make a lie sound plausible* ❹我国的本位货币单位。也作"元"(also written as 元) *yuan*, standard unit of Chinese currency

垣 yuán ㄩㄢˊ ❶墙，矮墙 wall; low wall: 断瓦颓～*debris; ruins* ❷城 city: 省～(省城) *provincial metropolis*

爰 yuán ㄩㄢˊ ❶于是 hence; thereupon; consequently: ～书其事以告。*Therefore I'm writing to you about it.* ❷何处，哪里 where: ～其适归? *Where am I to go?*

援 yuán ㄩㄢˊ ❶引，牵 to draw; to pull (㊁ ***doublet*** 一引 to quote; to cite; to invoke) ❷帮助，救助 to help; to rescue (㊁ ***doublet*** 一助 to aid): 孤立无～*to be isolated and helpless*｜支～前线 *to support the front* ❸引用 to quote; to cite: ～例 *to cite a precedent*

湲 yuán ㄩㄢˊ 见 74 页"潺"字条"潺湲"(chán—) see 潺湲 on p74

媛 ㊀ yuán ㄩㄢˊ ［婵媛］**1** (姿态)美好(of a lady) fair; lovely **2** 牵连，相连 linked; joined

㊁ yuàn 见 928 页 see p928

袁 yuán ㄩㄢˊ 姓 Yuan, a surname

猿(*猨) yuán ㄩㄢˊ 猴一类的动物，颊下没有囊，没有尾巴，猩猩、大猩

猩、长臂猿等都是 ape (*Pongidae*)

辕 yuán ㄩㄢˊ ❶车辕子，车前驾牲畜的部分 shafts (of a cart, carriage, etc) ❷辕门，旧时称军营的门 (in former times) outer gate of a barrack [引] ***extension*** 旧时军政大官的衙门 (in former times) outer gate of a government office

原 yuán ㄩㄢˊ ❶最初的，开始的 primary; original ([连] ***doublet*** 一始 original; primitive): ～稿 *original copy*; *manuscript* | ～创 *original* [引] ***extension*** 没有经过加工的 raw; crude; unrefined: ～油 *crude oil* | ～煤 *raw coal* [原子]构成元素的最小粒子 atom ❷原来，本来 formerly; originally: 这话～不错。*His words sounded OK at the time.* | ～打算去请他。*We had intended to invite him.* | 放还～处 *to put it back in its place* ❸谅解，宽容 to excuse; to pardon ([连] ***doublet*** 一谅 to forgive): 情有可～ *excusable*; *forgivable*; *pardonable* | 不可～谅的错误 *unpardonable mistake* ❹宽广平坦的地方 plain; levels; vast and flat land: ～野 *wild field* | 平～ *plain* | 高～ *plateau* | 大草～ *prairie*; *grassland* ❺同"塬" same as 塬

塬 yuán ㄩㄢˊ 我国西北部黄土高原地区因流水冲刷而形成的高地，四边陡，顶上平 tableland; terrace

源 yuán ㄩㄢˊ ❶水流所从出的地方 water source; fountainhead: 泉～ *fountainhead*; *springhead* | 河～ *source of a river*; *riverhead* [源源]继续不断 continuously: ～～而来 *to come in a steady and endless flow* ❷事物的根由，来路 source; cause: 来～ *source* | 货～ *source of goods*; *source of supplies* | 肥～ *source of manure*

嫄 yuán ㄩㄢˊ 用于人名。姜嫄，传说是周朝祖先后稷的母亲 (*yuan*, usually used in a given name) Jiang Yuan, mother of Hou Ji, ancestor of the Zhou Dynasty according to the legend

螈 yuán ㄩㄢˊ 见635页"蝾"字条"蝾螈"(róng—) see 蝾螈 on p635

羱 yuán ㄩㄢˊ 羱羊，即北山羊。似家畜山羊而大，生活在高山地带，吃草本植物 (i. e. 北山羊) ibex (*Capra ibex*)

缘 yuán ㄩㄢˊ ❶因由，原因 reason; cause ([连] ***doublet*** 一故 reason; cause | 一由 reason; cause): 无～无故 *without rhyme or reason*; *for no reason at all* | 没有～由 *without any reason* ❷过去宿命论者指人与人的遇合或结成关系的原因 destined relationship; predestined relationship: 姻～ *predestined marriage* | 有～相见 *to have the luck to meet* ❸沿，顺着 along: ～流而上 *to go upward along the river* | ～木求

鱼(喻必然得不到) *to climb a tree to catch a fish — it's bound to be fruitless.* ❹ 边 edge; rim (㊀ **doublet** 边— edge; brink) ❺因为 because: ～何至此? *Why did you come here?*

橼 yuán ㄩㄢˊ 见 370 页"枸"字条"枸橼"(jǔ—) see 枸橼 on p370

圜 ㊁ yuán ㄩㄢˊ 同"圆"same as 圆

㊀ huán 见 291 页 see p291

远(遠) yuǎn ㄩㄢˇ ❶ 跟"近"相对(the opposite of 近) **1** 距离长 distant; faraway; remote: 路～ *a long way; a long journey* | 住得～ *to live in a distant place; to live far from here* **2** 时间长 remote; distant (㊀ **doublet** 永— forever; permanent; everlasting; perpetual | 长—long-term; long-range): 作长～打算 *to take a long view; to make a long-term plan* ❷不亲密,不接近 distant; remote: ～亲 *distant relative* | 敬而～之 *to keep respectfully aloof from sb* ❸(差别)大(of difference) far: 差得～ *to be far inferior to* ❹深远 profound; abstruse: 言近旨～ *simple in language but profound in meaning*

苑 yuàn ㄩㄢˋ ❶养禽兽植林木的地方,旧时多指帝王的园林(usually used to denote the imperial garden in former times) enclosed ground for growing trees and keeping animals: 鹿～ *deer park* ❷(学术、文艺)荟萃之处(of academic research, art or literature) centre: 文～ *literary circle; literary world* | 艺～奇葩 *exquisite works of art; superb works of art*

怨 yuàn ㄩㄢˋ ❶仇恨 resentment; enmity (㊀ **doublet** —恨 resentment) ❷不满意,责备 to complain; to blame: 毫无～言 *without a word of complaint* | 任劳任～ *to bear hardships without grudge* | 这事不能～他。*He is not to be blamed for that.* [怨不得]怪不得 so that's why; no wonder; cannot blame

院 yuàn ㄩㄢˋ ❶(—子、—儿)围墙里房屋四周的空地 courtyard; yard; compound ❷某些机关和公共场所的名称 designation for certain government institutions and public places: 法～ *court* | 医～ *hospital* | 戏～ *theatre* ❸专指学院 college; university; institute: 高等～校 *colleges and universities; institutions of higher learning*

垸 yuàn ㄩㄢˋ 〈方 **dialect**〉(—子)湖南省、湖北省在江湖地带挡水用的堤圩(wéi) protective embankment built around houses or fields in riverside and lakeside areas in Hunan and Hubei Province

掾 yuàn ㄩㄢˋ 古代官署属员的通称 general term for ancient subordinates or minor officials

媛 ㊀ yuàn ㄩㄢˋ 美女 beautiful lady

㊁ yuán 见 925 页 see p925

瑗 yuàn ㄩㄢˋ 大孔的璧 fine jade with a big hole

愿(❶-❸願) yuàn ㄩㄢˋ ❶乐意 to be willing; to be ready; to be glad: 甘心情～ *to be most willing; to be perfectly happy* | 自觉自～ *of one's own free will; voluntarily* ❷希望 hope (㊀ **doublet** 一望 wish): 生平之～ *lifelong wish* | 如～以偿 *to have one's wish fulfilled; to achieve what one wishes* ❸迷信的人对神佛许下的酬谢 (to Buddha or God) vow: 许～ *to make a vow to a deity* | 还～ *to fulfill a vow to a deity* ❹恭谨 honest and prudent

YUE ㄩㄝ

曰 yuē ㄩㄝ ❶说 to say: 荀子～ *Xunzi says* | 其谁～不然? *Who said that it was wrong?* ❷叫作 to call; to name: 名之～农民学校 *to name it Farmers' School*

约 ㊀ yuē ㄩㄝ ❶拘束, 限制 to restrict; to restrain (㊀ **doublet** 一束 to restrain) ❷共同议定的要遵守的条款 pact; treaty; agreement: 条～ *treaty; pact* | 立～ *to conclude a treaty; to sign an agreement* | 爱国公～ *patriotic pledge* ❸预先说定 to make an appointment: 预～ *to make an appointment* | 和他～好了。*I have made an appointment with him.* ❹请 to invite: ～他来 *to invite him to come here* | 特～记者 *special correspondent* ❺算术上指用公因数去除分子和分母使分数简化 reduction of a fraction: 5/10 可以～成 1/2。*Five over ten can be reduced to one over two.* ❻俭省 economical; frugal; thrifty: 节～ *to economize; to save; to practise thrift* ❼简单, 简要 simple; brief; succinct: 简～ *brief; concise; sketchy* | 由博返～ *from complexity to simplicity* ❽大约, 大概, 不十分确定 about; around; approximately: ～计 *to come roughly to; to count roughly* | ～数 *approximate figure; appropriate number; divisor* | 大～有五十人 *about 50 people*

㊁ yāo 见 873 页 see p873

矱 yuē ㄩㄝ 尺度, 标准 yardstick; measure; scale

彟(彠) yuē ㄩㄝ 尺度 yardstick; measure; scale

哕(噦) yuě ㄩㄝˇ 呕吐 to vomit: 刚吃完药, 都～出来了。*All the medicine taken just now was thrown up.* [干哕] (gānyue) 要吐而吐不出东西来 to retch; to feel sick

月 yuè ㄩㄝˋ ❶月亮, 地球的卫星, 本身不发光, 它的光是反射太阳的光 moon [月食] (*月蚀) 地球在日、月中间成一条直线, 遮住太阳照到月亮上的光 lunar eclipse ❷计时单位,一年分十二个月 month［月子］（－zi）指妇女生产后一个月以内的时间（of woman）first month of confinement after giving birth to a child：坐～～*to be in confinement* ❸形状像月亮的，圆的 round：～饼 *moon cake*｜～琴 yueqin，*four-or-three stringed plucked musical instrument with a full-moon shaped sound box* ❹按月出现或完成的 monthly：～经 *menses；monthly period*｜～刊 *monthly；monthly publication*｜～票 *monthly ticket；monthly pass*｜～报表 *monthly report*
［月氏］（－zhī）我国古代西部民族名 the Yuezhi ethnic group，one of the western ethnic groups in ancient China

刖（**趴）yuè ㄩㄝˋ 古代的一种酷刑，把脚砍掉（in ancient China）cruel punishment of chopping off the feet

玥 yuè ㄩㄝˋ 古代传说中的一种神珠（in ancient legend）magic pearl

钥（鑰）㊀ yuè ㄩㄝˋ 锁 lock［锁钥］㊥ ***figurative*** **1** 重要关键 key **2** 边防要地 town of strategic importance：北门～～*northern town of strategic importance*

㊁ yào 见 876 页 see p876

乐（樂）㊁ yuè ㄩㄝˋ ❶音乐 music：奏～*to play music*［乐清］地名，在浙江省 Yueqing，a place，located in Zhejiang Province ❷姓 Yue，a surname

㊀ lè 见 422 页 see p422

栎（櫟）㊁ yuè ㄩㄝˋ［栎阳］古地名，在今陕西省临潼 Yueyang，an ancient place，located in today's Lintong，Shaanxi Province

㊀ lì 见 436 页 see p436

岳（❶*嶽）yuè ㄩㄝˋ ❶高大的山 lofty mountain［五岳］我国五座名山，即东岳泰山，西岳华山，南岳衡山，北岳恒山，中岳嵩山 Five Sacred Mountains in China — Mount Tai or Taishan Mountain，the Eastern Sacred Mountain in Shandong Province；Mount Heng or Hengshan Mountain，the Southern Sacred Mountain in Hunan Province；Mount Hua or Huashan Mountain，the Western Sacred Mountain in Shaanxi Province；Mount Heng or Hengshan Mountain，the Northern Sacred Mountain in Shanxi Province；Mount Song or Songshan Mountain，the Central Sacred Mountain in Henan Province ❷称妻的父母或妻的叔伯 wife's parents or uncle：～父 *wife's father；father-in-law*｜叔～ *wife's uncle；uncle-in-law*

说 ㊂ yuè ㄩㄝˋ 古同"悦" same as 悦 in ancient chinese

㊀ shuō 见 701 页 see p701

㊁ shuì 见 700 页 see p700

阅 yuè ㄩㄝˋ ❶看，察看 to read；to inspect（㊣ ***dou-***

blet 一览 to read)：～报 *to read newspapers*｜传～ *to circulate for perusal*｜检～军队 *to review troops; to inspect troops* ❷经历，经过 to experience; to pass through; to undergo：～历 *experience*｜～世 *to see the world*

悦 yuè ㄩㄝˋ ❶高兴，愉快 happy; pleased (㊟ **doublet** 喜一 happy; joyous)：和颜～色 *to be all smiles and sweetness; to have a genial expression*｜心～诚服 *to have a heartfelt admiration* ❷使愉快 to please; to delight：～耳 *to be pleasing to the ear*｜赏心～目 *to be pleasing to the eyes and mind; to rejoice the eyes and the heart*

钺(**戉) yuè ㄩㄝˋ 古代兵器名，像斧，比斧大些 (in ancient China) battleaxe, weapon shaped like but bigger than a broad axe

越 yuè ㄩㄝˋ ❶度过，超出 to go beyond **1** 度过阻碍 to surmount; to get over; to cross：爬山～岭 *to cross over hills and mountains* **2** 不按照一般的次序，超出范围 to exceed; to overstep：～级 *to bypass one's immediate superior*｜～权 *to overstep one's authority; to go beyond one's power*｜～俎(zǔ)代庖(páo)(喻越职做别人应做的事) *to exceed one's functions and meddle in other people's affairs; to take sb else's job into one's own hands* **3** 经过 to pass; to go through：～冬 *to live through the winter; to survive the winter* ❷扬起，昂扬(of one's voice or emotion) to be at high pitch：声音清～ *clear and melodious voice* ❸副词 **adverb**，越……越……，表示程度加深 the more ... the more ...：～快～好。*The faster, the better.*｜～跑～有劲儿。*The farther he ran, the more energetic he became.*｜我们的队伍～战～强。*Our army grew stronger and stronger with each battle.*｜天气～来～暖和。*It's getting warmer and warmer.*［越发］副词 **adverb**，更加 even more：今年的收成～～好了。*We are reaping an even better harvest this year.* ❹抢夺 to snatch; to seize：杀人～货 *to rob and kill* ❺周代诸侯国名，在今浙江省东部，后扩展到浙江省北部、江苏全省、安徽省南部及山东省南部。后来用作浙江省东部的别称 Yue, a princedom of the Zhou Dynasty, situated in the eastern part of today's Zhejiang Province, later expanded to the northern part of Zhejiang Province, the whole of Jiangsu Province, the southern part of Anhui and Shandong provinces; later used as another name for the eastern part of Zhejiang Province：～剧 Shaoxing *Opera*; Yueju *Opera*

樾 yuè ㄩㄝˋ 树阴凉儿 shade of a tree

跃(躍) yuè ㄩㄝˋ 跳 to jump; to leap (㊀ **doublet** 跳— to jump): 飞～ *to leap* | 龙腾虎～(喻生气勃勃、威武雄壮的姿态) *dragons rising and tigers leaping — scene of hustling and bustling activity* | ～～欲试 *to be eager to have a try; to itch to have a go* [跃进] **1** 跳着前进 to leap forward **2** 极快地前进 to advance rapidly: 向前～～*to develop by leaps and bounds*

粤 yuè ㄩㄝˋ 广东省的别称 Yue, another name for Guangdong Province [两粤]指广东省和广西壮族自治区 Guangdong Province and Guangxi Zhuang Autonomous Region

鹫(鸑) yuè ㄩㄝˋ [鹫鹭](—zhuó) 古书上指一种水鸟(in ancient Chinese texts) a kind of legendary aquatic bird

龠 yuè ㄩㄝˋ ❶古代管乐器(in ancient China) wind musical instrument ❷古代容量单位,两龠是一合(gě) *yue*, ancient unit of capacity, two *yue* is one *ge*

瀹 yuè ㄩㄝˋ ❶煮 to boil; to cook: ～茗(烹茶) *to make tea* ❷疏导(河道) to dredge: ～济(jǐ)漯(tà) *to dredge the Jita River*

籥 yuè ㄩㄝˋ 同"龠❶" same as 龠❶

篗(**簑) yuè ㄩㄝˋ 〈方 **dialect**〉(—子) 绕丝、纱等的工具 reel; spool; tools used to reel silk, yarn, etc

YUN ㄩㄣ

晕 ㊀ yūn ㄩㄣ 昏迷 to faint; to swoon; to lose consciousness: ～倒 *to faint* | ～过去了 *to lose consciousness* ㊁ **extension** 头脑不清 muddleheaded: 头～*dizzy; faint* | ～头转向 *muddleheaded; in a muddle*

㊁ yùn 见 934 页 see p934

氲 yūn ㄩㄣ 见 894 页"氤"字条"氤氲"(yīn—) see 氤氲 on p894

赟 yūn ㄩㄣ 美好。多用于人名(yun, ususlly used in a given name) fine

云(❸雲) yún ㄩㄣˊ ❶说 to say: 诗～*the poem says* | 人～亦～*to repeat what others say; to parrot others' words; to echo others' views without thinking* ❷文言助词 ***auxiliary in classical Chinese***,句首句中句末都用(used at the beginning, in the middle and at the end of a sentence): ～谁之思? *Whose idea is it?* | 岁～暮矣。*The year is drawing to its end.* | 盖记时也～。*This is a description of the season.* ❸水蒸气上升遇冷凝聚成微小的水点成团地在空中飘浮叫"云"cloud: ～彩 *cloud* | ～消雾散 *The clouds vanish and the mists disperse; to vanish* *into thin air*｜～集(喻许多人或事物聚集在一起) *to assemble*; *to gather*; *to converge*

芸(❷蕓) yún ㄩㄣˊ ❶芸香,多年生草本植物,花黄色,花、叶、茎有特殊气味,可入药 common rue (*Ruta graveolens*) ❷芸薹(tái),又叫"油菜"。二年生草本植物,花黄色,种子可榨油(also called 油菜) rape (*Brassica napus*)

[芸芸]形容众多 numerous; innumerable:～～众生 *all living things*; *all moral beings*; *common populace*

沄(❷澐) yún ㄩㄣˊ ❶[沄沄]形容水流动 (of water) flowing ❷大波浪 billow; surging wave; torrential wave

纭 yún ㄩㄣˊ [纷纭](fēn—)(言论、事情等)多而杂乱 numerous and disorderly; diverse and confused:众说～～ *Opinions are widely divergent*.

耘 yún ㄩㄣˊ 除草 to weed:～田 *to weed the fields*｜春耕夏～*to plough in spring and to weed in summer*

匀 yún ㄩㄣˊ ❶平均,使平均 even; to even up; to divide evenly (㊇ *doublet* 均—even):颜色涂得不～。*The colour is not evenly spread*.｜这两份儿多少不均,～—～吧。*The two portions are not equal, please even them up*. ❷从中抽出一部分给别人或做他用 to spare:把你买的纸～给我一些。*Would you spare me some of the paper you bought?*｜先～出两间房来给新来的同志。*Let's first spare two rooms for the newcomers*.

昀 yún ㄩㄣˊ 日光。多用于人名(yun, usually used in a given name) sunlight; sunshine

畇 yún ㄩㄣˊ 田地平坦整齐的样子(叠 ***reduplication***) (of fields) neat; tidy

筠 ㊀ yún ㄩㄣˊ ❶竹皮 skin of bamboo ❷竹子 bamboo

㊁ jūn 见378页 see p378

鋆 yún ㄩㄣˊ (在人名中也读 jūn also pronounced as jūn in a given name) 金子 gold

员 ㊁ yún ㄩㄣˊ 用于人名。伍员(即伍子胥),春秋时人 (yun, usually used in a given name) Wu Yun (Wu Zixu), living in the Spring and Autumn Period

㊀ yuán 见925页 see p925

㊂ yùn 见933页 see p933

郧 yún ㄩㄣˊ 郧县,地名,在湖北省 Yunxian County, Hubei Province

涢 yún ㄩㄣˊ 涢水,水名,在湖北省北部 Yunshui River in the northern part of Hubei Province

篔 yún ㄩㄣˊ [篔筜](—dāng)生长在水边的大竹子 tall bamboo growing by the waterside

允 yǔn ㄩㄣˇ ❶答应,认可 to allow; to consent (㊇ ***dou-***

blet 一许 to permit; to allow): ～诺 *to promise; to consent* | 应～*to agree; to promise; to consent* | 不～*to refuse to give consent; not to allow* ❷公平得当(dàng) fair; just: 公～ *impartial; fair and square*

狁 yǔn ㄩㄣˇ 见 814 页"猃"字条"猃狁"(xiǎn—) see 猃狁 on p814

陨 yǔn ㄩㄣˇ 坠落 to fall from the sky or outer space: ～石 *aerolite*

殒 yǔn ㄩㄣˇ 死亡 to perish; to die: ～命 *to die; to perish*

孕 yùn ㄩㄣˋ ❶怀胎 to be pregnant: ～妇 *pregnant woman* | ～期 *pregnancy; gestation* | ～育 *to nurture* ❷胎,身孕 foetus; embryo: 有～*to be pregnant* | 怀～ *to become pregnant*

运(運) yùn ㄩㄣˋ ❶旋转,循序移动 to rotate; to revolve: 日月～行 *revolution of the sun and the moon* [运动] **1** 物理学上指物体的位置连续不断地变化的现象(in physics) motion; movement **2** 哲学上指物质的存在形式和根本属性(in philosophy) motion; movement **3** 各种锻炼身体的活动,如体操、游泳等 sports; exercise; athletics **4** 政治、文化、生产等方面开展的有组织的群众性活动 movement; campaign; drive: 五四～～*May 4th Movement of 1919* | 增产节约～～*movement of increasing production and practicing economy* **5** (—dong) 为求达到某种目的而钻营奔走 to intrigue to gain ends; to arrange things through pull [运作](组织、机构等)进行工作;开展活动 to operate; to work; to implement: 正常～～ *proper working* | ～～方式很多 *various operating modes* ❷搬送 to carry; to transport; to ship (㊟ ***doublet*** 一输 to transport): ～货 *to transport cargo; to freight goods* | 客～*passenger transport* | 陆～*land transport* ❸运用,灵活使用 to use; to utilize; to wield: ～笔 *to wield the pen* | ～思 *to work out a concept; to exercise one's mind* | ～筹 *to draw up a plan; to map out a strategy* ❹指人的遭遇 fortune; luck; fate 特指迷信的人所说的命中注定的遭遇 destiny; lot; karma: 幸～*fortunate; lucky* | 走好～*to have good luck*

酝(醞) yùn ㄩㄣˋ 酿酒,也指酒(also used to denote wine) to ferment wine; to make wine; to brew beer: 佳～(好酒) *good wine* [酝酿](—niàng) 造酒材料加工后的发酵过程 fermentation ㊕ ***figurative*** 事前考虑或磋商使条件成熟 to deliberate on: 表决前要进行～～。*We should deliberate and consult on it before voting.*

员 ㊂ yùn ㄩㄣˋ 姓 Yun, a surname

㊀ yuán 见 925 页 see p925
㊁ yún 见 932 页 see p932

郓 yùn ㄩㄣˋ［郓城］地名，在山东省 Yuncheng, a place in Shandong Province

恽 yùn ㄩㄣˋ 姓 Yun, a surname

晕 ㊀ yùn ㄩㄣˋ ❶日光或月光通过云层时因折射作用而在太阳或月亮周围形成的光圈 halo; aureola：日～ *solar halo*｜月～而风。*The halo of the moon predicts the rising of wind*. ❷头发昏 dizzy; giddy; muddle-headed：一坐船就～ *to feel dizzy whenever on ship*

㊁ yūn 见 931 页 see p931

愠 yùn ㄩㄣˋ 怒，怨恨 angry; irritated：面有～色 *to appear angry; to look irritated*

缊 yùn ㄩㄣˋ ❶新旧混合的丝绵 silk wadding made of old and new floss：～袍 *floss-padded robe* ❷碎麻 bits of hemp, flax, etc

韫（韞） yùn ㄩㄣˋ 藏，收藏 to conceal; to collect; to store：～椟而藏诸（收在柜子里藏起来吗）？*Will it be stored up in the cabinet?*｜石～玉而山辉。*The stone that contains jade glorifies the mountain.*

蕴 yùn ㄩㄣˋ ❶包含，储藏 to contain; to hold in store（㊟ **doublet** 一藏 to hold in store）：我国石油～藏量很大。*Our country is rich in petroleum deposits*. ❷事理的深奥之处 profundity：底～ *profundity*｜精～ *profundity*

韵（*韻） yùn ㄩㄣˋ ❶语音名词 term of phonetics **1** 韵母，字音中声母、声调以外部分，包括介音在内，如"堂"（táng）的韵母是 ang，"皇"（huáng）的韵母是 uang vowel in a Chinese syllable, not including its consonant and tone, e.g. ang in 堂（táng）and uang in 皇（huáng）**2** 字音中声母、介音、声调以外的部分，如"堂皇"（táng-huáng）都是 ang 韵。又如 an、ian、uan、üan 是四个韵母，同是 an 韵 vowel in a Chinese syllable, excluding consonant, head vowel and tone, e.g. ang in 堂（táng）and uang in 皇（huáng）; an in an, ian, uan and üan：～文 *verse; rhymed prose*｜押～ *to rhyme; to be in rhyme*｜叶（xié）～ *to rhyme* ❷有节奏的声音 rhythmic sound：琴～悠扬 *melodious lute music* ❸风致，情趣 charm; appeal：风～ *graceful bearing; charm*｜～味 *lasting appeal; aroma*｜神～（*in literature and art*）*verve; romantic charm*

熨 ㊀ yùn ㄩㄣˋ 用烙铁、熨斗把衣布等烫平 to iron; to press［熨斗］（-dǒu）加热后用来烫平衣服的金属器具 flat iron; iron

㊁ yù 见 922 页 see p922

Z ㄗ

ZA ㄗㄚ

扎（*紮、*紥）㊂ zā ㄗㄚ ❶捆，缠束 to tie; to bind; to fasten：～辫子 *to plait one's hair*｜～腿 *to bind the bottoms of one's trouser legs* ❷把儿，捆儿 bundle; bunch：一～线 *a bundle of thread*

㊀ zhā 见 947 页 see p947
㊁ zhá 见 948 页 see p948

匝（*帀）zā ㄗㄚ ❶周 circle; circumference：绕树三～*to circle a tree three times* ❷满，环绕 full; surrounding：柳阴～地。*The willows shadowed the ground underneath.*

咂 zā ㄗㄚ ❶舌尖与腭接触发声 to make a tchick：～嘴 *to click the tongue* ❷吸，呷 to sip; to suck：～一口酒 *to take a sip of wine* ❸仔细辨别 to taste carefully：～滋味 *to savour*

拶 ㊀ zā ㄗㄚ 逼迫 to force; to compel

㊁ zǎn 见 938 页 see p938

杂（雜、*襍）zá ㄗㄚˊ ❶多种多样的，不单纯的 miscellaneous; sundry; mixed：～色 *variegated colours; a motley of colours*｜～事 *trifles; trivialities; odd jobs*｜～技表演 *acrobatic show; acrobatics*｜人多手～。*Too many cooks spoil the broth.*［杂志］把许多文章集在一起印行的期刊 magazine; periodical; journal ❷掺杂，混合 to mix; to mingle; to blend; to intersperse：夹～*to be mixed with; to be mingled with* ❸正项或正式以外的 extra; irregular：～费 *miscellaneous* (*or incidental*) *expenses*｜～牌儿军 *troop of promiscuous allegiances*

砸 zá ㄗㄚˊ ❶打，捣 to pound; to tamp; to ram：～钉子 *to drive in a nail; to knock in a nail*｜～地基 *to tamp* (*or ram*) *the foundation* ❷打坏，打破 to break; to smash; to shatter：碗～了。*The bowl is smashed.*｜～碎铁锁链 *to break the shackles* ㊕ ***transfer*** 失败 to fail：这件事搞～了。*The job was bungled.*

咋（**哫）㊁ zǎ ㄗㄚˇ〈方 ***dialect***〉代词 ***pronoun***，怎，怎么 what; how; why：～好？*What should we do?*｜～办？*What's to be done?*

㊀ zé 见 944 页 see p944
㊂ zhā 见 947 页 see p947

臜 za・ㄗㄚ 见 1 页"腌"字条"腌臜"(ā—) see 腌臜 on p1

Z ZAI ㄗㄞ

灾(*災、*烖) zāi ㄗㄞ ❶水、火、荒旱等所造成的祸害 disaster; calamity; catastrophe:战胜～害 *to overcome disasters*|旱～ *drought* ❷个人的不幸遭遇 misfortune; adversity; mishap:飞～*unexpected disaster*|招～惹祸 *to court disaster; to invite trouble*

甾 zāi ㄗㄞ 有机化合物的一类,广泛存在于动植物体内。胆固醇和许多种激素都属于甾类化合物。在医药上应用很广 steroid

哉 zāi ㄗㄞ 文言助词 ***auxiliary in classical Chinese*** **1** 表疑问或反问语气(used to ask a question or make a retort):有何难～? *What's so difficult about it?*|岂有他～? *What else can we do?* or *How could there be other ways?* **2** 表感叹语气(used to express interjection):呜呼哀～! *Alas!*|诚～斯言! *What a sincere remark!*

栽 zāi ㄗㄞ ❶种植 to plant; to grow:～菜 *to grow vegetables*|～树 *to plant trees* ㊁ ***extension*** 安上,插上 to insert; to plant:～绒 *tufted fabric*|～赃 *to frame sb; to fabricate a charge against sb* ❷(一子)秧子,可以移植的植物幼苗 seedling:桃～ *peach seedling*|树～子 *young tree* ❸跌倒 to tumble; to fall:～跟头 *to fall; to tumble; to topple*|～了一跤 *to trip and fall*

仔 ㊁ zǎi ㄗㄞˇ 〈方 ***dialect***〉同"崽"same as 崽

㊀ zǐ 见1011页 see p1011

㊂ zī 见1008页 see p1008

载 ㊁ zǎi ㄗㄞˇ ❶年 year:一年半～*in a year or so* ❷记在书报上 to record; to write down(㊎ ***doublet*** 记一 to record):历史记～*historical records*|登～*to publish; to carry*|刊～*to publish in a newspaper or a magazine*|转～*to reprint*

㊀ zài 见938页 see p938

宰 zǎi ㄗㄞˇ ❶杀牲畜 to slaughter; to butcher(㊎ ***doublet*** 一杀 to slaughter|屠一 to butcher):～猪 *to butcher pigs*|～鸡 *to kill chickens* ㊂ ***figurative*** 向买东西或接受服务的人索取高价 to overcharge; to soak:挨～ *to be fleeced*|～人 *to rip off; to soak sb* ❷主管,主持 to govern; to rule:主～*to dominate; to have the final say*|～制 *to rule; to dominate* ❸古代官名 ancient official title:太～*warden* [宰相]古代辅佐君王掌管国家大事的最高的官(in ancient China) prime minister; chancellor

崽 zǎi ㄗㄞˇ ❶〈方 ***dialect***〉小孩子 kid ❷(一子、一儿)幼小的动物 young animal; whelp; pup

再 zài ㄗㄞˋ ❶两次,第二次 twice; second time:一而～,～而三 *again and again;*

time and again ❷第二次出现，重复发生 to recur：良辰难～。*Opportunity knocks but once.*｜青春不～。*One's youth never returns.* ❸副词 ***adverb*** **1** 表示又一次 again：～版 *second edition*｜～接～厉 *to make persistent efforts; to continue to exert oneself*｜一错～错 *to make a series of mistakes; to repeat an error* [再三]副词 ***adverb***，不止一次地，一次又一次地 repeatedly; again and again：～～考虑 *with repeated consideration* **2** 表示事情或行为重复，继续，多指未然(与"又"不同)(different from 又)(used to indicate an action that will be repeated in future) again：明天～来。*Come again tomorrow.*｜雨不会～下了。*It won't rain any longer.* **3** 用在两个动词之间，表示动作的先后关系(used between two verbs to indicate one action taking place after the completion of another) then：吃完饭～去学习。*Have your meal and then go on with your studies.*｜把材料整理好了～动笔写。*Start writing after you have arranged your materials in good order.* **4** 更，更加(to a greater extent or degree)：～好没有了。*It couldn't be any better.*｜～大一点就好了。*It would be better if it's still bigger.* **5** 表示另外有所补充(used to indicate additional information)：～则 *furthermore; moreover; besides*｜盘里放着葡萄、鸭梨，～就是苹果。*On the plate are grapes, pears, and apples as well.*

在 zài ㄗㄞˋ ❶存在 to exist; to be alive：革命者青春常～。*The revolutionaries will keep their youthful vitality permanently.*｜人～阵地～。*Even if there is only one person left, he won't give up the position.* ❷存在于某地点(used to indicate where a person or a thing is)：书～桌子上呢。*The book is on the table.*｜我今天晚上～家。*I'll be at home this evening.* [引] ***extension*** 留在，处在 to remain：～职 *to be on the job; to be in active service* ❸在于，关系于某方面，指出着重点 to consist in; to rest with：事～人为。*Man disposes.* or *It all depends on human effort.*｜学习进步，主要～自己努力。*Progress in studies mainly comes from one's own efforts.* [在乎] **1** 同"在❸"same as 在❸ **2** (－hu)关心注意 to care about; to mind; to take to heart：满不～～ *not to care in the least; not to mind at all; to be totally unconcerned* ❹副词 ***adverb***，正在，表示动作的进行(used to indicate an action in progress)：会议～进行。*The meeting is in progress.*｜我～看报。*I'm reading newspapers.* ❺介词 ***preposition***，表示事情的时间、地点、情形、范围等(used to indicate time, place, condition, scope, etc) at; in;

Z

on:～晚上读书 *to study in the evening*|～礼堂开会 *to have a meeting in the auditorium*|～这种条件之下 *under such conditions* ❻"在"和"所"连用,表示强调(used in collocation with 所 for emphasis):～所不辞 *will not decline under any circumstances*|～所不计 *regardless of the risk; whatever the cost*|～所难免 *unavoidable; inevitable*

载 ㊀ zài ㄗㄞˋ ❶用交通工具装 to load; to carry:装～ *to load; to be laden with*|～货 *to carry cargo; to carry freight*|～重汽车 *lorry; truck*|满～而归 *to return with full load; to come back with fruitful results* ❷充满 to fill; to be all over:怨声～道。*Complaints are heard everywhere.* or *Voices of discontent are heard everywhere.*|风雨～途。*There is a snowstorm in the journey.* ❸载……载……,用在动词前,表示两个动作同时进行(used before verbs) and; as well as; at the same time:～歌～舞 *singing and dancing joyously; singing and dancing festively* ❹姓 Zai, a surname

㊁ zǎi 见 936 页 see p936

ZAN ㄗㄢ

糌 zān ㄗㄢ [糌粑](－ba)青稞麦炒熟后磨成的面,是藏族的主食 *zanba*, roasted *qingke* barley flour, a staple food of the Tibetan ethnic group

簪 zān ㄗㄢ ❶(－子、－儿)用来绾(wǎn)住头发的一种首饰,古时也用它把帽子别在头发上 hairpin ❷插,戴 to wear in one's hair:～花 *to wear flowers in one's hair*

咱(*喒、*偺) zán ㄗㄢˊ 代词 ***pronoun*** ❶我 I; me:～不懂他的话。*I don't understand what he is saying.* ❷咱们 we; us:～穷人都翻身了。*We poor people have now stood up.* [咱们]"我"的多数,跟"我们"不同,包括听话的人在内(including both the speaker and the person or persons spoken to) we; us; you and I (*or* you and me):同志,你别客气,～～军民是一家嘛! *Comrade, please don't stand on ceremony. The army and the people are all of one family.*

拶 ㊁ zǎn ㄗㄢˇ 压紧 to press hard; to squeeze hard [拶指]旧时用拶子夹手指的酷刑(in former times) torture of squeezing a person's fingers between sticks [拶子]旧时夹手指的刑具(in former times) finger squeezer

㊀ zā 见 935 页 see p935

昝 zǎn ㄗㄢˇ 姓 Zan, a surname

噆 zǎn ㄗㄢˇ ❶叼,衔 to hold in the mouth ❷咬 to bite

攒(**儧) ㊀ zǎn ㄗㄢˇ 积聚,积蓄 to accumulate; to hoard; to save (㊀ ***doublet*** 积— to hoard; to amass): ~粪 *to accumulate manure* | ~钱 *to save money*

㊁ cuán 见112页 see p112

趱 zǎn ㄗㄢˇ ❶赶,快走 to hurry; to rush through: ~路 *to hurry on with one's journey* | 紧~了一程 *to rush through one leg of a journey* ❷催促,催逼 to urge; to hasten; to press: ~马向前 *to prick a horse onward*

暂(*蹔) zàn ㄗㄢˋ ❶时间短,跟"久"相对 (the opposite of 久) transient; transitory: 短~ *transient; transitory* ❷副词 ***adverb***,暂时 temporarily; momentarily: ~停 *to suspend; to halt; to pause* | ~行条例 *provisional regulations* | 会议~不举行。*The meeting is postponed for the time being.*

錾 zàn ㄗㄢˋ ❶(—子)凿石头的小凿子 chisel ❷在金石上雕刻 to engrave on gold or stone: ~花 *to carve flowers; to engrave patterns* | ~字 *to inscribe characters*

赞(*賛、❷❸*讚) zàn ㄗㄢˋ ❶帮助 to support; to assist: ~助 *to sponsor; to patronize; to support* [赞成] **1** 表示同意 to agree with; to approve of: 大家都~~他的意见。*All agree with him.* **2** 助人成功 to help sb accomplish or achieve ❷夸奖,称扬 to praise; to commend; to extol (㊀ ***doublet*** —许 to praise; to commend | —扬 to praise; to commend; to acclaim | 称— to praise): ~不绝口 *to be profuse in praise; to be prodigal of praise* ❸旧时文体的一种 (in former times) eulogy: 像~ *inscription eulogizing the subject of a portrait* | 小~ *eulogy*

瓒 zàn ㄗㄢˋ 古代祭祀时用的一种像勺的玉器 (in ancient Chinese sacrifices) jade ladle

ZANG ㄗㄤ

赃(贜、**臟) zāng ㄗㄤ 赃物,贪污受贿或偷盗所得的财物 booty; spoils: 追~ *to recover stolen money or goods; to order the return of spoils* | 退~ *to disgorge spoils; to surrender booty*

脏(髒) ㊀ zāng ㄗㄤ 不干净 filthy; dirty: 衣服~了。*The clothes are dirty.* | 把~东西清除出去 *Get rid of those dirty things.*

㊁ zàng 见940页 see p940

牂 zāng ㄗㄤ 母羊 ewe

臧 zāng ㄗㄤ 善,好 good; right [臧否] (—pǐ)褒贬,评论,说好说坏 to appraise; to review; to comment: ~~人物 *to pass judgment on a person; to make comments on the merits and demerits of a person*

驵 zǎng ㄗㄤˇ 好马，壮马 fine horse; steed; courser [驵侩]（-kuài）马侩，进行牲畜交易的中间人，也泛指经纪人 horse broker; horse trader; broker

脏(臟) ㊀ zàng ㄗㄤˋ 身体内部器官的总称 general term for the internal organs of the body：内～*internal organs*; *entrails*; *viscera*｜五～六腑 *internal organs*

㊁ zāng 见939页 see p939

奘 ㊁ zàng ㄗㄤˋ ❶壮大，多用于人名(zang, usually used in a given name) strong; robust 玄奘，唐代一个和尚的名字 Xuan Zang, a monk of the Tang Dynasty ❷〈方 ***dialect***〉说话粗鲁，态度生硬 rude; stiff

㊀ zhuǎng 见1002页 see p1002

葬 zàng ㄗㄤˋ 掩埋死人，泛指处理死者遗体 to bury; to inter：埋～*to bury*; *to inter*｜火～*to cremate* [葬送] ⑩ ***figurative*** 断送，毁灭 to ruin; to wreck：～～前程 *to ruin one's prospects* (or *one's career*, *one's future*)｜～～幸福 *to ruin one's happiness*

藏 ㊁ zàng ㄗㄤˋ ❶储放东西的地方 storage; storehouse; depository：宝～*treasure*; *precious deposits* ❷佛教、道教经典的总称(general term for Buddhist or Taoist scriptures)：大～经 *Buddhist scriptures*｜道～*Taoist Canon* [三藏]佛教经典，包括"经"、"律"、"论"三部分，总称三藏(doctrinal records, writings on discipline and writings on metaphysics) Tripitaka; Threefold

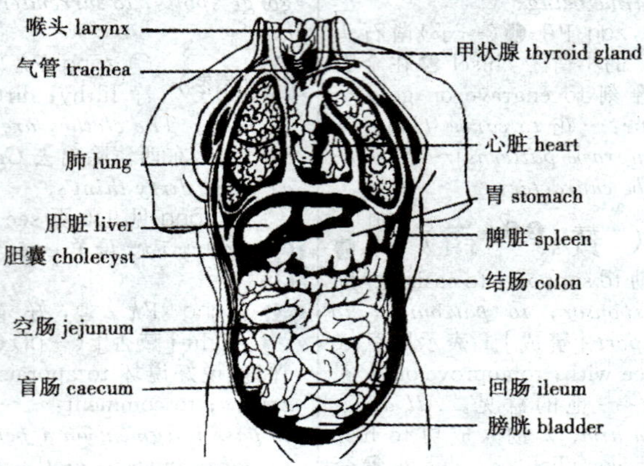

人体内脏 internal organs of human body

canon; three categories of the Buddhist classics 唐玄奘(zàng)号三藏法师 Tang monk Xuan Zang was named Master of the Threefold Canon ❸西藏自治区的简称 short for 西藏自治区

[藏族]我国少数民族,参看附表(see the appendix) the Tibetan ethnic group, one of the ethnic minorities of China

㊀ cáng 见 66 页 see p66

ZAO ㄗㄠ

遭 zāo ㄗㄠ ❶遇见,碰到 to meet with; to encounter (㊀ ***doublet*** 一遇 to meet with; to encounter):～灾 *to suffer disaster*|～难 *to meet with misfortune*|～殃 *to suffer calamity* ❷(一儿)量词 ***quantifier*** **1** 圈儿,周 round:用绳子多绕两～*to circle with the rope several times*|我去转了一～。*I've been out for a walk*. **2** 回,次 time; turn:一～生,两～熟。*Strangers at the first meeting, friends at the second*.

糟 zāo ㄗㄠ ❶做酒剩下的渣子 brewers' grains [糟粕]㊉ ***figurative*** 无价值的东西 dross; dregs:取其精华,去其～～*to discard the dross and to assimilate the essence* ❷用酒或酒糟腌制食品 to pickle with grain or in wine:～鱼 *fish pickled with grain or in wine*|～豆腐 *pickled tofu* (or *bean curd*) ❸腐烂,朽烂 rotten:木头～了。*The wood is rotten*.|布～了。*The cloth is decomposed*. ❹坏 in a wretched state; bad:事情～了。*It has been in a bad mess*.[糟蹋][糟踏](一ta)作践,不爱惜 to waste; to ruin; to spoil; to destroy:不许～～粮食。*Don't waste the grains*.

凿(鑿) záo ㄗㄠ ❶(一子)挖槽或穿孔用的工具 chisel ❷穿孔,挖掘 to chisel; to dig:～个眼 *to bore a hole*|～井 *to dig a well* [穿凿]对于讲不通的道理,牵强附会,以求其通 to give a farfetched interpretation ❸〈古 ***archaism***〉器物上的孔,是容纳枘(ruì)的 mortise; hole ❹明确,真实 certain; authentic (叠 ***reduplication***)(㊀ ***doublet*** 确一 irrefutable):证据确～。*The evidence is conclusive*.|言之～～*to say sth with certainty*

早 zǎo ㄗㄠ ❶太阳出来的时候 morning (㊀ ***doublet*** 一晨 morning):一大～就开会去了。*He went to a meeting early in the morning*.|～饭 *breakfast*|～操 *morning exercises* ❷时间靠前,在一定时间以前 early; in advance:～起～睡身体好。*Early to rise and early to bed makes a man healthy*.|那是很～的事了。*It happened a long time ago*.|我～就预备好了。*I've got ready in advance*.|开车还～着呢。*There is quite a while to go before the train leaves*.

Z

枣(棗) zǎo ㄗㄠˇ 枣树,落叶亚乔木,枝有刺,开小黄花,果实叫枣子或枣儿,椭圆形,熟时红色,可以吃 Chinese jujube; Chinese date (*Zizyphus zizyphus*) [黑枣儿] 黑枣树,落叶乔木,跟柿树同属一科,果实叫黑枣儿,可以吃 dateplum persimmon (*Diospyros lotus*)

蚤 zǎo ㄗㄠˇ ❶蛇蚤(gè-zao),跳蚤,昆虫名,赤褐色,善跳跃,寄生在人畜的身体上,吸血液,能传染鼠疫等疾病 flea (*Siphonaptera*) ❷古同"早" same as 早 in ancient Chinese

澡 zǎo ㄗㄠˇ 洗澡,沐浴,洗全身 to bathe:~盆 *bathtub; bath; tub* | ~堂 *bathhouse; public bath*

璪 zǎo ㄗㄠˇ ❶古代刻在玉上或画在衣裳上的水藻花纹 (in ancient China) algae-shaped pattern carved in a piece of jade or drawn on clothes ❷古代垂在冕上穿玉的五彩丝绦 (in ancient China) colourful ribbons hanging from a crown for threading pieces of jade

藻 zǎo ㄗㄠˇ ❶隐花植物的一大类,没有真正的根、茎、叶的分化,有叶绿素,可以自己制造养料。种类很多,大部生活在海水和淡水里 algae ❷华丽的文辞 literary embellishments:~饰 *embellishments in writing* | 辞~ *ornate diction; flowery language; rhetoric* [藻井]我国传统建筑中的一种顶棚形式,一般呈方形、多边形或圆形的凹面,上有各种花纹、雕刻和彩画 caisson ceiling; coffer; sunk panel

皂(*阜) zào ㄗㄠˋ ❶黑色 black:~鞋 *black shoes* | 不分~白(喻不问是非) *not to distinguish black and white — cannot tell right from wrong; to make no distinction between right and wrong* ❷差役 *yamen* runner:~隶 yamen *runner* ❸皂角,即皂荚。落叶乔木,枝上有刺,结的长荚也叫皂角或皂荚,可供洗衣去污用 (i. e. 皂荚) Chinese honey locust ❹有洗涤去污作用的日用化工制品 soap:肥~ *soap* | 香~ *scented soap; toilet soap* | 药~ *medicated soap*

唣(*啤) zào ㄗㄠˋ [啰唣] 吵闹 quarrelsome; argumentative

灶(竈) zào ㄗㄠˋ 用土坯、砖或金属等制成的生火做饭的设备 kitchen range; cooking stove:~台 *top of a cooking range* | 垒个~ *to make a kitchen range* | 煤气~ *gas range; gas cooker; gas ring*

造 zào ㄗㄠˋ ❶制作,做 to make (㊀ ***doublet*** 制 — to make):~船 *shipbuilding* | ~林 *afforestation* ㊁ ***extension*** 瞎编 to invent; to concoct:~谣 *to start a rumour; to cook up a story* | 捏~ *to fabricate* ❷成就 achievements; accomplishments; attainments:~诣(yì) *academic achievements; artistic attainments* ❸培养 to train; to cultivate: 深～*to pursue advanced studies* ❹到,去 to go to: ～访 *to pay a visit; to call on* | 登峰～极 *to reach the pinnacle; to reach the acme; to reach the peak of perfection* ❺相对两方面的人,法院里指诉讼的两方 one of the two parties in a legal agreement: 两～*both parties* | 甲～*party one; the first party* | 乙～*party two; the second party* ❻〈方 **dialect**〉稻子等作物从播种到收割一次叫一造 crop: 一年两～*two crops a year*

[造次] 仓卒,匆促 hurried; rash: ～～之间 *in a hurry; in a moment of haste* [引] **extension** 鲁莽,草率 rash; imprudent; impetuous: 不敢～～*dare not act rashly*

慥 zào ㄗㄠˋ (叠 **reduplication**)忠厚诚实的样子 honest and sincere

簉 zào ㄗㄠˋ 副,附属的 subsidiary; affiliated

噪 (❷ *譟) zào ㄗㄠˋ ❶许多鸟或虫子乱叫 chirping; chirruping: 鹊～*chattering of magpies* | 蝉～*chirping of cicadas* [引] **extension** 声音杂乱 noisy and confused: ～音 *noise* ❷许多人大声吵嚷 to clamour; to make an uproar: 聒～*noisy; clamorous* | 鼓～而进 *to advance with an uproar* ❸(名声)广为传扬 to be well-known: 名～一时 *to enjoy popular fame for a time*

燥 zào ㄗㄠˋ 干 dry; arid; parched (连 **doublet** 干—dry): ～热 *hot and dry* | 天气干～。*The weather is hot and dry.*

躁 zào ㄗㄠˋ 急躁,性急,不冷静 rash; impetuous; restless: 性情暴～*hot temper; explosive temper; violent temper* | 戒骄戒～*to guard against arrogance and rashness*

ZE ㄗㄜ

则 zé ㄗㄜˊ ❶模范 model; example: 以身作～*to set an example with one's own conduct* ❷规则,制度,规程 rule; regulation: 办事细～*detailed working rules* [法则]事物之间内在的必然的联系。也叫"规律"(also called 规律) rule; law [四则]算术里指加、减、乘、除四种方法 four fundamental arithmetic operations — addition, subtraction, multiplication and division ❸效法 to imitate; to follow: ～先烈之言行 *to follow the example of the martyrs in words and deeds* ❹连词 **conjunction** **1** 表示因果关系,就,便(used to denote the relation of cause and effect): 兼听～明,偏信～暗。*Listen to both sides and you will be enlightened; heed only one side and you will be benighted.* **2** 表示转折,却 but; however: 今～不然 *But it's different now.* **3** 表示两件事在时间上前后相

Z

承(used to denote one action following another):预备铃一响,～学生陆续走进教室。*When the preliminary bell rang, the students went into the classroom one after another.* ❺副词 ***adverb***,表示肯定的判断,就是 to be:此～余之罪也。*It's my fault.* or *I'm to blame.* ❻用在一、二、三等数字后,列举原因或理由(used to enumerate the reasons preceded with one, two, three, etc):一～房子太小,二～参加的人太多,以致室内拥挤不堪。*The room was overcrowded; for one thing it was too small, for another there were too many attendants.* ❼跟"做"义相近(similar to 做),宋、元、明小说戏剧里常用(usually used in novels or dramas in the Song, Yuan and Ming dynasties) to do:～甚(做什么)*What for?*|不～声 *to keep silence* ❽量词 ***quantifier***,用于成文的条数 piece; item:试题三～ *three questions*|新闻两～ *two items of news; two news stories*|随笔一～*an informal essay*

责 zé ㄗㄜˊ ❶责任,分(fèn)内应做的事 duty; responsibility:我们要对人民负～。*We should hold ourselves responsible to the people.*|尽～*to do one's duty*|爱护公物,人人有～。*It's everyone's duty to take good care of public property.* ❷要求 to demand; to require:求全～备 *to demand perfection; to try to round sth off*|～己严于～人 *to be stricter with oneself than with others* [责成]要求某人负责办好 to instruct sb to fulfil a task:这个问题已～～专人研究解决。*Someone has already been specially assigned to the study of this problem.* ❸指摘过失,责备 to reproach; to blame:～罚 *to punish; to penalize*|斥～*to rebuke; to denounce* ❹责问,质问,诘(jié)问 to question; to interrogate ❺旧指为惩罚而打(in former times) to beat for punishment:鞭～*to whip; to lash*|杖～*to flog with a stick*

〈古 ***archaism***〉又同"债"(zhài) also same as 债

啧 zé ㄗㄜˊ 争辩 to argue; to debate:～有烦言(很多人说不满意的话)。*There are a lot of complaints.* [啧啧] **1** 形容咂嘴或说话声 clicking the tongue or chattering:～～称羡 *to click the tongue in admiration; to praise highly*|人言～～*There are a lot of unfavourable comments.* **2** 鸟鸣声 chirping

帻 zé ㄗㄜˊ 古代的一种头巾 ancient man's headdress

箦 zé ㄗㄜˊ 床席 bamboo mat

赜 zé ㄗㄜˊ 深奥 subtle; abstruse; profound:探～索隐 *to delve into the abstruse; to unravel mysteries*

咋 ㊀ zé ㄗㄜˊ ❶大声呼叫 to cry out loudly ❷咬,啃 to

bite［咋舌］形容因惊讶、害怕而说不出话来 to be speechless with astonishment or horror

㊁ zǎ 见 935 页 see p935

㊂ zhā 见 947 页 see p947

迮 zé ㄗㄜˊ ❶〈古 ***archaism***〉狭窄 narrow：～狭 *narrow* ❷姓 Ze, a surname

笮 ㊁ zé ㄗㄜˊ 姓 Ze, a surname

㊀ zuó 见 1022 页 see p1022

舴 zé ㄗㄜˊ［舴艋］(—měng) 小船 small boat

择（擇） ㊀ zé ㄗㄜˊ 挑拣，挑选 to select; to choose; to pick（㊟ ***doublet*** 选一 to choose）：不～手段 *by fair means or foul; by hook or by crook; unscrupulously*｜～善而从 *to choose and follow what is good*｜～友 *to choose friends*｜～业 *to choose a job; to hunt for a job*

㊁ zhái 见 951 页 see p951

泽（澤） zé ㄗㄜˊ ❶水积聚的地方 pool; pond：大～ *vast marshes*｜水乡～国 *land crisscrossed with rivers and dotted with lakes; land that abounds in rivers and lakes* ❷光泽，金属或其他物体发出的光亮 luster：色～鲜明 *bright colour and luster* ❸湿 to moisten; to dampen：润～ *to moisten* ❹恩惠 favour; beneficence：恩～ *beneficence*

仄 zè ㄗㄜˋ ❶倾斜 slanting; sloping; inclined［仄声］古汉语里上声、去声、入声的总称（in classical Chinese pronunciation）oblique tones, a general term for the falling-rising tone, falling tone and entering tone ❷狭窄 narrow ❸心里不安 uneasy; sorry：歉～ *to feel sorry for*

昃 zè ㄗㄜˋ 太阳偏西 sun passing the meridian; sun inclining to the west; afternoon

侧 ㊂ zè ㄗㄜˋ 同"仄"same as 仄［侧声］同"仄声"same as 仄声

㊀ cè 见 68 页 see p68

㊁ zhāi 见 950 页 see p950

ZEI ㄗㄟ

贼 zéi ㄗㄟˊ ❶偷东西的人，盗匪 thief; burglar ㊞ ***extension*** 严重危害人民和国家的坏人 traitor; enemy：奸～ *conspirator; traitor*｜卖国～ *traitor to one's country* ❷伤害 to harm; to injure ❸邪的，不正派的 wicked; evil; furtive：～眼 *shifty eyes; furtive glance*｜～头～脑 *thievish; stealthy; furtive* ❹〈方 ***dialect***〉狡猾 cunning; wily; sly：老鼠真～。*Rats are really cunning.* ❺〈方 ***dialect***〉很，非常 very; rather：～冷 *very cold*｜～亮 *rather bright*

鲗 zéi ㄗㄟˊ 乌鲗，乌贼，又叫"墨鱼"或"墨斗鱼"。软体动物，有墨囊，遇危险放出黑色液体逃走，生活在海中。肉可吃。黑色液体叫鲗墨，可制颜料(also called 墨鱼 or 墨斗鱼) cuttlefish (*Sepiida*)

Z

ZEN ㄗㄣ

怎 zěn ㄗㄣˇ 如何 why; how; what:～样? *How is it?* | ～办? *What to do?* [怎么] (—me) 代词 ***pronoun***, 询问性质、状态、方式、原因等 what; why; how: 你～～也知道了? *How did you get to know it?* | 这是～～回事? *What's all this about?* | "难"字～～写? *How do you write the character* 难?

谮 zèn ㄗㄣˋ 说坏话诬陷别人 to slander; to defame; to calumniate: ～言 *slander; calumny; defamation* | ～害 *to calumniate* | ～毁 *to defame*

ZENG ㄗㄥ

曾 ㊀ zēng ㄗㄥ ❶ 重 (chóng), 用来指与自己中间隔着两代的亲属 relationship between great-grandchildren and great-grandparents: ～祖 *great-grandfather* | ～孙 *great-grandson* ❷ 古同"增" same as 增 in ancient Chinese ❸ 姓 Zeng, a surname

㊁ céng 见 69 页 see p69

增 zēng ㄗㄥ 加多, 添 to increase; to add ([连] ***doublet*** 一加 to increase): 为国～光 *to do credit to one's country* | ～产节约 *to boost production and practice economy; to increase output and practice economy* [增殖] 繁殖 to propagate; to breed; to reproduce: ～～耕牛 *to breed oxen* [引] ***extension*** 大量地增添 proliferation; multiplication: ～～财富 *to multiply one's wealth*

憎 zēng ㄗㄥ 厌恶(wù), 嫌, 跟"爱"相对 (the opposite of 爱) to hate; to detest; to abhor ([连] ***doublet*** 一恶 to abhor; to loathe; to abominate): 爱～分明 *to be clear about sympathy and antipathy*

缯 ㊀ zēng ㄗㄥ 古代丝织品的总称 (in ancient China) general term for silk fabrics

㊁ zèng 见 946 页 see p946

罾 zēng ㄗㄥ 一种用竹竿或木棍做支架的方形渔网 square-shaped fishing net with wooden or bamboo poles as supports

矰 zēng ㄗㄥ 古代射鸟用的一种拴着丝绳的箭 (in ancient China) retrievable arrow with a string attached to it for shooting birds

综 ㊁ zèng ㄗㄥˋ 织布机上使经线交错着上下分开以便梭子通过的装置 heddle; heald

㊀ zōng 见 1014 页 see p1014

锃 zèng ㄗㄥˋ 器物等经过擦磨或整理后闪光耀眼 shiny; polished: ～亮 *shiny* | ～光 *polished*

缯 ㊁ zèng ㄗㄥˋ 〈方 ***dialect***〉 捆, 扎 to bind; to fasten: 把那根裂了的棍子～起来 *to repair a broken cudgel by binding it up*

㊀ zēng 见 946 页 see p946

Z

赠 zèng ㄗㄥˋ 把东西无代价地送给别人 to present; to send as a gift: ～品 *giveaway; complimentary gift* | ～阅 *complimentary copy; (of a book, periodical, etc) given free by the publisher*

甑 zèng ㄗㄥˋ (旧读 formerly jìng) ❶古代蒸饭的一种瓦器。现在称蒸饭用的木制桶状物 ancient earthen utensil for steaming rice, now used to denote a modern barrel for steaming rice ❷蒸馏或使物体分解用的器皿 utensil for distilling water: 曲颈～ *retort; n-necked distiller*

ZHA ㄓㄚ

扎(❶❷*劄、❷*紮、❷*紥) ㊀ zhā ㄓㄚ ❶刺 to prick; to puncture: ～针 *to give (or have) an acupuncture treatment* | ～花(刺绣) *to embroider* ❷驻扎 to be stationed; to be quartered: ～营 *to camp; to pitch a camp* ❸钻 to plunge into; to get into: ～猛子(游泳时头朝下钻入水中) *to dive*

[扎煞] (—sha) 同"挓挲" same as 挓挲

㊁ zhá 见 948 页 see p948

㊂ zā 见 935 页 see p935

"劄"又 zhá 见 948 页"札" also pronounced zhá, see 札 on p948

吒 ㊀ zhā ㄓㄚ 用于神话中的人名,如金吒、木吒(used in names of mythical beings in ancient China, e. g. Jinzha, Muzha)

㊁ zhà 见 950 页"咤"see 咤 on p950

挓 zhā ㄓㄚ [挓挲] (—sha) 张开 to spread; to stretch out: ～～着手 *to spread out one's hand*

咋 ㊂ zhā ㄓㄚ [咋呼] (—hu) 〈方 **dialect**〉 **1** 吆喝 to shout blusteringly **2** 炫耀 to show off; to flaunt

㊀ zé 见 944 页 see p944

㊁ zǎ 见 935 页 see p935

哳 zhā ㄓㄚ 见 959 页"啁"字条"啁哳"(zhāo—) see 啁哳 on p959

查(*查) ㊁ zhā ㄓㄚ ❶同"楂㊀" same as 楂㊀ ❷姓 Zha, a surname

㊀ chá 见 70 页 see p70

揸(**摣、**齇) zhā ㄓㄚ ❶用手指撮东西 to pick up sth with one's fingers ❷把手指伸张开 to spread one's fingers

喳 ㊀ zhā ㄓㄚ [喳喳]拟声词 (**onomatopoeia**) chirping; chirruping; chittering: 唧唧～～ *chirping; chirming* | 喜鹊～～叫。*Magpies are chattering.*

㊁ chā 见 70 页 see p70

渣 zhā ㄓㄚ (—子、—儿) 提出精华或汁液后剩下的东西 dregs; residue; sediment (㊟ **doublet** —滓 dregs; residue; sediment): 豆腐～ *soybean residue* ㊀ **extension** 碎屑

crumbs; broken bits; dross:点心～儿 *biscuit crumbs*

楂(＊＊樝) ㊀ zhā ㄓㄚ [山楂](＊山查)落叶乔木,开白花。果实也叫山楂,红色有白点,味酸,可以吃,也可入药 Chinese hawthorn (*Crataegus pinnatifida*)

㊁ chá 见 70 页 see p70

奓 ㊁ zhā ㄓㄚ 奓山,地名,在湖北省武汉 Zhashan, a place in Wuhan, Hubei Province

㊀ zhà 见 950 页 see p950

齇(＊＊皻) zhā ㄓㄚ 鼻子上长的红色小疮,就是酒糟鼻上的红瘢 rosy acne on the nose

扎 ㊁ zhá ㄓㄚˊ [扎挣](— zheng)〈方 ***dialect***〉勉强支持 to move with difficulty; to struggle to maintain

㊀ zhā 见 947 页 see p947

㊂ zā 见 935 页 see p935

札(❶❸＊劄) zhá ㄓㄚˊ ❶古代写字用的木片(in ancient China) thin piece of wood used for writing on [札记]读书时摘记的要点和心得 reading notes; reading commentary ❷信件 letter; correspondence([连] ***doublet*** 信— letter|书— letter):手～ *personal letter*|来～ *incoming letter* ❸(—子)旧时的一种公文(in former times) official document

"劄"又 zhā 见 947 页"扎" also pronounced zhā, see 扎 on p947

轧 ㊁ zhá ㄓㄚˊ 义同"轧㊀",用于轧辊、轧钢、轧钢机等 same as 轧㊀, used in 轧辊, 轧钢, 轧钢机, etc [轧钢]把钢坯压成一定形状的钢材 to roll steel [轧辊](— gǔn)轧钢机中最主要的、直接完成轧制工作的部件 roll; roller

㊀ yà 见 860 页 see p860

㊂ gá 见 212 页 see p212

闸(△＊牐) zhá ㄓㄚˊ ❶拦住水流的建筑物,可以随时开关 floodgate; sluice; sluice gate; sluice valve:～口 *sluiceway*|河里有一道～。*There is a floodgate in the river.* ❷把水截住 to dam up a stream ❸使机械减速或停止运行的设备 brake:电～ *switch; main power (source) switch*|自行车～ *bicycle brakes*

炸(＊＊煠) ㊁ zhá ㄓㄚˊ 把食物放在煮沸的油或水里弄熟 to fry; to deep-fry; to scald:～糕 *fried cake*|～鱼 *fried fish*|把菠菜～一～ *to scald spinach in hot water*

㊀ zhà 见 949 页 see p949

铡 zhá ㄓㄚˊ ❶铡刀,一种切草或切其他东西的器具 hand hay cutter; fodder chopper ❷用铡刀切 to cut up with a hay cutter:～草 *to chop fodder; to cut hay*

喋 ㊁zhá ㄓㄚˊ 见650页"唼"字条"唼喋"(shà —) see 唼喋 on p650

㊀ dié 见 151 页 see p151

牐 zhá ㄓㄚˊ ❶古时防守城门的用具(in ancient China) tool for city gate defence ❷同"闸"same as 闸

拃 zhǎ ㄓㄚˇ ❶张开大拇指和中指量长度 to span; to measure by handspans ❷张开大拇指和中指两端的距离 span：两～宽 *two spans wide*

苲 zhǎ ㄓㄚˇ 苲草，指金鱼藻等水生植物 waterweed (*Elodea canadensis*); aquatic plant such as hornwort

砟 zhǎ ㄓㄚˇ (—子)某些坚硬成块的东西 tiny hard fragments：煤～子 *small coal fragments* | 炉灰～子 *cinder*

鲊 zhǎ ㄓㄚˇ 一种用盐和红曲(调制食品的材料)腌(yān)的鱼 salted fish

眨 zhǎ ㄓㄚˇ (—巴)眼睛很快地一闭一开 to blink; to wink：眼睛直～巴 *to blink one's eyes* | 一～眼(时间极短)就看不见了。*It disappeared in the twinkling of an eye.*

鲝 zhǎ ㄓㄚˇ ❶同"鲊"same as 鲊 ❷[鲝草滩]地名，在四川省乐山 Zhacaotan, a place in Leshan, Sichuan Province

乍 zhà ㄓㄚˋ ❶忽然 suddenly; abruptly; unexpectedly：～冷～热 *suddenly cold and suddenly hot* ❷刚刚 at first; at the beginning：新来～到 *to have just arrived; to be a newcomer* ❸张开 to spread; to stretch：～翅 *to spread the wings*

诈 zhà ㄓㄚˋ ❶假装 to pretend; to feign：～死 *to feign death* ❷使手段诓(kuāng)骗 to cheat; to swindle ([连] **doublet** 欺— to swindle; to defraud)：～财 *to defraud sb of money* | 你不必拿话～我。*You needn't try to draw me out.* [诈语] 骗人的话 lie; falsehood; fabrication

柞 ㊁ zhà ㄓㄚˋ [柞水]地名，在陕西省 Zhashui, a place in Shaanxi Province

㊀ zuò 见 1023 页 see p1023

炸 ㊀ zhà ㄓㄚˋ ❶突然破裂 to explode; to burst ([连] **doublet** 爆— to explode)：～弹 *bomb; bombshell* | 玻璃杯～了。*The glass has burst.* ❷用炸药、炸弹爆破 to blast; to bomb; to blow up：～碉堡 *to blow up a blockhouse* ❸发怒 to flare up; to fly into a rage：他一听就～了。*He flew into a towering rage at the words.* ❹因受惊而四处逃散 to scamper; to scurry away：～市(*of people in a marketplace*) *to flee in terror; to run away in all directions* | ～窝(*of birds, etc*) *to flee in fright*; (*of frightened people*) *to be thrown into confusion*

㊁ zhá 见 948 页 see p948

痄 zhà ㄓㄚˋ [痄腮](—sai)一种传染病，又叫"流行性腮腺炎"。耳朵下面肿胀疼痛，病原体是一种滤过性病毒(also called 流行性腮腺炎) epidemic parotitis; mumps

Z

蚱 zhà ㄓㄚˋ [蚱蜢](—měng) 一种有害的昆虫，身体绿色或褐色，触角短，吃稻叶等，不能远飞 grasshopper (*Orthoptera*)

榨(❷ *搾) zhà ㄓㄚˋ ❶压出物体里液汁的器具 press：油～ *oil press*｜酒～ *wine press* ❷用力压出 to press; to extract：～油 *to extract oil*｜压～ *to press; to squeeze*｜～汁机 *juicer; juice squeezer*

栅(*柵) ㊀ zhà ㄓㄚˋ 栅栏，用竹、木、铁条等做成的阻拦物 railing; palisade; paling; bar：篱笆～ *fence*｜铁～栏 *iron railing*

㊁ shān 见 652 页 see p652

奓 ㊀ zhà ㄓㄚˋ 张开 to open; to spread; to extend：头发～着 *with hair dishevelled*｜这件衣服下面太～了。*The hem of the dress is too full* (or *wide*).

㊁ zhā 见 948 页 see p948

砟 zhà ㄓㄚˋ [大水砟]地名，在甘肃省景泰 Dashuizha, a place in Jingtai, Gansu Province

咤(△ *吒) zhà ㄓㄚˋ 生气时对人大声嚷 to shout at when angry

"吒"又 zhā 见 947 页 also pronounced zhā, see p947

蛇 zhà ㄓㄚˋ 〈方 **dialect**〉海蜇 jellyfish (*Scyphozoa*)

溠 zhà ㄓㄚˋ 溠水，水名，在湖北省随州 Zhashui River, in Suizhou, Hubei Province

蜡(**褙) ㊁ zhà ㄓㄚˋ 古代年终的一种祭祀名 (in ancient China) sacrificial rite held at the end of a year

㊀ là 见 411 页 see p411

霅 zhà ㄓㄚˋ 霅溪，水名，在浙江省 Zhaxi River in Zhejiang Province

ZHAI ㄓㄞ

侧 ㊂ zhāi ㄓㄞ [侧棱](—leng) 向一边倾斜 inclining; slanting：～～着身子睡觉 *to sleep on one's side* [侧歪](—wai) 倾斜 tilting; slanting：车在山坡上～～着走。*The vehicles went slantingly along the hillside.*

㊀ cè 见 68 页 see p68

㊁ zè 见 945 页 see p945

斋(齋) zhāi ㄓㄞ ❶书房或校舍 study or school building：书～ *study; studio*｜第一～ *Studio No.1* ❷祭祀前整洁身心，以示虔诚 (before offering sacrifices to gods or ancestors) ablution and abstinence：～戒 *to fast* ㊂ ***extension*** 佛教、道教等教徒吃的素食 vegetarian diet adopted by Buddhists or Taoists：吃～ *to be on a vegetarian diet for religious purposes* ❸舍饭给僧人 to give alms to monks：～僧 *to give alms to Buddhist monks*

摘 zhāi ㄓㄞ ❶采下，拿下 to pick; to pluck; to take off：～瓜 *to pluck melons*｜～梨

to pick pears | ～帽子 *to take off one's cap* ❷选取 to select; to choose: ～要 *abstract; précis* | ～记 *to take notes* [指摘]指出缺点 to nitpick; to find fault with ❸借 to borrow: 东～西借 *to borrow all around*

宅 zhái ㄓㄞˊ 住所 residence; house; dwelling; abode: 住～*residence; dwelling* | 深～大院 *imposing dwellings and spacious courtyards; a compound of connecting courtyards*

择(擇) ㈡ zhái ㄓㄞˊ 义同"择㈠",用于口语(used in colloquial Chinese) same as 择㈠: ～菜 *to trim vegetables for cooking* | ～席(换个地方就睡不安稳) *to be unable to sleep well in a new place*

㈠ zé 见945页 see p945

翟 ㈡ zhái ㄓㄞˊ 姓 Zhai, a surname

㈠ dí 见141页 see p141

窄 zhǎi ㄓㄞˇ ❶狭,不宽,宽度小,跟"宽"相对(the opposite of 宽) narrow (㊟ **doublet** —狭 narrow | 狭— narrow): 路太～。*The road is too narrow.* | 地方太狭～。*There is not enough space here.* ㊀ **extension** 气量小,心胸不开阔 narrow-minded; petty: 他的心眼儿太～。*He's too narrow-minded.* ❷生活不宽裕 badly off: 以前的日子很～,现在可好了。*We were very badly off in the past, but are now pretty well-off.*

鉙 zhǎi ㄓㄞˇ (一儿) 器物残缺损坏的痕迹,水果伤损的痕迹 blemish; flaw: 碗上有块～儿。*There is a flaw in the bowl.* | 苹果没～儿。*The apple has no spots on it.*

债 zhài ㄓㄞˋ 所欠下的钱财 debt: 还～ *to pay debts* | 公～ *government bond*

寨(*砦) zhài ㄓㄞˋ ❶防守用的栅栏 stockade; fence [鹿寨] 军事上常用的一种障碍物,古代多用削尖的竹木,现多用铁蒺藜等做成 abatis ❷旧时军营(in former times) camp: 安营扎～ *to encamp; to pitch a camp* ❸村子 stockaded village: 村村～～ *hamlets and stockaded villages; all the villages*

搽 zhài ㄓㄞˋ 〈方 **dialects**〉缝纫方法,把衣服上附加的物件缝上 to sew sth on clothes: ～纽扣儿 *to sew on a button* | ～花边 *to trim with lace*

瘵 zhài ㄓㄞˋ 病,多指痨病(usually used to denote tuberculosis) disease

ZHAN ㄓㄢ

占 ㈠ zhān ㄓㄢ 古代用龟甲、蓍(shī)草等,后世用铜钱或牙牌等判断吉凶(in ancient China) to practice divination; to divine: ～卦 *to divine by means of the Eight Trigrams* | ～课 *to divine by drawing straws or tossing coins*

㈡ zhàn 见953页 see p953

Z

沾(❶ *霑) zhān ㄓㄢ ❶浸湿 to moisten; to wet:泪流～襟 *Tears wet the front of one's jacket.* |汗出～背 *to moisten one's back with sweat* ❷因接触而附着(zhuó)上 to be stained with:～水 *to get wet* ㊀ ***extension*** **1** 染上 to be infected with; to be contaminated by:～染了坏习气 *to be tainted with bad habits.* **2** 凭借某种关系而得到好处 to benefit from association with sb or sth:～光 *to profit from one's association with sb or sth; to avail oneself of a relationship with sb or sth* ❸稍微碰上或接触上 to touch:～边儿 *to touch on only slightly; to be slightly related to* |脚不～地 *with feet hardly touching the ground — to walk very fast; to be extremely busy*

[沾沾自喜] 形容自己觉得很好而得意的样子 to feel complacent; to be pleased with oneself; to be self-contented

毡(氈、*氊) zhān ㄓㄢ (一子)用兽毛砑成的片状物,可做防寒用品和工业上的垫衬材料 felt:炕～*bed felt* |～靴 *felt boots* |油毛～*asphalt felt*

粘 ㊀ zhān ㄓㄢ ❶黏的东西互相连接或附着在别的东西上 to stick:几块糖都～在一起了。*The sweets got glued together.* |不～锅 *nonstick pan (or cooker)* ❷用胶水或糨糊等把一种东西胶合在另一种东西上 to paste; to glue:～贴标语 *to paste slogans*

㊁ nián 见 534 页 see p534

旃 zhān ㄓㄢ 〈古 ***archaism***〉 ❶助词 ***auxiliary***,等于"之焉"两字连用的意义(fusion of 之 and 焉):勉～。*Do it as best as you can!* ❷同"毡"same as 毡

詹 zhān ㄓㄢ 姓 Zhan, a surname

谵 zhān ㄓㄢ 多说话。特指病中说胡话 to rave; to be delirious, especially during one's illness:～语 *delirious speech; wild talk; ravings* |～妄 *delirium*

瞻 zhān ㄓㄢ 往上或往前看 to look up or forward:～仰 *to look at sb or sth with reverence* |高～远瞩 *to look far ahead and aim high; to be farsighted*

邅 zhān ㄓㄢ ❶难走 difficult to walk ❷转变方向 to change direction:～彼南道兮 *to turn to the road southward*

鹯 zhān ㄓㄢ 古书中说的一种猛禽,似鹞(yào)鹰(in ancient Chinese texts) a kind of fierce bird similar to a sparrow hawk

鳣 zhān ㄓㄢ 古书上指鳇(huáng)鱼(in ancient Chinese texts) sturgeon

〈古 ***archaism***〉又同"鳝"(shàn)also same as 鳝

斩 zhǎn ㄓㄢˇ 砍断 to chop; to cut:～首 *to behead; to decapitate; to guillotine* |～草除

根 *to cut the weeds and dig up the roots — to stamp out the source of trouble; to eradicate the source of trouble* | ～钉截铁 *resolute and decisive; categorical*

崭 zhǎn ㄓㄢˇ ❶高峻，突出 towering：～露头角 *to begin to show one's brilliant talents; to begin to display remarkable abilities* ❷非常，极 very; extreme：～新(簇新) *brand-new*

㟻 zhǎn ㄓㄢˇ〈方 **dialect**〉眼皮开合，眨眼 to blink; to wink

飐 zhǎn ㄓㄢˇ 风吹物体使颤动 quivering in the wind

盏(盞) zhǎn ㄓㄢˇ ❶小杯子 small cup：酒～ *small wine cup* | 茶～ *small teacup with no handle* ❷量词 **quantifier**，用于灯(of lamps)：一～灯 *a lamp*

展 zhǎn ㄓㄢˇ ❶张开，舒张开 to open up; to spread out; to unfold; to unfurl：～翅 *to spread the wings* | ～望未来 *to look to the future* | ～开激烈斗争 *to wage a fierce struggle* [展览]把物品陈列起来让人参观 to exhibit; to display ❷施展 to put to good use; to give free play to：一筹莫～ *to be at one's wits' end; to be at a loss; to be at the end of one's tether* ❸放宽 to postpone; to extend：～缓 *to postpone; to extend; to prolong* | ～期 *to extend a time limit; to postpone; to put off* | ～限 *to extend a time limit*

搌 zhǎn ㄓㄢˇ 轻轻地擦抹 to wipe softly; to sop up liquid：～布 *dish cloth; dish towel* | 用药棉花～一～ *to soak up with absorbent cotton*

辗 zhǎn ㄓㄢˇ [辗转](*展转)(—zhuǎn) 翻来覆去地来回转动 to toss about：～～反侧 *to toss and turn* 喻 **figurative** 经过曲折，间接 to pass through many hands or places：～～传说 *to spread from place to place*

黵 zhǎn ㄓㄢˇ 弄脏，染上污点 to stain; to make dirty：墨水把纸～了。*The ink has stained the paper.* | 这种布颜色暗，禁(jīn)～(脏了不容易看出来)。*This dark cloth doesn't show the dirt.*

占(*佔) ㊁ zhàn ㄓㄢˋ ❶据有，用强力取得 to seize; to occupy (连 **doublet** —据 to occupy)：～领 *to capture; to occupy* | 攻～敌军据点 *to attack and occupy the enemy stronghold* ❷处于某种地位或情势 to hold a certain status; to be in a certain situation：～上风 *to get the upper hand* | ～优势 *to hold an advantage over; to be superior to* | 优等生～多数。*Top students constitute the majority.*

㊀ zhān 见 951 页 see p951

战(戰) zhàn ㄓㄢˋ ❶战争，通常指打仗 war; battle; fight (连 **doublet** —斗 fight; battle)：宣～ *to declare*

Z

war|～时 *wartime*|百～百胜 *to be ever-victorious; to win victory in every battle* [战略] **1** 指导战争全局的计划和策略 strategy **2** 比喻决定全局的策略 strategy that determines the overall trends of a situation; overall strategy [战术]进行战斗的原则和方法 tactics 喻 ***figurative*** 解决局部问题的方法 methods for solving concrete problems; concrete solution [战役]战争的一个段落。为实现一定的战略目的,在一定的方向上和一定的时间内进行的一系列战斗的总和 campaign: 淮海～～ *Huaihai Campaign* [战争]就是打仗,它是政治的继续,是民族和民族、国家和国家、阶级和阶级、政治集团和政治集团之间互相斗争的最高形式 war ❷发抖 to shiver: ～栗(害怕发抖) *to shudder; to tremble with fear*|打冷～ *to tremble*|寒～ *to shiver with cold*

站 zhàn ㄓㄢˋ ❶立 to stand; to be on one's feet: ～岗 *to stand guard; to stand sentry*|中国人民～起来了。*The Chinese people have risen to their feet.* ❷停 to stop; to halt: 不怕慢,就怕～。*We fear not slowness, but immobility.* ❸为乘客上下或货物装卸而设的停留的地方 station; stop: 车～ *railway station; bus stop* (or *station*)|起点～ *departing platform; starting point* ❹分支办事处 station or center for rendering certain services: 工作～ *working station*|保健～ *health centre*

栈(棧) zhàn ㄓㄢˋ ❶储存货物或供旅客住宿的房屋 inn; warehouse: 货～ *warehouse; storehouse*|客～ *inn* ❷养牲畜的竹木棚或栅栏 shed; pen; fold: 马～ *horse shed*

[栈道]古代在悬崖峭壁上凿孔架木桩,铺上木板而成的道路 plank road built on wooden brackets fixed into cliffs

绽 zhàn ㄓㄢˋ 裂开 to split; to burst: 破～ *flaw; weak-point*|鞋开～了。*The shoe bursts at a seam.*

湛 zhàn ㄓㄢˋ ❶深 profound; deep: 精～的演技 *excellent stage performance* ❷清澈 limpid; crystal clear: 清～ *lucid; limpid; crystal clear*

颤 ㊀ zhàn ㄓㄢˋ 同"战❷" same as 战❷

㊁ chàn 见 75 页 see p75

蘸 zhàn ㄓㄢˋ 在汁液或粉末里沾一下就拿出来 to dip in: ～墨水 *to dip in ink*|～酱 *to dip in sauce*

ZHANG ㄓㄤ

张(張) zhāng ㄓㄤ ❶展开,打开 to open; to spread: ～嘴 *to open one's mouth*|～弓搭箭 *to draw a bow to shoot; with bows drawn and arrows set*|纲举目～。*Once the headrope of a fishing*

net is pulled up, all its meshes open — once the key link is grasped, everything falls into place. or *When the general plan is laid out, the details are easy to arrange.* | ～牙舞爪 *to bare fangs and brandish claws; to make threatening gestures; rampant; truculent* ㊀ ***extension*** **1** 扩大,夸大 to magnify; to exaggerate: 虚～声势 *to make a false show of strength; to bluff and bluster* | ～大其词 *to exaggerate; to overstate* **2** 放纵,无拘束 self-indulgent; undisciplined: 乖～ *eccentric and unreasonable* | 嚣(xiāo)～ *rampant; arrogant* [张皇] **1** 扩大 to enlarge; to expand **2** 慌忙失措 alarmed; flurried; scared [张罗](—luo) 各方面照料,四处想办法 to attend to; to take care of; to get busy about: ～～事 *to take care of sth* [开张]开始营业 to begin doing business; to open a business ❷ 铺排陈设 to set out; to display: ～灯结彩 *to hang up lanterns and silk festoons; to be decorated with lanterns and coloured streamers* ❸ 看,望 to look; to see: 东～西望 *to look in all directions* ❹ 量词 ***quantifier***: 一～弓 *a bow* | 两～纸 *two pieces of paper* ❺ 星宿名,二十八宿之一 *zhang*, the 26th of the 28 constellations

章 zhāng ㄓㄤ ❶ 诗歌文辞的段落 chapter; section; division: 乐(yuè)～ *movement of a musical piece* | 篇～结构 *structure of an article* | 第一～ *Chapter One; the first chapter* ❷ 奏章,臣子呈给皇帝的意见书 memorial to the emperor ❸ 章程,法规 rule; regulation: 简～ *brief guide* | 党～ *Party Constitution* | 规～制度 *rules and regulations* ㊀ ***extension*** **1** 条理 order: 杂乱无～ *disorderly and unsystematic* **2** 条目 item; clause: 约法三～ *to agree on a three-point law — to make certain rules to be observed by all concerned* ❹ 戳记 seal; stamp: 图～ *stamp* | 盖～ *to affix a seal; to impress a seal* ❺ 佩带在身上的标志 badge; medal: 徽～ *insignia* | 袖～ *sleeve badge; armband*

鄣 zhāng ㄓㄤ 周朝国名,在今山东省东平东 Zhang, ancient state of the Zhou Dynasty, in the east of today's Dongping, Shandong Province

獐(*麞) zhāng ㄓㄤ (—子) 又叫河麂(jǐ)、牙獐。是一种小型的鹿,头上无角,雄的犬齿发达,形成獠牙,露出嘴外(also called 河麂 or 牙獐) Chinese water deer (*Hydropotes inermis*)

彰 zhāng ㄓㄤ ❶ 明显,显著 clear; evident; obvious: 欲盖弥～ *Try to conceal a mistake, only to make it more conspicuous.* or *The more one tries to hide, the more one exposes oneself.* | 相得益～ *each*

Z

shining more brilliantly in the other's company; to set off each other's merits ❷表彰 to make known; to commend: ～善瘅(dàn)恶 *to commend the good and denounce the evil; to uphold virtue and condemn vice*

漳 zhāng ㄓㄤ 漳河,发源于山西省,流至河北省入卫河 Zhanghe River, originating from Shanxi Province and running through Hebei Province into the Weihe River

嫜 zhāng ㄓㄤ [姑嫜]古时女子称丈夫的母亲和父亲 (address for husband's father and mother in ancient China) parents-in-law; husband's parents

璋 zhāng ㄓㄤ 一种玉器,形状像半个圭 a kind of jade article resembling half of a tablet

樟 zhāng ㄓㄤ 樟树,常绿乔木。木质坚固细致,有香气,做成箱柜,可以防蠹虫 camphor tree (*Cinnamomum camphora*) [樟脑]把樟树的根、茎、枝、叶蒸馏制成的白色结晶体,可做防腐驱虫剂,又可用来制造强心剂等 camphor

蟑 zhāng ㄓㄤ [蟑螂](—láng)一大类有害的昆虫,黑褐色,有光泽,常咬坏衣物、偷吃食物,能发臭气。也叫"蜚蠊"(fěilián) (also called 蜚蠊) cockroach (*Blattodea*)

长(長) ㊁ zhǎng ㄓㄤˇ ❶生,发育 to grow; to develop: ～疮 *to have a boil* | 庄稼～得很旺。*The crops are growing very well.* ❷增加 to boost; to increase; to enhance: ～见识 *to increase one's knowledge; to gain experience* | 在实践中增～才干 *to acquire ability in practice* ❸排行中第一的 eldest; oldest: ～兄 *eldest brother* | ～孙 *eldest grandson* [长子] **1** 排行第一的儿子 eldest son **2** 地名,在山西省 Zhangzi, a place in Shanxi Province ❹辈分高或年纪大的 older; elder; senior: 师～ *teacher* | ～者 *venerable elder* | ～辈 *elder member of a family* 敬辞 ***polite***: 学～ *schoolmate* ❺主持人,机关、团体等单位的负责人 chief; head: 部～ *minister* | 校～ *(of a school) headmaster; principal; (of a college or university) president*

㊀ cháng 见 76 页 see p76

涨(漲) ㊀ zhǎng ㄓㄤˇ ❶水量增加,水面高起来(of water) to rise; to go up: 水～船高 *When the water rises; the boat goes up.* | 河里～水了。*The river is rising.* ❷价格提高(of price) to go up; to rise: ～钱 *to rise in pay; to raise pay* | ～价 *to raise the price; to hike the price*

㊁ zhàng 见 958 页 see p958

仉 zhǎng ㄓㄤˇ 姓 Zhang, a surname

掌 zhǎng ㄓㄤˇ ❶巴掌,手心,握拳时指尖触着的一面

palm：鼓～*to clap one's hands*；*to applaud* ⓘ **extension** 脚的底面 sole：脚～子 *sole of the foot*｜熊～*bear's paw* ❷用巴掌打 to slap：～嘴 *to slap one's face* ❸把握，主持，主管 to be in charge of；to control；to wield：～印 *to keep the seal—to be in power*｜～舵 *to be at the helm*；*to operate the rudder*；*to steer a boat*｜～管档案 *to be in charge of files*｜～权 *to be in power*；*to exercise control* [掌故]关于古代人物、典章、制度等的故事 anecdote [掌握]把握，拿稳 to grasp；to master：～～政策 *to have a grasp of the policy*｜～～原则 *to hold to the principle* ❹(一儿)鞋底前后钉或缀上的皮子等 shoe sole；shoe heel：钉两块～儿 *to have shoes soled*；*to have shoes heeled* ❺马蹄铁，钉在马、驴、骡子等蹄子底下的铁 horseshoe：马～*horseshoe* ❻同"礃" same as 礃

礃 zhǎng ㄓㄤˇ [礃子]煤矿里掘进和采煤的工作面。也作"掌子"(also written as 掌子) working face

丈 zhàng ㄓㄤˋ ❶市制长度单位，1 丈是 10 尺，约合3.33米 *zhang*，traditional unit of length，one *zhang* is ten *chi*，approximately 3.33 metres ❷测量长度、面积 to measure length，area：～量 *to measure*｜～地 *to measure land* ❸对成年或老年男子的尊称(respectful form of address for grown-ups or old males) senior；elder：老～*old gentleman* [丈夫] **1** 成年男子的通称(general form of address for grown-up men) man **2** (—fu) 妇女的配偶，跟"妻子"相对(the opposite of 妻子) husband [丈人] **1** 旧称老年男子(in former times) old gentleman **2** (—ren) 称妻子的父亲 wife's father；father-in-law

仗 zhàng ㄓㄤˋ ❶古代兵器的总称 arms；weaponry；weapons：兵～*weapon*；*arms*｜仪～*flags，weapons，etc carried by guards of honour* ⓩ **transfer** 战争 war；battle：胜～*victorious battle*；*victory*；*triumph*｜败～*lost battle*；*defeat* [打仗]交战，发生战事 to fight a battle；to engage in a battle ❷凭借，依靠 to rely on；to depend on (ⓛ **doublet** 倚— to rely on；to count on｜—恃 to rely on；to count on)：～着大家的力量 *by dint of every one's effort*｜～势欺人 *to take advantage of one's or somebody else's power to bully people* ❸拿着(兵器) to hold (a weapon)：～剑 *to hold a sword*

杖 zhàng ㄓㄤˋ ❶拐杖，扶着走路的棍子 cane；stick：手～*(walking) stick* ❷泛指棍棒(general term for rod or staff used for a specific purpose)：擀面～*rolling pin*

帐(帳) zhàng ㄓㄤˋ ❶(一子)用布或其他材料做成的帷幕 curtain；canopy：

Z

蚊～*mosquito net*｜圆顶～子 *round-top bed-curtain*｜营～ *camp tent*｜～篷 *tent* ❷同"账" same as 账

账(賬) zhàng ㄓㄤˋ ❶关于银钱财物出入的记载 account：记～*to keep accounts*｜流水～*day-to-day account*；*daily account*；*running account* ❷指记载银钱财物出入的本子或单子 account book：一本～*an account book*｜一篇～*an account sheet* ❸债务 debt；credit：欠～*to owe a debt*｜不认～(喻不承认自己做的事) *not to acknowledge a debt*；*to deny what one has done*

胀(脹) zhàng ㄓㄤˋ ❶膨胀，体积变大 to expand；to distend：热～冷缩 *to expand when heated and contract when cooled*；*to expand with heat and contract with cold* ❷身体内壁受到压迫而产生不舒服的感觉 swollen；bloated：肚子～*to feel bloated in the stomach*｜肿～*bloated*；*swollen*

涨(漲) ㊁ zhàng ㄓㄤˋ ❶体积增大 to swell after absorbing water：豆子泡～了。*The beans swelled up after being soaked*. ❷弥漫 to be suffused with；to permeate：烟尘～天。*Smoke and dust fill the air*. ❸多出来 to be more than：～出十块钱 *to have ten yuan more than expected* ❹头部充血(of head) to be swollen by a rush of blood：头昏脑～*to feel one's head reeling* (or *swimming*)｜他气得～红了脸。*He flushed with anger*.

㊀ zhǎng 见 956 页 see p956

障 zhàng ㄓㄤˋ ❶阻隔 to block [障碍]阻挡进行的事物 barrier；hindrance：扫除～～*to clear away an obstacle* ❷用作遮蔽、防卫的东西 screen；barrier：风～*windbreak*｜屏～*screen*；*barrier*

嶂 zhàng ㄓㄤˋ 形势高险像屏障的山峰 screen-shaped precipitous mountain peak：层峦叠～*range upon range of hills*；*peaks rising one over another*

幛 zhàng ㄓㄤˋ (一子)上面题有词句的整幅绸布，用作庆贺或吊唁的礼物 large, oblong sheet of silk or cloth with an appropriate message inscribed, presented at a wedding, birthday or funeral

瘴 zhàng ㄓㄤˋ 瘴气，热带山林中的湿热空气 miasma, hot damp air in tropical forests

ZHAO ㄓㄠ

钊 zhāo ㄓㄠ 勉励 to encourage；to urge；to spur 多用于人名 zhao, usually used in a given name

招 zhāo ㄓㄠ ❶打手势叫人来 to beckon；to gesture：用手一～他就来了。*He came over at the beckoning*. [招待]应接宾客 to entertain；to serve; to receive [招呼](—hu) **1** 召唤 to call:有人～～你。*Someone's calling you.* **2** 照料,扶助 to take care of; to look after; to attend to:～～老人 *to take care of the old* ❷用公开的方式使人来 to recruit; to enlist; to enrol:～集 *to convene; to muster; to summon*|～生 *to enrol new students; to admit new students; to recruit students*|～兵买马 *to recruit men and buy horses — to raise or enlarge an army; to recruit personnel*|～商引资 *to attract investments from overseas* [引] ***extension*** **1** 惹起 to tease; to provoke:～事 *to invite trouble; to bring trouble on oneself*|～笑 *funny; laughable; comical*|别～他。*Don't try to provoke him.* **2** 引来 to invite; to attract:～蚂蚁 *to attract ants* ❸承认自己的罪状 to confess; to admit:不打自～*to confess without being tortured; to give oneself away; to make a confession of one's own accord* ❹武术上的动作 movement in *wushu* [喻] ***figurative*** 计策,办法 trick; device; tactic:花～儿 *trick; game*|绝～儿 *unique skill*

昭 zhāo ㄓㄠ ❶明显,显著 clear; obvious:罪恶～彰 *to commit towering crimes*|～然若揭 *all too clear; clear as daylight* ❷表明,显示 to show; to manifest:以～信守 *to show one's good faith* [昭昭] **1** 光明,明亮 bright:日月～～。*Bright are the sun and the moon.* **2** 明辨事理 to understand; to be clear-minded:使人～～*to enlighten others*

啁 ㊁ zhāo ㄓㄠ [啁哳][嘲哳](—zhā)形容声音杂乱细碎 twittering

㊀ zhōu 见 990 页 see p990

着 ㊂ zhāo ㄓㄠ ❶(—儿)下棋时下一子或走一步叫一着 move (in chess) [喻] ***figurative*** 计策,办法 trick; device; tactic:你出个高～儿。*You are to suggest a clever move.*|我没～儿了。*I'm at the end of my tether.* or *I'm at my wits' end.* ❷〈方 ***dialect***〉放,搁进去 to put in; to add:～点儿盐 *to put some salt in it* ❸〈方 ***dialect***〉用于应答,表示同意 all right; OK:～,你说得真对。*Quite right. That says it all.*

㊀ zhuó 见 1007 页 see p1007

㊁ zháo 见 960 页 see p960

㊃ zhe 见 965 页 see p965

朝 ㊀ zhāo ㄓㄠ 早晨 morning:只争～夕 *to seize the day and seize the hour; to seize every minute*|～思暮想 *to yearn all day long; to long day and night; to pine for sb or sth* [引] ***extension*** 日,天 day:今～*today; now* [朝气][喻] ***figurative*** 向上发展的气概 vigour; vitality; energy:～～蓬勃 *to be imbued with vitality; to be bursting with youthful spirit; vigorous*

㊀ cháo 见 79 页 see p79

嘲哳 ㊁ zhāo ㄓㄠ ［嘲哳］（—zhā）同"啁哳"same as 啁哳

㊀ cháo 见 80 页 see p80

着 ㊁ zháo ㄓㄠ ❶接触，挨上 to touch; to come in contact with：上不～天，下不～地 *to touch neither the sky nor the earth — to be utterly isolated* ❷感受，受到 to be affected by; to be troubled with; to suffer：～慌 *to get nervous; to get flustered; to get jittery*｜～凉 *to catch a cold*｜～急 *anxious* ❸燃烧，也指灯发光 to burn; to give off light：～火 *to catch fire*｜柴火～了。*The faggots are kindled.*｜天黑了，路灯都～了。*When it turned dark, the street lamps are all lit.* ❹入睡，睡着 to fall asleep; to be asleep：躺下就～了。*He fell asleep the moment he got into bed.* ❺用在动词后表示达到目的或有结果(used after a verb to denote the purpose or the result) to hit the mark; to succeed in：猜～了。(*You've*) *guessed it.*｜打～了。(*You've*) *hit it.*

㊀ zhuó 见 1007 页 see p1007

㊂ zhāo 见 959 页 see p959

㊃ zhe 见 965 页 see p965

爪 ㊀ zhǎo ㄓㄠ ❶指甲或趾甲 nail; toenail：手～ *fingernail* ❷鸟兽的脚指 claw; talon; paw：鹰～ *hawk talon* ［爪牙］[喻] ***figurative*** 党羽，狗腿子 underlings; lackeys

㊁ zhuǎ 见 999 页 see p999

找 zhǎo ㄓㄠ ❶寻求，想要得到或见到 to search; to seek：～东西 *to look for sth*｜～事做 *to hunt for a job*｜丢了不好～。*It's difficult to find what is missing.*｜～麻烦 *to ask for trouble*｜～人 *to look for sb*｜～经理 *to go find the manager; to see the manager* ❷退回，补还 to give change：～钱 *to give change*｜～零 *to give change*

沼 zhǎo ㄓㄠ 池子 pond ([连] ***doublet*** 池— pond; pool) ［沼气］有机物在地下隔绝空气的条件下分解而产生的气体，可以燃烧。多产生于池沼，也产生于煤矿井、石油井中。主要成分是甲烷 marsh gas; firedamp; methane ［沼泽］因湖泊淤浅等而形成的水草茂密的泥泞地带 marsh; swamp; bog

召 ㊀ zhào ㄓㄠ ❶呼唤，招呼 to call; to summon：号～ *to call; to appeal*｜～见 *to call in (one's subordinates) officially; to summon (a foreign envoy) for an audience*｜～唤 *to call; to summon*｜～集 *to convene; to assemble; to summon*｜～开会议 *to hold a convention; to summon a conference* ❷傣族姓 Zhao, a surname of the Dai ethnic group

㊁ shào 见 661 页 see p661

诏 zhào ㄓㄠ ❶告诉 to instruct; to warn; to exhort ❷皇帝所发的命令 imperial

Z

edict

照(❶ * 炤) zhào ㄓㄠˋ ❶光线射在物体上 to shine; to illuminate: 拿灯~一~ *to light it with a lamp* | 阳光普~ *The sun shines all over the land*. or *The land is bathed in the sun*. ❷对着镜子或其他反光的东西看自己或其他人物的影像 to reflect; to mirror: ~镜子 *to look in the mirror* ❸照相,摄影 to photograph; to film; to shoot: 天安门前~张相。*I had a picture taken in front of Tian'an Men*. ❹画像或相片 photograph; picture: 小~ *small-sized photo; miniature* ❺照管,看顾 to look after; to take care of: 请你~应一下。*Would you please keep an eye on it?* [照料]关心,料理 to attend (to); to tend: 病人需要~~ *The patient needs tending*. ❻查对,对比 to compare; to contrast: 比~ *in the light of; in conformity with* | 对~ *to contrast; to compare* | 参~ *to refer to; to consult* ❼凭证 licence; permit: 护~ *passport* | 牌~ *licence plate; licence tag* ❽知晓 to understand; to make out: 心~不宣 *to have a tacit understanding* ❾通告,通知 to notify; to inform: 知~ *to notify; to inform* | 请关~他一声,我明天来。*Please tell him that I'll be here tomorrow*. [照会]外交上用以表明立场、达成协议或通知事项的公文(of a government) note to another government ❿介词 ***preposition*** **1** 对着,向着 in the direction of; towards: ~敌人开枪 *to fire at the enemy* | ~着这个方向走 *to go in this direction* **2** 按照,依照 according to; in accordance with: ~计划执行 *to carry out in accordance with the plan* | ~他的意思办 *to follow his idea* ⓫副词 ***adverb***,表示按原样或某种标准做 to do accordingly: ~抄 *to copy; to duplicate; to replicate* | ~办 *to act accordingly; to act upon; to comply with*

兆 zhào ㄓㄠˋ ❶古代占验吉凶时灼龟甲所成的裂纹(迷信)(of superstition) cracks formed on the tortoise shell when it was burned for divination in ancient China ❷预兆 sign; omen; portent: 征~ *sign; omen* | 佳~ *auspicious omen* ❸预示 to foretell; to portend; to forebode; to augur: 瑞雪~丰年。*A timely snow promises a good harvest in the coming year*. ❹数目 numeral: **1** 百万 million; mega- **2** 古代指万亿(in ancient China) trillion; million million ❺法定计量单位中十进倍数单位词头之一,表示 10^6(符号 M) mega- (M)

赵(趙) zhào ㄓㄠˋ 战国国名,在今河北省南部和山西省中部、北部一带 Zhao, one of the seven major powers of the Warring States Period, covering the south of today's Henan Province and the middle and north of today's

Z

Shanxi Province

笊 zhào ㄓㄠˋ［笊篱］(—li) 用竹篾、柳条、铅丝等编成的一种用具，可以在汤水里捞东西 *zhaoli*, a strainer made of bamboo, wicker or wire

棹(*櫂) zhào ㄓㄠˋ 划船的一种工具，形状和桨差不多 oar ㉖ ***extension*** **1** 船 boat; ship **2**〈方 ***dialect***〉划(船) to row (a boat)

罩 zhào ㄓㄠˋ ❶(—子、—儿)覆盖物体的东西 cover: 口～ *mask* | 灯～子 *lampshade* ❷扣盖，覆盖 to cover; to overspread; to wrap: 把菜～起来 *to cover the dishes* ❸穿在其他衣服外面的单衣 overcoat; overall; overclothes: 外～ *overcoat* | ～衣 *overall; overclothes* | 袍～儿 *robe; dustcoat* ❹养鸡用的竹笼子 bamboo chicken coop ❺捕鱼用的竹器，圆筒形，无顶无底，下略大，上略小 bamboo fish trap

肇(**肈) zhào ㄓㄠˋ ❶开始 to commence; to initiate: ～端 *beginning; commencement* ❷发生 to cause; to lead to: ～祸(闯祸) *to cause trouble* | ～事 *to cause an accident; to create a disturbance*

曌 zhào ㄓㄠˋ 同"照"。唐朝女皇帝武则天为自己名字造的字(same as 照) *zhao*, a Chinese character coined by Empress Wu Zetian of the Tang Dynasty for her own given name

ZHE ㄓㄜ

折 ㊂ zhē ㄓㄜ 翻转，倒腾 to roll over; to turn over: ～跟头 *to somersault; to turn a somersault* | 用两个碗把开水～一～就凉了。*Water will soon turn cool if you pour it repeatedly from one bowl to another.*

㊀ zhé 见 962 页 see p962

㊁ shé 见 662 页 see p662

蜇 ㊁ zhē ㄓㄜ ❶有毒腺的虫子刺人或牲畜 to sting: 被蝎子～了 *to be stung by a scorpion* ❷某些东西刺激皮肤或器官使感觉不适 to smart; to prick: 切洋葱～眼睛。*Slicing onions makes one's eyes smart.*

㊀ zhé 见 963 页 see p963

遮 zhē ㄓㄜ 掩盖，掩蔽，挡 to cover; to conceal; to screen: ～丑 *to gloss over one's blemish; to cover up one's defect* | ～人耳目 *to throw dust in people's eyes* | 乌云～不住太阳的光辉。*The black clouds can never shut out the sunlight.*

螫 ㊁ zhē ㄓㄜ 同"蜇㊁❶"，用于口语(used in colloquial Chinese) same as 蜇㊁❶

㊀ shì 见 686 页 see p686

折(❹—❻△摺) ㊀ zhé ㄓㄜˊ ❶断，弄断 to break; to snap; to fracture: 禁止攀～花木。*No picking of flowers or climbing of trees.* ㉘ ***figurative*** 幼年死亡 to die young: 夭～ *to die young* ［折磨］(—mó) 使在肉体或精神

上受痛苦 torture; torment:解放前劳动人民受尽了～～。*The working people suffered greatly before liberation.* ❷损失 to suffer the loss of; to lose:损兵～将 *to suffer heavy casualties; to take a heavy toll* ❸弯转,屈曲 to bend; to twist:～腰 *to bend one's back* | 转～点 *turning point* ㊀ ***extension*** 返转,回转 to turn back:走到半路又～回来了 *to turn back halfway* [折中](*折衷)对不同意见采取调和态度 to compromise; to split the difference ❹叠 to fold (㊃ ***doublet*** 一叠 to fold):～衣服 *to fold clothes* | ～尺 *folding ruler* ❺(一子、一儿)用纸折叠起来的本子 booklet; folder:存～ *passbook; bankbook* ❻杂剧一本分四折,一折相当于现代戏曲的一场 scene, one of the four parts in a poetic drama in the Yuan Dynasty ❼心服 to be convinced; to be filled with admiration:～服 *to be fully convinced* | 心～ *to be deeply convinced; to be filled with heartfelt admiration* ❽折扣,按成数减少 discount; rebate:打～扣 *to sell at a discount* | 九～ *to give a 10% discount; 10% off* ❾抵作,对换,以此代彼 to convert into; to amount to:～账 *to pay a debt in kind* | ～变(变卖) *to sell off (one's property)* ❿汉字的一种笔形(㇀) *zhe*, one of the strokes of Chinese characters:"买"字的第一笔是～。*The first stroke of the character* 买 *is* zhe.

㊁ shé 见 662 页 see p662

㊂ zhē 见 962 页 see p962

哲(*喆) zhé ㄓㄜˊ ❶有智慧 wise; sagacious; sapient:～人 *sage; philosopher; oracle* [哲学]社会意识形态之一,它研究自然界、社会和思维的普遍规律,是关于自然知识和社会知识的概括和总结,是关于世界观的理论 philosophy ❷聪明智慧的人 wise man; sage:先～ *ancient sage*

注:"喆"多用于人名 *zhe*, usually used in a given name

晢(**晣) zhé ㄓㄜˊ 明亮 bright

蜇 ㊀ zhé ㄓㄜˊ 海蜇,在海里生活的一种腔肠动物,形状像张开的伞,可供食用 jellyfish (*Scyphozoa*)

㊁ zhē 见 962 页 see p962

簎 zhé ㄓㄜˊ 〈方 ***dialect***〉(一子)一种粗的竹席 coarse bamboo mat

辄(*輒) zhé ㄓㄜˊ 总是,就 always; often:每至此,～觉心旷神怡。*Whenever I come here, I always feel relaxed and happy.* | 所言～听 *always to heed sb's advice* | 动～得咎 *to be blamed for every move; to be frequently taken to task*

蛰(蟄) zhé ㄓㄜˊ 动物冬眠,藏起来不食不动 hibernation：～伏 *dormancy; hibernation*｜入～*to go into hibernation*｜～虫 *hibernating insect*

讋(讋) zhé ㄓㄜˊ 〈古 ***archaism***〉恐惧 fear; fright

谪(*讁) zhé ㄓㄜˊ ❶谴责，责罚 to censure; to blame; to reprimand ❷封建时代特指贬官(in feudal times) to relegate

摺 zhé ㄓㄜˊ 同"折㊀❹—❻" same as 折㊀❹—❻

磔 zhé ㄓㄜˊ ❶分裂肢体，古代的一种酷刑 dismemberment of the body as a cruel punishment in ancient China ❷汉字的笔画，即捺(nà)(i. e. 捺) *zhe*, right-falling stroke in Chinese written characters

辙 zhé ㄓㄜˊ 车辙，车轮轧的痕迹 rut; tyre track ㊀ ***extension*** **1** (一儿)车行的一定路线 track of traffic：戗(qiāng)～儿 *to drive in the wrong direction*｜顺～儿 *to go in the right direction; to follow the track* **2** 歌词、戏曲、杂曲所押的韵 rhyme：合～*to be rhymed; to be in rhyme*｜十三～*13 patterns with rhymes* **3** 〈方 ***dialect***〉办法 way; idea：没～了 *can find no way out; to be at the end of one's rope*

者 zhě ㄓㄜˇ ❶助词 ***auxiliary***，用在形容词、动词或词组后，指人或事物(used after a verb or an adjective or a phrase, to indicate a class of persons or things) one (or those) who; the person (or things) which：学～*scholar*｜读～*reader*｜作～*author*｜强～*the strong*｜符合标准～*those who have reached the standard* ❷助词 ***auxiliary***，表示语气停顿(used to indicate a pause)：陈胜～，阳城人也。*Chen Sheng is a man from Yangcheng City.*｜云～，水汽蒸腾而成。*Clouds are formed when water vapours rise into the sky.* ❸代词 ***pronoun***，这，此(多用在古诗词中)(usually used in ancient poetry) this：～回 *this time*｜～番 *on this occasion; this time*｜～边走。*This way, please!* ❹用在"二、三、数"等数词后，指上文所说的几件事(used with the numbers 二，三 or 数，etc to denote things mentioned above)：二～必居其一。*It must be either of the two.*｜三～缺一不可。*Of the three things, no one is dispensable.*

锗 zhě ㄓㄜˇ 一种金属元素，符号 Ge，银灰色，质脆，有光泽。是重要的半导体材料，主要用来制造半导体晶体管 germanium (Ge)

赭 zhě ㄓㄜˇ 红褐色 reddish brown; burnt ochre：～石(矿物名，可做颜料) *ochre*

褶(**襵) zhě ㄓㄜˇ (一子、一儿) ❶衣服折叠而形成的印痕 pleat; crease; wrinkle：百～裙 *pleated skirt* ❷泛指折皱的部分 crease; fold; wrinkle：衣服上净是～子。

There are lots of creases in the coat. |这张纸有好多～子。*The paper is wrinkled.*

这(這) ㊀ zhè ㄓㄜˋ ❶代词 ***pronoun***,此,指较近的时间、地方或事物,跟"那"相对(the opposite of 那) this; here; now:～里 *here* | ～些 *these* | ～个 *this one; this* | ～是英汉词典。*This is an English-Chinese dictionary.* [这么](—me) 代词 ***pronoun***,如此 so, such:～～办就好了。*It would be better to do like this.* ❷这时候,指说话的同时 now; at the moment:我～就走。*I'm leaving now.*

㊁ zhèi 见966页 see p966

柘 zhè ㄓㄜˋ 柘树,落叶灌木或小乔木,叶子卵形或椭圆形,前端有浅裂,可以喂蚕。柘木可以提取黄色染料,为柘黄 three-bristle cudrania (*Maclura tricuspidata*)

浙(*淛) zhè ㄓㄜˋ ❶浙江,古水名,又叫"渐江"、"之江"、"曲江",即今钱塘江,是浙江省第一大河流(also called 渐江, 之江 or 曲江, i.e. today's Qiantang River, the longest river in Zhejiang Province) Zhejiang River in ancient China ❷指浙江省 Zhejiang Province

蔗 zhè ㄓㄜˋ 甘蔗,多年生草本植物。茎有节,含甜汁很多,可以吃,也可制糖 sugarcane (*Saccharum*)

嗻 zhè ㄓㄜˋ 叹词 ***interjection***,旧时表示答应,"是"的意思(in ancient China) aye

鹧 zhè ㄓㄜˋ [鹧鸪](—gū) 鸟名,背部和腹部黑白两色相杂,头顶棕色,脚黄色。吃谷粒、昆虫、蚯蚓等 Chinese francolin (*Francolinus pintadeanus*)

䗪 zhè ㄓㄜˋ 䗪虫,即土鳖。体扁,棕黑色,雄的有翅,雌的无翅。雌的干制后可入药 (i.e. 土鳖) ground beetle (*Eupoly-phaga sinensis*)

着 ㊃ zhe ·ㄓㄜ 助词 ***auxiliary*** ❶在动词后(used after a verb) **1** 表示动作正进行 to be doing:走～*to be walking* | 等～*to be waiting* | 开～会呢 *to be having a meeting* **2** 表示状态的持续(used to indicate the continuation of a state):桌上放～一本书。*There is a book on the table.* | 墙上挂～一幅画。*A picture is hanging on the wall.* ❷表示程度深,常跟"呢"(ne)连用(usually used in collocation with 呢) very; quite:好～呢 *very good* | 这小孩儿精～呢! *The kid is smart indeed!* ❸用在动词或表示程度的形容词后表示祈使(used after a verb or an adjective of degree to indicate imperative mood):你听～。*Just listen!* | 步子大～点儿。*Walk in bigger strides, please.* ❹加在某些动词后,使变成介词(used after certain verbs as a preposition):顺～ *along* | 照～*according to* | 沿～ *along* | 朝～*towards*

㊀ zhuó 见1007页 see p1007

Z

㊂ zháo 见 960 页 see p960
㊃ zhāo 见 959 页 see p959

ZHEI ㄓㄟ

这(這) ㊁ zhèi ㄓㄟ "这(zhè)一"的合音,但指数量时不限于一(combined pronunciation of zhè and yī, but not limited to one when denoting number): ~个 *this one* | ~些 *these* | ~年 *this year* | ~三年 *these three years*

㊀ zhè 见 965 页 see p965

ZHEN ㄓㄣ

贞 zhēn ㄓㄣ (旧读 formerly zhēng) ❶坚定,有节操 loyal; faithful; staunch: 忠~ *loyal; staunch* | 坚~不屈 *to remain faithful and unyielding* ❷旧礼教中指女子不改嫁或不失身(in the feudal moral code) chastity; virginity: ~女 *virgin; chaste girl* ❸占,卜,问卦 divination: ~卜 *to tell fortune*

侦 zhēn ㄓㄣ (旧读 formerly zhēng) 探听,暗中察看 to detect; to scout; to investigate: ~探 *detective; spy* | ~查案件 *to investigate a case* | ~察机 *surveillance plane; reconnaissance plane; scout*

帧 zhēn ㄓㄣ (旧读 formerly zhēng) 量词 ***quantifier***,幅(用于字画、照片等)(of paintings or calligraphy, etc): 一~彩画 *a coloured painting* [装帧]书画等物的装潢设计 binding and layout design (of calligraphy, paintings, etc)

浈 zhēn ㄓㄣ (旧读 formerly zhēng) 浈江,水名,在广东省北部 Zhenjiang River in Guangdong Province

桢 zhēn ㄓㄣ (旧读 formerly zhēng) ❶坚硬的木头 hardwood ❷古代打土墙时所立的木柱(in ancient China) terminal posts used in building a wall [桢干](-gàn) ㊞ ***figurative*** 能胜重任的人才 backbone; pillar

祯 zhēn ㄓㄣ (旧读 formerly zhēng) 吉祥 auspicious; propitious

针(*鍼) zhēn ㄓㄣ ❶缝织衣物引线用的一种细长的工具 needle [针对]对准 to be aimed at; to be directed against: ~~着工作中的缺点,提出改进的办法 *to put forward a method of improvement as regards the weak points in the work* ❷细长像针形的东西 needle-shaped thing: 大头~ *pin* | 松~ *pine needle* | 钟表上有时~、分~和秒~。*The timepiece has an hour hand, a minute hand and a second hand.* [指南针]我国古代发明的一种利用磁石制成的指示方向的仪器 compass ❸用针扎治病 to acupuncture: ~灸 *acupuncture and moxibustion* [针刺麻醉]用针刺入人体的某些穴位,使人的某些部位暂时失去知觉,用以代替麻醉剂 acupuncture anaesthesia ❹西医注

射用的器具 hypodermic syringe：～头 *syringe needle* ❺针剂 injection medicine：打～ *to have an injection* | 防疫～ *prophylactic inoculation*

珍(*珎) zhēn ㄓㄣ ❶宝贝，宝贵的东西 treasure：奇～异宝 *rare treasures; treasures of priceless beauty and historical value* ❷贵重的，宝贵的 precious; valuable：～禽异兽 *rare birds and animals* ❸重视，看重 to value highly; to treasure：世人～之 *to be valued by the world at large* | ～惜 *to cherish; to treasure* | ～视 *to cherish; to treasure*

胗 zhēn ㄓㄣ 鸟类的胃 gizzard：鸡～肝儿 *chicken's gizzard and liver*

真 zhēn ㄓㄣ ❶真实，跟客观事物相符合，跟"假"相对(the opposite of 假) true; real：～相大白。*The whole truth has come out.* | 千～万确 *absolutely true* | 传～ *fax; facsimile* [真理]正确反映客观世界发展规律的思想 truth [天真] **1** 心地单纯，性格很直率 naïve; innocent **2** 头脑简单，容易被假象迷惑 naïve; simple-minded：这种想法太～～。*It's such a naïve idea.* ❷副词 ***adverb***，确实，的确 really; truly; indeed：～好 *really good* | ～高兴 *really happy* ❸清楚，显明 clearly; distinctly; unmistakably：字太小，看不～。*The characters are too small to see clearly.* | 听得很～ *to hear it unmistakably* ❹真书(楷书) *zhenshu*; regular script：～草隶篆 *regular, cursive, official and seal scripts* ❺本性，本原 nature; inherent quality：返朴归～ *to return to the natural state of man; to return to original purity and simplicity*

砧(*碪) zhēn ㄓㄣ 捶、砸或切东西的时候，垫在底下的器具 hammering block：铁～ *anvil* | ～板 *chopping block* [砧木]嫁接植物时把接穗接在另一个植物体上，这个植物体叫砧木 stock

蓁 zhēn ㄓㄣ ❶(叠 ***reduplication***)草木茂盛 luxuriant; lush：其叶～～ *with luxuriant leaves* ❷同"榛❷" same as 榛❷：深～(荆棘丛) *jungle*

獉 zhēn ㄓㄣ 同"榛❸" same as 榛❸：～狉(pī)(指草木丛杂，野兽出没) *densely wooded and frequented by wild animals*

溱 ㊀ zhēn ㄓㄣ 溱头河，水名，在河南省驻马店。今作"臻头河"(now written as 臻头河) Zhentou River in Zhumadian, Henan Province

㊁ qín 见607页 see p607

榛 zhēn ㄓㄣ ❶落叶灌木或小乔木，花黄褐色。果实叫榛子，果皮很坚硬，果仁可以吃 hazel (*Corylus heterophylla*) ❷泛指丛生的荆棘 overgrown brambles：～莽 *luxuriant vegetation* ❸草木丛杂(叠 ***reduplication***) to grow densely：草木～～ *with dense vegeta-*

Z

tion

臻 zhēn ㄓㄣ 到，达到 to reach; to arrive：日～完善 *to be perfected day by day*

斟 zhēn ㄓㄣ 往杯子里倒（酒或茶）to pour; to fill：～酒 *to fill a cup of wine* | ～茶 *to serve tea* | 给我～上碗水。*Pour me a bowl of water*.［斟酌］（— zhuó）㊕ ***transfer*** 度（duó）量，考虑 to consider; to deliberate：请你～～办理。*Please act at your discretion*.

椹 ㊀ zhēn ㄓㄣ 同"砧"same as 砧

㊁ shèn 见 669 页 see p669

甄 zhēn ㄓㄣ 审查 to discriminate; to distinguish：～别 *to examine and distinguish*; *to screen*; *to discriminate* | ～拔人才 *to select people of talent*

箴 zhēn ㄓㄣ ❶同"针❶"same as 针❶ ❷劝告，劝诫 to admonish; to exhort：～言 *maxim* ❸一种文体，以告诫规劝为主 genre of didactic literary composition

诊 zhěn ㄓㄣˇ 医生为断定病症而察看病人身体内部外部的情况（of a doctor）to examine：～断 *to diagnose* | ～脉 *to feel the pulse* | 门～*clinic*; *outpatient service* | 出～（*of a doctor*）*to visit a patient at home*

轸 zhěn ㄓㄣˇ ❶古代车后的横木 crossboard at the rear of an ancient carriage ❷悲痛 sorrowful; distressed：～悼 *to mourn with deep grief* | ～怀（痛念）*to sorrowfully cherish the memory of sb* | ～恤（怜悯）*to show great sympathy for sb* ❸星宿名，二十八宿之一 *zhen*, the 28th of the 28 constellations

畛 zhěn ㄓㄣˇ 田地间的小路 country path that divides a field ㊀ ***extension*** 界限 boundary：不分～域 *to make no distinctions*

疹 zhěn ㄓㄣˇ 病人皮肤上起的小疙瘩，通常是红色，小的像针尖，大的像豆粒，多由皮肤表层发炎浸润而起 rash：湿～*eczema*［疹子］（— zi）麻疹 measles

袗 zhěn ㄓㄣˇ ❶单衣 unlined jacket; thin clothes ❷（衣服）华美（of clothes）beautiful; gorgeous; resplendent

枕 zhěn ㄓㄣˇ ❶枕头，躺着时垫在头下的东西 pillow［枕木］铁路路基上承受铁轨的横木 railway sleeper; crosstie ❷躺着的时候把头放在枕头或器物上 to rest the head on a pillow or other things when lying：～着枕头 *to be resting one's head on a pillow* | ～戈待旦 *to lie with one's head pillowed on a spear waiting for the day to break*; *to be battle-ready all the night*

缜 zhěn ㄓㄣˇ 周密，细致 careful; deliberate（㊃ ***doublet*** 一密 careful; meticulous; deliberate）：～密的思考 *careful consideration*

稹 zhěn ㄓㄣˇ 同"缜"same as 缜

鬒（**黰） zhěn ㄓㄣˇ 头发浓密而黑（of hair）thick and dark：～发 *thick dark hair*

圳（**甽） zhèn ㄓㄣˋ〈方 *dialect*〉田边水沟。多用于地名（zhen，usually used in a place name）ditch between fields：深～（在广东省）*Shenzhen，a place in Guangdong Province*

阵 zhèn ㄓㄣˋ ❶军队作战时布置的局势 battle array；battle formation：～线 *front*｜严～以待 *to be ready in full battle array；to remain in combat readiness*｜一字长蛇～ *battle formation stretching out in a long single-file line* [引] ***extension*** 战场 battlefield：～亡 *to die on the battlefield* ［阵营］两军交战对立的阵势 camp [喻] ***figurative*** 利益和斗争目标相同的集团 camp：革命～～ *revolutionary camp* ❷量词 ***quantifier***，表示事情或动作经过的段落 period；spell：刮了一～风。*There was a gust of wind.* [转] ***transfer***（一子）一段时间 a period of time：这一～子工作正忙。*I am fully occupied with my work nowadays.*

纼 zhèn ㄓㄣˋ〈方 ***dialect***〉拴牛、马等的绳索 tether

鸩（❷❸$^{\triangle}$ *酖） zhèn ㄓㄣˋ ❶传说中的一种毒鸟，把它的羽毛泡在酒里，喝了可以毒死人 legendary bird with poisonous feathers ❷用鸩的羽毛泡成的毒酒 poisoned wine：饮～止渴（喻满足一时需要，不顾后果）*to quench thirst with poisoned wine — to seek temporary relief regardless of consequences* ❸用毒酒害人 to kill sb with poisoned wine

“酖”又 dān 见 126 页 also pronounced dān，see p 126

振 zhèn ㄓㄣˋ ❶摇动，挥动 to flap；to wield：～笔直书 *to wield the pen and write very fast*｜～铃 *ringing；peal*｜～臂高呼 *to raise one's arms and shout* ❷奋起，兴起 to boost；to brace up：～兴 *to revitalize*｜～作 *to bestir*｜精神一～ *to feel buoyed up* ❸救 to save；to rescue：～乏绝 *to save the rare and endangered species* ❹振动 vibration：共～ *resonance*｜谐～ *resonance*

赈 zhèn ㄓㄣˋ 赈济，救济 to aid；to relieve：～灾 *to provide relief to disaster-stricken areas*｜以工代～ *to provide work as a means of relief* 也作“振”also written as 振

震 zhèn ㄓㄣˋ ❶迅速或剧烈地颤动 to shake；to quake；to vibrate：地～ *earthquake*｜～耳 *deafening* ❷惊恐或情绪过分激动 excited；shocked：～惊 *shocked；astonished；amazed*｜～怒 *enraged；furious* ❸八卦之一，符号是☳，代表雷 one of the Eight Trigrams ☳，representing thunder

朕 zhèn ㄓㄣˋ ❶我，我的，由秦始皇时起专用作皇帝自称

Z

(used exclusively by the reigning emperor in feudal China from the first emperor of the Qin Dynasty) we; our ❷ 预兆 omen; portent

瑱 zhèn ㄓㄣˋ 古时戴在耳垂上的玉 jade earring

镇 zhèn ㄓㄣˋ ❶ 压 to apply weight to; to press with sth heavy:～尺 *paperweight in the shape of a ruler* ❷镇压 to suppress; to repress; to quell:～反(镇压反革命) *to suppress counter revolutionaries* ❸安定 calm; tranquil:～静 *calm; composed; sedate* | ～定 *calm; composed; sedate* ❹把饮料等同冰或冷水放在一起使凉 to cool with ice or in cold water:冰～汽水 *iced soda water; iced soda* ❺行政区划单位,一般由县一级领导 town:城～居民 *city and township residents* | 乡～企业 *township and village enterprises* ❻较大的集市 bazaar ❼时常 often:十年～相随。*For ten years we have been often together.*

ZHENG ㄓㄥ

丁 ㊁ zhēng ㄓㄥ [丁丁]拟声词 ***onomatopoeia***, 形容伐木、弹琴等声音 jingling; tinkling; clanging

㊀ dīng 见 151 页 see p151

正 ㊁ zhēng ㄓㄥ 正月,夏历一年的第一个月 first month by the lunar calendar:新～ *first month of the lunar year*

㊀ zhèng 见 972 页 see p972

征(❸－❻△徵) zhēng ㄓㄥ ❶ 远行 to make a long journey:～帆(远行的船) *ship on a long voyage* | 踏上～途 *to start on a journey; to embark on a journey* ❷用武力制裁 to go on an expedition; to go on a campaign:出～ *to set out on an expedition; to go out to battle* | ～讨 *to go on a punitive expedition* [征服]用力制服 to conquer; to subjugate:～～自然 *to conquer nature* ❸由国家召集或收用 to levy; to conscript; to draft:应(yìng)～入伍 *to be conscripted into the army; to be enlisted in the army* | ～税 *to levy taxes* ❹寻求,希望得到 to solicit (㊣ ***doublet*** 一求 to solicit):～稿 *to solicit contributions* | ～求群众意见 *to seek public opinion* ❺证明,证验 evidence; proof:有实物可～。*There is tangible evidence.* ❻现象,迹象 sign:特～ *characteristic; feature; trait* | ～兆 *sign; omen; portent*

"徵"又 zhǐ 见 981 页 also pronounced zhǐ, see p981

怔 zhēng ㄓㄥ [怔忡](—chōng) 中医所称的一种虚弱病,患者感到心脏跳动得很厉害(in traditional Chinese medicine) palpitation [怔忪](—zhōng) 惊惧 terrified; scared; panic-stricken

钲 ㊀ zhēng ㄓㄥ 古代的一种打击乐器,用铜做成,在行军时敲打 ancient bell-shaped percussion instrument made of copper used by troops on the march

㊁ zhèng 见 973 页 see p973

症(癥) ㊁ zhēng ㄓㄥ [症结]腹内结块的病 lump in the abdomen ㊞ *figurative* 事情难解决的关键所在 crux; nub; knotty point

㊀ zhèng 见 973 页 see p973

争 zhēng ㄓㄥ ❶力求获得,互不相让 to contend:~夺 *to vie; to contend* | ~先恐后 *to vie with one another lest one should lag behind* ❷争执 to dispute; to argue:意气之~ *biased dispute* | ~论 *to debate; to argue; to dispute* ❸〈方 *dialect*〉差,欠 short of; wanting ❹怎么,如何(多用在古诗词曲中)(usually used in ancient poetry and lyrics) why; how:~不 *why not* | ~知 *how does one know* | ~奈 *nevertheless; however*

挣 ㊁ zhēng ㄓㄥ [挣扎](—zhá)尽力支撑或摆脱 to struggle:垂死~~ *the last-ditch struggle*

㊀ zhèng 见 974 页 see p974

峥 zhēng ㄓㄥ [峥嵘](—róng) **1** 高峻,突出 lofty and steep; towering:山势~~ *mountains towering high* **2** 不平常 outstanding; extraordinary:~~岁月 *eventful times; turbulent years*

狰 zhēng ㄓㄥ [狰狞](—níng)样子凶恶 ferocious; hideous:面目~~ *hideous visage*

睁 zhēng ㄓㄥ 张开眼睛 to open eyes

铮 zhēng ㄓㄥ 拟声词 ***onomatopoeia***,金属相击的声音(叠 ***reduplication***) clanking; clanging

筝 zhēng ㄓㄥ 古代弦乐器 *zheng*, ancient stringed musical instrument [风筝](—zheng)玩具的一种,用竹篾做架,糊上纸,牵线放在空中,可以飞得很高。装上弓弦或哨子,迎着风能发声 kite

烝 zhēng ㄓㄥ ❶众多 multitude:~民 *masses of people* ❷古代冬祭名 term of winter sacrifice in ancient China ❸古同"蒸"same as 蒸 in ancient Chinese

蒸 zhēng ㄓㄥ ❶热气上升 to evaporate:~发 *to evaporate* | ~气 *vapour; steam* [蒸蒸]像气一样向上升 rising like vapour:~~日上 *to become more prosperous every day; to be thriving day by day* ❷利用水蒸气的热力使食物变熟或变热 to steam:~馒头 *to steam mantou*

拯 zhěng ㄓㄥˇ 援救,救助 to save; to rescue(㊟ ***doublet*** —救 to rescue; to deliver):~民于水火之中 *to deliver the*

people from an abyss of misery

整 zhěng ㄓㄥˇ ❶整齐,有秩序,不乱 orderly; neat; tidy:～洁 *clean and tidy*|仪容不～ *untidy in appearance* ❷不残缺,完全的,跟"零"相对(the opposite of 零) whole; complete; full (㊀ ***doublet*** 完一 whole; complete):完～无缺 *intact; integrated; integral*|～套的书 *a whole set of books*|忙了一～天 *to be busy for a whole day* [整数]算术上指不带分数、小数的数或不是分数、小数的数 integer 一般指没有零头的数目 round number; round figure ❸整理,整顿 to put in order; to consolidate:～装待发 *to get everything ready for departure*|～风 *to rectify incorrect styles of work and thinking* [整合]调整,重组,使和谐一致 to consolidate ㊁ ***extension*** 修理,搞,弄 to repair; to make:桌子坏了～一～ *to repair a damaged desk*|～旧如新 *to renovate* ❹使吃苦头 to make sb suffer:不要随便～人。*Don't discipline others at your will.*

正 ㊀ zhèng ㄓㄥˋ ❶不偏,不斜 straight; upright; perpendicular:～午 *noon; midday*|～中 *middle; center*|～南～北 *due south and north* ㊁ ***extension*** **1** 合于法则、规矩的 upright:～派 *upright; honest*|～当 *legitimate; justified*|～楷 *regular script* **2** 图形的各个边和各个角都相等的 regular:～方形 *square* [正经](-jing) **1** 端庄,正派 decent; honest:～～人 *decent person*|～～话 *honest words* **2** 正当 serious:～～事 *serious affairs* ❷副词 ***adverb***,恰 just; right; exactly:你来得～好。*You've come at the right time.*|时钟～打十二下。*The clock is striking twelve.* ❸副词 ***adverb***,表示动作在进行中 just (doing); just now:现在～开着会。*A meeting is being held now.*|我～出门,他来了。*I was about to go out when he came.* ❹改去偏差或错误 to correct (㊀ ***doublet*** 改一 to correct):～误 *to correct errors*|给他～音 *to correct his pronunciation* ❺纯,不杂(指色、味) pure:～黄 *pure yellow*|～色 *pure colour*|～味 *right flavour* ❻表示相对的两面的积极的一面 positive; obverse **1** 跟"反"相对(the opposite of 反) obverse:～面 *face; facade*|～比 *direct ratio; direct proportion* **2** 跟"负"相对(the opposite of 负) positive:～电 *positive electricity*|～极 *positive electrode; positive pole*|～数 *positive number* **3** 跟"副"相对(the opposite of 副):～本 *original; original copy*|～册 *regular register* ❼姓 Zheng, a surname

㊁ zhēng 见 970 页 see p970

证(證) zhèng ㄓㄥˋ ❶用人物、事实来表明或

断定 to prove; to demonstrate: ～明 *to demonstrate; to testify* | ～几何题 *to demonstrate a geometric problem* [公证]被授以权力的机关根据当事人的申请，证明法律行为或有法律意义的文书和事实的合法性、真实性 notarization [认证]证明产品达到某种质量标准的合格评定 attestation; authentication: 国际～～ *international attestation* | ～～书 *attestation certificate* [听证] **1** 法院为公正执法公开听取当事人的说明与证词 hearing of witnesses **2** 立法机关为保障法律、法规的合法性和合理性，直接听取各方面的意见 judicial hearing **3** 行政机关为实施行政决定公开听取公众意见和质询 administrative hearing ❷凭据，帮助断定事理或情况的东西 proof; evidence; testimony: ～据 *evidence; proof; testimony* | 工作～ *employee's identification card*

政 zhèng ㄓㄥˋ ❶政治 politics: ～党 *political party* | ～纲 *political programme* | 参～ *to be engaged in politics; to participate in government and political affairs* [政治]阶级、政党、社会集团、个人在国家生活和国际关系方面的活动。是经济的集中表现 politics [政府]国家权力机关的执行机关，即国家行政机关 government [政体]国家政权的构成形式。我国的政体是人民代表大会制 polity; regime [政权] **1** 指国家权力，即统治阶级实行阶级统治的权力 regime; state political power **2** 指政权机关，即国家机关。是行使国家权力，管理国家事务的机关。包括国家权力机关、国家行政机关、审判机关、检察机关和军队等 organ of political power; organ of state power [政策]国家、政党为了达到一定的目的，根据自己的政治路线，结合当前情况和历史条件制定的一切实际行动的准则 policy ❷国家某一部门主管的业务 administrative affairs of certain government departments: 财～ *finance; finance administration* | 民～ *civil affairs; civil administration* | 邮～ *postal service* ❸指集体的事务 affairs of an organization: 家～ *homemaking; household management* | 校～ *school administration*

钲 ㊀ zhèng ㄓㄥˋ 化学元素，镄(fèi)的旧称(former term for 镄) fermium

㊁ zhēng 见 971 页 see p971

症(**證) ㊀ zhèng ㄓㄥˋ 病 disease; illness: ～候 *symptom; disease* | 霍乱～ *cholera* | 急～ *acute disease* | 不治之～ *incurable disease* | 对～下药 *to prescribe the right remedy for an illness — to suit the remedy to the case*

㊁ zhēng 见 971 页 see p971

郑(鄭) zhèng ㄓㄥˋ 周代诸侯国名，在今河南省新郑一带 Zheng, a princedom of the Zhou Dynasty, covering today's Xinzheng and nearby areas in Henan province [郑重](—zhòng) 审慎,严肃 serious; solemn; earnest: ~~其事 *seriously; in earnest*

诤 zhèng ㄓㄥˋ 谏,照直说出人的过错,叫人改正 to criticize frankly: 谏~ *frank criticism*|~言 *forthright admonition* [诤友]能直言规劝的朋友 friend who gives forthright admonition

挣 ㊀ zhèng ㄓㄥˋ ❶用力支撑或摆脱 to struggle to hold on or get free: ~脱 *to break away from; to throw off*|~开 *to wriggle oneself free; to wrench oneself free* [挣揣](—chuài) 挣扎 to struggle; to strive hard [挣命]为保全性命而挣扎 to struggle for survival ❷出力量而取得报酬 to earn: ~钱 *to earn money; to make money*

㊁ zhēng 见 971 页 see p971

阐 zhèng ㄓㄥˋ [阐闼](—chuài) 同"挣揣"(多见于元曲)(usually seen in Yuan poetic plays) same as 挣揣

ZHI ㄓ

之 zhī ㄓ ❶助词 ***auxiliary*** **1** 表示修饰关系,在形容词、名词或数量词后(used after an adjective, a noun or a numeral to devote the descriptive function): 光荣~家 *honourable family*|淮河~南 *south of the Huaihe River*|百万~师 *a troop of one million bold warriors*|三分~一 *one third*|百万年(~)前 *a million years ago*|三天(~)后 *three days later* (例子中加括号的表示有时可省略不用。)(*The bracketed* 之 *in the examples can sometimes be omitted.*) **2** 表示领有、连属等关系,在名词或代词后(used after a noun or a pronoun to express possession, connection, etc): 人民~勤劳 *people's diligence*|余~生活 *my life* **3** 置于主谓结构之间,使其变成偏正结构(used between the subject and the predicate to turn the original structure onto a nominal phrase): 大道~行也,天下为公。*When the great doctrine prevails, the whole world is in one community.* ❷代词 ***pronoun***,代替人或事物,限于作宾语(used as an object): 爱~重~ *to cherish it so as to attach importance to it*|取~不尽 *inexhaustible*|偶一为~ *to do sth once in a while* ❸代词 ***pronoun***,虚指(used without definite reference): 久而久~ *with the passage of time; as time passes by; with the lapse of time* ❹文言代词 ***pronoun in classical Chinese***,这,这个 this: ~子于归。*The maiden goes to her future home.* ❺往,到 to go; to leave for: 由京~沪 *from Beijing to Shanghai*|尔将何~? *Where are you* *going?*

芝 zhī ㄓ ❶灵芝,长在枯树上的一种蕈,菌盖赤褐色,有光泽,可入药。古代以为瑞草 glossy ganoderma (*Ganoderma lucidum*) ❷古书上指白芷(in ancient Chinese texts) dahurian angelica (*Angelica dahurica*):～兰 *irises and orchids*

支 zhī ㄓ ❶撑持,支持 to prop up:把帐篷～起来 *to put up a tent* ㊀ ***extension*** 受得住 to bear; to sustain:乐不可～*to be overwhelmed with joy; to be overjoyed* [支援]支持,援助 to support; to aid:～～灾区 *to give aid to the disaster-stricken areas* | 互相～～ *to offer mutual support* ❷领款或付款 to draw or pay money:他已经～了工资。*He has drawn his wages.* | 把工资～给他。*Pay him his wages.* ❸用话敷衍,使人离开 to send sb away under a pretext:把他们都～出去。*Find an excuse and send them away.* [支配]指挥,调度 to allocate; to budget:人员由你～～。*The personnel are at your disposal.* ❹分支的,附属于总体的 branch:～流 *tributary; branch* | ～店 *branch store; sub-branch of a store* [支离] **1** 残缺不完整 fragmented; broken:～～破碎 *to be torn to pieces; to be all broken up* **2** 散乱不集中 jumbled; incoherent:言语～～ *in broken language* ❺量词 ***quantifier*** **1** 用于队伍、歌曲或杆形的东西等(used for troops, songs or thin objects, etc):一～军队 *an army* | 一～曲子 *a melody* | 一～笔 *a pen* **2** 各种纤维纺成的纱(如棉纱)粗细程度的计算单位,纱愈细,支数愈多,质量愈好 textile count ❻地支,历法中用的"子、丑、寅、卯、辰、巳、午、未、申、酉、戌、亥"十二个字(12 Earthly Branches, 子, 丑, 寅, 卯, 辰, 巳, 午, 未, 申, 酉, 戌 and 亥, used in combination with the 10 Heavenly Stems to designate years in the Chinese calendar)[支吾]用话搪塞、应付,说话含混躲闪 to prevaricate; to equivocate:～～其词 *to prevaricate; to hum and haw* | 一味～～*to hem and haw; to hum and ha*

吱 ㊀ zhī ㄓ 拟声词 ***onomatopoeia*** (叠 ***reduplication***) creaking:车轮～～地响。*The cartwheels are creaking.*

㊁ zī 见1008页 see p1008

枝 zhī ㄓ ❶(一子、一儿)由植物的主干上分出来的茎条 branch; twig:树～*tree branch* | 柳～*willow branch* | 节外生～(喻多生事端) *to complicate matters by raising side issues; to raise obstacles* [枝节] ㊃ ***figurative*** **1** 由一事件引起的其他问题 minor problems brought about by an event:这事又有了～～了。*New, unexpected difficulties cropped up again.* **2** 细碎的,不重要的 trivial; unimportant:～～问题

minor issues ❷量词 ***quantifier*** **1** 用于带枝子的花朵 for flowers with stems intact：一～杏花 *a spray of apricot blossoms* **2** 用于杆状物(for long, thin, inflexible objects)：一～铅笔 *a pencil*

肢 zhī ㄓ 手、脚、胳膊、腿的统称 limb：四～ *four limbs*｜断～再植 *replantation of a severed limb*

氏 ㊁ zhī ㄓ 见 862 页"阏"字条"阏氏"(yān—)、928 页"月"字条"月氏"(yuè—) see 阏氏 on p862 and 月氏 on p928

㊀ shì 见 680 页 see p680

泜 zhī ㄓ 泜河，水名，在河北省邢台 Zhihe River in Xingtai, Hebei Province

胝 zhī ㄓ 见 565 页"胼"字条"胼胝"(pián—) see 胼胝 on p565

祗 zhī ㄓ 恭敬 to venerate; to esteem：～仰 *to revere; to venerate*｜～候光临。*Your presence is respectfully requested.*

只(隻) ㊁ zhī ㄓ ❶量词 ***quantifier***：一～鸡 *a chicken*｜两～手 *two hands* ❷单独的，极少的 single; few：～身(一个人) *alone; all by oneself*｜片纸～字 *a character or two; a word or two* [只眼] ㊕ ***transfer*** 特别见解 unique view：独具～～ *to have exceptional insight*

㊀ zhǐ 见 979 页 see p979

织(織) zhī ㄓ 用丝、麻、棉纱、毛线等编成布或衣物等 to weave：～布 *to weave cotton cloth*｜～毛衣 *to knit a sweater*｜～席 *to weave a mat*

卮(*巵) zhī ㄓ 古代盛(chéng)酒的器皿(in ancient China) wine vessel

栀(*梔) zhī ㄓ 栀子树，常绿灌木，夏季开花，白色，很香。果实叫栀子，叶、花、果、根都可入药 cape jasmine (*Gardenia jasminoides*)

汁 zhī ㄓ 含有某种物质的液体 juice：墨～ *prepared Chinese ink*｜橘～ *orange juice*

知 zhī ㄓ ❶知道，晓得，明了 to know：～无不言 *to tell all one knows*｜人贵有自～之明。*Knowing oneself is wisdom.* [知觉]随着感觉而产生的反映客观物体或现象的心理过程 perception ❷使知道 to inform：通～ *to inform; to notify; to tell*｜～照 *to inform; to notify; to tell* ❸知识，学识，学问 knowledge; learning：求～ *to seek knowledge; to pursue knowledge*｜无～ *ignorant* ❹主管 to administer; to be in charge of：～县(主管县里的事务，旧时指县长)(also called 县长, who administered county aftairs) county magistrate｜～府 prefect ❺彼此相互了解而情谊深厚的人 bosom friend; intimate friend：新～ *new friend; new acquaintance*

〈古 ***archaism***〉又同“智”(zhì) also same as 智

枳 zhī ㄓ [槟枳](bīn—)越南地名。今作“槟知”(now written as 槟知) Binzhi, a place in Vietnam

蜘 zhī ㄓ [蜘蛛](—zhū)见993页“蛛”see 蛛 on p993

脂 zhī ㄓ ❶动物体内或油料植物种子内的油质 fat; grease; tallow (㊃ ***doublet*** —肪 fat | —膏 grease) ❷胭脂 rouge: ～粉 *rouge and powder* — *cosmetics*

稙 zhī ㄓ 庄稼种得较早或熟得较早(of crops) early-sown or early ripe: ～谷子*early sown millet* | 白玉米～(熟得早)。*The white maize ripens early*.

执(執) zhí ㄓˊ ❶拿着,掌握 to hold; to grasp: ～笔 *to write* | ～政 *to be in power; to be in office* ㊀ ***extension*** 固执,坚持(意见) to stick to; to persist in: ～意要去 *to insist on going* | ～迷不悟 *to obstinately stick to a wrong course; to refuse to come to one's senses* [争执]争论中各执己见,不肯相让 to argue; to dispute ❷行,施行 to conduct; to carry out: ～法 *to enforce the law; to execute the law* | ～礼甚恭 *to be punctilious in observing the etiquette; to stick to the etiquettes and to be polite to others* [执行]依据规定的原则、办法办事 to carry out; to execute; to implement ❸凭单 written acknowledgement: 回～ *return receipt* | 收～*receipt* [执照]由机关发给的正式凭证 license; permit ❹捕捉,逮捕 to catch; to capture

絷(縶) zhí ㄓˊ ❶拴,捆 to tie; to fasten; to bind ❷拘捕,拘禁 to take into custody ❸马缰绳 horse rein

直 zhí ㄓˊ ❶不弯曲 straight: ～线 *straight line* | ～立 *to stand erect* ㊄ ***figurative*** 公正合理 just; upright: 是非曲～ *rights and wrongs; merits and demerits; truth and falsehood* | 理～气壮 *to feel justified* [直接]事物的关系不必要经过第三者而发生,跟“间接”相对(the opposite of 间接) direct; immediate ❷使直,把弯曲的伸开 to straighten: ～起腰来 *to straighten one's back; to stand straight up* ❸爽快,坦率 frank; straight forward (㊃ ***doublet*** —爽 candid; forthright): ～言 *to speak bluntly; to state outright* | 心～口快 *frank and outspoken* ❹副词 ***adverb*** **1** 径直,一直 directly; straight: ～通北京 *to go straight to Beijing* | ～达客车 *through* (or *direct*) *passenger train* **2** 一个劲儿地,连续不断 continuously: ～哭 *to keep crying* | 逗得大家～笑。*He kept us all amused all the while*. ❺竖,跟“横”相对(the opposite of 横) vertical; perpendicular ❻汉字自上往下写的笔形(丨) vertical stroke in Chinese characters ❼古同“值”same as 值 in ancient Chinese

值 zhí ㄓˊ ❶价格,价钱 value; price: 两物之～相等。*The two things are of the same value.* ❷物和价相当 worth:～一百元 *to be worth 100 yuan* ㊀ ***extension*** 值得,有意义或有价值 to be worth; to be worthy; to deserve:不～一提 *not worth mentioning* ❸数学上指依照数学式演算所得结果 value ❹遇到 to happen to; to chance to: 相～*to run into; to run across; to come across*|正～新春佳节 *on the occasion of this Spring Festival* ㊀ ***extension*** 当,轮到 to be on duty; to take one's turn:～日 *to be on duty for the day*|～班 *to be on shift; to be on duty*

埴 zhí ㄓˊ 黏土 clay

植 zhí ㄓˊ ❶栽种 to plant; to grow (㊇ ***doublet*** 种一 to plant; to grow):～树 *to plant trees*|种～五谷 *to cultivate the cereals* [植物]谷类、花草、树木等的统称 plant; flora ❷戳住,立住 to set up; to establish:～其杖于门侧 *to put one's stick by the door*

殖 ㊀ zhí ㄓˊ 生息,滋生 to breed (㊇ ***doublet*** 生一 to breed; to multiply; to propagate): 繁～ *to reproduce; to propagate* [殖民地]被帝国主义国家剥夺了政治、经济的独立权力,并受它控制和掠夺的国家或地区 colony

㊁ shi 见 686 页 see p686

侄(*姪) zhí ㄓˊ 弟兄的儿子,同辈亲友的儿子 nephew

职(職) zhí ㄓˊ ❶职务,分(fèn)内应做的事 duty; job:尽～*to do one's duty; to exert oneself to fulfil one's responsibilities* ❷职位,执行事务所处的一定的地位 position; post; office: 调(diào)～ *to be transferred to another post*|兼～ *to hold two or more posts concurrently; pluralism; plurality* [职员]机关、企业、学校、团体里担任行政或业务工作的人员,也省称“职”(also 职 for short) clerk; staff member; office worker: ～工 *staff and workers* ❸旧时公文用语,下属对上司的自称(used in former official reports to superiors) your subordinate:～奉命前往 *Your humble subordinate acts on your instructions.* ❹由于 because of:～是之故 *for this particular reason*|～此 *so; for this reason* ❺掌管 to manage; to direct

跖(*蹠) zhí ㄓˊ ❶脚面上接近脚趾的部分 metatarsus:～骨 *phalanges* ❷脚掌 sole of the foot

摭 zhí ㄓˊ 摘取,拾取 to pick up: ～拾 *to pick; to collect; to gather*

踯(躑) zhí ㄓˊ [踯躅](—zhú)徘徊不进 to linger; to loiter:～～街头 *to tramp the streets; to wander*

the streets

蹢 ⊜ zhí ㄓˊ [蹢躅](—zhú) 同"踯躅"same as 踯躅
⊖ dí 见 141 页 see p141

止 zhǐ ㄓˇ ❶停住不动 to stop (㊀ ***doublet*** 停— to stop): ～步 *to halt; to stop*|血流不～ *to be bleeding profusely*|学无～境 *One can never learn too much.* or *There is no end in studying.* ❷拦阻,使停住 to stop; to check: 制～*to check; to curb*|～血 *to stop bleeding*|～痛 *to stop pain; to relieve pain* ❸截止 to terminate; to end: 报名日期自6月20日起至7月1日～。*The registration period is from June 20th to July 1st.* ❹仅,只 only: 不～一回 *more than once*

址(*阯) zhǐ ㄓˇ 地址,地基,地点 location; site; spot: 旧～ *former site*|住～*home address*

芷 zhǐ ㄓˇ 白芷,多年生草本植物,夏天开花,白色。根可入药 dahurian angelica (*Angelica dahurica*)

沚 zhǐ ㄓˇ 水中的小块陆地 isle; small island

祉 zhǐ ㄓˇ 福 happiness; bliss

趾 zhǐ ㄓˇ ❶脚 foot: ～高气扬(得意忘形的样子) *to be on one's high horse; to hold one's head high* ❷脚指头 toe: ～骨 *phalanges*|鸭的脚～中间有蹼。*Ducks are webbed-footed.*

只(衹、△*祇) ⊖ zhǐ ㄓˇ 副词 ***adverb*** ❶表示限于某个范围 only; just; merely: ～知其一,不知其二 *to know only one aspect of a thing but be ignorant of other aspects; to have only a one-sided view*|万事俱备,～欠东风。*All is ready except the east wind — all is ready except what is crucial.* ❷唯一,仅有 only; merely: 家里～我一个人。*I'm the only one at home.* [只是] **1** 连词 ***conjunction***,但是 but; only: 我很想看戏,～～没时间。*I really want to go to the theatre, but the trouble is that I have no time.* **2** 副词 ***adverb***,就是 simply: 人家问他,他～～不开口。*He kept silent and did not answer.* **3** 仅仅是 only; just: 对抗～～矛盾斗争的一种形式。*Antagonism is merely a form of contradiction and conflict.*
⊜ zhī 见 976 页 see p976
"祇"又 qí 见 583 页 also pronounced qi, see p583

枳 zhǐ ㄓˇ 落叶灌木或小乔木,通称"枸橘"。小枝多硬刺,叶为三小叶的复叶,果实球形,果实及叶可入药(generally called 枸橘) trifoliate orange (*Poncirus trifoliata*) [枳壳] 中药上指枳、香橼等成熟的果实 *dried ripe fruit of citron or trifoliate orange* [枳实] 中药上指枳、香橼等幼小的果实 *dried immature fruit of citron or trifoliate orange*

轵 zhǐ ㄓˇ 古代指车轴的末端 (in ancient China) axle

Z

end

咫 zhǐ ㄓˇ 古代指八寸 *zhi*, ancient unit of length, equal to eight *cun* [咫尺] ⊛喻 ***figurative*** 距离很近 very near; very close: 远在天边,近在~~ *to be as far away as beyond the horizon but as close as before one's eyes*

㕧 zhǐ ㄓˇ 殴伤 to beat and injure

旨(❶**恉) zhǐ ㄓˇ ❶意义,目的 purport; purpose (⊛连 ***doublet*** 意—purport): 要~*gist* | ~趣(目的和意义) *purport; objective* | 主~明确 *to have an explicit purport* | 执行党和人民的意~ *to fulfill the Party's and people's wishes* ❷封建时代称帝王的命令 decree: 圣~ *imperial decree* ❸美味 tasty; delicious: ~酒 *excellent wine*

指 zhǐ ㄓˇ ❶手指头 finger: 食~*index finger; forefinger* | 首屈一~ *to come first on the list; second to none* | 屈~可数 *can be counted on one's fingers—very few* ("脚趾"也写作"脚指") (脚趾 *also written as* 脚指) ❷一个手指头的宽度叫一指 finger-breadth; digit; finger: 下了四~雨 *to have four fingerbreadths of rain* ❸用尖端对着 to point at; to point to: 用手一~*by pointing one's finger at* | 时针~着十二点。*The hour hand points exactly to twelve.* ❹点明,告知 to indicate; to point out: ~导 *to guide; to direct* | ~出他的错误 *to point out his mistakes* [指示]上级对下级做有关原则和方法的说明,也指所做的说明 to instruct ❺仰仗,倚靠 to depend on; to count on: 不应~着别人生活。*One should not rely on others for a living.* | 单~着一个人是不能把事情做好的。*You cannot expect a single person to get the job done.* ❻直立起来 to bristle: 令人发(fà)~ *to get one's hackles up; to make one bristle with anger; to make one's blood boil* ❼向,意思上针对 to refer to; to direct at: 直~武夷山下 *to go straight to the foot of the* Wuyi *Mountain* | 他是~你说的。*His remarks were directed against you.*

酯 zhǐ ㄓˇ 有机化合物的一类,通式 R—COO—R′。脂肪的主要成分就是几种高级的酯 ester

抵 zhǐ ㄓˇ 侧手击 to attack sb's flank with one's hand [抵掌]击掌(表示高兴) to clap one's hands to show pleasure: ~~而谈 *to talk while clapping one's hands rhythmically; to have a heart-to-heart talk* ("抵"与"抵"(dǐ)形音义都不同。) (抵 is different from 抵 in spelling, pronunciation and meaning.)

纸(*帋) zhǐ ㄓˇ ❶纸张,多用植物纤维制成。造纸是我国四大发明之一,起源很早,东汉时蔡伦曾加

以改进 paper ❷量词 ***quantifier***：一～公文 *an official document*

黹 zhǐ ㄓˇ 缝纫、刺绣等针线活 needlework；embroidery：针～*needlework*

徵 ㊀ zhǐ ㄓˇ 古代五音"宫、商、角、徵、羽"之一 *zhi*，note of the ancient Chinese five-tone scale，corresponding to 5 in numbered musical notation

㊁ zhēng 见 970 页"征"see p970

至 zhì ㄓˋ ❶到 to；till：由南～北 *from south to north*｜～今未忘 *to be kept in mind till now*［至于］**1** 表示可能达到某种程度 to go so far as to：他还不～～不知道。*It would be unlikely for him to know nothing about it.* **2** 介词 ***preposition***，表示另提一事 as for；as to：～～个人得失，他根本不考虑。*As for personal gain and loss, he does not take them into consideration at all.*［以至］连词 ***conjunction***，一直到 down to；up to：自城市～～农村，爱国卫生运动普遍展开。*From cities to the countryside, the patriotic health campaign has developed widely.* ❷ 最好的 best：～宝 *most valuable treasure*｜～理名言 *maxim；famous dictum* ❸ 极，最 extremely；most：～尊 *most honoured and revered*｜～少 *at least*｜～高无上 *supreme；paramount*

厔 zhì ㄓˋ 见 990 页"盩"字条"盩厔"(zhōu—) see 盩厔 on p990

郅 zhì ㄓˋ 最，极 most；extremely

桎 zhì ㄓˋ 古代拘束犯人两脚的刑具 fetters［桎梏］(—gù)脚镣和手铐 fetters and handcuffs；shackles，喻束缚人或事物的东西 shackles；things that restrict or hinder

轾 zhì ㄓˋ 见 848 页"轩"字条"轩轾"(xuān—) see 轩轾 on p848

致(❹緻) zhì ㄓˋ ❶给予，送给 to extend；to deliver；to send：～函 *to write to；to send a letter to*｜～敬 *to extend a salute to；to pay one's respects to* ㊀ ***extension***（力量、意志等）集中于某个方面 to be concentrated on；to focus on：～力于学业 *to devote oneself to study*｜专心～志 *to be wholeheartedly devoted to；to be fully absorbed in；to be preoccupied with*［致命］可使丧失生命 fatal；deadly；lethal：～～伤 *mortal wound*［致意］向人表示问候的意思 to extend one's greetings；to send one's regards ❷招引，使达到 to incur；to lead to：～病 *to cause a disease*｜～富 *to become rich；to make a fortune*｜学以～用 *to study for the purpose of application；to put into practice what one has learned*［以致］连词 ***conjunction***，因而 so that；to such an extent that：由于没注意克服小缺点，～～犯了严重错误。*He was so ignorant*

Z

of his minor shortcomings that he made serious mistakes in the end. ❸样子,情趣 sentiment and interest:景～*scenery; view; scene* | 别～*novel; original; unique* | 风～*grace; charm* | 兴～*interest; mood to enjoy* | 雅～*elegance; refinement* | 错落有～*in picturesque disarray; in picturesque disorder* [大致]大概,大体情形 generally; on the whole:～～已结束 *almost finished* | ～～不差 *roughly the same* [一致]一样,没有分歧 unanimous; identical; uniform:行动～～*concerted action* | 全体～～通过 *to reach unanimity; to reach a consensus* ❹细密,精细 fine; delicate; exquisite ([连] ***doublet*** 细～ meticulous):他做事很细～。*He's very careful in working.* | 这东西做得真精～。*It's really an exquisite piece of work.*

铚 zhì ㄓˋ ❶古代一种短的镰刀 (in ancient China) short sickle ❷割禾穗 to cut ears of grain ❸古地名,在今安徽省宿州西南 Zhi, an ancient place in southeast of today's Suzhou, Anhui Province

窒 zhì ㄓˋ 阻塞不通 to block; to congest; to obstruct:～息(呼吸被阻停止) *to stifle; to choke; to suffocate*

蛭 zhì ㄓˋ ❶一类环节动物,俗称"蚂蟥"。大都吸其他动物的血或体液,生活在水里或山上,有的在医学上用来吸血治病 (popularly called 蚂蟥) leech (*Hirudinea*) ❷肝蛭,肝脏里的一种寄生虫,通常由螺蛳和鱼等传到人体内 fluke (*Trematoda*)

膣 zhì ㄓˋ 阴道,女性生殖器的一部分 vagina

志(❷❸❹*誌) zhì ㄓˋ ❶意向,要有所作为的决心 will; aspiration; ambition:立～*to be resolved; to be determined to* | ～同道合 *to cherish the same ideals and take the same course; to be like-minded* | 有～者事竟成。*Where there is a will, there is a way.* [意志]为了达到既定目的而自觉地努力的心理过程 will ❷记在心里 to keep in mind:永～不忘 *to bear in mind forever* [引] ***extension*** 表示不忘 to remember; to keep in mind:～喜 *celebration; congratulation* | ～哀 *expression of mourning* ❸记载的文字 records; annals; chronicles:杂～*magazine* | 地理～*geographical annals; gazetteer* ❹记号 mark; sign:标～*mark* ❺〈方 ***dialect***〉称轻重,量长短多少 to weigh; to measure:用秤～～*to weigh with a scale* | 拿碗～～*to measure with a bowl*

梽 zhì ㄓˋ [梽木山]地名,在湖南省邵阳 Zhimushan, a place in Shaoyang, Hunan Province

痣 zhì ㄓˋ 皮肤上生的斑痕,有青、红、褐等色,也有突起的 naevus; nevus; mole

豸 zhì ㄓˋ 古书上指没有脚的虫子 (in ancient Chinese texts) legless insect [虫豸]旧时对虫子的通称 (in former times) general term for insects

忮 zhì ㄓˋ 害，嫉妒 jealousy; envy

识(識) ㊁ zhì ㄓˋ ❶记住 to memorize; to bear in mind: 博闻强～ *to have wide learning and a retentive memory; to have encyclopaedic knowledge and extraordinary retention* ❷标志，记号 mark; sign; symbol: 款～ *inscriptions*
㊀ shí 见 677 页 see p677

帜(幟) zhì ㄓˋ 旗子 banner; flag (㊣ ***doublet*** 旗— banner; flag): 独树一～ *to fly one's own colours — to develop a school of one's own; to be unique* | 胜利的旗～ *victorious banner*

帙(*袠) zhì ㄓˋ ❶包书的布套子 cloth slip-case for a book ❷量词 ***quantifier***，用于装套的线装书 used for slip-cased, thread-bound books

秩 zhì ㄓˋ ❶秩序，有条理，不混乱的情况 order: 社会～序良好 *good social order* ❷十年 decade: 七～寿辰 *seventieth birthday* ❸旧时指俸禄，也指官的品级 former official salary or rank: 厚～ *handsome salary*

制(❹製) zhì ㄓˋ ❶规定，订立 to formulate; to stipulate: ～定计划 *to work out a plan* ❷限定，约束，管束 to restrict; to check; to control: ～止 *to stop; to curb; to refrain* | ～裁 *to apply* (or *impose*) *sanctions* | 限～ *to limit; to restrict; to confine* ❸制度，法度，法则 system: 民主集中～ *democratic centralism* | 全日～学校 *full-time school* [制服]依照规定样式做的衣服 uniform ❹造，作 to make; to manufacture (㊣ ***doublet*** —造 to make; to manufacture): 猪皮～革 *to tan pig skin* | ～版 *to make a plate* | ～图表 *to make a chart; to chart*

质(質) zhì ㄓˋ ❶本体，本性 nature; character: 物～ *matter; substance; material* | 流～ *liquid; fluid* | 铁～ *iron* | 问题的实～ *essence of the problem; substance of a matter* [质量] **1** 产品或工作的优劣程度 quality: 提高～～ *to improve* (or *better*) *the quality* **2** 物理学上指物体所含物质的量。过去习惯上称为重量 (habitually called 重量 in the past) mass [质子]原子核内带有正电的粒子，如氢原子核 proton [本质]与"现象"相对，指事物的内在联系，是这一事物和其他事物相区别的根本属性。它是由事物内部矛盾所规定的 (the opposite of 现象) essence ❷朴实 simple; plain (㊣ ***doublet*** —朴 plain) ❸依据事实来问明或辨别是非 to question: ～问 *to question; to interrogate* | ～疑 *to query; to question* | ～之高明 *to call his cleverness in*

Z

question ❹抵押，抵押品(to) pawn; (to) pledge

锧(鑕) zhì ㄓˋ ❶〈古 ***archaism***〉砧板 chopping block ❷铡刀座 executioner's block [斧锧]斩人的刑具 executioner's block and cleaver

踬(躓) zhì ㄓˋ 被东西绊倒 to trip; to stumble：颠～*to trip over* ㊀ ***extension*** 事情不顺利 to suffer a setback

炙 zhì ㄓˋ ❶烤 to broil; to roast; to grill [亲炙]直接得到某人的教诲或传授 to be directly under sb's tutorship; to study under sb'd direct guidance ❷烤熟的肉 barbecue：脍(kuài)～人口(喻诗文等受人欢迎) *delicious barbecue pleasant to everybody's taste —(of a piece of writing) to win universal praise; to enjoy great popularity*

治 zhì ㄓˋ ❶管理，处理 to govern; to manage (㊥ ***doublet*** 一理 to govern; to administer; to rule)：～国 *to govern a nation; to manage a state; to rule a country* | ～丧(sāng) *to make funeral arrangements; to arrange a funeral* | 自～*autonomy* [统治] **1** 凭借政权来控制、管理国家或地区 to rule; to govern; to reign **2** 占绝对优势，支配别的事物 to dominate ❷整理，治理 to control; to harness：～山 *to afforest mountains* | ～水 *to regulate rivers and watercourses; water control* | ～淮工程 *the project of harnessing the Huaihe River* ❸惩办 to penalize; to punish (㊥ ***doublet*** 惩一 to punish)：～罪 *to bring to justice* | 处(chǔ)～ *to penalize; to punish* ❹医疗 to treat：～病 *to treat an illness; to cure* | 不～之症 *incurable disease* ㊀ ***extension*** 消灭农作物的病虫害 to wipe out harmful insects：～蝗 *to eliminate locusts* | ～蚜虫 *to exterminate aphids* ❺从事研究 to study; to research：～学 *to pursue one's studies; to do scholarly research* ❻社会治理有序，与"乱"相对(the opposite of 乱) in good order; in peace：～世 *times of peace and prosperity; age of order and peace* | 天下大～*great order and peace in the world; well-ordered world* [治安]社会的秩序 public order; public security ❼旧称地方政府所在地(in former times) site of a local government：省～ *provincial capital* | 县～*county seat*

栉(櫛) zhì ㄓˋ ❶梳子和篦子的总称 comb：～比(像梳子齿那样挨着) *to be placed closely side by side (like the teeth of a comb)* ❷梳头 to comb：～风沐雨(喻辛苦勤劳) *to weather the storms; to be hardworking and diligent; to travel or work despite of wind and rain*

峙 ㊀ zhì ㄓˋ 直立，耸立 to stand erect; to stand towering：两峰相～。*The two mountain peaks are standing towering against each other.*
㊁ shì 见 683 页 see p683

庤 zhì ㄓˋ 储备 to store; to stock up

畤 zhì ㄓˋ 古时祭天、地、五帝的固定处所 (in ancient China) place where heaven and earth and ancient emperors were worshiped

痔 zhì ㄓˋ 痔疮，一种肛管疾病。因直肠静脉曲张、瘀血而形成 haemorrhoids; piles

陟 zhì ㄓˋ 登高，上升 to climb; to ascend：～山 *to climb a mountain*

骘 zhì ㄓˋ 排定 to evaluate; to assess：评～高低 *to evaluate; to assess; to pass judgement on*

贽(贄) zhì ㄓˋ 古时初次拜见人时所送的礼物 (in ancient China) gift presented to a senior as a mark of esteem at one's first visit：～见 *to call on sb with gifts* | ～敬 (*in former times*) *ceremonial gift presented to the teacher on one's first courtly call*

挚(摯) zhì ㄓˋ 亲密，诚恳 sincere; earnest (㊥ ***doublet*** 真－ sincere; cordial)：～友 *bosom friend; confidant; close friend; intimate friend*

鸷(鷙) zhì ㄓˋ 鸷鸟，凶猛的鸟，如鹰、雕等 ferocious birds; birds of prey ㊥ ***figurative*** 凶猛 ferocious; fierce：勇～ *valiant; violent*

掷(擲) zhì ㄓˋ 扔，投，抛 to throw; to cast; to fling：～铁饼 *to throw a discus* | ～手榴弹 *to throw a grenade*

智 zhì ㄓˋ 聪明，智慧，见识 wisdom; intelligence; resourcefulness：不经一事，不长(zhǎng)一～。*Wisdom comes from experience.* [智慧] 对事物能迅速、灵活、正确地理解和解决的能力 wisdom; intelligence

滞(滯) zhì ㄓˋ 凝积，积留，不流通 stagnant; sluggish：停～ *to stagnate; to be at a standstill* | ～销(销路不畅) *unsalable; unmarketable* | 沾～(拘泥) *to adhere rigidly to; to stick fast to*

彘 zhì ㄓˋ 〈古 ***archaism***〉猪 hog; pig; swine

置(*寘) zhì ㄓˋ ❶放，搁，摆 to place; to put; to set：～于桌上 *to place on the table* | ～之不理 *to turn one's back upon; to pay no heed to; to pay no attention* | ～若罔闻 *to turn a deaf ear to* ❷设立，装设 to install; to establish：装～电话 *to install a telephone* ❸购买 to purchase; to buy：～了一些家具 *to buy some furniture* | ～了一身衣裳 *to buy a suit*

雉 zhì ㄓˋ ❶鸟名，通称"野鸡"。雄的羽毛很美，尾长。雌的淡黄褐色，尾较短。

Z

善走，不能久飞（popularly called 野鸡）pheasant（*Phasianidae*）❷古代城墙长三丈高一丈叫一雉 *zhi*, a parapet section of an ancient city wall, which was three *zhang* long and one *zhang* high

稚（*稺） zhì 㞢 幼小 young; youngish：～子（*innocent*）*child*｜～气 *childishness*｜幼～*childish; infantile*

滍 zhì 㞢 滍水，古水名，在河南省平顶山市。现称沙河 Zhishui River（now named Shahe River），an ancient river in Pingdingshan City, Henan Province［滍阳］地名，在河南省平顶山市 Zhiyang, a place in Pingdingshan City, Henan Province

疐（**疐） zhì 㞢 ❶遇到障碍 to encounter obstacles ❷跌倒 to fall; to tumble：跋前～后（比喻进退两难）*to encounter obstacles ahead and behind; to be in a dilemma; to be at a nonplus*

瘈 ㊀ zhì 㞢 疯狂（特指狗）（especially of dogs）crazy; mad

㊁ chì 见 91 页 see p91

觯（觶） zhì 㞢 古时饮酒用的器皿（in ancient China）drinking vessel

ZHONG 㞢ㄨㄥ

中 ㊀ zhōng 㞢ㄨㄥ ❶和四方、上下或两端距离同等的地位 center; middle：～心 *center; core; heart*｜路～*in the middle of the road*［中人］为双方介绍买卖、调解纠纷等并做见证的人 broker; middleman; go-between［中央］**1** 中心的地方 center **2** 政党、国家等的最高领导机构 highest leading body（of a state, party, etc）：党～～*Central Committee of the Party; Party's Central Committee*［人中］人的上唇正中凹下的地方 philtrum ❷在一定的范围内，里面 in; among; amid：空～*in the sky; in the air*｜房～*in the room*｜水～*in the water* ❸性质、等级在两端之间的 middle; mid：～等 *medium-sized; secondary*｜～学 *middle school; secondary school; high school* ㊕ ***transfer*** 不偏不倚 impartial：～庸 *golden mean（of the Confucian school）*｜适～*moderate*［中子］构成原子核的一种不带电荷的微粒 neutron ❹用在动词后，表示动作正在进行［used after a verb］in the process of; in the course of：在研究～*to be under study*（or *research*）｜在印刷～*to be in printing*｜前进～*to be in progress*｜发展～*developing* ❺指中国 China：古今～外 *ancient and modern, Chinese and foreign; past and present, at home and abroad; at all times and in all countries*｜～文 *Chinese* ❻适于，合于 suitable; fit：～看 *pleasant to the eye*｜～听 *pleasant to the ear*

[中用]有用,有能力 useful ❼〈方 **dialect**〉成,行,好 all right; OK:~不~?~。*Is it all right? All right.*

㊁ zhòng 见 988 页 see p988

忠 zhōng ㄓㄨㄥ 赤诚无私,诚心尽力 loyal; devoted; faithful:~诚 *loyal; faithful; staunch* | ~言 *sincere advice; earnest exhortation* | ~告 *to advise sincerely; to admonish; to counsel* | ~于人民 *to be loyal to the people* | ~于祖国 *to be loyal to one's country*

盅 zhōng ㄓㄨㄥ 没有把儿的小杯子 small handleless cup:酒~ *wine cup* | 茶~ *tea cup*

钟(❶-❸ 鐘、❹❺ 鍾) zhōng ㄓㄨㄥ ❶金属制成的响器,中空,敲时发声 bell:警~ *alarm bell* ❷计时的器具 clock:座~ *desk clock* | 闹~ *alarm clock* ❸指钟点,时间 time (as measured in hours and minutes):两点~ *two o'clock* | 三个~头 *three hours* ❹杯子 cup ❺集中,专一 to concentrate on:~情 *to be in deep love with*

衷 zhōng ㄓㄨㄥ 内心 heart:由~之言 *words from the bottom of one's heart; sincere words* | 苦~ *private suffering, trouble or difficulty (that one is reluctant to discuss or mention or that is not easy for others to understand)* | ~心拥护 *to give wholehearted support*

忪 ㊁ zhōng ㄓㄨㄥ [怔忪] (zhēng—) 惊惧 terrified; scared; panic-stricken

㊀ sōng 见 706 页 see p706

终 zhōng ㄓㄨㄥ ❶末了(liǎo),完了 to end; to finish:~点 *termination; destination* | 年~ *end of a year* ㊕ **transfer** 人死 death:临~ *when one is dying; on one's deathbed* ❷到底,总归 eventually; ultimately:~将成功 *will succeed in the end* | ~必奏效 *will eventually take effect* ❸从开始到末了 whole:~日 *whole day* | ~年 *all the year round; throughout the year* | ~生 *all one's life* | ~身 *lifelong*

螽 zhōng ㄓㄨㄥ 螽斯,一类昆虫,身体绿色或褐色,善跳跃,有的危害农作物。雄的前翅有发声器,颤动翅膀能发声 katydid (*Microcentrum*)

肿(腫) zhǒng ㄓㄨㄥˇ 皮肉浮胀 swollen:他的手冻~了。*His hands were frost-bitten and swollen.*

种(種) ㊀ zhǒng ㄓㄨㄥˇ ❶(—子、—儿)植物果实中能长(zhǎng)成新植物的部分 seed:选~ *to select seeds* | 撒~ *to spread seeds evenly in the field* 泛指生物传代的东西 strain; breed:配~ *to breed; to mate* | 优良品~ *superior strains* [有种]有胆量或有骨气 to have guts; to have grit ❷人种,具有共同起源和共同遗传特征的人群 race:黄~ *yellow race* | 白~

Z

white race | ～族 *race* ❸事物的类别 kind; type: ～类 *sort; category* | 工～*type of work in production* | 军～*type of armed services* | 剧～*type* (or *genre*) *of traditional Chinese opera* | 语～*certain language* ❹生物的分类单位之一,在"属"之下,其下还可分出"亚种"、"变种" species ❺量词 ***quantifier***,表示种类,用于人和任何事物 type; kind; category: 两～面料 *two kinds of cloth* | 各～东西 *all kinds of things; a wide variety of things*

㊁ zhòng 见 988 页 see p988

㊂ chóng 见 93 页 see p93

冢(*塚) zhǒng ㄓㄨㄥˇ 坟墓 tomb; grave: 衣冠～*tomb containing personal effects of the deceased, whose remains are either missing or buried elsewhere*

踵 zhǒng ㄓㄨㄥˇ ❶脚后跟 heel: 继～而至 *to follow on one's heels; to come one after another* | 摩肩接～*to jostle each other in a crowd* (*with shoulder against shoulder, foot against foot*) ❷走到 to go in person: ～门相告 *to call in person to pass the news* | ～谢 *to pay a personal visit for thanks* ❸追随,继续 to follow; to carry on: ～至 *to arrive upon the heels of another; to arrive immediately after another*

中 ㊁ zhòng ㄓㄨㄥˋ ❶正对上,恰好合上 to hit; to fit exactly: ～的(dì) *to hit the target* | ～肯 *apropos; pertinent* | ～要害 *to go home; to hit sb's vital point* ❷感受,受到 to suffer: ～毒 *poisoning; toxicosis; toxication* | ～暑 *sunstroke; heatstroke; insolation* | ～弹(dàn) *to be hit by a bullet; to get shot*

㊀ zhōng 见 986 页 see p986

仲 zhòng ㄓㄨㄥˋ ❶兄弟排行常用伯、仲、叔、季为次序,仲是老二(of brothers) second in order of birth: ～兄 *second eldest brother* ❷在当中的 middle; intermediate: ～冬(冬季第二月) *midwinter* | ～裁(居间调停,裁判) *to arbitrate*

种(種) ㊁ zhòng ㄓㄨㄥˋ 种植,把种子或幼苗等埋在泥土里使生长 to grow; to plant; to cultivate: ～庄稼 *to grow crops* | ～瓜得瓜,～豆得豆。*As a man sows, so he shall reap.* or *You shall reap what you have sown.*

㊀ zhǒng 见 987 页 see p987

㊂ chóng 见 93 页 see p93

众(衆) zhòng ㄓㄨㄥˋ ❶许多 many; numerous: ～人 *many people; everybody present* | ～志成城(喻团结力量大)。*Unity of will is an impregnable fortress — unity is strength.* | 寡不敌～。*The few cannot beat the multitude.* ❷许多人 crowd; multitude: 从群～中来,到群～中去 *from the masses, and to the masses* | 大～

the public; the masses | 观～*audience; spectators; viewers*

重 ㊀ zhòng ㄓㄨㄥˋ ❶分量较大，跟"轻"相对(the opposite of 轻) heavy; weighty: 铁很～。*Iron is very heavy.* | ～于泰山 *to be weightier than Mount Tai—to be of great importance; to be of great significance* [重工业] 主要制造生产资料的工业，如冶金、电力、机械制造等工业 heavy industry [重力]物理学上称地球对物体的吸引力。也叫"地心吸引力"(also called 地心吸引力) gravity [重心] **1** 物体重量的集中作用点，不论物体的位置如何改变，物体的各部都围绕着这一点保持平衡 barycentre **2** 事物的主要部分 heart; core ❷程度深 deep; serious: 色～*deep-coloured* | ～病 *serious disease* | ～伤 *severe injury* ❸价格高(of price) high: ～金收买 *to buy sb over with a huge sum of money; to bribe sb with a large sum of money* ❹数量多 considerable: 眉毛～*to have thick eyebrows* | 工作很～*to have a heavy work load* ❺主要，要紧 important: ～镇 *place of strategic importance* | 军事～地 *place of military importance* | ～任 *heavy duty* ❻认为重要 to lay stress on; to attach importance to: ～视 *to attach importance to; to lay emphasis on* | ～男轻女是错误的。*It's wrong to regard men as superior to women.* or *It's wrong to value sons and belittle daughters.* ㊇ **extension** 敬重，尊重，尊敬 to respect; to revere: 人皆～之。*All show respect to him.* ❼言行不轻率 prudent; discreet: 慎～*prudent; discreet; circumspect*

㊁ chóng 见 93 页 see p93

ZHOU ㄓㄡ

舟 zhōu ㄓㄡ 船 boat: 轻～*skiff; cockle* | 一叶扁(piān)～ *a light boat*

侜(**譸) zhōu ㄓㄡ 欺诳 to deceive; to cheat [侜张]作伪，欺骗 to deceive; to cheat; to defraud: ～～为幻 *to delude*

辀 zhōu ㄓㄡ 车辕 shaft

鸼 zhōu ㄓㄡ 见 241 页"鹘"字条"鹘鸼"(gǔ—) see 鹘鸼 on p241

州 zhōu ㄓㄡ ❶旧时的一种行政区划。多用于地名，如杭州，柳州(former administration division) zhou, usually used in a place name, e. g. Hangzhou, Liuzhou ❷一种民族自治行政区划单位 autonomous prefecture

洲 zhōu ㄓㄡ ❶水中的陆地 islet; ait; shoal: 沙～*sandbank; sandbar* ❷大陆 continent: 亚～*Asia* | 地球上有七大～。*There are seven continents on the earth.*

Z

诌(謅) zhōu ㄓㄡ 随口编 to fabricate; to invent: 胡～ *to fudge; to cook up; to make up; tall talk* | 瞎～ *to spin a yarn; tall tale*

周(❶—❺*週) zhōu ㄓㄡ ❶周围,圈子 circumference; periphery; perimeter: 圆～ *circle; circumference* | 环绕地球一～ *to make a circuit of the earth* | 学校四～都种着树。*Trees are planted around the school.* ❷环绕,绕一圈 to make a circuit; to move in a circular course: ～而复始 *to go round and round; to move in circles* [周旋] **1** 打交道 to deal with **2** 交际,应酬 to socialize with; to hobnob with: 与客人～～ *to tackle guests (about sth)* ❸时期的一轮。特指一个星期 one of repeated periods of time; especially a week ❹普遍,全面 all; whole: 众所～知 *as is known to all* | ～身 *all over (the body)* ❺完备 thorough: ～到 *thoughtful; considerate* | 计划很～密 *well-conceived plan* ❻给,接济 to offer; to give: ～济 *to help out; to relieve* | ～急 *to relieve the badly needy* ❼朝代名 name of a dynasty **1** 周武王姬发所建立(公元前1046—公元前256年) Zhou Dynasty (1046BC—256 BC) founded by Jifa (Emperor Wu) **2** 北朝之一,宇文觉取代西魏称帝,国号周(公元557—581年),史称北周 Zhou (557—581), which was called the Northen Zhou by historians as it was one of the Northern Dynasties, founded by Yuwen Jue who took the place of the Western Wei emperor **3** 五代之一,郭威所建立(公元951—960年),史称后周 Later Zhou Dynasty (951—960), one of the five dynasties, founded by Guo Wei

啁 ㊀ zhōu ㄓㄡ [啁啾](—jiū) 拟声词 ***onomatopoeia***, 鸟叫的声音 twittering; chirping; warbling

㊁ zhāo 见959页 see p959

赒 zhōu ㄓㄡ 接济 to help out; to relieve: ～恤 *to sympathize and help out*

粥 zhōu ㄓㄡ 用米、面等煮成的比较稠的半流质食品 gruel; porridge; congee

〈古 ***archaism***〉又同"鬻"(yù) also same as 鬻

盩 zhōu ㄓㄡ [盩厔](—zhì) 地名,在陕西省。今作"周至"(now written as 周至) Zhouzhi, a place in Shaanxi Province

妯 zhóu ㄓㄡˊ [妯娌](—li) 兄和弟的妻子的合称 wives of brothers; sisters-in-law: 她们俩(liǎ)是～～。*They are sisters-in-law.*

轴 ㊀ zhóu ㄓㄡˊ ❶穿在轮子中间的圆柱形物件。(图见475页"轮"picture on p475) axle; shaft; spindle ❷(—儿)用来缠绕东西的像车轴的器物 axle-shaped thing: 线～儿

spool; bobbin | 画～ *painting scroll* ㊁ ***extension*** 量词 ***quantifier***：一～儿线 *a spool of thread* ❸把平面或立体分成对称部分的直线 axis; line along which a figure or a cube is symmetric

㊂ zhòu 见 991 页 see p991

肘 zhǒu ㄓㄡˇ 上臂与前臂相接处向外凸起的部分。(图见 741 页"体"picture on p741) elbow [肘子]指作食品的猪腿上半部 upper part of a leg of pork; ham

帚(*箒) zhǒu ㄓㄡˇ 扫除尘土、垃圾的用具 broom

纣 zhòu ㄓㄡˋ ❶牲口的后鞧(qiū) crupper:～棍(系在驴马等尾下的横木) *wood crupper* ❷古人名，殷朝末代君主 Zhou, an ancient person, the last ruler of the Yin Dynasty

葤 zhòu ㄓㄡˋ ❶用草包裹 to wrap with straw ❷量词 ***quantifier***，碗碟等用草绳束为一捆叫一葤(of bowls, plates, etc, tied together with a straw rope) bundle

酎 zhòu ㄓㄡˋ 醇酒 double-fermented wine

㑇(傷) zhòu ㄓㄡˋ 乖巧，伶俐，漂亮(元曲中常用)(usually used in the Yuan poetic plays) pretty; cute; handsome

㤘(懰) zhòu ㄓㄡˋ 〈方 ***dialect***〉性情固执，不易劝说 obstinate; stubborn

绉(縐) zhòu ㄓㄡˋ 一种有皱纹的丝织品 crepe

皱(皺) zhòu ㄓㄡˋ ❶脸上起的褶纹 wrinkle; crease ㊁ ***extension*** 物体上的褶纹 crease; crumple:～纹 *wrinkles; lines* ❷使生褶纹 to wrinkle; to rumple:～眉头 *to frown*

咒(*呪) zhòu ㄓㄡˋ ❶某些宗教或巫术中的密语 incantation; spell:～语 *incantation; spell* ❷说希望人不顺利的话 to curse:～骂 *to abuse; to swear; to execrate*

宙 zhòu ㄓㄡˋ ❶古往今来，指所有的时间 time conceived as past, present and future ❷地质年代分期的最高一级，在"代"之上 aeon; eon:显生～ *Phanerozoic Eonothem* | 元古～ *Proterozoic Eonothem* | 太古～ *Archean Eonothem*

轴 ㊁ zhòu ㄓㄡˋ [(大)轴子]一次戏曲演出的节目中排在最末的一出戏 last item in a theatrical performance:压～～(倒数第二出戏) *last but one item in a theatrical performance*

㊀ zhóu 见 990 页 see p990

胄 zhòu ㄓㄡˋ ❶盔，古代作战时戴的帽子(in ancient China) helmet ❷古代指帝王或贵族的后代(in ancient China) descendants of emperors or aristocrats

咮 zhòu ㄓㄡˋ 鸟嘴 beak

Z

昼（晝）zhòu ㄓㄡˋ 白天 daytime; daylight; day: ～夜不停 *to go on round the clock*

甃 zhòu ㄓㄡˋ ❶井壁 wall of a well ❷用砖砌 to lay bricks

繇 ㊂ zhòu ㄓㄡˋ 古时占卜的文辞 (in ancient China) divinatory words

㊀ yóu 见 910 页 see p910

㊁ yáo 见 875 页 see p875

骤 zhòu ㄓㄡˋ ❶快跑 to trot ([连] *doublet* 驰— to gallop) ❷急，疾速，突然 sudden; abrupt: 暴风～雨 *tempest; heavy storm* | 天气～冷。*There's a sudden drop in temperature.* | 狂风～起。*A sudden gale swept past.*

籀 zhòu ㄓㄡˋ ❶籀文，古代的一种字体，即大篆，相传是周宣王时太史籀所造 (i. e. 大篆, allegedly created by the official historian Zhou in the reign of Emperor Xuan of the Zhou Dynasty) seal script; ancient style of calligraphy ❷阅读 to read: ～绎 *to recite* | ～读 *to read aloud*

碡 zhou ·ㄓㄡ 见 459 页"碌"字条"碌碡"(liù—) see 碌碡 on p459

ZHU ㄓㄨ

朱（❷硃）zhū ㄓㄨ ❶大红色 bright red; vermilion ❷朱砂，即辰砂，矿物名。化学成分是硫化汞，颜色鲜红，是提炼汞的重要原料，又可做颜料或药材 (i. e. 辰砂) cinnabar; vermilion

邾 zhū ㄓㄨ 周代诸侯国名，后改称"邹"Zhu, a princedom of the Zhou Dynasty, later changed into 邹

侏 zhū ㄓㄨ [侏儒]身量特别矮小的人 dwarf; manikin; midget; pygmy

诛 zhū ㄓㄨ ❶把罪人杀死 to put (a criminal) to death; to execute: ～戮 *to kill* | 伏～*to be executed* | 罪不容～ *Even death cannot atone for the offence.* or *to be guilty of crimes for which even death is insufficient punishment* ❷责罚 to denounce and punish: 口～笔伐 *to condemn both in speech and in writing*

茱 zhū ㄓㄨ [茱萸](— yú) 植物名 (name of a plant) cornel **1** 山茱萸，落叶小乔木，开小黄花。果实椭圆形，红色，味酸，可入药 fruit of medicinal cornel (*Cornus officinalis*) **2** 吴茱萸，落叶乔木，开黄白色小花。果实红色，可入药 *medicinal evodia fruit* (*Evodia rutaecarpa*) **3** 食茱萸，落叶乔木，开淡绿色花。果实味苦，可入药 *ailanthus prickly ash* (*Zanthoxylum ailanthoides*)

洙 zhū ㄓㄨ 洙水河，在山东省西南部 Zhushui River in the southwest of Shandong Province

珠 zhū ㄓㄨ ❶(—子)珍珠(也作"真珠")，淡水里的

三角帆蚌和海水里的马氏珍珠贝等因沙粒窜入壳内,受到刺激而分泌珍珠质,逐层包起来形成的圆粒,有光泽,可入药,又可做装饰品(also written as 真珠) pearl:~宝 *jewellery* | 夜明~ *night-luminescent pearl* ❷(一儿)像珠子的东西 bead:眼~儿 *eyeball* | 水~儿 *water drops* [珠算]用算盘计算的方法 calculation with an abacus

株 zhū ㄓㄨ ❶露出地面的树根 stump:守~待兔(比喻妄想不劳而得,也比喻拘泥不知变通) *to stand by a tree stump waiting for a hare to dash itself against it — to wait for gains without pains; to be lacking in flexibility* [株连]指一人犯罪牵连到许多人 to implicate (*or* involve) others in a criminal case ❷棵儿,植物体 plant:植~ *plant* | 病~ *infected plant; diseased plant* [株距]种树或种庄稼时,同一行中相邻的两棵植株之间的距离 spacing between two plants in a row ❸量词 ***quantifier***,用于植物(of plants):一~桃树 *a peach tree*

铢 zhū ㄓㄨ 古代重量单位,二十四铢等于旧制一两 *zhu*, ancient unit of weight, equal to 1/24 tael:锱~ *trifles; small amount of money* | ~积寸累(lěi)(喻一点一滴地积累) *to accumulate little by little*

蛛 zhū ㄓㄨ 蜘蛛,节肢动物,俗叫"蛛蛛"。有足四对,腹部下方有丝腺开口,能分泌黏液,织网粘捕昆虫作食料,种类很多(popularly called 蛛蛛) spider:~网 *spiderweb; cobweb* | ~丝马迹(喻线索) *the thread of a spider and the trail of a horse — clues; traces*

诸 zhū ㄓㄨ ❶众,许多 many; numerous:~位 *ladies and gentlemen; everybody* | ~子百家 *various schools of thought and their exponents from pre-Qin times to the early Han Dynasty* ❷"之于"或"之乎"二字的合音(fusion of 之于 or 之乎):付~实施 *to put it into effect* | 藏~名山 *to hide sth in a famous mountain* | 公~社会 *to publicize to the society* | 有~? *Is it true?*

猪(*豬) zhū ㄓㄨ 一种家畜,体肥多肉,肉可吃,皮和鬃是工业原料,粪是很好的肥料 pig; hog; swine

槠 zhū ㄓㄨ 常绿乔木,初夏开花,黄绿色。木材坚硬,可做器具 sweet oak

潴(**瀦) zhū ㄓㄨ ❶(水)积聚(of water) to accumulate; to store ❷水停聚的地方 puddle; pool

橥(**櫫) zhū ㄓㄨ 拴牲口的小木桩 wooden stake for tethering domestic animals

术 ㊁ zhú ㄓㄨˊ 植物名 name of a plant **1** 白术,多年生草本植物,秋天开紫花。根状茎有香气,可入药 largeheaded atractylodes rhizome (*Atractylodes macrocephala rhizome*)

Z

2 苍术，多年生草本植物，秋天开白花，根状茎有香气，可入药 Chinese atractylodes (*Atractylodes lancea*)

㊀ shù 见 694 页 see p694

竹 zhú ㄓㄨˊ (一子)常绿多年生植物，茎节明显，节间多空，质地坚硬，可做器物，又可做建筑材料 bamboo：茂林修～ *dense forests and tall bamboos* | ～苞松茂 *luxuriant bamboos and pine trees*

竺 zhú ㄓㄨˊ 姓 Zhu, a surname［天竺］印度的古称 (ancient name) India

逐 zhú ㄓㄨˊ ❶追赶 to pursue; to chase：～鹿 *to chase the deer — to fight for the throne; to bid for the state power* | ～臭之夫 *person who runs after "stink" — person going after fame and personal gain; person of a worldly disposition* ❷赶走，强迫离开 to drive out; to expel (㊦ ***doublet*** 驱— to expel)：～客令 *order for guests to leave; showing sb the door* | 追亡～北 *to pursue and attack fleeing enemy* | 追～残敌 *to chase the remaining defeated enemy* ❸依照先后次序，一一挨着 one by one：～日 *day by day* | ～步进行 *to proceed step by step* | ～字讲解 *to explain word by word* | ～渐提高 *to improve gradually*

瘃 zhú ㄓㄨˊ 古书上指冻疮(in ancient Chinese texts) chilblain; frostbite

烛(燭) zhú ㄓㄨˊ ❶蜡烛，用线绳或苇子做中心，周围包上蜡油，点着取亮的东西 candle ❷照亮，照见 to illuminate; to light up：火光～天。*The sky lit up with raging flames.* ㊀ ***extension*** 明察 to see through：洞～其奸 *to see through one's treachery* (or *tricks*)

蠋 zhú ㄓㄨˊ 蝴蝶、蛾子等的幼虫 larva

躅 zhú ㄓㄨˊ ❶足迹 footprint ❷见 979 页"踯"字条"踯躅"(zhí—) see 踯躅 on p979

舳 zhú ㄓㄨˊ ［舳舻］(—lú) 船尾和船头，也指首尾相接的船只 stem and stern (of a ship); convoy：～～千里 *in stem-to-stern formation; in-line formation*

主 zhǔ ㄓㄨˇ ❶主人 master; host **1** 权力或财物的所有者 owner; possessor：人民是国家的～人。*The people are the masters of the country.* | 物～ *owner* **2** 接待客人的人，跟"宾、客"相对(the opposite of 宾 or 客) host; hostess：宾～ *guests and hosts* | 东道～ *host* **3** 事件中的当事人 person concerned：事～ *victim of a crime* | 失～ *owner of lost property*［主观］**1** 属于自我意识方面的，跟"客观"相对(the opposite of 客观) (of one's mind) subjective：人类意识属于～～，物质世界属于客观。*Human consciousness is subjective while the physical world is objective.* **2** 不依据客

观事物，单凭自己的偏见的（solely according to one's prejudice）subjective：他的意见太～～了。*His views are too subjective*. **3** 属于自身方面的（concerning oneself）subjective：～～努力 *subjective efforts*［主权］一个国家的独立自主的权力 sovereignty ❷旧社会占有奴隶或雇用仆役的人 master：奴隶～*slave owner*｜～仆 *master and servant* ❸主张，决定 to advocate；to decide：～见*one's own judgement*｜婚姻自～*marriage of one's own choice*［主席］**1** 开会时主持会议的人 chairman（of a meeting）**2** 某些国家、国家机关、党派、团体等的领导人（of a state，state administration，party，organization，etc）chairman；president［主义］**1** 人们对于自然界、社会以及学术、文艺等问题所持的有系统的理论与主张 doctrine；-ism；systematic theory and propositions on nature，society，science，arts，etc：马克思～～*Marxism*｜达尔文～～*Darwinism*｜现实～～*realism* **2** 思想作风 ideological style：革命乐观～～*revolutionary optimism*［主张］对事物的意见或认为应当如何处理 view；position；proposition；assertion：我们～～组织专门小组来研究这个问题。*We propose that a special team be formed to study this issue.*｜心里有～～*to have one's own stand* ❹最重要的，最基本的 main；primary；principal；major：～力 *main force*；*mainstay*；*backbone*｜以预防为～，治疗为辅 *to put prevention first*，*and treatment second*［主顾］商店称买货的人 customer；client；patron ❺主持，负主要责任 to preside over；to be in charge of：～办 *to sponsor*；*to host*；*to run*｜～讲 *chief lecturer* ❻预示 to indicate；to signify：早霞～雨，晚霞～晴。*Rainbow in the morning is the travellers' warning*；*rainbow at night is the travellers' delight*. ❼对事情的定见 definite view about sth：六神无～*all the six vital organs failing to function* — *to be at one's wit's end*；*to be at a loss*｜心里没～*not to know what to do*

拄 zhǔ ㄓㄨˇ 用手扶着杖或棍支持身体的平衡 to lean on（a stick，etc）：～拐棍 *to lean on a stick*

渚 zhǔ ㄓㄨˇ 水中间的小块陆地 islet

煮（*煑）zhǔ ㄓㄨˇ 把东西放在水里，用火把水烧开 to boil；to cook：～面 *to cook noodles*｜～饭 *to cook rice*｜病人的碗筷餐后要～一下。*Patients' tableware should be boiled after each meal.*

褚 ㊀ zhǔ ㄓㄨˇ ❶在衣服里铺丝绵 to pad（or wad）clothes with silk floss ❷囊，口袋 bag；satchel；sack

㊁ chǔ 见 98 页 see p98

Z

属(屬) ㊁ zhǔ ㄓㄨˇ ❶连缀 to join; to combine:～文 *to compose a piece of prose writing*|前后相～(*of two parts*) *to join together* ❷(意念)集中在一点 to focus on; to concentrate on:～意 *to fix one's mind on*|～望 *to centre one's hope on; to look forward to* ❸古同"嘱"same as 嘱 in ancient Chinese

㊀ shǔ 见 693 页 see p693

嘱(囑) zhǔ ㄓㄨˇ 托付 to entrust; to commit to sb's care:以事相～*to entrust sb with sth*|遗～*will; testament* [嘱咐]告诫 to tell; to exhort:母亲～～他好好学习。*His mother told him to study hard.*

瞩(矚) zhǔ ㄓㄨˇ 注视 to gaze; to look steadily:～目 *to fix one's eyes on; to focus one's attention upon*|～望 *to look forward to*|高瞻远～*to stand aloft and see afar; to take a broad and long-term view*

麈 zhǔ ㄓㄨˇ 古书上指鹿一类的动物,尾巴可以当作拂尘(in ancient Chinese texts) species of deer, whose tails can be used as whisks

伫(*佇、*竚) zhù ㄓㄨˋ 长时间站着 to stand for a long time:～候 *to stand waiting*

苎(△苧) zhù ㄓㄨˋ 苎麻,多年生草本植物,茎皮含纤维质很多,劈成细丝,可以做绳子,又可织夏布 ramie(*Boehmeria nivea*)

"苧"又 níng 见 538 页 also pronouced ning, see p 538

纻(紵) zhù ㄓㄨˋ ❶同"苎"same as 苎 ❷苎麻织成的布 cloth made from ramie; ramie cloth

贮(貯) zhù ㄓㄨˋ 储存 to store; to save; to lay aside(㊟ ***doublet*** 一存 to store; to keep in storage|一藏 to store up; to lay in; to preserve)

助 zhù ㄓㄨˋ 帮(㊟ ***doublet*** 帮一 to help),协助 to help; to assist:互～*to help each other*|～理 *assistant*|～我一臂之力 *to lend me a hand* [助词]不能独立使用,只能依附在别的词、词组或句子上表示一定语法意义的词,如"的"、"了"、"吗"等 auxiliary

住 zhù ㄓㄨˋ ❶长期居留或暂时歇息 to live; to reside; to dwell; to inhabit; to stay:～了一夜 *to stay overnight*|他家在这里～了好几代。*Several generations of his family have lived here.*|我家～在城外。*My family is in the suburbs.* ❷停,止 to stop; to cease:～手 *Stop!*|雨～了。*The rain stopped.* ❸用作动词的补语(used as a complement after a verb) **1** 表示稳当或牢固(used to indicate steadness or firmness):站～*Stop!*|把～方向盘 *to hold the wheel* **2** 表示停顿或静止(used to express a halt or stillness)：把他问～了。*He was stumped by the question.* **3** 表示力量够得上（跟"得"或"不"连用）(used in collocation with 得 or 不 to express being capable or incapable of)：禁得～*to be able to stand* | 支持不～*cannot withstand*

注(❸-❺*註) zhù ㄓㄨˋ ❶灌进去 to pour; to fill：～入 *to pour into* | ～射 *to inject* | 大雨如～。*It's raining cats and dogs.* ❷集中在一点 to concentrate on; to fix：～视 *to gaze at; to stare* | ～意 *to take notice of; to pay attention to* | 引人～目 *noticeable; conspicuous* | 精神贯～*to be concentrated on; to be absorbed in* ❸用文字来解释词句 to annotate：下边～了两行小注。*There are two lines of footnotes in a smaller type.* | ～解一篇文章 *to gloss a passage* ❹解释词、句所用的文字 note; annotation; commentary：加～*to add notes to* | 附～*appended notes; annotations* ❺记载，登记 to record; to register：～册 *to register; to enrol* | ～销 *to cancel; to annul; to write off* ❻赌博时所押的财物(in gambling) stakes：下～*to lay down a stake* | 孤～一掷(喻拿出所有的力量希望最后侥幸成功) *to put in a single bid; to make a last desperate effort*

驻 zhù ㄓㄨˋ ❶(车马等)停止 to stop; to halt：～足 *to halt; to make a temporary stay* ❷停留在一个地方 to be stationed：～军 *station troops* | ～外使节 *resident minister*

柱 zhù ㄓㄨˋ ❶(一子)支撑屋顶的构件，多用木、石等制成 pillar; column; post ❷像柱子的东西 column-shaped thing：水～*water column* | 花～*stylet; stylus* | 水银～*mercury column*

炷 zhù ㄓㄨˋ ❶灯心 wick ❷烧 to burn ❸量词 ***quantifier***，用于线香(of a joss stick)：一～香 *a burning joss stick*

砫 zhù ㄓㄨˋ [石砫]地名，在重庆市。今作"石柱"(now written as 石柱) Shizhu, a place in Chongqing

疰 zhù ㄓㄨˋ [疰夏] **1** 中医指夏季长期发烧的病，患者多为小儿，多由排汗机能发生障碍引起(in traditional Chinese medicine) chronic summer disease contracted by children and caused usually by malfunction of the sweat glands **2**〈方 ***dialect***〉苦夏 loss of appetite and weight in summer

蛀 zhù ㄓㄨˋ ❶蛀虫，咬木器、谷物或衣物的小虫 moth or any other insect that eats books, clothes, wood, etc ❷虫子咬坏 to eat into (*or* bore through) by the worm：这块木头被虫～了。*This piece of wood is worm-eaten.*

杼 zhù ㄓㄨˋ 织布机上的筘(kòu)。古代也指梭 reed; (in ancient China) shuttle

祝 zhù ㄓㄨˋ ❶削，断绝 to cut：～发为僧 *to shave one's*

Z

head and become a monk ❷衷心地表示对人对事的美好愿望 to express good wishes:～身体健康。*Wish you the best of health.*

著 ㊀ zhù ㄓㄨˋ ❶显明,显出 marked; outstanding ([连] ***doublet*** 显— striking; remarkable | 昭— distinct; evident; prominent):卓～*eminent; distinguished; distinct* | ～名 *famous; celebrated; well-known* | 颇～成效 *to prove most effective; to prove rather effective* ❷写文章,写书 to write; to compose:～书立说 *to write a book to expound a theory or doctrine; to write scholarly works* ❸著作,写出来的文章或书 work; book; writing:名～ *classic; masterpiece* | 大～ *your writing; your work* | 译～ *work of translation; translation* [土著] **1** 世代居住在一定的地方 to inhabit a place for generations **2** 世居本地的人 original inhabitants

㊁ zhuó 见 1007 页 see p1007

翥 zhù ㄓㄨˋ 鸟向上飞 to fly; to soar:龙翔凤～ *to fly like a phoenix and a dragon — (of calligraphy) to be beautifully written; to be written with flowing strokes*

箸(*筯) zhù ㄓㄨˋ 筷子 chopstick

铸(鑄) zhù ㄓㄨˋ 把金属熔化后倒在模子里制成器物 to cast; to found:～一口铁锅 *to cast an iron pan* | ～成大错(喻造成大错误) *to commit a gross error; to make an awful mistake* [铸铁] 又叫"铣(xiǎn)铁",是由铁矿砂最初炼出来的铁。含碳量在2.0%以上,质脆,易熔化,多用来铸造器物(also called 铣铁) cast iron

筑(❶築) zhù ㄓㄨˋ ❶建造,修盖 to build; to construct ([连] ***doublet*** 建— to construct; to build):～路 *to construct a road* | ～堤 *to build a dyke* | 建～楼房 *to construct high-rise buildings* ❷古代弦乐器,像琴,有十三根弦 *zhu*, ancient 13-stringed musical instrument played by striking with a bamboo stick ❸(旧读 formerly zhú) 贵州省贵阳的别称 Zhu, another name for Guiyang, Guizhou Province

ZHUA ㄓㄨㄚ

抓 zhuā ㄓㄨㄚ ❶用指或爪挠(náo) to scratch:～耳挠腮 *to tweak one's ears and scratch one's cheeks; to scratch one's head — to be anxious; to be delighted* ❷用手或爪拿取 to grab; to seize; to clutch; to grasp:老鹰～小鸡。*The hawk seized a chicken.* | ～一把米 *to take a handful of rice* [引] ***extension*** **1** 捉捕 to capture; to catch; to arrest:～贼 *to catch a thief* **2** 把握住,不放过 to take hold of; to seize:～工夫 *to* *make good use of one's time* | ～紧时间 *to make full use of one's time* ❸着力办理 to lay emphasis on; to stress: ～农业 *to pay great attention to agriculture* | ～工作 *to be engaged in work; to peg away at one's work* | ～重点 *to focus on the essential points* ❹引人注意 to attract; to draw one's attention: 这个演员一出场就～住了观众。*The actress caught the audience's attention as soon as she appeared on stage.*

挝(撾) ㊀ zhuā ㄓㄨㄚ 打，敲打 to knock; to beat

㊁ wō 见 791 页 see p791

髽 zhuā ㄓㄨㄚ [髽髻](—ji) [髽鬏](—jiu) 女孩子梳在头两旁的发结 two knots (*or* buns) worn on the sides of a girl's head

爪 ㊀ zhuǎ ㄓㄨㄚˇ ❶(—子、—儿)禽兽的脚(多指有尖甲的) (usually with nails) paw; claw; talon: 鸡～子 *chicken's claw* | 狗～儿 *dog's paw* ❷(—儿)像爪的东西 paw-shaped thing: 这个锅有三个～儿。*The pan stands on three hoof feet.*

㊁ zhǎo 见 960 页 see p960

ZHUAI ㄓㄨㄞ

拽 ㊀ zhuāi ㄓㄨㄞ ❶用力扔 to fling; to hurl: ～了吧，没用了。*Fling it out, for it's useless.* | 把球～过来。*Throw the ball to me.* ❷〈方 **dialect**〉胳膊有毛病，动转不灵 (of arm muscle) strained

㊁ zhuài 见 999 页 see p999

㊂ yè 见 880 页 see p880

跩 zhuǎi ㄓㄨㄞˇ 走路像鸭子似的摇摆 to waddle: 走路一～一～的 *to waddle*

拽(**攦) ㊁ zhuài ㄓㄨㄞˋ 拉，拖，牵引 to pull; to drag; to haul: ～不动 *to fail to be dragged* | 把门～上。*Shut the door behind you.* | 生拉硬～ *to drag sb along against his will*

㊀ zhuāi 见 999 页 see p999

㊂ yè 见 880 页 see p880

ZHUAN ㄓㄨㄢ

专(專、*耑) zhuān ㄓㄨㄢ ❶单纯，独一，集中在一件事上 only; unique; focused on one thing: ～心 *absorbed; concentrated; engrossed* | ～卖 *specialized* | ～修科 *special (training) course* [专家]学术技能有专长的人 expert; specialist ❷独自掌握或享有 to monopolize: ～权 *to monopolize power; to arrogate all powers to oneself* | ～政 *dictatorship; to exercise dictatorship over* ❸姓 Zhuan, a surname

"耑"又 duān 见 163 页"端" also pronounced duān, see 端

Z

on p163

肫(膞) zhuān ㄓㄨㄢ 〈方 *dialect*〉鸟类的胃 gizzard:鸡～*chicken gizzard*

砖(磚、*甎) zhuān ㄓㄨㄢ ❶用土坯烧成的建筑材料 brick ❷像砖的东西 brick-shaped thing:茶～*tea brick*|冰～(一种冷食) *ice-cream brick*|煤～*briquette*

颛 zhuān ㄓㄨㄢ ❶愚昧 ignorant; benighted ❷同"专" same as 专[颛顼](－xū)传说中上古帝王名 Zhuan Xu, legendary ruler in remote antiquity

转(轉) ㊀ zhuǎn ㄓㄨㄢˇ ❶旋动,改换方向或情势 to turn; to shift:～身 *to turn round*|运～*to work; to operate*|向左～*to turn left*|～眼之间 *in the twinkling of an eye; in an instant; in a flash*|情况好～。*The situation is taking a turn for the better.* ❷不直接地,中间再经过别人或别的地方 to pass on; to transfer:～送 *to pass on; to transmit*|～达 *to pass on; to convey; to relay*

㊁ zhuàn 见 1000 页 see p1000

传(傳) ㊁ zhuàn ㄓㄨㄢˋ ❶旧时一般指解说儒家经书的文字(in former times) commentaries on Confucian classics ❷记载。特指记载某人一生事迹的文字 biography:小～*profile; biographical sketch*|别～*supplementary biography*|外～*anecdotal (or unauthorized) biography* ❸叙述历史故事的作品 historical story or novel:《儿女英雄～》*The Story of Young Heroes and Heroines*|《水浒～》*Outlaws of the Marsh*

㊀ chuán 见 100 页 see p100

转(轉) ㊁ zhuàn ㄓㄨㄢˋ ❶旋转,绕着圈儿动,围绕着中心运动 to rotate; to revolve; to spin:轮子～得很快。*The wheels are turning swiftly.* ❷绕着某物移动,打转 to move about; to turn around:～圈子 *to go circling; to go round and round*|～来～去 *to hang around* ❸量词 ***quantifier***,绕几圈儿叫绕几转 revolution; rotation; turn

㊀ zhuǎn 见 1000 页 see p1000

啭(囀) zhuàn ㄓㄨㄢˋ 鸟婉转地叫 twittering; chirping:莺啼鸟～。*Orioles are singing and birds twittering.*

赚 ㊀ zhuàn ㄓㄨㄢˋ ❶做买卖得利 to make a profit; to gain:～钱 *to make money; to make a profit* ❷做买卖得的利 profit:～儿 *profit*|～头 *profit* ❸占便宜 to gain extra advantage; to profit at other people's expense:这回去香山真～,又得吃又得玩。*We profited a lot from this tour of Xiangshan Mountain, having both delicious food and fun.*

㊁ zuàn 见 1020 页 see

p1020

撰(*譔) zhuàn ㄓㄨㄢˋ 写文章,著书 to write; to compose:~文 *to write an article; to write an essay*|~稿 *to contribute*

馔 zhuàn ㄓㄨㄢˋ 饮食,吃喝 food:盛~*sumptuous feast*|设~招待 *to entertain sb to dinner*

篆 zhuàn ㄓㄨㄢˋ ❶篆字,古代的一种字体,有大篆、小篆[ancient style of Chinese calligraphy, including greater seal character (ancient calligraphy style current in the Zhou Dynasty) and lesser seal character (ancient calligraphy style current in the Qin Dynasty)] seal character ❷书写篆字 to write seal characters:~额 *to write seal characters on a horizontal tablet* ❸印章 seal:摄~(暂代某官) *to take the place of some office holder temporarily*

ZHUANG ㄓㄨㄤ

妆(妝、*粧) zhuāng ㄓㄨㄤ ❶修饰,打扮。特指妇女的装饰(especially used to denote woman's personal adornments) to make up ❷演员的衣装服饰 theatrical or stage costume and make-up:卸~*to remove one's make-up and costume* ❸出嫁女子的陪送衣物 trousseau; dowry:送~*to present a dowry*|嫁~*trousseau; dowry*

庄(莊) zhuāng ㄓㄨㄤ ❶村落,田舍 village (㊀ ***doublet*** 村— village) ❷商店的一种名称 name of a shop:布~*cloth store*|饭~*restaurant*|茶~*teahouse* ❸封建社会里君主、贵族等所占有的成片土地 manor:皇~*imperial manor*|~园 *estate; manor* ❹庄家,打牌时每一局的主持人(in gambling) banker ❺严肃,端重 serious; grave; solemn (㊀ ***doublet*** —严 solemn; dignified; stately|—重 grave; solemn; sedate):~严的五星红旗 *stately Five-Star Red Flag, national flag of the People's Republic of China*

桩(樁) zhuāng ㄓㄨㄤ ❶(—子)一头插入地里的木棍或石柱 stake; pile; post; peg:打~*to drive piles into the ground*|牲口~子 *stake for hitching domestic animals*|桥~*bridge piling* ❷量词 ***quantifier***,用于事件(of events):一~事 *an incident*

装(裝) zhuāng ㄓㄨㄤ ❶穿着的衣物 outfit; clothes (㊀ ***doublet*** 服— clothes):军~*military uniform*|春~*spring clothing*|泳~*swimsuit; swimwear* 特指演员演出时的打扮 stage makeup and costume:上~*to dress and make up*|卸~*to remove one's makeup and costume*[行装]出行时带的衣物 outfit for a journey; luggage; baggage ❷打扮,用服饰使人改变原来的外

貌 to dress up(㊀ **doublet** 一扮 to dress up)[装饰] **1** 加上一些附属的东西使美观 to decorate; to adorn; to ornament: ~~房间 *to decorate a room* **2** 事物的修饰点缀 decoration; adornment; ornament [化装] 改变装束 to make up; to disguise oneself ❸故意做作,假作 to pretend; to fake; to feign: ~听不见 *to pretend to hear nothing* | ~模作样 *to attitudinize; to strike an attitude; to strike a pose* ❹安置,安放,通常指放到器物里面去 to install; to fit; to load: ~电灯 *to install an electric lamp* | ~车 *to load a truck* | ~箱 *to pack a box; to crate sth* ㊂ **extension** 把零件或部件安在一起构成整体 to assemble; to install: ~配 *to assemble; to fit together* | ~了一架机器 *to fit together a machine* [装备] **1** 生产上或军事上必需的东西 equipment; outfit: 工业~~ *industrial equipment* | 军事~~ *military equipment* **2** 配备 to equip; to fit out: 学校正在~~多媒体教室。*The school is being equipped with multimedia classrooms.* ❺对书籍、字画加以修整或修整成的式样 to bind a book; to mount a picture on a scroll: ~订 *to bind* | 精~ *hardcover; hardback* | 线~书 *thread-bound book; thread-bound edition*

奘 ㊀ zhuǎng ㄓㄨㄤˇ 粗大 stout; robust: 这棵树很~。*The tree is very tall and thick.*

㊁ zàng 见 940 页 see p940

壮(壯) zhuàng ㄓㄨㄤˋ ❶健壮,有力 strong; robust; sturdy (㊀ **doublet** 强— strong): ~士 *brave man; hero; warrior* | 年轻力~ *young and vigorous* | 庄稼长得很~。*The crops are growing very well.* [壮年] 习惯指人三四十岁的时期 in one's thirties or forties — prime of life; meridian of life ❷雄伟,有气魄 magnificent; grand; splendid: ~观 *magnificent sight; splendid spectacle* | ~志凌云 *with lofty and soaring aspirations* ❸增加勇气或力量 to build up strength or courage: ~一~胆子 *to bolster sb's courage* [壮族] 我国少数民族,参看附表 (see the appendix) the Zhuang ethnic group, one of the ethnic minorities of China

状(狀) zhuàng ㄓㄨㄤˋ ❶形态 form; shape (㊀ **doublet** 形— form; shape | —态 state; condition): 奇形怪~ *grotesque in shape; fantastic in appearance* ❷事情表现出来的情形 state; condition (㊀ **doublet** —况 status; situation): 病~ *symptom* | 生活~况 *living conditions* ❸陈述或描摹 to describe: 写情~物 *to depict the scenery and objects and express feelings* | 风景奇丽,殆不可~。*The scenery is too beautiful to describe in words.* ❹叙述事件的文字 account; record: 行～(指死者传略) *brief biography of a deceased person* | 诉～*plaint; indictment* ❺褒奖、委任等的凭证 certificate: 奖～*certificate of merit* | 委任～*certificate of appointment*

僮 ㊀ zhuàng ㄓㄨㄤˋ 我国少数民族壮族的"壮"字旧作"僮" former written form of 壮, which means the Zhuang ethnic group in China

㊁ tóng 见 755 页 see p755

撞 zhuàng ㄓㄨㄤˋ ❶击打 to strike: ～钟 *to toll a bell* ❷碰 to collide; to crash: 别让汽车～了。*Be careful not to bump into the car.* ㊀ **extension** 无意中遇到 to run into; to come across; to bump into: 让我～见了。*I saw it by chance.* ❸莽撞地行动，闯 to rush; to dash; to barge: 横冲直～*to barge about wildly; to dash around madly*

幢 ㊁ zhuàng ㄓㄨㄤˋ 〈方 **dialect**〉量词 **quantifier**，用于房子(of buildings): 一～楼 *a building*

㊀ chuáng 见 102 页 see p102

戆 ㊀ zhuàng ㄓㄨㄤˋ 刚直 simple and blunt; honest and upright: 性情～直(*of nature*) *blunt and tactless*

㊁ gàng 见 220 页 see p220

ZHUI ㄓㄨㄟ

隹 zhuī ㄓㄨㄟ 短尾巴的鸟 bird with a short tail

骓 zhuī ㄓㄨㄟ 青白杂色的马 piebald

椎 ㊀ zhuī ㄓㄨㄟ 椎骨，脊椎骨，构成高等动物背部中央骨柱的短骨 vertebra: 颈～*cervical vertebra* | 胸～*thoracic vertebra*

㊁ chuí 见 103 页 see p103

锥 zhuī ㄓㄨㄟ ❶(～子)一头尖锐，可以扎窟窿的工具 awl: 针～*awl* | 无立～之地(喻赤贫) *to have not even enough land to stick an awl into* — *very poor; impoverished; penniless* ❷像锥子的东西 awl-shaped thing: 改～*screwdriver* ❸用锥子形的工具钻 to bore; to drill: 用锥子～个眼儿 *to drill a hole with an awl*

追 zhuī ㄓㄨㄟ ❶赶，紧跟着 to chase; to pursue (㊂ **doublet** 一逐 to chase; to pursue): ～随 *to follow* | ～击敌人 *to pursue and attack the enemy* | 急起直～*to summon all one's energies in an effort to catch up; to do one's utmost to overtake* | 他走得太快，我～不上他。*He walked so fast that I could hardly catch up with him.* ❷追溯过去，补做过去的事 to date back to; to trace back to; to date from: ～念 *to recall; to reminisce* | ～悼 *to mourn* | ～认 *to endorse subsequently; to confer* (or *admit*) *posthumously* | ～加预算 *to supplement a budget* | ～肥 *to add more manure* ❸竭力探求，寻求 to seek for; to go after;

Z

to hunt for; to pursue:～问 *to make a detailed enquiry; to question closely*|～根 *to get to the root of sth; to get to the bottom of sth*|这件事不必再～了。*It's unnecessary to dig into the matter.*|～求真理 *to seek truth; to pursue truth*

坠(墜) zhuì ㄓㄨㄟˋ ❶落,掉下 to fall; to drop:～马 *to fall off a horse*|摇摇欲～ *tottering; on the verge of collapse* ❷往下沉 to sink:船锚往下～。*The anchor sank into the water.* ❸(一儿)系在器物上垂着的东西 weight; hanging object:扇～ *fan pendant*|表～ *watch pendant* [坠子] **1** 耳朵上的一种装饰品。也叫"耳坠子"、"耳坠儿"(also called 耳坠子 or 耳坠儿) eardrop **2** 流行于河南、山东的一种曲艺 *zhuizi*, a ballad singing to the accompaniment of the *zhuiqin* (坠琴) popular in Henan and Shandong provinces

缀 zhuì ㄓㄨㄟˋ ❶缝 to sew; to stitch:把这个扣子～上。*Sew the button on.*|补～ *to patch; to mend* ❷连接 to compose:～字成文 *to put words together to produce a piece of writing* ❸装饰 to embellish; to decorate:点～ *to ornament; to adorn*

醊 zhuì ㄓㄨㄟˋ 祭奠 to offer sacrifices to gods or ancestors

惴 zhuì ㄓㄨㄟˋ 又忧愁,又恐惧 anxious and fearful:～～不安 *anxious and fearful; on tenterhooks*

缒 zhuì ㄓㄨㄟˋ 用绳子拴住人、物从上往下送 to let down (with a rope):工人们从楼顶上把空桶～下来。*The workers let down the empty barrel from the roof.*

膇 zhuì ㄓㄨㄟˋ 脚肿 (of the foot) swollen

赘 zhuì ㄓㄨㄟˋ ❶多余的,多而无用的 superfluous; redundant:～述 *to give unnecessary details; to say more than is needed*|～疣 *wart; anything superfluous or useless; superfluity* ❷男子到女家结婚并成为女家的家庭成员叫入赘,女家招女婿叫招赘 (of a man) to go to live in the household of his in-laws after marriage (which is called 入赘); (of the bride's parents) to gain a son-in-law who lives in the home of his wife's parents (which is calle 招赘):～婿 *to take a man into the family as a son-in-law*

ZHUN ㄓㄨㄣ

屯 ㊁ zhūn ㄓㄨㄣ 困难 difficulty [屯邅] (—zhān) 同"迍邅" same as 迍邅

㊀ tún 见 767 页 see p767

迍 zhūn ㄓㄨㄣ [迍邅] (—zhān) **1** 迟迟不前 to procrastinate in one's advance **2** 处在困难中,十分不得志 to be in a predicament; to be quite unsuccessful in one's career

肫 zhūn ㄓㄨㄣ ❶〈方 *dialect*〉鸟类的胃 gizzard：鸡～ *chicken gizzard* | 鸭～ *duck gizzard* ❷恳切，真挚(叠 ***reduplication***) sincere; genuine; earnest：～～*sincere* | ～笃 *genuine*

窀 zhūn ㄓㄨㄣ [窀穸](—xī) 墓穴 grave; tomb

谆 zhūn ㄓㄨㄣ 恳切 earnest; sincere [谆谆]恳切，不厌倦地 earnestly and ceaselessly：～～告诫 *to admonish repeatedly; to enjoin assiduously* | ～～教导 *to instruct earnestly*

衠 zhūn ㄓㄨㄣ〈方 ***dialect***〉纯粹，纯 pure; unadulterated

准(❷-❿準) zhǔn ㄓㄨㄣˇ ❶允许，许可 to allow; to permit; to grant：批～*to approve; to ratify; to sanction* | 不～他来。*He's not allowed to come.* ❷依照，依据 in accordance with：～此办理 *to do in accordance with this* ❸定平直的东西 thing that determines levelness and straightness：水～ *level; standard* | ～绳 *yardstick; criterion* ❹标准，法则，可以作为依据的 norm; rule：～则 *norm; criterion* | 以此为～。*Take this as the criterion.* ❺同"埻"same as 埻 ❻正确 accurate; correct (㊀ ***doublet*** —确 exact; precise)：瞄～*to aim at* ❼副词 ***adverb***，一定，确实 definitely; certainly; surely：我～来。*I'm sure to come.* | ～能完成任务 *to be sure to fulfil the task* ❽鼻子 nose：隆～(高鼻子) *prominent nose; high nose* ❾(—儿)把握 certain; sure：心里没～儿 *to be unsure about sth; to be unsure of* ❿和某类事物差不多的 quasi-; para-：～平原 *para-plain*

埻 zhǔn ㄓㄨㄣˇ 箭靶上的中心 bull's eye (of a target)

ZHUO ㄓㄨㄛ

拙 zhuō ㄓㄨㄛ 笨，不灵巧 clumsy; awkward (㊀ ***doublet*** —笨 clumsy; awkward)：～嘴笨舌 *clumsy-tongued; inarticulate* | 手～ *to be all thumbs* | 弄巧成～ *to try to be clever only to end up with a blunder* | 勤能补～。*Diligence can make up for one's clumsiness.* 谦辞(***humble***) I; my：～作 *my (poor) writing* | ～见 *my (humble) opinion*

捉 zhuō ㄓㄨㄛ ❶抓，逮 to catch; to capture：～老鼠 *to catch a rat* | ～蝗虫 *to catch locusts* | 捕风～影 *to chase shadow; to make groundless accusations* [捉弄]玩弄，戏弄 to tease; to make fun of ❷握 to clutch; to hold; to grasp：～刀 *to write for sb else; to ghostwrite* | ～笔 *to write*

桌(*槕) zhuō ㄓㄨㄛ ❶(—子、—儿)一种日用家具，上面可以放东西 table：书～ *desk* | 饭～ *dinner table* | 八仙～ *old-fashioned square table (for Eight Leg-*

endary Immortals）❷量词 ***quantifier***：一～酒席 *a table of dishes for feast*｜这些人可以坐三～。*These people can be seated at three tables.*

倬 zhuō ㄓㄨㄛ ❶显著 notable；striking ❷大 big；large

焯 ㊀ zhuō ㄓㄨㄛ 显明，明白 obvious；clear；evident

㊁ chāo 见 79 页 see p79

棁 zhuō ㄓㄨㄛ 梁上的短柱 short posts on a roof beam

涿 zhuō ㄓㄨㄛ 涿州，地名，在河北省 Zhuozhou，a place in Hebei Province

镨 zhuō ㄓㄨㄛ〈方 ***dialect***〉❶镨钩，刨地的镐（gǎo）pickaxe；pick ❷用小镐刨 to dig with a pick：～高粱 *to dig out Chinese sorghum stubbles with a pick*｜～玉米 *to dig out maize stubble with a pick*

灼 zhuó ㄓㄨㄛˊ ❶烧，炙 to burn；to scorch：～伤 *to get burnt*｜心如火～ *with a burning heart；to be extremely anxious* ❷明白，透彻 clear；profound：真知～见 *profound knowledge and penetrating insight*

酌 zhuó ㄓㄨㄛˊ ❶斟酒 to pour（wine）；to drink（wine）：自～自饮 *to enjoy wine all by oneself；to drink alone* ㊀ ***extension*** 酒饭 meal with wine or spirits：便～ *informal dinner* ❷度量，考虑 to weigh and consider（㊣ ***doublet*** 一量 to deliberate；to give due consideration）：～办 *to act according to one's judgement；to act at one's discretion；to do as one thinks fit*｜～情处理 *to settle a matter as one sees fit；to act at one's discretion*

茁 zhuó ㄓㄨㄛˊ 植物才生长出来的样子 thriving［茁壮］**1** 壮盛 healthy and strong：庄稼长得～～。*The crops are growing well.* **2** 壮健 sturdy：牛羊～～ *sturdy cattle and sheep*

卓 zhuó ㄓㄨㄛˊ ❶高而直 tall and erect：～立 *to stand upright* ❷高明，高超，杰出，不平凡 eminent；outstanding；prominent：～见 *brilliant idea*｜～越的成绩 *remarkable achievement*［卓绝］超过寻常，没有能比的 unsurpassed；outstanding；extreme：坚苦～～ *extremely hard and bitter*

斫（＊斲）zhuó ㄓㄨㄛˊ 砍削 to chop；to cut；to hack：～伐树木 *to hack down trees*｜～轮老手（喻经验多的人）*expert wheelwright — old hand；experienced person*［斫丧］（—sàng）摧残，伤害，特指因沉溺酒色以致伤害身体（used especially to indicate ruining one's health for indulging in sensual pleasures）to wreck；to damage

浊（濁）zhuó ㄓㄨㄛˊ ❶水不清，不干净，跟"清"相对（the opposite of 清）turbid；muddy；murky（㊣ ***doublet*** 浑一 turbid）❷混乱

confused; chaotic: ～世(旧时用以形容混乱的时代) *corrupted world; chaotic times; turbulent days* ❸(声音)低沉粗重(of voice) deep and thick: ～音 *voiced sound* | ～声～气 *in a deep, raucous voice* ❹浊音,发音时声带颤动的音 voiced sound; sound articulated by vibrating the vocal cords

镯(**鋜) zhuó ㄓㄨㄛˊ (一子)套在腕子上的环形装饰品 bracelet

涿 zhuó ㄓㄨㄛˊ 淋,使湿 to drench: 让雨～了 *to be drenched in rain*

诼 zhuó ㄓㄨㄛˊ 造谣毁谤 slander; calumny; defamation

啄 zhuó ㄓㄨㄛˊ 鸟类用嘴叩击并夹住东西 to peck: 鸡～米。*The chickens are pecking at the rice.* | ～木鸟 *woodpecker*

琢 ㊀ zhuó ㄓㄨㄛˊ 雕刻玉石,使成器物 to chisel; to carve: 精雕细～ *to sculpt with exquisite craftsmanship — to work at sth exquisitely; to work with meticulous care* [琢磨] **1** 雕刻和打磨(玉石) to carve and polish **2** 加工使精美(指文章等) to improve (literary works); to polish; to refine

㊁ zuó 见 1022 页 see p1022

椓 zhuó ㄓㄨㄛˊ ❶击 to strike; to hit ❷古代宫刑,割去男性的生殖器 castration, a torture in ancient China

著 ㊁ zhuó ㄓㄨㄛˊ 附着,穿着。后作"着"(zhuó) (later written as 着) to adhere to; to wear

㊀ zhù 见 998 页 see p998

着 ㊀ zhuó ㄓㄨㄛˊ ❶穿(衣) to wear; to dress: ～衣 *to put on clothes* ❷接触,挨上 to touch; to contact: 附～ *to adhere to; to attach to* | ～陆 *to land; to touch down* | 不～边际 *irrelevant; not to the point; off the point* ❸使接触别的事物,使附着在别的物体上 to adhere to; to attach to: ～眼 *to have sth in mind; to view from the angle of* | ～手 *to set about; to start doing* | ～色 *to apply colour; to colour* | 不～痕迹 *to leave no trace* ❹着落 whereabouts: 寻找无～ *nowhere to be found* [着落](—luò) 下落,来源 whereabouts; assured source: 遗失的东西有了～～了。*The lost thing has been found.* | 这笔费用还没有～～。*The expenses can be obtained from nowhere yet.* ❺派遣 to dispatch; to send: ～人前来办理。*Please send someone to handle the matter.* ❻公文用语,表示命令的语气(used in official documents, expressing peremptory tone) order: ～即施行 *must be enforced immediately*

㊁ zháo 见 960 页 see p960
㊂ zhāo 见 959 页 see p959
㊃ zhe 见 965 页 see p965

Z

禚 zhuó ㄓㄨㄛˊ 姓 Zhuo, a surname

鷟 zhuó ㄓㄨㄛˊ 见 931 页"鸑"字条"鸑鷟"(yuè—) see 鸑鷟 on p931

缴 ㊁ zhuó ㄓㄨㄛˊ 系在箭上的绳 string attached to an arrow

㊀ jiǎo 见 341 页 see p341

擢 zhuó ㄓㄨㄛˊ ❶拔 to pull out; to extract: ～发(fà)难数(喻罪恶多得像头发那样数不清)(*of crimes*) *to be as countless as the hairs on the head* ❷提拔 to promote: ～用 *to promote*

濯 zhuó ㄓㄨㄛˊ 洗 to wash: ～足 *to wash one's feet*

ZI ㄗ

仔 ㊂ zī ㄗ [仔肩]所担负的职务, 责任 official burdens; official responsibilities

㊀ zǐ 见 1011 页 see p1011

㊁ zǎi 见 936 页 see p936

孖 ㊀ zī ㄗ 双生子 twins

㊁ mā 见 480 页 see p480

孜 zī ㄗ [孜孜]勤勉, 不懈怠 diligent; industrious; hardworking: ～～不倦 *diligent; industrious; assiduous*

吱 ㊁ zī ㄗ 同"嗞"same as 嗞

㊀ zhī 见 975 页 see p975

呲 zī ㄗ 同"龇"same as 龇

赀(貲) zī ㄗ ❶计量(多用于否定)(usually used in negative sentences) to count; to calculate: 所费不～*to incur a considerable expense* | 不可～计 *cannot count clearly; innumerable* ❷同"资❶"same as 资❶

觜 ㊀ zī ㄗ 觜宿, 二十八宿之一 *zixiu*, 20th of the 28 constellations

㊁ zuǐ 见 1020 页 see p1020

訾 ㊁ zī ㄗ 姓 Zi, a surname

㊀ zǐ 见 1012 页 see p1012

龇 zī ㄗ 张开嘴露出牙 to bare one's teeth; to show one's teeth: ～牙咧嘴 *to show one's teeth; to look ferocious*

髭 zī ㄗ 嘴上边的胡子 moustache: ～须皆白 *with white hair and beard*

咨 zī ㄗ ❶跟别人商议, 询问 to consult; to take counsel (㊟ **doublet** —询 to consult): 有所～询 *to seek advice from; to hold counsel with* ❷咨文, 旧时用于同级机关的一种公文 official document between government offices of equal rank in former times

姿 zī ㄗ ❶容貌 appearance; looks: ～容 *appearance; looks* | 丰～ *graceful bearing; charm* ❷形态, 样子 gesture; posture; carriage (㊟ **doublet** —态 posture; carriage; bearing | —势 posture; pose; gesture): 雄～ *heroic posture* | 跳舞的～势 *dancer's posture and movements*

资(❶△*貲) zī ㄗ ❶财物, 钱财 treasure; wealth: ～源 *resources* | 投～ *investment* ㊡ **extension**

钱，费用 money; expenses：车～*fare*［资金］**1** 国民经济中物资的货币表现 funds **2** 经营工商业的本钱 capital［资料］**1** 生产、生活中必需的东西 means **2** 用作依据的材料 data; material：统计～～*statistical data*［工资］作为劳动报酬按期付给劳动者的货币或实物 wages; pay ❷供给 to supply：～助 *to give financial aid; to subsidize*｜以～参考 *for your reference* ❸智慧能力 endowment; aptitude; natural ability：天～聪明 *gifted; talented*［资质］人的素质；智力 natural endowments; intelligence; aptitude; credentials ㊀ ***extension*** 泛指从事某种工作或活动所应具备的条件、资格、能力等 qualifications and ability for certain work or certain task：管理～～*management endowments*｜设计～～*designing aptitude*｜～～等级 *grade of credentials* ❹资历，指出身、经历 qualifications; seniority：论～排辈 *to decide according to qualifications and seniority*［资格］从事某种活动应有的条件 qualifications for a certain task

谘 zī ㄗ 同"咨❶"same as 咨❶

粢 zī ㄗ 古代供祭祀用的谷类（in ancient China）cereals used as sacrifice

趑 zī ㄗ［趑趄］（－jū）❶行走困难 to walk with difficulty; to plough one's way ❷犹豫不前 to falter; to hesitate to advance：～～不前 *to hang back; to halt in hesitation*

兹（**茲） ㊀ zī ㄗ ❶这，这个 this; this one：～日 *today*｜～理易明。*The truth of the matter is easy to understand.* ❷现在 now; at present：～订于明日开全体职工大会。*This is to announce that a staff member conference will be held tomorrow.* ❸〈古 ***archaism***〉年 year：今～ *this year*｜来～*the coming year; the next year*

㊁ cí 见 107 页 see p107

嗞 zī ㄗ（－儿）拟声词 ***onomatopoeia***（叠 ***reduplication***）squeaking：老鼠～的一声跑了。*The rat squeaked and escaped.*｜小鸟～～地叫。*The birds were chirping.*

嵫 zī ㄗ 见 862 页"崦"字条"崦嵫"（yān－）see 崦嵫 on p862

孳 zī ㄗ 滋生，繁殖 to multiply; to breed; to propagate：～生得很快 *to breed quickly*

滋 zī ㄗ ❶生出，长 to grow：～芽 *to sprout; to germinate*｜～事 *to cause trouble; to provoke a dispute; to create a disturbance*｜～蔓 *to grow and spread; to grow vigorously* ❷益，增益，加多 to multiply; to add：～益 *to increase interest or profits*｜～补 *to nourish*［滋润］润泽，湿润，使不干枯 to moisten; to wet; to damp［滋味］味道 taste; flavour［滋养］补益身

体 to nourish ❸喷射 to spurt; to burst; to spout:水管往外～水。*Water is spurting from the pipe.*

镃 zī ㄗ 镃基,古代的锄头(in ancient China) hoe

菑 zī ㄗ ❶已经开垦了一年的田地 farmland cultivated for a year ❷除草 to weed ❸茂盛的草 luxuriant grass:～榛秽聚 *to be overgrown with grass and hazel*

〈古 **archaism**〉又同“灾”(zāi)also same as 灾

淄 zī ㄗ 淄河,水名,在山东省中部 Zihe River in the middle of Shandong Province

缁 zī ㄗ 黑色 black:～衣 *black dressing*

辎 zī ㄗ 辎车,有帷子的车(in ancient times) covered cart[辎重](—zhòng)行军时携带的器械、粮草、材料等 impedimenta; supplies and gear

锱 zī ㄗ 古代重量单位,六铢等于一锱,四锱等于一两 *zi*, an ancient unit of weight, equal to six *zhu* or one fourth of *liang* [锱铢](—zhū) ㊌ **figurative** 琐碎的事或极少的钱 trifle; farthing; small amount of money:～～必较 *to haggle over every penny; to dispute over trivialities*

鲻 zī ㄗ 鲻鱼,鱼名。背部青灰色,腹部白色,嘴宽而短。有的生活在海水和河水交界处,肉味美 mullet (*Mugilidae*)

鼒 zī ㄗ 上端收敛而口小的鼎 tripod tapering off towards the top

子 zǐ ㄗˇ ❶古代指儿女,现在专指儿子(in ancient China) children; (now) son [子弟]后辈人,年轻人 children; juniors ❷对人的称呼 person **1** 一般的人 average people:男～*man*|女～*woman* **2** 旧称某种行(háng)业的人(in former times) people in certain profession:士～*soldier; armyman*|舟～*boatman* **3** 古代指著书立说,代表一个流派的人(ancient title of respect for a learned man who wrote books and established theory, representing a school of thought):荀～*Xunzi, Master Xun*|诸～百家 *various schools of thought and their exponents from pre-Qin times to the early Han Dynasty* **4** 古代图书四部(经、史、子、集)分类法中的第三类“philosophy”, third of the four traditional categories of ancient Chinese writings as distinct from “Confucian classics”(经), “history”(史), and “belles-letters”(集):～部 *“philosophy” section, third of the four traditional categories of ancient Chinese writings, which contains works by the exponents of the various schools of thought other than Confucianism from the Spring and Autumn Period onwards*|～书 *works of ancient philosophers other than*

Confucius, which belong to the third traditional category of Chinese writings **5** 古代对对方的敬称，同现代汉语中代词“你”用法一样(ancient term of respect, same as the pronoun 你 in modern Chinese) you：～试为之。*You may have a try.*｜以～之矛，攻～之盾 *to pierce one's shield with one's own spear — to refute sb with his own argument* **6** 古代称老师(in ancient times) teacher：～墨子 *Master Mozi*［子虚］㊕ ***transfer*** 虚无的，不实在的 fictitious; unreal：事属～～。*It's sheer fiction.* ❸(一儿)植物的种子 seed：菜～ *vegetable seed*｜莲～*lotus seed*｜桐～*tung seed*｜瓜～儿 *melon seed*｜结～*to bear seed* ❹(一儿)动物的卵 egg：鱼～*roe*｜鸡～儿 *egg*｜蚕～*silkworm egg*｜下～儿 *to give birth to young; to lay eggs* ❺幼小的 young：～鸡 *chick*｜～姜 *tender ginger* ❻派生的，附属的 subsidiary; attached：～金 *interest*｜～公司 *subsidiary*［子音］见 206 页“辅”字条“辅音” see 辅音 on p206 ❼地支的第一位 *zi*, first of the 12 Earthly Branches ❽子时，指夜里十一点到一点 period of the day from 11 pm to 1 am［子夜］深夜 midnight ❾我国古代五等爵位(公、侯、伯、子、男)的第四等 viscount; fourth ranking of the five feudal titles of nobility in China (duke, marquis, count, viscount and baron) ❿ (zi) 名词词尾(noun suffix) **1** 加在名词性语素后(used after a noun)：孩～*child*｜珠～*pearl; bead*｜桌～*table*｜椅～*chair* **2** 加在形容词或动词性语素后(used after an adjective or a verb)：胖～*fat person*｜拐～*cripple*｜瞎～*blind man*｜乱～*disturbance; trouble*｜垫～*mat; cushion* ⓫ (zi) 个别量词词尾(suffix of a few quantifiers)：一档～事 *a thing (or matter) simitar to*｜敲了两下～门 *to knock twice at the door*

仔 ㊀ zǐ ㄗˇ 幼小的(多指家畜、家禽)(usually of domestic animals or poultry) young：～鸡 *chick*｜～猪 *piglet*［仔密］衣物等质地紧密 close-knit; close-woven：袜子织得十分～～。*The pair of socks is close-woven.*［仔细］**1** 周密，细致 careful; attentive：～～研究 *to study carefully*｜～～考虑 *to consider carefully* **2** 俭省 frugal; economical：日子过得～～ *to be frugal of one's expenses; to live with frugality* **3** 当心，注意 to take care; to look out; to watch out：路很滑，～～点儿。*The road is very slippery. Be careful!*

㊁ zǎi 见 936 页 see p936

㊂ zī 见 1008 页 see p1008

耔 zǐ ㄗˇ 培土 to hill up; to earth up

籽 zǐ ㄗˇ 同“子❸”same as 子❸

姊 zǐ ㄗˇ 姐姐 elder sister; sister［姊妹］**1** 姐姐和妹

Z

妹 sisters：她们一共～～三个。*The family has three daughters altogether.* **2** 同辈女朋友间亲热的称呼(intimate address between female friends of the same generation) sister

秭 zǐ ㄗˇ 古代数目，指一万亿，也指十亿或千亿等(ancient numeral) a thousand billion; also a billion or a hundred billion［秭归］地名，在湖北省 Zigui, a place in Hubei Province

笫 zǐ ㄗˇ 竹子编的床席 mat woven of fine bamboo strips：床～*bamboo bed mat*

茈 ㊀ zǐ ㄗˇ 茈草，即紫草，多年生草本植物。叶椭圆形或长卵形，开白色小花，根皮紫色。根可入药，又可作紫色染料(i. e. 紫草) Chinese gromwell (*Lithospermum erythrorhizon*)

㊁ cí 见 106 页 see p106

紫 zǐ ㄗˇ 蓝、红合成的颜色 purple

訾 ㊀ zǐ ㄗˇ 说别人的坏话，诋毁 to slander; to calumniate; to defame：不苟～议 *to make no casual slanderous remarks about others*

㊁ zī 见 1008 页 see p1008

梓 zǐ ㄗˇ ❶梓树，落叶乔木，开浅黄色花，木材可供建筑及制造器物用 Chinese catalpa (*Catalpa ovata*)［梓里］［桑梓］故乡 hometown ❷雕版，把木头刻成印书的版 to cut blocks for printing：付～*to send to the press; to put into print*｜～行 *block printing; printing; publishing*

滓 zǐ ㄗˇ 渣子，沉淀物 sediment; dregs; lees：渣～*dregs*

自 zì ㄗˋ ❶自己；己身，本人 self; oneself; one's own：～给～足 *to be self-supporting and self-sufficient*｜独立～主 *to maintain independence and keep the initiative in one's own hands; to be one's own master; to stand on one's own*｜～力更生 *to rely on one's own efforts*｜～动 *automatic*［自个儿］(*自各儿)(—gěr) oneself; by oneself〈方 **dialect**〉代词 **pronoun**，自己 oneself; by oneself［自然］**1** 一切天然存在的东西 nature：大～～*nature*｜～～景物 *natural scenery* **2** 不勉强 natural; unaffected：～～而然 *naturally; spontaneously; of oneself*｜功到～～成 *Constant efforts yield sure success.*｜他笑得很～～。*He puts on a natural smile.* **3** 当然，没有疑问 of course; naturally：学习不认真，～～就要落后。*If you do not study hard, you are bound to lag behind.*［自由］**1** 人们在法律规定的范围内，随意安排自己活动的权利 freedom; liberty **2** 哲学上指人们在实践中认识了客观规律，并能有意识地运用它来改造世界(of philosophy) freedom **3** 不受拘束和限制 free; unrestrained; unrestricted：～～活动 *to do as one likes*｜～～发言 *to talk freely*

[自在]（—zai）满意，舒服 comfortable; at ease：要勇挑重担，不图个人～～。*One should be brave enough to shoulder great responsibilities and seek no personal comforts.*｜逍遥～～ *leisurely and carefree* ❷介词 ***preposition***，从，由 from; since（㊣ ***doublet*** —从 since）：～古到今 *from ancient times to the present*｜～天津到北京 *from Tianjin to Beijing* ❸自然，当然 certainly; of course; naturally：～当努力 *will certainly do one's best*｜～不待言 *it is self-evident that; it goes without saying that; it's taken for granted that; needless to say*｜～属无碍。*It certainly does not matter.*｜公道～在人心。*People have a natural sense of justice.*｜久别重逢，～有许多话要讲。*It was quite natural that they should have a lot to say to each other after such a long separation.*

字 zì ㄗˋ ❶文字，用来记录语言的符号 word; character：汉～ *Chinese character*｜～眼儿 *wording; diction*｜～体 *script; typeface*｜常用～ *daily used characters; everyday words* [字典]注明文字的音义，列举词语说明用法的工具书 dictionary [字符]表示数据和信息的字母、数字及各种符号 character, a general term for letters, numbers and various symbols for statistics and information [字母]表语音的符号 letter：拼音～～ *phonetic alphabet*｜拉丁～～ *Latin letters* ❷字音 pronunciation：咬～清楚 *to pronounce clearly*｜～正腔圆 *to pronounce correctly and melodiously* ❸字体 style of calligraphy：篆～ *seal character*｜柳～ *style of calligraphy of Liu Gongquan* ❹书法作品 scripts; writings：～画 *calligraphy and painting* ❺根据人名中的字义另取的别名叫“字”，也叫“表字”，现在多称“号”（another name taken according to the meanings of the characters used in given names, called 字, also called 表字, now usually called 号） literary name：岳飞～鹏举。*Yue Fei had the literary name of Pengju.* ❻字据，合同，契约 written pledge; contract; deed：立～为凭 *to give a written pledge* ❼旧时称女子许嫁（of a girl in former times） to be betrothed to; to be engaged：待～闺中 *to remain unengaged; not to be betrothed to yet*

牸 zì ㄗˋ 雌性的牲畜 female livestock：～牛 *cow*

恣 zì ㄗˋ ❶放纵，无拘束 to do as one pleases; to be self-indulgent：～意 *unscrupulous; reckless; unbridled*｜～情 *to enjoy to one's heart's content; to indulge oneself as much as one likes* ❷〈方 ***dialect***〉舒服 comfortable：你看，你睡得多～。*See how comfortably you slept.*

眦（*眥）zì ㄗˋ 上下眼睑的接合处，靠近鼻子的叫内眦，靠近两鬓的叫外眦（The canthus close to the nose is called the inner canthus; while the canthus close to the temple is called the outer canthus.）canthus; corner of the eye

胔 zì ㄗˋ ❶带腐肉的尸骨 decayed body of a human being or an animal ❷腐烂的肉 rotten meat; putrid meat

渍 zì ㄗˋ ❶浸，沤 to steep; to soak; to ret: ～麻 *ret flax, jute, etc* ❷地面的积水 floodwater on a low-lying land: ～水 *accumulated floodwater* | 防洪排～ *prevention of floods and drainage of floodwater* ❸油、泥等积在上面难以除去 to be soiled with grease: 烟袋里～了很多油子。*The pipe is caked with tar.* | 手表的轮子～住了。*The wheel of the watch is soiled.*

胾 zì ㄗˋ 切成的大块肉 large chunk of meat

ZONG ㄗㄨㄥ

枞（樅）㊀ zōng ㄗㄨㄥ [枞阳]地名，在安徽省 Zongyang, a place in Anhui Province

㊁ cōng 见109页 see p109

宗 zōng ㄗㄨㄥ ❶旧指宗庙，祖庙 (in former times) ancestral temple or hall [祖宗]先人 ancestor ❷家族，同一家族的 clan: 同～ *of the same clan* | ～兄 *elder brother of the same clan* [宗法]封建社会以家族为中心，按血统远近区别亲疏的制度 patriarchal clan system: 破除～～观念 *to banish the concept of the patriarchism* ❸宗派，派别 faction; sect; school: 禅（chán）～ *Chan Sect of Chinese Buddhism* | 北～山水画 *landscape painting of the Northern Sect* ❹宗旨，主要的目的和意图 aim; purpose; tenet: 开～明义第一章 *to make clear the purpose from the very beginning* | 万变不离其～。*All changes, no matter how varied, centre on one purpose; to remain essentially the same despite all apparent changes* ❺尊奉，向往 to worship; to revere; to venerate: ～仰 *to hold in esteem* ❻量词 ***quantifier***, 件，批 piece; batch: 一～事 *a matter* | 大～货物 *a large batch of goods* ❼西藏地区旧行政区划单位，大致相当于县 old administrative district in Tibet, roughly corresponding to the county

综 ㊀ zōng ㄗㄨㄥ 总合 to sum up; to put together: 错～（纵横交错）*criss-cross; intricate* [综合] **1** 把各个独立而互相关联的事物或现象进行分析归纳整理 to synthesize; to colligate; to integrate; to subsume **2** 不同种类、不同性质的事物组合在一起 synthetical; comprehensive; composite: ～

～利用 *comprehensive utilization*｜～～大学 *university*

㊁ zèng 见 946 页 see p946

棕（*椶） zōng ㄗㄨㄥ 指棕榈（lǘ）树或棕毛 palm; palm fibre; coir［棕榈］常绿乔木，叶鞘上的毛叫棕毛，可以打绳、制刷子等。叶子可以做扇子。木材可以制器物 palm (*Palmae*)

腙 zōng ㄗㄨㄥ 有机化合物的一类，通式 $\frac{R}{R'}>C=N-NH_2$，是羰基与肼缩合而成的化合物 hydrazone

踪（*蹤） zōng ㄗㄨㄥ 人或动物走过留下的脚印 footprint; track（㊀ ***doublet*** 一迹 trace; trail）：～影 *trace; sign*｜追～*to follow the trail of; to track sb down; to trace; to pursue*｜失～*to be missing; to disappear*

鬃（*騌、*騣） zōng ㄗㄨㄥ 马、猪等兽类颈上的长毛，可制刷、帚等 mane; bristle

总（總、**縂） zǒng ㄗㄨㄥˇ ❶聚合，聚集在一起 to put together; to sum up：～在一起算 *to settle all the accounts*｜～共三万 *thirty thousand in all; thirty thousand altogether*｜～起来说 *to sum up*［总结］把一段工作过程中的经验教训分析、研究，归纳出结论 to sum up; to summarize：要认真～～经验。*You must learn your lessons seriously.* ❷概括全部的，主要的，为首的 general; chief; head：～纲 *general programme*｜～司令 *commander in chief* ❸副词 ***adverb***，经常，一直 always; invariably：为什么～是来晚？*Why are you always late?*｜～不肯听 *always to refuse to follow sb's advice* ❹副词 ***adverb***，一定，无论如何 anyway：这件事～是要办的。*It'll surely be done.*｜明天他～该回来了。*Tomorrow he'll be back anyway.*

傯（*偬） zǒng ㄗㄨㄥˇ 见 395 页"倥"字条"倥偬"（kǒng—）see 倥偬 on p395

纵（縱） zòng ㄗㄨㄥˋ ❶放 to release; to set free：～虎归山 *to let the tiger return to the mountain — to cause calamity for the future; to let go a deadly enemy unpunished* ❷放任，不加拘束 to indulge; to connive：～目四望 *to look into the distance in all directions*｜～情歌唱 *to sing to one's heart's content; to sing heartily* ❸身体猛然向前或向上 to jump up; to leap：～身一跳 *to jump in one leap*｜一～身就过去了 *to leap over* ❹连词 ***conjunction***，即使 even if; even though：～有千山万水，也拦不住不畏艰险的勘探队员。*Even the countless mountains and rivers cannot stop the dauntless prospectors.* ❺（旧读 formerly zōng）竖，直，南北的方向，跟

Z

"横"相对(the opposite of 横) vertical; longitudinal; lengthwise:～线 *vertical line*|排成～队 *to line up in a column*|～横各十里 *to lie ten* li *in length and breadth*|～剖面 *vertical section* ❻〈方 **dialect**〉起皱纹 to wrinkle; to crease; to crumple:这张纸都～了,怎么用来写字? *The paper got crumpled. How can you write on it?*|衣服压～了。*The dress is crumpled.*

疭(瘲) zòng ㄗㄨㄥˋ 见91页"瘛"字条"瘛疭"(chì—) see 瘛疭 on p91

粽(*糉) zòng ㄗㄨㄥˋ 粽子,用箬叶或苇叶裹糯米做成的多角形的食品。也叫"角黍"(also called 角黍) *zongzi*, pyramid-shaped dumpling made of glutinous rice wrapped in bamboo or reed leaves, usually eaten during the Dragon Boat Festival

糉 zòng ㄗㄨㄥˋ〈方 **dialect**〉公猪 boar

ZOU ㄗㄡ

邹(鄒) zōu ㄗㄡ 周代诸侯国名,在今山东省邹城东南 Zou, a princedom of the Zhou Dynasty, in the southeast of today's Toucheng, Shandong Province

驺(騶) zōu ㄗㄡ 驺从,封建时代贵族官僚出门时所带的骑马的侍从 groom

诹 zōu ㄗㄡ 在一起商量事情 to consult; to hold counsel with:～吉(商订好日子) *to select an auspicious day through consultation*|咨～(询问政事) *to inquire about government affairs*

陬 zōu ㄗㄡ 隅,角落 corner

緅 zōu ㄗㄡ 青赤色 dark red

鲰 zōu ㄗㄡ 小鱼 fingerling; fry [鲰生]古代称小子,小人(in ancient China) boy, mean or contemptible person

鄹(**郰) zōu ㄗㄡ ❶古地名,在今山东省曲阜东南 Zou, an ancient place in the southeast of today's Qufu, Shandong Province ❷古国名,即"邹"(i. e. 邹) Zou, an ancient state

走 zǒu ㄗㄡˇ ❶走路,步行 to walk:～得快 *to walk quickly*|小孩子会～路了。*The baby can walk now.* ㉿ **extension** **1** 往来 to visit; to call on:～亲戚 *to visit relatives* **2** 移动,挪动 to move:～棋 *to move (a piece)*|钟不～了。*The clock has stopped.* **3** 往来运送 to send; to deliver:～信 *to deliver letters*|～货 *to deliver goods* ❷离去 to leave; to go away:他刚～。*He's just left.*|我明天要～了。*I'm leaving tomorrow.* ❸通过,由 through; from:咱们～这个门出去吧。*Let's go out through this door.* ❹经过 to be noted in the account:这笔钱不～账了。*This sum of money won't be shown in the account.* ❺透漏出,越过范围 to leak; to let out:～漏消息 *to leak information*｜～气 *to go flat; to become stale*｜说话～了嘴 *to make a slip of the tongue; to let slip an inadvertent remark* ❻失去原样 to lose the original shape:衣服～样子了。*The coat has lost its shape.*｜茶叶～味了。*The tea has lost its flavour.* ❼古代指跑(in ancient China) to run ([连] ***doublet*** 奔— to run):～马看花 *to look at flowers while riding a horse — to gain a shallow understanding from a fleeting glance*［走狗］善跑的猎狗 hunting dog [喻] ***figurative*** 受人豢养而帮助作恶的人 lackey; stooge

奏 zòu ㄗㄡˋ ❶演奏,依照曲调吹弹乐器 to play; to perform:～乐 *to play music; to strike up a tune*｜提琴独～*violin solo*｜伴～*to accompany* ❷封建时代臣子对皇帝进言或上书 to submit a memorial to an emperor in feudal times:上～*to send a memorial to the emperor* ❸呈现,做出 to achieve; to produce:～效 *to prove effective*｜～功 *to achieve success; to yield result*

揍 zòu ㄗㄡˋ ❶打人 to beat; to hit; to strike ❷〈方 ***dialect***〉打碎 to smash; to break:小心别把玻璃～了。*Be careful not to break the glass.*

ZU ㄗㄨ

租 zū ㄗㄨ ❶出代价暂用别人的东西 to rent; to hire; to charter:～房 *to rent a house*｜～家具 *to rent furniture*［租界］帝国主义者强迫被侵略国家在通商都市以"租借"名义划给他们直接统治的地区 concession ❷出租 to let; to lease:～给人 *to be leased out to sb*｜～出去 *to let out*［出租］收取一定的代价,让别人暂时使用房地器物等 to let; to lease ❸出租所收取的钱或实物 rent; rental:房～*rent*｜收～*to collect rent* ❹田赋 land tax:～税 *land tax*

菹(**葅) zū ㄗㄨ ❶酸菜 pickled Chinese cabbages ❷多水草的沼泽地带 marshland［菹草］多年生水草,可做饲料 any of various types of perennial waterplants that can be used as forage ❸切碎(肉、菜) to cut into small pieces

足 zú ㄗㄨˊ ❶脚 foot:～迹 *footmark; footprint*｜画蛇添～*to draw a snake and add feet to it — to ruin the effect by adding sth superfluous; to paint the lily* [引] ***extension*** 器物下部的支撑部分 leg (of certain utensils):鼎～*three legs of a tripod* ❷满,充分,够量 enough; ample; sufficient ([连] ***doublet*** 充— sufficient):～数 *full amount; full number*｜心满意～*to be perfectly satisfied;*

to one's heart's content｜丰衣～食 *to have plenty of food and clothing; to be well-fed and well-clothed* ㊁ ***extension*** 副词 ***adverb*** **1** 尽情地，尽量地 fully; as much as：～玩了一天 *to have spent a whole day's good time* **2** 完全 enough：他～可以担任翻译工作。*He's fully qualified as an interpreter.*｜两天～能完成任务。*It's quite enough for us to finish the work within two days.* ❸值得 worthy：微不～道 *insignificant*

卒 ㊀ zú ㄗㄨˊ ❶古时指兵(in ancient China) soldier：小～*pawn*｜士～*rank and file; soldier; private* ❷旧称差役(in former times) servant：走～*lackey; underling; stooge*｜狱～*jailor; jailer; turnkey* ❸死亡 death：生～年月 *date of one's birth and death* ❹完毕，终了 to finish; to end：～业 *to graduate* ㊁ ***extension*** 究竟，终于 at last; finally; in the end：～胜敌军 *to defeat the enemy troops in the end*

㊁ cù 见111页 see p111

崒(**崪) zú ㄗㄨˊ 险峻 precipitous; steep

族 zú ㄗㄨˊ ❶民族 nationality; race; ethnic group：汉～*Han ethnic group; Han nationality*｜回～*Hui ethnic group; Hui ethnic minority*｜各～人民 *the people of all nationalities* ❷聚居而有血统关系的人群的统称 clan：宗～*patriarchal clan*｜家～*clan; family* ❸事物有共同属性的一大类 class or group of things with common features：水～*aquatic animals*｜芳香～*aromatic compounds* ㊇ ***figurative*** 有共同特点的某类人 group of people with common features：上班～*office worker*｜追星～*idolater; star fans* (or *chasers*) ❹灭族，古代的一种残酷刑法，一人有罪把全家或包括母家、妻家的人都杀死(in ancient China) death penalty, imposed on an offender and his whole family, or even the family of his mother and wife

䃚 zú ㄗㄨˊ 同"镞"，箭头，特指石制的箭头(same as 镞) arrowhead, especially stone arrowhead

镞 zú ㄗㄨˊ 箭镞，箭头 arrowhead

诅 zǔ ㄗㄨˇ ❶迷信的人求神加祸于别人 to curse; to swear [诅咒]咒骂，说希望人不顺利的话 to curse; to swear; to abuse ❷盟誓 oath of alliance

阻 zǔ ㄗㄨˇ 拦挡 to block; to impede (㊅ ***doublet*** 一挡 to hinder; to obstruct)：～止 *to prevent; to stop; to check*｜通行无～*smooth traffic; to go through without any hindrance*｜山川险～*dangerous and difficult mountains and rivers*

组 zǔ ㄗㄨˇ ❶结合，构成 to organize; to form：～成一队 *to form a team*｜改～*to reorganize; to restructure; to reconstitute* [组织] **1** 有目的、有

系统、有秩序地结合起来 to organize：～～群众 *to organize the masses* **2** 按照一定的政治目的、任务和系统建立起来的集体 organization：党团～～ *Party and Youth League organizations* **3** 有机体中由形状、性质和作用相同的若干细胞结合而成的单位 tissue：神经～～*nerve tissue*｜～～疗法 *tissue therapy; histotherapy* ❷由若干人员结合成的单位 group：学习小～*study group* ❸合成一组的（文学艺术作品）series；suite；cycle：～诗 *poems sequence*｜～画 *group paintings* ❹量词 ***quantifier***，用于成组的事物 set；series；suite：一～照片 *a set of photos*

俎 zǔ ㄗㄨˇ ❶古代祭祀时放祭品的器物 ancient sacrificial utensil ❷切肉或菜时垫在下面的砧（zhēn）板 chopping block for cutting meat and vegetables：刀～ *knife and chopping block*

祖 zǔ ㄗㄨˇ ❶父亲的上一辈 grandfather：～父 *paternal grandfather* ㊂ ***extension*** 先代 ancestor：～宗 *forefathers; forebears; ancestry; ancestors*｜始～*first ancestor* ［祖国］对自己国家的亲切称呼 motherland；homeland；nativeland ❷对跟祖父同辈的人的称呼（term of address for the people of the same generation with one's grandfather）：外～父 *maternal grandfather*｜外～母 *maternal grandmother*｜伯～ *grandfather's elder brother; grand uncle* ❸某种事业或流派的开创者（of a tradition，school of thought，etc）earliest ancestor； originator：鼻～ *founder; originator*｜不祧之～ *revered earliest ancestor; respected forerunner*｜开山～师 *earliest ancestor; originator*

ZUAN ㄗㄨㄢ

钻（鑽） ㊀ zuān ㄗㄨㄢ ❶用锥状的物体在另一物体上转动穿孔 to drill；to bore：～个眼儿 *to drill a hole*｜地质～探 *geological drilling* ㊂ ***extension*** 进入 to get into；to go through；to make one's way into：～山洞 *to go into a cave*｜～到水里 *to dive into the water*｜～空（kòng）子 *to avail oneself of loopholes* ［钻营］指攀附权势取得个人好处 to curry favour with sb in authority for personal gains；to fawn on sb in authority for personal gains ❷钻研，仔细深入研究 to make an intensive study；to dig into：～书本 *to dig into books*｜他肯～，学得快。*He studies hard so he learns quickly.*

㊁ zuàn 见 1020 页 see p1020

躜 zuān ㄗㄨㄢ 向上或向前冲 to jump up；to dash forward

缵 zuǎn ㄗㄨㄢˇ 继承 to inherit

Z

纂 zuǎn ㄗㄨㄢˇ ❶编纂,搜集材料编书 to compile; to edit:～修 *to compile; to edit* ❷(～儿)妇女梳在头后边的发髻 woman's hair worn in a knot at the nape; bun

钻(鑽) ㊁ zuàn ㄗㄨㄢˋ ❶穿孔洞的用具 drill; auger:～床 *drilling machine; driller*|电～*electrodrill; electric drill*|风～*pneumatic drill; air drill* ❷钻石,即金刚石,硬度很高(i. e. 金刚石) diamond:～戒 *diamond ring*|十七～的手表 *17-jewel watch* ❸义同"钻㊀❶" same as 钻㊀❶ in meaning

㊀ zuān 见 1019 页 see p1019

赚 ㊁ zuàn ㄗㄨㄢˋ 骗 to kid; to deceive; to hoax:～人 *to deceive; to hoax; to fool*

㊀ zhuàn 见 1000 页 see p1000

攥 zuàn ㄗㄨㄢˋ 用手握住 to hold; to grip; to grasp:手里～着一把斧子 *with an axe in one's hand*

ZUI ㄗㄨㄟ

咀 ㊁ zuǐ ㄗㄨㄟˇ "嘴"俗作"咀" popular form for 嘴

㊀ jǔ 见 369 页 see p369

觜 ㊁ zuǐ ㄗㄨㄟˇ 同"嘴" same as 嘴

㊀ zī 见 1008 页 see p1008

嘴 zuǐ ㄗㄨㄟˇ ❶口,人和动物吃东西、发声音的器官 mouth ❷(～子、～儿)形状或作用像嘴的东西 thing shaped or functioning like a mouth:山～*spur*|壶～儿 *spout of a pot* ❸指说话 to talk; to speak:别多～。*Keep your mouth shut.*

最 zuì ㄗㄨㄟˋ ❶副词 ***adverb***,极,无比的 most; -est:～大 *biggest*|～好 *best*|～要紧 *most important* ❷上(大)功 first-rate or superior achievements:殿～(指小功绩和大功绩)(*of political or military achievements in ancient China*) *inferior and superior achievements* ❸居首位的,没有比得上的 in the first place; at the very top:中华之～*best of China; greatest in China*|世界之～*best in the world; best of the world*|以此为～*to take this as the top*

蕞 zuì ㄗㄨㄟˋ 小的样子 small; tiny:～尔小国 *small country; tiny state*

晬 zuì ㄗㄨㄟˋ 婴儿周岁 first birthday of a baby; one full year after a child's birth

醉 zuì ㄗㄨㄟˋ ❶喝酒过多,神志不清 drunk; intoxicated; tipsy:他喝～了。*He's drunk.* ❷沉迷,过分地爱好 to be obsessed with; to be addicted to; to indulge oneself in:～心文学 *to be deeply engrossed in literature* ❸用酒泡制(食品) liquor-saturated:～蟹 *liquor-saturated crab*|～虾 *wine-soaked shrimp*|～枣 *wine-soaked red date*

罪(*辠) zuì ㄗㄨㄟˋ ❶犯法的行为 crime; guilt:犯～to commit a crime ㊟ *extension* 过失 fault; blame:不应该归～于人。*One should not shift the blame to others.* ❷刑罚 penalty:判～*to convict; to declare guilty*|死～*capital offense; death penalty* ❸苦难,痛苦 suffering; pain; hardship:受～*to suffer hardships* ❹把罪过归到某人身上 to blame; to put the blame on:～己 *to bear the blame by oneself*

槜(**檇) zuì ㄗㄨㄟˋ [槜李] **1** 一种李子,果皮鲜红,浆多味甜 a kind of plum of which the scarlet red fruit is juicy and sweet **2** 古地名,在今浙江省嘉兴一带 Zui, an ancient place covering today's Jiaxing, Zhejiang Province and nearby areas

ZUN ㄗㄨㄣ

尊 zūn ㄗㄨㄣ ❶地位或辈分高 senior; noble; of a senior generation:～卑 *seniors and juniors; superiors and inferiors*|～亲 *one's senior relatives*|～长(zhǎng) *elders and betters; elders and seniors* 敬辞 ***polite***:～姓 *your surname*|～著 *your works*|～府 *your residence* [令尊]对对方父亲的尊称 your father ❷敬重 to respect; to revere:～师爱徒 *to respect the master and love the apprentice* ❸量词 ***quantifier***:一～佛像 *a statue of Buddha*|一～大炮 *a cannon* ❹同"樽" same as 樽

遵 zūn ㄗㄨㄣ 依照,按照 to abide by; to obey; to observe:～守纪律 *to observe discipline*|～循着有中国特色的社会主义道路前进 *to follow the cause of socialism with Chinese characteristics*

樽(*罇) zūn ㄗㄨㄣ 古代的盛酒器具(in ancient China) wine vessel

鳟 zūn ㄗㄨㄣ 鳟鱼,体银白色,背略带黑色,肉可以吃 brown trout (*Salmo trutta*)

撙 zǔn ㄗㄨㄣˇ 撙节,从全部财物里节省下一部分 to save part of one's property; to cut down expenses; to retrench

ZUO ㄗㄨㄛ

作 ㊁ zuō ㄗㄨㄛ 作坊(fang),旧时手工业制造或加工的地方(in former times) workshop:油漆～*painter's workshop*|洗衣～*laundry*

㊀ zuò 见1022页 see p1022

嘬 ㊀ zuō ㄗㄨㄛ 聚缩嘴唇吸取 to suck:小孩～奶。*The baby is sucking its mother's breast.*

㊁ chuài 见100页 see p100

昨 zuó ㄗㄨㄛˊ ❶昨天,今天的前一天 yesterday:～夜 *last night* ❷泛指过去 past:觉今是而～非 *I begin to realize that what we did in the past was wrong and what we are*

doing now is right.

笮（**筰）㊀ zuó ㄗㄨㄛˊ 用竹子做成的索 rope woven with bamboo strips［笮桥］用竹索编成的桥 bridge made of bamboo rope; bamboo bridge

㊁ zé 见 945 页 see p945

捽 zuó ㄗㄨㄛˊ〈方 ***dialect***〉揪 to seize; to grasp：～他的头发 *to seize his hair*

琢 ㊁ zuó ㄗㄨㄛˊ［琢磨］(—mo) 反复思索、考虑 to think over; to turn over in one's mind; to ponder：这个问题我～～了很久。*I've been thinking about the problem for a long time.*｜你～～一下，是不是这个理ㄦ。*You'd better think it over and see if it's reasonable.*

㊀ zhuó 见 1007 页 see p1007

左 zuǒ ㄗㄨㄛˇ ❶面向南时靠东的一边，跟"右"相对(the opposite of 右) left：～手 *left hand* ㊕ ***transfer*** 东方(以面向南为准) east：山～*east of a mountain*｜江～*east of a river*［左右］**1** 上下 about; or so：三十岁～～*about thirty years old* **2** 横竖，反正 anyway; anyhow; in any case：～～是要去的，你还是早点去吧。*You'd better set out earlier, as you have to go there anyway.* **3** 身边跟从的人 attendant; retinue **4** 支配，操纵 to control; to manipulate：～～局势 *to have the situation under control* ❷政治思想上属于较激进的或进步的 radical; progressive：～派 *the Left*｜～翼 *Left Wing* ❸斜，偏，错 wrong; incorrect：～脾气 *queer temperament*｜越说越～。*The more you say, the more mistakes you are making.*｜你想～了。*You've got a wrong idea.*｜～道旁门 *heretical sect; heterodoxy; heresy* ❹相反 opposite; contrary：彼此意见相～ *to hold opposite views between the two persons*

佐 zuǒ ㄗㄨㄛˇ(旧读 formerly zuò) ❶辅佐，帮助 to assist; to help：～理 *to assist* ❷辅助别人的人 assistant：僚～ *assistant in a government*［佐证］(*左证)证据 evidence; proof

撮 ㊁ zuǒ ㄗㄨㄛˇ(一子、一ㄦ) 量词 ***quantifier***，用于成丛的毛发(used for hair) tuft：剪下一～子头发 *to cut off a tuft of hair*

㊀ cuō 见 115 页 see p115

作 ㊀ zuò ㄗㄨㄛˋ ❶起，兴起 to rise; to grow：振～精神 *to bestir oneself; to cheer up*｜锣鼓大～。*Gongs and drums sound deafeningly.*｜日出而～ *to begin a day's work at sunrise*｜一鼓～气 *at one fling; at a dash*［作用］功能，使事物发生变化的力量 function; effect：起～～*to be effective*｜带头～～ *to play a leading role* ❷劳作，制造 to work; to make：深耕细～ *deep ploughing and intensive cultivation; intensive and*

meticulous farming｜操～ *to operate* ❸写作 to write; to compose:～文 *to write a composition*｜～画 *to draw a picture*｜～曲 *to compose music*｜吟诗～赋 *to chant poetry and compose rhymed prose* ❹作品，指文学、艺术方面的创作 writings; works:佳～*fine piece of writing; excellent works*｜杰～ *masterpiece* ❺进行某种活动 to engage in an activity:～乱 *to stage an armed rebellion*｜～报告 *to deliver a speech; to make a report*｜向不良倾向～斗争 *to fight against harmful trends*
[作风]人们在工作或行动中表现出来的态度和风格 style; way

㊁ zuō 见 1021 页 see p1021

阼 zuò ㄗㄨㄛˋ 大堂前东面的台阶 eastern flight of steps in front of a hall

岞 zuò ㄗㄨㄛˋ [岞山]地名，在山东省昌邑 Zuoshan, a place in Changyi, Shandong Province

怍 zuò ㄗㄨㄛˋ 惭愧 ashamed (㊟ ***doublet*** 愧 — ashamed)

柞 ㊀ zuò ㄗㄨㄛˋ 柞树，即栎树 (i. e. 栎树) oak (*Quercus*):～蚕 *tussah* (*Antheraea paphia*)｜～丝(柞蚕吐的丝) *tussah silk* 参看 436 页"栎"(lì) see 栎 on p436

㊁ zhà 见 949 页 see p949

胙 zuò ㄗㄨㄛˋ 古代祭祀时供的肉 (in ancient China) sacrificial meat

祚 zuò ㄗㄨㄛˋ ❶福 blessing:门衰～薄。*The family is on the decline and its fortune running out.* ❷皇帝的地位 throne:卒践帝～ *to ascend* (or *mount*) *the throne*

酢 ㊀ zuò ㄗㄨㄛˋ 客人用酒回敬主人(of a guest) to propose a toast to the host

㊁ cù 见 111 页 see p111

坐 zuò ㄗㄨㄛˋ ❶臀部放在椅子等物体上以支持身体 to sit:席地而～*to sit on the floor*｜～在凳子上 *to sit on a stool* ㊂ ***extension*** **1** 乘，搭 to travel by; to take:～车 *to ride on the bus*｜～船 *to go by ship* **2** 坐落 to be situated in; to be located in:房屋～北朝南。*The house faces south.* ❷物体向后施压力 to sink; to subside:房子往后～了。*The house is slanting backward.*｜这枪～力很小。*The gun has little recoil.* ❸把锅、壶等放在炉火上 to put a pan, pot, kettle, etc on a fire:～锅 *to put a pot on a stove*｜～水 *to put a kettle of water on the fire* ❹因 because:～此解职 *to be dismissed on this account* ❺旧指定罪(in former times) to convict:连～(*of kinfolks, neighbours, etc*) *to be punished together with the criminal; to implicate others related to the one charged or found guilty*｜反～*to sentence the accuser to the punishment facing the person he falsely accused* ❻植物结实(of plants) to bear fruit:～果 *to bear fruit*; *to fructify*|～瓜 *to bear melon* ㊀ ***extension*** 形成(疾病) to cause disease; to become ill:打那以后就～下了病 *to have come down with illness since then* ❼自然而然 naturally; spontaneously:孤蓬自振,惊沙～飞。*The solitary bitter fleabane fluttered by itself, while the sand flew when disturbed.* ❽同"座❶" same as 座❶

唑 zuò ㄗㄨㄛˋ 见644页"噻"字条"噻唑"(sāi—) see 噻唑 on p644

座 zuò ㄗㄨㄛˋ ❶(一儿)座位 seat:入～*to take one' seat*|～无虚席 *All seats are occupied*. or *Every seat is taken*. or *There are no empty seats*. [座右铭]写出来放在座位旁边的格言。泛指警戒、激励自己的话 motto; maxim 敬辞 ***polite***,旧时称高级长官(in former times) senior officer:军～*your excellency army commander*|处～ *his excellency section chief* ❷(一子、一儿)托着器物的东西 stand; pedestal; base:钟～儿 *clock stand* ❸星座 constellation:天琴～*Lyra* ❹量词 ***quantifier***:一～山 *a mountain*|三～楼 *three buildings*

做 zuò ㄗㄨㄛˋ ❶干,进行工作或活动 to do; to conduct:～活 *to do manual labour*|～工 *to work*|～买卖 *to do business* ❷写作 to write:～诗 *to write a poem*|～文章 *to write an article* ❸制造 to make; to produce:～制服 *to make a uniform*|甘蔗能～糖。*The sugarcane can produce sugar.* ❹当,为(wéi) to be; to become:～父母的 *as parents*; *being (one's) parents*|～革命事业接班人 *to be successors to the revolutionary cause* ❺装,扮 to pretend; to feign; to affect:～样子 *to make a show*|～好～歹 *to try every possible way to persuade sb or to mediate* [做作]故意装出某种表情或神态 affected; unnatural ❻举行 to hold:～生日 *to celebrate one's birthday* ❼用为 to be used as:芦苇可以～造纸原料。*Reeds can be used as the raw material for paper.*

附录 Appendices

汉语拼音方案

Chinese Phonetic Alphabet

一　字母表

I The Alphabet

字母 Letter 名称 Name	Aa ㄚ	Bb ㄅㄝ	Cc ㄘㄝ	Dd ㄉㄝ	Ee ㄜ	Ff ㄝㄈ	Gg ㄍㄝ
	Hh ㄏㄚ	Ii ㄧ	Jj ㄐㄧㄝ	Kk ㄎㄝ	Ll ㄝㄌ	Mm ㄝㄇ	Nn ㄋㄝ
	Oo ㄛ	Pp ㄆㄝ	Qq ㄑㄧㄡ	Rr ㄚㄦ	Ss ㄝㄙ	Tt ㄊㄝ	
	Uu ㄨ	Vv ㄪㄝ	Ww ㄨㄚ	Xx ㄒㄧ	Yy ㄧㄚ	Zz ㄗㄝ	

v 只用来拼写外来语、少数民族语言和方言。
字母的手写体依照拉丁字母的一般书写习惯。
The letter v is only used in loan words, ethnic minority languages and dialects. The letters are written in the same way as the Latin alphabet.

二　声母表

II The Consonants

b	p	m	f	d	t	n	l
ㄅ玻	ㄆ坡	ㄇ摸	ㄈ佛	ㄉ得	ㄊ特	ㄋ讷	ㄌ勒
g	k	h		j	q	x	
ㄍ哥	ㄎ科	ㄏ喝		ㄐ基	ㄑ欺	ㄒ希	
zh	ch	sh	r	z	c	s	
ㄓ知	ㄔ蚩	ㄕ诗	ㄖ日	ㄗ资	ㄘ雌	ㄙ思	

在给汉字注音的时候，为了使拼式简短，zh ch sh可以省作 ẑ ĉ ŝ。

When phonetic notations are given to Chinese characters, zh, ch and sh can be abbreviated to ẑ, ĉ and ŝ to simplify the spelling.

三 韵母表
III The Vowels

	i 丨 衣	u ㄨ 乌	ü ㄩ 迂
a ㄚ 啊	ia 丨ㄚ 呀	ua ㄨㄚ 蛙	
o ㄛ 喔		uo ㄨㄛ 窝	
e ㄜ 鹅	ie 丨ㄝ 耶		üe ㄩㄝ 约
ai ㄞ 哀		uai ㄨㄞ 歪	
ei ㄟ 欸		uei ㄨㄟ 威	
ao ㄠ 熬	iao 丨ㄠ 腰		
ou ㄡ 欧	iou 丨ㄡ 忧		
an ㄢ 安	ian 丨ㄢ 烟	uan ㄨㄢ 弯	üan ㄩㄢ 冤
en ㄣ 恩	in 丨ㄣ 因	uen ㄨㄣ 温	ün ㄩㄣ 晕
ang ㄤ 昂	iang 丨ㄤ 央	uang ㄨㄤ 汪	
eng ㄥ 亨的韵母	ing 丨ㄥ 英	ueng ㄨㄥ 翁	
ong （ㄨㄥ） 轰的韵母	iong ㄩㄥ 雍		

(1) “知、蚩、诗、日、资、雌、思”等字的韵母用 i。

The vowel *i* is used in the syllables of 知，蚩，诗，日，资，雌，思，etc.

(2) 韵母儿写成 er，用作韵尾的时候写成 r。

The vowel 儿 is written as *er*，but as *r* when used as a tail vowel.

(3) 韵母ㄝ单用的时候写成 ê。

The vowel ㄝ is written as *ê* when used independently.

(4) i 行的韵母，前面没有声母的时候，写成 yi（衣），ya（呀），ye（耶），yao（腰），you（忧），yan（烟），yin（因），yang（央），ying（英），yong（雍）。

The vowels in the *i* row are written as *yi*（衣），*ya*（呀），*ye*（耶），*yao*（腰），*you*（忧），*yan*（烟），*yin*（因），*yang*（央），*ying*（英），*yong*（雍）if no consonants precede them.

u 行的韵母，前面没有声母的时候，写成 wu（乌），wa（蛙），wo（窝），wai（歪），wei（威），wan（弯），wen（温），wang（汪），weng（翁）。

The vowels in the *u* row are written as *wu*（乌），*wa*（蛙），*wo*（窝），*wai*（歪），*wei*（威），*wan*（弯），*wen*（温），*wang*（汪），*weng*（翁）if no consonants precede them.

ü 行的韵母，前面没有声母的时候，写成 yu（迂），yue（约），yuan（冤），yun（晕）。ü 上两点省略。

The vowels in the *ü* row are written as *yu*（迂），*yue*（约），*yuan*（冤），*yun*（晕）if no consonants precede them，and the two dots of *ü* are omitted.

ü 行的韵母跟声母 j，q，x 拼的时候，写成 ju（居），qu（区），xu（虚），ü 上两点也省略；但是跟声母 l，n 拼的时候，仍然写成 lü（吕），nü（女）。

When the vowels in the *ü* row are used together with the consonants of *j*，*q* and *x*，they are written as *ju*（居），*qu*（区），*xu*（虚），with the two dots of *ü* being omitted. When they are used together with the consonants of *l* and *n*，the two dots of *ü* are retained as in *lü*（吕）and *nü*（女）.

(5) iou，uei，uen 前面加声母的时候，写成 iu，ui，un。例如 niu（牛），gui（归），lun（论）。

When *iou*, *uei* and *uen* are preceded by consonants, they are written as *iu*, *ui* and *un*, such as in *niu*（牛）, *gui*（归）and *lun*（论）.

（6）在给汉字注音的时候，为了使拼式简短，ng 可以省作 ŋ。
When phonetic notations are added to Chinese characters, *ng* may be abbreviated to ŋ to simplify the spelling.

四　声调符号
IV The Symbols of Tones

阴平 high and level tone ˉ	阳平 rising tone ˊ
上声 falling-rising tone ˇ	去声 falling tone ˋ

声调符号标在音节的主要母音上，轻声不标。例如：
The symbol of each tone is marked on the main vowel of a syllable, but it is omitted when the pronunciation is light. For example:

妈 mā	麻 má	马 mǎ	骂 mà	吗 ma
（阴平）	（阳平）	（上声）	（去声）	（轻声）

五　隔音符号
V The Syllable-Dividing Mark

a，o，e 开头的音节连接在其他音节后面的时候，如果音节的界限发生混淆，用隔音符号（'）隔开，例如：pi'ao（皮袄）。

When a syllable beginning with *a*, *o*, *e* follows another syllable, and the boundary of the two syllables are confusing, the syllable-dividing mark (') is used to separate then, i. e. *pi'ao*（皮袄）.

常用标点符号用法简表*

Table for the Use of Punctuation Marks

一　基本定义 Basic Definitions

句子：前后都有停顿，并带有一定的句调，表示相对完整意义的语言单位。

Sentence: a tonal linguistic unit, with a pause before and after it, which conveys a relatively complete meaning.

陈述句：用来说明事实的句子。

Declarative sentence: a sentence that is used to state a fact.

祈使句：用来要求听话人做某件事情的句子。

Imperative sentence: a sentence that is used to request the hearer to do something.

疑问句：用来提出问题的句子。

Interrogative sentence: a sentence that is used to raise a question.

感叹句：用来抒发某种强烈感情的句子。

Exclamatory sentence: a sentence that is used to express some strong emotion.

复句、分句：意思上有密切联系的小句子组织在一起构成一个大句子。这样的大句子叫复句，复句中的每个小句子叫分句。

Composite sentence and clause: A composite sentence is a big sentence formed from small sentences that are closely related in meaning. Each of those small sentences is called a clause.

词语：词和短语（词组）。词，即最小的能独立运用的语言单位。短语，即由两个或两个以上的词按一定的语法规则组成的表达一定意义的语言单位，也叫词组。

Word and phrase (word group): A word is a minimum linguistic unit that can be used independently. A phrase (word

---

* 本表参考了中华人民共和国国家标准《标点符号用法》。

This table refers to the National Standard Use of Punctuation Marks of the People's Republic of China.

group) is a linguistic unit that is formed from two or more words and conveys certain meaning.

二 用法简表 Table of Uses

名称 Name	符号 Mark	用法说明 Use	举 例 Example
句号① Period	。	1. 用于陈述句的末尾。 Used at the end of a declarative sentence.	北京是中华人民共和国的首都。 Beijing is the capital of the People's Republic of China.
		2. 用于语气舒缓的祈使句末尾。 Used at the end of a mildly imperative sentence.	请您稍等一下。 Wait a moment, please.
问号 Question mark	?	1. 用于疑问句的末尾。 Used at the end of an interrogative sentence.	他叫什么名字? What's his name?
		2. 用于反问句的末尾。 Used at the end of a rhetorical sentence.	难道你还不了解我吗? Don't you understand me?
叹号 Exclamation mark	!	1. 用于感叹句的末尾。 Used at the end of an exclamatory sentence.	为祖国的繁荣昌盛而奋斗! Struggle for the thriving and prosperity of our motherland!
		2. 用于语气强烈的祈使句末尾。 Used at the end of a strong imperative sentence.	停止射击! Stop shooting!
		3. 用于语气强烈的反问句末尾。 Used at the end of a strong rhetorical sentence.	我哪里比得上他呀! How could I match him!

名称 Name	符号 Mark	用法说明 Use	举 例 Example
逗号 Comma	，	1. 句子内部主语与谓语之间如需停顿，用逗号。 Used when a pause is needed between the subject and its predicate in a sentence.	我们看得见的星星，绝大多数是恒星。 Most of the stars we see are fixed stars.
		2. 句子内部动词与宾语之间如需停顿，用逗号。 Used when a pause is needed between the verb and its object in a sentence.	应该看到，科学需要一个人贡献出毕生的精力。 We should know that scientific research needs a person's lifelong devotion.
		3. 句子内部状语后边如需停顿，用逗号。 Used when a pause is needed after an adverbial in a sentence.	对于这个城市，他并不陌生。 He is not unfamiliar with this city.
		4. 复句内各分句之间的停顿，除了有时要用分号外，都要用逗号。 Used for pauses between the clauses in a composite sentence except where the semicolon is required occasionally.	据说苏州园林有一百多处，我到过的不过十多处。 It is said that there are more than 100 gardens in Suzhou, but I have only visited over a dozen.
顿号 Slight-pause mark	、	用于句子内部并列词语之间的停顿。 Used for pauses between parallel words or phrases.	正方形是四边相等、四角均为直角的四边形。 A square is a quadrilateral with equal side lines and four right angles.

名称 Name	符号 Mark	用法说明 Use	举　例 Example
分号② Semi-colon	；	1. 用于复句内部并列分句之间的停顿。 Used for pauses between parallel clauses in a composite sentence.	语言，人们用来抒情达意；文字，人们用来记言记事。 Speech is used to express emotions and ideas while writing is used to record words and events.
		2. 用于分行列举的各项之间。 Used for items listed in separate lines.	中华人民共和国的行政区域划分如下： （一）全国分为省、自治区、直辖市； （二）省、自治区分为自治州、县、自治县、市； （三）县、自治县分为乡、民族乡、镇。 The administrative division of the People's Republic of China is as follows: (1) The country is divided into provinces, autonomous regions and municipalities directly under the Central Government; (2) Provinces and autonomous regions are divided into autonomous prefectures, counties, autonomous counties and cities; (3) Counties and autonomous counties are divided into townships, nationality townships and towns.

名称 Name	符号 Mark	用法说明 Use	举 例 Example
冒号 Colon	：	1. 用于称呼语后边，表示提起下文。 Used for a term of address to introduce what follows.	同志们，朋友们：现在开会了…… Comrades and friends, now the meeting begins ...
		2. 用于"说、想、是、证明、宣布、指出、透露、例如、如下"等词语后边，表示提起下文。 Used after such words or phrases as "说，想，是，证明，宣布，指出，透露，例如，如下，" etc. to introduce what follows.	他十分惊讶地说："啊，原来是你！" He says in great surprise: "Oh, it's you!"
		3. 用于总说性话语的后边，表示引起下文的分说。 Used after a summary expression to introduce a list of items.	北京紫禁城有四座城门：午门、神武门、东华门和西华门。 There are four gates in the Forbidden City of Beijing: *Wumen* Gate, *Shenwu* Gate, *Donghua* Gate and *Xihua* Gate.
		4. 用于需要解释的词语后边，表示引出解释或说明。 Used after a word or phrase that needs explanation or illustration.	外文图书展销会 日期：10 月 20 日至 11 月 10 日 时间：上午 8 时至下午 4 时 地点：北京朝阳区工体东路 16 号 主办单位：中国图书进出口总公司

名称 Name	符号 Mark	用法说明 Use	举 例 Example
冒号 Colon	：		Foreign Language Book Fair Dates：Oct. 20-Nov. 10 Time：8：00 a.m.-4：00 p.m. Location：16 East Gongti Road，Chaoyang District，Beijing Sponsor：China National Publications Import & Export（Group）Corporation
		5. 用于总括性话语的前边，以总结上文。 Used for a summarizing expression to sum up what has been discussed in the proceeding text.	张华考上了北京大学；李萍进了中等技术学校；我在百货公司当售货员：我们都有光明的前途。 Zhang Hua has been admitted into Beijing University，Li Ping is now attending a secondary technical school，and I have become a salesman in a department store. All of us have a bright future.
引号③ Quotation marks	“ ” ‘ ’	1. 用于行文中直接引用的部分。 Used for quotations in a text.	“满招损，谦受益”这句格言，流传到今天至少有两千年了。 The dictum “complacency spells loss，while modesty brings benefits” has been circulating for at least 2000 years.

名称 Name	符号 Mark	用法说明 Use	举 例 Example
引号③ Quotation marks	“ ” ‘ ’	2. 用于需要着重论述的对象。 Used for what needs to be emphasized in a discussion.	古人对于写文章有个基本要求，叫作“有物有序”。“有物”就是要有内容，“有序”就是要有条理。 There has been a basic requirement from the ancient times on how to write an article — “to have substance and be arranged in good order.” The former means that the article should have content while the latter means that the article should be well-organized.
		3. 用于具有特殊含义的词语。 Used for words or phrases with implied meaning.	这样的“聪明人”还是少一点好。 It is better to have fewer “wise persons” like these.
		4. 引号里面还要用引号时，外面一层用双引号，里面一层用单引号。 When quotation marks are embedded in quotation marks, single quotation marks are used for the embedded ones and double quotation marks for the embedding ones.	他站起来问：“老师，‘有条不紊’的‘紊’是什么意思？” He stands up and asks, “Professor, what does ‘紊’ in the idiom ‘有条不紊’ mean?”

名称 Name	符号 Mark	用法说明 Use	举 例 Example
括号④ Paren-theses	（ ）	用于行文中注释性的部分。注释句子中某些词语的，括注紧贴在被注释词语之后；注释整个句子的，括注放在句末标点之后。 Used for an annotation in a text. If the annotation in parentheses is applied to words or phrases, it is placed immediately after them; but if it is applied to a whole sentence, it is placed after the final punctuation mark of the sentence.	(1)中国猿人（全名为"中国猿人北京种"，或简称"北京人"）在我国的发现，是对古人类学的一个重大贡献。 The discovery of Chinese ape-men ("Beijing species of Chinese ape-men" for the full name or "Beijing men" for short) in our country is a great contribution to palaeoanthropology. (2)写研究性文章跟文学创作不同，不能摊开稿纸搞"即兴"。（其实文学创作也要有素养才能有"即兴"。） The research article writing, different from literary creation, is not to be done in an improvisational way. (In fact literary creation also depends on cultural attainment for "improvisation".)
破折号 Dash	——	1. 用于行文中解释说明的部分。 Used to introduce an explanation in a text.	迈进金黄色的大门，穿过宽阔的风门厅和衣帽厅，就到了大会堂建筑的枢纽部分——中央大厅。 Stepping into the great golden gate and passing through the lobby and the cloakroom, we came to the main quarters of the Great Hall of the People — the central hall.

名称 Name	符号 Mark	用法说明 Use	举例 Example
		2. 用于话题突然转变。Used for a sudden turn of topic.	"今天好热啊！——你什么时候去上海？"张强对刚刚进门的小王说。"How hot it is today! —When are you going to Shanghai?" Zhang Qiang said to Xiao Wang who had just entered the room.
		3. 用于声音延长的拟声词后面。Used after a prolonged onomatopoeic word.	"呜——"火车开动了。The train sets off with a "hoot—".
破折号 Dash	——	4. 用于事项列举分承的各项之前。Used before each of a list of items.	根据研究对象的不同，环境物理学分为以下五个分支学科： ——环境声学； ——环境光学； ——环境热学； ——环境电磁学； ——环境空气动力学。 According to the differences of its study objects, environmental physics is classified into five branches: —environmental acoustics —environmental optics —environmental thermodynamics —environmental electromagnetics —environmental aerodynamics.

名称 Name	符号 Mark	用法说明 Use	举　例 Example
省略号⑤ Ellipsis	……	1. 用于引文的省略。 Used for omissions in a quotation.	她轻轻地哼起了《摇篮曲》:"月儿明,风儿静,树叶儿遮窗棂啊……" "Bright is the moonlight, gentle is the wind, and shelter are the tree leaves ... " she hummed The Cradle Song.
		2. 用于列举的省略。 Used for omissions in listed items.	在广州的花市上,牡丹、吊钟、水仙、梅花、菊花、山茶、墨兰……春秋冬三季的鲜花都挤在一起啦! In the Guangzhou Flower Fair, there are peonies, bellflowers, narcissi, Chinese plum flowers, chrysanthemums, camellias, dark orchids ... . All the fresh flowers in spring, autumn and winter are displayed there.
		3. 用于话语中间,表示说话断断续续。 Used in a speech to indicate intermittence.	"我……对不起……大家,我……没有……完成……任务。" "I am sorry ... to all of you ... I have failed to ... fulfill ... my task. "
着重号 Emphasis mark	.	用于要求读者特别注意的字、词、句的下面。 Used under the Chinese characters, phrases or sentences to which the special attention is required of the readers.	事业是干出来的,不是吹出来的。 Your achievement in the cause lies in working hard, not in bragging.

名称 Name	符号 Mark	用法说明 Use	举　例 Example
连接号⑥ Hyphen	—	1. 两个相关的名词构成一个意义单位，中间用连接号。 Used between two related nouns to constitute a semantic unit.	我国秦岭—淮河以北地区属于温带季风气候区，夏季高温多雨，冬季寒冷干燥。 The North of Mount Qinling-Huaihe River is an area of temperate monsoon. It is hot and rainy in summer, and cold and dry in winter.
		2. 相关的时间、地点或数目之间用连接号，表示起止。 Used between related times, places, or numbers to indicate the beginning and the ending.	鲁迅(1881—1936)原名周树人，字豫才，浙江绍兴人。 Lu Xun (1881-1936), with the original name of Zhou Shuren and the style name of Yucai, was from Shaoxing County, Zhejiang Province.
		3. 相关的字母、阿拉伯数字等之间，用连接号，表示产品型号。 Used between related letters, Arabic numerals, etc. to indicate product model.	在太平洋地区，除了已建成投入使用的 HAW—4 和 TPC—3 海底光缆之外，又有 TPC—4 海底光缆投入运营。 In the Pacific Region, the optical cable TPC-4 has become operational in addition to HAW-4 and TPC-3.

名称 Name	符号 Mark	用法说明 Use	举　例 Example
连接号⑥ Hyphen	—	4. 几个相关的项目表示递进式发展,中间用连接号。 Used between related items to indicate progressive development.	人类的发展可以分为古猿—猿人—古人—新人这四个阶段。 The evolution of mankind can be divided into four stages: Aegyptopithecus, Pithecanthropus, Palaeoanthropus and Neoanthropus.
间隔号 Separation dot	·	1. 用于外国人和某些少数民族人名内各部分的分界。 Used to separate the different parts of the name of a foreigner or a person from certain minority ethnic group.	列奥纳多·达·芬奇 Leonardo da Vinci 爱新觉罗·努尔哈赤 Aisin Gioro Nurhachi
		2. 用于书名与篇(章、卷)名之间的分界。 Used to separate the title of a book and its chapter or volume.	《中国大百科全书·物理学》 Encyclopedia of China, Vol. Physics 《三国志·蜀书·诸葛亮传》 History of Three Kingdoms, History of Shuhan, A Biography of Zhuge Liang

名称 **Name**	符号 **Mark**	用法说明 **Use**	举 例 **Example**
书名号 Double angle brackets	《 》 〈 〉	用于书名、篇名、报纸名、刊物名等。 Used to enclose the title of a book, an article, a newspaper, a journal, etc.	(1)《红楼梦》的作者是曹雪芹。 The author of A Dream of Red Mansions is Cao Xueqin. (2)课文里有一篇鲁迅的《从百草园到三味书屋》。 In the textbook, there is an article entitled From the Garden of a Hundred Kinds of Grasses to Sanwei Study by Lu Xun. (3)他的文章在《人民日报》上发表了。 His article has been published in the People's Daily. (4)桌上放着一本《中国语文》。 There is a copy of Chinese Language and Writing on the desk. (5)《〈中国工人〉发刊词》发表于1940年2月7日。 Opening Remarks to *Chinese Workers* was published on Feb. 7th, 1940.
专名号⑦ Proper noun mark	——	用于人名、地名、朝代名等专名下面。 Used to underline the names of a person, place, dynasty, etc.	司马相如者,汉蜀郡成都人也,字长卿。 Sima Xiangru, with the style name of Changqing, was from Chengdu, Shu Prefecture, in the Han Dynasty.

附注 Notes：

① 句号还有一种形式，即一个小圆点“.”，一般在科技文献中使用。
Another form of full stop is a small dot “.”, which is usually used in scientific and technological writings.

② 非并列关系（如转折关系、因果关系等）的多重复句，第一层的前后两部分之间，也用分号。
The semicolon is also used between the two first-level clauses of a complex sentence (to express transition, cause-and-effect, etc.).

③ 直行文稿引号改用双引号“﹃﹄”和单引号“﹁﹂”。
The double quotation marks “﹃﹄” and single quotation marks “﹁﹂” are used in vertically written or printed text.

④ 此外还有方括号“[ ]”、六角括号“〔 〕”和方头括号“【 】”。
In addition, there are square brackets “[ ]”, hexagon brackets “〔 〕”, and square-head brackets “【 】”.

⑤ 如果是整段文章或诗行的省略，可以使用十二个小圆点来表示。
Twelve small dots (…………) can be used to indicate omission of whole paragraphs of a text or omission of whole lines of a poem.

⑥ 连接号另外还有三种形式，即长横“——”（占两个字的位置）、半字线“-”（占半个字的位置）和浪纹“～”（占一个字的位置）。
The hyphen has three more variants, i.e. a long horizontal line “——” (occupying a two-character space), a half-character line “-” (occupying a half-character space), a wavy line “～” (occupying a one-character space).

⑦ 专名号只用在古籍或某些文史著作里面。为了跟专名号配合，这类著作里的书名号可以用浪线“﹏﹏”。
The proper noun mark is only used in ancient books and certain literary and historical books. To go with the proper noun marks the wavy line “﹏﹏” can be used for double angle brackets in such books.

我国历史朝代公元对照简表

Dynastic Chronology of Chinese History

<table>
<tr><td colspan="2">夏 Xia Dynasty</td><td>约前 2070—前 1600
Around 2070 BC—1600 BC</td></tr>
<tr><td colspan="2">商 Shang Dynasty</td><td>前 1600—前 1046
1600 BC—1046 BC</td></tr>
<tr><td rowspan="2">周
Zhou
Dynasty</td><td>西周Western Zhou Dynasty</td><td>前 1046—前 771
1046 BC—771 BC</td></tr>
<tr><td>东周Eastern Zhou Dynasty
春秋时代 Spring and Autumn Period
战国时代 Warring States Period ①</td><td>前 770—前 256
770 BC—256 BC
前 770—前 476
770 BC—476 BC
前 475—前 221
475 BC—221 BC</td></tr>
<tr><td colspan="2">秦 Qin Dynasty</td><td>前 221—前 206
221 BC—206 BC</td></tr>
<tr><td rowspan="2">汉
Han
Dynasty</td><td>西汉Western Han Dynasty ②</td><td>前 206—公元 23
206 BC—23 AD</td></tr>
<tr><td>东汉Eastern Han Dynasty</td><td>25—220</td></tr>
<tr><td rowspan="3">三国 Three Kingdoms</td><td>魏 Kingdom of Wei</td><td>220—265</td></tr>
<tr><td>蜀 Kingdom of Shu</td><td>221—263</td></tr>
<tr><td>吴 Kingdom of Wu</td><td>222—280</td></tr>
<tr><td colspan="2">西晋 Western Jin Dynasty</td><td>265—316</td></tr>
<tr><td rowspan="2">东晋 Eastern Jin
十六国 Sixteen States</td><td>东晋 Eastern Jin Dynasty</td><td>317—420</td></tr>
<tr><td>十六国 Sixteen States Periods ③</td><td>304—439</td></tr>
</table>

<table>
<tr><td rowspan="9">南北朝
Southern and Northern Dynasties</td><td rowspan="4">南朝
Southern Dynasties</td><td>宋 Song Dynasty</td><td>420—479</td></tr>
<tr><td>齐 Qi Dynasty</td><td>479—502</td></tr>
<tr><td>梁 Liang Dynasty</td><td>502—557</td></tr>
<tr><td>陈 Chen Dynasty</td><td>557—589</td></tr>
<tr><td rowspan="5">北朝
Northern Dynasties</td><td>北魏 Northern Wei Dynasty</td><td>386—534</td></tr>
<tr><td>东魏 Eastern Wei Dynasty</td><td>534—550</td></tr>
<tr><td>北齐 Northern Qi Dynasty</td><td>550—577</td></tr>
<tr><td>西魏 Western Wei Dynasty</td><td>535—556</td></tr>
<tr><td>北周 Northern Zhou Dynasty</td><td>557—581</td></tr>
<tr><td colspan="3">隋 Sui Dynasty</td><td>581—618</td></tr>
<tr><td colspan="3">唐 Tang Dynasty</td><td>618—907</td></tr>
<tr><td rowspan="6">五代十国
Five Dynasties Ten States Periods</td><td colspan="2">后梁 Later Liang Dynasty</td><td>907—923</td></tr>
<tr><td colspan="2">后唐 Later Tang Dynasty</td><td>923—936</td></tr>
<tr><td colspan="2">后晋 Later Jin Dynasty</td><td>936—947</td></tr>
<tr><td colspan="2">后汉 Later Han Dynasty</td><td>947—950</td></tr>
<tr><td colspan="2">后周 Later Zhou Dynasty</td><td>951—960</td></tr>
<tr><td colspan="2">十国 Ten States Periods ④</td><td>902—979</td></tr>
<tr><td rowspan="2">宋 Song Dynasty</td><td colspan="2">北宋 Northern Song Dynasty</td><td>960—1127</td></tr>
<tr><td colspan="2">南宋 Southern Song Dynasty</td><td>1127—1279</td></tr>
<tr><td colspan="3">辽 Liao Dynasty</td><td>907—1125 ⑤</td></tr>
<tr><td colspan="3">西夏 Western Xia Dynasty</td><td>1038—1227</td></tr>
<tr><td colspan="3">金 Jin Dynasty</td><td>1115—1234</td></tr>
<tr><td colspan="3">元 Yuan Dynasty</td><td>1206—1368 ⑥</td></tr>
<tr><td colspan="3">明 Ming Dynasty</td><td>1368—1644</td></tr>
<tr><td colspan="3">清 Qing Dynasty</td><td>1616—1911</td></tr>
<tr><td colspan="3">中华民国 Republic of China</td><td>1912—1949</td></tr>
<tr><td colspan="4">中华人民共和国 1949 年 10 月 1 日成立
Founding of the People's Republic of China on October 1, 1949</td></tr>
</table>

附注 Notes：

① 这时期，主要有秦、魏、韩、赵、楚、燕、齐等国。
In this period，the main states are Qin，Wei，Han，Zhao，Chu，Yan，Qi，etc.

② 包括王莽建立的“新”王朝（公元 8 年—23 年）。王莽时期，爆发大规模的农民起义，建立了农民政权。公元 23 年，新莽王朝灭亡。公元 25 年，东汉王朝建立。
This period includes the “New” Dynasty（8－23）established by Wang Mang. Under Wang Mang's reign，a large-scale peasant uprising broke up and a peasant regime was established. In 23 AD，the new Dynasty of Wang Mang was overthrown. In 25 AD，Eastern Han Dynasty was established.

③ 这时期，在我国北方和巴蜀，先后存在过一些封建割据政权，其中有：汉（前赵）、成（成汉）、前凉、后赵（魏）、前燕、前秦、后燕、后秦、西秦、后凉、南凉、南燕、西凉、北凉、北燕、夏等国，历史上叫作“十六国”。
In this period，some feudal separatist regimes existed consecutively in the north and Bashu regions of China. Among them are Han（Former Zhao），Cheng（Cheng Han），Former Liang，Later Zhao（Wei），Former Yan，Former Qin，Later Yan，Later Qin，Western Qin，Later Liang，Southern Liang，Southern Yan，Western Liang，Northern Liang，Northern Yan，Xia etc. In history，these states are called “the Sixteen States”.

④ 这时期，除后梁、后唐、后晋、后汉、后周外，还先后存在过一些封建割据政权，其中有：吴、前蜀、吴越、楚、闽、南汉、荆南（南平）、后蜀、南唐、北汉等国，历史上叫作“十国”。
In this period，besides Later Liang，Later Tang，Later Jin，Later Han and Later Zhou，there were other feudal separatist regimes. They were Wu，Former Shu，Wu Yue，Chu，Min，Southern Han，Jing Nan（Nan Ping），Later Shu，Southern Tang，Northern Han，etc. In history，they are called “the Ten States”.

⑤ 辽建国于公元 907 年，国号契丹，916 年始建年号，938 年（一说 947 年）改国号为辽，983 年复称契丹，1066 年仍称辽。
The Liao Dynasty was known as the Qidan Kingdom when it was first established in 907. The dynasty began to use a

reign title in 916 and renamed itself Liao in 938 (or 947 according to another source), but it resumed the name of Qidan in 983, before changing back to Liao in 1066.

⑥ 铁木真于公元 1206 年建国;公元 1271 年忽必烈定国号为元,1279 年灭南宋。

Temuzin, a Mongol general, founded a kingdom in 1206. Kublai Khan renamed the kingdom Yuan in 1271, and overthrew the Southern Song Dynasty in 1279.

我国少数民族简表

Table of Ethnic Minorities in China

我国是一个统一的多民族的社会主义国家，由 56 个民族组成。除汉族外，有 55 个少数民族，约占全国总人口的 8%。

China is a unified, multi-ethnic, socialist country, which is made up of 56 ethnic groups. Other than Hans, there are 55 ethnic minorities, accounting for about 8% of the entire population in China.

民族名称 Names of Ethnic Groups	**主要分布地区 Main Distribution Areas**
蒙古族 Mongol	内蒙古、辽宁、新疆、黑龙江、吉林、青海、甘肃、河北、河南等地 Inner Mongolia, Liaoning, Xinjiang, Heilongjiang, Jilin, Qinghai, Gansu, Hebei, Henan, etc.
回族 Hui	宁夏、甘肃、河南、新疆、青海、云南、河北、山东、安徽、辽宁、北京、内蒙古、天津、黑龙江、陕西、吉林、江苏、贵州等地 Ningxia, Gansu, Henan, Xinjiang, Qinghai, Yunnan, Hebei, Shandong, Anhui, Liaoning, Beijing, Inner Mongolia, Tianjin, Heilongjiang, Shaanxi, Jilin, Jiangsu, Guizhou, etc.
藏族 Tibetan	西藏及四川、青海、甘肃、云南等地 Tibet, Sichuan, Qinghai, Gansu, Yunnan, etc.
维吾尔族 Uygur	新疆 Xinjiang
苗族 Miao	贵州、云南、湖南、重庆、广西、四川、海南、湖北等地 Guizhou, Yunnan, Hunan, Chongqing, Guangxi, Sichuan, Hainan, Hubei, etc.

民族名称 Names of Ethnic Groups	主要分布地区 Main Distribution Areas
彝族 Yi	云南、四川、贵州、广西等地 Yunnan, Sichuan, Guizhou, Guangxi, etc.
壮族 Zhuang	广西及云南、广东、贵州、湖南等地 Guangxi, Yunnan, Guangdong, Guizhou, Hunan, etc.
布依族 Bouyei	贵州 Guizhou
朝鲜族 Korean	吉林、黑龙江、辽宁等地 Jilin, Heilongjiang, Liaoning, etc.
满族 Manchu	辽宁及黑龙江、吉林、河北、内蒙古、北京等地 Liaoning, Heilongjiang, Jilin, Hebei, Inner Mongolia, Beijing, etc.
侗族 Dong	贵州、湖南、广西等地 Guizhou, Hunan, Guangxi, etc.
瑶族 Yao	广西、湖南、云南、广东、贵州等地 Guangxi, Hunan, Yunnan, Guangdong, Guizhou, etc.
白族 Bai	云南、贵州、湖南等地 Yunnan, Guizhou, Hunan, etc.
土家族 Tujia	湖北、湖南、重庆等地 Hubei, Hunan, Chongqing, etc.
哈尼族 Hani	云南 Yunnan
哈萨克族 Kazak	新疆、甘肃、青海等地 Xinjiang, Gansu, Qinghai, etc.
傣族 Dai	云南 Yunnan
黎族 Li	海南 Hainan
傈僳族 Lisu	云南、四川等地 Yunnan, Sichuan, etc.
佤族 Va	云南 Yunnan
畲族 She	福建、浙江、江西、广东等地 Fujian, Zhejiang, Jiangxi, Guangdong, etc.
高山族 Gaoshan	台湾及福建 Taiwan, Fujian

民族名称 Names of Ethnic Groups	主要分布地区 Main Distribution Areas
拉祜族 Lahu	云南 Yunnan
水族 Sui	贵州、广西 Guizhou，Guangxi
东乡族 Dongxiang	甘肃、新疆 Gansu，Xinjiang
纳西族 Naxi	云南、四川 Yunnan，Sichuan
景颇族 Jingpo	云南 Yunnan
柯尔克孜族 Kirgiz	新疆、黑龙江 Xinjiang，Heilongjiang
土族 Tu	青海、甘肃 Qinhai，Gansu
达斡尔族 Daur	内蒙古、黑龙江、新疆等地 Inner Mongolia，Heilongjiang，Xinjiang，etc.
仫佬族 Mulam	广西 Guangxi
羌族 Qiang	四川 Sichuan
布朗族 Blang	云南 Yunnan
撒拉族 Salar	青海、甘肃等地 Qinhai，Gansu，etc.
毛南族 Maonan	广西 Guangxi
仡佬族 Gelao	贵州、广西 Guizhou，Guangxi
锡伯族 Xibe	辽宁、新疆、吉林、黑龙江等地 Liaoning，Xinjiang，Jilin，Heilongjiang，etc.
阿昌族 Achang	云南 Yunnan
塔吉克族 Tajik	新疆 Xinjiang
普米族 Primi	云南 Yunnan
怒族 Nu	云南 Yunnan
乌孜别克族 Uzbek	新疆 Xinjiang
俄罗斯族 Russian	新疆、黑龙江 Xinjiang，Heilongjiang
鄂温克族 Ewenki	内蒙古和黑龙江 Inner Mongolia，Heilongjiang
德昂族 De'ang	云南 Yunnan
保安族 Bonan	甘肃 Gansu
裕固族 Yugur	甘肃 Gansu
京族 Gin	广西 Guangxi
塔塔尔族 Tatar	新疆 Xinjiang

民族名称 Names of Ethnic Groups	主要分布地区 Main Distribution Areas
独龙族 Derung	云南 Yunnan
鄂伦春族 Oroqen	内蒙古和黑龙江 Inner Mongolia，Heilongjiang
赫哲族 Hezhen	黑龙江 Heilongjiang
门巴族 Monba	西藏 Tibet
珞巴族 Lhoba	西藏 Tibet
基诺族 Jino	云南 Yunnan

我国各省、直辖市、自治区及省会(或首府)名称表

Table of Provinces, Municipalities, Autonomous Regions and Provincial Capitals in China

(按汉语拼音字母顺序排列)

(Arranged in Chinese phonetic alphabetical order)

省、市、自治区名 Province, Municipality, Autonomous Region	简称(或别称) Alternative Name	省会(或首府)名 Provincial Capital
安徽 Anhui	(皖)Wan	合肥 Hefei
北京 Beijing	京 Jing	
重庆 Chongqing	(渝)Yu	
福建 Fujian	(闽)Min	福州 Fuzhou
甘肃 Gansu	甘(陇)Gan (Long)	兰州 Lanzhou
广东 Guangdong	(粤)Yue	广州 Guangzhou
广西 Guangxi	(桂)Gui	南宁 Nanning
贵州 Guizhou	贵(黔)Gui (Qian)	贵阳 Guiyang
海南 Hainan	(琼)Qiong	海口 Haikou
河北 Hebei	(冀)Ji	石家庄 Shijiazhuang
河南 Henan	(豫)Yu	郑州 Zhengzhou
黑龙江 Heilongjiang	黑 Hei	哈尔滨 Harbin
湖北 Hubei	(鄂)E	武汉 Wuhan
湖南 Hunan	(湘)Xiang	长沙 Changsha
吉林 Jilin	吉 Ji	长春 Changchun

省、市、自治区名 Province, Municipality, Autonomous Region	简称(或别称) Alternative Name	省会(或首府)名 Provincial Capital
江苏 Jiangsu	苏 Su	南京 Nanjing
江西 Jiangxi	(赣)Gan	南昌 Nanchang
辽宁 Liaoning	辽 Liao	沈阳 Shenyang
内蒙古 Inner Mongolia	蒙 Meng	呼和浩特 Huhehaote
宁夏 Ningxia	宁 Ning	银川 Yinchuan
青海 Qinghai	青 Qing	西宁 Xining
山东 Shandong	(鲁)Lu	济南 Jinan
山西 Shanxi	(晋)Jin	太原 Taiyuan
陕西 Shaanxi	陕(秦)Shaan (Qin)	西安 Xi'an
上海 Shanghai	(沪)(申)Hu (Shen)	
四川 Sichuan	川(蜀)Chuan (Shu)	成都 Chengdu
台湾 Taiwan	台 Tai	台北 Taibei
天津 Tianjin	津 Jin	
西藏 Tibet	藏 Zang	拉萨 Lasa
新疆 Xinjiang	新 Xin	乌鲁木齐 Urumqi
云南 Yunnan	云(滇)Yun (Dian)	昆明 Kunming
浙江 Zhejiang	浙 Zhe	杭州 Hangzhou
香港 Hongkong (特别行政区 Special Administrative Region)	港 Gang	
澳门 Macao (特别行政区 Special Administrative Region)	澳 Ao	

世界各国和地区面积、人口、首都(或首府)一览表*

Table of Area, Population and Capitals for Countries and Regions Worldwide

国家或地区 Country / Region	面积(平方公里) Area (square kilometers)	人口(单位:千人) Population (unit: thousand)	首都(或首府) Capital
	亚洲 Asia		
中国 China (the People's Republic of China)	约 approx 9600000	1295330 ①	北京 Beijing
蒙古 Mongolia (the State of Mongolia)	1566500	2381	乌兰巴托 Ulan Bator
朝鲜 North Korea (the Democratic People's Republic of Korea)	122762	22114	平壤 Pyongyang
韩国 South Korea (the Republic of Korea)	99600	48293	首尔 Seoul
日本 Japan	377800	127310	东京 Tokyo

* 本资料主要依据 2002/2003《世界知识年鉴》(世界知识出版社,2003)整理。

This is mainly based on *The World Factbook* 2002/2003 by World Affairs Press, 2003.

老挝 Lao (the Lao People's Democratic Republic)	236800	5090	万象 Vientiane
越南 Vietnam (the Socialist Republic of Vietnam)	329556	77680	河内 Hanoi
柬埔寨 Cambodia (the Kingdom of Cambodia)	181035	11430	金边 Phnom Penh
缅甸 Myanmar (the Union of Myanmar)	676581	52000	仰光 Yangon
泰国 Thailand (the Kingdom of Thailand)	513115	62580	曼谷 Bangkok
马来西亚 Malaysia	329735	23275	吉隆坡 Kuala Lumpur
新加坡 Singapore (the Republic of Singapore)	683	3263	新加坡 Singapore City
文莱 Brunei (Negara Brunei Darussalam)	5765	345	斯里巴加湾市 Bandar Seri Begawan
菲律宾 Philippines (the Republic of the Philippines)	300000	80080	大马尼拉市 Manila
印度尼西亚 Indonesia (the Republic of Indonesia)	1904443	210000	雅加达 Jakarta
东帝汶 East Timor (the Democratic Republic of East Timor)	14874	742	帝力 Dili

尼泊尔 Nepal (the Kingdom of Nepal)	147181	23000	加德满都 Kathman-du
不丹 Bhutan (the Kingdom of Bhutan)	46000	782	廷布 Thimphu
孟加拉国 Bangladesh (the People's Republic of Bangladesh)	147570	129000	达卡 Dhaka
印度 India (the Republic of India)	约 approx 2980000	1020000	新德里 New Delhi
斯里兰卡 Sri Lanka (the Democratic Socialist Republic of Sri Lanka)	65610	16860	科伦坡 Colombo
马尔代夫 Maldives (the Republic of Maldives)	298	270	马累 Male
巴基斯坦 Pakistan (the Islamic Republic of Pakistan)	796095	140500	伊斯兰堡 Islamabad
阿富汗 Afghanistan (the Islamic State of Afghanistan)	652300	22000	喀布尔 Kabul
伊朗 Iran (the Islamic Republic of Iran)	1645000	63900	德黑兰 Tehran
科威特 Kuwait (the State of Kuwait)	17818	2240	科威特城 Kuwait City
沙特阿拉伯 Saudi Arabia (the Kingdom of Saudi Arabia)	2250000	22760	利雅得 Riyadh

巴林 Bahrain (the State of Bahrain)	706.5	690	麦纳麦 Manama
卡塔尔 Qatar (the State of Qatar)	11437	580	多哈 Doha
阿拉伯联合酋长国 United Arab Emirates (the United Arab Emirates)	83600	3108	阿布扎比 Abu Dhabi
阿曼 Oman (the Sultanate of Oman)	309500	2325	马斯喀特 Muscat
也门 Yemen (the Republic of Yemen)	555000	18300	萨那 Sana'a
伊拉克 Iraq (the Republic of Iraq)	441839	23100	巴格达 Baghdad
叙利亚 Syrian (the Syrian Arab Republic)	185180	18392	大马士革 Damascus
黎巴嫩 Lebanon (the Republic of Lebanon)	10452	4000	贝鲁特 Beirut
约旦 Jordan (the Hashemite Kingdom of Jordan)	89340	5040	安曼 Amman
巴勒斯坦 Palestine (the State of Palestine)	11500	8797	耶路撒冷 Jerusalem
以色列 Israel (the State of Israel)	14900	6458	特拉维夫 Tel Aviv-Jaffa
塞浦路斯 Cyprus (the Republic of Cyprus)	9251	864	尼科西亚 Nicosia

土耳其 Turkey (the Republic of Turkey)	779450	66500	安卡拉 Ankara
乌兹别克斯坦 Uzbekistan (the Republic of Uzbekistan)	447400	24967	塔什干 Tashkent
哈萨克斯坦 Kazakhstan (the Republic of Kazakhstan)	2717300	14821	阿斯塔纳 Astana
吉尔吉斯斯坦 Kyrgyzstan (the Kyrghyz Republic)	198500	4946	比什凯克 Bishkek
塔吉克斯坦 Tadzhikistan (the Republic of Tadzhikistan)	143100	6250	杜尚别 Dushanbe
亚美尼亚 Armenia (the Republic of Armenia)	29800	3800	埃里温 Yerevan
土库曼斯坦 Turkmenistan (the Republic of Turkmenistan)	491200	5370	阿什哈巴德 Ashkha-bad
阿塞拜疆 Azerbaijan (the Republic of Azerbaijan)	86600	8141	巴库 Baku
格鲁吉亚 Georgia (the Republic of Georgia)	69700	5438	第比利斯 Tbilisi
	欧洲 Europe		
冰岛 Iceland (the Republic of Iceland)	103000	283	雷克雅未克 Reykjavik
法罗群岛(丹) Faroe Islands (Danish Faroe Islands)	1399	45	托尔斯港 Torshavn

丹麦 Denmark (the Kingdom of Denmark)	43096	5350	哥本哈根 Copenhagen
挪威② Norway (the Kingdom of Norway)	385155	4504	奥斯陆 Oslo
瑞典 Sweden (the Kingdom of Sweden)	449964	8909	斯德哥尔摩 Stockholm
芬兰 Finland (the Republic of Finland)	338145	5181	赫尔辛基 Helsinki
俄罗斯联邦 Russia (the Russian Federation)	17075400	144000	莫斯科 Moscow
乌克兰 Ukraine	603700	48910	基辅 Kiev
白俄罗斯 Belarus (the Republic of Belarus)	207600	9951	明斯克 Minsk
摩尔多瓦 Moldova (the Republic of Moldova)	33800	4293	基希讷乌 Kishinev
立陶宛 Lithuania (the Republic of Lithuania)	65300	3482	维尔纽斯 Vilnius
爱沙尼亚 Estonia (the Republic of Estonia)	45200	1361	塔林 Tallinn
拉脱维亚 Latvia (the Republic of Latvia)	64589	2351	里加 Riga
波兰 Poland (the Republic of Poland)	312685	38644	华沙 Warsaw

捷克 Czech (the Czech Republic)	78866	10267	布拉格 Prague
匈牙利 Hungary (the Republic of Hungary)	93030	10197	布达佩斯 Budapest
德国 Germany (the Federal Republic of Germany)	357020	82370	柏林 Berlin
奥地利 Austria (the Republic of Austria)	83858	8110	维也纳 Vienna
列支敦士登 Liechtenstein (the Principality of Liechtenstein)	160	33	瓦杜兹 Vaduz
瑞士 Switzerland (the Confederation of Switzerland)	41284	7259	伯尔尼 Berne
荷兰 the Netherlands (the Kingdom of the Netherlands)	41864	16103	阿姆斯特丹 Amsterdam
比利时 Belgium (the Kingdom of Belgium)	32547	10263	布鲁塞尔 Brussels
卢森堡 Luxembourg (the Grand Duchy of Luxembourg)	2586	441	卢森堡 Luxembourg
英国 Britain (the United Kingdom of Great Britain and Northern Ireland)	244100	59760	伦敦 London
直布罗陀(英) Gibraltar (UK)	6.5	28	
爱尔兰 Ireland (the Republic of Ireland)	70282	3840	都柏林 Dublin

法国 France (the Republic of France)	551602	60628	巴黎 Paris
摩纳哥 Monaco (the Principality of Monaco)	1.95	35	摩纳哥 Monaco-Ville
安道尔 Andorra (the Principality of Andorra)	468	66	安道尔城 Andorra la Vella
西班牙 Spain (the Kingdom of Spain)	505925	41120	马德里 Madrid
葡萄牙 Portugal (the Portuguese Republic)	92142	10318	里斯本 Lisbon
意大利 Italy (the Italian Republic)	301318	57680	罗马 Rome
梵蒂冈 Vatican (the Vatican City State)	0.44	1.4	梵蒂冈城 the Vatican City
圣马力诺 San Marino (the Republic of San Marino)	61.2	25.5	圣马力诺 San Marino
马耳他 Malta (the Republic of Malta)	316	380	瓦莱塔 Valletta
克罗地亚 Croatia (the Republic of Croatia)	56538	4380	萨格勒布 Zagreb
斯洛伐克 Slovak (the Slovak Republic)	49035	5403	布拉迪斯拉发 Bratislava
斯洛文尼亚 Slovenia (the Republic of Slovenia)	20273	1990	卢布尔雅那 Ljubljana

波斯尼亚和黑塞哥维那,简称波黑 Bosnia and Herzegovina (the Republic of Bosnia and Herzegovina)	51129	3800	萨拉热窝 Sarajevo
马其顿 Macedonia (the Republic of Macedonia)	25713	2107	斯科普里 Skopje
塞尔维亚 Serbia (the Republic of Serbia)	88300	9900	贝尔格莱德 Belgrade
黑山 Montenegro (the Republic of Montenegro)	13800	620	波德戈里察 Podgorica
罗马尼亚 Romania	237500	22456	布加勒斯特 Bucharest
保加利亚 Bulgaria(the Republic of Bulgaria)	110994	7974	索非亚 Sofia
阿尔巴尼亚 Albania(the Republic of Albania)	28748	3080	地拉那 Tirana
希腊 Greece(the Republic of Greece)	131957	10900	雅典 Athens
	非洲 Africa		
埃及 Egypt (the Arab Republic of Egypt)	1001450	67886	开罗 Cairo
利比亚 Libya (the Great Socialist People's Libyan Arab Jamahiriya)	1760000	6220	的黎波里 Tripoli

突尼斯 Tunisia (the Republic of Tunisia)	164150	9700	突尼斯 Tunis
阿尔及利亚 Algeria (the Democratic People's Republic of Algeria)	2381741	29280	阿尔及尔 Algiers
摩洛哥 Morocco (the Kingdom of Morocco)	459000	29200	拉巴特 Rabat
西撒哈拉 West Sahara	266000	160	阿尤恩 Lá Youne
毛里塔尼亚 Mauritania (the Islamic Republic of Mauritania)	1030000	2548	努瓦克肖特 Nouak-chott
塞内加尔 Senegal (the Republic of Senegal)	196722	9800	达喀尔 Dakar
冈比亚 Gambia (the Republic of Gambia)	10380	1380	班珠尔 Banjul
马里 Mali (the Republic of Mali)	1241238	10400	巴马科 Bamako
布基纳法索 Burkina Faso	274200	12900	瓦加杜古 Quagado-ugou
佛得角 Cape Verde (the Republic of Cape Verde)	4033	434	普拉亚 Praia
几内亚比绍 Guinea-Bissau (the Republic of Guinea-Bissau)	36125	1210	比绍 Bissau
几内亚 Guinea (the Republic of Guinea)	245857	7300	科纳克里 Conakry

塞拉利昂 Sierra Leone (the Republic of Sierra Leone)	72326	5120	弗里敦 Freetown
利比里亚 Liberia (the Republic of Liberia)	111370	3010	蒙罗维亚 Monrovia
科特迪瓦 Cote d'Ivoire (the Republic of Cote d'Ivoire)	322463	17500	亚穆苏克罗③ Yamous-soukro
加纳 Ghana (the Republic of Ghana)	238537	18800	阿克拉 Accra
多哥 Togo (the Republic of Togo)	56785	5000	洛美 Lomé
贝宁 Benin (the Republic of Benin)	112622	6400	波多诺伏 Porto-No-vo
尼日尔 Niger (the Republic of Niger)	1267000	10640	尼亚美 Niamey
尼日利亚 Nigeria (the Federal Republic of Nigeria)	923768	120000	阿布贾 Abuja
喀麦隆 Cameroon (the Republic of Cameroon)	475650	15200	雅温得 Yaoundé
赤道几内亚 Equatorial Guinea (the Republic of Equatorial Guinea)	28051	476	马拉博 Malabo
乍得 Chad (the Republic of Chad)	1284000	8130	恩贾梅纳 N'Djamena

中非 Central Africa (the Central African Republic)	622984	3600	班吉 Bangui
苏丹 Sudan (the Republic of Sudan)	2500000	34470	喀土穆 Khartoum
埃塞俄比亚 Ethiopia (the Federal Democratic Republic of Ethiopia)	1103600	63495	亚的斯亚贝巴 Addis Ababa
吉布提 Djibouti (the Republic of Djibouti)	23200	740	吉布提市 Djibouti
索马里 Somali (the Somali Republic)	637660	8800	摩加迪沙 Mogadishu
肯尼亚 Kenya (the Republic of Kenya)	582646	29900	内罗毕 Nairobi
乌干达 Uganda (the Republic of Uganda)	241038	22200	坎帕拉 Kampala
坦桑尼亚 Tanzania (the Uninted Republic of Tanzania)	945087	34700	达累斯萨拉姆 Dar es Salaam
卢旺达 Rwanda (the Republic of Rwanda)	26338	8600	基加利 Kigali
布隆迪 Burundi (the Republic of Burundi)	27834	6800	布琼布拉 Bujumbura
刚果(金) Congo (K) (the Democratic Republic of Congo)	2344885	53000	金沙萨 Kinshasa

刚果(布) Congo (B) (the Republic of the Congo)	34200	3100	布拉柴维尔 Brazzaville
加蓬 Gabon (the Republic of Gabon)	267667	1210	利伯维尔 Libreville
圣多美和普林西比 Sao Tome and Principe (the Democratic Republic of Sao Tome and Principe)	1001	140	圣多美 Sao Tome
安哥拉 Angola (the Republic of Angola)	1246700	13100	罗安达 Luanda
赞比亚 Zambia (the Republic of Zambia)	752614	11000	卢萨卡 Lusaka
马拉维 Malawi (the Republic of Malawi)	119000	10180	利隆圭 Lilongwe
莫桑比克 Mozambique (the Republic of Mozambique)	799380	17242	马普托 Maputo
科摩罗 Comoros (the Federal Islamic Republic of the Comoros)	2336	700	莫罗尼 Moroni
马达加斯加 Madagascar (the Republic of Madagascar)	627000	16350	塔那那利佛 Antan-anarivo
塞舌尔 Seychelles (the Republic of Seychelles)	455	81	维多利亚 Victoria
毛里求斯 Mauritius (the Republic of Mauritius)	2040	1200	路易港 Port Louis

留尼汪(法) Reunion (Overseas Department and Region of France)	2512	728	圣但尼 Saint-Denis
津巴布韦 Zimbabwe (the Republic of Zimbabwe)	390580	12600	哈拉雷 Harare
博茨瓦纳 Botswana (the Republic of Botswana)	581730	1679	哈博罗内 Gaborone
纳米比亚 Namibia (the Republic of Namibia)	824269	1730	温得和克 Windhoek
南非 South Africa (the Republic of South Africa)	1221038	44600	比勒陀利亚④ Pretoria
斯威士兰 Swaziland (the Kingdom of Swaziland)	17363	980	姆巴巴内 Mbabane
莱索托 Lesotho (the Kingdom of Lesotho)	30344	2310	马塞卢 Maseru
圣赫勒拿(英)⑤ Saint Helena (UK)	122	7	詹姆斯敦 Jamestown
厄立特里亚 Eritrea (the State of Eritrea)	124320	4110	阿斯马拉 Asmara
法属南部领地 French Southern Territories	7796	0.093	
英属印度洋领地 British Indian Ocean Territory	60	⑥	
大洋洲 Oceania			
澳大利亚 Australia (the Commonwealth of Australia)	7692000	19200	堪培拉 Canberra

新西兰 New Zealand	270534	3881	惠灵顿 Wellington
巴布亚新几内亚 Papua New Guinea (the Independent State of Papua New Guinea)	462840	5130	莫尔斯比港 Port Moresby
所罗门群岛 Solomon Islands	28369	480	霍尼亚拉 Honiara
瓦努阿图 Vanuatu (the Republic of Vanuatu)	12190	191	维拉港 Port Vila
新喀里多尼亚(法) New Caledonia (France)	18575	209	努美阿 Noumea
斐济 Fiji (the Republic of the Fiji Islands)	18272	810	苏瓦 Suva
基里巴斯 Kiribati (the Republic of Kiribati)	812	84	塔拉瓦 Tarawa
瑙鲁 Nauru (the Republic of Nauru)	21.1	12	亚伦区⑦ Yaren District
密克罗尼西亚 Micronesia (the Federated States of Micronesia)	701	132	帕利基尔 Palikir
马绍尔群岛 Marshall Islands (the Republic of the Marshall Islands)	181.3	52	马朱罗 Majuro
北马里亚纳群岛⑧ the Northern Mariana Islands (the Commonwealth of the Northern Mariana Islands)	477	72	塞班岛 Saipan Island
关岛(美) Guam (US)	549	158	阿加尼亚 Agana

图瓦卢 Tuvalu	26	10.5	富纳富提 Funafuti
瓦利斯和富图纳(法) Wallis and Futuna Islands (France)	274	15	马塔乌图 Mata-Utu
萨摩亚 Samoa (the Independent State of Samoa)	2934	173	阿皮亚 Apia
美属萨摩亚⑨ American Samoa(Territory of American Samoa)	199	67	帕果帕果 Pago-Pago
纽埃(新) Niue (NZ)	260	1.9	阿洛菲 Alofi
诺福克岛 Norfolk Island	34.6	1.9	金斯敦 Kingstown
帕劳 Palau (the Republic of Palau)	458	19.2	科罗尔 Koror
托克劳(新) Tokelau (NZ)	12.2	1.4	⑩
库克群岛(新) the Cook Islands (NZ)	240	14.6	阿瓦鲁阿 Avarua
汤加 Tonga (the Kingdom of Tonga)	747	100	努库阿洛法 Nukualofa
法属波利尼西亚 French Polynesia	4167	232	帕皮提 Papeete
皮特凯恩群岛(英) Pitcairn Islands Groups (UK)	4.5	0.049	亚当斯敦 Adamston

赫德岛和麦克唐纳群岛 Heard Island and McDonald Islands (the Territory of Heard Island and McDonald Islands)	369	⑪	
科科斯(基林)群岛(澳) Cocos (Keeling) Islands (Australia)	14.2	0.633	西岛 West Island
美国本土外小岛屿⑫ United States Minor Outlying Islands			
圣诞岛(澳) Christmas Island (Australia)	135	1.9	
北美洲 North America			
格陵兰(丹) Greenland (Denmark)	2175600	56	努克,前称戈特霍布 Nuuk (formerly called Godthaab)
加拿大 Canada	9984670	31082	渥太华 Ottawa
圣皮埃尔和密克隆(法) The Islands of St. Pierre and Miquelon (France)	242	6.9	圣皮埃尔市 St. Pierre
美国 United States (the United States of America)	9372615	283000	华盛顿哥伦比亚特区 Washington D. C.
百慕大(英) the Bermuda Islands (UK)	53.3	63.5	汉密尔顿 Hamilton
墨西哥 Mexico (the United States of Mexico)	1964375	97480	墨西哥城 Mexico City

危地马拉 Guatemala (the Republic Guatemala)	108889	12974	危地马拉城 Guatemala City
伯利兹 Belize	22963	249.8	贝尔莫潘 Belmopan
萨尔瓦多 El Salvador (the Republic of El Salvador)	20720	6300	圣萨尔瓦多 San Salvador
洪都拉斯 Honduras (the Republic of Honduras)	112492	6600	特古西加尔巴 Tegucigalpa
尼加拉瓜 Nicaragua (the Republic of Nicaragua)	121428	4800	马那瓜 Managua
哥斯达黎加 Costa Rica (the Republic of Costa Rica)	51100	3820	圣何塞 San Jose
巴拿马 Panama (the Republic of Panama)	75517	2856	巴拿马城 Panama City
巴哈马 Bahamas (the Commonwealth of the Bahamas)	13939	304	拿骚 Nassau
特克斯和凯科斯群岛(英) Turks and Caicos Islands (UK)	430	24	科伯恩城 Cockburn Town
古巴 Cuba (the Republic of Cuba)	110860	11200	哈瓦那 La Havana
开曼群岛(英) the Cayman Islands (UK)	259	35.5	乔治敦 Georgetown
牙买加 Jamaica	10991	2610	金斯敦 Kingstown

海地 Haiti (the Republic of Haiti)	27797	7803	太子港 Port-au-Prince
多米尼加 the Dominican Republic	48734	8500	圣多明各 Santo Domingo
波多黎各(美) Puerto Rico (US) (the Commonwealth of Puerto Rico)	9104	3937	圣胡安 San Juan
美属维尔京群岛 the Virgin Islands of the United States	352	122	夏洛特·阿马里 Charlotte Amalie
英属维尔京群岛 the British Virgin Islands	153	19.8	罗德城 Road Town
圣基茨和尼维斯 Saint Kitts and Nevis (the Federation of Saint Kitts and Nevis)	267	42.5	巴斯特尔 Basseterre
安圭拉(英) Anguilla (UK)	96	11.6	瓦利 Valley
安提瓜和巴布达 Antigua and Barbuda	441.6	73	圣约翰 St. John's
蒙特塞拉特(英) Montserrat (UK)	102	5	普利茅斯 Plymouth
瓜德罗普(法) Guadeloupe (France)	1780	431	巴斯特尔 Basse-Terre
多米尼克 Dominica (the Commonwealth of Dominica)	751	77.6	罗索 Roseau

马提尼克(法) Martinique (France)	1100	418	法兰西堡 Fort-de-France
圣卢西亚 Saint Lucia	616	155	卡斯特里 Castries
圣文森特和格林纳丁斯 Saint Vincent and Grenadines	389	112	金斯敦 Kingstown
巴巴多斯 Barbados	431	280	布里奇顿 Bridge-town
格林纳达 Grenada	344	102	圣乔治 St. George's
特立尼达和多巴哥 Trinidad and Tobago (the Republic of Trinidad and Tobago)	5128	1300	西班牙港 Port of Spain
荷属安的列斯 the Netherlands Antilles	800	201.7	威廉斯塔德 Willem-stad
阿鲁巴(荷) Aruba (Dutch)	193	95	奥拉涅斯塔德 Oranjestad
	南美洲 South America		
哥伦比亚 Columbia (the Republic of Columbia)	1141748	42100	波哥大 Santa Fe Bogota
委内瑞拉 Venezuela (the Republic of Venezuela)	916700	24170	加拉加斯 Caracas
圭亚那 Guyana (the Cooperative Republic of Guyana)	214969	772	乔治敦 George-town

苏里南 Suriname (the Republic of Suriname)	163820⑬	431	帕拉马里博 Paramari-bo
法属圭亚那 French Guyana	91000	178	卡宴 Cayenne
厄瓜多尔 Ecuador (the Republic of Ecuador)	256370	12879	基多 Quito
秘鲁 Peru (the Republic of Peru)	1285216	25660	利马 Lima
巴西 Brazil (the Federative Republic of Brazil)	8547000	169600	巴西利亚 Brasilia
玻利维亚 Bolivia (the Republic of Bolivia)	1098581	8274	苏克雷⑭ Sucre
智利 Chile (the Republic of Chile)	756626	15402	圣地亚哥 Santiago
阿根廷 Argentina (the Republic of Argentina)	2780000	37000	布宜诺斯艾利斯 Buenos Aires
巴拉圭 Paraguay (the Republic of Paraguay)	407000	5600	亚松森 Asuncion
乌拉圭 Uruguay (the Oriental Republic of Uruguay)	177000	3360	蒙得维的亚 Montevid-eo
马尔维纳斯群岛⑮ Malvinas Islands	12173	2.9	斯坦利港 Port Stan-ley
南乔治亚和南桑德韦奇群岛(英) South Georgia and South Sandwich Islands (UK)	3903		

附注 Notes:

① 其中:祖国大陆 31 个省、自治区、直辖市(不包括福建省的金门、马祖等岛屿)的人口共 126583 万人。香港特别行政区人口为 678 万人。澳门特别行政区人口为 44 万人。台湾省和福建省的金门、马祖等岛屿人口为 2228 万人。
The population of the 31 provinces, autonomous regions and municipalities (excluding Jinmen and Mazu islands of Fujian Province) on the mainland of China totals 1 265.83 million. The population of Hong Kong Special Administrative Region is 6.78 million. The population of Macao Special Administrative Region is 440 thousand. The population of Tainwan Province and of Jinmen, Mazu and a few other islands of Fujian Province is 22.28 million.

② 包括斯瓦尔巴群岛、扬马延岛等属地。
This includes Svalbard and Jan Mayen.

③ 政治首都亚穆苏克罗,经济首都阿比让。
Its political capital is Yamoussoukro. Its economic capital is Abidjan.

④ 比勒陀利亚为行政首都,开普敦为立法首都,布隆方丹为司法首都。
Pretoria is the administrative capital. Cape Town the legislative capital, Bloemfontein the judicial capital.

⑤ 阿森松岛,特里斯坦——达库尼亚群岛为属岛。
Ascension and Tristan da Cunha are its dependencies.

⑥ 领地无常住人口。1998 年约 3100 名英美军事人员驻扎该地。
There are no permanent residents. In 1998, about 3100 English and American military personnel were stationed here.

⑦ 不设首都,行政管理中心在亚伦区。
There is no official capital. The government offices are located in the Yaren District.

⑧ 拥有美国联邦领土地位。
It has the status as a United States commonwealth territory.

⑨ 又称东萨摩亚。
It is also called Eastern Samoa.

⑩ 随着首席部长办公室轮流设于三个环礁岛。
The administrative center is located in turn at one of the three atolls (Atafu, Nukunoun and Fakaofo) with the chief executive office.

⑪ 无常住人口，为澳大利亚海外领地。
These islands are overseas territory of Australia and there are no permanent residents.

⑫ 包括豪兰和贝克群岛、贾维斯岛、约翰斯顿岛、中途岛、威克岛。
This includes Baker Island, Howland Island, Jarvis Island, Johnston Atoll, Midway Island, and Wake Atoll.

⑬ 包括同圭亚那有争议的17000平方公里。
This includes 17000 square kilometers which is disputable with Guyana.

⑭ 苏克雷为法定首都，政府、议会所在地在拉巴斯。
Sucre is the statutory capital. The government and Parliament are situated in La Paz.

⑮ 英国称福克兰群岛。
This is referred to as Falkland Islands by UK.

计量单位简表
Tables of Weights and Measures

一 法定计量单位表
I Tables of Legal Units of Weights and Measures

长度 Length

名称 Name	纳米 nano-metre	微米 micron	毫米 milli-metre	厘米 centi-metre	分米 deci-metre	米 metre	千米(公里) kilometre
符号 Symbol	nm	μm	mm	cm	dm	m	km
等数 Equi-valent		1000 纳米 nm	1000 微米 μm	10 毫米 mm	10 厘米 cm	10 分米 dm	1000 米 m

面积 Area

名称 Name	平方毫米 square millimetre	平方厘米 square centimetre	平方分米 square decimetre	平方米 square metre	平方千米(平方公里) square kilometre
符号 Symbol	mm^2	cm^2	dm^2	m^2	km^2
等数 Equi-valent		100 平方毫米 mm^2	100 平方厘米 cm^2	100 平方分米 dm^2	1000000 平方米 m^2

体积 Cubic Measure

名称 Name	立方毫米 cubic millimetre	立方厘米 cubic centimetre	立方分米 cubic decimetre	立方米 cubic metre
符号 Symbol	mm^3	cm^3	dm^3	m^3
等数 Equivalent		1000 立方毫米 mm^3	1000 立方厘米 cm^3	1000 立方分米 dm^3

容积(容量) Capacity (Volume)

名称 Name	毫升 millilitre	厘升 centiliter	分升 decilitre	升 litre
符号 Symbol	mL, ml	cL, cl	dL, dl	L, l
等数 Equivalent		10 毫升 ml	10 厘升 cl	10 分升 dl

质量(重量) Mass (Weight)

名称 Name	纳克 nano-gramme	微克 micro-gramme	毫克 milli-gramme	厘克 centi-gramme	分克 deci-gramme	克 gramme	千克(公斤) kilo-gramme	吨 ton
符号 Symbol	ng	μg	mg	cg	dg	g	kg	t
等数 Equivalent		1000 纳克 ng	1000 微克 μg	10 毫克 mg	10 厘克 cg	10 分克 dg	1000 克 g	1000 千克(公斤) kg

二 市制计量单位表
II Tables of Traditional Chinese Units of Weights and Measures

长度 Length

名称 Name	毫 *hao*	厘 *li*	分 *fen*	寸 *cun*	尺(市尺) *chi*	丈 *zhang*	里(市里) *li*
等数 Equivalent		10 毫 *hao*	10 厘 *li*	10 分 *fen*	10 寸 *cun*	10 尺 *chi*	150 丈 *zhang*

面积 Area

名称 Name	平方毫 square *hao*	平方厘 square *li*	平方分 square *fen*	平方寸 square *cun*	平方尺 square *chi*	平方丈 square *zhang*	平方里 square *li*
等数 Equivalent		100 平方毫 square *hao*	100 平方厘 square *li*	100 平方分 square *fen*	100 平方寸 square *cun*	100 平方尺 square *chi*	225000 平方丈 square *zhang*

地积 Acreage

名称 Name	毫 *hao*	厘 *li*	分 *fen*	亩 *mu*	顷 *qing*
等数 Equivalent		10 毫 *hao*	10 厘 *li*	10 分 *fen*	100 亩 *mu*

质量(重量) Mass (Weight)

名称 Name	丝 *si*	毫 *hao*	厘 *li*	分 *fen*	钱 *qian*	两 *liang*	斤 *jin*	担 *dan* (picul)
等数 Equivalent		10 丝 *si*	10 毫 *hao*	10 厘 *li*	10 分 *fen*	10 钱 *qian*	10 两 *liang*	100 斤 *jin*

容积(容量) Capacity (Volume)

名称 Name	撮 *cuo*	勺 *shao*	合 *he*	升 *sheng*	斗 *dou*	石 *shi*
等数 Equivalent		10 撮 *cuo*	10 勺 *shao*	10 合 *he*	10 升 *sheng*	10 斗 *dou*

三 计量单位比较表
III Conversion Tables of Legal Units of Weights and Measures

长度比较表
Conversion Table of Length

1 千米(公里)km=2 市里 *li*=0.621 英里 mi=0.540 海里 nautical mi 1 米(公尺)m=3 市尺 *chi*=3.281 英尺 ft 1 海里 nautical mi=1.852 千米(公里) km=3.704 市里 *li*=1.150 英里 mi
1 市里 *li*=150 丈 *zhang*=0.5 千米(公里) km=0.311 英里 mi=0.270海里 nautical mi 1 市尺 *chi*=10 市寸 *cun*=0.333 米 m=1.094 英尺 ft
1 英里 mi=1.609 千米(公里)km=3.219 市里 *li*=0.869 海里 nautical mi 1 英尺 ft=12 英寸 in=0.305 米 m=0.914 市尺 *chi*

面积比较表
Conversion Table of Area

1 平方千米(平方公里)km^2=100 公顷 ha=4 平方市里 square *li*=0.386 平方英里 mi^2 1 平方米 m^2=1 平米 m^2=9 平方市尺 square *chi*=10.764 平方英尺 ft^2
1 市顷 *qing*=100 市亩 *mu*=6.6667 公顷 ha 1 市亩 *mu*=10 市分 *fen*=60 平方市丈 square *zhang*=6.6667 公亩 a=666.67 平方米 m^2
1 公顷 ha=10000 平方米 m^2=100 公亩 a=15 市亩 *mu* 1 公亩 a=100 平方米 m^2=0.15 市亩 *mu*

质量(重量)比较表
Conversion Table of Mass (Weight)

1 千克(公斤)kg=2 市斤 *jin*=2.205 磅 lb
1 市斤 *jin*=10 *liang*=0.5 千克(公斤)kg=1.102 磅 lb
1 磅 lb=16 盎司 oz=0.454 千克(公斤) kg=0.907 市斤 *jin*

容积(容量)比较表
Conversion Table of Capacity (Volume)

1 升(公制)l=1 公升 l=1 立升 litre=1 市升 *sheng*=0.220 加仑(英制)UK gal 1 毫升 ml=1 西西 cc=0.001 升(公制)L
1 加仑(英制)Uk gal=4.546 升 L=4.546 *sheng*

地质年代简表

Table of the Geological Time Scale

宙 Eon	代 Era	纪 Period	符号 Symbol	同位素年龄 Isotopic age (单位:百万年) (million years) 开始时间 Start (距今 up to now)	持续时间 Duration	生物发展的阶段 Development of organism
显生宙 Phanerozoic (PH)	新生代 Cenozoic (Kz)	第四纪 Quaternary	Q	1.6	1.6	人类出现 appearance of man
		新近纪 Neogene	N	23	21.4	动植物都接近现代 fauna and flora approaching modern forms
		古近纪 Paleogen	E	65	42	哺乳动物迅速繁衍,被子植物繁盛 rapid mammal procreation; flourishing angiosperms

显生宙 Phanerozoic (PH)	中生代 Mesozoic (Mz)	白垩纪 Cretaceous	K	135	70	被子植物大量出现,爬行类后期急剧减少 appearance of abundant angiosperms; rapid decrease of reptiles in the Late Mesozoic
		侏罗纪 Jurassic	J	205	70	裸子植物繁盛,鸟类出现 flourishing gymnosperms; appearance of birds
		三叠纪 Triassic	T	250	45	哺乳动物出现,恐龙大量繁衍 appearance of mammals; abundant dinosaur procreation
	古生代 Palaeozoic (Pz)	二叠纪 Permian	P	290	40	松柏类开始发展 rise of pines and cypresses
		石炭纪 Carboniferous	C	355	65	爬行动物出现 appearance of reptiles
		泥盆纪 Devonian	D	410	55	裸子植物出现,昆虫和两栖动物出现 appearance of gymnosperms, insects and amphibians
		志留纪 Silurian	S	438	28	蕨类植物出现,鱼类出现 appearance of pteridophytes and fish

	中生代 Meso-zoic (Mz)	奥陶纪 Ordo-vician	O	510	72	藻类广泛发育，海生无脊椎动物繁盛 extensive development of algae; abundance of marine invertebrates
		寒武纪 Cam-brian	€	570	60	海生无脊椎动物门类大量增加 great increase of marine invertebrates
元古宙 Prote-rozoic (PT)				2500	1930	蓝藻和细菌开始繁盛，无脊椎动物出现 prosperity of blue green algae and bacteria; appearance of invertebrates
太古宙 Archeo-zoic (AR)				4000	1500	细菌和藻类出现 appearance of bacteria and algae

节　气　表

Table of Solar Terms

（按公元月日计算）
(Calculated according to the months and dates of the Christian Era)

春季 spring	立春 Beginning of Spring 2月3—5日交节 Reaching on 3—5 February	雨水 Rain Water 2月18—20日交节 Reaching on 18—20 February	惊蛰 Waking of Insects 3月5—7日交节 Reaching on 5—7 March
	春分 Spring Equinox 3月20—22日交节 Reaching on 20—22 March	清明 Pure Brightness 4月4—6日交节 Reaching on 4—6 April	谷雨 Grain Rain 4月19—21日交节 Reaching on 19—21 April
夏季 summer	立夏 Beginning of Summer 5月5—7日交节 Reaching on 5—7 May	小满 Grain Full 5月20—22日交节 Reaching on 20—22 May	芒种 Grain in Ear 6月5—7日交节 Reaching on 5—7 June
	夏至 Summer Solstice 6月21—22日交节 Reaching on 21—22 June	小暑 Slight Heat 7月6—8日交节 Reaching on 6—8 July	大暑 Great Heat 7月22—24日交节 Reaching on 22—24 July

秋季 autumn	立秋 Beginning of Autumn 8月7—9日交节 Reaching on 7－9 August	处暑 Limit of Heat 8月22—24日交节 Reaching on 22－24 August	白露 White Dew 9月7—9日交节 Reaching on 7－9 September
	秋分 Autumn Equinox 9月22—24日交节 Reaching on 22－24 September	寒露 Cold Dew 10月8—9日交节 Reaching on 8－9 October	霜降 Frost's Descent 10月23—24日交节 Reaching on 23－24 October
冬季 winter	立冬 Beginning of Winter 11月7—8日交节 Reaching on 7－8 November	小雪 Slight Snow 11月22—23日交节 Reaching on 22－23 November	大雪 Great Snow 12月6—8日交节 Reaching on 6－8 December
	冬至 Winter Solstice 12月21—23日交节 Reaching on 21－23 December	小寒 Slight Cold 1月5—7日交节 Reaching on 5－7 January	大寒 Great Cold 1月20—21日交节 Reaching on 20－21 January

二十四节气歌

Song of the Twenty-four Solar Terms

春雨惊春清谷天，夏满芒夏暑相连，
秋处露秋寒霜降，冬雪雪冬小大寒。
每月两节不变更，最多相差一两天，
上半年来六、廿一，下半年是八、廿三。
Beginning of Spring, Rain Water, and Waking of Insects,
Spring Equinox, Pure Brightness, and Grain Rain following,
Beginning of Summer, Grain Full, and Grain in Ear,
Summer Solstice, Slight Heat and Great Heat connecting,
Beginning of Autumn, Limit of Heat, and White Dew,
Autumn Equinox, Cold Dew, and Frost's Descent following,
Beginning of Winter, Slight Snow, and Great Snow,
Winter Solstice, Slight Cold, and Great Cold following.
Two solar terms always begin
On every 6th and 21st days,
In the first half of the year,
And on every 8th and 23rd days,
In the second half of the year,
With difference of only one or two days.